C# 2010 FOR PROGRAMMERS
FOURTH EDITION
DEITEL® DEVELOPER SERIES

The publisher offers excellent discounts on this book when ordered in quantity for bulk purchases or special sales, which may include electronic versions and/or custom covers and content particular to your business, training goals, marketing focus, and branding interests. For more information, please contact:

U. S. Corporate and Government Sales
(800) 382-3419
corpsales@pearsontechgroup.com

For sales outside the U. S., please contact:

International Sales
international@pearsoned.com

Visit us on the Web: informit.com/ph

Library of Congress Cataloging-in-Publication Data

On file

© 2011 Pearson Education, Inc.

ISBN-13: 978-0-13261820-5
ISBN-10: 0-13-261820-6

Text printed in the United States on recycled paper at RR Donnelley in Crawfordsville, Indiana.
First printing, October 2010

C# 2010 for Programmers
Fourth Edition
Deitel® Developer Series

Paul Deitel
Deitel & Associates, Inc.

Harvey Deitel
Deitel & Associates, Inc.

PRENTICE
HALL

Upper Saddle River, NJ • Boston • Indianapolis • San Francisco
New York • Toronto • Montreal • London • Munich • Paris • Madrid
Capetown • Sydney • Tokyo • Singapore • Mexico City

Trademarks

To Anders Hejlsberg,
    Chief Designer of Microsoft's
    C# Programming Language

Paul and Harvey Deitel

Contents

4 Introduction to Classes and Objects   66

5 Control Statements: Part 1   94

6 Control Statements: Part 2   120

7   Methods: A Deeper Look   149

8   Arrays   187

9   Introduction to LINQ and the List Collection   232

12 OOP: Polymorphism, Interfaces and Operator Overloading 332

13 Exception Handling 372

16 Strings and Characters   504

17 Files and Streams   543

18 Databases and LINQ   584

19 Web App Development with ASP.NET   620

20 Searching and Sorting   666

25 WPF Graphics and Multimedia   839

26 XML and LINQ to XML   881

27 Web App Development with ASP.NET: A Deeper Look   921

28   Web Services   948

29 Silverlight and Rich Internet Applications   1000

30 ATM Case Study, Part 1:
Object-Oriented Design with the UML   1044

31 ATM Case Study, Part 2:
Implementing an Object-Oriented Design   1087

A Operator Precedence Chart   1127

B Simple Types   1129

C ASCII Character Set   1131

D Number Systems   1132

E UML 2: Additional Diagram Types   1142

F Unicode®   1144

G Using the Visual C# 2010 Debugger   1152

Preface

"Live in fragments no longer, only connect."
—Edgar Morgan Forster

Welcome to Visual C#® 2010, C# 4 and the world of Microsoft® Windows® and Internet and web programming with Microsoft's .NET 4 Framework! This book presents leading-edge computing technologies for professional software developers. We believe the book will give you an informative, challenging and entertaining C# educational experience.

We use the Deitel signature **live-code approach**, presenting most concepts in the context of complete working Visual C# 2010 programs, rather than using code snippets. Each code example is immediately followed by one or more sample executions. All the source code is available at www.deitel.com/books/csharpfp4/.

At Deitel & Associates, we author programming-language professional books, Live-Lessons video courses and textbooks under the Prentice Hall imprint of Pearson Higher Education, and deliver our Dive Into® Series professional instructor-led training courses worldwide on site at corporations, government agencies, branches of the military and academic institutions.

As you read the book, if you have questions, send an e-mail to deitel@deitel.com; we'll respond promptly. For updates on this book and its supporting Visual C# software, visit www.deitel.com/books/csharpfp4/, follow us on Twitter (@deitel) and Facebook (www.deitel.com/deitelfan), and subscribe to the *Deitel® Buzz Online* newsletter (www.deitel.com/newsletter/subscribe.html). Check out our growing list of C# and related Resource Centers at www.deitel.com/ResourceCenters.html.

New and Updated Features

Here are some key features of *C# 2010 for Programmers, 4/e:*

- *LINQ.* LINQ provides a uniform syntax for querying data. Strong typing enables Visual Studio to provide *IntelliSense* support for LINQ operations and results. LINQ can be used on different types of data sources, including collections and files (LINQ to Objects, Chapters 9 and 17, respectively), databases (LINQ to SQL, Chapters 18, 19, 27 and 28) and XML (LINQ to XML, Chapters 26 and 29).

- *Early Introduction to Generic Collections and LINQ.* We introduce LINQ early so that you can begin using it with arrays. To enable you to work with more flexible data structures throughout the book, we introduce the List generic collection—a dynamic data structure—in close proximity to arrays. This enables us to demonstrate the power of LINQ and how it can be applied to most data structures. As a generic collection, the List class provides strong compile-time type safety—ensuring that all elements of the collection are of the appropriate type.

- *Databases.* We use the free Microsoft SQL Server Express Edition and real-world applications to present the fundamentals of database programming. Chapters 18, 27 and 28 discuss database and LINQ to SQL fundamentals, presented in the context of an address-book desktop application, a web-based bookstore application and a web-based airline reservation system. Chapter 18 also demonstrates using the Visual Studio 2010 tools to build a GUI application that accesses a database using LINQ to SQL.

- *Windows Presentation Foundation (WPF) GUI and Graphics.* We begin our GUI discussion with the traditional Windows Forms controls in Chapters 14–15. We extend our coverage in Chapters 24 and 25 with an introduction to Windows Presentation Foundation (WPF)—Microsoft's framework that integrates GUI, graphics and multimedia capabilities. We present many examples, including a painting application, a text editor, a color chooser, a book-cover viewer, a television video player, a 3-D rotating pyramid and various animations.

- *Windows Communication Foundation (WCF) Web Services.* Microsoft's .NET strategy embraces the Internet and web as integral to software development and deployment. Web-services technology enables information sharing, e-commerce and other interactions using standard Internet protocols and technologies, such as Hypertext Transfer Protocol (HTTP), Extensible Markup Language (XML), Simple Object Access Protocol (SOAP) and REST (Representational State Transfer). Web services enable you to package application functionality in a manner that turns the web into a library of reusable software components. We replaced our treatment of ASP.NET web services from an earlier edition with a discussion of Windows Communication Foundation (WCF) services in Chapter 28. WCF is a set of technologies for building distributed systems in which system components communicate with one another over networks. WCF uses a common framework for all communication between systems, so you need to learn only one programming model. Chapter 28 focuses on WCF web services that use either the SOAP protocol or REST architecture. The REST examples transmit both XML (eXtensible Markup Language) and JSON (JavaScript Object Notation).

- *ASP.NET 4 and ASP.NET AJAX.* The .NET platform enables you to create robust, scalable web-based applications. Microsoft's .NET server-side technology, ASP.NET 4, allows you to build web documents that respond to client requests. To enable interactive web pages, server-side programs process information that users input into HTML forms. ASP.NET provides enhanced visual programming capabilities, similar to those used in building Windows Forms for desktop programs. You can create web pages visually, by dragging and dropping web controls onto web forms. Chapters 19 and 27 introduce these powerful technologies. We present a sequence of examples in which you build several web applications, including a web-based bookstore. Chapter 27 culminates with an example that demonstrates the power of AJAX. We also discuss the ASP.NET Development Server (which enables you to test your web applications on your local computer), multitier architecture and web transactions. The chapter uses ASP.NET 4 and LINQ to build a guestbook application that retrieves information from a database and displays it in a web page. We use a `LinqDataSource` from a web application to manipulate a database. We use ASP.NET AJAX controls to add AJAX functionality to web applications to improve their responsiveness—in particular, we use the `UpdatePanel` control to perform partial-page updates.

- *Silverlight.* In Chapter 29, we introduce Silverlight, Microsoft's technology for building Rich Internet Applications (RIA). Silverlight, a competitor to JavaFX and Adobe's Flash and Flex technologies, allows you to create visually stunning, multimedia-intensive user interfaces for web applications using .NET languages such as Visual C#. Silverlight is a subset of WPF that runs in a web browser using a plug-in. One of Silverlight's most compelling features is its ability to stream high-definition video. The chapter presents powerful multimedia applications, including a weather viewer, Flickr® photo viewer, deep zoom book-cover collage and video viewer.

- *Language Features to Support LINQ.* Many of the Visual C# language features we cover in Chapter 10 were introduced to support LINQ. We show how to use extension methods to add functionality to a class without modifying the class's source code. We use delegates (objects that hold method references) to support our discussion of lambda expressions, which define anonymous functions. Lambda expressions can be used wherever delegates are needed—typically as arguments to method calls or to help create more powerful LINQ queries. You'll see how to use anonymous types to create simple classes that store data without writing a class definition—a feature used frequently in LINQ.

- *Implicitly Typed Local Variables.* When you initialize a local variable in its declaration, you can omit the variable's type—the compiler infers it from the type of the initializer value (introduced in Chapter 9). This is another feature used frequently in LINQ.

- *Object and Collection Initializers.* When creating an object, you can use the object initializer syntax (introduced in Chapter 9) to assign values to the new object's properties. Similarly, you can use the collection initializer syntax (Chapter 9) to specify values for the elements of collections, just as you do with arrays.

- *Auto-Implemented Properties.* For cases in which a property of a class has a `get` accessor that simply returns a `private` instance variable's value and a `set` accessor that simply assigns a value to the instance variable, C# provides automatically implemented properties (also known as auto-implemented properties; introduced in Chapter 4). With an auto-implemented property, the compiler automatically creates a `private` instance variable and the `get` and `set` accessors for manipulating it. This gives you the software engineering benefits of having a property, but enables you to implement the property trivially.

- **Other New Language Features.** We cover optional parameters, named parameters, covariance and contravariance.

- **Visual C# 2010 Express IDE.** All screenshots have been updated to the Visual C# 2010 Express IDE.

- **Contextual keywords.** The keywords table (Chapter 3) includes the contextual keywords—words that are considered keywords only in certain contexts. Outside those contexts, such keywords can still be used as valid identifiers. This minimizes the chance that older Visual C# code will break when upgrading to Visual C# 2010. Many of these contextual keywords are used with LINQ.

- *IntelliSense.* We point out additional ways in which the IDE's *IntelliSense* helps you write code.

- *Data Tips and Visualizers.* We use *DataTips* and visualizers to view object contents in the code window during debugging.

- *Tuned Treatment of Object-Oriented Programming.* The book offers a rich treatment of C#'s object-oriented programming features. Chapter 4 introduces how to create classes and objects. These concepts are extended in Chapter 10. Chapter 11 discusses how to create powerful new classes quickly by using inheritance to "absorb" the capabilities of existing classes. Chapter 12 presents the crucial concepts of polymorphism, abstract classes, concrete classes and interfaces, all of which facilitate powerful manipulations among objects in an inheritance hierarchy.

- *Visual Studio 2010 Debugger.* In Appendix G, we explain how to use key debugger features, such as setting "breakpoints" and "watches" and stepping into and out of methods. Most of the material in this appendix can be covered after Chapter 4. One example uses the conditional AND (&&) operator, which is explained in Chapter 6.

Case Studies

Among the hundreds of complete working C# programs we present are many case studies, including:

- GradeBook class in Chapters 4–8.
- OOD/UML ATM system in Chapters 30 and 31.
- Time class in Chapter 10.
- Employee payroll application in Chapters 11–12.
- WPF painter application in Chapter 24.
- WPF text-editor application in Chapter 24.
- WPF color-chooser application in Chapter 24.
- WPF book cover viewer application in Chapter 24.
- WPF television application in Chapter 25.
- Address-book application in Chapter 18.
- Guestbook ASP.NET application in Chapter 19.
- Password-protected books database ASP.NET application in Chapter 27.
- Airline reservation web service in Chapter 28.
- Blackjack web service in Chapter 28.
- Equation-generator web service and math-tutor application in Chapter 28.
- Silverlight weather-viewer application in Chapter 29.
- Silverlight Flickr® photo-viewer application in Chapter 29.
- Silverlight Deep Zoom book-cover collage application in Chapter 29.
- Silverlight video-viewer application in Chapter 29.

Object-Oriented Design Case Study: Designing and Implementing an ATM

In this case study, we design and fully implement the software for a simple automated teller machine (ATM). After completing this case study, you'll be familiar with an object-oriented design and implementation for a significant C# application.

The design was developed at Deitel & Associates, Inc., and reviewed by industry professionals and academics. We kept the design and the code small and simple so that they would work well in C# professional courses.

The Unified Modeling Language® (UML®) has become the preferred graphical modeling language for designing object-oriented systems. Chapters 30 and 31 present a carefully paced introduction to object-oriented design using the UML.

We employ a carefully developed, incremental object-oriented design process to produce a UML model for our ATM system. From this design, we produce a substantial working C# implementation using key programming notions, including classes, objects, encapsulation, visibility, composition, inheritance and polymorphism.

Here's what the sections of the case study cover:

Section 1.9—Introduction to Object Technology—presents basic concepts and terminology of object technology, including classes, objects, encapsulation and inheritance.

Section 30.2—Examining the ATM Requirements Document—discusses a *requirements document* specifying the requirements for a system that we'll design and implement —the software for a simple automated teller machine (ATM). We investigate the structure and behavior of object-oriented systems in general. We discuss how the UML facilitates the design process in subsequent Case Study sections by providing several additional types of diagrams to model our system. We discuss the interaction between the ATM system and its user. Specifically, we investigate the scenarios that may occur between the user and the system itself—called *use cases*. We model these interactions, using UML *use case diagrams*.

Section 30.3—Identifying the Classes in the ATM Requirements Documents— begins to design the ATM system. We identify its classes by extracting the nouns and noun phrases from the requirements document. We arrange these classes into a UML class diagram that describes the class structure of our system. The diagram also describes relationships, known as *associations*, among the classes.

Section 30.4—Identifying Class Attributes—focuses on the attributes of the classes discussed in Section 30.3. A class contains both *attributes* (data) and *operations* (behaviors). As we see in later sections, changes in an object's attributes often affect its behavior. To determine the attributes for the classes in our case study, we extract the adjectives describing the nouns and noun phrases (which defined our classes) from the requirements document, then place the attributes in the class diagram we created in Section 30.3.

Section 30.5—Identifying Objects' States and Activities—discusses how an object, at any given time, occupies a specific condition called a *state*. A *state transition* occurs when the object receives a message to change state. The UML provides the *state machine diagram*, which identifies the set of possible states that an object may occupy and models that object's state transitions. An object also has an *activity*—the work it performs in its lifetime. The UML provides the *activity diagram*—a flowchart that models an object's activity. This section uses both diagram types to model behavioral aspects of our ATM system, such as how it carries out a withdrawal transaction and how it responds when the user is authenticated.

Section 30.6—Identifying Class Operations—identifies the operations, or services, of our classes. We extract from the requirements document the verbs and verb phrases that specify the operations for each class. We then modify the class diagram of Section 30.3 to include each operation with its associated class. As future chapters introduce such topics as inheritance, we'll modify our classes and diagrams.

Section 30.7—Identifying Collaboration Among Objects—provides a "rough sketch" of the model for our ATM system. In this section, we see how it works. We investigate the behavior of the system by discussing *collaborations*—messages that objects send to each other to communicate. The class operations that we identified in Section 30.6 turn out to be the collaborations among the objects in our system. We determine the collaborations, then collect them into a *communication diagram*—the UML diagram for modeling collaborations. This diagram reveals which objects collaborate and when. We present a communication diagram of the collaborations among objects to perform an ATM balance inquiry. We then present the UML *sequence diagram* for modeling interactions in a system. This diagram emphasizes the chronological ordering of messages. A sequence diagram models how objects in the system interact to carry out withdrawal and deposit transactions.

Section 31.2—Starting to Program the Classes of the ATM System—takes a break from designing the behavior of our system. We begin the implementation process. Using the UML class diagram of Section 30.3 and the attributes and operations discussed in Section 30.4 and Section 30.6, we show how to implement a class in C# from a design. We do not implement all classes—because we have not completed the design process. Working from our UML diagrams, we create code for the Withdrawal class.

Section 31.3—Incorporating Inheritance and Polymorphism into the ATM System—continues our discussion of object-oriented programming. We consider inheritance: classes sharing common characteristics may inherit attributes and operations from a "base" class. In this section, we investigate how our ATM system can benefit from using inheritance. We document our discoveries in a class diagram that models inheritance relationships—the UML refers to these relationships as *generalizations*. We modify the class diagram of Section 30.3 by using inheritance to group classes with similar characteristics. This section concludes the design of the model portion of our simulation.

Section 31.4—ATM Case Study Implementation—The majority of the case study involves designing the model (i.e., the data and logic) of the ATM system. In this section, we fully implement that model in C#, working from the UML diagrams we created. We apply the concepts of object-oriented design with the UML and object-oriented programming in C# that you learned in the chapters. By the end of this case study, you'll have completed the design and implementation of a real-world system and should feel confident tackling larger systems.

Appendix E—UML: Additional Diagram Types—overviews the UML diagram types not discussed in the OOD/UML Case Study.

Dependency Charts

Figures 1–2 illustrate the dependencies among chapters in the book. An arrow pointing into a chapter indicates that it *depends on* the content of the chapter from which the arrow points. We've commented on some additional dependencies in the diagrams' footnotes.

Dependency Chart for Core Topics[1]

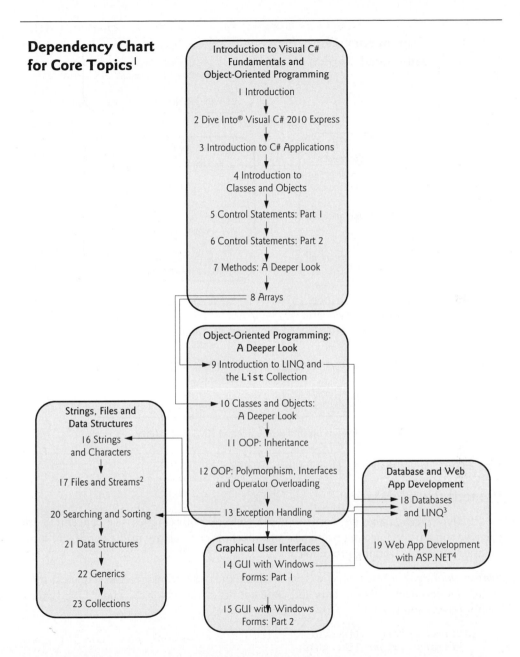

1. See Fig. 2 for the advanced topics chapters.
2. Requires Sections 14.1–14.5.
3. Requires Sections 14.1–14.6 and 15.8.
4. Requires general GUI and event-handling knowledge (Sections 14.1–14.3).

Fig. 1 | Chapter dependency chart for the core-topic chapters.

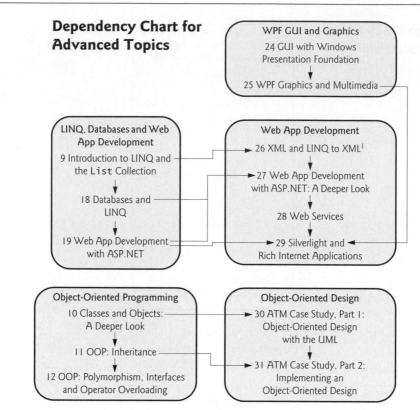

1. Chapter 26 depends on the introduction to XML in Chapter 24.

Fig. 2 | Chapter dependency chart for the advanced-topic chapters.

Presentation Features

C# 2010 for Programmers, 4/e, contains a rich collection of examples. We concentrate on effective software engineering principles and stress program clarity in the context of hundreds of complete, working programs.

Syntax Shading. For readability, we syntax shade the code, similar to the way most integrated-development environments and code editors syntax color the code. Our syntax-shading conventions are:

```
comments appear like this
keywords appear like this
constants and literal values appear like this
all other code appears in black
```

Code Highlighting. We place gray rectangles around each program's key code.

Programming Tips. We include programming tips to help you focus on important aspects of program development. These tips and practices represent the best we've gleaned from a combined seven decades of programming and teaching experience.

Good Programming Practice

The Good Programming Practices *call attention to techniques that will help you produce programs that are clearer, more understandable and more maintainable.*

Common Programming Error

Pointing out these Common Programming Errors *reduces the likelihood that you'll make them.*

Error-Prevention Tip

These tips contain suggestions for exposing and removing bugs from your programs; many of the tips describe aspects of Visual C# that prevent bugs from getting into programs.

Performance Tip

These tips highlight opportunities for making your programs run faster or minimizing the amount of memory that they occupy.

Portability Tip

The Portability Tips *help you write code that will run on a variety of platforms.*

Software Engineering Observation

The Software Engineering Observations *highlight architectural and design issues that affect the construction of software systems, especially large-scale systems.*

Look-and-Feel Observation

These observations help you design attractive, user-friendly graphical user interfaces that conform to industry norms.

Using Fonts for Emphasis. We place the key terms and the index's page reference for each defining occurrence in **bold** text for easier reference. On-screen components are emphasized in the **bold Helvetica** font (e.g., the **File** menu) and C# program text in the Lucida font (e.g., int x = 5).

Web Access. All of the source-code examples for *C# 2010 for Programmers, 4/e* are available for download from:

```
www.deitel.com/books/csharpfp4/
```

Site registration is quick and easy. Download all the examples, then run each program as you read the corresponding text discussions.

Objectives. Each chapter begins with a statement of objectives. This lets you know what to expect and gives you an opportunity, after reading the chapter, to determine if you've met the objectives.

Quotations. The learning objectives are accompanied by quotations. Some are humorous; some are philosophical; others offer interesting insights.

Outline. The chapter outline helps you approach the material in a top-down fashion, so you can anticipate what's to come and set an effective learning pace.

Illustrations/Figures. Abundant charts, tables, line drawings, programs and program output are included. We model the flow of control in control statements with UML activity diagrams. UML class diagrams model the fields, constructors and methods of classes. We make extensive use of six major UML diagram types in the OOD/UML ATM case study.

Wrap-Up Section. Each chapter ends with a brief "wrap-up" section that recaps the chapter content and transitions to the next chapter.

Thousands of Index Entries. We've included a comprehensive index, which is especially useful when you use the book as a reference.

Software for the Book

We use Microsoft Visual Studio 2010 development tools, including the free Visual C#® 2010 Express Edition, Visual Web Developer 2010 Express Edition and SQL Server 2008 Express Edition. The Express Editions provide rich functionality and can be used to build robust .NET applications. They are appropriate for professionals who do not have access to a complete version of Visual Studio 2010.

You may use the Express Editions to compile and execute *all* the example programs in the book. You may also use the full Visual Studio product to build and run the examples. All of the features supported by the Express Editions are also available in the complete Visual Studio 2010 editions.

You can download the latest versions of the Express Edition tools from:

```
www.microsoft.com/express/
```

When you install the software (discussed in the Before You Begin section that follows this Preface), you also should install the help documentation and SQL Server Express. Microsoft provides a dedicated forum for help using the Express Editions at:

```
social.msdn.microsoft.com/forums/en-US/Vsexpressinstall/threads/
```

Windows 7, Windows Vista and Windows XP
You can use Windows 7, Windows Vista or Windows XP. We used Windows 7 while developing the book. We use the Segoe UI font in the graphical user interfaces. This font is accessible to Windows XP users—we tell you how to get it in the Before You Begin section. Several of our reviewers tested all the programs on Windows XP and reported no problems. If any Windows XP-specific issues arise after the book is published, we'll post them at www.deitel.com/books/csharpfp4/ with appropriate instructions. Write to us at deitel@deitel.com if you encounter any problems, and we'll respond promptly.

Other Software Requirements
For Chapters 18, 19, 27 and 28 you'll need the SQL Server 2008 Express Edition. Chapters 19, 27 and 28 require Visual Web Developer 2010 Express (or a full Visual Studio 2008 edition). For updates on the software used in this book, subscribe to our free e-mail newsletter at www.deitel.com/newsletter/subscribe.html, visit the book's website at www.deitel.com/books/csharpfp4/, and follow us on Twitter (@deitel) and Facebook (www.deitel.com/deitelfan).

C# 2010 Fundamentals: Parts I, II and III LiveLessons Video Product

Our *C# 2010 Fundamentals: Parts I, II and III* LiveLessons Camtasia-based video training product shows you what you need to know to start building robust, powerful software with C# 2010 and .NET 4. It includes 20+ hours of expert training synchronized to *C# 2010 for Programmers, 4/e.*

Check out our growing list of LiveLessons video products:

- *C# 2010 Fundamentals I, II, and III*
- *C# 2008 Fundamentals I and II*
- *Java Fundamentals I and II*
- *C++ Fundamentals I and II*
- *iPhone App-Development Fundamentals I and II*
- *JavaScript Fundamentals I and II*
- *Visual Basic 2010 Fundamentals I and II*
- *C Fundamentals I and II*
- *Android Fundamentals I and II*

For additional information about Deitel LiveLessons video products, visit:

```
www.deitel.com/livelessons
```

Licensing Deitel Book and/or LiveLessons Video Content for Your Corporate Learning Management Systems

Corporations and organizations may purchase licenses for Deitel's best-selling book and LiveLessons video content to be placed on internal learning management systems. For more information, e-mail deitel@deitel.com.

The Deitel Online Resource Centers

We provide 100+ online Resource Centers on various topics of interest to our readers—see the list at www.deitel.com/ResourceCenters.html. We've found many exceptional resources online, including tutorials, documentation, software downloads, articles, blogs, podcasts, videos, code samples, books, e-books and more—most are free. Some of the Resource Centers you might find helpful while studying this book are Visual C#, ASP.NET, ASP.NET AJAX, LINQ, .NET, Silverlight, SQL Server, Web Services, Windows Communication Foundation, Windows Presentation Foundation, Windows 7, UML, Code Search Engines and Code Sites, Game Programming and Programming Projects.

Acknowledgments

It's a pleasure to acknowledge the efforts of people whose names do not appear on the cover, but whose hard work, cooperation, friendship and understanding were crucial to the book's production. Thanks especially to Abbey Deitel and Barbara Deitel.

We're fortunate to have worked on this project with the dedicated publishing professionals at Prentice Hall/Pearson. We appreciate the extraordinary efforts and 15-year mentorship of our friend and professional colleague Mark L. Taub, Editor-in-Chief of Pearson

Technology Group. Thanks to Sandra Schroeder and Chuti Prasertsith for their work on the cover, and to John Fuller for managing the production of the book.

We wish to acknowledge the efforts of our third and fourth edition reviewers. Adhering to tight schedules, they scrutinized the text and the programs and provided countless suggestions for improving the presentation:

Microsoft Reviewers

Vinay Ahuja (Architect), Dan Crevier, Marcelo Guerra Hahn, Helena Kotas, Eric Lippert, Kyrylo Osenkov (Visual C#) and Alex Turner (Visual C# Compiler Program Manager).

Other Industry Reviewers

Rizwan Ahmed a.k.a. RizwanSharp (C# MVP, Sr. Software Engineer, TEO), José Alarcón-Aguín (ASP.NET MVP, Krasis.com), Mostafa Arafa (C# MVP, Agility Logistics), Bonnie Berent (Microsoft C# MVP), Peter Bromberg (Senior Architect Merrill Lynch and C# MVP), Adam Calderon (C# MVP, InterKnowlogy), Stochio Goutsev (Independent Consultant, writer and developer and C# MVP), Octavio Hernandez (C# MVP, Advanced Bionics), Ged Mead (DevCity.Net, Microsoft VB MVP—Visual Developer) and José Antonio González Seco (Parliament of Andalusia).

Academic Reviewers

Mingsheng Hong (Cornell University), Stan Kurkovsky, Ph.D. (Central Connecticut State University), Markus Lumpe (Swinburne University of Technology), Gavin Osborne (Saskatchewan Institute of Applied Science and Technology) and Zijiang Yang (Western Michigan University).

Well, there you have it! Visual C# 2010 is a powerful programming language that will help you write programs quickly and effectively. It scales nicely into the realm of enterprise-systems development to help you build business-critical and mission-critical information systems. As you read the book, we'd appreciate your comments, criticisms, corrections and suggestions for improvement. Please address all correspondence to:

```
deitel@deitel.com
```

We'll respond promptly, and we'll post corrections and clarifications on the book's website:

```
www.deitel.com/books/csharpfp4/
```

We hope you enjoy reading *C# 2010 for Programmers, 4/e,* as much as we enjoyed writing it!

> *Paul J. Deitel*
> *Dr. Harvey M. Deitel*

About the Authors

Paul J. Deitel, CEO and Chief Technical Officer of Deitel & Associates, Inc., is a graduate of MIT, where he studied Information Technology. Through Deitel & Associates, Inc., he has delivered C#, Visual Basic, Java, C++, C and Internet programming courses to industry clients, including Cisco, IBM, Sun Microsystems, Dell, Siemens, Lucent Technologies, Fidelity, NASA at the Kennedy Space Center, the National Severe Storm Laboratory, White Sands Missile Range, Rogue Wave Software, Boeing, SunGard Higher Education, Stratus, Cambridge Technology Partners, One Wave, Hyperion Software,

Adra Systems, Entergy, CableData Systems, Nortel Networks, Puma, iRobot, Invensys and many more. He and his co-author, Dr. Harvey M. Deitel, are the world's best-selling programming-language textbook/professional book authors.

Dr. Harvey M. Deitel, Chairman and Chief Strategy Officer of Deitel & Associates, Inc., has 49 years of experience in the computer field. Dr. Deitel earned B.S. and M.S. degrees from MIT and a Ph.D. from Boston University. He has extensive industry and academic experience, including earning tenure and serving as the Chairman of the Computer Science Department at Boston College before founding Deitel & Associates, Inc., with his son, Paul J. Deitel. He and Paul are the co-authors of dozens of books and multimedia packages and they are writing many more. With translations published in Japanese, German, Russian, Chinese, Spanish, Koresan, French, Polish, Italian, Portuguese, Greek, Urdu and Turkish, the Deitels' texts have earned international recognition. Dr. Deitel has delivered hundreds of professional seminars to major corporations, academic institutions, government organizations and the military.

About Deitel & Associates, Inc.

Deitel & Associates, Inc., founded by Paul Deitel and Harvey Deitel, is an internationally recognized authoring, corporate training and software development organization specializing in computer programming languages, object technology, Android and iPhone app development, and Internet and web software technology. The company offers instructor-led training courses delivered at client sites worldwide on major programming languages and platforms, such as Visual C#®, Java™, C, C++, Visual Basic®, Objective-C and iPhone and iPad app development, Android app development, XML®, Python®, object technology, Internet and web programming, and a growing list of additional programming and software development courses. The company's clients include many of the world's largest companies, government agencies, branches of the military, and academic institutions.

Through its 34-year publishing partnership with Prentice Hall/Pearson, Deitel & Associates, Inc., publishes leading-edge programming professional books, college textbooks, and *LiveLessons* DVD- and web-based video courses. Deitel & Associates, Inc. and the authors can be reached at:

```
deitel@deitel.com
```

To learn more about Deitel's *Dive Into® Series* Corporate Training curriculum, visit:

```
www.deitel.com/training/
```

To request a proposal for on-site, instructor-led training at your company or organization, e-mail `deitel@deitel.com`.

Individuals wishing to purchase Deitel books and *LiveLessons* DVD training courses can do so through `www.deitel.com`. Bulk orders by corporations, the government, the military and academic institutions should be placed directly with Pearson. For more information, visit `www.pearsoned.com/professional/index.htm`.

Before You Begin

This section contains information you should review before using this book and instructions to ensure that your computer is set up properly for use with this book. We'll post updates to this Before You Begin section (if any) on the book's website:

```
www.deitel.com/books/csharpfp4/
```

Font and Naming Conventions

We use fonts to distinguish between features, such as menu names, menu items, and other elements that appear in the program-development environment. Our convention is to emphasize IDE features in a sans-serif bold **Helvetica** font (for example, **Properties** window) and to emphasize program text in a sans-serif Lucida font (for example, bool x = true).

A Note Regarding Software for the Book

This textbook includes a DVD which contains the Microsoft® Visual Studio® 2010 Express Edition integrated development environments for Visual C# 2010, Visual Basic 2010, Visual C++ 2010, Visual Web Developer 2010 and SQL Server 2008. The latest versions of these tools are also downloadable from www.microsoft.com/express. The Express Editions are fully functional, and there's no time limit for using the software. We discuss the setup of this software shortly. You do not need Visual Basic or Visual C++ for use with this book.

Hardware and Software Requirements for the Visual Studio 2010 Express Editions

To install and run the Visual Studio 2010 Express Editions, ensure that your system meets the minimum requirements specified at:

```
http://www.microsoft.com/express/support/default.aspx
```

Desktop Theme Settings for Windows 7 Users

If you are using Windows 7, we assume that your theme is set to **Windows 7**. Follow these steps to set **Windows 7** as your desktop theme:

1. Right click the desktop, then click **Personalize**.
2. Select the **Windows 7** theme.

Desktop Theme Settings for Windows Vista Users

If you are using Windows Vista, we assume that your theme is set to **Windows Vista**. Follow these steps to set **Windows Vista** as your desktop theme:

1. Right click the desktop, then click **Personalize**.
2. Click the **Theme** item. Select **Windows Vista** from the **Theme:** drop-down list.
3. Click **Apply** to save the settings.

Desktop Theme Settings for Windows XP Users

If you are using Windows XP, the windows you see on the screen will look slightly different from the screen captures in the book. We assume that your theme is set to **Windows XP**. Follow these steps to set **Windows XP** as your desktop theme:

1. Right click the desktop, then click **Properties**.

2. Click the **Themes** tab. Select **Windows XP** from the **Theme:** drop-down list.

3. Click **OK** to save the settings.

Viewing File Extensions

Several screenshots in *C# 2010 for Programmers, 4/e* display file names with file-name extensions (e.g., .txt, .cs or .png). Your system's settings may need to be adjusted to display file-name extensions. Follow these steps to configure your computer:

1. In the **Start** menu, select **All Programs**, then **Accessories**, then **Windows Explorer**.

2. In Windows 7 and Windows Vista, press *Alt* to display the menu bar, then select **Folder Options...** from **Windows Explorer**'s **Tools** menu. In Windows XP, simply select **Folder Options...** from **Windows Explorer**'s **Tools** menu.

3. In the dialog that appears, select the **View** tab.

4. In the **Advanced settings:** pane, uncheck the box to the left of the text **Hide extensions for known file types**. [*Note*: If this item is already unchecked, no action needs to be taken.]

5. Click OK to apply the setting and close the dialog.

Notes to Windows XP Users Regarding the Segoe UI Font Used in Many Applications

To make user interfaces more readable, Microsoft recommends using the Segoe UI font in Windows 7 and Windows Vista. This font is not available by default on Windows XP, but it is installed with the following software products: Windows Live Messenger, Windows Live Mail, Microsoft Office 2007 and Microsoft Office 2010. You can download Windows Live Messenger from explore.live.com/windows-live-messenger. You can downloadS Windows Live Mail from explore.live.com/windows-live-mail.

You must also enable ClearType on your system; otherwise, the font will not display correctly. ClearType is a technology for smoothing the edges of fonts displayed on the screen. To enable ClearType, perform the following steps:

1. Right click your desktop and select **Properties...** from the popup menu to view the **Display Properties** dialog.

2. In the dialog, click the **Appearance** tab, then click the **Effects...** button to display the **Effects** dialog.

3. In the **Effects** dialog, ensure that the **Use the following method to smooth edges of screen fonts** checkbox is checked, then select **ClearType** from the combobox below the checkbox.

4. Click **OK** to close the **Effects** dialog. Click **OK** to close the **Display Properties** dialog.

Obtaining the Code Examples

The examples for *C# 2010 for Programmers, 4/e* are available for download at

> www.deitel.com/books/csharpfp4q/

If you're not already registered at our website, go to www.deitel.com and click the **Register** link below our logo in the upper-left corner of the page. Fill in your information. There's no charge to register, and we do not share your information with anyone. We send you only account-management e-mails unless you register separately for our free e-mail newsletter at www.deitel.com/newsletter/subscribe.html. *You must enter a valid email address*. After registering, you'll receive a confirmation e-mail with your verification code. Click the link in the confirmation email to go to www.deitel.com and sign in.

Next, go to www.deitel.com/books/csharpfp4/. Click the **Examples** link to download the Examples.zip file to your computer. Write down the location where you choose to save the file on your computer.

We assume the examples are located at C:\Examples on your computer. Extract the contents of Examples.zip using a tool such as WinZip (www.winzip.com) or the built-in capabilities of Windows.

Installing the Software

Before you can run the applications in *C# 2010 for Programmers, 4/e* or build your own applications, you must install a development environment. We used Microsoft's free Visual C# 2010 Express Edition in the examples for most chapters and Visual Web Developer 2010 Express Edition for Chapters 19 and 27–29. Chapters 18, 27 and 28 also require SQL Server Express Edition. To install the Visual C# 2010 and Visual Web Developer 2010 Express Editions:

1. Insert the DVD that accompanies this book into your computer's DVD drive to launch the software installer. If the **Visual Studio 2010 Express Setup** window does not appear, use Windows Explorer to view the contents of the DVD drive and double click Setup.hta to launch the installer

2. In the **Visual Studio 2010 Express Setup** window, click **Visual C# 2010 Express** to display the **Visual C# 2010 Express Setup** window, then click **Next >**.

3. Carefully read the license agreement. Click the **I have read and accept the license terms** radio button to agree to the terms, then click **Next >**. [*Note:* If you do not accept the license agreement, the software will not install and you will not be able to create or execute Visual C# applications.]

4. Select the **MSDN Express Library for Visual Studio 2010, Microsoft SQL Server 2008 Express Edition (x86)** and **Microsoft Silverlight Runtime** options to install. Click **Next >**. [*Note:* Installing the MSDN documentation is not required but is highly recommended.]

5. Click **Next >**, then click **Finish >** to continue with the installation. The installer will now begin copying the files required by Visual C# 2010 Express Edition and SQL Server 2008 Express Edition. Wait for the installation to complete before proceeding—the installation process can be quite lengthy and might require you to reboot your computer. When the installation completes, click **Exit**.

6. In the **Visual Studio 2010 Express Setup** window, click **Visual Web Developer 2010 Express** to display the **Visual Web Developer 2010 Express Setup** window, then click **Next >**.

7. Carefully read the license agreement. Click the **I have read and accept the license terms** radio button to agree to the terms, then click **Next >**. [*Note:* If you do not accept the license agreement, the software will not install and you will not be able to create or execute web applications with Visual Web Developer.]

8. Click **Install >** to continue with the installation. The installer will now begin copying the files required by Visual Web Developer 2010 Express Edition. This portion of the install process should be much faster, since you've already installed most of the supporting software and files required by Visual Web Developer. When the installation completes, click **Exit**.

Miscellaneous Notes

- Some people like to change the workspace layout in the development tools. You can return the tools to their default layouts by selecting **Window > Reset Window Layout**.

- There are differences between the full Visual Studio 2010 products and the Express Edition products we use in this book, such as additional menu items. One key difference is that the **Database Explorer** we refer to in Chapters 18, 27 and 28 is called the **Server Explorer** in the full Visual Studio 2010 products.

- Many of the menu items we use in the book have corresponding icons shown with each menu item in the menus. Many of the icons also appear on one of the toolbars at the top of the development environment. As you become familiar with these icons, you can use the toolbars to help speed up your development time. Similarly, many of the menu items have keyboard shortcuts (also shown with each menu item in the menus) for accessing commands quickly.

Introduction

OBJECTIVES

In this chapter you'll learn:

■ The history of the Visual C# programming language.

■ Some basics of object technology.

■ The importance of XML as a data-representation scheme.

■ About Microsoft's .NET initiative, which involves the Internet in developing and using software systems.

■ About the .NET Framework and the Common Language Runtime.

■ To test-drive a Visual C# 2010 drawing application.

1.1 Introduction

Welcome to Visual C# 2010, one of the world's fastest-growing object-oriented programming languages! We hope that working with *C# 2010 for Programmers, 4/e* will be an informative, challenging and entertaining learning experience for you.

Perhaps most important, the book presents hundreds of complete, working C# programs and depicts their inputs and outputs. We call this the **live-code approach.** You can download all the book's source code from www.deitel.com/books/csharpfp4/.

As you proceed, if you have any questions, send an e-mail to

    deitel@deitel.com

To keep current with C# developments at Deitel & Associates and to receive updates to this book, subscribe to our e-mail newsletter, the *Deitel® Buzz Online,* at

    www.deitel.com/newsletter/subscribe.html

check out our growing list of C# and related Resource Centers at

    www.deitel.com/ResourceCenters.html

and follow us on Twitter (@deitel) and Facebook (www.deitel.com/deitelfan).

1.2 Microsoft's Windows® Operating System

Microsoft became the dominant software company in the 1980s and 1990s. In the mid-1980s, Microsoft developed the **Windows operating system**, consisting of a graphical user interface built on top of DOS (a personal computer operating system that users interacted with by typing commands). The Windows operating system became incredibly popular after the 1993 release of Windows 3.1, whose successors, Windows 95 and Windows 98, virtually cornered the desktop operating systems market by the late 1990s. These operating systems, which borrowed from many concepts (such as icons, menus and windows) popularized by early Apple Macintosh operating systems, enabled users to work with multiple applications simultaneously. Microsoft entered the corporate operating systems market with the 1993 release of Windows NT. Windows XP was released in 2001 and combined Microsoft's corporate and consumer operating system lines. Windows Vista, released in 2007, offered the attractive new Aero user interface, many powerful enhancements and new applications. A key focus of Windows Vista was enhanced security. Windows 7 is Microsoft's latest operating system—its features include enhancements to the Aero user interface, faster startup times, further refinement of Vista's security features, touch screen and multi-touch support, and more. This book is intended for Windows XP,

Windows Vista and Windows 7 users. Windows is by far the world's most widely used operating system.

1.3 C, C++, Objective-C and Java

The **C** programming language was developed in the early 1970s. C first gained widespread recognition as the development language of the UNIX operating system. C is a hardware-independent language, and, with careful design, it's possible to write C programs that are portable to most computers.

C++, developed in the early 1980s, provides several features that "spruce up" the C language, and, more importantly, capabilities for **object-oriented programming** (OOP). **Objects** are reusable software **components** that model items in the real world. A modular, object-oriented approach to design and implementation can make software development groups much more *productive* than is possible using earlier programming techniques.

The **Objective-C** programming language, also developed in the early 1980s, added capabilities for object-oriented programming (OOP) to the C programming language. It eventually became the software development language for Apple's Macintosh. Its use has exploded as the app development language for Apple's popular iPod, iPhone and iPad consumer devices.

Microprocessors are having a profound impact in intelligent consumer electronic devices. Recognizing this, Sun Microsystems in 1991 funded an internal corporate research project that resulted in the development of a C++-based language, which Sun eventually called **Java**. As the World Wide Web exploded in popularity in 1993, Sun saw the possibility of using Java to add **dynamic content** (for example, interactivity, animations and the like) to web pages. Sun announced the language in 1995. This generated immediate interest in the business community because of the commercial potential of the web. Java is now used to develop large-scale enterprise applications, to enhance the functionality of web servers, to provide applications for consumer devices (such as cell phones, pagers and smartphones) and for many other purposes.

1.4 C#

In 2000, Microsoft announced the **C#** (pronounced "C-Sharp") programming language—created specifically for the .NET platform (discussed in Sections 1.6–1.7). C# has roots in C, C++ and Java. Like Visual Basic, C# is object oriented and has access to the powerful **.NET Framework Class Library**—a vast collection of prebuilt components, enabling you to develop applications quickly. Both languages have similar capabilities to Java and are appropriate for the most demanding application development tasks, especially for building today's enterprise applications, and web-based and mobile applications.

C# is *object oriented*—you'll learn some basics of object technology shortly and will study a rich treatment later in the book. C# is **event driven**—you'll write programs that respond to user-initiated **events** such as mouse clicks, keystrokes and timer expirations. Microsoft's Visual C# is indeed a *visual programming language*—in addition to writing program statements to build portions of your applications, you'll also use Visual Studio's graphical user interface to conveniently drag and drop predefined objects like buttons and textboxes into place on your screen, and label and resize them. Visual Studio will write much of the GUI code for you.

C# has been standardized internationally, enabling other implementations of the language besides Microsoft's Visual C#, such as Mono (www.mono-project.com).

1.5 Extensible Markup Language (XML)

As the popularity of the web exploded, HTML's limitations became apparent. HTML's lack of **extensibility** (the ability to change or add features) frustrated developers, and its ambiguous definition allowed erroneous HTML to proliferate. The need for a standardized, fully extensible and structurally strict language was apparent. As a result, XML was developed by the W3C.

Data independence, the separation of content from its presentation, is the essential characteristic of XML. Because XML documents describe data, any application conceivably can process them. Software developers are integrating XML into their applications to improve web functionality and interoperability.

XML isn't limited to web applications. For example, it's increasingly used in databases—an XML document's structure enables it to be integrated easily with database applications. As applications become more web enabled, it's likely that XML will become the universal technology for data representation. Applications employing XML would be able to communicate with one another, provided that they could understand their respective XML markup schemes, or **vocabularies**. Microsoft's .NET technologies use XML to mark up and transfer data over the Internet, and to enable software components to interoperate.

1.6 Introduction to Microsoft .NET

In 2000, Microsoft announced its **.NET initiative** (www.microsoft.com/net), a broad new vision for using the Internet and the web in the development, engineering, distribution and use of software. Rather than forcing developers to use a single programming language, the .NET initiative permits developers to create .NET applications in *any* .NET-compatible language (such as C#, Visual Basic, and others). Part of the initiative includes Microsoft's **ASP.NET** technology, which allows you to create web applications.

The .NET strategy extends the idea of **software reuse** to the Internet by allowing you to concentrate on your specialties without having to implement every component of every application. Visual programming (which you'll learn throughout this book) has become popular because it enables you to create Windows and web applications easily, using such prepackaged controls as **buttons**, **textboxes** and **scrollbars**.

The **.NET Framework** is at the heart of Microsoft's .NET strategy. This framework executes applications, includes the .NET Framework Class Library and provides many other programming capabilities that you'll use to build C# applications.

1.7 The .NET Framework and the Common Language Runtime

The details of the .NET Framework are found in the **Common Language Infrastructure** (**CLI**), which contains information about the storage of data types (that is, data that has predefined characteristics such as a date, percentage or currency amount), objects and so on. The CLI has been standardized, making it easier to implement the .NET Framework for other platforms. This is like publishing the blueprints of the framework—anyone can build it by following the specifications.

The **Common Language Runtime (CLR)** is the central part of the .NET Framework—it executes .NET programs. Programs are compiled into machine-specific instructions in two steps. First, the program is compiled into **Microsoft Intermediate Language (MSIL)**, which defines instructions for the CLR. Code converted into MSIL from other languages and sources can be woven together by the CLR. The MSIL for an application's components is placed into the application's executable file. When the application executes, another compiler (known as the **just-in-time compiler** or **JIT compiler**) in the CLR translates the MSIL in the executable file into machine-language code (for a particular platform), then the machine-language code executes on that platform.

If the .NET Framework is installed on a platform, that platform can run any .NET program. A program's ability to run (without modification) across multiple platforms is known as **platform independence**. Code written once can be used on another type of computer without modification, saving time and money. Software can also target a wider audience—previously, companies had to decide whether converting their programs to different platforms (sometimes called **porting**) was worth the cost. With .NET, porting programs is no longer an issue (at least once .NET itself has been made available on the platforms).

The .NET Framework also provides a high level of **language interoperability**. Programs written in different languages (for example, C# and Visual Basic) are all compiled into MSIL—the different parts can be combined to create a single unified program. MSIL allows the .NET Framework to be **language independent**, because .NET programs are not tied to a particular programming language.

The .NET Framework Class Library can be used by any .NET language. The library contains a variety of reusable components, saving you the trouble of creating new components. This book explains how to develop .NET software with C#.

1.8 Test-Driving the Advanced Painter Application

In this section, you'll "test-drive" an existing application that enables you to draw on the screen using the mouse. The **Advanced Painter** application allows you to draw with different brush sizes and colors. The elements and functionality you see in this application are typical of what you'll learn to program in this text. The following steps show you how to test-drive the application. You'll run and interact with the working application.

1. *Checking your setup.* Confirm that you've set up your computer properly by reading the Before You Begin section located after the Preface.

2. *Locating the application directory.* Open a Windows Explorer window and navigate to the C:\examples\ch01 directory (Fig. 1.1)—we assume you placed the examples in the C:\examples folder.

3. *Running the Advanced Painter application.* Now that you're in the proper directory, double click the file name AdvancedPainter.exe (Fig. 1.1) to run the application (Fig. 1.2). [*Note:* Depending on your system configuration, Windows Explorer might not display file name extensions. To display file name extensions (like .exe in Fig. 1.1), type *Alt + T* in Windows Explorer to open the **Tools** menu, then select **Folder options....** In the **Folder Options** window, select the **View** tab, uncheck **Hide extensions for known file types** and click **OK.**]

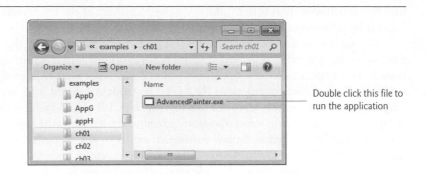

Double click this file to run the application

Fig. 1.1 | Contents of C:\examples\ch01.

Figure 1.2 labels several graphical elements—called **controls**. These include GroupBoxes, RadioButtons, a Panel and Buttons (these controls and many others are discussed in depth throughout the text). The application allows you to draw with a red, blue, green or black brush of small, medium or large size. You can also undo your previous operation or clear the drawing to start from scratch.

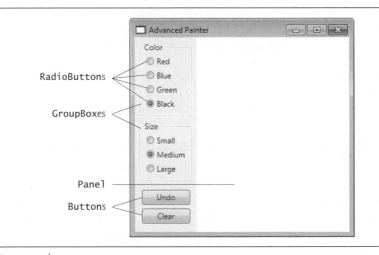

Fig. 1.2 | C# **Advanced Painter** application.

By using existing controls—which are objects—you can create powerful applications much faster than if you had to write all the code yourself.

The brush's properties, selected in the RadioButtons labeled **Black** and **Medium**, are *default settings*—the initial settings you see when you first run the application. Programmers include default settings to provide reasonable choices that the application will use if the user chooses not to change the settings. Default settings also provide visual cues for users to choose their own settings. Now you'll choose your own settings as a user of this application.

4. *Changing the brush color and size.* Click the RadioButton labeled **Red** to change the color of the brush, then click **Small** to change the size of the brush. Position

the mouse over the white Panel, then press and hold down the left mouse button to draw with the brush. Draw flower petals, as shown in Fig. 1.3.

Fig. 1.3 | Drawing with a new brush color.

5. *Changing the brush size.* Click the RadioButton labeled **Green** to change the color of the brush again. Then, click the RadioButton labeled **Large** to change the size of the brush. Draw grass and a flower stem, as shown in Fig. 1.4.

Fig. 1.4 | Drawing with a new brush size.

6. *Finishing the drawing.* Click the **Blue** and **Medium** RadioButtons. Draw raindrops, as shown in Fig. 1.5, to complete the drawing.

7. *Closing the application.* Close your running application by clicking its **close box**, ▣ (Fig. 1.5).

Close box

Fig. 1.5 | Finishing the drawing.

1.9 Introduction to Object Technology

When object-oriented programming became widely used in the 1980s and 1990s, it dramatically improved the software development process. What are objects, and why are they special? **Object technology** is a scheme for creating meaningful software units. There are date objects, time objects, paycheck objects, invoice objects, automobile objects, people objects, audio objects, video objects, file objects, record objects and so on. On your computer screen, there are button objects, textbox objects, menu objects and many more. In fact, almost any *noun* can be reasonably represented as a software object. Objects have **attributes** (also called **properties**), such as color, size, weight and speed; and perform **actions** (also called **methods** or **behaviors**), such as moving, sleeping or drawing.

Classes are types of related objects. For example, all cars belong to the "car" class, even though individual cars vary in make, model, color and options packages. A class specifies the attributes and actions available to an object of its class. An object is related to its class in much the same way as a building is related to the blueprint from which the building is constructed. Contractors can build many buildings from the same blueprint; programmers can instantiate (create) many objects from the same class.

With object technology, properly designed classes can be *reused* on future projects. Some organizations report that another key benefit they get from object-oriented programming is the production of software that's better organized and has fewer maintenance requirements than software produced with earlier technologies.

Object orientation allows you to focus on the "big picture." Instead of worrying about the details of how reusable objects are implemented, you focus on the behaviors and interactions of objects. A road map that showed every tree, house and driveway would be difficult to read. When such details are removed and only the essential information (roads) remains, the map becomes easier to understand. In the same way, an application that is divided into objects is easy to understand, modify and update because it hides much of the detail.

It's clear that object-oriented programming will be the key programming methodology for the next several decades. C# is one of the world's most widely used object-oriented languages, especially in the Microsoft software development community.

Basic Object-Technology Concepts

Object-oriented design (**OOD**) models software in terms similar to those that people use to describe real-world objects. It takes advantage of class relationships, where objects of a certain class, such as a class of vehicles, have the same characteristics—cars, trucks, little red wagons and roller skates have much in common. OOD takes advantage of **inheritance** relationships, where new classes of objects are derived by absorbing characteristics of existing classes and adding unique characteristics of their own. An object of class "convertible" certainly has the characteristics of the more general class "automobile," but more specifically, the roof goes up and down.

Object-oriented design provides a natural and intuitive way to view the software design process—namely, modeling objects by their attributes, behaviors and interrelationships, just as we describe real-world objects. OOD also models communication between objects. Just as people send messages to one another (for example, a sergeant commands a soldier to stand at attention), objects also communicate via messages. A bank-account object may receive a message to decrease its balance by a certain amount because the customer is withdrawing that amount of money.

OOD **encapsulates** (that is, wraps) attributes and **operations** (behaviors) into objects—an object's attributes and operations are intimately tied together. Objects have the property of **information hiding**. Objects may know how to communicate with one another across well-defined **interfaces**, but normally they're not allowed to know how other objects are implemented—such details are hidden within the objects themselves. You can drive a car effectively, for example, without knowing the details of how engines, transmissions, brakes and exhaust systems work internally—as long as you know how to use the accelerator pedal, the brake pedal, the steering wheel and so on. Information hiding, as you'll see, is crucial to good software engineering.

Classes, Fields and Methods

As a C# programmer, you'll concentrate on creating your own classes. Each class contains data as well as the set of methods that manipulate that data and provide services to **clients** (that is, other classes that *use* the class). The data components of a class are called attributes or **fields**. For example, a bank account class might include an account number and a balance. The operation components of a class are called methods. For example, a bank-account class might include methods to make a deposit (increase the balance), make a withdrawal (decrease the balance) and inquire what the current balance is.

Classes are to objects as blueprints are to houses—a class is a "plan" for building objects of the class. Just as we can build many houses from one blueprint, we can instantiate (create) many objects from one class. You *cannot* cook meals in the kitchen of a blueprint, but you *can* cook meals in the kitchen of a house. Packaging software as classes makes it possible for future software systems to reuse the classes.

Software Engineering Observation 1.1

Reuse of existing classes when building new classes and programs saves time, money and effort. Reuse also helps you build better systems, because existing classes and components often have gone through extensive testing, debugging and performance tuning.

You'll be *using existing classes and making objects of those classes* throughout the entire book. In Chapter 4, you'll begin building your own *customized* classes.

With object technology, you can build much of the new software you'll need by *combining existing classes*, just as automobile manufacturers combine *standardized interchangeable parts*. Each class you create will have the potential to become a valuable *software asset* that you and other programmers can reuse to speed future software development efforts.

Introduction to Object-Oriented Analysis and Design (OOAD)

To create the best solutions, you should follow a detailed process for determining your project's **requirements** (that is, *what* your system is supposed to do) and developing a **design** that satisfies them (that is, deciding *how* your system should do it). Ideally, you would go through this process and carefully review the design (and have your design reviewed by other software professionals) before writing any code. If this process involves analyzing and designing your system from an object-oriented point of view, it's called **object-oriented analysis and design** (**OOAD**). Proper analysis and design can help avoid an ill-planned system development approach that has to be abandoned partway through its implementation, possibly wasting considerable time, money and effort. Although many different OOAD processes exist, a single graphical language known as the **UML** (**Unified Modeling Language**) for communicating the results of *any* OOAD process has come into wide use. We introduce some simple UML diagrams in the early chapters and present a richer treatment in the ATM OOD case study (Chapters 30–31).

1.10 Wrap-Up

This chapter introduced basic object-technology concepts, including classes, objects, attributes and behaviors. We discussed the different types of programming languages and some widely used languages. We presented a brief history of Microsoft's Windows operating system. We discussed the history of the C# programming language and Microsoft's .NET initiative, which allows you to program Internet and web-based applications using C# (and other languages). You learned the steps for executing a C# application and you test-drove the **Advanced Painter** C# application that we create later in the book.

In the next chapter, you'll use the Visual Studio IDE (Integrated Development Environment) to create your first C# application, using the techniques of visual programming. You'll also become familiar with Visual Studio's help features.

2

Dive Into® Visual C# 2010 Express

Seeing is believing.
—Proverb

Form ever follows function.
—Louis Henri Sullivan

Intelligence ... is the faculty of making artificial objects, especially tools to make tools.
—Henri-Louis Bergson

OBJECTIVES

In this chapter you'll learn:

- The basics of the Visual Studio Integrated Development Environment (IDE) that assists you in writing, running and debugging your Visual C# programs.

- Visual Studio's help features.

- Key commands contained in the IDE's menus and toolbars.

- The purpose of the various kinds of windows in the Visual Studio 2010 IDE.

- What visual programming is and how it simplifies and speeds program development.

- To create, compile and execute a simple Visual C# program that displays text and an image using the Visual Studio IDE and the technique of visual programming.

2.1 Introduction

Visual Studio 2010 is Microsoft's Integrated Development Environment (IDE) for creating, running and debugging programs (also called **applications**) written in various .NET programming languages. This chapter provides an overview of the Visual Studio 2010 IDE and shows how to create a simple Visual C# program by dragging and dropping predefined building blocks into place—a technique known as **visual programming**.

2.2 Overview of the Visual Studio 2010 IDE

There are several Visual Studio versions. This book's examples are based on the **Visual C# 2010 Express Edition**. See the Before You Begin section that follows the Preface for information on installing the software. We assume that you're familiar with Windows.

Introduction to Microsoft Visual C# 2010 Express Edition
We use the > character to indicate the selection of a menu item from a menu. For example, we use the notation **File > Open File…** to indicate that you should select the **Open File…** menu item from the **File** menu.

To start Microsoft Visual C# 2010 Express Edition, select **Start > All Programs > Microsoft Visual Studio 2010 Express > Microsoft Visual C# 2010 Express**. Once the Express Edition begins execution, the **Start Page** displays (Fig. 2.1). Depending on your version of Visual Studio, your **Start Page** may look different. The **Start Page** contains a list of links to Visual Studio 2010 IDE resources and web-based resources. At any time, you can return to the **Start Page** by selecting **View > Start Page**.

Links on the Start Page
The **Start Page** links are organized into sections—**Recent Projects**, **Get Started** and **Latest News**—that contain links to helpful programming resources. Clicking any link on the **Start Page** displays relevant information associated with the specific link. [*Note:* An Internet connection is required for the IDE to access some of this information.] We refer to single clicking with the left mouse button as selecting or clicking. We refer to double clicking with the left mouse button simply as double clicking.

The **Recent Projects** section contains information on projects you've recently created or modified. You can also open existing projects or create new ones by clicking the links above this section. The **Get Started** section focuses on using the IDE for creating programs and learning Visual C#.

New Project button   Start Page tab   Latest News tab   Solution Explorer (no projects open)

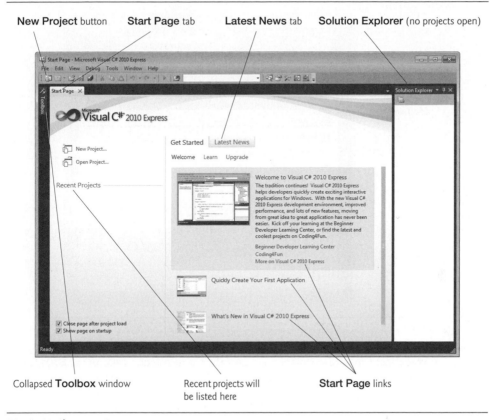

Collapsed **Toolbox** window   Recent projects will   **Start Page** links
                                be listed here

Fig. 2.1 | **Start Page** in Visual C# 2010 Express Edition.

The **Latest News** tab provides links to the latest Visual C# developments (such as updates and bug fixes) and to information on advanced programming topics. To access more extensive information on Visual Studio, you can browse the **MSDN (Microsoft Developer Network)** library at msdn.microsoft.com/en-us/library/default.aspx. The MSDN site contains articles, downloads and tutorials on technologies of interest to Visual Studio developers. You can also browse the web from the IDE by selecting **View > Other Windows > Web Browser**. To request a web page, type its URL into the location bar (Fig. 2.2) and press the *Enter* key—your computer, of course, must be connected to the Internet. The web page that you wish to view appears as another tab in the IDE (Fig. 2.2).

Customizing the IDE and Creating a New Project
To begin programming in Visual C#, you must create a new project or open an existing one. Select either **File > New Project...** to create a new project or **File > Open Project...** to open an existing project. From the **Start Page**, above the **Recent Projects** section, you can also click the links **New Project...** or **Open Project....** A **project** is a group of related files, such as the Visual C# code and any images that might make up a program. Visual Studio 2010 organizes programs into projects and **solutions**, which contain one or more projects. Multiple-project solutions are used to create large-scale programs. Most of the programs we create in this book consist of a single project.

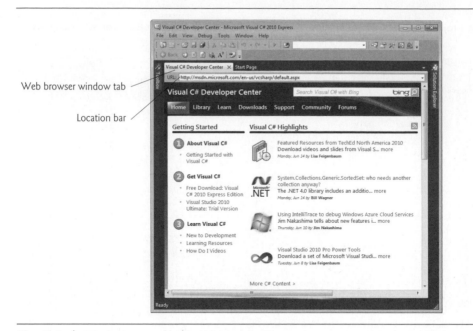

Web browser window tab

Location bar

Fig. 2.2 | Displaying a web page in Visual Studio.

When you select **File > New Project...** or click the **New Project...** link on the **Start Page**, the **New Project** dialog (Fig. 2.3) displays. **Dialogs** are windows that facilitate user–computer communication.

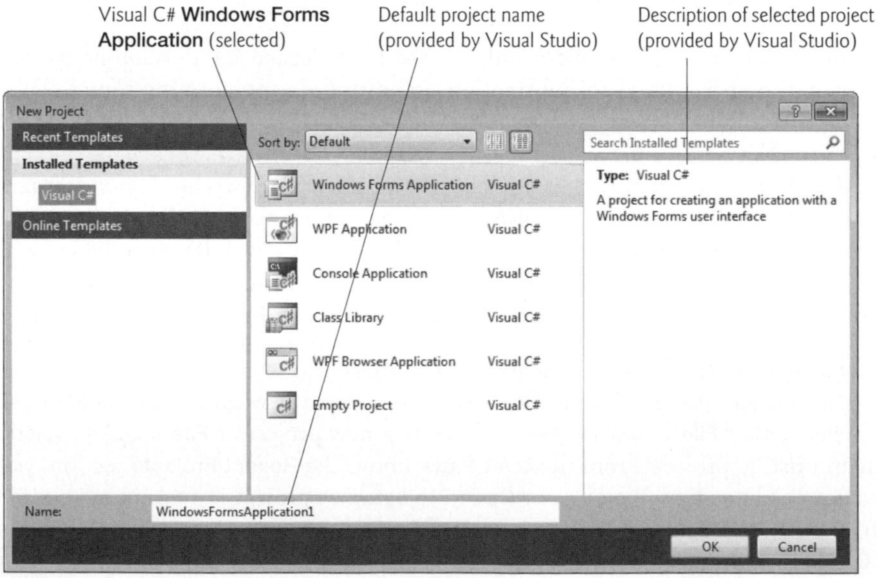

Visual C# **Windows Forms Application** (selected)

Default project name (provided by Visual Studio)

Description of selected project (provided by Visual Studio)

Fig. 2.3 | New Project dialog.

Visual Studio provides several templates (Fig. 2.3). **Templates** are the project types users can create in Visual C#—Windows Forms applications, console applications, WPF applications and others. In this chapter, we build a **Windows Forms Application**. Such an application executes within a Windows operating system (such as Windows 7) and typically has a **graphical user interface (GUI)**—the visual part of the program with which the user interacts. Windows applications include Microsoft software products like Microsoft Word, Internet Explorer and Visual Studio; software products created by other vendors; and customized software that you and other programmers create.

By default, Visual Studio assigns the name **WindowsFormsApplication1** to a new **Windows Forms Application** project and solution (Fig. 2.3). Select **Windows Forms Application**, then click **OK** to display the IDE in **Design view** (Fig. 2.4), which contains the features that enable you to create programs.

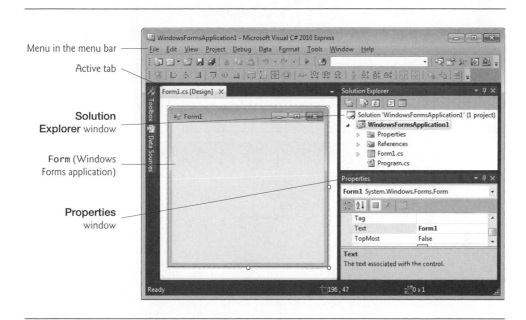

Fig. 2.4 | **Design** view of the IDE.

The rectangle in the **Design** area titled **Form1** (called a **Form**) represents the main window of the application that you're creating. Visual C# applications can have multiple Forms (windows)—however, most applications you'll create in this text will use only one Form. You'll learn how to customize the Form by adding GUI **controls**—in this example, you'll add a Label and a PictureBox (as you'll see in Fig. 2.25). A **Label** typically contains descriptive text (for example, "Welcome to Visual C#!"), and a **PictureBox** displays an image, such as the Deitel bug mascot. Visual C# Express has many preexisting controls and other components you can use to build and customize your programs.

In this chapter, you'll work with preexisting controls from the .NET Framework Class Library. As you place controls on the Form, you'll be able to modify their properties. For example, Fig. 2.5 shows where the Form's title can be modified and Fig. 2.6 shows a dialog in which a control's font properties can be modified.

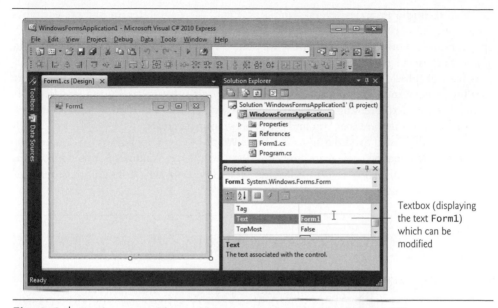

Fig. 2.5 | Textbox control for modifying a property in the Visual Studio IDE.

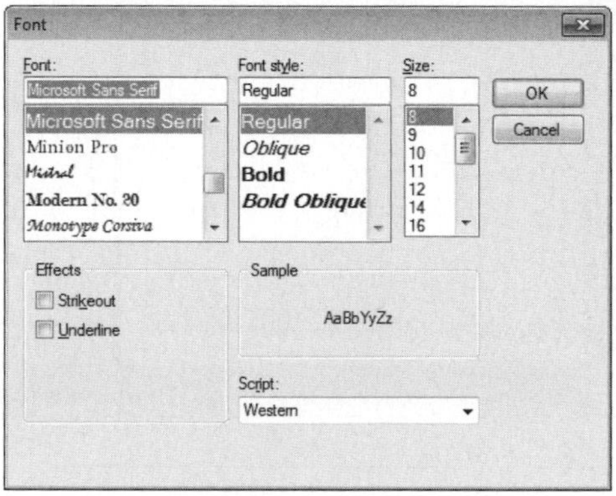

Fig. 2.6 | Dialog for modifying a control's font properties.

Collectively, the Form and controls make up the program's GUI. Users enter data (**inputs**) into the program by typing at the keyboard, by clicking the mouse buttons and in a variety of other ways. Programs use the GUI to display instructions and other information (**outputs**) for users to view. For example, the **New Project** dialog in Fig. 2.3 presents a GUI where the user clicks the mouse button to select a template type, then inputs a project name from the keyboard (the figure is still showing the default project name **WindowsFormsApplication1** supplied by Visual Studio).

Each open file name is listed on a tab. To view a document when multiple documents are open, click its tab. Tabs facilitate easy access to multiple open documents. The **active tab** (the tab of the currently displayed document) is highlighted in yellow (for example, **Form1.cs [Design]** in Fig. 2.4).

2.3 Menu Bar and Toolbar

Commands for managing the IDE and for developing, maintaining and executing programs are contained in **menus**, which are located on the **menu bar** of the IDE (Fig. 2.7). The set of menus displayed depends on what you're currently doing in the IDE.

| File | Edit | View | Project | Debug | Data | Format | Tools | Window | Help |

Fig. 2.7 | Visual Studio menu bar.

Menus contain groups of related commands (also called **menu items**) that, when selected, cause the IDE to perform specific actions. For example, new projects are created by selecting **File > New Project…**. The menus depicted in Fig. 2.7 are summarized in Fig. 2.8.

Menu	Description
File	Contains commands for opening, closing, adding and saving projects, as well as printing project data and exiting Visual Studio.
Edit	Contains commands for editing programs, such as cut, copy, paste, undo, redo, delete, find and select.
View	Contains commands for displaying IDE windows (for example, **Solution Explorer, Toolbox, Properties** window) and for adding toolbars to the IDE.
Project	Contains commands for managing projects and their files.
Debug	Contains commands for compiling, debugging (that is, identifying and correcting problems in programs) and running programs.
Data	Contains commands for interacting with databases (that is, organized collections of data stored on computers), which we discuss in Chapter 18, Databases and LINQ.
Format	Contains commands for arranging and modifying a **Form**'s controls. The **Format** menu appears only when a GUI component is selected in **Design** view.
Tools	Contains commands for accessing additional IDE tools and options for customizing the IDE.
Window	Contains commands for hiding, opening, closing and displaying IDE windows.
Help	Contains commands for accessing the IDE's help features.

Fig. 2.8 | Summary of Visual Studio 2010 IDE menus.

You can access many of the more common menu commands from the **toolbar** (Fig. 2.9), which contains graphics, called **icons**, that graphically represent commands. By default, the standard toolbar is displayed when you run Visual Studio for the first time—it contains icons for the most commonly used commands, such as opening a file, adding an item to a project, saving files and running applications (Fig. 2.9). The icons that appear on the standard toolbar may vary, depending on the version of Visual Studio you're using. Some commands are initially disabled (grayed out or unavailable to use). These commands are enabled by Visual Studio only when they're necessary. For example, Visual Studio enables the command for saving a file once you begin editing a file.

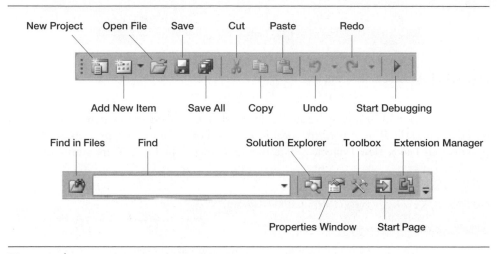

Fig. 2.9 | Standard Visual Studio toolbar.

You can customize the IDE's toolbars. Select **View > Toolbars** (Fig. 2.10). Each toolbar you select is displayed with the other toolbars at the top of the Visual Studio window. To execute a command via the toolbar, click its icon. Some icons contain a down arrow that you can click to display related commands, as shown in Fig. 2.11.

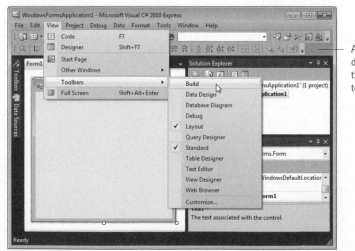

Additional toolbars are displayed at the top of the IDE with the other toolbars

Fig. 2.10 | Adding the **Build** toolbar to the IDE.

Fig. 2.11 | IDE toolbar icon showing additional commands.

It can be difficult to remember what each toolbar icon represents. Hovering the mouse pointer over an icon highlights it and, after a brief pause, displays a description of the icon called a tool tip (Fig. 2.12). **Tool tips** help you become familiar with the IDE's features and serve as useful reminders for each toolbar icon's functionality.

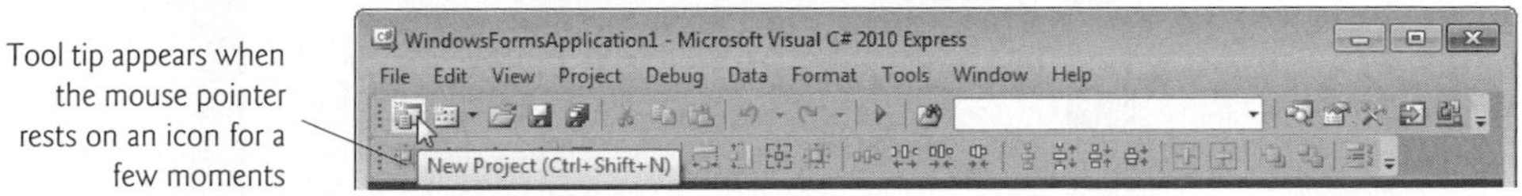

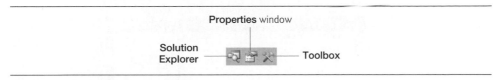

Fig. 2.12 | Tool tip demonstration.

2.4 Navigating the Visual Studio IDE

The IDE provides windows for accessing project files and customizing controls. This section introduces several windows that you'll use frequently when developing Visual C# programs. These windows can be accessed via the toolbar icons (Fig. 2.13) or by selecting the desired window's name from **View > Other Windows**.

Properties window

Solution Explorer ———— **Toolbox**

Fig. 2.13 | Toolbar icons for three Visual Studio windows.

Visual Studio provides a space-saving feature called **auto-hide**. When auto-hide is enabled, a tab appears along either the left, right or bottom edge of the IDE window (Fig. 2.14). This tab contains one or more icons, each of which identifies a hidden window. Placing the mouse pointer over one of these icons displays that window (Fig. 2.15). Moving the mouse pointer outside the window's area hides the window. To "pin down" a window (that is, to disable auto-hide and keep the window open), click the pin icon. When auto-hide is enabled, the pin icon is horizontal (Fig. 2.15)—when a window is "pinned down," the pin icon is vertical (Fig. 2.16).

The next few sections cover three of Visual Studio's main windows—the **Solution Explorer**, the **Properties** window and the **Toolbox**. These windows display project information and include tools that help you build your programs.

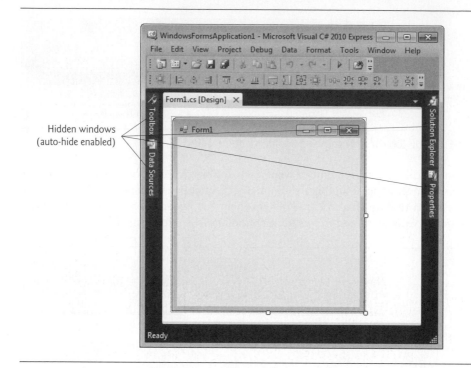

Hidden windows (auto-hide enabled)

Fig. 2.14 | Auto-hide feature demonstration.

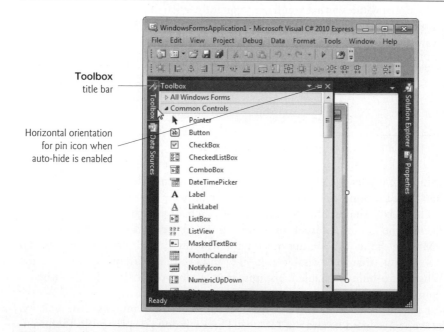

Toolbox title bar

Horizontal orientation for pin icon when auto-hide is enabled

Fig. 2.15 | Displaying a hidden window when auto-hide is enabled.

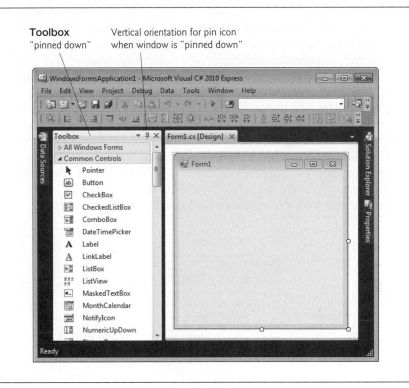

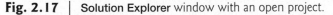

Fig. 2.16 | Disabling auto-hide ("pinning down" a window).

2.4.1 Solution Explorer

The **Solution Explorer** window (Fig. 2.17) provides access to all of a solution's files. If it's not shown in the IDE, click the **Solution Explorer** icon in the IDE (Fig. 2.13), select **View > Other Windows > Solution Explorer** or type *<Ctrl> <Alt> L*. When you open a new or existing solution, the **Solution Explorer** displays the solution's contents.

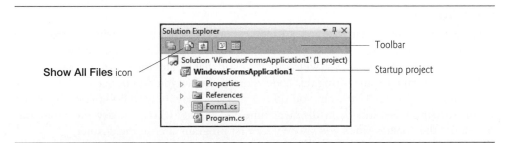

Fig. 2.17 | **Solution Explorer** window with an open project.

The solution's **startup project** is the one that runs when you select **Debug > Start Debugging** (or press the *F5* key). For a single-project solution like the examples in this book, the startup project is the only project (in this case, **WindowsFormsApplication1**) and the project name appears in bold text in the **Solution Explorer** window. When you create an application for the first time, the **Solution Explorer** window lists entries for the project's **Properties** and **References**, and the files Form1.cs and Program.cs (Fig. 2.17). The Visual C# file that corresponds to the Form shown in Fig. 2.4 is named Form1.cs (selected in Fig. 2.17). Visual C# files use the .cs file-name extension.

By default, the IDE displays only files that you may need to edit—other files that the IDE generates are hidden. The **Solution Explorer** window includes a toolbar that contains several icons. Clicking the **Show All Files** icon (Fig. 2.17) displays all the solution's files, including those generated by the IDE. Clicking the arrows to the left of a file or folder expands or collapses the project tree's nodes. Try clicking the arrow to the left of **References** to display items grouped under that heading (Fig. 2.18). Click the arrow again to collapse the tree. Other Visual Studio windows also use this convention.

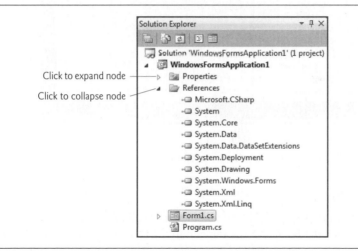

Fig. 2.18 | **Solution Explorer** with the **References** node expanded.

2.4.2 Toolbox

The **Toolbox** (**View > Other Windows > Toolbox**) contains icons representing controls used to customize Forms (Fig. 2.19). With visual programming, you can "drag and drop" controls onto the Form and the IDE will write the code that creates the controls for you. This is faster and simpler than writing this code yourself. Just as you do not need to know how to build an engine to drive a car, you do not need to know how to build controls to use them. Reusing preexisting controls saves time and money when you develop programs. You'll use the **Toolbox** when you create your first program later in the chapter.

The **Toolbox** groups the prebuilt controls into categories—**All Windows Forms, Common Controls, Containers, Menus & Toolbars, Data, Components, Printing, Dialogs, WPF Interoperability** and **General** are listed in Fig. 2.19. Again, note the use of arrows, which can expand or collapse a group of controls. We discuss many of the **Toolbox**'s controls and their functionality throughout the book.

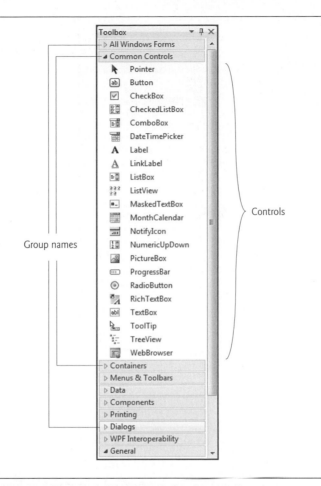

Group names

Controls

Fig. 2.19 | **Toolbox** window displaying controls for the **Common Controls** group.

2.4.3 Properties Window

To display the **Properties** window, select **View > Other Windows > Properties Window** or click the **Properties** window toolbar icon shown in Fig. 2.13. The **Properties window** displays the properties for the currently selected Form (Fig. 2.20), control or file in **Design** view. **Properties** specify information about the Form or control, such as its size, color and position. Each Form or control has its own set of properties—a property's description is displayed at the bottom of the **Properties** window whenever that property is selected.

Figure 2.20 shows Form1's **Properties** window. The left column lists the names of the Form's properties—the right column displays the current value of each property. You can sort the properties either alphabetically (by clicking the **Alphabetical icon**) or categorically (by clicking the **Categorized icon**). The properties can be sorted alphabetically from A to Z or Z to A—sorting by category groups the properties according to their use (that is, **Appearance**, **Behavior**, **Design**, etc.). Depending on the size of the **Properties** window, some of the properties may be hidden from view on the screen. Users can scroll through the list of properties by **dragging** the **scrollbox** up or down inside the **scrollbar**, or by

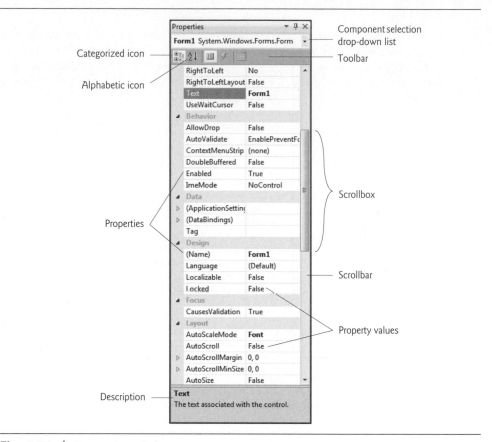

Fig. 2.20 | **Properties** window.

clicking the arrows at the top and bottom of the scrollbar. We show how to set individual properties later in this chapter.

The **Properties** window is crucial to visual programming—it allows you to modify a control's properties visually, without writing code. You can see which properties are available for modification and, in many cases, can learn the range of acceptable values for a given property. The **Properties** window displays a brief description of the selected property, helping you understand its purpose. A property can be set quickly using this window, and no code needs to be written.

At the top of the **Properties** window is the **component selection drop-down list**, which allows you to select the Form or control whose properties you wish to display in the **Properties** window (Fig. 2.20). Using the component selection drop-down list is an alternative way to display a Form's or control's properties without clicking the actual Form or control in the GUI.

2.5 Using Help

Microsoft provides extensive help documentation via the **Help menu**. Using **Help** is an excellent way to get information quickly about Visual Studio, Visual C# and more.

Before using **Help** the first time, you must configure it as follows:

1. Select **Help > Manage Help Settings** to display the **Help Library Manager**. The first time you do this, the dialog in Fig. 2.21 will appear. Simply click **OK** to select the default location for help content that's stored on your local computer. If a dialog appears with the message **Do you want to allow the following program to make changes to this computer?**, click **Yes**.

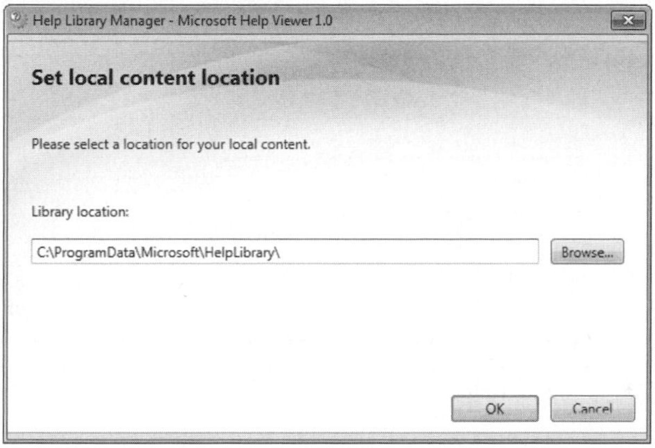

Fig. 2.21 | **Help Library Manager** window the first time you select **Help > Manage Help Settings**.

2. In the **Help Library Manager** window, click **Choose online or local help** (Fig. 2.22). Accessing online help requires an Internet connection, but gives you access to the most up-to-date documentation, as well as tutorials, downloads, support, forums and more. Accessing local help requires that you first download the help files, which can take considerable time and use a significant amount of disk space. If possible, we recommend that you use the online help.

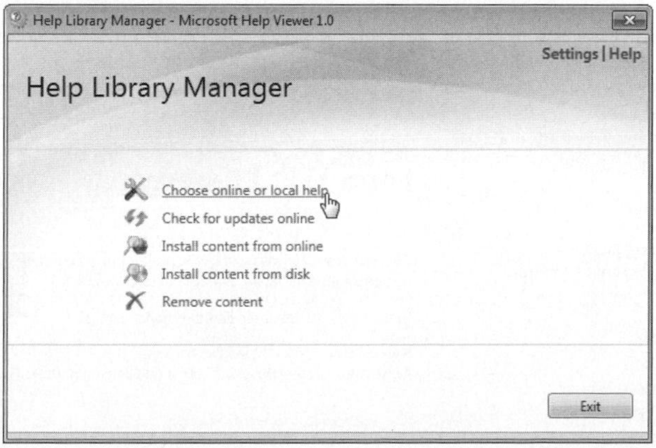

Fig. 2.22 | Preparing to select online or local help.

3. If it's not already selected, select **I want to use online help**, then click **OK**; otherwise, click **Cancel**. Next, click **Exit** in the **Help Library Manager** window. Your IDE is now configured to use online help.

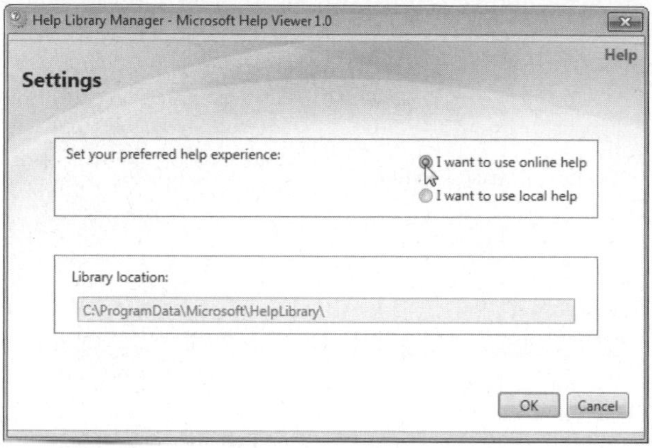

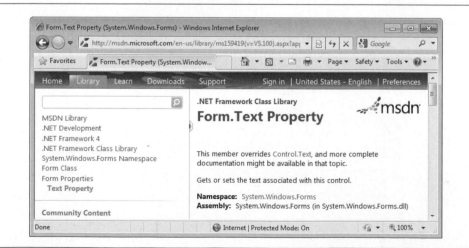

Fig. 2.23 | Selecting online help.

Context-Sensitive Help

Visual Studio provides **context-sensitive help** pertaining to the "current content" (that is, the items around the location of the mouse cursor). To use context-sensitive help, click an item, such as the Form, then press the *F1* key. The help documentation is displayed in a web browser window. To return to the IDE, either close the browser window or select the icon for the IDE in your Windows task bar. Figure 2.24 shows the help page for a Form's Text property. You can view this help by selecting the Form, clicking its Text property in the **Properties** window and pressing the *F1* key.

Fig. 2.24 | Using context-sensitive help.

2.6 Using Visual Programming to Create a Simple Program that Displays Text and an Image

Next, we create a program that displays the text "Welcome to Visual C#!" and an image of the Deitel & Associates bug mascot. The program consists of a single Form that uses a Label and a PictureBox. Figure 2.25 shows the result of the program as it executes. The program and the bug image are available with this chapter's examples, which you can download from www.deitel.com/books/csharpfp4/. We assume the examples are located at C:\examples on your computer.

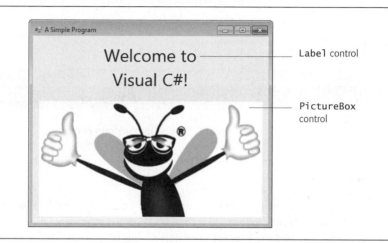

Label control

PictureBox control

Fig. 2.25 | Simple program executing.

You won't write a single line of program code. Instead, you'll use visual programming techniques. Visual Studio processes your actions (such as mouse clicking, dragging and dropping) to generate program code. Chapter 3 begins our discussion of writing program code. Throughout the book, you produce increasingly substantial and powerful programs that usually include a combination of code written by you and code generated by Visual Studio. The generated code can be difficult for novices to understand—but you'll rarely need to look at it.

Visual programming is useful for building GUI-intensive programs that require a significant amount of user interaction. To create, save, run and terminate this first program, perform the following steps:

1. *Closing the open project.* If a project is already open, close it by selecting **File > Close Solution**. A dialog asking whether to save the current solution might appear. Click **Save** to save your changes or **Discard** to ignore them.

2. *Creating the new project.* To create a new Windows Forms application for the program, select **File > New Project...** to display the **New Project** dialog (Fig. 2.26). Select **Windows Forms Application**. Name the project **ASimpleProgram** and click **OK**.

3. *Saving the project.* We mentioned earlier in this chapter that you must set the directory in which the project is saved. To specify the directory in Visual C# 2010 Express, select **File > Save All** to display the **Save Project** dialog (Fig. 2.27). By de-

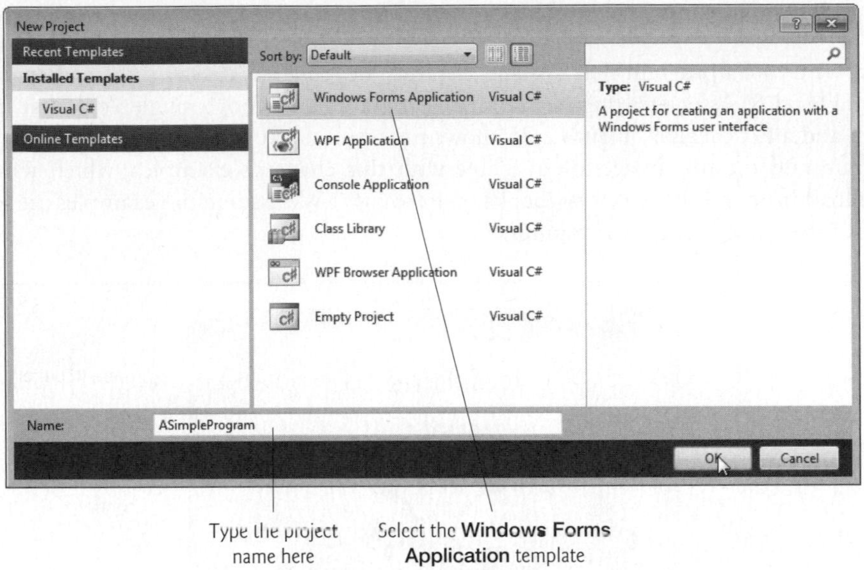

Type the project   Select the **Windows Forms**
name here   **Application** template

Fig. 2.26 | New Project dialog.

fault, projects are saved to your user directory in the folder My Documents\visual studio 2010\Projects. To change the project location, click the **Browse...** button, which opens the **Project Location dialog** (Fig. 2.28). Navigate through the directories, select one in which to place the project (in our example, we use the directory **C:\MyCSharpProjects**) and click **Select Folder** to close the dialog. Click **Save** in the **Save Project** dialog (Fig. 2.27) to save the project and close the dialog.

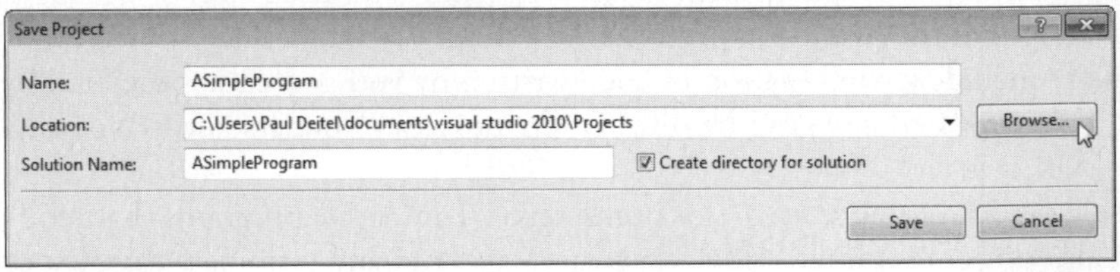

Fig. 2.27 | Save Project dialog.

When you first begin working in the IDE, it is in **design mode** (that is, the program is being designed and is not executing). This provides access to all the environment windows (for example, **Toolbox**, **Properties**), menus and toolbars, as you'll see shortly.

4. *Setting the text in the Form's title bar.* The text in the Form's title bar is determined by the Form's **Text property** (Fig. 2.29). If the **Properties** window is not open, click the properties icon in the toolbar or select **View > Other Windows > Properties Window**. Click anywhere in the Form to display the Form's properties in the **Properties** window. In the textbox to the right of the Text property, type

A Simple Program, as in Fig. 2.29. Press the *Enter* key—the Form's title bar is updated immediately (Fig. 2.30).

Selected project location

Click to set project location

Fig. 2.28 | Setting the project location in the **Project Location** dialog.

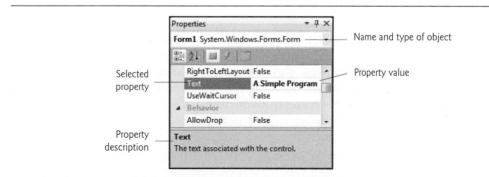

Selected property

Property description

Name and type of object

Property value

Fig. 2.29 | Setting the Form's Text property in the **Properties** window.

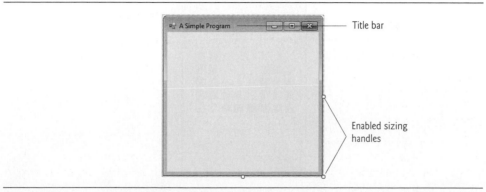

Title bar

Enabled sizing handles

Fig. 2.30 | Form with enabled sizing handles.

5. *Resizing the Form.* Click and drag one of the Form's enabled **sizing handles** (the small white squares that appear around the Form, as shown in Fig. 2.30). Using the mouse, select the bottom-right sizing handle and drag it down and to the right to make the Form larger (Fig. 2.31).

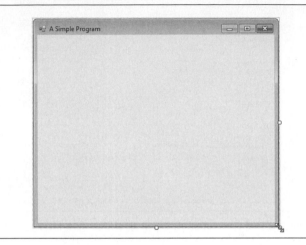

Fig. 2.31 | Resized Form.

6. *Changing the Form's background color.* The **BackColor property** specifies a Form's or control's background color. Clicking BackColor in the **Properties** window causes a down-arrow button to appear next to the value of the property (Fig. 2.32). When clicked, the down-arrow button displays other options, which vary depending on the property. In this case, the arrow displays tabs for **Custom**, **Web** and **System** (the default). Click the **Custom tab** to display the **palette** (a grid of colors). Select the box that represents light blue. Once you select the color, the palette closes and the Form's background color changes to light blue (Fig. 2.33).

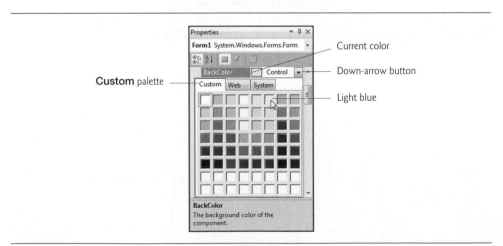

Fig. 2.32 | Changing the Form's BackColor property.

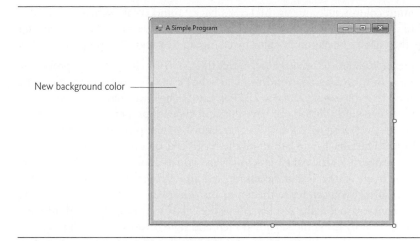

New background color ——

Fig. 2.33 | Form with new BackColor property applied.

7. *Adding a Label control to the Form.* If the **Toolbox** is not already open, select **View > Other Windows > Toolbox** to display the set of controls you'll use for creating your programs. For the type of program we're creating in this chapter, the typical controls we use are located in either the **All Windows Forms** group of the **Toolbox** or the **Common Controls** group. If either group name is collapsed, expand it by clicking the arrow to the left of the group name (the **All Windows Forms** and **Common Controls** groups are shown in Fig. 2.19). Next, double click the Label control in the **Toolbox**. This action causes a Label to appear in the upper-left corner of the Form (Fig. 2.34). [*Note:* If the Form is behind the **Toolbox**, you may need to hide the **Toolbox** to see the Label.] Although double clicking any **Toolbox** control places the control on the Form, you also can "drag" controls from the **Toolbox** to the Form—you may prefer dragging the control because you can position it wherever you want. The Label displays the text **label1** by default. The Label's

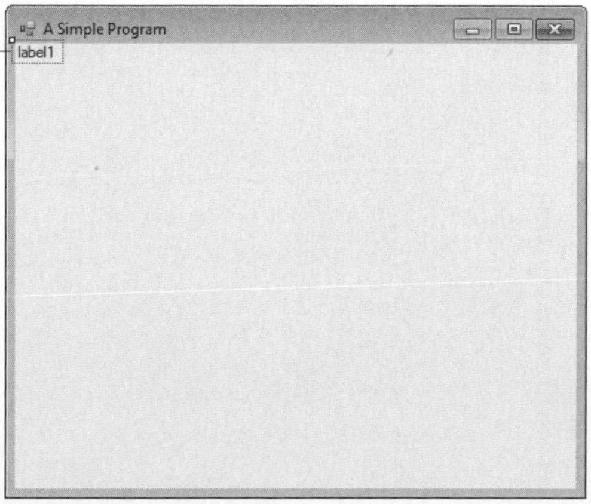

Label control ——

Fig. 2.34 | Adding a Label to the Form.

background color is the same as the Form's background color. When a control is added to the Form, its BackColor property is set to the Form's BackColor. You can change the Label's background color by changing its BackColor property.

8. *Customizing the **Label**'s appearance.* Select the Label by clicking it. Its properties now appear in the **Properties** window. The Label's Text property determines the text (if any) that the Label displays. The Form and Label each have their own Text property—Forms and controls can have the same types of properties (such as Back-Color, Text, etc.) without conflict. Set the Label's Text property to Welcome to Visual C#!. The Label resizes to fit all the typed text on one line. By default, the **AutoSize property** of the Label is set to True, which allows the Label to update its size to fit all of the text if necessary. Set the AutoSize property to False (Fig. 2.35) so that you can resize the Label on your own. Resize the Label (using the sizing handles) so that the text fits. Move the Label to the top center of the Form by dragging it or by using the keyboard's left and right arrow keys to adjust its position (Fig. 2.36). Alternatively, when the Label is selected, you can center the Label control horizontally by selecting **Format > Center In Form > Horizontally**.

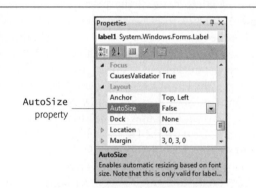

Fig. 2.35 | Changing the Label's AutoSize property to False.

Fig. 2.36 | GUI after the Form and Label have been customized.

9. *Setting the Label's font size.* To change the font type and appearance of the Label's text, select the value of the **Font property**, which causes an **ellipsis button** to appear next to the value (Fig. 2.37). When the ellipsis button is clicked, a dialog that provides additional values—in this case, the **Font dialog** (Fig. 2.38)—is displayed. You can select the font name (the font options may be different, depending on your system), font style (**Regular**, **Italic**, **Bold**, etc.) and font size (**16**, **18**, **20**, etc.) in this dialog. The **Sample** text shows the selected font settings. Under **Font**, select **Segoe UI**, Microsoft's recommended font for user interfaces. Under **Size**, select **24** points and click **OK**. If the Label's text does not fit on a single line, it wraps to the next line. Resize the Label so that it appears as shown in Fig. 2.25 if it's not large enough to hold the text. You may need to center the Label horizontally again after resizing.

Fig. 2.37 | **Properties** window displaying the Label's **Font** property.

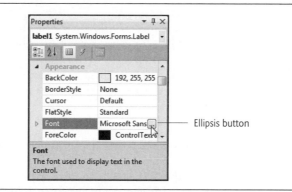

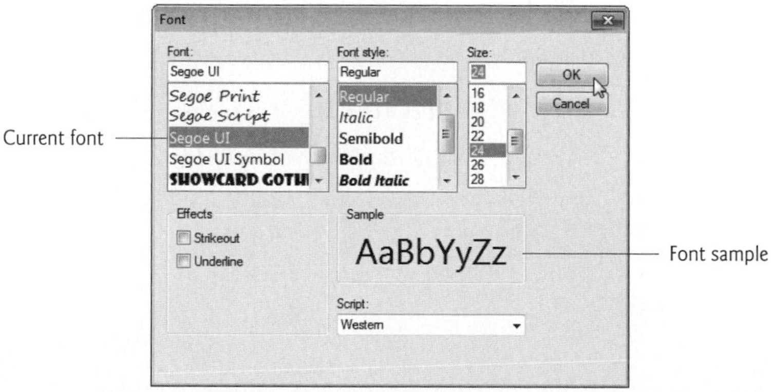

Fig. 2.38 | **Font** dialog for selecting fonts, styles and sizes.

10. *Aligning the Label's text.* Select the Label's **TextAlign** property, which determines how the text is aligned within the Label. A three-by-three grid of buttons representing alignment choices is displayed (Fig. 2.39). The position of each button corresponds to where the text appears in the Label. For this program, set the

TextAlign property to MiddleCenter in the three-by-three grid—this selection causes the text to appear centered in the middle of the Label, with equal spacing from the text to all sides of the Label. The other TextAlign values, such as Top-Left, TopRight, and BottomCenter, can be used to position the text anywhere within a Label. Certain alignment values may require that you resize the Label larger or smaller to better fit the text.

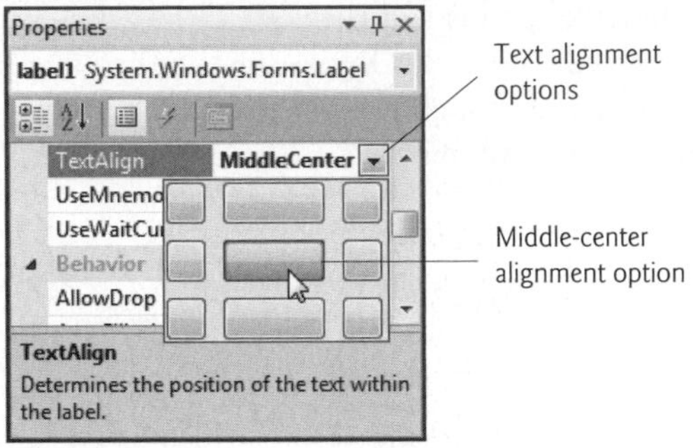

Fig. 2.39 | Centering the Label's text.

11. *Adding a **PictureBox** to the Form.* The PictureBox control displays images. The process involved in this step is similar to that of *Step 7*, in which we added a Label to the Form. Locate the PictureBox in the **Toolbox** (Fig. 2.19) and double click it to add it to the Form. When the PictureBox appears, move it underneath the Label, either by dragging it or by using the arrow keys (Fig. 2.40).

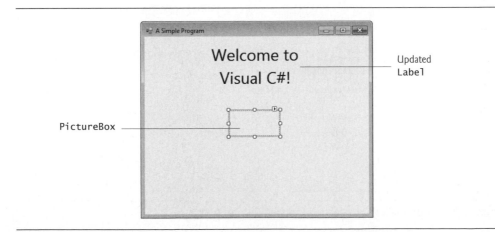

Fig. 2.40 | Inserting and aligning a PictureBox.

12. *Inserting an image.* Click the PictureBox to display its properties in the **Properties** window (Fig. 2.41). Locate the **Image property**, which displays a preview of

the selected image or **(none)** if no image is selected. Click the ellipsis button to display the **Select Resource dialog** (Fig. 2.42), which is used to import files, such as images, for use in a program. Click the **Import...** button to browse for an image to insert, select the image file and click **OK**. We used `bug.png` from this chapter's examples folder. The image is previewed in the **Select Resource** dialog (Fig. 2.43). Click **OK** to use the image. Supported image formats include PNG (Portable Network Graphics), GIF (Graphic Interchange Format), JPEG (Joint Photographic Experts Group) and BMP (Windows bitmap). To scale the image to the `PictureBox`'s size, change the **SizeMode property** to **StretchImage** (Fig. 2.44). Resize the `PictureBox`, making it larger (Fig. 2.45).

13. *Saving the project.* Select **File > Save All** to save the entire solution. The solution file (which has the file name extension `.sln`) contains the name and location of its project, and the project file (which has the file name extension `.csproj`) contains the names and locations of all the files in the project. If you want to reopen your project at a later time, simply open its `.sln` file.

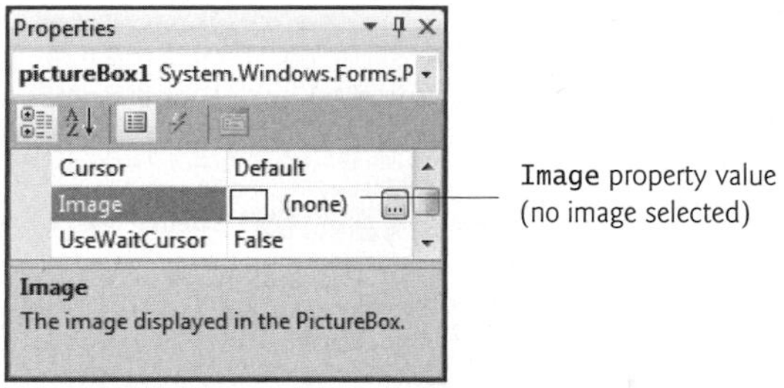

Fig. 2.41 | Image property of the `PictureBox`.

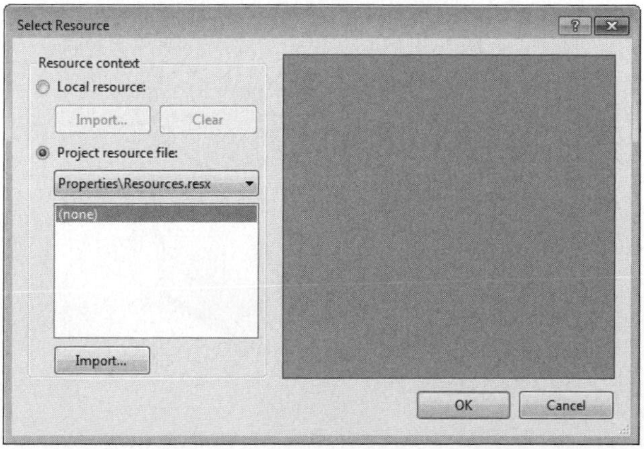

Fig. 2.42 | **Select Resource** dialog to select an image for the `PictureBox`.

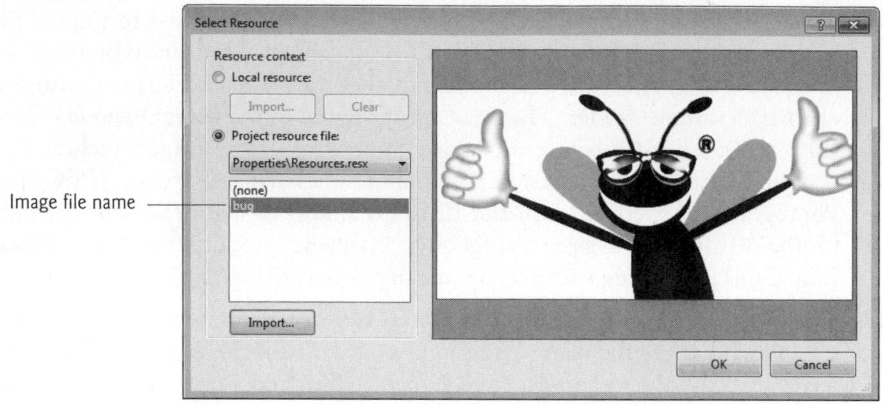

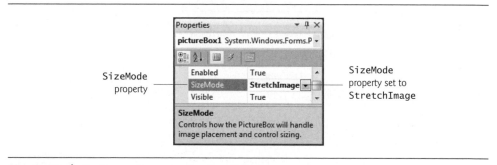

Fig. 2.43 | **Select Resource** dialog displaying a preview of selected image.

Image file name

SizeMode property

SizeMode property set to StretchImage

Fig. 2.44 | Scaling an image to the size of the PictureBox.

Newly inserted image

Fig. 2.45 | PictureBox displaying an image.

14. ***Running the project.*** Recall that up to this point we have been working in the IDE design mode (that is, the program being created is not executing). In **run mode**, the program is executing, and you can interact with only a few IDE features—features that are not available are disabled (grayed out). The text **Form1.cs [Design]** in the project tab (Fig. 2.46) means that we're designing the Form visually rather than programmatically. If we had been writing code, the tab would have contained only the text **Form1.cs**. If there's an asterisk (*) at the end of the text in the tab, the file has been changed and should be saved. Select **Debug > Start Debugging** to execute the program (or you can press the *F5* key). Figure 2.47 shows the IDE in run mode (indicated by the title-bar text **ASimpleProgram (Running) – Microsoft Visual C# 2010 Express Edition**). Many toolbar icons and menus are disabled, since they cannot be used while the program is running. The running program appears in a separate window outside the IDE as shown in the lower-right portion of Fig. 2.47.

15. ***Terminating execution.*** Click the running program's close box (⊠) in the top-right corner of the running program's window. This action stops the program's execution and returns the IDE to design mode. You can also select **Debug > Stop Debugging** to terminate the program.

Form1.cs [Design]   Debug menu

Fig. 2.46 | Debugging a solution.

IDE displays text **Running**, which
signifies that the program is executing

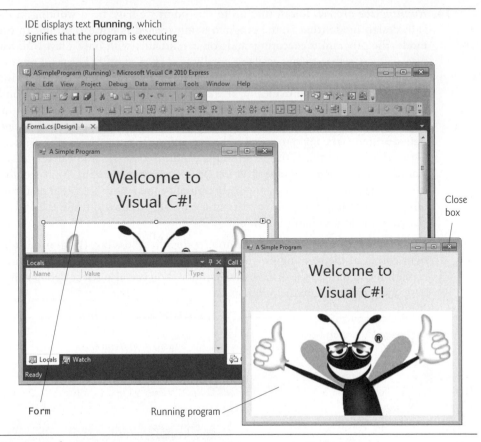

Close
box

Form   Running program

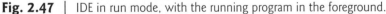

Fig. 2.47 | IDE in run mode, with the running program in the foreground.

2.7 Wrap-Up

In this chapter, we introduced key features of the Visual Studio Integrated Development Environment (IDE). You used the technique of visual programming to create a working Visual C# program without writing a single line of code. Visual C# programming is a mixture of the two styles: Visual programming allows you to develop GUIs easily and avoid tedious GUI programming. Conventional programming (which we introduce in Chapter 3) allows you to specify the behavior of your programs.

You created a Visual C# Windows Forms application with one Form. You worked with the **Solution Explorer**, **Toolbox** and **Properties** windows, which are essential to developing Visual C# programs. The **Solution Explorer** window allows you to manage your solution's files visually.

You explored Visual Studio's help features. You learned how to set **Help** options to display help resources internally or externally in a web browser. We also demonstrated context-sensitive help, which displays help topics related to selected controls or text.

You used visual programming to design the GUI portions of a program quickly and easily, by dragging and dropping controls (a Label and a PictureBox) onto a Form or by double clicking controls in the **Toolbox**.

In creating the **ASimpleProgram** program, you used the **Properties** window to set the `Text` and `BackColor` properties of the `Form`. You learned that `Label` controls display text and that `PictureBox`es display images. You displayed text in a `Label` and added an image to a `PictureBox`. You also worked with the `AutoSize`, `TextAlign` and `Font` properties of a `Label` and the `Image` and `SizeMode` properties of a `PictureBox`.

In the next chapter, we discuss "nonvisual," or "conventional," programming—you'll create your first programs that contain Visual C# code that you write, instead of having Visual Studio write the code. You'll study console applications (programs that display only text and do not have a GUI). You'll also learn memory concepts, arithmetic, decision making and how to use a dialog to display a message.

2.8 Web Resources

Please take a moment to visit each of these sites briefly.

`social.msdn.microsoft.com/forums/en-US/category/visualcsharp/`

This site provides access to the Microsoft Visual C# forums, which you can use to get your Visual C# language and IDE questions answered.

`www.deitel.com/VisualCSharp2010/`

This site lists many of the key web resources we used as we were preparing to write this book. There's lots of great stuff here to help you become familiar with the world of Visual C# 2010.

`msdn.microsoft.com/vstudio`

This site is the home page for Microsoft Visual Studio. The site includes news, documentation, downloads and other resources.

`msdn.microsoft.com/vcsharp`

This site provides information on the newest release of Visual C#, including downloads, community information and resources.

3

Introduction
to C# Applications

Objectives

In this chapter you'll learn:

- To write simple C# applications using code rather than visual programming.

- To write input/output statements.

- To declare and use data of various types.

- To store and retrieve data from memory.

- To use arithmetic operators.

- To determine the order in which operators are applied.

- To write decision-making statements.

- To use relational and equality operators.

- To use message dialogs to display messages.

*What's in a name?
That which we call a rose
by any other name
would smell as sweet.*
—William Shakespeare

*When faced with a
decision, I always ask,
"What would be the most
fun?"*
—Peggy Walker

*"Take some more tea," the
March Hare said to Alice,
very earnestly. "I've had
nothing yet," Alice replied
in an offended tone, "so I
can't take more." "You
mean you can't take less,"
said the Hatter: "it's very
easy to take more than
nothing."*
—Lewis Carroll

3.1 Introduction

In this chapter, we introduce **console applications**—these input and output text in a **console window**, which in Windows XP and Windows Vista is known as the **Command Prompt**. We use live-code examples to demonstrate input/output, text formatting and arithmetic, equality and relational operators. The optional Software Engineering Case Study section examines the requirements document that specifies what our ATM must do.

3.2 A Simple C# Application: Displaying a Line of Text

Let's consider an application that displays a line of text. (Later in this section we discuss how to compile and run an application.) The application and its output are shown in Fig. 3.1. The application illustrates several important C# language features. For your convenience, each program we present in this book includes line numbers, which are not part of actual C# code. In Section 3.3 we show how to display line numbers for your C# code in the IDE. We'll soon see that line 10 does the real work of the application—namely, displaying the phrase Welcome to C# Programming! on the screen. We now do a code walkthrough.

Line 1 begins with //, indicating that the remainder of the line is a comment. We begin every application with a comment indicating the figure number and the name of the file in which the application is stored.

```
1   // Fig. 3.1: Welcome1.cs
2   // Text-displaying application.
3   using System;
4
5   public class Welcome1
6   {
7      // Main method begins execution of C# application
8      public static void Main( string[] args )
9      {
10        Console.WriteLine( "Welcome to C# Programming!" );
11     } // end Main
12  } // end class Welcome1
```

```
Welcome to C# Programming!
```

Fig. 3.1 | Text-displaying application.

A comment that begins with // is called a **single-line comment**, because it terminates at the end of the line on which it appears. A // comment also can begin in the middle of a line and continue until the end of that line (as in lines 7, 11 and 12).

Delimited comments such as

```
/* This is a delimited comment.
   It can be split over many lines */
```

can be spread over several lines. This type of comment begins with the delimiter /* and ends with the delimiter */. All text between the delimiters is ignored by the compiler. C# incorporated delimited comments and single-line comments from the C and C++ programming languages, respectively. In this book, we use only single-line comments in our programs.

Common Programming Error 3.1

Forgetting one of the delimiters of a delimited comment is a syntax error.

Line 2 is a single-line comment that describes the purpose of the application. Line 3 is a **using directive** that tells the compiler where to look for a class that is used in this application. A great strength of Visual C# is its rich set of predefined classes that you can reuse rather than "reinventing the wheel." These classes are organized under **namespaces**—named collections of related classes. Collectively, .NET's namespaces are referred to as the **.NET Framework Class Library**. Each using directive identifies a namespace containing predefined classes that a C# application should be able to use. The using directive in line 3 indicates that this example uses classes from the System namespace, which contains the predefined Console class (discussed shortly) used in line 10, and many other useful classes.

Error-Prevention Tip 3.1

Forgetting to include a using directive for a namespace that contains a class used in your application typically results in a compilation error, containing a message such as "The name 'Console' does not exist in the current context." When this occurs, check that you provided the proper using directives and that the names in the using directives are spelled correctly, including proper use of uppercase and lowercase letters.

For each new .NET class we use, we indicate the namespace in which it's located. This information is important, because it helps you locate descriptions of each class in the .NET documentation. A web-based version of this documentation can be found at

```
msdn.microsoft.com/en-us/library/ms229335.aspx
```

You can also place the cursor on the name of any .NET class or method, then press the *F1* key to get more information.

Line 4 is simply a blank line. Blank lines, space characters and tab characters are **whitespace**. Space characters and tabs are known specifically as **whitespace characters**. Whitespace is ignored by the compiler. We use whitespace to enhance application readability.

Line 5 begins a **class declaration** for the class Welcome1. Every application you create consists of at least one class declaration that is defined by you. These are known as **user-defined classes**. The **class keyword** introduces a class declaration and is immediately followed by the **class name** (`Welcome1`). Keywords (also called **reserved words**) are reserved for use by C# and are always spelled with all lowercase letters. The complete list of C# keywords is shown in Fig. 3.2.

C# Keywords and contextual keywords				
abstract	as	base	bool	break
byte	case	catch	char	checked
class	const	continue	decimal	default
delegate	do	double	else	enum
event	explicit	extern	false	finally
fixed	float	for	foreach	goto
if	implicit	in	int	interface
internal	is	lock	long	namespace
new	null	object	operator	out
override	params	private	protected	public
readonly	ref	return	sbyte	sealed
short	sizeof	stackalloc	static	string
struct	switch	this	throw	true
try	typeof	uint	ulong	unchecked
unsafe	ushort	using	virtual	void
volatile	while			
Contextual Keywords				
add	alias	ascending	by	descending
equals	from	get	global	group
into	join	let	on	orderby
partial	remove	select	set	value
var	where	yield		

Fig. 3.2 | C# keywords and contextual keywords.

By convention, all class names begin with a capital letter and capitalize the first letter of each word they include (e.g., `SampleClassName`). This is frequently referred to as **Pascal casing**. A class name is an **identifier**—a series of characters consisting of letters, digits and underscores (_) that does not begin with a digit and does not contain spaces. Some valid identifiers are `Welcome1`, `identifier`, `_value` and `m_inputField1`. The name `7button` is not a valid identifier because it begins with a digit, and the name `input field` is not a valid identifier because it contains a space. Normally, an identifier that does not begin with a capital letter is not the name of a class. C# is **case sensitive**—that is, uppercase and lowercase letters are distinct, so `a1` and `A1` are different (but both valid) identifiers. Identifiers may also be preceded by the @ character. This indicates that a word should be interpreted as an identifier, even if it's a keyword (e.g., `@int`). This allows C# code to use code written in other .NET languages where an identifier might have the same name as a C# keyword.

The **contextual keywords** in Fig. 3.2 can be used as identifiers outside the contexts in which they're keywords, but for clarity this is not recommended.

Good Programming Practice 3.1

By convention, always begin a class name's identifier with a capital letter and start each subsequent word in the identifier with a capital letter.

Common Programming Error 3.2

C# is case sensitive. Not using the proper uppercase and lowercase letters for an identifier normally causes a compilation error.

In Chapters 3–9, every class we define begins with the keyword `public`. For now, we'll simply require this keyword. You'll learn more about `public` and non-`public` classes in Chapter 10, Classes and Objects: A Deeper Look. When you save your `public` class declaration in a file, the file name is usually the class name followed by the `.cs` file-name extension. For our application, the file name is `Welcome1.cs`.

Good Programming Practice 3.2

By convention, a file that contains a single `public` class should have a name that is identical to the class name (plus the `.cs` extension) in both spelling and capitalization. Naming your files in this way makes it easier for other programmers (and you) to determine where the classes of an application are located.

A **left brace** (in line 6 in Fig. 3.1), {, begins the **body** of every class declaration. A corresponding **right brace** (in line 12), }, must end each class declaration. Lines 7–11 are indented. This indentation is one of the spacing conventions mentioned earlier. We define each spacing convention as a *Good Programming Practice*.

Error-Prevention Tip 3.2

Whenever you type an opening left brace, {, in your application, immediately type the closing right brace, }, then reposition the cursor between the braces and indent to begin typing the body. This practice helps prevent errors due to missing braces.

Good Programming Practice 3.3

Indent the entire body of each class declaration one "level" of indentation between the left and right braces that delimit the body of the class. This format emphasizes the class declaration's structure and makes it easier to read. You can let the IDE format your code by selecting Edit > Advanced > Format Document

Good Programming Practice 3.4

Set a convention for the indent size you prefer, then uniformly apply that convention. The Tab key may be used to create indents, but tab stops vary among text editors. We recommend using three spaces to form each level of indentation. We show how to do this in Section 3.3.

Common Programming Error 3.3

It's a syntax error if braces do not occur in matching pairs.

Line 7 is a comment indicating the purpose of lines 8–11 of the application. Line 8 is the starting point of every application. The **parentheses** after the identifier Main indicate that it's an application building block called a method. Class declarations normally contain one or more methods. Method names usually follow the same Pascal casing capitalization conventions used for class names. For each application, one of the methods in a class must be called Main (which is typically defined as shown in line 8); otherwise, the application will not execute. Methods are able to perform tasks and return information when they complete their tasks. Keyword **void** (line 8) indicates that this method will not return any information after it completes its task. Later, we'll see that many methods do return information. You'll learn more about methods in Chapters 4 and 7. We discuss the contents of Main's parentheses in Chapter 8. For now, simply mimic Main's first line in your applications.

The left brace in line 9 begins the **body of the method declaration**. A corresponding right brace must end the method's body (line 11 of Fig. 3.1). Line 10 in the body of the method is indented between the braces.

Good Programming Practice 3.5

As with class declarations, indent the entire body of each method declaration one "level" of indentation between the left and right braces that define the method body. This format makes the structure of the method stand out and makes the method declaration easier to read.

Line 10 displays the **string** of characters contained between the double quotation marks. Whitespace characters in strings are *not* ignored by the compiler.

Class **Console** provides **standard input/output** capabilities that enable applications to read and display text in the console window from which the application executes. The **Console.WriteLine method** displays a line of text in the console window. The string in the parentheses in line 10 is the argument to the method. Method Console.WriteLine displays its argument in the console window. When Console.WriteLine completes its task, it positions the screen cursor at the beginning of the next line in the console window.

The entire line 10, including Console.WriteLine, the parentheses, the argument "Welcome to C# Programming!" in the parentheses and the **semicolon** (;), is called a **statement**. Most statements end with a semicolon. When the statement in line 10 executes, it displays the string Welcome to C# Programming! in the console window. A method is typically composed of one or more statements that perform the method's task.

Error-Prevention Tip 3.3

When the compiler reports a syntax error, the error may not be in the line indicated by the error message. First, check the line for which the error was reported. If that line does not contain syntax errors, check several preceding lines.

Some programmers find it difficult when reading or writing an application to match the left and right braces ({ and }) that delimit the body of a class declaration or a method declaration. For this reason, we include a comment after each closing right brace (}) that ends a method declaration and after each closing right brace that ends a class declaration. For example, line 11 specifies the closing right brace of method Main, and line 12 specifies the closing right brace of class Welcome1. Each of these comments indicates the method or class that the right brace terminates. Visual Studio can help you locate matching braces in your code. Simply place the cursor immediately in front of the left brace or immediately after the right brace, and Visual Studio will highlight both.

Good Programming Practice 3.6

Following the closing right brace of a method body or class declaration with a comment indicating the method or class declaration to which the brace belongs improves application readability.

3.3 Creating a Simple Application in Visual C# Express

Now that we have presented our first console application (Fig. 3.1), we provide a step-by-step explanation of how to compile and execute it using Visual C# Express.

Creating the Console Application

After opening Visual C# 2010Express, select **File > New Project...** to display the **New Project** dialog (Fig. 3.3), then select the **Console Application** template. In the dialog's **Name** field, type Welcome1. Click **OK** to create the project. The IDE now contains the open console application, as shown in Fig. 3.4. The editor window already contains some code provided by the IDE. Some of this code is similar to that of Fig. 3.1. Some is not, and uses features that we have not yet discussed. The IDE inserts this extra code to help organize the application and to provide access to some common classes in the .NET Framework Class Library—at this point in the book, this code is neither required nor relevant to the discussion of this application; delete all of it.

The code coloring scheme used by the IDE is called **syntax-color highlighting** and helps you visually differentiate application elements. For example, keywords appear in blue, and comments appear in green. When present, comments are green. In this black-and-white book, we syntax-shade our code similarly—bold for keywords, gray for comments, bold gray for literals and constants, and black for other text. One example of a literal is the string passed to Console.WriteLine in line 10 of Fig. 3.1. You can customize the colors shown in the code editor by selecting **Tools > Options....** This displays the **Options** dialog. Then expand the **Environment** node and select **Fonts and Colors**. Here you can change the colors for various code elements.

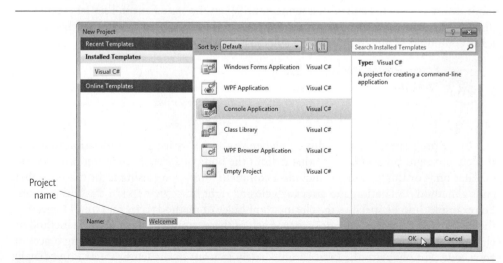

Fig. 3.3 | Creating a **Console Application** with the **New Project** dialog.

Editor window

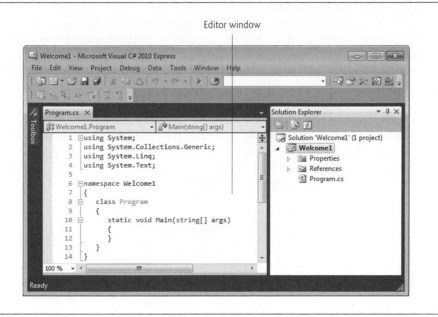

Fig. 3.4 | IDE with an open console application.

Modifying the Editor Settings to Display Line Numbers

Visual C# Express provides many ways to personalize your coding experience. In this step, you'll change the settings so that your code matches that of this book. To have the IDE display line numbers, select **Tools > Options...**. In the dialog that appears (Fig. 3.5), click the **Show all settings** checkbox on the lower left of the dialog, then expand the **Text Editor** node in the left pane and select **All Languages**. On the right, check the **Line numbers** checkbox. Keep the **Options** dialog open.

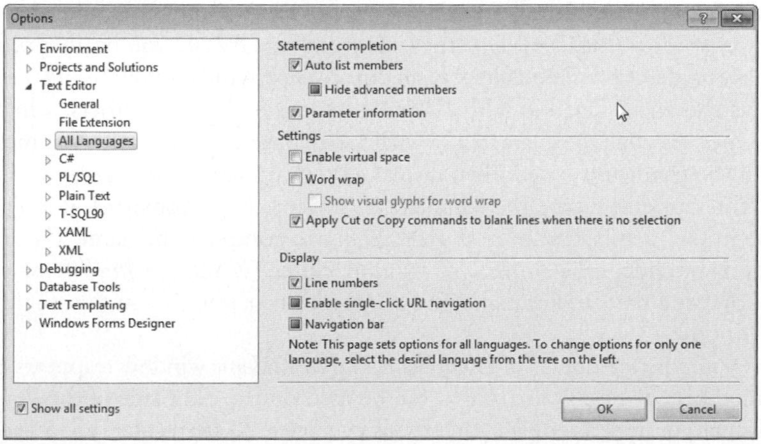

Fig. 3.5 | Modifying the IDE settings.

Setting Code Indentation to Three Spaces per Indent

In the **Options** dialog that you opened in the previous step (Fig. 3.5), expand the C# node in the left pane and select **Tabs**. Make sure that the option **Insert spaces** is selected. Enter **3** for both the **Tab size** and **Indent size** fields. Any new code you add will now use three spaces for each level of indentation. Click **OK** to save your settings, close the dialog and return to the editor window.

Changing the Name of the Application File

For applications we create in this book, we change the default name of the application file (i.e., `Program.cs`) to a more descriptive name. To rename the file, click `Program.cs` in the **Solution Explorer** window. This displays the application file's properties in the **Properties** window (Fig. 3.6). Change the **File Name property** to `Welcome1.cs`.

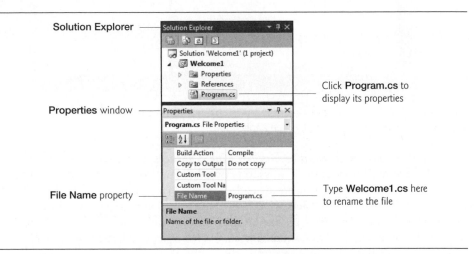

Fig. 3.6 | Renaming the program file in the **Properties** window.

Writing Code and Using IntelliSense

In the editor window (Fig. 3.4), type the code from Fig. 3.1. As you begin typing (in line 10) the class name class name `Console`, an *IntelliSense* window containing a scrollbar is displayed as shown in Fig. 3.7. This IDE feature lists a class's **members**, which include method names. As you type characters, Visual C# Express highlights the first member that matches all the characters typed, then displays a tool tip containing a description of that member. You can either type the complete item name (e.g., `Console`), double click the item name in the member list or press the *Tab* key to complete the name. Once the complete name is provided, the *IntelliSense* window closes. While the *IntelliSense* window is displayed, pressing the *Ctrl* key makes the window transparent so you can see the code behind the window.

When you type the dot (`.`) after `Console`, the *IntelliSense* window reappears and shows only the members of class `Console` that can be used on the right side of the dot (Fig. 3.7, part 1). When you type the open parenthesis character, `(`, after `Console.WriteLine`, the *Parameter Info* window is displayed (Fig. 3.8). This window contains information about the method's parameters. As you'll learn in Chapter 7, there can be several versions of a method.

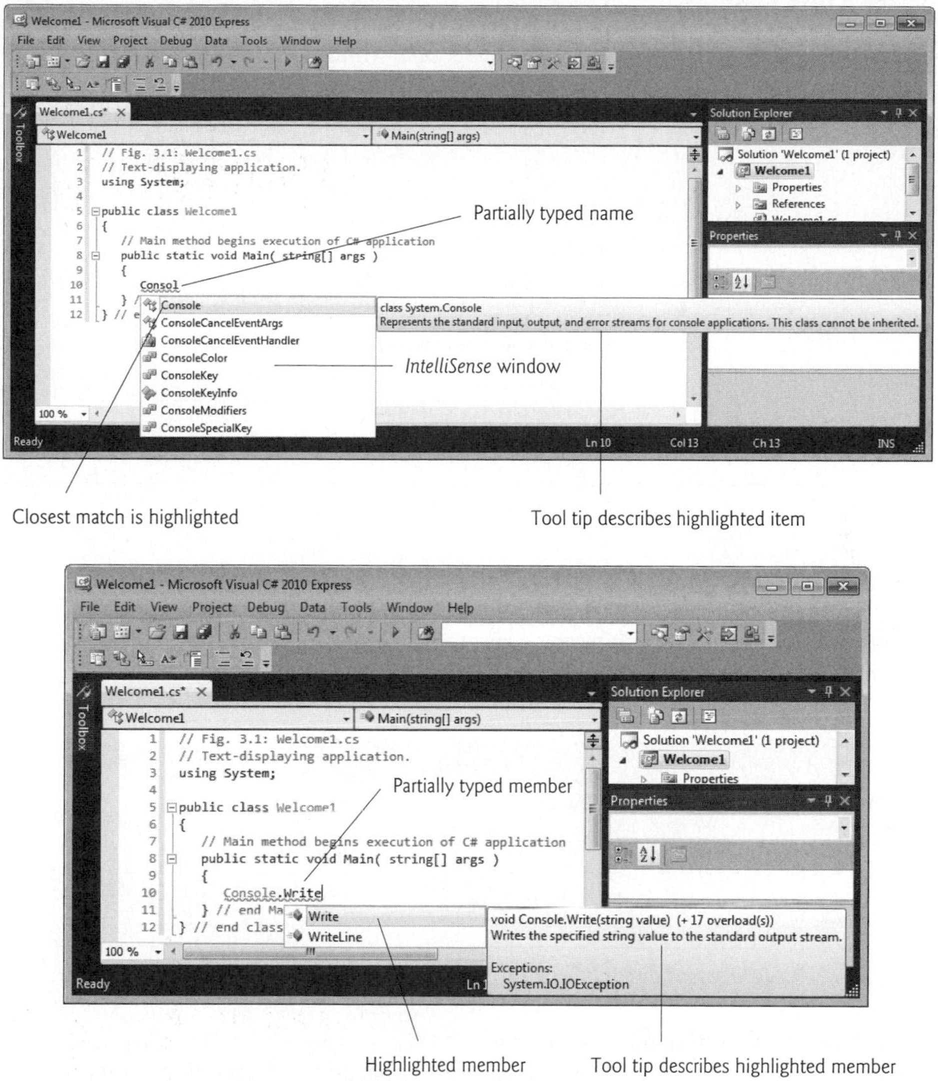

Fig. 3.7 | *IntelliSense* feature of Visual C# Express.

That is, a class can define several methods that have the same name, as long as they have different numbers and/or types of parameters—a concept known as overloaded methods. These methods normally all perform similar tasks. The *Parameter Info* window indicates how many versions of the selected method are available and provides up and down arrows for scrolling through the different versions. For example, there are 19 versions of the WriteLine method—we use one of these 19 versions in our application. The *Parameter Info* window is one of many features provided by the IDE to facilitate application development. In the next several chapters, you'll learn more about the information displayed in these windows. The *Parameter Info* window is especially helpful when you want to see the different ways in which a method can be used. From the code in Fig. 3.1, we already know that we intend to display one string with `WriteLine`, so, because you know exactly which version of `WriteLine` you want to use, you can simply close the *Parameter Info* window by pressing the *Esc* key.

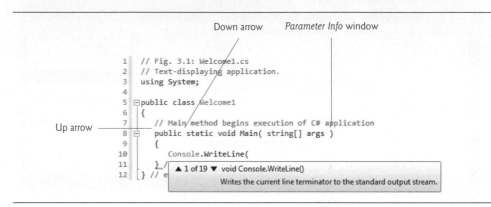

Fig. 3.8 | *Parameter Info* window.

Saving the Application

Select **File > Save All** to display the **Save Project** dialog (Fig. 3.9). In the **Location** textbox, specify the directory where you want to save this project. We chose the `MyProjects` directory on the `C:` drive. Select the **Create directory for solution** checkbox and click **Save**.

Fig. 3.9 | **Save Project** dialog.

Compiling and Running the Application

You're now ready to compile and execute your application. Depending on its type, the compiler may compile the code into files with a **.exe (executable) extension**, a **.dll (dynamically linked library) extension** or one of several other extensions. Such files are called **assemblies** and are the packaging units for compiled C# code. These assemblies contain the Microsoft Intermediate Language (MSIL) code for the application.

To compile the application, select **Debug > Build Solution**. If the application contains no syntax errors, this will compile your application and build it into an executable file (named `Welcome1.exe`, in one of the project's subdirectories). To execute it, type *Ctrl + F5*, which invokes the `Main` method (Fig. 3.1). (If you attempt to run the application before building it, the IDE will build the application first, then run it only if there are no compilation errors.) The statement in line 10 of `Main` displays `Welcome to C# Programming!`. Figure 3.10 shows the results of executing this application, displayed in a console (**Command Prompt**) window. Leave the application's project open in Visual C# Express;

we'll go back to it later in this section. [*Note:* Many environments show **Command Prompt** windows with black backgrounds and white text. We adjusted these settings in our environment to make our screen captures more readable.]

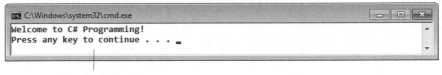

Console window

Fig. 3.10 | Executing the application shown in Fig. 3.1.

 Error-Prevention Tip 3.4

When learning how to program, sometimes it's helpful to "break" a working application so you can familiarize yourself with the compiler's syntax-error messages. Try removing a semicolon or brace from the code of Fig. 3.1, then recompiling the application to see the error messages generated by the omission.

Running the Application from the Command Prompt

As we mentioned at the beginning of the chapter, you can execute applications outside the IDE in a **Command Prompt**. This is useful when you simply want to run an application rather than open it for modification. To open the **Command Prompt**, select **Start > All Programs > Accessories > Command Prompt**. The window (Fig. 3.11) displays copyright information, followed by a prompt that indicates the current directory. By default, the prompt specifies the current user's directory on the local machine (in our case, C:\Users\paul). On your machine, the folder name paul will be replaced with your username.

Default prompt displays when
Command Prompt is opened

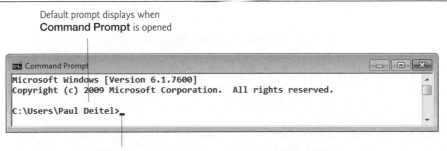

User enters the next command here

Fig. 3.11 | **Command Prompt** window when it's initially opened.

Enter the command cd (which stands for "change directory"), followed by the /d flag (to change drives if necessary), then the directory where the application's .exe file is located (i.e., your application's bin\Debug or bin\Release directory). For example, the command

```
cd /d C:\MyProjects\Welcome1\Welcome1\bin\Release
```

(Fig. 3.12) changes the current directory, to the `Welcome1` application's `Release` directory on the `C:` drive. The next prompt displays the new directory. After changing to the proper directory, you can run the application by entering the name of the `.exe` file— `Welcome1`. The application will run to completion, then the prompt will display again, awaiting the next command. To close the **Command Prompt**, type `exit` (Fig. 3.12) and press *Enter*.

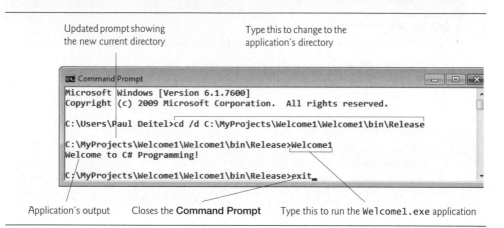

Updated prompt showing the new current directory

Type this to change to the application's directory

Application's output   Closes the **Command Prompt**   Type this to run the `Welcome1.exe` application

Fig. 3.12 | Executing the application shown in Fig. 3.1 from a **Command Prompt** window.

Visual C# 2010 Express maintains a `Debug` and a `Release` directory in each project's `bin` directory. The `Debug` directory contains a version of the application that can be used with the debugger (see Appendix G, Using the Visual C# 2010 Debugger). The `Release` directory contains an optimized version that you could provide to your clients. In the complete Visual Studio 2008, you can select the specific version you wish to build from the **Solution Configurations** drop-down list in the toolbars at the top of the IDE. The default is the `Release` version. The `Debug` version is created if you run the program with **Debug > Start Debugging**.

Syntax Errors, Error Messages and the Error List Window
Go back to the application in Visual C# Express. As you type code, the IDE responds either by applying syntax-color highlighting or by generating a **syntax error**, which indicates a violation of Visual C#'s rules for creating correct applications (i.e., one or more statements are not written correctly). Syntax errors occur for various reasons, such as missing parentheses and misspelled keywords.

When a syntax error occurs, the IDE underlines the error in red and provides a description of it in the **Error List** window (Fig. 3.13). If the **Error List** window is not visible in the IDE, select **View > Error List** to display it. In Figure 3.13, we intentionally omitted the comma between `"Welcome to"` and `"C# Programming!"` in line 10. The first error is simply indicating that line 10 is not a valid statement. The second error indicates that a right parenthesis is expected at character position 51 in the statement, because the compiler is confused by the unmatched left parenthesis from earlier in line 10. The third error has the text "**Invalid expression term ')'**", because the compiler thinks the closing right parenthesis should have appeared earlier in the line. The fourth error has the text "**; expected**", because the prior errors make the compiler think that the statement should have been terminated with a semicolon earlier in the line. Although we deleted only one comma in line 10, this caused the compiler to misinterpret several items in this line and to generate *four* error messages. You can double click an error message in the **Error List** to jump to the place in the code that caused the error.

> **Error-Prevention Tip 3.5**
> *One syntax error can lead to multiple entries in the **Error List** window. Each error that you address could eliminate several subsequent error messages when you recompile your application. So when you see an error you know how to fix, correct it and recompile—this may make several other errors disappear.*

Error List window   Intentionally omitted comma character (syntax error)

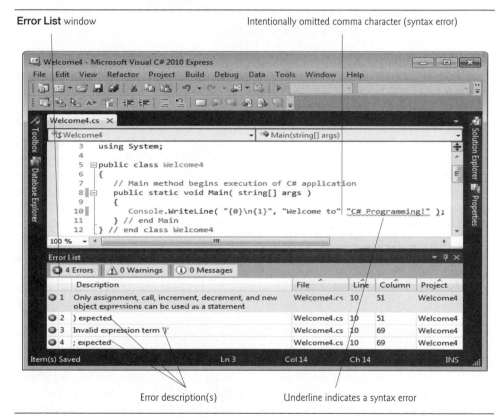

Error description(s)   Underline indicates a syntax error

Fig. 3.13 | Syntax errors indicated by the IDE.

3.4 Modifying Your Simple C# Application

This section continues our introduction to C# programming with two examples that modify the example of Fig. 3.1 to display text on one line by using several statements and to display text on several lines by using only one statement.

Displaying a Single Line of Text with Multiple Statements

"Welcome to C# Programming!" can be displayed several ways. Class Welcome2, shown in Fig. 3.14, uses two statements to produce the same output as that shown in Fig. 3.1. From this point forward, we highlight the new and key features in each code listing, as shown in lines 10–11 of Fig. 3.14.

```
 1   // Fig. 3.14: Welcome2.cs
 2   // Displaying one line of text with multiple statements.
 3   using System;
 4
 5   public class Welcome2
 6   {
 7      // Main method begins execution of C# application
 8      public static void Main( string[] args )
 9      {
10         Console.Write( "Welcome to " );
11         Console.WriteLine( "C# Programming!" );
12      } // end Main
13   } // end class Welcome2
```

```
Welcome to C# Programming!
```

Fig. 3.14 | Displaying one line of text with multiple statements.

The application is almost identical to Fig. 3.1. We discuss only the changes here. Line 2 is a comment stating the purpose of this application. Line 5 begins the Welcome2 class declaration. Lines 10–11 display one line of text in the console window. The first statement uses Console's method **Write** to display a string. Unlike WriteLine, after displaying its argument, Write does not position the screen cursor at the beginning of the next line in the console window—the next character the application displays will appear immediately after the last character that Write displays. Thus, line 11 positions the first character in its argument (the letter "C") immediately after the last character that line 10 displays (the space character before the string's closing double-quote character). Each Write statement resumes displaying characters from where the last Write statement displayed its last character.

Displaying Multiple Lines of Text with a Single Statement
A single statement can display multiple lines by using newline characters, which indicate to Console methods Write and WriteLine when they should position the screen cursor to the beginning of the next line in the console window. Like space characters and tab characters, newline characters are whitespace characters. The application of Fig. 3.15 outputs four lines of text, using newline characters to indicate when to begin each new line.

```
 1   // Fig. 3.15: Welcome3.cs
 2   // Displaying multiple lines with a single statement.
 3   using System;
 4
 5   public class Welcome3
 6   {
```

Fig. 3.15 | Displaying multiple lines with a single statement. (Part 1 of 2.)

```
 7        // Main method begins execution of C# application
 8        public static void Main( string[] args )
 9        {
10            Console.WriteLine( "Welcome\nto\nC#\nProgramming!" );
11        } // end Main
12    } // end class Welcome3
```

```
Welcome
to
C#
Programming!
```

Fig. 3.15 | Displaying multiple lines with a single statement. (Part 2 of 2.)

Most of the application is identical to the applications of Fig. 3.1 and Fig. 3.14, so we discuss only the changes here. Line 2 is a comment stating the purpose of this application. Line 5 begins the Welcome3 class declaration.

Line 10 displays four separate lines of text in the console window. Normally, the characters in a string are displayed exactly as they appear in the double quotes. Note, however, that the two characters \ and n (repeated three times in the statement) do not appear on the screen. The **backslash** (\) is called an **escape character**. It indicates to C# that a "special character" is in the string. When a backslash appears in a string of characters, C# combines the next character with the backslash to form an **escape sequence**. The escape sequence \n represents the **newline character**. When a newline character appears in a string being output with Console methods, the newline character causes the screen cursor to move to the beginning of the next line in the console window. Figure 3.16 lists several common escape sequences and describes how they affect the display of characters in the console window.

Escape sequence	Description
\n	Newline. Positions the screen cursor at the beginning of the next line.
\t	Horizontal tab. Moves the screen cursor to the next tab stop.
\r	Carriage return. Positions the screen cursor at the beginning of the current line—does not advance the cursor to the next line. Any characters output after the carriage return overwrite the characters previously output on that line.
\\	Backslash. Used to place a backslash character in a string.
\"	Double quote. Used to place a double-quote character (") in a string—e.g., `Console.Write( "\"in quotes\"" );` displays `"in quotes"`

Fig. 3.16 | Some common escape sequences.

3.5 Formatting Text with Console.Write and Console.WriteLine

Console methods Write and WriteLine also have the capability to display formatted data. Figure 3.17 outputs the strings "Welcome to" and "C# Programming!" with WriteLine.

```
 1   // Fig. 3.17: Welcome4.cs
 2   // Displaying multiple lines of text with string formatting.
 3   using System;
 4
 5   public class Welcome4
 6   {
 7      // Main method begins execution of C# application
 8      public static void Main( string[] args )
 9      {
10         Console.WriteLine( "{0}\n{1}", "Welcome to", "C# Programming!" );
11      } // end Main
12   } // end class Welcome4
```

```
Welcome to
C# Programming!
```

Fig. 3.17 | Displaying multiple lines of text with string formatting.

Line 10 calls method Console.WriteLine to display the application's output. The method call specifies three arguments. When a method requires multiple arguments, the arguments appear in a **comma-separated list**.

Good Programming Practice 3.7
Place a space after each comma (,) in an argument list to make applications more readable.

Most statements end with a semicolon (;). Therefore, line 10 represents only one statement. Large statements can be split over many lines, but there are some restrictions.

Common Programming Error 3.4
Splitting a statement in the middle of an identifier or a string is a syntax error.

Method WriteLine's first argument is a **format string** that may consist of **fixed text** and **format items**. Fixed text is output by WriteLine, as in Fig. 3.1. Each format item is a placeholder for a value. Format items also may include optional formatting information.

Format items are enclosed in curly braces and contain a sequence of characters that tell the method which argument to use and how to format it. For example, the format item {0} is a placeholder for the first additional argument (because C# starts counting from 0), {1} is a placeholder for the second, and so on. The format string in line 10 specifies that WriteLine should output two arguments and that the first one should be followed by a newline character. So this example substitutes "Welcome to" for the {0} and "C# Programming!" for the {1}. The output shows that two lines of text are displayed. Because braces in a formatted string normally indicate a placeholder for text substitution, you must type two left braces ({{) or two right braces (}}) to insert a single left or right brace into a formatted string, respectively. We introduce additional formatting features as they're needed in our examples.

3.6 Another C# Application: Adding Integers

Our next application reads (or inputs) two integers (whole numbers, like –22, 7, 0 and 1024) typed by a user at the keyboard, computes the sum of the values and displays the result. This application keeps track of the numbers supplied by the user in **variables**. The application of Fig. 3.18 demonstrates these concepts. In the sample output, we highlight data the user enters at the keyboard in bold.

```
 1   // Fig. 3.18: Addition.cs
 2   // Displaying the sum of two numbers input from the keyboard.
 3   using System;
 4
 5   public class Addition
 6   {
 7      // Main method begins execution of C# application
 8      public static void Main( string[] args )
 9      {
10         int number1; // declare first number to add
11         int number2; // declare second number to add
12         int sum; // declare sum of number1 and number2
13
14         Console.Write( "Enter first integer: " ); // prompt user
15         // read first number from user
16         number1 = Convert.ToInt32( Console.ReadLine() );
17
18         Console.Write( "Enter second integer: " ); // prompt user
19         // read second number from user
20         number2 = Convert.ToInt32( Console.ReadLine() );
21
22         sum = number1 + number2; // add numbers
23
24         Console.WriteLine( "Sum is {0}", sum ); // display sum
25      } // end Main
26   } // end class Addition
```

```
Enter first integer: 45
Enter second integer: 72
Sum is 117
```

Fig. 3.18 | Displaying the sum of two numbers input from the keyboard.

Lines 1–2 state the figure number, file name and purpose of the application. Line 5 begins the declaration of class Addition. Remember that the body of each class declaration starts with an opening left brace (line 6) and ends with a closing right brace (line 26).

The application begins execution with Main (lines 8–25). The left brace (line 9) marks the beginning of Main's body, and the corresponding right brace (line 25) marks the end of Main's body. Method Main is indented one level within the body of class Addition and the code in the body of Main is indented another level for readability.

Line 10 is a **variable declaration statement** (also called a **declaration**) that specifies the name and type of a variable (number1) used in this application. Variables are typically declared with a name and a type before they're used. The name of a variable can be any valid identifier. (See Section 3.2 for identifier naming requirements.) Declaration statements end with a semicolon (;).

The declaration in line 10 specifies that the variable named number1 is of type **int**—it will hold integer values . The range of values for an int is –2,147,483,648 (int.Min-Value) to +2,147,483,647 (int.MaxValue). We'll soon discuss types **float**, **double** and **decimal**, for specifying real numbers, and type **char**, for specifying characters. Real numbers contain decimal points, as in 3.4, 0.0 and –11.19. Variables of type float and double store approximations of real numbers in memory. Variables of type decimal store real numbers precisely (to 28–29 significant digits), so decimal variables are often used with monetary calculations. Variables of type char represent individual characters, such as an uppercase letter (e.g., A), a digit (e.g., 7), a special character (e.g., * or %) or an escape sequence (e.g., the newline character, \n). Types such as int, float, double, decimal and char are called **simple types**. Simple-type names are keywords and must appear in all lowercase letters. Appendix B summarizes the characteristics of the simple types (bool, byte, sbyte, char, short, ushort, int, uint, long, ulong, float, double and decimal).

The variable declaration statements at lines 11–12 similarly declare variables number2 and sum to be of type int. Variable declaration statements can be split over several lines, with the variable names separated by commas (i.e., a comma-separated list of variable names). Several variables of the same type may be declared in one declaration or in multiple declarations. For example, lines 10–12 can also be written as follows:

```
int number1, // declare first number to add
    number2, // declare second number to add
    sum; // declare sum of number1 and number2
```

Good Programming Practice 3.8
Declare each variable on a separate line. This format allows a comment to be easily inserted next to each declaration.

Good Programming Practice 3.9
Choosing meaningful variable names helps code to be self-documenting (i.e., one can understand the code simply by reading it rather than by reading documentation manuals or viewing an excessive number of comments).

Good Programming Practice 3.10
By convention, variable-name identifiers begin with a lowercase letter, and every word in the name after the first word begins with a capital letter. This naming convention is known as camel casing.

Line 14 uses Console.Write to display the message "Enter first integer: ". This message is a prompt—it directs the user to take a specific action. Line 16 first calls the Console's **ReadLine** method. This method waits for the user to type a string of characters at the keyboard and press the *Enter* key. As we mentioned, some methods perform a task, then return the result of that task. In this case, ReadLine returns the text the user entered. Then, the string is used as an argument to class **Convert**'s **ToInt32** method, which converts this sequence of characters into data of type int. In this case, method ToInt32 returns the int representation of the user's input.

Technically, the user can type anything as the input value. ReadLine will accept it and pass it off to the ToInt32 method. This method assumes that the string contains a valid integer value. In this application, if the user types a noninteger value, a runtime logic error called an exception will occur and the application will terminate. C# offers a technology called exception handling that will help you make your applications more robust by enabling them to handle exceptions and continue executing. This is also known as making your application **fault tolerant**. Chapter 13, Exception Handling, discusses how to make your applications more robust by enabling them to handle such errors and continue executing.

In line 16, the result of the call to method ToInt32 (an int value) is placed in variable number1 by using the **assignment operator**, =. The statement is read as "number1 gets the value returned by Convert.ToInt32." Operator = is a **binary operator**, because it works on two pieces of information. These are known as its **operands**—in this case, the operands are number1 and the result of the method call Convert.ToInt32. This statement is called an **assignment statement**, because it assigns a value to a variable. Everything to the right of the assignment operator, =, is always evaluated before the assignment is performed.

Good Programming Practice 3.11

Place spaces on either side of a binary operator to make it stand out and make the code more readable.

Line 18 prompts the user to enter the second integer. Line 20 reads a second integer and assigns it to the variable number2.

Line 22 calculates the sum of number1 and number2 and assigns the result to variable sum. In the preceding statement, the addition operator is a binary operator—its two operands are number1 and number2. Portions of statements that contain calculations are called **expressions**. In fact, an expression is any portion of a statement that has a value associated with it. For example, the value of the expression number1 + number2 is the sum of the numbers. Similarly, the value of the expression Console.ReadLine() is the string of characters typed by the user. After the calculation has been performed, line 24 uses method Console.WriteLine to display the sum. The format item {0} is a placeholder for the first argument after the format string. Other than the {0} format item, the remaining characters in the format string are all fixed text. So method WriteLine displays "Sum is ", followed by the value of sum (in the position of the {0} format item) and a newline.

Calculations can also be performed inside output statements. We could have combined the statements in lines 22 and 24 into the statement

```
Console.WriteLine( "Sum is {0}", ( number1 + number2 ) );
```

3.7 Arithmetic

The **arithmetic operators** are summarized in Fig. 3.19. Note the various special symbols not used in algebra. The **asterisk** (*) indicates multiplication, and the **percent sign** (%) is the **remainder operator** (called modulus in some languages), which we'll discuss shortly. The arithmetic operators in Fig. 3.19 are binary operators—for example, the expression f + 7 contains the binary operator + and the two operands f and 7.

C# operation	Arithmetic operator	Algebraic expression	C# expression
Addition	+	$f + 7$	f + 7
Subtraction	–	$p - c$	p - c
Multiplication	*	$b \cdot m$	b * m
Division	/	x / y or $\frac{x}{y}$ or $x \div y$	x / y
Remainder	%	$r \bmod s$	r % s

Fig. 3.19 | Arithmetic operators.

Integer division yields an integer quotient—for example, the expression 7 / 4 evaluates to 1, and the expression 17 / 5 evaluates to 3. Any fractional part in integer division is simply discarded (i.e., truncated)—no rounding occurs. C# provides the remainder operator, %, which yields the remainder after division. The expression x % y yields the remainder after x is divided by y. Thus, 7 % 4 yields 3, and 17 % 5 yields 2. This operator is most commonly used with integer operands but can also be used with floats, doubles, and decimals. We will consider several interesting applications of the remainder operator, such as determining whether one number is a multiple of another.

Arithmetic expressions must be written in **straight-line form** to facilitate entering applications into the computer. Thus, expressions such as "a divided by b" must be written as a / b, so that all constants, variables and operators appear in a straight line. The following algebraic notation is generally not acceptable to compilers:

$$\frac{a}{b}$$

Parentheses are used to group terms in C# expressions in the same manner as in algebraic expressions. For example, to multiply a times the quantity b + c, we write

```
a * ( b + c )
```

If an expression contains **nested parentheses**, such as

```
( ( a + b ) * c )
```

the expression in the innermost set of parentheses (a + b in this case) is evaluated first.

C# applies the operators in arithmetic expressions in a precise sequence determined by the following **rules of operator precedence**, which are generally the same as those followed in algebra (Fig. 3.20).

When we say that operators are applied from left to right, we're referring to their **associativity**. You'll see that some operators associate from right to left. Figure 3.20 summarizes these rules of operator precedence. We expand this table as additional operators are introduced. Appendix A provides the complete precedence chart.

Operators	Operations	Order of evaluation (associativity)
Evaluated first		
*	Multiplication	If there are several operators of this type,
/	Division	they're evaluated from left to right.
%	Remainder	
Evaluated next		
+	Addition	If there are several operators of this type,
–	Subtraction	they're evaluated from left to right.

Fig. 3.20 | Precedence of arithmetic operators.

3.8 Decision Making: Equality and Relational Operators

This section introduces a simple version of C#'s **if statement** that allows an application to make a decision based on the value of a condition. For example, the condition "grade is greater than or equal to 60" determines whether a student passed a test. If the condition in an if statement is true, the body of the if statement executes. If the condition is false, the body does not execute. We'll see an example shortly.

Conditions in if statements can be formed by using the **equality operators** (== and !=) and **relational operators** (>, <, >= and <=) summarized in Fig. 3.21. The two equality operators (== and !=) each have the same level of precedence, the relational operators (>, <, >= and <=) each have the same level of precedence, and the equality operators have lower precedence than the relational operators. They all associate from left to right.

> **Common Programming Error 3.5**
> *Confusing the equality operator, ==, with the assignment operator, =, can cause a logic error or a syntax error. The equality operator should be read as "is equal to," and the assignment operator should be read as "gets" or "gets the value of." To avoid confusion, some people read the equality operator as "double equals" or "equals equals."*

Standard algebraic equality and relational operators	C# equality or relational operator	Sample C# condition	Meaning of C# condition
Equality operators			
=	==	x == y	x is equal to y
≠	!=	x != y	x is not equal to y
Relational operators			
>	>	x > y	x is greater than y
<	<	x < y	x is less than y
≥	>=	x >= y	x is greater than or equal to y
≤	<=	x <= y	x is less than or equal to y

Fig. 3.21 | Equality and relational operators.

Figure 3.22 uses six if statements to compare two integers entered by the user. If the condition in any of these if statements is true, the assignment statement associated with that if statement executes. The application uses class Console to prompt for and read two lines of text from the user, extracts the integers from that text with the ToInt32 method of class Convert, and stores them in variables number1 and number2. Then the application compares the numbers and displays the results of the comparisons that are true.

The declaration of class Comparison begins at line 6. The class's Main method (lines 9–39) begins the execution of the application.

```
 1   // Fig. 3.22: Comparison.cs
 2   // Comparing integers using if statements, equality operators,
 3   // and relational operators.
 4   using System;
 5
 6   public class Comparison
 7   {
 8      // Main method begins execution of C# application
 9      public static void Main( string[] args )
10      {
11         int number1; // declare first number to compare
12         int number2; // declare second number to compare
13
14         // prompt user and read first number
15         Console.Write( "Enter first integer: " );
16         number1 = Convert.ToInt32( Console.ReadLine() );
17
18         // prompt user and read second number
19         Console.Write( "Enter second integer: " );
20         number2 = Convert.ToInt32( Console.ReadLine() );
21
22         if ( number1 == number2 )
23            Console.WriteLine( "{0} == {1}", number1, number2 );
24
25         if ( number1 != number2 )
26            Console.WriteLine( "{0} != {1}", number1, number2 );
27
28         if ( number1 < number2 )
29            Console.WriteLine( "{0} < {1}", number1, number2 );
30
31         if ( number1 > number2 )
32            Console.WriteLine( "{0} > {1}", number1, number2 );
33
34         if ( number1 <= number2 )
35            Console.WriteLine( "{0} <= {1}", number1, number2 );
36
37         if ( number1 >= number2 )
38            Console.WriteLine( "{0} >= {1}", number1, number2 );
39      } // end Main
40   } // end class Comparison
```

Fig. 3.22 | Comparing integers using if statements, equality operators and relational operators. (Part I of 2.)

```
Enter first integer: 42
Enter second integer: 42
42 == 42
42 <= 42
42 >= 42
```

```
Enter first integer: 1000
Enter second integer: 2000
1000 != 2000
1000 < 2000
1000 <= 2000
```

```
Enter first integer: 2000
Enter second integer: 1000
2000 != 1000
2000 > 1000
2000 >= 1000
```

Fig. 3.22 | Comparing integers using if statements, equality operators and relational operators. (Part 2 of 2.)

Lines 11–12 declare the int variables used to store the values entered by the user. Lines 14–16 prompt the user to enter the first integer and input the value. The input value is stored in variable number1. Lines 18-20 perform the same task, except that the input value is stored in variable number2.

Lines 22–23 compare the values of the variables number1 and number2 to determine whether they're equal. An if statement always begins with keyword if, followed by a condition in parentheses. An if statement expects one statement in its body. The indentation of the body statement shown here is not required, but it improves the code's readability by emphasizing that the statement in line 23 is part of the if statement that begins in line 22. Line 23 executes only if the numbers stored in variables number1 and number2 are equal (i.e., the condition is true). The if statements in lines 25–26, 28–29, 31–32, 34–35 and 37–38 compare number1 and number2 with the operators !=, <, >, <= and >=, respectively. If the condition in any of the if statements is true, the corresponding body statement executes.

Common Programming Error 3.6

Forgetting the left and/or right parentheses for the condition in an if statement is a syntax error—the parentheses are required.

Common Programming Error 3.7

Reversing the operators !=, >= and <=, as in =!, => and =<, can result in syntax or logic errors.

Common Programming Error 3.8

It's a syntax error if the operators ==, !=, >= and <= contain spaces between their symbols, as in = =, ! =, > = and < =, respectively.

Good Programming Practice 3.12

Indent an if statement's body to make it stand out and to enhance application readability.

There is no semicolon (;) at the end of the first line of each if statement. Such a semicolon would result in a logic error at execution time. For example,

```
if ( number1 == number2 ); // logic error
    Console.WriteLine( "{0} == {1}", number1, number2 );
```

would actually be interpreted by C# as

```
if ( number1 == number2 )
    ; // empty statement
Console.WriteLine( "{0} == {1}", number1, number2 );
```

where the semicolon in the line by itself—called the **empty statement**—is the statement to execute if the condition in the if statement is true. When the empty statement executes, no task is performed in the application. The application then continues with the output statement, which always executes, regardless of whether the condition is true or false, because the output statement is not part of the if statement.

Common Programming Error 3.9

Placing a semicolon immediately after the right parenthesis of the condition in an if statement is normally a logic error.

Note the use of whitespace in Fig. 3.22. Recall that whitespace characters, such as tabs, newlines and spaces, are normally ignored by the compiler. So statements may be split over several lines and may be spaced according to your preferences without affecting the meaning of an application. It's incorrect to split identifiers, strings, and multicharacter operators (like >=). Ideally, statements should be kept small, but this is not always possible.

Good Programming Practice 3.13

Place no more than one statement per line in an application. This format enhances readability.

Good Programming Practice 3.14

A lengthy statement can be spread over several lines. If a single statement must be split across lines, choose breaking points that make sense, such as after a comma in a comma-separated list, or after an operator in a lengthy expression. If a statement is split across two or more lines, indent all subsequent lines until the end of the statement.

Figure 3.23 shows the precedence of the operators introduced in this chapter. The operators are shown from top to bottom in decreasing order of precedence. All these operators, with the exception of the assignment operator, =, associate from left to right. Addition is left associative, so an expression like x + y + z is evaluated as if it had been written as (x + y) + z. The assignment operator, =, associates from right to left, so an expression like x = y = 0 is evaluated as if it had been written as x = (y = 0), which, as you'll soon see, first assigns the value 0 to variable y then assigns the result of that assignment, 0, to x.

Operators				Associativity	Type
*	/	%		left to right	multiplicative
+	-			left to right	additive
<	<=	>	>=	left to right	relational
==	!=			left to right	equality
=				right to left	assignment

Fig. 3.23 | Precedence and associativity of operations discussed so far.

Good Programming Practice 3.15

Refer to the operator precedence chart (the complete chart is in Appendix A) when writing expressions containing many operators. Confirm that the operations in the expression are performed in the order you expect. If you're uncertain about the order of evaluation in a complex expression, use parentheses to force the order, as you would do in algebraic expressions. Observe that some operators, such as assignment, =, associate from right to left rather than from left to right.

3.9 Wrap-Up

You learned many important features of C# in this chapter, including displaying data in a **Command Prompt**, inputting data from the keyboard, performing calculations and making decisions. The applications presented here introduced you to basic programming concepts. As you'll see in Chapter 4, C# applications typically contain just a few lines of code in method Main—these statements normally create the objects that perform the work of the application. In Chapter 4, you'll learn how to implement your own classes and use objects of those classes in applications.

Introduction to Classes and Objects

Objectives

In this chapter you'll learn:

- What classes, objects, methods and instance variables are.

- How to declare a class and use it to create an object.

- How to implement a class's behaviors as methods.

- How to implement a class's attributes as instance variables and properties.

- How to call an object's methods to make them perform their tasks.

- The differences between instance variables of a class and local variables of a method.

- How to use a constructor to ensure that an object's data is initialized when the object is created.

- The differences between value types and reference types.

Nothing can have value without being an object of utility.
—Karl Marx

Your public servants serve you right.
—Adlai E. Stevenson

*Knowing how to answer one who speaks,
To reply to one who sends a message.*
—Amenemope

*You'll see something new.
Two things. And I call them
Thing One and Thing Two.*
—Dr. Theodor Seuss Geisel

4.1 Introduction

In this chapter, we begin by explaining the concept of classes using a real-world example. Then we present five complete working applications to demonstrate how to create and use your own classes. The first four begin our case study on developing a grade book class that instructors can use to maintain student test scores. The last example introduces the type `decimal` and uses it to declare monetary amounts in the context of a bank account class that maintains a customer's balance.

4.2 Classes, Objects, Methods, Properties and Instance Variables

Let's begin with a simple analogy to help you understand classes and their contents. Suppose you want to drive a car and make it go faster by pressing down on its accelerator pedal. What must happen before you can do this? Well, before you can drive a car, someone has to design it. A car typically begins as engineering drawings, similar to the blueprints used to design a house. These engineering drawings include the design for an accelerator pedal to make the car go faster. The pedal "hides" the complex mechanisms that actually make the car go faster, just as the brake pedal "hides" the mechanisms that slow the car and the steering wheel "hides" the mechanisms that turn the car. This enables people with little or no knowledge of how engines work to drive a car easily.

Unfortunately, you can't drive the engineering drawings of a car. Before you can drive a car, it must be built from the engineering drawings that describe it. A completed car will have an actual accelerator pedal to make the car go faster, but even that's not enough—the car will not accelerate on its own, so the driver must press the accelerator pedal.

Methods

Now let's use our car example to introduce the key programming concepts of this section. Performing a task in an application requires a method. The **method** describes the mechanisms that actually perform its tasks. The method hides from its user the complex tasks that it performs, just as the accelerator pedal of a car hides from the driver the complex mechanisms of making the car go faster.

Classes

In C#, we begin by creating an application unit called a **class** to house (among other things) a method, just as a car's engineering drawings house (among other things) the design of an accelerator pedal. In a class, you provide one or more methods that are designed to perform the class's tasks. For example, a class that represents a bank account might contain one method to deposit money in an account, another to withdraw money from an account and a third to inquire what the current account balance is.

Objects

Just as you cannot drive an engineering drawing of a car, you cannot "drive" a class. Just as someone has to build a car from its engineering drawings before you can actually drive it, you must build an **object** of a class before you can make an application perform the tasks the class describes. That's one reason C# is known as an object-oriented programming language.

Method Calls

When you drive a car, pressing its gas pedal sends a message to the car to perform a task—make the car go faster. Similarly, you send **messages** to an object—each message is known as a **method call** and tells a method of the object to perform its task.

Attributes

Thus far, we've used the car analogy to introduce classes, objects and methods. In addition to a car's capabilities, it also has many **attributes**, such as its color, the number of doors, the amount of gas in its tank, its current speed and its total miles driven (i.e., its odometer reading). Like the car's capabilities, these attributes are represented as part of a car's design in its engineering diagrams. As you drive a car, these attributes are always associated with the car. Every car maintains its own attributes. For example, each car knows how much gas is in its own gas tank, but not how much is in the tanks of other cars. Similarly, an object has attributes that are carried with the object as it's used in an application. These attributes are specified as part of the object's class. For example, a bank-account object has a balance attribute that represents the amount of money in the account. Each bank-account object knows the balance in the account it represents, but not the balances of the other accounts in the bank. Attributes are specified by the class's **instance variables**.

Properties, Get Accessors and Set Accessors

Notice that these attributes are not necessarily accessible directly. The car manufacturer does not want drivers to take apart the car's engine to observe the amount of gas in its tank. Instead, the driver can check the fuel gauge on the dashboard. The bank does not want its customers to walk into the vault to count the amount of money in an account. Instead, the customers talk to a bank teller or check personalized online bank accounts. Similarly, you do not need to have access to an object's instance variables in order to use them. You can use the **properties** of an object. Properties contain **get accessors** for reading the values of variables, and **set accessors** for storing values into them.

4.3 Declaring a Class with a Method and Instantiating an Object of a Class

We begin with an example that consists of classes GradeBook (Fig. 4.1) and GradeBook-Test (Fig. 4.2). Class GradeBook (declared in file GradeBook.cs) will be used to display a message on the screen (Fig. 4.2) welcoming the instructor to the grade-book application. Class GradeBookTest (declared in the file GradeBookTest.cs) is a testing class in which the Main method will create and use an object of class GradeBook. By convention, we declare classes GradeBook and GradeBookTest in separate files, such that each file's name matches the name of the class it contains.

To start, select **File > New Project...** to open the **New Project** dialog, then create a GradeBook **Console Application**. Rename the Program.cs file to GradeBook.cs. Delete all the code provided automatically by the IDE and replace it with the code in Fig. 4.1.

```
 1   // Fig. 4.1: GradeBook.cs
 2   // Class declaration with one method.
 3   using System;
 4
 5   public class GradeBook
 6   {
 7      // display a welcome message to the GradeBook user
 8      public void DisplayMessage()
 9      {
10         Console.WriteLine( "Welcome to the Grade Book!" );
11      } // end method DisplayMessage
12   } // end class GradeBook
```

Fig. 4.1 | Class declaration with one method.

Class *GradeBook*

The GradeBook **class declaration** (Fig. 4.1) contains a DisplayMessage method (lines 8–11) that displays a message on the screen. Line 10 of the class displays the message. Recall that a class is like a blueprint—we need to make an object of this class and call its method to get line 10 to execute and display its message—we do this in Fig. 4.2.

The class declaration begins in line 5. The keyword public is an **access modifier**. Access modifiers determine the accessibility of an object's properties and methods to other methods in an application. For now, we simply declare every class public. Every class declaration contains keyword class followed by the class's name. Every class's body is enclosed in a pair of left and right braces ({ and }), as in lines 6 and 12 of class GradeBook.

In Chapter 3, each class we declared had one method named Main. Class GradeBook also has one method—DisplayMessage (lines 8–11). Recall that Main is a special method that's always called automatically when you execute an application. Most methods do not get called automatically. As you'll soon see, you must call method DisplayMessage to tell it to perform its task.

The method declaration begins with keyword public to indicate that the method is "available to the public"—that is, it can be called from outside the class declaration's body by methods of other classes. Keyword void—known as the method's **return type**—indicates that this method will not return (i.e., give back) any information to its **calling method** when it completes its task. When a method that specifies a return type other than void is called and completes its task, the method returns a result to its calling method. For example, when you go to an automated teller machine (ATM) and request your account balance, you expect the ATM to give you back a value that represents your balance. If you have a method Square that returns the square of its argument, you'd expect the statement

```
int result = Square( 2 );
```

to return 4 from method Square and assign 4 to variable result. If you have a method Maximum that returns the largest of three integer arguments, you'd expect the statement

```
int biggest = Maximum( 27, 114, 51 );
```

to return the value 114 from method Maximum and assign the value to variable biggest. You've already used methods that return information—for example, in Chapter 3 you used Console method ReadLine to input a string typed by the user at the keyboard. When ReadLine inputs a value, it returns that value for use in the application.

The name of the method, DisplayMessage, follows the return type (line 8). Generally, methods are named as verbs or verb phrases while classes are named as nouns. By convention, method names begin with an uppercase first letter, and all subsequent words in the name begin with an uppercase letter. This naming convention is referred to as Pascal case. The parentheses after the method name indicate that this is a method. An empty set of parentheses, as shown in line 8, indicates that this method does not require additional information to perform its task. Line 8 is commonly referred to as the **method header**. Every method's body is delimited by left and right braces, as in lines 9 and 11.

The body of a method contains statements that perform the method's task. In this case, the method contains one statement (line 10) that displays the message "Welcome to the Grade Book!", followed by a newline in the console window. After this statement executes, the method has completed its task.

Next, we'd like to use class GradeBook in an application. As you learned in Chapter 3, method Main begins the execution of every application. Class GradeBook cannot begin an application because it does not contain Main. This was not a problem in Chapter 3, because every class you declared had a Main method. To fix this problem for the Grade-Book, we must either declare a separate class that contains a Main method or place a Main method in class GradeBook. In preparation for the larger applications we'll encounter later in this book, we use a separate class (GradeBookTest in this example) containing method Main to test each new class we create in this chapter.

Adding a Class to a Visual C# Project

For each example in this chapter, you'll add a class to your console application. To do this, right click the project name in the **Solution Explorer** and select **Add > New Item...** from the pop-up menu. In the **Add New Item** dialog that appears, select **Code File** and enter the name of your new file (GradeBookTest.cs) then click the **Add** button. A new, blank file will be added to your project. Add the code from Fig. 4.2 to this file.

Class GradeBookTest

The GradeBookTest class declaration (Fig. 4.2) contains the Main method that controls our application's execution. Any class that contains a Main method (as shown in line 6) can be used to execute an application. This class declaration begins in line 3 and ends in line 14. The class contains only a Main method, which is typical of many classes that simply begin an application's execution.

Lines 6–13 declare method Main. A key part of enabling the method Main to begin the application's execution is the static keyword (line 6), which indicates that Main is a static method. A static method is special because it can be called without first creating an object of the class (in this case, GradeBookTest) in which the method is declared. We explain static methods in Chapter 7, Methods: A Deeper Look.

```
 1   // Fig. 4.2: GradeBookTest.cs
 2   // Create a GradeBook object and call its DisplayMessage method.
 3   public class GradeBookTest
 4   {
 5      // Main method begins program execution
 6      public static void Main( string[] args )
 7      {
 8         // create a GradeBook object and assign it to myGradeBook
 9         GradeBook myGradeBook = new GradeBook();
10
11         // call myGradeBook's DisplayMessage method
12         myGradeBook.DisplayMessage();
13      } // end Main
14   } // end class GradeBookTest
```

```
Welcome to the Grade Book!
```

Fig. 4.2 | Create a GradeBook object and call its DisplayMessage method.

In this application, we'd like to call class GradeBook's DisplayMessage method to display the welcome message in the console window. Typically, you cannot call a method that belongs to another class until you create an object of that class, as shown in line 9. We begin by declaring variable myGradeBook. The variable's type is GradeBook—the class we declared in Fig. 4.1. Each new class you create becomes a new type in C# that can be used to declare variables and create objects. New class types will be accessible to all classes in the same project. You can declare new class types as needed; this is one reason why C# is known as an **extensible language**.

Variable myGradeBook (line 9) is initialized with the result of the **object-creation expression** new GradeBook(). The new operator creates a new object of the class specified to the right of the keyword (i.e., GradeBook). The parentheses to the right of the Grade-Book are required. As you'll learn in Section 4.10, those parentheses in combination with a class name represent a call to a constructor, which is similar to a method, but is used only at the time an object is created to initialize the object's data. In that section you'll see that data can be placed in parentheses to specify initial values for the object's data. For now, we simply leave the parentheses empty.

We can now use myGradeBook to call its method DisplayMessage. Line 12 calls the method DisplayMessage (lines 8–11 of Fig. 4.1) using variable myGradeBook followed by a **member access (.) operator**, the method name DisplayMessage and an empty set of parentheses. This call causes the DisplayMessage method to perform its task. This method call differs from the method calls in Chapter 3 that displayed information in a console window—each of those method calls provided arguments that specified the data to display. At the beginning of line 12, "myGradeBook." indicates that Main should use the GradeBook object that was created in line 9. The empty parentheses in line 8 of Fig. 4.1 indicate that method DisplayMessage does not require additional information to perform its task. For this reason, the method call (line 12 of Fig. 4.2) specifies an empty set of parentheses after the method name to indicate that no arguments are being passed to method DisplayMessage. When method DisplayMessage completes its task, method Main continues executing at line 13. This is the end of method Main, so the application terminates.

UML Class Diagram for Class GradeBook

Figure 4.3 presents a **UML class diagram** for class GradeBook of Fig. 4.1. Recall from Section 1.9 that the UML is a graphical language used by programmers to represent their object-oriented systems in a standardized manner. In the UML, each class is modeled in a class diagram as a rectangle with three compartments. The top compartment contains the name of the class centered horizontally in boldface type. The middle compartment contains the class's attributes, which correspond to instance variables and properties in C#. In Fig. 4.3, the middle compartment is empty because the version of class GradeBook in Fig. 4.1 does not have any attributes. The bottom compartment contains the class's operations, which correspond to methods in C#. The UML models operations by listing the operation name followed by a set of parentheses. Class GradeBook has one method, DisplayMessage, so the bottom compartment of Fig. 4.3 lists one operation with this name. Method DisplayMessage does not require additional information to perform its tasks, so there are empty parentheses following DisplayMessage in the class diagram, just as they appeared in the method's declaration in line 8 of Fig. 4.1. The plus sign (+) in front of the operation name indicates that DisplayMessage is a public operation in the UML (i.e., a public method in C#). The plus sign is sometimes called the **public visibility symbol**. We'll often use UML class diagrams to summarize a class's attributes and operations.

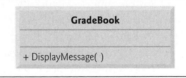

Fig. 4.3 | UML class diagram indicating that class GradeBook has a public DisplayMessage operation.

4.4 Declaring a Method with a Parameter

In our car analogy from Section 4.2, we discussed the fact that pressing a car's gas pedal sends a message to the car to perform a task—make the car go faster. But how fast should the car accelerate? As you know, the farther down you press the pedal, the faster the car accelerates. So the message to the car actually includes both the task to be performed and additional information that helps the car perform the task. This additional information is known as a **parameter**—the value of the parameter helps the car determine how fast to accelerate. Similarly, a method can require one or more parameters that represent additional information it needs to perform its task. A method call supplies values—called arguments—for each of the method's parameters. For example, the Console.WriteLine method requires an argument that specifies the data to be displayed in a console window. Similarly, to make a deposit into a bank account, a Deposit method specifies a parameter that represents the deposit amount. When the Deposit method is called, an argument value representing the deposit amount is assigned to the method's parameter. The method then makes a deposit of that amount, by increasing the account's balance.

Our next example declares class GradeBook (Fig. 4.4) with a DisplayMessage method that displays the course name as part of the welcome message. (See the sample execution in Fig. 4.5.) The new DisplayMessage method requires a parameter that represents the course name to output.

```
1   // Fig. 4.4: GradeBook.cs
2   // Class declaration with a method that has a parameter.
3   using System;
4
5   public class GradeBook
6   {
7      // display a welcome message to the GradeBook user
8      public void DisplayMessage( string courseName )
9      {
10         Console.WriteLine( "Welcome to the grade book for\n{0}!",
11            courseName );
12      } // end method DisplayMessage
13   } // end class GradeBook
```

Fig. 4.4 | Class declaration with a method that has a parameter.

Before discussing the new features of class GradeBook, let's see how the new class is used from the Main method of class GradeBookTest (Fig. 4.5). Line 12 creates an object of class GradeBook and assigns it to variable myGradeBook. Line 15 prompts the user to enter a course name. Line 16 reads the name from the user and assigns it to the variable nameOfCourse, using Console method ReadLine to perform the input. The user types the course name and presses *Enter* to submit the course name to the application. Pressing *Enter* inserts a newline character at the end of the characters typed by the user. Method ReadLine reads characters typed by the user until the newline character is encountered, then returns a string containing the characters up to, but not including, the newline. The newline character is discarded.

```
1   // Fig. 4.5: GradeBookTest.cs
2   // Create a GradeBook object and pass a string to
3   // its DisplayMessage method.
4   using System;
5
6   public class GradeBookTest
7   {
8      // Main method begins program execution
9      public static void Main( string[] args )
10     {
11        // create a GradeBook object and assign it to myGradeBook
12        GradeBook myGradeBook = new GradeBook();
13
14        // prompt for and input course name
15        Console.WriteLine( "Please enter the course name:" );
16        string nameOfCourse = Console.ReadLine(); // read a line of text
17        Console.WriteLine(); // output a blank line
18
19        // call myGradeBook's DisplayMessage method
20        // and pass nameOfCourse as an argument
21        myGradeBook.DisplayMessage( nameOfCourse );
22     } // end Main
23   } // end class GradeBookTest
```

Fig. 4.5 | Create GradeBook object and pass a string to its DisplayMessage method. (Part 1 of 2.)

```
Please enter the course name:
CS101 Introduction to C# Programming

Welcome to the grade book for
CS101 Introduction to C# Programming!
```

Fig. 4.5 | Create GradeBook object and pass a string to its DisplayMessage method. (Part 2 of 2.)

Line 21 calls myGradeBook's DisplayMessage method. The variable nameOfCourse in parentheses is the argument that's passed to method DisplayMessage so that the method can perform its task. Variable nameOfCourse's value in Main becomes the value of method DisplayMessage's parameter courseName in line 8 of Fig. 4.4. When you execute this application, notice that method DisplayMessage outputs the name you type as part of the welcome message (Fig. 4.5).

Software Engineering Observation 4.1

Normally, objects are created with new. One exception is a string literal that's contained in quotes, such as "hello". String literals are references to string objects that are implicitly created by C#.

More on Arguments and Parameters

When you declare a method, you must specify in the method's declaration whether the method requires data to perform its task. To do so, you place additional information in the method's **parameter list**, which is located in the parentheses that follow the method name. The parameter list may contain any number of parameters, including none at all. Each parameter is declared as a variable with a type and identifier in the parameter list. Empty parentheses following the method name (as in Fig. 4.1, line 8) indicate that a method does not require any parameters. In Fig. 4.4, DisplayMessage's parameter list (line 8) declares that the method requires one parameter. Each parameter must specify a type and an identifier. In this case, the type string and the identifier courseName indicate that method DisplayMessage requires a string to perform its task. At the time the method is called, the argument value in the call is assigned to the corresponding parameter (in this case, courseName) in the method header. Then, the method body uses the parameter courseName to access the value. Lines 10–11 of Fig. 4.4 display parameter courseName's value, using the {0} format item in WriteLine's first argument. The parameter variable's name (Fig. 4.4, line 8) can be the same or different from the argument variable's name (Fig. 4.5, line 21).

A method can specify multiple parameters by separating each parameter from the next with a comma. The number of arguments in a method call must match the number of parameters in the parameter list of the called method's declaration. Also, the types of the arguments in the method call must be consistent with the types of the corresponding parameters in the method's declaration. (As you'll learn in subsequent chapters, an argument's type and its corresponding parameter's type are not always required to be identical.) In our example, the method call passes one argument of type string (nameOfCourse is declared as a string in line 16 of Fig. 4.5), and the method declaration specifies one parameter of type string (line 8 in Fig. 4.4). So the type of the argument in the method call exactly matches the type of the parameter in the method header.

Common Programming Error 4.1

A compilation error occurs if the number and types of arguments in a method call do not match the number and types of parameters in the method declaration.

Updated UML Class Diagram for Class GradeBook

The UML class diagram of Fig. 4.6 models class GradeBook of Fig. 4.4. Like Fig. 4.4, this GradeBook class contains public operation DisplayMessage. However, this version of DisplayMessage has a parameter. The UML models a parameter a bit differently from C# by listing the parameter name, followed by a colon and the parameter type in the parentheses following the operation name. The UML has several data types that are similar to the C# types. For example, UML types String and Integer correspond to C# types string and int, respectively. Unfortunately, the UML does not provide types that correspond to every C# type. For this reason, and to avoid confusion between UML types and C# types, *we use only C# types in our UML diagrams.* Class Gradebook's method Display-Message (Fig. 4.4) has a string parameter named courseName, so Fig. 4.6 lists the parameter courseName : string between the parentheses following DisplayMessage.

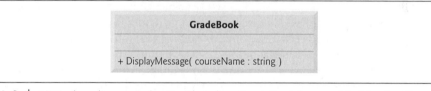

Fig. 4.6 | UML class diagram indicating that class GradeBook has a public DisplayMessage operation with a courseName parameter of type string.

Notes on using Directives

Notice the using directive in Fig. 4.5 (line 4). This indicates to the compiler that the application uses classes in the System namespace, like the Console class. Why do we need a using directive to use class Console, but not class GradeBook? There is a special relationship between classes that are compiled in the same project, like classes GradeBook and GradeBookTest. By default, such classes are considered to be in the same namespace. A using directive is not required when one class in a namespace uses another in the same namespace—such as when class GradeBookTest uses class GradeBook. For simplicity, our examples in this chapter do not declare a namespace. Any classes that are not explicitly placed in a namespace are implicitly placed in the so-called **global namespace**.

Actually, the using directive in line 4 is not required if we always refer to class Console as System.Console, which includes the full namespace and class name. This is known as the class's **fully qualified class name**. For example, line 15 could be written as

```
System.Console.WriteLine( "Please enter the course name:" );
```

Most C# programmers consider using fully qualified names to be cumbersome, and instead prefer to use using directives.

4.5 Instance Variables and Properties

In Chapter 3, we declared all of an application's variables in the application's Main method. Variables declared in the body of a method are known as **local variables** and can be used only in that method. When a method terminates, the values of its local variables are lost. Recall from Section 4.2 that an object has attributes that are carried with the object as it's used in an application. Such attributes exist before a method is called on an object and after the method completes execution.

Attributes are represented as variables in a class declaration. Such variables are called **fields** and are declared inside a class declaration but outside the bodies of the class's method declarations. When each object of a class maintains its own copy of an attribute, the field that represents the attribute is also known as an instance variable—each object (instance) of the class has a separate instance of the variable. In Chapter 10, Classes and Objects: A Deeper Look, we discuss another type of field called a static variable, where all objects of the same class share one variable.

A class normally contains one or more properties that manipulate the attributes that belong to a particular object of the class. The example in this section demonstrates a GradeBook class that contains a courseName instance variable to represent a particular GradeBook object's course name, and a CourseName property to manipulate courseName.

GradeBook Class with an Instance Variable and a Property
In our next application (Figs. 4.7–4.8), class GradeBook (Fig. 4.7) maintains the course name as an instance variable so that it can be used or modified at any time during an application's execution. The class also contains one method—DisplayMessage (lines 24–30)—and one property—CourseName (line 11–21). Recall from Chapter 2 that properties are used to manipulate an object's attributes. For example, in that chapter, we used a Label's Text property to specify the text to display on the Label. In this example, we use a property in code rather than in the **Properties** window of the IDE. To do this, we first declare a property as a member of the GradeBook class. As you'll soon see, the GradeBook's CourseName property can be used to store a course name in a GradeBook (in instance variable courseName) or retrieve the GradeBook's course name (from instance variable course-Name). Method DisplayMessage—which now specifies no parameters—still displays a welcome message that includes the course name. However, the method now uses the CourseName property to obtain the course name from instance variable courseName.

A typical instructor teaches more than one course, each with its own course name. Line 8 declares courseName as a variable of type string. Line 8 is a declaration for an instance variable, because the variable is declared in the class's body (lines 7–31) but outside the bodies of the class's method (lines 24–30) and property (lines 11–21). Every instance (i.e., object) of class GradeBook contains one copy of each instance variable. For example, if there are two GradeBook objects, each object has its own copy of courseName. All the methods and properties of class GradeBook can directly manipulate its instance variable courseName, but it's considered good practice for methods of a class to use that class's properties to manipulate instance variables (as we do in line 29 of method DisplayMessage). The software engineering reasons for this will soon become clear.

```
 1    // Fig. 4.7: GradeBook.cs
 2    // GradeBook class that contains a courseName instance variable,
 3    // and a property to get and set its value.
```

Fig. 4.7 | GradeBook class that contains a private instance variable, courseName and a public property to get and set its value. (Part 1 of 2.)

```
4    using System;
5
6    public class GradeBook
7    {
8       private string courseName; // course name for this GradeBook
9
10      // property to get and set the course name
11      public string CourseName
12      {
13         get
14         {
15            return courseName;
16         } // end get
17         set
18         {
19            courseName = value;
20         } // end set
21      } // end property CourseName
22
23      // display a welcome message to the GradeBook user
24      public void DisplayMessage()
25      {
26         // use property CourseName to get the
27         // name of the course that this GradeBook represents
28         Console.WriteLine( "Welcome to the grade book for\n{0}!",
29            CourseName ); // display property CourseName
30      } // end method DisplayMessage
31   } // end class GradeBook
```

Fig. 4.7 | GradeBook class that contains a private instance variable, courseName and a public property to get and set its value. (Part 2 of 2.)

Access Modifiers *public* and *private*

Most instance-variable declarations are preceded with the keyword private (as in line 8). Like public, keyword private is an access modifier. Variables, properties or methods declared with access modifier private are accessible only to properties and methods of the class in which they're declared. Thus, variable courseName can be used only in property CourseName and method DisplayMessage of class GradeBook.

Software Engineering Observation 4.2

Precede every field and method declaration with an access modifier. Generally, instance variables should be declared private and methods and properties should be declared public. If the access modifier is omitted before a member of a class, the member is implicitly declared private. (We'll see that it's appropriate to declare certain methods private, if they will be accessed only by other methods of the class.)

Software Engineering Observation 4.3

Declaring the instance variables of a class as private and the methods of the class as public facilitates debugging, because problems with data manipulations are localized to the class's methods and properties, since the private instance variables are accessible only to these methods and properties.

Declaring instance variables with access modifier `private` is known as **information hiding**. When an application creates (instantiates) an object of class `GradeBook`, variable `courseName` is encapsulated (hidden) in the object and can be accessed only by methods and properties of the object's class.

Setting and Getting the Values of `private` Instance Variables

How can we allow a program to manipulate a class's `private` instance variables but ensure that they remain in a valid state? We need to provide controlled ways for programmers to "get" (i.e., retrieve) the value in an instance variable and "set" (i.e., modify) the value in an instance variable. Although you can define methods like `GetCourseName` and `SetCourseName`, C# properties provide a more elegant solution. Next, we show how to declare and use properties.

GradeBook Class with a Property

The `GradeBook` class's `CourseName` **property declaration** is located in lines 11–21 of Fig. 4.7. The property begins in line 11 with an access modifier (in this case, `public`), followed by the type that the property represents (`string`) and the property's name (`Course-Name`). Properties use the same naming conventions as methods and classes.

Properties contain **accessors** that handle the details of returning and modifying data. A property declaration can contain a `get` accessor, a `set` accessor or both. The `get` accessor (lines 13–16) enables a client to read the value of `private` instance variable `courseName`; the `set` accessor (lines 17–20) enables a client to modify `courseName`.

After defining a property, you can use it like a variable in your code. For example, you can assign a value to a property using the = (assignment) operator. This executes the code in the property's `set` accessor to set the value of the corresponding instance variable. Similarly, referencing the property to use its value (for example, to display it on the screen) executes the code in the property's `get` accessor to obtain the corresponding instance variable's value. We show how to use properties shortly. By convention, we name each property with the capitalized name of the instance variable that it manipulates (e.g., `CourseName` is the property that represents instance variable `courseName`)—C# is case sensitive, so these are distinct identifiers.

get and set Accessors

Let's look more closely at property `CourseName`'s `get` and `set` accessors (Fig. 4.7). The `get` accessor (lines 13–16) begins with the identifier **get** and its body is delimited by braces. The accessor's body contains a **return statement**, which consists of the keyword **return** followed by an expression. The expression's value is returned to the client code that uses the property. In this example, the value of `courseName` is returned when the property `Course-Name` is referenced. For example, in the following statement

```
string theCourseName = gradeBook.CourseName;
```

the expression `gradeBook.CourseName` (where `gradeBook` is an object of class `GradeBook`) executes property `CourseName`'s `get` accessor, which returns the value of instance variable `courseName`. That value is then stored in variable `theCourseName`. Property `CourseName` can be used as simply as if it were an instance variable. The property notation allows the client to think of the property as the underlying data. Again, the client cannot directly manipulate instance variable `courseName` because it's `private`.

The set accessor (lines 17–20) begins with the identifier **set** and its body is delimited by braces. When the property CourseName appears in an assignment statement, as in

```
gradeBook.CourseName = "CS100 Introduction to Computers";
```

the text "CS100 Introduction to Computers" is assigned to the set accessor's contextual keyword named **value** and the set accessor executes. Note that value is implicitly declared and initialized in the set accessor—it's a compilation error to declare a local variable value in this body. Line 19 stores the contents of value in instance variable courseName. A set accessor does not return any data when it completes its task.

The statements inside the property in lines 15 and 19 (Fig. 4.7) each access course-Name even though it was declared outside the property. We can use instance variable courseName in the methods and properties of class GradeBook, because courseName is an instance variable of the class.

Using Property *CourseName* in Method *DisplayMessage*
Method DisplayMessage (lines 24–30 of Fig. 4.7) does not receive any parameters. Lines 28–29 output a welcome message that includes the value of instance variable courseName. We do not reference courseName directly. Instead, we access property CourseName (line 29), which executes the property's get accessor, returning the value of courseName.

GradeBookTest *Class That Demonstrates Class* GradeBook
Class GradeBookTest (Fig. 4.8) creates a GradeBook object and demonstrates property CourseName. Line 11 creates a GradeBook object and assigns it to local variable myGrade-Book. Lines 14–15 display the initial course name using the object's CourseName property—this executes the property's get accessor, which returns the value of courseName.

The first line of the output shows an empty name (marked by ' '). Unlike local variables, which are not automatically initialized, every field has a **default initial value**—a value provided by C# when you do not specify the initial value. Thus, fields are not required to be explicitly initialized before they're used in an application—unless they must be initialized to values other than their default values. The default value for an instance variable of type string (like courseName) is null. When you display a string variable that contains the value null, no text is displayed on the screen.

Line 18 prompts the user to enter a course name. Line 19 assigns the course name entered by the user to object myGradeBook's CourseName property. When a value is assigned to CourseName, the value specified (which is returned by ReadLine in this case) is assigned to implicit parameter value of CourseName's set accessor (lines 17–20, Fig. 4.7). Then parameter value is assigned by the set accessor to instance variable courseName (line 19 of Fig. 4.7). Line 20 (Fig. 4.8) displays a blank line, then line 23 calls myGradeBook's DisplayMessage method to display the welcome message containing the course name.

```
1   // Fig. 4.8: GradeBookTest.cs
2   // Create and manipulate a GradeBook object.
3   using System;
4
5   public class GradeBookTest
6   {
```

Fig. 4.8 | Create and manipulate a GradeBook object. (Part 1 of 2.)

```
 7      // Main method begins program execution
 8      public static void Main( string[] args )
 9      {
10         // create a GradeBook object and assign it to myGradeBook
11         GradeBook myGradeBook = new GradeBook();
12
13         // display initial value of CourseName
14         Console.WriteLine( "Initial course name is: '{0}'\n",
15            myGradeBook.CourseName );
16
17         // prompt for and read course name
18         Console.WriteLine( "Please enter the course name:" );
19         myGradeBook.CourseName = Console.ReadLine(); // set CourseName
20         Console.WriteLine(); // output a blank line
21
22         // display welcome message after specifying course name
23         myGradeBook.DisplayMessage();
24      } // end Main
25   } // end class GradeBookTest
```

```
Initial course name is: ''

Please enter the course name:
CS101 Introduction to C# Programming

Welcome to the grade book for
CS101 Introduction to C# Programming!
```

Fig. 4.8 | Create and manipulate a GradeBook object. (Part 2 of 2.)

4.6 UML Class Diagram with a Property

Figure 4.9 contains an updated UML class diagram for the version of class GradeBook in Fig. 4.7. We model properties in the UML as attributes—the property (in this case, CourseName) is listed as a public attribute—as indicated by the plus (+) sign—preceded by the word "property" in **guillemets** (« and »). Using descriptive words in guillemets (called **stereotypes** in the UML) helps distinguish properties from other attributes and operations. The UML indicates the type of the property by placing a colon and a type after the property name. The get and set accessors of the property are implied, so they're not listed in the UML diagram. Class GradeBook also contains one public method Display-Message, so the class diagram lists this operation in the third compartment. Recall that the plus (+) sign is the public visibility symbol.

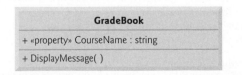

Fig. 4.9 | UML class diagram indicating that class GradeBook has a public CourseName property of type string and one public method.

A class diagram helps you design a class, so it's not required to show every implementation detail of the class. Since an instance variable that's manipulated by a property is really an implementation detail of that property, our class diagram does not show the courseName instance variable. A programmer implementing the GradeBook class based on this class diagram would create the instance variable courseName as part of the implementation process (as we did in Fig. 4.7).

In some cases, you may find it necessary to model the private instance variables of a class. Like properties, instance variables are attributes of a class and are modeled in the middle compartment of a class diagram. The UML represents instance variables as attributes by listing the attribute name, followed by a colon and the attribute type. To indicate that an attribute is private, a class diagram would list the **private visibility symbol**—a minus sign (–)—before the attribute's name. For example, the instance variable course-Name in Fig. 4.7 would be modeled as "- courseName : string" to indicate that it's a private attribute of type string.

4.7 Software Engineering with Properties and set and get Accessors

Using properties as described earlier in this chapter would seem to violate the notion of private data. Although providing a property with get and set accessors may appear to be the same as making its corresponding instance variable public, this is not the case. A public instance variable can be read or written by any property or method in the program. If an instance variable is private, the client code can access the instance variable only indirectly through the class's non-private properties or methods. This allows the class to control the manner in which the data is set or returned. For example, get and set accessors can translate between the format of the data stored in the private instance variable and the format of the data preferred by the client.

Consider a Clock class that represents the time of day as a private int instance variable time, containing the number of seconds since midnight. Suppose the class provides a Time property of type string to manipulate this instance variable. Although get accessors typically return data exactly as it's stored in an object, they need not expose the data in this "raw" format. When a client refers to a Clock object's Time property, the property's get accessor could use instance variable time to determine the number of hours, minutes and seconds since midnight, then return the time as a string of the form "HH:MM:SS". Similarly, suppose a Clock object's Time property is assigned a string of the form "HH:MM:SS". Using the string capabilities presented in Chapter 16, Strings and Characters, and the method Convert.ToInt32 presented in Section 3.6, the Time property's set accessor can convert this string to an int number of seconds since midnight and store the result in the Clock object's private instance variable time. The Time property's set accessor can also provide **data-validation** capabilities that scrutinize attempts to modify the instance variable's value to ensure that the value it receives represents a valid time (e.g., "12:30:45" is valid but "42:85:70" is not). We demonstrate data validation in Section 4.11. So, although a property's accessors enable clients to manipulate private data, they carefully control those manipulations, and the object's private data remains safely encapsulated (i.e., hidden) in the object. This is not possible with public instance variables, which can easily be set by clients to invalid values.

Properties of a class should also be used by the class's own methods to manipulate the class's private instance variables, even though the methods can directly access the private instance variables. Accessing an instance variable via a property's accessors—as in the body of method DisplayMessage (Fig. 4.7, lines 28–29)—creates a more robust class that's easier to maintain and less likely to malfunction. If we decide to change the representation of instance variable courseName in some way, the declaration of method DisplayMessage does not require modification—only the bodies of property Course-Name's get and set accessors that directly manipulate the instance variable will need to change. For example, suppose we want to represent the course name as two separate instance variables—courseNumber (e.g., "CS101") and courseTitle (e.g., "Introduction to C# Programming"). The DisplayMessage method can still use property CourseName's get accessor to obtain the full course name to display as part of the welcome message. In this case, the get accessor would need to build and return a string containing the courseNumber, followed by the courseTitle. Method DisplayMessage would continue to display the complete course title "CS101 Introduction to C# Programming," because it's unaffected by the change to the class's instance variables.

4.8 Auto-Implemented Properties

In Fig. 4.7, we created a GradeBook class with a private courseName instance variable and a public property CourseName to enable client code to access the courseName. When you look at the CourseName property's definition (Fig. 4.7, lines 11–21), notice that the get accessor simply returns private instance variable courseName's value and the set accessor simply assigns a value to the instance variable—no other logic appears in the accessors. For such cases, C# provides **automatically implemented properties** (also known as **auto-implemented properties**). With an auto-implemented property, the C# compiler creates a private instance variable, and the get and set accessors for returning and modifying the private instance variable. Unlike a user-defined property, an auto-implemented property, must have both a get and a set accessor. This enables you to implement the property trivially, which is handy when you're first designing a class. If you later decide to include other logic in the get or set accessors, you can simply modify the property's implementation. To use an auto-implemented property in the GradeBook class of Fig. 4.7, you can replace the private instance variable at line 8 and the property at lines 11–21 with the following code:

```
public string CourseName { get; set; }
```

Code Snippets for Auto-implemented Properties

The IDE has a feature called **code snippets** that allows you to insert predefined code templates into your source code. One such snippet enables you to insert a public auto-implemented property by typing the word "prop" in the code window and pressing the *Tab* key twice. Certain pieces of the inserted code are highlighted for you to easily change the property's type and name. You can press the *Tab* key to move from one highlighted piece of text to the next in the inserted code. By default, the new property's type is int and its name is MyProperty. To get a list of all available code snippets, type *Ctrl + k*, *Ctrl + x*. This displays the **Insert Snippet** window in the code editor. You can navigate through the Visual C# snippet folders with the mouse to see the snippets. This feature can also be accessed by right clicking in the source code editor and selecting the **Insert Snippet...** menu item.

4.9 Value Types vs. Reference Types

Types in C# are divided into two categories—**value types** and **reference types**. C#'s simple types are all value types. A variable of a value type simply contains a value of that type. For example, Fig. 4.10 shows an int variable named count that contains the value 7. Value types are implemented as structs, which are similar to classes and are discussed in more detail in Chapter 16.

`int count = 7;`

count

| 7 |

A variable (count) of a value type (int) contains a value (7) of that type

---

Fig. 4.10 | Value-type variable.

By contrast, a variable of a reference type (sometimes called a **reference**) contains the address of a location in memory where the data referred to by that variable is stored. Such a variable is said to **refer to an object** in the program. Line 11 of Fig. 4.8 creates a GradeBook object, places it in memory and stores the object's reference in variable myGradeBook of type GradeBook as shown in Fig. 4.11. The GradeBook object is shown with its courseName instance variable.

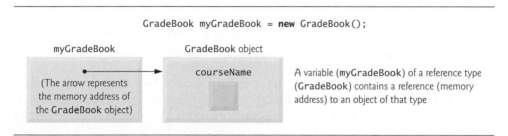

`GradeBook myGradeBook = new GradeBook();`

Fig. 4.11 | Reference-type variable.

Reference-type instance variables (such as myGradeBook in Fig. 4.11) are initialized by default to the value **null**. string is a reference type. For this reason, string variable courseName is shown in Fig. 4.11 with an empty box representing the null-valued variable. A string variable with the value null is not an empty string, which is represented by "" or **string.Empty**. The value null represents a reference that does not refer to an object. The empty string is a string object with no characters in it.

A client of an object must use a variable that refers to the object to **invoke** (i.e., call) the object's methods and access the object's properties. In Fig. 4.8, the statements in Main use variable myGradeBook, which contains the GradeBook object's reference, to send messages to the GradeBook object. These messages are calls to methods (like DisplayMessage) or references to properties (like CourseName) that enable the program to interact with GradeBook objects. For example, line 19 of Fig. 4.8 uses the reference myGradeBook to set the course name by assigning a value to property CourseName. This sends a message to the GradeBook object to invoke the CourseName property's set accessor. The message includes as an argument the value read from the user's input (in this case, "CS101 Introduction to C# Programming") that CourseName's set accessor requires to perform its task. The set accessor uses this information to set the courseName instance variable. In Section 7.16, we discuss value types and reference types in detail.

Software Engineering Observation 4.4

A variable's declared type (e.g., int, double or GradeBook) indicates whether the variable is of a value or a reference type. If a variable's type is not one of the thirteen simple types (Appendix B), or an enum or a struct type (which we discuss in Section 7.10 and Chapter 16, respectively), then it's a reference type. For example, Account account1 indicates that account1 is a variable that can refer to an Account object.

4.10 Initializing Objects with Constructors

As mentioned in Section 4.5, when a GradeBook (Fig. 4.7) object is created, its instance variable courseName is initialized to null by default. This is also true of the private instance variable that the compiler creates for the auto-implemented CourseName property discussed in Section 4.8. What if you want to provide a course name when you create a GradeBook object? Each class can provide a **constructor** that can be used to initialize an object of a class when the object is created. In fact, C# requires a constructor call for every object that's created. The new operator calls the class's constructor to perform the initialization. The constructor call is indicated by the class name, followed by parentheses. For example, line 11 of Fig. 4.8 first uses new to create a GradeBook object. The empty parentheses after "new GradeBook()" indicate a call without arguments to the class's constructor. The compiler provides a **public default constructor** with no parameters in any class that does not explicitly define a constructor, so *every* class has a constructor. The default constructor does not modify the default values of the instance variables.

When you declare a class, you can provide your own constructor (or several constructors, as you'll learn in Chapter 10) to specify custom initialization for objects of your class. For example, you might want to specify a course name for a GradeBook object when the object is created, as in

```
GradeBook myGradeBook =
    new GradeBook( "CS101 Introduction to C# Programming" );
```

In this case, the argument "CS101 Introduction to C# Programming" is passed to the GradeBook object's constructor and used to initialize the CourseName. Each time you create a new GradeBook object, you can provide a different course name. The preceding statement requires that the class provide a constructor with a string parameter. Figure 4.12 contains a modified GradeBook class with such a constructor.

```
1   // Fig. 4.12: GradeBook.cs
2   // GradeBook class with a constructor to initialize the course name.
3   using System;
4
5   public class GradeBook
6   {
```

Fig. 4.12 | GradeBook class with a constructor to initialize the course name. (Part 1 of 2.)

```
 7      // auto-implemented property CourseName implicitly created an
 8      // instance variable for this GradeBook's course name
 9      public string CourseName { get; set; }
10
11      // constructor initializes auto-implemented property
12      // CourseName with string supplied as argument
13      public GradeBook( string name )
14      {
15         CourseName = name; // set CourseName to name
16      } // end constructor
17
18      // display a welcome message to the GradeBook user
19      public void DisplayMessage()
20      {
21         // use auto-implemented property CourseName to get the
22         // name of the course that this GradeBook represents
23         Console.WriteLine( "Welcome to the grade book for\n{0}!",
24            CourseName );
25      } // end method DisplayMessage
26   } // end class GradeBook
```

Fig. 4.12 | GradeBook class with a constructor to initialize the course name. (Part 2 of 2.)

Lines 13–16 declare the constructor for class GradeBook. A constructor must have the same name as its class. Like a method, a constructor specifies in its parameter list the data it requires to perform its task. When you use new to create an object, you place this data in the parentheses that follow the class name. Unlike a method, a constructor doesn't specify a return type (not even void). Line 13 indicates that class GradeBook's constructor has a parameter called name of type string. In line 15, the name passed to the constructor is used to initialize auto-implemented property CourseName via its set accessor.

Figure 4.13 demonstrates initializing GradeBook objects using this constructor. Lines 12–13 create and initialize a GradeBook object. The constructor of class GradeBook is called with the argument "CS101 Introduction to C# Programming" to initialize the course name. The object-creation expression to the right of = in lines 12–13 returns a reference to the new object, which is assigned to variable gradeBook1. Lines 14–15 repeat this process for another GradeBook object, this time passing the argument "CS102 Data Structures in C#" to initialize the course name for gradeBook2. Lines 18–21 use each object's CourseName property to obtain the course names and show that they were indeed initialized when the objects were created. In Section 4.5, you learned that each instance (i.e., object) of a class contains its own copy of the class's instance variables. The output confirms that each GradeBook maintains its own course name.

```
1   // Fig. 4.13: GradeBookTest.cs
2   // GradeBook constructor used to specify the course name at the
3   // time each GradeBook object is created.
4   using System;
5
```

Fig. 4.13 | GradeBook constructor used to specify the course name at the time each GradeBook object is created. (Part 1 of 2.)

```
 6   public class GradeBookTest
 7   {
 8       // Main method begins program execution
 9       public static void Main( string[] args )
10       {
11           // create GradeBook object
12           GradeBook gradeBook1 = new GradeBook( // invokes constructor
13               "CS101 Introduction to C# Programming" );
14           GradeBook gradeBook2 = new GradeBook( // invokes constructor
15               "CS102 Data Structures in C#" );
16
17           // display initial value of courseName for each GradeBook
18           Console.WriteLine( "gradeBook1 course name is: {0}",
19               gradeBook1.CourseName );
20           Console.WriteLine( "gradeBook2 course name is: {0}",
21               gradeBook2.CourseName );
22       } // end Main
23   } // end class GradeBookTest
```

```
gradeBook1 course name is: CS101 Introduction to C# Programming
gradeBook2 course name is: CS102 Data Structures in C#
```

Fig. 4.13 | GradeBook constructor used to specify the course name at the time each GradeBook object is created. (Part 2 of 2.)

Normally, constructors are declared public. If a class does not explicitly define a constructor, the class's instance variables are initialized to their default values—0 for numeric types, false for type bool and null for reference types. If you declare any constructors for a class, C# will not create a default constructor for that class.

Error-Prevention Tip 4.1

Unless default initialization of your class's instance variables is acceptable, provide a constructor to ensure that your class's instance variables are properly initialized with meaningful values when each new object of your class is created.

Adding the Constructor to Class *GradeBook's* UML Class Diagram

The UML class diagram of Fig. 4.14 models class GradeBook of Fig. 4.12, which has a constructor that has a name parameter of type string. Like operations, the UML models constructors in the third compartment of a class in a class diagram. To distinguish a constructor from a class's operations, the UML places the word "constructor" between

GradeBook
+ «property» CourseName : string
+ «constructor» GradeBook(name : string) + DisplayMessage( )

Fig. 4.14 | UML class diagram indicating that class GradeBook has a constructor with a name parameter of type string.

guillemets (« and ») before the constructor's name. It's customary to list constructors before other operations in the third compartment.

4.11 Floating-Point Numbers and Type `decimal`

In our next application, we depart temporarily from our `GradeBook` case study to declare a class called `Account` that maintains a bank account's balance. Most account balances are not whole numbers (such as 0, −22 and 1024). For this reason, class `Account` represents the account balance as a real number (i.e., a number with a decimal point, such as 7.33, 0.0975 or 1000.12345). C# provides three simple types for storing real numbers—`float`, **`double`**, and `decimal`. Types `float` and `double` are called **floating-point** types. The primary difference between them and `decimal` is that `decimal` variables store a limited range of real numbers precisely, whereas floating-point variables store only approximations of real numbers, but across a much greater range of values. Also, `double` variables can store numbers with larger magnitude and finer detail (i.e., more digits to the right of the decimal point—also known as the number's **precision**) than `float` variables. A key application of type `decimal` is representing monetary amounts.

Real-Number Precision and Storage Requirements
Variables of type `float` represent **single-precision floating-point numbers** and have seven significant digits. Variables of type `double` represent **double-precision floating-point numbers**. These require twice as much storage as `float` variables and provide 15–16 significant digits—approximately double the precision of `float` variables. Furthermore, variables of type `decimal` require twice as much storage as `double` variables and provide 28–29 significant digits. In some applications, even variables of type `double` and `decimal` will be inadequate—such applications are beyond the scope of this book.

Most programmers represent floating-point numbers with type `double`. In fact, C# treats all real numbers you type in an application's source code (such as 7.33 and 0.0975) as `double` values by default. Such values in the source code are known as **floating-point literals**. To type a **`decimal` literal**, you must type the letter "M" or "m" (which stands for "money") at the end of a real number (for example, 7.33M is a `decimal` literal rather than a `double`). Integer literals are implicitly converted into type `float`, `double` or `decimal` when they're assigned to a variable of one of these types. See Appendix B, for the ranges of values for variables of types `float`, `double`, `decimal` and all the other simple types.

Although floating-point numbers are not always 100% precise, they have numerous applications. For example, when we speak of a "normal" body temperature of 98.6, we do not need to be precise to a large number of digits. When we read the temperature on a thermometer as 98.6, it may actually be 98.5999473210643. Calling this number simply 98.6 is fine for most applications involving body temperatures. Due to the imprecise nature of floating-point numbers, type `decimal` is preferred over the floating-point types whenever the calculations need to be exact, as with monetary calculations. In cases where approximation is enough, `double` is preferred over type `float` because `double` variables can represent floating-point numbers more accurately. For this reason, we use type `decimal` throughout the book for monetary amounts and type `double` for other real numbers.

Real numbers also arise as a result of division. In conventional arithmetic, for example, when we divide 10 by 3, the result is 3.3333333…, with the sequence of 3s repeating infinitely. The computer allocates only a fixed amount of space to hold such a value, so clearly the stored floating-point value can be only an approximation.

> **Common Programming Error 4.2**
> *Using floating-point numbers in a manner that assumes they're represented precisely can lead to logic errors.*

Account Class with an Instance Variable of Type `decimal`

Our next application (Figs. 4.15–4.16) contains a simple class named Account (Fig. 4.15) that maintains the balance of a bank account. A typical bank services many accounts, each with its own balance, so line 7 declares an instance variable named balance of type decimal. Variable balance is an instance variable because it's declared in the body of the class (lines 6–36) but outside the class's method and property declarations (lines 10–13, 16–19 and 22–35). Every instance (i.e., object) of class Account contains its own copy of balance.

Class Account contains a constructor, a method, and a property. Since it's common for someone opening an account to place money in the account immediately, the constructor (lines 10–13) receives a parameter initialBalance of type decimal that represents the account's starting balance. Line 12 assigns initialBalance to the property Balance, invoking Balance's set accessor to initialize the instance variable balance.

```
1   // Fig. 4.15: Account.cs
2   // Account class with a constructor to
3   // initialize instance variable balance.
4
5   public class Account
6   {
7      private decimal balance; // instance variable that stores the balance
8
9      // constructor
10     public Account( decimal initialBalance )
11     {
12        Balance = initialBalance; // set balance using property
13     } // end Account constructor
14
15     // credit (add) an amount to the account
16     public void Credit( decimal amount )
17     {
18        Balance = Balance + amount; // add amount to balance
19     } // end method Credit
20
21     // a property to get and set the account balance
22     public decimal Balance
23     {
24        get
25        {
26           return balance;
27        } // end get
28        set
29        {
```

Fig. 4.15 | Account class with a constructor to initialize instance variable balance.

```
30              // validate that value is greater than or equal to 0;
31              // if it is not, balance is left unchanged
32              if ( value >= 0 )
33                 balance = value;
34           } // end set
35        } // end property Balance
36     } // end class Account
```

Fig. 4.15 | Account class with a constructor to initialize instance variable balance.

```
1   // Fig. 4.16: AccountTest.cs
2   // Create and manipulate Account objects.
3   using System;
4
5   public class AccountTest
6   {
7      // Main method begins execution of C# application
8      public static void Main( string[] args )
9      {
10        Account account1 = new Account( 50.00M ); // create Account object
11        Account account2 = new Account( -7.53M ); // create Account object
12
13        // display initial balance of each object using a property
14        Console.WriteLine( "account1 balance: {0:C}",
15           account1.Balance ); // display Balance property
16        Console.WriteLine( "account2 balance: {0:C}\n",
17           account2.Balance ); // display Balance property
18
19        decimal depositAmount; // deposit amount read from user
20
21        // prompt and obtain user input
22        Console.Write( "Enter deposit amount for account1: " );
23        depositAmount = Convert.ToDecimal( Console.ReadLine() );
24        Console.WriteLine( "adding {0:C} to account1 balance\n",
25           depositAmount );
26        account1.Credit( depositAmount ); // add to account1 balance
27
28        // display balances
29        Console.WriteLine( "account1 balance: {0:C}",
30           account1.Balance );
31        Console.WriteLine( "account2 balance: {0:C}\n",
32           account2.Balance );
33
34        // prompt and obtain user input
35        Console.Write( "Enter deposit amount for account2: " );
36        depositAmount = Convert.ToDecimal( Console.ReadLine() );
37        Console.WriteLine( "adding {0:C} to account2 balance\n",
38           depositAmount );
39        account2.Credit( depositAmount ); // add to account2 balance
40
41        // display balances
42        Console.WriteLine( "account1 balance: {0:C}", account1.Balance );
```

Fig. 4.16 | Create and manipulate an Account object. (Part I of 2.)

```
43        Console.WriteLine( "account2 balance: {0:C}", account2.Balance );
44     } // end Main
45   } // end class AccountTest
```

```
account1 balance: $50.00
account2 balance: $0.00

Enter deposit amount for account1: 49.99
adding $49.99 to account1 balance

account1 balance: $99.99
account2 balance: $0.00

Enter deposit amount for account2: 123.21
adding $123.21 to account2 balance

account1 balance: $99.99
account2 balance: $123.21
```

Fig. 4.16 | Create and manipulate an `Account` object. (Part 2 of 2.)

Method `Credit` (lines 16–19) doesn't return data when it completes its task, so its return type is `void`. The method receives one parameter named `amount`—a `decimal` value that's added to the property `Balance`. Line 18 uses both the `get` and `set` accessors of `Balance`. The expression `Balance + amount` invokes property `Balance`'s `get` accessor to obtain the current value of instance variable `balance`, then adds `amount` to it. We then assign the result to instance variable `balance` by invoking the `Balance` property's `set` accessor (thus replacing the prior `balance` value).

Property `Balance` (lines 22–35) provides a `get` accessor, which allows clients of the class (i.e., other classes that use this class) to obtain the value of a particular `Account` object's `balance`. The property has type `decimal` (line 22). `Balance` also provides an enhanced `set` accessor.

In Section 4.5, we introduced properties whose `set` accessors allow clients of a class to modify the value of a `private` instance variable. In Fig. 4.7, class `GradeBook` defines property `CourseName`'s `set` accessor to assign the value received in its parameter `value` to instance variable `courseName` (line 19). This `CourseName` property does not ensure that `courseName` contains only valid data.

The application of Figs. 4.15–4.16 enhances the `set` accessor of class `Account`'s property `Balance` to perform this validity checking. Line 32 (Fig. 4.15) ensures that `value` is nonnegative. If the value is greater than or equal to 0, the amount stored in `value` is assigned to instance variable `balance` in line 33. Otherwise, `balance` is left unchanged.

AccountTest *Class to Use Class* Account

Class `AccountTest` (Fig. 4.16) creates two `Account` objects (lines 10–11) and initializes them respectively with `50.00M` and `-7.53M` (the decimal literals representing the real numbers 50.00 and -7.53). The `Account` constructor (lines 10–13 of Fig. 4.15) references property `Balance` to initialize `balance`. In previous examples, the benefit of referencing the property in the constructor was not evident. Now, however, the constructor takes advantage of the validation provided by the `set` accessor of the `Balance` property. The constructor simply assigns a value to `Balance` rather than duplicating the `set` accessor's validation code. When line 11 of Fig. 4.16 passes an initial balance of -7.53 to the Account constructor, the constructor passes this value to the set accessor of property Balance, where the actual initialization occurs. This value is less than 0, so the set accessor does not modify balance, leaving this instance variable with its default value of 0.

Lines 14–17 in Fig. 4.16 output the balance in each Account by using the Account's Balance property. When Balance is used for account1 (line 15), the value of account1's balance is returned by the get accessor in line 26 of Fig. 4.15 and displayed by the Console.WriteLine statement (Fig. 4.16, lines 14–15). Similarly, when property Balance is called for account2 from line 17, the value of the account2's balance is returned from line 26 of Fig. 4.15 and displayed by the Console.WriteLine statement (Fig. 4.16, lines 16–17). The balance of account2 is 0 because the constructor ensured that the account could not begin with a negative balance. The value is output by WriteLine with the format item {0:C}, which formats the account balance as a monetary amount. The : after the 0 indicates that the next character represents a **format specifier**, and the C format specifier after the : specifies a monetary amount (C is for currency). The cultural settings on the user's machine determine the format for displaying monetary amounts. For example, in the United States, 50 displays as $50.00. In Germany, 50 displays as 50,00€. Figure 4.17 lists a few other format specifiers in addition to C.

Format specifier	Description
C or c	Formats the string as currency. Displays an appropriate currency symbol ($ in the United States) next to the number. Separates digits with an appropriate separator character (comma in the United States) and sets the number of decimal places to two by default.
D or d	Formats the string as a decimal. Displays number as an integer.
N or n	Formats the string with a thousands separator and a default of two decimal places.
E or e	Formats the number using scientific notation with a default of six decimal places.
F or f	Formats the string with a fixed number of decimal places (two by default).
G or g	Formats the number normally with decimal places or using scientific notation, depending on context. If a format item does not contain a format specifier, format G is assumed implicitly.
X or x	Formats the string as hexadecimal.

Fig. 4.17 | `string` format specifiers.

Line 19 declares local variable depositAmount to store each deposit amount entered by the user. Unlike the instance variable balance in class Account, the local variable depositAmount in Main is *not* initialized to 0 by default. However, this variable does not need to be initialized here because its value will be determined by the user's input. The compiler does not allow a local variable's value to be read until it's initialized.

Line 22 prompts the user to enter a deposit amount for account1. Line 23 obtains the input from the user by calling the Console class's ReadLine method, then passing the string entered by the user to the Convert class's **ToDecimal** method, which returns the decimal value in this string. Lines 24–25 display the deposit amount. Line 26 calls object account1's Credit method and supplies depositAmount as the method's argument. When the method is called, the argument's value is assigned to parameter amount of method Credit (lines 16–19 of Fig. 4.15), then method Credit adds that value to the balance (line 18 of Fig. 4.15). Lines 29–32 (Fig. 4.16) output the balances of both Accounts again to show that only account1's balance changed.

Line 35 prompts the user to enter a deposit amount for account2. Line 36 obtains the input from the user by calling method Console.ReadLine, and passing the return value to the Convert class's ToDecimal method. Lines 37–38 display the deposit amount. Line 39 calls object account2's Credit method and supplies depositAmount as the method's argument, then method Credit adds that value to the balance. Finally, lines 42–43 output the balances of both Accounts again to show that only account2's balance changed.

set and *get* Accessors with Different Access Modifiers

By default, the get and set accessors of a property have the same access as the property—for example, for a public property, the accessors are public. It's possible to declare the get and set accessors with different access modifiers. In this case, one of the accessors must implicitly have the same access as the property and the other must be declared with a more restrictive access modifier than the property. For example, in a public property, the get accessor might be public and the set accessor might be private. We demonstrate this feature in Section 10.6.

> **Error-Prevention Tip 4.2**
>
> *The benefits of data integrity are not automatic simply because instance variables are made private—you must provide appropriate validity checking and report the errors.*

> **Error-Prevention Tip 4.3**
>
> *set accessors that set the values of private data should verify that the intended new values are proper; if they're not, the set accessors should leave the instance variables unchanged and indicate an error. We demonstrate how to indicate errors in Chapter 13, Exception Handling.*

UML Class Diagram for Class Account

The UML class diagram in Fig. 4.18 models class Account of Fig. 4.15. The diagram models the Balance property as a UML attribute of type decimal (because the corresponding C# property had type decimal). The diagram models class Account's constructor with a parameter initialBalance of type decimal in the third compartment of the class. The diagram models operation Credit in the third compartment with an amount

Account
+ «property» Balance : decimal
+ «constructor» Account(initialBalance : decimal) + Credit(amount : decimal)

Fig. 4.18 | UML class diagram indicating that class Account has a public Balance property of type decimal, a constructor and a method.

parameter of type decimal (because the corresponding method has an amount parameter of C# type decimal).

4.12 Wrap-Up

In this chapter, you learned the basic object-oriented concepts of classes, objects, methods, instance variables and properties—these will be used in most substantial C# applications you create. You learned how to declare instance variables of a class to maintain data for each object of the class, how to declare methods that operate on that data, and how to declare properties to obtain and set that data. We demonstrated how to call a method to tell it to perform its task and how to pass information to methods as arguments. We discussed the difference between a local variable of a method and an instance variable of a class and that only instance variables are initialized automatically. We discussed the difference between a value type and a reference type. You learned how to create auto-implemented properties. You also learned how to use a class's constructor to specify the initial values for an object's instance variables. We discussed some of the differences between value types and reference types. You learned about the value types float, double and decimal for storing real numbers.

We showed how the UML can be used to create class diagrams that model the constructors, methods, properties and attributes of classes. You learned the value of declaring instance variables private and using public properties to manipulate them. For example, we demonstrated how set accessors in properties can be used to validate an object's data and ensure that the object is maintained in a consistent state. You learned how to create auto-implemented properties.

In the next chapter we begin our introduction to control statements, which specify the order in which an application's actions are performed. You'll use these in your methods to specify how they should perform their tasks.

5

Control Statements:
Part 1

OBJECTIVES

In this chapter you'll learn:

- To use the `if` and `if...else` selection statements to choose between alternative actions.

- To use the `while` repetition statement to execute statements in an application repeatedly.

- To use counter-controlled repetition and sentinel-controlled repetition.

- To use the increment, decrement and compound assignment operators.

5.1 Introduction

In this chapter, we introduce C#'s if, if...else and while control statements,. We devote a portion of the chapter (and Chapters 6 and 8) to further developing the GradeBook class we introduced in Chapter 4. In particular, we add a method to the GradeBook class that uses control statements to calculate the average of a set of student grades. Another example demonstrates additional ways to combine control statements to solve a similar problem. We introduce C#'s compound assignment operators and explore its increment and decrement operators. These additional operators abbreviate and simplify many statements. Finally, we present an overview of C#'s simple types. In Chapter 6, Control Statements: Part 2, we present most of C#'s remaining control statements. Then we present C#'s last control statement, foreach, in Chapter 8, Arrays.

5.2 Control Structures

Normally, statements in an application are executed one after the other in the order in which they're written—this process is called sequential execution. Various C# statements enable you to specify that the next statement to execute is not necessarily the next one in sequence—this is called transfer of control.

During the 1960s, it became clear that the indiscriminate use of transfers of control was the root of much difficulty experienced by software development groups. The blame was pointed at the **goto statement** (used in most programming languages of the time), which allows programmers to specify a transfer of control to one of a wide range of possible destinations in an application (creating what is often called "spaghetti code"). The notion of so-called **structured programming** became almost synonymous with "goto elimination." We recommend that you avoid C#'s goto statement.

Research[1] had demonstrated that applications could be written without goto statements. The challenge of the era for programmers was to shift their styles to "goto-less programming." Not until the 1970s did programmers start taking structured programming seriously. The results were impressive because structured applications were clearer, easier to debug and modify, and more likely to be bug free in the first place.

Bohm and Jacopini's work demonstrated that all applications could be written in terms of only three control structures—the **sequence structure**, the **selection structure** and the **repetition structure**. When we introduce C#'s implementations of control structures, we'll refer to them in the terminology of the *C# Language Specification* as "control statements."

---

1. Bohm, C., and G. Jacopini, "Flow Diagrams, Turing Machines, and Languages with Only Two Formation Rules," *Communications of the ACM*, Vol. 9, No. 5, May 1966, pp. 336–371.

Sequence Structure in C#

The sequence structure is built into C#. Unless directed otherwise, the computer executes C# statements are executed one after the other in the order in which they're written—that is, in sequence. The UML **activity diagram** in Fig. 5.1 illustrates a typical sequence structure in which two calculations are performed in order. C# lets you have as many actions as you want in a sequence structure.

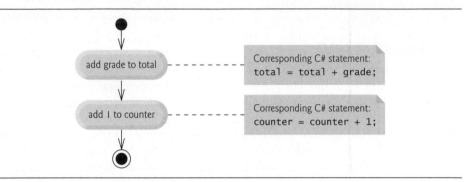

Fig. 5.1 | Sequence structure activity diagram.

An activity diagram models the **workflow** (also called the **activity**) of a portion of a software system. Such workflows may include a portion of an algorithm, such as the sequence structure in Fig. 5.1. Activity diagrams are composed of special-purpose symbols, such as **action-state symbols** (rectangles with their left and right sides replaced with arcs curving outward), **diamonds** and **small circles**. These symbols are connected by **transition arrows**, which represent the flow of the activity—that is, the order in which the actions should occur. Activity diagrams help you develop and represent algorithms. They also clearly show how control structures operate.

Consider the activity diagram for the sequence structure in Fig. 5.1. It contains two **action states** that represent actions to perform. Each action state contains an **action expression**—for example, "add grade to total" or "add 1 to counter"—that specifies an action to perform. Other actions might include calculations or input/output operations. The arrows in the activity diagram represent **transitions**, which indicate the order in which the actions occur. The portion of the application that implements the activities illustrated by the diagram in Fig. 5.1 first adds grade to total, then adds 1 to counter.

The **solid circle** at the activity diagram's top represents the activity's **initial state**—the beginning of the workflow before the application performs the modeled actions. The **solid circle surrounded by a hollow circle** that appears at the bottom of the diagram represents the **final state**—the end of the workflow after the application performs its actions.

Figure 5.1 also includes rectangles with the upper-right corners folded over. These are UML **notes** (like comments in C#) that describe the purpose of symbols in the diagram. Figure 5.1 uses UML notes to show the C# code associated with each action state in the activity diagram. A **dotted line** connects each note with the element that the note describes. Activity diagrams normally do not show the C# code that implements the activity. We use notes for this purpose here to illustrate how the diagram relates to C# code. For more information on the UML, see our optional case study, which appears in Chapters 30–31, and visit our UML Resource Center (www.deitel.com/UML/) and www.uml.org.

Selection Structures in C#

C# has three types of selection structures, which from this point forward we shall refer to as **selection statements**. The **if statement** either performs (selects) an action if a condition is true or skips the action if the condition is false. The **if...else** statement performs an action if a condition is true or performs a different action if the condition is false. The switch statement (Chapter 6) performs one of many different actions, depending on the value of an expression.

The if statement is called a **single-selection statement** because it selects or ignores a single action (or, as we'll soon see, a single group of actions). The if...else statement is called a **double-selection statement** because it selects between two different actions (or groups of actions). The switch statement is called a **multiple-selection statement** because it selects among many different actions (or groups of actions).

Repetition Structures in C#

C# provides four repetition structures, which from this point forward we shall refer to as **repetition statements**—these are the while, do...while, for and foreach statements. (Chapter 6 presents the do...while and for statements. Chapter 8 discusses the foreach statement.) The while, for and foreach statements perform the action (or group of actions) in their bodies zero or more times—if the loop-continuation condition is initially false, the action (or group of actions) will not execute. The do...while statement performs the action (or group of actions) in its body one or more times.

Summary of Control Statements in C#

C# has only three kinds of structured control statements: the sequence statement, selection statement (three types) and repetition statement (four types). We combine as many of each type of statement as necessary to make the program flow and work as required. As with the sequence statement in Fig. 5.1, we can model each control statement as an activity diagram. Each diagram contains one initial state and one final state that represent a control statement's entry point and exit point, respectively. **Single-entry/single-exit control statements** make it easy to build applications—the control statements are "attached" to one another by connecting the exit point of one to the entry point of the next. We call this **control-statement stacking**. There's only one other way in which control statements may be connected: **control-statement nesting**, in which one control statement appears inside another. Thus, algorithms in C# applications are constructed from only three kinds of structured control statements, combined in only two ways. This is the essence of simplicity.

5.3 if Single-Selection Statement

Applications use selection statements to choose among alternative courses of action. For example, suppose that the passing grade on an exam is 60. The C# statement

```
if ( grade >= 60 )
    Console.WriteLine( "Passed" );
```

determines whether the condition grade >= 60 is true or false. If the condition is true, "Passed" is displayed, and the next C# statement in order is performed. If the condition is false, the output statement is ignored, and the next C# statement in order is performed. The indentation of the second line of this selection statement is optional, but recommended, because it emphasizes the inherent structure of the if statement.

Figure 5.2 illustrates the single-selection if statement. This UML activity diagram contains what is perhaps the most important symbol in an activity diagram—the diamond, or **decision symbol**, which indicates that a decision is to be made. The workflow will continue along a path determined by the symbol's associated **guard conditions**, which can be true or false. Each transition arrow emerging from a decision symbol has a guard condition (specified in square brackets next to the transition arrow). If a guard condition is true, the workflow enters the action state to which the transition arrow points. In Fig. 5.2, if grade >= 60 is true, the application displays "Passed", then transitions to the final state of this activity. If grade < 60 is true, the application immediately transitions to the final state without displaying a message.

The if statement is a single-entry/single-exit control statement. The activity diagrams for the remaining control statements also contain initial states, transition arrows, action states that indicate actions to perform and decision symbols (with associated guard conditions) that indicate decisions to be made, and final states.

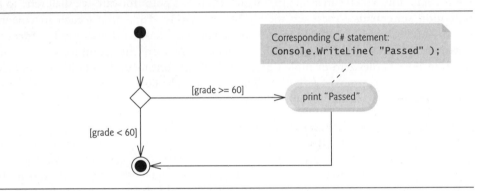

Fig. 5.2 | if single-selection statement UML activity diagram.

5.4 if...else Double-Selection Statement

The if single-selection statement performs an indicated action only when the condition is true; otherwise, the action is skipped. The if...else double-selection statement allows you to specify an action to perform when the condition is true and a different action when the condition is false. For example, the C# statement

```
if ( grade >= 60 )
    Console.WriteLine( "Passed" );
else
    Console.WriteLine( "Failed" );
```

displays "Passed" if grade >= 60 is true, but displays "Failed" if grade < 60 is true. In either case, after displaying occurs, the next statement in sequence is performed. The body of the else part is also indented. Whatever indentation convention you choose should be applied consistently throughout your applications. It's difficult to read applications that do not obey uniform spacing conventions.

Good Programming Practice 5.1

Indent both body statements of an if...else statement.

Good Programming Practice 5.2

If there are several levels of indentation, each level should be indented the same additional amount of space.

Figure 5.3 illustrates the flow of control in the if...else statement. Once again, the symbols in the UML activity diagram (besides the initial state, transition arrows and final state) represent action states and a decision.

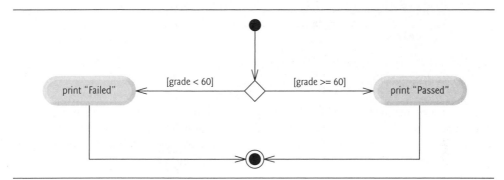

Fig. 5.3 | if...else double-selection statement UML activity diagram.

Conditional Operator (?:)

C# provides the **conditional operator** (?:), which can be used in place of an if...else statement. This is C#'s only **ternary operator**—it takes three operands. Together, the operands and the ?: symbols form a **conditional expression.** The first operand (to the left of the ?) is a **boolean** expression (i.e., an expression that evaluates to a bool-type value—**true** or **false**), the second operand (between the ? and :) is the value of the conditional expression if the boolean expression is true and the third operand (to the right of the :) is the value of the conditional expression if the boolean expression is false. For example, the statement

```
Console.WriteLine( grade >= 60 ? "Passed" : "Failed" );
```

displays the value of WriteLine's conditional-expression argument. The conditional expression in the preceding statement evaluates to the string "Passed" if the boolean expression grade >= 60 is true and evaluates to the string "Failed" if the boolean expression is false. Thus, this statement with the conditional operator performs essentially the same function as the if...else statement shown earlier in this section. You'll see that conditional expressions can be used in some situations where if...else statements cannot.

Good Programming Practice 5.3

When a conditional expression is inside a larger expression, it's good practice to parenthesize the conditional expression for clarity. Adding parentheses may also prevent operator-precedence problems that could cause syntax errors.

Nested if...else Statements

An application can test multiple cases by placing if...else statements inside other if...else statements to create **nested if...else statements.** For example, the following nested if...else statement displays A for exam grades greater than or equal to 90, B for grades in the range 80 to 89, C for grades in the range 70 to 79, D for grades in the range 60 to 69 and F for all other grades:

```
if ( grade >= 90 )
    Console.WriteLine( "A" );
else
    if ( grade >= 80 )
        Console.WriteLine( "B" );
    else
        if ( grade >= 70 )
            Console.WriteLine( "C" );
        else
            if ( grade >= 60 )
                Console.WriteLine( "D" );
            else
                Console.WriteLine( "F" );
```

If grade is greater than or equal to 90, the first four conditions will be true, but only the statement in the if-part of the first if...else statement will execute. After that statement executes, the else-part of the "outermost" if...else statement is skipped. Most C# programmers prefer to write the preceding if...else statement as

```
if ( grade >= 90 )
    Console.WriteLine( "A" );
else if ( grade >= 80 )
    Console.WriteLine( "B" );
else if ( grade >= 70 )
    Console.WriteLine( "C" );
else if ( grade >= 60 )
    Console.WriteLine( "D" );
else
    Console.WriteLine( "F" );
```

The two forms are identical except for the spacing and indentation, which the compiler ignores. The latter form is popular because it avoids deep indentation of the code to the right—such indentation often leaves little room on a line of code, forcing lines to be split and decreasing the readability of your code.

Dangling-else Problem

The C# compiler always associates an else with the immediately preceding if unless told to do otherwise by the placement of braces ({ and }). This behavior can lead to what is referred to as the **dangling-else problem**. For example,

```
if ( x > 5 )
    if ( y > 5 )
        Console.WriteLine( "x and y are > 5" );
else
    Console.WriteLine( "x is <= 5" );
```

appears to indicate that if x is greater than 5, the nested if statement determines whether y is also greater than 5. If so, the string "x and y are > 5" is output. Otherwise, it appears that if x is not greater than 5, the else part of the if...else outputs the string "x is <= 5".

Beware! This nested if...else statement does not execute as it appears. The compiler actually interprets the statement as

```
if ( x > 5 )
   if ( y > 5 )
      Console.WriteLine( "x and y are > 5" );
   else
      Console.WriteLine( "x is <= 5" );
```

in which the body of the first if is a nested if...else. The outer if statement tests whether x is greater than 5. If so, execution continues by testing whether y is also greater than 5. If the second condition is true, the proper string—"x and y are > 5"—is displayed. However, if the second condition is false, the string "x is <= 5" is displayed, even though we know that x is greater than 5.

To force the nested if...else statement to execute as it was originally intended, we must write it as follows:

```
if ( x > 5 )
{
   if ( y > 5 )
      Console.WriteLine( "x and y are > 5" );
}
else
   Console.WriteLine( "x is <= 5" );
```

The braces ({}) indicate to the compiler that the second if statement is in the body of the first if and that the else is associated with the *first* if.

Blocks

The if statement expects only one statement in its body. To include several statements in the body of an if (or the body of an else for an if...else statement), enclose the statements in braces ({ and }). A set of statements contained within a pair of braces is called a **block**. A block can be placed anywhere in an application that a single statement can be placed.

The following example includes a block in the else-part of an if...else statement:

```
if ( grade >= 60 )
   Console.WriteLine( "Passed" );
else
{
   Console.WriteLine( "Failed" );
   Console.WriteLine( "You must take this course again." );
}
```

In this case, if grade is less than 60, the application executes both statements in the body of the else and displays

```
Failed.
You must take this course again.
```

Note the braces surrounding the two statements in the else clause. These braces are important. Without the braces, the statement

```
Console.WriteLine( "You must take this course again." );
```

would be outside the body of the else-part of the if...else statement and would execute regardless of whether the grade was less than 60.

Good Programming Practice 5.4

Always using braces in an `if...else` (or other) statement helps prevent their accidental omission, especially when adding statements to the if-part or the `else`-part at a later time. To avoid omitting one or both of the braces, some programmers type the beginning and ending braces of blocks before typing the individual statements within them.

Just as a block can be placed anywhere a single statement can be placed, it's also possible to have an empty statement. Recall from Section 3.8 that the empty statement is represented by placing a semicolon (;) where a statement would normally be.

Common Programming Error 5.1

Placing a semicolon after the condition in an `if` or `if...else` statement leads to a logic error in single-selection `if` statements and a syntax error in double-selection `if...else` statements (when the if-part contains an actual body statement).

5.5 `while` Repetition Statement

A **repetition statement** allows you to specify that an application should repeat an action while some condition remains true. The statement(s) contained in the **while repetition statement** constitute its body, which may be a single statement or a block. Eventually, the condition will become false. At this point, the repetition terminates, and the first statement after the repetition statement executes.

Consider a code segment designed to find the first power of 3 larger than 100. When the following `while` statement finishes executing, `product` contains the result:

```
int product = 3;
while ( product <= 100 )
   product = 3 * product;
```

When this `while` statement begins execution, the value of variable `product` is 3. Each repetition of the `while` statement multiplies `product` by 3, so `product` takes on the subsequent values 9, 27, 81 and 243 successively. When variable `product` becomes 243, the `while` statement condition—product <= 100—becomes false. This terminates the repetition, so the final value of `product` is 243. At this point, application execution continues with the next statement after the `while` statement.

Common Programming Error 5.2

*Not providing in the body of a `while` statement an action that eventually causes the condition in the `while` to become false normally results in a logic error called an **infinite loop**, in which the loop never terminates.*

The UML activity diagram in Fig. 5.4 illustrates the flow of control for the preceding `while` statement. This diagram also introduces the UML's **merge symbol**. The UML represents both the merge and decision symbols as diamonds. The merge symbol joins two flows of activity into one. In this diagram, the merge symbol joins the transitions from the initial state and the action state, so they both flow into the decision that determines whether the loop should begin (or continue) executing. The decision and merge symbols can be distinguished by the number of "incoming" and "outgoing" transition arrows. A decision symbol has one transition arrow pointing to the diamond and two or more transition arrows pointing out from the diamond to indicate possible transitions from that point. Each transition arrow pointing out of a decision symbol has a guard condition. A merge symbol has two or more transition arrows pointing to the diamond and only one transition arrow pointing from the diamond, to indicate multiple activity flows merging to continue the activity. None of the transition arrows associated with a merge have guard conditions.

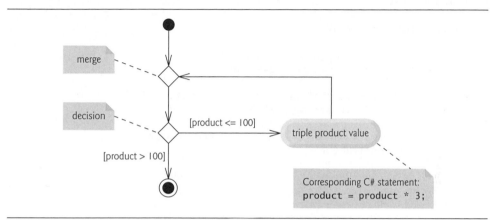

Fig. 5.4 | `while` repetition statement UML activity diagram.

Figure 5.4 clearly shows the repetition of the `while` statement discussed earlier in this section. The transition arrow emerging from the action state points back to the merge, from which program flow transitions back to the decision that's tested at the beginning of each repetition of the loop. The loop continues to execute until the guard condition `product > 100` becomes true. Then the `while` statement exits (reaches its final state), and control passes to the next statement in sequence in the application.

5.6 Counter-Controlled Repetition

Next, we modify the `GradeBook` class of Chapter 4 to solve two variations of a problem that averages student grades. Consider the following problem statement:

A class of 10 students took a quiz. The grades (integers in the range 0 to 100) for this quiz are available to you. Determine the class average on the quiz.

The class average is equal to the sum of the grades divided by the number of students. The algorithm for solving this problem must input each grade, keep track of the total of all grades input, perform the averaging calculation and display the result.

Implementing Counter-Controlled Repetition in Class *GradeBook*
Class `GradeBook` (Fig. 5.5) contains a constructor (lines 12–15) that assigns a value to the instance variable created by auto-implemented property `CourseName` in line 9. Lines 18–23 declare method `DisplayMessage`. Lines 26–52 declare method `DetermineClassAverage`, which meets the requirements of the problem statement. Lines 28–31 declare local variables `total`, `gradeCounter`, `grade` and `average` to be of type `int`. In this example, variable `total` accumulates the sum of the grades entered and `gradeCounter` counts the

number of grades entered. Variable grade stores the most recent grade value entered (line 41). Variable average stores the average grade.

```csharp
1   // Fig. 5.5: GradeBook.cs
2   // GradeBook class that solves class-average problem using
3   // counter-controlled repetition.
4   using System;
5
6   public class GradeBook
7   {\
8      // auto-implemented property CourseName
9      public string CourseName { get; set; }
10
11     // constructor initializes CourseName property
12     public GradeBook( string name )
13     {
14        CourseName = name; // set CourseName to name
15     } // end constructor
16
17     // display a welcome message to the GradeBook user
18     public void DisplayMessage()
19     {
20        // property CourseName gets the name of the course
21        Console.WriteLine( "Welcome to the grade book for\n{0}!\n",
22           CourseName );
23     } // end method DisplayMessage
24
25     // determine class average based on 10 grades entered by user
26     public void DetermineClassAverage()
27     {
28        int total; // sum of the grades entered by user
29        int gradeCounter; // number of the grade to be entered next
30        int grade; // grade value entered by the user
31        int average; // average of the grades
32
33        // initialization phase
34        total = 0; // initialize the total
35        gradeCounter = 1; // initialize the loop counter
36
37        // processing phase
38        while ( gradeCounter <= 10 ) // loop 10 times
39        {
40           Console.Write( "Enter grade: " ); // prompt the user
41           grade = Convert.ToInt32( Console.ReadLine() ); // read grade
42           total = total + grade; // add the grade to total
43           gradeCounter = gradeCounter + 1; // increment the counter by 1
44        } // end while
45
46        // termination phase
47        average = total / 10; // integer division yields integer result
48
```

Fig. 5.5 | GradeBook class that solves the class-average problem using counter-controlled repetition. (Part 1 of 2.)

```
49        // display total and average of grades
50        Console.WriteLine( "\nTotal of all 10 grades is {0}", total );
51        Console.WriteLine( "Class average is {0}", average );
52    } // end method DetermineClassAverage
53 } // end class GradeBook
```

Fig. 5.5 | GradeBook class that solves the class-average problem using counter-controlled repetition. (Part 2 of 2.)

The declarations (in lines 28–31) appear in method DetermineClassAverage's body. Variables declared in a method body are local variables and can be used only from the line of their declaration to the closing right brace of the block in which they're declared. A local variable's declaration must appear before the variable is used in that method. A local variable cannot be accessed outside the method in which it's declared.

The versions of class GradeBook in this chapter simply read and process a set of grades. The averaging calculation is performed in method DetermineClassAverage using local variables—we do not preserve any information about student grades in instance variables of the class. In later versions of the class (in Chapter 8), we store the grades using an instance variable that refers to an array. This allows a GradeBook object to perform various calculations on the same set of grades without requiring the user to enter the grades multiple times.

Good Programming Practice 5.5

Separate declarations from other statements in methods with a blank line for readability.

We say that a variable is **definitely assigned** when it's guaranteed to be assigned a value before it's used. Notice that each local variable declared in lines 28–31 is definitely assigned before it's used in calculations. The assignments (in lines 34–35) initialize total to 0 and gradeCounter to 1. Variables grade and average (for the user input and calculated average, respectively) need not be initialized here—their values are assigned as they're input or calculated later in the method.

Common Programming Error 5.3

Using the value of a local variable before it's definitely assigned results in a compilation error. All local variables must be definitely assigned before their values are used in expressions.

Error-Prevention Tip 5.1

Initialize each counter and total, either in its declaration or in an assignment statement. Totals are normally initialized to 0. Counters are normally initialized to 0 or 1, depending on how they're used (we'll show examples of each).

Line 38 indicates that the while statement should continue looping as long as the value of gradeCounter is less than or equal to 10. While this condition remains true, the while statement repeatedly executes the statements between the braces that delimit its body (lines 39–44).

Line 40 displays the prompt "Enter grade: ". Line 41 reads the grade entered by the user and assigns it to variable grade. Then line 42 adds the new grade entered by the user to the total and assigns the result to total, which replaces its previous value.

Line 43 increments gradeCounter to indicate that the application has processed a grade and is ready to input the next grade from the user. Incrementing gradeCounter eventually causes gradeCounter to exceed 10. At that point the while loop terminates, because its condition (line 38) becomes false.

When the loop terminates, line 47 performs the averaging calculation and assigns its result to the variable average. Line 50 uses Console's WriteLine method to display the text "Total of all 10 grades is " followed by variable total's value. Line 51 then displays the text "Class average is " followed by variable average's value. Method DetermineClassAverage returns control to the calling method (i.e., Main in GradeBookTest of Fig. 5.6) after reaching line 52.

Class *GradeBookTest*

Class GradeBookTest (Fig. 5.6) creates a GradeBook object and demonstrates its capabilities. Lines 9–10 create a new GradeBook object and assign it to variable myGradeBook. The string in line 10 is passed to the GradeBook constructor (lines 12–15 of Fig. 5.5). Line 12 calls myGradeBook's DisplayMessage method to display a welcome message to the user. Line 13 then calls myGradeBook's DetermineClassAverage method to allow the user to enter 10 grades, for which the method then calculates and displays the average.

```
1   // Fig. 5.6: GradeBookTest.cs
2   // Create GradeBook object and invoke its DetermineClassAverage method.
3   public class GradeBookTest
4   {
5      public static void Main( string[] args )
6      {
7         // create GradeBook object myGradeBook and
8         // pass course name to constructor
9         GradeBook myGradeBook = new GradeBook(
10           "CS101 Introduction to C# Programming" );
11
12        myGradeBook.DisplayMessage(); // display welcome message
13        myGradeBook.DetermineClassAverage(); // find average of 10 grades
14     } // end Main
15  } // end class GradeBookTest
```

```
Welcome to the grade book for
CS101 Introduction to C# Programming!

Enter grade: 88
Enter grade: 79
Enter grade: 95
Enter grade: 100
Enter grade: 48
Enter grade: 88
Enter grade: 92
Enter grade: 83
Enter grade: 90
Enter grade: 85

Total of all 10 grades is 848
Class average is 84
```

Fig. 5.6 | Create GradeBook object and invoke its DetermineClassAverage method.

Notes on Integer Division and Truncation

The averaging calculation performed by method DetermineClassAverage in response to the method call at line 13 in Fig. 5.6 produces an integer result. The application's output indicates that the sum of the grade values in the sample execution is 848, which, when divided by 10, should yield the floating-point number 84.8. However, the result of the calculation total / 10 (line 47 of Fig. 5.5) is the integer 84, because total and 10 are both integers. Dividing two integers results in integer division—any fractional part of the calculation is lost (i.e., truncated, not rounded). We'll see how to obtain a floating-point result from the averaging calculation in the next section.

Common Programming Error 5.4

Assuming that integer division rounds (rather than truncates) can lead to incorrect results. For example, 7 ÷ 4, which yields 1.75 in conventional arithmetic, truncates to 1 in integer arithmetic, rather than rounding to 2.

5.7 Sentinel-Controlled Repetition

Let us generalize Section 5.6's class-average problem. Consider the following problem:

> *Develop a class-averaging application that processes grades for an arbitrary number of students each time it's run.*

In the previous class-average example, the problem statement specified the number of students, so the number of grades (10) was known in advance. In this example, no indication is given of how many grades the user will enter during the application's execution. The application must process an arbitrary number of grades. How can it determine when to stop the input of grades? How will it know when to calculate and display the class average?

One way to solve this problem is to use a special value called a **sentinel value** (also called a **signal value**, a **dummy value** or a **flag value**) to indicate "end of data entry." The user enters grades until all legitimate grades have been entered. The user then types the sentinel value to indicate that no more grades will be entered. **Sentinel-controlled repetition** is often called **indefinite repetition** because the number of repetitions is not known by the application before the loop begins executing.

Clearly, a sentinel value must be chosen that cannot be confused with an acceptable input value. Grades on a quiz are nonnegative integers, so –1 is an acceptable sentinel value for this problem. Thus, a run of the class-average application might process a stream of inputs such as 95, 96, 75, 74, 89 and –1. The application would then compute and display the class average for the grades 95, 96, 75, 74 and 89. Since –1 is the sentinel value, it should not enter into the averaging calculation.

Common Programming Error 5.5

Choosing a sentinel value that's also a legitimate data value is a logic error.

*Implementing Sentinel-Controlled Repetition in Class **GradeBook***

Figure 5.7 shows the C# class GradeBook containing method DetermineClassAverage that meets the requirements of the problem statement. Although each grade is an integer, the averaging calculation is likely to produce a number with a decimal point—in other words, a real number or floating-point number. The type int cannot represent such a number, so this class uses type double to do so.

```csharp
1   // Fig. 5.7: GradeBook.cs
2   // GradeBook class that solves class-average problem using
3   // sentinel-controlled repetition.
4   using System;
5
6   public class GradeBook
7   {
8      // auto-implemented property CourseName
9      public string CourseName { get; set; }
10
11     // constructor initializes the CourseName property
12     public GradeBook( string name )
13     {
14        CourseName = name; // set CourseName to name
15     } // end constructor
16
17     // display a welcome message to the GradeBook user
18     public void DisplayMessage()
19     {
20        Console.WriteLine( "Welcome to the grade book for\n{0}!\n",
21           CourseName );
22     } // end method DisplayMessage
23
24     // determine the average of an arbitrary number of grades
25     public void DetermineClassAverage()
26     {
27        int total; // sum of grades
28        int gradeCounter; // number of grades entered
29        int grade; // grade value
30        double average; // number with decimal point for average
31
32        // initialization phase
33        total = 0; // initialize total
34        gradeCounter = 0; // initialize loop counter
35
36        // processing phase
37        // prompt for and read a grade from the user
38        Console.Write( "Enter grade or -1 to quit: " );
39        grade = Convert.ToInt32( Console.ReadLine() );
40
41        // loop until sentinel value is read from the user
42        while ( grade != -1 )
43        {
44           total = total + grade; // add grade to total
45           gradeCounter = gradeCounter + 1; // increment counter
46
47           // prompt for and read the next grade from the user
48           Console.Write( "Enter grade or -1 to quit: " );
```

Fig. 5.7 | GradeBook class that solves the class-average problem using sentinel-controlled repetition. (Part 1 of 2.)

```
49                grade = Convert.ToInt32( Console.ReadLine() );
50          } // end while
51
52          // termination phase
53          // if the user entered at least one grade...
54          if ( gradeCounter != 0 )
55          {
56             // calculate the average of all the grades entered
57             average = ( double ) total / gradeCounter;
58
59             // display the total and average (with two digits of precision)
60             Console.WriteLine( "\nTotal of the {0} grades entered is {1}",
61                gradeCounter, total );
62             Console.WriteLine( "Class average is {0:F}", average );
63          } // end if
64          else // no grades were entered, so output error message
65             Console.WriteLine( "No grades were entered" );
66       } // end method DetermineClassAverage
67    } // end class GradeBook
```

Fig. 5.7 | GradeBook class that solves the class-average problem using sentinel-controlled repetition. (Part 2 of 2.)

In this example, we see that control statements may be stacked on top of one another (in sequence)—the while statement (lines 42–50) is followed in sequence by an if...else statement (lines 54–65). Much of the code in this application is identical to the code in Fig. 5.5, so we concentrate on the new features and issues.

Line 30 declares double variable average. This variable allows us to store the calculated class average as a floating-point number. Line 34 initializes gradeCounter to 0, because no grades have been entered yet. Remember that this application uses sentinel-controlled repetition to input the grades from the user. To keep an accurate record of the number of grades entered, the application increments gradeCounter only when the user inputs a valid grade value.

Program Logic for Sentinel-Controlled Repetition vs. Counter-Controlled Repetition
Compare the program logic for sentinel-controlled repetition in this application with that for counter-controlled repetition in Fig. 5.5. In counter-controlled repetition, each repetition of the while statement (e.g., lines 38–44 of Fig. 5.5) reads a value from the user, for the specified number of repetitions. In sentinel-controlled repetition, the application reads the first value (lines 38–39 of Fig. 5.7) before reaching the while. This value determines whether the application's flow of control should enter the body of the while. If the condition of the while is false, the user entered the sentinel value, so the body of the while does not execute (because no grades were entered). If, on the other hand, the condition is true, the body begins execution, and the loop adds the grade value to the total (line 44) and adds 1 to gradeCounter (line 45). Then lines 48–49 in the loop's body input the next value from the user. Next, program control reaches the closing right brace of the body at line 50, so execution continues with the test of the while's condition (line 42). The condition uses the most recent grade input by the user to determine whether the loop's body should execute again. The value of variable grade is always input from the user immedi-

ately before the application tests the `while` condition. This allows the application to determine whether the value just input is the sentinel value *before* the application processes that value (i.e., adds it to the `total`). If the sentinel value is input, the loop terminates; the application does *not* add -1 to the `total`.

Good Programming Practice 5.6

In a sentinel-controlled loop, the prompts requesting data entry should explicitly remind the user of the sentinel value.

After the loop terminates, the `if...else` statement at lines 54–65 executes. The condition at line 54 determines whether any grades were input. If none were input, the `else` part (lines 64–65) of the `if...else` statement executes and displays the message "No grades were entered", and the method returns control to the calling method.

Error-Prevention Tip 5.2

When performing division by an expression whose value could be zero, explicitly test for this possibility and handle it appropriately in your application (e.g., by displaying an error message) rather than allowing the error to occur.

Notice the `while` statement's block in Fig. 5.7 (lines 43–50). Without the braces, the loop would consider its body to be only the first statement, which adds the `grade` to the `total`. The last three statements in the block would fall outside the loop's body, causing the computer to interpret the code incorrectly as follows:

```
while ( grade != -1 )
   total = total + grade; // add grade to total
gradeCounter = gradeCounter + 1; // increment counter

// prompt for input and read next grade from user
Console.Write( "Enter grade or -1 to quit: " );
grade = Convert.ToInt32( Console.ReadLine() );
```

The preceding code would cause an infinite loop in the application if the user did not enter the sentinel -1 at line 39 (before the `while` statement).

Error-Prevention Tip 5.3

Omitting the braces that delimit a block can lead to logic errors, such as infinite loops. To prevent this problem, some programmers enclose the body of every control statement in braces even if the body contains only a single statement.

Explicitly and Implicitly Converting Between Simple Types
If at least one grade was entered, line 57 of Fig. 5.7 calculates the average of the grades. Recall from Fig. 5.5 that integer division yields an integer result. Even though variable average is declared as a `double` (line 30), the calculation

```
average = total / gradeCounter;
```

loses the division's fractional part before the result is assigned to `average`. This occurs because `total` and `gradeCounter` are both integers, and integer division yields an integer result. To perform a floating-point calculation with integer values, we must temporarily treat these values as floating-point numbers for use in the calculation. C# provides the **unary cast operator** to accomplish this task. Line 57 uses the **(double)** cast operator—which has higher precedence than the arithmetic operators—to create a *temporary* floating-point copy of its operand `total` (which appears to the right of the operator). Using a cast operator in this manner is called **explicit conversion**. The value stored in `total` is still an integer.

The calculation now consists of a floating-point value (the temporary `double` version of `total`) divided by the integer `gradeCounter`. C# knows how to evaluate only arithmetic expressions in which the operands' types are identical. To ensure that the operands are of the same type, C# performs an operation called **promotion** (or **implicit conversion**) on selected operands. For example, in an expression containing values of the types `int` and `double`, the `int` values are promoted to `double` values for use in the expression. In this example, the value of `gradeCounter` is promoted to type `double`, then floating-point division is performed and the result of the calculation is assigned to `average`. As long as the (`double`) cast operator is applied to any variable in the calculation, the calculation will yield a `double` result.

> **Common Programming Error 5.6**
>
> *A cast operator can be used to convert between simple numeric types, such as int and double, and between related reference types (as we discuss in Chapter 12). Casting to the wrong type may cause compilation or runtime errors.*

Cast operators are available for all simple types. (We'll discuss cast operators for reference types in Chapter 12.) The cast operator is formed by placing parentheses around the name of a type. This operator is a **unary operator** (i.e., an operator that takes only one operand). In Chapter 3, we discussed the binary arithmetic operators. C# also supports unary versions of the plus (+) and minus (–) operators, so you can write expressions like +5 or -7. Cast operators associate from right to left and have the same precedence as other unary operators, such as unary + and unary –. This precedence is one level higher than that of the **multiplicative operators** *, / and %. (See the operator precedence chart in Appendix A.) We indicate the cast operator with the notation (*type*) in our precedence charts, to indicate that any type name can be used to form a cast operator.

Line 62 outputs the class average. In this example, we decided that we'd like to display the class average rounded to the nearest hundredth and output the average with exactly two digits to the right of the decimal point. The format specifier F in `WriteLine`'s format item (line 62) indicates that variable `average`'s value should be displayed as a real number. By default, numbers output with F have two digits to the right of the decimal point. The number of decimal places to the right of the decimal point is also known as the number's **precision**. Any floating-point value output with F will be rounded to the hundredths position—for example, 123.457 will be rounded to 123.46, and 27.333 will be rounded to 27.33. In this application, the three grades entered during the sample execution of class `GradeBookTest` (Fig. 5.8) total 263, which yields the average 87.66666.... The format item rounds the average to the hundredths position, and the average is displayed as 87.67.

```
1   // Fig. 5.8: GradeBookTest.cs
2   // Create GradeBook object and invoke its DetermineClassAverage method.
3   public class GradeBookTest
4   {
```

Fig. 5.8 | Create `GradeBook` object and invoke `DetermineClassAverage` method. (Part 1 of 2.)

```
 5      public static void Main( string[] args )
 6      {
 7         // create GradeBook object myGradeBook and
 8         // pass course name to constructor
 9         GradeBook myGradeBook = new GradeBook(
10            "CS101 Introduction to C# Programming" );
11
12         myGradeBook.DisplayMessage(); // display welcome message
13         myGradeBook.DetermineClassAverage(); // find average of grades
14      } // end Main
15   } // end class GradeBookTest
```

```
Welcome to the grade book for
CS101 Introduction to C# Programming!

Enter grade or -1 to quit: 96
Enter grade or -1 to quit: 88
Enter grade or -1 to quit: 79
Enter grade or -1 to quit: -1

Total of the 3 grades entered is 263
Class average is 87.67
```

Fig. 5.8 | Create GradeBook object and invoke DetermineClassAverage method. (Part 2 of 2.)

5.8 Nested Control Statements

We've seen that control statements can be stacked on top of one another (in sequence). In this case study, we examine the only other structured way control statements can be connected, namely, by **nesting** one control statement within another.

Consider the following problem statement:

> *A college offers a course that prepares students for the state licensing exam for real estate brokers. Last year, 10 of the students who completed this course took the exam. The college wants to know how well its students did on the exam. You've been asked to write an application to summarize the results. You've been given a list of these 10 students. Next to each name is written a 1 if the student passed the exam or a 2 if the student failed.*

> *Your application should analyze the results of the exam as follows:*

> 1. *Input each test result (i.e., a 1 or a 2). Display the message "Enter result" on the screen each time the application requests another test result.*

> 2. *Count the number of test results of each type.*

> 3. *Display a summary of the test results indicating the number of students who passed and the number who failed.*

> 4. *If more than eight students passed the exam, display the message "Bonus to instructor!"*

After reading the problem statement, we make the following observations:

1. The application must process test results for 10 students. A counter-controlled loop can be used because the number of test results is known in advance.

2. Each test result has a numeric value—either a 1 or a 2. Each time the application reads a test result, the application must determine whether the number is a 1 or a 2. We test for a 1 in our algorithm. If the number is not a 1, we assume that it's a 2.

3. Two counters are used to keep track of the exam results—one to count the number of students who passed the exam and one to count the number of students who failed the exam.

4. After the application has processed all the results, it must determine whether more than eight students passed the exam.

The C# class that meets these requirements is shown in Fig. 5.9. Lines 10–13 declare the variables that the program uses to process the examination results. Several of these declarations use C#'s ability to incorporate variable initialization into declarations (passes is assigned 0, failures is assigned 0 and studentCounter is assigned 1).

```
 1   // Fig. 5.9: Analysis.cs
 2   // Analysis of examination results, using nested control statements.
 3   using System;
 4
 5   public class Analysis
 6   {
 7      public static void Main( string[] args )
 8      {
 9         // initialize variables in declarations
10         int passes = 0; // number of passes
11         int failures = 0; // number of failures
12         int studentCounter = 1; // student counter
13         int result; // one exam result from user
14
15         // process 10 students using counter-controlled repetition
16         while ( studentCounter <= 10 )
17         {
18            // prompt user for input and obtain a value from the user
19            Console.Write( "Enter result (1 = pass, 2 = fail): " );
20            result = Convert.ToInt32( Console.ReadLine() );
21
22            // if...else nested in while
23            if ( result == 1 ) // if result 1,
24               passes = passes + 1; // increment passes
25            else // else result is not 1, so
26               failures = failures + 1; // increment failures
27
28            // increment studentCounter so loop eventually terminates
29            studentCounter = studentCounter + 1;
30         } // end while
31
32         // termination phase; prepare and display results
33         Console.WriteLine( "Passed: {0}\nFailed: {1}", passes, failures );
34
35         // determine whether more than 8 students passed
36         if ( passes > 8 )
37            Console.WriteLine( "Bonus to instructor!" );
38      } // end main
39   } // end class Analysis
```

Fig. 5.9 | Analysis of examination results, using nested control statements. (Part 1 of 2.)

```
Enter result (1 = pass, 2 = fail): 1
Enter result (1 = pass, 2 = fail): 2
Enter result (1 = pass, 2 = fail): 1
Enter result (1 = pass, 2 = fail): 1
Enter result (1 = pass, 2 = fail): 1
Enter result (1 = pass, 2 = fail): 1
Enter result (1 = pass, 2 = fail): 1
Enter result (1 = pass, 2 = fail): 1
Enter result (1 = pass, 2 = fail): 1
Enter result (1 = pass, 2 = fail): 1
Passed: 9
Failed: 1
Bonus to instructor!
```

```
Enter result (1 = pass, 2 = fail): 1
Enter result (1 = pass, 2 = fail): 2
Enter result (1 = pass, 2 = fail): 2
Enter result (1 = pass, 2 = fail): 2
Enter result (1 = pass, 2 = fail): 1
Enter result (1 = pass, 2 = fail): 1
Enter result (1 = pass, 2 = fail): 1
Enter result (1 = pass, 2 = fail): 1
Enter result (1 = pass, 2 = fail): 2
Enter result (1 = pass, 2 = fail): 2
Passed: 5
Failed: 5
```

Fig. 5.9 | Analysis of examination results, using nested control statements. (Part 2 of 2.)

The while statement (lines 16–30) loops 10 times. During each repetition, the loop inputs and processes one exam result. Notice that the if...else statement (lines 23–26) for processing each result is nested in the while statement. If the result is 1, the if...else statement increments passes; otherwise, it assumes the result is 2 and increments failures. Line 29 increments studentCounter before the loop condition is tested again at line 16. After 10 values have been input, the loop terminates and line 33 displays the number of passes and the number of failures. Lines 36–37 determine whether more than eight students passed the exam and, if so, outputs the message "Bonus to instructor!".

Error-Prevention Tip 5.4

Initializing local variables when they're declared helps you avoid compilation errors that might arise from attempts to use uninitialized data. While C# does not require that local-variable initializations be incorporated into declarations, it does require that local variables be initialized before their values are used in an expression.

Figure 5.9 shows the input and output from two sample executions of the application. During the first sample execution, the condition at line 36 is true—more than eight students passed the exam, so the application outputs a message indicating that the instructor should receive a bonus.

5.9 Compound Assignment Operators

C# provides several **compound assignment operators** for abbreviating assignment expressions. Any statement of the form

> *variable = variable operator expression*;

where *operator* is one of the binary operators +, -, *, / or % (or others we discuss later in the text) can be written in the form

> *variable operator= expression*;

For example, you can abbreviate the statement

> c = c + 3;

with the **addition compound assignment operator**, +=, as

> c += 3;

The += operator adds the value of the expression on the right of the operator to the value of the variable on the left of the operator and stores the result in the variable on the left of the operator. Thus, the assignment expression c += 3 adds 3 to c. Figure 5.10 shows the arithmetic compound assignment operators, sample expressions using the operators and explanations of what the operators do.

Assignment operator	Sample expression	Explanation	Assigns
Assume: **int** c = 3, d = 5, e = 4, f = 6, g = 12;			
+=	c += 7	c = c + 7	10 to c
-=	d -= 4	d = d - 4	1 to d
*=	e *= 5	e = e * 5	20 to e
/=	f /= 3	f = f / 3	2 to f
%=	g %= 9	g = g % 9	3 to g

Fig. 5.10 | Arithmetic compound assignment operators.

5.10 Increment and Decrement Operators

C# provides two unary operators for adding 1 to or subtracting 1 from the value of a numeric variable. These are the unary **increment operator**, ++, and the unary **decrement operator**, --, respectively, which are summarized in Fig. 5.11. An application can increment by 1 the value of a variable called c using the increment operator, ++, rather than the expression c = c + 1 or c += 1. An increment or decrement operator that's prefixed to (placed before) a variable is referred to as the **prefix increment operator** or **prefix decrement operator**, respectively. An increment or decrement operator that's postfixed to (placed after) a variable is referred to as the **postfix increment operator** or **postfix decrement operator**, respectively.

Incrementing (or decrementing) a variable with the prefix increment (or prefix decrement) operator causes it to be incremented (or decremented) by 1; then the new value of the variable is used in the expression in which it appears. Incrementing (or decrementing)

Operator	Called	Sample expression	Explanation
++	prefix increment	++a	Increments a by 1, then uses the new value of a in the expression in which a resides.
++	postfix increment	a++	Uses the current value of a in the expression in which a resides, then increments a by 1.
--	prefix decrement	--b	Decrements b by 1, then uses the new value of b in the expression in which b resides.
--	postfix decrement	b--	Uses the current value of b in the expression in which b resides, then decrements b by 1.

Fig. 5.11 | Increment and decrement operators.

the variable with the postfix increment (or postfix decrement) operator causes the variable's current value to be used in the expression in which it appears; then the variable's value is incremented (or decremented) by 1.

Good Programming Practice 5.7
Unlike binary operators, the unary increment and decrement operators should (by convention) be placed next to their operands, with no intervening spaces.

Figure 5.12 demonstrates the difference between the prefix increment and postfix increment versions of the ++ increment operator. The decrement operator (--) works similarly. In this example, we simply want to show the mechanics of the ++ operator, so we use only one class declaration containing method Main.

```
1   // Fig. 5.12: Increment.cs
2   // Prefix increment and postfix increment operators.
3   using System;
4
5   public class Increment
6   {
7      public static void Main( string[] args )
8      {
9         int c;
10
11        // demonstrate postfix increment operator
12        c = 5; // assign 5 to c
13        Console.WriteLine( c ); // display 5
14        Console.WriteLine( c++ ); // display 5 again, then increment
15        Console.WriteLine( c ); // display 6
16
17        Console.WriteLine(); // skip a line
18
19        // demonstrate prefix increment operator
20        c = 5; // assign 5 to c
```

Fig. 5.12 | Prefix increment and postfix increment operators. (Part I of 2.)

```
21          Console.WriteLine( c ); // display 5
22          Console.WriteLine( ++c ); // increment, then display
23          Console.WriteLine( c ); // display 6 again
24       } // end Main
25    } // end class Increment
```

```
5
5
6

5
6
6
```

Fig. 5.12 | Prefix increment and postfix increment operators. (Part 2 of 2.)

Line 12 initializes the variable c to 5, and line 13 outputs c's initial value. Line 14 outputs the value of the expression c++. This expression performs the postfix increment operation on the variable c, so c's original value (5) is output, then c's value is incremented. Thus, line 14 outputs c's initial value (5) again. Line 15 outputs c's new value (6) to prove that the variable's value was indeed incremented in line 14.

Line 20 resets c's value to 5, and line 21 outputs c's value. Line 22 outputs the value of the expression ++c. This expression performs the prefix increment operation on c, so its value is incremented; then the new value (6) is output. Line 23 outputs c's value again to show that the value of c is still 6 after line 22 executes.

The arithmetic compound assignment operators and the increment and decrement operators can be used to simplify statements. For example, the three assignment statements in Fig. 5.9 (lines 24, 26 and 29)

```
passes = passes + 1;
failures = failures + 1;
studentCounter = studentCounter + 1;
```

can be written more concisely with compound assignment operators as

```
passes += 1;
failures += 1;
studentCounter += 1;
```

and even more concisely with prefix increment operators as

```
++passes;
++failures;
++studentCounter;
```

or with postfix increment operators as

```
passes++;
failures++;
studentCounter++;
```

When incrementing or decrementing a variable in a statement by itself, the prefix increment and postfix increment forms have the same effect, and the prefix decrement and postfix decrement forms have the same effect. It's only when a variable appears in the context of a larger expression that the prefix increment and postfix increment have different effects (and similarly for the prefix decrement and postfix decrement).

Common Programming Error 5.7

Attempting to use the increment or decrement operator on an expression other than one to which a value can be assigned is a syntax error. For example, writing ++(x + 1) is a syntax error, because (x + 1) is not a variable.

Figure 5.13 shows the precedence and associativity of the operators introduced so far. The operators are shown from top to bottom in decreasing order of precedence. The second column describes the associativity of the operators at each level of precedence. The conditional operator (?:); the unary operators prefix increment (++), prefix decrement (--), plus (+) and minus (-); the cast operators; and the assignment operators =, +=, -=, *=, /= and %= associate from right to left. All the other operators in the operator precedence chart in Fig. 5.13 associate from left to right. The third column names the groups of operators.

Operators					Associativity	Type
.	new	++*(postfix)*	--*(postfix)*		left to right	highest precedence
++	--	+	-	*(type)*	right to left	unary prefix
*	/	%			left to right	multiplicative
+	-				left to right	additive
<	<=	>	>=		left to right	relational
==	!=				left to right	equality
?:					right to left	conditional
=	+=	-=	*=	/= %=	right to left	assignment

Fig. 5.13 | Precedence and associativity of the operators discussed so far.

5.11 Simple Types

The table in Appendix B lists the 13 **simple types** in C#. Like its predecessor languages C and C++, C# requires all variables to have a type. For this reason, C# is referred to as a **strongly typed language**.

In C and C++, programmers frequently have to write separate versions of applications to support different computer platforms, because the simple types are not guaranteed to be identical from computer to computer. For example, an int value on one machine might be represented by 16 bits (2 bytes) of storage, while an int value on another machine might be represented by 32 bits (4 bytes) of storage. In C#, int values are always 32 bits (4 bytes). In fact, *all* C# numeric types have fixed sizes, as is shown in Appendix B.

Each type in Appendix B is listed with its size in bits (there are eight bits to a byte) and its range of values. Because the designers of C# want it to be maximally portable, they use internationally recognized standards for both character formats (Unicode; for more information, see Appendix F) and floating-point numbers (IEEE 754; for more information, visit grouper.ieee.org/groups/754/).

Recall from Section 4.5 that variables of simple types declared outside of a method as fields of a class are automatically assigned default values unless explicitly initialized. Instance variables of types `char`, `byte`, `sbyte`, `short`, `ushort`, `int`, `uint`, `long`, `ulong`, `float`, `double`, and `decimal` are all given the value 0 by default. Instance variables of type `bool` are given the value `false` by default. Similarly, reference-type instance variables are initialized by default to the value `null`.

5.12 Wrap-Up

Only three types of control structures—sequence, selection and repetition—are needed to develop any problem-solving algorithm. Specifically, we demonstrated the `if` single-selection statement, the `if...else` double-selection statement and the `while` repetition statement. We used control-statement stacking to compute the total and the average of a set of student grades with counter- and sentinel-controlled repetition, and we used control-statement nesting to analyze and make decisions based on a set of exam results. We introduced C#'s compound assignment operators, unary cast operators, as well as its increment and decrement operators. Finally, we discussed the simple types available to C# programmers. In Chapter 6, Control Statements: Part 2, we continue our discussion of control statements, introducing the `for`, `do...while` and `switch` statements.

Control Statements: Part 2

OBJECTIVES

In this chapter you'll learn:

- The essentials of counter-controlled repetition.

- To use the `for` and `do...while` repetition statements to execute statements in an application repeatedly.

- To understand multiple selection using the `switch` selection statement.

- To use the `break` and `continue` program-control statements to alter the flow of control.

- To use the logical operators to form complex conditional expressions in control statements.

Not everything that can be counted counts, and not everything that counts can be counted.
—Albert Einstein

Who can control his fate?
—William Shakespeare

The used key is always bright.
—Benjamin Franklin

Every advantage in the past is judged in the light of the final issue.
—Demosthenes

6.1 Introduction

In this chapter, we introduce several of C#'s remaining control statements (the foreach statement is introduced in Chapter 8, Arrays). The control statements we study here and in Chapter 5 are helpful in building and manipulating objects.

Through a series of examples using while and for, we explore the essentials of counter-controlled repetition. We create a version of class GradeBook that uses a switch statement to count the number of A, B, C, D and F grade equivalents in a set of numeric grades entered by the user. We introduce the break and continue program-control statements. We discuss C#'s logical operators, which enable you to use more complex conditional expressions in control statements.

6.2 Essentials of Counter-Controlled Repetition

This section uses the while **repetition statement** to formalize the elements required to perform counter-controlled repetition. Counter-controlled repetition requires

1. a **control variable** (or loop counter)

2. the **initial value** of the control variable

3. the **increment** (or **decrement**) by which the control variable is modified each time through the loop (also known as each **iteration of the loop**)

4. the **loop-continuation condition** that determines whether to continue looping.

To see these elements of counter-controlled repetition, consider the application of Fig. 6.1, which uses a loop to display the numbers from 1 through 10.

In method Main of Fig. 6.1 (lines 7–18), the elements of counter-controlled repetition are defined in lines 9, 11 and 14. Line 9 declares the control variable (counter) as an int, reserves space for it in memory and sets its initial value to 1.

```
1   // Fig. 6.1: WhileCounter.cs
2   // Counter-controlled repetition with the while repetition statement.
3   using System;
4
5   public class WhileCounter
6   {
7      public static void Main( string[] args )
8      {
9         int counter = 1; // declare and initialize control variable
```

Fig. 6.1 | Counter-controlled repetition with the while repetition statement. (Part 1 of 2.)

```
10
11          while ( counter <= 10 ) // loop-continuation condition
12          {
13             Console.Write( "{0}  ", counter );
14             ++counter; // increment control variable
15          } // end while
16
17          Console.WriteLine(); // output a newline
18       } // end Main
19    } // end class WhileCounter
```

```
1  2  3  4  5  6  7  8  9  10
```

Fig. 6.1 | Counter-controlled repetition with the `while` repetition statement. (Part 2 of 2.)

Line 13 in the `while` statement displays control variable `counter`'s value during each iteration of the loop. Line 14 increments the control variable by 1 for each iteration of the loop. The loop-continuation condition in the `while` (line 11) tests whether the value of the control variable is less than or equal to 10 (the final value for which the condition is `true`). The application performs the body of this `while` even when the control variable is 10. The loop terminates when the control variable exceeds 10 (i.e., `counter` becomes 11).

Common Programming Error 6.1

Because floating-point values may be approximate, controlling loops with floating-point variables may result in imprecise counter values and inaccurate termination tests.

Error-Prevention Tip 6.1

Control counting loops with integers.

The application in Fig. 6.1 can be made more concise by initializing `counter` to 0 in line 9 and incrementing `counter` in the `while` condition with the prefix increment operator as follows:

```
while ( ++counter <= 10 ) // loop-continuation condition
   Console.Write( "{0}  ", counter );
```

This code saves a statement (and eliminates the need for braces around the loop's body), because the `while` condition performs the increment before testing the condition. (Recall from Section 5.10 that the precedence of `++` is higher than that of `<=`.) Code written in such a condensed fashion might be more difficult to read, debug, modify and maintain.

Software Engineering Observation 6.1

"Keep it simple" is good advice for most of the code you'll write.

6.3 for Repetition Statement

Section 6.2 presented the essentials of counter-controlled repetition. The `while` statement can be used to implement any counter-controlled loop. C# also provides the **for repeti-**

tion statement, which specifies the elements of counter-controlled-repetition in a single line of code. In general, counter-controlled repetition should be implemented with a for statement. Figure 6.2 reimplements the application in Fig. 6.1 using the for statement.

```
1   // Fig. 6.2: ForCounter.cs
2   // Counter-controlled repetition with the for repetition statement.
3   using System;
4
5   public class ForCounter
6   {
7      public static void Main( string[] args )
8      {
9         // for statement header includes initialization,
10        // loop-continuation condition and increment
11        for ( int counter = 1; counter <= 10; counter++ )
12           Console.Write( "{0}  ", counter );
13
14        Console.WriteLine(); // output a newline
15     } // end Main
16  } // end class ForCounter
```

```
1  2  3  4  5  6  7  8  9  10
```

Fig. 6.2 | Counter-controlled repetition with the for repetition statement.

When the lines 11–12 begin executing, control variable counter is declared and initialized to 1. Next, the loop-continuation condition, counter <= 10 (which is between the two required semicolons) is evaluated. The initial value of counter is 1, so the condition initially is true. Therefore, the body statement (line 12) displays control variable counter's value, which is 1. After executing the loop's body, the application increments counter in the expression counter++, which appears to the right of the second semicolon. Then the loop-continuation test is performed again to determine whether the application should continue with the next iteration of the loop. At this point, the control-variable value is 2, so the condition is still true—and the application performs the body statement again (i.e., the next iteration of the loop). This process continues until the numbers 1 through 10 have been displayed and the counter's value becomes 11, causing the loop-continuation test to fail and repetition to terminate (after 10 repetitions of the loop body at line 12). Then the application performs the first statement after the for—in this case, line 14.

Fig. 6.2 uses (in line 11) the loop-continuation condition counter <= 10. If you incorrectly specified counter < 10 as the condition, the loop would iterate only nine times—a common logic error called an **off-by-one error**.

Good Programming Practice 6.1

Using the final value in the condition of a while or for statement with the <= relational operator helps avoid off-by-one errors. For a loop that displays the values 1 to 10, the loop-continuation condition should be counter <= 10, rather than counter < 10 (which causes an off-by-one error) or counter < 11 (which is correct). Many programmers prefer so-called zero-based counting, in which, to count 10 times, counter would be initialized to zero and the loop-continuation test would be counter < 10.

Figure 6.3 takes a closer look at the for statement in Fig. 6.2. The for's first line (including the keyword for and everything in parentheses after for)—line 11 in Fig. 6.2—is sometimes called the **for statement header**, or simply the **for header**. The for header "does it all"—it specifies each of the items needed for counter-controlled repetition with a control variable. If there's more than one statement in the body of the for, braces are required to define the body of the loop.

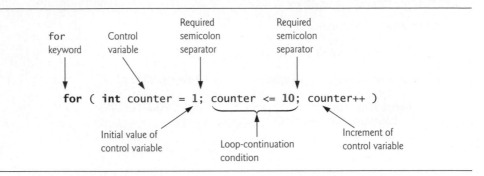

Fig. 6.3 | for statement header components.

The general format of the for statement is

> **for** (*initialization*; *loopContinuationCondition*; *increment*)
>   *statement*

where the *initialization* expression names the loop's control variable and provides its initial value, the *loopContinuationCondition* is the condition that determines whether looping should continue and the *increment* modifies the control variable's value (whether an increment or decrement), so that the loop-continuation condition eventually becomes false. The two semicolons in the for header are required. We don't include a semicolon after *statement*, because the semicolon is already assumed to be included in the notion of a *statement*.

Common Programming Error 6.2

Using commas instead of the two required semicolons in a for header is a syntax error.

In most cases, the for statement can be represented with an equivalent while statement as follows:

> *initialization*;
> **while** (*loopContinuationCondition*)
> {
>   *statement*
>   *increment*;
> }

In Section 6.7, we discuss a case in which a for statement cannot be represented with an equivalent while statement.

Typically, for statements are used for counter-controlled repetition, and while statements are used for sentinel-controlled repetition. However, while and for can each be used for either repetition type.

If the *initialization* expression in the for header declares the control variable (i.e., the control variable's type is specified before the variable name, as in Fig. 6.2), the control variable can be used only in that for statement—it will not exist outside it. This restricted use of the name of the control variable is known as the variable's **scope**. The scope of a variable defines where it can be used in an application. For example, a local variable can be used only in the method that declares the variable and only from the point of declaration through the end of the block in which the variable has been declared. Scope is discussed in detail in Chapter 7, Methods: A Deeper Look.

Common Programming Error 6.3

When a for statement's control variable is declared in the initialization section of the for's header, using the control variable after the for's body is a compilation error.

All three expressions in a for header are optional. If the *loopContinuationCondition* is omitted, the loop-continuation condition is always true, thus creating an infinite loop. You can omit the *initialization* expression if the control variable is initialized before the loop—in this case, the scope of the control variable will not be limited to the loop. You can omit the *increment* expression if the application calculates the increment with statements in the loop's body or if no increment is needed. The increment expression in a for acts as if it were a stand-alone statement at the end of the for's body. Therefore, the expressions

```
counter = counter + 1
counter += 1
++counter
counter++
```

are equivalent increment expressions in a for statement. Many programmers prefer counter++ because it's concise and because a for loop evaluates its increment expression after its body executes—so the postfix increment form seems more natural. In this case, the variable being incremented does not appear in a larger expression, so the prefix and postfix increment operators have the same effect.

Performance Tip 6.1

There's a slight performance advantage to using the prefix increment operator, but if you choose the postfix increment operator because it seems more natural (as in a for header), optimizing compilers will generate MSIL code that uses the more efficient form anyway.

Good Programming Practice 6.2

In many cases, the prefix and postfix increment operators are both used to add 1 to a variable in a statement by itself. In these cases, the effect is exactly the same, except that the prefix increment operator has a slight performance advantage. Given that the compiler typically optimizes your code to help you get the best performance, use the idiom (prefix or postfix) with which you feel most comfortable in these situations.

Error-Prevention Tip 6.2

Infinite loops occur when the loop-continuation condition in a repetition statement never becomes false. To prevent this situation in a counter-controlled loop, ensure that the control variable is incremented (or decremented) during each iteration of the loop. In a sentinel-controlled loop, ensure that the sentinel value is eventually input.

The initialization, loop-continuation condition and increment portions of a `for` statement can contain arithmetic expressions. For example, assume that x = 2 and y = 10; if x and y are not modified in the body of the loop, then the statement

```
for ( int j = x; j <= 4 * x * y; j += y / x )
```

is equivalent to the statement

```
for ( int j = 2; j <= 80; j += 5 )
```

The increment of a `for` statement may also be negative, in which case it's a decrement, and the loop counts downward.

If the loop-continuation condition is initially `false`, the application does not execute the `for` statement's body. Instead, execution proceeds with the statement following the `for`.

Applications frequently display the control variable value or use it in calculations in the loop body, but this use is not required. The control variable is commonly used to control repetition without being mentioned in the body of the `for`.

> **Error-Prevention Tip 6.3**
> *Although the value of the control variable can be changed in the body of a `for` loop, avoid doing so, because this practice can lead to subtle errors.*

Figure 6.4 shows the activity diagram of the `for` statement in Fig. 6.2. The diagram makes it clear that initialization occurs only once before the loop-continuation test is evaluated the first time, and that incrementing occurs each time through the loop after the body statement executes.

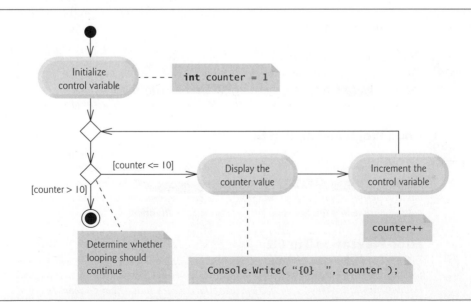

Fig. 6.4 | UML activity diagram for the `for` statement in Fig. 6.2.

6.4 Examples Using the **for** Statement

The following examples show techniques for varying the control variable in a for statement. In each case, we write the appropriate for header. Note the change in the relational operator for loops that decrement the control variable.

a) Vary the control variable from 1 to 100 in increments of 1.

```
for ( int i = 1; i <= 100; i++ )
```

b) Vary the control variable from 100 to 1 in decrements of 1.

```
for ( int i = 100; i >= 1; i-- )
```

c) Vary the control variable from 7 to 77 in increments of 7.

```
for ( int i = 7; i <= 77; i += 7 )
```

d) Vary the control variable from 20 to 2 in decrements of 2.

```
for ( int i = 20; i >= 2; i -= 2 )
```

e) Vary the control variable over the following sequence of values: 2, 5, 8, 11, 14, 17.

```
for ( int i = 2; i <= 17; i += 3 )
```

f) Vary the control variable over the following sequence of values: 99, 88, 77, 66, 55, 44, 33, 22, 11, 0.

```
for ( int i = 99; i >= 0; i -= 11 )
```

 Common Programming Error 6.4
Not using the proper relational operator in the loop-continuation condition of a loop that counts downward (e.g., using i <= 1 instead of i >= 1 in a loop counting down to 1) is a logic error.

Application: Summing the Even Integers from 2 to 20
We now consider two sample applications that demonstrate simple uses of for. The application in Fig. 6.5 uses a for statement to sum the even integers from 2 to 20 and store the result in an int variable called total.

```
1   // Fig. 6.5: Sum.cs
2   // Summing integers with the for statement.
3   using System;
4
5   public class Sum
6   {
7      public static void Main( string[] args )
8      {
9         int total = 0; // initialize total
10
11        // total even integers from 2 through 20
12        for ( int number = 2; number <= 20; number += 2 )
13           total += number;
```

Fig. 6.5 | Summing integers with the for statement. (Part 1 of 2.)

```
14
15        Console.WriteLine( "Sum is {0}", total ); // display results
16    } // end Main
17 } // end class Sum
```

```
Sum is 110
```

Fig. 6.5 | Summing integers with the for statement. (Part 2 of 2.)

The *initialization* and *increment* expressions can be comma-separated lists that enable you to use multiple initialization expressions or multiple increment expressions. For example, you could merge the body of the for statement in lines 12–13 of Fig. 6.5 into the increment portion of the for header by using a comma as follows:

```
for ( int number = 2; number <= 20; total += number, number += 2 )
    ; // empty statement
```

Good Programming Practice 6.3

Place only expressions involving the control variables in the initialization and increment sections of a for statement. Manipulations of other variables should appear either before the loop (if they execute only once, like initialization statements) or in the body of the loop (if they execute once per iteration of the loop, like increment or decrement statements).

Application: Compound-Interest Calculations

The next application uses the for statement to compute compound interest. Consider the following problem:

> *A person invests $1,000 in a savings account yielding 5% interest, compounded yearly. Assuming that all the interest is left on deposit, calculate and display the amount of money in the account at the end of each year for 10 years. Use the following formula to determine the amounts:*
>
> $$a = p\,(1 + r)^n$$
>
> *where*
>
> > *p is the original amount invested (i.e., the principal)*
> > *r is the annual interest rate (e.g., use 0.05 for 5%)*
> > *n is the number of years*
> > *a is the amount on deposit at the end of the nth year.*

This problem involves a loop that performs the indicated calculation for each of the 10 years the money remains on deposit. The solution is the application shown in Fig. 6.6. Lines 9–11 in method Main declare decimal variables amount and principal, and double variable rate. Lines 10–11 also initialize principal to 1000 (i.e., $1000.00) and rate to 0.05. C# treats real-number constants like 0.05 as type double. Similarly, C# treats whole-number constants like 7 and 1000 as type int. When principal is initialized to 1000, the value 1000 of type int is promoted to a decimal type implicitly—no cast is required.

Line 14 outputs the headers for the application's two columns of output. The first column displays the year, and the second column displays the amount on deposit at the end of that year. We use the format item {0,20} to output the string "Amount on deposit". The integer 20 after the comma indicates that the value output should be displayed with a

```
 1   // Fig. 6.6: Interest.cs
 2   // Compound-interest calculations with for.
 3   using System;
 4
 5   public class Interest
 6   {
 7      public static void Main( string[] args )
 8      {
 9         decimal amount; // amount on deposit at end of each year
10         decimal principal = 1000; // initial amount before interest
11         double rate = 0.05; // interest rate
12
13         // display headers
14         Console.WriteLine( "Year{0,20}", "Amount on deposit" );
15
16         // calculate amount on deposit for each of ten years
17         for ( int year = 1; year <= 10; year++ )
18         {
19            // calculate new amount for specified year
20            amount = principal *
21               ( ( decimal ) Math.Pow( 1.0 + rate, year ) );
22
23            // display the year and the amount
24            Console.WriteLine( "{0,4}{1,20:C}", year, amount );
25         } // end for
26      } // end Main
27   } // end class Interest
```

```
Year   Amount on deposit
  1          $1,050.00
  2          $1,102.50
  3          $1,157.63
  4          $1,215.51
  5          $1,276.28
  6          $1,340.10
  7          $1,407.10
  8          $1,477.46
  9          $1,551.33
 10          $1,628.89
```

Fig. 6.6 | Compound-interest calculations with for.

field width of 20—that is, WriteLine displays the value with at least 20 character positions. If the value to be output is less than 20 character positions wide (17 characters in this example), the value is **right justified** in the field by default (in this case the value is preceded by three blanks). If the year value to be output were more than four character positions wide, the field width would be extended to the right to accommodate the entire value—this would push the amount field to the right, upsetting the neat columns of our tabular output. To indicate that output should be **left justified**, simply use a negative field width.

The for statement (lines 17–25) executes its body 10 times, varying control variable year from 1 to 10 in increments of 1. This loop terminates when control variable year becomes 11. (Note that year represents n in the problem statement.)

Classes provide methods that perform common tasks on objects. In fact, most methods must be called on a specific object. For example, to output a greeting in Fig. 4.2, we called method `DisplayMessage` on the `myGradeBook` object. Many classes also provide methods that perform common tasks and cannot be called on objects—they must be called using a class name. Such methods are called **static methods**. For example, C# does not include an exponentiation operator, so the designers of C#'s `Math` class defined `static` method `Pow` for raising a value to a power. You can call a `static` method by specifying the class name followed by the member access (`.`) operator and the method name, as in

> *ClassName*.*methodName*(*arguments*)

`Console` methods `Write` and `WriteLine` are `static` methods. In Chapter 7, you'll learn how to implement `static` methods in your own classes.

We use `static` method `Pow` of class `Math` to perform the compound interest calculation. `Math.Pow(x, y)` calculates the value of *x* raised to the *y*th power. The method receives two `double` arguments and returns a `double` value. Lines 20–21 perform the calculation $a = p(1 + r)^n$, where *a* is the amount, *p* is the `principal`, *r* is the rate and *n* is the year. In this calculation, we need to multiply a `decimal` value (`principal`) by a `double` value (the return value of `Math.Pow`). C# will not implicitly convert a `double` to a `decimal`, or vice versa, because of the possible loss of information in either conversion, so line 21 uses a (`decimal`) cast operator to explicitly convert the `double` return value of `Math.Pow` to a `decimal`.

After each calculation, line 24 outputs the year and the amount on deposit at the end of that year. The year is output in a field width of four characters (as specified by `{0,4}`). The amount is output as a currency value with the format item `{1,20:C}`. The number 20 in the format item indicates that the value should be output right justified with a field width of 20 characters. The format specifier `C` specifies that the number should be formatted as currency.

Notice that we declared the variables `amount` and `principal` to be of type `decimal` rather than `double`. Recall that we introduced type `decimal` for monetary calculations in Section 4.11. We also use `decimal` in Fig. 6.6 for this purpose. You may be curious as to why we do this. We are dealing with fractional parts of dollars and thus need a type that allows decimal points in its values. Unfortunately, floating-point numbers of type `double` (or `float`) can cause trouble in monetary calculations. Two `double` dollar amounts stored in the machine could be 14.234 (which would normally be rounded to 14.23 for display purposes) and 18.673 (which would normally be rounded to 18.67 for display purposes). When these amounts are added, they produce the internal sum 32.907, which would normally be rounded to 32.91 for display purposes. Thus, your output could appear as

```
   14.23
 + 18.67
 -------
   32.91
```

but a person adding the individual numbers as displayed would expect the sum to be 32.90. You've been warned!

Good Programming Practice 6.4

Do not use variables of type double (or float) to perform precise monetary calculations; use type decimal instead. The imprecision of floating-point numbers can cause errors that will result in incorrect monetary values.

The body of the for statement contains the calculation 1.0 + rate, which appears as an argument to the Math.Pow method. In fact, this calculation produces the same result each time through the loop, so repeating the calculation in every iteration of the loop is wasteful.

> **Performance Tip 6.2**
>
> *In loops, avoid calculations for which the result never changes—such calculations should typically be placed before the loop.* [Note: *Optimizing compilers will typically place such calculations outside loops in the compiled code.*]

6.5 do...while Repetition Statement

The **do...while repetition statement** is similar to the while statement. In the while, the application tests the loop-continuation condition at the beginning of the loop, before executing the loop's body. If the condition is false, the body never executes. The do...while statement tests the loop-continuation condition *after* executing the loop's body; therefore, the body always executes at least once. When a do...while statement terminates, execution continues with the next statement in sequence. Figure 6.7 uses a do...while (lines 11–15) to output the numbers 1–10.

```
1   // Fig. 6.7: DoWhileTest.cs
2   // do...while repetition statement.
3   using System;
4
5   public class DoWhileTest
6   {
7      public static void Main( string[] args )
8      {
9         int counter = 1; // initialize counter
10
11         do
12         {
13            Console.Write( "{0}  ", counter );
14            ++counter;
15         } while ( counter <= 10 ); // end do...while
16
17         Console.WriteLine(); // outputs a newline
18      } // end Main
19   } // end class DoWhileTest
```

```
1  2  3  4  5  6  7  8  9  10
```

Fig. 6.7 | do...while repetition statement.

Line 9 declares and initializes control variable counter. Upon entering the do...while statement, line 13 outputs counter's value, and line 14 increments counter. Then the application evaluates the loop-continuation test at the bottom of the loop (line 15). If the condition is true, the loop continues from the first body statement in the do...while (line 13). If the condition is false, the loop terminates, and the application continues with the next statement after the loop.

Figure 6.8 contains the UML activity diagram for the do...while statement. This diagram makes it clear that the loop-continuation condition is not evaluated until after the loop performs the action state at least once. Compare this activity diagram with that of the while statement (Fig. 5.4). It's not necessary to use braces in the do...while repetition statement if there's only one statement in the body. However, most programmers include the braces to avoid confusion between the while and do...while statements. For example,

```
while ( condition )
```

is normally the first line of a while statement. A do...while statement with no braces around a single-statement body appears as:

```
do
    statement
while ( condition );
```

which can be confusing. Some people misinterpret the last line—while(*condition*);—as a while statement containing an empty statement (the semicolon by itself). To avoid confusion, a do...while statement with one body statement can be written as follows:

```
do
{
    statement
} while ( condition );
```

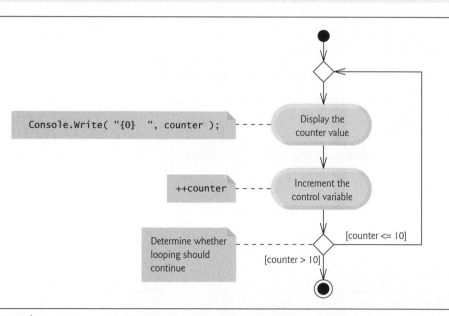

Fig. 6.8 | do...while repetition statement UML activity diagram.

6.6 switch Multiple-Selection Statement

We discussed the if single-selection statement and the if...else double-selection statement in Chapter 5. C# provides the **switch multiple-selection** statement to perform different actions based on the possible values of an expression. Each action is associated with the value of a **constant integral expression** or a **constant string expression** that the variable or expression on which the switch is based may assume. A constant integral expression is any expression involving character and integer constants that evaluates to an integer value—i.e., values of type sbyte, byte, short, ushort, int, uint, long, ulong and char, or a constant from an enum type (enum is discussed in Section 7.10). A constant string expression is any expression composed of string literals that always results in the same string.

GradeBook Class with switch Statement to Count A, B, C, D and F Grades.

Figure 6.9 contains an enhanced version of the GradeBook class introduced in Chapter 4 and further developed in Chapter 5. The version of the class we now present not only calculates the average of a set of numeric grades entered by the user, but uses a switch statement to determine whether each grade is the equivalent of an A, B, C, D or F, then increments the appropriate grade counter. The class also displays a summary of the number of students who received each grade. Figure 6.10 shows sample input and output of the GradeBookTest application that uses class GradeBook to process a set of grades.

```csharp
1   // Fig. 6.9: GradeBook.cs
2   // GradeBook class uses switch statement to count letter grades.
3   using System;
4
5   public class GradeBook
6   {
7      private int total; // sum of grades
8      private int gradeCounter; // number of grades entered
9      private int aCount; // count of A grades
10     private int bCount; // count of B grades
11     private int cCount; // count of C grades
12     private int dCount; // count of D grades
13     private int fCount; // count of F grades
14
15     // automatic property CourseName
16     public string CourseName { get; set; }
17
18     // constructor initializes automatic property CourseName;
19     // int instance variables are initialized to 0 by default
20     public GradeBook( string name )
21     {
22        CourseName = name; // set CourseName to name
23     } // end constructor
24
25     // display a welcome message to the GradeBook user
26     public void DisplayMessage()
27     {
28        // CourseName gets the name of the course
29        Console.WriteLine( "Welcome to the grade book for\n{0}!\n",
30           CourseName );
31     } // end method DisplayMessage
32
```

Fig. 6.9 | GradeBook class that uses a switch statement to count A, B, C, D and F grades. (Part 1 of 3.)

```csharp
33      // input arbitrary number of grades from user
34      public void InputGrades()
35      {
36         int grade; // grade entered by user
37         string input; // text entered by the user
38
39         Console.WriteLine( "{0}\n{1}",
40            "Enter the integer grades in the range 0-100.",
41            "Type <Ctrl> z and press Enter to terminate input:" );
42
43         input = Console.ReadLine(); // read user input
44
45         // loop until user enters the end-of-file indicator (<Ctrl> z)
46         while ( input != null )
47         {
48            grade = Convert.ToInt32( input ); // read grade off user input
49            total += grade; // add grade to total
50            ++gradeCounter; // increment number of grades
51
52            // call method to increment appropriate counter
53            IncrementLetterGradeCounter( grade );
54
55            input = Console.ReadLine(); // read user input
56         } // end while
57      } // end method InputGrades
58
59      // add 1 to appropriate counter for specified grade
60      private void IncrementLetterGradeCounter( int grade )
61      {
62         // determine which grade was entered
63         switch ( grade / 10 )
64         {
65            case 9: // grade was in the 90s
66            case 10: // grade was 100
67               ++aCount; // increment aCount
68               break; // necessary to exit switch
69            case 8: // grade was between 80 and 89
70               ++bCount; // increment bCount
71               break; // exit switch
72            case 7: // grade was between 70 and 79
73               ++cCount; // increment cCount
74               break; // exit switch
75            case 6: // grade was between 60 and 69
76               ++dCount; // increment dCount
77               break; // exit switch
78            default: // grade was less than 60
79               ++fCount; // increment fCount
80               break; // exit switch
81         } // end switch
82      } // end method IncrementLetterGradeCounter
83
```

Fig. 6.9 | GradeBook class that uses a `switch` statement to count A, B, C, D and F grades. (Part 2 of 3.)

```
84      // display a report based on the grades entered by the user
85      public void DisplayGradeReport()
86      {
87         Console.WriteLine( "\nGrade Report:" );
88
89         // if user entered at least one grade...
90         if ( gradeCounter != 0 )
91         {
92            // calculate average of all grades entered
93            double average = ( double ) total / gradeCounter;
94
95            // output summary of results
96            Console.WriteLine( "Total of the {0} grades entered is {1}",
97               gradeCounter, total );
98            Console.WriteLine( "Class average is {0:F}", average );
99            Console.WriteLine( "{0}A: {1}\nB: {2}\nC: {3}\nD: {4}\nF: {5}",
100              "Number of students who received each grade:\n",
101              aCount, // display number of A grades
102              bCount, // display number of B grades
103              cCount, // display number of C grades
104              dCount, // display number of D grades
105              fCount ); // display number of F grades
106        } // end if
107        else // no grades were entered, so output appropriate message
108           Console.WriteLine( "No grades were entered" );
109     } // end method DisplayGradeReport
110  } // end class GradeBook
```

Fig. 6.9 | GradeBook class that uses a switch statement to count A, B, C, D and F grades. (Part 3 of 3.)

Instance Variables

Class GradeBook (Fig. 6.9) declares instance variables total (line 7) and gradeCounter (line 8), which keep track of the sum of the grades entered by the user and the number of grades entered, respectively. Lines 9–13 declare counter variables for each grade category. Class GradeBook maintains total, gradeCounter and the five letter-grade counters as instance variables so that they can be used or modified in any of the class's methods.

Property CourseName, Method DisplayMessage and the Constructor

Like earlier versions of the class, class GradeBook declares automatic property CourseName (line 16) and method DisplayMessage (lines 26–31) to display a welcome message to the user. The class also contains a constructor (lines 20–23) that initializes the course name. The constructor sets only the course name—the remaining seven instance variables are ints and are initialized to 0 by default.

Methods InputGrades and DisplayGradeReport

Class GradeBook contains three additional methods—InputGrades, IncrementLetter-GradeCounter and DisplayGradeReport. Method InputGrades (lines 34–57) reads an arbitrary number of integer grades from the user using sentinel-controlled repetition and updates instance variables total and gradeCounter. Method InputGrades calls method IncrementLetterGradeCounter (lines 60–82) to update the appropriate letter-grade counter for each grade entered. Class GradeBook also contains method DisplayGradeReport (lines 85–109), which outputs a report containing the total of all grades entered, the average of the grades and the number of students who received each letter grade. Let's examine these methods in more detail.

Lines 36–37 in method InputGrades declare variables grade and input, which will first store the user's input as a string (in the variable input), then convert it to an int to store in the variable grade. Lines 39–41 prompt the user to enter integer grades and to type *Ctrl + z*, then press *Enter* to terminate the input. The notation *Ctrl + z* means to simultaneously press both the *Ctrl* key and the *z* key when typing in a **Command Prompt**. *Ctrl + z* is the Windows key sequence for typing the **end-of-file indicator**. This is one way to inform an application that there's no more data to input. If *Ctrl + z* is entered while the application is awaiting input with a ReadLine method, null is returned. (The end-of-file indicator is a system-dependent keystroke combination. On many non-Windows systems, end-of-file is entered by typing *Ctrl + d*.) In Chapter 17, Files and Streams, we'll see how the end-of-file indicator is used when an application reads its input from a file. [*Note:* Windows typically displays the characters ^Z in a **Command Prompt** when the end-of-file indicator is typed, as shown in the output of Fig. 6.10.]

Line 43 uses the ReadLine method to get the first line that the user entered and store it in variable input. The while statement (lines 46–56) processes this user input. The condition at line 46 checks whether the value of input is a null reference. The Console class's ReadLine method will return null only if the user typed an end-of-file indicator. As long as the end-of-file indicator has not been typed, input will not contain a null reference, and the condition will pass.

Line 48 converts the string in input to an int type. Line 49 adds grade to total. Line 50 increments gradeCounter. The class's DisplayGradeReport method uses these variables to compute the average of the grades. Line 53 calls the class's IncrementLetterGradeCounter method (declared in lines 60–82) to increment the appropriate letter-grade counter, based on the numeric grade entered.

Method IncrementLetterGradeCounter and the Constructor

Method IncrementLetterGradeCounter contains a switch statement (lines 63–81) that determines which counter to increment. In this example, we assume that the user enters a valid grade in the range 0–100. A grade in the range 90–100 represents A, 80–89 represents B, 70–79 represents C, 60–69 represents D and 0–59 represents F. The switch statement consists of a block that contains a sequence of **case labels** and an optional **default label**. These are used in this example to determine which counter to increment based on the grade.

When the flow of control reaches the switch statement, the application evaluates the expression in the parentheses (grade / 10) following keyword switch—this is called the **switch expression**. The application attempts to match the value of the switch expression with one of the case labels. The switch expression in line 63 performs integer division, which truncates the fractional part of the result. Thus, when we divide any value in the range 0–100 by 10, the result is always a value from 0 to 10. We use several of these values in our case labels. For example, if the user enters the integer 85, the switch expression evaluates to int value 8. If a match occurs between the switch expression and a case (case 8: at line 69), the application executes the statements for that case. For the integer 8, line

70 increments bCount, because a grade in the 80s is a B. The **break statement** (line 71) causes program control to proceed with the first statement after the switch—in this application, we reach the end of method IncrementLetterGradeCounter's body, so control returns to line 55 in method InputGrades (the first line after the call to IncrementLetterGradeCounter). This line uses the ReadLine method to read the next line entered by the user and assign it to the variable input. Line 56 marks the end of the body of the while statement that inputs grades (lines 46–56), so control flows to the while's condition (line 46) to determine whether the loop should continue executing based on the value just assigned to the variable input.

The cases in our switch explicitly test for the values 10, 9, 8, 7 and 6. Note the case labels at lines 65–66 that test for the values 9 and 10 (both of which represent the grade A). Listing case labels consecutively in this manner with no statements between them enables the cases to perform the same set of statements—when the switch expression evaluates to 9 or 10, the statements in lines 67–68 execute. The switch statement does not provide a mechanism for testing ranges of values, so every value to be tested must be listed in a separate case label. Each case can have multiple statements. The switch statement differs from other control statements in that it does not require braces around multiple statements in each case.

In C, C++, and many other programming languages that use the switch statement, the break statement is not required at the end of a case. Without break statements, each time a match occurs in the switch, the statements for that case and subsequent cases execute until a break statement or the end of the switch is encountered. This is often referred to as "falling through" to the statements in subsequent cases. This frequently leads to logic errors when you forget the break statement. For this reason, C# has a "no fall through" rule for cases in a switch—after the statements in a case, you are required to include a statement that terminates the case, such as a break, a return or a throw. (We discuss the throw statement in Chapter 13, Exception Handling.)

If no match occurs between the switch expression's value and a case label, the statements after the default label (lines 79–80) execute. We use the default label in this example to process all switch-expression values that are less than 6—that is, all failing grades. If no match occurs and the switch does not contain a default label, program control simply continues with the first statement (if there is one) after the switch statement.

GradeBookTest Class That Demonstrates Class GradeBook

Class GradeBookTest (Fig. 6.10) creates a GradeBook object (lines 10–11). Line 13 invokes the object's DisplayMessage method to output a welcome message to the user. Line 14 invokes the object's InputGrades method to read a set of grades from the user and keep track of the sum of all the grades entered and the number of grades. Recall that method InputGrades also calls method IncrementLetterGradeCounter to keep track of the number of students who received each letter grade. Line 15 invokes method DisplayGradeReport of class GradeBook, which outputs a report based on the grades entered. Line 90 of class GradeBook (Fig. 6.9) determines whether the user entered at least one grade—this avoids dividing by zero. If so, line 93 calculates the average of the grades. Lines 96–105 then output the total of all the grades, the class average and the number of students who received each letter grade. If no grades were entered, line 108 outputs an appropriate message. The output in Fig. 6.10 shows a sample grade report based on 9 grades.

```
1   // Fig. 6.10: GradeBookTest.cs
2   // Create GradeBook object, input grades and display grade report.
3
4   public class GradeBookTest
5   {
6      public static void Main( string[] args )
7      {
8         // create GradeBook object myGradeBook and
9         // pass course name to constructor
10        GradeBook myGradeBook = new GradeBook(
11           "CS101 Introduction to C# Programming" );
12
13        myGradeBook.DisplayMessage(); // display welcome message
14        myGradeBook.InputGrades(); // read grades from user
15        myGradeBook.DisplayGradeReport(); // display report based on grades
16     } // end Main
17  } // end class GradeBookTest
```

```
Welcome to the grade book for
CS101 Introduction to C# Programming!

Enter the integer grades in the range 0-100.
Type <Ctrl> z and press Enter to terminate input:
99
92
45
100
57
63
76
14
92
^Z

Grade Report:
Total of the 9 grades entered is 638
Class average is 70.89
Number of students who received each grade:
A: 4
B: 0
C: 1
D: 1
F: 3
```

Fig. 6.10 | Create GradeBook object, input grades and display grade report.

Class GradeBookTest (Fig. 6.10) does not directly call GradeBook method IncrementLetterGradeCounter (lines 60–82 of Fig. 6.9). This method is used exclusively by method InputGrades of class GradeBook to update the appropriate letter-grade counter as each new grade is entered by the user. Method IncrementLetterGradeCounter exists solely to support the operations of class GradeBook's other methods and thus is declared private. Members of a class declared with access modifier private can be accessed only by members of the class in which the private members are declared. When a private member is a method, it's commonly referred to as a **utility method** or **helper method**, because it can be called only by other members of that class and is used to support the operation of those other members.

switch *Statement UML Activity Diagram*

Figure 6.11 shows the UML activity diagram for the general switch statement. Every set of statements after a case label normally ends its execution with a break or return statement to terminate the switch statement after processing the case. Typically, you'll use break statements. Figure 6.11 emphasizes this by including break statements in the activity diagram. The diagram makes it clear that the break statement at the end of a case causes control to exit the switch statement immediately.

> **Good Programming Practice 6.5**
> *Although each case and the default label in a switch can occur in any order, place the default label last for clarity.*

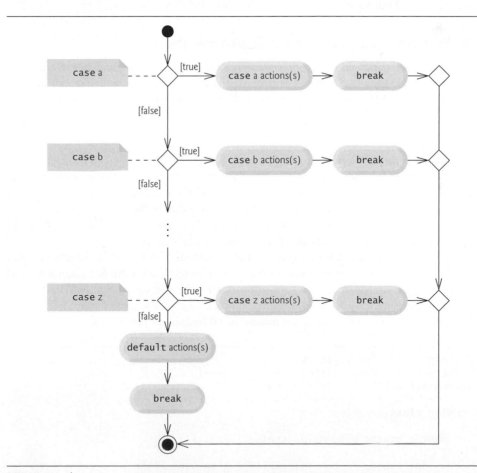

Fig. 6.11 | switch multiple-selection statement UML activity diagram with break statements.

When using the switch statement, remember that the expression after each case can be only a constant integral expression or a constant string expression—that is, any combination of constants that evaluates to a constant value of an integral or string type. An integer constant is simply an integer value (e.g., –7, 0 or 221). In addition, you can use **character constants**—specific characters in single quotes, such as 'A', '7' or '$'—which represent the integer values of characters. (Appendix C shows the integer values of the characters in the ASCII character set, which is a subset of the Unicode character set used by C#.) A string constant (or string literal) is a sequence of characters in double quotes, such as "Welcome to C# Programming!".

The expression in each case also can be a **constant**—a value which does not change for the entire application. Constants are declared with the keyword const (discussed in Chapter 7). C# also has a feature called enumerations, which we also present in Chapter 7. Enumeration constants can also be used in case labels. In Chapter 12, we present a more elegant way to implement switch logic—we use a technique called polymorphism to create applications that are often clearer, easier to maintain and easier to extend than applications using switch logic.

6.7 break and continue Statements

In addition to selection and repetition statements, C# provides statements break and continue to alter the flow of control. The preceding section showed how break can be used to terminate a switch statement's execution. This section discusses how to use break to terminate any repetition statement.

break *Statement*

The break statement, when executed in a while, for, do...while, switch, or foreach, causes immediate exit from that statement. Execution typically continues with the first statement after the control statement—you'll see that there are other possibilities as you learn about additional statement types in C#. Common uses of the break statement are to escape early from a repetition statement or to skip the remainder of a switch (as in Fig. 6.9). Figure 6.12 demonstrates a break statement exiting a for.

When the if nested at line 13 in the for statement (lines 11–17) determines that count is 5, the break statement at line 14 executes. This terminates the for statement, and the application proceeds to line 19 (immediately after the for statement), which displays a message indicating the value of the control variable when the loop terminated. The loop fully executes its body only four times instead of 10 because of the break.

```
1   // Fig. 6.12: BreakTest.cs
2   // break statement exiting a for statement.
3   using System;
4
5   public class BreakTest
6   {
7      public static void Main( string[] args )
8      {
9         int count; // control variable also used after loop terminates
```

Fig. 6.12 | break statement exiting a for statement. (Part 1 of 2.)

```
10
11          for ( count = 1; count <= 10; count++ ) // loop 10 times
12          {
13             if ( count == 5 ) // if count is 5,
14                break; // terminate loop
15
16             Console.Write( "{0} ", count );
17          } // end for
18
19          Console.WriteLine( "\nBroke out of loop at count = {0}", count );
20       } // end Main
21    } // end class BreakTest
```

```
1 2 3 4
Broke out of loop at count = 5
```

Fig. 6.12 | break statement exiting a for statement. (Part 2 of 2.)

continue *Statement*

The **continue statement**, when executed in a while, for, do...while, or foreach, skips the remaining statements in the loop body and proceeds with the next iteration of the loop. In while and do...while statements, the application evaluates the loop-continuation test immediately after the continue statement executes. In a for statement, the increment expression normally executes next, then the application evaluates the loop-continuation test.

```
1    // Fig. 6.13: ContinueTest.cs
2    // continue statement terminating an iteration of a for statement.
3    using System;
4
5    public class ContinueTest
6    {
7       public static void Main( string[] args )
8       {
9          for ( int count = 1; count <= 10; count++ ) // loop 10 times
10         {
11            if ( count == 5 ) // if count is 5,
12               continue; // skip remaining code in loop
13
14            Console.Write( "{0} ", count );
15         } // end for
16
17         Console.WriteLine( "\nUsed continue to skip displaying 5" );
18      } // end Main
19   } // end class ContinueTest
```

```
1 2 3 4 6 7 8 9 10
Used continue to skip displaying 5
```

Fig. 6.13 | continue statement terminating an iteration of a for statement.

Figure 6.13 uses the continue statement in a for to skip the statement at line 14 when the nested if (line 11) determines that the value of count is 5. When the continue statement executes, program control continues with the increment of the control variable in the for statement (line 9).

In Section 6.3, we stated that a while can be used in most cases in place of for. One exception occurs when the increment expression in the while follows a continue statement. In this case, the increment doesn't execute before the repetition-continuation condition evaluates, so the while does not execute in the same manner as the for.

6.8 Logical Operators

The if, if...else, while, do...while and for statements each require a condition to determine how to continue an application's flow of control. So far, we have studied only **simple conditions**, such as count <= 10, number != sentinelValue and total > 1000. Simple conditions are expressed in terms of the relational operators >, <, >= and <=, and the equality operators == and !=. Each expression tests only one condition. To test multiple conditions in the process of making a decision, we performed these tests in separate statements or in nested if or if...else statements. Sometimes, control statements require more complex conditions to determine an application's flow of control.

C# provides **logical operators** to enable you to form more complex conditions by combining simple conditions. The logical operators are && (conditional AND), || (conditional OR), & (boolean logical AND), | (boolean logical inclusive OR), ∧ (boolean logical exclusive OR) and ! (logical negation).

Conditional AND (&&) Operator

Suppose that we wish to ensure at some point in an application that two conditions are *both* true before we choose a certain path of execution. In this case, we can use the **&&** (**conditional AND**) operator, as follows:

```
if ( gender == "F" && age >= 65 )
   ++seniorFemales;
```

This if statement contains two simple conditions. The condition gender == "F" determines whether a person is female. The condition age >= 65 might be evaluated to determine whether a person is a senior citizen. The if statement considers the combined condition

```
gender == "F" && age >= 65
```

which is true if and only if *both* simple conditions are true. If the combined condition is true, the if statement's body increments seniorFemales by 1. If either or both of the simple conditions are false, the application skips the increment. Some programmers find that the preceding combined condition is more readable when redundant parentheses are added, as in:

```
( gender == "F" ) && ( age >= 65 )
```

The table in Fig. 6.14 summarizes the && operator. The table shows all four possible combinations of false and true values for *expression1* and *expression2*. Such tables are called **truth tables**. C# evaluates all expressions that include relational operators, equality operators or logical operators to bool values—which are either true or false.

expression1	expression2	expression1 && expression2
false	false	false
false	true	false
true	false	false
true	true	true

Fig. 6.14 | && (conditional AND) operator truth table.

Conditional OR (||) Operator

Now suppose we wish to ensure that *either or both* of two conditions are true before we choose a certain path of execution. In this case, we use the **|| (conditional OR) operator**, as in the following application segment:

```
if ( ( semesterAverage >= 90 ) || ( finalExam >= 90 ) )
    Console.WriteLine ( "Student grade is A" );
```

This statement also contains two simple conditions. The condition `semesterAverage >= 90` is evaluated to determine whether the student deserves an A in the course because of a solid performance throughout the semester. The condition `finalExam >= 90` is evaluated to determine whether the student deserves an A in the course because of an outstanding performance on the final exam. The `if` statement then considers the combined condition

```
( semesterAverage >= 90 ) || ( finalExam >= 90 )
```

and awards the student an A if either or both of the simple conditions are true. The only time the message `"Student grade is A"` is *not* displayed is when both of the simple conditions are false. Figure 6.15 is a truth table for operator conditional OR (||). Operator && has a higher precedence than operator ||. Both operators associate from left to right.

expression1	expression2	expression1 || expression2
false	false	false
false	true	true
true	false	true
true	true	true

Fig. 6.15 | || (conditional OR) operator truth table.

Short-Circuit Evaluation of Complex Conditions

The parts of an expression containing && or || operators are evaluated only until it's known whether the condition is true or false. Thus, evaluation of the expression

```
( gender == "F" ) && ( age >= 65 )
```

stops immediately if `gender` is not equal to `"F"` (i.e., at that point, it's certain that the entire expression is `false`) and continues if `gender` *is* equal to `"F"` (i.e., the entire expression could still be `true` if the condition `age >= 65` is `true`). This feature of conditional AND and conditional OR expressions is called **short-circuit evaluation**.

Common Programming Error 6.5

In expressions using operator &&, a condition—which we refer to as the dependent condition—may require another condition to be true for the evaluation of the dependent condition to be meaningful. In this case, the dependent condition should be placed after the other condition, or an error might occur. For example, in the expression (i != 0) && (10 / i == 2), the second condition must appear after the first condition, or a divide-by-zero error might occur.

Boolean Logical AND (&) and Boolean Logical OR (|) Operators

The **boolean logical AND** (&) and **boolean logical inclusive OR** (|) operators work identically to the && (conditional AND) and || (conditional OR) operators, with one exception—the boolean logical operators always evaluate both of their operands (i.e., they do not perform short-circuit evaluation). Therefore, the expression

```
( gender == "F" ) & ( age >= 65 )
```

evaluates age >= 65 regardless of whether gender is equal to "F". This is useful if the right operand of the boolean logical AND or boolean logical inclusive OR operator has a required **side effect**—a modification of a variable's value. For example, the expression

```
( birthday == true ) | ( ++age >= 65 )
```

guarantees that ++age >= 65 will be evaluated. Thus, the variable age is incremented in the preceding expression, regardless of whether the overall expression is true or false.

Error-Prevention Tip 6.4

For clarity, avoid expressions with side effects in conditions. The side effects may look clever, but they can make it harder to understand code and can lead to subtle logic errors.

Boolean Logical Exclusive OR (∧)

A complex condition containing the **boolean logical exclusive OR** (∧) operator (also called the **logical XOR operator**) is true *if and only if one of its operands is true and the other is false*. If both operands are true or both are false, the entire condition is false. Figure 6.16 is a truth table for the boolean logical exclusive OR operator (∧). This operator is also guaranteed to evaluate both of its operands.

expression1	expression2	expression1 ∧ expression2
false	false	false
false	true	true
true	false	true
true	true	false

Fig. 6.16 | ∧ (boolean logical exclusive OR) operator truth table.

Logical Negation (!) Operator

The ! (**logical negation** or **not**) operator enables you to "reverse" the meaning of a condition. Unlike the logical operators &&, ||, &, | and ∧, which are binary operators that combine two conditions, the logical negation operator is a unary operator that has only a single condition as an operand. The logical negation operator is placed before a condition to choose a path of execution if the original condition (without the logical negation operator) is `false`, as in the code segment

```
if ( ! ( grade == sentinelValue ) )
   Console.WriteLine( "The next grade is {0}", grade );
```

which executes the `WriteLine` call only if `grade` is not equal to `sentinelValue`. The parentheses around the condition `grade == sentinelValue` are needed because the logical negation operator has a higher precedence than the equality operator.

In most cases, you can avoid using logical negation by expressing the condition differently with an appropriate relational or equality operator. For example, the previous statement may also be written as follows:

```
if ( grade != sentinelValue )
   Console.WriteLine( "The next grade is {0}", grade );
```

This flexibility can help you express a condition in a more convenient manner. Figure 6.17 is a truth table for the logical negation operator.

expression	!expression
false	true
true	false

Fig. 6.17 | ! (logical negation) operator truth table.

Logical Operators Example

Figure 6.18 demonstrates the logical operators and boolean logical operators by producing their truth tables. The output shows the expression that was evaluated and the `bool` result of that expression. Lines 10–14 produce the truth table for `&&` (conditional AND). Lines 17–21 produce the truth table for `||` (conditional OR). Lines 24–28 produce the truth table for `&` (boolean logical AND). Lines 31–36 produce the truth table for `|` (boolean logical inclusive OR). Lines 39–44 produce the truth table for `^` (boolean logical exclusive OR). Lines 47–49 produce the truth table for `!` (logical negation).

```
1   // Fig. 6.18: LogicalOperators.cs
2   // Logical operators.
3   using System;
4
5   public class LogicalOperators
6   {
7      public static void Main( string[] args )
8      {
```

Fig. 6.18 | Logical operators. (Part 1 of 3.)

```
 9          // create truth table for && (conditional AND) operator
10          Console.WriteLine( "{0}\n{1}: {2}\n{3}: {4}\n{5}: {6}\n{7}: {8}\n",
11             "Conditional AND (&&)", "false && false", ( false && false ),
12             "false && true", ( false && true ),
13             "true && false", ( true && false ),
14             "true && true", ( true && true ) );
15
16          // create truth table for || (conditional OR) operator
17          Console.WriteLine( "{0}\n{1}: {2}\n{3}: {4}\n{5}: {6}\n{7}: {8}\n",
18             "Conditional OR (||)", "false || false", ( false || false ),
19             "false || true", ( false || true ),
20             "true || false", ( true || false ),
21             "true || true", ( true || true ) );
22
23          // create truth table for & (boolean logical AND) operator
24          Console.WriteLine( "{0}\n{1}: {2}\n{3}: {4}\n{5}: {6}\n{7}: {8}\n",
25             "Boolean logical AND (&)", "false & false", ( false & false ),
26             "false & true", ( false & true ),
27             "true & false", ( true & false ),
28             "true & true", ( true & true ) );
29
30          // create truth table for | (boolean logical inclusive OR) operator
31          Console.WriteLine( "{0}\n{1}: {2}\n{3}: {4}\n{5}: {6}\n{7}: {8}\n",
32             "Boolean logical inclusive OR (|)",
33             "false | false", ( false | false ),
34             "false | true", ( false | true ),
35             "true | false", ( true | false ),
36             "true | true", ( true | true ) );
37
38          // create truth table for ^ (boolean logical exclusive OR) operator
39          Console.WriteLine( "{0}\n{1}: {2}\n{3}: {4}\n{5}: {6}\n{7}: {8}\n",
40             "Boolean logical exclusive OR (^)",
41             "false ^ false", ( false ^ false ),
42             "false ^ true", ( false ^ true ),
43             "true ^ false", ( true ^ false ),
44             "true ^ true", ( true ^ true ) );
45
46          // create truth table for ! (logical negation) operator
47          Console.WriteLine( "{0}\n{1}: {2}\n{3}: {4}",
48             "Logical negation (!)", "!false", ( !false ),
49             "!true", ( !true ) );
50      } // end Main
51   } // end class LogicalOperators
```

```
Conditional AND (&&)
false && false: False
false && true: False
true && false: False
true && true: True

Conditional OR (||)
false || false: False
```

Fig. 6.18 | Logical operators. (Part 2 of 3.)

```
false || true: True
true || false: True
true || true: True

Boolean logical AND (&)
false & false: False
false & true: False
true & false: False
true & true: True

Boolean logical inclusive OR (|)
false | false: False
false | true: True
true | false: True
true | true: True

Boolean logical exclusive OR (^)
false ^ false: False
false ^ true: True
true ^ false: True
true ^ true: False

Logical negation (!)
!false: True
!true: False
```

Fig. 6.18 | Logical operators. (Part 3 of 3.)

Figure 6.19 shows the precedence and associativity of the C# operators introduced so far. The operators are shown from top to bottom in decreasing order of precedence.

Operators						Associativity	Type
.	new	++*(postfix)*	--*(postfix)*			left to right	highest precedence
++	--	+	-	!	*(type)*	right to left	unary prefix
*	/	%				left to right	multiplicative
+	-					left to right	additive
<	<=	>	>=			left to right	relational
==	!=					left to right	equality
&						left to right	boolean logical AND
^						left to right	boolean logical exclusive OR
|						left to right	boolean logical inclusive OR
&&						left to right	conditional AND
||						left to right	conditional OR
?:						right to left	conditional
=	+=	-=	*=	/=	%=	right to left	assignment

Fig. 6.19 | Precedence/associativity of the operators discussed so far.

6.9 Wrap-Up

Chapter 5 discussed the if, if...else and while control statements. In this chapter, we discussed the for, do...while and switch control statements. (We'll discuss the foreach statement in Chapter 8.) You learned that any algorithm can be developed using combinations of sequence (i.e., statements listed in the order in which they should execute), the three selection statements—if, if...else and switch—and the four repetition statements—while, do...while, for and foreach. You saw that the for and do...while statements are simply more convenient ways to express certain types of repetition. Similarly, we showed that the switch statement is a convenient notation for multiple selection, rather than using nested if...else statements. We discussed how you can combine various control statements by stacking and nesting them. We showed how to use the break and continue statements to alter the flow of control in repetition statements. You also learned about the logical operators, which enable you to use more complex conditional expressions in control statements.

In Chapter 4, we introduced the basic concepts of objects, classes and methods. Chapters 5 and 6 provided a thorough introduction to the control statements that you use to specify application logic in methods. In Chapter 7, we examine methods in greater depth.

7

Methods:
A Deeper Look

Form ever follows function.
—Louis Henri Sullivan

E pluribus unum.
(One composed of many.)
—Virgil

O! call back yesterday, bid
time return.
—William Shakespeare

Call me Ishmael.
—Herman Melville

When you call me that,
smile!
—Owen Wister

Answer me in one word.
—William Shakespeare

There is a point at which
methods devour themselves.
—Frantz Fanon

Life can only be understood
backwards; but it must be
lived forwards.
—Soren Kierkegaard

OBJECTIVES

In this chapter you'll learn:

- How **static** methods and variables are associated with a class rather than specific instances of the class.

- How the method call/return mechanism is supported by the method-call stack and activation records.

- How to use random-number generation to implement game-playing applications.

- How the visibility of declarations is limited to specific regions of applications.

- What method overloading is and how to create overloaded methods.

- What recursive methods are.

- The differences between passing method arguments by value and by reference.

7.1 Introduction

We introduced methods in Chapter 4. In this chapter we study methods in more depth. We emphasize how to declare and use methods to facilitate the design, implementation, operation and maintenance of large applications.

You'll see that it's possible for certain methods, called static methods, to be called without the need for an object of the class to exist. You'll learn how to declare a method with more than one parameter. You'll also learn how C# is able to keep track of which method is currently executing, how value-type and reference-type arguments are passed to methods, how local variables of methods are maintained in memory and how a method knows where to return after it completes execution.

We discuss **simulation** techniques with random-number generation and develop a version of the casino dice game called craps that uses most of the programming techniques you've learned to this point in the book. In addition, you'll learn to declare values that cannot change (i.e., constants). You'll also learn to write methods that call themselves—this is called **recursion**.

Many of the classes you'll use or create while developing applications will have more than one method of the same name. This technique, called **method overloading**, is used to implement methods that perform similar tasks but with different types and/or different numbers of arguments.

7.2 Packaging Code in C#

Common ways of packaging code are properties, methods, classes and namespaces. C# applications are written by combining new properties, methods and classes that you write with predefined properties, methods and classes available in the .NET Framework Class Library and in various other class libraries. Related classes are often grouped into namespaces and compiled into class libraries so that they can be reused in other applications. You'll learn how to create your own namespaces and class libraries in Chapter 10. The .NET Framework Class Library provides many predefined classes that contain methods for performing common mathematical calculations, string manipulations, character manipulations, input/output operations, database operations, networking operations, file processing, error checking, web-application development and more.

Good Programming Practice 7.1

Familiarize yourself with the classes and methods provided by the .NET Framework Class Library (msdn.microsoft.com/en-us/library/ms229335.aspx).

Software Engineering Observation 7.1

Don't try to "reinvent the wheel." When possible, reuse .NET Framework Class Library classes and methods. This reduces application-development time, avoids introducing programming errors and contributes to good application performance.

Software Engineering Observation 7.2

To promote software reusability, every method should be limited to performing a single, well-defined task, and the name of the method should express that task effectively. Such methods make applications easier to write, debug, maintain and modify.

Software Engineering Observation 7.3

If you cannot choose a concise name that expresses a method's task, your method might be attempting to perform too many diverse tasks. It's usually best to break such a method into several smaller methods.

7.3 static Methods, static Variables and Class Math

Although most methods execute on specific objects in response to method calls, this is not always the case. Sometimes a method performs a task that does not depend on the contents of any object. Such a method applies to the class in which it's declared as a whole and is known as a static method. It's not uncommon for a class to contain a group of static methods to perform common tasks. For example, recall that we used static method Pow of class Math to raise a value to a power in Fig. 6.6. To declare a method as static, place the keyword static before the return type in the method's declaration. You call any static method by specifying the name of the class in which the method is declared, followed by the member access (.) operator and the method name, as in

ClassName.*MethodName*(*arguments*)

We use various methods of the Math class here to present the concept of static methods. Class Math (from the System namespace) provides a collection of methods that enable you to perform common mathematical calculations. For example, you can calculate the square root of 900.0 with the static method call

```
Math.Sqrt( 900.0 )
```

The preceding expression evaluates to 30.0. Method Sqrt takes an argument of type double and returns a result of type double. To output the value of the preceding method call in the console window, you might write the statement

```
Console.WriteLine( Math.Sqrt( 900.0 ) );
```

In this statement, the value that Sqrt returns becomes the argument to method Write-Line. We did not create a Math object before calling method Sqrt. Also *all* of Math's methods are static—therefore, each is called by preceding the name of the method with the class name Math and the member access (.) operator. Similarly, Console method Write-Line is a static method of class Console, so we invoke the method by preceding its name with the class name Console and the member access (.) operator.

Method arguments may be constants, variables or expressions. If c = 13.0, d = 3.0 and f = 4.0, then the statement

```
Console.WriteLine( Math.Sqrt( c + d * f ) );
```

calculates and displays the square root of 13.0 + 3.0 * 4.0 = 25.0—namely, 5.0. Figure 7.1 summarizes several Math class methods. In the figure, *x* and *y* are of type double.

Method	Description	Example
Abs(*x*)	absolute value of *x*	Abs(23.7) is 23.7 Abs(0.0) is 0.0 Abs(-23.7) is 23.7
Ceiling(*x*)	rounds *x* to the smallest integer not less than *x*	Ceiling(9.2) is 10.0 Ceiling(-9.8) is -9.0
Cos(*x*)	trigonometric cosine of *x* (*x* in radians)	Cos(0.0) is 1.0
Exp(*x*)	exponential method e^x	Exp(1.0) is 2.71828 Exp(2.0) is 7.38906
Floor(*x*)	rounds *x* to the largest integer not greater than *x*	Floor(9.2) is 9.0 Floor(-9.8) is -10.0
Log(*x*)	natural logarithm of *x* (base *e*)	Log(Math.E) is 1.0 Log(Math.E * Math.E) is 2.0
Max(*x*, *y*)	larger value of *x* and *y*	Max(2.3, 12.7) is 12.7 Max(-2.3, -12.7) is -2.3
Min(*x*, *y*)	smaller value of *x* and *y*	Min(2.3, 12.7) is 2.3 Min(-2.3, -12.7) is -12.7
Pow(*x*, *y*)	*x* raised to the power *y* (i.e., x^y)	Pow(2.0, 7.0) is 128.0 Pow(9.0, 0.5) is 3.0
Sin(*x*)	trigonometric sine of *x* (*x* in radians)	Sin(0.0) is 0.0
Sqrt(*x*)	square root of *x*	Sqrt(900.0) is 30.0
Tan(*x*)	trigonometric tangent of *x* (*x* in radians)	Tan(0.0) is 0.0

Fig. 7.1 | Math class methods.

Math Class Constants PI and E

Class Math also declares two static constants that represent commonly used mathematical values: **Math.PI** and **Math.E**. The constant Math.PI (3.14159265358979323846) is the ratio of a circle's circumference to its diameter. The constant Math.E (2.7182818284590452354) is the base value for natural logarithms (calculated with static Math method Log). These constants are declared in class Math with the modifiers public and const. Making them public allows other programmers to use these variables in their own classes. A constant is declared with the keyword **const**—its value cannot be changed after the constant is declared. Both PI and E are declared const because their values never change.

Common Programming Error 7.1

Every constant declared in a class, but not inside a method of the class is implicitly static, so it's a syntax error to declare such a constant with keyword static explicitly.

Because these constants are static, you can access them via the class name Math and the member access (.) operator, just like class Math's methods. Recall from Section 4.5 that when each object of a class maintains its own copy of an attribute, the variable that represents the attribute is also known as an instance variable—each object (instance) of the class has a separate instance of the variable. There are also variables for which each object of a class does *not* have a separate instance of the variable. That's the case with static variables. When objects of a class containing static variables are created, all the objects of that class share one copy of the class's static variables. Together the static variables and instance variables represent the **fields** of a class.

Why Is Method Main Declared static?

Why must Main be declared static? During application startup, when no objects of the class have been created, the Main method must be called to begin program execution. The Main method is sometimes called the application's **entry point**. Declaring Main as static allows the execution environment to invoke Main without creating an instance of the class. Method Main is often declared with the header:

```
public static void Main( string args[] )
```

When you execute your application from the command line, you type the application name, as in

ApplicationName argument1 argument2 ...

where *argument1* and *argument2* are the **command-line arguments** to the application that specify a list of strings (separated by spaces) the execution environment will pass to the Main method of your application. Such arguments might be used to specify options (e.g., a file name) to run the application. As you'll learn in Chapter 8, Arrays, your application can access those command-line arguments and use them to customize the application.

Additional Comments about Method Main

The header of a Main method does not need to appear exactly as we've shown. Applications that do not take command-line arguments may omit the string[] args parameter. The public keyword may also be omitted. In addition, you can declare Main with return type int (instead of void) to enable Main to return an error code with the return statement. A Main method declared with any one of these headers can be used as the application's entry point—but you can declare only one such Main method in each class.

In earlier chapters, most applications had one class that contained only Main, and some examples had a second class that was used by Main to create and manipulate objects. Actually, any class can contain a Main method. In fact, each of our two-class examples could have been implemented as one class. For example, in the application in Figs. 6.9 and

6.10, method Main (lines 6–16 of Fig. 6.10) could have been taken as is and placed in class GradeBook (Fig. 6.9). The application results would have been identical to those of the two-class version. You can place a Main method in every class you declare. Some programmers take advantage of this to build a small test application into each class they declare. However, if you declare more than one Main method among the classes of your project, you'll need to indicate to the IDE which one you would like to be the application's entry point. You can do this by selecting **Project > [ProjectName] Properties...** (where **[Project-Name]** is the name of your project) and selecting the class containing the Main method that should be the entry point from the **Startup object** list box.

7.4 Declaring Methods with Multiple Parameters

Figure 7.2 uses a user-defined method called Maximum to determine and return the largest of three double values that are input by the user. Lines 11–15 prompt the user to enter three double values and read them from the user. Line 18 calls method Maximum (declared in lines 25–38) to determine the largest of the three double values passed as arguments to the method. When method Maximum returns the result to line 18, the application assigns Maximum's return value to local variable result. Then line 21 outputs result. At the end of this section, we'll discuss the use of operator + in line 21.

```
1   // Fig. 7.2: MaximumFinder.cs
2   // User-defined method Maximum.
3   using System;
4
5   public class MaximumFinder
6   {
7      // obtain three floating-point values and determine maximum value
8      public static void Main( string[] args )
9      {
10        // prompt for and input three floating-point values
11        Console.WriteLine( "Enter three floating-point values,\n"
12           + "  pressing 'Enter' after each one: " );
13        double number1 = Convert.ToDouble( Console.ReadLine() );
14        double number2 = Convert.ToDouble( Console.ReadLine() );
15        double number3 = Convert.ToDouble( Console.ReadLine() );
16
17        // determine the maximum value
18        double result = Maximum( number1, number2, number3 );
19
20        // display maximum value
21        Console.WriteLine( "Maximum is: " + result );
22     } // end Main
23
24     // returns the maximum of its three double parameters
25     public static double Maximum( double x, double y, double z )
26     {
27        double maximumValue = x; // assume x is the largest to start
28
```

Fig. 7.2 | User-defined method Maximum. (Part 1 of 2.)

```
29          // determine whether y is greater than maximumValue
30          if ( y > maximumValue )
31             maximumValue = y;
32
33          // determine whether z is greater than maximumValue
34          if ( z > maximumValue )
35             maximumValue = z;
36
37          return maximumValue;
38       } // end method Maximum
39    } // end class MaximumFinder
```

Fig. 7.2 | User-defined method `Maximum`. (Part 2 of 2.)

The *public* and *static* Keywords

Method `Maximum`'s declaration begins with keyword `public` to indicate that the method is "available to the public"—it can be called from methods of other classes. The keyword `static` enables the `Main` method (another `static` method) to call `Maximum` as shown in line 18 without qualifying the method name with the class name `MaximumFinder`—`static` methods in the same class can call each other directly. Any other class that uses `Maximum` must fully qualify the method name with the class name.

Method *Maximum*

Consider the declaration of method `Maximum` (lines 25–38). Line 25 indicates that the method returns a `double` value, that the method's name is `Maximum` and that the method requires three `double` parameters (x, y and z) to accomplish its task. When a method has more than one parameter, the parameters are specified as a comma-separated list. When `Maximum` is called in line 18, the parameter x is initialized with the value of the argument number1, the parameter y is initialized with the value of the argument number2 and the parameter z is initialized with the value of the argument number3. There must be one argument in the method call for each required parameter (sometimes called a **formal parameter**) in the method declaration. Also, each argument must be consistent with the type of the corresponding parameter. For example, a parameter of type `double` can receive values like `7.35` (a `double`), `22` (an `int`) or `–0.03456` (a `double`), but not `strings` like `"hello"`. Section 7.7 discusses the argument types that can be provided in a method call for each parameter of a simple type.

To determine the maximum value, we begin with the assumption that parameter x contains the largest value, so line 27 declares local variable `maximumValue` and initializes it with the value of parameter x. Of course, it's possible that parameter y or z contains the largest value, so we must compare each of these values with `maximumValue`. The `if` statement at lines 30–31 determines whether y is greater than `maximumValue`. If so, line 31 assigns y to `maximumValue`. The `if` statement at lines 34–35 determines whether z is greater than `maximumValue`. If so, line 35 assigns z to `maximumValue`. At this point, the largest of the three values resides in `maximumValue`, so line 37 returns that value to line 18. When program control returns to the point in the application where `Maximum` was called, `Maximum`'s parameters x, y and z are no longer accessible. Methods can return at most one value; the returned value can be a value type that contains many values (implemented as a `struct`) or a reference to an object that contains many values.

Variable `result` is a local variable in method `Main` because it's declared in the block that represents the method's body. Variables should be declared as fields of a class (i.e., as either instance variables or `static` variables of the class) only if they're required for use in more than one method of the class or if the application should save their values between calls to the class's methods.

Common Programming Error 7.2

Declaring method parameters of the same type as `float x, y` *instead of* `float x, float y` *is a syntax error—a type is required for each parameter in the parameter list.*

Implementing Method `Maximum` by Reusing Method `Math.Max`

Recall from Fig. 7.1 that class `Math` has a `Max` method that can determine the larger of two values. The entire body of our maximum method could also be implemented with nested calls to `Math.Max`, as follows:

```
return Math.Max( x, Math.Max( y, z ) );
```

The leftmost call to `Math.Max` specifies arguments x and `Math.Max( y, z )`. Before any method can be called, all its arguments must be evaluated to determine their values. If an argument is a method call, the method call must be performed to determine its return value. So, in the preceding statement, `Math.Max( y, z )` is evaluated first to determine the maximum of y and z. Then the result is passed as the second argument to the other call to `Math.Max`, which returns the larger of its two arguments. Using `Math.Max` in this manner is a good example of software reuse—we find the largest of three values by reusing `Math.Max`, which finds the larger of two values. Note how concise this code is compared to lines 27–37 of Fig. 7.2.

Assembling Strings with String Concatenation

C# allows `string` objects to be created by assembling smaller `strings` into larger `strings` using operator + (or the compound assignment operator +=). This is known as **string concatenation**. When both operands of operator + are `string` objects, operator + creates a new `string` object in which a copy of the characters of the right operand is placed at the end of a copy of the characters in the left operand. For example, the expression `"hello " + "there"` creates the `string` `"hello there"` without disturbing the original `strings`.

In line 21 of Fig. 7.2, the expression `"Maximum is: " + result` uses operator + with operands of types `string` and `double`. Every value of a simple type in C# has a `string` representation. When one of the + operator's operands is a `string`, the other is implicitly converted to a `string`, then the two are concatenated. In line 21, the `double` value is implicitly converted to its `string` representation and placed at the end of the `string` `"Maximum is: "`. If there are any trailing zeros in a `double` value, these will be discarded when the number is converted to a `string`. Thus, the number 9.3500 would be represented as 9.35 in the resulting `string`.

For values of simple types used in `string` concatenation, the values are converted to `strings`. If a `bool` is concatenated with a `string`, the `bool` is converted to the `string` `"True"` or `"False"` (note that each is capitalized). All objects have a `ToString` method that returns a `string` representation of the object. When an object is concatenated with a `string`, the object's `ToString` method is implicitly called to obtain the `string` representation of the object. If the object is `null`, an empty string is written.

Line 21 of Fig. 7.2 could also be written using `string` formatting as

```
Console.WriteLine( "Maximum is: {0}", result );
```

As with `string` concatenation, using a format item to substitute an object into a `string` implicitly calls the object's `ToString` method to obtain the object's `string` representation. You'll learn more about method `ToString` in Chapter 8, Arrays.

When a large `string` literal is typed into an application's source code, you can break that `string` into several smaller `strings` and place them on multiple lines for readability. The `strings` can be reassembled using either string concatenation or string formatting. We discuss the details of `strings` in Chapter 16.

Common Programming Error 7.3

It's a syntax error to break a `string` literal across multiple lines in an application. If a string does not fit on one line, split the `string` into several smaller `strings` and use concatenation to form the desired `string`. C# also provides so-called verbatim `string` literals, which are preceded by the @ character. Such literals can be split over multiple lines and the characters in the literal are processed exactly as they appear in the literal.

Common Programming Error 7.4

Confusing the + operator used for string concatenation with the + operator used for addition can lead to strange results. The + operator is left-associative. For example, if integer variable y has the value 5, the expression "y + 2 = " + y + 2 results in the string "y + 2 = 52", not "y + 2 = 7", because first the value of y (5) is concatenated with the string "y + 2 = ", then the value 2 is concatenated with the new larger string "y + 2 = 5". The expression "y + 2 = " + (y + 2) produces the desired result "y + 2 = 7".

7.5 Notes on Declaring and Using Methods

You've seen three ways to call a method:

1. Using a method name by itself to call a method of the same class—such as `Maximum(number1, number2, number3)` in line 18 of Fig. 7.2.

2. Using a variable that contains a reference to an object, followed by the member access (`.`) operator and the method name to call a non-`static` method of the referenced object—such as the method call in line 13 of Fig. 6.10, `myGradeBook.DisplayMessage()`, which calls a method of class `GradeBook` from the `Main` method of `GradeBookTest`.

3. Using the class name and the member access (`.`) operator to call a `static` method of a class—such as `Convert.ToDouble( Console.ReadLine() )` in lines 13–15 of Fig. 7.2 or `Math.Sqrt( 900.0 )` in Section 7.3.

A `static` method can call only other `static` methods of the same class directly (i.e., using the method name by itself) and can manipulate only `static` variables in the same class directly. To access the class's non-`static` members, a `static` method must use a reference to an object of the class. Recall that `static` methods relate to a class as a whole, whereas non-`static` methods are associated with a specific instance (object) of the class and may manipulate the instance variables of that object. Many objects of a class, each with its own copies of the instance variables, may exist at the same time. Suppose a `static` method were to invoke a non-static method directly. How would the method know which object's instance variables to manipulate? What would happen if no objects of the class existed at the time the non-static method was invoked? Thus, C# does not allow a static method to access non-static members of the same class directly.

There are three ways to return control to the statement that calls a method. If the method does not return a result, control returns when the program flow reaches the method-ending right brace or when the statement

```
return;
```

is executed. If the method returns a result, the statement

```
return expression;
```

evaluates the *expression*, then returns the result (and control) to the caller.

Common Programming Error 7.5
Declaring a method outside the body of a class declaration or inside the body of another method is a syntax error.

Common Programming Error 7.6
Omitting the return type in a method declaration is a syntax error.

Common Programming Error 7.7
Redeclaring a method parameter as a local variable in the method's body is a compilation error.

Common Programming Error 7.8
Forgetting to return a value from a method that should return one is a compilation error. If a return type other than void is specified, the method must contain a return statement in each possible execution path through the method and each return statement must return a value consistent with the method's return type. Returning a value from a method whose return type has been declared void is a compilation error.

7.6 Method-Call Stack and Activation Records

To understand how C# performs method calls, we first need to consider a data structure (i.e., collection of related data items) known as a **stack** (we discuss data structures in more detail in Chapters 21–23). You can think of a stack as analogous to a pile of dishes. When a dish is placed on the pile, it's normally placed at the top (referred to as **pushing** the dish onto the stack). Similarly, when a dish is removed from the pile, it's always removed from the top (referred to as **popping** the dish off the stack). Stacks are known as **last-in, first-out (LIFO) data structures**—the last item pushed (inserted) on the stack is the first item popped off (removed from) the stack.

When an application calls a method, the called method must know how to return to its caller, so the return address of the calling method is pushed onto the **program-execution stack** (sometimes referred to as the **method-call stack**). If a series of method calls occurs, the successive return addresses are pushed onto the stack in last-in, first-out order so that each method can return to its caller.

The program-execution stack also contains the memory for the local variables used in each invocation of a method during an application's execution. This data, stored as a portion of the program-execution stack, is known as the **activation record** or **stack frame** of the method call. When a method call is made, the activation record for it is pushed onto the program-execution stack. When the method returns to its caller, the activation record for this method call is popped off the stack, and those local variables are no longer known to the application. If a local variable holding a reference to an object is the only variable in the application with a reference to that object, when the activation record containing that local variable is popped off the stack, the object can no longer be accessed by the application and will eventually be deleted from memory during "garbage collection." We'll discuss garbage collection in Section 10.9.

Of course, the amount of memory in a computer is finite, so only a certain amount of memory can be used to store activation records on the program-execution stack. If more method calls occur than can have their activation records stored on the program-execution stack, an error known as a **stack overflow** occurs.

7.7 Argument Promotion and Casting

Another important feature of method calls is **argument promotion**—implicitly converting an argument's value to the type that the method expects to receive in its corresponding parameter. For example, an application can call `Math` method `Sqrt` with an integer argument even though the method expects to receive a `double` argument. The statement

```
Console.WriteLine( Math.Sqrt( 4 ) );
```

correctly evaluates `Math.Sqrt( 4 )` and displays the value `2.0`. Sqrt's parameter list causes C# to convert the `int` value 4 to the `double` value 4.0 before passing the value to `Sqrt`. Such conversions may lead to compilation errors if C#'s **promotion rules** are not satisfied. The promotion rules specify which conversions are allowed—that is, which conversions can be performed without losing data. In the `Sqrt` example above, an `int` is converted to a `double` without changing its value. However, converting a `double` to an `int` truncates the fractional part of the `double` value—thus, part of the value is lost. Also, `double` variables can hold values much larger (and much smaller) than `int` variables, so assigning a `double` to an `int` can cause a loss of information when the `double` value doesn't fit in the `int`. Converting large integer types to small integer types (e.g., `long` to `int`) can also result in changed values.

The promotion rules apply to expressions containing values of two or more simple types and to simple-type values passed as arguments to methods. Each value is promoted to the appropriate type in the expression. (Actually, the expression uses a temporary copy of each value—the types of the original values remain unchanged.) Figure 7.3 lists the simple types alphabetically and the types to which each can be promoted. Note that values of all simple types can also be implicitly converted to type `object`. We demonstrate such implicit conversions in Chapter 21, Data Structures.

By default, C# does not allow you to implicitly convert values between simple types if the target type cannot represent the value of the original type (e.g., the `int` value 2000000 cannot be represented as a `short`, and any floating-point number with digits after its decimal point cannot be represented in an integer type such as `long`, `int` or `short`). Therefore, to prevent a compilation error in cases where information may be lost due to an implicit

Type	Conversion types
bool	no possible implicit conversions to other simple types
byte	ushort, short, uint, int, ulong, long, decimal, float or double
char	ushort, int, uint, long, ulong, decimal, float or double
decimal	no possible implicit conversions to other simple types
double	no possible implicit conversions to other simple types
float	double
int	long, decimal, float or double
long	decimal, float or double
sbyte	short, int, long, decimal, float or double
short	int, long, decimal, float or double
uint	ulong, long, decimal, float or double
ulong	decimal, float or double
ushort	uint, int, ulong, long, decimal, float or double

Fig. 7.3 | Implicit conversions between simple types.

conversion between simple types, the compiler requires you to use a cast operator (introduced in Section 5.7) to explicitly force the conversion. This enables you to "take control" from the compiler. You essentially say, "I know this conversion might cause loss of information, but for my purposes here, that's fine." Suppose you create a method Square that calculates the square of an integer and thus requires an int argument. To call Square with a double argument named doubleValue, you would write Square((int) doubleValue). This method call explicitly casts (converts) the value of doubleValue to an integer for use in method Square. Thus, if doubleValue's value is 4.5, the method receives the value 4 and returns 16, not 20.25 (which does, unfortunately, result in the loss of information).

Common Programming Error 7.9
Converting a simple-type value to a value of another simple type may change the value if the promotion is not allowed. For example, converting a floating-point value to an integral value may introduce truncation errors (loss of the fractional part) in the result.

7.8 The .NET Framework Class Library

Many predefined classes are grouped into categories of related classes called namespaces. Together, these namespaces are referred to as the .NET Framework Class Library.

Throughout the text, using directives allow us to use library classes from the .NET Framework Class Library without specifying their fully qualified names. For example, an application includes the declaration

```
using System;
```

in order to use the class names from the System namespace without fully qualifying their names. This allows you to use the **unqualified class name** Console, rather than the fully qualified class name System.Console, in your code. A great strength of C# is the large number of classes in the namespaces of the .NET Framework Class Library. Some key .NET Framework Class Library namespaces are described in Fig. 7.4, which represents only a small portion of the reusable classes in the .NET Framework Class Library.

Namespace	Description
`System.Windows.Forms`	Contains the classes required to create and manipulate GUIs. (Various classes in this namespace are discussed in Chapters 14–15.)
`System.Windows.Controls` `System.Windows.Input` `System.Windows.Media` `System.Windows.Shapes`	Contain the classes of the Windows Presentation Foundation for GUIs, 2-D and 3-D graphics, multimedia and animation. (You'll learn more about these namespaces in Chapter 24, GUI with Windows Presentation Foundation, Chapter 25, WPF Graphics and Multimedia and Chapter 29, Silverlight and Rich Internet Applications.)
`System.Linq`	Contains the classes that support Language Integrated Query (LINQ). (You'll learn more about this namespace in Chapter 9, Introduction to LINQ and the `List` Collection, and several other chapters throughout the book.)
`System.Data` `System.Data.Linq`	Contain the classes for manipulating data in databases (i.e., organized collections of data), including support for LINQ to SQL. (You'll learn more about these namespaces in Chapter 18, Databases and LINQ.)
`System.IO`	Contains the classes that enable programs to input and output data. (You'll learn more about this namespace in Chapter 17, Files and Streams.)
`System.Web`	Contains the classes used for creating and maintaining web applications, which are accessible over the Internet. (You'll learn more about this namespace in Chapter 19, Web App Development with ASP.NET and Chapter 27, Web App Development with ASP.NET: A Deeper Look.)
`System.Xml.Linq`	Contains the classes that support Language Integrated Query (LINQ) for XML documents. (You'll learn more about this namespace in Chapter 26, XML and LINQ to XML, and several other chapters throughout the book.)
`System.Xml`	Contains the classes for creating and manipulating XML data. Data can be read from or written to XML files. (You'll learn more about this namespace in Chapter 26.)
`System.Collections` `System.Collections.Generic`	Contain the classes that define data structures for maintaining collections of data. (You'll learn more about these namespaces in Chapter 23, Collections.)
`System.Text`	Contains the classes that enable programs to manipulate characters and strings. (You'll learn more about this namespace in Chapter 16, Strings and Characters.)

Fig. 7.4 | .NET Framework Class Library namespaces (a subset).

The set of namespaces available in the .NET Framework Class Library is quite large. Besides those summarized in Fig. 7.4, the .NET Framework Class Library contains namespaces for complex graphics, advanced graphical user interfaces, printing, advanced networking, security, database processing, multimedia, accessibility (for people with disabilities) and many other capabilities—over 100 namespaces in all.

You can locate additional information about a predefined C# class's methods in the *.NET Framework Class Library* reference (msdn.microsoft.com/en-us/library/ms229335.aspx). When you visit this site, you'll see an alphabetical listing of all the namespaces in the .NET Framework Class Library. Locate the namespace and click its link to see an alphabetical listing of all its classes, with a brief description of each. Click a class's link to see a more complete description of the class. Click the **Methods** link in the left-hand column to see a listing of the class's methods.

> **Good Programming Practice 7.2**
>
> *The online .NET Framework documentation is easy to search and provides many details about each class. As you learn each class in this book, you should review the class in the online documentation for additional information.*

7.9 Case Study: Random-Number Generation

In this and the next section, we develop a nicely structured game-playing application with multiple methods. The application uses most of the control statements presented thus far in the book and introduces several new C# programming concepts.

There is something in the air of a casino that invigorates people—from the high rollers at the plush mahogany-and-felt craps tables to the quarter poppers at the one-armed bandits. It's the **element of chance**, the possibility that luck will convert a pocketful of money into a mountain of wealth. The element of chance can be introduced in an application via an object of class Random (of namespace System). Objects of class **Random** can produce random byte, int and double values. In the next several examples, we use objects of class Random to produce random numbers.

A new random-number generator object can be created as follows:

```
Random randomNumbers = new Random();
```

The random-number generator object can then be used to generate random byte, int and double values—we discuss only random int values here.

Consider the following statement:

```
int randomValue = randomNumbers.Next();
```

Method Next of class Random generates a random int value from 0 to +2,147,483,646, inclusive. If the Next method truly produces values at random, then every value in that range should have an equal chance (or probability) of being chosen each time method Next is called. The values returned by Next are actually **pseudorandom numbers**—a sequence of values produced by a complex mathematical calculation. The calculation uses the current time of day (which, of course, changes constantly) to **seed** the random-number generator such that each execution of an application yields a different sequence of random values.

The range of values produced directly by method Next often differs from the range of values required in a particular C# application. For example, an application that simulates coin tossing might require only 0 for "heads" and 1 for "tails." An application that simulates the rolling of a six-sided die might require random integers in the range 1–6. A video game that randomly predicts the next type of spaceship (out of four possibilities) that will fly across the horizon might require random integers in the range 1–4. For cases like these, class Random provides other versions of method Next. One receives an int argument and returns a value from 0 up to, but not including, the argument's value. For example, you might use the statement

```
int randomValue = randomNumbers.Next( 6 );
```

which returns 0, 1, 2, 3, 4 or 5. The argument 6—called the **scaling factor**—represents the number of unique values that Next should produce (in this case, six—0, 1, 2, 3, 4 and 5). This manipulation is called **scaling** the range of values produced by Random method Next.

Suppose we wanted to simulate a six-sided die that has the numbers 1–6 on its faces, not 0–5. Scaling the range of values alone is not enough. So we **shift** the range of numbers produced. We could do this by adding a **shifting value**—in this case 1—to the result of method Next, as in

```
face = 1 + randomNumbers.Next( 6 );
```

The shifting value (1) specifies the first value in the desired set of random integers. The preceding statement assigns to face a random integer in the range 1–6.

The third alternative of method Next provides a more intuitive way to express both shifting and scaling. This method receives two int arguments and returns a value from the first argument's value up to, but not including, the second argument's value. We could use this method to write a statement equivalent to our previous statement, as in

```
face = randomNumbers.Next( 1, 7 );
```

Rolling a Six-Sided Die

To demonstrate random numbers, let's develop an application that simulates 20 rolls of a six-sided die and displays each roll's value. Figure 7.5 shows two sample outputs, which confirm that the results of the preceding calculation are integers in the range 1–6 and that each run of the application can produce a different sequence of random numbers. The using directive (line 3) enables us to use class Random without fully qualifying its name. Line 9 creates the Random object randomNumbers to produce random values. Line 16 executes 20 times in a loop to roll the die. The if statement (lines 21–22) starts a new line of output after every five numbers, so the results can be presented on multiple lines.

```
1    // Fig. 7.5: RandomIntegers.cs
2    // Shifted and scaled random integers.
3    using System;
4
5    public class RandomIntegers
6    {
7       public static void Main( string[] args )
8       {
9          Random randomNumbers = new Random(); // random-number generator
10         int face; // stores each random integer generated
```

Fig. 7.5 | Shifted and scaled random integers. (Part 1 of 2.)

```
11
12          // loop 20 times
13          for ( int counter = 1; counter <= 20; counter++ )
14          {
15              // pick random integer from 1 to 6
16              face = randomNumbers.Next( 1, 7 );
17
18              Console.Write( "{0}  ", face ); // display generated value
19
20              // if counter is divisible by 5, start a new line of output
21              if ( counter % 5 == 0 )
22                  Console.WriteLine();
23          } // end for
24      } // end Main
25  } // end class RandomIntegers
```

```
3  3  3  1  1
2  1  2  4  2
2  3  6  2  5
3  4  6  6  1
```

```
6  2  5  1  3
5  2  1  6  5
4  1  6  1  3
3  1  4  3  4
```

Fig. 7.5 | Shifted and scaled random integers. (Part 2 of 2.)

Rolling a Six-Sided Die 6000 Times

To show that the numbers produced by Next occur with approximately equal likelihood, let's simulate 6000 rolls of a die (Fig. 7.6). Each integer from 1 to 6 should appear approximately 1000 times.

```
1   // Fig. 7.6: RollDie.cs
2   // Roll a six-sided die 6000 times.
3   using System;
4
5   public class RollDie
6   {
7       public static void Main( string[] args )
8       {
9           Random randomNumbers = new Random(); // random-number generator
10
11          int frequency1 = 0; // count of 1s rolled
12          int frequency2 = 0; // count of 2s rolled
13          int frequency3 = 0; // count of 3s rolled
14          int frequency4 = 0; // count of 4s rolled
15          int frequency5 = 0; // count of 5s rolled
16          int frequency6 = 0; // count of 6s rolled
17
```

Fig. 7.6 | Roll a six-sided die 6000 times. (Part 1 of 2.)

```
18          int face; // stores most recently rolled value
19
20          // summarize results of 6000 rolls of a die
21          for ( int roll = 1; roll <= 6000; roll++ )
22          {
23             face = randomNumbers.Next( 1, 7 ); // number from 1 to 6
24
25             // determine roll value 1-6 and increment appropriate counter
26             switch ( face )
27             {
28                case 1:
29                   ++frequency1; // increment the 1s counter
30                   break;
31                case 2:
32                   ++frequency2; // increment the 2s counter
33                   break;
34                case 3:
35                   ++frequency3; // increment the 3s counter
36                   break;
37                case 4:
38                   ++frequency4; // increment the 4s counter
39                   break;
40                case 5:
41                   ++frequency5; // increment the 5s counter
42                   break;
43                case 6:
44                   ++frequency6; // increment the 6s counter
45                   break;
46             } // end switch
47          } // end for
48
49          Console.WriteLine( "Face\tFrequency" ); // output headers
50          Console.WriteLine(
51             "1\t{0}\n2\t{1}\n3\t{2}\n4\t{3}\n5\t{4}\n6\t{5}", frequency1,
52             frequency2, frequency3, frequency4, frequency5, frequency6 );
53       } // end Main
54    } // end class RollDie
```

Face	Frequency
1	1039
2	994
3	991
4	970
5	978
6	1028

Face	Frequency
1	985
2	985
3	1001
4	1017
5	1002
6	1010

Fig. 7.6 | Roll a six-sided die 6000 times. (Part 2 of 2.)

As the sample outputs show, the values produced by Next enable the application to realistically simulate rolling a six-sided die. We used nested control statements (the switch is nested inside the for) to determine the number of times each side of the die occurred. Lines 21–47 iterate 6000 times. Line 23 produces a random value from 1 to 6. This face value is then used as the switch expression (line 26) in the switch statement (lines 26–46). Based on the face value, the switch statement increments one of the six counter variables during each iteration of the loop. (In Chapter 8, we show an elegant way to replace the entire switch statement in this application with a single statement.) The switch statement has no default label because we have a case label for every possible die value that the expression in line 23 can produce. Run the application several times and observe the results. You'll see that every time you execute this application, it produces different results.

7.9.1 Scaling and Shifting Random Numbers

Previously, we demonstrated the statement

```
face = randomNumbers.Next( 1, 7 );
```

which simulates the rolling of a six-sided die. This statement always assigns to variable face an integer in the range 1 ≤ face < 7. The width of this range (i.e., the number of consecutive integers in the range) is 6, and the starting number in the range is 1. Referring to the preceding statement, we see that the width of the range is determined by the difference between the two integers passed to Random method Next, and the starting number of the range is the value of the first argument. We can generalize this result as

```
number = randomNumbers.Next( shiftingValue, shiftingValue + scalingFactor );
```

where *shiftingValue* specifies the first number in the desired range of consecutive integers and *scalingFactor* specifies how many numbers are in the range.

It's also possible to choose integers at random from sets of values other than ranges of consecutive integers. For this purpose, it's simpler to use the version of the Next method that takes only one argument. For example, to obtain a random value from the sequence 2, 5, 8, 11 and 14, you could use the statement

```
number = 2 + 3 * randomNumbers.Next( 5 );
```

In this case, randomNumberGenerator.Next(5) produces values in the range 0–4. Each value produced is multiplied by 3 to produce a number in the sequence 0, 3, 6, 9 and 12. We then add 2 to that value to shift the range of values and obtain a value from the sequence 2, 5, 8, 11 and 14. We can generalize this result as

```
number = shiftingValue +
    differenceBetweenValues * randomNumbers.Next( scalingFactor );
```

where *shiftingValue* specifies the first number in the desired range of values, *differenceBetweenValues* represents the difference between consecutive numbers in the sequence and *scalingFactor* specifies how many numbers are in the range.

7.9.2 Random-Number Repeatability for Testing and Debugging

As we mentioned earlier in Section 7.9, the methods of class Random actually generate pseudorandom numbers based on complex mathematical calculations. Repeatedly calling any of Random's methods produces a sequence of numbers that appears to be random. The calculation that produces the pseudorandom numbers uses the time of day as a **seed value** to change the sequence's starting point. Each new Random object seeds itself with a value based on the computer system's clock at the time the object is created, enabling each execution of an application to produce a different sequence of random numbers.

When debugging an application, it's sometimes useful to repeat the exact same sequence of pseudorandom numbers during each execution of the application. This repeatability enables you to prove that your application is working for a specific sequence of random numbers before you test the application with different sequences of random numbers. When repeatability is important, you can create a Random object as follows:

```
Random randomNumbers = new Random( seedValue );
```

The seedValue argument (type int) seeds the random-number calculation. If the same seedValue is used every time, the Random object produces the same sequence of numbers.

Error-Prevention Tip 7.1

While an application is under development, create the Random object with a specific seed value to produce a repeatable sequence of random numbers each time the application executes. If a logic error occurs, fix the error and test the application again with the same seed value—this allows you to reconstruct the same sequence of random numbers that caused the error. Once the logic errors have been removed, create the Random object without using a seed value, causing the Random object to generate a new sequence of random numbers each time the application executes.

7.10 Case Study: A Game of Chance (Introducing Enumerations)

One popular game of chance is the dice game known as "craps," which is played in casinos and back alleys throughout the world. The rules of the game are straightforward:

> *You roll two dice. Each die has six faces, which contain one, two, three, four, five and six spots, respectively. After the dice have come to rest, the sum of the spots on the two upward faces is calculated. If the sum is 7 or 11 on the first throw, you win. If the sum is 2, 3 or 12 on the first throw (called "craps"), you lose (i.e., "the house" wins). If the sum is 4, 5, 6, 8, 9 or 10 on the first throw, that sum becomes your "point." To win, you must continue rolling the dice until you "make your point" (i.e., roll that same point value). You lose by rolling a 7 before making your point.*

The application in Fig. 7.7 simulates the game of craps, using methods to define the logic of the game. The Main method (lines 24–70) calls the RollDice method (lines 73–85) as needed to roll the two dice and compute their sum. The four sample outputs in show winning on the first roll, losing on the first roll, winning on a subsequent roll and losing on a subsequent roll, respectively. Variable randomNumbers (line 8) is declared static so it can be created once during the program's execution and used in method RollDice.

```
1   // Fig. 7.7: Craps.cs
2   // Craps class simulates the dice game craps.
3   using System;
```

Fig. 7.7 | Craps class simulates the dice game craps. (Part 1 of 4.)

```
4
5    public class Craps
6    {
7       // create random-number generator for use in method RollDice
8       private static Random randomNumbers = new Random();
9
10      // enumeration with constants that represent the game status
11      private enum Status { CONTINUE, WON, LOST }
12
13      // enumeration with constants that represent common rolls of the dice
14      private enum DiceNames
15      {
16         SNAKE_EYES = 2,
17         TREY = 3,
18         SEVEN = 7,
19         YO_LEVEN = 11,
20         BOX_CARS = 12
21      }
22
23      // plays one game of craps
24      public static void Main( string[] args )
25      {
26         // gameStatus can contain CONTINUE, WON or LOST
27         Status gameStatus = Status.CONTINUE;
28         int myPoint = 0; // point if no win or loss on first roll
29
30         int sumOfDice = RollDice(); // first roll of the dice
31
32         // determine game status and point based on first roll
33         switch ( ( DiceNames ) sumOfDice )
34         {
35            case DiceNames.SEVEN: // win with 7 on first roll
36            case DiceNames.YO_LEVEN: // win with 11 on first roll
37               gameStatus = Status.WON;
38               break;
39            case DiceNames.SNAKE_EYES: // lose with 2 on first roll
40            case DiceNames.TREY: // lose with 3 on first roll
41            case DiceNames.BOX_CARS: // lose with 12 on first roll
42               gameStatus = Status.LOST;
43               break;
44            default: // did not win or lose, so remember point
45               gameStatus = Status.CONTINUE; // game is not over
46               myPoint = sumOfDice; // remember the point
47               Console.WriteLine( "Point is {0}", myPoint );
48               break;
49         } // end switch
50
51         // while game is not complete
52         while ( gameStatus == Status.CONTINUE ) // game not WON or LOST
53         {
54            sumOfDice = RollDice(); // roll dice again
55
```

Fig. 7.7 | Craps class simulates the dice game craps. (Part 2 of 4.)

```
56              // determine game status
57              if ( sumOfDice == myPoint ) // win by making point
58                 gameStatus = Status.WON;
59              else
60                 // lose by rolling 7 before point
61                 if ( sumOfDice == ( int ) DiceNames.SEVEN )
62                    gameStatus = Status.LOST;
63           } // end while
64
65           // display won or lost message
66           if ( gameStatus == Status.WON )
67              Console.WriteLine( "Player wins" );
68           else
69              Console.WriteLine( "Player loses" );
70        } // end Main
71
72        // roll dice, calculate sum and display results
73        public static int RollDice()
74        {
75           // pick random die values
76           int die1 = randomNumbers.Next( 1, 7 ); // first die roll
77           int die2 = randomNumbers.Next( 1, 7 ); // second die roll
78
79           int sum = die1 + die2; // sum of die values
80
81           // display results of this roll
82           Console.WriteLine( "Player rolled {0} + {1} = {2}",
83              die1, die2, sum );
84           return sum; // return sum of dice
85        } // end method RollDice
86  } // end class Craps
```

```
Player rolled 2 + 5 = 7
Player wins
```

```
Player rolled 2 + 1 = 3
Player loses
```

```
Player rolled 4 + 6 = 10
Point is 10
Player rolled 1 + 3 = 4
Player rolled 1 + 3 = 4
Player rolled 2 + 3 = 5
Player rolled 4 + 4 = 8
Player rolled 6 + 6 = 12
Player rolled 4 + 4 = 8
Player rolled 4 + 5 = 9
Player rolled 2 + 6 = 8
Player rolled 6 + 6 = 12
Player rolled 6 + 4 = 10
Player wins
```

Fig. 7.7 | Craps class simulates the dice game craps. (Part 3 of 4.)

```
Player rolled 2 + 4 = 6
Point is 6
Player rolled 3 + 1 = 4
Player rolled 5 + 5 = 10
Player rolled 6 + 1 = 7
Player loses
```

Fig. 7.7 | Craps class simulates the dice game craps. (Part 4 of 4.)

Method RollDice

In the rules of the game, the player must roll two dice on the first roll and must do the same on all subsequent rolls. We declare method RollDice (lines 73–85) to roll the dice and compute and display their sum. Method RollDice is declared once, but it's called from two places (lines 30 and 54) in method Main, which contains the logic for one complete game of craps. Method RollDice takes no arguments, so it has an empty parameter list. Each time it's called, RollDice returns the sum of the dice, so the return type int is indicated in the method header (line 73). Although lines 76 and 77 look the same (except for the die names), they do not necessarily produce the same result. Each of these statements produces a random value in the range 1–6. Note that randomNumbers (used in lines 76 and 77) is not declared in the method. Rather it's declared as a private static variable of the class and initialized in line 8. This enables us to create one Random object that's reused in each call to RollDice.

Method Main's Local Variables

The game is reasonably involved. The player may win or lose on the first roll or may win or lose on any subsequent roll. Method Play (lines 24–70) uses local variable gameStatus (line 27) to keep track of the overall game status, local variable myPoint (line 28) to store the "point" if the player does not win or lose on the first roll and local variable sumOfDice (line 30) to maintain the sum of the dice for the most recent roll. Note that myPoint is initialized to 0 to ensure that the application will compile. If you do not initialize myPoint, the compiler issues an error, because myPoint is not assigned a value in every branch of the switch statement—thus, the application could try to use myPoint before it's definitely assigned a value. By contrast, gameStatus does not require initialization because it *is* assigned a value in every branch of the switch statement—thus, it's guaranteed to be initialized before it's used. However, as good programming practice, we initialize it anyway.

enum *Type* Status

Local variable gameStatus is declared to be of a new type called Status, which we declared in line 11. Type Status is declared as a private member of class Craps, because Status will be used only in that class. Status is a user-defined type called an **enumeration**, which declares a set of constants represented by identifiers. An enumeration is introduced by the keyword **enum** and a type name (in this case, Status). As with a class, braces ({ and }) delimit the body of an enum declaration. Inside the braces is a comma-separated list of **enumeration constants**. The enum constant names must be unique, but the value associated with each constant need not be.

Good Programming Practice 7.3

Use only uppercase letters in the names of constants. This makes the constants stand out in an application and reminds you that enumeration constants are not variables.

Variables of type `Status` should be assigned only one of the three constants declared in the enumeration. When the game is won, the application sets local variable `gameStatus` to `Status.WON` (lines 37 and 58). When the game is lost, the application sets local variable `gameStatus` to `Status.LOST` (lines 42 and 62). Otherwise, the application sets local variable `gameStatus` to `Status.CONTINUE` (line 45) to indicate that the dice must be rolled again.

Good Programming Practice 7.4

Using enumeration constants (like `Status.WON`, `Status.LOST` and `Status.CONTINUE`) rather than literal integer values (such as 0, 1 and 2) can make code easier to read and maintain.

*Logic of the **Main** Method*

Line 30 in method `Play` calls `RollDice`, which picks two random values from 1 to 6, displays the value of the first die, the value of the second die and the sum of the dice, and returns the sum of the dice. Method `Main` next enters the `switch` statement at lines 33–49, which uses the `sumOfDice` value from line 30 to determine whether the game has been won or lost, or whether it should continue with another roll.

The sums of the dice that would result in a win or loss on the first roll are declared in the `DiceNames` enumeration in lines 14–21. These are used in the `cases` of the `switch` statement. The identifier names use casino parlance for these sums. Notice that in the `DiceNames` enumeration, a value is explicitly assigned to each identifier name. When the enum is declared, each constant in the enum declaration is a constant value of type `int`. If you do not assign a value to an identifier in the enum declaration, the compiler will do so. If the first enum constant is unassigned, the compiler gives it the value 0. If any other enum constant is unassigned, the compiler gives it a value equal to one more than the value of the preceding enum constant. For example, in the `Status` enumeration, the compiler implicitly assigns 0 to `Status.WON`, 1 to `Status.CONTINUE` and 2 to `Status.LOST`.

You could also declare an enum's underlying type to be `byte`, `sbyte`, `short`, `ushort`, `int`, `uint`, `long` or `ulong` by writing

```
private enum MyEnum : typeName { Constant1, Constant2, ... }
```

where *typeName* represents one of the integral simple types.

If you need to compare a simple integral type value to the underlying value of an enumeration constant, you must use a cast operator to make the two types match. In the `switch` statement at lines 33–49, we use the cast operator to convert the `int` value in `sumOfDice` to type `DiceNames` and compare it to each of the constants in `DiceNames`. Lines 35–36 determine whether the player won on the first roll with `SEVEN` (7) or `YO_LEVEN` (11). Lines 39–41 determine whether the player lost on the first roll with `SNAKE_EYES` (2), `TREY` (3) or `BOX_CARS` (12). After the first roll, if the game is not over, the `default` case (lines 44–48) saves `sumOfDice` in `myPoint` (line 46) and displays the point (line 47).

If we're still trying to "make our point" (i.e., the game is continuing from a prior roll), the loop in lines 52–63 executes. Line 54 rolls the dice again. If `sumOfDice` matches `myPoint` in line 57, line 58 sets `gameStatus` to `Status.WON`, and the loop terminates because the game is complete. In line 61, we use the cast operator (int) to obtain the underlying value of DiceNames.SEVEN so that we can compare it to sumOfDice. If sumOfDice is equal to SEVEN (7), line 62 sets gameStatus to Status.LOST, and the loop terminates because the game is over. When the game completes, lines 66–69 display a message indicating whether the player won or lost, and the application terminates.

Summary of the **Craps** Example

Note the use of the various program-control mechanisms we have discussed. The Craps class uses two methods—Main and RollDice (called twice from Main)—and the switch, while, if...else and nested if control statements. Also, notice that we use multiple case labels in the switch statement to execute the same statements for sums of SEVEN and YO_LEVEN (lines 35–36) and for sums of SNAKE_EYES, TREY and BOX_CARS (lines 39–41). To easily create a switch statement with all possible values for an enum type, you can use the switch code snippet. Type switch in the C# code then press *Tab* twice. If you enter an enum type into the switch statement's expression (the highlighted code of the snippet) and press *Enter*, a case for each enum constant will be generated automatically.

7.11 Scope of Declarations

You've seen declarations of C# entities, such as classes, methods, properties, variables and parameters. Declarations introduce names that can be used to refer to such C# entities. The **scope** of a declaration is the portion of the application that can refer to the declared entity by its unqualified name. Such an entity is said to be "in scope" for that portion of the application. This section introduces several important scope issues.

1. The scope of a parameter declaration is the body of the method in which the declaration appears.

2. The scope of a local-variable declaration is from the point at which the declaration appears to the end of the block containing the declaration.

3. The scope of a local-variable declaration that appears in the initialization section of a for statement's header is the body of the for statement and the other expressions in the header.

4. The scope of a method, property or field of a class is the entire body of the class. This enables non-static methods and properties of a class to use any of the class's fields, methods and properties, regardless of the order in which they're declared. Similarly, static methods and properties can use any of the static members of the class.

Any block may contain variable declarations. If a local variable or parameter in a method has the same name as a field, the field is hidden until the block terminates. In Chapter 10, we discuss how to access hidden fields. The application in Fig. 7.8 demonstrates scoping issues with fields and local variables.

Error-Prevention Tip 7.2

Use different names for fields and local variables to help prevent subtle logic errors that occur when a method is called and a local variable of the method hides a field of the same name in the class.

Line 8 declares and initializes the static variable x to 1. This static variable is hidden in any block (or method) that declares local variable named x. Method Main (lines 12–31) declares local variable x (line 14) and initializes it to 5. This local variable's value is output to show that static variable x (whose value is 1) is hidden in method Main. The application declares two other methods—UseLocalVariable (lines 34–43) and UseStaticVariable (lines 46–53)—that each take no arguments and do not return results. Method Main calls each method twice (lines 19–28). Method UseLocalVariable declares local variable x (line 36). When UseLocalVariable is first called (line 19), it creates local variable x and initializes it to 25 (line 36), outputs the value of x (lines 38–39), increments x (line 40) and outputs the value of x again (lines 41–42). When UseLocalVariable is called a second time (line 25), it re-creates local variable x and reinitializes it to 25, so the output of each UseLocalVariable call is identical.

```
1   // Fig. 7.8: Scope.cs
2   // Scope class demonstrates static and local variable scopes.
3   using System;
4
5   public class Scope
6   {
7      // static variable that is accessible to all methods of this class
8      private static int x = 1;
9
10     // Main creates and initializes local variable x
11     // and calls methods UseLocalVariable and UseStaticVariable
12     public static void Main( string[] args )
13     {
14        int x = 5; // method's local variable x hides static variable x
15
16        Console.WriteLine( "local x in method Main is {0}", x );
17
18        // UseLocalVariable has its own local x
19        UseLocalVariable();
20
21        // UseStaticVariable uses class Scope's static variable x
22        UseStaticVariable();
23
24        // UseLocalVariable reinitializes its own local x
25        UseLocalVariable();
26
27        // class Scope's static variable x retains its value
28        UseStaticVariable();
29
30        Console.WriteLine( "\nlocal x in method Main is {0}", x );
31     } // end Main
32
33     // create and initialize local variable x during each call
34     public static void UseLocalVariable()
35     {
36        int x = 25; // initialized each time UseLocalVariable is called
37
```

Fig. 7.8 | Scope class demonstrates static and local variable scopes. (Part I of 2.)

```
38          Console.WriteLine(
39             "\nlocal x on entering method UseLocalVariable is {0}", x );
40          ++x; // modifies this method's local variable x
41          Console.WriteLine(
42             "local x before exiting method UseLocalVariable is {0}", x );
43       } // end method UseLocalVariable
44
45       // modify class Scope's static variable x during each call
46       public static void UseStaticVariable()
47       {
48          Console.WriteLine( "\nstatic variable x on entering {0} is {1}",
49             "method UseStaticVariable", x );
50          x *= 10; // modifies class Scope's static variable x
51          Console.WriteLine( "static variable x before exiting {0} is {1}",
52             "method UseStaticVariable", x );
53       } // end method UseStaticVariable
54    } // end class Scope
```

```
local x in method Main is 5

local x on entering method UseLocalVariable is 25
local x before exiting method UseLocalVariable is 26

static variable x on entering method UseStaticVariable is 1
static variable x before exiting method UseStaticVariable is 10

local x on entering method UseLocalVariable is 25
local x before exiting method UseLocalVariable is 26

static variable x on entering method UseStaticVariable is 10
static variable x before exiting method UseStaticVariable is 100

local x in method Main is 5
```

Fig. 7.8 | Scope class demonstrates static and local variable scopes. (Part 2 of 2.)

Method UseStaticVariable does not declare any local variables. Therefore, when it refers to x, static variable x (line 8) of the class is used. When method UseStaticVariable is first called (line 22), it outputs the value (1) of static variable x (lines 48–49), multiplies the static variable x by 10 (line 50) and outputs the value (10) of static variable x again (lines 51–52) before returning. The next time method UseStaticVariable is called (line 28), the static variable has its modified value, 10, so the method outputs 10, then 100. Finally, in method Main, the application outputs the value of local variable x again (line 30) to show that none of the method calls modified Main's local variable x, because the methods all referred to variables named x in other scopes.

7.12 Method Overloading

Methods of the same name can be declared in the same class, as long as they have different sets of parameters (determined by the number, types and order of the parameters). This is called **method overloading**. When an **overloaded method** is called, the C# compiler selects the appropriate method by examining the number, types and order of the arguments in the call. Method overloading is commonly used to create several methods with the same name that perform the same or similar tasks, but on different types or different numbers of arguments. For example, Math methods Min and Max (summarized in Section 7.3) are overloaded with 11 versions. These find the minimum and maximum, respectively, of two values of each of the 11 numeric simple types. Our next example demonstrates declaring and invoking overloaded methods. You'll see examples of overloaded constructors in Chapter 10.

Declaring Overloaded Methods

In class MethodOverload (Fig. 7.9), we include two overloaded versions of a method called Square—one that calculates the square of an int (and returns an int) and one that calculates the square of a double (and returns a double). Although these methods have the same name and similar parameter lists and bodies, you can think of them simply as *different* methods. It may help to think of the method names as "Square of int" and "Square of double," respectively.

```csharp
1   // Fig. 7.9: MethodOverload.cs
2   // Overloaded method declarations.
3   using System;
4
5   public class MethodOverload
6   {
7      // test overloaded square methods
8      public static void Main( string[] args )
9      {
10         Console.WriteLine( "Square of integer 7 is {0}", Square( 7 ) );
11         Console.WriteLine( "Square of double 7.5 is {0}", Square( 7.5 ) );
12      } // end Main
13
14      // square method with int argument
15      public static int Square( int intValue )
16      {
17         Console.WriteLine( "Called square with int argument: {0}",
18            intValue );
19         return intValue * intValue;
20      } // end method Square with int argument
21
22      // square method with double argument
23      public static double Square( double doubleValue )
24      {
25         Console.WriteLine( "Called square with double argument: {0}",
26            doubleValue );
27         return doubleValue * doubleValue;
28      } // end method Square with double argument
29   } // end class MethodOverload
```

```
Called square with int argument: 7
Square of integer 7 is 49
Called square with double argument: 7.5
Square of double 7.5 is 56.25
```

Fig. 7.9 | Overloaded method declarations.

Line 10 in Main invokes method Square with the argument 7. Literal integer values are treated as type int, so the method call in line 10 invokes the version of Square at lines 15–20 that specifies an int parameter. Similarly, line 11 invokes method Square with the argument 7.5. Literal real-number values are treated as type double, so the method call in line 11 invokes the version of Square at lines 23–28 that specifies a double parameter. Each method first outputs a line of text to prove that the proper method was called in each case.

Notice that the overloaded methods in Fig. 7.9 perform the same calculation, but with two different types. C#'s generics feature provides a mechanism for writing a single "generic method" that can perform the same tasks as an entire set of overloaded methods. We discuss generic methods in Chapter 22.

Distinguishing Between Overloaded Methods

The compiler distinguishes overloaded methods by their **signature**—a combination of the method's name and the number, types and order of its parameters. The signature also includes the way those parameters are passed, which can be modified by the ref and out keywords (discussed in Section 7.16). If the compiler looked only at method names during compilation, the code in Fig. 7.9 would be ambiguous—the compiler would not know how to distinguish between the Square methods (lines 15–20 and 23–28). Internally, the compiler uses signatures to determine whether a class's methods are unique in that class.

For example, in Fig. 7.9, the compiler will use the method signatures to distinguish between the "Square of int" method (the Square method that specifies an int parameter) and the "Square of double" method (the Square method that specifies a double parameter). If Method1's declaration begins as

```
void Method1( int a, float b )
```

then that method will have a different signature than the method declared beginning with

```
void Method1( float a, int b )
```

The order of the parameter types is important—the compiler considers the preceding two Method1 headers to be distinct.

Return Types of Overloaded Methods

In discussing the logical names of methods used by the compiler, we did not mention the return types of the methods. This is because method *calls* cannot be distinguished by return type. The application in Fig. 7.10 illustrates the compiler errors generated when two methods have the same signature but different return types. Overloaded methods can have the same or different return types if the methods have different parameter lists. Also, overloaded methods need not have the same number of parameters.

```
1   // Fig. 7.10: MethodOverload.cs
2   // Overloaded methods with identical signatures
3   // cause compilation errors, even if return types are different.
4   public class MethodOverloadError
5   {
```

Fig. 7.10 | Overloaded methods with identical signatures cause compilation errors, even if return types are different. (Part 1 of 2.)

```
 6      // declaration of method Square with int argument
 7      public int Square( int x )
 8      {
 9         return x * x;
10      } // end method Square
11
12      // second declaration of method Square with int argument
13      // causes compilation error even though return types are different
14      public double Square( int y )
15      {
16         return y * y;
17      } // end method Square
18  } // end class MethodOverloadError
```

Error List						
⊗ 1 Error	⚠ 0 Warnings	ⓘ 0 Messages				
	Description		File	Line	Column	Project
⊗ 1	Type 'MethodOverloadError' already defines a member called 'Square' with the same parameter types		MethodOverloadError	14	25	MethodOverloadError

Fig. 7.10 | Overloaded methods with identical signatures cause compilation errors, even if return types are different. (Part 2 of 2.)

Common Programming Error 7.10

Declaring overloaded methods with identical parameter lists is a compilation error regardless of whether the return types are different.

7.13 Optional Parameters

As of Visual C# 2010, methods can have **optional parameters** that allow the calling method to vary the number of arguments to pass. An optional parameter specifies a **default value** that's assigned to the parameter if the optional argument is omitted.

You can create methods with one or more optional parameters. *All optional parameters must be placed to the right of the method's non-optional parameters*—that is, at the end of the parameter list.

Common Programming Error 7.11

Declaring a non-optional parameter to the right of an optional one is a compilation error.

When a parameter has a default value, the caller has the *option* of passing that particular argument. For example, the method header

```
public int Power( int baseValue, int exponentValue = 2 )
```

specifies an optional second parameter. A call to Power must pass at least an argument for the parameter baseValue, or a compilation error occurs. Optionally, a second argument (for the exponentValue parameter) can be passed to Power. Consider the following calls to Power:

```
Power()
Power(10)
Power(10, 3)
```

The first call generates a compilation error because this method requires a minimum of one argument. The second call is valid because one argument (10) is being passed—the optional `exponentValue` is not specified in the method call. The last call is also valid—10 is passed as the required argument and 3 is passed as the optional argument.

In the call that passes only one argument (10), parameter `exponentValue` defaults to 2, which is the default value specified in the method's header. Each optional parameter must specify a default value by using an equal (=) sign followed by the value. For example, the header for `Power` sets 2 as `exponentValue`'s default value.

Figure 7.11 demonstrates an optional parameter. The program calculates the result of raising a base value to an exponent. Method `Power` (Fig. 7.11, lines 15–23) specifies that its second parameter is optional. In method `DisplayPowers`, lines 10–11 of Fig. 7.11 call method `Power`. Line 10 calls the method without the optional second argument. In this case, the compiler provides the second argument, 2, using the default value of the optional argument, which is not visible to you in the call.

```vb
1   // Fig. 7.11: Power.vb
2   // Optional argument demonstration with method Power.
3   using System;
4
5   class CalculatePowers
6   {
7      // call Power with and without optional arguments
8      public static void Main( string[] args )
9      {
10        Console.WriteLine( "Power(10) = {0}", Power( 10 ) ) ;
11        Console.WriteLine( "Power(2, 10) = {0}", Power( 2, 10 ) );
12     } // end Main
13
14     // use iteration to calculate power
15     public int Power( int baseValue, int exponentValue = 2 )
16     {
17        int result = 1; // initialize total
18
19        for ( int i = 1; i <= exponentValue; i++ )
20           result *= baseValue;
21
22        return result;
23     } // end method Power
24  } // end class CalculatePowers
```

```
Power(10) = 100
Power(2, 10) = 1024
```

Fig. 7.11 | Optional argument demonstration with method `Power`.

7.14 Named Parameters

Normally, when calling a method that has optional parameters, the argument values—in order—are assigned to the parameters from left to right in the parameter list. Consider a `Time` class that stores the time of day in 24-hour clock format as `int` values representing the hour (0–23), minute (0–59) and second (0–59). Such a class might provide a SetTime method with optional parameters like

```
public void SetTime( int hour = 0, int minute = 0, int second = 0 )
```

In the preceding method header, all of three of SetTime's parameters are optional. Assuming that we have a Time object named t, we can call SetTime as follows:

```
t.SetTime(); // sets the time to 12:00:00 AM
t.SetTime( 12 ); // sets the time to 12:00:00 PM
t.SetTime( 12, 30 ); // sets the time to 12:30:00 PM
t.SetTime( 12, 30, 22 ); // sets the time to 12:30:22 PM
```

In the first call, no arguments are specified, so the compiler assigns 0 to each parameter. In the second call, the compiler assigns the argument, 12, to the first parameter, hour, and assigns default values of 0 to the minute and second parameters. In the third call, the compiler assigns the two arguments, 12 and 30, to the parameters hour and minute, respectively, and assigns the default value 0 to the parameter second. In the last call, the compiler assigns the three arguments, 12, 30 and 22, to the parameters hour, minute and second, respectively.

What if you wanted to specify only arguments for the hour and second? You might think that you could call the method as follows:

```
t.SetTime( 12, , 22 ); // COMPILATION ERROR
```

Unlike some programming languages, C# doesn't allow you to skip an argument as shown in the preceding statement. However, Visual C# 2010 provides a new feature called **named parameters**, which enable you to call methods that receive optional parameters by providing only the optional arguments you wish to specify. To do so, you explicitly specify the parameter's name and value—separated by a colon (:)—in the argument list of the method call. For example, the preceding statement can be implemented in Visual C# 2010 as follows:

```
t.SetTime( hour: 12, second: 22 ); // sets the time to 12:00:22
```

In this case, the compiler assigns parameter hour the argument 12 and parameter second the argument 22. The parameter minute is not specified, so the compiler assigns it the default value 0. It's also possible to specify the arguments out of order when using named parameters. The arguments for the required parameters must always be supplied.

7.15 Recursion

The applications we have discussed thus far are generally structured as methods that call one another in a disciplined, hierarchical manner. For some problems, however, it's useful to have a method call itself. A **recursive method** is a method that calls itself, either directly or indirectly through another method.

We consider recursion conceptually first. Then we examine an application containing a recursive method. Recursive problem-solving approaches have a number of elements in common. When a recursive method is called to solve a problem, it actually is capable of solving only the simplest case(s), or **base case(s)**. If the method is called with a base case, it returns a result. If the method is called with a more complex problem, it divides the problem into two conceptual pieces: a piece that the method knows how to do and a piece that it does not know how to do. To make recursion feasible, the latter piece must resemble the original problem, but be a slightly simpler or slightly smaller version of it. Because this new problem looks like the original problem, the method calls a fresh copy of itself to work on the smaller problem; this is referred to as a **recursive call** and is also called the **recursion step**. The recursion step normally includes a `return` statement, because its result will be combined with the portion of the problem the method knew how to solve to form a result that will be passed back to the original caller.

The recursion step executes while the original call to the method is still active (i.e., while it has not finished executing). The recursion step can result in many more recursive calls, as the method divides each new subproblem into two conceptual pieces. For the recursion to terminate eventually, each time the method calls itself with a slightly simpler version of the original problem, the sequence of smaller and smaller problems must converge on the base case. At that point, the method recognizes the base case and returns a result to the previous copy of the method. A sequence of returns ensues until the original method call returns the result to the caller. This process sounds complex compared with the conventional problem solving we have performed to this point.

Recursive Factorial Calculations

As an example of recursion concepts at work, let's write a recursive application to perform a popular mathematical calculation. Consider the factorial of a nonnegative integer n, written $n!$ (and pronounced "n factorial"), which is the product

$$n \cdot (n-1) \cdot (n-2) \cdot \ldots \cdot 1$$

$1!$ is equal to 1 and $0!$ is defined to be 1. For example, $5!$ is the product $5 \cdot 4 \cdot 3 \cdot 2 \cdot 1$, which is equal to 120.

The factorial of an integer, `number`, greater than or equal to 0 can be calculated iteratively (nonrecursively) using the `for` statement as follows:

```
factorial = 1;

for ( int counter = number; counter >= 1; counter-- )
   factorial *= counter;
```

A recursive declaration of the factorial method is arrived at by observing the following relationship:

$$n! = n \cdot (n-1)!$$

For example, $5!$ is clearly equal to $5 \cdot 4!$, as is shown by the following equations:

$$5! = 5 \cdot 4 \cdot 3 \cdot 2 \cdot 1$$
$$5! = 5 \cdot (4 \cdot 3 \cdot 2 \cdot 1)$$
$$5! = 5 \cdot (4!)$$

The evaluation of $5!$ would proceed as shown in Fig. 7.12. Figure 7.12(a) shows how the succession of recursive calls proceeds until $1!$ is evaluated to be 1, which terminates the recursion. Figure 7.12(b) shows the values returned from each recursive call to its caller until the value is calculated and returned.

Figure 7.13 uses recursion to calculate and display the factorials of the integers from 0 to 10. The recursive method `Factorial` (lines 16–24) first tests to determine whether a

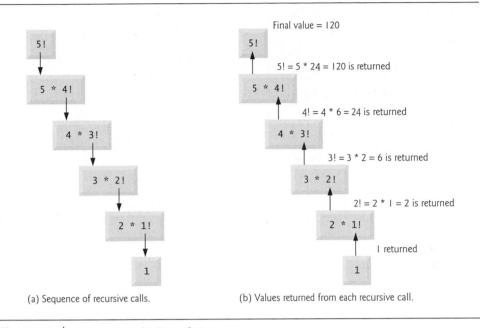

(a) Sequence of recursive calls. (b) Values returned from each recursive call.

Fig. 7.12 | Recursive evaluation of 5!.

terminating condition (line 19) is true. If number is less than or equal to 1 (the base case), Factorial returns 1, no further recursion is necessary and the method returns. If number is greater than 1, line 23 expresses the problem as the product of number and a recursive call to Factorial evaluating the factorial of number - 1, which is a slightly simpler problem than the original calculation, Factorial(number).

Method Factorial (lines 16–24) receives a parameter of type long and returns a result of type long. As you can see in Fig. 7.13, factorial values become large quickly. We chose type long (which can represent relatively large integers) so that the application could calculate factorials greater than 20!. Unfortunately, the Factorial method produces large values so quickly that factorial values soon exceed even the maximum value that can be stored in a long variable. Due to the restrictions on the integral types, variables of type float, double or decimal might ultimately be needed to calculate factorials of larger numbers. This situation points to a weakness in many programming languages—the languages are not easily extended to handle the unique requirements of various applications. As you know, C# allows you to create a type that supports arbitrarily large integers if you wish. For example, you could create a HugeInteger class that would enable an application to calculate the factorials of arbitrarily large numbers. You can also use the new type BigInteger from the .NET Framework's class library.

Common Programming Error 7.12

*Either omitting the base case or writing the recursion step incorrectly so that it does not converge on the base case will cause **infinite recursion**, eventually exhausting memory. This error is analogous to the problem of an infinite loop in an iterative (nonrecursive) solution.*

```
1   // Fig. 7.13: FactorialTest.cs
2   // Recursive Factorial method.
3   using System;
4
5   public class FactorialTest
6   {
7      public static void Main( string[] args )
8      {
9         // calculate the factorials of 0 through 10
10        for ( long counter = 0; counter <= 10; counter++ )
11           Console.WriteLine( "{0}! = {1}",
12              counter, Factorial( counter ) );
13     } // end Main
14
15     // recursive declaration of method Factorial
16     public static long Factorial( long number )
17     {
18        // base case
19        if ( number <= 1 )
20           return 1;
21        // recursion step
22        else
23           return number * Factorial( number - 1 );
24     } // end method Factorial
25  } // end class FactorialTest
```

```
0! = 1
1! = 1
2! = 2
3! = 6
4! = 24
5! = 120
6! = 720
7! = 5040
8! = 40320
9! = 362880
10! = 3628800
```

Fig. 7.13 | Recursive Factorial method.

7.16 Passing Arguments: Pass-by-Value vs. Pass-by-Reference

Two ways to pass arguments to functions in many programming languages are **pass-by-value** and **pass-by-reference**. When an argument is passed by value (the default in C#), a *copy* of its value is made and passed to the called function. Changes to the copy do not affect the original variable's value in the caller. This prevents the accidental side effects that so greatly hinder the development of correct and reliable software systems. Each argument that has been passed in the programs in this chapter so far has been passed by value. When an argument is passed by reference, the caller gives the method the ability to access and modify the caller's original variable.

Software Engineering Observation 7.4

Pass-by-reference can weaken security, because the called function can corrupt the caller's data.

To pass an object by reference into a method, simply provide as an argument in the method call the variable that refers to the object. Then, in the method body, reference the object using the parameter name. The parameter refers to the original object in memory, so the called method can access the original object directly.

Previously, we discussed the difference between value types and reference types. A major difference between them is that value-type variables store values, so specifying a value-type variable in a method call passes a copy of that variable's value to the method. Reference-type variables store references to objects, so specifying a reference-type variable as an argument passes the method a copy of the actual reference that refers to the object. Even though the reference itself is passed by value, the method can still use the reference it receives to interact with—and possibly modify—the original object. Similarly, when returning information from a method via a `return` statement, the method returns a copy of the value stored in a value-type variable or a copy of the reference stored in a reference-type variable. When a reference is returned, the calling method can use that reference to interact with the referenced object.

What if you would like to pass a variable by reference so the called method can modify the variable's value? To do this, C# provides keywords **ref** and **out**. Applying the `ref` keyword to a parameter declaration allows you to pass a variable to a method by reference—the called method will be able to modify the original variable in the caller. The `ref` keyword is used for variables that already have been initialized in the calling method. Normally, when a method call contains an uninitialized variable as an argument, the compiler generates an error. Preceding a parameter with keyword `out` creates an **output parameter**. This indicates to the compiler that the argument will be passed into the called method by reference and that the called method will assign a value to the original variable in the caller. If the method does not assign a value to the output parameter in every possible path of execution, the compiler generates an error. This also prevents the compiler from generating an error message for an uninitialized variable that's passed as an argument to a method. A method can return only one value to its caller via a return statement, but can return many values by specifying multiple output (`ref` and/or `out`) parameters.

You can also pass a reference-type variable by reference, which allows you to modify reference-type variable so that it refers to a new object. Passing a reference by reference is a tricky but powerful technique that we discuss in Section 8.8.

The application in Fig. 7.14 uses the `ref` and `out` keywords to manipulate integer values. The class contains three methods that calculate the square of an integer. Method `SquareRef` (lines 37–40) multiplies its parameter x by itself and assigns the new value to x. `SquareRef`'s parameter is declared as `ref int`, which indicates that the argument passed to this method must be an integer that's passed by reference. Because the argument is passed by reference, the assignment at line 39 modifies the original argument's value in the caller.

Method `SquareOut` (lines 44–48) assigns its parameter the value 6 (line 46), then squares that value. `SquareOut`'s parameter is declared as `out int`, which indicates that the argument passed to this method must be an integer that's passed by reference and that the argument does not need to be initialized in advance.

```
 1   // Fig. 7.14: ReferenceAndOutputParameters.cs
 2   // Reference, output and value parameters.
 3   using System;
 4
 5   class ReferenceAndOutputParameters
 6   {
 7      // call methods with reference, output and value parameters
 8      public static void Main( string[] args )
 9      {
10         int y = 5; // initialize y to 5
11         int z; // declares z, but does not initialize it
12
13         // display original values of y and z
14         Console.WriteLine( "Original value of y: {0}", y );
15         Console.WriteLine( "Original value of z: uninitialized\n" );
16
17         // pass y and z by reference
18         SquareRef( ref y ); // must use keyword ref
19         SquareOut( out z ); // must use keyword out
20
21         // display values of y and z after they are modified by
22         // methods SquareRef and SquareOut, respectively
23         Console.WriteLine( "Value of y after SquareRef: {0}", y );
24         Console.WriteLine( "Value of z after SquareOut: {0}\n", z );
25
26         // pass y and z by value
27         Square( y );
28         Square( z );
29
30         // display values of y and z after they are passed to method Square
31         // to demonstrate that arguments passed by value are not modified
32         Console.WriteLine( "Value of y after Square: {0}", y );
33         Console.WriteLine( "Value of z after Square: {0}", z );
34      } // end Main
35
36      // uses reference parameter x to modify caller's variable
37      static void SquareRef( ref int x )
38      {
39         x = x * x; // squares value of caller's variable
40      } // end method SquareRef
41
42      // uses output parameter x to assign a value
43      // to an uninitialized variable
44      static void SquareOut( out int x )
45      {
46         x = 6; // assigns a value to caller's variable
47         x = x * x; // squares value of caller's variable
48      } // end method SquareOut
49
50      // parameter x receives a copy of the value passed as an argument,
51      // so this method cannot modify the caller's variable
52      static void Square( int x )
53      {
```

Fig. 7.14 | Reference, output and value parameters. (Part 1 of 2.)

```
54              x = x * x;
55        } // end method Square
56  } // end class ReferenceAndOutputParameters
```

```
Original value of y: 5
Original value of z: uninitialized

Value of y after SquareRef: 25
Value of z after SquareOut: 36

Value of y after Square: 25
Value of z after Square: 36
```

Fig. 7.14 | Reference, output and value parameters. (Part 2 of 2.)

Method Square (lines 52–55) multiplies its parameter x by itself and assigns the new value to x. When this method is called, a copy of the argument is passed to the parameter x. Thus, even though parameter x is modified in the method, the original value in the caller is not modified.

Method Main (lines 8–34) invokes methods SquareRef, SquareOut and Square. We begin by initializing variable y to 5 and declaring, but not initializing, variable z. Lines 18–19 call methods SquareRef and SquareOut. Notice that when you pass a variable to a method with a reference parameter, you must precede the argument with the same keyword (ref or out) that was used to declare the reference parameter. Lines 23–24 display the values of y and z after the calls to SquareRef and SquareOut. Notice that y has been changed to 25 and z has been set to 36.

Lines 27–28 call method Square with y and z as arguments. In this case, both variables are passed by value—only copies of their values are passed to Square. As a result, the values of y and z remain 25 and 36, respectively. Lines 32–33 output the values of y and z to show that they were not modified.

Common Programming Error 7.13
The ref and out arguments in a method call must match the parameters specified in the method declaration; otherwise, a compilation error occurs.

Software Engineering Observation 7.5
By default, C# does not allow you to choose whether to pass each argument by value or by reference. Value types are passed by value. Objects are not passed to methods; rather, references to objects are passed to methods. The references themselves are passed by value. When a method receives a reference to an object, the method can manipulate the object directly, but the reference value cannot be changed to refer to a new object. In Section 8.8, you'll see that references also can be passed by reference.

7.17 Wrap-Up

In this chapter, we discussed the difference between non-static and static methods, and we showed how to call static methods by preceding the method name with the name of the class in which it appears and the member access (.) operator. You saw that the Math class in the .NET Framework Class Library provides many static methods to perform mathematical calculations. We presented several commonly used .NET Framework Class Library namespaces. You learned how to use operator + to perform string concatenations. You also learned how to declare constant values in two ways—with the const keyword and with enum types. We demonstrated simulation techniques and used class Random to generate sets of random numbers. We discussed the scope of fields and local variables in a class. You saw how to overload methods in a class by providing methods with the same name but different signatures. We discussed how recursive methods call themselves, breaking larger problems into smaller subproblems until eventually the original problem is solved. You learned the differences between value types and reference types with respect to how they're passed to methods, and how to use the ref and out keywords to pass arguments by reference.

In Chapter 8, you'll learn how to maintain lists and tables of data in arrays. You'll see a more elegant implementation of the application that rolls a die 6000 times and two enhanced versions of our GradeBook case study. You'll also learn how to access an application's command-line arguments that are passed to method Main when a console application begins execution.

8

Arrays

*Begin at the beginning, …
and go on till you come to
the end: then stop.*
—Lewis Carroll

*Now go, write it
before them in a table,
and note it in a book.*
—Isaiah 30:8

*To go beyond is as
wrong as to fall short.*
—Confucius

OBJECTIVES

In this chapter you'll learn:

■ To use arrays to store data in and retrieve data from lists
and tables of values.

■ To declare arrays, initialize arrays and refer to individual
elements of arrays.

■ To use the `foreach` statement to iterate through arrays.

■ To use implicitly typed local variables.

■ To pass arrays to methods.

■ To declare and manipulate multidimensional arrays.

8.1 Introduction

This chapter introduces the important topic of **data structures**—collections of related data items. **Arrays** are data structures consisting of related data items of the same type. Arrays are fixed-length entities—they remain the same length once they're created, although an array variable may be reassigned such that it refers to a new array of a different length.

After discussing how arrays are declared, created and initialized, we present a series of examples that demonstrate several common array manipulations. We use arrays to simulate shuffling and dealing playing cards. The chapter demonstrates C#'s last structured control statement—the foreach repetition statement—which provides a concise notation for accessing data in arrays (and other data structures, as you'll see in Chapter 9 and later in the book). We enhance the GradeBook case study using arrays to enable the class to store a set of grades and analyze student grades from multiple exams.

8.2 Arrays

An array is a group of variables (called **elements**) containing values that all have the same type. Recall that types are divided into two categories—value types and reference types. Arrays are reference types. As you'll see, what we typically think of as an array is actually a reference to an array object. The elements of an array can be either value types or reference types, including other arrays. To refer to a particular element in an array, we specify the name of the reference to the array and the position number of the element in the array, which is known as the element's **index**.

Figure 8.1 shows a logical representation of an integer array called c. This array contains 12 elements. An application refers to any one of these elements with an **array-access expression** that includes the name of the array, followed by the index of the particular element in **square brackets** ([]). The first element in every array has **index zero** and is sometimes called the **zeroth element**. Thus, the elements of array c are c[0], c[1], c[2] and so on. The highest index in array c is 11, which is one less than the number of elements in the array, because indices begin at 0. Array names follow the same conventions as other variable names.

An index must be a nonnegative integer and can be an expression. For example, if we assume that variable a is 5 and variable b is 6, then the statement

```
c[ a + b ] += 2;
```

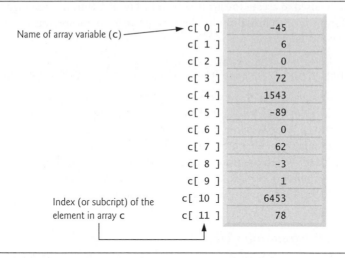

Fig. 8.1 | A 12-element array.

adds 2 to array element c[11]. An indexed array name is an array-access expression. Such expressions can be used on the left side of an assignment to place a new value into an array element. The array index must be a value of type int, uint, long or ulong, or a value of a type that can be implicitly promoted to one of these types.

Let's examine array c in Fig. 8.1 more closely. The **name** of the variable that references the array is c. Every array instance knows its own length and provides access to this information with the Length property. For example, the expression c.Length uses array c's Length property to determine the length of the array (that is, 12). The Length property of an array cannot be changed, because it does not provide a set accessor. The array's 12 elements are referred to as c[0], c[1], c[2], ..., c[11]. Referring to elements outside of this range, such as c[-1] or c[12] is a runtime error. The value of c[0] is -45, the value of c[1] is 6, the value of c[2] is 0, the value of c[7] is 62 and the value of c[11] is 78. To calculate the sum of the values contained in the first three elements of array c and store the result in variable sum, we would write

```
sum = c[ 0 ] + c[ 1 ] + c[ 2 ];
```

To divide the value of c[6] by 2 and assign the result to the variable x, we would write

```
x = c[ 6 ] / 2;
```

8.3 Declaring and Creating Arrays

Arrays occupy space in memory. Since they're objects, they're typically created with keyword new. To create an array object, you specify the type and the number of array elements as part of an **array-creation expression** that uses keyword new. Such an expression returns a reference that can be stored in an array variable. The following declaration and array-creation expression create an array object containing 12 int elements and store the array's reference in variable c:

```
int[] c = new int[ 12 ];
```

This expression can be used to create the array shown in Fig. 8.1 (but not the initial values in the array—we'll show how to initialize the elements of an array momentarily). This task also can be performed as follows:

```
int[] c; // declare the array variable
c = new int[ 12 ]; // create the array; assign to array variable
```

In the declaration, the square brackets following the type `int` indicate that `c` is a variable that will refer to an array of `int`s (i.e., `c` will store a reference to an array object). In the assignment statement, the array variable `c` receives the reference to a new array object of 12 `int` elements. The number of elements can also be specified as an expression that's calculated at execution time. When an array is created, each element of the array receives a default value—0 for the numeric simple-type elements, `false` for `bool` elements and `null` for references. As we'll soon see, we can provide specific, nondefault initial element values when we create an array.

Common Programming Error 8.1

In the declaration of a variable that will refer to an array, specifying the number of elements in the square brackets (e.g., `int[12] c;`) is a syntax error.

An application can create several arrays in a single declaration. The following statement reserves 100 elements for `string` array b and 27 elements for `string` array x:

```
string[] b = new string[ 100 ], x = new string[ 27 ];
```

In this statement, `string[]` applies to each variable. For readability and ease of commenting, we prefer to split the preceding statement into two statements, as in:

```
string[] b = new string[ 100 ]; // create string array b
string[] x = new string[ 27 ]; // create string array x
```

An application can declare variables that will refer to arrays of value-type elements or reference-type elements. For example, every element of an `int` array is an `int` value, and every element of a `string` array is a reference to a `string` object.

Resizing an Array

Though arrays are fixed-length entities, you can use the `static` `Array` method `Resize`, which takes two arguments—the array to be resized and the new length—to create a new array with the specified length. This method copies the contents of the old array into the new array and sets the variable it receives as its first argument to reference the new array. For example, consider the following statements:

```
int[] newArray = new int[ 5 ];
Array.Resize( ref newArray, 10 );
```

The variable `newArray` initially refers to a five-element array. The resize method sets `newArray` to refer to a new 10-element array. If the new array is smaller than the old array, any content that cannot fit into the new array is truncated without warning.

8.4 Examples Using Arrays

This section presents several examples that demonstrate declaring arrays, creating arrays, initializing arrays and manipulating array elements.

Creating and Initializing an Array

The application of Fig. 8.2 uses keyword new to create an array of five int elements that are initially 0 (the default for int variables).

```
1   // Fig. 8.2: InitArray.cs
2   // Creating an array.
3   using System;
4
5   public class InitArray
6   {
7      public static void Main( string[] args )
8      {
9         int[] array; // declare array named array
10
11        // create the space for array and initialize to default zeros
12        array = new int[ 5 ]; // 5 int elements
13
14        Console.WriteLine( "{0}{1,8}", "Index", "Value" ); // headings
15
16        // output each array element's value
17        for ( int counter = 0; counter < array.Length; counter++ )
18           Console.WriteLine( "{0,5}{1,8}", counter, array[ counter ] );
19     } // end Main
20  } // end class InitArray
```

```
Index   Value
    0       0
    1       0
    2       0
    3       0
    4       0
```

Fig. 8.2 | Creating an array.

Line 9 declares array—a variable capable of referring to an array of int elements. Line 12 creates the five-element array object and assigns its reference to variable array. Line 14 outputs the column headings. The first column contains the index (0–9) of each array element, and the second column contains the default value (0) of each array element and has a field width of 8.

The for statement in lines 17–18 outputs the index number (represented by counter) and the value (represented by array[counter]) of each array element. The loop-control variable counter is initially 0—index values start at 0, so using zero-based counting allows the loop to access every element of the array. The for statement's loop-continuation condition uses the property array.Length (line 17) to obtain the length of the array. In this example, the length of the array is 10, so the loop continues executing as long as the value of control variable counter is less than 10. The highest index value of a 10-element array is 9, so using the less-than operator in the loop-continuation condition guarantees that the loop does not attempt to access an element beyond the end of the array (i.e., during the final iteration of the loop, counter is 9). We'll soon see what happens when such an out-of-range index is encountered at execution time.

Using an Array Initializer

An application can create an array and initialize its elements with an **array initializer**, which is a comma-separated list of expressions (called an **initializer list**) enclosed in braces. In this case, the array length is determined by the number of elements in the initializer list. For example, the declaration

```
int[] n = { 10, 20, 30, 40, 50 };
```

creates a five-element array with index values 0, 1, 2, 3 and 4. Element n[0] is initialized to 10, n[1] is initialized to 20 and so on. This statement does not require new to create the array object. When the compiler encounters an array initializer list, the compiler counts the number of initializers in the list to determine the size of the array, then sets up the appropriate new operation "behind the scenes." The application in Fig. 8.3 initializes an integer array with 10 values (line 10) and displays the array in tabular format. The code for displaying the array elements (lines 15–16) is identical to that in Fig. 8.2 (lines 17–18).

```
1   // Fig. 8.3: InitArray.cs
2   // Initializing the elements of an array with an array initializer.
3   using System;
4
5   public class InitArray
6   {
7      public static void Main( string[] args )
8      {
9         // initializer list specifies the value for each element
10        int[] array = { 32, 27, 64, 18, 95, 14, 90, 70, 60, 37 };
11
12        Console.WriteLine( "{0}{1,8}", "Index", "Value" ); // headings
13
14        // output each array element's value
15        for ( int counter = 0; counter < array.Length; counter++ )
16           Console.WriteLine( "{0,5}{1,8}", counter, array[ counter ] );
17     } // end Main
18  } // end class InitArray
```

```
Index   Value
    0      32
    1      27
    2      64
    3      18
    4      95
    5      14
    6      90
    7      70
    8      60
    9      37
```

Fig. 8.3 | Initializing the elements of an array with an array initializer.

Calculating a Value to Store in Each Array Element

Some applications calculate the value to be stored in each array element. The application in Fig. 8.4 creates a 10-element array and assigns to each element one of the even integers from 2 to 20 (2, 4, 6, ..., 20). Then the application displays the array in tabular format. The for statement at lines 13–14 calculates an array element's value by multiplying the current value of the for loop's control variable counter by 2, then adding 2.

```
1    // Fig. 8.4: InitArray.cs
2    // Calculating values to be placed into the elements of an array.
3    using System;
4
5    public class InitArray
6    {
7       public static void Main( string[] args )
8       {
9          const int ARRAY_LENGTH = 10; // create a named constant
10         int[] array = new int[ ARRAY_LENGTH ]; // create array
11
12         // calculate value for each array element
13         for ( int counter = 0; counter < array.Length; counter++ )
14            array[ counter ] = 2 + 2 * counter;
15
16         Console.WriteLine( "{0}{1,8}", "Index", "Value" ); // headings
17
18         // output each array element's value
19         for ( int counter = 0; counter < array.Length; counter++ )
20            Console.WriteLine( "{0,5}{1,8}", counter, array[ counter ] );
21      } // end Main
22   } // end class InitArray
```

```
Index   Value
    0       2
    1       4
    2       6
    3       8
    4      10
    5      12
    6      14
    7      16
    8      18
    9      20
```

Fig. 8.4 | Calculating values to be placed into the elements of an array.

Line 9 uses the modifier const to declare the constant ARRAY_LENGTH, whose value is 10. Constants must be initialized when they're declared and cannot be modified thereafter. We declare constants with all capital letters by convention to make them stand out in the code.

Good Programming Practice 8.1

*Constants also are called **named constants**. Applications using constants often are more readable than those that use literal values (e.g., 10)—a named constant such as ARRAY_LENGTH clearly indicates its purpose, whereas a literal value could have different meanings based on the context in which it's used. Another advantage to using named constants is that if the value of the constant must be changed, the change is necessary only in the declaration, thus reducing the cost of maintaining the code.*

Common Programming Error 8.2

Assigning a value to a named constant after it has been initialized is a compilation error.

Common Programming Error 8.3

Attempting to declare a named constant without initializing it is a compilation error.

Summing the Elements of an Array

Often, the elements of an array represent a series of values to be used in a calculation. For example, if the elements of an array represent exam grades, an instructor may wish to total the elements and use that total to calculate the class average for the exam. The GradeBook examples later in the chapter (Fig. 8.15 and Fig. 8.20) use this technique.

The application in Fig. 8.5 sums the values contained in a 10-element integer array. The application creates and initializes the array at line 9. The for statement performs the calculations. [*Note:* The values supplied as array initializers are often read into an application, rather than specified in an initializer list. For example, an application could input the values from a user or from a file on disk (as discussed in Chapter 17, Files and Streams). Reading the data into an application makes the application more reusable, because it can be used with different sets of data.]

```csharp
1   // Fig. 8.5: SumArray.cs
2   // Computing the sum of the elements of an array.
3   using System;
4
5   public class SumArray
6   {
7      public static void Main( string[] args )
8      {
9         int[] array = { 87, 68, 94, 100, 83, 78, 85, 91, 76, 87 };
10        int total = 0;
11
12        // add each element's value to total
13        for ( int counter = 0; counter < array.Length; counter++ )
14           total += array[ counter ];
15
16        Console.WriteLine( "Total of array elements: {0}", total );
17     } // end Main
18  } // end class SumArray
```

```
Total of array elements: 849
```

Fig. 8.5 | Computing the sum of the elements of an array.

Using Bar Charts to Display Array Data Graphically

Many applications present data to users in a graphical manner. For example, numeric values are often displayed as bars in a bar chart. In such a chart, longer bars represent proportionally larger numeric values. One simple way to display numeric data graphically is with a bar chart that shows each numeric value as a bar of asterisks (*).

An instructor might graph the number of grades in each of several categories to visualize the grade distribution for the exam. Suppose the grades on an exam were 87, 68, 94, 100, 83, 78, 85, 91, 76 and 87. There was one grade of 100, two grades in the 90s, four grades in the 80s, two grades in the 70s, one grade in the 60s and no grades below 60. Our next application (Fig. 8.6) stores this grade distribution data in an array of 11 elements, each corresponding to a category of grades. For example, array[0] indicates the number of grades in the range 0–9, array[7] the number of grades in the range 70–79 and array[10] the number of 100 grades. The two versions of class GradeBook later in the chapter (Figs. 8.15 and 8.20) contain code that calculates these grade frequencies based on a set of grades. For now, we manually create array by examining the set of grades and initializing the elements of array to the number of values in each range (line 9).

The application reads the numbers from the array and graphs the information as a bar chart. Each grade range is followed by a bar of asterisks indicating the number of grades in that range. To label each bar, lines 17–21 output a grade range (e.g., "70-79: ") based on the current value of counter. When counter is 10, line 18 outputs " 100: " to align the colon with the other bar labels. When counter is not 10, line 20 uses the format items {0:D2} and {1:D2} to output the label of the grade range. The format specifier D indicates that the value should be formatted as an integer, and the number after the D indicates how

```
1   // Fig. 8.6: BarChart.cs
2   // Bar chart displaying application.
3   using System;
4
5   public class BarChart
6   {
7      public static void Main( string[] args )
8      {
9         int[] array = { 0, 0, 0, 0, 0, 0, 1, 2, 4, 2, 1 };
10
11        Console.WriteLine( "Grade distribution:" );
12
13        // for each array element, output a bar of the chart
14        for ( int counter = 0; counter < array.Length; counter++ )
15        {
16           // output bar labels ( "00-09: ", ..., "90-99: ", "100: " )
17           if ( counter == 10 )
18              Console.Write( "  100: " );
19           else
20              Console.Write( "{0:D2}-{1:D2}: ",
21                 counter * 10, counter * 10 + 9 );
22
23           // display bar of asterisks
24           for ( int stars = 0; stars < array[ counter ]; stars++ )
25              Console.Write( "*" );
26
27           Console.WriteLine(); // start a new line of output
28        } // end outer for
29     } // end Main
30  } // end class BarChart
```

Fig. 8.6 | Bar chart displaying application. (Part 1 of 2.)

```
Grade distribution:
00-09:
10-19:
20-29:
30-39:
40-49:
50-59:
60-69: *
70-79: **
80-89: ****
90-99: **
  100: *
```

Fig. 8.6 | Bar chart displaying application. (Part 2 of 2.)

many digits this formatted integer must contain. The 2 indicates that values with fewer than two digits should begin with a leading 0.

The nested for statement (lines 24–25) outputs the bars. Note the loop-continuation condition at line 24 (stars < array[counter]). Each time the application reaches the inner for, the loop counts from 0 up to one less than array[counter], thus using a value in array to determine the number of asterisks to display. In this example, array[0]–array[5] contain 0s because no students received a grade below 60. Thus, the application displays no asterisks next to the first six grade ranges.

Using the Elements of an Array as Counters

Sometimes, applications use counter variables to summarize data, such as the results of a survey. In Fig. 7.6, we used separate counters in our die-rolling application to track the number of times each face of a six-sided die appeared as the application rolled the die 6000 times. An array version of the application in Fig. 7.6 is shown in Fig. 8.7.

Figure 8.7 uses array frequency (line 10) to count the occurrences of each side of the die. *The single statement in line 14 of this application replaces lines 26–46 of Fig. 7.6.* Line 14 uses the random value to determine which frequency element to increment during each iteration of the loop. The calculation in line 14 produces random numbers from 1 to 6, so array frequency must be large enough to store six counters. We use a seven-element array in which we ignore frequency[0]—it's more logical to have the face value 1 increment frequency[1] than frequency[0]. Thus, each face value is used as an index for array frequency. We also replaced lines 50–52 of Fig. 7.6 by looping through array frequency to output the results (Fig. 8.7, lines 19–20).

```
1   // Fig. 8.7: RollDie.cs
2   // Roll a six-sided die 6000 times.
3   using System;
4
5   public class RollDie
6   {
7      public static void Main( string[] args )
8      {
9         Random randomNumbers = new Random(); // random-number generator
```

Fig. 8.7 | Roll a six-sided die 6000 times. (Part 1 of 2.)

```
10                int[] frequency = new int[ 7 ]; // array of frequency counters
11
12                // roll die 6000 times; use die value as frequency index
13                for ( int roll = 1; roll <= 6000; roll++ )
14                   ++frequency[ randomNumbers.Next( 1, 7 ) ];
15
16                Console.WriteLine( "{0}{1,10}", "Face", "Frequency" );
17
18                // output each array element's value
19                for ( int face = 1; face < frequency.Length; face++ )
20                   Console.WriteLine( "{0,4}{1,10}", face, frequency[ face ] );
21          } // end Main
22    } // end class RollDie
```

Face	Frequency
1	956
2	981
3	1001
4	1030
5	1035
6	997

Fig. 8.7 | Roll a six-sided die 6000 times. (Part 2 of 2.)

Using Arrays to Analyze Survey Results

Our next example uses arrays to summarize data collected in a survey:

> *Forty students were asked to rate the quality of the food in the student cafeteria on a scale of 1 to 10 (where 1 means awful and 10 means excellent). Place the 40 responses in an integer array and summarize the results of the poll.*

This is a typical array-processing application (see Fig. 8.8). We wish to summarize the number of responses of each type (i.e., 1 through 10). The array responses (lines 10–12) is a 40-element int array of the students' responses to the survey. We use 11-element array frequency (line 13) to count the number of occurrences of each response. Each element of the array is used as a counter for one of the survey responses and is initialized to 0 by default. As in Fig. 8.7, we ignore frequency[0].

```
1    // Fig. 8.8: StudentPoll.cs
2    // Poll analysis application.
3    using System;
4
5    public class StudentPoll
6    {
7       public static void Main( string[] args )
8       {
9          // array of survey responses
10         int[] responses = { 1, 2, 6, 4, 8, 5, 9, 7, 8, 10, 1, 6, 3, 8, 6,
11            10, 3, 8, 2, 7, 6, 5, 7, 6, 8, 6, 7, 5, 6, 6, 5, 6, 7, 5, 6,
12            4, 8, 6, 8, 10 };
```

Fig. 8.8 | Poll analysis application. (Part 1 of 2.)

```
13          int[] frequency = new int[ 11 ]; // array of frequency counters
14
15          // for each answer, select responses element and use that value
16          // as frequency index to determine element to increment
17          for ( int answer = 0; answer < responses.Length; answer++ )
18             ++frequency[ responses[ answer ] ];
19
20          Console.WriteLine( "{0}{1,10}", "Rating", "Frequency" );
21
22          // output each array element's value
23          for ( int rating = 1; rating < frequency.Length; rating++ )
24             Console.WriteLine( "{0,6}{1,10}", rating, frequency[ rating ] );
25       } // end Main
26    } // end class StudentPoll
```

```
Rating Frequency
    1         2
    2         2
    3         2
    4         2
    5         5
    6        11
    7         5
    8         7
    9         1
   10         3
```

Fig. 8.8 | Poll analysis application. (Part 2 of 2.)

Lines 17–18 take the responses one at a time from array responses and increments one of the 10 counters frequency[1] to frequency[10]; we ignore frequency[0] because the survey responses are limited to the range 1–10. The key statement in the loop appears in line 18, which increments the appropriate frequency counter, depending on the value of responses[answer].

Let's consider several iterations of the for statement. When control variable answer is 0, the value of responses[answer] is the value of responses[0] (i.e., 1 in line 10), so the application interprets ++frequency[responses[answer]] as

```
    ++frequency[ 1 ]
```

which increments the value in frequency array element 1. To evaluate the expression, start with the value in the innermost set of square brackets, answer. Once you know answer's value (which is the value of the loop-control variable in line 17), plug it into the expression and evaluate the next outer set of square brackets—i.e., responses[answer], which is a value selected from the responses array in lines 10–12. Then use the resulting value as the index for the frequency array to specify which counter to increment (line 18).

When answer is 1, responses[answer] is the value of responses[1], which is 2, so the application interprets ++frequency[responses[answer]] as

```
    ++frequency[ 2 ]
```

which increments the frequency array element 2.

When answer is 2, responses[answer] is the value of responses[2], which is 6, so the application interprets ++frequency[responses[answer]] as

```
++frequency[ 6 ]
```

which increments frequency array element 6, and so on. Regardless of the number of responses processed in the survey, the application requires only an 11-element array (in which we ignore element 0) to summarize the results, because all the response values are between 1 and 10, inclusive, and the index values for an 11-element array are 0 through 10.

If the data in the responses array had contained invalid values, such as 13, the application would have attempted to add 1 to frequency[13], which is outside the bounds of the array. In many programming languages, like C and C++, writing outside the bounds of an array is actually allowed and would overwrite arbitrary information in memory, often causing disastrous results. C# does not allow this—accessing any array element forces a check on the array index to ensure that it's valid (i.e., it must be greater than or equal to 0 and less than the length of the array). This is called **bounds checking**. If an application uses an invalid index, the Common Language Runtime generates an exception (specifically, an **IndexOutOfRangeException**) to indicate that an error occurred in the application at execution time. The condition in a control statement could determine whether an index is valid before allowing it to be used in an *array-access expression*, thus avoiding the exception.

Error-Prevention Tip 8.1
An exception indicates that an error has occurred in an application. You often can write code to recover from an exception and continue application execution, rather than abnormally terminating the application. Exception handling is discussed in Chapter 13.

Error-Prevention Tip 8.2
When writing code to loop through an array, ensure that the array index remains greater than or equal to 0 and less than the length of the array. The loop-continuation condition should prevent the accessing of elements outside this range.

8.5 Case Study: Card Shuffling and Dealing Simulation

So far, this chapter's examples have used arrays of value-type elements. This section uses random-number generation and an array of reference-type elements—namely, objects representing playing cards—to develop a class that simulates card shuffling and dealing. This class can then be used to implement applications that play card games.

We first develop class Card (Fig. 8.9), which represents a playing card that has a face (e.g., "Ace", "Deuce", "Three", ..., "Jack", "Queen", "King") and a suit (e.g., "Hearts", "Diamonds", "Clubs", "Spades"). Next, we develop class DeckOfCards (Fig. 8.10), which creates a deck of 52 playing cards in which each element is a Card object. Then we build an application (Fig. 8.11) that uses class DeckOfCards's card-shuffling-and-dealing capabilities.

Class Card

Class Card (Fig. 8.9) contains two string instance variables—face and suit—that are used to store references to the face value and suit name for a specific Card. The constructor for the class (lines 9–13) receives two strings that it uses to initialize face and suit. Method ToString (lines 16–19) creates a string consisting of the face of the card, the string " of " and the suit of the card. Recall from Chapter 7 that the + operator can be used to concatenate (i.e., combine) several strings to form one larger string. Card's To-String method can be invoked explicitly to obtain a string representation of a Card object (e.g., "Ace of Spades"). The ToString method of an object is called implicitly in many cases when the object is used where a string is expected (e.g., when WriteLine outputs the object or when the object is concatenated to a string using the + operator). For this behavior to occur, ToString must be declared with the header exactly as shown in line 16 of Fig. 8.9. We'll explain the purpose of the override keyword in more detail when we discuss inheritance in Chapter 11.

```
1   // Fig. 8.9: Card.cs
2   // Card class represents a playing card.
3   public class Card
4   {
5      private string face; // face of card ("Ace", "Deuce", ...)
6      private string suit; // suit of card ("Hearts", "Diamonds", ...)
7
8      // two-parameter constructor initializes card's face and suit
9      public Card( string cardFace, string cardSuit )
10     {
11        face = cardFace; // initialize face of card
12        suit = cardSuit; // initialize suit of card
13     } // end two-parameter Card constructor
14
15     // return string representation of Card
16     public override string ToString()
17     {
18        return face + " of " + suit;
19     } // end method ToString
20  } // end class Card
```

Fig. 8.9 | Card class represents a playing card.

Class DeckOfCards

Class DeckOfCards (Fig. 8.10) declares an instance-variable named deck that will refer to an array of Card objects (line 7). Like simple-type array variable declarations, the declaration of a variable for an array of objects includes the type of the elements in the array, followed by square brackets and the name of the array variable. Class DeckOfCards also declares int instance variable currentCard (line 8), representing the next Card to be dealt from the deck array, and named constant NUMBER_OF_CARDS (line 9), indicating the number of Cards in the deck (52).

```
1   // Fig. 8.10: DeckOfCards.cs
2   // DeckOfCards class represents a deck of playing cards.
3   using System;
4
5   public class DeckOfCards
6   {
```

Fig. 8.10 | DeckOfCards class represents a deck of playing cards. (Part 1 of 2.)

```
7     private Card[] deck; // array of Card objects
8     private int currentCard; // index of next Card to be dealt
9     private const int NUMBER_OF_CARDS = 52; // constant number of Cards
10    private Random randomNumbers; // random-number generator
11
12    // constructor fills deck of Cards
13    public DeckOfCards()
14    {
15       string[] faces = { "Ace", "Deuce", "Three", "Four", "Five", "Six",
16          "Seven", "Eight", "Nine", "Ten", "Jack", "Queen", "King" };
17       string[] suits = { "Hearts", "Diamonds", "Clubs", "Spades" };
18
19       deck = new Card[ NUMBER_OF_CARDS ]; // create array of Card objects
20       currentCard = 0; // set currentCard so deck[ 0 ] is dealt first
21       randomNumbers = new Random(); // create random-number generator
22
23       // populate deck with Card objects
24       for ( int count = 0; count < deck.Length; count++ )
25          deck[ count ] =
26             new Card( faces[ count % 13 ], suits[ count / 13 ] );
27    } // end DeckOfCards constructor
28
29    // shuffle deck of Cards with one-pass algorithm
30    public void Shuffle()
31    {
32       // after shuffling, dealing should start at deck[ 0 ] again
33       currentCard = 0; // reinitialize currentCard
34
35       // for each Card, pick another random Card and swap them
36       for ( int first = 0; first < deck.Length; first++ )
37       {
38          // select a random number between 0 and 51
39          int second = randomNumbers.Next( NUMBER_OF_CARDS );
40
41          // swap current Card with randomly selected Card
42          Card temp = deck[ first ];
43          deck[ first ] = deck[ second ];
44          deck[ second ] = temp;
45       } // end for
46    } // end method Shuffle
47
48    // deal one Card
49    public Card DealCard()
50    {
51       // determine whether Cards remain to be dealt
52       if ( currentCard < deck.Length )
53          return deck[ currentCard++ ]; // return current Card in array
54       else
55          return null; // indicate that all Cards were dealt
56    } // end method DealCard
57 } // end class DeckOfCards
```

Fig. 8.10 | DeckOfCards class represents a deck of playing cards. (Part 2 of 2.)

The class's constructor instantiates the deck array (line 19) to be of size NUMBER_OF_CARDS. When first created, the elements of the deck array are null by default, so the constructor uses a for statement (lines 24–26) to fill the deck array with Cards. The for statement initializes control variable count to 0 and loops while count is less than deck.Length, causing count to take on each integer value from 0 to 51 (the indices of the deck array). Each Card is instantiated and initialized with two strings—one from the faces array (which contains the strings "Ace" through "King") and one from the suits array (which contains the strings "Hearts", "Diamonds", "Clubs" and "Spades"). The calculation count % 13 always results in a value from 0 to 12 (the 13 indices of the faces array in lines 15–16), and the calculation count / 13 always results in a value from 0 to 3 (the four indices of the suits array in line 17). When the deck array is initialized, it contains the Cards with faces "Ace" through "King" in order for each suit.

Method Shuffle (lines 30–46) shuffles the Cards in the deck. The method loops through all 52 Cards (array indices 0 to 51). For each Card, a number between 0 and 51 is picked randomly to select another Card. Next, the current Card object and the randomly selected Card object are swapped in the array. This exchange is performed by the three assignments in lines 42–44. The extra variable temp temporarily stores one of the two Card objects being swapped. The swap cannot be performed with only the two statements

```
deck[ first ] = deck[ second ];
deck[ second ] = deck[ first ];
```

If deck[first] is the "Ace" of "Spades" and deck[second] is the "Queen" of "Hearts", then after the first assignment, both array elements contain the "Queen" of "Hearts", and the "Ace" of "Spades" is lost—hence, the extra variable temp is needed. After the for loop terminates, the Card objects are randomly ordered. Only 52 swaps are made in a single pass of the entire array, and the array of Card objects is shuffled. [*Note:* It's recommended that you use a so-called unbiased shuffling algorithm for real card games. Such an algorithm ensures that all possible shuffled card sequences are equally likely to occur. A popular unbiased shuffling algorithm is the Fisher-Yates algorithm—en.wikipedia.org/wiki/Fisher%E2%80%93Yates_shuffle. This page also shows how to implement the algorithm in several programming languages.]

Method DealCard (lines 49–56) deals one Card in the array. Recall that currentCard indicates the index of the next Card to be dealt (i.e., the Card at the top of the deck). Thus, line 52 compares currentCard to the length of the deck array. If the deck is not empty (i.e., currentCard is less than 52), line 53 returns the top Card and increments currentCard to prepare for the next call to DealCard—otherwise, null is returned.

Shuffling and Dealing Cards

The application of Fig. 8.11 demonstrates the card shuffling and dealing capabilities of class DeckOfCards (Fig. 8.10). Line 10 creates a DeckOfCards object named myDeckOfCards. Recall that the DeckOfCards constructor creates the deck with the 52 Card objects in order by suit and face. Line 11 invokes myDeckOfCards's Shuffle method to rearrange the Card objects. The for statement in lines 14–20 deals all 52 Cards in the deck and displays them in four columns of 13 Cards each. Line 16 deals and displays a Card object by invoking myDeckOfCards's DealCard method. When Console.Write outputs a Card with string formatting, the Card's ToString method (declared in lines 16–19 of Fig. 8.9) is invoked implicitly. Because the field width is negative, the result is output *left* justified in a field of width 19.

```
 1   // Fig. 8.11: DeckOfCardsTest.cs
 2   // Card shuffling and dealing application.
 3   using System;
 4
 5   public class DeckOfCardsTest
 6   {
 7      // execute application
 8      public static void Main( string[] args )
 9      {
10         DeckOfCards myDeckOfCards = new DeckOfCards();
11         myDeckOfCards.Shuffle(); // place Cards in random order
12
13         // display all 52 Cards in the order in which they are dealt
14         for ( int i = 0; i < 52; i++ )
15         {
16            Console.Write( "{0,-19}", myDeckOfCards.DealCard() );
17
18            if ( ( i + 1 ) % 4 == 0 )
19               Console.WriteLine();
20         } // end for
21      } // end Main
22   } // end class DeckOfCardsTest
```

Eight of Clubs	Ten of Clubs	Ten of Spades	Four of Spades
Ace of Spades	Jack of Spades	Three of Spades	Seven of Spades
Three of Diamonds	Five of Clubs	Eight of Spades	Five of Hearts
Ace of Hearts	Ten of Hearts	Deuce of Hearts	Deuce of Clubs
Jack of Hearts	Nine of Spades	Four of Hearts	Seven of Clubs
Queen of Spades	Seven of Diamonds	Five of Diamonds	Ace of Clubs
Four of Clubs	Ten of Diamonds	Jack of Clubs	Six of Diamonds
Eight of Diamonds	King of Hearts	Three of Clubs	King of Spades
King of Diamonds	Six of Spades	Deuce of Spades	Five of Spades
Queen of Clubs	King of Clubs	Queen of Hearts	Seven of Hearts
Ace of Diamonds	Deuce of Diamonds	Four of Diamonds	Nine of Clubs
Queen of Diamonds	Jack of Diamonds	Six of Hearts	Nine of Diamonds
Nine of Hearts	Three of Hearts	Six of Clubs	Eight of Hearts

Fig. 8.11 | Card shuffling and dealing application.

8.6 foreach Statement

In previous examples, we demonstrated how to use counter-controlled for statements to iterate through the elements in an array. In this section, we introduce the **foreach state-ment**, which iterates through the elements of an entire array or collection. This section dis-cusses how to use the foreach statement to loop through an array. We show how to use it with collections in Chapter 23. The syntax of a foreach statement is:

> **foreach** (*type identifier* **in** *arrayName*)
> *statement*

where *type* and *identifier* are the type and name (e.g., int number) of the **iteration variable**, and *arrayName* is the array through which to iterate. The type of the iteration variable must be consistent with the type of the elements in the array. As the next example illustrates, the iteration variable represents successive values in the array on successive iterations of the foreach statement.

Figure 8.12 uses the foreach statement (lines 13–14) to calculate the sum of the integers in an array of student grades. The type specified is int, because array contains int values—therefore, the loop will select one int value from the array during each iteration. The foreach statement iterates through successive values in the array one by one. The foreach header can be read concisely as "for each iteration, assign the next element of array to int variable number, then execute the following statement." Thus, for each iteration, identifier number represents the next int value in the array. Lines 13–14 are equivalent to the following counter-controlled repetition used in lines 13–14 of Fig. 8.5 to total the integers in array:

```
for ( int counter = 0; counter < array.Length; counter++ )
    total += array[ counter ];
```

Common Programming Error 8.4

The foreach statement can be used only to access array elements—it cannot be used to modify elements. Any attempt to change the value of the iteration variable in the body of a foreach statement will cause a compilation error.

```
1   // Fig. 8.12: ForEachTest.cs
2   // Using the foreach statement to total integers in an array.
3   using System;
4
5   public class ForEachTest
6   {
7      public static void Main( string[] args )
8      {
9         int[] array = { 87, 68, 94, 100, 83, 78, 85, 91, 76, 87 };
10        int total = 0;
11
12        // add each element's value to total
13        foreach ( int number in array )
14           total += number;
15
16        Console.WriteLine( "Total of array elements: {0}", total );
17     } // end Main
18  } // end class ForEachTest
```

```
Total of array elements: 849
```

Fig. 8.12 | Using the foreach statement to total integers in an array.

The foreach statement can be used in place of the for statement whenever code looping through an array does not require access to the counter indicating the index of the current array element. For example, totaling the integers in an array requires access only to the element values—the index of each element is irrelevant. However, if an application must use a counter for some reason other than simply to loop through an array (e.g., to display an index number next to each array element value, as in the examples earlier in this chapter), use the for statement.

Implicitly Typed Local Variables

In each for statement presented so far and in the foreach statement of Fig. 8.12, we declared the type of the control variable either in the for or foreach statement's header. C# provides a new feature—called **implicitly typed local variables**—that enables the compiler to infer a local variable's type based on the type of the variable's initializer. To distinguish such an initialization from a simple assignment statement, the **var** keyword is used in place of the variable's type. Recall that a local variable is any variable declared in the body of a method. In the declaration

```
var x = 7;
```

the compiler infers that the variable x should be of type int, because the compiler assumes that whole-number values, like 7, are of type int. Similarly, in the declaration

```
var y = -123.45;
```

the compiler infers that the variable y should be of type double, because the compiler assumes that floating-point number values, like -123.45, are of type double.

You can also use local type inference with control variables in the header of a for or foreach statement. For example, the for statement header

```
for ( int counter = 1; counter < 10; counter++ )
```

can be written as

```
for ( var counter = 1; counter < 10; counter++ )
```

In this case, counter is of type int because it's initialized with a whole-number value (1). Similarly, assuming that myArray is an array of ints, the foreach statement header

```
foreach ( int number in myArray )
```

can be written as

```
foreach ( var number in myArray )
```

In this case, number is of type int because it's used to process elements of the int array myArray. The implicitly typed local-variable feature is one of several new Visual C# 2010 features that support Language Integrated Query (LINQ).

Implicitly typed local variables can be also used to initialize arrays without explicitly giving their type. For example, the following statement creates an array of int values:

```
var array = new[] { 32, 27, 64, 18, 95, 14, 90, 70, 60, 37 };
```

There are no square brackets on the left side of the assignment operator, and that new[] is used to specify that the variable is an array. We'll use implicitly typed local variables when we present LINQ examples in Chapter 9 and several later chapters.

8.7 Passing Arrays and Array Elements to Methods

To pass an array argument to a method, specify the name of the array without any brackets. For example, if hourlyTemperatures is declared as

```
double[] hourlyTemperatures = new double[ 24 ];
```

then the method call

```
    ModifyArray( hourlyTemperatures );
```

passes the reference of array `hourlyTemperatures` to method `ModifyArray`. Every array object "knows" its own length (and makes it available via its `Length` property). Thus, when we pass an array object's reference to a method, we need not pass the array length as an additional argument.

For a method to receive an array reference through a method call, the method's parameter list must specify an array parameter. For example, the method header for method `ModifyArray` might be written as

```
    void ModifyArray( double[] b )
```

indicating that `ModifyArray` receives the reference of an array of `double`s in parameter `b`. The method call passes array `hourlyTemperature`'s reference, so when the called method uses the array variable `b`, it refers to the same array object as `hourlyTemperatures` in the calling method.

When an argument to a method is an entire array or an individual array element of a reference type, the called method receives a copy of the reference. However, when an argument to a method is an individual array element of a value type, the called method receives a copy of the element's value. To pass an individual array element to a method, use the indexed name of the array as an argument in the method call. If you want to pass a value-type array element to a method by reference, you must use the `ref` keyword as shown in Section 7.16.

Figure 8.13 demonstrates the difference between passing an entire array and passing a value-type array element to a method. The `foreach` statement at lines 17–18 outputs the five elements of array (an array of `int` values). Line 20 invokes method `ModifyArray`, passing array as an argument. Method `ModifyArray` (lines 37–41) receives a copy of array's reference and uses the reference to multiply each of array's elements by 2. To prove that array's elements (in `Main`) were modified, the `foreach` statement at lines 24–25 outputs the five elements of array again. As the output shows, method `ModifyArray` doubled the value of each element.

```
 1   // Fig. 8.13: PassArray.cs
 2   // Passing arrays and individual array elements to methods.
 3   using System;
 4
 5   public class PassArray
 6   {
 7      // Main creates array and calls ModifyArray and ModifyElement
 8      public static void Main( string[] args )
 9      {
10         int[] array = { 1, 2, 3, 4, 5 };
11
12         Console.WriteLine(
13            "Effects of passing reference to entire array:\n" +
14            "The values of the original array are:" );
15
```

Fig. 8.13 | Passing arrays and individual array elements to methods. (Part 1 of 2.)

```
16          // output original array elements
17          foreach ( int value in array )
18             Console.Write( "   {0}", value );
19
20          ModifyArray( array ); // pass array reference
21          Console.WriteLine( "\n\nThe values of the modified array are:" );
22
23          // output modified array elements
24          foreach ( int value in array )
25             Console.Write( "   {0}", value );
26
27          Console.WriteLine(
28             "\n\nEffects of passing array element value:\n" +
29             "array[3] before ModifyElement: {0}", array[ 3 ] );
30
31          ModifyElement( array[ 3 ] ); // attempt to modify array[ 3 ]
32          Console.WriteLine(
33             "array[3] after ModifyElement: {0}", array[ 3 ] );
34       } // end Main
35
36       // multiply each element of an array by 2
37       public static void ModifyArray( int[] array2 )
38       {
39          for ( int counter = 0; counter < array2.Length; counter++ )
40             array2[ counter ] *= 2;
41       } // end method ModifyArray
42
43       // multiply argument by 2
44       public static void ModifyElement( int element )
45       {
46          element *= 2;
47          Console.WriteLine(
48             "Value of element in ModifyElement: {0}", element );
49       } // end method ModifyElement
50    } // end class PassArray
```

```
Effects of passing reference to entire array:
The values of the original array are:
   1    2    3    4    5

The values of the modified array are:
   2    4    6    8    10

Effects of passing array element value:
array[3] before ModifyElement: 8
Value of element in ModifyElement: 16
array[3] after ModifyElement: 8
```

Fig. 8.13 | Passing arrays and individual array elements to methods. (Part 2 of 2.)

Figure 8.13 next demonstrates that when a copy of an individual value-type array element is passed to a method, modifying the copy in the called method does not affect the original value of that element in the calling method's array. To show the value of array[3] before invoking method ModifyElement, lines 27–29 output the value of array[3], which is 8. Line 31 calls method ModifyElement and passes array[3] as an argument. Remember that array[3] is actually one int value (8) in array. Therefore, the application passes a copy of the value of array[3]. Method ModifyElement (lines 44–49) multiplies the value received as an argument by 2, stores the result in its parameter element, then outputs the value of element (16). Since method parameters, like local variables, cease to exist when the method in which they're declared completes execution, the method parameter element is destroyed when method ModifyElement terminates. Thus, when the application returns control to Main, lines 32–33 output the unmodified value of array[3] (i.e., 8).

8.8 Passing Arrays by Value and by Reference

In C#, a variable that "stores" an object, such as an array, does not actually store the object itself. Instead, such a variable stores a reference to the object. The distinction between reference-type variables and value-type variables raises some subtle issues that you must understand to create secure, stable programs.

As you know, when an application passes an argument to a method, the called method receives a copy of that argument's value. Changes to the local copy in the called method do not affect the original variable in the caller. If the argument is of a reference type, the method makes a copy of the reference, not a copy of the actual object that's referenced. The local copy of the reference also refers to the original object, which means that changes to the object in the called method affect the original object.

Performance Tip 8.1

Passing arrays and other objects by reference makes sense for performance reasons. If arrays were passed by value, a copy of each element would be passed. For large, frequently passed arrays, this would waste time and would consume considerable storage for the copies of the arrays—both of these problems cause poor performance.

In Section 7.16, you learned that C# allows variables to be passed by reference with keyword ref. You can also use keyword ref to pass a reference-type variable *by reference*, which allows the called method to modify the original variable in the caller and make that variable refer to a different object. This is a subtle capability, which, if misused, can lead to problems. For instance, when a reference-type object like an array is passed with ref, the called method actually gains control over the reference itself, allowing the called method to replace the original reference in the caller with a reference to a different object, or even with null. Such behavior can lead to unpredictable effects, which can be disastrous in mission-critical applications. The application in Fig. 8.14 demonstrates the subtle difference between passing a reference by value and passing a reference by reference with keyword ref.

```
1   // Fig. 8.14: ArrayReferenceTest.cs
2   // Testing the effects of passing array references
3   // by value and by reference.
4   using System;
5
6   public class ArrayReferenceTest
7   {
```

Fig. 8.14 | Passing an array reference by value and by reference. (Part 1 of 4.)

```
 8      public static void Main( string[] args )
 9      {
10         // create and initialize firstArray
11         int[] firstArray = { 1, 2, 3 };
12
13         // copy the reference in variable firstArray
14         int[] firstArrayCopy = firstArray;
15
16         Console.WriteLine(
17            "Test passing firstArray reference by value" );
18
19         Console.Write( "\nContents of firstArray " +
20            "before calling FirstDouble:\n\t" );
21
22         // display contents of firstArray
23         for ( int i = 0; i < firstArray.Length; i++ )
24            Console.Write( "{0} ", firstArray[ i ] );
25
26         // pass variable firstArray by value to FirstDouble
27         FirstDouble( firstArray );
28
29         Console.Write( "\n\nContents of firstArray after " +
30            "calling FirstDouble\n\t" );
31
32         // display contents of firstArray
33         for ( int i = 0; i < firstArray.Length; i++ )
34            Console.Write( "{0} ", firstArray[ i ] );
35
36         // test whether reference was changed by FirstDouble
37         if ( firstArray == firstArrayCopy )
38            Console.WriteLine(
39               "\n\nThe references refer to the same array" );
40         else
41            Console.WriteLine(
42               "\n\nThe references refer to different arrays" );
43
44         // create and initialize secondArray
45         int[] secondArray = { 1, 2, 3 };
46
47         // copy the reference in variable secondArray
48         int[] secondArrayCopy = secondArray;
49
50         Console.WriteLine( "\nTest passing secondArray " +
51            "reference by reference" );
52
53         Console.Write( "\nContents of secondArray " +
54            "before calling SecondDouble:\n\t" );
55
56         // display contents of secondArray before method call
57         for ( int i = 0; i < secondArray.Length; i++ )
58            Console.Write( "{0} ", secondArray[ i ] );
59
```

Fig. 8.14 | Passing an array reference by value and by reference. (Part 2 of 4.)

```
60          // pass variable secondArray by reference to SecondDouble
61          SecondDouble( ref secondArray );
62
63          Console.Write( "\n\nContents of secondArray " +
64             "after calling SecondDouble:\n\t" );
65
66          // display contents of secondArray after method call
67          for ( int i = 0; i < secondArray.Length; i++ )
68             Console.Write( "{0} ", secondArray[ i ] );
69
70          // test whether reference was changed by SecondDouble
71          if ( secondArray == secondArrayCopy )
72             Console.WriteLine(
73                "\n\nThe references refer to the same array" );
74          else
75             Console.WriteLine(
76                "\n\nThe references refer to different arrays" );
77       } // end Main
78
79       // modify elements of array and attempt to modify reference
80       public static void FirstDouble( int[] array )
81       {
82          // double each element's value
83          for ( int i = 0; i < array.Length; i++ )
84             array[ i ] *= 2;
85
86          // create new object and assign its reference to array
87          array = new int[] { 11, 12, 13 };
88       } // end method FirstDouble
89
90       // modify elements of array and change reference array
91       // to refer to a new array
92       public static void SecondDouble( ref int[] array )
93       {
94          // double each element's value
95          for ( int i = 0; i < array.Length; i++ )
96             array[ i ] *= 2;
97
98          // create new object and assign its reference to array
99          array = new int[] { 11, 12, 13 };
100      } // end method SecondDouble
101   } // end class ArrayReferenceTest
```

```
Test passing firstArray reference by value

Contents of firstArray before calling FirstDouble:
      1 2 3

Contents of firstArray after calling FirstDouble
      2 4 6

The references refer to the same array
```

Fig. 8.14 | Passing an array reference by value and by reference. (Part 3 of 4.)

```
Test passing secondArray reference by reference

Contents of secondArray before calling SecondDouble:
     1 2 3

Contents of secondArray after calling SecondDouble:
     11 12 13

The references refer to different arrays
```

Fig. 8.14 | Passing an array reference by value and by reference. (Part 4 of 4.)

Lines 11 and 14 declare two integer array variables, firstArray and firstArrayCopy. Line 11 initializes firstArray with the values 1, 2 and 3. The assignment statement at line 14 copies the reference stored in firstArray to variable firstArrayCopy, causing these variables to reference the same array object. We make the copy of the reference so that we can determine later whether reference firstArray gets overwritten. The for statement at lines 23–24 displays the contents of firstArray before it's passed to method FirstDouble (line 27) so that we can verify that the called method indeed changes the array's contents.

The for statement in method FirstDouble (lines 83–84) multiplies the values of all the elements in the array by 2. Line 87 creates a new array containing the values 11, 12 and 13, and assigns the array's reference to parameter array in an attempt to overwrite reference firstArray in the caller—this, of course, does not happen, because the reference was passed by value. After method FirstDouble executes, the for statement at lines 33–34 displays the contents of firstArray, demonstrating that the values of the elements have been changed by the method. The if...else statement at lines 37–42 uses the == operator to compare references firstArray (which we just attempted to overwrite) and firstArrayCopy. The expression in line 37 evaluates to true if the operands of operator == reference the same object. In this case, the object represented by firstArray is the array created in line 11—not the array created in method FirstDouble (line 87)—so the original reference stored in firstArray was not modified.

Lines 45–76 perform similar tests, using array variables secondArray and secondArrayCopy, and method SecondDouble (lines 92–100). Method SecondDouble performs the same operations as FirstDouble, but receives its array argument using keyword ref. In this case, the reference stored in secondArray after the method call is a reference to the array created in line 99 of SecondDouble, demonstrating that a variable passed with keyword ref can be modified by the called method so that the variable in the caller actually points to a different object—in this case, an array created in SecondDouble. The if...else statement in lines 71–76 confirms that secondArray and secondArrayCopy no longer refer to the same array.

Software Engineering Observation 8.1

When a method receives a reference-type parameter by value, a copy of the object's reference is passed. This prevents a method from overwriting references passed to that method. In the vast majority of cases, protecting the caller's reference from modification is the desired behavior. If you encounter a situation where you truly want the called procedure to modify the caller's reference, pass the reference-type parameter using keyword ref—but, again, such situations are rare.

Software Engineering Observation 8.2

In C#, objects (including arrays) are effectively passed by reference, because references to objects are passed to called methods. A called method receiving a reference to an object in a caller can interact with, and possibly change, the caller's object.

8.9 Case Study: Class GradeBook Using an Array to Store Grades

This section further evolves class GradeBook, introduced in Chapter 4 and expanded in Chapters 5–6. Recall that this class represents a grade book used by an instructor to store and analyze a set of student grades. Previous versions of the class process a set of grades entered by the user, but do not maintain the individual grade values in instance variables of the class. Thus, repeat calculations require the user to re-enter the same grades. One way to solve this problem would be to store each grade entered in an individual instance of the class. For example, we could create instance variables grade1, grade2, ..., grade10 in class GradeBook to store 10 student grades. However, the code to total the grades and determine the class average would be cumbersome, and the class would not be able to process any more than 10 grades at a time. In this section, we solve this problem by storing grades in an array.

*Storing Student Grades in an Array in Class **GradeBook***

The version of class GradeBook (Fig. 8.15) presented here uses an array of integers to store the grades of several students on a single exam. This eliminates the need to repeatedly input the same set of grades. Variable grades (which will refer to an array of ints) is declared as an instance variable in line 7—therefore, each GradeBook object maintains its own set of grades. The class's constructor (lines 14–18) has two parameters—the name of the course and an array of grades. When an application (e.g., class GradeBookTest in Fig. 8.16) creates a GradeBook object, the application passes an existing int array to the constructor, which assigns the array's reference to instance variable grades (line 17). The size of array grades is determined by the class that passes the array to the constructor.

```
 1   // Fig. 8.15: GradeBook.cs
 2   // Grade book using an array to store test grades.
 3   using System;
 4
 5   public class GradeBook
 6   {
 7      private int[] grades; // array of student grades
 8
 9      // auto-implemented property CourseName
10      public string CourseName { get; set; }
11
12      // two-parameter constructor initializes
13      // auto-implemented property CourseName and grades array
14      public GradeBook( string name, int[] gradesArray )
15      {
16         CourseName = name; // set CourseName to name
```

Fig. 8.15 | Grade book using an array to store test grades. (Part 1 of 4.)

```
17            grades = gradesArray; // initialize grades array
18        } // end two-parameter GradeBook constructor
19
20        // display a welcome message to the GradeBook user
21        public void DisplayMessage()
22        {
23            // auto-implemented property CourseName gets the name of course
24            Console.WriteLine( "Welcome to the grade book for\n{0}!\n",
25                CourseName );
26        } // end method DisplayMessage
27
28        // perform various operations on the data
29        public void ProcessGrades()
30        {
31            // output grades array
32            OutputGrades();
33
34            // call method GetAverage to calculate the average grade
35            Console.WriteLine( "\nClass average is {0:F}", GetAverage() );
36
37            // call methods GetMinimum and GetMaximum
38            Console.WriteLine( "Lowest grade is {0}\nHighest grade is {1}\n",
39                GetMinimum(), GetMaximum() );
40
41            // call OutputBarChart to display grade distribution chart
42            OutputBarChart();
43        } // end method ProcessGrades
44
45        // find minimum grade
46        public int GetMinimum()
47        {
48            int lowGrade = grades[ 0 ]; // assume grades[ 0 ] is smallest
49
50            // loop through grades array
51            foreach ( int grade in grades )
52            {
53                // if grade lower than lowGrade, assign it to lowGrade
54                if ( grade < lowGrade )
55                    lowGrade = grade; // new lowest grade
56            } // end for
57
58            return lowGrade; // return lowest grade
59        } // end method GetMinimum
60
61        // find maximum grade
62        public int GetMaximum()
63        {
64            int highGrade = grades[ 0 ]; // assume grades[ 0 ] is largest
65
66            // loop through grades array
67            foreach ( int grade in grades )
68            {
```

Fig. 8.15 | Grade book using an array to store test grades. (Part 2 of 4.)

```
69            // if grade greater than highGrade, assign it to highGrade
70            if ( grade > highGrade )
71               highGrade = grade; // new highest grade
72         } // end for
73
74         return highGrade; // return highest grade
75      } // end method GetMaximum
76
77      // determine average grade for test
78      public double GetAverage()
79      {
80         int total = 0; // initialize total
81
82         // sum grades for one student
83         foreach ( int grade in grades )
84            total += grade;
85
86         // return average of grades
87         return ( double ) total / grades.Length;
88      } // end method GetAverage
89
90      // output bar chart displaying grade distribution
91      public void OutputBarChart()
92      {
93         Console.WriteLine( "Grade distribution:" );
94
95         // stores frequency of grades in each range of 10 grades
96         int[] frequency = new int[ 11 ];
97
98         // for each grade, increment the appropriate frequency
99         foreach ( int grade in grades )
100           ++frequency[ grade / 10 ];
101
102        // for each grade frequency, display bar in chart
103        for ( int count = 0; count < frequency.Length; count++ )
104        {
105           // output bar label ( "00-09: ", ..., "90-99: ", "100: " )
106           if ( count == 10 )
107              Console.Write( "  100: " );
108           else
109              Console.Write( "{0:D2}-{1:D2}: ",
110                 count * 10, count * 10 + 9 );
111
112           // display bar of asterisks
113           for ( int stars = 0; stars < frequency[ count ]; stars++ )
114              Console.Write( "*" );
115
116           Console.WriteLine(); // start a new line of output
117        } // end outer for
118     } // end method OutputBarChart
119
```

Fig. 8.15 | Grade book using an array to store test grades. (Part 3 of 4.)

```
120      // output the contents of the grades array
121      public void OutputGrades()
122      {
123         Console.WriteLine( "The grades are:\n" );
124
125         // output each student's grade
126         for ( int student = 0; student < grades.Length; student++ )
127            Console.WriteLine( "Student {0,2}: {1,3}",
128               student + 1, grades[ student ] );
129      } // end method OutputGrades
130   } // end class GradeBook
```

Fig. 8.15 | Grade book using an array to store test grades. (Part 4 of 4.)

Thus, a GradeBook object can process a variable number of grades—as many as are in the array in the caller. The grade values in the passed array could have been input from a user at the keyboard or read from a file on disk (as discussed in Chapter 17). In our test application, we simply initialize an array with a set of grade values (Fig. 8.16, line 9). Once the grades are stored in instance variable grades of class GradeBook, all the class's methods can access the elements of grades as needed to perform various calculations.

Method ProcessGrades (lines 29–43) contains a series of method calls that result in the output of a report summarizing the grades. Line 32 calls method OutputGrades to display the contents of array grades. Lines 126–128 in method OutputGrades use a for statement to output the student grades. A for statement, rather than a foreach, must be used in this case, because lines 127–128 use counter variable student's value to output each grade next to a particular student number (see Fig. 8.16). Although array indices start at 0, an instructor would typically number students starting at 1. Thus, lines 127–128 output student + 1 as the student number to produce grade labels "Student 1: ", "Student 2: " and so on.

Method ProcessGrades next calls method GetAverage (line 35) to obtain the average of the grades in the array. Method GetAverage (lines 78–88) uses a foreach statement to total the values in array grades before calculating the average. The iteration variable in the foreach's header (e.g., int grade) indicates that for each iteration, int variable grade takes on a value in array grades. The averaging calculation in line 87 uses grades.Length to determine the number of grades being averaged.

Lines 38–39 in method ProcessGrades call methods GetMinimum and GetMaximum to determine the lowest and highest grades of any student on the exam, respectively. Each of these methods uses a foreach statement to loop through array grades. Lines 51–56 in method GetMinimum loop through the array, and lines 54–55 compare each grade to lowGrade. If a grade is less than lowGrade, lowGrade is set to that grade. When line 58 executes, lowGrade contains the lowest grade in the array. Method GetMaximum (lines 62–75) works the same way as method GetMinimum.

Finally, line 42 in method ProcessGrades calls method OutputBarChart to display a distribution chart of the grade data, using a technique similar to that in Fig. 8.6. In that example, we manually calculated the number of grades in each category (i.e., 0–9, 10–19, ..., 90–99 and 100) by simply looking at a set of grades. In this example, lines 99–100 use a technique similar to that in Figs. 8.7 and 8.8 to calculate the frequency of grades in each category. Line 96 declares variable frequency and initializes it with an array of 11 ints to store the frequency of grades in each grade category. For each grade in array grades, lines 99–100 increment the appropriate element of the frequency array. To determine which element to increment, line 100 divides the current grade by 10, using integer division. For example, if grade is 85, line 100 increments frequency[8] to update the count of grades in the range 80–89. Lines 103–117 next display the bar chart (see Fig. 8.6) based on the values in array frequency. Like lines 24–25 of Fig. 8.6, lines 113–114 of Fig. 8.15 use a value in array frequency to determine the number of asterisks to display in each bar.

Class *GradeBookTest* That Demonstrates Class *GradeBook*

The application of Fig. 8.16 creates an object of class GradeBook (Fig. 8.15) using int array gradesArray (declared and initialized in line 9). Lines 11–12 pass a course name and gradesArray to the GradeBook constructor. Line 13 displays a welcome message, and line 14 invokes the GradeBook object's ProcessGrades method. The output reveals the summary of the 10 grades in myGradeBook.

Software Engineering Observation 8.3

A test harness (or test application) is responsible for creating an object of the class being tested and providing it with data. This data could come from any of several sources. Test data can be placed directly into an array with an array initializer, it can come from the user at the keyboard or it can come from a file (as you'll see in Chapter 17). After passing this data to the class's constructor to instantiate the object, the test harness should call the object to test its methods and manipulate its data. Gathering data in the test harness like this allows the class to manipulate data from several sources.

```
1  // Fig. 8.16: GradeBookTest.cs
2  // Create GradeBook object using an array of grades.
3  public class GradeBookTest
4  {
5     // Main method begins application execution
6     public static void Main( string[] args )
7     {
8        // one-dimensional array of student grades
9        int[] gradesArray = { 87, 68, 94, 100, 83, 78, 85, 91, 76, 87 };
10
11       GradeBook myGradeBook = new GradeBook(
12          "CS101 Introduction to C# Programming", gradesArray );
13       myGradeBook.DisplayMessage();
14       myGradeBook.ProcessGrades();
15    } // end Main
16 } // end class GradeBookTest
```

```
Welcome to the grade book for
CS101 Introduction to C# Programming!

The grades are:

Student  1:  87
Student  2:  68
Student  3:  94
```

Fig. 8.16 | Create a GradeBook object using an array of grades. (Part 1 of 2.)

```
Student  4: 100
Student  5:  83
Student  6:  78
Student  7:  85
Student  8:  91
Student  9:  76
Student 10:  87

Class average is 84.90
Lowest grade is 68
Highest grade is 100

Grade distribution:
00-09:
10-19:
20-29:
30-39:
40-49:
50-59:
60-69: *
70-79: **
80-89: ****
90-99: **
  100: *
```

Fig. 8.16 | Create a `GradeBook` object using an array of grades. (Part 2 of 2.)

8.10 Multidimensional Arrays

Multidimensional arrays with two dimensions are often used to represent **tables of values** consisting of information arranged in **rows** and **columns**. To identify a particular table element, we must specify two indices. By convention, the first identifies the element's row and the second its column. Arrays that require two indices to identify a particular element are called **two-dimensional arrays**. (Multidimensional arrays can have more than two dimensions, but such arrays are beyond the scope of this book.) C# supports two types of two-dimensional arrays—**rectangular arrays** and **jagged arrays**.

Rectangular Arrays
Rectangular arrays are used to represent tables of information in the form of rows and columns, where each row has the same number of columns. Figure 8.17 illustrates a rectangular array named a containing three rows and four columns—a three-by-four array. In general, an array with m rows and n columns is called an *m-by-n* **array**.

Every element in array a is identified in Fig. 8.17 by an array-access expression of the form a[*row*, *column*]; a is the name of the array, and *row* and *column* are the indices that uniquely identify each element in array a by row and column number. The names of the elements in row 0 all have a first index of 0, and the names of the elements in column 3 all have a second index of 3.

Like one-dimensional arrays, multidimensional arrays can be initialized with array initializers in declarations. A rectangular array b with two rows and two columns could be declared and initialized with **nested array initializers** as follows:

```
int[ , ] b = { { 1, 2 }, { 3, 4 } };
```

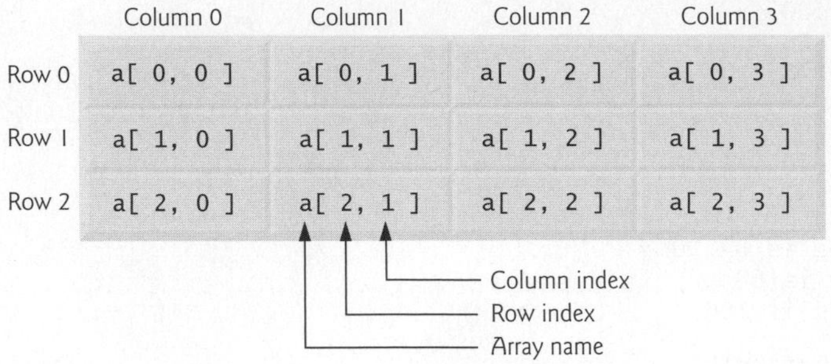

Fig. 8.17 | Rectangular array with three rows and four columns.

The initializer values are grouped by row in braces. So 1 and 2 initialize b[0, 0] and b[0, 1], respectively, and 3 and 4 initialize b[1, 0] and b[1, 1], respectively. The compiler counts the number of nested array initializers (represented by sets of two inner braces within the outer braces) in the initializer list to determine the number of rows in array b. The compiler counts the initializer values in the nested array initializer for a row to determine the number of columns (two) in that row. The compiler will generate an error if the number of initializers in each row is not the same, because every row of a rectangular array must have the same length.

Jagged Arrays

A **jagged array** is maintained as a one-dimensional array in which each element refers to a one-dimensional array. The manner in which jagged arrays are represented makes them quite flexible, because the lengths of the rows in the array need not be the same. For example, jagged arrays could be used to store a single student's exam grades across multiple classes, where the number of exams may vary from class to class.

We can access the elements in a jagged array by an array-access expression of the form *arrayName*[*row*] [*column*]—similar to the array-access expression for rectangular arrays, but with a separate set of square brackets for each dimension. A jagged array with three rows of different lengths could be declared and initialized as follows:

```
int[][] jagged = { new int[] { 1, 2 },
                   new int[] { 3 },
                   new int[] { 4, 5, 6 } };
```

In this statement, 1 and 2 initialize jagged[0][0] and jagged[0][1], respectively; 3 initializes jagged[1][0]; and 4, 5 and 6 initialize jagged[2][0], jagged[2][1] and jagged[2][2], respectively. Therefore, array jagged in the preceding declaration is actually composed of four separate one-dimensional arrays—one that represents the rows, one containing the values in the first row ({1, 2}), one containing the value in the second row ({3}) and one containing the values in the third row ({4, 5, 6}). Thus, array jagged itself is an array of three elements, each a reference to a one-dimensional array of int values.

Observe the differences between the array-creation expressions for rectangular arrays and for jagged arrays. Two sets of square brackets follow the type of jagged, indicating that this is an array of int arrays. Furthermore, in the array initializer, C# requires the keyword new to create an array object for each row. Figure 8.18 illustrates the array reference jagged after it's been declared and initialized.

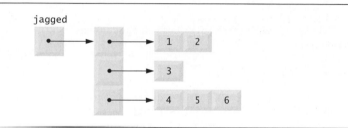

Fig. 8.18 | Jagged array with three rows of different lengths.

Creating Two-Dimensional Arrays with Array-Creation Expressions
A rectangular array can be created with an array-creation expression. For example, the following lines declare variable b and assign it a reference to a three-by-four rectangular array:

```
int[ , ] b;
b = new int[ 3, 4 ];
```

In this case, we use the literal values 3 and 4 to specify the number of rows and number of columns, respectively, but this is not required—applications can also use variables and expressions to specify array dimensions. As with one-dimensional arrays, the elements of a rectangular array are initialized when the array object is created.

A jagged array cannot be completely created with a single array-creation expression. The following statement is a syntax error:

```
int[][] c = new int[ 2 ][ 5 ]; // error
```

Instead, each one-dimensional array in the jagged array must be initialized separately. A jagged array can be created as follows:

```
int[][] c;
c = new int[ 2 ][ ]; // create 2 rows
c[ 0 ] = new int[ 5 ]; // create 5 columns for row 0
c[ 1 ] = new int[ 3 ]; // create 3 columns for row 1
```

The preceding statements create a jagged array with two rows. Row 0 has five columns, and row 1 has three columns.

Two-Dimensional Array Example: Displaying Element Values
Figure 8.19 demonstrates initializing rectangular and jagged arrays with array initializers and using nested for loops to **traverse** the arrays (i.e., visit every element of each array).

Class InitArray's Main method creates two arrays. Line 12 uses nested array initializers to initialize variable rectangular with an array in which row 0 has the values 1, 2 and 3, and row 1 has the values 4, 5 and 6. Lines 17–19 uses nested initializers of different lengths to initialize variable jagged. In this case, the initializer uses the keyword new to create a one-dimensional array for each row. Row 0 is initialized to have two elements with values 1 and 2, respectively. Row 1 is initialized to have one element with value 3. Row 2 is initialized to have three elements with the values 4, 5 and 6, respectively.

Method OutputArray has been overloaded with two versions. The first version (lines 27–40) specifies the array parameter as int[,] array to indicate that it takes a rectangular array. The second version (lines 43–56) takes a jagged array, because its array parameter is listed as int[][] array.

```csharp
 1    // Fig. 8.19: InitArray.cs
 2    // Initializing rectangular and jagged arrays.
 3    using System;
 4
 5    public class InitArray
 6    {
 7       // create and output rectangular and jagged arrays
 8       public static void Main( string[] args )
 9       {
10          // with rectangular arrays,
11          // every column must be the same length.
12          int[ , ] rectangular = { { 1, 2, 3 }, { 4, 5, 6 } };
13
14          // with jagged arrays,
15          // we need to use "new int[]" for every row,
16          // but every column does not need to be the same length.
17          int[][] jagged = { new int[] { 1, 2 },
18                             new int[] { 3 },
19                             new int[] { 4, 5, 6 } };
20
21          OutputArray( rectangular ); // displays array rectangular by row
22          Console.WriteLine(); // output a blank line
23          OutputArray( jagged ); // displays array jagged by row
24       } // end Main
25
26       // output rows and columns of a rectangular array
27       public static void OutputArray( int[ , ] array )
28       {
29          Console.WriteLine( "Values in the rectangular array by row are" );
30
31          // loop through array's rows
32          for ( int row = 0; row < array.GetLength( 0 ); row++ )
33          {
34             // loop through columns of current row
35             for ( int column = 0; column < array.GetLength( 1 ); column++ )
36                Console.Write( "{0}  ", array[ row, column ] );
37
38             Console.WriteLine(); // start new line of output
39          } // end outer for
40       } // end method OutputArray
41
42       // output rows and columns of a jagged array
43       public static void OutputArray( int[][] array )
44       {
45          Console.WriteLine( "Values in the jagged array by row are" );
46
47          // loop through each row
48          foreach ( var row in array )
49          {
50             // loop through each element in current row
51             foreach ( var element in row )
52                Console.Write( "{0}  ", element );
53
```

Fig. 8.19 | Initializing jagged and rectangular arrays. (Part 1 of 2.)

```
54                  Console.WriteLine(); // start new line of output
55              } // end outer foreach
56          } // end method OutputArray
57      } // end class InitArray
```

```
Values in the rectangular array by row are
1  2  3
4  5  6

Values in the jagged array by row are
1  2
3
4  5  6
```

Fig. 8.19 | Initializing jagged and rectangular arrays. (Part 2 of 2.)

Line 21 invokes method OutputArray with argument rectangular, so the version of OutputArray at lines 27–40 is called. The nested for statement (lines 32–39) outputs the rows of a rectangular array. The loop-continuation condition of each for statement (lines 32 and 35) uses the rectangular array's GetLength method to obtain the length of each dimension. Dimensions are numbered starting from 0, so the method call GetLength(0) on array returns the size of the first dimension of the array (the number of rows), and the call GetLength(1) returns the size of the second dimension (the number of columns).

Line 23 invokes method OutputArray with argument jagged, so the version of OutputArray at lines 43–56 is called. The nested foreach statement (lines 48–55) outputs the rows of a jagged array. The inner foreach statement (lines 51–52) iterates through each element in the current row of the array. This allows the loop to determine the exact number of columns in each row. Since the jagged array is created as an array of arrays, we can use nested foreach statements to output the elements in the console window. The outer loop iterates through the elements of array, which are references to one-dimensional arrays of int values that represent each row. The inner loop iterates through the elements of the current row. A foreach statement can also iterate through all the elements in a rectangular array. In this case, foreach iterates through all the rows and columns starting from row 0, as if the elements were in a one-dimensional array.

*Common Multidimensional-Array Manipulations Performed with **for** Statements*
Many common array manipulations use for statements. As an example, the following for statement sets all the elements in row 2 of rectangular array a in Fig. 8.17 to 0:

```
for ( int column = 0; column < a.GetLength( 1 ); column++)
    a[ 2, column ] = 0;
```

We specified row 2; therefore, we know that the first index is always 2 (0 is the first row, and 1 is the second row). This for loop varies only the second index (i.e., the column index). The preceding for statement is equivalent to the assignment statements

```
a[ 2, 0 ] = 0;
a[ 2, 1 ] = 0;
a[ 2, 2 ] = 0;
a[ 2, 3 ] = 0;
```

The following nested for statement totals the values of all the elements in array a:

```
int total = 0;
for ( int row = 0; row < a.GetLength( 0 ); row++ )
{
    for ( int column = 0; column < a.GetLength( 1 ); column++ )
        total += a[ row, column ];
} // end outer for
```

These nested for statements total the array elements one row at a time. The outer for statement begins by setting the row index to 0 so that row 0's elements can be totaled by the inner for statement. The outer for then increments row to 1 so that row 1's elements can be totaled. Then the outer for increments row to 2 so that row 2's elements can be totaled. The variable total can be displayed when the outer for statement terminates. In the next example, we show how to process a rectangular array in a more concise manner using foreach statements.

8.11 Case Study: GradeBook Using a Rectangular Array

In Section 8.9, we presented class GradeBook (Fig. 8.15), which used a one-dimensional array to store student grades on a single exam. In most courses, students take several exams. Instructors are likely to want to analyze grades across the entire course, both for a single student and for the class as a whole.

*Storing Student Grades in a Rectangular Array in Class **GradeBook***
Figure 8.20 contains a version of class GradeBook that uses a rectangular array grades to store the grades of a number of students on multiple exams. Each row of the array represents a single student's grades for the entire course, and each column represents the grades for the whole class on one of the exams the students took during the course. An application such as GradeBookTest (Fig. 8.21) passes the array as an argument to the GradeBook constructor. In this example, we use a 10-by-3 array containing 10 students' grades on three exams. Five methods perform array manipulations to process the grades. Each method is similar to its counterpart in the earlier one-dimensional-array version of class GradeBook (Fig. 8.15). Method GetMinimum (lines 44–58) determines the lowest grade of any student for the semester. Method GetMaximum (lines 61–75) determines the highest grade of any student for the semester. Method GetAverage (lines 78–90) determines a particular student's semester average. Method OutputBarChart (lines 93–122) outputs a bar chart of the distribution of all student grades for the semester. Method OutputGrades (lines 125–149) outputs the two-dimensional array in tabular format, along with each student's semester average.

```
1   // Fig. 8.20: GradeBook.cs
2   // Grade book using rectangular array to store grades.
3   using System;
4
5   public class GradeBook
6   {
7       private int[ , ] grades; // rectangular array of student grades
```

Fig. 8.20 | Grade book using rectangular array to store grades. (Part 1 of 4.)

```
 8
 9      // auto-implemented property CourseName
10      public string CourseName { get; set; }
11
12      // two-parameter constructor initializes
13      // auto-implemented property CourseName and grades array
14      public GradeBook( string name, int[ , ] gradesArray )
15      {
16         CourseName = name; // set CourseName to name
17         grades = gradesArray; // initialize grades array
18      } // end two-parameter GradeBook constructor
19
20      // display a welcome message to the GradeBook user
21      public void DisplayMessage()
22      {
23         // auto-implemented property CourseName gets the name of course
24         Console.WriteLine( "Welcome to the grade book for\n{0}!\n",
25            CourseName );
26      } // end method DisplayMessage
27
28      // perform various operations on the data
29      public void ProcessGrades()
30      {
31         // output grades array
32         OutputGrades();
33
34         // call methods GetMinimum and GetMaximum
35         Console.WriteLine( "\n{0} {1}\n{2} {3}\n",
36            "Lowest grade in the grade book is", GetMinimum(),
37            "Highest grade in the grade book is", GetMaximum() );
38
39         // output grade distribution chart of all grades on all tests
40         OutputBarChart();
41      } // end method ProcessGrades
42
43      // find minimum grade
44      public int GetMinimum()
45      {
46         // assume first element of grades array is smallest
47         int lowGrade = grades[ 0, 0 ];
48
49         // loop through elements of rectangular grades array
50         foreach ( int grade in grades )
51         {
52            // if grade less than lowGrade, assign it to lowGrade
53            if ( grade < lowGrade )
54               lowGrade = grade;
55         } // end foreach
56
57         return lowGrade; // return lowest grade
58      } // end method GetMinimum
59
```

Fig. 8.20 | Grade book using rectangular array to store grades. (Part 2 of 4.)

```
60      // find maximum grade
61      public int GetMaximum()
62      {
63         // assume first element of grades array is largest
64         int highGrade = grades[ 0, 0 ];
65
66         // loop through elements of rectangular grades array
67         foreach ( int grade in grades )
68         {
69            // if grade greater than highGrade, assign it to highGrade
70            if ( grade > highGrade )
71               highGrade = grade;
72         } // end foreach
73
74         return highGrade; // return highest grade
75      } // end method GetMaximum
76
77      // determine average grade for particular student
78      public double GetAverage( int student )
79      {
80         // get the number of grades per student
81         int amount = grades.GetLength( 1 );
82         int total = 0; // initialize total
83
84         // sum grades for one student
85         for ( int exam = 0; exam < amount; exam++ )
86            total += grades[ student, exam ];
87
88         // return average of grades
89         return ( double ) total / amount;
90      } // end method GetAverage
91
92      // output bar chart displaying overall grade distribution
93      public void OutputBarChart()
94      {
95         Console.WriteLine( "Overall grade distribution:" );
96
97         // stores frequency of grades in each range of 10 grades
98         int[] frequency = new int[ 11 ];
99
100        // for each grade in GradeBook, increment the appropriate frequency
101        foreach ( int grade in grades )
102        {
103           ++frequency[ grade / 10 ];
104        } // end foreach
105
106        // for each grade frequency, display bar in chart
107        for ( int count = 0; count < frequency.Length; count++ )
108        {
109           // output bar label ( "00-09: ", ..., "90-99: ", "100: " )
110           if ( count == 10 )
111              Console.Write( "  100: " );
```

Fig. 8.20 | Grade book using rectangular array to store grades. (Part 3 of 4.)

```
112             else
113                 Console.Write( "{0:D2}-{1:D2}: ",
114                     count * 10, count * 10 + 9 );
115
116             // display bar of asterisks
117             for ( int stars = 0; stars < frequency[ count ]; stars++ )
118                 Console.Write( "*" );
119
120             Console.WriteLine(); // start a new line of output
121         } // end outer for
122     } // end method OutputBarChart
123
124     // output the contents of the grades array
125     public void OutputGrades()
126     {
127         Console.WriteLine( "The grades are:\n" );
128         Console.Write( "                " ); // align column heads
129
130         // create a column heading for each of the tests
131         for ( int test = 0; test < grades.GetLength( 1 ); test++ )
132             Console.Write( "Test {0}  ", test + 1 );
133
134         Console.WriteLine( "Average" ); // student average column heading
135
136         // create rows/columns of text representing array grades
137         for ( int student = 0; student < grades.GetLength( 0 ); student++ )
138         {
139             Console.Write( "Student {0,2}", student + 1 );
140
141             // output student's grades
142             for ( int grade = 0; grade < grades.GetLength( 1 ); grade++ )
143                 Console.Write( "{0,8}", grades[ student, grade ] );
144
145             // call method GetAverage to calculate student's average grade;
146             // pass row number as the argument to GetAverage
147             Console.WriteLine( "{0,9:F}", GetAverage( student ) );
148         } // end outer for
149     } // end method OutputGrades
150 } // end class GradeBook
```

Fig. 8.20 | Grade book using rectangular array to store grades. (Part 4 of 4.)

Methods GetMinimum, GetMaximum and OutputBarChart each loop through array grades using the foreach statement—for example, the foreach statement from method GetMinimum (lines 50–55). To find the lowest overall grade, this foreach statement iterates through rectangular array grades and compares each element to variable lowGrade. If a grade is less than lowGrade, lowGrade is set to that grade.

When the foreach statement traverses the elements of the array grades, it looks at each element of the first row in order by index, then each element of the second row in order by index and so on. The foreach statement in lines 50–55 traverses the elements of grade in the same order as the following equivalent code, expressed with nested for statements:

```
        for ( int row = 0; row < grades.GetLength( 0 ); row++ )
           for ( int column = 0; column < grades.GetLength( 1 ); column++ )
           {
               if ( grades[ row, column ] < lowGrade )
                   lowGrade = grades[ row, column ];
           }
```

When the foreach statement completes, lowGrade contains the lowest grade in the rectangular array. Method GetMaximum works similarly to method GetMinimum.

Method OutputBarChart (lines 93–122) displays the grade distribution as a bar chart. The syntax of the foreach statement (lines 101–104) is identical for one-dimensional and two-dimensional arrays.

Method OutputGrades (lines 125–149) uses nested for statements to output values of the array grades, in addition to each student's semester average. The output in Fig. 8.21 shows the result, which resembles the tabular format of an instructor's physical grade book. Lines 131–132 display the column headings for each test. We use the for statement rather than the foreach statement here so that we can identify each test with a number. Similarly, the for statement in lines 137–148 first outputs a row label using a counter variable to identify each student (line 139). Although array indices start at 0, lines 132 and 139 output test + 1 and student + 1, respectively, to produce test and student numbers starting at 1 (see Fig. 8.21). The inner for statement in lines 142–143 uses the outer for statement's counter variable student to loop through a specific row of array grades and output each student's test grade. Finally, line 147 obtains each student's semester average by passing the row index of grades (i.e., student) to method GetAverage.

Method GetAverage (lines 78–90) takes one argument—the row index for a particular student. When line 147 calls GetAverage, the argument is int value student, which specifies the particular row of rectangular array grades. Method GetAverage calculates the sum of the array elements on this row, divides the total by the number of test results and returns the floating-point result as a double value (line 89).

Class *GradeBookTest* That Demonstrates Class *GradeBook*
The application in Fig. 8.21 creates an object of class GradeBook (Fig. 8.20) using the two-dimensional array of ints that gradesArray references (lines 9–18). Lines 20–21 pass a course name and gradesArray to the GradeBook constructor. Lines 22–23 then invoke myGradeBook's DisplayMessage and ProcessGrades methods to display a welcome message and obtain a report summarizing the students' grades for the semester, respectively.

```
 1   // Fig. 8.21: GradeBookTest.cs
 2   // Create GradeBook object using a rectangular array of grades.
 3   public class GradeBookTest
 4   {
 5      // Main method begins application execution
 6      public static void Main( string[] args )
 7      {
 8         // rectangular array of student grades
 9         int[ , ] gradesArray = { { 87, 96, 70 },
10                                  { 68, 87, 90 },
```

Fig. 8.21 | Create GradeBook object using a rectangular array of grades. (Part 1 of 2.)

```
11                              { 94, 100, 90 },
12                              { 100, 81, 82 },
13                              { 83, 65, 85 },
14                              { 78, 87, 65 },
15                              { 85, 75, 83 },
16                              { 91, 94, 100 },
17                              { 76, 72, 84 },
18                              { 87, 93, 73 } };
19
20          GradeBook myGradeBook = new GradeBook(
21             "CS101 Introduction to C# Programming", gradesArray );
22          myGradeBook.DisplayMessage();
23          myGradeBook.ProcessGrades();
24       } // end Main
25    } // end class GradeBookTest
```

```
Welcome to the grade book for
CS101 Introduction to C# Programming!

The grades are:

           Test 1  Test 2  Test 3  Average
Student  1     87      96      70    84.33
Student  2     68      87      90    81.67
Student  3     94     100      90    94.67
Student  4    100      81      82    87.67
Student  5     83      65      85    77.67
Student  6     78      87      65    76.67
Student  7     85      75      83    81.00
Student  8     91      94     100    95.00
Student  9     76      72      84    77.33
Student 10     87      93      73    84.33

Lowest grade in the grade book is 65
Highest grade in the grade book is 100

Overall grade distribution:
00-09:
10-19:
20-29:
30-39:
40-49:
50-59:
60-69: ***
70-79: ******
80-89: ***********
90-99: *******
  100: ***
```

Fig. 8.21 | Create GradeBook object using a rectangular array of grades. (Part 2 of 2.)

8.12 Variable-Length Argument Lists

Variable-length argument lists allow you to create methods that receive an arbitrary number of arguments. A one-dimensional array-type argument preceded by the keyword

params in a method's parameter list indicates that the method receives a variable number of arguments with the type of the array's elements. This use of a params modifier can occur only in the last entry of the parameter list. While you can use method overloading and array passing to accomplish much of what is accomplished with variable-length argument lists, using the params modifier is more concise.

Figure 8.22 demonstrates method Average (lines 8–17), which receives a variable-length sequence of doubles (line 8). C# treats the variable-length argument list as a one-dimensional array whose elements are all of the same type. Hence, the method body can manipulate the parameter numbers as an array of doubles. Lines 13–14 use the foreach loop to walk through the array and calculate the total of the doubles in the array. Line 16 accesses numbers.Length to obtain the size of the numbers array for use in the averaging calculation. Lines 31, 33 and 35 in Main call method Average with two, three and four arguments, respectively. Method Average has a variable-length argument list, so it can average as many double arguments as the caller passes. The output reveals that each call to method Average returns the correct value.

Common Programming Error 8.5

The params modifier may be used only with the last parameter of the parameter list.

```
1   // Fig. 8.22: ParamArrayTest.cs
2   // Using variable-length argument lists.
3   using System;
4
5   public class ParamArrayTest
6   {
7      // calculate average
8      public static double Average( params double[] numbers )
9      {
10        double total = 0.0; // initialize total
11
12        // calculate total using the foreach statement
13        foreach ( double d in numbers )
14           total += d;
15
16        return total / numbers.Length;
17     } // end method Average
18
19     public static void Main( string[] args )
20     {
21        double d1 = 10.0;
22        double d2 = 20.0;
23        double d3 = 30.0;
24        double d4 = 40.0;
25
26        Console.WriteLine(
27           "d1 = {0:F1}\nd2 = {1:F1}\nd3 = {2:F1}\nd4 = {3:F1}\n",
28           d1, d2, d3, d4 );
29
```

Fig. 8.22 | Using variable-length argument lists. (Part 1 of 2.)

```
30          Console.WriteLine( "Average of d1 and d2 is {0:F1}",
31             Average( d1, d2 ) );
32          Console.WriteLine( "Average of d1, d2 and d3 is {0:F1}",
33             Average( d1, d2, d3 ) );
34          Console.WriteLine( "Average of d1, d2, d3 and d4 is {0:F1}",
35             Average( d1, d2, d3, d4 ) );
36      } // end Main
37   } // end class ParamArrayTest
```

```
d1 = 10.0
d2 = 20.0
d3 = 30.0
d4 = 40.0

Average of d1 and d2 is 15.0
Average of d1, d2 and d3 is 20.0
Average of d1, d2, d3 and d4 is 25.0
```

Fig. 8.22 | Using variable-length argument lists. (Part 2 of 2.)

8.13 Using Command-Line Arguments

On many systems, it's possible to pass arguments from the command line (these are known as **command-line arguments**) to an application by including a parameter of type `string[]` (i.e., an array of `string`s) in the parameter list of `Main`, exactly as we have done in every application in the book. By convention, this parameter is named `args` (Fig. 8.23, line 7). When an application is executed from the **Command Prompt**, the execution environment passes the command-line arguments that appear after the application name to the application's `Main` method as `string`s in the one-dimensional array `args`. The number of arguments passed from the command line is obtained by accessing the array's `Length` property. For example, the command `"MyApplication a b"` passes two command-line arguments to application `MyApplication`. Command-line arguments are separated by white space, not commas. When the preceding command executes, the `Main` method entry point receives the two-element array `args` (i.e., `args.Length` is 2) in which `args[0]` contains the `string` `"a"` and `args[1]` contains the `string` `"b"`. Common uses of command-line arguments include passing options and file names to applications.

Figure 8.23 uses three command-line arguments to initialize an array. When the application executes, if `args.Length` is not 3, the application displays an error message and terminates (lines 10–13). Otherwise, lines 16–32 initialize and display the array based on the values of the command-line arguments.

```
1    // Fig. 8.23: InitArray.cs
2    // Using command-line arguments to initialize an array.
3    using System;
4
5    public class InitArray
6    {
7       public static void Main( string[] args )
8       {
```

Fig. 8.23 | Using command-line arguments to initialize an array. (Part 1 of 2.)

```
 9          // check number of command-line arguments
10          if ( args.Length != 3 )
11             Console.WriteLine(
12                "Error: Please re-enter the entire command, including\n" +
13                "an array size, initial value and increment." );
14          else
15          {
16             // get array size from first command-line argument
17             int arrayLength = Convert.ToInt32( args[ 0 ] );
18             int[] array = new int[ arrayLength ]; // create array
19
20             // get initial value and increment from command-line argument
21             int initialValue = Convert.ToInt32( args[ 1 ] );
22             int increment = Convert.ToInt32( args[ 2 ] );
23
24             // calculate value for each array element
25             for ( int counter = 0; counter < array.Length; counter++ )
26                array[ counter ] = initialValue + increment * counter;
27
28             Console.WriteLine( "{0}{1,8}", "Index", "Value" );
29
30             // display array index and value
31             for ( int counter = 0; counter < array.Length; counter++ )
32                Console.WriteLine( "{0,5}{1,8}", counter, array[ counter ] );
33          } // end else
34       } // end Main
35    } // end class InitArray
```

```
C:\Examples\ch08\fig08_23>InitArray.exe
Error: Please re-enter the entire command, including
an array size, initial value and increment.
```

```
C:\Examples\ch08\fig08_23>InitArray.exe 10 1 2
Index   Value
    0       1
    1       3
    2       5
    3       7
    4       9
    5      11
    6      13
    7      15
    8      17
    9      19
```

```
C:\Examples\ch08\fig08_23>InitArray.exe 5 0 4
Index   Value
    0       0
    1       4
    2       8
    3      12
    4      16
```

Fig. 8.23 | Using command-line arguments to initialize an array. (Part 2 of 2.)

The command-line arguments become available to Main as strings in args. Line 17 gets args[0]—a string that specifies the array size—and converts it to an int value, which the application uses to create the array in line 18. The static method ToInt32 of class Convert converts its string argument to an int. Lines 21–22 convert the args[1] and args[2] command-line arguments to int values and store them in initialValue and increment, respectively. Lines 25–26 calculate the value for each array element.

The first sample execution indicates that the application received an insufficient number of command-line arguments. The second sample execution uses command-line arguments 5, 0 and 4 to specify the size of the array (5), the value of the first element (0) and the increment of each value in the array (4), respectively. The corresponding output indicates that these values create an array containing the integers 0, 4, 8, 12 and 16. The output from the third sample execution illustrates that the command-line arguments 10, 1 and 2 produce an array whose 10 elements are the nonnegative odd integers from 1 to 19.

8.14 Wrap-Up

This chapter began our data structures introduction. We used arrays to store data in and retrieve data from lists and tables of values. We demonstrated how to declare array variables, initialize arrays and refer to individual array elements. We introduced foreach as an additional means (besides the for statement) for iterating through arrays. We showed how to pass arrays to methods and how to declare and manipulate multidimensional arrays. Finally, the chapter showed how to write methods that use variable-length argument lists and how to read arguments passed to an application from the command line.

We continue our data structures coverage in Chapter 9 where we discuss List collections—dynamically resizable array-based collections. Chapter 21, Data Structures, introduces dynamic data structures, such as lists, queues, stacks and trees, that can grow and shrink as applications execute. Chapter 22, Generics, presents generics, which provide the means to create general models of methods and classes that can be declared once, but used with many data types. Chapter 23, Collections, introduces the data structure classes provided by the .NET Framework Class Library, some of which use generics to allow you to specify the exact types of objects that a particular data structure will store. You can use these predefined data structures instead of building your own. The .NET Framework Class Library also provides class Array, which contains utility methods for array manipulation. Chapter 23 uses several static methods of class Array to perform such manipulations as sorting and searching the data in an array.

In Chapter 9 we introduce Language Integrated Query (LINQ), which enables you to write expressions that can retrieve information from a wide variety of data sources, such as arrays and collections. You'll see how to search, sort and filter data using LINQ.

9

Introduction to LINQ and the **List** Collection

OBJECTIVES

In this chapter you'll learn:

■ Basic LINQ concepts.

■ How to query an array using LINQ.

■ Basic .NET collections concepts.

■ How to create and use a generic **List** collection.

■ How to query a generic **List** collection using LINQ.

To write it, it took three months; to conceive it three minutes; to collect the data in it—all my life.
—F. Scott Fitzgerald

Science is feasible when the variables are few and can be enumerated …
—Paul Valéry

You shall listen to all sides and filter them from your self.
—Walt Whitman

The portraitist can select one tiny aspect of everything shown at a moment to incorporate into the final painting.
—Robert Nozick

List, list, O, list!
—William Shakespeare

9.1 Introduction

The preceding chapter introduced arrays—simple data structures used to store data items of a specific type. Although commonly used, arrays have limited capabilities. For instance, you must specify an array's size, and if at execution time, you wish to modify it, you must do so manually by creating a new array or by using the `Array` class's `Resize` method, which creates a new array and copies the existing elements into the new array for you.

Here, we introduce a set of *prepackaged* data structures—the .NET Framework's collection classes—that offer greater capabilities than traditional arrays. They're reusable, reliable, powerful and efficient and have been carefully designed and tested to ensure quality and performance. This chapter focuses on the `List` collection. `List`s are similar to arrays but provide additional functionality, such as **dynamic resizing**—they automatically increase their size at execution time to accommodate additional elements. We use the `List` collection to implement several examples similar to those used in the preceding chapter.

Large amounts of data are often stored in a database—an organized collection of data. (We discuss databases in detail in Chapter 18.) A database management system (DBMS) provides mechanisms for storing, organizing, retrieving and modifying data in the database. A language called SQL—pronounced "sequel"—is the international standard used to perform **queries** (i.e., to request information that satisfies given criteria) and to manipulate data. For years, programs accessing a relational database passed SQL queries to the database management system, then processed the results. This chapter introduces C#'s new **LINQ** (**Language Integrated Query**) capabilities. LINQ allows you to write **query expressions**, similar to SQL queries, that retrieve information from a wide variety of data sources, not just databases. We use **LINQ to Objects** in this chapter to query arrays and `List`s, selecting elements that satisfy a set of conditions—this is known as **filtering**. Figure 9.1 shows where and how we use LINQ throughout the book to retrieve information from many data sources.

Chapter	Used to
Chapter 9, Introduction to LINQ and the `List` Collection	Query arrays and `List`s.
Chapter 16, Strings and Characters	Select GUI controls in a Windows Forms application.
Chapter 17, Files and Streams	Search a directory and manipulate text files.

Fig. 9.1 | LINQ usage throughout the book. (Part 1 of 2.)

Chapter	Used to
Chapter 18, Databases and LINQ	Retrieve information from a database.
Chapter 19, Web App Development with ASP.NET	Retrieve information from a database to be used in a web-based application.
Chapter 26, XML and LINQ to XML	Query an XML document.
Chapter 28, Web Services	Query and update a database. Process XML returned by WCF services.
Chapter 29, Silverlight and Rich Internet Applications	Process XML returned by web services to a Silverlight application.

Fig. 9.1 | LINQ usage throughout the book. (Part 2 of 2.)

LINQ Providers

The syntax of LINQ is built into C#, but LINQ queries may be used in many different contexts because of libraries known as providers. A **LINQ provider** is a set of classes that implement LINQ operations and enable programs to interact with data sources to perform tasks such as sorting, grouping and filtering elements.

In this book, we discuss LINQ to SQL and LINQ to XML, which allow you to query databases and XML documents using LINQ. These providers, along with LINQ to Objects, mentioned above, are included with Visual Studio and the .NET Framework. There are many providers that are more specialized, allowing you to interact with a specific website or data format. An extensive list of available providers is located at:

```
blogs.msdn.com/charlie/archive/2006/10/05/Links-to-LINQ.aspx
```

9.2 Querying an Array of int Values Using LINQ

Figure 9.2 demonstrates querying an array of integers using LINQ. Repetition statements that filter arrays focus on the process of getting the results—iterating through the elements and checking whether they satisfy the desired criteria. LINQ specifies the conditions that selected elements must satisfy. This is known as **declarative programming**—as opposed to **imperative programming** (which we've been doing so far) in which you specify the actual steps to perform a task. The query in lines 20–22 specifies that the results should consist of all the ints in the values array that are greater than 4. It *does not* specify *how* those results are obtained—the C# compiler generates all the necessary code automatically, which is one of the great strengths of LINQ. To use LINQ to Objects, you must import the System.Linq namespace (line 4).

```
1   // Fig. 9.2: LINQWithSimpleTypeArray.cs
2   // LINQ to Objects using an int array.
3   using System;
4   using System.Linq;
```

Fig. 9.2 | LINQ to Objects using an int array. (Part 1 of 3.)

```
 5
 6   class LINQWithSimpleTypeArray
 7   {
 8      public static void Main( string[] args )
 9      {
10         // create an integer array
11         int[] values = { 2, 9, 5, 0, 3, 7, 1, 4, 8, 5 };
12
13         // display original values
14         Console.Write( "Original array:" );
15         foreach ( var element in values )
16            Console.Write( " {0}", element );
17
18         // LINQ query that obtains values greater than 4 from the array
19         var filtered =
20            from value in values
21            where value > 4
22            select value;
23
24         // display filtered results
25         Console.Write( "\nArray values greater than 4:" );
26         foreach ( var element in filtered )
27            Console.Write( " {0}", element );
28
29         // use orderby clause to sort original array in ascending order
30         var sorted =
31            from value in values
32            orderby value
33            select value;
34
35         // display sorted results
36         Console.Write( "\nOriginal array, sorted:" );
37         foreach ( var element in sorted )
38            Console.Write( " {0}", element );
39
40         // sort the filtered results into descending order
41         var sortFilteredResults =
42            from value in filtered
43            orderby value descending
44            select value;
45
46         // display the sorted results
47         Console.Write(
48            "\nValues greater than 4, descending order (separately):" );
49         foreach ( var element in sortFilteredResults )
50            Console.Write( " {0}", element );
51
52         // filter original array and sort in descending order
53         var sortAndFilter =
54            from value in values
55            where value > 4
56            orderby value descending
57            select value;
```

Fig. 9.2 | LINQ to Objects using an `int` array. (Part 2 of 3.)

```
58
59          // display the filtered and sorted results
60          Console.Write(
61             "\nValues greater than 4, descending order (one query):" );
62          foreach ( var element in sortAndFilter )
63             Console.Write( " {0}", element );
64
65          Console.WriteLine();
66       } // end Main
67    } // end class LINQWithSimpleTypeArray
```

```
Original array: 2 9 5 0 3 7 1 4 8 5
Array values greater than 4: 9 5 7 8 5
Original array, sorted: 0 1 2 3 4 5 5 7 8 9
Values greater than 4, descending order (separately): 9 8 7 5 5
Values greater than 4, descending order (one query): 9 8 7 5 5
```

Fig. 9.2 | LINQ to Objects using an int array. (Part 3 of 3.)

The *from Clause and Implicitly Typed Local Variables*

A LINQ query begins with a **from clause** (line 20), which specifies a **range variable** (value) and the data source to query (values). The range variable represents each item in the data source (one at a time), much like the control variable in a foreach statement. We do not specify the range variable's type. Since it is assigned one element at a time from the array values, which is an int array, the compiler determines that the range variable value should be of type int. This is a C# feature called **implicitly typed local variables**, which enables the compiler to *infer* a local variable's type based on the context in which it's used.

Introducing the range variable in the from clause at the beginning of the query allows the IDE to provide *IntelliSense* while you write the rest of the query. The IDE knows the range variable's type, so when you enter the range variable's name followed by a dot (.) in the code editor, the IDE can display the range variable's methods and properties.

The *var Keyword and Implicitly Typed Local Variables*

You can also declare a local variable and let the compiler infer the variable's type based on the variable's initializer. To do so, the **var keyword** is used in place of the variable's type when declaring the variable. Consider the declaration

```
var x = 7;
```

Here, the compiler *infers* that the variable x should be of type int, because the compiler assumes that whole-number values, like 7, are of type int. Similarly, in the declaration

```
var y = -123.45;
```

the compiler infers that y should be of type double, because the compiler assumes that floating-point number values, like -123.45, are of type double. Typically, implicitly typed local variables are used for more complex types, such as the collections of data returned by LINQ queries. We use this feature in lines 19, 30, 41 and 53 to enable the compiler to determine the type of each variable that stores the results of a LINQ query. We also use this feature to declare the control variable in the foreach statements at lines 15–16, 26–27, 37–38, 49–50 and 62–63. In each case, the compiler infers that the control variable is of type int because the array values and the LINQ query results all contain int values.

The *where Clause*

If the condition in the **where clause** (line 21) evaluates to `true`, the element is *selected*—i.e., it's included in the results. Here, the `int`s in the array are included only if they're greater than 4. An expression that takes an element of a collection and returns `true` or `false` by testing a condition on that element is known as a **predicate**.

The `select` *Clause*

For each item in the data source, the **select clause** (line 22) determines what value appears in the results. In this case, it's the `int` that the range variable currently represents. A LINQ query typically ends with a `select` clause.

Iterating Through the Results of the LINQ Query

Lines 26–27 use a `foreach` statement to display the query results. As you know, a `foreach` statement can iterate through the contents of an array, allowing you to process each element in the array. Actually, the `foreach` statement can iterate through the contents arrays, collections and the results of LINQ queries. The `foreach` statement in lines 26–27 iterates over the query result `filtered`, displaying each of its items.

LINQ vs. Repetition Statements

It would be simple to display the integers greater than 4 using a repetition statement that tests each value before displaying it. However, this would intertwine the code that selects elements and the code that displays them. With LINQ, these are kept separate, making the code easier to understand and maintain.

The *orderby Clause*

The **orderby clause** (line 32) sorts the query results in ascending order. Lines 43 and 56 use the **descending** modifier in the `orderby` clause to sort the results in descending order. An **ascending** modifier also exists but isn't normally used, because it's the default. Any value that can be compared with other values of the same type may be used with the orderby clause. A value of a simple type (e.g., `int`) can always be compared to another value of the same type; we'll say more about comparing values of reference types in Chapter 12.

The queries in lines 42–44 and 54–57 generate the same results, but in different ways. The first query uses LINQ to sort the results of the query from lines 20–22. The second query uses both the `where` and `orderby` clauses. Because queries can operate on the results of other queries, it's possible to build a query one step at a time, and pass the results of queries between methods for further processing.

More on Implicitly Typed Local Variables

Implicitly typed local variables can also be used to initialize arrays without explicitly giving their type. For example, the following statement creates an array of `int` values:

```
var array = new[] { 32, 27, 64, 18, 95, 14, 90, 70, 60, 37 };
```

There are no square brackets on the left side of the assignment operator, and that `new[]` is used to specify that the variable is an array.

An Aside: Interface `IEnumerable<T>`

As we mentioned, the `foreach` statement can iterate through the contents of arrays, collections and LINQ query results. Actually, `foreach` iterates over any so-called `IEnumerable<T>` object, which just happens to be what a LINQ query returns.

IEnumerable<T> is an **interface**. Interfaces define and standardize the ways in which people and systems can interact with one another. For example, the controls on a radio serve as an interface between radio users and the radio's internal components. The controls allow users to perform a limited set of operations (e.g., changing the station, adjusting the volume, and choosing between AM and FM), and different radios may implement the controls in different ways (e.g., using push buttons, dials or voice commands). The interface specifies *what* operations a radio permits users to perform but does not specify *how* the operations are implemented. Similarly, the interface between a driver and a car with a manual transmission includes the steering wheel, the gear shift, the clutch, the gas pedal and the brake pedal. This same interface is found in nearly all manual-transmission cars, enabling someone who knows how to drive one manual-transmission car to drive another.

Software objects also communicate via interfaces. A C# interface describes a set of methods that can be called on an object—to tell the object, for example, to perform some task or return some piece of information. The IEnumerable<T> interface describes the functionality of any object that can be iterated over and thus offers methods to access each element. A class that implements an interface must define each method in the interface with a signature identical to the one in the interface definition. Implementing an interface is like signing a contract with the compiler that states, "I will declare all the methods specified by the interface." Chapter 12 covers use of interfaces in more detail, as well as how to define your own interfaces.

Arrays are IEnumerable<T> objects, so a foreach statement can iterate over an array's elements. Similarly, each LINQ query returns an IEnumerable<T> object. Therefore, you can use a foreach statement to iterate over the results of any LINQ query. The notation <T> indicates that the interface is a generic interface that can be used with any type of data (for example, ints, strings or Employees). You'll learn more about the <T> notation in Section 9.4. You'll learn more about interfaces in Section 12.7.

9.3 Querying an Array of Employee Objects Using LINQ

LINQ is not limited to querying arrays of primitive types such as ints. It can be used with most data types, including strings and user-defined classes. It cannot be used when a query does not have a defined meaning—for example, you cannot use orderby on objects that are not comparable. Comparable types in .NET are those that implement the IComparable interface, which is discussed in Section 22.4. All built-in types, such as string, int and double implement IComparable. Figure 9.3 presents the Employee class. Figure 9.4 uses LINQ to query an array of Employee objects.

```
 1   // Fig. 9.3: Employee.cs
 2   // Employee class with FirstName, LastName and MonthlySalary properties.
 3   public class Employee
 4   {
 5      private decimal monthlySalaryValue; // monthly salary of employee
 6
 7      // auto-implemented property FirstName
 8      public string FirstName { get; set; }
 9
```

Fig. 9.3 | Employee class. (Part 1 of 2.)

```
10      // auto-implemented property LastName
11      public string LastName { get; set; }
12
13      // constructor initializes first name, last name and monthly salary
14      public Employee( string first, string last, decimal salary )
15      {
16         FirstName = first;
17         LastName = last;
18         MonthlySalary = salary;
19      } // end constructor
20
21      // property that gets and sets the employee's monthly salary
22      public decimal MonthlySalary
23      {
24         get
25         {
26            return monthlySalaryValue;
27         } // end get
28         set
29         {
30            if ( value >= 0M ) // if salary is nonnegative
31            {
32               monthlySalaryValue = value;
33            } // end if
34         } // end set
35      } // end property MonthlySalary
36
37      // return a string containing the employee's information
38      public override string ToString()
39      {
40         return string.Format( "{0,-10} {1,-10} {2,10:C}",
41            FirstName, LastName, MonthlySalary );
42      } // end method ToString
43   } // end class Employee
```

Fig. 9.3 | Employee class. (Part 2 of 2.)

```
1    // Fig. 9.4: LINQWithArrayOfObjects.cs
2    // LINQ to Objects using an array of Employee objects.
3    using System;
4    using System.Linq;
5
6    public class LINQWithArrayOfObjects
7    {
8       public static void Main( string[] args )
9       {
10         // initialize array of employees
11         Employee[] employees = {
12            new Employee( "Jason", "Red", 5000M ),
13            new Employee( "Ashley", "Green", 7600M ),
14            new Employee( "Matthew", "Indigo", 3587.5M ),
```

Fig. 9.4 | LINQ to Objects using an array of Employee objects. (Part 1 of 3.)

```
15            new Employee( "James", "Indigo", 4700.77M ),
16            new Employee( "Luke", "Indigo", 6200M ),
17            new Employee( "Jason", "Blue", 3200M ),
18            new Employee( "Wendy", "Brown", 4236.4M ) }; // end init list
19
20         // display all employees
21         Console.WriteLine( "Original array:" );
22         foreach ( var element in employees )
23            Console.WriteLine( element );
24
25         // filter a range of salaries using && in a LINQ query
26         var between4K6K =
27            from e in employees
28            where e.MonthlySalary >= 4000M && e.MonthlySalary <= 6000M
29            select e;
30
31         // display employees making between 4000 and 6000 per month
32         Console.WriteLine( string.Format(
33            "\nEmployees earning in the range {0:C}-{1:C} per month:",
34            4000, 6000 ) );
35         foreach ( var element in between4K6K )
36            Console.WriteLine( element );
37
38         // order the employees by last name, then first name with LINQ
39         var nameSorted =
40            from e in employees
41            orderby e.LastName, e.FirstName
42            select e;
43
44         // header
45         Console.WriteLine( "\nFirst employee when sorted by name:" );
46
47         // attempt to display the first result of the above LINQ query
48         if ( nameSorted.Any() )
49            Console.WriteLine( nameSorted.First() );
50         else
51            Console.WriteLine( "not found" );
52
53         // use LINQ to select employee last names
54         var lastNames =
55            from e in employees
56            select e.LastName;
57
58         // use method Distinct to select unique last names
59         Console.WriteLine( "\nUnique employee last names:" );
60         foreach ( var element in lastNames.Distinct() )
61            Console.WriteLine( element );
62
63         // use LINQ to select first and last names
64         var names =
65            from e in employees
66            select new { e.FirstName, Last = e.LastName };
67
```

Fig. 9.4 | LINQ to Objects using an array of Employee objects. (Part 2 of 3.)

```
68              // display full names
69              Console.WriteLine( "\nNames only:" );
70              foreach ( var element in names )
71                 Console.WriteLine( element );
72
73              Console.WriteLine();
74          } // end Main
75      } // end class LINQWithArrayOfObjects
```

```
Original array:
Jason      Red         $5,000.00
Ashley     Green       $7,600.00
Matthew    Indigo      $3,587.50
James      Indigo      $4,700.77
Luke       Indigo      $6,200.00
Jason      Blue        $3,200.00
Wendy      Brown       $4,236.40

Employees earning in the range $4,000.00-$6,000.00 per month:
Jason      Red         $5,000.00
James      Indigo      $4,700.77
Wendy      Brown       $4,236.40

First employee when sorted by name:
Jason      Blue        $3,200.00

Unique employee last names:
Red
Green
Indigo
Blue
Brown

Names only:
{ FirstName = Jason, Last = Red }
{ FirstName = Ashley, Last = Green }
{ FirstName = Matthew, Last = Indigo }
{ FirstName = James, Last = Indigo }
{ FirstName = Luke, Last = Indigo }
{ FirstName = Jason, Last = Blue }
{ FirstName = Wendy, Last = Brown }
```

Fig. 9.4 | LINQ to Objects using an array of Employee objects. (Part 3 of 3.)

Accessing the Properties of a LINQ Query's Range Variable

Line 28 of Fig. 9.4 shows a where clause that accesses the properties of the range variable. In this example, the compiler infers that the range variable is of type Employee based on its knowledge that employees was defined as an array of Employee objects (lines 11–18). Any bool expression can be used in a where clause. Line 28 uses the conditional AND (&&) operator to combine conditions. Here, only employees that have a salary between $4,000 and $6,000 per month, inclusive, are included in the query result, which is displayed in lines 35–36.

Sorting a LINQ Query's Results By Multiple Properties

Line 41 uses an orderby clause to sort the results according to multiple properties—specified in a comma-separated list. In this query, the employees are sorted alphabetically by last name. Each group of Employees that have the same last name is then sorted within the group by first name.

Any, First and Count Extension Methods

Line 48 introduces the query result's **Any** method, which returns true if there's at least one element, and false if there are no elements. The query result's **First** method (line 49) returns the first element in the result. You should check that the query result is not empty (line 48) before calling First.

We've not specified the class that defines methods First and Any. Your intuition probably tells you they're methods declared in the IEnumerable<T> interface, but they aren't. They're actually extension methods, but they can be used as if they were methods of IEnumerable<T>.

LINQ defines many more extension methods, such as **Count**, which returns the number of elements in the results. Rather than using Any, we could have checked that Count was nonzero, but it's more efficient to determine whether there's at least one element than to count all the elements. The LINQ query syntax is actually transformed by the compiler into extension method calls, with the results of one method call used in the next. It's this design that allows queries to be run on the results of previous queries, as it simply involves passing the result of a method call to another method.

Selecting a Portion of an Object

Line 56 uses the select clause to select the range variable's LastName property rather than the range variable itself. This causes the results of the query to consist of only the last names (as strings), instead of complete Employee objects. Lines 60–61 display the unique last names. The **Distinct extension method** (line 60) removes duplicate elements, causing all elements in the result to be unique.

Creating New Types in the select Clause of a LINQ Query

The last LINQ query in the example (lines 65–66) selects the properties FirstName and LastName. The syntax

```
new { e.FirstName, Last = e.LastName }
```

creates a new object of an **anonymous type** (a type with no name), which the compiler generates for you based on the properties listed in the curly braces ({}). In this case, the anonymous type consists of properties for the first and last names of the selected Employee. The LastName property is assigned to the property Last in the select clause. This shows how you can specify a new name for the selected property. If you don't specify a new name, the property's original name is used—this is the case for FirstName in this example. The preceding query is an example of a **projection**—it performs a transformation on the data. In this case, the transformation creates new objects containing only the FirstName and Last properties. Transformations can also manipulate the data. For example, you could give all employees a 10% raise by multiplying their MonthlySalary properties by 1.1.

When creating a new anonymous type, you can select any number of properties by specifying them in a comma-separated list within the curly braces ({}) that delineate the anonymous type definition. In this example, the compiler automatically creates a new class having properties FirstName and Last, and the values are copied from the Employee objects. These selected properties can then be accessed when iterating over the results.

Implicitly typed local variables allow you to use anonymous types because you do not have to explicitly state the type when declaring such variables.

When the compiler creates an anonymous type, it automatically generates a `ToString` method that returns a `string` representation of the object. You can see this in the program's output—it consists of the property names and their values, enclosed in braces. Anonymous types are discussed in more detail in Chapter 18.

9.4 Introduction to Collections

The .NET Framework Class Library provides several classes, called collections, used to store groups of related objects. These classes provide efficient methods that organize, store and retrieve your data without requiring knowledge of how the data is being stored. This reduces application-development time.

You've used arrays to store sequences of objects. Arrays do not automatically change their size at execution time to accommodate additional elements—you must do so manually by creating a new array or by using the `Array` class's `Resize` method.

The collection class **List<T>** (from namespace `System.Collections.Generic`) provides a convenient solution to this problem. The `T` is a placeholder—when declaring a new `List`, replace it with the type of elements that you want the `List` to hold. This is similar to specifying the type when declaring an array. For example,

```
List< int > list1;
```

declares `list1` as a `List` collection that can store only `int` values, and

```
List< string > list2;
```

declares `list2` as a `List` of `string`s. Classes with this kind of placeholder that can be used with any type are called **generic classes**. Generic classes and additional generic collection classes are discussed in Chapters 22 and 23, respectively. Figure 23.2 provides a table of collection classes. Figure 9.5 shows some common methods and properties of class `List<T>`.

Method or property	Description
Add	Adds an element to the end of the `List`.
Capacity	Property that gets or sets the number of elements a `List` can store without resizing.
Clear	Removes all the elements from the `List`.
Contains	Returns `true` if the `List` contains the specified element; otherwise, returns `false`.
Count	Property that returns the number of elements stored in the `List`.
IndexOf	Returns the index of the first occurrence of the specified value in the `List`.
Insert	Inserts an element at the specified index.
Remove	Removes the first occurrence of the specified value.

Fig. 9.5 | Some methods and properties of class `List<T>`. (Part 1 of 2.)

Method or property	Description
RemoveAt	Removes the element at the specified index.
RemoveRange	Removes a specified number of elements starting at a specified index.
Sort	Sorts the List.
TrimExcess	Sets the Capacity of the List to the number of elements the List currently contains (Count).

Fig. 9.5 | Some methods and properties of class List<T>. (Part 2 of 2.)

Figure 9.6 demonstrates dynamically resizing a List object. The Add and Insert methods add elements to the List (lines 13–14). The **Add** method appends its argument to the end of the List. The **Insert** method inserts a new element at the specified position. The first argument is an index—as with arrays, collection indices start at zero. The second argument is the value that's to be inserted at the specified index. All elements at the specified index and above are shifted up by one position. This is usually slower than adding an element to the end of the List.

```csharp
1   // Fig. 9.6: ListCollection.cs
2   // Generic List collection demonstration.
3   using System;
4   using System.Collections.Generic;
5
6   public class ListCollection
7   {
8      public static void Main( string[] args )
9      {
10        // create a new List of strings
11        List< string > items = new List< string >();
12
13        items.Add( "red" ); // append an item to the List
14        items.Insert( 0, "yellow" ); // insert the value at index 0
15
16        // display the colors in the list
17        Console.Write(
18           "Display list contents with counter-controlled loop:" );
19        for ( int i = 0; i < items.Count; i++ )
20           Console.Write( " {0}", items[ i ] );
21
22        // display colors using foreach
23        Console.Write(
24           "\nDisplay list contents with foreach statement:" );
25        foreach ( var item in items )
26           Console.Write( " {0}", item );
27
28        items.Add( "green" ); // add "green" to the end of the List
29        items.Add( "yellow" ); // add "yellow" to the end of the List
30
```

Fig. 9.6 | Generic List<T> collection demonstration. (Part 1 of 2.)

```
31          // display the List
32          Console.Write( "\nList with two new elements:" );
33          foreach ( var item in items )
34             Console.Write( " {0}", item );
35
36          items.Remove( "yellow" ); // remove the first "yellow"
37
38          // display the List
39          Console.Write( "\nRemove first instance of yellow:" );
40          foreach ( var item in items )
41             Console.Write( " {0}", item );
42
43          items.RemoveAt( 1 ); // remove item at index 1
44
45          // display the List
46          Console.Write( "\nRemove second list element (green):" );
47          foreach ( var item in items )
48             Console.Write( " {0}", item );
49
50          // check if a value is in the List
51          Console.WriteLine( "\n\"red\" is {0}in the list",
52             items.Contains( "red" ) ? string.Empty : "not " );
53
54          // display number of elements in the List
55          Console.WriteLine( "Count: {0}", items.Count );
56
57          // display the capacity of the List
58          Console.WriteLine( "Capacity: {0}", items.Capacity );
59       } // end Main
60    } // end class ListCollection
```

```
Display list contents with counter-controlled loop: yellow red
Display list contents with foreach statement: yellow red
List with two new elements: yellow red green yellow
Remove first instance of yellow: red green yellow
Remove second list element (green): red yellow
"red" is in the list
Count: 2
Capacity: 4
```

Fig. 9.6 | Generic List<T> collection demonstration. (Part 2 of 2.)

Lines 19–20 display the items in the List. The **Count** property returns the number of elements currently in the List. Lists can be indexed like arrays by placing the index in square brackets after the List variable's name. The indexed List expression can be used to modify the element at the index. Lines 25–26 output the List by using a foreach statement. More elements are then added to the List, and it's displayed again (lines 28–34).

The **Remove** method is used to remove the *first* element with a specific value (line 36). If no such element is in the List, Remove does nothing. A similar method, **RemoveAt**, removes the element at the specified index (line 43). When an element is removed through either of these methods, all elements above that index are shifted down by one—the opposite of the Insert method.

Line 52 uses the **Contains** method to check if an item is in the List. The Contains method returns true if the element is found in the List, and false otherwise. The method compares its argument to each element of the List in order until the item is found, so using Contains on a large List is inefficient.

Lines 55 and 58 display the List's Count and Capacity. Recall that the Count property (line 55) indicates the number of items in the List. The **Capacity** property (line 58) indicates how many items the List can hold without growing. List is implemented using an array behind the scenes. When the List grows, it must create a larger internal array and copy each element to the new array. This is a time-consuming operation. It would be inefficient for the List to grow each time an element is added. Instead, the List grows only when an element is added *and* the Count and Capacity properties are equal—there's no space for the new element.

9.5 Querying a Generic Collection Using LINQ

You can use LINQ to Objects to query Lists just as arrays. In Fig. 9.7, a List of strings is converted to uppercase and searched for those that begin with "R".

```csharp
1   // Fig. 9.7: LINQWithListCollection.cs
2   // LINQ to Objects using a List< string >.
3   using System;
4   using System.Linq;
5   using System.Collections.Generic;
6
7   public class LINQWithListCollection
8   {
9      public static void Main( string[] args )
10     {
11        // populate a List of strings
12        List< string > items = new List< string >();
13        items.Add( "aQua" ); // add "aQua" to the end of the List
14        items.Add( "RusT" ); // add "RusT" to the end of the List
15        items.Add( "yElLow" ); // add "yElLow" to the end of the List
16        items.Add( "rEd" ); // add "rEd" to the end of the List
17
18        // convert all strings to uppercase; select those starting with "R"
19        var startsWithR =
20           from item in items
21           let uppercaseString = item.ToUpper()
22           where uppercaseString.StartsWith( "R" )
23           orderby uppercaseString
24           select uppercaseString;
25
26        // display query results
27        foreach ( var item in startsWithR )
28           Console.Write( "{0} ", item );
29
30        Console.WriteLine(); // output end of line
```

Fig. 9.7 | LINQ to Objects using a List<string>. (Part I of 2.)

```
31
32          items.Add( "rUbY" ); // add "rUbY" to the end of the List
33          items.Add( "SaFfRon" ); // add "SaFfRon" to the end of the List
34
35          // display updated query results
36          foreach ( var item in startsWithR )
37             Console.Write( "{0} ", item );
38
39          Console.WriteLine(); // output end of line
40       } // end Main
41    } // end class LINQWithListCollection
```

```
RED RUST
RED RUBY RUST
```

Fig. 9.7 | LINQ to Objects using a `List<string>`. (Part 2 of 2.)

Line 21 uses LINQ's **let clause** to create a new range variable. This is useful if you need to store a temporary result for use later in the LINQ query. Typically, `let` declares a new range variable to which you assign the result of an expression that operates on the query's original range variable. In this case, we use `string` method **ToUpper** to convert each `item` to uppercase, then store the result in the new range variable `uppercaseString`. We then use the new range variable `uppercaseString` in the where, `orderby` and `select` clauses. The `where` clause (line 22) uses `string` method **StartsWith** to determine whether `uppercaseString` starts with the character `"R"`. Method `StartsWith` performs a case-sensitive comparison to determine whether a `string` starts with the `string` received as an argument. If `uppercaseString` starts with `"R"`, method `StartsWith` returns `true`, and the element is included in the query results. More powerful `string` matching can be done using the regular-expression capabilities introduced in Chapter 16, Strings and Characters.

The query is created only once (lines 20–24), yet iterating over the results (lines 27–28 and 36–37) gives two different lists of colors. This demonstrates LINQ's **deferred execution**—the query executes only when you access the results—such as iterating over them or using the `Count` method—not when you define the query. This allows you to create a query once and execute it many times. Any changes to the data source are reflected in the results each time the query executes.

There may be times when you do not want this behavior, and want to retrieve a collection of the results immediately. LINQ provides extension methods `ToArray` and `ToList` for this purpose. These methods execute the query on which they're called and give you the results as an array or `List<T>`, respectively. These methods can also improve efficiency if you'll be iterating over the results multiple times, as you execute the query only once.

C# has a feature called **collection initializers**, which provide a convenient syntax (similar to array initializers) for initializing a collection. For example, lines 12–16 of Fig. 9.7 could be replaced with the following statement:

```
List< string > items =
   new List< string > { "aQua", "RusT", "yElLow", "rEd" };
```

9.6 Wrap-Up

This chapter introduced LINQ (Language Integrated Query), a powerful feature for querying data. We showed how to filter an array or collection using LINQ's where clause, and how to sort the query results using the orderby clause. We used the select clause to select specific properties of an object, and the let clause to introduce a new range variable to make writing queries more convenient. The StartsWith method of class string was used to filter strings starting with a specified character or series of characters. We used several LINQ extension methods to perform operations not provided by the query syntax—the Distinct method to remove duplicates from the results, the Any method to determine if the results contain any items, and the First method to retrieve the first element in the results.

We introduced the List<T> generic collection, which provides all the functionality of arrays, along with other useful capabilities such as dynamic resizing. We used method Add to append new items to the end of the List, method Insert to insert new items into specified locations in the List, method Remove to remove the first occurrence of a specified item, method RemoveAt to remove an item at a specified index and method Contains to determine if an item was in the List. We used property Count to get the number of items in the List, and property Capacity to determine the size the List can grow to without reallocating the internal array. In Chapter 10 we take a deeper look at classes and objects.

9.7 Deitel LINQ Resource Center

We use more advanced features of LINQ in later chapters. We've also created a LINQ Resource Center (www.deitel.com/LINQ/) that contains many links to additional information, including blogs by Microsoft LINQ team members, books, sample chapters, FAQs, tutorials, videos, webcasts and more. We encourage you to browse the LINQ Resource Center to learn more about this powerful technology.

10

Classes and Objects:
A Deeper Look

Instead of this absurd division into sexes, they ought to class people as static and dynamic.
—Evelyn Waugh

Is it a world to hide virtues in?
—William Shakespeare

But what, to serve our private ends, Forbids the cheating of our friends?
—Charles Churchill

This above all: to thine own self be true.
—William Shakespeare

Don't be "consistent," but be simply true.
—Oliver Wendell Holmes, Jr.

OBJECTIVES

In this chapter you'll learn:

- Encapsulation and data hiding.
- The concepts of data abstraction and abstract data types (ADTs).
- To use keyword `this`.
- To use indexers to access members of a class.
- To use `static` variables and methods.
- To use `readonly` fields.
- To take advantage of C#'s memory-management features.
- How to create a class library.
- When to use the `internal` access modifier.
- To use object initializers to set property values as you create a new object.
- To add functionality to existing classes with extension methods.
- To use delegates and lambda expressions to pass methods to other methods for execution at a later time.
- To create objects of anonymous types.

10.1 Introduction

In this chapter, we take a deeper look at building classes, controlling access to members of a class and creating constructors. We discuss composition—a capability that allows a class to have references to objects of other classes as members. We reexamine properties and explore indexers as an alternative notation for accessing the members of a class. The chapter also discusses static class members and readonly instance variables in detail. We investigate issues such as software reusability, data abstraction and encapsulation. Finally, we explain how to organize classes in assemblies to help manage large applications and promote reuse, then show a special relationship between classes in the same assembly.

10.2 Time Class Case Study

Time1 Class Declaration

Our first example consists of two classes—Time1 (Fig. 10.1) and Time1Test (Fig. 10.2). Class Time1 represents the time of day. Class Time1Test is a testing class in which the Main method creates an object of class Time1 and invokes its methods. The output of this application appears in Fig. 10.2.

Class Time1 contains three private instance variables of type int (Fig. 10.1, lines 5–7)—hour, minute and second—that represent the time in universal-time format (24-hour clock format, in which hours are in the range 0–23). Class Time1 contains public methods SetTime (lines 11–16), ToUniversalString (lines 19–23) and ToString (lines 26–31). These are the **public services** or the **public interface** that the class provides to its clients.

```
1   // Fig. 10.1: Time1.cs
2   // Time1 class declaration maintains the time in 24-hour format.
3   public class Time1
4   {
```

Fig. 10.1 | Time1 class declaration maintains the time in 24-hour format. (Part 1 of 2.)

```
 5      private int hour; // 0 - 23
 6      private int minute; // 0 - 59
 7      private int second; // 0 - 59
 8
 9      // set a new time value using universal time; ensure that
10      // the data remains consistent by setting invalid values to zero
11      public void SetTime( int h, int m, int s )
12      {
13          hour = ( ( h >= 0 && h < 24 ) ? h : 0 ); // validate hour
14          minute = ( ( m >= 0 && m < 60 ) ? m : 0 ); // validate minute
15          second = ( ( s >= 0 && s < 60 ) ? s : 0 ); // validate second
16      } // end method SetTime
17
18      // convert to string in universal-time format (HH:MM:SS)
19      public string ToUniversalString()
20      {
21          return string.Format( "{0:D2}:{1:D2}:{2:D2}",
22              hour, minute, second );
23      } // end method ToUniversalString
24
25      // convert to string in standard-time format (H:MM:SS AM or PM)
26      public override string ToString()
27      {
28          return string.Format( "{0}:{1:D2}:{2:D2} {3}",
29              ( ( hour == 0 || hour == 12 ) ? 12 : hour % 12 ),
30              minute, second, ( hour < 12 ? "AM" : "PM" ) );
31      } // end method ToString
32  } // end class Time1
```

Fig. 10.1 | `Time1` class declaration maintains the time in 24-hour format. (Part 2 of 2.)

In this example, class `Time1` does not declare a constructor, so the class has a default constructor that's supplied by the compiler. Each instance variable implicitly receives the default value 0 for an `int`. When instance variables are declared in the class body, they can be initialized using the same initialization syntax as a local variable.

Method *SetTime*

Method `SetTime` (lines 11–16) is a `public` method that declares three `int` parameters and uses them to set the time. A conditional expression tests each argument to determine whether the value is in a specified range. For example, the `hour` value (line 13) must be greater than or equal to 0 and less than 24, because universal-time format represents hours as integers from 0 to 23 (e.g., 1 PM is hour 13 and 11 PM is hour 23; midnight is hour 0 and noon is hour 12). Similarly, both `minute` and `second` values (lines 14 and 15) must be greater than or equal to 0 and less than 60. Any out-of-range values are set to 0 to ensure that a `Time1` object always contains consistent data—that is, the object's data values are always kept in range, even if the values provided as arguments to method `SetTime` are incorrect. In this example, 0 is a consistent value for `hour`, `minute` and `second`.

A value passed to `SetTime` is a correct value if that value is in the allowed range for the member it's initializing. So, any number in the range 0–23 would be a correct value for the hour. A correct value is always a consistent value. However, a consistent value is not necessarily a correct value. If `SetTime` sets `hour` to 0 because the argument received was out of range, then SetTime is taking an incorrect value and making it consistent, so the object remains in a consistent state at all times. In this case, the application might want to indicate that the object is incorrect. In Chapter 13, Exception Handling, you'll learn techniques that enable your classes to indicate when incorrect values are received.

Software Engineering Observation 10.1

Methods and properties that modify the values of private variables should verify that the intended new values are valid. If they're not, they should place the private variables in an appropriate consistent state.

Method ToUniversalString

Method ToUniversalString (lines 19–23) takes no arguments and returns a string in universal-time format, consisting of six digits—two for the hour, two for the minute and two for the second. For example, if the time were 1:30:07 PM, method ToUniversal-String would return 13:30:07. The return statement (lines 21–22) uses static method **Format** of class string to return a string containing the formatted hour, minute and second values, each with two digits and, where needed, a leading 0 (specified with the D2 format specifier—which pads the integer with 0s if it has less than two digits). Method Format is similar to the string formatting in method Console.Write, except that Format returns a formatted string rather than displaying it in a console window. The formatted string is returned by method ToUniversalString.

Method ToString

Method ToString (lines 26–31) takes no arguments and returns a string in standard-time format, consisting of the hour, minute and second values separated by colons and followed by an AM or PM indicator (e.g., 1:27:06 PM). Like method ToUniversalString, method ToString uses static string method Format to format the minute and second as two-digit values with leading 0s, if necessary. Line 29 uses a conditional operator (?:) to determine the value for hour in the string—if the hour is 0 or 12 (AM or PM), it appears as 12—otherwise, it appears as a value from 1 to 11. The conditional operator in line 30 determines whether AM or PM will be returned as part of the string.

Recall from Section 7.4 that all objects in C# have a ToString method that returns a string representation of the object. We chose to return a string containing the time in standard-time format. Method ToString is called implicitly when an object's value is output with a format item in a call to Console.Write. Remember that to enable objects to be converted to their string representations, we need to declare method ToString with keyword override—the reason for this will become clear when we discuss inheritance in Chapter 11.

Using Class Time1

As you learned in Chapter 4, each class you declare represents a new type in C#. Therefore, after declaring class Time1, we can use it as a type in declarations such as

```
Time1 sunset; // sunset can hold a reference to a Time1 object
```

The Time1Test application class (Fig. 10.2) uses class Time1. Line 10 creates a Time1 object and assigns it to local variable time. Note that new invokes class Time1's default constructor, since Time1 does not declare any constructors. Lines 13–17 output the time, first in universal-time format (by invoking time's ToUniversalString method in line 14), then in standard-time format (by explicitly invoking time's ToString method in line 16) to confirm that the Time1 object was initialized properly.

Line 20 invokes method SetTime of the time object to change the time. Then lines 21–25 output the time again in both formats to confirm that the time was set correctly.

```
1   // Fig. 10.2: Time1Test.cs
2   // Time1 object used in an application.
3   using System;
4
5   public class Time1Test
6   {
7      public static void Main( string[] args )
8      {
9         // create and initialize a Time1 object
10        Time1 time = new Time1(); // invokes Time1 constructor
11
12        // output string representations of the time
13        Console.Write( "The initial universal time is: " );
14        Console.WriteLine( time.ToUniversalString() );
15        Console.Write( "The initial standard time is: " );
16        Console.WriteLine( time.ToString() );
17        Console.WriteLine(); // output a blank line
18
19        // change time and output updated time
20        time.SetTime( 13, 27, 6 );
21        Console.Write( "Universal time after SetTime is: " );
22        Console.WriteLine( time.ToUniversalString() );
23        Console.Write( "Standard time after SetTime is: " );
24        Console.WriteLine( time.ToString() );
25        Console.WriteLine(); // output a blank line
26
27        // set time with invalid values; output updated time
28        time.SetTime( 99, 99, 99 );
29        Console.WriteLine( "After attempting invalid settings:" );
30        Console.Write( "Universal time: " );
31        Console.WriteLine( time.ToUniversalString() );
32        Console.Write( "Standard time: " );
33        Console.WriteLine( time.ToString() );
34     } // end Main
35  } // end class Time1Test
```

```
The initial universal time is: 00:00:00
The initial standard time is: 12:00:00 AM

Universal time after SetTime is: 13:27:06
Standard time after SetTime is: 1:27:06 PM

After attempting invalid settings:
Universal time: 00:00:00
Standard time: 12:00:00 AM
```

Fig. 10.2 | Time1 object used in an application.

To illustrate that method SetTime maintains the object in a consistent state, line 28 calls method SetTime with invalid arguments of 99 for the hour, minute and second. Lines 29–33 output the time again in both formats to confirm that SetTime maintains the object's consistent state, then the application terminates. The last two lines of the application's output show that the time is reset to midnight—the initial value of a Time1 object—after an attempt to set the time with three out-of-range values.

*Notes on the **Time1** Class Declaration*

Consider several issues of class design with respect to class Time1. The instance variables hour, minute and second are each declared private. The actual data representation used within the class is of no concern to the class's clients. For example, it would be perfectly reasonable for Time1 to represent the time internally as the number of seconds since midnight or the number of minutes and seconds since midnight. Clients could use the same public methods and properties to get the same results without being aware of this.

Software Engineering Observation 10.2

Classes simplify programming because the client can use only the public members exposed by the class. Such members are usually client oriented rather than implementation oriented. Clients are neither aware of, nor involved in, a class's implementation. Clients generally care about what *the class does but not* how *the class does it. (Clients do, of course, care that the class operates correctly and efficiently.)*

Software Engineering Observation 10.3

Interfaces change less frequently than implementations. When an implementation changes, implementation-dependent code must change accordingly. Hiding the implementation reduces the possibility that other application parts become dependent on class-implementation details.

10.3 Controlling Access to Members

The access modifiers public and private control access to a class's variables and methods. (In Section 10.14 and Chapter 11, we'll introduce the additional access modifiers internal and protected, respectively.) As we stated in Section 10.2, the primary purpose of public methods is to present to the class's clients a view of the services the class provides (that is, the class's public interface). Clients of the class need not be concerned with how the class accomplishes its tasks. For this reason, a class's private variables, properties and methods (i.e., the class's implementation details) are not directly accessible to the class's clients.

Figure 10.3 demonstrates that private class members are not directly accessible outside the class. Lines 9–11 attempt to directly access private instance variables hour, minute and second of Time1 object time. When this application is compiled, the compiler generates error messages stating that these private members are not accessible. [*Note:* This application uses the Time1 class from Fig. 10.1.]

Notice that members of a class—for instance, properties, methods and instance variables—do not need to be explicitly declared private. If a class member is not declared with an access modifier, it has private access by default. For clarity, we always explicitly declare private members.

```
1   // Fig. 10.3: MemberAccessTest.cs
2   // Private members of class Time1 are not accessible.
3   public class MemberAccessTest
4   {
5      public static void Main( string[] args )
6      {
7         Time1 time = new Time1(); // create and initialize Time1 object
8
9         time.hour = 7; // error: hour has private access in Time1
10        time.minute = 15; // error: minute has private access in Time1
11        time.second = 30; // error: second has private access in Time1
12     } // end Main
13  } // end class MemberAccessTest
```

		Description	File	Line	Column	Project
		Error List				▾ ╄ ×
		🚫 3 Errors ⚠ 0 Warnings ① 0 Messages				
🚫	1	'Time1.hour' is inaccessible due to its protection level	MemberAccessTest.cs	9	12	MemberAccessTest
🚫	2	'Time1.minute' is inaccessible due to its protection level	MemberAccessTest.cs	10	12	MemberAccessTest
🚫	3	'Time1.second' is inaccessible due to its protection level	MemberAccessTest.cs	11	12	MemberAccessTest

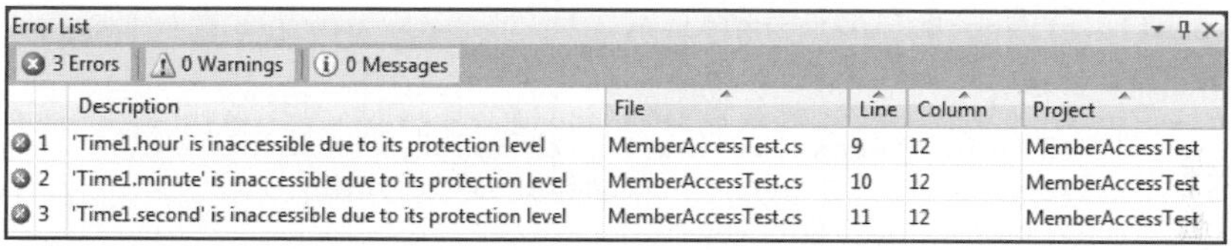

Fig. 10.3 | Private members of class Time1 are not accessible.

10.4 Referring to the Current Object's Members with the this Reference

Every object can access a reference to itself with keyword **this** (also called the **this refer-ence**). When a non-static method is called for a particular object, the method's body implicitly uses keyword this to refer to the object's instance variables and other methods. As you'll see in Fig. 10.4, you can also use keyword this *explicitly* in a non-static method's body. Section 10.5 and Section 10.6 shows a more interesting use of keyword this. Section 10.10 explains why keyword this cannot be used in a static method.

```
1   // Fig. 10.4: ThisTest.cs
2   // this used implicitly and explicitly to refer to members of an object.
3   using System;
4
5   public class ThisTest
6   {
7      public static void Main( string[] args )
8      {
9         SimpleTime time = new SimpleTime( 15, 30, 19 );
10        Console.WriteLine( time.BuildString() );
11     } // end Main
12  } // end class ThisTest
13
14  // class SimpleTime demonstrates the "this" reference
15  public class SimpleTime
16  {
17     private int hour; // 0-23
```

Fig. 10.4 | this used implicitly and explicitly to refer to members of an object. (Part 1 of 2.)

```
18      private int minute; // 0-59
19      private int second; // 0-59
20
21      // if the constructor uses parameter names identical to
22      // instance-variable names, the "this" reference is
23      // required to distinguish between names
24      public SimpleTime( int hour, int minute, int second )
25      {
26         this.hour = hour; // set "this" object's hour instance variable
27         this.minute = minute; // set "this" object's minute
28         this.second = second; // set "this" object's second
29      } // end SimpleTime constructor
30
31      // use explicit and implicit "this" to call ToUniversalString
32      public string BuildString()
33      {
34         return string.Format( "{0,24}: {1}\n{2,24}: {3}",
35            "this.ToUniversalString()", this.ToUniversalString(),
36            "ToUniversalString()", ToUniversalString() );
37      } // end method BuildString
38
39      // convert to string in universal-time format (HH:MM:SS)
40      public string ToUniversalString()
41      {
42         // "this" is not required here to access instance variables,
43         // because method does not have local variables with same
44         // names as instance variables
45         return string.Format( "{0:D2}:{1:D2}:{2:D2}",
46            this.hour, this.minute, this.second );
47      } // end method ToUniversalString
48   } // end class SimpleTime
```

```
this.ToUniversalString(): 15:30:19
    ToUniversalString(): 15:30:19
```

Fig. 10.4 | this used implicitly and explicitly to refer to members of an object. (Part 2 of 2.)

We now demonstrate implicit and explicit use of the this reference to enable class ThisTest's Main method to display the private data of a class SimpleTime object (Fig. 10.4). For the sake of brevity, we declare two classes in one file—class ThisTest is declared in lines 5–12, and class SimpleTime is declared in lines 15–48.

Class SimpleTime (lines 15–48) declares three private instance variables—hour, minute and second (lines 17–19). The constructor (lines 24–29) receives three int arguments to initialize a SimpleTime object. For the constructor we used parameter names that are identical to the class's instance-variable names (lines 17–19). We don't recommend this practice, but we intentionally did it here to hide the corresponding instance variables so that we could illustrate explicit use of the this reference. Recall from Section 7.11 that if a method contains a local variable with the same name as a field, that method will refer to the local variable rather than the field. In this case, the parameter hides the field in the method's scope. However, the method can use the this reference to refer to the hidden instance variable explicitly, as shown in lines 26–28 for SimpleTime's hidden instance variables.

Method `BuildString` (lines 32–37) returns a `string` created by a statement that uses the `this` reference explicitly and implicitly. Line 35 uses the `this` reference explicitly to call `ToUniversalString`. Line 36 uses the `this` reference implicitly to call the same method. Programmers typically do not use the `this` reference explicitly to reference other methods in the current object. Also, line 46 in method `ToUniversalString` explicitly uses the `this` reference to access each instance variable. This is not necessary here, because the method does not have any local variables that hide the instance variables of the class.

Common Programming Error 10.1

It's often a logic error when a method contains a parameter or local variable that has the same name as an instance variable of the class. In such a case, use reference `this` if you wish to access the instance variable of the class—otherwise, the method parameter or local variable will be referenced.

Error-Prevention Tip 10.1

Avoid method-parameter names or local-variable names that conflict with field names. This helps prevent subtle, hard-to-locate bugs.

Class `ThisTest` (Fig. 10.4, lines 5–12) demonstrates class `SimpleTime`. Line 9 creates an instance of class `SimpleTime` and invokes its constructor. Line 10 invokes the object's `BuildString` method, then displays the results.

Performance Tip 10.1

C# conserves memory by maintaining only one copy of each method per class—this method is invoked by every object of the class. Each object, on the other hand, has its own copy of the class's instance variables (i.e., non-`static` variables). Each method of the class implicitly uses the `this` reference to determine the specific object of the class to manipulate.

10.5 Indexers

Chapter 4 introduced properties as a way to access a class's `private` data in a controlled manner via the properties' `get` and `set` accessors. Sometimes a class encapsulates lists of data such as arrays. Such a class can use keyword `this` to define property-like class members called **indexers** that allow array-style indexed access to lists of elements. With "conventional" C# arrays, the index must be an integer value. A benefit of indexers is that you can define both integer indices and noninteger indices. For example, you could allow client code to manipulate data using `string`s as indices that represent the data items' names or descriptions. When manipulating "conventional" C# array elements, the array element-access operator always returns a value of the same type—i.e., the type of the array's elements. Indexers are more flexible—they can return any type, even one that's different from the type of the underlying data.

Although an indexer's element-access operator is used like an array element-access operator, indexers are defined like properties in a class. Unlike properties, for which you can choose an appropriate property name, indexers must be defined with keyword `this`. Indexers have the general form:

```
accessModifier  returnType this[ IndexType1 name1, IndexType2 name2, ... ]
{
    get
    {
        // use name1, name2, ... here to get data
    }
    set
    {
        // use name1, name2, ... here to set data
    }
}
```

The *IndexType* parameters specified in the brackets ([]) are accessible to the get and set accessors. These accessors define how to use the index (or indices) to retrieve or modify the appropriate data member. As with properties, the indexer's get accessor must return a value of type *returnType*, and the set accessor can use the implicit parameter value to reference the value that should be assigned to the element.

 Common Programming Error 10.2
Declaring indexers as static is a syntax error.

The application of Figs. 10.5 and 10.6 contains two classes—class Box represents a box with a length, a width and a height, and class BoxTest demonstrates class Box's indexers.

```
1   // Fig. 10.5: Box.cs
2   // Box class definition represents a box with length,
3   // width and height dimensions with indexers.
4   public class Box
5   {
6       private string[] names = { "length", "width", "height" };
7       private double[] dimensions = new double[ 3 ];
8
9       // constructor
10      public Box( double length, double width, double height )
11      {
12          dimensions[ 0 ] = length;
13          dimensions[ 1 ] = width;
14          dimensions[ 2 ] = height;
15      }
16
17      // indexer to access dimensions by integer index number
18      public double this[ int index ]
19      {
20          get
21          {
22              // validate index to get
23              if ( ( index < 0 ) || ( index >= dimensions.Length ) )
24                  return -1;
```

Fig. 10.5 | Box class definition represents a box with length, width and height dimensions with indexers. (Part 1 of 2.)

```
25              else
26                 return dimensions[ index ];
27          } // end get
28          set
29          {
30             if ( index >= 0 && index < dimensions.Length )
31                dimensions[ index ] = value;
32          } // end set
33       } // end numeric indexer
34
35       // indexer to access dimensions by their string names
36       public double this[ string name ]
37       {
38          get
39          {
40             // locate element to get
41             int i = 0;
42             while ( ( i < names.Length ) &&
43                ( name.ToLower() != names[ i ] ) )
44                ++i;
45
46             return ( i == names.Length ) ? -1 : dimensions[ i ];
47          } // end get
48          set
49          {
50             // locate element to set
51             int i = 0;
52             while ( ( i < names.Length ) &&
53                ( name.ToLower() != names[ i ] ) )
54                ++i;
55
56             if ( i != names.Length )
57                dimensions[ i ] = value;
58          } // end set
59       } // end string indexer
60    } // end class Box
```

Fig. 10.5 | Box class definition represents a box with length, width and height dimensions with indexers. (Part 2 of 2.)

The private data members of class Box are string array names (line 6), which contains the names (i.e., "length", "width" and "height") for the dimensions of a Box, and double array dimensions (line 7), which contains the size of each dimension. Each element in array names corresponds to an element in array dimensions (e.g., dimensions[2] contains the height of the Box).

Box defines two indexers (lines 18–33 and lines 36–59) that each return a double value representing the size of the dimension specified by the indexer's parameter. Indexers can be overloaded like methods. The first indexer uses an int index to manipulate an element in the dimensions array. The second indexer uses a string index representing the name of the dimension to manipulate an element in the dimensions array. Each indexer returns -1 if its get accessor encounters an invalid index. Each indexer's set accessor assigns value to the appropriate element of the array dimensions only if the index specified is valid. Normally, you would have an indexer throw an exception if it receives an invalid index. We discuss how to throw exceptions and process them in Chapter 13, Exception Handling.

The indexer that receives a string argument uses a while statement to search for a matching string in the names array (lines 42–44 and lines 52–54). If it finds a match, the indexer manipulates the corresponding element in array dimensions (lines 46 and 57).

Class BoxTest (Fig. 10.6) manipulates class Box's private data members through Box's indexers. Local variable box is declared at line 10 and initialized to a new instance of class Box. We use the Box class's constructor to initialize box with dimensions of 30, 30, and 30. Lines 14–16 use the indexer declared with parameter int to obtain the three dimensions of box and display them with WriteLine. The expression box[0] (line 14) implicitly calls the indexer's get accessor to obtain the value of box's private instance variable dimensions[0]. Similarly, the assignment to box0] in line 20 implicitly calls the indexer's set accessor in lines 28–32 of Fig. 10.5. The set accessor implicitly sets its value parameter to 10, then sets dimensions[0] to value (10). Lines 24 and 28–30 in Fig. 10.6 take similar actions, using the overloaded indexer with a string parameter to manipulate the Box's properties.

```
 1   // Fig. 10.6: BoxTest.cs
 2   // Indexers provide access to a Box object's members.
 3   using System;
 4
 5   public class BoxTest
 6   {
 7      public static void Main( string[] args )
 8      {
 9         // create a box
10         Box box = new Box( 30, 30, 30 );
11
12         // show dimensions with numeric indexers
13         Console.WriteLine( "Created a box with the dimensions:" );
14         Console.WriteLine( "box[ 0 ] = {0}", box[ 0 ] );
15         Console.WriteLine( "box[ 1 ] = {0}", box[ 1 ] );
16         Console.WriteLine( "box[ 2 ] = {0}", box[ 2 ] );
17
18         // set a dimension with the numeric indexer
19         Console.WriteLine( "\nSetting box[ 0 ] to 10...\n" );
20         box[ 0 ] = 10;
21
22         // set a dimension with the string indexer
23         Console.WriteLine( "Setting box[ \"width\" ] to 20...\n" );
24         box[ "width" ] = 20;
25
26         // show dimensions with string indexers
27         Console.WriteLine( "Now the box has the dimensions:" );
28         Console.WriteLine( "box[ \"length\" ] = {0}", box[ "length" ] );
29         Console.WriteLine( "box[ \"width\" ] = {0}", box[ "width" ] );
30         Console.WriteLine( "box[ \"height\" ] = {0}", box[ "height" ] );
31      } // end Main
32   } // end class BoxTest
```

Fig. 10.6 | Indexers provide access to an object's members. (Part 1 of 2.)

```
Created a box with the dimensions:
box[ 0 ] = 30
box[ 1 ] = 30
box[ 2 ] = 30

Setting box[ 0 ] to 10...

Setting box[ "width" ] to 20...

Now the box has the dimensions:
box[ "length" ] = 10
box[ "width" ] = 20
box[ "height" ] = 30
```

Fig. 10.6 | Indexers provide access to an object's members. (Part 2 of 2.)

10.6 Time Class Case Study: Overloaded Constructors

As you know, you can declare your own constructor to specify how objects of a class should be initialized. Next, we demonstrate a class with several **overloaded constructors** that enable objects of that class to be initialized in different ways. To overload constructors, simply provide multiple constructor declarations with different signatures.

Class *Time2* with Overloaded Constructors

By default, instance variables hour, minute and second of class Time1 (Fig. 10.1) are initialized to their default values of 0—midnight in universal time. Class Time1 does not enable the class's clients to initialize the time with specific nonzero values. Class Time2 (Fig. 10.7) contains overloaded constructors for conveniently initializing its objects in a variety of ways. The constructors ensure that each Time2 object begins in a consistent state. In this application, four of the constructors invoke a fifth constructor, which in turn calls method SetTime. Method SetTime invokes the **set** accessors of properties Hour, Minute and Second, which ensure that the value supplied for hour is in the range 0 to 23 and that the values for minute and second are each in the range 0 to 59. If a value is out of range, it's set to 0 by the corresponding property (once again ensuring that each instance variable remains in a consistent state). The compiler invokes the appropriate constructor by matching the number and types of the arguments specified in the constructor call with the number and types of the parameters specified in each constructor declaration. We could have combined the constructors in lines 11–23 into a single constructor with optional parameters. Class Time2 also provides properties for each instance variable.

```
1   // Fig. 10.7: Time2.cs
2   // Time2 class declaration with overloaded constructors.
3   public class Time2
4   {
5      private int hour; // 0 - 23
6      private int minute; // 0 - 59
7      private int second; // 0 - 59
8
```

Fig. 10.7 | Time2 class declaration with overloaded constructors. (Part 1 of 3.)

```
 9      // Time2 no-argument constructor: initializes each instance variable
10      // to zero; ensures that Time2 objects start in a consistent state
11      public Time2() : this( 0, 0, 0 ) { }
12
13      // Time2 constructor: hour supplied, minute and second defaulted to 0
14      public Time2( int h ) : this( h, 0, 0 ) { }
15
16      // Time2 constructor: hour and minute supplied, second defaulted to 0
17      public Time2( int h, int m ) : this( h, m, 0 ) { }
18
19      // Time2 constructor: hour, minute and second supplied
20      public Time2( int h, int m, int s )
21      {
22         SetTime( h, m, s ); // invoke SetTime to validate time
23      } // end Time2 three-argument constructor
24
25      // Time2 constructor: another Time2 object supplied
26      public Time2( Time2 time )
27         : this( time.Hour, time.Minute, time.Second ) { }
28
29      // set a new time value using universal time; ensure that
30      // the data remains consistent by setting invalid values to zero
31      public void SetTime( int h, int m, int s )
32      {
33         Hour = h; // set the Hour property
34         Minute = m; // set the Minute property
35         Second = s; // set the Second property
36      } // end method SetTime
37
38      // Properties for getting and setting
39      // property that gets and sets the hour
40      public int Hour
41      {
42         get
43         {
44            return hour;
45         } // end get
46         // make writing inaccessible outside the class
47         private set
48         {
49            hour = ( ( value >= 0 && value < 24 ) ? value : 0 );
50         } // end set
51      } // end property Hour
52
53      // property that gets and sets the minute
54      public int Minute
55      {
56         get
57         {
58            return minute;
59         } // end get
60         // make writing inaccessible outside the class
```

Fig. 10.7 | Time2 class declaration with overloaded constructors. (Part 2 of 3.)

```
61            private set
62            {
63               minute = ( ( value >= 0 && value < 60 ) ? value : 0 );
64            } // end set
65         } // end property Minute
66
67         // property that gets and sets the second
68         public int Second
69         {
70            get
71            {
72               return second;
73            } // end get
74            // make writing inaccessible outside the class
75            private set
76            {
77               second = ( ( value >= 0 && value < 60 ) ? value : 0 );
78            } // end set
79         } // end property Second
80
81         // convert to string in universal-time format (HH:MM:SS)
82         public string ToUniversalString()
83         {
84            return string.Format(
85               "{0:D2}:{1:D2}:{2:D2}", Hour, Minute, Second );
86         } // end method ToUniversalString
87
88         // convert to string in standard-time format (H:MM:SS AM or PM)
89         public override string ToString()
90         {
91            return string.Format( "{0}:{1:D2}:{2:D2} {3}",
92               ( ( Hour == 0 || Hour == 12 ) ? 12 : Hour % 12 ),
93               Minute, Second, ( Hour < 12 ? "AM" : "PM" ) );
94         } // end method ToString
95      } // end class Time2
```

Fig. 10.7 | Time2 class declaration with overloaded constructors. (Part 3 of 3.)

Class *Time2's Constructors*

Line 11 declares a **parameterless constructor**—a constructor invoked without arguments. This constructor has an empty body, as indicated by the empty set of curly braces after the constructor header. Instead, we introduce a use of the this reference that's allowed only in the constructor's header. In line 11, the usual constructor header is followed by a colon (:), then the keyword this. The this reference is used in method-call syntax (along with the three int arguments) to invoke the Time2 constructor that takes three int arguments (lines 20–23). The parameterless constructor passes values of 0 for the hour, minute and second to the constructor with three int parameters. The use of the this reference as shown here is called a **constructor initializer**. Constructor initializers are a popular way to reuse initialization code provided by one of the class's constructors rather than defining similar code in another constructor's body. We use this syntax in four of the five Time2 constructors to make the class easier to maintain. If we needed to change how objects of class Time2 are initialized, only the constructor that the class's other constructors call would need to be modified. Even that constructor might not need modification—it simply calls the SetTime method to perform the actual initialization, so it's possible that the changes the class might require would be localized to this method.

Line 14 declares a Time2 constructor with a single int parameter representing the hour, which is passed with 0 for the minute and second to the constructor at lines 20–23. Line 17 declares a Time2 constructor that receives two int parameters representing the hour and minute, which are passed with 0 for the second to the constructor at lines 20–23. Like the parameterless constructor, each of these constructors invokes the constructor at lines 20–23 to minimize code duplication. Lines 20–23 declare the Time2 constructor that receives three int parameters representing the hour, minute and second. This constructor calls SetTime to initialize the instance variables to consistent values. SetTime, in turn, invokes the set accessors of properties Hour, Minute and Second.

Common Programming Error 10.3

A constructor can call methods of the class. Be aware that the instance variables might not yet be in a consistent state, because the constructor is in the process of initializing the object. Using instance variables before they have been initialized properly is a logic error.

Lines 26–27 declare a Time2 constructor that receives a reference to another Time2 object. In this case, the values from the Time2 argument are passed to the three-parameter constructor at lines 20–23 to initialize the hour, minute and second. Line 27 could have directly accessed the hour, minute and second instance variables of the constructor's time argument with the expressions time.hour, time.minute and time.second—even though hour, minute and second are declared as private variables of class Time2.

Software Engineering Observation 10.4

When one object of a class has a reference to another object of the same class, the first object can access all the second object's data and methods (including those that are private).

Notes Regarding Class *Time2*'s Methods, Properties and Constructors

Time2's properties are accessed throughout the body of the class. In particular, method SetTime assigns values to properties Hour, Minute and Second in lines 33–35, and methods ToUniversalString and ToString use properties Hour, Minute and Second in line 85 and lines 92–93, respectively. In each case, these methods could have accessed the class's private data directly without using the properties. However, consider changing the representation of the time from three int values (requiring 12 bytes of memory) to a single int value representing the total number of seconds that have elapsed since midnight (requiring only 4 bytes of memory). If we make such a change, only the bodies of the methods that access the private data directly would need to change—in particular, the individual properties Hour, Minute and Second. There would be no need to modify the bodies of methods SetTime, ToUniversalString or ToString, because they do not access the private data directly. Designing the class in this manner reduces the likelihood of programming errors when altering the class's implementation.

Similarly, each Time2 constructor could be written to include a copy of the appropriate statements from method SetTime. Doing so may be slightly more efficient, because the extra constructor call and the call to SetTime are eliminated. However, duplicating statements in multiple methods or constructors makes changing the class's internal data representation more difficult and error-prone. Having the Time2 constructors call the three-parameter constructor (or even call SetTime directly) requires any changes to the implementation of SetTime to be made only once.

Software Engineering Observation 10.5

When implementing a method of a class, use the class's properties to access the class's private data. This simplifies code maintenance and reduces the likelihood of errors.

Also notice that class Time2 takes advantage of access modifiers to ensure that clients of the class must use the appropriate methods and properties to access private data. In particular, the properties Hour, Minute and Second declare private set accessors (lines 47, 61 and 75, respectively) to restrict the use of the set accessors to members of the class. We declare these private for the same reasons that we declare the instance variables private—to simplify code maintenance and ensure that the data remains in a consistent state. Although the methods in class Time2 still have all the advantages of using the set accessors to perform validation, clients of the class must use the SetTime method to modify this data. The get accessors of properties Hour, Minute and Second are implicitly declared public because their properties are declared public—when there is no access modifier before a get or set accessor, the accessor inherits the access modifier preceding the property name.

Using Class Time2's Overloaded Constructors
Class Time2Test (Fig. 10.8) creates six Time2 objects (lines 9–14) to invoke the overloaded Time2 constructors. Line 9 shows that the parameterless constructor (line 11 of Fig. 10.7) is invoked by placing an empty set of parentheses after the class name when allocating a Time2 object with new. Lines 10–14 of the application demonstrate passing arguments to the other Time2 constructors. C# invokes the appropriate overloaded constructor by matching the number and types of the arguments specified in the constructor call with the number and types of the parameters specified in each constructor declaration. Line 10 invokes the constructor at line 14 of Fig. 10.7. Line 11 invokes the constructor at line 17 of Fig. 10.7. Lines 12–13 invoke the constructor at lines 20–23 of Fig. 10.7. Line 14 invokes the constructor at lines 26–27 of Fig. 10.7. The application displays the string representation of each initialized Time2 object to confirm that each was initialized properly.

```csharp
1   // Fig. 10.8: Time2Test.cs
2   // Overloaded constructors used to initialize Time2 objects.
3   using System;
4
5   public class Time2Test
6   {
7      public static void Main( string[] args )
8      {
9         Time2 t1 = new Time2(); // 00:00:00
10        Time2 t2 = new Time2( 2 ); // 02:00:00
11        Time2 t3 = new Time2( 21, 34 ); // 21:34:00
12        Time2 t4 = new Time2( 12, 25, 42 ); // 12:25:42
13        Time2 t5 = new Time2( 27, 74, 99 ); // 00:00:00
14        Time2 t6 = new Time2( t4 ); // 12:25:42
```

Fig. 10.8 | Overloaded constructors used to initialize Time2 objects. (Part 1 of 2.)

```
15
16          Console.WriteLine( "Constructed with:\n" );
17          Console.WriteLine( "t1: all arguments defaulted" );
18          Console.WriteLine( "   {0}", t1.ToUniversalString() ); // 00:00:00
19          Console.WriteLine( "   {0}\n", t1.ToString() ); // 12:00:00 AM
20
21          Console.WriteLine(
22             "t2: hour specified; minute and second defaulted" );
23          Console.WriteLine( "   {0}", t2.ToUniversalString() ); // 02:00:00
24          Console.WriteLine( "   {0}\n", t2.ToString() ); // 2:00:00 AM
25
26          Console.WriteLine(
27             "t3: hour and minute specified; second defaulted" );
28          Console.WriteLine( "   {0}", t3.ToUniversalString() ); // 21:34:00
29          Console.WriteLine( "   {0}\n", t3.ToString() ); // 9:34:00 PM
30
31          Console.WriteLine( "t4: hour, minute and second specified" );
32          Console.WriteLine( "   {0}", t4.ToUniversalString() ); // 12:25:42
33          Console.WriteLine( "   {0}\n", t4.ToString() ); // 12:25:42 PM
34
35          Console.WriteLine( "t5: all invalid values specified" );
36          Console.WriteLine( "   {0}", t5.ToUniversalString() ); // 00:00:00
37          Console.WriteLine( "   {0}\n", t5.ToString() ); // 12:00:00 AM
38
39          Console.WriteLine( "t6: Time2 object t4 specified" );
40          Console.WriteLine( "   {0}", t6.ToUniversalString() ); // 12:25:42
41          Console.WriteLine( "   {0}", t6.ToString() ); // 12:25:42 PM
42       } // end Main
43    } // end class Time2Test
```

```
Constructed with:

t1: all arguments defaulted
   00:00:00
   12:00:00 AM

t2: hour specified; minute and second defaulted
   02:00:00
   2:00:00 AM

t3: hour and minute specified; second defaulted
   21:34:00
   9:34:00 PM

t4: hour, minute and second specified
   12:25:42
   12:25:42 PM

t5: all invalid values specified
   00:00:00
   12:00:00 AM

t6: Time2 object t4 specified
   12:25:42
   12:25:42 PM
```

Fig. 10.8 | Overloaded constructors used to initialize Time2 objects. (Part 2 of 2.)

10.7 Default and Parameterless Constructors

Every class must have at least one constructor. Recall from Section 4.10 that if you do not provide any constructors in a class's declaration, the compiler creates a default constructor that takes no arguments when it's invoked. In Section 11.4.2, you'll learn that the default constructor implicitly performs a special task.

The compiler will not create a default constructor for a class that explicitly declares at least one constructor. In this case, if you want to be able to invoke the constructor with no arguments, you must declare a parameterless constructor—as in line 11 of Fig. 10.7. Like a default constructor, a parameterless constructor is invoked with empty parentheses. The Time2 parameterless constructor explicitly initializes a Time2 object by passing to the three-parameter constructor 0 for each parameter. Since 0 is the default value for int instance variables, the parameterless constructor in this example could actually omit the constructor initializer. In this case, each instance variable would receive its default value when the object is created. If we omit the parameterless constructor, clients of this class would not be able to create a Time2 object with the expression new Time2().

Common Programming Error 10.4

If a class has constructors, but none of the public constructors are parameterless constructors, and an application attempts to call a parameterless constructor to initialize an object of the class, a compilation error occurs. A constructor can be called with no arguments only if the class does not have any constructors (in which case the default constructor is called) or if the class has a public parameterless constructor.

10.8 Composition

A class can have references to objects of other classes as members. This is called **composition** and is sometimes referred to as a *has-a* **relationship**. For example, an object of class AlarmClock needs to know the current time and the time when it's supposed to sound its alarm, so it's reasonable to include two references to Time objects in an AlarmClock object.

Software Engineering Observation 10.6

One form of software reuse is composition, in which a class has as members references to objects of other classes.

Our example of composition contains three classes—Date (Fig. 10.9), Employee (Fig. 10.10) and EmployeeTest (Fig. 10.11). Class Date (Fig. 10.9) declares instance variables month and day (lines 7–9) and auto-implemented property Year (line 11) to represent a date. The constructor receives three int parameters. Line 17 invokes the set accessor of property Month (lines 24–40) to validate the month—an out-of-range value is set to 1 to maintain a consistent state. Line 18 uses property Year to set the year. Since Year is an auto-implemented property, we're assuming in this example that the value for Year is correct. Line 19 uses property Day (lines 43–67), which validates and assigns the value for day based on the current month and Year (by using properties Month and Year in turn to obtain the values of month and Year). The order of initialization is important, because the set accessor of property Day validates the value for day based on the assumption that month and Year are correct. Line 55 determines whether the day is correct based on the number of days in the particular Month. If the day is not correct, lines 58–59 determine whether the Month is February, the day is 29 and the Year is a leap year. Otherwise, if the parameter value does not contain a correct value for day, line 64 sets day to 1 to maintain the Date in a consistent state. Line 20 in the constructor outputs the this reference as a string. Since this is a reference to the current Date object, the object's ToString method (lines 70–73) is called implicitly to obtain the object's string representation.

```csharp
1   // Fig. 10.9: Date.cs
2   // Date class declaration.
3   using System;
4
5   public class Date
6   {
7      private int month; // 1-12
8      private int day; // 1-31 based on month
9
10     // auto-implemented property Year
11     public int Year { get; set; }
12
13     // constructor: use property Month to confirm proper value for month;
14     // use property Day to confirm proper value for day
15     public Date( int theMonth, int theDay, int theYear )
16     {
17        Month = theMonth; // validate month
18        Year = theYear; // could validate year
19        Day = theDay; // validate day
20        Console.WriteLine( "Date object constructor for date {0}", this );
21     } // end Date constructor
22
23     // property that gets and sets the month
24     public int Month
25     {
26        get
27        {
28           return month;
29        } // end get
30        private set // make writing inaccessible outside the class
31        {
32           if ( value > 0 && value <= 12 ) // validate month
33              month = value;
34           else // month is invalid
35           {
36              Console.WriteLine( "Invalid month ({0}) set to 1.", value );
37              month = 1; // maintain object in consistent state
38           } // end else
39        } // end set
40     } // end property Month
41
42     // property that gets and sets the day
43     public int Day
44     {
45        get
46        {
```

Fig. 10.9 | Date class declaration. (Part 1 of 2.)

```
47          return day;
48       } // end get
49       private set // make writing inaccessible outside the class
50       {
51          int[] daysPerMonth = { 0, 31, 28, 31, 30, 31, 30,
52                                  31, 31, 30, 31, 30, 31 };
53
54          // check if day in range for month
55          if ( value > 0 && value <= daysPerMonth[ Month ] )
56             day = value;
57          // check for leap year
58          else if ( Month == 2 && value == 29 &&
59             ( Year % 400 == 0 || ( Year % 4 == 0 && Year % 100 != 0 ) ) )
60             day = value;
61          else
62          {
63             Console.WriteLine( "Invalid day ({0}) set to 1.", value );
64             day = 1; // maintain object in consistent state
65          } // end else
66       } // end set
67    } // end property Day
68
69    // return a string of the form month/day/year
70    public override string ToString()
71    {
72       return string.Format( "{0}/{1}/{2}", Month, Day, Year );
73    } // end method ToString
74 } // end class Date
```

Fig. 10.9 | Date class declaration. (Part 2 of 2.)

Class Employee (Fig. 10.10) has instance variables firstName, lastName, birthDate and hireDate. Members birthDate and hireDate (lines 7–8) are references to Date objects, demonstrating that a class can have as instance variables references to objects of other classes. The Employee constructor (lines 11–18) takes four parameters—first, last, dateOfBirth and dateOfHire. The objects referenced by parameters dateOfBirth and dateOfHire are assigned to the Employee object's birthDate and hireDate instance variables, respectively. When class Employee's ToString method is called, it returns a string containing the string representations of the two Date objects. Each of these strings is obtained with an implicit call to the Date class's ToString method.

```
1   // Fig. 10.10: Employee.cs
2   // Employee class with references to other objects.
3   public class Employee
4   {
5      private string firstName;
6      private string lastName;
7      private Date birthDate;
8      private Date hireDate;
9
```

Fig. 10.10 | Employee class with references to other objects. (Part 1 of 2.)

```
10       // constructor to initialize name, birth date and hire date
11       public Employee( string first, string last,
12          Date dateOfBirth, Date dateOfHire )
13       {
14          firstName = first;
15          lastName = last;
16          birthDate = dateOfBirth;
17          hireDate = dateOfHire;
18       } // end Employee constructor
19
20       // convert Employee to string format
21       public override string ToString()
22       {
23          return string.Format( "{0}, {1}  Hired: {2}  Birthday: {3}",
24             lastName, firstName, hireDate, birthDate );
25       } // end method ToString
26    } // end class Employee
```

Fig. 10.10 | Employee class with references to other objects. (Part 2 of 2.)

Class `EmployeeTest` (Fig. 10.11) creates two `Date` objects (lines 9–10) to represent an `Employee`'s birthday and hire date, respectively. Line 11 creates an `Employee` and initializes its instance variables by passing to the constructor two `strings` (representing the `Employee`'s first and last names) and two `Date` objects (representing the birthday and hire date). Line 13 implicitly invokes the `Employee`'s `ToString` method to display the values of its instance variables and demonstrate that the object was initialized properly.

```
1    // Fig. 10.11: EmployeeTest.cs
2    // Composition demonstration.
3    using System;
4
5    public class EmployeeTest
6    {
7       public static void Main( string[] args )
8       {
9          Date birth = new Date( 7, 24, 1949 );
10         Date hire = new Date( 3, 12, 1988 );
11         Employee employee = new Employee( "Bob", "Blue", birth, hire );
12
13         Console.WriteLine( employee );
14      } // end Main
15   } // end class EmployeeTest
```

```
Date object constructor for date 7/24/1949
Date object constructor for date 3/12/1988
Blue, Bob  Hired: 3/12/1988  Birthday: 7/24/1949
```

Fig. 10.11 | Composition demonstration.

10.9 Garbage Collection and Destructors

Every object you create uses various system resources, such as memory. In many programming languages, these system resources are reserved for the object's use until they're explicitly released by the programmer. If all the references to the object that manages the resource are lost before the resource is explicitly released, the application can no longer access the resource to release it. This is known as a **resource leak**.

We need a disciplined way to give resources back to the system when they're no longer needed, thus avoiding resource leaks. The Common Language Runtime (CLR) performs automatic memory management by using a **garbage collector** to reclaim the memory occupied by objects that are no longer in use, so the memory can be used for other objects. When there are no more references to an object, the object becomes **eligible for destruction**. Every object has a special member, called a **destructor**, that is invoked by the garbage collector to perform **termination housekeeping** on an object before the garbage collector reclaims the object's memory. A destructor is declared like a parameterless constructor, except that its name is the class name, preceded by a tilde (~), and it has no access modifier in its header. After the garbage collector calls the object's destructor, the object becomes **eligible for garbage collection**. The memory for such an object can be reclaimed by the garbage collector. With .NET 4, Microsoft has introduced a new background garbage collector that manages memory more efficiently than the garbage collectors in earlier .NET versions.

Memory leaks, which are common in other languages such as C and C++ (because memory is not automatically reclaimed in those languages), are less likely in C# (but some can still happen in subtle ways). Other types of resource leaks can occur. For example, an application could open a file on disk to modify its contents. If the application does not close the file, no other application can modify (or possibly even use) the file until the application that opened it terminates.

A problem with the garbage collector is that it doesn't guarantee that it will perform its tasks at a specified time. Therefore, the garbage collector may call the destructor any time after the object becomes eligible for destruction, and may reclaim the memory any time after the destructor executes. In fact, it's possible that neither will happen before the application terminates. Thus, it's unclear whether, or when, the destructor will be called. For this reason, destructors are rarely used.

> **Software Engineering Observation 10.7**
>
> *A class that uses system resources, such as files on disk, should provide a method to eventually release the resources. Many Framework Class Library classes provide Close or Dispose methods for this purpose. Section 13.5 introduces the Dispose method, which is then used in many later examples. Close methods are typically used with objects that are associated with files (Chapter 17) and other types of so-called streams of data.*

10.10 static Class Members

Every object has its own copy of all the instance variables of the class. In certain cases, only one copy of a particular variable should be shared by all objects of a class. A static **variable** is used in such cases. A static variable represents **classwide information**—all objects of the class share the same piece of data. The declaration of a static variable begins with the keyword static.

Let's motivate static data with an example. Suppose that we have a video game with Martians and other space creatures. Each Martian tends to be brave and willing to attack other space creatures when it's aware that there are at least four other Martians present. If fewer than five Martians are present, each Martian becomes cowardly. Thus each Martian needs to know the martianCount. We could endow class Martian with martianCount as an instance variable. If we do this, every Martian will have a separate copy of the instance variable, and every time we create a new Martian, we'll have to update the instance variable martianCount in every Martian. This wastes space on redundant copies, wastes time updating the separate copies and is error prone. Instead, we declare martianCount to be static, making martianCount classwide data. Every Martian can access the martianCount as if it were an instance variable of class Martian, but only one copy of the static martianCount is maintained. This saves space. We save time by having the Martian constructor increment the static martianCount—there is only one copy, so we do not have to increment separate copies of martianCount for each Martian object.

Software Engineering Observation 10.8

Use a static variable when all objects of a class must use the same copy of the variable.

The scope of a static variable is the body of its class. A class's public static members can be accessed by qualifying the member name with the class name and the member access (.) operator, as in Math.PI. A class's private static class members can be accessed only through the methods and properties of the class. Actually, static class members exist even when no objects of the class exist—they're available as soon as the class is loaded into memory at execution time. To access a private static member from outside its class, a public static method or property can be provided.

Common Programming Error 10.5

It's a compilation error to access or invoke a static member by referencing it through an instance of the class, like a non-static member.

Software Engineering Observation 10.9

Static variables and methods exist, and can be used, even if no objects of that class have been instantiated.

Our next application declares two classes—Employee (Fig. 10.12) and EmployeeTest (Fig. 10.13). Class Employee declares private static variable count (Fig. 10.12, line 8) and public static property Count (lines 38–44). We omit the set accessor of property Count to make the property read-only—we do not want clients of the class to be able to modify count. The static variable count is initialized to 0 in line 8. If a static variable is not initialized, the compiler assigns a default value to the variable—in this case 0, the default value for type int. Variable count maintains a count of the number of objects of class Employee that have been created.

```
1   // Fig. 10.12: Employee.cs
2   // Static variable used to maintain a count of the number of
3   // Employee objects that have been created.
4   using System;
5
```

Fig. 10.12 | static variable used to maintain a count of the number of Employee objects in memory. (Part 1 of 2.)

```
 6   public class Employee
 7   {
 8      private static int count = 0; // number of objects in memory
 9
10      // read-only auto-implemented property FirstName
11      public string FirstName { get; private set; }
12
13      // read-only auto-implemented property LastName
14      public string LastName { get; private set; }
15
16      // initialize employee, add 1 to static count and
17      // output string indicating that constructor was called
18      public Employee( string first, string last )
19      {
20         FirstName = first;
21         LastName = last;
22         count++; // increment static count of employees
23         Console.WriteLine( "Employee constructor: {0} {1}; count = {2}",
24            FirstName, LastName, Count );
25      } // end Employee constructor
26
27      // read-only property that gets the employee count
28      public static int Count
29      {
30         get
31         {
32            return count;
33         } // end get
34      } // end property Count
35   } // end class Employee
```

Fig. 10.12 | static variable used to maintain a count of the number of Employee objects in memory. (Part 2 of 2.)

When Employee objects exist, member count can be used in any method of an Employee object—this example increments count in the constructor (line 22). When no objects of class Employee exist, member count can still be referenced, but only through a call to public static property Count (lines 28–34), as in Employee.Count, which evaluates to the number of Employee objects currently in memory.

EmployeeTest method Main (Fig. 10.13) instantiates two Employee objects (lines 14–15). When each Employee object's constructor is invoked, lines 20–21 of Fig. 10.12 assign the Employee's first name and last name to properties FirstName and LastName. These two statements do not make copies of the original string arguments. Actually, string objects in C# are immutable—they cannot be modified after they're created. Therefore, it's safe to have many references to one string object. This is not normally the case for objects of most other classes in C#. If string objects are immutable, you might wonder why we're able to use operators + and += to concatenate string objects. String-concatenation operations actually result in a new string object containing the concatenated values. The original string objects are not modified.

Lines 18–19 display the updated Count. When Main has finished using the two Employee objects, references e1 and e2 are set to null at lines 29–30, so they no longer

```
1   // Fig. 10.13: EmployeeTest.cs
2   // Static member demonstration.
3   using System;
4
5   public class EmployeeTest
6   {
7      public static void Main( string[] args )
8      {
9         // show that count is 0 before creating Employees
10        Console.WriteLine( "Employees before instantiation: {0}",
11           Employee.Count );
12
13        // create two Employees; count should become 2
14        Employee e1 = new Employee( "Susan", "Baker" );
15        Employee e2 = new Employee( "Bob", "Blue" );
16
17        // show that count is 2 after creating two Employees
18        Console.WriteLine( "\nEmployees after instantiation: {0}",
19           Employee.Count );
20
21        // get names of Employees
22        Console.WriteLine( "\nEmployee 1: {0} {1}\nEmployee 2: {2} {3}\n",
23           e1.FirstName, e1.LastName,
24           e2.FirstName, e2.LastName );
25
26        // in this example, there is only one reference to each Employee,
27        // so the following statements cause the CLR to mark each
28        // Employee object as being eligible for garbage collection
29        e1 = null; // good practice: mark object e1 no longer needed
30        e2 = null; // good practice: mark object e2 no longer needed
31     } // end Main
32  } // end class EmployeeTest
```

```
Employees before instantiation: 0
Employee constructor: Susan Baker; count = 1
Employee constructor: Bob Blue; count = 2

Employees after instantiation: 2

Employee 1: Susan Baker
Employee 2: Bob Blue
```

Fig. 10.13 | static member demonstration.

refer to the objects that were instantiated in lines 14–15. The objects become "eligible for destruction" because there are no more references to them in the application. After the objects' destructors are called, the objects become "eligible for garbage collection."

Eventually, the garbage collector might reclaim the memory for these objects (or the operating system will reclaim the memory when the application terminates). C# does not guarantee when, or even whether, the garbage collector will execute. When the garbage collector does run, it's possible that no objects or only a subset of the eligible objects will be collected.

A method declared static cannot access non-static class members directly, because a static method can be called even when no objects of the class exist. For the same reason, the this reference cannot be used in a static method—the this reference must refer to a specific object of the class, and when a static method is called, there might not be any objects of its class in memory.

10.11 readonly Instance Variables

The **principle of least privilege** is fundamental to good software engineering. In the context of an application, the principle states that *code should be granted the amount of privilege and access needed to accomplish its designated task, but no more.* Let's see how this principle applies to instance variables.

Some instance variables need to be modifiable, and some do not. In Section 8.4, we used keyword const for declaring constants. These constants must be initialized to a constant value when they're declared. Suppose, however, we want to initialize a constant belonging to an object in the object's constructor. C# provides keyword **readonly** to specify that an instance variable of an object is not modifiable and that any attempt to modify it after the object is constructed is an error. For example,

```
    private readonly int INCREMENT;
```

declares readonly instance variable INCREMENT of type int. Like constants, readonly variables are declared with all capital letters by convention. Although readonly instance variables can be initialized when they're declared, this isn't required. Readonly variables should be initialized *by each* of the class's constructors. Each constructor can assign values to a readonly instance variable multiple times—the variable doesn't become unmodifiable until after the constructor completes execution. A constructor does not initialize the readonly variable, the variable receives the same default value as any other instance variable (0 for numeric simple types, false for bool type and null for reference types), and the compiler generates a warning.

> **Software Engineering Observation 10.10**
> *Declaring an instance variable as readonly helps enforce the principle of least privilege. If an instance variable should not be modified after the object is constructed, declare it to be readonly to prevent modification.*

Members that are declared as const must be assigned values at compile time. Therefore, const members can be initialized *only* with other constant values, such as integers, string literals, characters and other const members. Constant members with values that cannot be determined at compile time must be declared with keyword readonly, so they can be initialized at *execution time*. Variables that are readonly can be initialized with more complex expressions, such as an array initializer or a method call that returns a value or a reference to an object.

> **Common Programming Error 10.6**
> *Attempting to modify a readonly instance variable anywhere but in its declaration or the object's constructors is a compilation error.*

Error-Prevention Tip 10.2

Attempts to modify a `readonly` instance variable are caught at compilation time rather than causing execution-time errors. It's always preferable to get bugs out at compile time, if possible, rather than allowing them to slip through to execution time (where studies have found that repairing bugs is often many times more costly).

Software Engineering Observation 10.11

If a `readonly` instance variable is initialized to a constant only in its declaration, it's not necessary to have a separate copy of the instance variable for every object of the class. The variable should be declared `const` instead. Constants declared with `const` are implicitly `static`, so there will only be one copy for the entire class.

10.12 Data Abstraction and Encapsulation

Classes normally hide the details of their implementation from their clients. This is called **information hiding**. As an example, let's consider the **stack data structure** introduced in Section 7.6. Recall that a stack is a **last-in, first-out (LIFO)** data structure—the last item pushed (inserted) on the stack is the first item popped (removed) off the stack.

Stacks can be implemented with arrays and with other data structures, such as linked lists. (We discuss stacks and linked lists in Chapters 21 and 23.) A client of a stack class need not be concerned with the stack's implementation. The client knows only that when data items are placed in the stack, they'll be recalled in last-in, first-out order. The client cares about *what* functionality a stack offers, not about *how* that functionality is implemented. This concept is referred to as **data abstraction**. Even if you know the details of a class's implementation, you shouldn't write code that depends on these details as they may later change. This enables a particular class (such as one that implements a stack and its *push* and *pop* operations) to be replaced with another version—perhaps one that runs faster or uses less memory—without affecting the rest of the system. As long as the `public` services of the class do not change (i.e., every original method still has the same name, return type and parameter list in the new class declaration), the rest of the system is not affected.

Earlier non-object-oriented programming languages like C emphasize actions. In these languages, data exists to support the actions that applications must take. Data is "less interesting" than actions. Data is "crude." Only a few simple types exist, and it's difficult for programmers to create their own types. C# and the object-oriented style of programming elevate the importance of data. The primary activities of object-oriented programming in C# are creating types (e.g., classes) and expressing the interactions among objects of those types. To create languages that emphasize data, the programming-languages community needed to formalize some notions about data. The formalization we consider here is the notion of **abstract data types (ADTs)**, which improve the application-development process.

Consider the type `int`, which most people associate with an integer in mathematics. Actually, an `int` is an *abstract representation of an integer*. Unlike mathematical integers, computer `int`s are *fixed* in size. Type `int` in C# is limited to the range −2,147,483,648 to +2,147,483,647. If the result of a calculation falls *outside* this range, an error occurs, and the computer responds in some appropriate manner. It might "quietly" produce an incorrect result, such as a value too large to fit in an `int` variable—commonly called **arithmetic overflow**. It also might throw an exception, called an `OverflowException`. (We show how to deal with arithmetic overflow in Section 13.8.) *Mathematical* integers do not have this problem. Therefore, the computer int is only an *approximation* of the real-world integer. Simple types like int, double, and char are all examples of abstract data types—*representations of real-world concepts to some satisfactory level of precision within a computer system.*

An ADT actually captures two notions: a **data representation** and the **operations** that can be performed on that data. For example, in C#, an int contains an integer value (data) and provides addition, subtraction, multiplication, division and remainder operations—division by zero is undefined.

Software Engineering Observation 10.12

Programmers create types through the class mechanism. New types can be designed to be as convenient to use as the simple types. Although the language is easy to extend via new types, you cannot alter the base language itself.

Another ADT we discuss is a **queue**, which is similar to a "waiting line." Computer systems use many queues internally. A queue offers well-understood behavior to its clients: Clients place items in a queue one at a time via an *enqueue* operation, then retrieve them one at a time via a *dequeue* operation. A queue returns items in **first-in, first-out (FIFO)** order—the first item inserted in a queue is the first removed. Conceptually, a queue can become infinitely long, but real queues are finite.

The queue hides an internal data representation that keeps track of the items currently waiting in line, and it offers *enqueue* and *dequeue* operations to its clients. The clients are not concerned about the implementation of the queue—they simply depend on the queue to operate "as advertised." When a client enqueues an item, the queue should accept that item and place it in some kind of internal FIFO data structure. Similarly, when the client wants the next item from the front of the queue, the queue should remove the item from its internal representation and deliver it in FIFO order—the item that has been in the queue the longest should be returned by the next dequeue operation.

The queue ADT guarantees the integrity of its internal data structure. Clients cannot manipulate this data structure directly—only the queue ADT has access to its internal data. Clients are able to perform only allowable operations on the data representation—the ADT rejects operations that its public interface does not provide. We'll discuss stacks and queues in greater depth in Chapter 21, Data Structures.

10.13 Time Class Case Study: Creating Class Libraries

In almost every example in the book, we have seen that classes from preexisting libraries, such as the .NET Framework Class Library, can be imported into a C# application. Each class belongs to a namespace that contains a group of related classes. As applications become more complex, namespaces help you manage the complexity of application components. Class libraries and namespaces also facilitate software reuse by enabling applications to add classes from other namespaces (as we have done in most examples). This section introduces how to create your own class libraries.

Steps for Declaring and Using a Reusable Class

Before a class can be used in multiple applications, it must be placed in a class library to make it reusable. Figure 10.14 shows how to specify the namespace in which a class should be placed in the library. Figure 10.17 shows how to use our class library in an application. The steps for creating a reusable class are:

1. Declare a `public` class. If the class is not `public`, it can be used only by other classes in the same assembly.

2. Choose a namespace name and add a **namespace declaration** to the source-code file for the reusable class declaration.

3. Compile the class into a class library.

4. Add a reference to the class library in an application.

5. Specify a `using` directive for the namespace of the reusable class and use the class.

Step 1: Creating a `public` Class

For *Step 1* in this discussion, we use the `public` class `Time1` declared in Fig. 10.1. No modifications have been made to the implementation of the class, so we'll not discuss its implementation details again here.

Step 2: Adding the `namespace` Declaration

For *Step 2*, we add a `namespace` declaration to Fig. 10.1. The new version is shown in Fig. 10.14. Line 3 declares a namespace named `Chapter10`. Placing the `Time1` class inside the `namespace` declaration indicates that the class is part of the specified namespace. The namespace name is part of the fully qualified class name, so the name of class `Time1` is actually `Chapter10.Time1`. You can use this fully qualified name in your applications, or you can write a `using` directive (as we'll see shortly) and use its **simple name** (the unqualified class name—`Time1`) in the application. If another namespace also contains a `Time1` class, the fully qualified class names can be used to distinguish between the classes in the application and prevent a **name conflict** (also called a **name collision**).

```
1   // Fig. 10.14: Time1.cs
2   // Time1 class declaration in a namespace.
3   namespace Chapter10
4   {
5      public class Time1
6      {
7         private int hour; // 0 - 23
8         private int minute; // 0 - 59
9         private int second; // 0 - 59
10
11        // set a new time value using universal time; ensure that
12        // the data remains consistent by setting invalid values to zero
13        public void SetTime( int h, int m, int s )
14        {
15           hour = ( ( h >= 0 && h < 24 ) ? h : 0 ); // validate hour
16           minute = ( ( m >= 0 && m < 60 ) ? m : 0 ); // validate minute
17           second = ( ( s >= 0 && s < 60 ) ? s : 0 ); // validate second
18        } // end method SetTime
19
20        // convert to string in universal-time format (HH:MM:SS)
21        public string ToUniversalString()
22        {
```

Fig. 10.14 | `Time1` class declaration in a namespace. (Part 1 of 2.)

```
23            return string.Format( "{0:D2}:{1:D2}:{2:D2}",
24                hour, minute, second );
25        } // end method ToUniversalString
26
27        // convert to string in standard-time format (H:MM:SS AM or PM)
28        public override string ToString()
29        {
30            return string.Format( "{0}:{1:D2}:{2:D2} {3}",
31                ( ( hour == 0 || hour == 12 ) ? 12 : hour % 12 ),
32                minute, second, ( hour < 12 ? "AM" : "PM" ) );
33        } // end method ToString
34    } // end class Time1
35 } // end namespace Chapter10
```

Fig. 10.14 | `Time1` class declaration in a namespace. (Part 2 of 2.)

Most language elements must appear inside the braces of a type declaration (e.g., classes and enumerations). Some exceptions are `namespace` declarations, `using` directives, comments and C# attributes (first used in Chapter 17). Only class declarations declared `public` will be reusable by clients of the class library. Non-`public` classes are typically placed in a library to support the `public` reusable classes in that library.

Step 3: Compiling the Class Library

Step 3 is to compile the class into a class library. To create a class library in Visual C# Express, we must create a new project by clicking the **File** menu, selecting **New Project...** and choosing **Class Library** from the list of templates, as shown in Fig. 10.15. Then add the code from Fig. 10.14 into the new project (either by copying our code from the book's examples or by typing the code yourself). In the projects you've created so far, the C# compiler created an executable `.exe` containing the application. When you compile a **Class Library** project, the compiler creates a **`.dll` file**, known as a **dynamically linked library**—a type of assembly that you can reference from other applications.

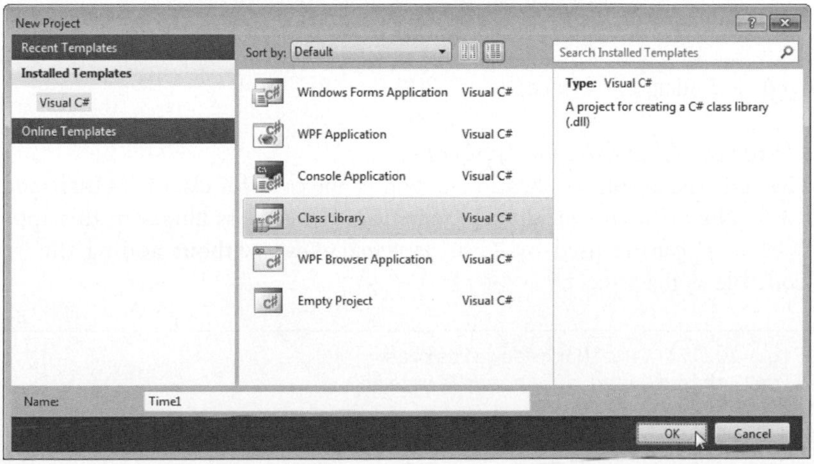

Fig. 10.15 | Creating a **Class Library** Project.

Step 4: Adding a Reference to the Class Library

Once the class is compiled and stored in the class library file, the library can be referenced from any application by indicating to the Visual C# Express IDE where to find the class library file. Create a new (empty) project and right-click the project name in the **Solution Explorer** window. Select **Add Reference...** from the pop-up menu that appears. The dialog box that appears will contain a list of class libraries from the .NET Framework. Some class libraries, like the one containing the System namespace, are so common that they're added to your application by the IDE. The ones in this list are not.

In the **Add Reference...** dialog box, click the **Browse** tab. Recall from Section 3.3 that when you build an application, Visual C# 2010places the .exe file in the bin\Release folder in the directory of your application. When you build a class library, Visual C# places the .dll file in the same place. In the **Browse** tab, you can navigate to the directory containing the class library file you created in *Step 3*, as shown in Fig. 10.16. Select the .dll file and click **OK**.

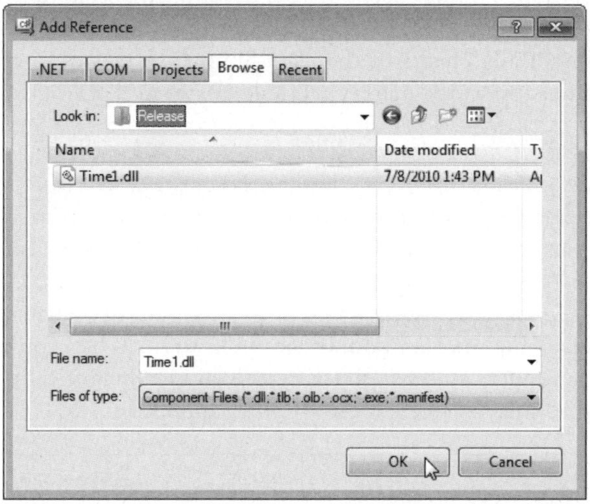

Fig. 10.16 | Adding a Reference.

Step 5: Using the Class from an Application

Add a new code file to your application and enter the code for class Time1NamespaceTest (Fig. 10.17). Now that you've added a reference to your class library in this application, your Time1 class can be used by Time1NamespaceTest without adding the Time1.cs source-code file to the project.

```
1   // Fig. 10.17: Time1NamespaceTest.cs
2   // Time1 object used in an application.
3   using Chapter10;
4   using System;
```

Fig. 10.17 | Time1 object used in an application. (Part 1 of 2.)

```
 5
 6   public class Time1NamespaceTest
 7   {
 8      public static void Main( string[] args )
 9      {
10         // create and initialize a Time1 object
11         Time1 time = new Time1(); // calls Time1 constructor
12
13         // output string representations of the time
14         Console.Write( "The initial universal time is: " );
15         Console.WriteLine( time.ToUniversalString() );
16         Console.Write( "The initial standard time is: " );
17         Console.WriteLine( time.ToString() );
18         Console.WriteLine(); // output a blank line
19
20         // change time and output updated time
21         time.SetTime( 13, 27, 6 );
22         Console.Write( "Universal time after SetTime is: " );
23         Console.WriteLine( time.ToUniversalString() );
24         Console.Write( "Standard time after SetTime is: " );
25         Console.WriteLine( time.ToString() );
26         Console.WriteLine(); // output a blank line
27
28         // set time with invalid values; output updated time
29         time.SetTime( 99, 99, 99 );
30         Console.WriteLine( "After attempting invalid settings:" );
31         Console.Write( "Universal time: " );
32         Console.WriteLine( time.ToUniversalString() );
33         Console.Write( "Standard time: " );
34         Console.WriteLine( time.ToString() );
35      } // end Main
36   } // end class Time1NamespaceTest
```

```
The initial universal time is: 00:00:00
The initial standard time is: 12:00:00 AM

Universal time after SetTime is: 13:27:06
Standard time after SetTime is: 1:27:06 PM

After attempting invalid settings:
Universal time: 00:00:00
Standard time: 12:00:00 AM
```

Fig. 10.17 | Time1 object used in an application. (Part 2 of 2.)

In Fig. 10.17, the using directive in line 3 specifies that we'd like to use the class(es) of namespace Chapter10 in this file. Class Time1NamespaceTest is in the global namespace of this application, because the class's file does not contain a namespace declaration. Since the two classes are in different namespaces, the using directive at line 3 allows class Time1NamespaceTest to use class Time1 as if it were in the same namespace.

Recall from Section 4.4 that we could omit the using directive in line 4 if we always referred to class Console by its fully qualified class name, System.Console. Similarly, we could omit the using directive in line 3 for namespace Chapter10 if we changed the Time1 declaration in line 11 of Fig. 10.17 to use class Time1's fully qualified name, as in:

```
Chapter10.Time1 time = new Chapter10.Time1();
```

10.14 internal Access

Classes like the ones we've defined so far can be declared with only two access modifiers—public and internal. Such classes are sometimes called top-level classes. C# also supports nested classes—classes defined inside other classes. In addition to public and internal, such classes can be declared private or protected. If there is no access modifier in the class declaration, the class defaults to **internal access**. This allows the class to be used by all code in the same assembly as the class, but not by code in other assemblies. Within the same assembly as the class, this is equivalent to public access. However, if a class library is referenced from an application, the library's internal classes will be inaccessible from the code of the application. Similarly, methods, instance variables and other members of a class declared internal are accessible to all code compiled in the same assembly, but not to code in other assemblies.

The application in Fig. 10.18 demonstrates internal access. The application contains two classes in one source-code file—the InternalAccessTest application class (lines 6–22) and the InternalData class (lines 25–43).

```
1   // Fig. 10.18: InternalAccessTest.cs
2   // Members declared internal in a class are accessible by other classes
3   // in the same assembly.
4   using System;
5
6   public class InternalAccessTest
7   {
8      public static void Main( string[] args )
9      {
10        InternalData internalData = new InternalData();
11
12        // output string representation of internalData
13        Console.WriteLine( "After instantiation:\n{0}", internalData );
14
15        // change internal-access data in internalData
16        internalData.number = 77;
17        internalData.message = "Goodbye";
18
19        // output string representation of internalData
20        Console.WriteLine( "\nAfter changing values:\n{0}", internalData );
21     } // end Main
22  } // end class InternalAccessTest
23
24  // class with internal-access instance variables
25  class InternalData
26  {
```

Fig. 10.18 | Members declared internal in a class are accessible by other classes in the same assembly. (Part 1 of 2.)

```
27        internal int number; // internal-access instance variable
28        internal string message; // internal-access instance variable
29
30        // constructor
31        public InternalData()
32        {
33           number = 0;
34           message = "Hello";
35        } // end InternalData constructor
36
37        // return InternalData object string representation
38        public override string ToString()
39        {
40           return string.Format(
41              "number: {0}; message: {1}", number, message );
42        } // end method ToString
43     } // end class InternalData
```

```
After instantiation:
number: 0; message: Hello

After changing values:
number: 77; message: Goodbye
```

Fig. 10.18 | Members declared `internal` in a class are accessible by other classes in the same assembly. (Part 2 of 2.)

In the `InternalData` class declaration, lines 27–28 declare the instance variables `number` and `message` with the `internal` access modifier—class `InternalData` has access `internal` by default, so there is no need for an access modifier. The `InternalAccessTest`'s `static Main` method creates an instance of the `InternalData` class (linc 10) to demonstrate modifying the `InternalData` instance variables directly (as shown in lines 16–17). Within the same assembly, `internal` access is equivalent to `public` access. The results can be seen in the output window. If we compile this class into a `.dll` class library file and reference it from a new application, that application will have access to `public` class `InternalAccessTest`, but not to `internal` class `InternalData`, or its `internal` members.

10.15 Class View and Object Browser

Now that we have introduced key concepts of object-oriented programming, we present two features that Visual Studio provides to facilitate the design of object-oriented applications—**Class View** and **Object Browser**.

Using the Class View Window
The **Class View** displays the fields, methods and properties for all classes in a project. To access this feature, you must first enable the IDE's "expert features." To do so, select **Tools > Settings > Expert Settings**. Next, select **View > Class View**. Figure 10.19 shows the **Class View** for the `Time1` project of Fig. 10.1 (class `Time1`) and Fig. 10.2 (class `Time1Test`). The view follows a hierarchical structure, positioning the project name (`Time1`) as the *root* and

including a series of nodes that represent the classes, variables, methods and properties in the project. If a ▷ appears to the left of a node, that node can be expanded to show other nodes. If a ◢ appears to the left of a node, that node can be collapsed. According to the **Class View**, project Time1 contains class Time1 and class Time1Test as children. When class Time1 is selected, the class's members appear in the lower half of the window. Class Time1 contains methods SetTime, ToString and ToUniversalString (indicated by purple boxes, ≡●) and instance variables hour, minute and second (indicated by blue boxes, ▱●). The lock icons to the left of the blue box icons for the instance variables specify that the variables are private. Both class Time1 and class Time1Test contain the **Base Types** node. If you expand this node, you'll see class Object in each case, because each class *inherits* from class System.Object (discussed in Chapter 11).

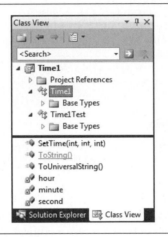

Fig. 10.19 | **Class View** of class Time1 (Fig. 10.1) and class Time1Test (Fig. 10.2).

Using the Object Browser
Visual C# Express's **Object Browser** lists all classes in the C# library. You can use the **Object Browser** to learn about the functionality provided by a specific class. To open the **Object Browser**, select **Other Windows** from the **View** menu and click **Object Browser**. Figure 10.20 depicts the **Object Browser** when the user navigates to the Math class in namespace System. To do this, we expanded the node for mscorlib (Microsoft Core Library) in the upper-left pane of the **Object Browser**, then expanded its subnode for System. [*Note:* The most common classes from the System namespace, such as System.Math, are in mscorlib.]

The **Object Browser** lists all methods provided by class Math in the upper-right frame—this offers you "instant access" to information regarding the functionality of various objects. If you click the name of a member in the upper-right frame, a description of that member appears in the lower-right frame. The **Object Browser** lists all the classes of the Framework Class Library. The **Object Browser** can be a quick mechanism to learn about a class or one of its methods. Remember that you can also view the complete description of a class or a method in the online documentation available through the **Help** menu in Visual C# Express.

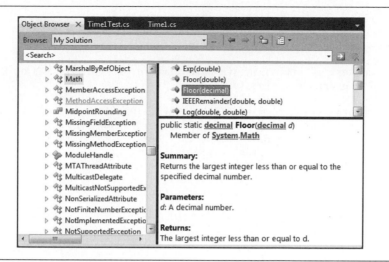

Fig. 10.20 | Object Browser for class Math.

10.16 Object Initializers

Object initializers allow you to create an object and initialize its properties in the same statement. This is useful when a class does not provide an appropriate constructor to meet your needs. For this example, we created a version of the Time class (Fig. 10.21) in which we did not define any constructors—so this class's only constructor is the default one provided by the compiler, which does not allow client code to specify hour, minute and second values in the constructor call. Figure 10.22 demonstrates object initializers.

```
1   // Fig. 10.21: Time.cs
2   // Time class declaration maintains the time in 24-hour format.
3   public class Time
4   {
5      private int hour; // 0 - 23
6      private int minute; // 0 - 59
7      private int second; // 0 - 59
8
9      // set a new time value using universal time; ensure that
10     // the data remains consistent by setting invalid values to zero
11     public void SetTime( int h, int m, int s )
12     {
13        Hour = h; // validate hour
14        Minute = m; // validate minute
15        Second = s; // validate second
16     } // end method SetTime
17
18     // convert to string in universal-time format (HH:MM:SS)
19     public string ToUniversalString()
20     {
```

Fig. 10.21 | Time class declaration maintains the time in 24-hour format. (Part 1 of 2.)

```
21          return string.Format( "{0:D2}:{1:D2}:{2:D2}",
22             hour, minute, second );
23       } // end method ToUniversalString
24
25       // convert to string in standard-time format (H:MM:SS AM or PM)
26       public override string ToString()
27       {
28          return string.Format( "{0}:{1:D2}:{2:D2} {3}",
29             ( ( hour == 0 || hour == 12 ) ? 12 : hour % 12 ),
30             minute, second, ( hour < 12 ? "AM" : "PM" ) );
31       } // end method ToString
32
33       // Properties for getting and setting
34       // property that gets and sets the hour
35       public int Hour
36       {
37          get
38          {
39             return hour;
40          } // end get
41          set
42          {
43             hour = ( ( value >= 0 && value < 24 ) ? value : 0 );
44          } // end set
45       } // end property Hour
46
47       // property that gets and sets the minute
48       public int Minute
49       {
50          get
51          {
52             return minute;
53          } // end get
54          set
55          {
56             minute = ( ( value >= 0 && value < 60 ) ? value : 0 );
57          } // end set
58       } // end property Minute
59
60       // property that gets and sets the second
61       public int Second
62       {
63          get
64          {
65             return second;
66          } // end get
67          set
68          {
69             second = ( ( value >= 0 && value < 60 ) ? value : 0 );
70          } // end set
71       } // end property Second
72    } // end class Time
```

Fig. 10.21 | Time class declaration maintains the time in 24-hour format. (Part 2 of 2.)

Line 12 (Fig. 10.22) creates a Time object and initializes it with class Time's parameterless constructor, then uses an object initializer to set its Hour, Minute and Second properties. Notice that new Time is immediately followed by an **object-initializer list**—a comma-separated list in curly braces ({ }) of properties and their values. Each property name can appear only once in the object-initializer list.

```
1   // Fig. 10.22: ObjectInitializerTest.cs
2   // Demonstrate object initializers using class Time.
3   using System;
4
5   class ObjectInitializerTest
6   {
7      static void Main( string[] args )
8      {
9         Console.WriteLine( "Time object created with object initializer" );
10
11        // create a Time object and initialize its properties
12        Time aTime = new Time { Hour = 14, Minute = 145, Second = 12 };
13
14        // display the time in both standard and universal format
15        Console.WriteLine( "Standard time: {0}", aTime.ToString() );
16        Console.WriteLine( "Universal time: {0}\n",
17           aTime.ToUniversalString() );
18
19        Console.WriteLine( "Time object created with Minute property set" );
20
21        // create a Time object and initialize its Minute property only
22        Time anotherTime = new Time { Minute = 45 };
23
24        // display the time in both standard and universal format
25        Console.WriteLine( "Standard time: {0}", anotherTime.ToString() );
26        Console.WriteLine( "Universal time: {0}",
27           anotherTime.ToUniversalString() );
28     } // end Main
29  } // end class ObjectInitializerTest
```

```
Time object created with object initializer
Standard time: 2:00:12 PM
Universal time: 14:00:12

Time object created with Minute property set
Standard time: 12:45:00 AM
Universal time: 00:45:00
```

Fig. 10.22 | Demonstrate object initializers using class Time.

The object initializer executes the property initializers in the order in which they appear. Lines 15–17 display the Time object in standard and universal time formats. The Minute property's value is 0. The value supplied for the Minute property in the object initializer (145) is invalid. The Minute property's set accessor validates the supplied value, setting the Minute property to 0.

Line 22 uses an object initializer to create a new Time object (anotherTime) and set only its Minute property. Lines 25–27 display the Time object in both standard and universal time formats. The time is set to 12:45:00 AM. Recall that an object initializer first calls the class's constructor. The Time constructor initializes the time to midnight (00:00:00). The object initializer then sets each specified property to the supplied value. In this case, the Minute property is set to 45. The Hour and Second properties retain their default values, because no values are specified for them in the object initializer.

10.17 Time Class Case Study: Extension Methods

Sometimes it's useful to add new functionality to an existing class. However, you cannot modify code for classes in the .NET Framework Class Library or other class libraries that you did not create. In Visual C# 2010, you can use **extension methods** to add functionality to an existing class without modifying the class's source code. Many LINQ capabilities are also available as extension methods.

Figure 10.23 uses extension methods to add functionality to class Time (from Section 10.16). The extension method DisplayTime (lines 35–38) displays the time in the console window using the Time object's ToString method. The key new feature of method DisplayTime is the this keyword that precedes the Time object parameter in the method header (line 35). The this keyword notifies the compiler that the DisplayTime method extends an existing class. The C# compiler uses this information to inject additional code into the compiled program that enables extension methods to work with existing types. The type of an extension method's first parameter specifies the class that's being extended—extension methods must define at least one parameter. Also, extension methods must be defined as static methods in a static top-level class such as TimeExtensions (lines 32–53). A static class can contain only static members and cannot be instantiated.

```
1   // Fig. 10.23: TimeExtensionsTest.cs
2   // Demonstrating extension methods.
3   using System;
4
5   class TimeExtensionsTest
6   {
7      static void Main( string[] args )
8      {
9         Time myTime = new Time(); // call Time constructor
10        myTime.SetTime( 11, 34, 15 ); // set the time to 11:34:15
11
12        // test the DisplayTime extension method
13        Console.Write( "Use the DisplayTime method: " );
14        myTime.DisplayTime();
15
16        // test the AddHours extension method
17        Console.Write( "Add 5 hours to the Time object: " );
18        Time timeAdded = myTime.AddHours( 5 ); // add five hours
19        timeAdded.DisplayTime(); // display the new Time object
20
```

Fig. 10.23 | Demonstrating extension methods. (Part 1 of 2.)

```
21          // add hours and display the time in one statement
22          Console.Write( "Add 15 hours to the Time object: " );
23          myTime.AddHours( 15 ).DisplayTime(); // add hours and display time
24
25          // use fully qualified extension-method name to display the time
26          Console.Write( "Use fully qualified extension-method name: " );
27          TimeExtensions.DisplayTime( myTime );
28       } // end Main
29    } // end class TimeExtensionsTest
30
31    // extension-methods class
32    static class TimeExtensions
33    {
34       // display the Time object in console
35       public static void DisplayTime( this Time aTime )
36       {
37          Console.WriteLine( aTime.ToString() );
38       } // end method DisplayTime
39
40       // add the specified number of hours to the time
41       // and return a new Time object
42       public static Time AddHours( this Time aTime, int hours )
43       {
44          Time newTime = new Time(); // create a new Time object
45          newTime.Minute = aTime.Minute; // set the minutes
46          newTime.Second = aTime.Second; // set the seconds
47
48          // add the specified number of hours to the given time
49          newTime.Hour = ( aTime.Hour + hours ) % 24;
50
51          return newTime; // return the new Time object
52       } // end method AddHours
53    } // end class TimeExtensions
```

```
Use the DisplayTime method: 11:34:15 AM
Add 5 hours to the Time object: 4:34:15 PM
Add 15 hours to the Time object: 2:34:15 AM
Use fully qualified extension-method name: 11:34:15 AM
```

Fig. 10.23 | Demonstrating extension methods. (Part 2 of 2.)

The parameter list for the DisplayTime method (line 35) contains a single parameter of type Time, indicating that this method extends class Time. Line 14 of Fig. 10.23 uses Time object myTime to call the DisplayTime extension method. Line 14 does not provide an argument to the method call. The compiler implicitly passes the object that's used to call the method (myTime in this case) as the extension method's first argument. This allows you to call an extension method as if it were an instance method of the extended class. In fact, *IntelliSense* displays extension methods with the extended class's instance methods and identifies them with a distinct icon (Fig. 10.24). Note the blue down-arrow in the icon to the left of the method name in the *IntelliSense* window—this denotes an extension method. The tool tip shown to the right of the *IntelliSense* window includes the text (**exten-**

sion) to indicate that `DisplayTime` is an extension method. Also note in the tool tip that the method's signature shows an empty parameter list.

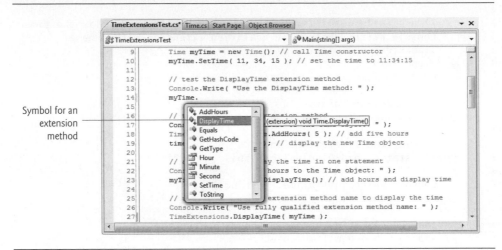

Symbol for an extension method

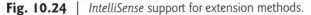

Fig. 10.24 | *IntelliSense* support for extension methods.

Lines 42–52 of Fig. 10.23 define the `AddHours` extension method. Again, the method parameter contains the `this` keyword (line 42). The first parameter of `AddHours` is a `Time` object, indicating that the method extends class `Time`. The second parameter is an `int` value specifying the number of hours to add to the time. The `AddHours` method returns a new `Time` object with the specified number of hours added. Line 44 creates the new `Time` object. Lines 45–46 set the new `Time`'s `Minute` and `Second` properties using the values of the `Time` object received as an argument. Line 49 adds the specified number of hours to the value of the original `Time` object's `Hour` property, then uses the `%` operator to ensure the value is in the range 0–23. This value is assigned to the new `Time` object's `Hour` property. Line 51 returns the new `Time` object to the caller. Line 18 calls the `AddHours` extension method to add five hours to the `myTime` object's hour value. The method call receives one argument—the number of hours to add. Again, the compiler implicitly passes the object that's used to call the method (`myTime`) as the extension method's first argument. The `Time` object returned by `AddHours` is assigned to a local variable (`timeAdded`) and displayed in the console using the `DisplayTime` extension method (line 19). Line 23 uses both extension methods (`DisplayTime` and `AddHours`) in a single statement to add 15 hours to `myTime` and display the result in the console. Extension methods, as well as instance methods, allow **cascaded method calls**—that is, invoking multiple methods in the same statement (line 23). The methods are called from left to right. In line 23, the `DisplayTime` method is called on the `Time` object returned by method `AddHours`.

Line 27 calls extension method `DisplayTime` using its fully qualified name—the name of the `class` in which the extension method is defined (`TimeExtensions`), followed by the method name (`DisplayTime`) and its argument list. Note in line 27 that the call to `DisplayTime` passes a `Time` object as an argument to the method. When using the fully qualified method name, you must specify an argument for extension method's first parameter. This use of the extension method resembles a call to a `static` method.

Extension Method Notes

Be careful when using extension methods to add functionality to preexisting classes. If the type being extended defines an instance method with the same name as your extension method and a compatible signature, the instance method will shadow the extension method. If a predefined class is later updated to include an instance method that shadows an extension method, the compiler does not report any errors and the extension method does not appear in *IntelliSense*.

10.18 Delegates

A **delegate** is an object that holds a reference to a method. Delegates allow you to treat methods as data—via delegates, you can assign methods to variables, and pass methods to and from other methods. You can also call methods through variables of delegate types. Figure 10.25 uses delegates to customize the functionality of a method that filters an `int` array. Line 9 defines a delegate type named `NumberPredicate`. A variable of this type can store a reference to any method that takes an `int` argument and returns a `bool`. A delegate type is declared by preceeding a method header with keyword **delegate** (placed after any access specifiers, such as `public` or `private`). The `delegate` type declaration includes the method header only—the `delegate` type simply describes a set of methods with specific parameters and a specific return type.

```
 1   // Fig. 10.25: Delegates.cs
 2   // Using delegates to pass functions as arguments.
 3   using System;
 4   using System.Collections.Generic;
 5
 6   class Delegates
 7   {
 8      // delegate for a function that receives an int and returns a bool
 9      public delegate bool NumberPredicate( int number );
10
11      static void Main( string[] args )
12      {
13         int[] numbers = { 1, 2, 3, 4, 5, 6, 7, 8, 9, 10 };
14
15         // create an instance of the NumberPredicate delegate type
16         NumberPredicate evenPredicate = IsEven;
17
18         // call IsEven using a delegate variable
19         Console.WriteLine( "Call IsEven using a delegate variable: {0}",
20            evenPredicate( 4 ) );
21
22         // filter the even numbers using method IsEven
23         List< int > evenNumbers = FilterArray( numbers, evenPredicate );
24
25         // display the result
26         DisplayList( "Use IsEven to filter even numbers: ", evenNumbers );
27
```

Fig. 10.25 | Using delegates to pass functions as arguments. (Part 1 of 3.)

```
28          // filter the odd numbers using method IsOdd
29          List< int > oddNumbers = FilterArray( numbers, IsOdd );
30
31          // display the result
32          DisplayList( "Use IsOdd to filter odd numbers: ", oddNumbers );
33
34          // filter numbers greater than 5 using method IsOver5
35          List< int > numbersOver5 = FilterArray( numbers, IsOver5 );
36
37          // display the result
38          DisplayList( "Use IsOver5 to filter numbers over 5: ",
39             numbersOver5 );
40       } // end Main
41
42       // select an array's elements that satisfy the predicate
43       private static List< int > FilterArray( int[] intArray,
44          NumberPredicate predicate )
45       {
46          // hold the selected elements
47          List< int > result = new List< int >();
48
49          // iterate over each element in the array
50          foreach ( int item in intArray )
51          {
52             // if the element satisfies the predicate
53             if ( predicate( item ) )
54                result.Add( item ); // add the element to the result
55          } // end foreach
56
57          return result; // return the result
58       } // end method FilterArray
59
60       // determine whether an int is even
61       private static bool IsEven( int number )
62       {
63          return ( number % 2 == 0 );
64       } // end method IsEven
65
66       // determine whether an int is odd
67       private static bool IsOdd( int number )
68       {
69          return ( number % 2 == 1 );
70       } // end method IsOdd
71
72       // determine whether an int is positive
73       private static bool IsOver5( int number )
74       {
75          return ( number > 5 );
76       } // end method IsOver5
77
78       // display the elements of a List
79       private static void DisplayList( string description, List< int > list )
80       {
```

Fig. 10.25 | Using delegates to pass functions as arguments. (Part 2 of 3.)

```
81          Console.Write( description ); // display the output's description
82
83          // iterate over each element in the List
84          foreach ( int item in list )
85             Console.Write( "{0} ", item ); // print item followed by a space
86
87          Console.WriteLine(); // add a new line
88       } // end method DisplayList
89    } // end class Delegates
```

```
Call IsEven using a delegate variable: True
Use IsEven to filter even numbers: 2 4 6 8 10
Use IsOdd to filter odd numbers: 1 3 5 7 9
Use IsOver5 to filter numbers over 5: 6 7 8 9 10
```

Fig. 10.25 | Using delegates to pass functions as arguments. (Part 3 of 3.)

Line 16 declares evenPredicate as a variable of type NumberPredicate and assigns to it a reference to the IsEven method (defined in lines 61–64). Since method IsEven's signature matches the NumberPredicate delegate's signature, IsEven can be referenced by a variable of type NumberPredicate. Variable evenPredicate can now be used as an alias for method IsEven. A NumberPredicate variable can hold a reference to any method that receives an int and returns a bool. Lines 19–20 use variable evenPredicate to call method IsEven, then display the result. The method referenced by the delegate is called using the delegate variable's name in place of the method's name (i.e., evenPredicate(4)).

The real power of delegates is the ability to pass a method reference as an argument to another method, as shown by method FilterArray (lines 43–58). FilterArray takes as arguments an int array and a NumberPredicate that references a method used to filter the array elements. The foreach statement (lines 50–55) calls the method referenced by the NumberPredicate delegate (line 53) on each element of the array. If the method call returns true, the element is included in the result. The NumberPredicate is guaranteed to return either true or false, because any method referenced by a NumberPredicate must return a bool—as specified by the definition of the NumberPredicate delegate type. Line 23 passes FilterArray the int array (numbers) and the NumberPredicate that references the IsEven method (evenPredicate). FilterArray calls the NumberPredicate delegate on each array element. FilterArray returns a List of ints, because we don't know in advance how many elements will be selected. Line 23 assigns the List returned by FilterArray to variable evenNumbers and line 26 calls method DisplayList to display the results.

Line 29 calls method FilterArray to select the odd numbers in the array. We reference method IsOdd (defined in lines 67–70) in FilterArray's second argument, rather than creating a NumberPredicate variable. Line 32 displays the results. Line 35 calls method FilterArray to select the numbers greater than five in the array. Method IsOver5 is referenced by a NumberPredicate delegate and passed to method FilterArray (line 35). The filtered list is then displayed in lines 38–39.

10.19 Lambda Expressions

Lambda expressions (new in Visual C# 2010) allow you to define simple, **anonymous functions**. Figure 10.26 uses lambda expressions to reimplement the previous example that introduced delegates. A lambda expression (line 17) begins with a parameter list. The parameter list is followed by the => **lambda operator** (read as "goes to") and an expression that represents the body of the function. The lambda expression in line 17 uses the % operator to determine whether the parameter's number value is an even int. The value produced by the expression—true if the int is even, false otherwise—is implicitly returned by the lambda expression. We do not specify a return type for the lambda expression—the return type is inferred from the return value or, in some cases, from the delegate's return type. The lambda expression in line 17 produces the same results as the IsEven method in Fig. 10.25. In fact, the expression used in the body of the IsEven method is the same one used in the lambda expression.

```
1   // Fig. 10.26: Lambdas.cs
2   // Using lambda expressions.
3   using System;
4   using System.Collections.Generic;
5
6   class Lambdas
7   {
8      // delegate for a function that receives an int and returns a bool
9      public delegate bool NumberPredicate( int number );
10
11     static void Main( string[] args )
12     {
13        int[] numbers = { 1, 2, 3, 4, 5, 6, 7, 8, 9, 10 };
14
15        // create an instance of the NumberPredicate delegate type using an
16        // implicit lambda expression
17        NumberPredicate evenPredicate = number => ( number % 2 == 0 );
18
19        // call a lambda expression through a variable
20        Console.WriteLine( "Use a lambda-expression variable: {0}",
21           evenPredicate( 4 ) );
22
23        // filter the even numbers using a lambda expression
24        List< int > evenNumbers = FilterArray( numbers, evenPredicate );
25
26        // display the result
27        DisplayList( "Use a lambda expression to filter even numbers: ",
28           evenNumbers );
29
30        // filter the odd numbers using an explicitly typed lambda
31        // expression
32        List< int > oddNumbers = FilterArray( numbers,
33           ( int number ) => ( number % 2 == 1 ) );
34
35        // display the result
36        DisplayList( "Use a lambda expression to filter odd numbers: ",
37           oddNumbers );
38
```

Fig. 10.26 | Using lambda expressions. (Part 1 of 2.)

```
39            // filter numbers greater than 5 using an implicit lambda statement
40            List< int > numbersOver5 = FilterArray( numbers,
41               number => { return number > 5; } );
42
43            // display the result
44            DisplayList( "Use a lambda expression to filter numbers over 5: ",
45               numbersOver5 );
46         } // end Main
47
48         // select an array's elements that satisfy the predicate
49         private static List< int > FilterArray( int[] intArray,
50            NumberPredicate predicate )
51         {
52            // hold the selected elements
53            List< int > result = new List< int >();
54
55            // iterate over each element in the array
56            foreach ( int item in intArray )
57            {
58               // if the element satisfies the predicate
59               if ( predicate( item ) )
60                  result.Add( item ); // add the element to the result
61            } // end foreach
62
63            return result; // return the result
64         } // end method FilterArray
65
66         // display the elements of a List
67         private static void DisplayList( string description, List< int > list )
68         {
69            Console.Write( description ); // display the output's description
70
71            // iterate over each element in the List
72            foreach ( int item in list )
73               Console.Write( "{0} ", item ); // print item followed by a space
74
75            Console.WriteLine(); // add a new line
76         } // end method DisplayList
77      } // end class Lambdas
```

```
Use a lambda expression variable: True
Use a lambda expression to filter even numbers: 2 4 6 8 10
Use a lambda expression to filter odd numbers: 1 3 5 7 9
Use a lambda expression to filter numbers over 5: 6 7 8 9 10
```

Fig. 10.26 | Using lambda expressions. (Part 2 of 2.)

In line 17, the lambda expression is assigned to a variable of type NumberPredicate (defined in line 9). Recall that NumberPredicate is the delegate type used in the previous example. A delegate can hold a reference to a lambda expression. As with traditional methods, a method defined by a lambda expression must have a signature that's compatible with the delegate type. The NumberPredicate delegate can hold a reference to any method that takes an int as an argument and returns a bool. Based on this, the compiler is able to infer that the lambda expression in line 17 defines a method that implicitly takes an int as an argument and returns the bool result of the expression in its body. Lambda expressions are often used as arguments to methods with parameters of delegate types, rather than defining and referencing a separate method.

Lines 20–21 display the result of calling the lambda expression defined in line 17. The lambda expression is called via the variable that references it (evenPredicate). Line 24 passes evenPredicate to method FilterArray (lines 49–64), which is identical to the method used in Fig. 10.25—it uses the NumberPredicate delegate to determine whether an array element should be included in the result. Lines 27–28 display the filtered results.

Lines 32–33 select the odd array elements and store the results. The lambda expression's input parameter number is explicitly typed as an int, rather than implicitly typed like the lambda expression in line 17. The lambda expressions in lines 17 and 33 are called **expression lambdas** because they have an expression to the right of the lambda operator. In this case, the lambda expression is passed directly to method FilterArray and is implicitly converted to a NumberPredicate delegate. The lambda expression in line 33 is equivalent to the IsOdd method defined in Fig. 10.25. Lines 36–37 display the filtered results.

Lines 40–41 filter ints greater than 5 from the array and store the results. The lambda expression in line 41 is equivalent to the IsOver5 method in Fig. 10.25. This lambda expression is called a **statement lambda**, because it contains a statement block—a set of statements enclosed in braces ({})—to the right of the lambda operator. The statement block of a statement lambda can contain multiple statements. The lambda expression's signature is compatible with the NumberPredicate delegate, because the parameter's type is inferred to be int and the statement in the lambda returns a bool.

Lambda expressions can help reduce the size of your code and the complexity of working with delegates—the program in Fig. 10.26 performs the same actions as the one in Fig. 10.25 but is 12 lines shorter. Lambda expressions are particularly powerful when combined with the where clause in LINQ queries.

10.20 Anonymous Types

Anonymous types (new in Visual C# 2010) allow you to create simple classes used to store data without writing a class definition. An anonymous type declaration (line 10 of Fig. 10.27)—known formally as an **anonymous object-creation expression**—is similar to an object initializer (discussed in Section 10.16). The anonymous type declaration begins with the keyword new followed by a member-initializer list in braces ({}). Notice that no class name is specified after the new keyword. The compiler generates a new class definition based on the anonymous object-creation expression. The new class contains the properties specified in the member-initializer list—Name and Age. All properties of an anonymous type are public and immutable. Anonymous type properties are read-only—you cannot modify a property's value once the object is created. Each property's type is inferred from the values assigned to it. The class definition is generated automatically by the compiler, so you don't know the class's type name (hence the term anonymous type). Thus, you must use implicitly typed local variables to store references to objects of anonymous types (e.g., line 10). Line 13 uses the anonymous type's ToString method to display the object's information on the console. The compiler defines the ToString method when creating the anonymous type's class definition. The method returns a string in curly braces containing a comma-separated list of *PropertyName* = *value* pairs.

```
 1   // Fig. 10.27: AnonymousTypes.cs
 2   // Using anonymous types.
 3   using System;
 4
 5   class AnonymousTypes
 6   {
 7      static void Main( string[] args )
 8      {
 9         // create a "person" object using an anonymous type
10         var bob = new { Name = "Bob Smith", Age = 37 };
11
12         // display Bob's information
13         Console.WriteLine( "Bob: " + bob.ToString() );
14
15         // create another "person" object using the same anonymous type
16         var steve = new { Name = "Steve Jones", Age = 26 };
17
18         // display Steve's information
19         Console.WriteLine( "Steve: " + steve.ToString() );
20
21         // determine if objects of the same anonymous type are equal
22         Console.WriteLine( "\nBob and Steve are {0}",
23            ( bob.Equals( steve ) ? "equal" : "not equal" ) );
24
25         // create a "person" object using an anonymous type
26         var bob2 = new { Name = "Bob Smith", Age = 37 };
27
28         // display Bob's information
29         Console.WriteLine( "\nBob2: " + bob2.ToString() );
30
31         // determine whether objects of the same anonymous type are equal
32         Console.WriteLine( "\nBob and Bob2 are {0}\n",
33            ( bob.Equals( bob2 ) ? "equal" : "not equal" ) );
34      } // end Main
35   } // end class AnonymousTypes
```

```
Bob: { Name = Bob Smith, Age = 37 }
Steve: { Name = Steve Jones, Age = 26 }

Bob and Steve are not equal

Bob2: { Name = Bob Smith, Age = 37 }

Bob and Bob2 are equal
```

Fig. 10.27 | Using anonymous types.

Line 16 creates another anonymous object and assigns it to variable steve. The anonymous object-creation expression uses the same property names (Name and Age) and types in the member-initializer list as the anonymous type defined in line 10. Two anonymous objects that specify the same property names and types, in the same order, use the same anonymous class definition and are considered to be of the same type.

Lines 22–23 determine if the two anonymous objects, bob and steve, are equal and display the results. When anonymous objects are compared for equality, all properties are considered. Line 23 uses the anonymous type's `Equals` method (also defined by the compiler), which compares the properties of the anonymous object that calls the method and the anonymous object that it receives as an argument. Since bob's `Name` and `Age` properties are not equal to steve's `Name` and `Age` properties, the two objects are not equal.

Line 26 creates an object of the same anonymous type as bob and steve and assigns it to variable bob2. This object specifies the same property values as bob. Line 33 uses the anonymous type's `Equals` method to determine that bob and bob2 are equal—both have the same `Name` and `Age` property values and the properties are declared in the same order.

Anonymous Types in LINQ
Anonymous types are frequently used in LINQ queries to select specific properties from the items being queried. Recall the `Employee` class used in Section 9.3. The class defines three properties—`FirstName`, `LastName` and `MonthlySalary`. The statement

```
var names =
   from e in employees
   select new { e.FirstName, Last = e.LastName };
```

from lines 64–66 of Fig. 9.4 uses a LINQ query to select properties `FirstName` and `LastName` of each `Employee` object (e) in an array of `Employee`s (employees). The `select` clause creates an anonymous type with properties `FirstName` and `Last` to store the selected property values. The syntax used in the `select` clause to create the anonymous type is different than what you've seen in this section. The member-initializer list doesn't specify a name for the `FirstName` property. As explained in Chapter 9, the compiler implicitly uses the name of the selected property unless you specify otherwise.

10.21 Wrap-Up

In this chapter, we discussed additional class concepts. The `Time` class case study presented a complete class declaration consisting of `private` data, overloaded `public` constructors for initialization flexibility, properties for manipulating the class's data and methods that returned `string` representations of a `Time` object in two different formats. You learned that every class can declare a `ToString` method that returns a `string` representation of an object of the class and that this method is invoked implicitly when an object of a class is output as a `string` or concatenated with a `string`.

You learned that the `this` reference is used implicitly in a class's non-`static` methods to access the class's instance variables and other non-`static` methods. You saw explicit uses of the `this` reference to access the class's members (including hidden fields) and learned how to use keyword `this` in a constructor to call another constructor of the class. You also learned how to declare indexers with the `this` keyword, allowing you to access the data of an object in much the same manner as you access the elements of an array.

You saw that composition enables a class to have references to objects of other classes as members. You learned about C#'s garbage-collection capability and how it reclaims the memory of objects that are no longer used. We explained the motivation for `static` variables in a class and demonstrated how to declare and use `static` variables and methods in your own classes. You also learned how to declare and initialize `readonly` variables.

We showed how to create a class library for reuse and how to use the classes of the library in an application. You learned that classes declared without an access modifier are given `internal` access by default. You saw that classes in an assembly can access the `internal`-access members of the other classes in the same assembly. We also showed how to use Visual Studio's **Class View** and **Object Browser** windows to navigate the classes of the .NET Framework Class Library and your own applications to discover information about those classes.

You learned how to initialize an object's properties as you create it with an object-initializer list. We used extension methods to add functionality to a class without modifying the class's source code. You then learned that a delegate is an object that holds a method reference. We showed you how to use delegates to assign methods to variables and pass methods to other methods. Next we demonstrated lambda expressions for defining simple, anonymous methods that can also be used with delegates. Finally, you learned how to use anonymous types to create simple classes that store data without writing a class definition.

In the next chapter, you'll learn about inheritance. You'll see that all classes in C# are related directly or indirectly to the `object` class and begin to understand how inheritance enables you to build more powerful applications faster.

Object-Oriented Programming: Inheritance

OBJECTIVES

In this chapter you'll learn:

- How inheritance promotes software reusability.

- To create a derived class that inherits attributes and behaviors from a base class.

- To use access modifier **protected** to give derived-class methods access to base-class members.

- To access base-class members with **base**.

- How constructors are used in inheritance hierarchies.

- The methods of class **object**, the direct or indirect base class of all classes.

11.1 Introduction

This chapter continues our discussion of object-oriented programming (OOP) by introducing one of its primary features—**inheritance,** a form of software reuse in which a new class is created by absorbing an existing class's members and enhancing them with new or modified capabilities. Inheritance lets you save time during application development by reusing proven and debugged high-quality software. This also increases the likelihood that a system will be implemented effectively.

The existing class from which a new class inherits members is called the **base class,** and the new class is the **derived class.** Each derived class can become the base class for future derived classes.

A derived class normally adds its own fields and methods. Therefore, it's more specific than its base class and represents a more specialized group of objects. Typically, the derived class exhibits the behaviors of its base class and additional ones that are specific to itself.

The **direct base class** is the base class from which the derived class explicitly inherits. An **indirect base class** is any class above the direct base class in the **class hierarchy,** which defines the inheritance relationships among classes. The class hierarchy begins with class **object** (which is the C# alias for System.Object in the Framework Class Library), which *every* class directly or indirectly **extends** (or "inherits from"). Section 11.7 lists the methods of class object, which *every* other class inherits. In the case of **single inheritance,** a class is derived from one direct base class. C#, unlike C++, does not support multiple inheritance (which occurs when a class is derived from more than one direct base class). In Chapter 12, OOP: Polymorphism, Interfaces and Operator Overloading, we explain how you can use interfaces to realize many of the benefits of multiple inheritance while avoiding the associated problems.

Experience in building software systems indicates that significant amounts of code deal with closely related special cases. When you're preoccupied with special cases, the details can obscure the big picture. With object-oriented programming, you can, when appropriate, focus on the commonalities among objects in the system rather than the special cases.

We distinguish between the *is-a* **relationship** and the *has-a* **relationship.** *Is-a* represents inheritance. In an *is-a* relationship, an object of a derived class can also be treated as an object of its base class. For example, a car *is a* vehicle, and a truck *is a* vehicle. By contrast, *has-a* represents composition (see Chapter 10). In a *has-a* relationship, an object contains as members references to other objects. For example, a car *has a* steering wheel, and a car object *has a* reference to a steering-wheel object.

New classes can inherit from classes in **class libraries**. Organizations develop their own class libraries and can take advantage of others available worldwide. Some day, most new software likely will be constructed from **standardized reusable components**, just as automobiles and most computer hardware are constructed today. This will facilitate the development of more powerful, abundant and economical software.

11.2 Base Classes and Derived Classes

Often, an object of one class *is an* object of another class as well. For example, in geometry, a rectangle *is a* quadrilateral (as are squares, parallelograms and trapezoids). Thus, class `Rectangle` can be said to inherit from class `Quadrilateral`. In this context, class `Quadrilateral` is a base class and class `Rectangle` is a derived class. A rectangle *is a* specific type of quadrilateral, but it's incorrect to claim that every quadrilateral *is a* rectangle—the quadrilateral could be a parallelogram or some other shape. Figure 11.1 lists several simple examples of base classes and derived classes—base classes tend to be "more general," and derived classes tend to be "more specific."

Base class	Derived classes
Student	GraduateStudent, UndergraduateStudent
Shape	Circle, Triangle, Rectangle
Loan	CarLoan, HomeImprovementLoan, MortgageLoan
Employee	Faculty, Staff, HourlyWorker, CommissionWorker
BankAccount	CheckingAccount, SavingsAccount

Fig. 11.1 | Inheritance examples.

Because every derived-class object *is an* object of its base class, and one base class can have many derived classes, the set of objects represented by a base class is typically larger than the set of objects represented by any of its derived classes. For example, the base class `Vehicle` represents all vehicles—cars, trucks, boats, bicycles and so on. By contrast, derived class `Car` represents a smaller, more specific subset of vehicles.

Inheritance relationships form treelike hierarchical structures (Figs. 11.2 and 11.3). A base class exists in a hierarchical relationship with its derived classes. When classes participate in inheritance relationships, they become "affiliated" with other classes. A class becomes either a base class, supplying members to other classes, or a derived class, inheriting its members from another class. Sometimes, a class is both a base and a derived class.

Let us develop a sample class hierarchy, also called an **inheritance hierarchy** (Fig. 11.2). The UML class diagram of Fig. 11.2 shows a university community that has many types of members, including employees, students and alumni. Employees are either faculty members or staff members. Faculty members are either administrators (such as deans and department chairpersons) or teachers. The hierarchy could contain many other classes. For example, students can be graduate or undergraduate students. Undergraduate students can be freshmen, sophomores, juniors or seniors.

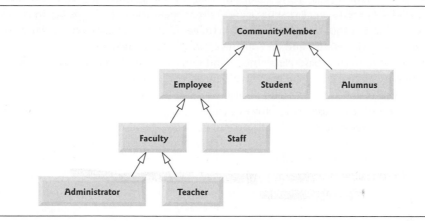

Fig. 11.2 | UML class diagram showing an inheritance hierarchy for university `CommunityMember`s.

Each arrow with a hollow triangular arrowhead in the hierarchy diagram represents an *is-a* relationship. As we follow the arrows, we can state, for instance, that "an `Employee` *is a* `CommunityMember`" and "a `Teacher` *is a* `Faculty` member." `CommunityMember` is the *direct* base class of `Employee`, `Student` and `Alumnus` and is an *indirect* base class of all the other classes in the diagram. Starting from the bottom, the reader can follow the arrows and apply the *is-a* relationship up to the topmost base class. For example, an `Administrator` *is a* `Faculty` member, *is an* `Employee` and *is a* `CommunityMember`.

Now consider the `Shape` hierarchy in Fig. 11.3, which begins with base class `Shape`. This class is extended by derived classes `TwoDimensionalShape` and `ThreeDimensionalShape`—a `Shape` is either a `TwoDimensionalShape` or a `ThreeDimensionalShape`. The third level of this hierarchy contains specific `TwoDimensionalShape`s and `ThreeDimensionalShape`s. We can follow the arrows from the bottom to the topmost base class in this hierarchy to identify the *is-a* relationships. For instance, a `Triangle` *is a* `TwoDimensionalShape` and *is a* `Shape`, while a `Sphere` *is a* `ThreeDimensionalShape` and *is a* `Shape`. This hierarchy could contain many other classes. For example, ellipses and trapezoids also are `TwoDimensionalShape`s.

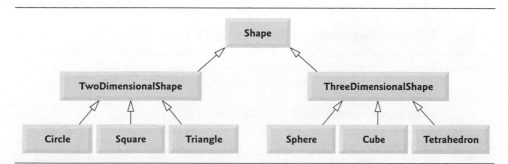

Fig. 11.3 | UML class diagram showing an inheritance hierarchy for `Shape`s.

Not every class relationship is an inheritance relationship. In Chapter 10 we discussed the *has-a* relationship, in which classes have members that are references to objects of other classes. Such relationships create classes by *composition* of existing classes. For example, given the classes Employee, BirthDate and TelephoneNumber, it's improper to say that an Employee *is a* BirthDate or that an Employee *is a* TelephoneNumber. However, an Employee *has a* BirthDate, and an Employee *has a* TelephoneNumber.

It's possible to treat base-class objects and derived-class objects similarly—their commonalities are expressed in the base class's members. Objects of all classes that extend a common base class can be treated as objects of that base class—such objects have an *is-a* relationship with the base class. However, *base-class objects cannot be treated as objects of their derived classes*. For example, all cars are vehicles, but not all vehicles are cars (other vehicles could be trucks, planes, bicycles, etc.). This chapter and Chapter 12 consider many examples of *is-a* relationships.

A derived class can customize methods it inherits from its base class. In such cases, the derived class can **override** (redefine) the base-class method with an appropriate implementation, as we'll see often in the chapter's code examples.

11.3 protected Members

Chapter 10 discussed access modifiers public and private. A class's public members are accessible wherever the application has a reference to an object of that class or one of its derived classes. A class's private members are accessible *only* within the class itself. A base class's private members *are* inherited by its derived classes, but are *not* directly accessible by derived-class methods and properties. In this section, we introduce access modifier protected. Using protected access offers an intermediate level of access between public and private. A base class's protected members can be accessed by members of that base class *and* by members of its derived classes.

All non-private base-class members retain their original access modifier when they become members of the derived class—public members of the base class become public members of the derived class, and protected members of the base class become protected members of the derived class.

Derived-class methods can refer to public and protected members inherited from the base class simply by using the member names. When a derived-class method overrides a base-class method, the base-class version can be accessed from the derived class by preceding the base-class method name with the keyword base and the member access (.) operator. We discuss accessing overridden members of the base class in Section 11.4.

Software Engineering Observation 11.1

Properties and methods of a derived class cannot directly access private members of the base class. A derived class can change the state of private base-class fields only through non-private methods and properties provided in the base class.

Software Engineering Observation 11.2

Declaring private fields in a base class helps you test, debug and correctly modify systems. If a derived class could access its base class's private fields, classes that inherit from that base class could access the fields as well. This would propagate access to what should be private fields, and the benefits of information hiding would be lost.

11.4 Relationship between Base Classes and Derived Classes

In this section, we use an inheritance hierarchy containing types of employees in a company's payroll application to discuss the relationship between a base class and its derived classes. In this company, commission employees (who will be represented as objects of a base class) are paid a percentage of their sales, while base-salaried commission employees (who will be represented as objects of a derived class) receive a base salary *plus* a percentage of their sales.

We divide our discussion of the relationship between commission employees and base-salaried commission employees into five examples:

1. The first example creates class CommissionEmployee, which directly inherits from class object and declares as private instance variables a first name, last name, social security number, commission rate and gross (i.e., total) sales amount.

2. The second example declares class BasePlusCommissionEmployee, which also directly inherits from class object and declares as private instance variables a first name, last name, social security number, commission rate, gross sales amount *and* base salary. We create the latter class by writing *every* line of code the class requires—we'll soon see that it's much more efficient to create this class by inheriting from class CommissionEmployee.

3. The third example declares a separate BasePlusCommissionEmployee class that extends class CommissionEmployee (i.e., a BasePlusCommissionEmployee *is a* CommissionEmployee who also has a base salary). We show that base-class methods must be explicitly declared virtual if they're to be overridden by methods in derived classes. BasePlusCommissionEmployee attempts to access class CommissionEmployee's private members, but this results in compilation errors because a derived class cannot access its base class's private instance variables.

4. The fourth example shows that if base class CommissionEmployee's instance variables are declared as protected, a BasePlusCommissionEmployee class that inherits from class CommissionEmployee can access that data directly. For this purpose, we declare class CommissionEmployee with protected instance variables.

5. After we discuss the convenience of using protected instance variables, we create the fifth example, which sets the CommissionEmployee instance variables back to private in class CommissionEmployee to enforce good software engineering. Then we show how a separate BasePlusCommissionEmployee class, which inherits from class CommissionEmployee, can use CommissionEmployee's public methods to manipulate CommissionEmployee's private instance variables.

11.4.1 Creating and Using a CommissionEmployee Class

We begin by declaring class CommissionEmployee (Fig. 11.4). Line 5 begins the class declaration. The colon (:) followed by class name object at the end of the declaration header indicates that class CommissionEmployee extends (i.e., inherits from) class object (System.Object in the Framework Class Library). C# programmers use inheritance to create classes from existing classes. In fact, every class in C# (except object) extends an existing class. Because class CommissionEmployee extends class object, class CommissionEmployee inherits the methods of class object—class object has no fields. Every C# class directly or indirectly inherits object's methods. If a class does not specify that it inherits from another class, the new class implicitly inherits from object. For this reason, you typically do not include ": object" in your code—we do so in this example for demonstration purposes.

> **Software Engineering Observation 11.3**
>
> *The compiler sets the base class of a class to object when the class declaration does not explicitly extend a base class.*

```
1   // Fig. 11.4: CommissionEmployee.cs
2   // CommissionEmployee class represents a commission employee.
3   using System;
4
5   public class CommissionEmployee : object
6   {
7      private string firstName;
8      private string lastName;
9      private string socialSecurityNumber;
10     private decimal grossSales; // gross weekly sales
11     private decimal commissionRate; // commission percentage
12
13     // five-parameter constructor
14     public CommissionEmployee( string first, string last, string ssn,
15        decimal sales, decimal rate )
16     {
17        // implicit call to object constructor occurs here
18        firstName = first;
19        lastName = last;
20        socialSecurityNumber = ssn;
21        GrossSales = sales; // validate gross sales via property
22        CommissionRate = rate; // validate commission rate via property
23     } // end five-parameter CommissionEmployee constructor
24
25     // read-only property that gets commission employee's first name
26     public string FirstName
27     {
28        get
29        {
30           return firstName;
31        } // end get
32     } // end property FirstName
33
34     // read-only property that gets commission employee's last name
35     public string LastName
36     {
37        get
38        {
39           return lastName;
40        } // end get
41     } // end property LastName
42
```

Fig. 11.4 | CommissionEmployee class represents a commission employee. (Part 1 of 3.)

```
43        // read-only property that gets
44        // commission employee's social security number
45        public string SocialSecurityNumber
46        {
47           get
48           {
49              return socialSecurityNumber;
50           } // end get
51        } // end property SocialSecurityNumber
52
53        // property that gets and sets commission employee's gross sales
54        public decimal GrossSales
55        {
56           get
57           {
58              return grossSales;
59           } // end get
60           set
61           {
62              if ( value >= 0 )
63                 grossSales = value;
64              else
65                 throw new ArgumentOutOfRangeException(
66                    "GrossSales", value, "GrossSales must be >= 0" );
67           } // end set
68        } // end property GrossSales
69
70        // property that gets and sets commission employee's commission rate
71        public decimal CommissionRate
72        {
73           get
74           {
75              return commissionRate;
76           } // end get
77           set
78           {
79              if ( value > 0 && value < 1 )
80                 commissionRate = value;
81              else
82                 throw new ArgumentOutOfRangeException( "CommissionRate",
83                    value, "CommissionRate must be > 0 and < 1" );
84           } // end set
85        } // end property CommissionRate
86
87        // calculate commission employee's pay
88        public decimal Earnings()
89        {
90           return commissionRate * grossSales;
91        } // end method Earnings
92
93        // return string representation of CommissionEmployee object
94        public override string ToString()
95        {
```

Fig. 11.4 | CommissionEmployee class represents a commission employee. (Part 2 of 3.)

```
96          return string.Format(
97              "{0}: {1} {2}\n{3}: {4}\n{5}: {6:C}\n{7}: {8:F2}",
98              "commission employee", FirstName, LastName,
99              "social security number", SocialSecurityNumber,
100             "gross sales", GrossSales, "commission rate", CommissionRate );
101     } // end method ToString
102 } // end class CommissionEmployee
```

Fig. 11.4 | CommissionEmployee class represents a commission employee. (Part 3 of 3.)

CommissionEmployee *Class Overview*
CommissionEmployee's public services include a constructor (lines 14–23), methods Earnings (lines 88–91) and ToString (lines 94–101), and the public properties (lines 26–85) for manipulating the class's instance variables firstName, lastName, socialSecurityNumber, grossSales and commissionRate (declared in lines 7–11). Each of its instance variable is private, so objects of other classes cannot directly access these variables. Declaring instance variables as private and providing public properties to manipulate and validate them helps enforce good software engineering. The set accessors of properties GrossSales and CommissionRate, for example, *validate* their arguments before assigning the values to instance variables grossSales and commissionRate, respectively.

CommissionEmployee *Constructor*
Constructors are *not* inherited, so class CommissionEmployee does not inherit class object's constructor. However, class CommissionEmployee's constructor calls class object's constructor implicitly. In fact, before executing the code in its own body, the derived class's constructor calls its direct base class's constructor, either explicitly or implicitly (if no constructor call is specified), to ensure that the instance variables inherited from the base class are initialized properly. The syntax for calling a base-class constructor explicitly is discussed in Section 11.4.3. If the code does not include an explicit call to the base-class constructor, the compiler generates an implicit call to the base class's default or parameterless constructor. The comment in line 17 indicates where the implicit call to the base class object's default constructor is made (you do not write the code for this call). Class object's default (empty) constructor does nothing. Even if a class does not have constructors, the default constructor that the compiler implicitly declares for the class will call the base class's default or parameterless constructor. Class object is the *only* class that does not have a base class.

After the implicit call to object's constructor occurs, lines 18–22 in the constructor assign values to the class's instance variables. We do *not* validate the values of arguments first, last and ssn before assigning them to the corresponding instance variables. We certainly could validate the first and last names—perhaps by ensuring that they're of a reasonable length. Similarly, a social security number could be validated to ensure that it contains nine digits, with or without dashes (e.g., 123-45-6789 or 123456789).

CommissionEmployee *GrossSales and* CommissionRate *Properties*
In Chapter 10, when the client code provided incorrect data to set a particular instance variable, we maintained the object in a consistent state by assigning a default value to the instance variable. In this example, properties GrossSales and CommissionRate **throw an exception** of type **ArgumentOutOfRangeException** (lines 65–66 and 82–83), which notifies the client code that an invalid argument was passed to the corresponding property's

set accessor. The **throw statement** creates a new object of type ArgumentOutOfRangeException. The parentheses following the class name indicate a call to the ArgumentOutOfRangeException constructor. After the exception object is created, the throw statement immediately exits the set accessor and the exception is returned to the code that attempted to set the time. As you'll learn in Chapter 13, you can use exception handling in the client code to "catch" such exceptions and attempt to recover from them.

CommissionEmployee Method Earnings
Method Earnings (lines 88–91) calculates a CommissionEmployee's earnings. Line 90 multiplies the commissionRate by the grossSales and returns the result.

CommissionEmployee Method ToString
Method ToString (lines 94–101) is special—it's one of the methods that every class inherits directly or indirectly from class object, which is the root of the C# class hierarchy. Section 11.7 summarizes class object's methods. Method ToString returns a string representing an object. It's called implicitly by an application whenever an object must be converted to a string representation, such as in Console's Write method or string method Format using a format item. Class object's ToString method returns a string that includes the name of the object's class. It's primarily a placeholder that can be (and typically should be) overridden by a derived class to specify an appropriate string representation of the data in a derived class object. Method ToString of class CommissionEmployee overrides (redefines) class object's ToString method. When invoked, CommissionEmployee's ToString method uses string method Format to return a string containing information about the CommissionEmployee. We use the format specifier C to format grossSales as currency and the format specifier F2 to format the commissionRate with two digits of precision to the right of the decimal point. To override a base-class method, a derived class must declare a method with keyword **override** and with the same signature (method name, number of parameters and parameter types) *and* return type as the base-class method—object's ToString method takes no parameters and returns type string, so CommissionEmployee declares ToString with no parameters and returns type string.

Common Programming Error 11.1
It's a compilation error to override a method with one that has a different access modifier. Overriding a method with a more restrictive access modifier would break the is-a relationship. If a public method could be overridden as a protected or private method, the derived-class objects would not be able to respond to the same method calls as base-class objects. Once a method is declared in a base class, the method must *have the same access modifier for all that class's direct and indirect derived classes.*

Class CommissionEmployeeTest
Figure 11.5 tests class CommissionEmployee. Lines 10–11 create a CommissionEmployee object and invoke its constructor (lines 14–23 of Fig. 11.4) to initialize it. We append the M suffix to the gross sales amount and the commission rate to indicate that the compiler should treat these as decimal literals, rather than doubles. Lines 16–22 use CommissionEmployee's properties to retrieve the object's instance-variable values for output. Line 23 outputs the amount calculated by the Earnings method. Lines 25–26 invoke the set accessors of the object's GrossSales and CommissionRate properties to change the values of instance variables grossSales and commissionRate. Lines 28–29 output the string rep-

resentation of the updated CommissionEmployee. When an object is output using a format item, the object's ToString method is invoked implicitly to obtain the object's string representation. Line 30 outputs the earnings again.

```
1   // Fig. 11.5: CommissionEmployeeTest.cs
2   // Testing class CommissionEmployee.
3   using System;
4
5   public class CommissionEmployeeTest
6   {
7      public static void Main( string[] args )
8      {
9         // instantiate CommissionEmployee object
10        CommissionEmployee employee = new CommissionEmployee( "Sue",
11           "Jones", "222-22-2222", 10000.00M, .06M );
12
13        // display commission-employee data
14        Console.WriteLine(
15           "Employee information obtained by properties and methods: \n" );
16        Console.WriteLine( "First name is {0}", employee.FirstName );
17        Console.WriteLine( "Last name is {0}", employee.LastName );
18        Console.WriteLine( "Social security number is {0}",
19           employee.SocialSecurityNumber );
20        Console.WriteLine( "Gross sales are {0:C}", employee.GrossSales );
21        Console.WriteLine( "Commission rate is {0:F2}",
22           employee.CommissionRate );
23        Console.WriteLine( "Earnings are {0:C}", employee.Earnings() );
24
25        employee.GrossSales = 5000.00M; // set gross sales
26        employee.CommissionRate = .1M; // set commission rate
27
28        Console.WriteLine( "\n{0}:\n\n{1}",
29           "Updated employee information obtained by ToString", employee );
30        Console.WriteLine( "earnings: {0:C}", employee.Earnings() );
31     } // end Main
32  } // end class CommissionEmployeeTest
```

```
Employee information obtained by properties and methods:

First name is Sue
Last name is Jones
Social security number is 222-22-2222
Gross sales are $10,000.00
Commission rate is 0.06
Earnings are $600.00

Updated employee information obtained by ToString:

commission employee: Sue Jones
social security number: 222-22-2222
gross sales: $5,000.00
commission rate: 0.10
earnings: $500.00
```

Fig. 11.5 | Testing class CommissionEmployee.

11.4.2 Creating a BasePlusCommissionEmployee Class without Using Inheritance

We now discuss the second part of our introduction to inheritance by declaring and testing the (completely new and independent) class BasePlusCommissionEmployee (Fig. 11.6), which contains a first name, last name, social security number, gross sales amount, commission rate *and* base salary. Class BasePlusCommissionEmployee's public services include a BasePlusCommissionEmployee constructor (lines 16–26), methods Earnings (lines 113–116) and ToString (lines 119–127), and public properties (lines 30–110) for the class's private instance variables firstName, lastName, socialSecurityNumber, grossSales, commissionRate and baseSalary (declared in lines 8–11). These variables, properties and methods encapsulate all the necessary features of a base-salaried commission employee. Note the similarity between this class and class CommissionEmployee (Fig. 11.4)—in this example, *we do not yet exploit that similarity*.

Class BasePlusCommissionEmployee does not specify that it extends object with the syntax ": object" in line 6, so the class *implicitly* extends object. Also, like class CommissionEmployee's constructor (lines 14–23 of Fig. 11.4), class BasePlusCommissionEmployee's constructor invokes class object's default constructor implicitly, as noted in the comment in line 19 of Fig. 11.6.

Class BasePlusCommissionEmployee's Earnings method (lines 113–116) computes the earnings of a base-salaried commission employee. Line 115 adds the employee's base salary to the product of the commission rate and the gross sales, and returns the result.

Class BasePlusCommissionEmployee overrides object method ToString to return a string containing the BasePlusCommissionEmployee's information (lines 119–127). Once again, we use format specifier C to format the gross sales and base salary as currency and format specifier F2 to format the commission rate with two digits of precision to the right of the decimal point (line 122).

```csharp
1   // Fig. 11.6: BasePlusCommissionEmployee.cs
2   // BasePlusCommissionEmployee class represents an employee that receives
3   // a base salary in addition to a commission.
4   using System;
5
6   public class BasePlusCommissionEmployee
7   {
8      private string firstName;
9      private string lastName;
10     private string socialSecurityNumber;
11     private decimal grossSales; // gross weekly sales
12     private decimal commissionRate; // commission percentage
13     private decimal baseSalary; // base salary per week
14
15     // six-parameter constructor
16     public BasePlusCommissionEmployee( string first, string last,
17        string ssn, decimal sales, decimal rate, decimal salary )
18     {
```

Fig. 11.6 | BasePlusCommissionEmployee class represents an employee that receives a base salary in addition to a commission. (Part 1 of 4.)

```
19            // implicit call to object constructor occurs here
20            firstName = first;
21            lastName = last;
22            socialSecurityNumber = ssn;
23            GrossSales = sales; // validate gross sales via property
24            CommissionRate = rate; // validate commission rate via property
25            BaseSalary = salary; // validate base salary via property
26         } // end six-parameter BasePlusCommissionEmployee constructor
27
28         // read-only property that gets
29         // BasePlusCommissionEmployee's first name
30         public string FirstName
31         {
32            get
33            {
34               return firstName;
35            } // end get
36         } // end property FirstName
37
38         // read-only property that gets
39         // BasePlusCommissionEmployee's last name
40         public string LastName
41         {
42            get
43            {
44               return lastName;
45            } // end get
46         } // end property LastName
47
48         // read-only property that gets
49         // BasePlusCommissionEmployee's social security number
50         public string SocialSecurityNumber
51         {
52            get
53            {
54               return socialSecurityNumber;
55            } // end get
56         } // end property SocialSecurityNumber
57
58         // property that gets and sets
59         // BasePlusCommissionEmployee's gross sales
60         public decimal GrossSales
61         {
62            get
63            {
64               return grossSales;
65            } // end get
66            set
67            {
68               if ( value >= 0 )
69                  grossSales = value;
```

Fig. 11.6 | BasePlusCommissionEmployee class represents an employee that receives a base salary in addition to a commission. (Part 2 of 4.)

```
70                else
71                    throw new ArgumentOutOfRangeException(
72                        "GrossSales", value, "GrossSales must be >= 0" );
73            } // end set
74        } // end property GrossSales
75
76        // property that gets and sets
77        // BasePlusCommissionEmployee's commission rate
78        public decimal CommissionRate
79        {
80            get
81            {
82                return commissionRate;
83            } // end get
84            set
85            {
86                if ( value > 0 && value < 1 )
87                    commissionRate = value;
88                else
89                    throw new ArgumentOutOfRangeException( "CommissionRate",
90                        value, "CommissionRate must be > 0 and < 1" );
91            } // end set
92        } // end property CommissionRate
93
94        // property that gets and sets
95        // BasePlusCommissionEmployee's base salary
96        public decimal BaseSalary
97        {
98            get
99            {
100                return baseSalary;
101            } // end get
102            set
103            {
104                if ( value >= 0 )
105                    baseSalary = value;
106                else
107                    throw new ArgumentOutOfRangeException( "BaseSalary",
108                        value, "BaseSalary must be >= 0" );
109            } // end set
110        } // end property BaseSalary
111
112        // calculate earnings
113        public decimal Earnings()
114        {
115            return baseSalary + ( commissionRate * grossSales );
116        } // end method earnings
117
118        // return string representation of BasePlusCommissionEmployee
119        public override string ToString()
120        {
```

Fig. 11.6 | BasePlusCommissionEmployee class represents an employee that receives a base salary in addition to a commission. (Part 3 of 4.)

```
121        return string.Format(
122            "{0}: {1} {2}\n{3}: {4}\n{5}: {6:C}\n{7}: {8:F2}\n{9}: {10:C}",
123            "base-salaried commission employee", firstName, lastName,
124            "social security number", socialSecurityNumber,
125            "gross sales", grossSales, "commission rate", commissionRate,
126            "base salary", baseSalary );
127        } // end method ToString
128    } // end class BasePlusCommissionEmployee
```

Fig. 11.6 | BasePlusCommissionEmployee class represents an employee that receives a base salary in addition to a commission. (Part 4 of 4.)

Class *BasePlusCommissionEmployeeTest*
Figure 11.7 tests class BasePlusCommissionEmployee. Lines 10–12 instantiate a Base-PlusCommissionEmployee object and pass "Bob", "Lewis", "333-33-3333", 5000.00M, .04M and 300.00M to the constructor as the first name, last name, social security number, gross sales, commission rate and base salary, respectively. Lines 17–25 use BasePlusCommissionEmployee's properties and methods to retrieve the values of the object's instance variables and calculate the earnings for output. Line 27 invokes the object's BaseSalary property to *change* the base salary. Property BaseSalary's set accessor (Fig. 11.6, lines 102–109) ensures that instance variable baseSalary is not assigned a negative value, because an employee's base salary cannot be negative. Lines 29–30 of Fig. 11.7 invoke the object's ToString method implicitly to get the object's string representation.

```
1    // Fig. 11.7: BasePlusCommissionEmployeeTest.cs
2    // Testing class BasePlusCommissionEmployee.
3    using System;
4
5    public class BasePlusCommissionEmployeeTest
6    {
7        public static void Main( string[] args )
8        {
9            // instantiate BasePlusCommissionEmployee object
10           BasePlusCommissionEmployee employee =
11               new BasePlusCommissionEmployee( "Bob", "Lewis",
12               "333-33-3333", 5000.00M, .04M, 300.00M );
13
14           // display BasePlusCommissionEmployee's data
15           Console.WriteLine(
16               "Employee information obtained by properties and methods: \n" );
17           Console.WriteLine( "First name is {0}", employee.FirstName );
18           Console.WriteLine( "Last name is {0}", employee.LastName );
19           Console.WriteLine( "Social security number is {0}",
20               employee.SocialSecurityNumber );
21           Console.WriteLine( "Gross sales are {0:C}", employee.GrossSales );
22           Console.WriteLine( "Commission rate is {0:F2}",
23               employee.CommissionRate );
24           Console.WriteLine( "Earnings are {0:C}", employee.Earnings() );
25           Console.WriteLine( "Base salary is {0:C}", employee.BaseSalary );
```

Fig. 11.7 | Testing class BasePlusCommissionEmployee. (Part 1 of 2.)

```
26
27          employee.BaseSalary = 1000.00M; // set base salary
28
29          Console.WriteLine( "\n{0}:\n\n{1}",
30             "Updated employee information obtained by ToString", employee );
31          Console.WriteLine( "earnings: {0:C}", employee.Earnings() );
32       } // end Main
33    } // end class BasePlusCommissionEmployeeTest
```

```
Employee information obtained by properties and methods:

First name is Bob
Last name is Lewis
Social security number is 333-33-3333
Gross sales are $5,000.00
Commission rate is 0.04
Earnings are $500.00
Base salary is $300.00

Updated employee information obtained by ToString:

base-salaried commission employee: Bob Lewis
social security number: 333-33-3333
gross sales: $5,000.00
commission rate: 0.04
base salary: $1,000.00
earnings: $1,200.00
```

Fig. 11.7 | Testing class BasePlusCommissionEmployee. (Part 2 of 2.)

Much of the code for class BasePlusCommissionEmployee (Fig. 11.6) is similar, if not identical, to the code for class CommissionEmployee (Fig. 11.4). For example, in class BasePlusCommissionEmployee, private instance variables firstName and lastName and properties FirstName and LastName are identical to those of class CommissionEmployee. Classes CommissionEmployee and BasePlusCommissionEmployee also both contain private instance variables socialSecurityNumber, commissionRate and grossSales, as well as properties to manipulate these variables. In addition, the BasePlusCommissionEmployee constructor is almost identical to that of class CommissionEmployee, except that BasePlusCommissionEmployee's constructor also sets the baseSalary. The other additions to class BasePlusCommissionEmployee are private instance variable baseSalary and property BaseSalary. Class BasePlusCommissionEmployee's Earnings method is nearly identical to that of class CommissionEmployee, except that BasePlusCommissionEmployee's also adds the baseSalary. Similarly, class BasePlusCommissionEmployee's ToString method is nearly identical to that of class CommissionEmployee, except that BasePlusCommissionEmployee's ToString also formats the value of instance variable baseSalary as currency.

We literally *copied* the code from class CommissionEmployee and *pasted* it into class BasePlusCommissionEmployee, then modified class BasePlusCommissionEmployee to include a base salary and methods and properties that manipulate the base salary. This "copy-and-paste" approach is often error prone and time consuming. Worse yet, it can spread many physical copies of the same code throughout a system, creating a code-maintenance nightmare. Is there a way to "absorb" the members of one class in a way that makes them part of other classes without copying code? In the next several examples we answer this question, using a more elegant approach to building classes—namely, inheritance.

Error-Prevention Tip 11.1

Copying and pasting code from one class to another can spread errors across multiple source-code files. To avoid duplicating code (and possibly errors) in situations where you want one class to "absorb" the members of another class, use inheritance rather than the "copy-and-paste" approach.

Software Engineering Observation 11.4

With inheritance, the common members of all the classes in the hierarchy are declared in a base class. When changes are required for these common features, you need to make the changes only in the base class—derived classes then inherit the changes. Without inheritance, changes would need to be made to all the source-code files that contain a copy of the code in question.

11.4.3 Creating a CommissionEmployee–BasePlusCommissionEmployee Inheritance Hierarchy

Now we declare class BasePlusCommissionEmployee (Fig. 11.8), which extends class CommissionEmployee (Fig. 11.4). A BasePlusCommissionEmployee object *is a* CommissionEmployee (because inheritance passes on the capabilities of class CommissionEmployee), but class BasePlusCommissionEmployee also has instance variable baseSalary (Fig. 11.8, line 7). The colon (:) in line 5 of the class declaration indicates inheritance. As a derived class, BasePlusCommissionEmployee inherits the members of class CommissionEmployee and can access those members that are non-private. The constructor of class CommissionEmployee is *not* inherited. Thus, the public services of BasePlusCommissionEmployee include its constructor (lines 11–16), public methods and properties inherited from class CommissionEmployee, property BaseSalary (lines 20–34), method Earnings (lines 37–41) and method ToString (lines 44–53).

```
1   // Fig. 11.8: BasePlusCommissionEmployee.cs
2   // BasePlusCommissionEmployee inherits from class CommissionEmployee.
3   using System;
4
5   public class BasePlusCommissionEmployee : CommissionEmployee
6   {
7      private decimal baseSalary; // base salary per week
8
9      // six-parameter derived-class constructor
10     // with call to base class CommissionEmployee constructor
11     public BasePlusCommissionEmployee( string first, string last,
12        string ssn, decimal sales, decimal rate, decimal salary )
13        : base( first, last, ssn, sales, rate )
14     {
```

Fig. 11.8 | BasePlusCommissionEmployee inherits from class CommissionEmployee. (Part 1 of 2.)

```
15          BaseSalary = salary; // validate base salary via property
16       } // end six-parameter BasePlusCommissionEmployee constructor
17
18       // property that gets and sets
19       // BasePlusCommissionEmployee's base salary
20       public decimal BaseSalary
21       {
22          get
23          {
24             return baseSalary;
25          } // end get
26          set
27          {
28             if ( value >= 0 )
29                baseSalary = value;
30             else
31                throw new ArgumentOutOfRangeException( "BaseSalary",
32                   value, "BaseSalary must be >= 0" );
33          } // end set
34       } // end property BaseSalary
35
36       // calculate earnings
37       public override decimal Earnings()
38       {
39          // not allowed: commissionRate and grossSales private in base class
40          return baseSalary + ( commissionRate * grossSales );
41       } // end method Earnings
42
43       // return string representation of BasePlusCommissionEmployee
44       public override string ToString()
45       {
46          // not allowed: attempts to access private base-class members
47          return string.Format(
48             "{0}: {1} {2}\n{3}: {4}\n{5}: {6:C}\n{7}: {8:F2}\n{9}: {10:C}",
49             "base-salaried commission employee", firstName, lastName,
50             "social security number", socialSecurityNumber,
51             "gross sales", grossSales, "commission rate", commissionRate,
52             "base salary", baseSalary );
53       } // end method ToString
54    } // end class BasePlusCommissionEmployee
```

Error List						▼ ᴚ ×
⊗ 1 Error	⚠ 0 Warnings	ⓘ 0 Messages				
	Description		File	Line	Column	Project
⊗ 1	'BasePlusCommissionEmployee.Earnings()': cannot override inherited member 'CommissionEmployee.Earnings()' because it is not marked virtual, abstract, or override		BasePlusCommissionEmployee.cs	37	28	BasePlusCommissionEmployee

Fig. 11.8 | BasePlusCommissionEmployee inherits from class CommissionEmployee. (Part 2 of 2.)

A Derived Class's Constructor Must Call Its Base Class's Constructor

Each derived-class constructor *must* implicitly or explicitly call its base-class constructor to ensure that the instance variables inherited from the base class are initialized properly.

BasePlusCommissionEmployee's six-parameter constructor explicitly calls class Commis-sionEmployee's five-parameter constructor to initialize the base-class portion of a Base-PlusCommissionEmployee object—that is, the instance variables firstName, lastName, socialSecurityNumber, grossSales and commissionRate. Line 13 in the header of BasePlusCommissionEmployee's six-parameter constructor invokes the CommissionEm-ployee's five-parameter constructor (declared at lines 14–23 of Fig. 11.4) by using a con-structor initializer. In Section 10.6, we used constructor initializers with keyword this to call overloaded constructors in the same class. In line 13 of Fig. 11.8, we use a constructor initializer with keyword **base** to invoke the base-class constructor. The arguments first, last, ssn, sales and rate are used to initialize base-class members firstName, lastName, socialSecurityNumber, grossSales and commissionRate, respectively. If BasePlus-CommissionEmployee's constructor did not invoke CommissionEmployee's constructor ex-plicitly, C# would attempt to invoke class CommissionEmployee's parameterless or default constructor—but the class does not have such a constructor, so the compiler would issue an error. When a base class contains a parameterless constructor, you can use base() in the constructor initializer to call that constructor explicitly, but this is rarely done.

Common Programming Error 11.2

A compilation error occurs if a derived-class constructor calls one of its base-class construc-tors with arguments that do not match the number and types of parameters specified in one of the base-class constructor declarations.

BasePlusCommissionEmployee Method Earnings

Lines 37–41 of Fig. 11.8 declare method Earnings using keyword override to override the CommissionEmployee's Earnings method, as we did with method ToString in previ-ous examples. Line 37 causes a compilation error indicating that we cannot override the base class's Earnings method because it was not explicitly "marked virtual, abstract, or override." The **virtual** and abstract keywords indicate that a base-class method can be overridden in derived classes. (As you'll learn in Section 12.4, abstract methods are im-plicitly virtual.) The override modifier declares that a derived-class method overrides a virtual or abstract base-class method. This modifier also implicitly declares the derived-class method virtual and allows it to be overridden in derived classes further down the inheritance hierarchy.

If we add the keyword virtual to the declaration of method Earnings in Fig. 11.4 and recompile, other compilation errors appear. As shown in Fig. 11.9, the compiler gen-erates additional errors for line 40 of Fig. 11.8 because base class CommissionEmployee's instance variables commissionRate and grossSales are private—derived class Base-PlusCommissionEmployee's methods are not allowed to access base class CommissionEm-ployee's private instance variables. The compiler issues additional errors at lines 49–51 of BasePlusCommissionEmployee's ToString method for the same reason. The errors in BasePlusCommissionEmployee could have been prevented by using the public properties inherited from class CommissionEmployee. For example, line 40 could have invoked the get accessors of properties CommissionRate and GrossSales to access CommissionEm-ployee's private instance variables commissionRate and grossSales, respectively. Lines 49–51 also could have used appropriate properties to retrieve the values of the base class's instance variables.

Error List

7 Errors | 0 Warnings | 0 Messages

	Description	File	Line	Column	Project
1	'CommissionEmployee.commissionRate' is inaccessible due to its protection level	BasePlusCommissionEmployee.cs	40	29	BasePlusCommissionEmployee
2	'CommissionEmployee.grossSales' is inaccessible due to its protection level	BasePlusCommissionEmployee.cs	40	46	BasePlusCommissionEmployee
3	'CommissionEmployee.firstName' is inaccessible due to its protection level	BasePlusCommissionEmployee.cs	49	47	BasePlusCommissionEmployee
4	'CommissionEmployee.lastName' is inaccessible due to its protection level	BasePlusCommissionEmployee.cs	49	58	BasePlusCommissionEmployee
5	'CommissionEmployee.socialSecurityNumber' is inaccessible due to its protection level	BasePlusCommissionEmployee.cs	50	36	BasePlusCommissionEmployee
6	'CommissionEmployee.grossSales' is inaccessible due to its protection level	BasePlusCommissionEmployee.cs	51	25	BasePlusCommissionEmployee
7	'CommissionEmployee.commissionRate' is inaccessible due to its protection level	BasePlusCommissionEmployee.cs	51	56	BasePlusCommissionEmployee

Fig. 11.9 | Compilation errors generated by `BasePlusCommissionEmployee` (Fig. 11.8) after declaring the `Earnings` method in Fig. 11.4 with keyword `virtual`.

11.4.4 CommissionEmployee-BasePlusCommissionEmployee Inheritance Hierarchy Using protected Instance Variables

To enable class `BasePlusCommissionEmployee` to directly access base-class instance variables `firstName`, `lastName`, `socialSecurityNumber`, `grossSales` and `commissionRate`, we can declare those members as `protected` in the base class. As we discussed in Section 11.3, a base class's `protected` members *are* inherited by all derived classes of that base class. Class `CommissionEmployee` in this example is a modification of the version from Fig. 11.4 that declares its instance variables `firstName`, `lastName`, `socialSecurityNumber`, `grossSales` and `commissionRate` as `protected` rather than `private`. We also declare the `Earnings` method `virtual` as in

```
public virtual decimal Earnings()
```

so that `BasePlusCommissionEmployee` can override the method. The rest of the class declaration in this example is identical to that of Fig. 11.4. The complete source code for class `CommissionEmployee` is included in this example's project.

`public` vs. `protected` Data

We could have declared base class `CommissionEmployee`'s instance variables `firstName`, `lastName`, `socialSecurityNumber`, `grossSales` and `commissionRate` as `public` to enable derived class `BasePlusCommissionEmployee` to access the base-class instance variables. However, declaring `public` instance variables is poor software engineering, because it allows unrestricted access to the instance variables, greatly increasing the chance of errors. With `protected` instance variables, the derived class gets access to the instance variables, but classes that are not derived from the base class cannot access its variables directly.

Class `BasePlusCommissionEmployee`

Class `BasePlusCommissionEmployee` (Fig. 11.10) in this example extends the version of class `CommissionEmployee` with `protected` data rather than the one with `private` data in Fig. 11.4. Each `BasePlusCommissionEmployee` object inherits `CommissionEmployee`'s `protected` instance variables `firstName`, `lastName`, `socialSecurityNumber`, `grossSales` and commissionRate—all these variables are now protected members of BasePlusCommissionEmployee. As a result, the compiler does not generate errors when compiling line 40 of method Earnings and lines 48–50 of method ToString. If another class extends BasePlusCommissionEmployee, the new derived class also inherits the protected members.

Class BasePlusCommissionEmployee does *not* inherit class CommissionEmployee's constructor. However, class BasePlusCommissionEmployee's six-parameter constructor (lines 12–17) calls class CommissionEmployee's five-parameter constructor with a constructor initializer. BasePlusCommissionEmployee's six-parameter constructor must explicitly call the five-parameter constructor of class CommissionEmployee, because CommissionEmployee does not provide a parameterless constructor that could be invoked implicitly.

```
1   // Fig. 11.10: BasePlusCommissionEmployee.cs
2   // BasePlusCommissionEmployee inherits from CommissionEmployee and has
3   // access to CommissionEmployee's protected members.
4   using System;
5
6   public class BasePlusCommissionEmployee : CommissionEmployee2
7   {
8      private decimal baseSalary; // base salary per week
9
10     // six-parameter derived-class constructor
11     // with call to base class CommissionEmployee constructor
12     public BasePlusCommissionEmployee( string first, string last,
13        string ssn, decimal sales, decimal rate, decimal salary )
14        : base( first, last, ssn, sales, rate )
15     {
16        BaseSalary = salary; // validate base salary via property
17     } // end six-parameter BasePlusCommissionEmployee constructor
18
19     // property that gets and sets
20     // BasePlusCommissionEmployee's base salary
21     public decimal BaseSalary
22     {
23        get
24        {
25           return baseSalary;
26        } // end get
27        set
28        {
29           if ( value >= 0 )
30              baseSalary = value;
31           else
32              throw new ArgumentOutOfRangeException( "BaseSalary",
33                 value, "BaseSalary must be >= 0" );
34        } // end set
35     } // end property BaseSalary
36
37     // calculate earnings
38     public override decimal Earnings()
39     {
```

Fig. 11.10 | BasePlusCommissionEmployee inherits from CommissionEmployee and has access to CommissionEmployee's protected members. (Part 1 of 2.)

```
40            return baseSalary + ( commissionRate * grossSales );
41       } // end method Earnings
42
43       // return string representation of BasePlusCommissionEmployee
44       public override string ToString()
45       {
46            return string.Format(
47               "{0}: {1} {2}\n{3}: {4}\n{5}: {6:C}\n{7}: {8:F2}\n{9}: {10:C}",
48               "base-salaried commission employee", firstName, lastName,
49               "social security number", socialSecurityNumber,
50               "gross sales", grossSales, "commission rate", commissionRate,
51               "base salary", baseSalary );
52       } // end method ToString
53    } // end class BasePlusCommissionEmployee
```

Fig. 11.10 | BasePlusCommissionEmployee inherits from CommissionEmployee and has access to CommissionEmployee's protected members. (Part 2 of 2.)

Class *BasePlusCommissionEmployeeTest*

Figure 11.11 uses a BasePlusCommissionEmployee object to perform the same tasks that Fig. 11.7 performed on the version of the class from Fig. 11.6. The outputs of the two applications are identical. Although we declared the version of the class in Fig. 11.6 without using inheritance and declared the version in Fig. 11.10 using inheritance, both classes provide the same functionality. The source code in Fig. 11.10 (which is 53 lines) is considerably shorter than version in Fig. 11.6 (which is 128 lines), because the new class inherits most of its functionality from CommissionEmployee, whereas the version in Fig. 11.6 inherits only class object's functionality. Also, there's now only one copy of the commission-employee functionality declared in class CommissionEmployee. This makes the code easier to maintain, modify and debug, because the code related to a commission employee exists only in class CommissionEmployee.

```
1    // Fig. 11.11: BasePlusCommissionEmployee.cs
2    // Testing class BasePlusCommissionEmployee.
3    using System;
4
5    public class BasePlusCommissionEmployeeTest
6    {
7       public static void Main( string[] args )
8       {
9          // instantiate BasePlusCommissionEmployee object
10         BasePlusCommissionEmployee basePlusCommissionEmployee =
11            new BasePlusCommissionEmployee( "Bob", "Lewis",
12            "333-33-3333", 5000.00M, .04M, 300.00M );
13
14         // display BasePlusCommissionEmployee's data
15         Console.WriteLine(
16            "Employee information obtained by properties and methods: \n" );
17         Console.WriteLine( "First name is {0}",
18            basePlusCommissionEmployee.FirstName );
```

Fig. 11.11 | Testing class BasePlusCommissionEmployee. (Part 1 of 2.)

```
19          Console.WriteLine( "Last name is {0}",
20             basePlusCommissionEmployee.LastName );
21          Console.WriteLine( "Social security number is {0}",
22             basePlusCommissionEmployee.SocialSecurityNumber );
23          Console.WriteLine( "Gross sales are {0:C}",
24             basePlusCommissionEmployee.GrossSales );
25          Console.WriteLine( "Commission rate is {0:F2}",
26             basePlusCommissionEmployee.CommissionRate );
27          Console.WriteLine( "Earnings are {0:C}",
28             basePlusCommissionEmployee.Earnings() );
29          Console.WriteLine( "Base salary is {0:C}",
30             basePlusCommissionEmployee.BaseSalary );
31
32          basePlusCommissionEmployee.BaseSalary = 1000.00M; // set base salary
33
34          Console.WriteLine( "\n{0}:\n\n{1}",
35             "Updated employee information obtained by ToString",
36             basePlusCommissionEmployee );
37          Console.WriteLine( "earnings: {0:C}",
38             basePlusCommissionEmployee.Earnings() );
39       } // end Main
40    } // end class BasePlusCommissionEmployee
```

```
Employee information obtained by properties and methods:

First name is Bob
Last name is Lewis
Social security number is 333-33-3333
Gross sales are $5,000.00
Commission rate is 0.04
Earnings are $500.00
Base salary is $300.00

Updated employee information obtained by ToString:

base-salaried commission employee: Bob Lewis
social security number: 333-33-3333
gross sales: $5,000.00
commission rate: 0.04
base salary: $1,000.00
earnings: $1,200.00
```

Fig. 11.11 | Testing class BasePlusCommissionEmployee. (Part 2 of 2.)

In this example, we declared base-class instance variables as protected so that derived classes could access them. Inheriting protected instance variables enables you to directly access the variables in the derived class without invoking the set or get accessors of the corresponding property. In most cases, however, it's better to use private instance variables to encourage proper software engineering. Your code will be easier to maintain, modify and debug.

Using protected instance variables creates several potential problems. First, the derived-class object can set an inherited variable's value directly without using a property's set accessor. Therefore, a derived-class object can assign an invalid value to the variable.

For example, if we were to declare CommissionEmployee's instance variable grossSales as protected, a derived-class object (e.g., BasePlusCommissionEmployee) could then assign a negative value to grossSales. The second problem with using protected instance variables is that derived-class methods are more likely to be written to depend on the base class's data implementation. In practice, derived classes should depend only on the base-class services (i.e., non-private methods and properties) and not on the base-class data implementation. With protected instance variables in the base class, we may need to modify all the derived classes of the base class if the base-class implementation changes. For example, if for some reason we were to change the names of instance variables first-Name and lastName to first and last, then we would have to do so for all occurrences in which a derived class directly references base-class instance variables firstName and last-Name. In such a case, the software is said to be **fragile** or **brittle**, because a small change in the base class can "break" derived-class implementation. You should be able to change the base-class implementation while still providing the same services to the derived classes. Of course, if the base-class services change, we must reimplement our derived classes.

> **Software Engineering Observation 11.5**
>
> *Declaring base-class instance variables private (as opposed to protected) enables the base-class implementation of these instance variables to change without affecting derived-class implementations.*

11.4.5 CommissionEmployee–BasePlusCommissionEmployee Inheritance Hierarchy Using private Instance Variables

We now reexamine our hierarchy once more, this time using the best software engineering practices. Class CommissionEmployee (Fig. 11.12) declares instance variables firstName, lastName, socialSecurityNumber, grossSales and commissionRate as private (lines 7–11) and provides public properties FirstName, LastName, SocialSecurityNumber, GrossSales and GrossSales for manipulating these values. Methods Earnings (lines 88–91) and ToString (lines 94–101) use the class's properties to obtain the values of its instance variables. If we decide to change the instance-variable names, the Earnings and ToString declarations will not require modification—only the bodies of the properties that directly manipulate the instance variables will need to change. These changes occur solely within the base class—no changes to the derived class are needed. Localizing the effects of changes like this is a good software engineering practice. Derived class BasePlusCommissionEmployee (Fig. 11.13) inherits from CommissionEmployee's and can access the private base-class members via the inherited public properties.

```
1   // Fig. 11.12: CommissionEmployee.cs
2   // CommissionEmployee class represents a commission employee.
3   using System;
4
5   public class CommissionEmployee
6   {
7       private string firstName;
8       private string lastName;
```

Fig. 11.12 | CommissionEmployee class represents a commission employee. (Part 1 of 3.)

```
 9     private string socialSecurityNumber;
10     private decimal grossSales; // gross weekly sales
11     private decimal commissionRate; // commission percentage
12
13     // five-parameter constructor
14     public CommissionEmployee( string first, string last, string ssn,
15        decimal sales, decimal rate )
16     {
17        // implicit call to object constructor occurs here
18        firstName = first;
19        lastName = last;
20        socialSecurityNumber = ssn;
21        GrossSales = sales; // validate gross sales via property
22        CommissionRate = rate; // validate commission rate via property
23     } // end five-parameter CommissionEmployee constructor
24
25     // read-only property that gets commission employee's first name
26     public string FirstName
27     {
28        get
29        {
30           return firstName;
31        } // end get
32     } // end property FirstName
33
34     // read-only property that gets commission employee's last name
35     public string LastName
36     {
37        get
38        {
39           return lastName;
40        } // end get
41     } // end property LastName
42
43     // read-only property that gets
44     // commission employee's social security number
45     public string SocialSecurityNumber
46     {
47        get
48        {
49           return socialSecurityNumber;
50        } // end get
51     } // end property SocialSecurityNumber
52
53     // property that gets and sets commission employee's gross sales
54     public decimal GrossSales
55     {
56        get
57        {
58           return grossSales;
59        } // end get
60        set
61        {
```

Fig. II.I2 | CommissionEmployee class represents a commission employee. (Part 2 of 3.)

```
62          if ( value >= 0 )
63              grossSales = value;
64          else
65              throw new ArgumentOutOfRangeException(
66                  "GrossSales", value, "GrossSales must be >= 0" );
67      } // end set
68    } // end property GrossSales
69
70    // property that gets and sets commission employee's commission rate
71    public decimal CommissionRate
72    {
73      get
74      {
75          return commissionRate;
76      } // end get
77      set
78      {
79          if ( value > 0 && value < 1 )
80              commissionRate = value;
81          else
82              throw new ArgumentOutOfRangeException( "CommissionRate",
83                  value, "CommissionRate must be > 0 and < 1" );
84      } // end set
85    } // end property CommissionRate
86
87    // calculate commission employee's pay
88    public virtual decimal Earnings()
89    {
90      return CommissionRate * GrossSales;
91    } // end method Earnings
92
93    // return string representation of CommissionEmployee object
94    public override string ToString()
95    {
96      return string.Format(
97          "{0}: {1} {2}\n{3}: {4}\n{5}: {6:C}\n{7}: {8:F2}",
98          "commission employee", FirstName, LastName,
99          "social security number", SocialSecurityNumber,
100         "gross sales", GrossSales, "commission rate", CommissionRate );
101   } // end method ToString
102 } // end class CommissionEmployee
```

Fig. 11.12 | CommissionEmployee class represents a commission employee. (Part 3 of 3.)

Class BasePlusCommissionEmployee (Fig. 11.13) has several changes to its method implementations that distinguish it from the version in Fig. 11.10. Methods Earnings (Fig. 11.13, lines 39–42) and ToString (lines 45–49) each invoke property BaseSalary's get accessor to obtain the base-salary value, rather than accessing baseSalary directly. If we decide to rename instance variable baseSalary, only the body of property BaseSalary will need to change.

```
 1   // Fig. 11.13: BasePlusCommissionEmployee.cs
 2   // BasePlusCommissionEmployee inherits from CommissionEmployee and has
 3   // access to CommissionEmployee's private data via
 4   // its public properties.
 5   using System;
 6
 7   public class BasePlusCommissionEmployee : CommissionEmployee
 8   {
 9      private decimal baseSalary; // base salary per week
10
11      // six-parameter derived class constructor
12      // with call to base class CommissionEmployee constructor
13      public BasePlusCommissionEmployee( string first, string last,
14         string ssn, decimal sales, decimal rate, decimal salary )
15         : base( first, last, ssn, sales, rate )
16      {
17         BaseSalary = salary; // validate base salary via property
18      } // end six-parameter BasePlusCommissionEmployee constructor
19
20      // property that gets and sets
21      // BasePlusCommissionEmployee's base salary
22      public decimal BaseSalary
23      {
24         get
25         {
26            return baseSalary;
27         } // end get
28         set
29         {
30            if ( value >= 0 )
31               baseSalary = value;
32            else
33               throw new ArgumentOutOfRangeException( "BaseSalary",
34                  value, "BaseSalary must be >= 0" );
35         } // end set
36      } // end property BaseSalary
37
38      // calculate earnings
39      public override decimal Earnings()
40      {
41         return BaseSalary + base.Earnings();
42      } // end method Earnings
43
44      // return string representation of BasePlusCommissionEmployee
45      public override string ToString()
46      {
47         return string.Format( "base-salaried {0}\nbase salary: {1:C}",
48            base.ToString(), BaseSalary );
49      } // end method ToString
50   } // end class BasePlusCommissionEmployee
```

Fig. 11.13 | BasePlusCommissionEmployee inherits from CommissionEmployee and has access to CommissionEmployee's private data via its public properties.

BasePlusCommissionEmployee Method Earnings

Class `BasePlusCommissionEmployee`'s `Earnings` method (Fig. 11.13, lines 39–42) overrides class `CommissionEmployee`'s `Earnings` method (Fig. 11.12, lines 88–91) to calculate a `BasePlusCommissionEmployee`'s earnings. The method obtains the portion of the employee's earnings based on commission alone by calling `CommissionEmployee`'s `Earnings` method with `base.Earnings()` (Fig. 11.13, line 41), then adds the base salary to this value to calculate the total earnings of the employee. Note the syntax used to invoke an overridden base-class method from a derived class—place the keyword base and the member access (.) operator before the base-class method name. This method invocation is a good software engineering practice—by having `BasePlusCommissionEmployee`'s `Earnings` method invoke `CommissionEmployee`'s `Earnings` method to calculate part of a `BasePlusCommissionEmployee` object's earnings, we avoid duplicate code and reduce code-maintenance problems.

> ### Common Programming Error 11.3
> *When a base-class method is overridden in a derived class, the derived-class version often calls the base-class version to do a portion of the work. Failure to prefix the base-class method name with the keyword* base *and the member access (.) operator when referencing the base class's method from the derived-class version causes the derived-class method to call itself, creating infinite recursion.*

BasePlusCommissionEmployee Method ToString

Similarly, `BasePlusCommissionEmployee`'s `ToString` method (Fig. 11.13, lines 45–49) overrides class `CommissionEmployee`'s version (Fig. 11.12, lines 94–101) to return a `string` representation that's appropriate for a base-salaried commission employee. The method creates part of a `BasePlusCommissionEmployee` object's `string` representation (i.e., the string `"commission employee"` and the values of `CommissionEmployee`'s `private` instance variables) by calling `CommissionEmployee`'s `ToString` method with `base.ToString()` (Fig. 11.13, line 48). The derived class's method then outputs the remainder of the object's `string` representation (i.e., the value of class `BasePlusCommissionEmployee`'s base salary).

Class BasePlusCommissionEmployeeTest

Figure 11.14 performs the same manipulations on a `BasePlusCommissionEmployee` object as did Figs. 11.7 and 11.11, respectively. Although each "base-salaried commission employee" class behaves identically, the `BasePlusCommissionEmployee` in this example is the best engineered. By using inheritance and by using properties that hide the data and ensure consistency, we have efficiently and effectively constructed a well-engineered class.

```
1   // Fig. 11.14: BasePlusCommissionEmployeeTest.cs
2   // Testing class BasePlusCommissionEmployee.
3   using System;
4
5   public class BasePlusCommissionEmployeeTest
6   {
7      public static void Main( string[] args )
8      {
```

Fig. 11.14 | Testing class `BasePlusCommissionEmployee`. (Part 1 of 2.)

```
 9          // instantiate BasePlusCommissionEmployee object
10          BasePlusCommissionEmployee employee =
11             new BasePlusCommissionEmployee( "Bob", "Lewis",
12             "333-33-3333", 5000.00M, .04M, 300.00M );
13
14          // display BasePlusCommissionEmployee's data
15          Console.WriteLine(
16             "Employee information obtained by properties and methods: \n" );
17          Console.WriteLine( "First name is {0}", employee.FirstName );
18          Console.WriteLine( "Last name is {0}", employee.LastName );
19          Console.WriteLine( "Social security number is {0}",
20             employee.SocialSecurityNumber );
21          Console.WriteLine( "Gross sales are {0:C}", employee.GrossSales );
22          Console.WriteLine( "Commission rate is {0:F2}",
23             employee.CommissionRate );
24          Console.WriteLine( "Earnings are {0:C}", employee.Earnings() );
25          Console.WriteLine( "Base salary is {0:C}", employee.BaseSalary );
26
27          employee.BaseSalary = 1000.00M; // set base salary
28
29          Console.WriteLine( "\n{0}:\n\n{1}",
30             "Updated employee information obtained by ToString", employee );
31          Console.WriteLine( "earnings: {0:C}", employee.Earnings() );
32       } // end Main
33    } // end class BasePlusCommissionEmployeeTest
```

```
Employee information obtained by properties and methods:

First name is Bob
Last name is Lewis
Social security number is 333-33-3333
Gross sales are $5,000.00
Commission rate is 0.04
Earnings are $500.00
Base salary is $300.00

Updated employee information obtained by ToString:

base-salaried commission employee: Bob Lewis
social security number: 333-33-3333
gross sales: $5,000.00
commission rate: 0.04
base salary: $1,000.00
earnings: $1,200.00
```

Fig. 11.14 | Testing class `BasePlusCommissionEmployee`. (Part 2 of 2.)

In this section, you saw an evolutionary set of examples that was carefully designed to teach key capabilities for good software engineering with inheritance. You learned how to create a derived class using inheritance, how to use protected base-class members to enable a derived class to access inherited base-class instance variables and how to override base-class methods to provide versions that are more appropriate for derived-class objects. In addition, you applied software engineering techniques from Chapter 4, Chapter 10 and this chapter to create classes that are easy to maintain, modify and debug.

11.5 Constructors in Derived Classes

As we explained in the preceding section, instantiating a derived-class object begins a chain of constructor calls. The derived-class constructor, before performing its own tasks, invokes its direct base class's constructor either explicitly (via a constructor initializer with the base reference) or implicitly (calling the base class's default constructor or parameterless constructor). Similarly, if the base class is derived from another class (as every class except object is), the base-class constructor invokes the constructor of the next class up in the hierarchy, and so on. The last constructor called in the chain is always the constructor for class object. The original derived-class constructor's body finishes executing last. Each base class's constructor manipulates the base-class instance variables that the derived-class object inherits. For example, consider again the CommissionEmployee–BasePlusCommissionEmployee hierarchy from Figs. 11.12 and 11.13. When an application creates a BasePlusCommissionEmployee object, the BasePlusCommissionEmployee constructor is called. That constructor immediately calls CommissionEmployee's constructor, which in turn immediately calls object's constructor implicitly. Class object's constructor has an empty body, so it immediately returns control to CommissionEmployee's constructor, which then initializes the private instance variables of CommissionEmployee that are part of the BasePlusCommissionEmployee object. When CommissionEmployee's constructor completes execution, it returns control to BasePlusCommissionEmployee's constructor, which initializes the BasePlusCommissionEmployee object's baseSalary.

11.6 Software Engineering with Inheritance

This section discusses customizing existing software with inheritance. When a new class extends an existing class, the new class inherits the members of the existing class. We can customize the new class to meet our needs by including additional members and by overriding base-class members. Doing this does not require the derived-class programmer to change the base class's source code. C# simply requires access to the compiled base-class code, so it can compile and execute any application that uses or extends the base class. This powerful capability is attractive to independent software vendors (ISVs), who can develop proprietary classes for sale or license and make them available to users in class libraries. Users then can derive new classes from these library classes rapidly, without accessing the ISVs' proprietary source code.

Software Engineering Observation 11.6

Although inheriting from a class does not require access to the class's source code, developers often insist on seeing the source code to understand how the class is implemented. They may, for example, want to ensure that they're extending a class that performs well and is implemented securely.

Students sometimes have difficulty appreciating the scope of the problems faced by designers who work on large-scale software projects in industry. People experienced with such projects say that effective software reuse improves the software-development process. Object-oriented programming facilitates software reuse, potentially shortening development time. The availability of substantial and useful class libraries delivers the maximum benefits of software reuse through inheritance.

Software Engineering Observation 11.7

At the design stage in an object-oriented system, the designer often finds that certain classes are closely related. The designer should "factor out" common members and place them in a base class. Then the designer should use inheritance to develop derived classes, specializing them with capabilities beyond those inherited from the base class.

Software Engineering Observation 11.8

Declaring a derived class does not affect its base class's source code. Inheritance preserves the integrity of the base class.

Reading derived-class declarations can be confusing, because inherited members are not declared explicitly in the derived classes, but are nevertheless present in them. A similar problem exists in documenting derived-class members.

11.7 Class object

As we discussed earlier in this chapter, all classes inherit directly or indirectly from the object class (System.Object in the Framework Class Library), so its seven methods are inherited by all other classes. Figure 11.15 summarizes object's methods. You can learn more about object's methods at:

> msdn.microsoft.com/en-us/library/system.object_members.aspx

Method	Description
Equals	This method compares two objects for equality and returns true if they're equal and false otherwise. It takes any object as an argument. When objects of a particular class must be compared for equality, the class should override method Equals to compare the *contents* of the two objects. The method's implementation should meet the following requirements: • It should return false if the argument is null. • It should return true if an object is compared to itself, as in object1.Equals(object1). • It should return true only if both object1.Equals(object2) and object2.Equals(object1) would return true. • For three objects, if object1.Equals(object2) returns true and object2.Equals(object3) returns true, then object1.Equals(object3) should also return true. • A class that overrides the method Equals should also override the method GetHashCode to ensure that equal objects have identical hashcodes. The default Equals implementation determines only whether two references *refer to the same object.*

Fig. 11.15 | object methods that are inherited directly or indirectly by all classes. (Part 1 of 2.)

Method	Description
Finalize	This method cannot be explicitly declared or called. When a class contains a destructor, the compiler implicitly renames it to override the protected method Finalize, which is called only by the garbage collector before it reclaims an object's memory. The garbage collector is not guaranteed to reclaim an object, thus it's not guaranteed that an object's Finalize method will execute. When a derived class's Finalize method executes, it performs its task, then invokes the base class's Finalize method. In general, you should avoid using Finalize.
GetHashCode	A hashtable data structure relates one object, called the key, to another object, called the value. We discuss Hashtable in Chapter 23, Collections. When a value is initially inserted in a hashtable, the key's GetHashCode method is called. The value returned is used by the hashtable to determine the location at which to insert the corresponding value. The key's hashcode is also used by the hashtable to locate the key's corresponding value.
GetType	Every object knows its own type at execution time. Method GetType (used in Section 12.5) returns an object of class Type (namespace System) that contains information about the object's type, such as its class name (obtained from Type property FullName).
Memberwise-Clone	This protected method, which takes no arguments and returns an object reference, makes a copy of the object on which it's called. The implementation of this method performs a **shallow copy**—instance-variable values in one object are copied into another object of the same type. For reference types, only the references are copied.
Reference-Equals	This static method receives two objects and returns true if two they're the same instance or if they're null references. Otherwise, it returns false.
ToString	This method (introduced in Section 7.4) returns a string representation of an object. The default implementation of this method returns the namespace followed by a dot and the class name of the object's class.

Fig. 11.15 | object methods that are inherited directly or indirectly by all classes. (Part 2 of 2.)

11.8 Wrap-Up

This chapter introduced inheritance—the ability to create classes by absorbing an existing class's members and enhancing them with new capabilities. You learned the notions of base classes and derived classes and created a derived class that inherits members from a base class. The chapter introduced access modifier protected; derived-class members can access protected base-class members. You learned how to access base-class members with base. You also saw how constructors are used in inheritance hierarchies. Finally, you learned about the methods of class object, the direct or indirect base class of *all* classes.

In Chapter 12, we build on our discussion of inheritance by introducing polymorphism—an object-oriented concept that enables us to write applications that handle, in a more general manner, objects of a wide variety of classes related by inheritance. After studying Chapter 12, you'll be familiar with classes, objects, encapsulation, inheritance and polymorphism—the most essential aspects of object-oriented programming.

OOP: Polymorphism, Interfaces and Operator Overloading

OBJECTIVES

In this chapter you'll learn:

- How polymorphism enables you to "program in the general" and make systems extensible.

- To use overridden methods to effect polymorphism.

- To create abstract classes and methods.

- To determine an object's type at execution time.

- To create `sealed` methods and classes.

- To declare and implement interfaces.

- To overload operators to enable them to manipulate objects.

One Ring to rule them all,
One Ring to find them,
One Ring to bring them all
and in the darkness bind
them.
—John Ronald Reuel Tolkien

General propositions do not
decide concrete cases.
—Oliver Wendell Holmes

A philosopher of imposing
stature doesn't think in a
vacuum. Even his most
abstract ideas are, to some
extent, conditioned by
what is or is not known
in the time when he lives.
—Alfred North Whitehead

12.1 Introduction

We now continue our study of object-oriented programming by explaining and demonstrating **polymorphism** with inheritance hierarchies. Polymorphism enables us to "program in the general" rather than "program in the specific." In particular, polymorphism enables us to write applications that process objects that share the same base class in a class hierarchy as if they were all objects of the base class.

Let's consider a polymorphism example. Suppose we create an application that simulates moving several types of animals for a biological study. Classes Fish, Frog and Bird represent the types of animals under investigation. Imagine that each class extends base class Animal, which contains a method Move and maintains an animal's current location as *x–y–z* coordinates. Each derived class implements method Move. Our application maintains an array of references to objects of the various Animal-derived classes. To simulate an animal's movements, the application sends each object the *same* message once per second—namely, Move. Each specific type of Animal responds to a Move message in a unique way—a Fish might swim three feet, a Frog might jump five feet and a Bird might fly 10 feet. The application issues the Move message to each animal object generically, but each object modifies its *x–y–z* coordinates appropriately for its specific type of movement. Relying on each object to know how to "do the right thing" in response to the *same* method call is the key concept of polymorphism. The *same* message (in this case, Move) sent to a variety of objects has "many forms" of results—hence the term polymorphism.

Systems Are Easy to Extend
With polymorphism, we can design and implement systems that are easily extensible—new classes can be added with little or no modification to the general portions of the application, as long as the new classes are part of the inheritance hierarchy that the applica-

tion processes generically. The only parts of an application that must be altered to accommodate new classes are those that require direct knowledge of the new classes that you add to the hierarchy. For example, if we extend class Animal to create class Tortoise (which might respond to a Move message by crawling one inch), we need to write only the Tortoise class and the part of the simulation that instantiates a Tortoise object. The portions of the simulation that process each Animal generically can remain the same.

This chapter has several parts. First, we discuss common examples of polymorphism. We then provide a live-code example demonstrating polymorphic behavior. As you'll soon see, you'll use base-class references to manipulate both base-class objects and derived-class objects polymorphically.

Polymorphic *Employee* Inheritance Hierarchy
We then present a case study that revisits the employee hierarchy of Section 11.4.5. We develop a simple payroll application that polymorphically calculates the weekly pay of several different types of employees using each employee's Earnings method. Though the earnings of each type of employee are calculated in a specific way, polymorphism allows us to process the employees "in the general." In the case study, we enlarge the hierarchy to include two new classes—SalariedEmployee (for people paid a fixed weekly salary) and HourlyEmployee (for people paid an hourly salary and "time-and-a-half" for overtime). We declare a *common set of functionality* for all the classes in the updated hierarchy in an "abstract" class, Employee, from which classes SalariedEmployee, HourlyEmployee and CommissionEmployee *inherit directly* and class BasePlusCommissionEmployee *inherits indirectly*. As you'll soon see, when we invoke each employee's Earnings method off a base-class Employee reference, the correct earnings calculation is performed due to C#'s polymorphic capabilities.

Determining the Type of an Object at Execution Time
Occasionally, when performing polymorphic processing, we need to program "in the specific." Our Employee case study demonstrates that an application can determine the type of an object at execution time and act on that object accordingly. In the case study, we use these capabilities to determine whether a particular employee object *is a* BasePlus-CommissionEmployee. If so, we increase that employee's base salary by 10%.

Interfaces
The chapter continues with an introduction to C# interfaces. An interface describes a set of methods and properties that can be called on an object, but does not provide concrete implementations for them. You can declare classes that **implement** (i.e., provide concrete implementations for the methods and properties of) one or more interfaces. Each interface member must be defined for all the classes that implement the interface. Once a class implements an interface, all objects of that class have an *is-a* relationship with the interface type, and all objects of the class are guaranteed to provide the functionality described by the interface. This is true of all derived classes of that class as well.

Interfaces are particularly useful for assigning common functionality to possibly unrelated classes. This allows objects of unrelated classes to be processed polymorphically—objects of classes that implement the same interface can respond to the same method calls. To demonstrate creating and using interfaces, we modify our payroll application to create a general accounts-payable application that can calculate payments due for the earnings of company employees and for invoice amounts to be billed for purchased goods. As you'll see, interfaces enable polymorphic capabilities similar to those enabled by inheritance.

Operator Overloading

This chapter ends with an introduction to operator overloading. In previous chapters, we declared our own classes and used methods to perform tasks on objects of those classes. Operator overloading allows us to define the behavior of the built-in operators, such as +, – and <, when used on objects of our own classes. This provides a much more convenient notation than calling methods for performing tasks on objects.

12.2 Polymorphism Examples

We now consider several additional examples of polymorphism.

Quadrilateral *Inheritance Hierachy*

If class `Rectangle` is derived from class `Quadrilateral` (a four-sided shape), then a `Rectangle` *is a* more specific version of a `Quadrilateral`. Any operation (e.g., calculating the perimeter or the area) that can be performed on a `Quadrilateral` object can also be performed on a `Rectangle` object. These operations also can be performed on other `Quadrilaterals`, such as `Squares`, `Parallelograms` and `Trapezoids`. The polymorphism occurs when an application invokes a method through a base-class variable—at execution time, the correct derived-class version of the method is called, based on the type of the referenced object. You'll see a simple code example that illustrates this process in Section 12.3.

Video Game `SpaceObject` *Inheritance Hierarchy*

As another example, suppose we design a video game that manipulates objects of many different types, including objects of classes `Martian`, `Venusian`, `Plutonian`, `SpaceShip` and `LaserBeam`. Imagine that each class inherits from the common base class `SpaceObject`, which contains method `Draw`. Each derived class implements this method. A screen-manager application maintains a collection (e.g., a `SpaceObject` array) of references to objects of the various classes. To refresh the screen, the screen manager periodically sends each object the *same message*—namely, `Draw`. However, each object responds in a unique way. For example, a `Martian` object might *draw itself* in red with the appropriate number of antennae. A `SpaceShip` object might *draw itself* as a bright silver flying saucer. A `LaserBeam` object might *draw itself* as a bright red beam across the screen. Again, the *same message* (in this case, `Draw`) sent to a variety of objects has *many forms* of results.

A polymorphic screen manager might use polymorphism to facilitate adding new classes to a system with minimal modifications to the system's code. Suppose we want to add `Mercurian` objects to our video game. To do so, we must build a `Mercurian` class that extends `SpaceObject` and provides its own `Draw` method implementation. When objects of class `Mercurian` appear in the `SpaceObject` collection, the screen-manager code invokes method `Draw`, exactly as it does for every other object in the collection, *regardless of its type*, so the new `Mercurian` objects simply "plug right in" without any modification of the screen-manager code by the programmer. Thus, without modifying the system (other than to build new classes and modify the code that creates new objects), you can use polymorphism to include additional types that might not have been envisioned when the system was created.

Software Engineering Observation 12.1

Polymorphism promotes extensibility: Software that invokes polymorphic behavior is independent of the object types to which messages are sent. New object types that can respond to existing method calls can be incorporated into a system without requiring modification of the base system. Only client code that instantiates new objects must be modified to accommodate new types.

12.3 Demonstrating Polymorphic Behavior

Section 11.4 created a commission-employee class hierarchy, in which class BasePlusCommissionEmployee inherited from class CommissionEmployee. The examples in that section manipulated CommissionEmployee and BasePlusCommissionEmployee objects by using references to them to invoke their methods. We aimed base-class references at base-class objects and derived-class references at derived-class objects. These assignments are natural and straightforward—base-class references are intended to refer to base-class objects, and derived-class references are intended to refer to derived-class objects. However, other assignments are possible.

In the next example, we aim a base-class reference at a derived-class object. We then show how invoking a method on a derived-class object via a base-class reference can invoke the derived-class functionality—*the type of the actual referenced object, not the type of the reference, determines which method is called*. This example demonstrates the key concept that an object of a derived class can be treated as an object of its base class. This enables various interesting manipulations. An application can create an array of base-class references that refer to objects of many derived-class types. This is allowed because each derived-class object *is an* object of its base class. For instance, we can assign the reference of a BasePlusCommissionEmployee object to a base-class CommissionEmployee variable because a BasePlusCommissionEmployee *is a* CommissionEmployee—so we can treat a BasePlusCommissionEmployee as a CommissionEmployee.

A base-class object is not an object of any of its derived classes. For example, we cannot directly assign the reference of a CommissionEmployee object to a derived-class BasePlusCommissionEmployee variable, because a CommissionEmployee *is not* a BasePlusCommissionEmployee—a CommissionEmployee does not, for example, have a baseSalary instance variable and does not have a BaseSalary property. The *is-a* relationship applies from a derived class to its direct and indirect base classes, but not vice versa.

The compiler allows the assignment of a base-class reference to a derived-class variable *if* we explicitly cast the base-class reference to the derived-class type—a technique we discuss in greater detail in Section 12.5.6. Why would we ever want to perform such an assignment? *A base-class reference can be used to invoke only the methods declared in the base class*—attempting to invoke derived-class-only methods through a base-class reference results in compilation errors. If an application needs to perform a derived-class-specific operation on a derived-class object referenced by a base-class variable, the application must first cast the base-class reference to a derived-class reference through a technique known as **downcasting**. This enables the application to invoke derived-class methods that are not in the base class. We present an example of downcasting in Section 12.5.6.

Figure 12.1 demonstrates three ways to use base-class and derived-class variables to store references to base-class and derived-class objects. The first two are straightforward—as in Section 11.4, we assign a base-class reference to a base-class variable, and we assign a derived class reference to a derived class variable. Then we demonstrate the relationship between derived classes and base classes (i.e., the *is-a* relationship) by assigning a derived-class reference to a base-class variable. [*Note:* This application uses classes CommissionEmployee and BasePlusCommissionEmployee from Fig. 11.12 and Fig. 11.13, respectively.]

```csharp
1   // Fig. 12.1: PolymorphismTest.cs
2   // Assigning base-class and derived-class references to base-class and
3   // derived-class variables.
4   using System;
5
6   public class PolymorphismTest
7   {
8      public static void Main( string[] args )
9      {
10        // assign base-class reference to base-class variable
11        CommissionEmployee commissionEmployee = new CommissionEmployee(
12           "Sue", "Jones", "222-22-2222", 10000.00M, .06M );
13
14        // assign derived-class reference to derived-class variable
15        BasePlusCommissionEmployee basePlusCommissionEmployee =
16           new BasePlusCommissionEmployee( "Bob", "Lewis",
17           "333-33-3333", 5000.00M, .04M, 300.00M );
18
19        // invoke ToString and Earnings on base-class object
20        // using base-class variable
21        Console.WriteLine( "{0} {1}:\n\n{2}\n{3}: {4:C}\n",
22           "Call CommissionEmployee's ToString and Earnings methods ",
23           "with base-class reference to base class object",
24           commissionEmployee.ToString(),
25           "earnings", commissionEmployee.Earnings() );
26
27        // invoke ToString and Earnings on derived-class object
28        // using derived-class variable
29        Console.WriteLine( "{0} {1}:\n\n{2}\n{3}: {4:C}\n",
30           "Call BasePlusCommissionEmployee's ToString and Earnings ",
31           "methods with derived class reference to derived-class object",
32           basePlusCommissionEmployee.ToString(),
33           "earnings", basePlusCommissionEmployee.Earnings() );
34
35        // invoke ToString and Earnings on derived-class object
36        // using base-class variable
37        CommissionEmployee commissionEmployee2 =
38           basePlusCommissionEmployee;
39        Console.WriteLine( "{0} {1}:\n\n{2}\n{3}: {4:C}",
40           "Call BasePlusCommissionEmployee's ToString and Earnings ",
41           "with base class reference to derived-class object",
42           commissionEmployee2.ToString(), "earnings",
43           commissionEmployee2.Earnings() );
44     } // end Main
45  } // end class PolymorphismTest
```

Fig. 12.1 | Assigning base-class and derived-class references to base-class and derived-class variables. (Part 1 of 2.)

```
Call CommissionEmployee's ToString and Earnings methods with base class refer-
ence to base class object:

commission employee: Sue Jones
social security number: 222-22-2222
gross sales: $10,000.00
commission rate: 0.06
earnings: $600.00

Call BasePlusCommissionEmployee's ToString and Earnings methods with derived
class reference to derived class object:

base-salaried commission employee: Bob Lewis
social security number: 333-33-3333
gross sales: $5,000.00
commission rate: 0.04
base salary: $300.00
earnings: $500.00

Call BasePlusCommissionEmployee's ToString and Earnings methods with base
class reference to derived class object:

base-salaried commission employee: Bob Lewis
social security number: 333-33-3333
gross sales: $5,000.00
commission rate: 0.04
base salary: $300.00
earnings: $500.00
```

Fig. 12.1 | Assigning base-class and derived-class references to base-class and derived-class variables. (Part 2 of 2.)

In Fig. 12.1, lines 11–12 create a new CommissionEmployee object and assign its reference to a CommissionEmployee variable. Lines 15–17 create a new BasePlus-CommissionEmployee object and assign its reference to a BasePlusCommissionEmployee variable. These assignments are *natural*—for example, a CommissionEmployee variable's primary purpose is to hold a reference to a CommissionEmployee object. Lines 21–25 use the reference commissionEmployee to invoke methods ToString and Earnings. Because commissionEmployee refers to a CommissionEmployee object, *base class* Commission-Employee's version of the methods are called. Similarly, lines 29–33 use the reference basePlusCommissionEmployee to invoke the methods ToString and Earnings on the BasePlusCommissionEmployee object. This invokes *derived class* BasePlusCommission-Employee's version of the methods.

Lines 37–38 then assign the reference to derived-class object basePlusCommission-Employee to a base-class CommissionEmployee variable, which lines 39–43 use to invoke methods ToString and Earnings. *A base-class variable that contains a reference to a derived-class object and is used to call a* virtual *method actually calls the overriding derived-class version of the method.* Hence, commissionEmployee2.ToString() in line 42 actually calls *derived* class BasePlusCommissionEmployee's ToString method. The compiler allows this "crossover" because an object of a derived class *is an* object of its base class (but not vice versa). When the compiler encounters a method call made through a variable, the compiler determines if the method can be called by checking the *variable's* class type. If that class contains the proper method declaration (or inherits one), the compiler allows the call to be compiled. At execution time, *the type of the object to which the variable refers* determines the actual method to use.

12.4 Abstract Classes and Methods

When we think of a class type, we assume that applications will create objects of that type. In some cases, however, it's useful to declare *classes for which you never intend to instantiate objects*. Such classes are called **abstract classes**. Because they're used only as base classes in inheritance hierarchies, we refer to them as **abstract base classes**. These classes cannot be used to instantiate objects, because, as you'll soon see, abstract classes are *incomplete*—derived classes must define the "missing pieces." We demonstrate abstract classes in Section 12.5.1.

The purpose of an abstract class is primarily to provide an appropriate base class from which other classes can inherit, and thus share a common design. In the Shape hierarchy of Fig. 11.3, for example, derived classes inherit the notion of what it means to be a Shape— common attributes such as location, color and borderThickness, and behaviors such as Draw, Move, Resize and ChangeColor. Classes that can be used to instantiate objects are called **concrete classes**. Such classes provide implementations of *every* method they declare (some of the implementations can be inherited). For example, we could derive concrete classes Circle, Square and Triangle from abstract base class TwoDimensionalShape. Similarly, we could derive concrete classes Sphere, Cube and Tetrahedron from abstract base class ThreeDimensionalShape. Abstract base classes are *too general* to create real objects—they specify only what is common among derived classes. We need to be more *specific* before we can create objects. For example, if you send the Draw message to abstract class TwoDimensionalShape, the class knows that two-dimensional shapes should be drawable, but it does not know what *specific* shape to draw, so it cannot implement a real Draw method. *Concrete* classes provide the *specifics* that make it reasonable to instantiate objects.

Not all inheritance hierarchies contain abstract classes. However, you'll often write client code that uses only abstract base-class types to reduce client code's dependencies on a range of specific derived-class types. For example, you can write a method with a parameter of an abstract base-class type. When called, such a method can be passed an object of any concrete class that directly or indirectly extends the base class specified as the parameter's type.

Abstract classes sometimes constitute several levels of the hierarchy. For example, the Shape hierarchy of Fig. 11.3 begins with abstract class Shape. On the next level of the hierarchy are two more abstract classes, TwoDimensionalShape and ThreeDimensionalShape. The next level of the hierarchy declares concrete classes for TwoDimensionalShapes (Circle, Square and Triangle) and for ThreeDimensionalShapes (Sphere, Cube and Tetrahedron).

You make a class abstract by declaring it with the keyword **abstract**. An abstract class normally contains one or more **abstract methods**. An abstract method is one with keyword abstract in its declaration, as in

```
public abstract void Draw(); // abstract method
```

Abstract methods are implicitly virtual and do not provide implementations. A class that contains abstract methods must be declared as an abstract class even if it contains some concrete (nonabstract) methods. Each concrete derived class of an abstract base class also must provide concrete implementations of the base class's abstract methods. We show an example of an abstract class with an abstract method in Fig. 12.4.

Properties can also be declared abstract or virtual, then overridden in derived classes with the override keyword, just like methods. This allows an abstract base class to specify common properties of its derived classes. Abstract property declarations have the form:

```
public abstract PropertyType MyProperty
{
    get;
    set;
} // end abstract property
```

The semicolons after the get and set keywords indicate that we provide *no implementation* for these accessors. An abstract property may omit implementations for the get accessor or the set accessor. Concrete derived classes must provide implementations for *every* accessor declared in the abstract property. When both get and set accessors are specified, every concrete derived class must implement both. If one accessor is omitted, the derived class is not allowed to implement that accessor. Doing so causes a compilation error.

Constructors and static methods cannot be declared abstract. Constructors are not inherited, so an abstract constructor could never be implemented. Similarly, derived classes cannot override static methods, so an abstract static method could never be implemented.

Software Engineering Observation 12.2

An abstract class declares common attributes and behaviors of the various classes that inherit from it, either directly or indirectly, in a class hierarchy. An abstract class typically contains one or more abstract methods or properties that concrete derived classes must override. The instance variables, concrete methods and concrete properties of an abstract class are subject to the normal rules of inheritance.

Common Programming Error 12.1

Attempting to instantiate an object of an abstract class is a compilation error.

Common Programming Error 12.2

Failure to implement a base class's abstract methods and properties in a derived class is a compilation error unless the derived class is also declared abstract

Although we cannot instantiate objects of abstract base classes, you'll soon see that we *can* use abstract base classes to declare variables that can hold references to objects of any concrete classes derived from those abstract classes. Applications typically use such variables to manipulate derived-class objects polymorphically. Also, you can use abstract base-class names to invoke static methods declared in those abstract base classes.

Polymorphism and Device Drivers
Polymorphism is particularly effective for implementing so-called *layered software systems*. In operating systems, for example, each type of physical device could operate quite differently from the others. Even so, common commands can read or write data from and to the devices. For each device, the operating system uses a piece of software called a *device driver* to control all communication between the system and the device. The write message

sent to a device driver object needs to be interpreted specifically in the context of that driver and how it manipulates a specific device. However, the write call itself really is no different from the write to any other device in the system: Place some number of bytes from memory onto that device. An object-oriented operating system might use an abstract base class to provide an "interface" appropriate for all device drivers. Then, through inheritance from that abstract base class, derived classes are formed that all behave similarly. The device-driver methods are declared as abstract methods in the abstract base class. The implementations of these abstract methods are provided in the derived classes that correspond to the specific types of device drivers. New devices are always being developed, often long after the operating system has been released. When you buy a new device, it comes with a device driver provided by the device vendor. The device is immediately operational after you connect it to your computer and install the device driver. This is another elegant example of how polymorphism makes systems extensible.

Iterators

It's common in object-oriented programming to declare an **iterator class** that can traverse all the objects in a collection, such as an array (Chapter 8) or a `List` (Chapter 9). For example, an application can print a `List` of objects by creating an iterator object and using it to obtain the next list element each time the iterator is called. Iterators often are used in polymorphic programming to traverse a collection that contains references to objects of various classes in an inheritance hierarchy. (Chapters 22–23 present a thorough treatment of C#'s "generics" capabilities and iterators.) A `List` of references to objects of class `TwoDimensionalShape`, for example, could contain references to objects from derived classes `Square`, `Circle`, `Triangle` and so on. Calling method `Draw` for each `TwoDimensionalShape` object off a `TwoDimensionalShape` variable would polymorphically draw each object correctly on the screen.

12.5 Case Study: Payroll System Using Polymorphism

This section reexamines the `CommissionEmployee-BasePlusCommissionEmployee` hierarchy that we explored throughout Section 11.4. Now we use an abstract method and polymorphism to perform payroll calculations based on the type of employee. We create an enhanced employee hierarchy to solve the following problem:

> *A company pays its employees on a weekly basis. The employees are of four types: Salaried employees are paid a fixed weekly salary regardless of the number of hours worked, hourly employees are paid by the hour and receive "time-and-a-half" overtime pay for all hours worked in excess of 40 hours, commission employees are paid a percentage of their sales, and salaried-commission employees receive a base salary plus a percentage of their sales. For the current pay period, the company has decided to reward salaried-commission employees by adding 10% to their base salaries. The company wants to implement a C# application that performs its payroll calculations polymorphically.*

We use `abstract` class `Employee` to represent the general concept of an employee. The classes that extend `Employee` are `SalariedEmployee`, `CommissionEmployee` and `HourlyEmployee`. Class `BasePlusCommissionEmployee`—which extends `CommissionEmployee`—represents the last employee type. The UML class diagram in Fig. 12.2 shows the inheritance hierarchy for our polymorphic employee payroll application. Abstract class `Employee` is *italicized*, as per the convention of the UML.

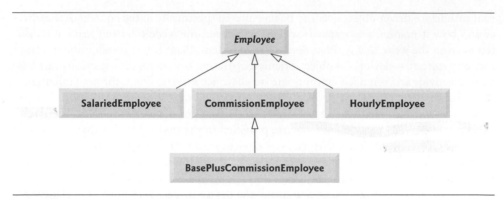

Fig. 12.2 | `Employee` hierarchy UML class diagram.

Abstract base class `Employee` declares the "interface" to the hierarchy—that is, the set of methods that an application can invoke on all `Employee` objects. We use the term "interface" here in a general sense to refer to the various ways applications can communicate with objects of any `Employee` derived class. Be careful not to confuse the general notion of an "interface" with the formal notion of a C# interface, the subject of Section 12.7. Each employee, regardless of the way his or her earnings are calculated, has a first name, a last name and a social security number, so those pieces of data appear in abstract base class `Employee`.

Software Engineering Observation 12.3

*A derived class can inherit "interface" or "implementation" from a base class. Hierarchies designed for **implementation inheritance** tend to have their functionality high in the hierarchy—each new derived class inherits one or more methods that were implemented in a base class, and the derived class uses the base-class implementations. Hierarchies designed for **interface inheritance** tend to have their functionality lower in the hierarchy—a base class specifies one or more abstract methods that must be declared for each concrete class in the hierarchy, and the individual derived classes override these methods to provide derived-class-specific implementations.*

The following sections implement the `Employee` class hierarchy. The first section implements `abstract` base class `Employee`. The next four sections each implement one of the concrete classes. The sixth section implements a test application that builds objects of all these classes and processes those objects polymorphically.

12.5.1 Creating Abstract Base Class `Employee`

Class `Employee` (Fig. 12.4) provides methods `Earnings` and `ToString`, in addition to the auto-implemented properties that manipulate `Employee`'s data. An `Earnings` method certainly applies generically to all employees. But each earnings calculation depends on the employee's class. So we declare `Earnings` as `abstract` in base class `Employee`, because a default implementation does not make sense for that method—there's not enough information to determine what amount `Earnings` should return. Each derived class overrides `Earnings` with an appropriate implementation. To calculate an employee's earnings, the application assigns a reference to the employee's object to a base class Employee variable, then invokes the Earnings method on that variable. We maintain an array of Employee variables, each of which holds a reference to an Employee object (of course, there *cannot* be Employee objects because Employee is an *abstract* class—because of inheritance, however, all objects of all derived classes of Employee may nevertheless be thought of as Employee objects). The application iterates through the array and calls method Earnings for each Employee object. C# processes these method calls polymorphically. Including Earnings as an abstract method in Employee forces every directly derived *concrete* class of Employee to override Earnings with a method that performs an appropriate pay calculation.

Method ToString in class Employee returns a string containing the employee's first name, last name and social security number. Each derived class of Employee overrides method ToString to create a string representation of an object of that class containing the employee's type (e.g., "salaried employee:"), followed by the rest of the employee's information.

The diagram in Fig. 12.3 shows each of the five classes in the hierarchy down the left side and methods Earnings and ToString across the top. For each class, the diagram shows the desired results of each method. [*Note:* We do not list base class Employee's properties because they're not overridden in any of the derived classes—each of these properties is inherited and used "as is" by each of the derived classes.]

	Earnings	ToString
Employee	abstract	*firstName lastName* social security number: *SSN*
Salaried-Employee	weeklySalary	salaried employee: *firstName lastName* social security number: *SSN* weekly salary: *weeklysalary*

Hourly-Employee	*If hours <= 40*
	  wage * hours
	If hours > 40
	  40 * wage +
	  (hours - 40) *
	  wage * 1.5
		hourly employee: *firstName lastName*
		social security number: *SSN*
		hourly wage: *wage*
		hours worked: *hours*

Commission-Employee	commissionRate * grossSales	commission employee: *firstName lastName* social security number: *SSN* gross sales: *grossSales* commission rate: *commissionRate*
BasePlus-Commission-Employee	(commissionRate * grossSales) + baseSalary	base salaried commission employee: *firstName lastName* social security number: *SSN* gross sales: *grossSales* commission rate: *commissionRate* base salary: *baseSalary*

Fig. 12.3 | Polymorphic interface for the Employee hierarchy classes.

Let's consider class Employee's declaration (Fig. 12.4). The class includes a constructor that takes the first name, last name and social security number as arguments (lines 15–20); read-only properties for obtaining the first name, last name and social security number (lines 6, 9 and 12, respectively); method ToString (lines 23–27), which uses properties to return the string representation of the Employee; and abstract method Earnings (line 30), which *must* be implemented by *concrete* derived classes. The Employee constructor does not validate the social security number in this example. Normally, such validation should be provided.

```
1   // Fig. 12.4: Employee.cs
2   // Employee abstract base class.
3   public abstract class Employee
4   {
5      // read-only property that gets employee's first name
6      public string FirstName { get; private set; }
7
8      // read-only property that gets employee's last name
9      public string LastName { get; private set; }
10
11     // read-only property that gets employee's social security number
12     public string SocialSecurityNumber { get; private set; }
13
14     // three-parameter constructor
15     public Employee( string first, string last, string ssn )
16     {
17        FirstName = first;
18        LastName = last;
19        SocialSecurityNumber = ssn;
20     } // end three-parameter Employee constructor
21
22     // return string representation of Employee object, using properties
23     public override string ToString()
24     {
25        return string.Format( "{0} {1}\nsocial security number: {2}",
26           FirstName, LastName, SocialSecurityNumber );
27     } // end method ToString
28
29     // abstract method overridden by derived classes
30     public abstract decimal Earnings(); // no implementation here
31  } // end abstract class Employee
```

Fig. 12.4 | Employee abstract base class.

Why did we declare Earnings as an abstract method? As explained earlier, it simply does not make sense to provide an implementation of this method in class Employee. We cannot calculate the earnings for a general Employee—we first must know the *specific* Employee type to determine the appropriate earnings calculation. By declaring this method abstract, we indicate that each *concrete* derived class *must* provide an appropriate Earnings implementation and that an application will be able to use base-class Employee variables to invoke method Earnings polymorphically for *any* type of Employee.

12.5.2 Creating Concrete Derived Class SalariedEmployee

Class SalariedEmployee (Fig. 12.5) extends class Employee (line 5) and overrides Earn-ings (lines 34–37), which makes SalariedEmployee a concrete class. The class includes a constructor (lines 10–14) that takes a first name, a last name, a social security number and a weekly salary as arguments; property WeeklySalary (lines 17–31) to manipulate instance variable weeklySalary, including a set accessor that ensures we assign only nonnegative values to weeklySalary; method Earnings (lines 34–37) to calculate a SalariedEmploy-ee's earnings; and method ToString (lines 40–44), which returns a string including the employee's type, namely, "salaried employee: ", followed by employee-specific infor-mation produced by base class Employee's ToString method and SalariedEmployee's WeeklySalary property. Class SalariedEmployee's constructor passes the first name, last name and social security number to the Employee constructor (line 11) via a constructor initializer to initialize the base class's data. Method Earnings overrides Employee's abstract method Earnings to provide a concrete implementation that returns the SalariedEm-ployee's weekly salary. If we do not implement Earnings, class SalariedEmployee must be declared abstract—otherwise, a compilation error occurs (and, of course, we want SalariedEmployee to be a concrete class).

```
1   // Fig. 12.5: SalariedEmployee.cs
2   // SalariedEmployee class that extends Employee.
3   using System;
4
5   public class SalariedEmployee : Employee
6   {
7      private decimal weeklySalary;
8
9      // four-parameter constructor
10     public SalariedEmployee( string first, string last, string ssn,
11        decimal salary ) : base( first, last, ssn )
12     {
13        WeeklySalary = salary; // validate salary via property
14     } // end four-parameter SalariedEmployee constructor
15
16     // property that gets and sets salaried employee's salary
17     public decimal WeeklySalary
18     {
19        get
20        {
21           return weeklySalary;
22        } // end get
23        set
24        {
25           if ( value >= 0 ) // validation
26              weeklySalary = value;
27           else
28              throw new ArgumentOutOfRangeException( "WeeklySalary",
29                 value, "WeeklySalary must be >= 0" );
30        } // end set
31     } // end property WeeklySalary
```

Fig. 12.5 | SalariedEmployee class that extends Employee. (Part 1 of 2.)

```
32
33      // calculate earnings; override abstract method Earnings in Employee
34      public override decimal Earnings()
35      {
36         return WeeklySalary;
37      } // end method Earnings
38
39      // return string representation of SalariedEmployee object
40      public override string ToString()
41      {
42         return string.Format( "salaried employee: {0}\n{1}: {2:C}",
43            base.ToString(), "weekly salary", WeeklySalary );
44      } // end method ToString
45   } // end class SalariedEmployee
```

Fig. 12.5 | SalariedEmployee class that extends Employee. (Part 2 of 2.)

SalariedEmployee method ToString (lines 40–44) overrides Employee's version. If class SalariedEmployee did not override ToString, SalariedEmployee would have inherited the Employee version. In that case, SalariedEmployee's ToString method would simply return the employee's full name and social security number, which does not adequately represent a SalariedEmployee. To produce a complete string representation of a SalariedEmployee, the derived class's ToString method returns "salaried employee: ", followed by the base-class Employee-specific information (i.e., first name, last name and social security number) obtained by invoking the base class's ToString (line 43)—this is a nice example of code reuse. The string representation of a SalariedEmployee also contains the employee's weekly salary, obtained by using the class's WeeklySalary property.

12.5.3 Creating Concrete Derived Class HourlyEmployee

Class HourlyEmployee (Fig. 12.6) also extends class Employee (line 5). The class includes a constructor (lines 11–17) that takes as arguments a first name, a last name, a social security number, an hourly wage and the number of hours worked. Lines 20–34 and 37–51 declare properties Wage and Hours for instance variables wage and hours, respectively. The set accessor in property Wage ensures that wage is nonnegative, and the set accessor in property Hours ensures that hours is in the range 0–168 (the total number of hours in a week) inclusive. The class overrides method Earnings (lines 54–60) to calculate an HourlyEmployee's earnings and method ToString (lines 63–68) to return the employee's string representation. The HourlyEmployee constructor, similarly to the SalariedEmployee constructor, passes the first name, last name and social security number to the base-class Employee constructor (line 13) to initialize the base class's data. Also, method ToString calls base-class method ToString (line 67) to obtain the Employee-specific information (i.e., first name, last name and social security number.

```
1    // Fig. 12.6: HourlyEmployee.cs
2    // HourlyEmployee class that extends Employee.
3    using System;
4
```

Fig. 12.6 | HourlyEmployee class that extends Employee. (Part 1 of 3.)

```
5   public class HourlyEmployee : Employee
6   {
7      private decimal wage; // wage per hour
8      private decimal hours; // hours worked for the week
9
10     // five-parameter constructor
11     public HourlyEmployee( string first, string last, string ssn,
12        decimal hourlyWage, decimal hoursWorked )
13        : base( first, last, ssn )
14     {
15        Wage = hourlyWage; // validate hourly wage via property
16        Hours = hoursWorked; // validate hours worked via property
17     } // end five-parameter HourlyEmployee constructor
18
19     // property that gets and sets hourly employee's wage
20     public decimal Wage
21     {
22        get
23        {
24           return wage;
25        } // end get
26        set
27        {
28           if ( value >= 0 ) // validation
29              wage = value;
30           else
31              throw new ArgumentOutOfRangeException( "Wage",
32                 value, "Wage must be >= 0" );
33        } // end set
34     } // end property Wage
35
36     // property that gets and sets hourly employee's hours
37     public decimal Hours
38     {
39        get
40        {
41           return hours;
42        } // end get
43        set
44        {
45           if ( value >= 0 && value <= 168 ) // validation
46              hours = value;
47           else
48              throw new ArgumentOutOfRangeException( "Hours",
49                 value, "Hours must be >= 0 and <= 168" );
50        } // end set
51     } // end property Hours
52
53     // calculate earnings; override Employee's abstract method Earnings
54     public override decimal Earnings()
55     {
56        if ( Hours <= 40 ) // no overtime
57           return Wage * Hours;
```

Fig. 12.6 | HourlyEmployee class that extends Employee. (Part 2 of 3.)

```
58          else
59              return ( 40 * Wage ) + ( ( Hours - 40 ) * Wage * 1.5M );
60      } // end method Earnings
61
62      // return string representation of HourlyEmployee object
63      public override string ToString()
64      {
65          return string.Format(
66              "hourly employee: {0}\n{1}: {2:C}; {3}: {4:F2}",
67              base.ToString(), "hourly wage", Wage, "hours worked", Hours );
68      } // end method ToString
69  } // end class HourlyEmployee
```

Fig. 12.6 | HourlyEmployee class that extends Employee. (Part 3 of 3.)

12.5.4 Creating Concrete Derived Class CommissionEmployee

Class CommissionEmployee (Fig. 12.7) extends class Employee (line 5). The class includes a constructor (lines 11–16) that takes a first name, a last name, a social security number, a sales amount and a commission rate; properties (lines 19–33 and 36–50) for instance variables grossSales and commissionRate, respectively; method Earnings (lines 53–56) to calculate a CommissionEmployee's earnings; and method ToString (lines 59–64), which returns the employee's string representation. The CommissionEmployee's constructor also passes the first name, last name and social security number to the Employee constructor (line 12) to initialize Employee's data. Method ToString calls base-class method ToString (line 62) to obtain the Employee-specific information (i.e., first name, last name and social security number).

```
1   // Fig. 12.7: CommissionEmployee.cs
2   // CommissionEmployee class that extends Employee.
3   using System;
4
5   public class CommissionEmployee : Employee
6   {
7       private decimal grossSales; // gross weekly sales
8       private decimal commissionRate; // commission percentage
9
10      // five-parameter constructor
11      public CommissionEmployee( string first, string last, string ssn,
12          decimal sales, decimal rate ) : base( first, last, ssn )
13      {
14          GrossSales = sales; // validate gross sales via property
15          CommissionRate = rate; // validate commission rate via property
16      } // end five-parameter CommissionEmployee constructor
17
18      // property that gets and sets commission employee's gross sales
19      public decimal GrossSales
20      {
21          get
22          {
```

Fig. 12.7 | CommissionEmployee class that extends Employee. (Part 1 of 2.)

```
23              return grossSales;
24           } // end get
25           set
26           {
27              if ( value >= 0 )
28                 grossSales = value;
29              else
30                 throw new ArgumentOutOfRangeException(
31                    "GrossSales", value, "GrossSales must be >= 0" );
32           } // end set
33        } // end property GrossSales
34
35        // property that gets and sets commission employee's commission rate
36        public decimal CommissionRate
37        {
38           get
39           {
40              return commissionRate;
41           } // end get
42           set
43           {
44              if ( value > 0 && value < 1 )
45                 commissionRate = value;
46              else
47                 throw new ArgumentOutOfRangeException( "CommissionRate",
48                    value, "CommissionRate must be > 0 and < 1" );
49           } // end set
50        } // end property CommissionRate
51
52        // calculate earnings; override abstract method Earnings in Employee
53        public override decimal Earnings()
54        {
55           return CommissionRate * GrossSales;
56        } // end method Earnings
57
58        // return string representation of CommissionEmployee object
59        public override string ToString()
60        {
61           return string.Format( "{0}: {1}\n{2}: {3:C}\n{4}: {5:F2}",
62              "commission employee", base.ToString(),
63              "gross sales", GrossSales, "commission rate", CommissionRate );
64        } // end method ToString
65     } // end class CommissionEmployee
```

Fig. 12.7 | CommissionEmployee class that extends Employee. (Part 2 of 2.)

12.5.5 Creating Indirect Concrete Derived Class BasePlusCommissionEmployee

Class BasePlusCommissionEmployee (Fig. 12.8) extends class CommissionEmployee (line 5) and therefore is an *indirect* derived class of class Employee. Class BasePlusCommission-Employee has a constructor (lines 10–15) that takes as arguments a first name, a last name, a social security number, a sales amount, a commission rate and a base salary. It then passes the first name, last name, social security number, sales amount and commission rate to the

CommissionEmployee constructor (line 12) to initialize the base class's data. BasePlusCommissionEmployee also contains property BaseSalary (lines 19–33) to manipulate instance variable baseSalary. Method Earnings (lines 36–39) calculates a BasePlusCommissionEmployee's earnings. Line 38 in method Earnings calls base class CommissionEmployee's Earnings method to calculate the commission-based portion of the employee's earnings. Again, this shows the benefits of code reuse. BasePlusCommissionEmployee's ToString method (lines 42–46) creates a string representation of a BasePlusCommissionEmployee that contains "base-salaried", followed by the string obtained by invoking base class CommissionEmployee's ToString method (another example of code reuse), then the base salary. The result is a string beginning with "base-salaried commission employee", followed by the rest of the BasePlusCommissionEmployee's information. Recall that CommissionEmployee's ToString method obtains the employee's first name, last name and social security number by invoking the ToString method of *its* base class (i.e., Employee)—a further demonstration of code reuse. BasePlusCommissionEmployee's ToString initiates a chain of method calls that spans all three levels of the Employee hierarchy.

```
1   // Fig. 12.8: BasePlusCommissionEmployee.cs
2   // BasePlusCommissionEmployee class that extends CommissionEmployee.
3   using System;
4
5   public class BasePlusCommissionEmployee : CommissionEmployee
6   {
7      private decimal baseSalary; // base salary per week
8
9      // six-parameter constructor
10     public BasePlusCommissionEmployee( string first, string last,
11        string ssn, decimal sales, decimal rate, decimal salary )
12        : base( first, last, ssn, sales, rate )
13     {
14        BaseSalary = salary; // validate base salary via property
15     } // end six-parameter BasePlusCommissionEmployee constructor
16
17     // property that gets and sets
18     // base-salaried commission employee's base salary
19     public decimal BaseSalary
20     {
21        get
22        {
23           return baseSalary;
24        } // end get
25        set
26        {
27           if ( value >= 0 )
28              baseSalary = value;
29           else
30              throw new ArgumentOutOfRangeException( "BaseSalary",
31                 value, "BaseSalary must be >= 0" );
32        } // end set
33     } // end property BaseSalary
```

Fig. 12.8 | BasePlusCommissionEmployee class that extends CommissionEmployee. (Part 1 of 2.)

```
34
35      // calculate earnings; override method Earnings in CommissionEmployee
36      public override decimal Earnings()
37      {
38         return BaseSalary + base.Earnings();
39      } // end method Earnings
40
41      // return string representation of BasePlusCommissionEmployee object
42      public override string ToString()
43      {
44         return string.Format( "base-salaried {0}; base salary: {1:C}",
45            base.ToString(), BaseSalary );
46      } // end method ToString
47   } // end class BasePlusCommissionEmployee
```

Fig. 12.8 | BasePlusCommissionEmployee class that extends CommissionEmployee. (Part 2 of 2.)

12.5.6 Polymorphic Processing, Operator is and Downcasting

To test our Employee hierarchy, the application in Fig. 12.9 creates an object of each of the four concrete classes SalariedEmployee, HourlyEmployee, CommissionEmployee and BasePlusCommissionEmployee. The application manipulates these objects, first via variables of each object's own type, then polymorphically, using an array of Employee variables. While processing the objects polymorphically, the application increases the base salary of each BasePlusCommissionEmployee by 10% (this, of course, requires determining the object's type at execution time). Finally, the application polymorphically determines and outputs the type of each object in the Employee array. Lines 10–20 create objects of each of the four concrete Employee derived classes. Lines 24–32 output the string representation and earnings of each of these objects. Each object's ToString method is called implicitly by WriteLine when the object is output as a string with format items.

Assigning Derived-Class Objects to Base-Class References
Line 35 declares employees and assigns it an array of four Employee variables. Lines 38–41 assign a SalariedEmployee object, an HourlyEmployee object, a CommissionEmployee object and a BasePlusCommissionEmployee object to employees[0], employees[1], employees[2] and employees[3], respectively. Each assignment is allowed, because a SalariedEmployee *is an* Employee, an HourlyEmployee *is an* Employee, a CommissionEmployee *is an* Employee and a BasePlusCommissionEmployee *is an* Employee. Therefore, we can assign the references of SalariedEmployee, HourlyEmployee, CommissionEmployee and BasePlusCommissionEmployee objects to base-class Employee variables, even though Employee is an abstract class.

```
1    // Fig. 12.9: PayrollSystemTest.cs
2    // Employee hierarchy test application.
3    using System;
4
```

Fig. 12.9 | Employee hierarchy test application. (Part 1 of 4.)

```
5   public class PayrollSystemTest
6   {
7      public static void Main( string[] args )
8      {
9         // create derived-class objects
10        SalariedEmployee salariedEmployee =
11           new SalariedEmployee( "John", "Smith", "111-11-1111", 800.00M );
12        HourlyEmployee hourlyEmployee =
13           new HourlyEmployee( "Karen", "Price",
14           "222-22-2222", 16.75M, 40.0M );
15        CommissionEmployee commissionEmployee =
16           new CommissionEmployee( "Sue", "Jones",
17           "333-33-3333", 10000.00M, .06M );
18        BasePlusCommissionEmployee basePlusCommissionEmployee =
19           new BasePlusCommissionEmployee( "Bob", "Lewis",
20           "444-44-4444", 5000.00M, .04M, 300.00M );
21
22        Console.WriteLine( "Employees processed individually:\n" );
23
24        Console.WriteLine( "{0}\nearned: {1:C}\n",
25           salariedEmployee, salariedEmployee.Earnings() );
26        Console.WriteLine( "{0}\nearned: {1:C}\n",
27           hourlyEmployee, hourlyEmployee.Earnings() );
28        Console.WriteLine( "{0}\nearned: {1:C}\n",
29           commissionEmployee, commissionEmployee.Earnings() );
30        Console.WriteLine( "{0}\nearned: {1:C}\n",
31           basePlusCommissionEmployee,
32           basePlusCommissionEmployee.Earnings() );
33
34        // create four-element Employee array
35        Employee[] employees = new Employee[ 4 ];
36
37        // initialize array with Employees of derived types
38        employees[ 0 ] = salariedEmployee;
39        employees[ 1 ] = hourlyEmployee;
40        employees[ 2 ] = commissionEmployee;
41        employees[ 3 ] = basePlusCommissionEmployee;
42
43        Console.WriteLine( "Employees processed polymorphically:\n" );
44
45        // generically process each element in array employees
46        foreach ( Employee currentEmployee in employees )
47        {
48           Console.WriteLine( currentEmployee ); // invokes ToString
49
50           // determine whether element is a BasePlusCommissionEmployee
51           if ( currentEmployee is BasePlusCommissionEmployee )
52           {
53              // downcast Employee reference to
54              // BasePlusCommissionEmployee reference
55              BasePlusCommissionEmployee employee =
56                 ( BasePlusCommissionEmployee ) currentEmployee;
57
```

Fig. 12.9 | Employee hierarchy test application. (Part 2 of 4.)

```
58              employee.BaseSalary *= 1.10M;
59              Console.WriteLine(
60                 "new base salary with 10% increase is: {0:C}",
61                 employee.BaseSalary );
62          } // end if
63
64          Console.WriteLine(
65             "earned {0:C}\n", currentEmployee.Earnings() );
66       } // end foreach
67
68       // get type name of each object in employees array
69       for ( int j = 0; j < employees.Length; j++ )
70          Console.WriteLine( "Employee {0} is a {1}", j,
71             employees[ j ].GetType() );
72    } // end Main
73 } // end class PayrollSystemTest
```

```
Employees processed individually:

salaried employee: John Smith
social security number: 111-11-1111
weekly salary: $800.00
earned: $800.00

hourly employee: Karen Price
social security number: 222-22-2222
hourly wage: $16.75; hours worked: 40.00
earned: $670.00

commission employee: Sue Jones
social security number: 333-33-3333
gross sales: $10,000.00
commission rate: 0.06
earned: $600.00

base-salaried commission employee: Bob Lewis
social security number: 444-44-4444
gross sales: $5,000.00
commission rate: 0.04; base salary: $300.00
earned: $500.00


Employees processed polymorphically:

salaried employee: John Smith
social security number: 111-11-1111
weekly salary: $800.00
earned $800.00

hourly employee: Karen Price
social security number: 222-22-2222
hourly wage: $16.75; hours worked: 40.00
earned $670.00
```

Fig. 12.9 | Employee hierarchy test application. (Part 3 of 4.)

```
commission employee: Sue Jones
social security number: 333-33-3333
gross sales: $10,000.00
commission rate: 0.06
earned $600.00

base-salaried commission employee: Bob Lewis
social security number: 444-44-4444
gross sales: $5,000.00
commission rate: 0.04; base salary: $300.00
new base salary with 10% increase is: $330.00
earned $530.00

Employee 0 is a SalariedEmployee
Employee 1 is a HourlyEmployee
Employee 2 is a CommissionEmployee
Employee 3 is a BasePlusCommissionEmployee
```

Fig. 12.9 | Employee hierarchy test application. (Part 4 of 4.)

Polymorphically Processing Employees

Lines 46–66 iterate through array employees and invoke methods ToString and Earnings with Employee variable currentEmployee, which is assigned the reference to a different Employee during each iteration. The output illustrates that the appropriate methods for each class are indeed invoked. All calls to virtual methods ToString and Earnings are resolved at execution time, based on the type of the object to which currentEmployee refers. This process is known as **dynamic binding** or **late binding**. For example, line 48 implicitly invokes method ToString of the object to which currentEmployee refers. Only the methods of class Employee can be called via an Employee variable—and Employee includes class object's methods, such as ToString. (Section 11.7 discussed the methods that all classes inherit from class object.) A base-class reference can be used to invoke only methods of the base class.

Giving BasePlusCommissionEmployees 10% Raises

We perform special processing on BasePlusCommissionEmployee objects—as we encounter them, we increase their base salary by 10%. When processing objects polymorphically, we typically do not need to worry about the "specifics," but to adjust the base salary, we do have to determine the specific type of each Employee object at execution time. Line 51 uses the is operator to determine whether a particular Employee object's type is Base-PlusCommissionEmployee. The condition in line 51 is true if the object referenced by currentEmployee *is a* BasePlusCommissionEmployee. This would also be true for any object of a BasePlusCommissionEmployee derived class (if there were any), because of the *is-a* relationship a derived class has with its base class. Lines 55–56 downcast current-Employee from type Employee to type BasePlusCommissionEmployee—this cast is allowed only if the object has an *is-a* relationship with BasePlusCommissionEmployee. The condition at line 51 ensures that this is the case. This cast is required if we are to use derived class BasePlusCommissionEmployee's BaseSalary property on the current Employee object—*attempting to invoke a derived-class-only method directly on a base class reference is a compilation error.*

Common Programming Error 12.3

Assigning a base-class variable to a derived-class variable (without an explicit downcast) is a compilation error.

Software Engineering Observation 12.4

If at execution time the reference to a derived-class object has been assigned to a variable of one of its direct or indirect base classes, it's acceptable to cast the reference stored in that base-class variable back to a reference of the derived-class type. Before performing such a cast, use the is operator to ensure that the object is indeed an object of an appropriate derived-class type.

When downcasting an object, an InvalidCastException (of namespace *System*) occurs if at execution time the object does not have an *is a* relationship with the type specified in the cast operator. An object can be cast only to its own type or to the type of one of its base classes. You can avoid a potential InvalidCastException by using the **as** operator to perform a downcast rather than a cast operator. For example, in the statement

```
BasePlusCommissionEmployee employee =
    currentEmployee as BasePlusCommissionEmployee;
```

employee is assigned a reference to an object that *is a* BasePlusCommissionEmployee, or the value null if currentEmployee is not a BasePlusCommissionEmployee. You can then compare employee with null to determine whether the cast succeeded.

If the is expression in line 51 is true, the if statement (lines 51–62) performs the special processing required for the BasePlusCommissionEmployee object. Using BasePlusCommissionEmployee variable employee, line 58 accesses the derived-class-only property BaseSalary to retrieve and update the employee's base salary with the 10% raise.

Lines 64–65 invoke method Earnings on currentEmployee, which calls the appropriate derived-class object's Earnings method polymorphically. Obtaining the earnings of the SalariedEmployee, HourlyEmployee and CommissionEmployee polymorphically in lines 64–65 produces the same result as obtaining these employees' earnings individually in lines 24–29. However, the earnings amount obtained for the BasePlusCommissionEmployee in lines 64–65 is higher than that obtained in lines 30–32, due to the 10% increase in its base salary.

Every Object Knows Its Own Type

Lines 69–71 display each employee's type as a string. Every object in C# knows its own type and can access this information through method **GetType**, which all classes inherit from class object. Method GetType returns an object of class Type (of namespace System), which contains information about the object's type, including its class name, the names of its methods, and the name of its base class. Line 71 invokes method GetType on the object to get its runtime class (i.e., a Type object that represents the object's type). Then method ToString is implicitly invoked on the object returned by GetType. The Type class's ToString method returns the class name.

Avoiding Compilation Errors with Downcasting

In the previous example, we avoid several compilation errors by downcasting an Employee variable to a BasePlusCommissionEmployee variable in lines 55–56. If we remove the cast operator (BasePlusCommissionEmployee) from line 56 and attempt to assign Employee variable currentEmployee directly to BasePlusCommissionEmployee variable employee, we receive a "Cannot implicitly convert type" compilation error. This error indicates that the attempt to assign the reference of base-class object commissionEmployee to derived-class variable basePlusCommissionEmployee is not allowed without an appropriate cast operator. The compiler prevents this assignment, because a CommissionEmployee is *not* a BasePlusCommissionEmployee—again, the *is-a* relationship applies only between the derived class and its base classes, not vice versa.

Similarly, if lines 58 and 61 use base-class variable currentEmployee, rather than derived-class variable employee, to use derived-class-only property BaseSalary, we receive an "'Employee' does not contain a definition for 'BaseSalary'" compilation error on each of these lines. *Attempting to invoke derived-class-only methods on a base-class reference is not allowed.* While lines 58 and 61 execute only if is in line 51 returns true to indicate that currentEmployee has been assigned a reference to a BasePlusCommissionEmployee object, we cannot attempt to use derived-class BasePlusCommissionEmployee property BaseSalary with base-class Employee reference currentEmployee. The compiler would generate errors in lines 58 and 61, because BaseSalary is not a base-class member and cannot be used with a base-class variable. Although the actual method that's called depends on the object's type at execution time, *a variable can be used to invoke only those methods that are members of that variable's type*, which the compiler verifies. Using a base-class Employee variable, we can invoke only methods and properties found in class Employee—methods Earnings and ToString, and properties FirstName, LastName and SocialSecurityNumber—and method methods inherited from class object.

12.5.7 Summary of the Allowed Assignments Between Base-Class and Derived-Class Variables

Now that you've seen a complete application that processes diverse derived-class objects polymorphically, we summarize what you can and cannot do with base-class and derived-class objects and variables. Although a derived-class object also *is a* base-class object, the two are nevertheless different. As discussed previously, derived-class objects can be treated as if they were base-class objects. However, the derived class can have additional derived-class-only members. For this reason, assigning a base-class reference to a derived-class variable is not allowed without an explicit cast—such an assignment would leave the derived-class members undefined for a base-class object.

We've discussed four ways to assign base-class and derived-class references to variables of base-class and derived-class types:

1. Assigning a base-class reference to a base-class variable is straightforward.

2. Assigning a derived-class reference to a derived-class variable is straightforward.

3. Assigning a derived-class reference to a base-class variable is safe, because the derived-class object *is an* object of its base class. However, this reference can be used to refer *only* to base-class members. If this code refers to derived-class-only members through the base-class variable, the compiler reports errors.

4. Attempting to assign a base-class reference to a derived-class variable is a compilation error. To avoid this error, the base-class reference must be cast to a derived-class type explicitly or must be converted using the as operator. At execution

time, if the object to which the reference refers is *not* a derived-class object, an exception will occur. The is operator can be used to ensure that such a cast is performed *only* if the object is a derived-class object.

12.6 sealed Methods and Classes

Only methods declared virtual, override or abstract can be overridden in derived classes. A method declared **sealed** in a base class cannot be overridden in a derived class. Methods that are declared private are implicitly sealed, because it's impossible to override them in a derived class (though the derived class can declare a new method with the same signature as the private method in the base class). Methods that are declared static also are implicitly sealed, because static methods cannot be overridden either. A derived-class method declared both override and sealed can override a base-class method, but cannot be overridden in derived classes further down the inheritance hierarchy.

A sealed method's declaration can never change, so all derived classes use the same method implementation, and calls to sealed methods are resolved at compile time—this is known as **static binding**. Since the compiler knows that sealed methods cannot be overridden, it can often optimize code by removing calls to sealed methods and replacing them with the expanded code of their declarations at each method-call location—a technique known as **inlining the code**.

Performance Tip 12.1
The compiler can decide to inline a sealed method call and will do so for small, simple sealed methods. Inlining does not violate encapsulation or information hiding, but does improve performance, because it eliminates the overhead of making a method call.

A class that's declared sealed cannot be a base class (i.e., a class cannot extend a sealed class). All methods in a sealed class are implicitly sealed. Class string is a sealed class. This class cannot be extended, so applications that use strings can rely on the functionality of string objects as specified in the Framework Class Library.

Common Programming Error 12.4
Attempting to declare a derived class of a sealed class is a compilation error.

12.7 Case Study: Creating and Using Interfaces

Our next example (Figs. 12.11–12.15) reexamines the payroll system of Section 12.5. Suppose that the company involved wishes to perform several accounting operations in a single accounts-payable application—in addition to calculating the payroll earnings that must be paid to each employee, the company must also calculate the payment due on each of several invoices (i.e., bills for goods purchased). Though applied to unrelated things (i.e., employees and invoices), both operations have to do with calculating some kind of payment amount. For an employee, the payment refers to the employee's earnings. For an invoice, the payment refers to the total cost of the goods listed on the invoice. Can we calculate such different things as the payments due for employees and invoices polymorphically in a single application? Does C# offer a capability that requires that *unrelated* classes implement a set of common methods (e.g., a method that calculates a payment amount)? C# interfaces offer exactly this capability.

Interfaces define and standardize the ways in which people and systems can interact with one another. For example, the controls on a radio serve as an interface between a radio's users and its internal components. The controls allow users to perform a limited set of operations (e.g., changing the station, adjusting the volume, choosing between AM and FM), and different radios may implement the controls in different ways (e.g., using push buttons, dials, voice commands). The interface specifies *what* operations a radio must permit users to perform but does not specify *how* they're performed. Similarly, the interface between a driver and a car with a manual transmission includes the steering wheel, the gear shift, the clutch pedal, the gas pedal and the brake pedal. This same interface is found in nearly all manual-transmission cars, enabling someone who knows how to drive one particular manual-transmission car to drive just about any other. The components of each car may look a bit different, but the general purpose is the same—to allow people to drive the car.

Software objects also communicate via interfaces. A C# interface describes a set of methods and properties that can be called on an object—to tell it, for example, to perform some task or return some piece of information. The next example introduces an interface named `IPayable` that describes the functionality of any object that must be capable of being paid and thus must offer a method to determine the proper payment amount due. An **interface declaration** begins with the keyword **interface** and can contain only abstract methods, properties, indexers and events (events are discussed in Chapter 14, Graphical User Interfaces with Windows Forms: Part 1.) All interface members are implicitly declared both `public` and `abstract`. In addition, each interface can extend one or more other interfaces to create a more elaborate interface that other classes can implement.

Common Programming Error 12.5

It's a compilation error to declare an interface member public or abstract explicitly, because they're redundant in interface-member declarations. It's also a compilation error to specify any implementation details, such as concrete method declarations, in an interface.

To use an interface, a class must specify that it **implements** the interface by listing the interface after the colon (:) in the class declaration. This is the same syntax used to indicate inheritance from a base class. A concrete class implementing the interface must declare each member of the interface with the signature specified in the interface declaration. A class that implements an interface but does not implement all its members is an abstract class—it must be declared `abstract` and must contain an `abstract` declaration for each unimplemented member of the interface. Implementing an interface is like signing a contract with the compiler that states, "I will provide an implementation for all the members specified by the interface, or I will declare them `abstract`."

Common Programming Error 12.6

Failing to define or declare any member of an interface in a class that implements the interface results in a compilation error.

An interface is typically used when unrelated classes need to share common methods. This allows objects of unrelated classes to be processed polymorphically—objects of classes that implement the same interface can respond to the same method calls. You can create an interface that describes the desired functionality, then implement this interface in any classes requiring that functionality. For example, in the accounts-payable application developed in this section, we implement interface `IPayable` in any class that must be able to calculate a payment amount (e.g., `Employee`, `Invoice`).

An interface often is used in place of an `abstract` class when there's no default implementation to inherit—that is, no fields and no default method implementations. Like `abstract` classes, interfaces are typically `public` types, so they're normally declared in files by themselves with the same name as the interface and the `.cs` file-name extension.

12.7.1 Developing an `IPayable` Hierarchy

To build an application that can determine payments for employees and invoices alike, we first create an interface named `IPayable`. Interface `IPayable` contains method `Get-PaymentAmount` that returns a `decimal` amount to be paid for an object of any class that implements the interface. Method `GetPaymentAmount` is a general-purpose version of method `Earnings` of the `Employee` hierarchy—method `Earnings` calculates a payment amount specifically for an `Employee`, while `GetPaymentAmount` can be applied to a broad range of unrelated objects. After declaring interface `IPayable`, we introduce class `Invoice`, which implements interface `IPayable`. We then modify class `Employee` such that it also implements interface `IPayable`. Finally, we update `Employee` derived class `SalariedEmployee` to "fit" into the `IPayable` hierarchy (i.e., we rename `SalariedEmployee` method `Earnings` as `GetPaymentAmount`).

Good Programming Practice 12.1

By convention, the name of an interface begins with "`I`". This helps distinguish interfaces from classes, improving code readability.

Good Programming Practice 12.2

When declaring a method in an interface, choose a name that describes the method's purpose in a general manner, because the method may be implemented by a broad range of unrelated classes.

Classes `Invoice` and `Employee` both represent things for which the company must be able to calculate a payment amount. Both classes implement `IPayable`, so an application can invoke method `GetPaymentAmount` on `Invoice` objects and `Employee` objects alike. This enables the polymorphic processing of `Invoices` and `Employees` required for our company's accounts-payable application.

The UML class diagram in Fig. 12.10 shows the interface and class hierarchy used in our accounts-payable application. The hierarchy begins with interface `IPayable`. The UML distinguishes an interface from a class by placing the word "interface" in guillemets (« and ») above the interface name. The UML expresses the relationship between a class and an interface through a **realization**. A class is said to "realize," or implement, an interface. A class diagram models a realization as a dashed arrow with a hollow arrowhead pointing from the implementing class to the interface. The diagram in Fig. 12.10 indicates that classes `Invoice` and `Employee` each realize (i.e., implement) interface `IPayable`. As in the class diagram of Fig. 12.2, class `Employee` appears in italics, indicating that it's an abstract class. Concrete class `SalariedEmployee` extends `Employee` and inherits its base class's realization relationship with interface `IPayable`.

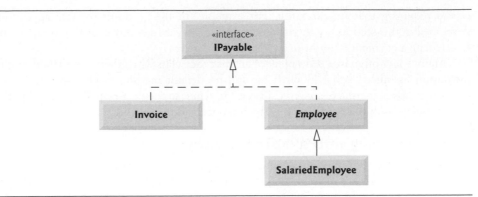

Fig. 12.10 | IPayable interface and class hierarchy UML class diagram.

12.7.2 Declaring Interface IPayable

The declaration of interface IPayable begins in Fig. 12.11 at line 3. Interface IPayable contains public abstract method GetPaymentAmount (line 5). The method cannot be *explicitly* declared public or abstract. Interfaces can have any number of members and interface methods can have parameters.

```
1   // Fig. 12.11: IPayable.cs
2   // IPayable interface declaration.
3   public interface IPayable
4   {
5      decimal GetPaymentAmount(); // calculate payment; no implementation
6   } // end interface IPayable
```

Fig. 12.11 | IPayable interface declaration.

12.7.3 Creating Class Invoice

We now create class Invoice (Fig. 12.12) to represent a simple invoice that contains billing information for one kind of part. The class contains properties PartNumber (line 11), PartDescription (line 14), Quantity (lines 27–41) and PricePerItem (lines 44–58) that indicate the part number, the description of the part, the quantity of the part ordered and the price per item. Class Invoice also contains a constructor (lines 17–24) and a ToString method (lines 61–67) that returns a string representation of an Invoice object. The set accessors of properties Quantity and PricePerItem ensure that quantity and pricePerItem are assigned only nonnegative values.

```
1   // Fig. 12.12: Invoice.cs
2   // Invoice class implements IPayable.
3   using System;
4
5   public class Invoice : IPayable
6   {
```

Fig. 12.12 | Invoice class implements IPayable. (Part 1 of 3.)

```
 7       private int quantity;
 8       private decimal pricePerItem;
 9
10       // property that gets and sets the part number on the invoice
11       public string PartNumber { get; set; }
12
13       // property that gets and sets the part description on the invoice
14       public string PartDescription { get; set; }
15
16       // four-parameter constructor
17       public Invoice( string part, string description, int count,
18          decimal price )
19       {
20          PartNumber = part;
21          PartDescription = description;
22          Quantity = count; // validate quantity via property
23          PricePerItem = price; // validate price per item via property
24       } // end four-parameter Invoice constructor
25
26       // property that gets and sets the quantity on the invoice
27       public int Quantity
28       {
29          get
30          {
31             return quantity;
32          } // end get
33          set
34          {
35             if ( value >= 0 ) // validate quantity
36                quantity = value;
37             else
38                throw new ArgumentOutOfRangeException( "Quantity",
39                   value, "Quantity must be >= 0" );
40          } // end set
41       } // end property Quantity
42
43       // property that gets and sets the price per item
44       public decimal PricePerItem
45       {
46          get
47          {
48             return pricePerItem;
49          } // end get
50          set
51          {
52             if ( value >= 0 ) // validate price
53                quantity = value;
54             else
55                throw new ArgumentOutOfRangeException( "PricePerItem",
56                   value, "PricePerItem must be >= 0" );
57          } // end set
58       } // end property PricePerItem
59
```

Fig. 12.12 | Invoice class implements IPayable. (Part 2 of 3.)

```
60      // return string representation of Invoice object
61      public override string ToString()
62      {
63         return string.Format(
64            "{0}: \n{1}: {2} ({3}) \n{4}: {5} \n{6}: {7:C}",
65            "invoice", "part number", PartNumber, PartDescription,
66            "quantity", Quantity, "price per item", PricePerItem );
67      } // end method ToString
68
69      // method required to carry out contract with interface IPayable
70      public decimal GetPaymentAmount()
71      {
72         return Quantity * PricePerItem; // calculate total cost
73      } // end method GetPaymentAmount
74   } // end class Invoice
```

Fig. 12.12 | Invoice class implements IPayable. (Part 3 of 3.)

Line 5 of Fig. 12.12 indicates that class Invoice implements interface IPayable. Like all classes, class Invoice also implicitly inherits from class object. *C# does not allow derived classes to inherit from more than one base class, but it does allow a class to inherit from a base class and implement* any *number of interfaces*. All objects of a class that implement multiple interfaces have the *is-a* relationship with each implemented interface type. To implement more than one interface, use a comma-separated list of interface names after the colon (:) in the class declaration, as in:

> **public class** *ClassName* : *BaseClassName*, *FirstInterface*, *SecondInterface*, ...

When a class inherits from a base class and implements one or more interfaces, the class declaration *must* list the base-class name before any interface names.

Class Invoice implements the one method in interface IPayable—method GetPaymentAmount is declared in lines 70–73. The method calculates the amount required to pay the invoice. The method multiplies the values of quantity and pricePerItem (obtained through the appropriate properties) and returns the result (line 72). This method satisfies the implementation requirement for the method in interface IPayable—we've fulfilled the interface contract with the compiler.

12.7.4 Modifying Class Employee to Implement Interface IPayable

We now modify class Employee to implement interface IPayable. Figure 12.13 contains the modified Employee class. This class declaration is identical to that of Fig. 12.4 with two exceptions. First, line 3 of Fig. 12.13 indicates that class Employee now implements interface IPayable. Because of this, we must rename Earnings to GetPaymentAmount throughout the Employee hierarchy. As with method Earnings in the version of class Employee in Fig. 12.4, however, it does not make sense to implement method GetPaymentAmount in class Employee, because we cannot calculate the earnings payment owed to a *general* Employee—first, we must know the *specific* type of Employee. In Fig. 12.4, we declared method Earnings as abstract for this reason, and as a result, class Employee had to be declared abstract. This forced each Employee derived class to override Earnings with a concrete implementation.

```
 1   // Fig. 12.13: Employee.cs
 2   // Employee abstract base class.
 3   public abstract class Employee : IPayable
 4   {
 5      // read-only property that gets employee's first name
 6      public string FirstName { get; private set; }
 7
 8      // read-only property that gets employee's last name
 9      public string LastName { get; private set; }
10
11      // read-only property that gets employee's social security number
12      public string SocialSecurityNumber { get; private set; }
13
14      // three-parameter constructor
15      public Employee( string first, string last, string ssn )
16      {
17         FirstName = first;
18         LastName = last;
19         SocialSecurityNumber = ssn;
20      } // end three-parameter Employee constructor
21
22      // return string representation of Employee object
23      public override string ToString()
24      {
25         return string.Format( "{0} {1}\nsocial security number: {2}",
26            FirstName, LastName, SocialSecurityNumber );
27      } // end method ToString
28
29      // Note: We do not implement IPayable method GetPaymentAmount here, so
30      // this class must be declared abstract to avoid a compilation error.
31      public abstract decimal GetPaymentAmount();
32   } // end abstract class Employee
```

Fig. 12.13 | Employee abstract base class.

In Fig. 12.13, we handle this situation the same way. Recall that when a class implements an interface, the class makes a contract with the compiler stating that the class either will implement *each* of the methods in the interface *or* will declare them abstract. If the latter option is chosen, we must also declare the class abstract. As we discussed in Section 12.4, any concrete derived class of the abstract class must implement the abstract methods of the base class. If the derived class does not do so, it too must be declared abstract. As indicated by the comments in lines 29–30, class Employee of Fig. 12.13 does not implement method GetPaymentAmount, so the class is declared abstract.

12.7.5 Modifying Class SalariedEmployee for Use with IPayable

Figure 12.14 contains a modified version of class SalariedEmployee that extends Employee and implements method GetPaymentAmount. This version of SalariedEmployee is identical to that of Fig. 12.5 with the exception that the version here implements method GetPaymentAmount (lines 35–38) instead of method Earnings. The two methods contain the same functionality but have different names. Recall that the IPayable version of the method has a more general name to be applicable to possibly disparate classes. The remaining Employee derived classes (e.g., HourlyEmployee, CommissionEmployee and BasePlusCommissionEmployee) also must be modified to contain method GetPaymentAmount in place of Earnings to reflect the fact that Employee now implements IPayable. We leave these modifications to try on your own and use only SalariedEmployee in our test application in this section.

```
1   // Fig. 12.14: SalariedEmployee.cs
2   // SalariedEmployee class that extends Employee.
3   using System;
4
5   public class SalariedEmployee : Employee
6   {
7      private decimal weeklySalary;
8
9      // four-parameter constructor
10     public SalariedEmployee( string first, string last, string ssn,
11        decimal salary ) : base( first, last, ssn )
12     {
13        WeeklySalary = salary; // validate salary via property
14     } // end four-parameter SalariedEmployee constructor
15
16     // property that gets and sets salaried employee's salary
17     public decimal WeeklySalary
18     {
19        get
20        {
21           return weeklySalary;
22        } // end get
23        set
24        {
25           if ( value >= 0 ) // validation
26              weeklySalary = value;
27           else
28              throw new ArgumentOutOfRangeException( "WeeklySalary",
29                 value, "WeeklySalary must be >= 0" );
30        } // end set
31     } // end property WeeklySalary
32
33     // calculate earnings; implement interface IPayable method
34     // that was abstract in base class Employee
35     public override decimal GetPaymentAmount()
36     {
37        return WeeklySalary;
38     } // end method GetPaymentAmount
39
40     // return string representation of SalariedEmployee object
41     public override string ToString()
42     {
43        return string.Format( "salaried employee: {0}\n{1}: {2:C}",
44           base.ToString(), "weekly salary", WeeklySalary );
45     } // end method ToString
46  } // end class SalariedEmployee
```

Fig. 12.14 | SalariedEmployee class that extends Employee.

When a class implements an interface, the same *is-a* relationship provided by inheritance applies. Class Employee implements IPayable, so we can say that an Employee *is an* IPayable, as are any classes that extend Employee. As such, SalariedEmployee objects are IPayable objects. An object of a class that implements an interface may be thought of as an object of the interface type. Objects of any classes derived from the class that implements the interface can also be thought of as objects of the interface type. Thus, just as we can assign the reference of a SalariedEmployee object to a base-class Employee variable, we can assign the reference of a SalariedEmployee object to an interface IPayable variable. Invoice implements IPayable, so an Invoice object also *is an* IPayable object, and we can assign the reference of an Invoice object to an IPayable variable.

Software Engineering Observation 12.5

Inheritance and interfaces are similar in their implementation of the is-a *relationship. An object of a class that implements an interface may be thought of as an object of that interface type. An object of any derived classes of a class that implements an interface also can be thought of as an object of the interface type.*

Software Engineering Observation 12.6

The is-a *relationship that exists between base classes and derived classes, and between interfaces and the classes that implement them, holds when passing an object to a method. When a method parameter receives an argument of a base class or interface type, the method polymorphically processes the object received as an argument.*

12.7.6 Using Interface IPayable to Process Invoices and Employees Polymorphically

PayableInterfaceTest (Fig. 12.15) illustrates that interface IPayable can be used to process a set of Invoices and Employees polymorphically in a single application. Line 10 declares payableObjects and assigns it an array of four IPayable variables. Lines 13–14 assign the references of Invoice objects to the first two elements of payableObjects. Lines 15–18 assign the references of SalariedEmployee objects to the remaining two elements of payableObjects. These assignments are allowed because an Invoice *is an* IPayable, a SalariedEmployee *is an* Employee and an Employee *is an* IPayable. Lines 24–29 use a foreach statement to process each IPayable object in payableObjects polymorphically, printing the object as a string, along with the payment due. Lines 27–28 implicitly invokes method ToString off an IPayable interface reference, even though ToString is not declared in interface IPayable—all references (including those of interface types) refer to objects that extend object and therefore have a ToString method. Line 28 invokes IPayable method GetPaymentAmount to obtain the payment amount for each object in payableObjects, regardless of the actual type of the object. The output reveals that the method calls in lines 27–28 invoke the appropriate class's implementation of methods ToString and GetPayment-Amount. For instance, when currentPayable refers to an Invoice during the first iteration of the foreach loop, class Invoice's ToString and GetPaymentAmount methods execute.

Software Engineering Observation 12.7

All methods of class object can be called by using a reference of an interface type—the reference refers to an object, and all objects inherit the methods of class object.

```
 1   // Fig. 12.15: PayableInterfaceTest.cs
 2   // Tests interface IPayable with disparate classes.
 3   using System;
 4
 5   public class PayableInterfaceTest
 6   {
 7      public static void Main( string[] args )
 8      {
 9         // create four-element IPayable array
10         IPayable[] payableObjects = new IPayable[ 4 ];
11
12         // populate array with objects that implement IPayable
13         payableObjects[ 0 ] = new Invoice( "01234", "seat", 2, 375.00M );
14         payableObjects[ 1 ] = new Invoice( "56789", "tire", 4, 79.95M );
15         payableObjects[ 2 ] = new SalariedEmployee( "John", "Smith",
16            "111-11-1111", 800.00M );
17         payableObjects[ 3 ] = new SalariedEmployee( "Lisa", "Barnes",
18            "888-88-8888", 1200.00M );
19
20         Console.WriteLine(
21            "Invoices and Employees processed polymorphically:\n" );
22
23         // generically process each element in array payableObjects
24         foreach ( var currentPayable in payableObjects )
25         {
26            // output currentPayable and its appropriate payment amount
27            Console.WriteLine( "payment due {0}: {1:C}\n",
28               currentPayable, currentPayable.GetPaymentAmount() );
29         } // end foreach
30      } // end Main
31   } // end class PayableInterfaceTest
```

```
Invoices and Employees processed polymorphically:

invoice:
part number: 01234 (seat)
quantity: 2
price per item: $375.00
payment due: $750.00

invoice:
part number: 56789 (tire)
quantity: 4
price per item: $79.95
payment due: $319.80

salaried employee: John Smith
social security number: 111-11-1111
weekly salary: $800.00
payment due: $800.00

salaried employee: Lisa Barnes
social security number: 888-88-8888
weekly salary: $1,200.00
payment due: $1,200.00
```

Fig. 12.15 | Tests interface IPayable with disparate classes.

12.7.7 Common Interfaces of the .NET Framework Class Library

In this section, we overview several common interfaces defined in the .NET Framework Class Library. These interfaces are implemented and used in the same manner as those you create (e.g., interface IPayable in Section 12.7.2). The Framework Class Library's interfaces enable you to extend many important aspects of C# with your own classes. Figure 12.16 overviews several commonly used Framework Class Library interfaces.

Interface	Description
IComparable	C# contains several comparison operators (e.g., <, <=, >, >=, ==, !=) that allow you to compare simple-type values. In Section 12.8 you'll see that these operators can be defined to compare two objects. Interface IComparable can also be used to allow objects of a class that implements the interface to be compared to one another. The interface contains one method, CompareTo, that compares the object that calls the method to the object passed as an argument to the method. Classes must implement CompareTo to return a value indicating whether the object on which it's invoked is less than (negative integer return value), equal to (0 return value) or greater than (positive integer return value) the object passed as an argument, using any criteria you specify. For example, if class Employee implements IComparable, its CompareTo method could compare Employee objects by their earnings amounts. Interface IComparable is commonly used for ordering objects in a collection such as an array. We use IComparable in Chapter 22, Generics, and Chapter 23, Collections.
IComponent	Implemented by any class that represents a component, including Graphical User Interface (GUI) controls (such as buttons or labels). Interface IComponent defines the behaviors that components must implement. We discuss IComponent and many GUI controls that implement this interface in Chapter 14, Graphical User Interfaces with Windows Forms: Part 1, and Chapter 15, Graphical User Interfaces with Windows Forms: Part 2.
IDisposable	Implemented by classes that must provide an explicit mechanism for releasing resources. Some resources can be used by only one program at a time. In addition, some resources, such as files on disk, are unmanaged resources that, unlike memory, cannot be released by the garbage collector. Classes that implement interface IDisposable provide a Dispose method that can be called to explicitly release resources. We discuss IDisposable briefly in Chapter 13, Exception Handling. You can learn more about this interface at msdn.microsoft.com/en-us/library/system.idisposable.aspx. The MSDN article *Implementing a Dispose Method* at msdn.microsoft.com/en-us/library/fs2xkftw.aspx discusses the proper implementation of this interface in your classes.
IEnumerator	Used for iterating through the elements of a collection (such as an array) one element at a time. Interface IEnumerator contains method MoveNext to move to the next element in a collection, method Reset to move to the position before the first element and property Current to return the object at the current location. We use IEnumerator in Chapter 23.

Fig. 12.16 | Common interfaces of the .NET Framework Class Library.

12.8 Operator Overloading

Object manipulations are accomplished by sending messages (in the form of method calls) to the objects. This method-call notation is cumbersome for certain kinds of classes, especially mathematical classes. For these classes, it would be convenient to use C#'s rich set of built-in operators to specify object manipulations. In this section, we show how to enable these operators to work with class objects—via a process called **operator overloading**.

C# enables you to overload most operators to make them sensitive to the context in which they're used. Some operators are overloaded more frequently than others, especially the various arithmetic operators, such as + and -, where operator notation often is more natural. Figures 12.17 and 12.18 provide an example of using operator overloading with a ComplexNumber class. For a list of overloadable operators, see msdn.microsoft.com/en-us/library/8edha89s.aspx.

Class ComplexNumber (Fig. 12.17) overloads the plus (+), minus (–) and multiplication (*) operators to enable programs to add, subtract and multiply instances of class ComplexNumber using common mathematical notation. Lines 9 and 12 define properties for the Real and Imaginary components of the complex number.

```
 1   // Fig. 12.17: ComplexNumber.cs
 2   // Class that overloads operators for adding, subtracting
 3   // and multiplying complex numbers.
 4   using System;
 5
 6   public class ComplexNumber
 7   {
 8      // read-only property that gets the real component
 9      public double Real { get; private set; }
10
11      // read-only property that gets the imaginary component
12      public double Imaginary { get; private set; }
13
14      // constructor
15      public ComplexNumber( double a, double b )
16      {
17         Real = a;
18         Imaginary = b;
19      } // end constructor
20
21      // return string representation of ComplexNumber
22      public override string ToString()
23      {
24         return string.Format( "({0} {1} {2}i)",
25            Real, ( Imaginary < 0 ? "-" : "+" ), Math.Abs( Imaginary ) );
26      } // end method ToString
27
28      // overload the addition operator
29      public static ComplexNumber operator+ (
30         ComplexNumber x, ComplexNumber y )
31      {
```

Fig. 12.17 | Class that overloads operators for adding, subtracting and multiplying complex numbers. (Part 1 of 2.)

```
32          return new ComplexNumber( x.Real + y.Real,
33             x.Imaginary + y.Imaginary );
34       } // end operator +
35
36       // overload the subtraction operator
37       public static ComplexNumber operator- (
38          ComplexNumber x, ComplexNumber y )
39       {
40          return new ComplexNumber( x.Real - y.Real,
41             x.Imaginary - y.Imaginary );
42       } // end operator -
43
44       // overload the multiplication operator
45       public static ComplexNumber operator* (
46          ComplexNumber x, ComplexNumber y )
47       {
48          return new ComplexNumber(
49             x.Real * y.Real - x.Imaginary * y.Imaginary,
50             x.Real * y.Imaginary + y.Real * x.Imaginary );
51       } // end operator *
52    } // end class ComplexNumber
```

Fig. 12.17 | Class that overloads operators for adding, subtracting and multiplying complex numbers. (Part 2 of 2.)

Lines 29–34 overload the plus operator (+) to perform addition of ComplexNumbers. Keyword **operator**, followed by an operator symbol, indicates that a method overloads the specified operator. Methods that overload binary operators must take two arguments. The first argument is the left operand, and the second argument is the right operand. Class ComplexNumber's overloaded plus operator takes two ComplexNumber references as arguments and returns a ComplexNumber that represents the sum of the arguments. This method is marked public and static, which is required for overloaded operators. The body of the method (lines 32–33) performs the addition and returns the result as a new ComplexNumber. Notice that we do not modify the contents of either of the original operands passed as arguments x and y. This matches our intuitive sense of how this operator should behave—adding two numbers does not modify either of the original numbers. Lines 37–51 provide similar overloaded operators for subtracting and multiplying ComplexNumbers.

Software Engineering Observation 12.8

Overload operators to perform the same function or similar functions on class objects as the operators perform on objects of simple types. Avoid nonintuitive use of operators.

Software Engineering Observation 12.9

At least one parameter of an overloaded operator method must be a reference to an object of the class in which the operator is overloaded. This prevents you from changing how operators work on simple types.

Class ComplexTest (Fig. 12.18) demonstrates the overloaded ComplexNumber operators +, - and *. Lines 14–27 prompt the user to enter two complex numbers, then use this input to create two ComplexNumbers and assign them to variables x and y.

```
 1    // Fig. 12.18: OperatorOverloading.cs
 2    // Overloading operators for complex numbers.
 3    using System;
 4
 5    public class ComplexTest
 6    {
 7       public static void Main( string[] args )
 8       {
 9          // declare two variables to store complex numbers
10          // to be entered by user
11          ComplexNumber x, y;
12
13          // prompt the user to enter the first complex number
14          Console.Write( "Enter the real part of complex number x: " );
15          double realPart = Convert.ToDouble( Console.ReadLine() );
16          Console.Write(
17             "Enter the imaginary part of complex number x: " );
18          double imaginaryPart = Convert.ToDouble( Console.ReadLine() );
19          x = new ComplexNumber( realPart, imaginaryPart );
20
21          // prompt the user to enter the second complex number
22          Console.Write( "\nEnter the real part of complex number y: " );
23          realPart = Convert.ToDouble( Console.ReadLine() );
24          Console.Write(
25             "Enter the imaginary part of complex number y: " );
26          imaginaryPart = Convert.ToDouble( Console.ReadLine() );
27          y = new ComplexNumber( realPart, imaginaryPart );
28
29          // display the results of calculations with x and y
30          Console.WriteLine();
31          Console.WriteLine( "{0} + {1} = {2}", x, y, x + y );
32          Console.WriteLine( "{0} - {1} = {2}", x, y, x - y );
33          Console.WriteLine( "{0} * {1} = {2}", x, y, x * y );
34       } // end method Main
35    } // end class ComplexTest
```

```
Enter the real part of complex number x: 2
Enter the imaginary part of complex number x: 4

Enter the real part of complex number y: 4
Enter the imaginary part of complex number y: -2

(2 + 4i) + (4 - 2i) = (6 + 2i)
(2 + 4i) - (4 - 2i) = (-2 + 6i)
(2 + 4i) * (4 - 2i) = (16 + 12i)
```

Fig. 12.18 | Overloading operators for complex numbers.

Lines 31–33 add, subtract and multiply x and y with the overloaded operators, then output the results. In line 31, we perform the addition by using the plus operator with ComplexNumber operands x and y. Without operator overloading, the expression x + y wouldn't make sense—the compiler wouldn't know how two objects of class Complex-Number should be added. This expression makes sense here because we've defined the plus operator for two ComplexNumbers in lines 29–34 of Fig. 12.17. When the two Complex-

Numbers are "added" in line 31 of Fig. 12.18, this invokes the `operator+` declaration, passing the left operand as the first argument and the right operand as the second argument. When we use the subtraction and multiplication operators in lines 32–33, their respective overloaded operator declarations are invoked similarly.

Each calculation's result is a reference to a new `ComplexNumber` object. When this new object is passed to the `Console` class's `WriteLine` method, its `ToString` method (Fig. 12.17, lines 22–26) is implicitly invoked. Line 31 of Fig. 12.18 could be rewritten to explicitly invoke the `ToString` method of the object created by the overloaded plus operator, as in:

```
Console.WriteLine( "{0} + {1} = {2}", x, y, ( x + y ).ToString() );
```

12.9 Wrap-Up

This chapter introduced polymorphism—the ability to process objects that share the same base class in a class hierarchy as if they were all objects of the base class. The chapter discussed how polymorphism makes systems extensible and maintainable, then demonstrated how to use overridden methods to effect polymorphic behavior. We introduced the notion of an abstract class, which allows you to provide an appropriate base class from which other classes can inherit. You learned that an abstract class can declare abstract methods that each derived class must implement to become a concrete class, and that an application can use variables of an abstract class to invoke derived class implementations of abstract methods polymorphically. You also learned how to determine an object's type at execution time. We showed how to create `sealed` methods and classes. The chapter discussed declaring and implementing an interface as another way to achieve polymorphic behavior, often among objects of different classes. Finally, you learned how to define the behavior of the built-in operators on objects of your own classes with operator overloading.

You should now be familiar with classes, objects, encapsulation, inheritance, interfaces and polymorphism—the most essential aspects of object-oriented programming. Next, we take a deeper look at using exception handling to deal with runtime errors.

13

Exception Handling

OBJECTIVES

In this chapter you'll learn:

- What exceptions are and how they're handled.
- When to use exception handling.
- To use **try** blocks to delimit code in which exceptions might occur.
- To **throw** exceptions to indicate a problem.
- To use **catch** blocks to specify exception handlers.
- To use the **finally** block to release resources.
- The .NET exception class hierarchy.
- **Exception** properties.
- To create user-defined exceptions.

It is common sense to take a method and try it. If it fails, admit it frankly and try another. But above all, try something.
—Franklin Delano Roosevelt

O! throw away the worser part of it, And live the purer with the other half.
—William Shakespeare

If they're running and they don't look where they're going I have to come out from somewhere and catch them.
—J. D. Salinger

13.1 Introduction

In this chapter, we take a deeper look at **exception handling**. An **exception** indicates that a problem occurred during a program's execution. The name "exception" comes from the fact that, although the problem can occur, it occurs infrequently. If the "rule" is that a statement normally executes correctly, then the occurrence of a problem represents the "exception to the rule." Exception handling enables you to create applications that can handle exceptions—in many cases allowing a program to continue executing as if no problems were encountered. More severe problems may prevent a program from continuing normal execution, instead requiring the program to notify the user of the problem, then terminate in a controlled manner. The features presented in this chapter enable you to write clear, **robust** and more **fault-tolerant programs** (i.e., programs that are able to deal with problems that may arise and continue executing). The style and details of C# exception handling are based in part on the work of Andrew Koenig and Bjarne Stroustrup. "Best practices" for exception handling in Visual C# are specified in the Visual Studio documentation.[1]

After reviewing exception-handling concepts and basic exception-handling techniques, we overview .NET's exception-handling class hierarchy. Programs typically request and release resources (such as files on disk) during program execution. Often, the supply of these resources is limited, or the resources can be used by only one program at a time. We demonstrate a part of the exception-handling mechanism that enables a program to use a resource, then guarantee that it will be released for use by other programs, even if an exception occurs. We show several properties of class System.Exception (the base class of all exception classes) and discuss how you can create and use your own exception classes.

13.2 Example: Divide by Zero without Exception Handling

Let's see what happens when errors arise in a console application that does not use exception handling. Figure 13.1 inputs two integers from the user, then divides the first integer by the second using integer division to obtain an int result. In this example, an exception

---

1. "Best Practices for Handling Exceptions [C#]," *.NET Framework Developer's Guide*, Visual Studio .NET Online Help. Available at msdn.microsoft.com/en-us/library/seyhszts.aspx.

is **thrown** (i.e., an exception occurs) when a method detects a problem and is unable to handle it.

Running the Application

In most of our examples, the application appears to run the same with or without debugging. As we discuss shortly, the example in Fig. 13.1 might cause errors, depending on the user's input. If you run this application using the **Debug > Start Debugging** menu option, the program pauses at the line where an exception occurs, displays the Exception Assistant and allows you to analyze the current state of the program and debug it. We discuss the Exception Assistant in Section 13.3.3. We discuss debugging in detail in Appendix G.

In this example, we do not wish to debug the application; we simply want to see what happens when errors arise. For this reason, we execute this application from a **Command**

```
1   // Fig. 13.1: DivideByZeroNoExceptionHandling.cs
2   // Integer division without exception handling.
3   using System;
4
5   class DivideByZeroNoExceptionHandling
6   {
7      static void Main()
8      {
9         // get numerator and denominator
10        Console.Write( "Please enter an integer numerator: " );
11        int numerator = Convert.ToInt32( Console.ReadLine() );
12        Console.Write( "Please enter an integer denominator: " );
13        int denominator = Convert.ToInt32( Console.ReadLine() );
14
15        // divide the two integers, then display the result
16        int result = numerator / denominator;
17        Console.WriteLine( "\nResult: {0:D} / {1:D} = {2:D}",
18           numerator, denominator, result );
19     } // end Main
20  } // end class DivideByZeroNoExceptionHandling
```

```
Please enter an integer numerator: 100
Please enter an integer denominator: 7

Result: 100 / 7 = 14
```

```
Please enter an integer numerator: 100
Please enter an integer denominator: 0

Unhandled Exception: System.DivideByZeroException:
   Attempted to divide by zero.
   at DivideByZeroNoExceptionHandling.Main()
      in C:\examples\ch13\Fig13_01\DivideByZeroNoExceptionHandling\
      DivideByZeroNoExceptionHandling\
      DivideByZeroNoExceptionHandling.cs:line 16
```

Fig. 13.1 | Integer division without exception handling. (Part 1 of 2.)

```
Please enter an integer numerator: 100
Please enter an integer denominator: hello

Unhandled Exception: System.FormatException:
   Input string was not in a correct format.
   at System.Number.StringToNumber(String str, NumberStyles options,
      NumberBuffer& number, NumberFormatInfo info, Boolean parseDecimal)
   at System.Number.ParseInt32(String s, NumberStyles style,
      NumberFormatInfo info)
   at DivideByZeroNoExceptionHandling.Main()
      in C:\examples\ch13\Fig13_01\DivideByZeroNoExceptionHandling\
      DivideByZeroNoExceptionHandling\
      DivideByZeroNoExceptionHandling.cs:line 13
```

Fig. 13.1 | Integer division without exception handling. (Part 2 of 2.)

Prompt window. Select **Start > All Programs > Accessories > Command Prompt** to open a **Command Prompt** window, then use the cd command to change to the application's Debug directory. For example, if this application resides in the directory C:\examples\ ch13\Fig13_01\DivideByZeroNoExceptionHandling on your system, you will type

```
cd /d C:\examples\ch13\Fig13_01\DivideByZeroNoExceptionHandling\
      DivideByZeroNoExceptionHandling\bin\Debug
```

in the **Command Prompt**, then press *Enter* to change to the application's Debug directory. To execute the application, type

```
DivideByZeroNoExceptionHandling.exe
```

in the **Command Prompt**, then press *Enter*. If an error arises during execution, a dialog is displayed indicating that the application encountered a problem and needs to close. In Windows Vista and Windows 7, the system tries to find a solution to the problem, then asks you to choose between looking online for a solution to the problem and closing the program. [*Note:* On some systems a **Just-In-Time Debugging** dialog is displayed instead. If this occurs, simply click the **No** button to dismiss the dialog.] At this point, an error message describing the problem is displayed in the **Command Prompt**. We formatted the error messages in Fig. 13.1 for readability. [*Note:* Selecting **Debug > Start Without Debugging** (or *<Ctrl> F5*) to run the application from Visual Studio executes the application's so-called release version. The error messages produced by this version of the application may differ from those shown in Fig. 13.1, because of optimizations that the compiler performs to create an application's release version.]

Analyzing the Results

The first sample execution shows a successful division. In the second, the user enters 0 as the denominator. Several lines of information are displayed in response to the invalid input. This information—known as a **stack trace**—includes the name of the exception class (System.DivideByZeroException) in a message indicating the problem that occurred and the path of execution that led to the exception, method by method. This information helps you debug a program. The first line of the error message specifies that a DivideByZeroException occurred. When a program divides an integer by 0, the CLR throws a **DivideByZeroException** (namespace System). The text after the name of the exception,

"`Attempted to divide by zero,`" indicates why this exception occurred. Division by zero is not allowed in integer arithmetic. [*Note:* Division by zero with floating-point values *is* allowed and results in the value infinity—represented by either constant **Double.PositiveInfinity** or constant **Double.NegativeInfinity**, depending on whether the numerator is positive or negative. These values are displayed as `Infinity` or `-Infinity`. If both the numerator and denominator are zero, the result of the calculation is the constant **Double.NaN** ("not a number"), which is returned when a calculation's result is undefined.]

Each "`at`" line in a stack trace indicates a line of code in the particular method that was executing when the exception occurred. The "`at`" line contains the namespace, class and method in which the exception occurred (`DivideByZeroNoExceptionHandling.Main`), the location and name of the file containing the code (`C:\examples\ch13\Fig13_01\DivideByZeroNoExceptionHandling\DivideByZeroNoExceptionHandling\DivideByZeroNoExceptionHandling.cs`) and the line number (`:line 16`) where the exception occurred. In this case, the stack trace indicates that the `DivideByZeroException` occurred when the program was executing line 16 of method `Main`. The first "`at`" line in the stack trace indicates the exception's **throw point**—the initial point at which the exception occurred (i.e., line 16 in `Main`). This information makes it easy for you to see where the exception originated, and what method calls were made to get to that point in the program.

In the third sample execution, the user enters the string `"hello"` as the denominator. This causes a `FormatException`, and another stack trace is displayed. Our earlier examples that read numeric values from the user assumed that the user would input an integer value, but a noninteger value could be entered. A **FormatException** (namespace `System`) occurs, for example, when `Convert` method `ToInt32` receives a string that does not represent a valid integer. Starting from the last "`at`" line in the stack trace, we see that the exception was detected in line 13 of method `Main`. The stack trace also shows the other methods that led to the exception being thrown. To perform its task, `Convert.ToInt32` calls method `Number.ParseInt32`, which in turn calls `Number.StringToNumber`. The throw point occurs in `Number.StringToNumber`, as indicated by the first "`at`" line in the stack trace. Method `Convert.ToInt32` is not in the stack trace because the compiler optimized this call out of the code—all it does forward its arguments to `Number.ParseInt32`.

In the sample executions in Fig. 13.1, the program terminates when exceptions occur and stack traces are displayed. This does not always happen—sometimes a program may continue executing even though an exception has occurred and a stack trace has been printed. In such cases, the application may produce incorrect results. The next section demonstrates how to handle exceptions to enable the program to run to normal completion.

13.3 Example: Handling DivideByZeroExceptions and FormatExceptions

Now, let's consider a simple example of exception handling. The application in Fig. 13.2 uses exception handling to process any `DivideByZeroExceptions` and `FormatExceptions` that might arise. The application reads two integers from the user (lines 18–21). Assuming that the user provides integers as input and does not specify 0 as the denominator for the division, line 25 performs the division and lines 28–29 display the result. However, if the user inputs a noninteger value or supplies 0 as the denominator, an exception occurs. This program demonstrates how to **catch** and **handle** such exceptions—in this case, displaying an error message and allowing the user to enter another set of values.

```
1    // Fig. 13.2: DivideByZeroExceptionHandling.cs
2    // FormatException and DivideByZeroException handlers.
3    using System;
4
5    class DivideByZeroExceptionHandling
6    {
7       static void Main( string[] args )
8       {
9          bool continueLoop = true; // determines whether to keep looping
10
11         do
12         {
13            // retrieve user input and calculate quotient
14            try
15            {
16               // Convert.ToInt32 generates FormatException
17               // if argument cannot be converted to an integer
18               Console.Write( "Enter an integer numerator: " );
19               int numerator = Convert.ToInt32( Console.ReadLine() );
20               Console.Write( "Enter an integer denominator: " );
21               int denominator = Convert.ToInt32( Console.ReadLine() );
22
23               // division generates DivideByZeroException
24               // if denominator is 0
25               int result = numerator / denominator;
26
27               // display result
28               Console.WriteLine( "\nResult: {0} / {1} = {2}",
29                  numerator, denominator, result );
30               continueLoop = false;
31            } // end try
32            catch ( FormatException formatException )
33            {
34               Console.WriteLine( "\n" + formatException.Message );
35               Console.WriteLine(
36                  "You must enter two integers. Please try again.\n" );
37            } // end catch
38            catch ( DivideByZeroException divideByZeroException )
39            {
40               Console.WriteLine( "\n" + divideByZeroException.Message );
41               Console.WriteLine(
42                  "Zero is an invalid denominator. Please try again.\n" );
43            } // end catch
44         } while ( continueLoop ); // end do...while
45      } // end Main
46   } // end class DivideByZeroExceptionHandling
```

```
Please enter an integer numerator: 100
Please enter an integer denominator: 7

Result: 100 / 7 = 14
```

Fig. 13.2 | FormatException and DivideByZeroException handlers. (Part 1 of 2.)

```
Enter an integer numerator: 100
Enter an integer denominator: 0

Attempted to divide by zero.
Zero is an invalid denominator. Please try again.

Enter an integer numerator: 100
Enter an integer denominator: 7

Result: 100 / 7 = 14
```

```
Enter an integer numerator: 100
Enter an integer denominator: hello

Input string was not in a correct format.
You must enter two integers. Please try again.

Enter an integer numerator: 100
Enter an integer denominator: 7

Result: 100 / 7 = 14
```

Fig. 13.2 | `FormatException` and `DivideByZeroException` handlers. (Part 2 of 2.)

Sample Outputs
Before we discuss the details of the program, let's consider the sample outputs in Fig. 13.2. The first sample output shows a successful calculation in which the user enters the numerator 100 and the denominator 7. The result (14) is an `int`, because integer division always yields an `int` result. The second sample output demonstrates the result of an attempt to divide by zero. In integer arithmetic, the CLR tests for division by zero and generates a `DivideByZeroException` if the denominator is zero. The program detects the exception and displays an error message indicating the attempt to divide by zero. The last sample output depicts the result of inputting a non-`int` value—in this case, the user enters "hello" as the denominator. The program attempts to convert the input `string`s to `int`s using method `Convert.ToInt32` (lines 19 and 21). If an argument cannot be converted to an `int`, the method throws a `FormatException`. The program catches the exception and displays an error message indicating that the user must enter two `int`s.

Another Way to Convert Strings to Integers
Another way to validate the input is to use the **`Int32.TryParse`** method, which converts a `string` to an `int` value if possible. All of the numeric types have `TryParse` methods. The method requires two arguments—one is the `string` to parse and the other is the variable in which the converted value is to be stored. The method returns a `bool` value that's `true` only if the `string` was parsed successfully. If the `string` could not be converted, the value 0 is assigned to the second argument, which is passed by reference so its value can be modified in the calling method. Method `TryParse` can be used to validate input in code rather than allowing the code to throw an exception.

13.3.1 Enclosing Code in a try Block
Now we consider the user interactions and flow of control that yield the results shown in the sample output windows. Lines 14–31 define a **try block** enclosing the code that might

throw exceptions, as well as the code that's skipped when an exception occurs. For example, the program should not display a new result (lines 28–29) unless the calculation in line 25 completes successfully.

The user inputs values that represent the numerator and denominator. The two statements that read the ints (lines 19 and 21) call method Convert.ToInt32 to convert strings to int values. This method throws a FormatException if it cannot convert its string argument to an int. If lines 19 and 21 convert the values properly (i.e., no exceptions occur), then line 25 divides the numerator by the denominator and assigns the result to variable result. If denominator is 0, line 25 causes the CLR to throw a DivideByZero-Exception. If line 25 does not cause an exception to be thrown, then lines 28–29 display the result of the division.

13.3.2 Catching Exceptions

Exception-handling code appears in a **catch block**. In general, when an exception occurs in a try block, a corresponding catch block catches the exception and handles it. The try block in this example is followed by two catch blocks—one that handles a Format-Exception (lines 32–37) and one that handles a DivideByZeroException (lines 38–43). A catch block specifies an exception parameter representing the exception that the catch block can handle. The catch block can use the parameter's identifier (which you choose) to interact with a caught exception object. If there's no need to use the exception object in the catch block, the exception parameter's identifier can be omitted. The type of the catch's parameter is the type of the exception that the catch block handles. Optionally, you can include a catch block that does not specify an exception type—such a catch block (known as a **general catch clause**) catches all exception types. At least one catch block and/or a **finally block** (discussed in Section 13.5) must immediately follow a try block.

In Fig. 13.2, the first catch block catches FormatExceptions (thrown by method Convert.ToInt32), and the second catch block catches DivideByZeroExceptions (thrown by the CLR). If an exception occurs, the program executes only the first matching catch block. Both exception handlers in this example display an error-message dialog. After either catch block terminates, program control continues with the first statement after the last catch block (the end of the method, in this example). We'll soon take a deeper look at how this flow of control works in exception handling.

13.3.3 Uncaught Exceptions

An **uncaught exception** (or **unhandled exception**) is an exception for which there's no matching catch block. You saw the results of uncaught exceptions in the second and third outputs of Fig. 13.1. Recall that when exceptions occur in that example, the application terminates early (after displaying the exception's stack trace). The result of an uncaught exception depends on how you execute the program—Fig. 13.1 demonstrated the results of an uncaught exception when an application is executed in a **Command Prompt**. If you run the application from Visual Studio with debugging, and the runtime environment detects an uncaught exception, the application pauses, and a window called the **Exception Assistant** appears indicating where the exception occurred, the type of the exception and links to helpful information on handling the exception. Figure 13.3 shows the Exception Assistant that's displayed if the user attempts to divide by zero in the application of Fig. 13.1.

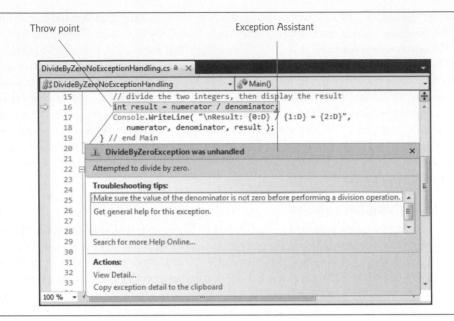

Throw point   Exception Assistant

Fig. 13.3 | Exception Assistant.

13.3.4 Termination Model of Exception Handling

When a method called in a program or the CLR detects a problem, the method or the CLR throws an exception. Recall that the point in the program at which an exception occurs is called the throw point—this is an important location for debugging purposes (as we demonstrate in Section 13.7). If an exception occurs in a try block (such as a FormatException being thrown as a result of the code in lines 19 and 21 in Fig. 13.2), the try block terminates immediately, and program control transfers to the first of the following catch blocks in which the exception parameter's type matches the type of the thrown exception. In Fig. 13.2, the first catch block catches FormatExceptions (which occur if input of an invalid type is entered); the second catch block catches DivideByZeroExceptions (which occur if an attempt is made to divide by zero). After the exception is handled, program control does not return to the throw point because the try block has expired (which also causes any of its local variables to go out of scope). Rather, control resumes after the last catch block. This is known as the **termination model of exception handling**. [*Note:* Some languages use the **resumption model of exception handling**, in which, after an exception is handled, control resumes just after the throw point.]

If no exceptions occur in the try block, the program of Fig. 13.2 successfully completes the try block by ignoring the catch blocks in lines 32–37 and 38–43, and passing line 43. Then the program executes the first statement following the try and catch blocks. In this example, the program reaches the end of the do…while loop (line 44), so the method terminates, and the program awaits the next user interaction.

The try block and its corresponding catch and finally blocks together form a **try statement**. It's important not to confuse the terms "try block" and "try statement"—the term "try block" refers to the block of code following the keyword try (but before any catch or finally blocks), while the term "try statement" includes all the code from the opening try keyword to the end of the last catch or finally block. This includes the try block, as well as any associated catch blocks and finally block.

When a try block terminates, local variables defined in the block go out of scope. If a try block terminates due to an exception, the CLR searches for the first catch block that can process the type of exception that occurred. The CLR locates the matching catch by comparing the type of the thrown exception to each catch's parameter type. A match occurs if the types are identical or if the thrown exception's type is a derived class of the catch's parameter type. Once an exception is matched to a catch block, the code in that block executes and the other catch blocks in the try statement are ignored.

13.3.5 Flow of Control When Exceptions Occur

In the third sample output of Fig. 13.2, the user inputs hello as the denominator. When line 21 executes, Convert.ToInt32 cannot convert this string to an int, so the method throws a FormatException object to indicate that the method was unable to convert the string to an int. When the exception occurs, the try block expires (terminates). Next, the CLR attempts to locate a matching catch block. A match occurs with the catch block in line 32, so the exception handler displays the exception's Message property (to retrieve the error message associated with the exception) and the program ignores all other exception handlers following the try block. Program control then continues with line 44.

Common Programming Error 13.1

Specifying a comma-separated list of parameters in a catch *block is a syntax error. A* catch *block can have at most one parameter.*

In the second sample output of Fig. 13.2, the user inputs 0 as the denominator. When the division in line 25 executes, a DivideByZeroException occurs. Once again, the try block terminates, and the program attempts to locate a matching catch block. In this case, the first catch block does not match—the exception type in the catch-handler declaration is not the same as the type of the thrown exception, and FormatException is not a base class of DivideByZeroException. Therefore the program continues to search for a matching catch block, which it finds in line 38. Line 40 displays the exception's Message property. Again, program control then continues with line 44.

13.4 .NET Exception Hierarchy

In C#, the exception-handling mechanism allows only objects of class **Exception** (namespace System) and its derived classes to be thrown and caught. Note, however, that C# programs may interact with software components written in other .NET languages (such as C++) that do not restrict exception types. The general catch clause can be used to catch such exceptions.

This section overviews several of the .NET Framework's exception classes and focuses exclusively on exceptions that derive from class Exception. In addition, we discuss how to determine whether a particular method throws exceptions.

13.4.1 Class SystemException

Class Exception (namespace System) is the base class of .NET's exception class hierarchy. An important derived class is **SystemException**. The CLR generates SystemExceptions.

Many of these can be avoided if applications are coded properly. For example, if a program attempts to access an **out-of-range array index**, the CLR throws an exception of type **IndexOutOfRangeException** (a derived class of SystemException). Similarly, an exception occurs when a program uses a reference-type variable to call a method when the reference has a value of null. This causes a **NullReferenceException** (another derived class of SystemException). You saw earlier in this chapter that a DivideByZeroException occurs in integer division when a program attempts to divide by zero.

Other exceptions thrown by the CLR include **OutOfMemoryException**, **StackOverflowException** and **ExecutionEngineException**, which are thrown when something goes wrong that causes the CLR to become unstable. Sometimes such exceptions cannot even be caught. It's best to simply log such exceptions, then terminate your application.

A benefit of the exception class hierarchy is that a catch block can catch exceptions of a particular type or—because of the *is-a* relationship of inheritance—can use a base-class type to catch exceptions in a hierarchy of related exception types. For example, Section 13.3.2 discussed the catch block with no parameter, which catches exceptions of all types (including those that are not derived from Exception). A catch block that specifies a parameter of type Exception can catch all exceptions that derive from Exception, because Exception is the base class of all exception classes. The advantage of this approach is that the exception handler can access the caught exception's information via the parameter in the catch. We'll say more about accessing exception information in Section 13.7.

Using inheritance with exceptions enables an catch block to catch related exceptions using a concise notation. A set of exception handlers could catch each derived-class exception type individually, but catching the base-class exception type is more concise. However, this technique makes sense only if the handling behavior is the same for a base class and all derived classes. Otherwise, catch each derived-class exception individually.

Common Programming Error 13.2

The compiler issues an error if a catch block that catches a base-class exception is placed before a catch block for any of that class's derived-class types. In this case, the base-class catch block would catch all base-class and derived-class exceptions, so the derived-class exception handler would never execute.

13.4.2 Determining Which Exceptions a Method Throws

How do we determine that an exception might occur in a program? For methods contained in the .NET Framework classes, read the detailed descriptions of the methods in the online documentation. If a method throws an exception, its description contains a section called **Exceptions** that specifies the types of exceptions the method throws and briefly describes what causes them. For an example, search for "Convert.ToInt32 method" in the Visual Studio online documentation. The **Exceptions** section of this method's web page indicates that method Convert.ToInt32 throws two exception types—FormatException and OverflowException—and describes the reason why each might occur. [*Note:* You can also find this information in the **Object Browser** described in Section 10.15.]

Software Engineering Observation 13.1

If a method throws exceptions, statements that invoke the method directly or indirectly should be placed in try blocks, and those exceptions should be caught and handled.

It's more difficult to determine when the CLR throws exceptions. Such information appears in the *C# Language Specification* (available from bit.ly/CSharp4Spec). This document defines C#'s syntax and specifies cases in which exceptions are thrown.

13.5 finally Block

Programs frequently request and release resources dynamically (i.e., at execution time). For example, a program that reads a file from disk first makes a file-open request (as we'll see in Chapter 17, Files and Streams). If that request succeeds, the program reads the contents of the file. Operating systems typically prevent more than one program from manipulating a file at once. Therefore, when a program finishes processing a file, the program should close the file (i.e., release the resource) so other programs can use it. If the file is not closed, a **resource leak** occurs. In such a case, the file resource is not available to other programs, possibly because a program using the file has not closed it.

In programming languages such as C and C++, in which the programmer is responsible for dynamic memory management, the most common type of resource leak is a **memory leak**. A memory leak occurs when a program allocates memory (as C# programmers do via keyword new), but does not deallocate the memory when it's no longer needed. Normally, this is not an issue in C#, because the CLR performs garbage collection of memory that's no longer needed by an executing program (Section 10.9). However, other kinds of resource leaks (such as unclosed files) can occur.

Error-Prevention Tip 13.1

The CLR does not completely eliminate memory leaks. The CLR will not garbage collect an object until the program contains no more references to that object, and even then there may be a delay until the memory is required. Thus, memory leaks can occur if you inadvertently keep references to unwanted objects.

Moving Resource-Release Code to a finally Block

Typically, exceptions occur when processing resources that require explicit release. For example, a program that processes a file might receive IOExceptions during the processing. For this reason, file-processing code normally appears in a try block. Regardless of whether a program experiences exceptions while processing a file, the program should close the file when it's no longer needed. Suppose a program places all resource-request and resource-release code in a try block. If no exceptions occur, the try block executes normally and releases the resources after using them. However, if an exception occurs, the try block may expire before the resource-release code can execute. We could duplicate all the resource-release code in each of the catch blocks, but this would make the code more difficult to modify and maintain. We could also place the resource-release code after the try statement; however, if the try block terminated due to a return statement, code following the try statement would never execute.

To address these problems, C#'s exception-handling mechanism provides the finally block, which is guaranteed to execute regardless of whether the try block executes successfully or an exception occurs. This makes the finally block an ideal location in which to place resource-release code for resources that are acquired and manipulated in the corresponding try block. If the try block executes successfully, the finally block executes immediately after the try block terminates. If an exception occurs in the try block, the `finally` block executes immediately after a `catch` block completes. If the exception is not caught by a `catch` block associated with the `try` block, or if a `catch` block associated with the `try` block throws an exception itself, the `finally` block executes before the exception is processed by the next enclosing `try` block, which could be in the calling method. By placing the resource-release code in a `finally` block, we ensure that even if the program terminates due to an uncaught exception, the resource will be deallocated. Local variables in a `try` block cannot be accessed in the corresponding `finally` block. For this reason, variables that must be accessed in both a `try` block, and its corresponding `finally` block should be declared before the `try` block.

Error-Prevention Tip 13.2

A `finally` block typically contains code to release resources acquired in the corresponding `try` block, which makes the `finally` block an effective mechanism for eliminating resource leaks.

Performance Tip 13.1

As a rule, resources should be released as soon as they're no longer needed in a program. This makes them available for reuse promptly.

If one or more `catch` blocks follow a `try` block, the `finally` block is optional. However, if no `catch` blocks follow a `try` block, a `finally` block must appear immediately after the `try` block. If any `catch` blocks follow a `try` block, the `finally` block (if there is one) appears *after* the last `catch` block. Only whitespace and comments can separate the blocks in a `try` statement.

Demonstrating the `finally` Block

The application in Fig. 13.4 demonstrates that the `finally` block always executes, regardless of whether an exception occurs in the corresponding `try` block. The program consists of method `Main` (lines 8–47) and four other methods that `Main` invokes to demonstrate `finally`. These methods are `DoesNotThrowException` (lines 50–67), `ThrowException-WithCatch` (lines 70–89), `ThrowExceptionWithoutCatch` (lines 92–108) and `ThrowExceptionCatchRethrow` (lines 111–136).

```
 1   // Fig. 13.4: UsingExceptions.cs
 2   // Using finally blocks.
 3   // finally blocks always execute, even when no exception occurs.
 4   using System;
 5
 6   class UsingExceptions
 7   {
 8      static void Main()
 9      {
10         // Case 1: No exceptions occur in called method
11         Console.WriteLine( "Calling DoesNotThrowException" );
12         DoesNotThrowException();
13
14         // Case 2: Exception occurs and is caught in called method
15         Console.WriteLine( "\nCalling ThrowExceptionWithCatch" );
```

Fig. 13.4 | `finally` blocks always execute, even when no exception occurs. (Part 1 of 4.)

```
16              ThrowExceptionWithCatch();
17
18              // Case 3: Exception occurs, but is not caught in called method
19              // because there is no catch block.
20              Console.WriteLine( "\nCalling ThrowExceptionWithoutCatch" );
21
22              // call ThrowExceptionWithoutCatch
23              try
24              {
25                  ThrowExceptionWithoutCatch();
26              } // end try
27              catch
28              {
29                  Console.WriteLine( "Caught exception from " +
30                      "ThrowExceptionWithoutCatch in Main" );
31              } // end catch
32
33              // Case 4: Exception occurs and is caught in called method,
34              // then rethrown to caller.
35              Console.WriteLine( "\nCalling ThrowExceptionCatchRethrow" );
36
37              // call ThrowExceptionCatchRethrow
38              try
39              {
40                  ThrowExceptionCatchRethrow();
41              } // end try
42              catch
43              {
44                  Console.WriteLine( "Caught exception from " +
45                      "ThrowExceptionCatchRethrow in Main" );
46              } // end catch
47          } // end method Main
48
49          // no exceptions thrown
50          static void DoesNotThrowException()
51          {
52              // try block does not throw any exceptions
53              try
54              {
55                  Console.WriteLine( "In DoesNotThrowException" );
56              } // end try
57              catch
58              {
59                  Console.WriteLine( "This catch never executes" );
60              } // end catch
61              finally
62              {
63                  Console.WriteLine( "finally executed in DoesNotThrowException" );
64              } // end finally
65
66              Console.WriteLine( "End of DoesNotThrowException" );
67          } // end method DoesNotThrowException
68
```

Fig. 13.4 | finally blocks always execute, even when no exception occurs. (Part 2 of 4.)

```
69   // throws exception and catches it locally
70   static void ThrowExceptionWithCatch()
71   {
72      // try block throws exception
73      try
74      {
75         Console.WriteLine( "In ThrowExceptionWithCatch" );
76         throw new Exception( "Exception in ThrowExceptionWithCatch" );
77      } // end try
78      catch ( Exception exceptionParameter )
79      {
80         Console.WriteLine( "Message: " + exceptionParameter.Message );
81      } // end catch
82      finally
83      {
84         Console.WriteLine(
85            "finally executed in ThrowExceptionWithCatch" );
86      } // end finally
87
88      Console.WriteLine( "End of ThrowExceptionWithCatch" );
89   } // end method ThrowExceptionWithCatch
90
91   // throws exception and does not catch it locally
92   static void ThrowExceptionWithoutCatch()
93   {
94      // throw exception, but do not catch it
95      try
96      {
97         Console.WriteLine( "In ThrowExceptionWithoutCatch" );
98         throw new Exception( "Exception in ThrowExceptionWithoutCatch" );
99      } // end try
100     finally
101     {
102        Console.WriteLine( "finally executed in " +
103           "ThrowExceptionWithoutCatch" );
104     } // end finally
105
106     // unreachable code; logic error
107     Console.WriteLine( "End of ThrowExceptionWithoutCatch" );
108  } // end method ThrowExceptionWithoutCatch
109
110  // throws exception, catches it and rethrows it
111  static void ThrowExceptionCatchRethrow()
112  {
113     // try block throws exception
114     try
115     {
116        Console.WriteLine( "In ThrowExceptionCatchRethrow" );
117        throw new Exception( "Exception in ThrowExceptionCatchRethrow" );
118     } // end try
119     catch ( Exception exceptionParameter )
120     {
121        Console.WriteLine( "Message: " + exceptionParameter.Message );
```

Fig. 13.4 | finally blocks always execute, even when no exception occurs. (Part 3 of 4.)

```
122
123          // rethrow exception for further processing
124          throw;
125
126          // unreachable code; logic error
127      } // end catch
128      finally
129      {
130          Console.WriteLine( "finally executed in " +
131              "ThrowExceptionCatchRethrow" );
132      } // end finally
133
134      // any code placed here is never reached
135      Console.WriteLine( "End of ThrowExceptionCatchRethrow" );
136   } // end method ThrowExceptionCatchRethrow
137 } // end class UsingExceptions
```

```
Calling DoesNotThrowException
In DoesNotThrowException
finally executed in DoesNotThrowException
End of DoesNotThrowException

Calling ThrowExceptionWithCatch
In ThrowExceptionWithCatch
Message: Exception in ThrowExceptionWithCatch
finally executed in ThrowExceptionWithCatch
End of ThrowExceptionWithCatch

Calling ThrowExceptionWithoutCatch
In ThrowExceptionWithoutCatch
finally executed in ThrowExceptionWithoutCatch
Caught exception from ThrowExceptionWithoutCatch in Main

Calling ThrowExceptionCatchRethrow
In ThrowExceptionCatchRethrow
Message: Exception in ThrowExceptionCatchRethrow
finally executed in ThrowExceptionCatchRethrow
Caught exception from ThrowExceptionCatchRethrow in Main
```

Fig. 13.4 | finally blocks always execute, even when no exception occurs. (Part 4 of 4.)

Line 12 of Main invokes method DoesNotThrowException. This method's try block outputs a message (line 55). Because the try block does not throw any exceptions, program control ignores the catch block (lines 57–60) and executes the finally block (lines 61–64), which outputs a message. At this point, program control continues with the first statement after the close of the finally block (line 66), which outputs a message indicating that the end of the method has been reached. Then, program control returns to Main.

*Throwing Exceptions Using the **throw** Statement*
Line 16 of Main invokes method ThrowExceptionWithCatch (lines 70–89), which begins in its try block (lines 73–77) by outputting a message. Next, the try block creates an Exception object and uses a **throw statement** to throw it (line 76). Executing the throw statement indicates that a problem has occurred in the code. As you've seen in earlier chapters, you can throw exceptions by using the throw statement. Just as with exceptions

thrown by the Framework Class Library's methods and the CLR, this indicates to client applications that an error has occurred. A throw statement specifies an object to be thrown. The operand of a throw statement can be of type Exception or of any type derived from class Exception.

The string passed to the constructor becomes the exception object's error message. When a throw statement in a try block executes, the try block expires immediately, and program control continues with the first matching catch block (lines 78–81) following the try block. In this example, the type thrown (Exception) matches the type specified in the catch, so line 80 outputs a message indicating the exception that occurred. Then, the finally block (lines 82–86) executes and outputs a message. At this point, program control continues with the first statement after the close of the finally block (line 88), which outputs a message indicating that the end of the method has been reached. Program control then returns to Main. In line 80, we use the exception object's Message property to retrieve the error message associated with the exception (i.e., the message passed to the Exception constructor). Section 13.7 discusses several properties of class Exception.

Lines 23–31 of Main define a try statement in which Main invokes method Throw-ExceptionWithoutCatch (lines 92–108). The try block enables Main to catch any exceptions thrown by ThrowExceptionWithoutCatch. The try block in lines 95–99 of ThrowExceptionWithoutCatch begins by outputting a message. Next, the try block throws an Exception (line 98) and expires immediately.

Normally, program control would continue at the first catch following this try block. However, this try block does not have any catch blocks. Therefore, the exception is not caught in method ThrowExceptionWithoutCatch. Program control proceeds to the finally block (lines 100–104), which outputs a message. At this point, program control returns to Main—any statements appearing after the finally block (e.g., line 107) do not execute. In this example, such statements could cause logic errors, because the exception thrown in line 98 is not caught. In Main, the catch block in lines 27–31 catches the exception and displays a message indicating that the exception was caught in Main.

Rethrowing Exceptions
Lines 38–46 of Main define a try statement in which Main invokes method Throw-ExceptionCatchRethrow (lines 111–136). The try statement enables Main to catch any exceptions thrown by ThrowExceptionCatchRethrow. The try statement in lines 114–132 of ThrowExceptionCatchRethrow begins by outputting a message. Next, the try block throws an Exception (line 117). The try block expires immediately, and program control continues at the first catch (lines 119–127) following the try block. In this example, the type thrown (Exception) matches the type specified in the catch, so line 121 outputs a message indicating where the exception occurred. Line 124 uses the throw statement to **rethrow** the exception. This indicates that the catch block performed partial processing of the exception and now is throwing the exception again (in this case, back to the method Main) for further processing. In general, it's considered better practice to throw a new exception and pass the original one to the new exception's constructor. This maintains all of the stack-trace information from the original exception. Rethrowing an exception loses the original exception's stack-trace information.

You can also rethrow an exception with a version of the throw statement which takes an operand that is the reference to the exception that was caught. It's important to note, however, that this form of throw statement resets the throw point, so the original throw point's stack-trace information is lost. Section 13.7 demonstrates using a throw statement with an operand from a catch block. In that section, you'll see that after an exception is caught, you can create and throw a different type of exception object from the catch block and you can include the original exception as part of the new exception object. Class library designers often do this to customize the exception types thrown from methods in their class libraries or to provide additional debugging information.

The exception handling in method ThrowExceptionCatchRethrow does not complete, because the throw statement in line 124 immediately terminates the catch block—if there were any code between line 124 and the end of the block, it would not execute. When line 124 executes, method ThrowExceptionCatchRethrow terminates and returns control to Main. Once again, the finally block (lines 128–132) executes and outputs a message before control returns to Main. When control returns to Main, the catch block in lines 42–46 catches the exception and displays a message indicating that the exception was caught. Then the program terminates.

Returning After a *finally* Block

The next statement to execute after a finally block terminates depends on the exception-handling state. If the try block successfully completes, or if a catch block catches and handles an exception, the program continues its execution with the next statement after the finally block. However, if an exception is not caught, or if a catch block rethrows an exception, program control continues in the next enclosing try block. The enclosing try could be in the calling method or in one of its callers. It also is possible to nest a try statement in a try block; in such a case, the outer try statement's catch blocks would process any exceptions that were not caught in the inner try statement. If a try block executes and has a corresponding finally block, the finally block executes even if the try block terminates due to a return statement. The return occurs after the execution of the finally block.

Common Programming Error 13.3

If an uncaught exception is awaiting processing when the finally block executes, and the finally block throws a new exception that's not caught in the finally block, the first exception is lost, and the new exception is passed to the next enclosing try block.

Error-Prevention Tip 13.3

When placing code that can throw an exception in a finally block, always enclose the code in a try statement that catches the appropriate exception types. This prevents the loss of any uncaught and rethrown exceptions that occur before the finally block executes.

Software Engineering Observation 13.2

Do not place try blocks around every statement that might throw an exception—this can make programs difficult to read. Instead, place one try block around a significant portion of code, and follow this try block with catch blocks that handle each possible exception. Then follow the catch blocks with a single finally block. Use separate try blocks to distinguish between multiple statements that can throw the same exception type.

13.6 The `using` Statement

Typically resource-release code should be placed in a finally block to ensure that a resource is released, regardless of whether there were exceptions when the resource was used in the corresponding `try` block. An alternative notation—the **using** statement (not to be confused with the `using` directive for using namespaces)—simplifies writing code in which you obtain a resource, use the resource in a `try` block and release the resource in a corresponding `finally` block. For example, a file-processing application (Chapter 17) could process a file with a `using` statement to ensure that the file is closed properly when it's no longer needed. The resource must be an object that implements the `IDisposable` interface and therefore has a `Dispose` method. The general form of a `using` statement is

```
using ( ExampleObject exampleObject = new ExampleObject() )
{
    exampleObject.SomeMethod();
}
```

where `ExampleObject` is a class that implements the `IDisposable` interface. This code creates an object of type `ExampleObject` and uses it in a statement, then calls its `Dispose` method to release any resources used by the object. The `using` statement implicitly places the code in its body in a `try` block with a corresponding `finally` block that calls the object's `Dispose` method. For instance, the preceding code is equivalent to

```
{
    ExampleObject exampleObject = new ExampleObject();

    try
    {
        exampleObject.SomeMethod();
    }
    finally
    {
        if ( exampleObject != null )
            ( ( IDisposable ) exampleObject ).Dispose();
    }
}
```

The `if` statement ensures that `exampleObject` still references an object; otherwise, a `NullReferenceException` might occur.

13.7 Exception Properties

As we discussed in Section 13.4, exception types derive from class `Exception`, which has several properties. These frequently are used to formulate error messages indicating a caught exception. Two important properties are `Message` and **StackTrace**. Property `Message` stores the error message associated with an `Exception` object. This message can be a default message associated with the exception type or a customized message passed to an `Exception` object's constructor when the `Exception` object is thrown. Property `StackTrace` contains a `string` that represents the **method-call stack**. Recall that the runtime environment at all times keeps a list of open method calls that have been made but have not yet returned. The `StackTrace` represents the series of methods that have not finished processing at the time the exception occurs. If the debugging information that is generated by the compiler for the method is accessible to the IDE, the stack trace also includes line numbers; the first line number indicates the throw point, and subsequent line numbers indicate the locations from which the methods in the stack trace were called. PDB files are created by the IDE to maintain the debugging information for your projects.

*Property **InnerException***

Another property used frequently by class-library programmers is **InnerException**. Typically, class library programmers "wrap" exception objects caught in their code so that they then can throw new exception types that are specific to their libraries. For example, a programmer implementing an accounting system might have some account-number processing code in which account numbers are input as strings but represented as ints in the code. Recall that a program can convert strings to int values with Convert.ToInt32, which throws a FormatException when it encounters an invalid number format. When an invalid account-number format occurs, the accounting-system programmer might wish to employ a different error message than the default message supplied by FormatException or might wish to indicate a new exception type, such as InvalidAccountNumberFormat-Exception. In such cases, you would provide code to catch the FormatException, then create an appropriate type of Exception object in the catch block and pass the original exception as one of the constructor arguments. The original exception object becomes the InnerException of the new exception object. When an InvalidAccountNumberFormat-Exception occurs in code that uses the accounting system library, the catch block that catches the exception can obtain a reference to the original exception via property Inner-Exception. Thus the exception indicates both that the user specified an invalid account number and that the problem was an invalid number format. If the InnerException property is null, this indicates that the exception was not caused by another exception.

*Other **Exception** Properties*

Class Exception provides other properties, including **HelpLink**, **Source** and **TargetSite**. Property HelpLink specifies the location of the help file that describes the problem that occurred. This property is null if no such file exists. Property Source specifies the name of the application or object that caused the exception. Property TargetSite specifies the method where the exception originated.

*Demonstrating **Exception** Properties and Stack Unwinding*

Our next example (Fig. 13.5) demonstrates properties Message, StackTrace and Inner-Exception of class Exception. In addition, the example introduces **stack unwinding**—when an exception is thrown but not caught in a particular scope, the method-call stack is "unwound," and an attempt is made to catch the exception in the next outer try block. We keep track of the methods on the call stack as we discuss property StackTrace and the stack-unwinding mechanism. To see the proper stack trace, you should execute this program using steps similar to those presented in Section 13.2.

```
 1   // Fig. 13.5: Properties.cs
 2   // Stack unwinding and Exception class properties.
 3   // Demonstrates using properties Message, StackTrace and InnerException.
 4   using System;
 5
 6   class Properties
 7   {
 8      static void Main()
 9      {
```

Fig. 13.5 | Stack unwinding and Exception class properties. (Part 1 of 3.)

```
10          // call Method1; any Exception generated is caught
11          // in the catch block that follows
12          try
13          {
14             Method1();
15          } // end try
16          catch ( Exception exceptionParameter )
17          {
18             // output the string representation of the Exception, then output
19             // properties Message, StackTrace and InnerException
20             Console.WriteLine( "exceptionParameter.ToString: \n{0}\n",
21                exceptionParameter );
22             Console.WriteLine( "exceptionParameter.Message: \n{0}\n",
23                exceptionParameter.Message );
24             Console.WriteLine( "exceptionParameter.StackTrace: \n{0}\n",
25                exceptionParameter.StackTrace );
26             Console.WriteLine( "exceptionParameter.InnerException: \n{0}\n",
27                exceptionParameter.InnerException );
28          } // end catch
29       } // end method Main
30
31       // calls Method2
32       static void Method1()
33       {
34          Method2();
35       } // end method Method1
36
37       // calls Method3
38       static void Method2()
39       {
40          Method3();
41       } // end method Method2
42
43       // throws an Exception containing an InnerException
44       static void Method3()
45       {
46          // attempt to convert string to int
47          try
48          {
49             Convert.ToInt32( "Not an integer" );
50          } // end try
51          catch ( FormatException formatExceptionParameter )
52          {
53             // wrap FormatException in new Exception
54             throw new Exception( "Exception occurred in Method3",
55                formatExceptionParameter );
56          } // end catch
57       } // end method Method3
58    } // end class Properties
```

```
exceptionParameter.ToString:
System.Exception: Exception occurred in Method3 --->
   System.FormatException: Input string was not in a correct format.
```

Fig. 13.5 | Stack unwinding and Exception class properties. (Part 2 of 3.)

```
    at System.Number.StringToNumber(String str, NumberStyles options,
       NumberBuffer& number, NumberFormatInfo info, Boolean parseDecimal)
    at System.Number.ParseInt32(String s, NumberStyles style,
       NumberFormatInfo info)
    at Properties.Method3() in C:\examples\ch13\Fig13_05\Properties\
       Properties\Properties.cs:line 49
    --- End of inner exception stack trace ---
    at Properties.Method3() in C:\examples\ch13\Fig13_05\Properties\
       Properties\Properties.cs:line 54
    at Properties.Method2() in C:\examples\ch13\Fig13_05\Properties\
       Properties\Properties.cs:line 40
    at Properties.Method1() in C:\examples\ch13\Fig13_05\Properties\
       Properties\Properties.cs:line 34
    at Properties.Main() in C:\examples\ch13\Fig13_05\Properties\
       Properties\Properties.cs:line 14

exceptionParameter.Message:
Exception occurred in Method3

exceptionParameter.StackTrace:
    at Properties.Method3() in C:\examples\ch13\Fig13_05\Properties\
       Properties\Properties.cs:line 54
    at Properties.Method2() in C:\examples\ch13\Fig13_05\Properties\
       Properties\Properties.cs:line 40
    at Properties.Method1() in C:\examples\ch13\Fig13_05\Properties\
       Properties\Properties.cs:line 34
    at Properties.Main() in C:\examples\ch13\Fig13_05\Properties\
       Properties\Properties.cs:line 14

exceptionParameter.InnerException:
System.FormatException: Input string was not in a correct format.
    at System.Number.StringToNumber(String str, NumberStyles options,
       NumberBuffer& number, NumberFormatInfo info, Boolean parseDecimal)
    at System.Number.ParseInt32(String s, NumberStyles style,
       NumberFormatInfo info)
    at Properties.Method3() in C:\examples\ch13\Fig13_05\Properties\
       Properties\Properties.cs:line 49
```

Fig. 13.5 | Stack unwinding and Exception class properties. (Part 3 of 3.)

Program execution begins with Main, which becomes the first method on the method-call stack. Line 14 of the try block in Main invokes Method1 (declared in lines 32–35), which becomes the second method on the stack. If Method1 throws an exception, the catch block in lines 16–28 handles the exception and outputs information about the exception that occurred. Line 34 of Method1 invokes Method2 (lines 38–41), which becomes the third method on the stack. Then line 40 of Method2 invokes Method3 (lines 44–57), which becomes the fourth method on the stack.

At this point, the method-call stack (from top to bottom) for the program is:

```
    Method3
    Method2
    Method1
    Main
```

The method called most recently (Method3) appears at the top of the stack; the first method called (Main) appears at the bottom. The try statement (lines 47–56) in Method3 invokes method `Convert.ToInt32` (line 49), which attempts to convert a `string` to an `int`. At this point, `Convert.ToInt32` becomes the fifth and final method on the call stack.

Throwing an *Exception* with an *InnerException*

Because the argument to `Convert.ToInt32` is not in `int` format, line 49 throws a `Format-Exception` that's caught in line 51 of `Method3`. The exception terminates the call to `Convert.ToInt32`, so the method is removed (or unwound) from the method-call stack. The `catch` block in `Method3` then creates and throws an `Exception` object. The first argument to the `Exception` constructor is the custom error message for our example, "Exception occurred in `Method3`." The second argument is the `InnerException`—the `Format-Exception` that was caught. The `StackTrace` for this new exception object reflects the point at which the exception was thrown (lines 54–55). Now `Method3` terminates, because the exception thrown in the `catch` block is not caught in the method body. Thus, control returns to the statement that invoked `Method3` in the prior method in the call stack (`Method2`). This removes, or **unwinds**, `Method3` from the method-call stack.

When control returns to line 40 in `Method2`, the CLR determines that line 40 is not in a `try` block. Therefore the exception cannot be caught in `Method2`, and `Method2` terminates. This unwinds `Method2` from the call stack and returns control to line 34 in `Method1`.

Here again, line 34 is not in a `try` block, so `Method1` cannot catch the exception. The method terminates and is unwound from the call stack, returning control to line 14 in `Main`, which *is* located in a `try` block. The `try` block in `Main` expires and the `catch` block (lines 16–28) catches the exception. The `catch` block uses properties `Message`, `StackTrace` and `InnerException` to create the output. Stack unwinding continues until a `catch` block catches the exception or the program terminates.

Displaying Information About the *Exception*

The first block of output (which we reformatted for readability) in Fig. 13.5 contains the exception's `string` representation, which is returned from an implicit call to method `To-String`. The `string` begins with the name of the exception class followed by the `Message` property value. The next four items present the stack trace of the `InnerException` object. The remainder of the block of output shows the `StackTrace` for the exception thrown in `Method3`. The `StackTrace` represents the state of the method-call stack at the throw point of the exception, rather than at the point where the exception eventually is caught. Each `StackTrace` line that begins with "`at`" represents a method on the call stack. These lines indicate the method in which the exception occurred, the file in which the method resides and the line number of the throw point in the file. The inner-exception information includes the inner-exception stack trace.

 Error-Prevention Tip 13.4
When catching and rethrowing an exception, provide additional debugging information in the rethrown exception. To do so, create an `Exception` object containing more specific debugging information, then pass the original caught exception to the new exception object's constructor to initialize the `InnerException` property.

The next block of output (two lines) simply displays the `Message` property's value (`Exception occurred in Method3`) of the exception thrown in `Method3`.

The third block of output displays the `StackTrace` property of the exception thrown in `Method3`. This `StackTrace` property contains the stack trace starting from line 54 in

`Method3`, because that's the point at which the `Exception` object was created and thrown. The stack trace always begins from the exception's throw point.

Finally, the last block of output displays the `string` representation of the `Inner-Exception` property, which includes the namespace and class name of the exception object, as well as its `Message` and `StackTrace` properties.

13.8 User-Defined Exception Classes

In many cases, you can use existing exception classes from the .NET Framework Class Library to indicate exceptions that occur in your programs. In some cases, however, you might wish to create new exception classes specific to the problems that occur in your programs. **User-defined exception classes** should derive directly or indirectly from class `Exception` of namespace `System`. When you create code that throws exceptions, they should be well documented, so that other developers who use your code will know how to handle them.

Good Programming Practice 13.1
Associating each type of malfunction with an appropriately named exception class improves program clarity.

Software Engineering Observation 13.3
Before creating a user-defined exception class, investigate the existing exceptions in the .NET Framework Class Library to determine whether an appropriate exception type already exists.

Class *NegativeNumberException*
Figures 13.6–13.7 demonstrate a user-defined exception class. `NegativeNumberException` (Fig. 13.6) represents exceptions that occur when a program performs an illegal operation on a negative number, such as attempting to calculate its square root.

```
1   // Fig. 13.6: NegativeNumberException.cs
2   // NegativeNumberException represents exceptions caused by
3   // illegal operations performed on negative numbers.
4   using System;
5
6   class NegativeNumberException : Exception
7   {
8      // default constructor
9      public NegativeNumberException()
10        : base( "Illegal operation for a negative number" )
11     {
12        // empty body
13     } // end default constructor
14
15     // constructor for customizing error message
16     public NegativeNumberFxception( string messageValue )
17        : base( messageValue )
18     {
```

Fig. 13.6 | `NegativeNumberException` represents exceptions caused by illegal operations performed on negative numbers. (Part 1 of 2.)

```
19        // empty body
20     } // end one-argument constructor
21
22     // constructor for customizing the exception's error
23     // message and specifying the InnerException object
24     public NegativeNumberException( string messageValue,
25        Exception inner )
26        : base( messageValue, inner )
27     {
28        // empty body
29     } // end two-argument constructor
30  } // end namespace SquareRootTest
```

Fig. 13.6 | NegativeNumberException represents exceptions caused by illegal operations performed on negative numbers. (Part 2 of 2.)

According to Microsoft's docuemtn on "Best Practices for Handling Exceptions" (bit.ly/ExceptionsBestPractices), user-defined exceptions should typically extend class Exception, have a class name that ends with "Exception" and define three constructors: a parameterless constructor; a constructor that receives a string argument (the error message); and a constructor that receives a string argument and an Exception argument (the error message and the inner-exception object). Defining these three constructors makes your exception class more flexible, allowing other programmers to easily use and extend it.

NegativeNumberExceptions most frequently occur during arithmetic operations, so it seems logical to derive class NegativeNumberException from class ArithmeticException. However, class ArithmeticException derives from class SystemException—the category of exceptions thrown by the CLR. Per Microsoft's best practices for exception handling, user-defined exception classes should inherit from Exception rather than SystemException. In this case, we could have used the built-in ArgumentException class, which is recommended in the best practices for invalid argument values. We create our own exception type here simply for demonstration purposes.

Class *NegativeNumberException*
Class SquareRootTest (Fig. 13.7) demonstrates our user-defined exception class. The application enables the user to input a numeric value, then invokes method SquareRoot (lines 40–48) to calculate the square root of that value. To perform this calculation, SquareRoot invokes class Math's Sqrt method, which receives a double value as its argument. Normally, if the argument is negative, method Sqrt returns NaN. In this program, we'd like to prevent the user from calculating the square root of a negative number. If the numeric value that the user enters is negative, method SquareRoot throws a NegativeNumberException (lines 44–45). Otherwise, SquareRoot invokes class Math's method Sqrt to compute the square root (line 47).

When the user inputs a value, the try statement (lines 14–34) attempts to invoke SquareRoot using the value input by the user. If the user input is not a number, a FormatException occurs, and the catch block in lines 25–29 processes the exception. If the user inputs a negative number, method SquareRoot throws a NegativeNumberException (lines 44–45); the catch block in lines 30–34 catches and handles this type of exception.

```
 1    // Fig. 13.7: SquareRootTest.cs
 2    // Demonstrating a user-defined exception class.
 3    using System;
 4
 5    class SquareRootTest
 6    {
 7       static void Main( string[] args )
 8       {
 9          bool continueLoop = true;
10
11          do
12          {
13             // catch any NegativeNumberException thrown
14             try
15             {
16                Console.Write(
17                   "Enter a value to calculate the square root of: " );
18                double inputValue = Convert.ToDouble( Console.ReadLine() );
19                double result = SquareRoot( inputValue );
20
21                Console.WriteLine( "The square root of {0} is {1:F6}\n",
22                   inputValue, result );
23                continueLoop = false;
24             } // end try
25             catch ( FormatException formatException )
26             {
27                Console.WriteLine( "\n" + formatException.Message );
28                Console.WriteLine( "Please enter a double value.\n" );
29             } // end catch
30             catch ( NegativeNumberException negativeNumberException )
31             {
32                Console.WriteLine( "\n" + negativeNumberException.Message );
33                Console.WriteLine( "Please enter a non-negative value.\n" );
34             } // end catch
35          } while ( continueLoop );
36       } // end Main
37
38       // computes square root of parameter; throws
39       // NegativeNumberException if parameter is negative
40       public static double SquareRoot( double value )
41       {
42          // if negative operand, throw NegativeNumberException
43          if ( value < 0 )
44             throw new NegativeNumberException(
45                "Square root of negative number not permitted" );
46          else
47             return Math.Sqrt( value ); // compute square root
48       } // end method SquareRoot
49    } // end class SquareRootTest
```

```
Enter a value to calculate the square root of: 30
The square root of 30 is 5.477226
```

Fig. 13.7 | Demonstrating a user-defined exception class. (Part 1 of 2.)

```
Enter a value to calculate the square root of: hello

Input string was not in a correct format.
Please enter a double value.

Enter a value to calculate the square root of: 25
The square root of 25 is 5.000000
```

```
Enter a value to calculate the square root of: -2

Square root of negative number not permitted
Please enter a non-negative value.

Enter a value to calculate the square root of: 2
The square root of 2 is 1.414214
```

Fig. 13.7 | Demonstrating a user-defined exception class. (Part 2 of 2.)

13.9 Wrap-Up

In this chapter, you learned how to use exception handling to deal with errors in an application. We demonstrated that exception handling enables you to remove error-handling code from the "main line" of the program's execution. You saw exception handling in the context of a divide-by-zero example. You learned how to use try blocks to enclose code that may throw an exception, and how to use catch blocks to deal with exceptions that may arise. We explained the termination model of exception handling, in which, after an exception is handled, program control does not return to the throw point. We discussed several important classes of the .NET Exception hierarchy, including Exception (from which user-defined exception classes are derived) and SystemException. Next you learned how to use the finally block to release resources whether or not an exception occurs, and how to throw and rethrow exceptions with the throw statement. We showed how the using statement can be used to automate the process of releasing a resource. You then learned how to obtain information about an exception using Exception properties Message, StackTrace and InnerException, and method ToString. You learned how to create your own exception classes. In the next two chapters, we present an in-depth treatment of graphical user interfaces. In these chapters and throughout the rest of the book, we use exception handling to make our examples more robust, while demonstrating new features of the language.

Graphical User Interfaces with Windows Forms: Part 1

OBJECTIVES

In this chapter you'll learn:

- Design principles of graphical user interfaces (GUIs).

- How to create graphical user interfaces.

- How to process events in response to user interactions with GUI controls.

- The namespaces that contain the classes for GUI controls and event handling.

- How to create and manipulate various controls.

- How to add descriptive ToolTips to GUI controls.

- How to process mouse and keyboard events.

14.1 Introduction

A graphical user interface (GUI) allows a user to interact visually with a program. A GUI (pronounced "GOO-ee") gives a program a distinctive "look" and "feel." Providing different applications with a consistent set of intuitive user-interface components enables users to become productive with each application faster.

> **Look-and-Feel Observation 14.1**
> *Consistent user interfaces enable a user to learn new applications more quickly because the applications have the same "look" and "feel."*

As an example of a GUI, consider Fig. 14.1, which shows a Visual C# Express Edition window containing various GUI controls. Near the top of the window, there's a menu bar containing the menus **File**, **Edit**, **View**, **Project**, **Build**, **Debug**, **Data**, **Tools**, **Window**, and **Help**. Below the menu bar is a tool bar of buttons, each with a defined task, such as creating

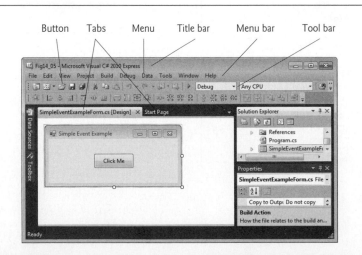

Fig. 14.1 │ GUI controls in the Visual C# IDE window.

a new project or opening an existing project. There are two tabs below the tool bar—these present information in a tabbed view and allow users to switch between them. These controls form a user-friendly interface through which you have been interacting with the IDE.

GUIs are built from GUI controls (which are sometimes called **components** or **widgets**—short for **window gadgets**). GUI controls are objects that can display information on the screen or enable users to interact with an application via the mouse, keyboard or some other form of input (such as voice commands). Several common GUI controls are listed in Fig. 14.2—in the sections that follow and in Chapter 15, we discuss each of these in detail. Chapter 15 also explores the features and properties of additional GUI controls.

Control	Description
Label	Displays images or uneditable text.
TextBox	Enables the user to enter data via the keyboard. It can also be used to display editable or uneditable text.
Button	Triggers an event when clicked with the mouse.
CheckBox	Specifies an option that can be selected (checked) or unselected (not checked).
ComboBox	Provides a drop-down list of items from which the user can make a selection either by clicking an item in the list or by typing in a box.
ListBox	Provides a list of items from which the user can make a selection by clicking one or more items.
Panel	A container in which controls can be placed and organized.
NumericUpDown	Enables the user to select from a range of numeric input values.

Fig. 14.2 | Some basic GUI controls.

14.2 Windows Forms

Windows Forms are used to create the GUIs for programs. A Form is a graphical element that appears on your computer's desktop; it can be a dialog, a window or an **MDI window** (**multiple document interface window**)—discussed in Chapter 15. A component is an instance of a class that implements the **IComponent interface**, which defines the behaviors that components must implement, such as how the component is loaded. A control, such as a Button or Label, has a graphical representation at runtime. Some components lack graphical representations (e.g., class Timer of namespace System.Windows.Forms—see Chapter 15). Such components are not visible at run time.

Figure 14.3 displays the Windows Forms controls and components from the C# **Toolbox**. The controls and components are organized into categories by functionality. Selecting the category **All Windows Forms** at the top of the **Toolbox** allows you to view all the controls and components from the other tabs in one list (as shown in Fig. 14.3). In this chapter and the next, we discuss many of these controls and components. To add a control or component to a Form, select that control or component from the **Toolbox** and drag it on the Form. To deselect a control or component, select the **Pointer** item in the **Toolbox** (the icon at the top of the list). When the **Pointer** item is selected, you cannot accidentally add a new control to the Form.

Display all controls and components

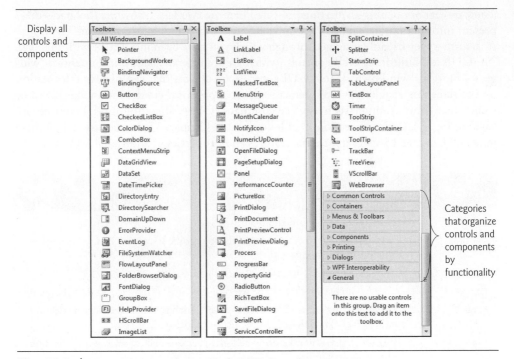

Categories that organize controls and components by functionality

Fig. 14.3 | Components and controls for Windows Forms.

When there are several windows on the screen, the **active window** is the frontmost and has a highlighted title bar. A window becomes the active window when the user clicks somewhere inside it. The active window is said to "have the **focus**." For example, in Visual Studio the active window is the **Toolbox** when you're selecting an item from it, or the **Properties** window when you're editing a control's properties.

A Form is a **container** for controls and components. When you drag items from the **Toolbox** onto the Form, Visual Studio generates code that creates the object and sets its basic properties. This code is updated when the control or component's properties are modified in the IDE. Removing a control or component from the Form deletes the corresponding generated code. The IDE maintains the generated code in a separate file using **partial classes**—classes that are split among multiple files and assembled into a single class by the compiler. We could write this code ourselves, but it's much easier to allow Visual Studio to handle the details. We introduced visual programming concepts in Chapter 2. In this chapter and the next, we use visual programming to build more substantial GUIs.

Each control or component we present in this chapter is located in namespace System.Windows.Forms. To create a Windows application, you generally create a Windows Form, set its properties, add controls to the Form, set their properties and implement event handlers (methods) that respond to events generated by the controls. Figure 14.4 lists common Form properties, methods and a common event.

When we create controls and event handlers, Visual Studio generates much of the GUI-related code. In visual programming, the IDE maintains GUI-related code and you write the bodies of the event handlers to indicate what actions the program should take when particular events occur.

Form properties, methods and an event	Description
Common Properties	
AcceptButton	Button that is clicked when *Enter* is pressed.
AutoScroll	bool value that allows or disallows scrollbars when needed.
CancelButton	Button that is clicked when the *Escape* key is pressed.
FormBorderStyle	Border style for the Form (e.g., none, single, three-dimensional).
Font	Font of text displayed on the Form, and the default font for controls added to the Form.
Text	Text in the Form's title bar.
Common Methods	
Close	Closes a Form and releases all resources, such as the memory used for the Form's contents. A closed Form cannot be reopened.
Hide	Hides a Form, but does not destroy the Form or release its resources.
Show	Displays a hidden Form.
Common Event	
Load	Occurs before a Form is displayed to the user. The handler for this event is displayed in the Visual Studio editor when you double click the Form in the Visual Studio designer.

Fig. 14.4 | Common Form properties, methods and an event.

14.3 Event Handling

Normally, a user interacts with an application's GUI to indicate the tasks that the application should perform. For example, when you write an e-mail in an e-mail application, clicking the **Send** button tells the application to send the e-mail to the specified e-mail addresses. GUIs are **event driven**. When the user interacts with a GUI component, the interaction—known as an **event**—drives the program to perform a task. Common events (user interactions) that might cause an application to perform a task include clicking a Button, typing in a TextBox, selecting an item from a menu, closing a window and moving the mouse. All GUI controls have events associated with them. Objects of other types can also have associated events as well. A method that performs a task in response to an event is called an **event handler**, and the overall process of responding to events is known as **event handling**.

14.3.1 A Simple Event-Driven GUI

The Form in the application of Fig. 14.5 contains a Button that a user can click to display a MessageBox. In line 6, notice the namespace declaration, which is inserted for every class you create. We've been removing these from earlier simple examples because they were unnecessary. Namespaces organize groups of related classes. Each class's name is actually a combination of its namespace name, a dot (.) and the class name. This is known as the class's **fully qualified class name**. You can use the class's **simple name** (the unqualified class name—SimpleEventExample) in the application. If you were to reuse this class in another application, you'd use the fully qualified name or write a using directive so that you could refer to the class by its simple name. We'll use namespaces like this in Chapters 15 and Chapters 21. If another namespace also contains a class with the same name, the fully qualified class names can be used to distinguish between the classes in the application and prevent a **name conflict** (also called a **name collision**).

```
1   // Fig. 14.5: SimpleEventExampleForm.cs
2   // Simple event handling example.
3   using System;
4   using System.Windows.Forms;
5
6   namespace SimpleEventExample
7   {
8      // Form that shows a simple event handler
9      public partial class SimpleEventExampleForm : Form
10     {
11        // default constructor
12        public SimpleEventExampleForm()
13        {
14           InitializeComponent();
15        } // end constructor
16
17        // handles click event of Button clickButton
18        private void clickButton_Click( object sender, EventArgs e )
19        {
20           MessageBox.Show( "Button was clicked." );
21        } // end method clickButton_Click
22     } // end class SimpleEventExampleForm
23  } // end namespace SimpleEventExample
```

Fig. 14.5 | Simple event-handling example.

Using the techniques presented in Chapter 2, create a Form containing a Button. First, create a new Windows application. Next, rename the Form1.cs file to SimpleEventExample.cs in the **Solution Explorer**. Click the Form in the designer, then use the **Properties** window to set the Form's Text property to "Simple Event Example". Set the Form's Font property to Segoe UI, 9pt. To do so, select the Font property in the **Properties** window, then click the ellipsis (...) button in the property's value field to display a font dialog.

Drag a Button from the **Toolbox** onto the Form. In the **Properties** window for the Button, set the (Name) property to clickButton and the Text property to Click Me. You'll notice that we use a convention in which each variable name we create for a control ends with the control's type. For example, in the variable name clickButton, "Button" is the control's type.

When the user clicks the Button in this example, we want the application to respond by displaying a MessageBox. To do this, you must create an event handler for the Button's Click event. You can create this event handler by double clicking the Button on the Form, which declares the following empty event handler in the program code:

```
private void clickButton_Click( object sender, EventArgs e )
{
}
```

By convention, the IDE names the event-handler method as *objectName_eventName* (e.g., clickButton_Click). The clickButton_Click event handler executes when the user clicks the clickButton control.

Each event handler receives two parameters when it's called. The first—an object reference typically named sender—is a reference to the object that generated the event. The second is a reference to an event arguments object of type EventArgs (or one of its derived classes), which is typically named e. This object contains additional information about the event that occurred. EventArgs is the base class of all classes that represent event information.

To display a MessageBox in response to the event, insert the statement

```
MessageBox.Show( "Button was clicked." );
```

in the event handler's body. The resulting event handler appears in lines 18–21 of Fig. 14.5. When you execute the application and click the Button, a MessageBox appears displaying the text "Button was clicked".

14.3.2 Visual Studio Generated GUI Code

Visual Studio places the auto-generated GUI code in the Designer.cs file of the Form (SimpleEventExampleForm.Designer.cs in this example). You can open this file by expanding the node in the **Solution Explorer** window for the file you're currently working in (SimpleEventExampleForm.cs) and double clicking the file name that ends with Designer.cs. Figs. 14.6 and 14.7 show this file's contents. The IDE collapses the code in lines

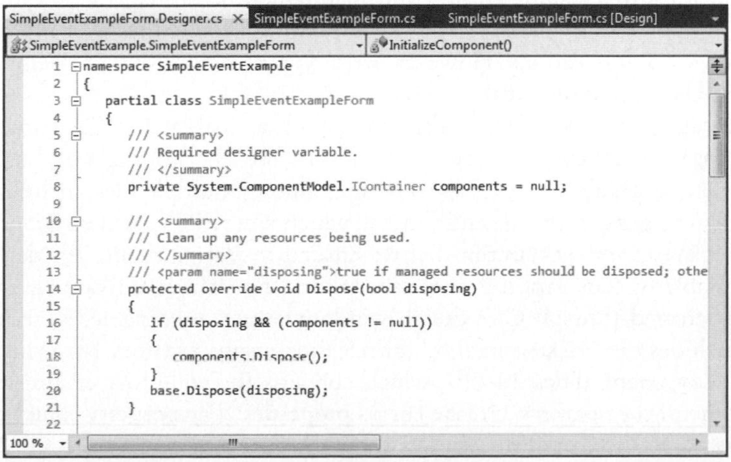

Fig. 14.6 | First half of the Visual Studio generated code file.

```
SimpleEventExampleForm.Designer.cs  X   Program.cs      SimpleEventExampleForm.cs
SimpleEventExample.SimpleEventExampleForm                     components
23         #region Windows Form Designer generated code
24
25         /// <summary>
26         /// Required method for Designer support - do not modify
27         /// the contents of this method with the code editor.
28         /// </summary>
29         private void InitializeComponent()
30         {
31             this.clickButton = new System.Windows.Forms.Button();
32             this.SuspendLayout();
33             //
34             // clickButton
35             //
36             this.clickButton.Location = new System.Drawing.Point(104, 37);
37             this.clickButton.Name = "clickButton";
38             this.clickButton.Size = new System.Drawing.Size(75, 23);
39             this.clickButton.TabIndex = 0;
40             this.clickButton.Text = "Click Me";
41             this.clickButton.UseVisualStyleBackColor = true;
42             this.clickButton.Click += new System.EventHandler(this.clickButton_Click);
43             //
44             // SimpleEventExampleForm
45             //
46             this.AutoScaleDimensions = new System.Drawing.SizeF(7F, 15F);
47             this.AutoScaleMode = System.Windows.Forms.AutoScaleMode.Font;
48             this.ClientSize = new System.Drawing.Size(282, 97);
49             this.Controls.Add(this.clickButton);
50             this.Font = new System.Drawing.Font("Segoe UI", 9F, System.Drawing.FontStyl
51             this.Name = "SimpleEventExampleForm";
52             this.Text = "Simple Event Example";
53             this.ResumeLayout(false);
54
55         }
56
57         #endregion
58
59         private System.Windows.Forms.Button clickButton;
60     }
61 }
100 %
```

Fig. 14.7 | Second half of the Visual Studio generated code file.

23–57 of Fig. 14.7 by default—you can click the + icon next to line 23 to expand the code, then click the – icon next to that line to collapse it.

Now that you have studied classes and objects in detail, this code will be easier to understand. Since this code is created and maintained by Visual Studio, you generally don't need to look at it. In fact, you do not need to understand most of the code shown here to build GUI applications. However, we now take a closer look to help you understand how GUI applications work.

The auto-generated code that defines the GUI is actually part of the Form's class—in this case, SimpleEventExample. Line 3 of Fig. 14.6 (and line 9 of Fig. 14.5) uses the partial modifier, which allows this class to be split among multiple files, including the files that contain auto-generated code and those in which you write your own code. Line 59 of Fig. 14.7 declares the clickButton that we created in **Design** mode. It's declared as an instance variable of class SimpleEventExampleForm. By default, all variable declarations for controls created through C#'s design window have a private access modifier. The code also includes the Dispose method for releasing resources (lines 14–21) and method InitializeComponent (lines 29–55), which contains the code that creates the Button, then sets some of the Button's and the Form's properties. The property values correspond to the values set in the **Properties** window for each control. Visual Studio adds comments to the code that it generates, as in lines 33–35. Line 42 was generated when we created the event handler for the Button's Click event.

Method `InitializeComponent` is called when the `Form` is created, and establishes such properties as the `Form` title, the `Form` size, control sizes and text. Visual Studio also uses the code in this method to create the GUI you see in design view. Changing the code in `InitializeComponent` may prevent Visual Studio from displaying the GUI properly.

> **Error-Prevention Tip 14.1**
>
> *The code generated by building a GUI in Design mode is not meant to be modified directly, which is why this code is placed in a separate file. Modifying this code can prevent the GUI from being displayed correctly in Design mode and might cause an application to function incorrectly. Modify control properties only through the Properties window.*

14.3.3 Delegates and the Event-Handling Mechanism

The control that generates an event is known as the **event sender**. An event-handling method—known as the event handler—responds to a particular event that a control generates. When the event occurs, the event sender calls its event handler to perform a task (i.e., to "handle the event").

The .NET event-handling mechanism allows you to choose your own names for event-handling methods. However, each event-handling method must declare the proper parameters to receive information about the event that it handles. Since you can choose your own method names, an event sender such as a `Button` cannot know in advance which method will respond to its events. So, we need a mechanism to indicate which method is the event handler for an event.

Delegates

Event handlers are connected to a control's events via special objects called **delegates**. A delegate object holds a reference to a method with a signature that is specified by the delegate type's declaration. GUI controls have predefined delegates that correspond to every event they can generate. For example, the delegate for a `Button`'s `Click` event is of type `EventHandler` (namespace `System`). If you look at this type in the online help documentation, you'll see that it's declared as follows:

```
public delegate void EventHandler( object sender, EventArgs e );
```

This uses the **delegate** keyword to declare a delegate type named `EventHandler`, which can hold references to methods that return `void` and receive two parameters—one of type `object` (the event sender) and one of type `EventArgs`. If you compare the delegate declaration with `clickButton_Click`'s header (Fig. 14.5, line 18), you'll see that this event handler indeed meets the requirements of the `EventHandler` delegate. The preceding declaration actually creates an entire class for you. The details of this special class's declaration are handled by the compiler.

Indicating the Method that a Delegate Should Call

An event sender calls a delegate object like a method. Since each event handler is declared as a delegate, the event sender can simply call the appropriate delegate when an event occurs—a `Button` calls the `EventHandler` delegate that corresponds to its `Click` event in response to a click. The delegate's job is to invoke the appropriate method. To enable the `clickButton_Click` method to be called, Visual Studio assigns `clickButton_Click` to the delegate, as shown in line 42 of Fig. 14.7. This code is added by Visual Studio when you double click the Button control in **Design** mode. The expression

```
new System.EventHandler(this.clickButton_Click);
```

creates an EventHandler delegate object and initializes it with the clickButton_Click method. Line 42 uses the += operator to add the delegate to the Button's Click event. This indicates that clickButton_Click will respond when a user clicks the Button. The += operator is overloaded by the delegate class that is created by the compiler.

You can actually specify that several different methods should be invoked in response to an event by adding other delegates to the Button's Click event with statements similar to line 42 of Fig. 14.7. Event delegates are **multicast**—they represent a set of delegate objects that all have the same signature. Multicast delegates enable several methods to be called in response to a single event. When an event occurs, the event sender calls every method referenced by the multicast delegate. This is known as **event multicasting**. Event delegates derive from class **MulticastDelegate**, which derives from class **Delegate** (both from namespace System).

14.3.4 Another Way to Create Event Handlers

For the GUI application in Fig. 14.5, you double clicked the Button control on the Form to create its event handler. This technique creates an event handler for a control's **default event**—the event that is most frequently used with that control. Controls can generate many different events, and each one can have its own event handler. For instance, your application can also provide an event handler for a Button's MouseHover event, which occurs when the mouse pointer remains positioned over the Button for a short period of time. We now discuss how to create an event handler for an event that is not a control's default event.

Using the Properties Window to Create Event Handlers
You can create additional event handlers through the **Properties** window. If you select a control on the Form, then click the **Events** icon (the lightning bolt icon in Fig. 14.8) in the **Properties** window, all the events for that control are listed in the window. You can double click an event's name to display the event handler in the editor, if the event handler already exists, or to create the event handler. You can also select an event, then use the drop-down list to its right to choose an existing method that should be used as the event handler for that event. The methods that appear in this drop-down list are the Form class's methods that have the proper signature to be an event handler for the selected event. You can return to viewing the properties of a control by selecting the **Properties** icon (Fig. 14.8).

A single method can handle multiple events from multiple controls. For example, the Click events of three Buttons could all be handled by the same method. You can specify an event handler for multiple events by selecting multiple controls and selecting a single method in the **Properties** window. If you create a new event handler this way, you should rename it appropriately. You could also select each control individually and specify the same method for each one's event.

14.3.5 Locating Event Information

Read the Visual Studio documentation to learn about the different events raised by each control. To do this, select a control in the IDE and press the *F1* key to display that control's online help (Fig. 14.9). The web page that is displayed contains basic information

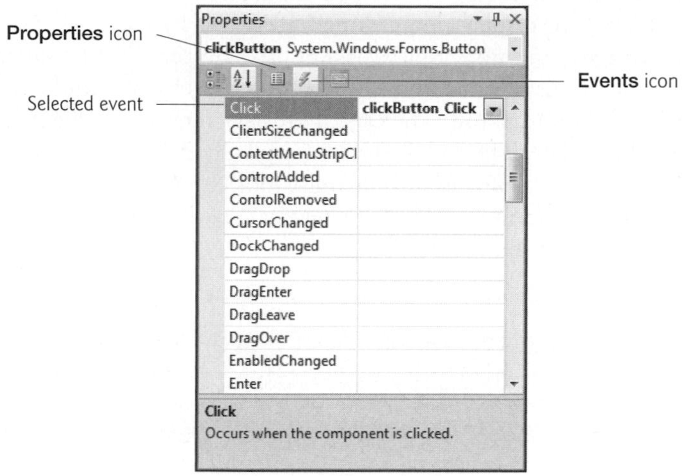

Fig. 14.8 | Viewing events for a Button control in the **Properties** window.

about the control's class. In the left column of the page are several links to more information about the class—**Members**, **Constructor**, **Methods**, **Properties** and **Events**. This list may vary by class. The **Members** link displays a complete list of the class's members. This list includes the events that the class can generate. Each of the other links displays a subset of the class's members. Click the link to the list of events for that control (**Button Events** in this case) to display the supported events for that control.

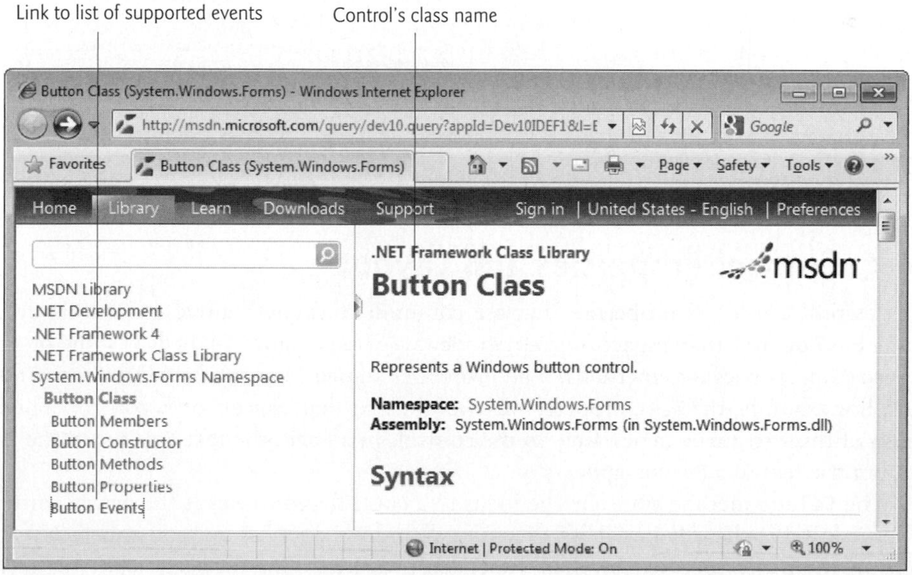

Fig. 14.9 | List of Button events.

Next, click the name of an event to view its description and examples of its use. We selected the Click event to display the information in Fig. 14.10. The Click event is a member of class Control, an indirect base class of class Button. The **Remarks** section of the page discusses the details of the selected event. Alternatively, you could use the **Object Browser** to look up this information. The **Object Browser** shows only the members originally defined in a given class. The Click event is originally defined in class Control and inherited into Button. For this reason, you must look at class Control in the **Object Browser** to see the documentation for the Click event. See Section 10.15 for more information regarding the **Object Browser.**

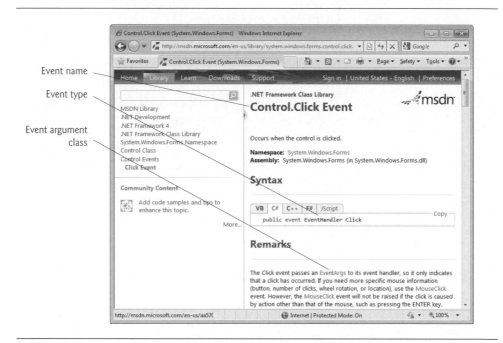

Fig. 14.10 | Click event details.

14.4 Control Properties and Layout

This section overviews properties that are common to many controls. Controls derive from class **Control** (namespace System.Windows.Forms). Figure 14.11 lists some of class Control's properties and methods. The properties shown here can be set for many controls. For example, the Text property specifies the text that appears on a control. The location of this text varies depending on the control. In a Form, the text appears in the title bar, but the text of a Button appears on its face.

The **Select** method transfers the focus to a control and makes it the **active control**. When you press the *Tab* key in an executing Windows application, controls receive the focus in the order specified by their **TabIndex** property. This property is set by Visual Studio based on the order in which controls are added to a Form, but you can change the tabbing order. TabIndex is helpful for users who enter information in many controls, such

Class `Control` properties and methods	Description
Common Properties	
`BackColor`	The control's background color.
`BackgroundImage`	The control's background image.
`Enabled`	Specifies whether the control is enabled (i.e., if the user can interact with it). Typically, portions of a disabled control appear "grayed out" as a visual indication to the user that the control is disabled.
`Focused`	Indicates whether the control has the focus.
`Font`	The `Font` used to display the control's text.
`ForeColor`	The control's foreground color. This usually determines the color of the text in the `Text` property.
`TabIndex`	The tab order of the control. When the *Tab* key is pressed, the focus transfers between controls based on the tab order. You can set this order.
`TabStop`	If `true`, then a user can give focus to this control via the *Tab* key.
`Text`	The text associated with the control. The location and appearance of the text vary depending on the type of control.
`Visible`	Indicates whether the control is visible.
Common Methods	
`Hide`	Hides the control (sets the `Visible` property to `false`).
`Select`	Acquires the focus.
`Show`	Shows the control (sets the `Visible` property to `true`).

Fig. 14.11 | Class `Control` properties and methods.

as a set of `TextBoxes` that represent a user's name, address and telephone number. The user can enter information, then quickly select the next control by pressing the *Tab* key.

The **Enabled** property indicates whether the user can interact with a control to generate an event. Often, if a control is disabled, it's because an option is unavailable to the user at that time. For example, text editor applications often disable the "paste" command until the user copies some text. In most cases, a disabled control's text appears in gray (rather than in black). You can also hide a control from the user without disabling the control by setting the `Visible` property to `false` or by calling method `Hide`. In each case, the control still exists but is not visible on the `Form`.

Anchoring and Docking
You can use anchoring and docking to specify the layout of controls inside a container (such as a `Form`). **Anchoring** causes controls to remain at a fixed distance from the sides of the container even when the container is resized. Anchoring enhances the user experience. For example, if the user expects a control to appear in a particular corner of the application, anchoring ensures that the control will always be in that corner—even if the user resizes the `Form`. **Docking** attaches a control to a container such that the control stretches

across an entire side or fills an entire area. For example, a button docked to the top of a container stretches across the entire top of that container, regardless of the width of the container.

When parent containers are resized, anchored controls are moved (and possibly resized) so that the distance from the sides to which they're anchored does not vary. By default, most controls are anchored to the top-left corner of the Form. To see the effects of anchoring a control, create a simple Windows application that contains two Buttons. Anchor one control to the right and bottom sides by setting the **Anchor** property as shown in Fig. 14.12. Leave the other control with its default anchoring (top, left). Execute the application and enlarge the Form. Notice that the Button anchored to the bottom-right corner is always the same distance from the Form's bottom-right corner (Fig. 14.13), but that the other control stays its original distance from the top-left corner of the Form.

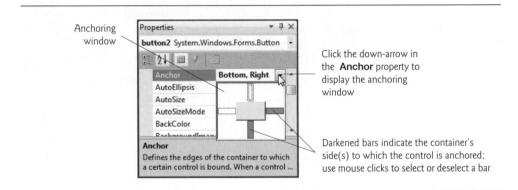

Fig. 14.12 | Manipulating the **Anchor** property of a control.

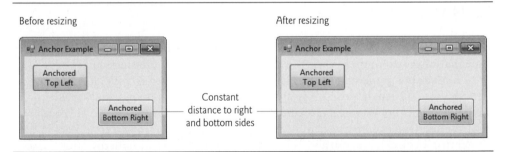

Fig. 14.13 | Anchoring demonstration.

Sometimes, it's desirable for a control to span an entire side of the Form, even when the Form is resized. For example, a control such as a status bar typically should remain at the bottom of the Form. Docking allows a control to span an entire side (left, right, top or bottom) of its parent container or to fill the entire container. When the parent control is resized, the docked control resizes as well. In Fig. 14.14, a Button is docked at the top of the Form (spanning the top portion). When the Form is resized, the Button is resized to the Form's new width. Forms have a **Padding** property that specifies the distance between the docked controls and the Form edges. This property specifies four values (one for each side), and each value is set to 0 by default. Some common control layout properties are summarized in Fig. 14.15.

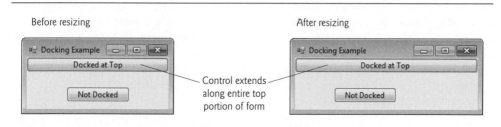

Fig. 14.14 | Docking a `Button` to the top of a `Form`.

Control layout properties	Description
Anchor	Causes a control to remain at a fixed distance from the side(s) of the container even when the container is resized.
Dock	Allows a control to span one side of its container or to fill the remaining space in the container.
Padding	Sets the space between a container's edges and docked controls. The default is 0, causing the control to appear flush with the container's sides.
Location	Specifies the location (as a set of coordinates) of the upper-left corner of the control, in relation to its container's upper-left corner.
Size	Specifies the size of the control in pixels as a `Size` object, which has properties `Width` and `Height`.
MinimumSize, MaximumSize	Indicates the minimum and maximum size of a `Control`, respectively.

Fig. 14.15 | `Control` layout properties.

The Anchor and Dock properties of a Control are set with respect to the Control's parent container, which could be a Form or another parent container (such as a Panel; discussed in Section 14.6). The minimum and maximum Form (or other Control) sizes can be set via properties **MinimumSize** and **MaximumSize**, respectively. Both are of type **Size**, which has properties **Width** and **Height** to specify the size of the Form. Properties MinimumSize and MaximumSize allow you to design the GUI layout for a given size range. The user cannot make a Form smaller than the size specified by property MinimumSize and cannot make a Form larger than the size specified by property MaximumSize. To set a Form to a fixed size (where the Form cannot be resized by the user), set its minimum and maximum size to the same value.

Look-and-Feel Observation 14.2

For resizable Forms, ensure that the GUI layout appears consistent across various Form sizes.

Using Visual Studio To Edit a GUI's Layout

Visual Studio helps you with GUI layout. When you drag a control across a Form, blue **snap lines** appear to help you position the control with respect to others (Fig. 14.16) and the Form's edges. This feature makes the control you're dragging appear to "snap into place" alongside other controls. Visual Studio also provides the **Format** menu, which contains options for modifying your GUI's layout. The **Format** menu does not appear in the IDE unless you select one or more controls in design view. When you select multiple controls, you can align them with the **Format** menu's **Align** submenu. The **Format** menu also enables you to modify the space between controls or to center a control on the Form.

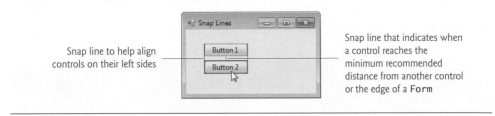

Fig. 14.16 | Snap lines for aligning controls.

14.5 Labels, TextBoxes and Buttons

Labels provide text information (as well as optional images) and are defined with class Label (a derived class of Control). A Label displays text that the user cannot directly modify. A Label's text can be changed programmatically by modifying the Label's Text property. Figure 14.17 lists common Label properties.

Common Label properties	Description
Font	The font of the text on the Label.
Text	The text on the Label.
TextAlign	The alignment of the Label's text on the control—horizontally (left, center or right) and vertically (top, middle or bottom). The default is top, left.

Fig. 14.17 | Common Label properties.

A textbox (class TextBox) is an area in which either text can be displayed by a program or the user can type text via the keyboard. A **password TextBox** is a TextBox that hides the information entered by the user. As the user types characters, the password TextBox masks the user input by displaying a password character. If you set the property **UseSystemPasswordChar** to true, the TextBox becomes a password TextBox. Users often encounter both types of TextBoxes, when logging into a computer or website—the username TextBox allows users to input their usernames; the password TextBox allows users to enter their passwords. Figure 14.18 lists the common properties and a common event of TextBoxes.

TextBox properties and an event	Description
Common Properties	
AcceptsReturn	If true in a multiline TextBox, pressing *Enter* in the TextBox creates a new line. If false (the default), pressing *Enter* is the same as pressing the default Button on the Form. The default Button is the one assigned to a Form's AcceptButton property.
Multiline	If true, the TextBox can span multiple lines. The default value is false.
ReadOnly	If true, the TextBox has a gray background, and its text cannot be edited. The default value is false.
ScrollBars	For multiline textboxes, this property indicates which scrollbars appear (None—the default, Horizontal, Vertical or Both).
Text	The TextBox's text content.
UseSystem- PasswordChar	When true, the TextBox becomes a password TextBox, and the system-specified character masks each character the user types.
Common Event	
TextChanged	Generated when the text changes in a TextBox (i.e., when the user adds or deletes characters). When you double click the TextBox control in **Design** mode, an empty event handler for this event is generated.

Fig. 14.18 | TextBox properties and an event.

A button is a control that the user clicks to trigger a specific action or to select an option in a program. As you'll see, a program can use several types of buttons, such as **checkboxes** and **radio buttons**. All the button classes derive from class **ButtonBase** (namespace System.Windows.Forms), which defines common button features. In this section, we discuss class Button, which typically enables a user to issue a command to an application. Figure 14.19 lists common properties and a common event of class Button.

Button properties and an event	Description
Common Properties	
Text	Specifies the text displayed on the Button face.
FlatStyle	Modifies a Button's appearance—attribute Flat (for the Button to display without a three-dimensional appearance), Popup (for the Button to appear flat until the user moves the mouse pointer over the Button), Standard (three-dimensional) and System, where the Button's appearance is controlled by the operating system. The default value is Standard.
Common Event	
Click	Generated when the user clicks the Button. When you double click a Button in design view, an empty event handler for this event is created.

Fig. 14.19 | Button properties and an event.

Figure 14.20 uses a TextBox, a Button and a Label. The user enters text into a password box and clicks the Button, causing the text input to be displayed in the Label. Normally, we would not display this text—the purpose of password TextBoxes is to hide the text being entered by the user. When the user clicks the **Show Me** Button, this application retrieves the text that the user typed in the password TextBox and displays it in a Label.

```csharp
 1   // Fig. 14.20: LabelTextBoxButtonTestForm.cs
 2   // Using a TextBox, Label and Button to display
 3   // the hidden text in a password TextBox.
 4   using System;
 5   using System.Windows.Forms;
 6
 7   namespace LabelTextBoxButtonTest
 8   {
 9      // Form that creates a password TextBox and
10      // a Label to display TextBox contents
11      public partial class LabelTextBoxButtonTestForm : Form
12      {
13         // default constructor
14         public LabelTextBoxButtonTestForm()
15         {
16            InitializeComponent();
17         } // end constructor
18
19         // display user input in Label
20         private void displayPasswordButton_Click(
21            object sender, EventArgs e )
22         {
23            // display the text that the user typed
24            displayPasswordLabel.Text = inputPasswordTextBox.Text;
25         } // end method displayPasswordButton_Click
26      } // end class LabelTextBoxButtonTestForm
27   } // end namespace LabelTextBoxButtonTest
```

Fig. 14.20 | Program to display hidden text in a password box.

First, create the GUI by dragging the controls (a TextBox, a Button and a Label) on the Form. Once the controls are positioned, change their names in the **Properties** window from the default values—textBox1, button1 and label1—to the more descriptive displayPasswordLabel, displayPasswordButton and inputPasswordTextBox. The (Name) property in the **Properties** window enables us to change the variable name for a control. Visual Studio creates the necessary code and places it in method InitializeComponent of the partial class in the file LabelTextBoxButtonTestForm.Designer.cs.

We set `displayPasswordButton`'s `Text` property to "Show Me" and clear the `Text` of `displayPasswordLabel` so that it's blank when the program begins executing. The `BorderStyle` property of `displayPasswordLabel` is set to `Fixed3D`, giving our `Label` a three-dimensional appearance. We also changed its `TextAlign` property to `MiddleLeft` so that the `Label`'s text is displayed centered between its top and bottom. The password character for `inputPasswordTextBox` is determined by the user's system settings when you set `UseSystemPasswordChar` to `true`. This property accepts only one character.

We create an event handler for `displayPasswordButton` by double clicking this control in **Design** mode. We added line 24 to the event handler's body. When the user clicks the **Show Me** `Button` in the executing application, line 24 obtains the text entered by the user in `inputPasswordTextBox` and displays the text in `displayPasswordLabel`.

14.6 GroupBoxes and Panels

GroupBoxes and **Panels** arrange controls on a GUI. `GroupBoxes` and `Panels` are typically used to group several controls of similar functionality or several controls that are related in a GUI. All of the controls in a `GroupBox` or `Panel` move together when the `GroupBox` or `Panel` is moved. Furthermore, a `GroupBoxes` and `Panels` can also be used to show or hide a set of controls at once. When you modify a container's `Visible` property, it toggles the visibility of all the controls within it.

The primary difference between these two controls is that `GroupBoxes` can display a caption (i.e., text) and do not include scrollbars, whereas `Panels` can include scrollbars and do not include a caption. `GroupBoxes` have thin borders by default; `Panels` can be set so that they also have borders by changing their `BorderStyle` property. Figures 14.21–14.22 list the common properties of `GroupBoxes` and `Panels`, respectively.

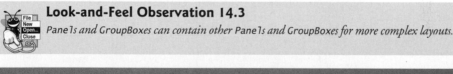

Look-and-Feel Observation 14.3

Panels and GroupBoxes can contain other Panels and GroupBoxes for more complex layouts.

GroupBox properties	Description
Controls	The set of controls that the `GroupBox` contains.
Text	Specifies the caption text displayed at the top of the `GroupBox`.

Fig. 14.21 | GroupBox properties.

Panel properties	Description
AutoScroll	Indicates whether scrollbars appear when the `Panel` is too small to display all of its controls. The default value is `false`.
BorderStyle	Sets the border of the `Panel`. The default value is `None`; other options are `Fixed3D` and `FixedSingle`.
Controls	The set of controls that the `Panel` contains.

Fig. 14.22 | Panel properties.

Look-and-Feel Observation 14.4
You can organize a GUI by anchoring and docking controls inside a GroupBox or Panel. The GroupBox or Panel then can be anchored or docked inside a Form. This divides controls into functional "groups" that can be arranged easily.

To create a GroupBox, drag its icon from the **Toolbox** onto a Form. Then, drag new controls from the **Toolbox** into the GroupBox. These controls are added to the GroupBox's **Controls** property and become part of the GroupBox. The GroupBox's Text property specifies the caption.

To create a Panel, drag its icon from the **Toolbox** onto the Form. You can then add controls directly to the Panel by dragging them from the **Toolbox** onto the Panel. To enable the scrollbars, set the Panel's AutoScroll property to true. If the Panel is resized and cannot display all of its controls, scrollbars appear (Fig. 14.23). The scrollbars can be used to view all the controls in the Panel—both at design time and at execution time. In Fig. 14.23, we set the Panel's BorderStyle property to FixedSingle so that you can see the Panel in the Form.

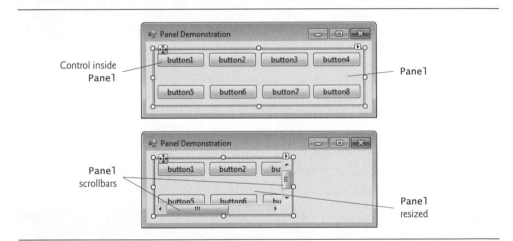

Fig. 14.23 | Creating a Panel with scrollbars.

Look-and-Feel Observation 14.5
Use Panels with scrollbars to avoid cluttering a GUI and to reduce the GUI's size.

The program in Fig. 14.24 uses a GroupBox and a Panel to arrange Buttons. When these Buttons are clicked, their event handlers change the text on a Label.

```
1   // Fig. 14.24: GroupboxPanelExampleForm.cs
2   // Using GroupBoxes and Panels to arrange Buttons.
3   using System;
4   using System.Windows.Forms;
```

Fig. 14.24 | Using GroupBoxes and Panels to arrange Buttons. (Part 1 of 2.)

```
5
6   namespace GroupBoxPanelExample
7   {
8      // Form that displays a GroupBox and a Panel
9      public partial class GroupBoxPanelExampleForm : Form
10     {
11        // default constructor
12        public GroupBoxPanelExampleForm()
13        {
14           InitializeComponent();
15        } // end constructor
16
17        // event handler for Hi Button
18        private void hiButton_Click( object sender, EventArgs e )
19        {
20           messageLabel.Text = "Hi pressed"; // change text in Label
21        } // end method hiButton_Click
22
23        // event handler for Bye Button
24        private void byeButton_Click( object sender, EventArgs e )
25        {
26           messageLabel.Text = "Bye pressed"; // change text in Label
27        } // end method byeButton_Click
28
29        // event handler for Far Left Button
30        private void leftButton_Click( object sender, EventArgs e )
31        {
32           messageLabel.Text = "Far left pressed"; // change text in Label
33        } // end method leftButton_Click
34
35        // event handler for Far Right Button
36        private void rightButton_Click( object sender, EventArgs e )
37        {
38           messageLabel.Text = "Far right pressed"; // change text in Label
39        } // end method rightButton_Click
40     } // end class GroupBoxPanelExampleForm
41  } // end namespace GroupBoxPanelExample
```

Fig. 14.24 | Using GroupBoxes and Panels to arrange Buttons. (Part 2 of 2.)

The mainGroupBox has two Buttons—hiButton (which displays the text **Hi**) and bye-Button (which displays the text **Bye**). The Panel (named mainPanel) also has two Buttons, leftButton (which displays the text **Far Left**) and rightButton (which displays the text **Far Right**). The mainPanel has its AutoScroll property set to true, allowing scrollbars to appear when the contents of the Panel require more space than the Panel's visible area. The Label (named messageLabel) is initially blank. To add controls to mainGroupBox or mainPanel, Visual Studio calls method Add of each container's Controls property. This code is placed in the partial class located in the file GroupBoxPanelExample.Designer.cs.

The event handlers for the four Buttons are located in lines 18–39. Lines 20, 26, 32 and 38 change the text of messageLabel to indicate which Button the user pressed.

14.7 CheckBoxes and RadioButtons

C# has two types of **state buttons** that can be in the on/off or true/false states—**CheckBoxes** and **RadioButtons**. Like class Button, classes CheckBox and RadioButton are derived from class ButtonBase.

CheckBoxes

A CheckBox is a small square that either is blank or contains a check mark. When the user clicks a CheckBox to select it, a check mark appears in the box. If the user clicks the CheckBox again to deselect it, the check mark is removed. You can also configure a CheckBox to toggle between three states (checked, unchecked and indeterminate) by setting its **ThreeState** property to true. Any number of CheckBoxes can be selected at a time. A list of common CheckBox properties and events appears in Fig. 14.25.

CheckBox properties and events	Description
Common Properties	
Appearance	By default, this property is set to Normal, and the CheckBox displays as a traditional checkbox. If it's set to Button, the CheckBox displays as a Button that looks pressed when the CheckBox is checked.
Checked	Indicates whether the CheckBox is checked (contains a check mark) or unchecked (blank). This property returns a bool value. The default is false (unchecked).
CheckState	Indicates whether the CheckBox is checked or unchecked with a value from the CheckState enumeration (Checked, Unchecked or Indeterminate). Indeterminate is used when it's unclear whether the state should be Checked or Unchecked. When CheckState is set to Indeterminate, the CheckBox is usually shaded.
Text	Specifies the text displayed to the right of the CheckBox.
ThreeState	When this property is true, the CheckBox has three states—checked, unchecked and indeterminate. By default, this property is false and the CheckBox has only two states—checked and unchecked.
Common Events	
CheckedChanged	Generated when the Checked property changes. This is a CheckBox's default event. When a user double clicks the CheckBox control in design view, an empty event handler for this event is generated.
CheckStateChanged	Generated when the CheckState property changes.

Fig. 14.25 | CheckBox properties and events.

The program in Fig. 14.26 allows the user to select CheckBoxes to change a Label's font style. The event handler for one CheckBox applies bold and the event handler for the other applies italic. If both CheckBoxes are selected, the font style is set to bold and italic. Initially, neither CheckBox is checked.

```
1   // Fig. 14.26: CheckBoxTestForm.cs
2   // Using CheckBoxes to toggle italic and bold styles.
3   using System;
4   using System.Drawing;
5   using System.Windows.Forms;
6
7   namespace CheckBoxTest
8   {
9      // Form contains CheckBoxes to allow the user to modify sample text
10     public partial class CheckBoxTestForm : Form
11     {
12        // default constructor
13        public CheckBoxTestForm()
14        {
15           InitializeComponent();
16        } // end constructor
17
18        // toggle the font style between bold and
19        // not bold based on the  current setting
20        private void boldCheckBox_CheckedChanged(
21           object sender, EventArgs e )
22        {
23           outputLabel.Font = new Font( outputLabel.Font,
24              outputLabel.Font.Style ^ FontStyle.Bold );
25        } // end method boldCheckBox_CheckedChanged
26
27        // toggle the font style between italic and
28        // not italic based on the current setting
29        private void italicCheckBox_CheckedChanged(
30           object sender, EventArgs e )
31        {
32           outputLabel.Font = new Font( outputLabel.Font,
33              outputLabel.Font.Style ^ FontStyle.Italic );
34        } // end method italicCheckBox_CheckedChanged
35     } // end class CheckBoxTestForm
36  } // end namespace CheckBoxTest
```

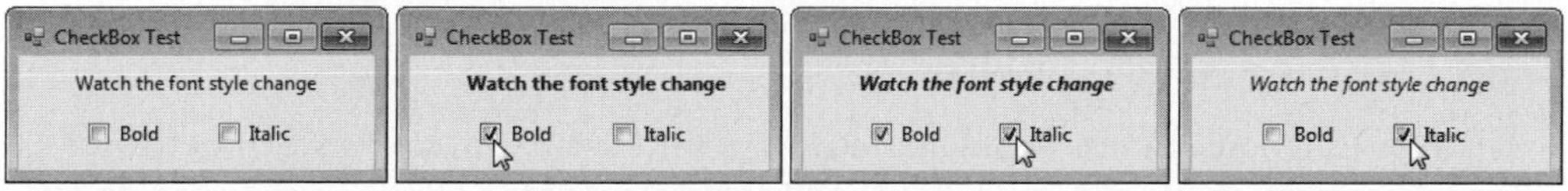

Fig. 14.26 | Using CheckBoxes to change font styles.

The boldCheckBox has its Text property set to Bold. The italicCheckBox has its Text property set to Italic. The Text property of outputLabel is set to Watch the font style change. After creating the controls, we define their event handlers. Double clicking the CheckBoxes at design time creates empty CheckedChanged event handlers.

To change a Label's font style, set its Font property to a new **Font object** (lines 23–24 and 32–33). Class Font is in the System.Drawing namespace. The Font constructor that we use here takes the current font and new style as arguments. The first argument—output-Label.Font—uses outputLabel's original font name and size. The style is specified with a member of the **FontStyle enumeration**, which contains Regular, Bold, Italic, Strikeout and Underline. (The Strikeout style displays text with a line through it.) A Font object's **Style** property is read-only, so it can be set only when the Font object is created.

Combining Font Styles with Bitwise Operators

Styles can be combined via **bitwise operators**—operators that perform manipulation on bits of information. Recall from Chapter 1 that all data is represented in the computer as combinations of 0s and 1s. Each 0 or 1 represents a bit. The FontStyle (namespace System.Drawing) is represented as a set of bits that are selected in a way that allows us to combine different FontStyle elements to create compound styles, using bitwise operators. These styles are not mutually exclusive, so we can combine different styles and remove them without affecting the combination of previous FontStyle elements. We can combine these various font styles, using either the logical OR (|) operator or the logical exclusive OR (^) operator (also called XOR). When the logical OR operator is applied to two bits, if at least one bit of the two has the value 1, then the result is 1. Combining styles using the logical OR operator works as follows. Assume that FontStyle.Bold is represented by bits 01 and that FontStyle.Italic is represented by bits 10. When we use the logical OR (|) to combine the styles, we obtain the bits 11.

```
01   =   Bold
10   =   Italic
--
11   =   Bold and Italic
```

The logical OR operator helps create style combinations. However, what happens if we want to undo a style combination, as we did in Fig. 14.26?

The logical exclusive OR operator enables us to combine styles and to undo existing style settings. When logical exclusive OR is applied to two bits, if both bits have the same value, then the result is 0. If both bits are different, then the result is 1.

Combining styles using logical exclusive OR works as follows. Assume, again, that FontStyle.Bold is represented by bits 01 and that FontStyle.Italic is represented by bits 10. When we use logical exclusive OR (^) on both styles, we obtain the bits 11.

```
01   =   Bold
10   =   Italic
--
11   =   Bold and Italic
```

Now, suppose that we would like to remove the FontStyle.Bold style from the previous combination of FontStyle.Bold and FontStyle.Italic. The easiest way to do so is to reapply the logical exclusive OR (^) operator to the compound style and FontStyle.Bold.

```
11   =   Bold and Italic
01   =   Bold
--
10   =   Italic
```

This is a simple example. The advantages of using bitwise operators to combine FontStyle values become more evident when we consider that there are five FontStyle values (Bold, Italic, Regular, Strikeout and Underline), resulting in 16 FontStyle combinations. Using bitwise operators to combine font styles greatly reduces the amount of code required to check all possible font combinations.

In Fig. 14.26, we need to set the FontStyle so that the text appears in bold if it was not bold originally, and vice versa. Line 24 uses the bitwise logical exclusive OR operator to do this. If outputLabel.Font.Style is bold, then the resulting style is not bold. If the text is originally italic, the resulting style is bold and italic, rather than just bold. The same applies for FontStyle.Italic in line 33.

If we didn't use bitwise operators to compound FontStyle elements, we'd have to test for the current style and change it accordingly. In boldCheckBox_CheckedChanged, we could test for the regular style and make it bold; test for the bold style and make it regular; test for the italic style and make it bold italic; and test for the italic bold style and make it italic. This is cumbersome because, for every new style we add, we double the number of combinations. Adding a CheckBox for underline would require testing eight additional styles. Adding a CheckBox for strikeout would require testing 16 additional styles.

RadioButtons

Radio buttons (defined with class RadioButton) are similar to CheckBoxes in that they also have two states—**selected** and **not selected** (also called **deselected**). However, RadioButtons normally appear as a **group**, in which only one RadioButton can be selected at a time. Selecting one RadioButton in the group forces all the others to be deselected. Therefore, RadioButtons are used to represent a set of **mutually exclusive** options (i.e., a set in which multiple options cannot be selected at the same time).

Look-and-Feel Observation 14.6
Use RadioButtons when the user should choose only one option in a group.

Look-and-Feel Observation 14.7
Use CheckBoxes when the user should be able to choose multiple options in a group.

All RadioButtons added to a container become part of the same group. To divide RadioButtons into several groups, they must be added to separate containers, such as GroupBoxes or Panels. The common properties and a common event of class RadioButton are listed in Fig. 14.27.

RadioButton properties and an event	Description
Common Properties	
Checked	Indicates whether the RadioButton is checked.
Text	Specifies the RadioButton's text.

Fig. 14.27 | RadioButton properties and an event. (Part 1 of 2.)

RadioButton properties and an event	Description
Common Event	
CheckedChanged	Generated every time the RadioButton is checked or unchecked. When you double click a RadioButton control in design view, an empty event handler for this event is generated.

Fig. 14.27 | RadioButton properties and an event. (Part 2 of 2.)

Software Engineering Observation 14.1

Forms, GroupBoxes, and Panels can act as logical groups for RadioButtons. The RadioButtons within each group are mutually exclusive to each other, but not to RadioButtons in different logical groups.

The program in Fig. 14.28 uses RadioButtons to enable users to select options for a MessageBox. After selecting the desired attributes, the user presses the **Display** Button to display the MessageBox. A Label in the lower-left corner shows the result of the MessageBox (i.e., which Button the user clicked—**Yes, No, Cancel**, etc.).

To store the user's choices, we create and initialize the iconType and buttonType objects (lines 13–14). Object iconType is of type MessageBoxIcon, and can have values Asterisk, Error, Exclamation, Hand, Information, None, Question, Stop and Warning. The sample output shows only Error, Exclamation, Information and Question icons.

Object buttonType is of type MessageBoxButtons, and can have values AbortRetryIgnore, OK, OKCancel, RetryCancel, YesNo and YesNoCancel. The name indicates the options that are presented to the user in the MessageBox. The sample output windows show MessageBoxes for all of the MessageBoxButtons enumeration values.

```
1   // Fig. 14.28: RadioButtonsTestForm.cs
2   // Using RadioButtons to set message window options.
3   using System;
4   using System.Windows.Forms;
5
6   namespace RadioButtonsTest
7   {
8      // Form contains several RadioButtons--user chooses one
9      // from each group to create a custom MessageBox
10     public partial class RadioButtonsTestForm : Form
11     {
12        // create variables that store the user's choice of options
13        private MessageBoxIcon iconType;
14        private MessageBoxButtons buttonType;
15
16        // default constructor
17        public RadioButtonsTestForm()
18        {
```

Fig. 14.28 | Using RadioButtons to set message-window options. (Part 1 of 4.)

```
19              InitializeComponent();
20          } // end constructor
21
22          // change Buttons based on option chosen by sender
23          private void buttonType_CheckedChanged(
24             object sender, EventArgs e )
25          {
26             if ( sender == okRadioButton ) // display OK Button
27                buttonType = MessageBoxButtons.OK;
28
29             // display OK and Cancel Buttons
30             else if ( sender == okCancelRadioButton )
31                buttonType = MessageBoxButtons.OKCancel;
32
33             // display Abort, Retry and Ignore Buttons
34             else if ( sender == abortRetryIgnoreRadioButton )
35                buttonType = MessageBoxButtons.AbortRetryIgnore;
36
37             // display Yes, No and Cancel Buttons
38             else if ( sender == yesNoCancelRadioButton )
39                buttonType = MessageBoxButtons.YesNoCancel;
40
41             // display Yes and No Buttons
42             else if ( sender == yesNoRadioButton )
43                buttonType = MessageBoxButtons.YesNo;
44
45             // only on option left--display Retry and Cancel Buttons
46             else
47                buttonType = MessageBoxButtons.RetryCancel;
48          } // end method buttonType_CheckedChanged
49
50          // change Icon based on option chosen by sender
51          private void iconType_CheckedChanged( object sender, EventArgs e )
52          {
53             if ( sender == asteriskRadioButton ) // display asterisk Icon
54                iconType = MessageBoxIcon.Asterisk;
55
56             // display error Icon
57             else if ( sender == errorRadioButton )
58                iconType = MessageBoxIcon.Error;
59
60             // display exclamation point Icon
61             else if ( sender == exclamationRadioButton )
62                iconType = MessageBoxIcon.Exclamation;
63
64             // display hand Icon
65             else if ( sender == handRadioButton )
66                iconType = MessageBoxIcon.Hand;
67
68             // display information Icon
69             else if ( sender == informationRadioButton )
70                iconType = MessageBoxIcon.Information;
```

Fig. 14.28 | Using RadioButtons to set message-window options. (Part 2 of 4.)

```
71
72          // display question mark Icon
73          else if ( sender == questionRadioButton )
74             iconType = MessageBoxIcon.Question;
75
76          // display stop Icon
77          else if ( sender == stopRadioButton )
78             iconType = MessageBoxIcon.Stop;
79
80          // only one option left--display warning Icon
81          else
82             iconType = MessageBoxIcon.Warning;
83       } // end method iconType_CheckedChanged
84
85       // display MessageBox and Button user pressed
86       private void displayButton_Click( object sender, EventArgs e )
87       {
88          // display MessageBox and store
89          // the value of the Button that was pressed
90          DialogResult result = MessageBox.Show(
91             "This is your Custom MessageBox.", "Custom MessageBox",
92             buttonType, iconType );
93
94          // check to see which Button was pressed in the MessageBox
95          // change text displayed accordingly
96          switch (result)
97          {
98             case DialogResult.OK:
99                displayLabel.Text = "OK was pressed.";
100               break;
101            case DialogResult.Cancel:
102               displayLabel.Text = "Cancel was pressed.";
103               break;
104            case DialogResult.Abort:
105               displayLabel.Text = "Abort was pressed.";
106               break;
107            case DialogResult.Retry:
108               displayLabel.Text = "Retry was pressed.";
109               break;
110            case DialogResult.Ignore:
111               displayLabel.Text = "Ignore was pressed.";
112               break;
113            case DialogResult.Yes:
114               displayLabel.Text = "Yes was pressed.";
115               break;
116            case DialogResult.No:
117               displayLabel.Text = "No was pressed.";
118               break;
119         } // end switch
120      } // end method displayButton_Click
121   } // end class RadioButtonsTestForm
122 } // end namespace RadioButtonsTest
```

Fig. 14.28 | Using RadioButtons to set message-window options. (Part 3 of 4.)

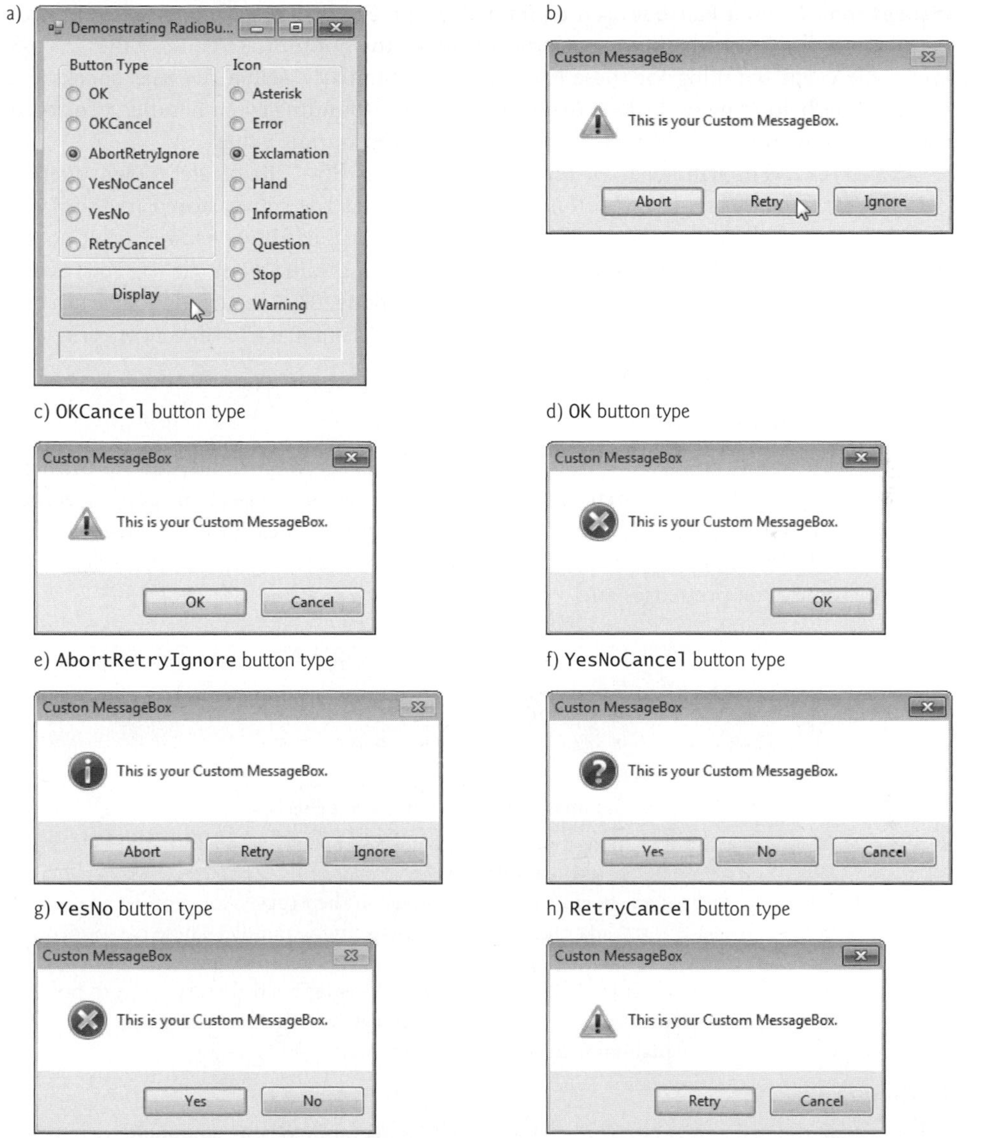

a)

b)

c) OKCancel button type

d) OK button type

e) AbortRetryIgnore button type

f) YesNoCancel button type

g) YesNo button type

h) RetryCancel button type

Fig. 14.28 | Using RadioButtons to set message-window options. (Part 4 of 4.)

We created two GroupBoxes, one for each set of enumeration values. The GroupBox captions are **Button Type** and **Icon**. The GroupBoxes contain RadioButtons for the corresponding enumeration options, and the RadioButtons' Text properties are set appropriately. Because the RadioButtons are grouped, only one RadioButton can be selected from each GroupBox. There's also a Button (displayButton) labeled **Display**. When a user clicks this Button, a customized MessageBox is displayed. A Label (displayLabel) displays which Button the user pressed within the MessageBox.

The event handler for the RadioButtons handles the CheckedChanged event of each RadioButton. When a RadioButton contained in the **Button Type** GroupBox is checked, the corresponding event handler sets buttonType to the appropriate value. Lines 23–48 contain the event handling for these RadioButtons. Similarly, when the user checks the RadioButtons belonging to the **Icon** GroupBox, the corresponding event handler associated with these events (lines 51–83) sets iconType to the appropriate value.

The Click event handler for displayButton (lines 86–120) creates a MessageBox (lines 90–93). The MessageBox options are specified with the values stored in iconType and buttonType. When the user clicks one of the MessageBox's buttons, the result of the message box is returned to the application. This result is a value from the **DialogResult enumeration** that contains Abort, Cancel, Ignore, No, None, OK, Retry or Yes. The switch statement in lines 96–119 tests for the result and sets displayLabel.Text appropriately.

14.8 PictureBoxes

A PictureBox displays an image. The image can be one of several formats, such as bitmap, GIF (Graphics Interchange Format) and JPEG. A PictureBox's Image property specifies the image that is displayed, and the SizeMode property indicates how the image is displayed (Normal, StretchImage, Autosize, CenterImage or Zoom). Figure 14.29 describes common PictureBox properties and a common event.

PictureBox properties and an event	Description
Common Properties	
Image	Sets the image to display in the PictureBox.
SizeMode	Enumeration that controls image sizing and positioning. Values are Normal (default), StretchImage, AutoSize, CenterImage, and Zoom. Normal places the image in the PictureBox's top-left corner, and CenterImage puts the image in the middle. These two options truncate the image if it's too large. StretchImage resizes the image to fit in the PictureBox. AutoSize resizes the PictureBox to hold the image. Zoom resizes the image to to fit the PictureBox but maintains the original aspect ratio.
Common Event	
Click	Occurs when the user clicks a control. When you double click this control in the designer, an event handler is generated for this event.

Fig. 14.29 | PictureBox properties and an event.

Figure 14.30 uses a PictureBox named imagePictureBox to display one of three bitmap images—image0.bmp, image1.bmp or image2.bmp. These images are provided in the Images subdirectory of this chapter's examples directory. Whenever a user clicks the **Next Image** Button, the image changes to the next image in sequence. When the last image is displayed and the user clicks the **Next Image** Button, the first image is displayed again.

```csharp
 1   // Fig. 14.30: PictureBoxTestForm.cs
 2   // Using a PictureBox to display images.
 3   using System;
 4   using System.Drawing;
 5   using System.Windows.Forms;
 6
 7   namespace PictureBoxTest
 8   {
 9      // Form to display different images when PictureBox is clicked
10      public partial class PictureBoxTestForm : Form
11      {
12         private int imageNum = -1; // determines which image is displayed
13
14         // default constructor
15         public PictureBoxTestForm()
16         {
17            InitializeComponent();
18         } // end constructor
19
20         // change image whenever Next Button is clicked
21         private void nextButton_Click( object sender, EventArgs e )
22         {
23            imageNum = ( imageNum + 1 ) % 3; // imageNum cycles from 0 to 2
24
25            // retrieve image from resources and load into PictureBox
26            imagePictureBox.Image = ( Image )
27               ( Properties.Resources.ResourceManager.GetObject(
28               string.Format( "image{0}", imageNum ) ) );
29         } // end method nextButton_Click
30      } // end class PictureBoxTestForm
31   } // end namespace PictureBoxTest
```

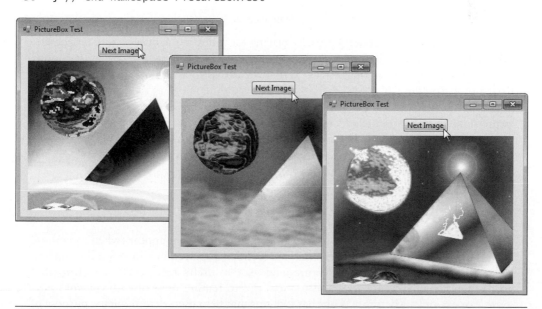

Fig. 14.30 | Using a PictureBox to display images.

Using Resources Programmatically

In this example, we added the images to the project as **resources**. This causes the compiler to embed the images in the application's executable file and enables the application to access the images through the project's Properties namespace. By embedding the images in the application, you don't need to worry about wrapping the images with the application when you move it to another location or computer.

If you're creating a new project, use the following steps to add images to the project as resources:

1. After creating your project, right click the project's **Properties** node in the **Solution Explorer** and select **Open** to display the project's properties.

2. From the tabs on the left, click the **Resources** tab.

3. At the top of the **Resources** tab, click the down arrow next to **Add Resource** and select **Add Existing File...** to display the **Add existing file to resources** dialog.

4. Locate the image files you wish to add as resources and click the **Open** button. We provided three sample images in the Images folder with this chapter's examples.

5. Save your project.

The files now appear in a folder named **Resources** in the **Solution Explorer**. We'll use this technique in most examples that use images going forward.

A project's resources are stored in its **Resources** class (of the project's Properties namespace). The Resources class contains a **ResourceManager** object for interacting with the resources programmatically. To access an image, you can use the method **GetObject**, which takes as an argument the resource name as it appears in the **Resources** tab (e.g., "image0") and returns the resource as an Object. Lines 27–28 invoke GetObject with the result of the expression

```
string.Format( "image{0}", imageNum )
```

which builds the name of the resource by placing the index of the next picture (imageNum, which was obtained earlier in line 23) at the end of the word "image". You must convert this Object to type Image (namespace System.Drawing) to assign it to the PictureBox's Image property (line 26).

The Resources class also provides direct access to the resources you define with expressions of the form Resources.*resourceName*, where *resourceName* is the name you provided to the resource when you created it. When using such an expression, the resource returned already has the appropriate type. For example, Properties.Resources.image0 is an Image object representing the first image.

14.9 ToolTips

In Chapter 2, we demonstrated tool tips—the helpful text that appears when the mouse hovers over an item in a GUI. Recall that the tool tips displayed in Visual Studio help you become familiar with the IDE's features and serve as useful reminders for each toolbar icon's functionality. Many programs use tool tips to remind users of each control's purpose. For example, Microsoft Word has tool tips that help users determine the purpose of the application's icons. This section demonstrates how to use the **ToolTip component** to add tool tips to your applications. Figure 14.31 describes common properties and a common event of class `ToolTip`.

ToolTip properties and an event	Description
Common Properties	
AutoPopDelay	The amount of time (in milliseconds) that the tool tip appears while the mouse is over a control.
InitialDelay	The amount of time (in milliseconds) that a mouse must hover over a control before a tool tip appears.
ReshowDelay	The amount of time (in milliseconds) between which two different tool tips appear (when the mouse is moved from one control to another).
Common Event	
Draw	Raised when the tool tip is displayed. This event allows programmers to modify the appearance of the tool tip.

Fig. 14.31 | `ToolTip` properties and an event.

When you add a `ToolTip` component from the **Toolbox**, it appears in the **component tray**—the gray region below the `Form` in **Design** mode. Once a `ToolTip` is added to a `Form`, a new property appears in the **Properties** window for the `Form`'s other controls. This property appears in the **Properties** window as **ToolTip on**, followed by the name of the `ToolTip` component. For instance, if our `Form`'s `ToolTip` were named `helpfulToolTip`, you would set a control's **ToolTip on helpfulToolTip** property value to specify the control's tool tip text. Figure 14.32 demonstrates the `ToolTip` component. For this example, we create a GUI containing two `Label`s, so we can demonstrate different tool tip text for each `Label`. To make the sample outputs clearer, we set the `BorderStyle` property of each `Label` to `FixedSingle`, which displays a solid border. Since there's no event-handling code in this example, we did not show the code for the `Form` class.

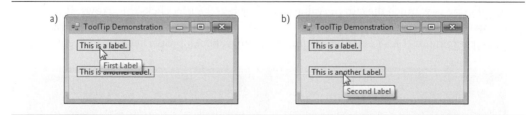

Fig. 14.32 | Demonstrating the `ToolTip` component.

In this example, we named the `ToolTip` component `labelsToolTip`. Figure 14.33 shows the `ToolTip` in the component tray. We set the tool tip text for the first `Label` to `"First Label"` and the tool tip text for the second `Label` to `"Second Label"`. Figure 14.34 demonstrates setting the tool tip text for the first `Label`.

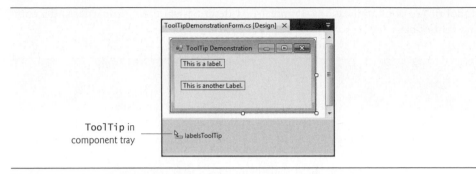

Fig. 14.33 | Demonstrating the component tray.

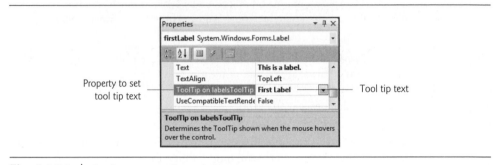

Fig. 14.34 | Setting a control's tool tip text.

14.10 NumericUpDown Control

At times, you'll want to restrict a user's input choices to a specific range of numeric values. This is the purpose of the **NumericUpDown control**. This control appears as a TextBox, with two small Buttons on the right side—one with an up arrow and one with a down arrow. By default, a user can type numeric values into this control as if it were a TextBox or click the up and down arrows to increase or decrease the value in the control, respectively. The largest and smallest values in the range are specified with the **Maximum** and **Minimum** properties, respectively (both of type decimal). The **Increment** property (also of type decimal) specifies by how much the current value changes when the user clicks the arrows. Property **DecimalPlaces** specifies the number of decimal places that the control should display as an integer. Figure 14.35 describes common NumericUpDown properties and an event.

NumericUpDown properties and an event	Description
Common Properties	
DecimalPlaces	Specifies how many decimal places to display in the control.
Increment	Specifies by how much the current number in the control changes when the user clicks the control's up and down arrows.

Fig. 14.35 | NumericUpDown properties and an event. (Part 1 of 2.)

NumericUpDown properties and an event	Description
Maximum	Largest value in the control's range.
Minimum	Smallest value in the control's range.
UpDownAlign	Modifies the alignment of the up and down Buttons on the NumericUpDown control. This property can be used to display these Buttons either to the left or to the right of the control.
Value	The numeric value currently displayed in the control.
Common Event	
ValueChanged	This event is raised when the value in the control is changed. This is the default event for the NumericUpDown control.

Fig. 14.35 | NumericUpDown properties and an event. (Part 2 of 2.)

Figure 14.36 demonstrates a NumericUpDown control in a GUI that calculates interest rate. The calculations performed in this application are similar to those in Fig. 6.6. Text-Boxes are used to input the principal and interest rate amounts, and a NumericUpDown control is used to input the number of years for which we want to calculate interest.

```
1   // Fig. 14.36: InterestCalculatorForm.cs
2   // Demonstrating the NumericUpDown control.
3   using System;
4   using System.Windows.Forms;
5
6   namespace NumericUpDownTest
7   {
8      public partial class InterestCalculatorForm : Form
9      {
10        // default constructor
11        public InterestCalculatorForm()
12        {
13           InitializeComponent();
14        } // end constructor
15
16        private void calculateButton_Click(
17           object sender, EventArgs e )
18        {
19           // declare variables to store user input
20           decimal principal; // store principal
21           double rate; // store interest rate
22           int year; // store number of years
23           decimal amount; // store amount
24           string output; // store output
25
26           // retrieve user input
27           principal = Convert.ToDecimal( principalTextBox.Text );
```

Fig. 14.36 | Demonstrating the NumericUpDown control. (Part 1 of 2.)

```
28          rate = Convert.ToDouble( interestTextBox.Text );
29          year = Convert.ToInt32( yearUpDown.Value );
30
31          // set output header
32          output = "Year\tAmount on Deposit\r\n";
33
34          // calculate amount after each year and append to output
35          for ( int yearCounter = 1; yearCounter <= year;  yearCounter++ )
36          {
37             amount =  principal * ( ( decimal )
38                Math.Pow( ( 1 + rate / 100 ), yearCounter ) );
39             output += ( yearCounter + "\t" +
40                string.Format( "{0:C}", amount ) + "\r\n" );
41          } // end for
42
43          displayTextBox.Text = output; // display result
44       } // end method calculateButton_Click
45    } // end class InterestCalculatorForm
46 } // end namespace NumericUpDownTest
```

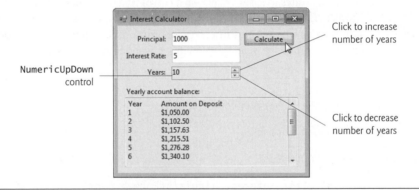

Fig. 14.36 | Demonstrating the NumericUpDown control. (Part 2 of 2.)

For the NumericUpDown control named yearUpDown, we set the Minimum property to 1 and the Maximum property to 10. We left the Increment property set to 1, its default value. These settings specify that users can enter a number of years in the range 1 to 10 in increments of 1. If we had set the Increment to 0.5, we could also input values such as 1.5 or 2.5. If you don't modify the DecimalPlaces property (0 by default), 1.5 and 2.5 display as 2 and 3, respectively. We set the NumericUpDown's **ReadOnly property** to true to indicate that the user cannot type a number into the control to make a selection. Thus, the user must click the up and down arrows to modify the value in the control. By default, the ReadOnly property is set to false, but the IDE changes this to true when you drag a NumericUpDown onto the Form. The output for this application is displayed in a multiline read-only TextBox with a vertical scrollbar, so the user can scroll through the entire output.

14.11 Mouse-Event Handling

This section explains how to handle **mouse events**, such as **clicks** and **moves**, which are generated when the user interacts with a control via the mouse. Mouse events can be handled for any control that derives from class System.Windows.Forms.Control. For most mouse events, information about the event is passed to the event-handling method through an object of class **MouseEventArgs**, and the delegate used to create the mouse-event handlers is **MouseEventHandler**. Each mouse-event-handling method for these events requires an object and a MouseEventArgs object as arguments.

Class MouseEventArgs contains information related to the mouse event, such as the mouse pointer's *x*- and *y*-coordinates, the mouse button pressed (Right, Left or Middle) and the number of times the mouse was clicked. The *x*- and *y*-coordinates of the Mouse-EventArgs object are relative to the control that generated the event—i.e., point *(0,0)* represents the upper-left corner of the control where the mouse event occurred. Several common mouse events and event arguments are described in Fig. 14.37.

Mouse events and event arguments
Mouse Events with Event Argument of Type EventArgs
MouseEnter — Occurs when the mouse cursor enters the control's boundaries.
MouseHover — Occurs when the mouse cursor hovers within the control's boundaries.
MouseLeave — Occurs when the mouse cursor leaves the control's boundaries.
Mouse Events with Event Argument of Type MouseEventArgs
MouseDown — Occurs when a mouse button is pressed while the mouse cursor is within a control's boundaries.
MouseMove — Occurs when the mouse cursor is moved while in the control's boundaries.
MouseUp — Occurs when a mouse button is released when the cursor is over the control's boundaries.
Class MouseEventArgs Properties
Button — Specifies which mouse button was pressed (Left, Right, Middle or None).
Clicks — The number of times that the mouse button was clicked.
X — The *x*-coordinate within the control where the event occurred.
Y — The *y*-coordinate within the control where the event occurred.

Fig. 14.37 | Mouse events and event arguments.

Figure 14.38 uses mouse events to draw on a Form. Whenever the user drags the mouse (i.e., moves the mouse while a mouse button is pressed), small circles appear on the Form at the position where each mouse event occurs during the drag operation.

```
1   // Fig. 14.38: PainterForm.cs
2   // Using the mouse to draw on a Form.
3   using System;
4   using System.Drawing;
5   using System.Windows.Forms;
6
7   namespace Painter
8   {
```

Fig. 14.38 | Using the mouse to draw on a Form. (Part 1 of 2.)

```
 9      // creates a Form that is a drawing surface
10      public partial class PainterForm : Form
11      {
12         bool shouldPaint = false; // determines whether to paint
13
14         // default constructor
15         public PainterForm()
16         {
17            InitializeComponent();
18         } // end constructor
19
20         // should paint when mouse button is pressed down
21         private void PainterForm_MouseDown(
22            object sender, MouseEventArgs e )
23         {
24            // indicate that user is dragging the mouse
25            shouldPaint = true;
26         } // end method PainterForm_MouseDown
27
28         // stop painting when mouse button is released
29         private void PainterForm_MouseUp( object sender, MouseEventArgs e )
30         {
31            // indicate that user released the mouse button
32            shouldPaint = false;
33         } // end method PainterForm_MouseUp
34
35         // draw circle whenever mouse moves with its button held down
36         private void PainterForm_MouseMove(
37            object sender, MouseEventArgs e )
38         {
39            if ( shouldPaint ) // check if mouse button is being pressed
40            {
41               // draw a circle where the mouse pointer is present
42               using ( Graphics graphics = CreateGraphics() )
43               {
44                  graphics.FillEllipse(
45                     new SolidBrush( Color.BlueViolet ), e.X, e.Y, 4, 4 );
46               } // end using; calls graphics.Dispose()
47            } // end if
48         } // end method PainterForm_MouseMove
49      } // end class PainterForm
50   } // end namespace Painter
```

Fig. 14.38 | Using the mouse to draw on a Form. (Part 2 of 2.)

In line 12, the program declares variable `shouldPaint`, which determines whether to draw on the `Form`. We want the program to draw only while the mouse button is pressed (i.e., held down). Thus, when the user clicks or holds down a mouse button, the system generates a `MouseDown` event, and the event handler (lines 21–26) sets `shouldPaint` to `true`. When the user releases the mouse button, the system generates a `MouseUp` event, `shouldPaint` is set to `false` in the `PainterForm_MouseUp` event handler (lines 29–33) and the program stops drawing. Unlike `MouseMove` events, which occur continuously as the user moves the mouse, the system generates a `MouseDown` event only when a mouse button is first pressed and generates a `MouseUp` event only when a mouse button is released.

Whenever the mouse moves over a control, the `MouseMove` event for that control occurs. Inside the `PainterForm_MouseMove` event handler (lines 36–48), the program draws only if `shouldPaint` is `true` (i.e., a mouse button is pressed). In the `using` statement, line 42 calls inherited `Form` method `CreateGraphics` to create a **`Graphics`** object that allows the program to draw on the `Form`. Class `Graphics` provides methods that draw various shapes. For example, lines 44–45 use method **`FillEllipse`** to draw a circle. The first parameter to method `FillEllipse` in this case is an object of class **`SolidBrush`**, which specifies the solid color that will fill the shape. The color is provided as an argument to class `SolidBrush`'s constructor. Type **`Color`** contains numerous predefined color constants—we selected `Color.BlueViolet`. `FillEllipse` draws an oval in a bounding rectangle that is specified by the *x*- and *y*-coordinates of its upper-left corner, its width and its height—the final four arguments to the method. The *x*- and *y*-coordinates represent the location of the mouse event and can be taken from the mouse-event arguments (`e.X` and `e.Y`). To draw a circle, we set the width and height of the bounding rectangle so that they're equal—in this example, both are 4 pixels. `Graphics`, `SolidBrush` and `Color` are all part of the namespace `System.Drawing`. Recall from Chapter 13 that the `using` statement automatically calls `Dispose` on the object that was created in the parentheses following keyword `using`. This is important because `Graphics` objects are a limited resource. Calling `Dispose` on a `Graphics` object ensures that its resources are returned to the system for reuse.

14.12 Keyboard-Event Handling

Key events occur when keyboard keys are pressed and released. Such events can be handled for any control that inherits from `System.Windows.Forms.Control`. There are three key events—`KeyPress`, `KeyUp` and `KeyDown`. The **`KeyPress`** event occurs when the user presses a key that represents an ASCII character. The specific key can be determined with property **`KeyChar`** of the event handler's **`KeyPressEventArgs`** argument. ASCII is a 128-character set of alphanumeric symbols, a full listing of which can be found in Appendix C.

The `KeyPress` event does not indicate whether **modifier keys** (e.g., *Shift*, *Alt* and *Ctrl*) were pressed when a key event occurred. If this information is important, the **`KeyUp`** or **`KeyDown`** events can be used. The **`KeyEventArgs`** argument for each of these events contains information about modifier keys. Figure 14.39 lists important key event information. Several properties return values from the **`Keys`** **enumeration**, which provides constants that specify the various keys on a keyboard. Like the `FontStyle` enumeration (Section 14.7), the `Keys` enumeration is represented with a set of bits, so the enumeration's constants can be combined to indicate multiple keys pressed at the same time.

Keyboard events and event arguments	
Key Events with Event Arguments of Type `KeyEventArgs`	
KeyDown	Generated when a key is initially pressed.
KeyUp	Generated when a key is released.
Key Event with Event Argument of Type `KeyPressEventArgs`	
KeyPress	Generated when a key is pressed. Raised after KeyDown and before KeyUp.
Class `KeyPressEventArgs` Properties	
KeyChar	Returns the ASCII character for the key pressed.
Class `KeyEventArgs` Properties	
Alt	Indicates whether the *Alt* key was pressed.
Control	Indicates whether the *Ctrl* key was pressed.
Shift	Indicates whether the *Shift* key was pressed.
KeyCode	Returns the key code for the key as a value from the Keys enumeration. This does not include modifier-key information. It's used to test for a specific key.
KeyData	Returns the key code for a key combined with modifier information as a Keys value. This property contains all information about the pressed key.
KeyValue	Returns the key code as an int, rather than as a value from the Keys enumeration. This property is used to obtain a numeric representation of the pressed key. The int value is known as a Windows virtual key code.
Modifiers	Returns a Keys value indicating any pressed modifier keys (*Alt*, *Ctrl* and *Shift*). This property is used to determine modifier-key information only.

Fig. 14.39 | Keyboard events and event arguments.

Figure 14.40 demonstrates the use of the key-event handlers to display a key pressed by a user. The program is a Form with two Labels that displays the pressed key on one Label and modifier key information on the other.

```
 1   // Fig. 14.40: KeyDemo.cs
 2   // Displaying information about the key the user pressed.
 3   using System;
 4   using System.Windows.Forms;
 5
 6   namespace KeyDemo
 7   {
 8      // Form to display key information when key is pressed
 9      public partial class KeyDemo : Form
10      {
11         // default constructor
12         public KeyDemo()
13         {
```

Fig. 14.40 | Demonstrating keyboard events. (Part 1 of 2.)

```
14                  InitializeComponent();
15          } // end constructor
16
17          // display the character pressed using KeyChar
18          private void KeyDemo_KeyPress(
19             object sender, KeyPressEventArgs e )
20          {
21             charLabel.Text = "Key pressed: " + e.KeyChar;
22          } // end method KeyDemo_KeyPress
23
24          // display modifier keys, key code, key data and key value
25          private void KeyDemo_KeyDown( object sender, KeyEventArgs e )
26          {
27             keyInfoLabel.Text =
28                "Alt: " + ( e.Alt ? "Yes" : "No" ) + '\n' +
29                "Shift: " + ( e.Shift ? "Yes" : "No" ) + '\n' +
30                "Ctrl: " + ( e.Control ? "Yes" : "No" ) + '\n' +
31                "KeyCode: " + e.KeyCode + '\n' +
32                "KeyData: " + e.KeyData + '\n' +
33                "KeyValue: " + e.KeyValue;
34          } // end method KeyDemo_KeyDown
35
36          // clear Labels when key released
37          private void KeyDemo_KeyUp( object sender, KeyEventArgs e )
38          {
39             charLabel.Text = "";
40             keyInfoLabel.Text = "";
41          } // end method KeyDemo_KeyUp
42       } // end class KeyDemo
43    } // end namespace KeyDemo
```

a) *H pressed*   b) *F7 pressed*   c) *$ pressed*   d) *Tab pressed*

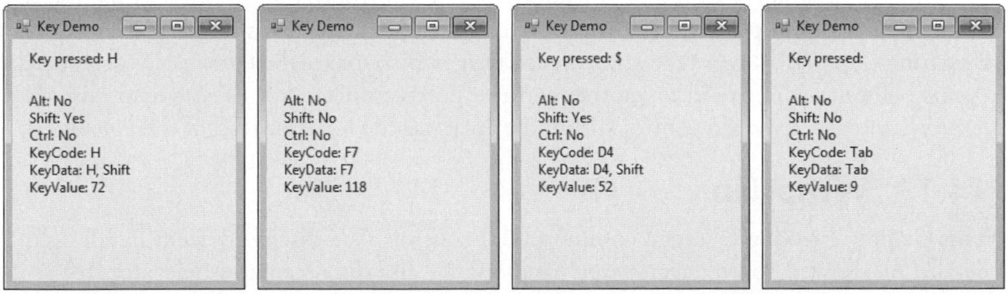

Fig. 14.40 | Demonstrating keyboard events. (Part 2 of 2.)

Control charLabel displays the character value of the key pressed, whereas keyInfo-Label displays information relating to the pressed key. Because the KeyDown and KeyPress events convey different information, the Form (KeyDemo) handles both.

The KeyPress event handler (lines 18–22) accesses the KeyChar property of the Key-PressEventArgs object. This returns the pressed key as a char, which we then display in charLabel (line 21). If the pressed key is not an ASCII character, then the KeyPress event will not occur, and charLabel will not display any text. ASCII is a common encoding format for letters, numbers, punctuation marks and other characters. It does not support keys such as the **function keys** (like *F1*) or the modifier keys (*Alt*, *Ctrl* and *Shift*).

The KeyDown event handler (lines 25–34) displays information from its KeyEventArgs object. The event handler tests for the *Alt*, *Shift* and *Ctrl* keys by using the Alt, Shift and Control properties, each of which returns a bool value—true if the corresponding key is pressed and false otherwise. The event handler then displays the KeyCode, KeyData and KeyValue properties.

The KeyCode property returns a Keys enumeration value (line 31). The KeyCode property returns the pressed key, but does not provide any information about modifier keys. Thus, both a capital and a lowercase "a" are represented as the *A* key.

The KeyData property (line 32) also returns a Keys enumeration value, but this property includes data about modifier keys. Thus, if "A" is input, the KeyData shows that both the *A* key and the *Shift* key were pressed. Lastly, KeyValue (line 33) returns an int representing a pressed key. This int is the **key code**. The key code is useful when testing for non-ASCII keys like *F12*.

The KeyUp event handler (lines 37–41) clears both Labels when the key is released. As we can see from the output, non-ASCII keys are not displayed in charLabel, because the KeyPress event is not generated. For example, charLabel does not display any text when you press the *F7* or *Tab* keys, as shown in Fig. 14.40(b) and (d). However, the KeyDown event still is generated, and keyInfoLabel displays information about the key that is pressed. The Keys enumeration can be used to test for specific keys by comparing the key pressed to a specific KeyCode.

> ### Software Engineering Observation 14.2
> *To cause a control to react when a particular key is pressed (such as* Enter*), handle a key event and test for the pressed key. To cause a* Button *to be clicked when the* Enter *key is pressed on a* Form*, set the* Form's AcceptButton *property.*

By default, a keyboard event is handled by the control that currently has the focus. Sometimes it's appropriate to have the Form handle these events. This can be accomplished by setting the Form's KeyPreview property to true, which makes the Form receive keyboard events before they're passed to another control. For example, a key press would raise the Form's KeyPress, even if a control within the Form has the focus instead of the Form itself.

14.13 Wrap-Up

This chapter introduced several common GUI controls. We discussed event handling in detail, and showed how to create event handlers. We also discussed how delegates are used to connect event handlers to the events of specific controls. You learned how to use a control's properties and Visual Studio to specify the layout of your GUI. We then demonstrated several controls, beginning with Labels, Buttons and TextBoxes. You learned how to use GroupBoxes and Panels to organize other controls. We then demonstrated CheckBoxes and RadioButtons, which are state buttons that allow users to select among several options. We displayed images in PictureBox controls, displayed helpful text on a GUI with ToolTip components and specified a range of numeric input values for users with a NumericUpDown control. We then demonstrated how to handle mouse and keyboard events. The next chapter introduces additional GUI controls. You'll learn how to add menus to your GUIs and create Windows applications that display multiple Forms.

Graphical User
Interfaces with
Windows Forms: Part 2

*I claim not to have
controlled events, but
confess plainly that events
have controlled me.*
—Abraham Lincoln

Capture its reality in paint!
—Paul Cézanne

*An actor entering through
the door, you've got nothing.
But if he enters through the
window, you've got a
situation.*
—Billy Wilder

*But, soft! what light
through yonder window
breaks?
It is the east, and Juliet is
the sun!*
—William Shakespeare

OBJECTIVES

In this chapter you'll learn:

- To create menus, tabbed windows and multiple
  document interface (MDI) programs.

- To use the `ListView` and `TreeView` controls for
  displaying information.

- To create hyperlinks using the `LinkLabel` control.

- To display lists of information in `ListBox` and
  `ComboBox` controls.

- To input date and time data with the
  `DateTimePicker`.

- To create custom controls.

15.1 Introduction

This chapter continues our study of GUIs. We start with menus, which present users with logically organized commands (or options). We show how to develop menus with the tools provided by Visual Studio. Next, we discuss how to input and display dates and times using the MonthCalendar and DateTimePicker controls. We also introduce LinkLabels—powerful GUI components that enable the user to access one of several destinations, such as a file on the current machine or a web page, by simply clicking the mouse.

We demonstrate how to manipulate a list of values via a ListBox and how to combine several checkboxes in a CheckedListBox. We also create drop-down lists using ComboBoxes and display data hierarchically with a TreeView control. You'll learn two other important GUI elements—tab controls and multiple document interface (MDI) windows. These components enable you to create real-world programs with sophisticated GUIs.

Visual Studio provides many GUI components, several of which are discussed in this (and the previous) chapter. You can also design custom controls and add them to the **ToolBox**, as we demonstrate in this chapter's last example. The techniques presented here form the groundwork for creating more substantial GUIs and custom controls.

15.2 Menus

Menus provide groups of related commands for Windows applications. Although these commands depend on the program, some—such as **Open** and **Save**—are common to many applications. Menus are an integral part of GUIs, because they organize commands without "cluttering" the GUI.

In Fig. 15.1, an expanded menu from the Visual C# IDE lists various commands (called **menu items**), plus **submenus** (menus within a menu). The top-level menus appear in the left portion of the figure, whereas any submenus or menu items are displayed to the right. The menu that contains a menu item is called that menu item's **parent menu**. A menu item that contains a submenu is considered to be the parent of that submenu.

Menus can have *Alt* key shortcuts (also called **access shortcuts**, **keyboard shortcuts** or **hotkeys**), which are accessed by pressing *Alt* and the underlined letter—for example, *Alt F* typically expands the **File** menu. Menu items can have shortcut keys as well (combinations of *Ctrl, Shift, Alt, F1, F2,* letter keys, and so on). Some menu items display checkmarks, usually indicating that multiple options on the menu can be selected at once.

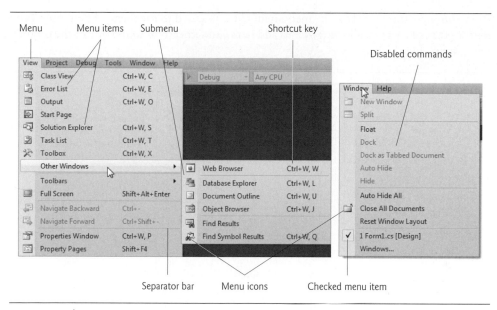

Fig. 15.1 | Menus, submenus and menu items.

To create a menu, open the **Toolbox** and drag a **MenuStrip** control onto the Form. This creates a menu bar across the top of the Form (below the title bar) and places a MenuStrip icon in the component tray. To select the MenuStrip, click this icon. You can now use **Design** mode to create and edit menus for your application. Menus, like other controls, have properties and events, which can be accessed through the **Properties** window.

To add menu items to the menu, click the **Type Here** TextBox (Fig. 15.2) and type the menu item's name. This action adds an entry to the menu of type **ToolStripMenuItem**.

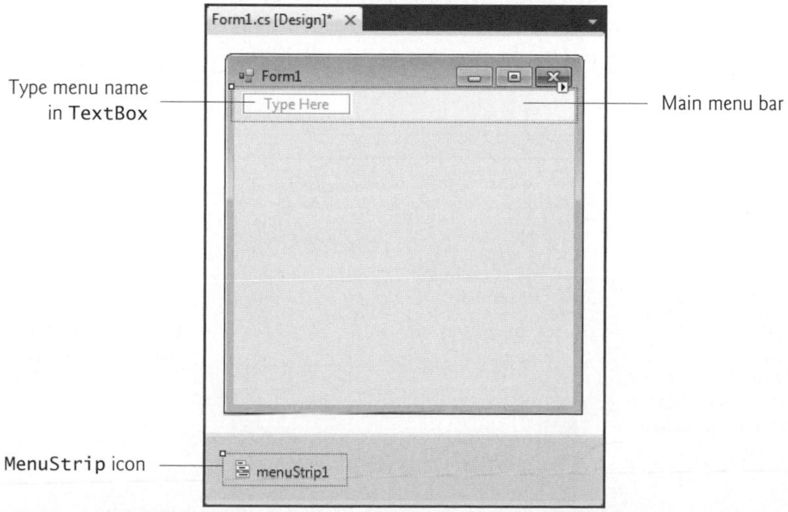

Fig. 15.2 | Editing menus in Visual Studio.

After you press the *Enter* key, the menu item name is added to the menu. Then more **Type Here** TextBoxes appear, allowing you to add items underneath or to the side of the original menu item (Fig. 15.3).

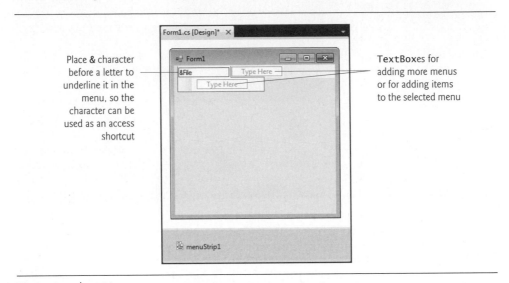

Place & character before a letter to underline it in the menu, so the character can be used as an access shortcut

TextBoxes for adding more menus or for adding items to the selected menu

Fig. 15.3 | Adding ToolStripMenuItems to a MenuStrip.

To create an access shortcut, type an ampersand (&) before the character to be underlined. For example, to create the **File** menu item with the letter **F** underlined, type &File. To display an ampersand, type &&. To add other shortcut keys (e.g., *<Ctrl> F9*) for menu items, set the **ShortcutKeys** property of the appropriate ToolStripMenuItems. To do this, select the down arrow to the right of this property in the **Properties** window. In the window that appears (Fig. 15.4), use the CheckBoxes and drop-down list to select the shortcut keys. When you are finished, click elsewhere on the screen. You can hide the shortcut keys by setting property **ShowShortcutKeys** to false, and you can modify how the shortcut keys are displayed in the menu item by modifying property **ShortcutKeyDisplayString**.

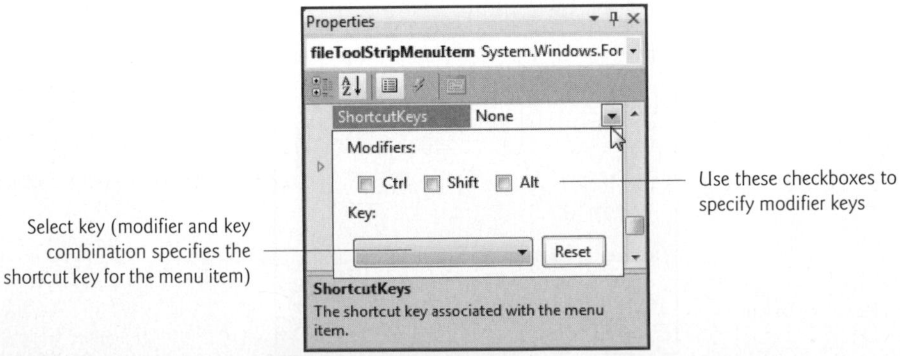

Select key (modifier and key combination specifies the shortcut key for the menu item)

Use these checkboxes to specify modifier keys

Fig. 15.4 | Setting a menu item's shortcut keys.

Look-and-Feel Observation 15.1

Buttons can have access shortcuts. Place the & symbol immediately before the desired character in the Button's text. To press the button by using its access key in the running application, the user presses Alt and the underlined character. If the underline is not visible when the application runs, press the Alt key to display the underlines.

You can remove a menu item by selecting it with the mouse and pressing the *Delete* key. Menu items can be grouped logically by **separator bars**, which are inserted by right clicking the menu and selecting **Insert > Separator** or by typing "-" for the text of a menu item.

In addition to text, Visual Studio allows you to easily add `TextBox`es and `ComboBox`es (drop-down lists) as menu items. When adding an item in **Design** mode, you may have noticed that before you enter text for a new item, you are provided with a drop-down list. Clicking the down arrow (Fig. 15.5) allows you to select the type of item to add—**MenuItem** (of type `ToolStripMenuItem`, the default), **ComboBox** (of type `ToolStripComboBox`) and **TextBox** (of type `ToolStripTextBox`). We focus on `ToolStripMenuItems`. [*Note:* If you view this drop-down list for menu items that are not on the top level, a fourth option appears, allowing you to insert a separator bar.]

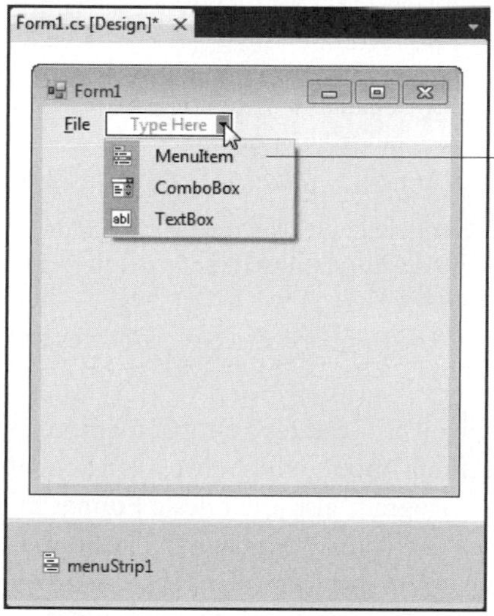

Fig. 15.5 | Menu-item options.

`ToolStripMenuItems` generate a **Click** event when selected. To create an empty **Click** event handler, double click the menu item in **Design** mode. Common actions in response to these events include displaying dialogs and setting properties. Common menu properties and a common event are summarized in Fig. 15.6.

Look-and-Feel Observation 15.2

*It is a convention to place an ellipsis (…) after the name of a menu item (e.g., **Save As…**) that requires the user to provide more information—typically through a dialog. A menu item that produces an immediate action without prompting the user for more information (e.g., **Save**) should not have an ellipsis following its name.*

MenuStrip and ToolStripMenuItem properties and an event	Description
MenuStrip Properties	
RightToLeft	Causes text to display from right to left. This is useful for languages that are read from right to left.
ToolStripMenuItem Properties	
Checked	Indicates whether a menu item is checked. The default value is false, meaning that the menu item is unchecked.
CheckOnClick	Indicates that a menu item should appear checked or unchecked as it is clicked.
ShortcutKey-DisplayString	Specifies text that should appear beside a menu item for a shortcut key. If left blank, the key names are displayed. Otherwise, the text in this property is displayed for the shortcut key.
ShortcutKeys	Specifies the shortcut key for the menu item (e.g., *<Ctrl>-F9* is equivalent to clicking a specific item).
ShowShortcutKeys	Indicates whether a shortcut key is shown beside menu item text. The default is true, which displays the shortcut key.
Text	Specifies the menu item's text. To create an *Alt* access shortcut, precede a character with & (e.g., &File to specify a menu named **File** with the letter **F** underlined).
Common ToolStripMenuItem Event	
Click	Generated when an item is clicked or a shortcut key is used. This is the default event when the menu is double clicked in the designer.

Fig. 15.6 | MenuStrip and ToolStripMenuItem properties and an event.

Class MenuTestForm (Fig. 15.7) creates a simple menu on a Form. The Form has a top-level **File** menu with menu items **About** (which displays a MessageBox) and **Exit** (which terminates the program). The program also includes a **Format** menu, which contains menu items that change the format of the text on a Label. The **Format** menu has submenus **Color** and **Font**, which change the color and font of the text on a Label.

Create the GUI
To create this GUI, begin by dragging the MenuStrip from the **ToolBox** onto the Form. Then use **Design** mode to create the menu structure shown in the sample outputs. The **File** menu (fileToolStripMenuItem) has menu items **About** (aboutToolStripMenuItem) and **Exit** (exitToolStripMenuItem); the **Format** menu (formatToolStripMenuItem) has two submenus. The first submenu, **Color** (colorToolStripMenuItem), contains menu items **Black** (blackToolStripMenuItem), **Blue** (blueToolStripMenuItem), **Red** (redToolStrip-MenuItem) and **Green** (greenToolStripMenuItem). The second submenu, **Font** (fontTool-StripMenuItem), contains menu items **Times New Roman** (timesToolStripMenuItem), **Courier** (courierToolStripMenuItem), **Comic Sans** (comicToolStripMenuItem), a separator bar (dashToolStripMenuItem), **Bold** (boldToolStripMenuItem) and **Italic** (italic-ToolStripMenuItem).

```
 1   // Fig. 15.7: MenuTestForm.cs
 2   // Using Menus to change font colors and styles.
 3   using System;
 4   using System.Drawing;
 5   using System.Windows.Forms;
 6
 7   namespace MenuTest
 8   {
 9      // our Form contains a Menu that changes the font color
10      // and style of the text displayed in Label
11      public partial class MenuTestForm : Form
12      {
13         // constructor
14         public MenuTestForm()
15         {
16            InitializeComponent();
17         } // end constructor
18
19         // display MessageBox when About ToolStripMenuItem is selected
20         private void aboutToolStripMenuItem_Click(
21            object sender, EventArgs e )
22         {
23            MessageBox.Show( "This is an example\nof using menus.", "About",
24               MessageBoxButtons.OK, MessageBoxIcon.Information );
25         } // end method aboutToolStripMenuItem_Click
26
27         // exit program when Exit ToolStripMenuItem is selected
28         private void exitToolStripMenuItem_Click(
29            object sender, EventArgs e )
30         {
31            Application.Exit();
32         } // end method exitToolStripMenuItem_Click
33
34         // reset checkmarks for Color ToolStripMenuItems
35         private void ClearColor()
36         {
37            // clear all checkmarks
38            blackToolStripMenuItem.Checked = false;
39            blueToolStripMenuItem.Checked = false;
40            redToolStripMenuItem.Checked = false;
41            greenToolStripMenuItem.Checked = false;
42         } // end method ClearColor
43
44         // update Menu state and color display black
45         private void blackToolStripMenuItem_Click(
46            object sender, EventArgs e )
47         {
48            // reset checkmarks for Color ToolStripMenuItems
49            ClearColor();
50
51            // set color to Black
52            displayLabel.ForeColor = Color.Black;
```

Fig. 15.7 | Menus for changing text font and color. (Part 1 of 4.)

```
53              blackToolStripMenuItem.Checked = true;
54          } // end method blackToolStripMenuItem_Click
55
56          // update Menu state and color display blue
57          private void blueToolStripMenuItem_Click(
58              object sender, EventArgs e )
59          {
60              // reset checkmarks for Color ToolStripMenuItems
61              ClearColor();
62
63              // set color to Blue
64              displayLabel.ForeColor = Color.Blue;
65              blueToolStripMenuItem.Checked = true;
66          } // end method blueToolStripMenuItem_Click
67
68          // update Menu state and color display red
69          private void redToolStripMenuItem_Click(
70              object sender, EventArgs e )
71          {
72              // reset checkmarks for Color ToolStripMenuItems
73              ClearColor();
74
75              // set color to Red
76              displayLabel.ForeColor = Color.Red;
77              redToolStripMenuItem.Checked = true;
78          } // end method redToolStripMenuItem_Click
79
80          // update Menu state and color display green
81          private void greenToolStripMenuItem_Click(
82              object sender, EventArgs e )
83          {
84              // reset checkmarks for Color ToolStripMenuItems
85              ClearColor();
86
87              // set color to Green
88              displayLabel.ForeColor = Color.Green;
89              greenToolStripMenuItem.Checked = true;
90          } // end method greenToolStripMenuItem_Click
91
92          // reset checkmarks for Font ToolStripMenuItems
93          private void ClearFont()
94          {
95              // clear all checkmarks
96              timesToolStripMenuItem.Checked = false;
97              courierToolStripMenuItem.Checked = false;
98              comicToolStripMenuItem.Checked = false;
99          } // end method ClearFont
100
101         // update Menu state and set Font to Times New Roman
102         private void timesToolStripMenuItem_Click(
103             object sender, EventArgs e )
104         {
105             // reset checkmarks for Font ToolStripMenuItems
```

Fig. 15.7 | Menus for changing text font and color. (Part 2 of 4.)

```
106            ClearFont();
107
108            // set Times New Roman font
109            timesToolStripMenuItem.Checked = true;
110            displayLabel.Font = new Font( "Times New Roman", 14,
111               displayLabel.Font.Style );
112         } // end method timesToolStripMenuItem_Click
113
114         // update Menu state and set Font to Courier
115         private void courierToolStripMenuItem_Click(
116            object sender, EventArgs e )
117         {
118            // reset checkmarks for Font ToolStripMenuItems
119            ClearFont();
120
121            // set Courier font
122            courierToolStripMenuItem.Checked = true;
123            displayLabel.Font = new Font( "Courier", 14,
124               displayLabel.Font.Style );
125         } // end method courierToolStripMenuItem_Click
126
127         // update Menu state and set Font to Comic Sans MS
128         private void comicToolStripMenuItem_Click(
129            object sender, EventArgs e )
130         {
131            // reset checkmarks for Font ToolStripMenuItems
132            ClearFont();
133
134            // set Comic Sans font
135            comicToolStripMenuItem.Checked = true;
136            displayLabel.Font = new Font( "Comic Sans MS", 14,
137               displayLabel.Font.Style );
138         } // end method comicToolStripMenuItem_Click
139
140         // toggle checkmark and toggle bold style
141         private void boldToolStripMenuItem_Click(
142            object sender, EventArgs e )
143         {
144            // toggle checkmark
145            boldToolStripMenuItem.Checked = !boldToolStripMenuItem.Checked;
146
147            // use Xor to toggle bold, keep all other styles
148            displayLabel.Font = new Font( displayLabel.Font
149               displayLabel.Font.Style ^ FontStyle.Bold );
150         } // end method boldToolStripMenuItem_Click
151
152         // toggle checkmark and toggle italic style
153         private void italicToolStripMenuItem_Click(
154            object sender, EventArgs e )
155         {
156            // toggle checkmark
157            italicToolStripMenuItem.Checked =
158               !italicToolStripMenuItem.Checked;
```

Fig. 15.7 | Menus for changing text font and color. (Part 3 of 4.)

```
159
160              // use Xor to toggle italic, keep all other styles
161              displayLabel.Font = new Font( displayLabel.Font
162                 displayLabel.Font.Style ^ FontStyle.Italic );
163          } // end method italicToolStripMenuItem_Click
164       } // end class MenuTestForm
165    } // end namespace MenuTest
```

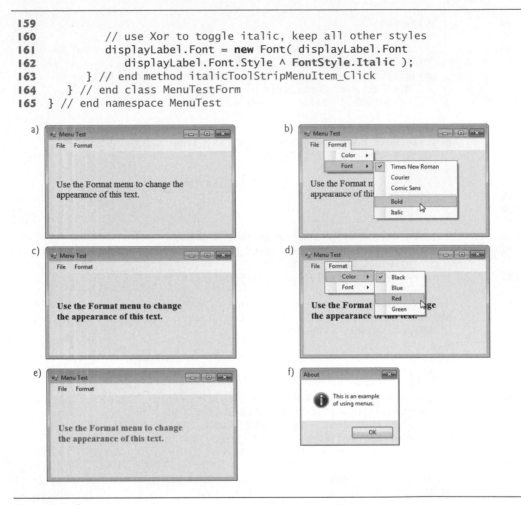

Fig. 15.7 | Menus for changing text font and color. (Part 4 of 4.)

Handling the *Click Events for the* About *and* Exit *Menu Items*

The **About** menu item in the **File** menu displays a MessageBox when clicked (lines 20–25). The **Exit** menu item closes the application through static method **Exit** of class **Application** (line 31). Class Application's static methods control program execution. Method Exit causes our application to terminate.

Color *Submenu Events*

We made the items in the **Color** submenu (**Black**, **Blue**, **Red** and **Green**) mutually exclusive—the user can select only one at a time (we explain how we did this shortly). To indicate that a menu item is selected, we will set each **Color** menu item's **Checked** property to true. This causes a check to appear to the left of a menu item.

Each **Color** menu item has its own Click event handler. The method handler for color **Black** is blackToolStripMenuItem_Click (lines 45–54). Similarly, the event handlers for colors **Blue**, **Red** and **Green** are `blueToolStripMenuItem_Click` (lines 57–66), `redTool-StripMenuItem_Click` (lines 69–78) and `greenToolStripMenuItem_Click` (lines 81–90), respectively. Each **Color** menu item must be mutually exclusive, so each event handler calls method `ClearColor` (lines 35–42) before setting its corresponding `Checked` property to `true`. Method `ClearColor` sets the `Checked` property of each color `ToolStripMenuItem` to `false`, effectively preventing more than one menu item from being selected at a time. In the designer, we initially set the **Black** menu item's `Checked` property to `true`, because at the start of the program, the text on the `Form` is black.

Software Engineering Observation 15.1

The mutual exclusion of menu items is not enforced by the MenuStrip, *even when the* Checked *property is* true. *You must program this behavior.*

Font Submenu Events

The **Font** menu contains three menu items for fonts (**Courier**, **Times New Roman** and **Comic Sans**) and two menu items for font styles (**Bold** and **Italic**). We added a separator bar between the font and font-style menu items to indicate that these are separate options. A `Font` object can specify only one font at a time but can set multiple styles at once (e.g., a font can be both bold and italic). We set the font menu items to display checks. As with the **Color** menu, we must enforce mutual exclusion of these items in our event handlers.

Event handlers for font menu items **Times New Roman**, **Courier** and **Comic Sans** are `timesToolStripMenuItem_Click` (lines 102–112), `courierToolStripMenuItem_Click` (lines 115–125) and `comicToolStripMenuItem_Click` (lines 128–138), respectively. These event handlers behave in a manner similar to that of the event handlers for the **Color** menu items. Each event handler clears the `Checked` properties for all font menu items by calling method `ClearFont` (lines 93–99), then sets the `Checked` property of the menu item that raised the event to `true`. This enforces the mutual exclusion of the font menu items. In the designer, we initially set the **Times New Roman** menu item's `Checked` property to `true`, because this is the original font for the text on the `Form`. The event handlers for the **Bold** and **Italic** menu items (lines 141–163) use the bitwise logical exclusive OR (∧) operator to combine font styles, as we discussed in Chapter 14.

15.3 MonthCalendar Control

Many applications must perform date and time calculations. The .NET Framework provides two controls that allow an application to retrieve date and time information—the `MonthCalendar` and `DateTimePicker` (Section 15.4) controls.

The **MonthCalendar** (Fig. 15.8) control displays a monthly calendar on the `Form`. The user can select a date from the currently displayed month or can use the provided arrows to navigate to another month. When a date is selected, it is highlighted. Multiple dates can be selected by clicking dates on the calendar while holding down the *Shift* key. The default event for this control is the **DateChanged** event, which is generated when a new date is selected. Properties are provided that allow you to modify the appearance of the calendar, how many dates can be selected at once, and the minimum date and maximum date that may be selected. `MonthCalendar` properties and a common `MonthCalendar` event are summarized in Fig. 15.9.

Current day is outlined

Selected day is highlighted

Fig. 15.8 | MonthCalendar control.

MonthCalendar properties and an event	Description
MonthCalendar Properties	
FirstDayOfWeek	Sets which day of the week is the first displayed for each week in the calendar.
MaxDate	The last date that can be selected.
MaxSelectionCount	The maximum number of dates that can be selected at once.
MinDate	The first date that can be selected.
MonthlyBoldedDates	An array of dates that will displayed in bold in the calendar.
SelectionEnd	The last of the dates selected by the user.
SelectionRange	The dates selected by the user.
SelectionStart	The first of the dates selected by the user.
Common MonthCalendar Event	
DateChanged	Generated when a date is selected in the calendar.

Fig. 15.9 | MonthCalendar properties and an event.

15.4 DateTimePicker Control

The **DateTimePicker** control (see output of Fig. 15.11) is similar to the MonthCalendar control but displays the calendar when a down arrow is selected. The DateTimePicker can be used to retrieve date and time information from the user. A DateTimePicker's **Value** property stores a DateTime object, which always contains both date and time information. You can retrieve the date information from the DateTime object by using property **Date**, and you can retrieve only the time information by using the **TimeOfDay** property.

The DateTimePicker is also more customizable than a MonthCalendar control— more properties are provided to edit the look and feel of the drop-down calendar. Property **Format** specifies the user's selection options using the **DateTimePickerFormat** enumeration. The values in this enumeration are Long (displays the date in long format, as in **Thursday, July 10, 2010**), Short (displays the date in short format, as in **7/10/2010**), Time (displays a time value, as in **5:31:02 PM**) and Custom (indicates that a custom format will be used). If value Custom is used, the display in the DateTimePicker is specified using property **CustomFormat**. The default event for this control is **ValueChanged**, which occurs when the selected value (whether a date or a time) is changed. DateTimePicker properties and a common event are summarized in Fig. 15.10.

DateTimePicker properties and an event	Description
DateTimePicker Properties	
CalendarForeColor	Sets the text color for the calendar.
CalendarMonth-Background	Sets the calendar's background color.
CustomFormat	Sets the custom format string for the user's options.
Format	Sets the format of the date and/or time used for the user's options.
MaxDate	The maximum date and time that can be selected.
MinDate	The minimum date and time that can be selected.
ShowCheckBox	Indicates if a CheckBox should be displayed to the left of the selected date and time.
ShowUpDown	Indicates whether the control displays up and down Buttons. Helpful when the DateTimePicker is used to select a time—the Buttons can be used to increase or decrease hour, minute and second.
Value	The data selected by the user.
Common DateTimePicker Event	
ValueChanged	Generated when the Value property changes, including when the user selects a new date or time.

Fig. 15.10 | DateTimePicker properties and an event.

Figure 15.11 demonstrates using a DateTimePicker to select an item's drop-off time. Many companies use such functionality—several online DVD rental companies specify the day a movie is sent out and the estimated time that it will arrive at your home. The user selects a drop-off day, then an estimated arrival date is displayed. The date is always two days after drop-off, three days if a Sunday is reached (mail is not delivered on Sunday).

```
1   // Fig. 15.11: DateTimePickerForm.cs
2   // Using a DateTimePicker to select a drop-off time.
3   using System;
4   using System.Windows.Forms;
5
6   namespace DateTimePickerTest
7   {
```

Fig. 15.11 | Demonstrating DateTimePicker. (Part 1 of 3.)

```
 8      // Form lets user select a drop-off date using a DateTimePicker
 9      // and displays an estimated delivery date
10      public partial class DateTimePickerForm : Form
11      {
12         // constructor
13         public DateTimePickerForm()
14         {
15            InitializeComponent();
16         } // end constructor
17
18         private void dateTimePickerDropOff_ValueChanged(
19            object sender, EventArgs e )
20         {
21            DateTime dropOffDate = dateTimePickerDropOff.Value;
22
23            // add extra time when items are dropped off around Sunday
24            if ( dropOffDate.DayOfWeek == DayOfWeek.Friday ||
25               dropOffDate.DayOfWeek == DayOfWeek.Saturday ||
26               dropOffDate.DayOfWeek == DayOfWeek.Sunday )
27
28               //estimate three days for delivery
29               outputLabel.Text =
30                  dropOffDate.AddDays( 3 ).ToLongDateString();
31            else
32               // otherwise estimate only two days for delivery
33               outputLabel.Text =
34                  dropOffDate.AddDays( 2 ).ToLongDateString();
35         } // end method dateTimePickerDropOff_ValueChanged
36
37         private void DateTimePickerForm_Load( object sender, EventArgs e )
38         {
39            // user cannot select days before today
40            dateTimePickerDropOff.MinDate = DateTime.Today;
41
42            // user can only select days of this year
43            dateTimePickerDropOff.MaxDate = DateTime.Today.AddYears( 1 );
44         } // end method DateTimePickerForm_Load
45      } // end class DateTimePickerForm
46   } // end namespace DateTimePickerTest
```

a)

DateTimePickerTest

Drop Off Date:

Friday , July 16, 2010

Estimated Delivery Date:

b)

DateTimePickerTest

Drop Off Date:

Friday , July 16, 2010

◄   July, 2010   ►
Sun Mon Tue Wed Thu Fri Sat

                         16   17
18 19 20 21 22 23   24
25 26 27 28 29 30   31
 1   2   3   4   5   6   7
        Today: 7/16/2010

Fig. 15.11 | Demonstrating DateTimePicker. (Part 2 of 3.)

c) 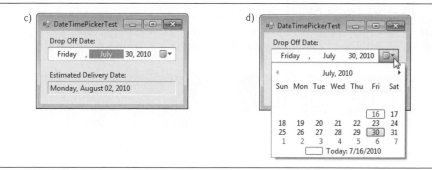 d)

Fig. 15.11 | Demonstrating DateTimePicker. (Part 3 of 3.)

The DateTimePicker (dropOffDateTimePicker) has its Format property set to Long, so the user can select a date and not a time in this application. When the user selects a date, the ValueChanged event occurs. The event handler for this event (lines 18–35) first retrieves the selected date from the DateTimePicker's Value property (line 21). Lines 24–26 use the DateTime structure's **DayOfWeek** property to determine the day of the week on which the selected date falls. The day values are represented using the **DayOfWeek** enumeration. Lines 29–30 and 33–34 use DateTime's **AddDays** method to increase the date by three days or two days, respectively. The resulting date is then displayed in Long format using method **ToLongDateString**.

In this application, we do not want the user to be able to select a drop-off day before the current day, or one that is more than a year into the future. To enforce this, we set the DateTimePicker's **MinDate** and **MaxDate** properties when the Form is loaded (lines 40 and 43). Property Today returns the current day, and method **AddYears** (with an argument of 1) is used to specify a date one year in the future.

Let's take a closer look at the output. This application begins by displaying the current date (Fig. 15.11(a)). In Fig. 15.11(b), we selected the 30th of July. In Fig. 15.11(c), the estimated arrival date is displayed as the 2nd of August. Figure 15.11(d) shows that the 30th, after it is selected, is highlighted in the calendar.

15.5 LinkLabel Control

The **LinkLabel** control displays links to other resources, such as files or web pages (Fig. 15.12). A LinkLabel appears as underlined text (colored blue by default). When the mouse moves over the link, the pointer changes to a hand; this is similar to the behavior of a hyperlink in a web page. The link can change color to indicate whether it is not yet visited, previously visited or active. When clicked, the LinkLabel generates a **LinkClicked** event (see Fig. 15.13). Class LinkLabel is derived from class Label and therefore inherits all of class Label's functionality.

LinkLabel on a Form ⸻ Hand image displays when mouse moves over LinkLabel

Fig. 15.12 | LinkLabel control in running program.

Look-and-Feel Observation 15.3

A LinkLabel is the preferred control for indicating that the user can click a link to jump to a resource such as a web page, though other controls can perform similar tasks.

LinkLabel properties and an event	Description
Common Properties	
ActiveLinkColor	Specifies the color of the active link when the user is in the process of clicking the link. The default color (typically red) is set by the system.
LinkArea	Specifies which portion of text in the LinkLabel is part of the link.
LinkBehavior	Specifies the link's behavior, such as how the link appears when the mouse is placed over it.
LinkColor	Specifies the original color of the link before it's been visited. The default color (typically blue) is set by the system.
LinkVisited	If true, the link appears as though it has been visited (its color is changed to that specified by property VisitedLinkColor). The default value is false.
Text	Specifies the control's text.
UseMnemonic	If true, the & character in the Text property acts as a shortcut (similar to the *Alt* shortcut in menus).
VisitedLinkColor	Specifies the color of a visited link. The default color (typically purple) is set by the system.
Common Event	*(Event arguments LinkLabelLinkClickedEventArgs)*
LinkClicked	Generated when the link is clicked. This is the default event when the control is double clicked in **Design** mode.

Fig. 15.13 | LinkLabel properties and an event.

Class LinkLabelTestForm (Fig. 15.14) uses three LinkLabels to link to the C: drive, the Deitel website (www.deitel.com) and the Notepad application, respectively. The Text properties of the LinkLabel's cDriveLinkLabel, deitelLinkLabel and notepadLink-Label describe each link's purpose.

```
 1   // Fig. 15.14: LinkLabelTestForm.cs
 2   // Using LinkLabels to create hyperlinks.
 3   using System;
 4   using System.Windows.Forms;
 5
 6   namespace LinkLabelTest
 7   {
 8      // Form using LinkLabels to browse the C:\ drive,
 9      // load a web page and run Notepad
10      public partial class LinkLabelTestForm : Form
11      {
```

Fig. 15.14 | LinkLabels used to link to a drive, a web page and an application. (Part 1 of 3.)

```
12          // constructor
13          public LinkLabelTestForm()
14          {
15              InitializeComponent();
16          } // end constructor
17
18          // browse C:\ drive
19          private void cDriveLinkLabel_LinkClicked( object sender,
20              LinkLabelLinkClickedEventArgs e )
21          {
22              // change LinkColor after it has been clicked
23              driveLinkLabel.LinkVisited = true;
24
25              System.Diagnostics.Process.Start( @"C:\" );
26          } // end method cDriveLinkLabel_LinkClicked
27
28          // load www.deitel.com in web browser
29          private void deitelLinkLabel_LinkClicked( object sender,
30              LinkLabelLinkClickedEventArgs e )
31          {
32              // change LinkColor after it has been clicked
33              deitelLinkLabel.LinkVisited = true;
34
35              System.Diagnostics.Process.Start( "http://www.deitel.com" );
36          } // end method deitelLinkLabel_LinkClicked
37
38          // run application Notepad
39          private void notepadLinkLabel_LinkClicked( object sender,
40              LinkLabelLinkClickedEventArgs e )
41          {
42              // change LinkColor after it has been clicked
43              notepadLinkLabel.LinkVisited = true;
44
45              // program called as if in run
46              // menu and full path not needed
47              System.Diagnostics.Process.Start( "notepad" );
48          } // end method driveLinkLabel_LinkClicked
49      } // end class LinkLabelTestForm
50  } // end namespace LinkLabelTest
```

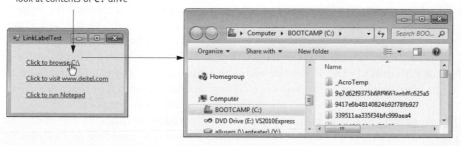

Click first LinkLabel to
look at contents of C: drive

Fig. 15.14 | LinkLabels used to link to a drive, a web page and an application. (Part 2 of 3.)

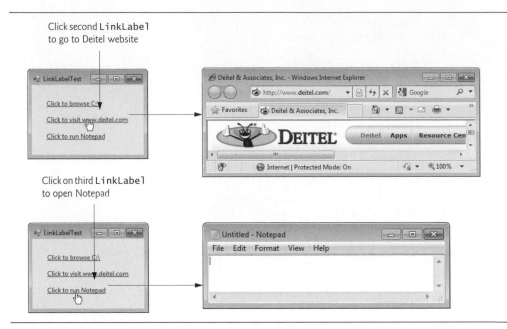

Fig. 15.14 | LinkLabels used to link to a drive, a web page and an application. (Part 3 of 3.)

The event handlers for the LinkLabels call method **Start** of class **Process** (namespace **System.Diagnostics**), which allows you to execute other programs, or load documents or web sites from an application. Method Start can take one argument, the file to open, or two arguments, the application to run and its command-line arguments. Method Start's arguments can be in the same form as if they were provided for input to the Windows **Run** command (**Start > Run...**). For applications that are known to Windows, full path names are not needed, and the file extension often can be omitted. To open a file of a type that Windows recognizes (and knows how to handle), simply use the file's full path name. For example, if you a pass the method a .doc file, Windows will open it in Microsoft Word (or whatever program is registered to open .doc files, if any). The Windows operating system must be able to use the application associated with the given file's extension to open the file.

The event handler for cDriveLinkLabel's LinkClicked event browses the C: drive (lines 19–26). Line 23 sets the LinkVisited property to true, which changes the link's color from blue to purple (the LinkVisited colors can be configured through the **Properties** window in Visual Studio). The event handler then passes @"C:\" to method Start (line 25), which opens a **Windows Explorer** window. The @ symbol that we placed before "C:\" indicates that all characters in the string should be interpreted literally—this is known as a **verbatim string**. Thus, the backslash within the string is not considered to be the first character of an escape sequence. This simplifies strings that represent directory paths, since you do not need to use \\ for each \ character in the path.

The event handler for deitelLinkLabel's LinkClicked event (lines 29–36) opens the web page www.deitel.com in the user's default web browser. We achieve this by passing the web-page address as a string (line 35), which opens the web page in a new web browser window or tab. Line 33 sets the LinkVisited property to true.

The event handler for notepadLinkLabel's LinkClicked event (lines 39–48) opens the Notepad application. Line 43 sets the LinkVisited property to true so that the link appears as a visited link. Line 47 passes the argument "notepad" to method Start, which runs notepad.exe. In line 47, neither the full path nor the .exe extension is required—Windows automatically recognizes the argument given to method Start as an executable file.

15.6 ListBox Control

The **ListBox** control allows the user to view and select from multiple items in a list. List-Boxes are static GUI entities, which means that users cannot directly edit the list of items. The user can be provided with TextBoxes and Buttons with which to specify items to be added to the list, but the actual additions must be performed in code. The **CheckedList-Box** control (Section 15.7) extends a ListBox by including CheckBoxes next to each item in the list. This allows users to place checks on multiple items at once, as is possible with CheckBox controls. (Users also can select multiple items from a ListBox by setting the ListBox's **SelectionMode** property, which is discussed shortly.) Figure 15.15 displays a ListBox and a CheckedListBox. In both controls, scrollbars appear if the number of items exceeds the ListBox's viewable area.

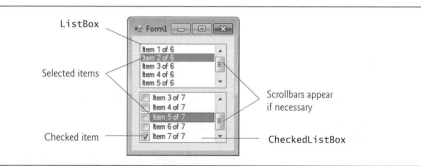

Fig. 15.15 | ListBox and CheckedListBox on a Form.

Figure 15.16 lists common ListBox properties and methods and a common event. The SelectionMode property determines the number of items that can be selected. This property has the possible values None, One, MultiSimple and MultiExtended (from the **SelectionMode** enumeration)—the differences among these settings are explained in Fig. 15.16. The **SelectedIndexChanged** event occurs when the user selects a new item.

ListBox properties, methods and an event	Description
Common Properties	
Items	The collection of items in the ListBox.
MultiColumn	Indicates whether the ListBox can display multiple columns. Multiple columns eliminate vertical scrollbars from the display.

Fig. 15.16 | ListBox properties, methods and an event. (Part 1 of 2.)

ListBox properties, methods and an event	Description
SelectedIndex	Returns the index of the selected item. If no items have been selected, the property returns -1. If the user selects multiple items, this property returns only one of the selected indices. If multiple items are selected, use property SelectedIndices.
SelectedIndices	Returns a collection containing the indices for all selected items.
SelectedItem	Returns a reference to the selected item. If multiple items are selected, it returns the item with the lowest index number.
SelectedItems	Returns a collection of the selected item(s).
SelectionMode	Determines the number of items that can be selected and the means through which multiple items can be selected. Values None, One (the default), MultiSimple (multiple selection allowed) or MultiExtended (multiple selection allowed using a combination of arrow keys or mouse clicks and *Shift* and *Ctrl* keys).
Sorted	Indicates whether items are sorted alphabetically. Setting this property's value to true sorts the items. The default value is false.
Common Methods	
ClearSelected	Deselects every item.
GetSelected	Returns true if the item at the specified index is selected.
Common Event	
SelectedIndexChanged	Generated when the selected index changes. This is the default event when the control is double clicked in the designer.

Fig. 15.16 | ListBox properties, methods and an event. (Part 2 of 2.)

Both the ListBox and CheckedListBox have properties Items, SelectedItem and SelectedIndex. Property **Items** returns a collection of the list items. Collections are a common way to manage lists of objects in the .NET framework. Many .NET GUI components (e.g., ListBoxes) use collections to expose lists of internal objects (e.g., items in a ListBox). We discuss collections further in Chapter 23. The collection returned by property Items is represented as an object of type ListBox.ObjectCollection. Property **SelectedItem** returns the ListBox's currently selected item. If the user can select multiple items, use collection **SelectedItems** to return all the selected items as a ListBox.SelectedObjectColection. Property **SelectedIndex** returns the index of the selected item—if there could be more than one, use property **SelectedIndices**, which returns a ListBox.SelectedIndexColection. If no items are selected, property SelectedIndex returns -1. Method **GetSelected** takes an index and returns true if the corresponding item is selected.

Adding Items to ListBoxes and CheckedListBoxes
To add items to a ListBox or to a CheckedListBox, we must add objects to its Items collection. This can be accomplished by calling method Add to add a string to the ListBox's or CheckedListBox's Items collection. For example, we could write

```
myListBox.Items.Add( myListItem );
```

to add string *myListItem* to ListBox *myListBox*. To add multiple objects, you can either call method Add multiple times or call method AddRange to add an array of objects. Classes ListBox and CheckedListBox each call the submitted object's ToString method to determine the Label for the corresponding object's entry in the list. This allows you to add different objects to a ListBox or a CheckedListBox that later can be returned through properties SelectedItem and SelectedItems.

Alternatively, you can add items to ListBoxes and CheckedListBoxes visually by examining the Items property in the **Properties** window. Clicking the ellipsis button opens the **String Collection Editor**, which contains a text area for adding items; each item appears on a separate line (Fig. 15.17). Visual Studio then writes code to add these strings to the Items collection inside method InitializeComponent.

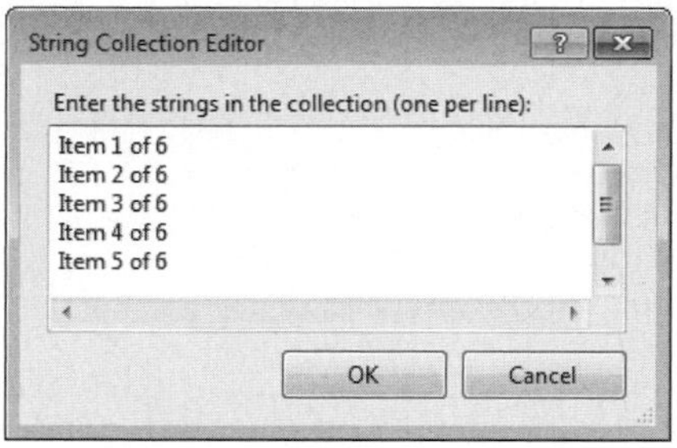

Fig. 15.17 | String Collection Editor.

Figure 15.18 uses class ListBoxTestForm to add, remove and clear items from ListBox displayListBox. Class ListBoxTestForm uses TextBox inputTextBox to allow the user to type in a new item. When the user clicks the **Add** Button, the new item appears in displayListBox. Similarly, if the user selects an item and clicks **Remove**, the item is deleted. When clicked, **Clear** deletes all entries in displayListBox. The user terminates the application by clicking **Exit**.

The addButton_Click event handler (lines 20–24) calls method Add of the Items collection in the ListBox. This method takes a string as the item to add to displayListBox. In this case, the string used is the user input from the inputTextBox (line 22). After the item is added, inputTextBox.Text is cleared (line 23).

```
1   // Fig. 15.18: ListBoxTestForm.cs
2   // Program to add, remove and clear ListBox items
3   using System;
4   using System.Windows.Forms;
5
6   namespace ListBoxTest
7   {
8      // Form uses a TextBox and Buttons to add,
9      // remove, and clear ListBox items
10     public partial class ListBoxTestForm : Form
11     {
```

Fig. 15.18 | Program that adds, removes and clears ListBox items. (Part 1 of 3.)

```
12          // constructor
13          public ListBoxTestForm()
14          {
15             InitializeComponent();
16          } // end constructor
17
18          // add new item to ListBox (text from input TextBox)
19          // and clear input TextBox
20          private void addButton_Click( object sender, EventArgs e )
21          {
22             displayListBox.Items.Add( inputTextBox.Text );
23             inputTextBox.Clear();
24          } // end method addButton_Click
25
26          // remove item if one is selected
27          private void removeButton_Click( object sender, EventArgs e )
28          {
29             // check whether item is selected, remove if
30             if ( displayListBox.SelectedIndex != -1 )
31                displayListBox.Items.RemoveAt(
32                   displayListBox.SelectedIndex );
33          } // end method removeButton_Click
34
35          // clear all items in ListBox
36          private void clearButton_Click( object sender, EventArgs e )
37          {
38             displayListBox.Items.Clear();
39          } // end method clearButton_Click
40
41          // exit application
42          private void exitButton_Click( object sender, EventArgs e )
43          {
44             Application.Exit();
45          } // end method exitButton_Click
46       } // end class ListBoxTestForm
47    } // end namespace ListBoxTest
```

Fig. 15.18 | Program that adds, removes and clears ListBox items. (Part 2 of 3.)

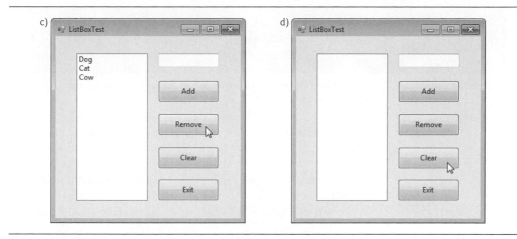

Fig. 15.18 | Program that adds, removes and clears ListBox items. (Part 3 of 3.)

The removeButton_Click event handler (lines 27–33) uses method RemoveAt to remove an item from the ListBox. Event handler removeButton_Click first uses property SelectedIndex to determine which index is selected. If SelectedIndex is not –1 (i.e., an item is selected), lines 31–32 remove the item that corresponds to the selected index.

The clearButton_Click event handler (lines 36–39) calls method Clear of the Items collection (line 38). This removes all the entries in displayListBox. Finally, event handler exitButton_Click (lines 42–45) terminates the application by calling method Application.Exit (line 44).

15.7 CheckedListBox Control

The CheckedListBox control derives from ListBox and displays a CheckBox with each item. Items can be added via methods Add and AddRange or through the **String Collection Editor.** CheckedListBoxes allow multiple items to be checked, but item selection is more restrictive. The only values for the SelectionMode property are None and One. One allows a single selection, whereas None allows no selections. Because an item must be selected to be checked, you must set the SelectionMode to be One if you wish to allow users to check items. Thus, toggling property SelectionMode between One and None effectively switches between enabling and disabling the user's ability to check list items. Common properties, a method and an event of CheckedListBoxes appear in Fig. 15.19.

> **Common Programming Error 15.1**
> *The IDE displays an error message if you attempt to set the SelectionMode property to MultiSimple or MultiExtended in the **Properties** window of a CheckedListBox. If this value is set programmatically, a runtime error occurs.*

Event **ItemCheck** occurs whenever a user checks or unchecks a CheckedListBox item. Event-argument properties CurrentValue and NewValue return CheckState values for the current and new state of the item, respectively. A comparison of these values allows you to determine whether the CheckedListBox item was checked or unchecked. The CheckedListBox control retains the SelectedItems and SelectedIndices properties (it inherits

CheckedListBox properties, a method and an event	Description
Common Properties	*(All the ListBox properties, methods and events are inherited by CheckedListBox.)*
CheckedItems	Returns the collection of items that are checked as a CheckedList-Box.CheckedItemCollection. This is distinct from the selected item, which is highlighted (but not necessarily checked). [*Note:* There can be at most one selected item at any given time.]
CheckedIndices	Returns indices for all checked items as a CheckedListBox.Checked-IndexCollection.
CheckOnClick	When true and the user clicks an item, the item is both selected and checked or unchecked. By default, this property is false, which means that the user must select an item, then click it again to check or uncheck it.
SelectionMode	Determines whether items can be selected and checked. The possible values are One (the default; allows multiple checks to be placed) or None (does not allow any checks to be placed).
Common Method	
GetItemChecked	Takes an index and returns true if the corresponding item is checked.
Common Event	*(Event arguments ItemCheckEventArgs)*
ItemCheck	Generated when an item is checked or unchecked.
ItemCheckEventArgs Properties	
CurrentValue	Indicates whether the current item is checked or unchecked. Possible values are Checked, Unchecked and Indeterminate.
Index	Returns the zero-based index of the item that changed.
NewValue	Specifies the new state of the item.

Fig. 15.19 | CheckedListBox properties, a method and an event.

them from class ListBox). However, it also includes properties CheckedItems and CheckedIndices, which return information about the checked items and indices.

In Fig. 15.20, class CheckedListBoxTestForm uses a CheckedListBox and a ListBox to display a user's selection of books. The CheckedListBox allows the user to select multiple titles. In the **String Collection Editor**, items were added for some Deitel books: C, C++, Java™, Internet & WWW, VB 2008, Visual C++ and Visual C# 2008 (the acronym HTP stands for "How to Program"). The ListBox (named displayListBox) displays the user's selection. In the screenshots accompanying this example, the CheckedListBox appears to the left, the ListBox on the right.

When the user checks or unchecks an item in itemCheckedListBox_ItemCheck, an ItemCheck event occurs and event handler itemCheckedListBox_ItemCheck (lines 19–31) executes. An if...else statement (lines 27–30) determines whether the user checked or unchecked an item in the CheckedListBox. Line 27 uses the NewValue property to deter-

```
 1    // Fig. 15.20: CheckedListBoxTestForm.cs
 2    // Using a CheckedListBox to add items to a display ListBox
 3    using System;
 4    using System.Windows.Forms;
 5
 6    namespace CheckedListBoxTest
 7    {
 8       // Form uses a checked ListBox to add items to a display ListBox
 9       public partial class CheckedListBoxTestForm : Form
10       {
11          // constructor
12          public CheckedListBoxTestForm()
13          {
14             InitializeComponent();
15          } // end constructor
16
17          // item about to change
18          // add or remove from display ListBox
19          private void itemCheckedListBox_ItemCheck(
20             object sender, ItemCheckEventArgs e )
21          {
22             // obtain reference of selected item
23             string item = itemCheckedListBox.SelectedItem.ToString();
24
25             // if item checked, add to ListBox
26             // otherwise remove from ListBox
27             if ( e.NewValue == CheckState.Checked )
28                displayListBox.Items.Add( item );
29             else
30                displayListBox.Items.Remove( item );
31          } // end method itemCheckedListBox_ItemCheck
32       } // end class CheckedListBoxTestForm
33    } // end namespace CheckedListBoxTest
```

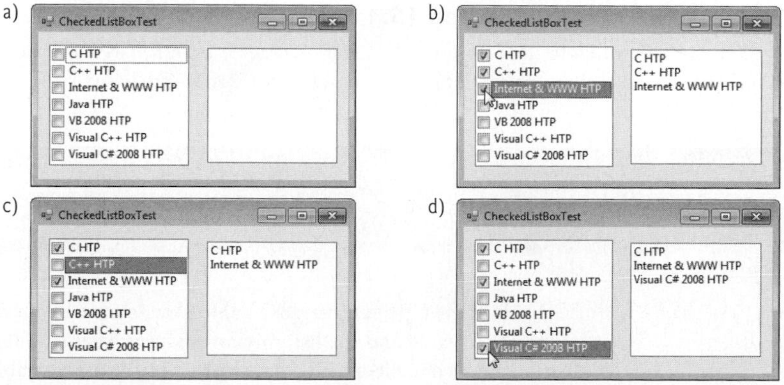

Fig. 15.20 | CheckedListBox and ListBox used in a program to display a user selection.

mine whether the item is being checked (CheckState.Checked). If the user checks an item, line 28 adds the checked entry to the ListBox displayListBox. If the user unchecks an item, line 30 removes the corresponding item from displayListBox. This event handler was created by selecting the CheckedListBox in **Design** mode, viewing the control's events in the **Properties** window and double clicking the ItemCheck event. The default event for a CheckedListBox is a SelectedIndexChanged event.

15.8 ComboBox Control

The **ComboBox** control combines TextBox features with a **drop-down list**—a GUI component that contains a list from which a value can be selected. A ComboBox usually appears as a TextBox with a down arrow to its right. By default, the user can enter text into the TextBox or click the down arrow to display a list of predefined items. If a user chooses an element from this list, that element is displayed in the TextBox. If the list contains more elements than can be displayed in the drop-down list, a scrollbar appears. The maximum number of items that a drop-down list can display at one time is set by property **MaxDropDownItems**. Figure 15.21 shows a sample ComboBox in three different states.

Click the down arrow to display items in drop-down list

Selecting an item from drop-down list changes text in **TextBox** portion

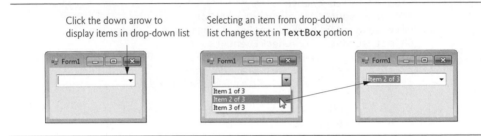

Fig. 15.21 | ComboBox demonstration.

As with the ListBox control, you can add objects to collection Items programmatically, using methods Add and AddRange, or visually, with the **String Collection Editor**. Figure 15.22 lists common properties and a common event of class ComboBox.

Look-and-Feel Observation 15.4
Use a ComboBox to save space on a GUI. A disadvantage is that, unlike with a ListBox, the user cannot see available items without expanding the drop-down list.

ComboBox properties and an event	Description
Common Properties	
DropDownStyle	Determines the type of ComboBox. Value Simple means that the text portion is editable and the list portion is always visible. Value DropDown (the default) means that the text portion is editable but the user must click an arrow button to see the list portion. Value DropDownList means that the text portion is not editable and the user must click the arrow button to see the list portion.
Items	The collection of items in the ComboBox control.

Fig. 15.22 | ComboBox properties and an event. (Part 1 of 2.)

ComboBox properties and an event	Description
MaxDropDownItems	Specifies the maximum number of items (between 1 and 100) that the drop-down list can display. If the number of items exceeds the maximum number of items to display, a scrollbar appears.
SelectedIndex	Returns the index of the selected item, or -1 if none are selected.
SelectedItem	Returns a reference to the selected item.
Sorted	Indicates whether items are sorted alphabetically. Setting this property's value to true sorts the items. The default is false.
Common Event	
SelectedIndexChanged	Generated when the selected index changes (such as when a different item is selected). This is the default event when control is double clicked in the designer.

Fig. 15.22 | ComboBox properties and an event. (Part 2 of 2.)

Property **DropDownStyle** determines the type of ComboBox and is represented as a value of the **ComboBoxStyle** enumeration, which contains values Simple, DropDown and DropDownList. Option Simple does not display a drop-down arrow. Instead, a scrollbar appears next to the control, allowing the user to select a choice from the list. The user also can type in a selection. Style DropDown (the default) displays a drop-down list when the down arrow is clicked (or the down arrow key is pressed). The user can type a new item in the ComboBox. The last style is DropDownList, which displays a drop-down list but does not allow the user to type in the TextBox.

The ComboBox control has properties **Items** (a collection), **SelectedItem** and **SelectedIndex**, which are similar to the corresponding properties in ListBox. There can be at most one selected item in a ComboBox. If no items are selected, then SelectedIndex is -1. When the selected item changes, a **SelectedIndexChanged** event occurs.

Class ComboBoxTestForm (Fig. 15.23) allows users to select a shape to draw—circle, ellipse, square or pie (in both filled and unfilled versions)—by using a ComboBox. The ComboBox in this example is uneditable, so the user cannot type in the TextBox.

Look-and-Feel Observation 15.5

Make lists (such as ComboBoxes) editable only if the program is designed to accept user-submitted elements. Otherwise, the user might try to enter a custom item that is improper for the purposes of your application.

```
1   // Fig. 15.23: ComboBoxTestForm.cs
2   // Using ComboBox to select a shape to draw.
3   using System;
4   using System.Drawing;
5   using System.Windows.Forms;
```

Fig. 15.23 | ComboBox used to draw a selected shape. (Part 1 of 3.)

```
 6
 7    namespace ComboBoxTest
 8    {
 9       // Form uses a ComboBox to select different shapes to draw
10       public partial class ComboBoxTestForm : Form
11       {
12          // constructor
13          public ComboBoxTestForm()
14          {
15             InitializeComponent();
16          } // end constructor
17
18          // get index of selected shape, draw shape
19          private void imageComboBox_SelectedIndexChanged(
20             object sender, EventArgs e )
21          {
22             // create graphics object, Pen and SolidBrush
23             Graphics myGraphics = base.CreateGraphics();
24
25             // create Pen using color DarkRed
26             Pen myPen = new Pen( Color.DarkRed );
27
28             // create SolidBrush using color DarkRed
29             SolidBrush mySolidBrush = new SolidBrush( Color.DarkRed );
30
31             // clear drawing area, setting it to color white
32             myGraphics.Clear( Color.White );
33
34             // find index, draw proper shape
35             switch ( imageComboBox.SelectedIndex )
36             {
37                case 0: // case Circle is selected
38                   myGraphics.DrawEllipse( myPen, 50, 50, 150, 150 );
39                   break;
40                case 1: // case Rectangle is selected
41                   myGraphics.DrawRectangle( myPen, 50, 50, 150, 150 );
42                   break;
43                case 2: // case Ellipse is selected
44                   myGraphics.DrawEllipse( myPen, 50, 85, 150, 115 );
45                   break;
46                case 3: // case Pie is selected
47                   myGraphics.DrawPie( myPen, 50, 50, 150, 150, 0, 45 );
48                   break;
49                case 4: // case Filled Circle is selected
50                   myGraphics.FillEllipse( mySolidBrush, 50, 50, 150, 150 );
51                   break;
52                case 5: // case Filled Rectangle is selected
53                   myGraphics.FillRectangle( mySolidBrush, 50, 50, 150,
54                      150 );
55                   break;
56                case 6: // case Filled Ellipse is selected
57                   myGraphics.FillEllipse( mySolidBrush, 50, 85, 150, 115 );
58                   break;
```

Fig. 15.23 | ComboBox used to draw a selected shape. (Part 2 of 3.)

```
59              case 7: // case Filled Pie is selected
60                  myGraphics.FillPie( mySolidBrush, 50, 50, 150, 150, 0,
61                      45 );
62                  break;
63          } // end switch
64
65          myGraphics.Dispose(); // release the Graphics object
66      } // end method imageComboBox_SelectedIndexChanged
67  } // end class ComboBoxTestForm
68 } // end namespace ComboBoxTest
```

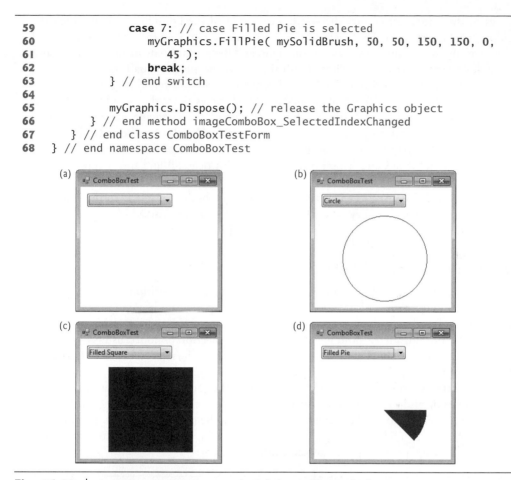

Fig. 15.23 | ComboBox used to draw a selected shape. (Part 3 of 3.)

After creating ComboBox imageComboBox, make it uneditable by setting its DropDown-Style to DropDownList in the **Properties** window. Next, add items Circle, Square, Ellipse, Pie, Filled Circle, Filled Square, Filled Ellipse and Filled Pie to the Items collection using the **String Collection Editor**. Whenever the user selects an item from imageComboBox, a SelectedIndexChanged event occurs and event handler imageCombo-Box_SelectedIndexChanged (lines 19–66) executes. Lines 23–29 create a Graphics object, a Pen and a SolidBrush, which are used to draw on the Form. The Graphics object (line 23) allows a pen or brush to draw on a component, using one of several Graphics methods. The Pen object (line 26) is used by methods DrawEllipse, DrawRectangle and DrawPie (lines 38, 41, 44 and 47) to draw the outlines of their corresponding shapes. The SolidBrush object (line 29) is used by methods FillEllipse, FillRectangle and FillPie (lines 50, 53–54, 57 and 60–61) to fill their corresponding solid shapes. Line 32 colors the entire Form White, using Graphics method **Clear**.

The application draws a shape based on the selected item's index. The switch statement (lines 35–63) uses imageComboBox.SelectedIndex to determine which item the user selected. Graphics method **DrawEllipse** (line 38) takes a Pen, and the x- and y-coordinates of the upper-left corner, the width and height of the bounding box in which the ellipse will be displayed. The origin of the coordinate system is in the upper-left corner of the Form; the *x*-coordinate increases to the right, and the *y*-coordinate increases downward. A circle is a special case of an ellipse (with the width and height equal). Line 38 draws a circle. Line 44 draws an ellipse that has different values for width and height.

Class Graphics method **DrawRectangle** (line 41) takes a Pen, the *x*- and *y*-coordinates of the upper-left corner and the width and height of the rectangle to draw. Method **DrawPie** (line 47) draws a pie as a portion of an ellipse. The ellipse is bounded by a rectangle. Method DrawPie takes a Pen, the *x*- and *y*-coordinates of the upper-left corner of the rectangle, its width and height, the start angle (in degrees) and the sweep angle (in degrees) of the pie. Angles increase clockwise. The **FillEllipse** (lines 50 and 57), **Fill-Rectangle** (line 53–54) and **FillPie** (line 60–61) methods are similar to their unfilled counterparts, except that they take a Brush (e.g., SolidBrush) instead of a Pen. Some of the drawn shapes are illustrated in the screenshots of Fig. 15.23.

15.9 TreeView Control

The **TreeView** control displays **nodes** hierarchically in a **tree**. Traditionally, nodes are objects that contain values and can refer to other nodes. A **parent node** contains **child nodes**, and the child nodes can be parents to other nodes. Two child nodes that have the same parent node are considered **sibling nodes**. A tree is a collection of nodes, usually organized in a hierarchical manner. The first parent node of a tree is the **root** node (a TreeView can have multiple roots). For example, the file system of a computer can be represented as a tree. The top-level directory (perhaps C:) would be the root, each subfolder of C: would be a child node and each child folder could have its own children. TreeView controls are useful for displaying hierarchical information, such as the file structure that we just mentioned. We cover nodes and trees in greater detail in Chapter 21, Data Structures. Figure 15.24 displays a sample TreeView control on a Form.

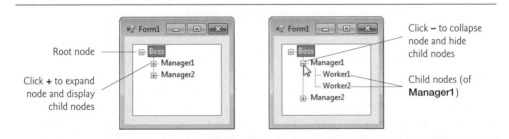

Fig. 15.24 | TreeView displaying a sample tree.

A parent node can be expanded or collapsed by clicking the plus box or minus box to its left. Nodes without children do not have these boxes.

The nodes in a TreeView are instances of class **TreeNode**. Each TreeNode has a **Nodes** collection (type **TreeNodeCollection**), which contains a list of other TreeNodes—known as its children. The Parent property returns a reference to the parent node (or null if the node is a root node). Figure 15.25 and Fig. 15.26 list the common properties of TreeViews and TreeNodes, common TreeNode methods and a common TreeView event.

TreeView properties and an event	Description
Common Properties	
CheckBoxes	Indicates whether CheckBoxes appear next to nodes. A value of true displays CheckBoxes. The default value is false.
ImageList	Specifies an ImageList object containing the node icons. An **ImageList** object is a collection that contains Image objects.
Nodes	Returns the collection of TreeNodes in the control as a TreeNodeCollection. It contains methods Add (adds a TreeNode object), Clear (deletes the entire collection) and Remove (deletes a specific node). Removing a parent node deletes all of its children.
SelectedNode	The selected node.
*Common Event (Event arguments **TreeViewEventArgs**)*	
AfterSelect	Generated after selected node changes. This is the default event when the control is double clicked in the designer.

Fig. 15.25 | TreeView properties and an event.

TreeNode properties and methods	Description
Common Properties	
Checked	Indicates whether the TreeNode is checked (CheckBoxes property must be set to true in the parent TreeView).
FirstNode	Specifies the first node in the Nodes collection (i.e., the first child in the tree).
FullPath	Indicates the path of the node, starting at the root of the tree.
ImageIndex	Specifies the index in the TreeView's ImageList of the image shown when the node is deselected.
LastNode	Specifies the last node in the Nodes collection (i.e., the last child in the tree).
NextNode	Next sibling node.
Nodes	Collection of TreeNodes contained in the current node (i.e., all the children of the current node). It contains methods Add (adds a TreeNode object), Clear (deletes the entire collection) and Remove (deletes a specific node). Removing a parent node deletes all of its children.
PrevNode	Previous sibling node.
SelectedImageIndex	Specifies the index in the TreeView's ImageList of the image to use when the node is selected.
Text	Specifies the TreeNode's text.
Common Methods	
Collapse	Collapses a node.

Fig. 15.26 | TreeNode properties and methods. (Part 1 of 2.)

TreeNode properties and methods	Description
Expand	Expands a node.
ExpandAll	Expands all the children of a node.
GetNodeCount	Returns the number of child nodes.

Fig. 15.26 | TreeNode properties and methods. (Part 2 of 2.)

To add nodes to the TreeView visually, click the ellipsis next to the Nodes property in the **Properties** window. This opens the **TreeNode Editor** (Fig. 15.27), which displays an empty tree representing the TreeView. There are Buttons to create a root and to add or delete a node. To the right are the properties of current node. Here you can rename the node.

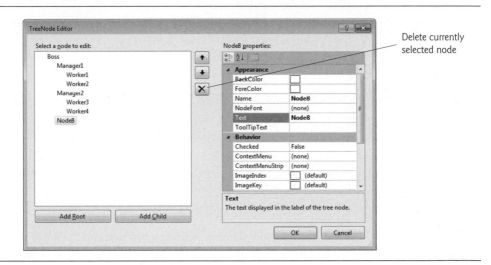

Fig. 15.27 | TreeNode Editor.

To add nodes programmatically, first create a root node. Create a new TreeNode object and pass it a string to display. Then call method Add to add this new TreeNode to the TreeView's Nodes collection. Thus, to add a root node to TreeView *myTreeView*, write

> *myTreeView*.Nodes.Add(**new** TreeNode(*rootLabel*));

where *myTreeView* is the TreeView to which we are adding nodes, and *rootLabel* is the text to display in *myTreeView*. To add children to a root node, add new TreeNodes to its Nodes collection. We select the appropriate root node from the TreeView by writing

> *myTreeView*.Nodes[*myIndex*]

where *myIndex* is the root node's index in *myTreeView*'s Nodes collection. We add nodes to child nodes through the same process by which we added root nodes to *myTreeView*. To add a child to the root node at index *myIndex*, write

> *myTreeView*.Nodes[*myIndex*].Nodes.Add(**new** TreeNode(*ChildLabel*));

Class TreeViewDirectoryStructureForm (Fig. 15.28) uses a TreeView to display the contents of a directory chosen by the user. A TextBox and a Button are used to specify the directory. First, enter the full path of the directory you want to display. Then click the Button to set the specified directory as the root node in the TreeView. Each subdirectory of this directory becomes a child node. This layout is similar to that used in **Windows Explorer**. Folders can be expanded or collapsed by clicking the plus or minus boxes that appear to their left.

When the user clicks the enterButton, all the nodes in directoryTreeView are cleared (line 68). Then, if the directory exists (line 73), the path entered in inputTextBox is used to create the root node. Line 76 adds the directory to directoryTreeView as the root node, and lines 79–80 call method PopulateTreeView (lines 21–62), which takes a directory (a string) and a parent node. Method PopulateTreeView then creates child nodes corresponding to the subdirectories of the directory it receives as an argument.

```
 1   // Fig. 15.28: TreeViewDirectoryStructureForm.cs
 2   // Using TreeView to display directory structure.
 3   using System;
 4   using System.Windows.Forms;
 5   using System.IO;
 6
 7   namespace TreeViewDirectoryStructure
 8   {
 9      // Form uses TreeView to display directory structure
10      public partial class TreeViewDirectoryStructureForm : Form
11      {
12         string substringDirectory; // store last part of full path name
13
14         // constructor
15         public TreeViewDirectoryStructureForm()
16         {
17            InitializeComponent();
18         } // end constructor
19
20         // populate current node with subdirectories
21         public void PopulateTreeView(
22            string directoryValue, TreeNode parentNode )
23         {
24            // array stores all subdirectories in the directory
25            string[] directoryArray =
26               Directory.GetDirectories( directoryValue );
27
28            // populate current node with subdirectories
29            try
30            {
31               // check to see if any subdirectories are present
32               if ( directoryArray.Length != 0 )
33               {
34                  // for every subdirectory, create new TreeNode,
35                  // add as a child of current node and recursively
36                  // populate child nodes with subdirectories
```

Fig. 15.28 | TreeView used to display directories. (Part 1 of 3.)

```
37                    foreach ( string directory in directoryArray )
38                    {
39                        // obtain last part of path name from the full path
40                        // name by calling the GetFileNameWithoutExtension
41                        // method of class Path
42                        substringDirectory =
43                            Path.GetFileNameWithoutExtension( directory );
44
45                        // create TreeNode for current directory
46                        TreeNode myNode = new TreeNode( substringDirectory );
47
48                        // add current directory node to parent node
49                        parentNode.Nodes.Add( myNode );
50
51                        // recursively populate every subdirectory
52                        PopulateTreeView( directory, myNode );
53                    } // end foreach
54                } // end if
55            } //end try
56
57            // catch exception
58            catch ( UnauthorizedAccessException )
59            {
60                parentNode.Nodes.Add( "Access denied" );
61            } // end catch
62        } // end method PopulateTreeView
63
64        // handles enterButton click event
65        private void enterButton_Click( object sender, EventArgs e )
66        {
67            // clear all nodes
68            directoryTreeView.Nodes.Clear();
69
70            // check if the directory entered by user exists
71            // if it does, then fill in the TreeView,
72            // if not, display error MessageBox
73            if ( Directory.Exists( inputTextBox.Text ) )
74            {
75                // add full path name to directoryTreeView
76                directoryTreeView.Nodes.Add( inputTextBox.Text );
77
78                // insert subfolders
79                PopulateTreeView(
80                    inputTextBox.Text, directoryTreeView.Nodes[ 0 ] );
81            }
82            // display error MessageBox if directory not found
83            else
84                MessageBox.Show( inputTextBox.Text + " could not be found.",
85                    "Directory Not Found", MessageBoxButtons.OK,
86                    MessageBoxIcon.Error );
87        } // end method enterButton_Click
88    } // end class TreeViewDirectoryStructureForm
89 } // end namespace TreeViewDirectoryStructure
```

Fig. 15.28 | TreeView used to display directories. (Part 2 of 3.)

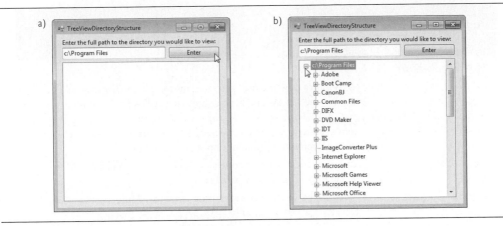

Fig. 15.28 | TreeView used to display directories. (Part 3 of 3.)

Method PopulateTreeView (lines 21–62) obtains a list of subdirectories, using method **GetDirectories** of class Directory (namespace System.IO) in lines 25–26. Method GetDirectories takes a string (the current directory) and returns an array of strings (the subdirectories). If a directory is not accessible for security reasons, an UnauthorizedAccessException is thrown. Lines 58–61 catch this exception and add a node containing "Access denied" instead of displaying the subdirectories.

If there are accessible subdirectories, lines 42–43 use method GetFileNameWithoutExtension of class Path to increase readability by shortening the full path name to just the directory name. The **Path** class provides functionality for working with strings that are file or directory paths. Next, each string in the directoryArray is used to create a new child node (line 46). We use method Add (line 49) to add each child node to the parent. Then method PopulateTreeView is called recursively on every subdirectory (line 52), which eventually populates the TreeView with the entire directory structure. Our recursive algorithm may cause a delay when the program loads large directories. However, once the folder names are added to the appropriate Nodes collection, they can be expanded and collapsed without delay. In the next section, we present an alternate algorithm to solve this problem.

15.10 ListView **Control**

The **ListView** control is similar to a ListBox in that both display lists from which the user can select one or more items (an example of a ListView can be found in Fig. 15.31). ListView is more versatile and can display items in different formats. For example, a ListView can display icons next to the list items (controlled by its SmallImageList, LargeImageList or StateImageList properties) and show the details of items in columns. Property **MultiSelect** (a bool) determines whether multiple items can be selected. CheckBoxes can be included by setting property **CheckBoxes** (a bool) to true, making the ListView's appearance similar to that of a CheckedListBox. The **View** property specifies the layout of the ListBox. Property **Activation** determines the method by which the user selects a list item. The details of these properties and the ItemActivate event are explained in Fig. 15.29.

ListView allows you to define the images used as icons for ListView items. To display images, an ImageList component is required. Create one by dragging it to a Form from

ListView properties and events	Description
Common Properties	
Activation	Determines how the user activates an item. This property takes a value in the ItemActivation enumeration. Possible values are OneClick (single-click activation), TwoClick (double-click activation, item changes color when selected) and Standard (the default; double-click activation, item does not change color).
CheckBoxes	Indicates whether items appear with CheckBoxes. true displays CheckBoxes. The default is false.
LargeImageList	Specifies the ImageList containing large icons for display.
Items	Returns the collection of ListViewItems in the control.
MultiSelect	Determines whether multiple selection is allowed. The default is true, which enables multiple selection.
SelectedItems	Returns the collection of selected items as a ListView.SelectedListViewItemCollection.
SmallImageList	Specifies the ImageList containing small icons for display.
View	Determines appearance of ListViewItems. Possible values are LargeIcon (the default; large icon displayed, items can be in multiple columns), SmallIcon (small icon displayed, items can be in multiple columns), List (small icons displayed, items appear in a single column), Details (like List, but multiple columns of information can be displayed per item) and Tile (large icons displayed, information provided to right of icon; valid only in Windows XP or later).
Common Events	
Click	Generated when an item is clicked. This is the default event.
ItemActivate	Generated when an item in the ListView is activated (clicked or double clicked). Does not contain the specifics of which item is activated.

Fig. 15.29 | ListView properties and events.

the **ToolBox**. Then, select the **Images** property in the **Properties** window to display the **Image Collection Editor** (Fig. 15.30). Here you can browse for images that you wish to add to the ImageList, which contains an array of Images. Adding images this way embeds them into the application (like resources), so they do not need to be included separately with the published application. They're not however part of the project. In this example, we added images to the ImageList programmatically rather than using the **Image Collection Editor** so that we could use image resources. After creating an empty ImageList, add the file and folder icon images to the project as resources. Next, set property SmallImageList of the ListView to the new ImageList object. Property **SmallImageList** specifies the image list for the small icons. Property **LargeImageList** sets the ImageList for large icons. The items in a ListView are each of type **ListViewItem**. Icons for the ListView items are selected by setting the item's **ImageIndex** property to the appropriate index.

Class ListViewTestForm (Fig. 15.31) displays files and folders in a ListView, along with small icons representing each file or folder. If a file or folder is inaccessible because of

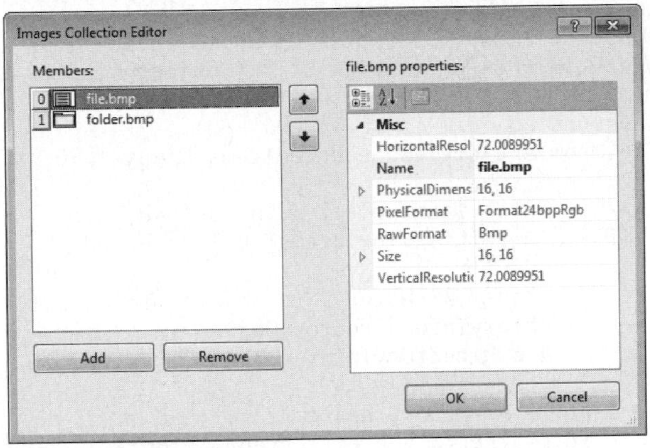

Fig. 15.30 | Image Collection Editor window for an ImageList component.

permission settings, a MessageBox appears. The program scans the contents of the directory as it browses, rather than indexing the entire drive at once.

Method *ListViewTestForm_Load*

Method ListViewTestForm_Load (lines 114–123) handles the Form's Load event. When the application loads, the folder and file icon images are added to the Images collection of fileFolderImageList (lines 117–118). Since the ListView's SmallImageList property is set to this ImageList, the ListView can display these images as icons for each item. Because the folder icon was added first, it has array index 0, and the file icon has array index 1. The application also loads its home directory (obtained at line 14) into the ListView when it first loads (line 121) and displays the directory path (line 122).

```
1   // Fig. 15.31: ListViewTestForm.cs
2   // Displaying directories and their contents in ListView.
3   using System;
4   using System.Windows.Forms;
5   using System.IO;
6
7   namespace ListViewTest
8   {
9      // Form contains a ListView which displays
10     // folders and files in a directory
11     public partial class ListViewTestForm : Form
12     {
13        // store current directory
14        string currentDirectory = Directory.GetCurrentDirectory();
15
16        // constructor
17        public ListViewTestForm()
18        {
19           InitializeComponent();
20        } // end constructor
```

Fig. 15.31 | ListView displaying files and folders. (Part 1 of 4.)

```
21
22       // browse directory user clicked or go up one level
23       private void browserListView_Click( object sender, EventArgs e )
24       {
25          // ensure an item is selected
26          if ( browserListView.SelectedItems.Count != 0 )
27          {
28             // if first item selected, go up one level
29             if ( browserListView.Items[ 0 ].Selected )
30             {
31                // create DirectoryInfo object for directory
32                DirectoryInfo directoryObject =
33                   new DirectoryInfo( currentDirectory );
34
35                // if directory has parent, load it
36                if ( directoryObject.Parent != null )
37                {
38                   LoadFilesInDirectory(
39                      directoryObject.Parent.FullName );
40                } // end if
41             } // end if
42
43             // selected directory or file
44             else
45             {
46                // directory or file chosen
47                string chosen = browserListView.SelectedItems[ 0 ].Text;
48
49                // if item selected is directory, load selected directory
50                if ( Directory.Exists(
51                   Path.Combine( currentDirectory, chosen ) ) )
52                {
53                   LoadFilesInDirectory(
54                      Path.Combine( currentDirectory, chosen ) );
55                } // end if
56             } // end else
57
58             // update displayLabel
59             displayLabel.Text = currentDirectory;
60          } // end if
61       } // end method browserListView_Click
62
63       // display files/subdirectories of current directory
64       public void LoadFilesInDirectory( string currentDirectoryValue )
65       {
66          // load directory information and display
67          try
68          {
69             // clear ListView and set first item
70             browserListView.Items.Clear();
71             browserListView.Items.Add( "Go Up One Level" );
72
```

Fig. 15.31 | ListView displaying files and folders. (Part 2 of 4.)

```
73              // update current directory
74              currentDirectory = currentDirectoryValue;
75              DirectoryInfo newCurrentDirectory =
76                 new DirectoryInfo( currentDirectory );
77
78              // put files and directories into arrays
79              DirectoryInfo[] directoryArray =
80                 newCurrentDirectory.GetDirectories();
81              FileInfo[] fileArray = newCurrentDirectory.GetFiles();
82
83              // add directory names to ListView
84              foreach ( DirectoryInfo dir in directoryArray )
85              {
86                 // add directory to ListView
87                 ListViewItem newDirectoryItem =
88                    browserListView.Items.Add( dir.Name );
89
90                 newDirectoryItem.ImageIndex = 0;  // set directory image
91              } // end foreach
92
93              // add file names to ListView
94              foreach ( FileInfo file in fileArray )
95              {
96                 // add file to ListView
97                 ListViewItem newFileItem =
98                    browserListView.Items.Add( file.Name );
99
100                newFileItem.ImageIndex = 1;  // set file image
101             } // end foreach
102          } // end try
103
104          // access denied
105          catch ( UnauthorizedAccessException )
106          {
107             MessageBox.Show( "Warning: Some fields may not be " +
108                "visible due to permission settings",
109                "Attention", 0, MessageBoxIcon.Warning );
110          } // end catch
111       } // end method LoadFilesInDirectory
112
113       // handle load event when Form displayed for first time
114       private void ListViewTestForm_Load( object sender, EventArgs e )
115       {
116          // add icon images to ImageList
117          fileFolderImageList.Images.Add( Properties.Resources.folder );
118          fileFolderImageList.Images.Add( Properties.Resources.file );
119
120          // load current directory into browserListView
121          LoadFilesInDirectory( currentDirectory );
122          displayLabel.Text = currentDirectory;
123       } // end method ListViewTestForm_Load
124    } // end class ListViewTestForm
125 } // end namespace ListViewTest
```

Fig. 15.31 | ListView displaying files and folders. (Part 3 of 4.)

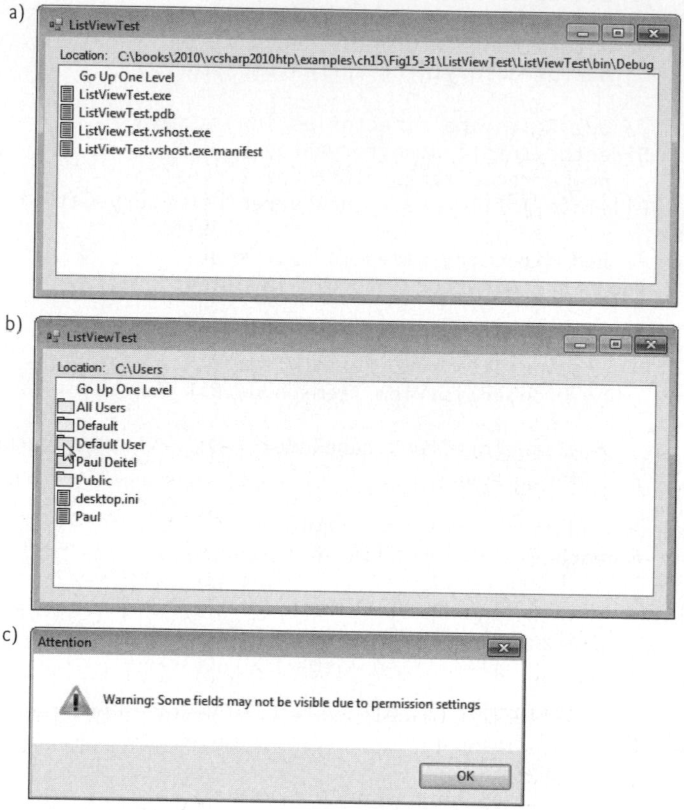

a)

```
ListViewTest                                    ─ ▢ ✕
Location:   C:\books\2010\vcsharp2010htp\examples\ch15\Fig15_31\ListViewTest\ListViewTest\bin\Debug
            Go Up One Level
        📄 ListViewTest.exe
        📄 ListViewTest.pdb
        📄 ListViewTest.vshost.exe
        📄 ListViewTest.vshost.exe.manifest
```

b)

```
ListViewTest                                    ─ ▢ ✕
Location:   C:\Users
            Go Up One Level
        📁 All Users
        📁 Default
        📁 Default User
        📁 Paul Deitel
        📁 Public
        📄 desktop.ini
        📄 Paul
```

c)

```
Attention                                        ✕

    ⚠  Warning: Some fields may not be visible due to permission settings


                                          [ OK ]
```

Fig. 15.31 │ ListView displaying files and folders. (Part 4 of 4.)

Method *LoadFilesInDirectory*

The LoadFilesInDirectory method (lines 64–111) populates browserListView with the directory passed to it (currentDirectoryValue). It clears browserListView and adds the element "Go Up One Level". When the user clicks this element, the program attempts to move up one level (we see how shortly). The method then creates a DirectoryInfo object initialized with the string currentDirectory (lines 75–76). If permission is not given to browse the directory, an exception is thrown (and caught in line 105). Method Load-FilesInDirectory works differently from method PopulateTreeView in the previous program (Fig. 15.28). Instead of loading all the folders on the hard drive, method Load-FilesInDirectory loads only the folders in the current directory.

Class **DirectoryInfo** (namespace System.IO) enables us to browse or manipulate the directory structure easily. Method **GetDirectories** (line 80) returns an array of Direc-toryInfo objects containing the subdirectories of the current directory. Similarly, method **GetFiles** (line 81) returns an array of class **FileInfo** objects containing the files in the current directory. Property **Name** (of both class DirectoryInfo and class FileInfo) contains only the directory or file name, such as temp instead of C:\myfolder\temp. To access the full name, use property **FullName**.

Lines 84–91 and lines 94–101 iterate through the subdirectories and files of the current directory and add them to browserListView. Lines 90 and 100 set the ImageIndex properties of the newly created items. If an item is a directory, we set its icon to a directory icon (index 0); if an item is a file, we set its icon to a file icon (index 1).

Method *browserListView_Click*

Method browserListView_Click (lines 23–61) responds when the user clicks control browserListView. Line 26 checks whether anything is selected. If a selection has been made, line 29 determines whether the user chose the first item in browserListView. The first item in browserListView is always **Go Up One Level**; if it is selected, the program attempts to go up a level. Lines 32–33 create a DirectoryInfo object for the current directory. Line 36 tests property Parent to ensure that the user is not at the root of the directory tree. Property **Parent** indicates the parent directory as a DirectoryInfo object; if no parent directory exists, Parent returns the value null. If a parent directory does exist, lines 38–39 pass the parent directory's full name to LoadFilesInDirectory.

If the user did not select the first item in browserListView, lines 44–56 allow the user to continue navigating through the directory structure. Line 47 creates string chosen and assigns it the text of the selected item (the first item in collection SelectedItems). Lines 50–51 determine whether the user selected a valid directory (rather than a file). Using the Combine method of class Path, the program combines strings currentDirectory and chosen to form the new directory path. The Combine method automatically adds a backslash (\), if necessary, between the two pieces. This value is passed to the **Exists** method of class Directory. Method Exists returns true if its string parameter is a valid directory. If so, the program passes the string to method LoadFilesInDirectory (lines 53–54). Finally, displayLabel is updated with the new directory (line 59).

This program loads quickly, because it indexes only the files in the current directory. A small delay may occur when a new directory is loaded. In addition, changes in the directory structure can be shown by reloading a directory. The previous program (Fig. 15.28) may have a large initial delay, as it loads an entire directory structure. This type of trade-off is typical in the software world.

Software Engineering Observation 15.2

When designing applications that run for long periods of time, you might choose a large initial delay to improve performance throughout the rest of the program. However, in applications that run for only short periods, developers often prefer fast initial loading times and small delays after each action.

15.11 TabControl Control

The **TabControl** creates tabbed windows, such as those in Visual Studio (Fig. 15.32). This enables you to specify more information in the same space on a Form and group displayed data logically. TabControls contain **TabPage** objects, which are similar to Panels and GroupBoxes in that TabPages also can contain controls. You first add controls to the Tab-Page objects, then add the TabPages to the TabControl. Only one TabPage is displayed at a time. To add objects to the TabPage and the TabControl, write

```
myTabPage.Controls.Add( myControl );
myTabControl.TabPages.Add( myTabPage );
```

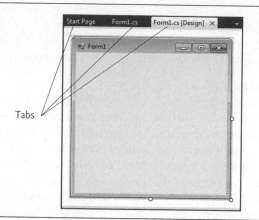

Fig. 15.32 | Tabbed windows in Visual Studio.

The preceding statements call method Add of the Controls collection and method Add of the TabPages collection. The example adds TabControl *myControl* to TabPage *myTab-Page*, then adds *myTabPage* to *myTabControl*. Alternatively, we can use method AddRange to add an array of TabPages or controls to a TabControl or TabPage, respectively. Figure 15.33 depicts a sample TabControl.

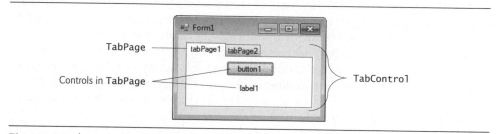

Fig. 15.33 | TabControl with TabPages example.

You can add TabControls visually by dragging and dropping them onto a Form in **Design** mode. To add TabPages in **Design** mode, right click the TabControl and select **Add Tab** (Fig. 15.34). Alternatively, click the **TabPages** property in the **Properties** window and add tabs in the dialog that appears. To change a tab label, set the **Text** property of the TabPage. Clicking the tabs selects the TabControl—to select the TabPage, click the control area underneath the tabs. You can add controls to the TabPage by dragging and dropping items from the **ToolBox**. To view different TabPages, click the appropriate tab (in either design or run mode). Common properties and a common event of TabControls are described in Fig. 15.35.

Each TabPage generates a Click event when its tab is clicked. Event handlers for this event can be created by double clicking the body of the TabPage.

Class UsingTabsForm (Fig. 15.36) uses a TabControl to display various options relating to the text on a label (**Color**, **Size** and **Message**). The last TabPage displays an **About** message, which describes the use of TabControls.

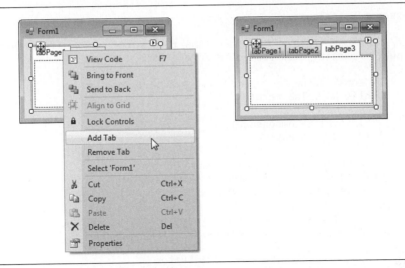

Fig. 15.34 | TabPages added to a TabControl.

TabControl properties and an event	Description
Common Properties	
ImageList	Specifies images to be displayed on tabs.
ItemSize	Specifies the tab size.
Multiline	Indicates whether multiple rows of tabs can be displayed.
SelectedIndex	Index of the selected TabPage.
SelectedTab	The selected TabPage.
TabCount	Returns the number of tab pages.
TabPages	Returns the collection of TabPages within the TabControl as a TabControl.TabPageCollection.
Common Event	
SelectedIndexChanged	Generated when SelectedIndex changes (i.e., another TabPage is selected).

Fig. 15.35 | TabControl properties and an event.

```
1   // Fig. 15.36: UsingTabsForm.cs
2   // Using TabControl to display various font settings.
3   using System;
4   using System.Drawing;
5   using System.Windows.Forms;
6
```

Fig. 15.36 | TabControl used to display various font settings. (Part 1 of 3.)

```
 7    namespace UsingTabs
 8    {
 9       // Form uses Tabs and RadioButtons to display various font settings
10       public partial class UsingTabsForm : Form
11       {
12          // constructor
13          public UsingTabsForm()
14          {
15             InitializeComponent();
16          } // end constructor
17
18          // event handler for Black RadioButton
19          private void blackRadioButton_CheckedChanged(
20             object sender, EventArgs e )
21          {
22             displayLabel.ForeColor = Color.Black; // change color to black
23          } // end method blackRadioButton_CheckedChanged
24
25          // event handler for Red RadioButton
26          private void redRadioButton_CheckedChanged(
27             object sender, EventArgs e )
28          {
29             displayLabel.ForeColor = Color.Red; // change color to red
30          } // end method redRadioButton_CheckedChanged
31
32          // event handler for Green RadioButton
33          private void greenRadioButton_CheckedChanged(
34             object sender, EventArgs e )
35          {
36             displayLabel.ForeColor = Color.Green; // change color to green
37          } // end method greenRadioButton_CheckedChanged
38
39          // event handler for 12 point RadioButton
40          private void size12RadioButton_CheckedChanged(
41             object sender, EventArgs e )
42          {
43             // change font size to 12
44             displayLabel.Font = new Font( displayLabel.Font.Name, 12 );
45          } // end method size12RadioButton_CheckedChanged
46
47          // event handler for 16 point RadioButton
48          private void size16RadioButton_CheckedChanged(
49             object sender, EventArgs e )
50          {
51             // change font size to 16
52             displayLabel.Font = new Font( displayLabel.Font.Name, 16 );
53          } // end method size16RadioButton_CheckedChanged
54
55          // event handler for 20 point RadioButton
56          private void size20RadioButton_CheckedChanged(
57             object sender, EventArgs e )
58          {
```

Fig. 15.36 | TabControl used to display various font settings. (Part 2 of 3.)

```
59              // change font size to 20
60              displayLabel.Font = new Font( displayLabel.Font.Name, 20 );
61           } // end method size20RadioButton_CheckedChanged
62
63           // event handler for Hello! RadioButton
64           private void helloRadioButton_CheckedChanged(
65              object sender, EventArgs e )
66           {
67              displayLabel.Text = "Hello!"; // change text to Hello!
68           } // end method helloRadioButton_CheckedChanged
69
70           // event handler for Goodbye! RadioButton
71           private void goodbyeRadioButton_CheckedChanged(
72              object sender, EventArgs e )
73           {
74              displayLabel.Text = "Goodbye!"; // change text to Goodbye!
75           } // end method goodbyeRadioButton_CheckedChanged
76        } // end class UsingTabsForm
77     } // end namespace UsingTabs
```

Fig. 15.36 | TabControl used to display various font settings. (Part 3 of 3.)

The textOptionsTabControl and the colorTabPage, sizeTabPage, messageTabPage and aboutTabPage are created in the designer (as described previously). The colorTabPage contains three RadioButtons for the colors black (blackRadioButton), red (red-RadioButton) and green (greenRadioButton). This TabPage is displayed in Fig. 15.36(a). The CheckedChanged event handler for each RadioButton updates the color of the text in displayLabel (lines 22, 29 and 36). The sizeTabPage (Fig. 15.36(b)) has three RadioBut-tons, corresponding to font sizes 12 (size12RadioButton), 16 (size16RadioButton) and 20 (size20RadioButton), which change the font size of displayLabel—lines 44, 52 and 60, respectively. The messageTabPage (Fig. 15.36(c)) contains two RadioButtons for the messages **Hello!** (helloRadioButton) and **Goodbye!** (goodbyeRadioButton). The two RadioButtons determine the text on displayLabel (lines 67 and 74, respectively). The aboutTabPage (Fig. 15.36(d)) contains a Label (messageLabel) describing the purpose of TabControls.

Software Engineering Observation 15.3

A TabPage can act as a container for a single logical group of RadioButtons, enforcing their mutual exclusivity. To place multiple RadioButton groups inside a single TabPage, you should group RadioButtons within Panels or GroupBoxes contained within the TabPage.

15.12 Multiple Document Interface (MDI) Windows

In previous chapters, we have built only **single document interface** (SDI) applications. Such programs (including Microsoft's Notepad and Paint) can support only one open window or document at a time. SDI applications usually have limited abilities—Paint and Notepad, for example, have limited image- and text-editing features. To edit multiple documents, the user must execute another instance of the SDI application.

Many complex applications are **multiple document interface** (MDI) programs, which allow users to edit multiple documents at once (e.g., Microsoft Office products). MDI programs also tend to be more complex—Paint Shop Pro and Photoshop have a greater number of image-editing features than does Paint.

An MDI program's main window is called the **parent window**, and each window inside the application is referred to as a **child window**. Although an MDI application can have many child windows, each has only one parent window. Furthermore, a maximum of one child window can be active at once. Child windows cannot be parents themselves and cannot be moved outside their parent. Otherwise, a child window behaves like any other window (with regard to closing, minimizing, resizing, and so on). A child window's functionality can differ from that of other child windows of the parent. For example, one child window might allow the user to edit images, another might allow the user to edit text and a third might display network traffic graphically, but all could belong to the same MDI parent. Figure 15.37 depicts a sample MDI application with two child windows.

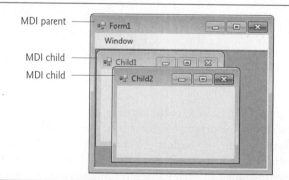

Fig. 15.37 | MDI parent window and MDI child windows.

To create an MDI Form, create a new Form and set its **IsMdiContainer** property to true. The Form changes appearance, as in Fig. 15.38. Next, create a child Form class to be added to the Form. To do this, right click the project in the **Solution Explorer**, select **Project > Add Windows Form...** and name the file. Edit the Form as you like. To add the

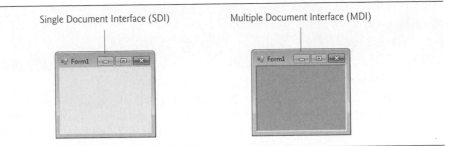

Fig. 15.38 | SDI and MDI forms.

child Form to the parent, we must create a new child Form object, set its **MdiParent** property to the parent Form and call the child Form's Show method. In general, to add a child Form to a parent, write

```
ChildFormClass childForm = New ChildFormClass();
childForm.MdiParent = parentForm;
childForm.Show();
```

In most cases, the parent Form creates the child, so the *parentForm* reference is this. The code to create a child usually lies inside an event handler, which creates a new window in response to a user action. Menu selections (such as **File**, followed by a submenu option of **New**, followed by a submenu option of **Window**) are common techniques for creating new child windows.

Class Form property **MdiChildren** returns an array of child Form references. This is useful if the parent window wants to check the status of all its children (for example, ensuring that all are saved before the parent closes). Property **ActiveMdiChild** returns a reference to the active child window; it returns null if there are no active child windows. Other features of MDI windows are described in Fig. 15.39.

MDI Form properties, a method and an event	Description
Common MDI Child Properties	
IsMdiChild	Indicates whether the Form is an MDI child. If true, Form is an MDI child (read-only property).
MdiParent	Specifies the MDI parent Form of the child.
Common MDI Parent Properties	
ActiveMdiChild	Returns the Form that is the currently active MDI child (returns null if no children are active).
IsMdiContainer	Indicates whether a Form can be an MDI parent. If true, the Form can be an MDI parent. The default value is false.
MdiChildren	Returns the MDI children as an array of Forms.

Fig. 15.39 | MDI parent and MDI child properties, a method and an event. (Part 1 of 2.)

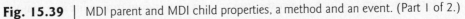

MDI Form properties, a method and an event	Description
Common Method	
LayoutMdi	Determines the display of child forms on an MDI parent. The method takes as a parameter an MdiLayout enumeration with possible values ArrangeIcons, Cascade, TileHorizontal and TileVertical. Figure 15.42 depicts the effects of these values.
Common Event	
MdiChildActivate	Generated when an MDI child is closed or activated.

Fig. 15.39 | MDI parent and MDI child properties, a method and an event. (Part 2 of 2.)

Child windows can be minimized, maximized and closed independently of the parent window. Figure 15.40 shows two images: one containing two minimized child windows and a second containing a maximized child window. When the parent is minimized or closed, the child windows are minimized or closed as well. Notice that the title bar in Fig. 15.40(b) is **Form1 - [Child1]**. When a child window is maximized, its title-bar text is inserted into the parent window's title bar. When a child window is minimized or maximized, its title bar displays a restore icon, which can be used to return the child window to its previous size (its size before it was minimized or maximized).

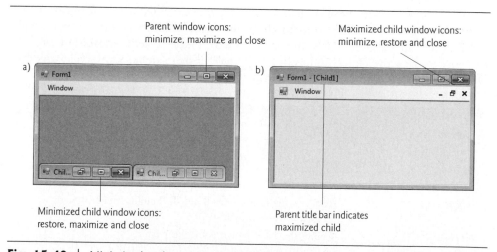

Fig. 15.40 | Minimized and maximized child windows.

C# provides a property that helps track which child windows are open in an MDI container. Property **MdiWindowListItem** of class MenuStrip specifies which menu, if any, displays a list of open child windows that the user can select to bring the corresponding window to the foreground. When a new child window is opened, an entry is added to the end of the list (Fig. 15.41). If ten or more child windows are open, the list includes the option **More Windows...**, which allows the user to select a window from a list in a dialog.

Good Programming Practice 15.1

When creating MDI applications, include a menu that displays a list of the open child windows. This helps the user select a child window quickly, rather than having to search for it in the parent window.

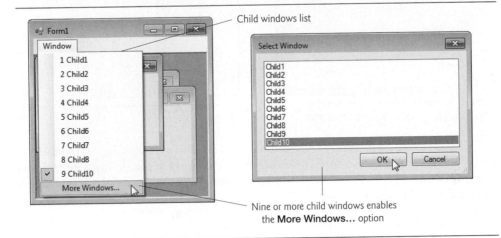

Child windows list

Nine or more child windows enables
the **More Windows...** option

Fig. 15.41 | MenuStrip property MdiWindowListItem example.

MDI containers allow you to organize the placement of its child windows. The child windows in an MDI application can be arranged by calling method **LayoutMdi** of the parent Form. Method LayoutMdi takes an **MdiLayout** enumeration, which can have values Arrange-Icons, Cascade, TileHorizontal and TileVertical. **Tiled windows** completely fill the parent and do not overlap; such windows can be arranged horizontally (value TileHorizontal) or vertically (value TileVertical). **Cascaded windows** (value Cascade) overlap—each is the same size and displays a visible title bar, if possible. Value ArrangeIcons arranges the icons for any minimized child windows. If minimized windows are scattered around the parent window, value ArrangeIcons orders them neatly at the bottom-left corner of the parent window. Figure 15.42 illustrates the values of the MdiLayout enumeration.

a) ArrangeIcons b) Cascade

Fig. 15.42 | MdiLayout enumeration values. (Part 1 of 2.)

c) TileHorizontal

d) TileVertical

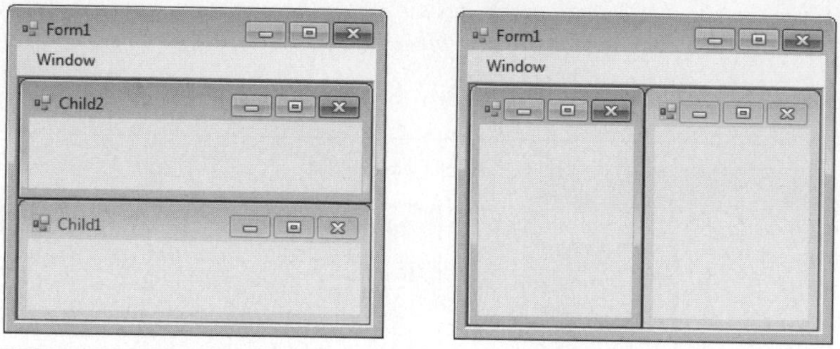

Fig. 15.42 | MdiLayout enumeration values. (Part 2 of 2.)

Class UsingMDIForm (Fig. 15.43) demonstrates MDI windows. Class UsingMDIForm uses three instances of child Form ChildForm (Fig. 15.44), each containing a PictureBox that displays an image. The parent MDI Form contains a menu enabling users to create and arrange child Forms.

MDI Parent Form

Figure 15.43 presents class UsingMDIForm—the application's MDI parent Form. This Form, which is created first, contains two top-level menus. The first of these menus, **File** (fileToolStripMenuItem), contains both an **Exit** item (exitToolStripMenuItem) and a **New** submenu (newToolStripMenuItem) consisting of items for each child window. The second menu, **Window** (windowToolStripMenuItem), provides options for laying out the MDI children, plus a list of the active MDI children.

In the **Properties** window, we set the Form's IsMdiContainer property to true, making the Form an MDI parent. In addition, we set the MenuStrip's MdiWindowListItem property to windowToolStripMenuItem. This enables the **Window** menu to contain the list of child MDI windows.

```
1   // Fig. 15.43: UsingMDIForm.cs
2   // Demonstrating use of MDI parent and child windows.
3   using System;
4   using System.Windows.Forms;
5
6   namespace UsingMDI
7   {
8      // Form demonstrates the use of MDI parent and child windows
9      public partial class UsingMDIForm : Form
10     {
11        // constructor
12        public UsingMDIForm()
13        {
14           InitializeComponent();
15        } // end constructor
16
```

Fig. 15.43 | MDI parent-window class. (Part 1 of 3.)

```
17        // create Lavender Flowers image window
18        private void lavenderToolStripMenuItem_Click(
19           object sender, EventArgs e )
20        {
21           // create new child
22           ChildForm child = new ChildForm(
23              "Lavender Flowers", "lavenderflowers" );
24           child.MdiParent = this; // set parent
25           child.Show(); // display child
26        } // end method lavenderToolStripMenuItem_Click
27
28        // create Purple Flowers image window
29        private void purpleToolStripMenuItem_Click(
30           object sender, EventArgs e )
31        {
32           // create new child
33           ChildForm child = new ChildForm(
34              "Purple Flowers", "purpleflowers" );
35           child.MdiParent = this; // set parent
36           child.Show(); // display child
37        } // end method purpleToolStripMenuItem_Click
38
39        // create Yellow Flowers image window
40        private void yellowToolStripMenuItem_Click(
41           object sender, EventArgs e )
42        {
43           // create new child
44           Child child = new ChildForm(
45              "Yellow Flowers", "yellowflowers" );
46           child.MdiParent = this; // set parent
47           child.Show(); // display child
48        } // end method yellowToolStripMenuItem_Click
49
50        // exit application
51        private void exitToolStripMenuItem_Click(
52           object sender, EventArgs e )
53        {
54           Application.Exit();
55        } // end method exitToolStripMenuItem_Click
56
57        // set Cascade layout
58        private void cascadeToolStripMenuItem_Click(
59           object sender, EventArgs e )
60        {
61           this.LayoutMdi( MdiLayout.Cascade );
62        } // end method cascadeToolStripMenuItem_Click
63
64        // set TileHorizontal layout
65        private void tileHorizontalToolStripMenuItem_Click(
66           object sender, EventArgs e )
67        {
68           this.LayoutMdi( MdiLayout.TileHorizontal );
69        } // end method tileHorizontalToolStripMenuItem
```

Fig. 15.43 | MDI parent-window class. (Part 2 of 3.)

```
70
71        // set TileVertical layout
72        private void tileVerticalToolStripMenuItem_Click(
73           object sender, EventArgs e )
74        {
75           this.LayoutMdi( MdiLayout.TileVertical );
76        } // end method tileVerticalToolStripMenuItem_Click
77     } // end class UsingMDIForm
78  } // end namespace UsingMDI
```

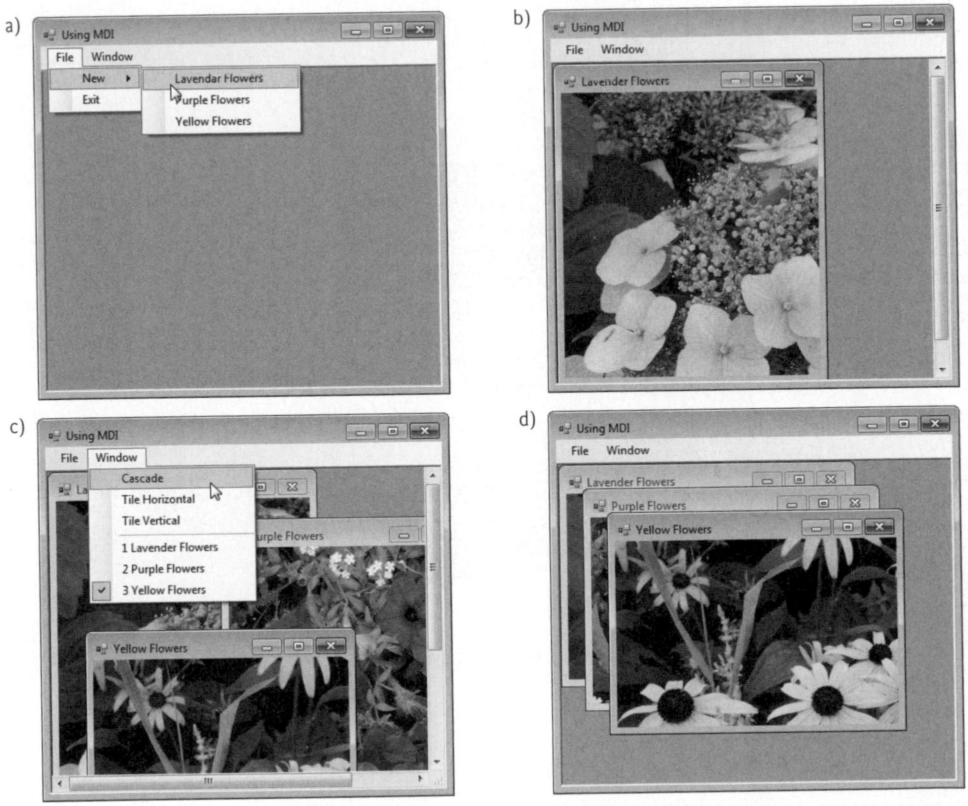

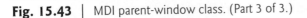

Fig. 15.43 | MDI parent-window class. (Part 3 of 3.)

The **Cascade** menu item (cascadeToolStripMenuItem) has an event handler (cascadeToolStripMenuItem_Click, lines 58–62) that arranges the child windows in a cascading manner. The event handler calls method LayoutMdi with the argument Cascade from the MdiLayout enumeration (line 61).

The **Tile Horizontal** menu item (tileHorizontalToolStripMenuItem) has an event handler (tileHorizontalToolStripMenuItem_Click, lines 65–69) that arranges the child windows in a horizontal manner. The event handler calls method LayoutMdi with the argument TileHorizontal from the MdiLayout enumeration (line 68).

Finally, the **Tile Vertical** menu item (tileVerticalToolStripMenuItem) has an event handler (tileVerticalToolStripMenuItem_Click, lines 72–76) that arranges the child windows in a vertical manner. The event handler calls method LayoutMdi with the argument TileVertical from the MdiLayout enumeration (line 75).

MDI Child *Form*

At this point, the application is still incomplete—we must define the MDI child class. To do this, right click the project in the **Solution Explorer** and select **Add > Windows Form....** Then name the new class in the dialog as ChildForm (Fig. 15.44). Next, we add a PictureBox (displayPictureBox) to ChildForm. In ChildForm's constructor, line 16 sets the title-bar text. Lines 19–21 retrieve the appropriate image resource, cast it to an Image and set displayPictureBox's Image property. The images that are used can be found in the Images subfolder of this chapter's examples directory.

```
1   // Fig. 15.44: ChildForm.cs
2   // Child window of MDI parent.
3   using System;
4   using System.Drawing;
5   using System.Windows.Forms;
6
7   namespace UsingMDI
8   {
9      public partial class ChildForm : Form
10     {
11        public ChildForm( string title, string resourceName )
12        {
13           // Required for Windows Form Designer support
14           InitializeComponent();
15
16           Text = title; // set title text
17
18           // set image to display in PictureBox
19           displayPictureBox.Image =
20              ( Image ) ( Properties.Resources.ResourceManager.GetObject(
21                 resourceName );
22        } // end constructor
23     } // end class ChildForm
24  } // end namespace UsingMDI
```

Fig. 15.44 | MDI child ChildForm.

After the MDI child class is defined, the parent MDI Form (Fig. 15.43) can create new child windows. The event handlers in lines 18–48 create a new child Form corresponding to the menu item clicked. Lines 22–23, 33–34 and 44–45 create new instances of Child-Form. Lines 24, 35 and 46 set each Child's MdiParent property to the parent Form. Lines 25, 36 and 47 call method Show to display each child Form.

15.13 Visual Inheritance

Chapter 11 discussed how to create classes by inheriting from other classes. We have also used inheritance to create Forms that display a GUI, by deriving our new Form classes from class System.Windows.Forms.Form. This is an example of **visual inheritance**. The derived Form class contains the functionality of its Form base class, including any base-class properties, methods, variables and controls. The derived class also inherits all visual aspects—such as sizing, component layout, spacing between GUI components, colors and fonts—from its base class.

Visual inheritance enables you to achieve visual consistency across applications. For example, you could define a base Form that contains a product's logo, a specific background color, a predefined menu bar and other elements. You then could use the base Form throughout an application for uniformity and branding. You can also create controls that inherit from other controls. For example, you might create a custom UserControl (discussed in Section 15.14) that is derived from an existing control.

Creating a Base *Form*

Class VisualInheritanceBaseForm (Fig. 15.45) derives from Form. The output depicts the workings of the program. The GUI contains two Labels with text **Bugs, Bugs, Bugs** and **Copyright 2010, by Deitel & Associates, Inc.**, as well as one Button displaying the text **Learn More**. When a user presses the **Learn More** Button, method learnMoreButton_Click (lines 18–24) is invoked. This method displays a MessageBox that provides some informative text.

```
1   // Fig. 15.45: VisualInheritanceBaseForm.cs
2   // Base Form for use with visual inheritance.
3   using System;
4   using System.Windows.Forms;
5
6   namespace VisualInheritanceBase
7   {
8      // base Form used to demonstrate visual inheritance
9      public partial class VisualInheritanceBaseForm : Form
10     {
11        // constructor
12        public VisualInheritanceForm()
13        {
14           InitializeComponent();
15        } // end constructor
16
17        // display MessageBox when Button is clicked
18        private void learnMoreButton_Click( object sender, EventArgs e )
19        {
20           MessageBox.Show(
21              "Bugs, Bugs, Bugs is a product of deitel.com",
22              "Learn More", MessageBoxButtons.OK,
23              MessageBoxIcon.Information );
24        } // end method learnMoreButton_Click
25     } // end class VisualInheritanceBaseForm
26  } // end namespace VisualInheritanceBase
```

Fig. 15.45 | Class VisualInheritanceBaseForm, which inherits from class Form, contains a Button (**Learn More**). (Part 1 of 2.)

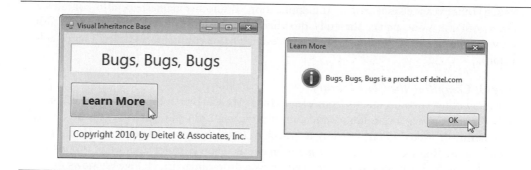

Fig. 15.45 | Class `VisualInheritanceBaseForm`, which inherits from class `Form`, contains a Button (**Learn More**). (Part 2 of 2.)

Steps for Declaring and Using a Reusable Class

Before a `Form` (or any class) can be used in multiple applications, it must be placed in a class library to make it reusable. The steps for creating a reusable class are:

1. Declare a `public` class. If the class is not `public`, it can be used only by other classes in the same assembly—that is, compiled into the same DLL or EXE file.

2. Choose a namespace name and add a `namespace` declaration to the source-code file for the reusable class declaration.

3. Compile the class into a class library.

4. Add a reference to the class library in an application.

5. Use the class.

Let's take a look at these steps in the context of this example.

Step 1: Creating a `public` Class

For *Step 1* in this discussion, we use the `public` class `VisualInheritanceBaseForm` declared in Fig. 15.45. By default, every new `Form` class you create is declares as a public class.

Step 2: Adding the `namespace` Declaration

For *Step 2*, we use the `namespace` declaration that was created for us by the IDE. By default, every new class you define is placed in a `namespace` with the same name as the project. In almost every example in the text, we've seen that classes from preexisting libraries, such as the .NET Framework Class Library, can be imported into a C# application. Each class belongs to a namespace that contains a group of related classes. As applications become more complex, namespaces help you manage the complexity of application components. Class libraries and namespaces also facilitate software reuse by enabling applications to add classes from other namespaces (as we've done in most examples). We removed the namespace declarations in earlier chapters because they were not necessary.

Placing a class inside a `namespace` declaration indicates that the class is part of the specified namespace. The `namespace` name is part of the fully qualified class name, so the name of class `VisualInheritanceTestForm` is actually `VisualInheritanceBase.VisualInheritanceBaseForm`. You can use this fully qualified name in your applications, or you can write a `using` directive and use the class's simple name (the unqualified class name—

VisualInheritanceBaseForm) in the application. If another namespace also contains a class with the same name, the fully qualified class names can be used to distinguish between the classes in the application and prevent a name conflict (also called a name collision).

Step 3: Compiling the Class Library

To allow other Forms to inherit from VisualInheritanceForm, we must package Visual-InheritanceForm as a class library and compile it into a **.dll file**. Such as file is known as a **dynamically linked library**—a way to package classes that you can reference from other applications. Right click the project name in the **Solution Explorer** and select **Properties**, then choose the **Application** tab. In the **Output type** drop-down list, change **Windows Application** to **Class Library**. Building the project produces the .dll. You can configure a project to be a class library when you first create it by selecting the **Class Library** template in the **New Project** dialog. [*Note:* A class library cannot execute as a stand-alone application. The screen captures in Fig. 15.45 were taken before changing the project to a class library.]

Step 4: Adding a Reference to the Class Library

Once the class is compiled and stored in the class library file, the library can be referenced from any application by indicating to the Visual C# Express IDE where to find the class library file. To visually inherit from VisualInheritanceBaseForm, first create a new Windows application. Right-click the project name in the **Solution Explorer** window and select **Add Reference...** from the pop-up menu that appears. The dialog box that appears will contain a list of class libraries from the .NET Framework. Some class libraries, like the one containing the System namespace, are so common that they're added to your application by the IDE. The ones in this list are not.

In the **Add Reference...** dialog box, click the **Browse** tab. When you build a class library, Visual C# places the .dll file in the project's bin\Release folder. In the **Browse** tab, you can navigate to the directory containing the class library file you created in *Step 3*, as shown in Fig. 15.46. Select the .dll file and click **OK**.

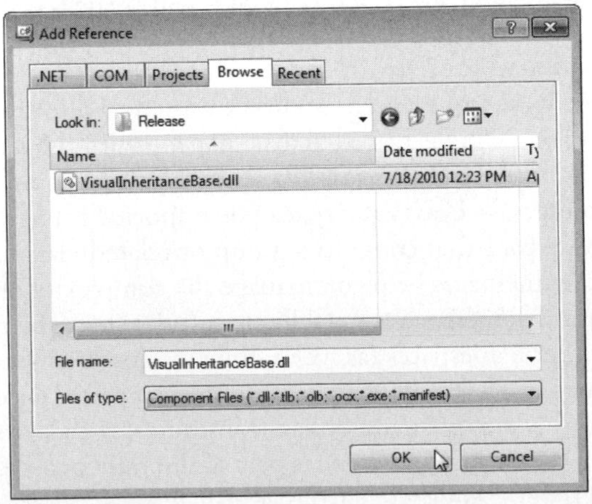

Fig. 15.46 | Adding a reference.

Step 5: Using the Class—Deriving From a Base *Form*

Open the file that defines the new application's GUI and modify the line that defines the class to indicate that the application's Form should inherit from class VisualInheritanceBaseForm. The class-declaration line should now appear as follows:

```
public partial class VisualInheritanceTestForm :
    VisualInheritanceBase.VisualInheritanceBaseForm
```

Unless you specify namespace VisualInheritanceBase in a using directive, you must use the fully qualified name VisualInheritanceBase.VisualInheritanceBaseForm. In **Design** view, the new application's Form should now display the controls inherited from the base Form (Fig. 15.47). We can now add more components to the Form.

Fig. 15.47 | Form demonstrating visual inheritance.

Class *VisualInheritanceTestForm*

Class VisualInheritanceTestForm (Fig. 15.48) is a derived class of VisualInheritanceBaseForm. The output illustrates the functionality of the program. The components, their layouts and the functionality of base class VisualInheritanceBaseForm (Fig. 15.45) are inherited by VisualInheritanceTestForm. We added an additional Button with text **About this Program**. When a user presses this Button, method aboutButton_Click (lines 19–25) is invoked. This method displays another MessageBox providing different informative text (lines 21–24).

```
1   // Fig. 15.48: VisualInheritanceTestForm.cs
2   // Derived Form using visual inheritance.
3   using System;
4   using System.Windows.Forms;
5
6   namespace VisualInheritanceTest
7   {
8      // derived form using visual inheritance
9      public partial class VisualInheritanceTestForm :
10        VisualInheritanceBase.VisualInheritanceBaseForm
11     {
```

Fig. 15.48 | Class VisualInheritanceTestForm, which inherits from class VisualInheritanceBaseForm, contains an additional Button. (Part 1 of 2.)

```
12          // constructor
13          public VisualInheritanceTestForm()
14          {
15             InitializeComponent();
16          } // end constructor
17
18          // display MessageBox when Button is clicked
19          private void aboutButton_Click(object sender, EventArgs e)
20          {
21             MessageBox.Show(
22                "This program was created by Deitel & Associates.",
23                "About This Program", MessageBoxButtons.OK,
24                MessageBoxIcon.Information );
25          } // end method aboutButton_Click
26       } // end class VisualInheritanceTestForm
27    } // end namespace VisualInheritanceTest
```

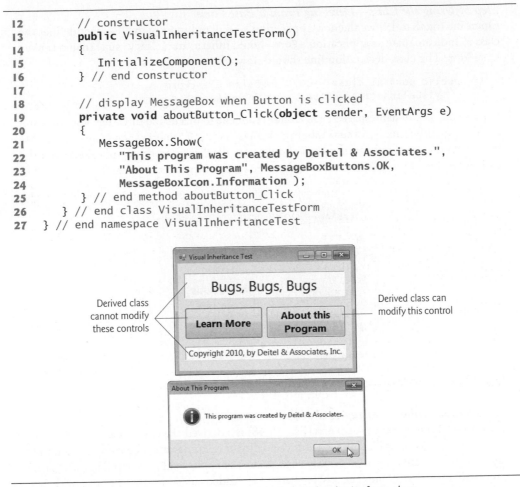

Fig. 15.48 | Class `VisualInheritanceTestForm`, which inherits from class `VisualInheritanceBaseForm`, contains an additional `Button`. (Part 2 of 2.)

If a user clicks the **Learn More** button, the event is handled by the base-class event handler `learnMoreButton_Click`. Because `VisualInheritanceBaseForm` uses a private access modifier to declare its controls, `VisualInheritanceTestForm` cannot modify the controls inherited from class `VisualInheritanceBaseForm` visually or programmatically. You can, however, add event handlers for the inherited controls. The IDE displays a small icon at the top left of the visually inherited controls to indicate that they're inherited and cannot be altered.

15.14 User-Defined Controls

The .NET Framework allows you to create **custom controls**. These custom controls appear in the user's **Toolbox** and can be added to `Forms`, `Panels` or `GroupBoxes` in the same way that we add `Buttons`, `Labels` and other predefined controls. The simplest way to create a custom control is to derive a class from an existing control, such as a `Label`. This is useful if you want to add functionality to an existing control, rather than replacing it with one that provides the desired functionality. For example, you can create a new type of Label that behaves like a normal Label but has a different appearance. You accomplish this by inheriting from class Label and overriding method OnPaint.

Method OnPaint

All controls have an **OnPaint** method, which the system calls when a component must be redrawn (such as when the component is resized). The method receives a **PaintEventArgs** object, which contains graphics information—property **Graphics** is the graphics object used to draw, and property **ClipRectangle** defines the rectangular boundary of the control. Whenever the system raises a Paint event to draw the control on the screen, the control catches the event and calls its OnPaint method. The base class's OnPaint should be called explicitly from an overridden OnPaint implementation before executing custom-paint code. In most cases, you want to do this to ensure that the original painting code executes in addition to the code you define in the custom control's class. Alternately, if we do not wish to let the base-class OnPaint method execute, we do not call it.

Creating New Controls

To create a new control composed of existing controls, use class **UserControl**. Controls added to a custom control are called **constituent controls**. For example, a programmer could create a UserControl composed of a Button, a Label and a TextBox, each associated with some functionality (for example, the Button setting the Label's text to that contained in the TextBox). The UserControl acts as a container for the controls added to it. The UserControl contains constituent controls, but it does not determine how these constituent controls are displayed. To control the appearance of each constituent control, you can handle each control's Paint event or override OnPaint. Both the Paint event handler and OnPaint are passed a PaintEventArgs object, which can be used to draw graphics (lines, rectangles, and so on) on the constituent controls.

Using another technique, a programmer can create a brand-new control by inheriting from class Control. This class does not define any specific behavior; that's left to you. Instead, class Control handles the items associated with all controls, such as events and sizing handles. Method OnPaint should contain a call to the base class's OnPaint method, which calls the Paint event handlers. You add code that draws custom graphics inside the overridden OnPaint method. This technique allows for the greatest flexibility but also requires the most planning. All three approaches are summarized in Fig. 15.49.

Custom-control techniques and PaintEventArgs properties	Description
Custom-Control Techniques	
Inherit from Windows Forms control	You can do this to add functionality to a preexisting control. If you override method OnPaint, call the base class's OnPaint method. You only can add to the original control's appearance, not redesign it.

Fig. 15.49 | Custom-control creation. (Part 1 of 2.)

Custom-control techniques and PaintEventArgs properties	Description
Create a UserControl	You can create a UserControl composed of multiple preexisting controls (e.g., to combine their functionality). You place drawing code in a Paint event handler or overridden OnPaint method.
Inherit from class Control	Define a brand new control. Override method OnPaint, then call base-class method OnPaint and include methods to draw the control. With this method you can customize control appearance and functionality.
PaintEventArgs Properties	
Graphics	The control's graphics object. It is used to draw on the control.
ClipRectangle	Specifies the rectangle indicating the boundary of the control.

Fig. 15.49 | Custom-control creation. (Part 2 of 2.)

Clock Control

We create a "clock" control in Fig. 15.50. This is a UserControl composed of a Label and a Timer—whenever the Timer raises an event (once per second in this example), the Label is updated to reflect the current time.

```
1   // Fig. 15.50: ClockUserControl.cs
2   // User-defined control with a timer and a Label.
3   using System;
4   using System.Windows.Forms;
5
6   namespace ClockExample
7   {
8      // UserControl that displays the time on a Label
9      public partial class ClockUserControl : UserControl
10     {
11        // constructor
12        public ClockUserControl()
13        {
14           InitializeComponent();
15        } // end constructor
16
17        // update Label at every tick
18        private void clockTimer_Tick(object sender, EventArgs e)
19        {
20           // get current time (Now), convert to string
21           displayLabel.Text = DateTime.Now.ToLongTimeString();
22        } // end method clockTimer_Tick
23     } // end class ClockUserControl
24  } // end namespace ClockExample
```

Fig. 15.50 | UserControl-defined clock. (Part 1 of 2.)

Fig. 15.50 | UserControl-defined clock. (Part 2 of 2.)

Timers

Timers (System.Windows.Forms namespace) are non-visual components that generate Tick events at a set interval. This interval is set by the Timer's **Interval** property, which defines the number of milliseconds (thousandths of a second) between events. By default, timers are disabled and do not generate events.

Adding a User Control

This application contains a user control (ClockUserControl) and a Form that displays the user control. Create a Windows application, then create a UserControl class by selecting **Project > Add User Control....** This displays a dialog from which we can select the type of control to add—user controls are already selected. We then name the file (and the class) ClockUserControl. Our empty ClockUserControl is displayed as a grey rectangle.

Designing the User Control

You can treat this control like a Windows Form, meaning that you can add controls using the **ToolBox** and set properties using the **Properties** window. However, instead of creating an application, you are simply creating a new control composed of other controls. Add a Label (displayLabel) and a Timer (clockTimer) to the UserControl. Set the Timer interval to 1000 milliseconds and set displayLabel's text with each Tick event (lines 18–22). To generate events, clockTimer must be enabled by setting property Enabled to true in the **Properties** window.

Structure **DateTime** (namespace System) contains property **Now**, which returns the current time. Method **ToLongTimeString** converts Now to a string containing the current hour, minute and second (along with AM or PM, depending on your locale). We use this to set the time in displayLabel in line 21.

Once created, our clock control appears as an item on the **ToolBox** in the section titled *ProjectName* **Components**, where *ProjectName* is your project's name. *You may need to switch to the application's Form before the item appears in the **ToolBox**.* To use the control, simply drag it to the Form and run the Windows application. We gave the ClockUserControl object a white background to make it stand out in the Form. Figure 15.50 shows the output of Clock, which contains our ClockUserControl. There are no event handlers in Clock, so we show only the code for ClockUserControl.

Sharing Custom Controls with Other Developers

Visual Studio allows you to share custom controls with other developers. To create a User-Control that can be exported to other solutions, do the following:

1. Create a new **Class Library** project.

2. Delete Class1.cs, initially provided with the application.

3. Right click the project in the **Solution Explorer** and select **Add > User Control...**. In the dialog that appears, name the user-control file and click **Add**.

4. Inside the project, add controls and functionality to the UserControl (Fig. 15.51).

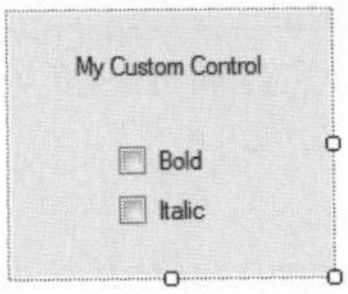

Fig. 15.51 | Custom-control creation.

5. Build the project. Visual Studio creates a .dll file for the UserControl in the output directory (bin/Release). The file is not executable; class libraries are used to define classes that are reused in other executable applications.

6. Create a new Windows application.

7. In the new Windows application, right click the **ToolBox** and select **Choose Items...**. In the **Choose Toolbox Items** dialog that appears, click **Browse...**. Browse for the .dll file from the class library created in *Steps 1–5*. The item will then appear in the **Choose Toolbox Items** dialog (Fig. 15.52). If it is not already checked, check this item. Click **OK** to add the item to the **Toolbox**. This control can now be added to the Form as if it were any other control.

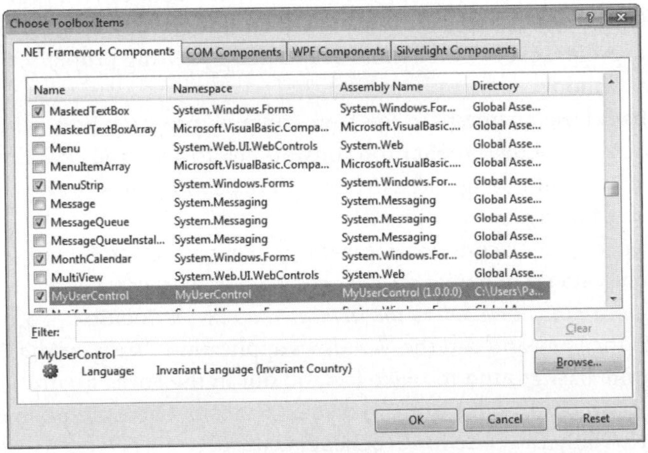

Fig. 15.52 | Custom control added to the **ToolBox**.

15.15 Wrap-Up

Many of today's commercial applications provide GUIs that are easy to use and manipulate. Because of this demand for user-friendly GUIs, the ability to design sophisticated

GUIs is an essential programming skill. Visual Studio's IDE makes GUI development quick and easy. In Chapters 14 and 15, we presented basic Windows Forms GUI development techniques. In Chapter 15, we demonstrated how to create menus, which provide users easy access to an application's functionality. You learned the `DateTimePicker` and `MonthCalendar` controls, which allow users to input date and time values. We demonstrated `LinkLabels`, which are used to link the user to an application or a web page. You used several controls that provide lists of data to the user—`ListBoxes`, `CheckedListBoxes` and `ListViews`. We used the `ComboBox` control to create drop-down lists, and the `TreeView` control to display data in hierarchical form. We then introduced complex GUIs that use tabbed windows and multiple document interfaces. The chapter concluded with demonstrations of visual inheritance and creating custom controls. In Chapter 16, we introduce `string` and character processing.

16

Strings and Characters

OBJECTIVES

In this chapter you'll learn:

■ To create and manipulate immutable character-string objects of class `string` and mutable character-string objects of class `StringBuilder`.

■ To manipulate character objects of `struct Char`.

■ To use regular-expression classes `Regex` and `Match`.

■ To iterate through matches to a regular expression.

■ To use character classes to match any character from a set of characters.

■ To use quantifiers to match a pattern multiple times.

■ To search for patterns in text using regular expressions.

■ To validate data using regular expressions and LINQ.

■ To modify `string`s using regular expressions and class `Regex`.

The chief defect of Henry King
Was chewing little bits of string.
—Hilaire Belloc

The difference between the almost-right word and the right word is really a large matter—it's the difference between the lightning bug and the lightning.
—Mark Twain

16.1 Introduction

This chapter introduces the .NET Framework Class Library's string- and character-processing capabilities and demonstrates how to use regular expressions to search for patterns in text. The techniques it presents can be employed in text editors, word processors, page-layout software, computerized typesetting systems and other kinds of text-processing software. Previous chapters presented some basic string-processing capabilities. Now we discuss in detail the text-processing capabilities of class string and type char from the System namespace and class StringBuilder from the System.Text namespace.

We begin with an overview of the fundamentals of characters and strings in which we discuss character constants and string literals. We then provide examples of class string's many constructors and methods. The examples demonstrate how to determine the length of strings, copy strings, access individual characters in strings, search strings, obtain substrings from larger strings, compare strings, concatenate strings, replace characters in strings and convert strings to uppercase or lowercase letters.

Next, we introduce class StringBuilder, which is used to build strings dynamically. We demonstrate StringBuilder capabilities for determining and specifying the size of a StringBuilder, as well as appending, inserting, removing and replacing characters in a StringBuilder object. We then introduce the character-testing methods of struct Char that enable a program to determine whether a character is a digit, a letter, a lowercase letter, an uppercase letter, a punctuation mark or a symbol other than a punctuation mark. Such methods are useful for validating individual characters in user input. In addition, type Char provides methods for converting a character to uppercase or lowercase.

We discuss regular expressions. We present classes Regex and Match from the System.Text.RegularExpressions namespace as well as the symbols that are used to form regular expressions. We then demonstrate how to find patterns in a string, match entire strings to patterns, replace characters in a string that match a pattern and split strings at delimiters specified as a pattern in a regular expression.

16.2 Fundamentals of Characters and Strings

Characters are the fundamental building blocks of C# source code. Every program is composed of characters that, when grouped together meaningfully, create a sequence that the compiler interprets as instructions describing how to accomplish a task. In addition to normal characters, a program also can contain **character constants**. A character constant is a character that's represented as an integer value, called a *character code*. For example, the integer value 122 corresponds to the character constant 'z'. The integer value 10 corresponds to the newline character '\n'. Character constants are established according to the **Unicode character set**, an international character set that contains many more symbols and letters than does the ASCII character set (listed in Appendix C). To learn more about Unicode, see Appendix F.

A string is a series of characters treated as a unit. These characters can be uppercase letters, lowercase letters, digits and various **special characters**: +, -, *, /, $ and others. A string is an object of class string in the System namespace.[1] We write **string literals**, also called **string constants**, as sequences of characters in double quotation marks, as follows:

```
"John Q. Doe"
"9999 Main Street"
"Waltham, Massachusetts"
"(201) 555-1212"
```

A declaration can assign a string literal to a string reference. The declaration

```
string color = "blue";
```

initializes string reference color to refer to the string literal object "blue".

> **Performance Tip 16.1**
>
> *If there are multiple occurrences of the same string literal object in an application, a single copy of it will be referenced from each location in the program that uses that string literal. It's possible to share the object in this manner, because string literal objects are implicitly constant. Such sharing conserves memory.*

On occasion, a string will contain multiple backslash characters (this often occurs in the name of a file). To avoid excessive backslash characters, it's possible to exclude escape sequences and interpret all the characters in a string literally, using the @ character. Backslashes within the double quotation marks following the @ character are not considered escape sequences, but rather regular backslash characters. Often this simplifies programming and makes the code easier to read. For example, consider the string "C:\MyFolder\MySubFolder\MyFile.txt" with the following assignment:

```
string file = "C:\\MyFolder\\MySubFolder\\MyFile.txt";
```

Using the verbatim string syntax, the assignment can be altered to

```
string file = @"C:\MyFolder\MySubFolder\MyFile.txt";
```

This approach also has the advantage of allowing string literals to span multiple lines by preserving all newlines, spaces and tabs.

---

1. C# provides the string keyword as an alias for class String. In this book, we use the term string.

16.3 string Constructors

Class string provides eight constructors for initializing strings in various ways. Figure 16.1 demonstrates three of the constructors.

```
1   // Fig. 16.1: StringConstructor.cs
2   // Demonstrating string class constructors.
3   using System;
4
5   class StringConstructor
6   {
7      public static void Main( string[] args )
8      {
9         // string initialization
10        char[] characterArray =
11           { 'b', 'i', 'r', 't', 'h', ' ', 'd', 'a', 'y' };
12        string originalString = "Welcome to C# programming!";
13        string string1 = originalString;
14        string string2 = new string( characterArray );
15        string string3 = new string( characterArray, 6, 3 );
16        string string4 = new string( 'C', 5 );
17
18        Console.WriteLine( "string1 = " + "\"" + string1 + "\"\n" +
19           "string2 = " + "\"" + string2 + "\"\n" +
20           "string3 = " + "\"" + string3 + "\"\n" +
21           "string4 = " + "\"" + string4 + "\"\n" );
22     } // end Main
23  } // end class StringConstructor
```

```
string1 = "Welcome to C# programming!"
string2 = "birth day"
string3 = "day"
string4 = "CCCCC"
```

Fig. 16.1 | string constructors.

Lines 10–11 allocate the char array characterArray, which contains nine characters. Lines 12–16 declare the strings originalString, string1, string2, string3 and string4. Line 12 assigns string literal "Welcome to C# programming!" to string reference originalString. Line 13 sets string1 to reference the same string literal.

Line 14 assigns to string2 a new string, using the string constructor with a character array argument. The new string contains a copy of the array's characters.

Line 15 assigns to string3 a new string, using the string constructor that takes a char array and two int arguments. The second argument specifies the starting index position (the *offset*) from which characters in the array are to be copied. The third argument specifies the number of characters (the *count*) to be copied from the specified starting position in the array. The new string contains a copy of the specified characters in the array. If the specified offset or count indicates that the program should access an element outside the bounds of the character array, an ArgumentOutOfRangeException is thrown.

Line 16 assigns to string4 a new string, using the string constructor that takes as arguments a character and an int specifying the number of times to repeat that character in the string.

Software Engineering Observation 16.1

In most cases, it's not necessary to make a copy of an existing string. All strings are immutable—their character contents cannot be changed after they're created. Also, if there are one or more references to a string (or any object for that matter), the object cannot be reclaimed by the garbage collector.

16.4 string Indexer, Length Property and CopyTo Method

The application in Fig. 16.2 presents the string indexer, which facilitates the retrieval of any character in the string, and the string property Length, which returns the length of the string. The string method CopyTo copies a specified number of characters from a string into a char array.

```
1   // Fig. 16.2: StringMethods.cs
2   // Using the indexer, property Length and method CopyTo
3   // of class string.
4   using System;
5
6   class StringMethods
7   {
8      public static void Main( string[] args )
9      {
10        string string1 = "hello there";
11        char[] characterArray = new char[ 5 ];
12
13        // output string1
14        Console.WriteLine( "string1: \"" + string1 + "\"" );
15
16        // test Length property
17        Console.WriteLine( "Length of string1: " + string1.Length );
18
19        // loop through characters in string1 and display reversed
20        Console.Write( "The string reversed is: " );
21
22        for ( int i = string1.Length - 1; i >= 0; i-- )
23           Console.Write( string1[ i ] );
24
25        // copy characters from string1 into characterArray
26        string1.CopyTo( 0, characterArray, 0, characterArray.Length );
27        Console.Write( "\nThe character array is: " );
28
29        for ( int i = 0; i < characterArray.Length; i++ )
30           Console.Write( characterArray[ i ] );
31
32        Console.WriteLine( "\n" );
33     } // end Main
34  } // end class StringMethods
```

Fig. 16.2 | string indexer, Length property and CopyTo method. (Part 1 of 2.)

```
string1: "hello there"
Length of string1: 11
The string reversed is: ereht olleh
The character array is: hello
```

Fig. 16.2 | `string` indexer, `Length` property and `CopyTo` method. (Part 2 of 2.)

This application determines the length of a `string`, displays its characters in reverse order and copies a series of characters from the `string` to a character array. Line 17 uses `string` property `Length` to determine the number of characters in `string1`. Like arrays, `strings` always know their own size.

Lines 22–23 write the characters of `string1` in reverse order using the `string` indexer. The `string` indexer treats a `string` as an array of `char`s and returns each character at a specific position in the `string`. The indexer receives an integer argument as the *position number* and returns the character at that position. As with arrays, the first element of a `string` is considered to be at position 0.

Common Programming Error 16.1

Attempting to access a character that's outside a `string`'s bounds results in an `Index-OutOfRangeException`.

Line 26 uses `string` method `CopyTo` to copy the characters of `string1` into a character array (`characterArray`). The first argument given to method `CopyTo` is the index from which the method begins copying characters in the `string`. The second argument is the character array into which the characters are copied. The third argument is the index specifying the starting location at which the method begins placing the copied characters into the character array. The last argument is the number of characters that the method will copy from the `string`. Lines 29–30 output the `char` array contents one character at a time.

16.5 Comparing `strings`

The next two examples demonstrate various methods for comparing `strings`. To understand how one `string` can be "greater than" or "less than" another, consider the process of alphabetizing a series of last names. The reader would, no doubt, place `"Jones"` before `"Smith"`, because the first letter of `"Jones"` comes before the first letter of `"Smith"` in the alphabet. The alphabet is more than just a set of 26 letters—it's an ordered list of characters in which each letter occurs in a specific position. For example, Z is more than just a letter of the alphabet; it's specifically the twenty-sixth letter of the alphabet. Computers can order characters alphabetically because they're represented internally as Unicode numeric codes.

*Comparing Strings with **Equals**, **CompareTo** and the Equality Operator (**==**)*
Class `string` provides several ways to compare `strings`. The application in Fig. 16.3 demonstrates the use of method `Equals`, method `CompareTo` and the equality operator (`==`).

The condition in line 21 uses `string` method `Equals` to compare `string1` and literal `string` `"hello"` to determine whether they're equal. Method `Equals` (inherited from `object` and overridden in `string`) tests any two objects for equality (i.e., checks whether the objects have identical contents). The method returns `true` if the objects are equal and false otherwise. In this case, the condition returns true, because string1 references string literal object "hello". Method Equals uses word sorting rules that depend on your system's currently selected culture. Comparing "hello" with "HELLO" would return false, because the lowercase letters are different from the those of corresponding upper-case letters.

```
 1   // Fig. 16.3: StringCompare.cs
 2   // Comparing strings
 3   using System;
 4
 5   class StringCompare
 6   {
 7      public static void Main( string[] args )
 8      {
 9         string string1 = "hello";
10         string string2 = "good bye";
11         string string3 = "Happy Birthday";
12         string string4 = "happy birthday";
13
14         // output values of four strings
15         Console.WriteLine( "string1 = \"" + string1 + "\"" +
16            "\nstring2 = \"" + string2 + "\"" +
17            "\nstring3 = \"" + string3 + "\"" +
18            "\nstring4 = \"" + string4 + "\"\n" );
19
20         // test for equality using Equals method
21         if ( string1.Equals( "hello" ) )
22            Console.WriteLine( "string1 equals \"hello\"" );
23         else
24            Console.WriteLine( "string1 does not equal \"hello\"" );
25
26         // test for equality with ==
27         if ( string1 == "hello" )
28            Console.WriteLine( "string1 equals \"hello\"" );
29         else
30            Console.WriteLine( "string1 does not equal \"hello\"" );
31
32         // test for equality comparing case
33         if ( string.Equals( string3, string4 ) ) // static method
34            Console.WriteLine( "string3 equals string4" );
35         else
36            Console.WriteLine( "string3 does not equal string4" );
37
38         // test CompareTo
39         Console.WriteLine( "\nstring1.CompareTo( string2 ) is " +
40            string1.CompareTo( string2 ) + "\n" +
41            "string2.CompareTo( string1 ) is " +
42            string2.CompareTo( string1 ) + "\n" +
43            "string1.CompareTo( string1 ) is " +
44            string1.CompareTo( string1 ) + "\n" +
45            "string3.CompareTo( string4 ) is " +
```

Fig. 16.3 | string test to determine equality. (Part 1 of 2.)

```
46                   string3.CompareTo( string4 ) + "\n" +
47                   "string4.CompareTo( string3 ) is " +
48                   string4.CompareTo( string3 ) + "\n\n" );
49      } // end Main
50   } // end class StringCompare
```

```
string1 = "hello"
string2 = "good bye"
string3 = "Happy Birthday"
string4 = "happy birthday"

string1 equals "hello"
string1 equals "hello"
string3 does not equal string4

string1.CompareTo( string2 ) is 1
string2.CompareTo( string1 ) is -1
string1.CompareTo( string1 ) is 0
string3.CompareTo( string4 ) is 1
string4.CompareTo( string3 ) is -1
```

Fig. 16.3 | string test to determine equality. (Part 2 of 2.)

The condition in line 27 uses the overloaded equality operator (==) to compare string string1 with the literal string "hello" for equality. In C#, the equality operator also compares the contents of two strings. Thus, the condition in the if statement evaluates to true, because the values of string1 and "hello" are equal.

Line 33 tests whether string3 and string4 are equal to illustrate that comparisons are indeed case sensitive. Here, static method Equals is used to compare the values of two strings. "Happy Birthday" does not equal "happy birthday", so the condition of the if statement fails, and the message "string3 does not equal string4" is output (line 36).

Lines 40–48 use string method CompareTo to compare strings. Method CompareTo returns 0 if the strings are equal, a negative value if the string that invokes CompareTo is less than the string that's passed as an argument and a positive value if the string that invokes CompareTo is greater than the string that's passed as an argument.

Notice that CompareTo considers string3 to be greater than string4. The only difference between these two strings is that string3 contains two uppercase letters in positions where string4 contains lowercase letters.

Determining Whether a String Begins or Ends with a Specified String

Figure 16.4 shows how to test whether a string instance begins or ends with a given string. Method StartsWith determines whether a string instance starts with the string text passed to it as an argument. Method EndsWith determines whether a string instance ends with the string text passed to it as an argument. Class stringStartEnd's Main method defines an array of strings (called strings), which contains "started", "starting", "ended" and "ending". The remainder of method Main tests the elements of the array to determine whether they start or end with a particular set of characters.

Line 13 uses method StartsWith, which takes a string argument. The condition in the if statement determines whether the string at index i of the array starts with the characters "st". If so, the method returns true, and strings[i] is output along with a message.

```
 1    // Fig. 16.4: StringStartEnd.cs
 2    // Demonstrating StartsWith and EndsWith methods.
 3    using System;
 4
 5    class StringStartEnd
 6    {
 7       public static void Main( string[] args )
 8       {
 9          string[] strings = { "started", "starting", "ended", "ending" };
10
11          // test every string to see if it starts with "st"
12          for ( int i = 0; i < strings.Length; i++ )
13             if ( strings[ i ].StartsWith( "st" ) )
14                Console.WriteLine( "\"" + strings[ i ] + "\"" +
15                   " starts with \"st\"" );
16
17          Console.WriteLine();
18
19          // test every string to see if it ends with "ed"
20          for ( int i = 0; i < strings.Length; i++ )
21             if ( strings[ i ].EndsWith( "ed" ) )
22                Console.WriteLine( "\"" + strings[ i ] + "\"" +
23                   " ends with \"ed\"" );
24
25          Console.WriteLine();
26       } // end Main
27    } // end class StringStartEnd
```

```
"started" starts with "st"
"starting" starts with "st"

"started" ends with "ed"
"ended" ends with "ed"
```

Fig. 16.4 | StartsWith and EndsWith methods.

Line 21 uses method EndsWith to determine whether the string at index i of the array ends with the characters "ed". If so, the method returns true, and strings[i] is displayed along with a message.

16.6 Locating Characters and Substrings in strings

In many applications, it's necessary to search for a character or set of characters in a string. For example, a programmer creating a word processor would want to provide capabilities for searching through documents. The application in Fig. 16.5 demonstrates some of the many versions of string methods IndexOf, IndexOfAny, LastIndexOf and LastIndexOfAny, which search for a specified character or substring in a string. We perform all searches in this example on the string letters (initialized with "abcdefghijklmabcdefghijklm") located in method Main of class StringIndexMethods.

Lines 14, 16 and 18 use method IndexOf to locate the first occurrence of a character or substring in a string. If it finds a character, IndexOf returns the index of the specified

```
1   // Fig. 16.5: StringIndexMethods.cs
2   // Using string-searching methods.
3   using System;
4
5   class StringIndexMethods
6   {
7      public static void Main( string[] args )
8      {
9         string letters = "abcdefghijklmabcdefghijklm";
10        char[] searchLetters = { 'c', 'a', '$' };
11
12        // test IndexOf to locate a character in a string
13        Console.WriteLine( "First 'c' is located at index " +
14           letters.IndexOf( 'c' ) );
15        Console.WriteLine( "First 'a' starting at 1 is located at index " +
16           letters.IndexOf( 'a', 1 ) );
17        Console.WriteLine( "First '$' in the 5 positions starting at 3 " +
18           "is located at index " + letters.IndexOf( '$', 3, 5 ) );
19
20        // test LastIndexOf to find a character in a string
21        Console.WriteLine( "\nLast 'c' is located at index " +
22           letters.LastIndexOf( 'c' ) );
23        Console.WriteLine( "Last 'a' up to position 25 is located at " +
24           "index " + letters.LastIndexOf( 'a', 25 ) );
25        Console.WriteLine( "Last '$' in the 5 positions starting at 15 " +
26           "is located at index " + letters.LastIndexOf( '$', 15, 5 ) );
27
28        // test IndexOf to locate a substring in a string
29        Console.WriteLine( "\nFirst \"def\" is located at index " +
30           letters.IndexOf( "def" ) );
31        Console.WriteLine( "First \"def\" starting at 7 is located at " +
32           "index " + letters.IndexOf( "def", 7 ) );
33        Console.WriteLine( "First \"hello\" in the 15 positions " +
34           "starting at 5 is located at index " +
35           letters.IndexOf( "hello", 5, 15 ) );
36
37        // test LastIndexOf to find a substring in a string
38        Console.WriteLine( "\nLast \"def\" is located at index " +
39           letters.LastIndexOf( "def" ) );
40        Console.WriteLine( "Last \"def\" up to position 25 is located " +
41           "at index " + letters.LastIndexOf( "def", 25 ) );
42        Console.WriteLine( "Last \"hello\" in the 15 positions " +
43           "ending at 20 is located at index " +
44           letters.LastIndexOf( "hello", 20, 15 ) );
45
46        // test IndexOfAny to find first occurrence of character in array
47        Console.WriteLine( "\nFirst 'c', 'a' or '$' is " +
48           "located at index " + letters.IndexOfAny( searchLetters ) );
49        Console.WriteLine("First 'c', 'a' or '$' starting at 7 is " +
50           "located at index " + letters.IndexOfAny( searchLetters, 7 ) );
51        Console.WriteLine( "First 'c', 'a' or '$' in the 5 positions " +
52           "starting at 7 is located at index " +
53           letters.IndexOfAny( searchLetters, 7, 5 ) );
```

Fig. 16.5 | Searching for characters and substrings in strings. (Part 1 of 2.)

```
54
55        // test LastIndexOfAny to find last occurrence of character
56        // in array
57        Console.WriteLine( "\nLast 'c', 'a' or '$' is " +
58           "located at index " + letters.LastIndexOfAny( searchLetters ) );
59        Console.WriteLine( "Last 'c', 'a' or '$' up to position 1 is " +
60           "located at index " +
61           letters.LastIndexOfAny( searchLetters, 1 ) );
62        Console.WriteLine( "Last 'c', 'a' or '$' in the 5 positions " +
63           "ending at 25 is located at index " +
64           letters.LastIndexOfAny( searchLetters, 25, 5 ) );
65     } // end Main
66  } // end class StringIndexMethods
```

```
First 'c' is located at index 2
First 'a' starting at 1 is located at index 13
First '$' in the 5 positions starting at 3 is located at index -1

Last 'c' is located at index 15
Last 'a' up to position 25 is located at index 13
Last '$' in the 5 positions starting at 15 is located at index -1

First "def" is located at index 3
First "def" starting at 7 is located at index 16
First "hello" in the 15 positions starting at 5 is located at index -1

Last "def" is located at index 16
Last "def" up to position 25 is located at index 16
Last "hello" in the 15 positions ending at 20 is located at index -1

First 'c', 'a' or '$' is located at index 0
First 'c', 'a' or '$' starting at 7 is located at index 13
First 'c', 'a' or '$' in the 5 positions starting at 7 is located at index -1

Last 'c', 'a' or '$' is located at index 15
Last 'c', 'a' or '$' up to position 1 is located at index 0
Last 'c', 'a' or '$' in the 5 positions ending at 25 is located at index -1
```

Fig. 16.5 | Searching for characters and substrings in `strings`. (Part 2 of 2.)

character in the `string`; otherwise, `IndexOf` returns –1. The expression in line 16 uses a version of method `IndexOf` that takes two arguments—the character to search for and the starting index at which the search of the `string` should begin. The method does not examine any characters that occur prior to the starting index (in this case, 1). The expression in line 18 uses another version of method `IndexOf` that takes three arguments—the character to search for, the index at which to start searching and the number of characters to search.

Lines 22, 24 and 26 use method `LastIndexOf` to locate the last occurrence of a character in a `string`. Method `LastIndexOf` performs the search from the end of the `string` to the beginning of the `string`. If it finds the character, `LastIndexOf` returns the index of the specified character in the `string`; otherwise, `LastIndexOf` returns –1. There are three versions of method `LastIndexOf`. The expression in line 22 uses the version that takes as an argument the character for which to search. The expression in line 24 uses the version that takes two arguments—the character for which to search and the highest index from which to begin searching backward for the character. The expression in line 26 uses a third version of method `LastIndexOf` that takes three arguments—the character for which to search, the starting index from which to start searching backward and the number of characters (the portion of the `string`) to search.

Lines 29–44 use versions of `IndexOf` and `LastIndexOf` that take a `string` instead of a character as the first argument. These versions of the methods perform identically to those described above except that they search for sequences of characters (or substrings) that are specified by their `string` arguments.

Lines 47–64 use methods `IndexOfAny` and `LastIndexOfAny`, which take an array of characters as the first argument. These versions of the methods also perform identically to those described above, except that they return the index of the first occurrence of any of the characters in the character-array argument.

> **Common Programming Error 16.2**
>
> *In the overloaded methods `LastIndexOf` and `LastIndexOfAny` that take three parameters, the second argument must be greater than or equal to the third. This might seem counterintuitive, but remember that the search moves from the end of the string toward the start of the string.*

16.7 Extracting Substrings from `strings`

Class `string` provides two `Substring` methods, which create a new `string` by copying part of an existing `string`. Each method returns a new `string`. The application in Fig. 16.6 demonstrates the use of both methods.

```
1   // Fig. 16.6: SubString.cs
2   // Demonstrating the string Substring method.
3   using System;
4
5   class SubString
6   {
7      public static void Main( string[] args )
8      {
9         string letters = "abcdefghijklmabcdefghijklm";
10
11        // invoke Substring method and pass it one parameter
12        Console.WriteLine( "Substring from index 20 to end is \"" +
13           letters.Substring( 20 ) + "\"" );
14
15        // invoke Substring method and pass it two parameters
16        Console.WriteLine( "Substring from index 0 of length 6 is \"" +
17           letters.Substring( 0, 6 ) + "\"" );
18     } // end method Main
19  } // end class SubString
```

```
Substring from index 20 to end is "hijklm"
Substring from index 0 of length 6 is "abcdef"
```

Fig. 16.6 | Substrings generated from `strings`.

The statement in line 13 uses the Substring method that takes one int argument. The argument specifies the starting index from which the method copies characters in the original string. The substring returned contains a copy of the characters from the starting index to the end of the string. If the index specified in the argument is outside the bounds of the string, the program throws an ArgumentOutOfRangeException.

The second version of method Substring (line 17) takes two int arguments. The first argument specifies the starting index from which the method copies characters from the original string. The second argument specifies the length of the substring to copy. The substring returned contains a copy of the specified characters from the original string. If the supplied length of the substring is too large (i.e., the substring tries to retrieve characters past the end of the original string), an ArgumentOutOfRangeException is thrown.

16.8 Concatenating strings

The + operator is not the only way to perform string concatenation. The static method Concat of class string (Fig. 16.7) concatenates two strings and returns a new string containing the combined characters from both original strings. Line 16 appends the characters from string2 to the end of a copy of string1, using method Concat. The statement in line 16 does not modify the original strings.

```
1   // Fig. 16.7: SubConcatenation.cs
2   // Demonstrating string class Concat method.
3   using System;
4
5   class StringConcatenation
6   {
7      public static void Main( string[] args )
8      {
9         string string1 = "Happy ";
10        string string2 = "Birthday";
11
12        Console.WriteLine( "string1 = \"" + string1 + "\"\n" +
13           "string2 = \"" + string2 + "\"" );
14        Console.WriteLine(
15           "\nResult of string.Concat( string1, string2 ) = " +
16           string.Concat( string1, string2 ) );
17        Console.WriteLine( "string1 after concatenation = " + string1 );
18     } // end Main
19  } // end class StringConcatenation
```

```
string1 = "Happy "
string2 = "Birthday"

Result of string.Concat( string1, string2 ) = Happy Birthday
string1 after concatenation = Happy
```

Fig. 16.7 | Concat static method.

16.9 Miscellaneous string Methods

Class string provides several methods that return modified copies of strings. The application in Fig. 16.8 demonstrates the use of these methods, which include string methods Replace, ToLower, ToUpper and Trim.

```
1   // Fig. 16.8: StringMethods2.cs
2   // Demonstrating string methods Replace, ToLower, ToUpper, Trim,
3   // and ToString.
4   using System;
5
6   class StringMethods2
7   {
8      public static void Main( string[] args )
9      {
10         string string1 = "cheers!";
11         string string2 = "GOOD BYE ";
12         string string3 = "   spaces   ";
13
14         Console.WriteLine( "string1 = \"" + string1 + "\"\n" +
15            "string2 = \"" + string2 + "\"\n" +
16            "string3 = \"" + string3 + "\"" );
17
18         // call method Replace
19         Console.WriteLine(
20            "\nReplacing \"e\" with \"E\" in string1: \"" +
21            string1.Replace( 'e', 'E' ) + "\"" );
22
23         // call ToLower and ToUpper
24         Console.WriteLine( "\nstring1.ToUpper() = \"" +
25            string1.ToUpper() + "\"\nstring2.ToLower() = \"" +
26            string2.ToLower() + "\"" );
27
28         // call Trim method
29         Console.WriteLine( "\nstring3 after trim = \"" +
30            string3.Trim() + "\"" );
31
32         Console.WriteLine( "\nstring1 = \"" + string1 + "\"" );
33      } // end Main
34   } // end class StringMethods2
```

```
string1 = "cheers!"
string2 = "GOOD BYE "
string3 = "   spaces   "

Replacing "e" with "E" in string1: "chEErs!"

string1.ToUpper() = "CHEERS!"
string2.ToLower() = "good bye "

string3 after trim = "spaces"

string1 = "cheers!"
```

Fig. 16.8 | string methods Replace, ToLower, ToUpper and Trim.

Line 21 uses `string` method `Replace` to return a new `string`, replacing every occurrence in `string1` of character `'e'` with `'E'`. Method `Replace` takes two arguments—a `char` for which to search and another `char` with which to replace all matching occurrences of the first argument. The original `string` remains unchanged. If there are no occurrences of the first argument in the `string`, the method returns the original `string`. An overloaded version of this method allows you to provide two `strings` as arguments.

The `string` method `ToUpper` generates a new `string` (line 25) that replaces any lowercase letters in `string1` with their uppercase equivalents. The method returns a new `string` containing the converted `string`; the original `string` remains unchanged. If there are no characters to convert, the original `string` is returned. Line 26 uses `string` method `ToLower` to return a new `string` in which any uppercase letters in `string2` are replaced by their lowercase equivalents. The original `string` is unchanged. As with `ToUpper`, if there are no characters to convert to lowercase, method `ToLower` returns the original `string`.

Line 30 uses `string` method `Trim` to remove all whitespace characters that appear at the beginning and end of a `string`. Without otherwise altering the original `string`, the method returns a new `string` that contains the `string`, but omits leading and trailing whitespace characters. This method is particularly useful for retrieving user input (i.e., via a `TextBox`). Another version of method `Trim` takes a character array and returns a copy of the `string` that does not begin or end with any of the characters in the array argument.

16.10 Class `StringBuilder`

The `string` class provides many capabilities for processing `strings`. However a `string`'s contents can never change. Operations that seem to concatenate `strings` are in fact assigning `string` references to newly created `strings` (e.g., the += operator creates a new `string` and assigns the initial `string` reference to the newly created `string`).

The next several sections discuss the features of class `StringBuilder` (namespace `System.Text`), used to create and manipulate dynamic string information—i.e., mutable strings. Every `StringBuilder` can store a certain number of characters that's specified by its capacity. Exceeding the capacity of a `StringBuilder` causes the capacity to expand to accommodate the additional characters. As we'll see, members of class `StringBuilder`, such as methods `Append` and `AppendFormat`, can be used for concatenation like the operators + and += for class `string`. `StringBuilder` is particularly useful for manipulating in place a large number of `strings`, as it's much more efficient than creating individual immutable `strings`.

Performance Tip 16.2

Objects of class `string` are immutable (i.e., constant strings), whereas objects of class `StringBuilder` are mutable. C# can perform certain optimizations involving strings (such as the sharing of one string among multiple references), because it knows these objects will not change.

Class `StringBuilder` provides six overloaded constructors. Class `StringBuilderConstructor` (Fig. 16.9) demonstrates three of these overloaded constructors.

Line 10 employs the no-parameter `StringBuilder` constructor to create a `StringBuilder` that contains no characters and has an implementation-specific default initial capacity. Line 11 uses the `StringBuilder` constructor that takes an `int` argument to create a `StringBuilder` that contains no characters and has the initial capacity specified in the `int` argument (i.e., 10). Line 12 uses the `StringBuilder` constructor that takes a `string` argument to create a StringBuilder containing the characters of the string argument. Lines 14–16 implicitly use StringBuilder method ToString to obtain string representations of the StringBuilders' contents.

```
1   // Fig. 16.9: StringBuilderConstructor.cs
2   // Demonstrating StringBuilder class constructors.
3   using System;
4   using System.Text;
5
6   class StringBuilderConstructor
7   {
8      public static void Main( string[] args )
9      {
10        StringBuilder buffer1 = new StringBuilder();
11        StringBuilder buffer2 = new StringBuilder( 10 );
12        StringBuilder buffer3 = new StringBuilder( "hello" );
13
14        Console.WriteLine( "buffer1 = \"" + buffer1 + "\"" );
15        Console.WriteLine( "buffer2 = \"" + buffer2 + "\"" );
16        Console.WriteLine( "buffer3 = \"" + buffer3 + "\"" );
17     } // end Main
18  } // end class StringBuilderConstructor
```

```
buffer1 = ""
buffer2 = ""
buffer3 = "hello"
```

Fig. 16.9 | StringBuilder class constructors.

16.11 Length and Capacity Properties, EnsureCapacity Method and Indexer of Class StringBuilder

Class StringBuilder provides the Length and Capacity properties to return the number of characters currently in a StringBuilder and the number of characters that a StringBuilder can store without allocating more memory, respectively. These properties also can increase or decrease the length or the capacity of the StringBuilder. Method EnsureCapacity allows you to reduce the number of times that a StringBuilder's capacity must be increased. The method ensures that the StringBuilder's capacity is at least the specified value. The program in Fig. 16.10 demonstrates these methods and properties.

```
1   // Fig. 16.10: StringBuilderFeatures.cs
2   // Demonstrating some features of class StringBuilder.
3   using System;
4   using System.Text;
5
6   class StringBuilderFeatures
7   {
```

Fig. 16.10 | StringBuilder size manipulation. (Part 1 of 2.)

```
 8        public static void Main( string[] args )
 9        {
10            StringBuilder buffer =
11               new StringBuilder( "Hello, how are you?" );
12
13            // use Length and Capacity properties
14            Console.WriteLine( "buffer = " + buffer +
15               "\nLength = " + buffer.Length +
16               "\nCapacity = " + buffer.Capacity );
17
18            buffer.EnsureCapacity( 75 ); // ensure a capacity of at least 75
19            Console.WriteLine( "\nNew capacity = " +
20               buffer.Capacity );
21
22            // truncate StringBuilder by setting Length property
23            buffer.Length = 10;
24            Console.Write( "\nNew length = " +
25               buffer.Length + "\nbuffer = " );
26
27            // use StringBuilder indexer
28            for ( int i = 0; i < buffer.Length; i++ )
29               Console.Write( buffer[ i ] );
30
31            Console.WriteLine( "\n" );
32        } // end Main
33     } // end class StringBuilderFeatures
```

```
buffer = Hello, how are you?
Length = 19
Capacity = 19
New length = 10
buffer = Hello, how
```

Fig. 16.10 | StringBuilder size manipulation. (Part 2 of 2.)

The program contains one StringBuilder, called buffer. Lines 10–11 of the program use the StringBuilder constructor that takes a string argument to instantiate the StringBuilder and initialize its value to "Hello, how are you?". Lines 14–16 output the content, length and capacity of the StringBuilder.

Line 18 expands the capacity of the StringBuilder to a minimum of 75 characters. If new characters are added to a StringBuilder so that its length exceeds its capacity, the capacity grows to accommodate the additional characters in the same manner as if method EnsureCapacity had been called.

Line 23 uses property Length to set the length of the StringBuilder to 10. If the specified length is less than the current number of characters in the StringBuilder, the contents of the StringBuilder are truncated to the specified length. If the specified length is greater than the number of characters currently in the StringBuilder, null characters are appended to the StringBuilder until the total number of characters in the StringBuilder is equal to the specified length.

16.12 Append and AppendFormat Methods of Class StringBuilder

Class StringBuilder provides 19 overloaded Append methods that allow various types of values to be added to the end of a StringBuilder. The Framework Class Library provides versions for each of the simple types and for character arrays, strings and objects. (Remember that method ToString produces a string representation of any object.) Each method takes an argument, converts it to a string and appends it to the StringBuilder. Figure 16.11 demonstrates the use of several Append methods.

```
1   // Fig. 16.11: StringBuilderAppend.cs
2   // Demonstrating StringBuilder Append methods.
3   using System;
4   using System.Text;
5
6   class StringBuilderAppend
7   {
8      public static void Main( string[] args )
9      {
10        object objectValue = "hello";
11        string stringValue = "good bye";
12        char[] characterArray = { 'a', 'b', 'c', 'd', 'e', 'f' };
13        bool booleanValue = true;
14        char characterValue = 'Z';
15        int integerValue = 7;
16        long longValue = 1000000;
17        float floatValue = 2.5F; // F suffix indicates that 2.5 is a float
18        double doubleValue = 33.333;
19        StringBuilder buffer = new StringBuilder();
20
21        // use method Append to append values to buffer
22        buffer.Append( objectValue );
23        buffer.Append( "  " );
24        buffer.Append( stringValue );
25        buffer.Append( "  " );
26        buffer.Append( characterArray );
27        buffer.Append( "  ");
28        buffer.Append( characterArray, 0, 3 );
29        buffer.Append( "  " );
30        buffer.Append( booleanValue );
31        buffer.Append( "  " );
32        buffer.Append( characterValue );
33        buffer.Append( "  " );
34        buffer.Append( integerValue );
35        buffer.Append( "  " );
36        buffer.Append( longValue );
37        buffer.Append( "  " );
38        buffer.Append( floatValue );
39        buffer.Append( "  " );
40        buffer.Append( doubleValue );
41
```

Fig. 16.11 | Append methods of StringBuilder. (Part 1 of 2.)

```
42              Console.WriteLine( "buffer = " + buffer.ToString() + "\n" );
43          } // end Main
44      } // end class StringBuilderAppend
```

```
buffer = hello  good bye  abcdef  abc  True  Z  7  1000000  2.5  33.333
```

Fig. 16.11 | Append methods of `StringBuilder`. (Part 2 of 2.)

Lines 22–40 use 10 different overloaded `Append` methods to attach the string representations of objects created in lines 10–18 to the end of the `StringBuilder`.

Class `StringBuilder` also provides method `AppendFormat`, which converts a `string` to a specified format, then appends it to the `StringBuilder`. The example in Fig. 16.12 demonstrates the use of this method.

```
 1   // Fig. 16.12: StringBuilderAppendFormat.cs
 2   // Demonstrating method AppendFormat.
 3   using System;
 4   using System.Text;
 5
 6   class StringBuilderAppendFormat
 7   {
 8      public static void Main( string[] args )
 9      {
10         StringBuilder buffer = new StringBuilder();
11
12         // formatted string
13         string string1 = "This {0} costs: {1:C}.\n";
14
15         // string1 argument array
16         object[] objectArray = new object[ 2 ];
17
18         objectArray[ 0 ] = "car";
19         objectArray[ 1 ] = 1234.56;
20
21         // append to buffer formatted string with argument
22         buffer.AppendFormat( string1, objectArray );
23
24         // formatted string
25         string string2 = "Number:{0:d3}.\n" +
26            "Number right aligned with spaces:{0, 4}.\n" +
27            "Number left aligned with spaces:{0, -4}.";
28
29         // append to buffer formatted string with argument
30         buffer.AppendFormat( string2, 5 );
31
32         // display formatted strings
33         Console.WriteLine( buffer.ToString() );
34      } // end Main
35   } // end class StringBuilderAppendFormat
```

Fig. 16.12 | `StringBuilder`'s `AppendFormat` method. (Part 1 of 2.)

```
This car costs: $1,234.56.
Number:005.
Number right aligned with spaces:   5.
Number left aligned with spaces:5   .
```

Fig. 16.12 | StringBuilder's AppendFormat method. (Part 2 of 2.)

Line 13 creates a string that contains formatting information. The information enclosed in braces specifies how to format a specific piece of data. Formats have the form {X[,Y][:FormatString]}, where X is the number of the argument to be formatted, counting from zero. Y is an optional argument, which can be positive or negative, indicating how many characters should be in the result. If the resulting string is less than the number Y, it will be padded with spaces to make up for the difference. A positive integer aligns the string to the right; a negative integer aligns it to the left. The optional Format-String applies a particular format to the argument—currency, decimal or scientific, among others. In this case, "{0}" means the first argument will be printed out. "{1:C}" specifies that the second argument will be formatted as a currency value.

Line 22 shows a version of AppendFormat that takes two parameters—a string specifying the format and an array of objects to serve as the arguments to the format string. The argument referred to by "{0}" is in the object array at index 0.

Lines 25–27 define another string used for formatting. The first format "{0:d3}", specifies that the first argument will be formatted as a three-digit decimal, meaning that any number having fewer than three digits will have leading zeros placed in front to make up the difference. The next format, "{0, 4}", specifies that the formatted string should have four characters and be right aligned. The third format, "{0, -4}", specifies that the strings should be aligned to the left.

Line 30 uses a version of AppendFormat that takes two parameters—a string containing a format and an object to which the format is applied. In this case, the object is the number 5. The output of Fig. 16.12 displays the result of applying these two versions of AppendFormat with their respective arguments.

16.13 Insert, Remove and Replace Methods of Class StringBuilder

Class StringBuilder provides 18 overloaded Insert methods to allow various types of data to be inserted at any position in a StringBuilder. The class provides versions for each of the simple types and for character arrays, strings and objects. Each method takes its second argument, converts it to a string and inserts the string into the StringBuilder in front of the character in the position specified by the first argument. The index specified by the first argument must be greater than or equal to 0 and less than the length of the StringBuilder; otherwise, the program throws an ArgumentOutOfRangeException.

Class StringBuilder also provides method Remove for deleting any portion of a StringBuilder. Method Remove takes two arguments—the index at which to begin deletion and the number of characters to delete. The sum of the starting index and the number of characters to be deleted must always be less than the length of the StringBuilder; otherwise, the program throws an ArgumentOutOfRangeException. The Insert and Remove methods are demonstrated in Fig. 16.13.

```
1   // Fig. 16.13: StringBuilderInsertRemove.cs
2   // Demonstrating methods Insert and Remove of the
3   // StringBuilder class.
4   using System;
5   using System.Text;
6
7   class StringBuilderInsertRemove
8   {
9      public static void Main( string[] args )
10     {
11        object objectValue = "hello";
12        string stringValue = "good bye";
13        char[] characterArray = { 'a', 'b', 'c', 'd', 'e', 'f' };
14        bool booleanValue = true;
15        char characterValue = 'K';
16        int integerValue = 7;
17        long longValue = 10000000;
18        float floatValue = 2.5F; // F suffix indicates that 2.5 is a float
19        double doubleValue = 33.333;
20        StringBuilder buffer = new StringBuilder();
21
22        // insert values into buffer
23        buffer.Insert( 0, objectValue );
24        buffer.Insert( 0, "   " );
25        buffer.Insert( 0, stringValue );
26        buffer.Insert( 0, "   " );
27        buffer.Insert( 0, characterArray );
28        buffer.Insert( 0, "   " );
29        buffer.Insert( 0, booleanValue );
30        buffer.Insert( 0, "   " );
31        buffer.Insert( 0, characterValue );
32        buffer.Insert( 0, "   " );
33        buffer.Insert( 0, integerValue );
34        buffer.Insert( 0, "   " );
35        buffer.Insert( 0, longValue );
36        buffer.Insert( 0, "   " );
37        buffer.Insert( 0, floatValue );
38        buffer.Insert( 0, "   " );
39        buffer.Insert( 0, doubleValue );
40        buffer.Insert( 0, "   " );
41
42        Console.WriteLine( "buffer after Inserts: \n" + buffer + "\n" );
43
44        buffer.Remove( 10, 1 ); // delete 2 in 2.5
45        buffer.Remove( 4, 4 );  // delete .333 in 33.333
46
47        Console.WriteLine( "buffer after Removes:\n" + buffer );
48     } // end Main
49  } // end class StringBuilderInsertRemove
```

```
buffer after Inserts:
   33.333   2.5   10000000   7   K   True   abcdef   good bye   hello
```

Fig. 16.13 | StringBuilder text insertion and removal. (Part 1 of 2.)

```
buffer after Removes:
  33  .5  10000000  7  K  True  abcdef  good bye  hello
```

Fig. 16.13 | StringBuilder text insertion and removal. (Part 2 of 2.)

Another useful method included with StringBuilder is Replace. Replace searches for a specified string or character and substitutes another string or character in its place. Figure 16.14 demonstrates this method.

```
1   // Fig. 16.14: StringBuilderReplace.cs
2   // Demonstrating method Replace.
3   using System;
4   using System.Text;
5
6   class StringBuilderReplace
7   {
8      public static void Main( string[] args )
9      {
10        StringBuilder builder1 =
11           new StringBuilder( "Happy Birthday Jane" );
12        StringBuilder builder2 =
13           new StringBuilder( "good bye greg" );
14
15        Console.WriteLine( "Before replacements:\n" +
16           builder1.ToString() + "\n" + builder2.ToString() );
17
18        builder1.Replace( "Jane", "Greg" );
19        builder2.Replace( 'g', 'G', 0, 5 );
20
21        Console.WriteLine( "\nAfter replacements:\n" +
22           builder1.ToString() + "\n" + builder2.ToString() );
23     } // end Main
24  } // end class StringBuilderReplace
```

```
Before Replacements:
Happy Birthday Jane
good bye greg

After replacements:
Happy Birthday Greg
Good bye greg
```

Fig. 16.14 | StringBuilder text replacement.

Line 18 uses method Replace to replace all instances "Jane" with the "Greg" in builder1. Another overload of this method takes two characters as parameters and replaces each occurrence of the first character with the second. Line 19 uses an overload of Replace that takes four parameters, of which the first two are characters and the second two are ints. The method replaces all instances of the first character with the second character, beginning at the index specified by the first int and continuing for a count specified by the second int. Thus, in this case, Replace looks through only five characters, starting with the character at index 0. As the output illustrates, this version of Replace replaces g with G in the word "good", but not in "greg". This is because the gs in "greg" are not in the range indicated by the int arguments (i.e., between indexes 0 and 4).

16.14 Char Methods

C# provides a concept called a **struct** (short for "structure") that's similar to a class. Although structs and classes are comparable, structs represent value types. Like classes, structs can have methods and properties, and can use the access modifiers public and private. Also, struct members are accessed via the member access operator (.).

The simple types are actually aliases for struct types. For instance, an int is defined by struct System.Int32, a long by System.Int64 and so on. All struct types derive from class **ValueType**, which derives from object. Also, all struct types are implicitly sealed, so they do not support virtual or abstract methods, and their members cannot be declared protected or protected internal.

In the struct **Char**,[2] which is the struct for characters, most methods are static, take at least one character argument and perform either a test or a manipulation on the character. We present several of these methods in the next example. Figure 16.15 demonstrates static methods that test characters to determine whether they're of a specific character type and static methods that perform case conversions on characters.

```
1   // Fig. 16.15: StaticCharMethods.cs
2   // Demonstrates static character-testing and case-conversion methods
3   // from Char struct
4   using System;
5
6   class StaticCharMethods
7   {
8      static void Main( string[] args )
9      {
10        Console.Write( "Enter a character: " );
11        char character = Convert.ToChar( Console.ReadLine() );
12
13        Console.WriteLine( "is digit: {0}", Char.IsDigit( character ) );
14        Console.WriteLine( "is letter: {0}", Char.IsLetter( character )  );
15        Console.WriteLine( "is letter or digit: {0}",
16           Char.IsLetterOrDigit( character ) );
17        Console.WriteLine( "is lower case: {0}",
18           Char.IsLower( character ) );
19        Console.WriteLine( "is upper case: {0}",
20           Char.IsUpper( character ) );
21        Console.WriteLine( "to upper case: {0}",
22           Char.ToUpper( character ) );
23        Console.WriteLine( "to lower case: {0}",
24           Char.ToLower( character ) );
```

Fig. 16.15 | Char's static character-testing and case-conversion methods. (Part 1 of 3.)

2. Just as keyword string is an alias for class String, keyword char is an alias for struct Char. In this text, we use the term Char when calling a static method of struct Char and the term char elsewhere.

```
25            Console.WriteLine( "is punctuation: {0}",
26               Char.IsPunctuation( character ) );
27            Console.WriteLine( "is symbol: {0}", Char.IsSymbol( character ) );
28         } // end Main
29      } // end class StaticCharMethods
```

```
Enter a character: A
is digit: False
is letter: True
is letter or digit: True
is lower case: False
is upper case: True
to upper case: A
to lower case: a
is punctuation: False
is symbol: False
```

```
Enter a character: 8
is digit: True
is letter: False
is letter or digit: True
is lower case: False
is upper case: False
to upper case: 8
to lower case: 8
is punctuation: False
is symbol: False
```

```
Enter a character: @
is digit: False
is letter: False
is letter or digit: False
is lower case: False
is upper case: False
to upper case: @
to lower case: @
is punctuation: True
is symbol: False
```

```
Enter a character: m
is digit: False
is letter: True
is letter or digit: True
is lower case: True
is upper case: False
to upper case: M
to lower case: m
is punctuation: False
is symbol: False
```

Fig. 16.15 | Char's static character-testing and case-conversion methods. (Part 2 of 3.)

```
Enter a character: +
is digit: False
is letter: False
is letter or digit: False
is lower case: False
is upper case: False
to upper case: +
to lower case: +
is punctuation: False
is symbol: True
```

Fig. 16.15 | Char's static character-testing and case-conversion methods. (Part 3 of 3.)

After the user enters a character, lines 13–27 analyze it. Line 13 uses Char method IsDigit to determine whether character is defined as a digit. If so, the method returns true; otherwise, it returns false (note again that bool values are output capitalized). Line 14 uses Char method IsLetter to determine whether character character is a letter. Line 16 uses Char method IsLetterOrDigit to determine whether character character is a letter or a digit.

Line 18 uses Char method IsLower to determine whether character character is a lowercase letter. Line 20 uses Char method IsUpper to determine whether character character is an uppercase letter. Line 22 uses Char method ToUpper to convert character character to its uppercase equivalent. The method returns the converted character if the character has an uppercase equivalent; otherwise, the method returns its original argument. Line 24 uses Char method ToLower to convert character character to its lowercase equivalent. The method returns the converted character if the character has a lowercase equivalent; otherwise, the method returns its original argument.

Line 26 uses Char method IsPunctuation to determine whether character is a punctuation mark, such as "!", ":" or ")". Line 27 uses Char method IsSymbol to determine whether character character is a symbol, such as "+", "=" or "^".

Structure type Char also contains other methods not shown in this example. Many of the static methods are similar—for instance, IsWhiteSpace is used to determine whether a certain character is a whitespace character (e.g., newline, tab or space). The struct also contains several public instance methods; many of these, such as methods ToString and Equals, are methods that we have seen before in other classes. This group includes method CompareTo, which is used to compare two character values with one another.

16.15 Regular Expressions

We now introduce **regular expressions**—specially formatted strings used to find patterns in text. They can be used to ensure that data is in a particular format. For example, a U.S. zip code must consist of five digits, or five digits followed by a dash followed by four more digits. Compilers use regular expressions to validate program syntax. If the program code does not match the regular expression, the compiler indicates that there's a syntax error. We discuss classes Regex and Match from the System.Text.RegularExpressions namespace as well as the symbols used to form regular expressions. We then demonstrate how to find patterns in a string, match entire strings to patterns, replace characters in a string that match a pattern and split strings at delimiters specified as a pattern in a regular expression.

16.15.1 Simple Regular Expressions and Class Regex

The .NET Framework provides several classes to help developers manipulate regular expressions. Figure 16.16 demonstrates the basic regular-expression classes. To use these classes, add a using statement for the namespace System.Text.RegularExpressions (line 4). Class **Regex** represents a regular expression. We create a Regex object named expression (line 16) to represent the regular expression "e". This regular expression matches the literal character "e" anywhere in an arbitrary string. Regex *method* **Match** returns an object of *class* **Match** that represents a single regular-expression match. Class Match's To-String method returns the substring that matched the regular expression. The call to method Match (line 17) matches the leftmost occurrence of the character "e" in testString. Class Regex also provides method **Matches** (line 21), which finds all matches of the regular expression in an arbitrary string and returns a MatchCollection object containing all the Matches. A **MatchCollection** is a collection, similar to an array, and can be used with a foreach statement to iterate through the collection's elements. We introduced collections in Chapter 9 and discuss them in more detail in Chapter 23, Collections. We use a foreach statement (lines 21–22) to display all the matches to expression in testString. The elements in the MatchCollection are Match objects, so the foreach statement infers variable myMatch to be of type Match. For each Match, line 22 outputs the text that matched the regular expression.

```
1   // Fig. 16.16: BasicRegex.cs
2   // Demonstrate basic regular expressions.
3   using System;
4   using System.Text.RegularExpressions;
5
6   class BasicRegex
7   {
8      static void Main( string[] args )
9      {
10        string testString =
11           "regular expressions are sometimes called regex or regexp";
12        Console.WriteLine( "The test string is\n   \"{0}\"", testString );
13        Console.Write( "Match 'e' in the test string: " );
14
15        // match 'e' in the test string
16        Regex expression = new Regex( "e" );
17        Console.WriteLine( expression.Match( testString ) );
18        Console.Write( "Match every 'e' in the test string: " );
19
20        // match 'e' multiple times in the test string
21        foreach ( var myMatch in expression.Matches( testString ) )
22           Console.Write( "{0} ", myMatch );
23
24        Console.Write( "\nMatch \"regex\" in the test string: " );
25
26        // match 'regex' in the test string
27        foreach ( var myMatch in Regex.Matches( testString, "regex" ) )
28           Console.Write( "{0} ", myMatch );
29
```

Fig. 16.16 | Demonstrating basic regular expressions. (Part 1 of 2.)

```
30          Console.Write(
31             "\nMatch \"regex\" or \"regexp\" using an optional 'p': " );
32
33          // use the ? quantifier to include an optional 'p'
34          foreach ( var myMatch in Regex.Matches( testString, "regexp?" ) )
35             Console.Write( "{0} ", myMatch );
36
37          // use alternation to match either 'cat' or 'hat'
38          expression = new Regex( "(c|h)at" );
39          Console.WriteLine(
40             "\n\"hat cat\" matches {0}, but \"cat hat\" matches {1}",
41             expression.Match( "hat cat" ), expression.Match( "cat hat" ) );
42       } // end Main
43    } // end class BasicRegex
```

```
The test string is
   "regular expressions are sometimes called regex or regexp"
Match 'e' in the test string: e
Match every 'e' in the test string: e e e e e e e e e
Match "regex" in the test string: regex regex
Match "regex" or "regexp" using an optional 'p': regex regexp
"hat cat" matches hat, but "cat hat" matches cat
```

Fig. 16.16 | Demonstrating basic regular expressions. (Part 2 of 2.)

Regular expressions can also be used to match a sequence of literal characters anywhere in a string. Lines 27–28 display all the occurrences of the character sequence "regex" in testString. Here we use the Regex static method Matches. Class Regex provides static versions of both methods Match and Matches. The static versions take a regular expression as an argument in addition to the string to be searched. This is useful when you want to use a regular expression only once. The call to method Matches (line 27) returns two matches to the regular expression "regex". Notice that "regexp" in the testString matches the regular expression "regex", but the "p" is excluded. We use the regular expression "regexp?" (line 34) to match occurrences of both "regex" and "regexp". The question mark (?) is a **metacharacter**—a character with special meaning in a regular expression. More specifically, the question mark is a **quantifier**—a metacharacter that describes how many times a part of the pattern may occur in a match. The **? quantifier** matches zero or one occurrence of the pattern to its left. In line 34, we apply the ? quantifier to the character "p". This means that a match to the regular expression contains the sequence of characters "regex" and may be followed by a "p". Notice that the foreach statement (lines 34–35) displays both "regex" and "regexp".

Metacharacters allow you to create more complex patterns. The "|" (**alternation**) metacharacter matches the expression to its left or to its right. We use alternation in the regular expression "(c|h)at" (line 38) to match either "cat" or "hat". Parentheses are used to group parts of a regular expression, much as you group parts of a mathematical expression. The "|" causes the pattern to match a sequence of characters starting with either "c" or "h", followed by "at". The "|" character attempts to match the entire expression to its left or to its right. If we didn't use the parentheses around "c|h", the regular expression would match either the single character "c" or the sequence of characters "hat". Line 41 uses the regular expression (line 38) to search the strings "hat cat" and "cat hat". Notice in the output that the first match in "hat cat" is "hat", while the first match in "cat hat" is "cat". Alternation chooses the leftmost match in the string for either of the alternating expressions—the order of the expressions doesn't matter.

Regular-Expression Character Classes and Quantifiers

The table in Fig. 16.17 lists some character classes that can be used with regular expressions. A **character class** represents a group of characters that might appear in a string. For example, a **word character** (**\w**) is any alphanumeric character (a-z, A-Z and 0-9) or underscore. A **whitespace character** (**\s**) is a space, a tab, a carriage return, a newline or a form feed. A **digit** (**\d**) is any numeric character.

Character class	Matches	Character class	Matches
\d	any digit	\D	any nondigit
\w	any word character	\W	any nonword character
\s	any whitespace	\S	any nonwhitespace

Fig. 16.17 | Character classes.

Figure 16.18 uses character classes in regular expressions. For this example, we use method DisplayMatches (lines 53–59) to display all matches to a regular expression. Method DisplayMatches takes two strings representing the string to search and the regular expression to match. The method uses a foreach statement to display each Match in the MatchCollection object returned by the static method Matches of class Regex.

```
1   // Fig. 16.18: CharacterClasses.cs
2   // Demonstrate using character classes and quantifiers.
3   using System;
4   using System.Text.RegularExpressions;
5
6   class CharacterClasses
7   {
8      static void Main( string[] args )
9      {
10        string testString = "abc, DEF, 123";
11        Console.WriteLine( "The test string is: \"{0}\"", testString );
12
13        // find the digits in the test string
14        Console.WriteLine( "Match any digit" );
15        DisplayMatches( testString, @"\d" );
16
17        // find anything that isn't a digit
18        Console.WriteLine( "\nMatch any nondigit" );
19        DisplayMatches( testString, @"\D" );
20
```

Fig. 16.18 | Demonstrating using character classes and quantifiers. (Part 1 of 3.)

```
21          // find the word characters in the test string
22          Console.WriteLine( "\nMatch any word character" );
23          DisplayMatches( testString, @"\w" );
24
25          // find sequences of word characters
26          Console.WriteLine(
27             "\nMatch a group of at least one word character" );
28          DisplayMatches( testString, @"\w+" );
29
30          // use a lazy quantifier
31          Console.WriteLine(
32             "\nMatch a group of at least one word character (lazy)" );
33          DisplayMatches( testString, @"\w+?" );
34
35          // match characters from 'a' to 'f'
36          Console.WriteLine( "\nMatch anything from 'a' - 'f'" );
37          DisplayMatches( testString, "[a-f]" );
38
39          // match anything that isn't in the range 'a' to 'f'
40          Console.WriteLine( "\nMatch anything not from 'a' - 'f'" );
41          DisplayMatches( testString, "[^a-f]" );
42
43          // match any sequence of letters in any case
44          Console.WriteLine( "\nMatch a group of at least one letter" );
45          DisplayMatches( testString, "[a-zA-Z]+" );
46
47          // use the . (dot) metacharacter to match any character
48          Console.WriteLine( "\nMatch a group of any characters" );
49          DisplayMatches( testString, ".*" );
50       } // end Main
51
52       // display the matches to a regular expression
53       private static void DisplayMatches( string input, string expression )
54       {
55          foreach ( var regexMatch in Regex.Matches( input, expression ) )
56             Console.Write( "{0} ", regexMatch );
57
58          Console.WriteLine(); // move to the next line
59       } // end method DisplayMatches
60    } // end class CharacterClasses
```

```
The test string is: "abc, DEF, 123"
Match any digit
1 2 3

Match any nondigit
a b c ,   D E F ,

Match any word character
a b c D E F 1 2 3

Match a group of at least one word character
abc DEF 123
```

Fig. 16.18 | Demonstrating using character classes and quantifiers. (Part 2 of 3.)

```
Match a group of at least one word character (lazy)
a b c D E F 1 2 3

Match anything from 'a' - 'f'
a b c

Match anything not from 'a' - 'f'
,   D E F ,   1 2 3

Match a group of at least one letter
abc DEF

Match a group of any characters
abc, DEF, 123
```

Fig. 16.18 | Demonstrating using character classes and quantifiers. (Part 3 of 3.)

The first regular expression (line 15) matches digits in the testString. We use the digit character class (\d) to match any digit (0–9). We precede the regular expression string with @. Recall that backslashes within the double quotation marks following the @ character are regular backslash characters, not the beginning of escape sequences. To define the regular expression without prefixing @ to the string, you would need to escape every backslash character, as in

```
"\\d"
```

which makes the regular expression more difficult to read.

The output shows that the regular expression matches 1, 2, and 3 in the testString. You can also match anything that *isn't* a member of a particular character class using an uppercase instead of a lowercase letter. For example, the regular expression "\D" (line 19) matches any character that isn't a digit. Notice in the output that this includes punctuation and whitespace. Negating a character class matches *everything* that *isn't* a member of the character class.

The next regular expression (line 23) uses the character class \w to match any word character in the testString. Notice that each match consists of a single character. It would be useful to match a sequence of word characters rather than a single character. The regular expression in line 28 uses the + quantifier to match a sequence of word characters. The **+ quantifier** matches one or more occurrences of the pattern to its left. There are three matches for this expression, each three characters long. Quantifiers are **greedy**—they match the *longest* possible occurrence of the pattern. You can follow a quantifier with a question mark (?) to make it **lazy**—it matches the *shortest* possible occurrence of the pattern. The regular expression "\w+?" (line 33) uses a lazy + quantifier to match the shortest sequence of word characters possible. This produces nine matches of length one instead of three matches of length three. Figure 16.19 lists other quantifiers that you can place after a pattern in a regular expression, and the purpose of each.

Regular expressions are not limited to the character classes in Fig. 16.17. You can create your own character class by listing the members of the character class between square brackets, [and]. [*Note:* Metacharacters in square brackets are treated as literal characters.] You can include a range of characters using the "-" character. The regular expression in line 37 of Fig. 16.18 creates a character class to match any lowercase letter

Quantifier	Matches
*	Matches zero or more occurrences of the preceding pattern.
+	Matches one or more occurrences of the preceding pattern.
?	Matches zero or one occurrences of the preceding pattern.
.	Matches any single character.
{n}	Matches exactly n occurrences of the preceding pattern.
{n,}	Matches at least n occurrences of the preceding pattern.
{n,m}	Matches between n and m (inclusive) occurrences of the preceding pattern.

Fig. 16.19 | Quantifiers used in regular expressions.

from a to f. These custom character classes match a single character that's a member of the class. The output shows three matches, a, b and c. Notice that D, E and F don't match the character class [a-f] because they're uppercase. You can negate a custom character class by placing a "^" character after the opening square bracket. The regular expression in line 41 matches any character that *isn't* in the range a-f. As with the predefined character classes, negating a custom character class matches *everything* that isn't a member, including punctuation and whitespace. You can also use quantifiers with custom character classes. The regular expression in line 45 uses a character class with two ranges of characters, a-z and A-Z, and the + quantifier to match a sequence of lowercase or uppercase letters. You can also use the "." (dot) character to match any character other than a newline. The regular expression ".*" (line 49) matches any sequence of characters. The * quantifier matches zero or more occurrences of the pattern to its left. Unlike the + quantifier, the * quantifier can be used to match an empty string.

16.15.2 Complex Regular Expressions

The program of Fig. 16.20 tries to match birthdays to a regular expression. For demonstration purposes, the expression matches only birthdays that do not occur in April and that belong to people whose names begin with "J". We can do this by combining the basic regular-expression techniques we've already discussed.

```
1   // Fig. 16.20: RegexMatches.cs
2   // A more complex regular expression.
3   using System;
4   using System.Text.RegularExpressions;
5
6   class RegexMatches
7   {
8      static void Main( string[] args )
9      {
10        // create a regular expression
11        Regex expression = new Regex( @"J.*\d[\d-[4]]-\d\d-\d\d" );
12
```

Fig. 16.20 | A more complex regular expression. (Part 1 of 2.)

```
13          string testString =
14              "Jane's Birthday is 05-12-75\n" +
15              "Dave's Birthday is 11-04-68\n" +
16              "John's Birthday is 04-28-73\n" +
17              "Joe's Birthday is 12-17-77";
18
19          // display all matches to the regular expression
20          foreach ( var regexMatch in expression.Matches( testString ) )
21              Console.WriteLine( regexMatch );
22      } // end Main
23   } // end class RegexMatches
```

```
Jane's Birthday is 05-12-75
Joe's Birthday is 12-17-77
```

Fig. 16.20 | A more complex regular expression. (Part 2 of 2.)

Line 11 creates a `Regex` object and passes a regular-expression pattern `string` to its constructor. The first character in the regular expression, `"J"`, is a literal character. Any `string` matching this regular expression must start with `"J"`. The next part of the regular expression (`".*"`) matches any number of unspecified characters except newlines. The pattern `"J.*"` matches a person's name that starts with J and any characters that may come after that.

Next we match the person's birthday. We use the `\d` character class to match the first digit of the month. Since the birthday must not occur in April, the second digit in the month can't be 4. We could use the character class `"[0-35-9]"` to match any digit other than 4. However, .NET regular expressions allow you to subtract members from a character class, called **character-class subtraction**. In line 11, we use the pattern `"[\d-[4]]"` to match any digit other than 4. When the `"-"` character in a character class is followed by a character class instead of a literal character, the `"-"` is interpreted as subtraction instead of a range of characters. The members of the character class following the `"-"` are removed from the character class preceding the `"-"`. When using character-class subtraction, the class being subtracted (`[4]`) must be the last item in the enclosing brackets (`[\d-[4]]`). This notation allows you to write shorter, easier-to-read regular expressions.

Although the `"-"` character indicates a range or character-class subtraction when it's enclosed in square brackets, instances of the `"-"` character outside a character class are treated as literal characters. Thus, the regular expression in line 11 searches for a `string` that starts with the letter `"J"`, followed by any number of characters, followed by a two-digit number (of which the second digit cannot be 4), followed by a dash, another two-digit number, a dash and another two-digit number.

Lines 20–21 use a `foreach` statement to iterate through the `MatchCollection` object returned by method `Matches`, which received `testString` as an argument. For each `Match`, line 21 outputs the text that matched the regular expression. The output in Fig. 16.20 displays the two matches that were found in `testString`. Notice that both matches conform to the pattern specified by the regular expression.

16.15.3 Validating User Input with Regular Expressions and LINQ

The application in Fig. 16.21 presents a more involved example that uses regular expressions to validate name, address and telephone-number information input by a user.

```
 1    // Fig. 16.21: Validate.cs
 2    // Validate user information using regular expressions.
 3    using System;
 4    using System.Linq;
 5    using System.Text.RegularExpressions;
 6    using System.Windows.Forms;
 7
 8    namespace Validate
 9    {
10       public partial class ValidateForm : Form
11       {
12          public ValidateForm()
13          {
14             InitializeComponent();
15          } // end constructor
16
17          // handles OK Button's Click event
18          private void okButton_Click( object sender, EventArgs e )
19          {
20             // find blank TextBoxes and order by TabIndex
21             var emptyBoxes =
22                from Control currentControl in Controls
23                where currentControl is TextBox
24                let box = currentControl as TextBox
25                where string.IsNullOrEmpty( box.Text )
26                orderby box.TabIndex
27                select box;
28
29             // if there are any empty TextBoxes
30             if ( emptyBoxes.Count() > 0 )
31             {
32                // display message box indicating missing information
33                MessageBox.Show( "Please fill in all fields",
34                   "Missing Information", MessageBoxButtons.OK,
35                   MessageBoxIcon.Error );
36
37                emptyBoxes.First().Select(); // select first empty TextBox
38             } // end if
39             else
40             {
41                // check for invalid input
42                if ( !ValidateInput( lastNameTextBox.Text,
43                   "^[A-Z][a-zA-Z]*$", "Invalid last name" ) )
44
45                   lastNameTextBox.Select(); // select invalid TextBox
46                else if ( !ValidateInput( firstNameTextBox.Text,
47                   "^[A-Z][a-zA-Z]*$", "Invalid first name" ) )
48
49                   firstNameTextBox.Select(); // select invalid TextBox
50                else if ( !ValidateInput( addressTextBox.Text,
51                   @"^[0-9]+\s+([a-zA-Z]+|[a-zA-Z]+\s[a-zA-Z]+)$",
52                   "Invalid address" ) )
```

Fig. 16.21 | Validating user information using regular expressions. (Part 1 of 4.)

```
53
54                  addressTextBox.Select(); // select invalid TextBox
55               else if ( !ValidateInput( cityTextBox.Text,
56                  @"^([a-zA-Z]+|[a-zA-Z]+\s[a-zA-Z]+)$", "Invalid city" ) )
57
58                  cityTextBox.Select(); // select invalid TextBox
59               else if ( !ValidateInput( stateTextBox.Text,
60                  @"^([a-zA-Z]+|[a-zA-Z]+\s[a-zA-Z]+)$", "Invalid state" ) )
61
62                  stateTextBox.Select(); // select invalid TextBox
63               else if ( !ValidateInput( zipCodeTextBox.Text,
64                  @"^\d{5}$", "Invalid zip code" ) )
65
66                  zipCodeTextBox.Select(); // select invalid TextBox
67               else if ( !ValidateInput( phoneTextBox.Text,
68                  @"^[1-9]\d{2}-[1-9]\d{2}-\d{4}$",
69                  "Invalid phone number" ) )
70
71                  phoneTextBox.Select(); // select invalid TextBox
72               else // if all input is valid
73               {
74                  this.Hide(); // hide main window
75                  MessageBox.Show( "Thank You!", "Information Correct",
76                     MessageBoxButtons.OK, MessageBoxIcon.Information );
77                  Application.Exit(); // exit the application
78               } // end else
79            } // end else
80         } // end method okButton_Click
81
82         // use regular expressions to validate user input
83         private bool ValidateInput(
84            string input, string expression, string message )
85         {
86            // store whether the input is valid
87            bool valid = Regex.Match( input, expression ).Success;
88
89            // if the input doesn't match the regular expression
90            if ( !valid )
91            {
92               // signal the user that input was invalid
93               MessageBox.Show( message, "Invalid Input",
94                  MessageBoxButtons.OK, MessageBoxIcon.Error );
95            } // end if
96
97            return valid; // return whether the input is valid
98         } // end method ValidateInput
99      } // end class ValidateForm
100  } // end namespace Validate
```

Fig. 16.21 | Validating user information using regular expressions. (Part 2 of 4.)

Fig. 16.21 | Validating user information using regular expressions. (Part 3 of 4.)

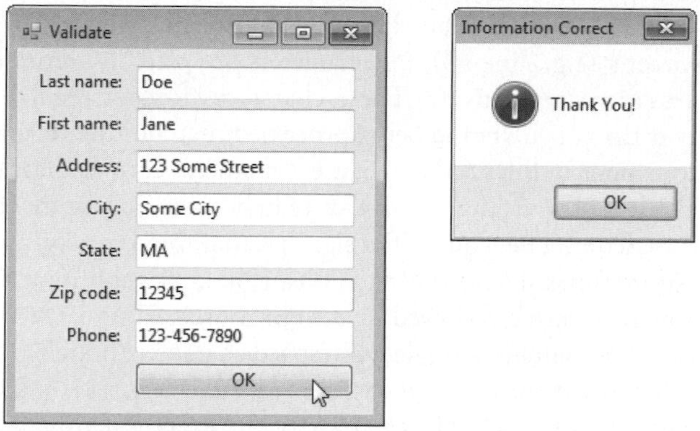

Fig. 16.21 | Validating user information using regular expressions. (Part 4 of 4.)

When a user clicks **OK**, the program uses a LINQ query to select any empty TextBoxes (lines 22–27) from the Controls collection. Notice that we explicitly declare the type of the range variable in the from clause (line 22). When working with nongeneric collections, such as Controls, you must explicitly type the range variable. The first where clause (line 23) determines whether the currentControl is a TextBox. The let clause (line 24) creates and initializes a variable in a LINQ query for use later in the query. Here, we use the let clause to define variable box as a TextBox, which contains the Control object cast to a TextBox. This allows us to use the control in the LINQ query as a TextBox, enabling access to its properties (such as Text). You may include a second where clause after the let clause. The second where clause determines whether the TextBox's Text property is empty. If one or more TextBoxes are empty (line 30), the program displays a message to the user (lines 33–35) that all fields must be filled in before the program can validate the information. Line 37 calls the Select method of the first TextBox in the query result so that the user can begin typing in that TextBox. The query sorted the TextBoxes by TabIndex (line 26) so the first TextBox in the query result is the first empty TextBox on the Form. If there are no empty fields, lines 39–71 validate the user input.

We call method ValidateInput to determine whether the user input matches the specified regular expressions. ValidateInput (lines 83–98) takes as arguments the text input by the user (input), the regular expression the input must match (expression) and a message to display if the input is invalid (message). Line 87 calls Regex static method Match, passing both the string to validate and the regular expression as arguments. The **Success** property of class Match indicates whether method Match's first argument matched the pattern specified by the regular expression in the second argument. If the value of Success is false (i.e., there was no match), lines 93–94 display the error message passed as an argument to method ValidateInput. Line 97 then returns the value of the Success property. If ValidateInput returns false, the TextBox containing invalid data is selected so the user can correct the input. If all input is valid—the else statement (lines 72–78) displays a message dialog stating that all input is valid, and the program terminates when the user dismisses the dialog.

In the previous example, we searched a string for substrings that matched a regular expression. In this example, we want to ensure that the entire string for each input conforms to a particular regular expression. For example, we want to accept "Smith" as a last name, but not "9@Smith#". In a regular expression that begins with a "^" character and ends with a "$" character (e.g., line 43), the characters "^" and "$" represent the beginning and end of a string, respectively. These characters force a regular expression to return a match only if the entire string being processed matches the regular expression.

The regular expressions in lines 43 and 47 use a character class to match an uppercase first letter followed by letters of any case—a-z matches any lowercase letter, and A-Z matches any uppercase letter. The * quantifier signifies that the second range of characters may occur zero or more times in the string. Thus, this expression matches any string consisting of one uppercase letter, followed by zero or more additional letters.

The \s character class matches a single whitespace character (lines 51, 56 and 60). In the expression "\d{5}", used for the zipCode string (line 64), {5} is a quantifier (see Fig. 16.19). The pattern to the left of {n} must occur exactly n times. Thus "\d{5}" matches any five digits. Recall that the character "|" (lines 51, 56 and 60) matches the expression to its left or the expression to its right. In line 51, we use the character "|" to indicate that the address can contain a word of one or more characters or a word of one or more characters followed by a space and another word of one or more characters. Note the use of parentheses to group parts of the regular expression. This ensures that "|" is applied to the correct parts of the pattern.

The **Last Name:** and **First Name:** TextBoxes each accept strings that begin with an uppercase letter (lines 43 and 47). The regular expression for the **Address:** TextBox (line 51) matches a number of at least one digit, followed by a space and then either one or more letters or else one or more letters followed by a space and another series of one or more letters. Therefore, "10 Broadway" and "10 Main Street" are both valid addresses. As currently formed, the regular expression in line 51 doesn't match an address that does not start with a number, or that has more than two words. The regular expressions for the **City:** (line 56) and **State:** (line 60) TextBoxes match any word of at least one character or, alternatively, any two words of at least one character if the words are separated by a single space. This means both Waltham and West Newton would match. Again, these regular expressions would not accept names that have more than two words. The regular expression for the **Zip code:** TextBox (line 64) ensures that the zip code is a five-digit number. The regular expression for the **Phone:** TextBox (line 68) indicates that the phone number must be of the form xxx-yyy-yyyy, where the xs represent the area code and the ys the number. The first x and the first y cannot be zero, as specified by the range [1–9] in each case.

16.15.4 Regex Methods Replace and Split

Sometimes it's useful to replace parts of one string with another or to split a string according to a regular expression. For this purpose, class Regex provides static and instance versions of methods Replace and Split, which are demonstrated in Fig. 16.22.

```
1   // Fig. 16.22: RegexSubstitution.cs
2   // Using Regex methods Replace and Split.
3   using System;
4   using System.Text.RegularExpressions;
```

Fig. 16.22 | Using Regex methods Replace and Split. (Part 1 of 2.)

```
 5
 6   class RegexSubstitution
 7   {
 8      static void Main( string[] args )
 9      {
10         string testString1 = "This sentence ends in 5 stars *****";
11         string testString2 = "1, 2, 3, 4, 5, 6, 7, 8";
12         Regex testRegex1 = new Regex( @"\d" );
13         string output = string.Empty;
14
15         Console.WriteLine( "First test string: {0}", testString1 );
16
17         // replace every '*' with a '^' and display the result
18         testString1 = Regex.Replace( testString1, @"\*", "^" );
19         Console.WriteLine( "^ substituted for *: {0}", testString1 );
20
21         // replace the word "stars" with "carets" and display the result
22         testString1 = Regex.Replace( testString1, "stars", "carets" );
23         Console.WriteLine( "\"carets\" substituted for \"stars\": {0}",
24            testString1 );
25
26         // replace every word with "word" and display the result
27         Console.WriteLine( "Every word replaced by \"word\": {0}",
28            Regex.Replace( testString1, @"\w+", "word" ) );
29
30         Console.WriteLine( "\nSecond test string: {0}", testString2 );
31
32         // replace the first three digits with the word "digit"
33         Console.WriteLine( "Replace first 3 digits by \"digit\": {0}",
34            testRegex1.Replace( testString2, "digit", 3 ) );
35
36         Console.Write( "string split at commas [" );
37
38         // split the string into individual strings, each containing a digit
39         string[] result = Regex.Split( testString2, @",\s" );
40
41         // add each digit to the output string
42         foreach( var resultString in result )
43            output += "\"" + resultString + "\", ";
44
45         // delete ", " at the end of output string
46         Console.WriteLine( output.Substring( 0, output.Length - 2 ) + "]" );
47      } // end Main
48   } // end class RegexSubstitution
```

```
First test string: This sentence ends in 5 stars *****
^ substituted for *: This sentence ends in 5 stars ^^^^^
"carets" substituted for "stars": This sentence ends in 5 carets ^^^^^
Every word replaced by "word": word word word word word word ^^^^^

Second test string: 1, 2, 3, 4, 5, 6, 7, 8
Replace first 3 digits by "digit": digit, digit, digit, 4, 5, 6, 7, 8
String split at commas ["1", "2", "3", "4", "5", "6", "7", "8"]
```

Fig. 16.22 | Using Regex methods Replace and Split. (Part 2 of 2.)

Regex method **Replace** replaces text in a `string` with new text wherever the original `string` matches a regular expression. We use two versions of this method in Fig. 16.22. The first version (line 18) is a `static` method and takes three parameters—the `string` to modify, the `string` containing the regular expression to match and the replacement `string`. Here, `Replace` replaces every instance of "`*`" in `testString1` with "`^`". Notice that the regular expression ("`\*`") precedes character `*` with a backslash (`\`). Normally, `*` is a quantifier indicating that a regular expression should match any number of occurrences of a preceding pattern. However, in line 18, we want to find all occurrences of the literal character `*`; to do this, we must escape character `*` with character `\`. By escaping a special regular-expression character, we tell the regular-expression matching engine to find the actual character `*` rather than use it as a quantifier.

The second version of method `Replace` (line 34) is an instance method that uses the regular expression passed to the constructor for `testRegex1` (line 12) to perform the replacement operation. Line 12 instantiates `testRegex1` with argument `@"\d"`. The call to instance method `Replace` in line 34 takes three arguments—a `string` to modify, a `string` containing the replacement text and an integer specifying the number of replacements to make. In this case, line 34 replaces the first three instances of a digit ("`\d`") in `testString2` with the text "`digit`".

Method **Split** divides a `string` into several substrings. The original `string` is broken at delimiters that match a specified regular expression. Method `Split` returns an `array` containing the substrings. In line 39, we use `static` method `Split` to separate a `string` of comma-separated integers. The first argument is the `string` to split; the second argument is the regular expression that represents the delimiter. The regular expression "`,\s`" separates the substrings at each comma. By matching a whitespace character (`\s` in the regular expression), we eliminate the extra spaces from the resulting substrings.

16.16 Wrap-Up

In this chapter, you learned about the Framework Class Library's string- and character-processing capabilities. We overviewed the fundamentals of characters and strings. You saw how to determine the length of strings, copy strings, access the individual characters in strings, search strings, obtain substrings from larger strings, compare strings, concatenate strings, replace characters in strings and convert strings to uppercase or lowercase letters.

We showed how to use class `StringBuilder` to build strings dynamically. You learned how to determine and specify the size of a `StringBuilder` object, and how to append, insert, remove and replace characters in a `StringBuilder` object. We then introduced the character-testing methods of type `Char` that enable a program to determine whether a character is a digit, a letter, a lowercase letter, an uppercase letter, a punctuation mark or a symbol other than a punctuation mark, and the methods for converting a character to uppercase or lowercase.

Finally, we discussed classes `Regex`, `Match` and `MatchCollection` from namespace `System.Text.RegularExpressions` and the symbols that are used to form regular expressions. You learned how to find patterns in a `string` and match entire `strings` to patterns with `Regex` methods `Match` and `Matches`, how to replace characters in a `string` with `Regex` method `Replace` and how to split `strings` at delimiters with `Regex` method `Split`. In the next chapter, you'll learn how to read data from and write data to files.

Files and Streams

I can only assume that a "Do Not File" document is filed in a "Do Not File" file.
—Senator Frank Church
Senate Intelligence Subcommittee
Hearing, 1975

Consciousness ... does not appear to itself chopped up in bits. ... A "river" or a "stream" are the metaphors by which it is most naturally described.
—William James

I read part of it all the way through.
—Samuel Goldwyn

OBJECTIVES

In this chapter you'll learn:

- To create, read, write and update files.

- To use classes `File` and `Directory` to obtain information about files and directories on your computer.

- To use LINQ to search through directories.

- To become familiar with sequential-access file processing.

- To use classes `FileStream`, `StreamReader` and `StreamWriter` to read text from and write text to files.

- To use classes `FileStream` and `BinaryFormatter` to read objects from and write objects to files.

17.1 Introduction

Variables and arrays offer only temporary storage of data—the data is lost when a local variable "goes out of scope" or when the program terminates. By contrast, **files** (and databases, which we cover in Chapter 18) are used for long-term retention of large amounts of data, even after the program that created the data terminates. Data maintained in files often is called **persistent data**. Computers store files on **secondary storage devices**, such as magnetic disks, optical disks, flash memory and magnetic tapes. In this chapter, we explain how to create, update and process data files in C# programs.

We begin with an overview of the data hierarchy from bits to files. Next, we overview some of the Framework Class Library's file-processing classes. We then present two examples that show how you can determine information about the files and directories on your computer. The remainder of the chapter shows how to write to and read from text files that are human readable and binary files that store entire objects in binary format.

17.2 Data Hierarchy

Ultimately, all data items that computers process are reduced to combinations of 0s and 1s. This occurs because it's simple and economical to build electronic devices that can assume two stable states—one state represents 0 and the other represents 1. It's remarkable that the impressive functions performed by computers involve only the most fundamental manipulations of 0s and 1s.

Bits
The smallest data item that computers support is called a **bit** (short for "**binary digit**"—a digit that can assume one of two values). Each bit can assume either the value 0 or the value 1. Computer circuitry performs various simple **bit manipulations**, such as examining the value of a bit, setting the value of a bit and reversing a bit (from 1 to 0 or from 0 to 1).

Characters
Programming with data in the low-level form of bits is cumbersome. It's preferable to program with data in forms such as **decimal digits** (i.e., 0, 1, 2, 3, 4, 5, 6, 7, 8 and 9), **letters** (i.e., A–Z and a–z) and **special symbols** (i.e., $, @, %, &, *, (,), -, +, ", :, ?, / and many others). Digits, letters and special symbols are referred to as **characters**. The set of all characters used to write programs and represent data items on a particular computer is called

that computer's **character set**. Because computers can process only 0s and 1s, every character in a computer's character set is represented as a pattern of 0s and 1s. **Bytes** are composed of eight bits. C# uses the **Unicode® character set** (www.unicode.org) in which characters are composed of 2 bytes. Programmers create programs and data items with characters; computers manipulate and process these characters as patterns of bits.

Fields

Just as characters are composed of bits, fields are composed of characters. A **field** is a group of characters that conveys meaning. For example, a field consisting of uppercase and lowercase letters can represent a person's name.

Data items processed by computers form a **data hierarchy** (Fig. 17.1), in which data items become larger and more complex in structure as we progress from bits to characters to fields to larger data aggregates.

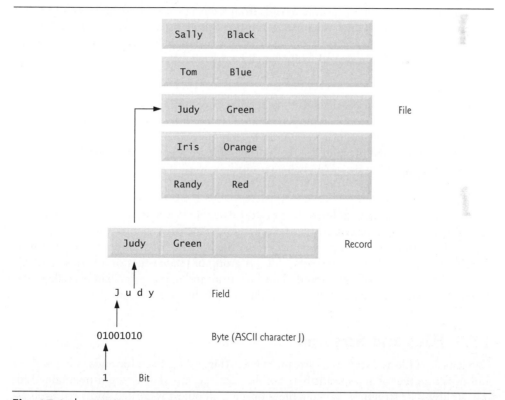

Fig. 17.1 | Data hierarchy.

Records and Files

Typically, a **record** (which can be represented as a class) is composed of several related fields. In a payroll system, for example, a record for a particular employee might include the following fields:

1. Employee identification number
2. Name

3. Address

4. Hourly pay rate

5. Number of exemptions claimed

6. Year-to-date earnings

7. Amount of taxes withheld

In the preceding example, each field is associated with the same employee. A file is a group of related records.[1] A company's payroll file normally contains one record for each employee. A payroll file for a small company might contain only 22 records, whereas one for a large company might contain 100,000. It's not unusual for a company to have many files, some containing millions, billions or even trillions of characters of information.

Record Key

To facilitate the retrieval of specific records from a file, at least one field in each record is chosen as a **record key,** which identifies a record as belonging to a particular person or entity and distinguishes that record from all others. For example, in a payroll record, the employee identification number normally would be the record key.

Sequential Files

There are many ways to organize records in a file. A common organization is called a **sequential file,** in which records typically are stored in order by a record-key field. In a payroll file, records usually are placed in order by employee identification number. The first employee record in the file contains the lowest employee identification number, and subsequent records contain increasingly higher ones.

Databases

Most businesses use many different files to store data. For example, a company might have payroll files, accounts-receivable files (listing money due from clients), accounts-payable files (listing money due to suppliers), inventory files (listing facts about all the items handled by the business) and many other files. A group of related files often are stored in a **database.** A collection of programs designed to create and manage databases is called a **database management system (DBMS).** We discuss databases in Chapter 18.

17.3 Files and Streams

C# views each file as a sequential **stream** of bytes (Fig. 17.2). Each file ends either with an **end-of-file marker** or at a specific byte number that's recorded in a system-maintained administrative data structure. When a file is opened, an object is created and a stream is associated with the object. When a console application executes, the runtime environment creates three stream objects that are accessible via properties **Console.Out, Console.In** and **Console.Error,** respectively. These objects facilitate communication between a program and a particular file or device. **Console.In** refers to the **standard input stream ob-**

---

1. Generally, a file can contain arbitrary data in arbitrary formats. In some operating systems, a file is viewed as nothing more than a collection of bytes, and any organization of the bytes in a file (such as organizing the data into records) is a view created by the application programmer.

ject, which enables a program to input data from the keyboard. Console.Out refers to the **standard output stream object**, which enables a program to output data to the screen. Console.Error refers to the **standard error stream object**, which enables a program to output error messages to the screen. We have been using Console.Out and Console.In in our console applications, Console methods Write and WriteLine use Console.Out to perform output, and Console methods Read and ReadLine use Console.In to perform input.

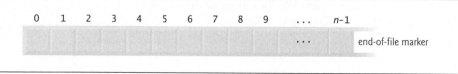

Fig. 17.2 | C#'s view of an *n*-byte file.

There are many file-processing classes in the Framework Class Library. The **System.IO namespace** includes stream classes such as **StreamReader** (for text input from a file), **StreamWriter** (for text output to a file) and **FileStream** (for both input from and output to a file). These stream classes inherit from abstract classes **TextReader**, **TextWriter** and Stream, respectively. Actually, properties Console.In and Console.Out are of type TextReader and TextWriter, respectively. The system creates objects of TextReader and TextWriter derived classes to initialize Console properties Console.In and Console.Out.

Abstract class **Stream** provides functionality for representing streams as bytes. Classes FileStream, **MemoryStream** and **BufferedStream** (all from namespace System.IO) inherit from class Stream. Class FileStream can be used to write data to and read data from files. Class MemoryStream enables the transfer of data directly to and from memory—this is much faster than reading from and writing to external devices. Class BufferedStream uses **buffering** to transfer data to or from a stream. Buffering is an I/O performance-enhancement technique, in which each output operation is directed to a region in memory, called a **buffer**, that's large enough to hold the data from many output operations. Then actual transfer to the output device is performed in one large **physical output operation** each time the buffer fills. The output operations directed to the output buffer in memory often are called **logical output operations**. Buffering can also be used to speed input operations by initially reading more data than is required into a buffer, so subsequent reads get data from memory rather than an external device.

In this chapter, we use key stream classes to implement file-processing programs that create and manipulate sequential-access files.

17.4 Classes File and Directory

Information is stored in files, which are organized in directories (also called folders). Classes File and Directory enable programs to manipulate files and directories on disk. Class **File** can determine information about files and can be used to open files for reading or writing. We discuss techniques for writing to and reading from files in subsequent sections.

Figure 17.3 lists several of class File's static methods for manipulating and determining information about files. We demonstrate several of these methods in Fig. 17.5.

static Method	Description
AppendText	Returns a StreamWriter that appends text to an existing file or creates a file if one does not exist.
Copy	Copies a file to a new file.
Create	Creates a file and returns its associated FileStream.
CreateText	Creates a text file and returns its associated StreamWriter.
Delete	Deletes the specified file.
Exists	Returns true if the specified file exists and false otherwise.
GetCreationTime	Returns a DateTime object representing when the file was created.
GetLastAccessTime	Returns a DateTime object representing when the file was last accessed.
GetLastWriteTime	Returns a DateTime object representing when the file was last modified.
Move	Moves the specified file to a specified location.
Open	Returns a FileStream associated with the specified file and equipped with the specified read/write permissions.
OpenRead	Returns a read-only FileStream associated with the specified file.
OpenText	Returns a StreamReader associated with the specified file.
OpenWrite	Returns a write FileStream associated with the specified file.

Fig. 17.3 | File class static methods (partial list).

Class **Directory** provides capabilities for manipulating directories. Figure 17.4 lists some of class Directory's static methods for directory manipulation. Figure 17.5 demonstrates several of these methods, as well. The **DirectoryInfo** object returned by method **CreateDirectory** contains information about a directory. Much of the information contained in class DirectoryInfo also can be accessed via the methods of class Directory.

static Method	Description
CreateDirectory	Creates a directory and returns its associated DirectoryInfo object.
Delete	Deletes the specified directory.
Exists	Returns true if the specified directory exists and false otherwise.
GetDirectories	Returns a string array containing the names of the subdirectories in the specified directory.
GetFiles	Returns a string array containing the names of the files in the specified directory.
GetCreationTime	Returns a DateTime object representing when the directory was created.
GetLastAccessTime	Returns a DateTime object representing when the directory was last accessed.
GetLastWriteTime	Returns a DateTime object representing when items were last written to the directory.
Move	Moves the specified directory to a specified location.

Fig. 17.4 | Directory class static methods.

Demonstrating Classes File and Directory

Class FileTestForm (Fig. 17.5) uses File and Directory methods to access file and directory information. This Form contains the control inputTextBox, in which the user enters a file or directory name. For each key that the user presses while typing in the TextBox, the program calls event handler inputTextBox_KeyDown (lines 19–75). If the user presses the *Enter* key (line 22), this method displays either the file's or directory's contents, depending on the text the user input. (If the user does not press the *Enter* key, this method returns without displaying any content.) Line 28 uses File method Exists to determine whether the user-specified text is the name of an existing file. If so, line 31 invokes private method GetInformation (lines 79–97), which calls File methods GetCreationTime (line 88), GetLastWriteTime (line 92) and GetLastAccessTime (line 96) to access file information. When method GetInformation returns, line 38 instantiates a StreamReader for reading text from the file. The StreamReader constructor takes as an argument a string containing the name of the file to open. Line 40 calls StreamReader method ReadToEnd to read the entire contents of the file as a string, then appends the string to outputTextBox. Once the file has been read, the using block terminates, closes the file and disposes of the corresponding object.

```
 1    // Fig. 17.5: FileTestForm.cs
 2    // Using classes File and Directory.
 3    using System;
 4    using System.Windows.Forms;
 5    using System.IO;
 6
 7    namespace FileTest
 8    {
 9       // displays contents of files and directories
10       public partial class FileTestForm : Form
11       {
12          // parameterless constructor
13          public FileTestForm()
14          {
15             InitializeComponent();
16          } // end constructor
17
18          // invoked when user presses key
19          private void inputTextBox_KeyDown( object sender, KeyEventArgs e )
20          {
21             // determine whether user pressed Enter key
22             if ( e.KeyCode == Keys.Enter )
23             {
24                // get user-specified file or directory
25                string fileName = inputTextBox.Text;
26
27                // determine whether fileName is a file
28                if ( File.Exists( fileName ) )
29                {
30                   // get file's creation date, modification date, etc.
31                   GetInformation( fileName );
32                   StreamReader stream = null; // declare StreamReader
33
```

Fig. 17.5 | Using classes File and Directory. (Part 1 of 3.)

```
34                    // display file contents through StreamReader
35                    try
36                    {
37                        // obtain reader and file contents
38                        using ( stream = new StreamReader( fileName ) )
39                        {
40                            outputTextBox.AppendText( stream.ReadToEnd() );
41                        } // end using
42                    } // end try
43                    catch ( IOException )
44                    {
45                        MessageBox.Show( "Error reading from file",
46                            "File Error", MessageBoxButtons.OK,
47                            MessageBoxIcon.Error );
48                    } // end catch
49                } // end if
50                // determine whether fileName is a directory
51                else if ( Directory.Exists( fileName ) )
52                {
53                    // get directory's creation date,
54                    // modification date, etc.
55                    GetInformation( fileName );
56
57                    // obtain file/directory list of specified directory
58                    string[] directoryList =
59                        Directory.GetDirectories( fileName );
60
61                    outputTextBox.AppendText( "Directory contents:\n" );
62
63                    // output directoryList contents
64                    foreach ( var directory in directoryList )
65                        outputTextBox.AppendText( directory + "\n" );
66                } // end else if
67                else
68                {
69                    // notify user that neither file nor directory exists
70                    MessageBox.Show( inputTextBox.Text +
71                        " does not exist", "File Error",
72                        MessageBoxButtons.OK, MessageBoxIcon.Error );
73                } // end else
74            } // end if
75        } // end method inputTextBox_KeyDown
76
77        // get information on file or directory,
78        // and output it to outputTextBox
79        private void GetInformation( string fileName )
80        {
81            outputTextBox.Clear();
82
83            // output that file or directory exists
84            outputTextBox.AppendText( fileName + " exists\n" );
85
```

Fig. 17.5 | Using classes `File` and `Directory`. (Part 2 of 3.)

```
86              // output when file or directory was created
87              outputTextBox.AppendText( "Created: " +
88                  File.GetCreationTime( fileName ) + "\n" );
89
90              // output when file or directory was last modified
91              outputTextBox.AppendText( "Last modified: " +
92                  File.GetLastWriteTime( fileName ) + "\n" );
93
94              // output when file or directory was last accessed
95              outputTextBox.AppendText( "Last accessed: " +
96                  File.GetLastAccessTime( fileName ) + "\n" );
97          } // end method GetInformation
98      } // end class FileTestForm
99  } // end namespace FileTest
```

a) Viewing the contents of file "quotes.txt" b) Viewing all files in directory C:\Program Files\

c) User gives invalid input d) Error message is displayed

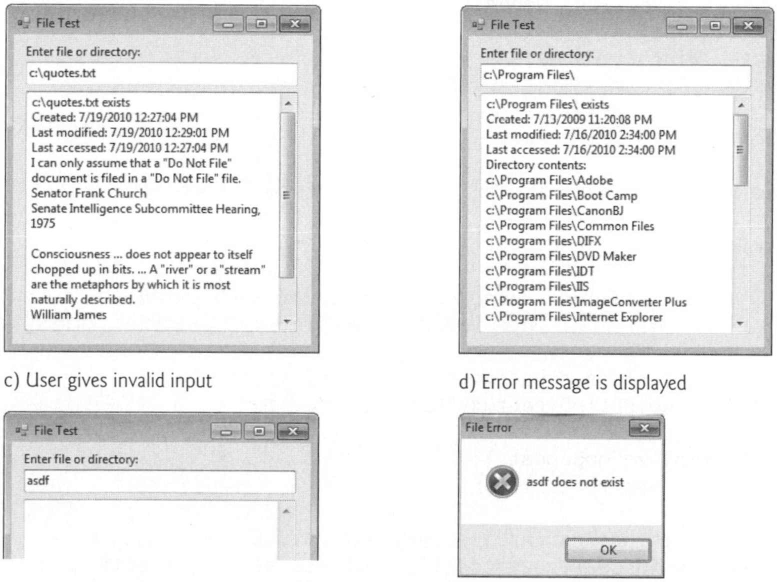

Fig. 17.5 | Using classes File and Directory. (Part 3 of 3.)

If line 28 determines that the user-specified text is not a file, line 51 determines whether it's a directory using Directory method **Exists**. If the user specified an existing directory, line 55 invokes method GetInformation to access the directory information. Line 59 calls Directory method **GetDirectories** to obtain a string array containing the names of subdirectories in the specified directory. Lines 64–65 display each element in the string array. Note that, if line 51 determines that the user-specified text is not a directory name, lines 70–72 notify the user (via a MessageBox) that the name the user entered does not exist as a file or directory.

Searching Directories with LINQ
We now consider another example that uses file- and directory-manipulation capabilities. Class LINQToFileDirectoryForm (Fig. 17.6) uses LINQ with classes File, Path and

Directory to report the number of files of each file type that exist in the specified directory path. The program also serves as a "clean-up" utility—when it finds a file that has the .bak file-name extension (i.e., a backup file), the program displays a MessageBox asking the user whether that file should be removed, then responds appropriately to the user's input. This example also uses LINQ to Objects to help delete the backup files.

When the user clicks **Search Directory**, the program invokes searchButton_Click (lines 25–65), which searches recursively through the directory path specified by the user. If the user inputs text in the TextBox, line 29 calls Directory method Exists to determine whether that text is a valid directory. If it's not, lines 32–33 notify the user of the error.

```csharp
1   // Fig. 17.6: LINQToFileDirectoryForm.cs
2   // Using LINQ to search directories and determine file types.
3   using System;
4   using System.Collections.Generic;
5   using System.Linq;
6   using System.Windows.Forms;
7   using System.IO;
8
9   namespace LINQToFileDirectory
10  {
11     public partial class LINQToFileDirectoryForm : Form
12     {
13        string currentDirectory; // directory to search
14
15        // store extensions found, and number of each extension found
16        Dictionary<string, int> found = new Dictionary<string, int>();
17
18        // parameterless constructor
19        public LINQToFileDirectoryForm()
20        {
21           InitializeComponent();
22        } // end constructor
23
24        // handles the Search Directory Button's Click event
25        private void searchButton_Click( object sender, EventArgs e )
26        {
27           // check whether user specified path exists
28           if ( pathTextBox.Text != string.Empty &&
29              !Directory.Exists( pathTextBox.Text ) )
30           {
31              // show error if user does not specify valid directory
32              MessageBox.Show( "Invalid Directory", "Error",
33                 MessageBoxButtons.OK, MessageBoxIcon.Error );
34           } // end if
35           else
36           {
37              // use current directory if no directory is specified
38              if ( pathTextBox.Text == string.Empty )
39                 currentDirectory = Directory.GetCurrentDirectory();
```

Fig. 17.6 | Using LINQ to search directories and determine file types. (Part 1 of 4.)

```
40              else
41                  currentDirectory = pathTextBox.Text;
42
43              directoryTextBox.Text = currentDirectory; // show directory
44
45              // clear TextBoxes
46              pathTextBox.Clear();
47              resultsTextBox.Clear();
48
49              SearchDirectory( currentDirectory ); // search the directory
50
51              // allow user to delete .bak files
52              CleanDirectory( currentDirectory );
53
54              // summarize and display the results
55              foreach ( var current in found.Keys )
56              {
57                  // display the number of files with current extension
58                  resultsTextBox.AppendText( string.Format(
59                      "* Found {0} {1} files.\r\n",
60                      found[ current ], current ) );
61              } // end foreach
62
63              found.Clear(); // clear results for new search
64          } // end else
65      } // end method searchButton_Click
66
67      // search directory using LINQ
68      private void SearchDirectory( string folder )
69      {
70          // files contained in the directory
71          string[] files = Directory.GetFiles( folder );
72
73          // subdirectories in the directory
74          string[] directories = Directory.GetDirectories( folder );
75
76          // find all file extensions in this directory
77          var extensions =
78              ( from file in files
79                select Path.GetExtension( file ) ).Distinct();
80
81          // count the number of files using each extension
82          foreach ( var extension in extensions )
83          {
84              var temp = extension;
85
86              // count the number of files with the extension
87              var extensionCount =
88                  ( from file in files
89                    where Path.GetExtension( file ) == temp
90                    select file ).Count();
91
```

Fig. 17.6 | Using LINQ to search directories and determine file types. (Part 2 of 4.)

```
 92              // if the Dictionary already contains a key for the extension
 93              if ( found.ContainsKey( extension ) )
 94                 found[ extension ] += extensionCount; // update the count
 95              else
 96                 found.Add( extension, extensionCount ); // add new count
 97           } // end foreach
 98
 99           // recursive call to search subdirectories
100           foreach ( var subdirectory in directories )
101              SearchDirectory( subdirectory );
102        } // end method SearchDirectory
103
104        // allow user to delete backup files (.bak)
105        private void CleanDirectory( string folder )
106        {
107           // files contained in the directory
108           string[] files = Directory.GetFiles( folder );
109
110           // subdirectories in the directory
111           string[] directories = Directory.GetDirectories( folder );
112
113           // select all the backup files in this directory
114           var backupFiles =
115              from file in files
116              where Path.GetExtension( file ) == ".bak"
117              select file;
118
119           // iterate over all backup files (.bak)
120           foreach ( var backup in backupFiles )
121           {
122              DialogResult result = MessageBox.Show( "Found backup file " +
123                 Path.GetFileName( backup ) + ". Delete?", "Delete Backup",
124                 MessageBoxButtons.YesNo, MessageBoxIcon.Question );
125
126              // delete file if user clicked 'yes'
127              if ( result == DialogResult.Yes )
128              {
129                 File.Delete( backup ); // delete backup file
130                 --found[ ".bak" ]; // decrement count in Dictionary
131
132                 // if there are no .bak files, delete key from Dictionary
133                 if ( found[ ".bak" ] == 0 )
134                    found.Remove( ".bak" );
135              } // end if
136           } // end foreach
137
138           // recursive call to clean subdirectories
139           foreach ( var subdirectory in directories )
140              CleanDirectory( subdirectory );
141        } // end method CleanDirectory
142     } // end class LINQToFileDirectoryForm
143  } // end namespace LINQToFileDirectory
```

Fig. 17.6 | Using LINQ to search directories and determine file types. (Part 3 of 4.)

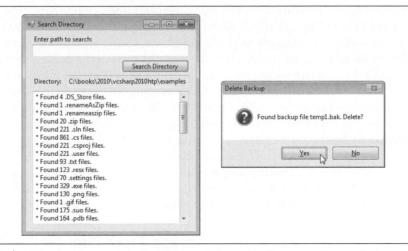

Fig. 17.6 | Using LINQ to search directories and determine file types. (Part 4 of 4.)

*Method **SearchDirectory***

Lines 38–41 get the current directory (if the user did not specify a path) or the specified directory. Line 49 passes the directory name to recursive method SearchDirectory (lines 68–102). Line 71 calls Directory method **GetFiles** to get a string array containing file names in the specified directory. Line 74 calls Directory method GetDirectories to get a string array containing the subdirectory names in the specified directory.

Lines 78–79 use LINQ to get the Distinct file-name extensions in the files array. **Path** method **GetExtension** obtains the extension for the specified file name. For each file-name extension returned by the LINQ query, lines 82–97 determine the number of occurrences of that extension in the files array. The LINQ query at lines 88–90 compares each file-name extension in the files array with the current extension being processed (line 89). All matches are included in the result. We then use LINQ method Count to determine the total number of files that matched the current extension.

Class LINQToFileDirectoryForm uses a Dictionary (declared in line 16) to store each file-name extension and the corresponding number of file names with that extension. A **Dictionary** (namespace System.Collections.Generic) is a collection of key/value pairs, in which each key has a corresponding value. Class Dictionary is a generic class like class List (presented in Section 9.4). Line 16 indicates that the Dictionary found contains pairs of strings and ints, which represent the file-name extensions and the number of files with those extensions, respectively. Line 93 uses Dictionary method **ContainsKey** to determine whether the specified file-name extension has been placed in the Dictionary previously. If this method returns true, line 94 adds the extensionCount determined in lines 88–90 to the current total for that extension that's stored in the Dictionary. Otherwise, line 96 uses Dictionary method **Add** to insert a new key/value pair into the Dictionary for the new file-name extension and its extensionCount. Lines 100–101 recursively call SearchDirectory for each subdirectory in the current directory.

*Method **CleanDirectory***

When method SearchDirectory returns, line 52 calls CleanDirectory (defined at lines 105–141) to search for all files with extension .bak. Lines 108 and 111 obtain the list of file names and list of directory names in the current directory, respectively. The LINQ query in lines 115–117 locates all file names in the current directory that have the .bak extension. Lines 120–136 iterate through the query's results and prompt the user to determine whether each file should be deleted. If the user clicks **Yes** in the dialog, line 129 uses File method **Delete** to remove the file from disk, and line 130 subtracts 1 from the total number of .bak files. If the number of .bak files remaining is 0, line 134 uses Dictionary method **Remove** to delete the key/value pair for .bak files from the Dictionary. Lines 139–140 recursively call CleanDirectory for each subdirectory in the current directory. After each subdirectory has been checked for .bak files, method CleanDirectory returns, and lines 55–61 display the summary of file-name extensions and the number of files with each extension. Line 55 uses Dictionary property **Keys** to get all the keys in the Dictionary. Line 60 uses the Dictionary's indexer to get the value for the current key. Finally, line 63 uses Dictionary method **Clear** to delete the contents of the Dictionary.

17.5 Creating a Sequential-Access Text File

C# imposes no structure on files. Thus, the concept of a "record" does not exist in C# files. This means that you must structure files to meet the requirements of your applications. The next few examples use text and special characters to organize our own concept of a "record."

Class *BankUIForm*

The following examples demonstrate file processing in a bank-account maintenance application. These programs have similar user interfaces, so we created reusable class BankUI-Form (Fig. 17.7) to encapsulate a base-class GUI (see the screen capture in Fig. 17.7). Class BankUIForm contains four Labels and four TextBoxes. Methods ClearTextBoxes (lines 28–40), SetTextBoxValues (lines 43–64) and GetTextBoxValues (lines 67–78) clear, set the values of and get the values of the text in the TextBoxes, respectively.

```csharp
1   // Fig. 17.7: BankUIForm.cs
2   // A reusable Windows Form for the examples in this chapter.
3   using System;
4   using System.Windows.Forms;
5
6   namespace BankLibrary
7   {
8      public partial class BankUIForm : Form
9      {
10        protected int TextBoxCount = 4; // number of TextBoxes on Form
11
12        // enumeration constants specify TextBox indices
13        public enum TextBoxIndices
14        {
15           ACCOUNT,
16           FIRST,
17           LAST,
18           BALANCE
19        } // end enum
20
```

Fig. 17.7 | Base class for GUIs in our file-processing applications. (Part 1 of 3.)

```
21          // parameterless constructor
22          public BankUIForm()
23          {
24              InitializeComponent();
25          } // end constructor
26
27          // clear all TextBoxes
28          public void ClearTextBoxes()
29          {
30              // iterate through every Control on form
31              foreach ( Control guiControl in Controls )
32              {
33                  // determine whether Control is TextBox
34                  if ( guiControl is TextBox )
35                  {
36                      // clear TextBox
37                      ( ( TextBox ) guiControl ).Clear();
38                  } // end if
39              } // end for
40          } // end method ClearTextBoxes
41
42          // set text box values to string-array values
43          public void SetTextBoxValues( string[] values )
44          {
45              // determine whether string array has correct length
46              if ( values.Length != TextBoxCount )
47              {
48                  // throw exception if not correct length
49                  throw ( new ArgumentException( "There must be " +
50                      ( TextBoxCount + 1 ) + " strings in the array" ) );
51              } // end if
52              // set array values if array has correct length
53              else
54              {
55                  // set array values to TextBox values
56                  accountTextBox.Text =
57                      values[ ( int ) TextBoxIndices.ACCOUNT ];
58                  firstNameTextBox.Text =
59                      values[ ( int ) TextBoxIndices.FIRST ];
60                  lastNameTextBox.Text = values[ ( int ) TextBoxIndices.LAST ];
61                  balanceTextBox.Text =
62                      values[ ( int ) TextBoxIndices.BALANCE ];
63              } // end else
64          } // end method SetTextBoxValues
65
66          // return TextBox values as string array
67          public string[] GetTextBoxValues()
68          {
69              string[] values = new string[ TextBoxCount ];
70
71              // copy TextBox fields to string array
72              values[ ( int ) TextBoxIndices.ACCOUNT ] = accountTextBox.Text;
73              values[ ( int ) TextBoxIndices.FIRST ] = firstNameTextBox.Text;
```

Fig. 17.7 | Base class for GUIs in our file-processing applications. (Part 2 of 3.)

```
74                  values[ ( int ) TextBoxIndices.LAST ] = lastNameTextBox.Text;
75                  values[ ( int ) TextBoxIndices.BALANCE ] = balanceTextBox.Text;
76
77                  return values;
78              } // end method GetTextBoxValues
79          } // end class BankUIForm
80      } // end namespace BankLibrary
```

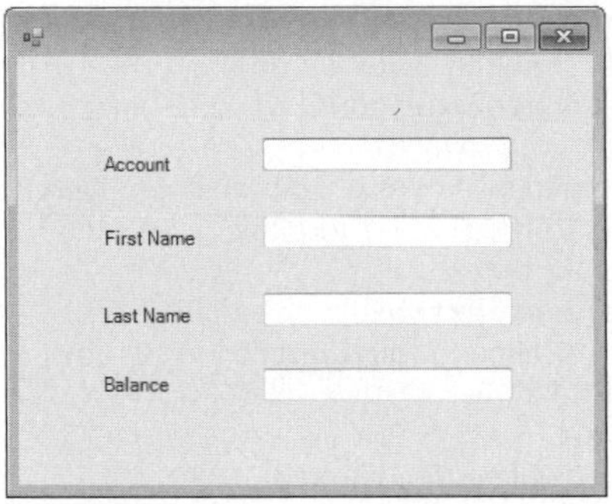

Fig. 17.7 | Base class for GUIs in our file-processing applications. (Part 3 of 3.)

Using visual inheritance (Section 15.13), you can extend this class to create the GUIs for several examples in this chapter. Recall that to reuse class BankUIForm, you must compile the GUI into a class library, then add a reference to the new class library in each project that will reuse it. This library (BankLibrary) is provided with the code for this chapter. You might need to re-add the references to this library in our examples when you copy them to your system, since the library most likely will reside in a different location on your system.

Class Record

Figure 17.8 contains class Record that Figs. 17.9, 17.11 and 17.12 use for maintaining the information in each record that's written to or read from a file. This class also belongs to the BankLibrary DLL, so it's located in the same project as class BankUIForm.

```
 1    // Fig. 17.8: Record.cs
 2    // Class that represents a data record.
 3
 4    namespace BankLibrary
 5    {
 6       public class Record
 7       {
 8          // auto-implemented Account property
 9          public int Account { get; set; }
10
11          // auto-implemented FirstName property
12          public string FirstName { get; set; }
13
14          // auto-implemented LastName property
15          public string LastName { get; set; }
```

Fig. 17.8 | Record for sequential-access file-processing applications. (Part 1 of 2.)

```
16
17        // auto-implemented Balance property
18        public decimal Balance { get; set; }
19
20        // parameterless constructor sets members to default values
21        public Record()
22           : this( 0, string.Empty, string.Empty, 0M )
23        {
24        } // end constructor
25
26        // overloaded constructor sets members to parameter values
27        public Record( int accountValue, string firstNameValue,
28           string lastNameValue, decimal balanceValue )
29        {
30           Account = accountValue;
31           FirstName = firstNameValue;
32           LastName = lastNameValue;
33           Balance = balanceValue;
34        } // end constructor
35     } // end class Record
36  } // end namespace BankLibrary
```

Fig. 17.8 | Record for sequential-access file-processing applications. (Part 2 of 2.)

Class `Record` contains auto-implemented properties for instance variables `Account`, `FirstName`, `LastName` and `Balance` (lines 9–18), which collectively represent all the information for a record. The parameterless constructor (lines 21–24) sets these members by calling the four-argument constructor with 0 for the account number, `string.Empty` for the first and last name and `0.0M` for the balance. The four-argument constructor (lines 27–34) sets these members to the specified parameter values.

Using a Character Stream to Create an Output File

Class `CreateFileForm` (Fig. 17.9) uses instances of class `Record` to create a sequential-access file that might be used in an accounts-receivable system—i.e., a program that organizes data regarding money owed by a company's credit clients. For each client, the program obtains an account number and the client's first name, last name and balance (i.e., the amount of money that the client owes to the company for previously received goods and services). The data obtained for each client constitutes a record for that client. In this application, the account number is used as the record key—files are created and maintained in account-number order. This program assumes that the user enters records in account-number order. However, a comprehensive accounts-receivable system would provide a sorting capability, so the user could enter the records in any order.

```
1   // Fig. 17.9: CreateFileForm.cs
2   // Creating a sequential-access file.
3   using System;
4   using System.Windows.Forms;
5   using System.IO;
```

Fig. 17.9 | Creating and writing to a sequential-access file. (Part 1 of 5.)

```
 6   using BankLibrary;
 7
 8   namespace CreateFile
 9   {
10      public partial class CreateFileForm : BankUIForm
11      {
12         private StreamWriter fileWriter; // writes data to text file
13
14         // parameterless constructor
15         public CreateFileForm()
16         {
17            InitializeComponent();
18         } // end constructor
19
20         // event handler for Save Button
21         private void saveButton_Click( object sender, EventArgs e )
22         {
23            // create and show dialog box enabling user to save file
24            DialogResult result; // result of SaveFileDialog
25            string fileName; // name of file containing data
26
27            using ( SaveFileDialog fileChooser = new SaveFileDialog() )
28            {
29               fileChooser.CheckFileExists = false; // let user create file
30               result = fileChooser.ShowDialog();
31               fileName = fileChooser.FileName; // name of file to save data
32            } // end using
33
34            // ensure that user clicked "OK"
35            if ( result == DialogResult.OK )
36            {
37               // show error if user specified invalid file
38               if ( fileName == string.Empty )
39                  MessageBox.Show( "Invalid File Name", "Error",
40                     MessageBoxButtons.OK, MessageBoxIcon.Error );
41               else
42               {
43                  // save file via FileStream if user specified valid file
44                  try
45                  {
46                     // open file with write access
47                     FileStream output = new FileStream( fileName,
48                        FileMode.OpenOrCreate, FileAccess.Write );
49
50                     // sets file to where data is written
51                     fileWriter = new StreamWriter( output );
52
53                     // disable Save button and enable Enter button
54                     saveButton.Enabled = false;
55                     enterButton.Enabled = true;
56                  } // end try
57                  // handle exception if there is a problem opening the file
```

Fig. 17.9 | Creating and writing to a sequential-access file. (Part 2 of 5.)

```
58              catch ( IOException )
59              {
60                  // notify user if file does not exist
61                  MessageBox.Show( "Error opening file", "Error",
62                      MessageBoxButtons.OK, MessageBoxIcon.Error );
63              } // end catch
64          } // end else
65      } // end if
66  } // end method saveButton_Click
67
68  // handler for enterButton Click
69  private void enterButton_Click( object sender, EventArgs e )
70  {
71      // store TextBox values string array
72      string[] values = GetTextBoxValues();
73
74      // Record containing TextBox values to output
75      Record record = new Record();
76
77      // determine whether TextBox account field is empty
78      if ( values[ ( int ) TextBoxIndices.ACCOUNT ] != string.Empty )
79      {
80          // store TextBox values in Record and output it
81          try
82          {
83              // get account-number value from TextBox
84              int accountNumber = Int32.Parse(
85                  values[ ( int ) TextBoxIndices.ACCOUNT ] );
86
87              // determine whether accountNumber is valid
88              if ( accountNumber > 0 )
89              {
90                  // store TextBox fields in Record
91                  record.Account = accountNumber;
92                  record.FirstName = values[ ( int )
93                      TextBoxIndices.FIRST ];
94                  record.LastName = values[ ( int )
95                      TextBoxIndices.LAST ];
96                  record.Balance = Decimal.Parse(
97                      values[ ( int ) TextBoxIndices.BALANCE ] );
98
99                  // write Record to file, fields separated by commas
100                 fileWriter.WriteLine(
101                     record.Account + "," + record.FirstName + "," +
102                     record.LastName + "," + record.Balance );
103             } // end if
104             else
105             {
106                 // notify user if invalid account number
107                 MessageBox.Show( "Invalid Account Number", "Error",
108                     MessageBoxButtons.OK, MessageBoxIcon.Error );
109             } // end else
110         } // end try
```

Fig. 17.9 | Creating and writing to a sequential-access file. (Part 3 of 5.)

```
111                    // notify user if error occurs during the output operation
112                    catch ( IOException )
113                    {
114                        MessageBox.Show( "Error Writing to File", "Error",
115                            MessageBoxButtons.OK, MessageBoxIcon.Error );
116                    } // end catch
117                    // notify user if error occurs regarding parameter format
118                    catch ( FormatException )
119                    {
120                        MessageBox.Show( "Invalid Format", "Error",
121                            MessageBoxButtons.OK, MessageBoxIcon.Error );
122                    } // end catch
123                } // end if
124
125                ClearTextBoxes(); // clear TextBox values
126            } // end method enterButton_Click
127
128            // handler for exitButton Click
129            private void exitButton_Click( object sender, EventArgs e )
130            {
131                // determine whether file exists
132                if ( fileWriter != null )
133                {
134                    try
135                    {
136                        // close StreamWriter and underlying file
137                        fileWriter.Close();
138                    } // end try
139                    // notify user of error closing file
140                    catch ( IOException )
141                    {
142                        MessageBox.Show( "Cannot close file", "Error",
143                            MessageBoxButtons.OK, MessageBoxIcon.Error );
144                    } // end catch
145                } // end if
146
147                Application.Exit();
148            } // end method exitButton_Click
149        } // end class CreateFileForm
150    } // end namespace CreateFile
```

a) BankUI graphical user interface with three additional controls

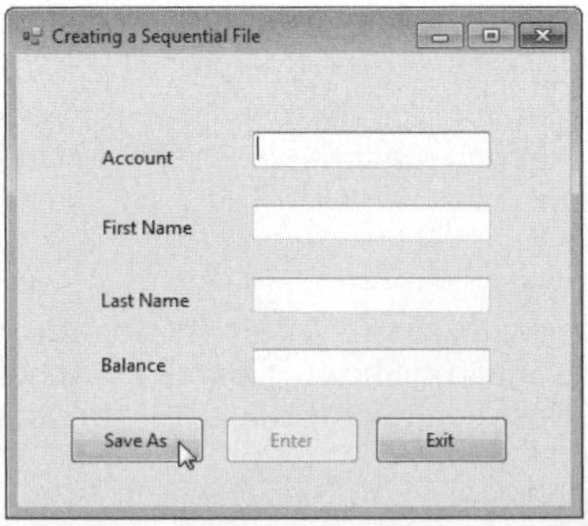

Fig. 17.9 | Creating and writing to a sequential-access file. (Part 4 of 5.)

b) Save File dialog

Files and directories

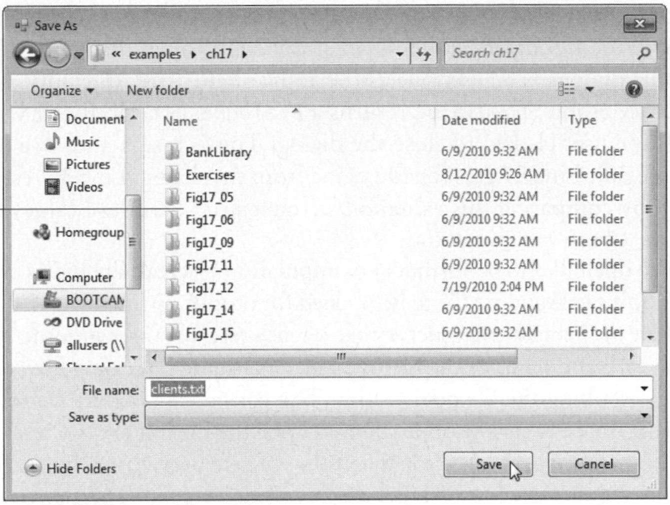

c) Account 100, "Nancy Brown", saved with a balance of -25.54

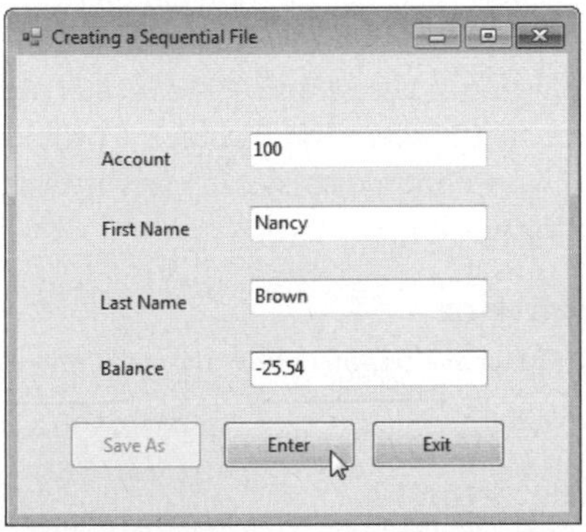

Fig. 17.9 | Creating and writing to a sequential-access file. (Part 5 of 5.)

Class `CreateFileForm` either creates or opens a file (depending on whether one exists), then allows the user to write records to it. The `using` directive in line 6 enables us to use the classes of the `BankLibrary` namespace; this namespace contains class `BankUI-Form`, from which class `CreateFileForm` inherits (line 10). Class `CreateFileForm`'s GUI enhances that of class `BankUIForm` with buttons **Save As**, **Enter** and **Exit**.

Method *saveButton_Click*
When the user clicks the **Save As** button, the program invokes the event handler `saveButton_Click` (lines 21–66). Line 27 instantiates an object of class **SaveFileDialog** (namespace `System.Windows.Forms`). By placing this object in a `using` statement (lines 27–32), we can ensure that the dialog's `Dispose` method is called to release its resources as soon as the program has retrieved user input from it. `SaveFileDialog` objects are used for selecting files (see the second screen in Fig. 17.9). Line 29 indicates that the dialog should not check if the file name specified by the user already exists. Line 30 calls `SaveFileDialog`

method ShowDialog to display the dialog. When displayed, a SaveFileDialog prevents the user from interacting with any other window in the program until the user closes the SaveFileDialog by clicking either **Save** or **Cancel**. Dialogs that behave in this manner are called **modal dialogs**. The user selects the appropriate drive, directory and file name, then clicks **Save**. Method **ShowDialog** returns a DialogResult specifying which button (**Save** or **Cancel**) the user clicked to close the dialog. This is assigned to DialogResult variable result (line 30). Line 31 gets the file name from the dialog. Line 35 tests whether the user clicked **OK** by comparing this value to DialogResult.OK. If the values are equal, method saveButton_Click continues.

You can open files to perform text manipulation by creating objects of class FileStream. In this example, we want the file to be opened for output, so lines 47–48 create a FileStream object. The FileStream constructor that we use receives three arguments—a string containing the path and name of the file to open, a constant describing how to open the file and a constant describing the file permissions. The constant FileMode.OpenOrCreate (line 48) indicates that the FileStream object should open the file if it exists or create the file if it does not exist. Note that the contents of an existing file are overwritten by the StreamWriter. To preserve the original contents of a file, use FileMode.Append. There are other FileMode constants describing how to open files; we introduce these constants as we use them in examples. The constant FileAccess.Write indicates that the program can perform only write operations with the FileStream object. There are two other constants for the third constructor parameter—FileAccess.Read for read-only access and FileAccess.ReadWrite for both read and write access. Line 58 catches an **IOException** if there's a problem opening the file or creating the StreamWriter. If so, the program displays an error message (lines 61–62). If no exception occurs, the file is open for writing.

Good Programming Practice 17.1

*When opening files, use the **FileAccess enumeration** to control user access to these files.*

Common Programming Error 17.1

Failure to open a file before attempting to use it in a program is a logic error.

Method enterButton_Click

After typing information into each TextBox, the user clicks the **Enter** button, which calls event handler enterButton_Click (lines 69–126) to save the data from the TextBoxes into the user-specified file. If the user entered a valid account number (i.e., an integer greater than zero), lines 91–97 store the TextBox values in an object of type Record (created at line 75). If the user entered invalid data in one of the TextBoxes (such as nonnumeric characters in the **Balance** field), the program throws a FormatException. The catch block in lines 118–122 handles such exceptions by notifying the user (via a MessageBox) of the improper format.

If the user entered valid data, lines 100–102 write the record to the file by invoking method WriteLine of the StreamWriter object that was created at line 51. Method WriteLine writes a sequence of characters to a file. The StreamWriter object is constructed with a FileStream argument that specifies the file to which the StreamWriter will output text. Class StreamWriter belongs to the System.IO namespace.

Method *exitButton_Click*

When the user clicks **Exit**, exitButton_Click (lines 129–148) executes. Line 137 closes the StreamWriter, which automatically closes the FileStream. Then, line 147 terminates the program. Note that method Close is called in a try block. Method Close throws an IOException if the file or stream cannot be closed properly. In this case, it's important to notify the user that the information in the file or stream might be corrupted.

Performance Tip 17.1

Close each file explicitly when the program no longer needs to use it. This can reduce resource usage in programs that continue executing long after they finish using a specific file. The practice of explicitly closing files also improves program clarity.

Performance Tip 17.2

Releasing resources explicitly when they're no longer needed makes them immediately available for reuse by other programs, thus improving resource utilization.

Sample Data

To test the program, we entered information for the accounts shown in Fig. 17.10. The program does not depict how the data records are stored in the file. To verify that the file has been created successfully, we create a program in the next section to read and display the file. Since this is a text file, you can actually open it in any text editor to see its contents.

Account number	First name	Last name	Balance
100	Nancy	Brown	-25.54
200	Stacey	Dunn	314.33
300	Doug	Barker	0.00
400	Dave	Smith	258.34
500	Sam	Stone	34.98

Fig. 17.10 | Sample data for the program of Fig. 17.9.

17.6 Reading Data from a Sequential-Access Text File

The previous section demonstrated how to create a file for use in sequential-access applications. In this section, we discuss how to read (or retrieve) data sequentially from a file.

Class ReadSequentialAccessFileForm (Fig. 17.11) reads records from the file created by the program in Fig. 17.9, then displays the contents of each record. Much of the code in this example is similar to that of Fig. 17.9, so we discuss only the unique aspects of the application.

```
1   // Fig. 17.11: ReadSequentialAccessFileForm.cs
2   // Reading a sequential-access file.
3   using System;
```

Fig. 17.11 | Reading sequential-access files. (Part 1 of 4.)

```
 4  using System.Windows.Forms;
 5  using System.IO;
 6  using BankLibrary;
 7
 8  namespace ReadSequentialAccessFile
 9  {
10     public partial class ReadSequentialAccessFileForm : BankUIForm
11     {
12        private StreamReader fileReader; // reads data from a text file
13
14        // parameterless constructor
15        public ReadSequentialAccessFileForm()
16        {
17           InitializeComponent();
18        } // end constructor
19
20        // invoked when user clicks the Open button
21        private void openButton_Click( object sender, EventArgs e )
22        {
23           // create and show dialog box enabling user to open file
24           DialogResult result; // result of OpenFileDialog
25           string fileName; // name of file containing data
26
27           using ( OpenFileDialog fileChooser = new OpenFileDialog() )
28           {
29              result = fileChooser.ShowDialog();
30              fileName = fileChooser.FileName; // get specified name
31           } // end using
32
33           // ensure that user clicked "OK"
34           if ( result == DialogResult.OK )
35           {
36              ClearTextBoxes();
37
38              // show error if user specified invalid file
39              if ( fileName == string.Empty )
40                 MessageBox.Show( "Invalid File Name", "Error",
41                    MessageBoxButtons.OK, MessageBoxIcon.Error );
42              else
43              {
44                 try
45                 {
46                    // create FileStream to obtain read access to file
47                    FileStream input = new FileStream(
48                       fileName, FileMode.Open, FileAccess.Read );
49
50                    // set file from where data is read
51                    fileReader = new StreamReader( input );
52
53                    openButton.Enabled = false; // disable Open File button
54                    nextButton.Enabled = true; // enable Next Record button
55                 } // end try
```

Fig. 17.11 | Reading sequential-access files. (Part 2 of 4.)

```
56                       catch ( IOException )
57                       {
58                           MessageBox.Show( "Error reading from file",
59                               "File Error", MessageBoxButtons.OK,
60                               MessageBoxIcon.Error );
61                       } // end catch
62                   } // end else
63               } // end if
64           } // end method openButton_Click
65
66           // invoked when user clicks Next button
67           private void nextButton_Click( object sender, EventArgs e )
68           {
69               try
70               {
71                   // get next record available in file
72                   string inputRecord = fileReader.ReadLine();
73                   string[] inputFields; // will store individual pieces of data
74
75                   if ( inputRecord != null )
76                   {
77                       inputFields = inputRecord.Split( ',' );
78
79                       Record record = new Record(
80                           Convert.ToInt32( inputFields[ 0 ] ), inputFields[ 1 ],
81                           inputFields[ 2 ],
82                           Convert.ToDecimal( inputFields[ 3 ] ) );
83
84                       // copy string-array values to TextBox values
85                       SetTextBoxValues( inputFields );
86                   } // end if
87                   else
88                   {
89                       // close StreamReader and underlying file
90                       fileReader.Close();
91                       openButton.Enabled = true; // enable Open File button
92                       nextButton.Enabled = false; // disable Next Record button
93                       ClearTextBoxes();
94
95                       // notify user if no records in file
96                       MessageBox.Show( "No more records in file", string.Empty,
97                           MessageBoxButtons.OK, MessageBoxIcon.Information );
98                   } // end else
99               } // end try
100              catch ( IOException )
101              {
102                  MessageBox.Show( "Error Reading from File", "Error",
103                      MessageBoxButtons.OK, MessageBoxIcon.Error );
104              } // end catch
105          } // end method nextButton_Click
106      } // end class ReadSequentialAccessFileForm
107  } // end namespace ReadSequentialAccessFile
```

Fig. 17.11 | Reading sequential-access files. (Part 3 of 4.)

a) BankUI graphical user interface with an Open File button

b) OpenFileDialog window

c) Reading account 100

d) User is shown a messagebox when all records have been read

Fig. 17.11 | Reading sequential-access files. (Part 4 of 4.)

Method **openButton_Click**

When the user clicks the **Open File** button, the program calls event handler open-Button_Click (lines 21–64). Line 27 creates an **OpenFileDialog**, and line 29 calls its ShowDialog method to display the **Open** dialog (see the second screenshot in Fig. 17.11). The behavior and GUI for the **Save** and **Open** dialog types are identical, except that **Save** is replaced by **Open**. If the user selects a valid file name, lines 47–48 create a FileStream object and assign it to reference input. We pass constant FileMode.Open as the second argument to the FileStream constructor to indicate that the FileStream should open the file if it exists or throw a **FileNotFoundException** if it does not. (In this example, the FileStream constructor will *not* throw a FileNotFoundException, because the OpenFile-Dialog is configured to check that the file exists.) In the last example (Fig. 17.9), we wrote text to the file using a FileStream object with write-only access. In this example (Fig. 17.11), we specify read-only access to the file by passing constant FileAccess.Read as the third argument to the FileStream constructor. This FileStream object is used to create a StreamReader object in line 51. The FileStream object specifies the file from which the StreamReader object will read text.

Error-Prevention Tip 17.1

Open a file with the FileAccess.Read file-open mode if its contents should not be modified. This prevents unintentional modification of the contents.

Method **nextButton_Click**

When the user clicks the **Next Record** button, the program calls event handler nextButton_Click (lines 67–104), which reads the next record from the user-specified file. (The user must click **Next Record** after opening the file to view the first record.) Line 72 calls StreamReader method ReadLine to read the next record. If an error occurs while reading the file, an IOException is thrown (caught at line 99), and the user is notified (lines 101–102). Otherwise, line 75 determines whether StreamReader method ReadLine returned null (i.e., there's no more text in the file). If not, line 77 uses method Split of class string to separate the stream of characters that was read from the file into strings that represent the Record's properties. These properties are then stored by constructing a Record object using the properties as arguments (lines 79–81). Line 84 displays the Record values in the TextBoxes. If ReadLine returns null, the program closes the StreamReader object (line 90), automatically closing the FileStream object, then notifies the user that there are no more records (lines 96–97).

17.7 Case Study: Credit Inquiry Program

To retrieve data sequentially from a file, programs normally start from the beginning of the file, reading consecutively until the desired data is found. It sometimes is necessary to process a file sequentially several times (from the beginning of the file) during the execution of a program. A FileStream object can reposition its **file-position pointer** (which contains the byte number of the next byte to be read from or written to the file) to any position in the file. When a FileStream object is opened, its file-position pointer is set to byte position 0 (i.e., the beginning of the file)

We now present a program that builds on the concepts employed in Fig. 17.11. Class CreditInquiryForm (Fig. 17.12) is a credit-inquiry program that enables a credit manager to search for and display account information for those customers with credit balances (i.e., customers to whom the company owes money), zero balances (i.e., customers who do not owe the company money) and debit balances (i.e., customers who owe the company money for previously received goods and services). We use a RichTextBox in the program to display the account information. RichTextBoxes provide more functionality than regular TextBoxes—for example, RichTextBoxes offer method Find for searching individual strings and method LoadFile for displaying file contents. Classes RichTextBox and TextBox both inherit from abstract class System.Windows.Forms.TextBoxBase. In this example, we chose a RichTextBox, because it displays multiple lines of text by default, whereas a regular TextBox displays only one. Alternatively, we could have specified that a TextBox object display multiple lines of text by setting its Multiline property to true.

The program displays buttons that enable a credit manager to obtain credit information. The **Open File** button opens a file for gathering data. The **Credit Balances** button displays a list of accounts that have credit balances, the **Debit Balances** button displays a list of accounts that have debit balances and the **Zero Balances** button displays a list of accounts that have zero balances. The **Done** button exits the application.

```csharp
1   // Fig. 17.12: CreditInquiryForm.cs
2   // Read a file sequentially and display contents based on
3   // account type specified by user ( credit, debit or zero balances ).
4   using System;
5   using System.Windows.Forms;
6   using System.IO;
7   using BankLibrary;
8
9   namespace CreditInquiry
10  {
11     public partial class CreditInquiryForm : Form
12     {
13        private FileStream input; // maintains the connection to the file
14        private StreamReader fileReader; // reads data from text file
15
16        // name of file that stores credit, debit and zero balances
17        private string fileName;
18
19        // parameterless constructor
20        public CreditInquiryForm()
21        {
22           InitializeComponent();
23        } // end constructor
24
25        // invoked when user clicks Open File button
26        private void openButton_Click( object sender, EventArgs e )
27        {
28           // create dialog box enabling user to open file
29           DialogResult result;
30
31           using ( OpenFileDialog fileChooser = new OpenFileDialog() )
32           {
```

Fig. 17.12 | Credit-inquiry program. (Part 1 of 5.)

```
33                  result = fileChooser.ShowDialog();
34                  fileName = fileChooser.FileName;
35            } // end using
36
37            // exit event handler if user clicked Cancel
38            if ( result == DialogResult.OK )
39            {
40               // show error if user specified invalid file
41               if ( fileName == string.Empty )
42                  MessageBox.Show( "Invalid File Name", "Error",
43                     MessageBoxButtons.OK, MessageBoxIcon.Error );
44               else
45               {
46                  // create FileStream to obtain read access to file
47                  input = new FileStream( fileName,
48                     FileMode.Open, FileAccess.Read );
49
50                  // set file from where data is read
51                  fileReader = new StreamReader( input );
52
53                  // enable all GUI buttons, except for Open File button
54                  openButton.Enabled = false;
55                  creditButton.Enabled = true;
56                  debitButton.Enabled = true;
57                  zeroButton.Enabled = true;
58               } // end else
59            } // end if
60         } // end method openButton_Click
61
62         // invoked when user clicks credit balances,
63         // debit balances or zero balances button
64         private void getBalances_Click( object sender, System.EventArgs e )
65         {
66            // convert sender explicitly to object of type button
67            Button senderButton = ( Button ) sender;
68
69            // get text from clicked Button, which stores account type
70            string accountType = senderButton.Text;
71
72            // read and display file information
73            try
74            {
75               // go back to the beginning of the file
76               input.Seek( 0, SeekOrigin.Begin );
77
78               displayTextBox.Text = "The accounts are:\r\n";
79
80               // traverse file until end of file
81               while ( true )
82               {
83                  string[] inputFields; // stores individual pieces of data
84                  Record record; // store each Record as file is read
85                  decimal balance; // store each Record's balance
```

Fig. 17.12 | Credit-inquiry program. (Part 2 of 5.)

```
86
87                    // get next Record available in file
88                    string inputRecord = fileReader.ReadLine();
89
90                    // when at the end of file, exit method
91                    if ( inputRecord == null )
92                       return;
93
94                    inputFields = inputRecord.Split( ',' ); // parse input
95
96                    // create Record from input
97                    record = new Record(
98                       Convert.ToInt32( inputFields[ 0 ] ), inputFields[ 1 ],
99                       inputFields[ 2 ], Convert.ToDecimal(inputFields[ 3 ]));
100
101                    // store record's last field in balance
102                    balance = record.Balance;
103
104                    // determine whether to display balance
105                    if ( ShouldDisplay( balance, accountType ) )
106                    {
107                       // display record
108                       string output = record.Account + "\t" +
109                          record.FirstName + "\t" + record.LastName + "\t";
110
111                       // display balance with correct monetary format
112                       output += String.Format( "{0:F}", balance ) + "\r\n";
113
114                       // copy output to screen
115                       displayTextBox.AppendText( output );
116                    } // end if
117                 } // end while
118              } // end try
119              // handle exception when file cannot be read
120              catch ( IOException )
121              {
122                 MessageBox.Show( "Cannot Read File", "Error",
123                    MessageBoxButtons.OK, MessageBoxIcon.Error );
124              } // end catch
125           } // end method getBalances_Click
126
127           // determine whether to display given record
128           private bool ShouldDisplay( decimal balance, string accountType )
129           {
130              if ( balance > 0M )
131              {
132                 // display credit balances
133                 if ( accountType == "Credit Balances" )
134                    return true;
135              } // end if
136              else if ( balance < 0M )
137              {
```

Fig. 17.12 | Credit-inquiry program. (Part 3 of 5.)

```
138              // display debit balances
139              if ( accountType == "Debit Balances" )
140                  return true;
141          } // end else if
142          else // balance == 0
143          {
144              // display zero balances
145              if ( accountType == "Zero Balances" )
146                  return true;
147          } // end else
148
149          return false;
150      } // end method ShouldDisplay
151
152      // invoked when user clicks Done button
153      private void doneButton_Click( object sender, EventArgs e )
154      {
155          if ( input != null )
156          {
157              // close file and StreamReader
158              try
159              {
160                  // close StreamReader and underlying file
161                  fileReader.Close();
162              } // end try
163              // handle exception if FileStream does not exist
164              catch ( IOException )
165              {
166                  // notify user of error closing file
167                  MessageBox.Show( "Cannot close file", "Error",
168                      MessageBoxButtons.OK, MessageBoxIcon.Error );
169              } // end catch
170          } // end if
171
172          Application.Exit();
173      } // end method doneButton_Click
174  } // end class CreditInquiryForm
175 } // end namespace CreditInquiry
```

a)

Fig. 17.12 | Credit-inquiry program. (Part 4 of 5.)

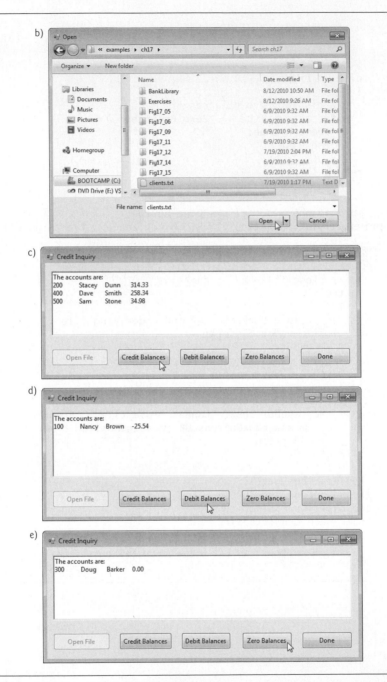

Fig. 17.12 | Credit-inquiry program. (Part 5 of 5.)

When the user clicks the **Open File** button, the program calls the event handler openButton_Click (lines 26–60). Line 31 creates an OpenFileDialog, and line 33 calls its ShowDialog method to display the **Open** dialog, in which the user selects the file to open.

Lines 47–48 create a `FileStream` object with read-only file access and assign it to reference `input`. Line 51 creates a `StreamReader` object that we use to read text from the `FileStream`.

When the user clicks **Credit Balances**, **Debit Balances** or **Zero Balances**, the program invokes method `getBalances_Click` (lines 64–125). Line 67 casts the `sender` parameter, which is an `object` reference to the control that generated the event, to a `Button` object. Line 70 extracts the `Button` object's text, which the program uses to determine which type of accounts to display. Line 76 uses `FileStream` method **Seek** to reset the file-position pointer back to the beginning of the file. `FileStream` method Seek allows you to reset the file-position pointer by specifying the number of bytes it should be offset from the file's beginning, end or current position. The part of the file you want to be offset from is chosen using constants from the **SeekOrigin** enumeration. In this case, our stream is offset by 0 bytes from the file's beginning (`SeekOrigin.Begin`). Lines 81–117 define a `while` loop that uses `private` method `ShouldDisplay` (lines 128–150) to determine whether to display each record in the file. The `while` loop obtains each record by repeatedly calling `StreamReader` method `ReadLine` (line 88) and splitting the text into tokens (line 94) that are used to initialize object `record` (lines 97–99). Line 91 determines whether the file-position pointer has reached the end of the file, in which case `ReadLine` returns `null`. If so, the program returns from method `getBalances_Click` (line 92).

17.8 Serialization

Section 17.5 demonstrated how to write the individual fields of a `Record` object to a text file, and Section 17.6 demonstrated how to read those fields from a file and place their values in a `Record` object in memory. In the examples, `Record` was used to aggregate the information for one record. When the instance variables for a `Record` were output to a disk file, certain information was lost, such as the type of each value. For instance, if the value `"3"` is read from a file, there's no way to tell if the value came from an `int`, a `string` or a `decimal`. We have only data, not type information, on disk. If the program that's going to read this data "knows" what object type the data corresponds to, then the data can be read directly into objects of that type. For example, in Fig. 17.11, we know that we are inputting an `int` (the account number), followed by two `string`s (the first and last name) and a `decimal` (the balance). We also know that these values are separated by commas, with only one record on each line. So, we are able to parse the strings and convert the account number to an `int` and the balance to a `decimal`. Sometimes it would be easier to read or write entire objects. C# provides such a mechanism, called **object serialization**. A **serialized object** is an object represented as a sequence of bytes that includes the object's data, as well as information about the object's type and the types of data stored in the object. After a serialized object has been written to a file, it can be read from the file and **deserialized**—that is, the type information and bytes that represent the object and its data can be used to recreate the object in memory.

Class **BinaryFormatter** (namespace **System.Runtime.Serialization.Formatters. Binary**) enables entire objects to be written to or read from a stream. BinaryFormatter method **Serialize** writes an object's representation to a file. BinaryFormatter method **Deserialize** reads this representation from a file and reconstructs the original object. Both methods throw a **SerializationException** if an error occurs during serialization or deserialization. Both methods require a `Stream` object (e.g., the `FileStream`) as a parameter so that the `BinaryFormatter` can access the correct stream.

In Sections 17.9–17.10, we create and manipulate sequential-access files using object serialization. Object serialization is performed with byte-based streams, so the sequential files created and manipulated will be binary files. Binary files are not human readable. For this reason, we write a separate application that reads and displays serialized objects.

17.9 Creating a Sequential-Access File Using Object Serialization

We begin by creating and writing serialized objects to a sequential-access file. In this section, we reuse much of the code from Section 17.5, so we focus only on the new features.

Defining the RecordSerializable Class
Let's begin by modifying our Record class (Fig. 17.8) so that objects of this class can be serialized. Class RecordSerializable (Fig. 17.13) is marked with the **[Serializable]** attribute (line 7), which indicates to the CLR that objects of class RecordSerializable can be serialized. The classes for objects that we wish to write to or read from a stream must include this attribute in their declarations or must implement interface **ISerializable**.

```
 1   // Fig. 17.13: RecordSerializable.cs
 2   // Serializable class that represents a data record.
 3   using System;
 4
 5   namespace BankLibrary
 6   {
 7      [Serializable]
 8      public class RecordSerializable
 9      {
10         // automatic Account property
11         public int Account { get; set; }
12
13         // automatic FirstName property
14         public string FirstName { get; set; }
15
16         // automatic LastName property
17         public string LastName { get; set; }
18
19         // automatic Balance property
20         public decimal Balance { get; set; }
21
22         // default constructor sets members to default values
23         public RecordSerializable()
24            : this( 0, string.Empty, string.Empty, 0M )
25         {
26         } // end constructor
27
28         // overloaded constructor sets members to parameter values
29         public RecordSerializable( int accountValue, string firstNameValue,
30            string lastNameValue, decimal balanceValue )
31         {
32            Account = accountValue;
```

Fig. 17.13 | RecordSerializable class for serializable objects. (Part 1 of 2.)

```
33                FirstName = firstNameValue;
34                LastName = lastNameValue;
35                Balance = balanceValue;
36          } // end constructor
37      } // end class RecordSerializable
38  } // end namespace BankLibrary
```

Fig. 17.13 | RecordSerializable class for serializable objects. (Part 2 of 2.)

In a class that's marked with the [Serializable] attribute or that implements interface ISerializable, you must ensure that every instance variable of the class is also serializable. All simple-type variables and strings are serializable. For variables of reference types, you must check the class declaration (and possibly its base classes) to ensure that the type is serializable. By default, array objects are serializable. However, if the array contains references to other objects, those objects may or may not be serializable.

Using a Serialization Stream to Create an Output File

Next, we'll create a sequential-access file with serialization (Fig. 17.14). To test this program, we used the sample data from Fig. 17.10 to create a file named clients.ser. Since the sample screen captures are the same as Fig. 17.9, they are not shown here. Line 15 creates a BinaryFormatter for writing serialized objects. Lines 53–54 open the FileStream to which this program writes the serialized objects. The string argument that's passed to the FileStream's constructor represents the name and path of the file to be opened. This specifies the file to which the serialized objects will be written.

This program assumes that data is input correctly and in the proper record-number order. Event handler enterButton_Click (lines 72–127) performs the write operation. Line 78 creates a RecordSerializable object, which is assigned values in lines 94–100. Line 103 calls method Serialize to write the RecordSerializable object to the output file. Method Serialize takes the FileStream object as the first argument so that the BinaryFormatter can write its second argument to the correct file. Only one statement is required to write the entire object. If a problem occurs during serialization, a SerializationException occurs—we catch this exception in lines 113–117.

In the sample execution for the program in Fig. 17.14, we entered information for five accounts—the same information shown in Fig. 17.10. The program does not show how the data records actually appear in the file. Remember that we are now using binary files, which are not human readable. To verify that the file was created successfully, the next section presents a program to read the file's contents.

```
1   // Fig. 17.14: CreateFileForm.cs
2   // Creating a sequential-access file using serialization.
3   using System;
4   using System.Windows.Forms;
5   using System.IO;
6   using System.Runtime.Serialization.Formatters.Binary;
7   using System.Runtime.Serialization;
8   using BankLibrary;
9
```

Fig. 17.14 | Sequential file created using serialization. (Part 1 of 4.)

```
10   namespace CreateFile
11   {
12      public partial class CreateFileForm : BankUIForm
13      {
14         // object for serializing RecordSerializables in binary format
15         private BinaryFormatter formatter = new BinaryFormatter();
16         private FileStream output; // stream for writing to a file
17
18         // parameterless constructor
19         public CreateFileForm()
20         {
21            InitializeComponent();
22         } // end constructor
23
24         // handler for saveButton_Click
25         private void saveButton_Click( object sender, EventArgs e )
26         {
27            // create and show dialog box enabling user to save file
28            DialogResult result;
29            string fileName; // name of file to save data
30
31            using ( SaveFileDialog fileChooser = new SaveFileDialog() )
32            {
33               fileChooser.CheckFileExists = false; // let user create file
34
35               // retrieve the result of the dialog box
36               result = fileChooser.ShowDialog();
37               fileName = fileChooser.FileName; // get specified file name
38            } // end using
39
40            // ensure that user clicked "OK"
41            if ( result == DialogResult.OK )
42            {
43               // show error if user specified invalid file
44               if ( fileName == string.Empty )
45                  MessageBox.Show( "Invalid File Name", "Error",
46                     MessageBoxButtons.OK, MessageBoxIcon.Error );
47               else
48               {
49                  // save file via FileStream if user specified valid file
50                  try
51                  {
52                     // open file with write access
53                     output = new FileStream( fileName,
54                        FileMode.OpenOrCreate, FileAccess.Write );
55
56                     // disable Save button and enable Enter button
57                     saveButton.Enabled = false;
58                     enterButton.Enabled = true;
59                  } // end try
60                  // handle exception if there is a problem opening the file
61                  catch ( IOException )
62                  {
```

Fig. 17.14 | Sequential file created using serialization. (Part 2 of 4.)

```
63                            // notify user if file could not be opened
64                            MessageBox.Show( "Error opening file", "Error",
65                               MessageBoxButtons.OK, MessageBoxIcon.Error );
66                       } // end catch
67                    } // end else
68                 } // end if
69            } // end method saveButton_Click
70
71            // handler for enterButton Click
72            private void enterButton_Click( object sender, EventArgs e )
73            {
74                // store TextBox values string array
75                string[] values = GetTextBoxValues();
76
77                // RecordSerializable containing TextBox values to serialize
78                RecordSerializable record = new RecordSerializable();
79
80                // determine whether TextBox account field is empty
81                if ( values[ ( int ) TextBoxIndices.ACCOUNT ] != string.Empty )
82                {
83                    // store TextBox values in RecordSerializable and serialize it
84                    try
85                    {
86                        // get account-number value from TextBox
87                        int accountNumber = Int32.Parse(
88                            values[ ( int ) TextBoxIndices.ACCOUNT ] );
89
90                        // determine whether accountNumber is valid
91                        if ( accountNumber > 0 )
92                        {
93                            // store TextBox fields in RecordSerializable
94                            record.Account = accountNumber;
95                            record.FirstName = values[ ( int )
96                                TextBoxIndices.FIRST ];
97                            record.LastName = values[ ( int )
98                                TextBoxIndices.LAST ];
99                            record.Balance = Decimal.Parse( values[
100                               ( int ) TextBoxIndices.BALANCE ] );
101
102                           // write RecordSerializable to FileStream
103                           formatter.Serialize( output, record );
104                       } // end if
105                       else
106                       {
107                           // notify user if invalid account number
108                           MessageBox.Show( "Invalid Account Number", "Error",
109                               MessageBoxButtons.OK, MessageBoxIcon.Error );
110                       } // end else
111                   } // end try
112                   // notify user if error occurs in serialization
113                   catch ( SerializationException )
114                   {
```

Fig. 17.14 | Sequential file created using serialization. (Part 3 of 4.)

```
115              MessageBox.Show( "Error Writing to File", "Error",
116                 MessageBoxButtons.OK, MessageBoxIcon.Error );
117           } // end catch
118           // notify user if error occurs regarding parameter format
119           catch ( FormatException )
120           {
121              MessageBox.Show( "Invalid Format", "Error",
122                 MessageBoxButtons.OK, MessageBoxIcon.Error );
123           } // end catch
124        } // end if
125
126        ClearTextBoxes(); // clear TextBox values
127     } // end method enterButton_Click
128
129     // handler for exitButton Click
130     private void exitButton_Click( object sender, EventArgs e )
131     {
132        // determine whether file exists
133        if ( output != null )
134        {
135           // close file
136           try
137           {
138              output.Close(); // close FileStream
139           } // end try
140           // notify user of error closing file
141           catch ( IOException )
142           {
143              MessageBox.Show( "Cannot close file", "Error",
144                 MessageBoxButtons.OK, MessageBoxIcon.Error );
145           } // end catch
146        } // end if
147
148        Application.Exit();
149     } // end method exitButton_Click
150  } // end class CreateFileForm
151 } // end namespace CreateFile
```

Fig. 17.14 | Sequential file created using serialization. (Part 4 of 4.)

17.10 Reading and Deserializing Data from a Binary File

The preceding section showed how to create a sequential-access file using object serialization. In this section, we discuss how to read serialized objects sequentially from a file.

Figure 17.15 reads and displays the contents of the clients.ser file created by the program in Fig. 17.14. The sample screen captures are identical to those of Fig. 17.11, so they are not shown here. Line 15 creates the BinaryFormatter that will be used to read objects. The program opens the file for input by creating a FileStream object (lines 49–50). The name of the file to open is specified as the first argument to the FileStream constructor.

The program reads objects from a file in event handler nextButton_Click (lines 59–92). We use method Deserialize (of the BinaryFormatter created in line 15) to read the data (lines 65–66). Note that we cast the result of Deserialize to type RecordSerializ-

able (line 66)—this cast is necessary, because Deserialize returns a reference of type
object and we need to access properties that belong to class RecordSerializable. If an
error occurs during deserialization, a SerializationException is thrown, and the
FileStream object is closed (line 82).

```
1   // Fig. 17.15: ReadSequentialAccessFileForm.cs
2   // Reading a sequential-access file using deserialization.
3   using System;
4   using System.Windows.Forms;
5   using System.IO;
6   using System.Runtime.Serialization.Formatters.Binary;
7   using System.Runtime.Serialization;
8   using BankLibrary;
9
10  namespace ReadSequentialAccessFile
11  {
12     public partial class ReadSequentialAccessFileForm : BankUIForm
13     {
14        // object for deserializing RecordSerializable in binary format
15        private BinaryFormatter reader = new BinaryFormatter();
16        private FileStream input; // stream for reading from a file
17
18        // parameterless constructor
19        public ReadSequentialAccessFileForm()
20        {
21           InitializeComponent();
22        } // end constructor
23
24        // invoked when user clicks the Open button
25        private void openButton_Click( object sender, EventArgs e )
26        {
27           // create and show dialog box enabling user to open file
28           DialogResult result; // result of OpenFileDialog
29           string fileName; // name of file containing data
30
31           using ( OpenFileDialog fileChooser = new OpenFileDialog() )
32           {
33              result = fileChooser.ShowDialog();
34              fileName = fileChooser.FileName; // get specified name
35           } // end using
36
37           // ensure that user clicked "OK"
38           if ( result == DialogResult.OK )
39           {
40              ClearTextBoxes();
41
42              // show error if user specified invalid file
43              if ( fileName == string.Empty )
44                 MessageBox.Show( "Invalid File Name", "Error",
45                    MessageBoxButtons.OK, MessageBoxIcon.Error );
46              else
47              {
```

Fig. 17.15 | Sequential file read using deserialization. (Part 1 of 2.)

```
48                    // create FileStream to obtain read access to file
49                    input = new FileStream(
50                       fileName, FileMode.Open, FileAccess.Read );
51
52                    openButton.Enabled = false; // disable Open File button
53                    nextButton.Enabled = true;  // enable Next Record button
54                 } // end else
55              } // end if
56           } // end method openButton_Click
57
58           // invoked when user clicks Next button
59           private void nextButton_Click( object sender, EventArgs e )
60           {
61              // deserialize RecordSerializable and store data in TextBoxes
62              try
63              {
64                 // get next RecordSerializable available in file
65                 RecordSerializable record =
66                    ( RecordSerializable ) reader.Deserialize( input );
67
68                 // store RecordSerializable values in temporary string array
69                 string[] values = new string[] {
70                    record.Account.ToString(),
71                    record.FirstName.ToString(),
72                    record.LastName.ToString(),
73                    record.Balance.ToString()
74                 };
75
76                 // copy string-array values to TextBox values
77                 SetTextBoxValues( values );
78              } // end try
79              // handle exception when there are no RecordSerializables in file
80              catch ( SerializationException )
81              {
82                 input.Close(); // close FileStream
83                 openButton.Enabled = true; // enable Open File button
84                 nextButton.Enabled = false; // disable Next Record button
85
86                 ClearTextBoxes();
87
88                 // notify user if no RecordSerializables in file
89                 MessageBox.Show( "No more records in file", string.Empty,
90                    MessageBoxButtons.OK, MessageBoxIcon.Information );
91              } // end catch
92           } // end method nextButton_Click
93        } // end class ReadSequentialAccessFileForm
94     } // end namespace ReadSequentialAccessFile
```

Fig. 17.15 | Sequential file read using deserialization. (Part 2 of 2.)

17.11 Wrap-Up

In this chapter, you learned how to use file processing to manipulate persistent data. You learned that data is stored in computers as 0s and 1s, and that combinations of these values are used to form bytes, fields, records and eventually files. We overviewed several file-processing classes from the `System.IO` namespace. You used class `File` to manipulate files, and classes `Directory` and `DirectoryInfo` to manipulate directories. Next, you learned how to use sequential-access file processing to manipulate records in text files. We then discussed the differences between text-file processing and object serialization, and used serialization to store entire objects in and retrieve entire objects from files.

In Chapter 18, we begin our discussion of databases, which organize data in such a way that the data can be selected and updated quickly. We introduce Structured Query Language (SQL) for writing simple database queries. We then introduce LINQ to SQL, which allows you to write LINQ queries that are automatically converted into SQL queries. These SQL queries are then used to query the database.

18

Databases and LINQ

Now go, write it before them in a table, and note it in a book, that it may be for the time to come for ever and ever.
—Isaiah 30:8

It is a capital mistake to theorize before one has data.
—Arthur Conan Doyle

OBJECTIVES

In this chapter you'll learn:

- The relational database model.

- To use LINQ to retrieve and manipulate data from a database.

- To add data sources to projects.

- To use the Object Relational Designer to create LINQ to SQL classes.

- To use the IDE's drag-and-drop capabilities to display database tables in applications.

- To use data binding to move data seamlessly between GUI controls and databases.

- To create Master/Detail views that enable you to select a record and display its details.

18.1 Introduction

A **database** is an organized collection of data. A **database management system** (**DBMS**) provides mechanisms for storing, organizing, retrieving and modifying data. Today's most popular DBMSs manage relational databases, which organize data simply as tables with *rows* and *columns*.

Some popular proprietary DBMSs are Microsoft SQL Server, Oracle, Sybase and IBM DB2. PostgreSQL and MySQL are popular *open-source* DBMSs that can be downloaded and used *freely* by anyone. In this chapter, we use Microsoft's free **SQL Server Express**, which is installed with Visual C# Express and Visual Studio. It can also be downloaded separately from Microsoft (www.microsoft.com/express/sql).

SQL Server Express provides many features of Microsoft's full (fee-based) SQL Server product, but has some limitations, such as a maximum database size. A SQL Server Express database can be easily migrated to a full version of SQL Server—we did this with our deitel.com website once our database became too large for SQL Server Express. You can learn more about the SQL Server versions at bit.ly/SQLServerEditions.

Today's most popular database systems are relational databases. A language called **Structured Query Language (SQL)**—pronounced "sequel"—is an international standard used with relational databases to perform **queries** (that is, to request information that satisfies given criteria) and to manipulate data. For years, programs that accessed a relational database passed SQL queries as Strings to the database management system, then processed the results.

A logical extension of querying and manipulating data in databases is to perform similar operations on any sources of data, such as arrays, collections (like the Items collection of a ListBox) and files. Chapter 9 introduced LINQ to Objects and used it to to manipulate data stored in arrays. **LINQ to SQL** allows you to manipulate data stored in a *SQL Server* or *SQL Server Express* relational database. The SQL in LINQ to SQL stands for *SQL Server, not Structured Query Language*. As with LINQ to Objects, the IDE provides *IntelliSense* for your LINQ to SQL queries.

This chapter introduces general concepts of relational databases, then explores LINQ to SQL and the IDE's tools for working with databases. In later chapters, you'll see other practical database and LINQ to SQL applications, such as a web-based bookstore and a web-based airline reservation service. Databases are at the heart of almost all "industrial strength" applications.

[*Note:* In previous editions of this book, this chapter included an introduction to Structured Query Language (SQL). We now perform all of the database interactions in this chapter using LINQ, so we've moved the introduction to SQL to this book's website at www.deitel.com/books/csharphtp4/.]

18.2 Relational Databases

A **relational database** organizes data simply in **tables**. Figure 18.1 illustrates a sample Employees table that might be used in a personnel system. The table stores the attributes of employees. Tables are composed of **rows** (also called records) and **columns** (also called **fields**) in which values are stored. This table consists of six rows (one per employee) and five columns (one per attribute). The attributes are the employee's ID, name, department, salary and location. The ID column of each row is the table's **primary key**—a column (or group of columns) requiring a *unique* value that cannot be duplicated in other rows. This guarantees that each primary key value can be used to identify *one* row. A primary key composed of two or more columns is known as a **composite key**. Good examples of primary-key columns in other applications are a book's ISBN number in a book information system or a part number in an inventory system—values in each of these columns must be unique. LINQ to SQL *requires every table to have a primary key* to support updating the data in tables. The rows in Fig. 18.1 are displayed in ascending order by primary key. But they could be listed in decreasing (descending) order or in no particular order at all.

Table Employees

	ID	Name	Department	Salary	Location
	23603	Jones	413	1100	New Jersey
	24568	Kerwin	413	2000	New Jersey
Row {	34589	Larson	642	1800	Los Angeles
	35761	Myers	611	1400	Orlando
	47132	Neumann	413	9000	New Jersey
	78321	Stephens	611	8500	Orlando
	Primary key		Column		

Fig. 18.1 | Employees table sample data.

Each *column* represents a different data *attribute*. Some column values may be duplicated between rows. For example, three different rows in the Employees table's Department column contain the number 413, indicating that these employees work in the same department.

You can use LINQ to SQL to define queries that select subsets of the data from a table. For example, a program might select data from the Employees table to create a query result that shows where each department is located, in increasing order by Department number (Fig. 18.2).

Department	Location
413	New Jersey
611	Orlando
642	Los Angeles

Fig. 18.2 | Distinct `Department` and `Location` data from the `Employees` table.

18.3 A Books Database

We now consider a simple `Books` database that stores information about some Deitel publications. First, we overview the database's tables. A database's tables, their fields and the relationships among them are collectively known as a **database schema**. LINQ to SQL uses a database's schema to define classes that enable you to interact with the database. Next, we show how to use LINQ to SQL to retrieve information from the `Books` database. The database file—`Books.mdf`—is provided with this chapter's examples. SQL Server database files have the `.mdf` ("master data file") file-name extension.

Authors *Table of the* Books *Database*

The database consists of three tables: `Authors`, `Titles` and `AuthorISBN`. The `Authors` table (described in Fig. 18.3) consists of three columns that maintain each author's unique ID number, first name and last name, respectively. Figure 18.4 contains the data from the Authors table.

Column	Description
AuthorID	Author's ID number in the database. In the `Books` database, this integer column is defined as an **identity** column, also known as an **autoincremented** column—for each row inserted in the table, the `AuthorID` value is increased by 1 automatically to ensure that each row has a unique `AuthorID`. This is the *primary key*.
FirstName	Author's first name (a string).
LastName	Author's last name (a string).

Fig. 18.3 | Authors table of the Books database.

AuthorID	FirstName	LastName
1	Harvey	Deitel
2	Paul	Deitel
3	Greg	Ayer
4	Dan	Quirk

Fig. 18.4 | Data from the `Authors` table of the Books database.

Titles *Table of the* Books *Database*

The Titles table (described in Fig. 18.5) consists of four columns that maintain information about each book in the database, including its ISBN, title, edition number and copyright year. Figure 18.6 contains the data from the Titles table.

Column	Description
ISBN	ISBN of the book (a string). The table's primary key. ISBN is an abbreviation for "International Standard Book Number"—a numbering scheme that publishers worldwide use to give every book a *unique* identification number.
Title	Title of the book (a string).
EditionNumber	Edition number of the book (an integer).
Copyright	Copyright year of the book (a string).

Fig. 18.5 | Titles table of the Books database.

ISBN	Title	Edition-Number	Copy-right
0131752421	Internet & World Wide Web How to Program	4	2008
0132222205	Java How to Program	7	2007
0132404168	C How to Program	5	2007
0136053033	Simply Visual Basic 2008	3	2009
013605305X	Visual Basic 2008 How to Program	4	2009
013605322X	Visual C# 2008 How to Program	3	2009
0136151574	Visual C++ 2008 How to Program	2	2008
0136152503	C++ How to Program	6	2008

Fig. 18.6 | Data from the Titles table of the Books database.

AuthorISBN *Table of the* Books *Database*

The AuthorISBN table (described in Fig. 18.7) consists of two columns that maintain ISBNs for each book and their corresponding authors' ID numbers. This table associates authors with their books. The AuthorID column is a **foreign key**—a column in this table that matches the primary-key column in another table (that is, AuthorID in the Authors table). The ISBN column is also a foreign key—it matches the primary-key column (that is, ISBN) in the Titles table. Together the AuthorID and ISBN columns in this table form a *composite primary key*. Every row in this table uniquely matches one author to one book's ISBN. Figure 18.8 contains the data from the AuthorISBN table of the Books database.

Foreign Keys

A database might consist of many tables. A goal when designing a database is to minimize the amount of duplicated data among the database's tables. Foreign keys, which are specified when a database table is created, link the data in multiple tables.

Column	Description
AuthorID	The author's ID number, a foreign key to the Authors table.
ISBN	The ISBN for a book, a foreign key to the Titles table.

Fig. 18.7 | AuthorISBN table of the Books database.

AuthorID	ISBN	AuthorID	ISBN
1	0131752421	*(continued)*	
1	0132222205	2	0132222205
1	0132404168	2	0132404168
1	0136053033	2	0136053033
1	013605305X	2	013605305X
1	013605322X	2	013605322X
1	0136151574	2	0136151574
1	0136152503	2	0136152503
2	0131752421	3	0136053033
(continued)		4	0136151574

Fig. 18.8 | Data from the AuthorISBN table of the Books database.

Every foreign-key value must appear as another table's primary-key value so the DBMS can ensure that the foreign key value is valid. For example, the DBMS ensures that the AuthorID value for a particular row of the AuthorISBN table (Fig. 18.8) is valid by checking that there is a row in the Authors table with that AuthorID as the primary key.

Foreign keys also allow related data in multiple tables to be selected from those tables—this is known as **joining** the data. There is a **one-to-many relationship** between a primary key and a corresponding foreign key (for example, one author can write many books and one book can be written by many authors). This means that a foreign key can appear *many* times in its own table but only *once* (as the primary key) in another table. For example, the ISBN 0131450913 can appear in several rows of AuthorISBN (because this book has several authors) but only once in Titles, where ISBN is the primary key.

*Entity-Relationship Diagram for the **Books** Database*
Figure 18.9 is an **entity-relationship (ER) diagram** for the Books database. This diagram shows the tables in the database and the relationships among them. The first compartment in each box contains the table's name. The names in italic font are primary keys—*AuthorID* in the Authors table, AuthorID and ISBN in the AuthorISBN table, and ISBN in the Titles table. Every row *must* have a value in the primary-key column (or group of columns), and the value of the key must be *unique* in the table; otherwise, the DBMS will report an error. The names AuthorID and ISBN in the AuthorISBN table are *both* italic—together these form a *composite primary key* for the AuthorISBN table.

Fig. 18.9 | Entity-relationship diagram for the Books database.

The lines connecting the tables in Fig. 18.9 represent the relationships among the tables. Consider the line between the Authors and AuthorISBN tables. On the Authors end of the line, there's a 1, and on the AuthorISBN end, an infinity symbol (∞). This indicates a one-to-many relationship—for *each* author in the Authors table, there can be an *arbitrary number* of ISBNs for books written by that author in the AuthorISBN table (that is, an author can write any number of books). Note that the relationship line links the AuthorID column in the Authors table (where AuthorID is the primary key) to the AuthorID column in the AuthorISBN table (where AuthorID is a foreign key)—the line between the tables links the primary key to the matching foreign key.

The line between the Titles and AuthorISBN tables illustrates a one-to-many relationship—one book can be written by many authors. Note that the line between the tables links the primary key ISBN in table Titles to the corresponding foreign key in table AuthorISBN. The relationships in Fig. 18.9 illustrate that the sole purpose of the AuthorISBN table is to provide a **many-to-many relationship** between the Authors and Titles tables—an author can write *many* books, and a book can have *many* authors.

18.4 LINQ to SQL

LINQ to SQL enables you to access data in *SQL Server databases* using the same LINQ syntax introduced in Chapter 9. You interact with the database via classes that are automatically generated from the database schema by the IDE's **LINQ to SQL Designer**. For each table in the database, the IDE creates two classes:

- A class that represents a row of the table: This class contains properties for each column in the table. LINQ to SQL creates objects of this class—called **row objects**—to store the data from individual rows of the table.

- A class that represents the table: LINQ to SQL creates an object of this class to store a collection of row objects that correspond to all of the rows in the table.

Relationships between tables are also taken into account in the generated classes:

- In a row object's class, an additional property is created for each foreign key. This property returns the row object of the corresponding primary key in another table. For example, the class that represents the rows of the Books database's AuthorISBN table also contains an Author property and a Title property—from any AuthorISBN row object, you can access the full author and title information.

- In the class for a row object, an additional property is created for the collection of row objects with foreign-keys that reference the row object's primary key. For example, the LINQ to SQL class that represents the rows of the Books database's Authors table contains an AuthorISBNs property that you can use to get all of the books written by that author. The IDE automatically adds the "s" to "Author-ISBN" to indicate that this property represents a collection of AuthorISBN objects. Similarly, the LINQ to SQL class that represents the rows of the Titles table also contains an AuthorISBNs property that you can use to get all of the co-authors of a particular title.

Once generated, the LINQ to SQL classes have full *IntelliSense* support in the IDE. Section 18.7 demonstrates queries that use the relationships among the Books database's tables to join data.

IQueryable *Interface*
LINQ to SQL works through the **IQueryable interface**, which inherits from the IEnumerable interface introduced in Chapter 9. When a LINQ to SQL query on an IQueryable object executes against the database, the results are loaded into objects of the corresponding LINQ to SQL classes for convenient access in your code.

DataContext *Class*
All LINQ to SQL queries occur via a **DataContext class**, which controls the flow of data between the program and the database. A specific DataContext derived class, which inherits from the class System.Data.Linq.DataContext, is created when the LINQ to SQL classes representing each row of the table are generated by the IDE. This derived class has properties for each table in the database, which can be used as data sources in LINQ queries. Any changes made to the DataContext can be saved back to the database using the DataContext's **SubmitChanges method**, so with LINQ to SQL you can modify the database's contents.

18.5 Querying a Database with LINQ

In this section, we demonstrate how to *connect* to a database, *query* it and *display* the results of the query. There is little code in this section—the IDE provides *visual programming* tools and *wizards* that simplify accessing data in applications. These tools establish database connections and create the objects necessary to view and manipulate the data through Windows Forms GUI controls—a technique known as **data binding**.

Our first example performs a simple query on the Books database from Section 18.3. We retrieve the entire Authors table and use data binding to display its data in a **DataGridView**—a control from namespace System.Windows.Forms that can display data from a data source in tabular format. The basic steps we'll perform are:

* Connect to the Books database.
* Create the LINQ to SQL classes required to use the database.
* Add the Authors table as a data source.
* Drag the Authors table data source onto the **Design** view to create a GUI for displaying the table's data.
* Add a few statements to the program to allow it to interact with the database.

The GUI for the program is shown in Fig. 18.10. All of the controls in this GUI are automatically generated when we drag a data source that represents the Authors table onto the Form in **Design** view. The BindingNavigator at the top of the window is a collection of controls that allow you to navigate through the records in the DataGridView that fills the rest of the window. The BindingNavigator controls also allow you to add records, delete records and save your changes to the database. If you add a new record, note that empty values are not allowed in the Books database, so attempting to save a new record without specifying a value for each field will cause an error.

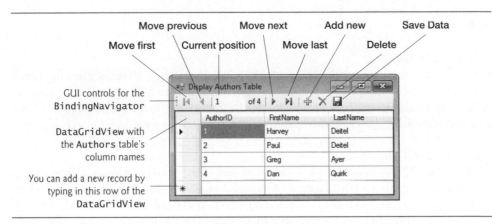

Fig. 18.10 | GUI for the **Display Authors Table** application.

18.5.1 Creating LINQ to SQL Classes

This section presents the steps required to create LINQ to SQL classes for a database.

Step 1: Creating the Project

Create a new **Windows Forms Application** named DisplayTable. Change the name of the source file to DisplayAuthorsTable.cs. The IDE updates the Form's class name to match the source file. Set the Form's **Text** property to Display Authors Table.

Step 2: Adding a Database to the Project and Connecting to the Database

To interact with a database, you must create a **connection** to the database. This will also give you the option of copying the database file to your project.

1. In Visual C# 2010 Express, select **View > Other Windows > Database Explorer** to display the **Database Explorer** window. By default, it appears on the left side of the IDE. If you're using a full version of Visual Studio, select **View > Server Explorer** to display the **Server Explorer**. From this point forward, we'll refer to the Database Explorer. If you have a full version of Visual Studio, substitute **Server Explorer** for **Database Explorer** in the steps.

2. Click the **Connect to Database** icon () at the top of the **Database Explorer**. If the **Choose Data Source** dialog appears (Fig. 18.11), select **Microsoft SQL Server Database File** from the **Data source:** list. If you check the **Always use this selection** CheckBox, the IDE will use this type of database file by default when you connect to databases in the future. Click **Continue** to display the **Add Connection** dialog.

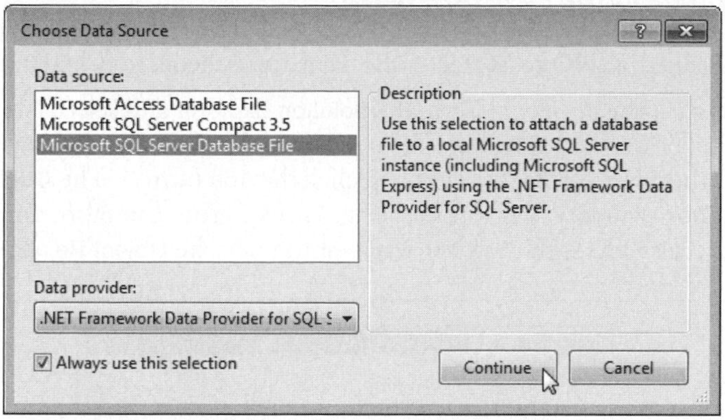

Fig. 18.11 | **Choose Data Source** dialog.

3. In the **Add Connection** dialog (Fig. 18.12), the **Data source:** TextBox reflects your selection from the **Choose Data Source** dialog. You can click the **Change...** Button to select a different type of database. Next, click **Browse...** to locate and select the Books.mdf file in the Databases directory included with this chapter's examples. You can click **Test Connection** to verify that the IDE can connect to the database through SQL Server Express. Click **OK** to create the connection.

Error-Prevention Tip 18.1
Ensure that no other program is using the database file before you attempt to add it to the project. Connecting to the database requires exclusive access.

Fig. 18.12 | **Add Connection** dialog.

Step 3: Generating the LINQ to SQL classes
After adding the database, you must select the database tables from which the LINQ to SQL classes will be created. LINQ to SQL uses the database's schema to help define the classes.

1. Right click the project name in the **Solution Explorer** and select **Add > New Item...** to display the **Add New Item** dialog. Select the **LINQ to SQL Classes** template, name the new item Books.dbml and click the **Add** button. The **Object Relational Designer** window will appear (Fig. 18.13). You can also double click the Books.dbml file in the **Solution Explorer** to open the **Object Relational Designer**.

Drag the database's tables here to generate the LINQ to SQL classes

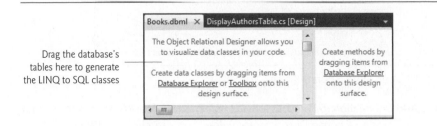

Fig. 18.13 | **Object Relational Designer** window.

2. Expand the Books.mdf database node in the **Database Explorer**, then expand the **Tables** node. Drag the Authors, Titles and AuthorISBN tables onto the **Object Relational Designer**. The IDE prompts whether you want to copy the database to the project directory. Select **Yes**. The **Object Relational Designer** will display the tables that you dragged from the **Database Explorer** (Fig. 18.14). Notice that the **Object Relational Designer** named the class that represents items from the Authors table as Author, and named the class that represents the Titles table as Title. This is because one object of the Author class represents one author—a single row from the Authors table. Similarly, one object of the Title class represents one book—a single row from the Titles table. Because the class name Title conflicts with one of the column names in the Titles table, the IDE renames that column's property in the Title class as Title1.

3. Save the Books.dbml file.

Fig. 18.14 | **Object Relational Designer** window showing the selected tables from the Books database and their relationships.

When you save Books.dbml, the IDE generates the LINQ to SQL classes that you can use to interact with the database. These include a class for each table you selected from the database and a derived class of DataContext named BooksDataContext that enables you to programmatically interact with the database.

Error-Prevention Tip 18.2
Be sure to save the file in the **Object Relational Designer** *before trying to use the LINQ to SQL classes in code. The IDE* does not *generate the classes until you save the file.*

18.5.2 Data Bindings Between Controls and the LINQ to SQL Classes

The IDE's automatic data binding capabilities simplify creating applications that can view and modify the data in a database. You must write a small amount of code to enable the autogenerated data-binding classes to interact with the autogenerated LINQ to SQL classes. You'll now perform the steps to display the contents of the Authors table in a GUI.

*Step 1: Adding the **Author** LINQ to SQL Class as a Data Source*
To use the LINQ to SQL classes for data binding, you must first add them as a data source.

1. Select Data > Add New Data Source... to display the **Data Source Configuration Wizard**.

2. The LINQ to SQL classes are used to create objects representing the tables in the database, so we'll use an **Object** data source. In the dialog, select **Object** and click **Next >**. Expand the tree view as shown in Fig. 18.15 and ensure that **Author** is checked. An object of this class will be used as the data source.

3. Click **Finish**.

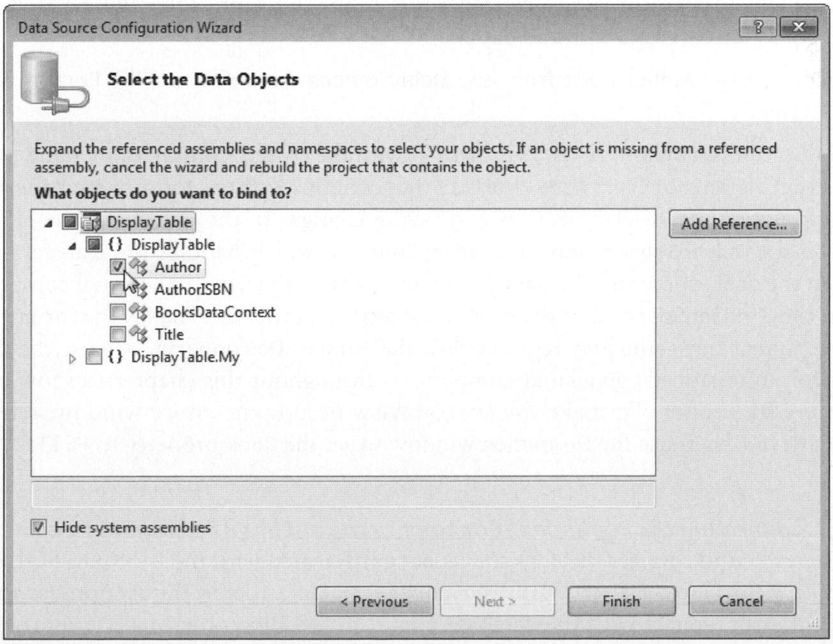

Data Source Configuration Wizard   [?] [X]

Select the Data Objects

Expand the referenced assemblies and namespaces to select your objects. If an object is missing from a referenced assembly, cancel the wizard and rebuild the project that contains the object.

What objects do you want to bind to?

- ▲ ☐ 🗔 DisplayTable   [Add Reference...]
  - ▲ ☐ { } DisplayTable
    - ☑ 🕸 Author
    - ☐ 🕸 AuthorISBN
    - ☐ 🕸 BooksDataContext
    - ☐ 🕸 Title
  - ▷ ☐ { } DisplayTable.My

☑ Hide system assemblies

[< Previous] [Next >] [Finish] [Cancel]

Fig. 18.15 | Selecting the Author LINQ to SQL class as the data source.

The Authors table in the database is now a data source that can be used by the bindings. Open the **Data Sources window** (Fig. 18.16) by selecting **Data > Show Data Sources**—the window is displayed at the left side of the IDE. You can see the Author class that you added in the previous step. The columns of the database's Authors table should appear below it, as well as an AuthorISBNs entry representing the relationship between the database's Authors and AuthorISBN tables.

Fig. 18.16 | **Data Sources** window showing the Author class as a data source.

Step 2: Creating GUI Elements

Next, you'll use the **Design** view to create a GUI control that can display the Authors table's data.

1. Switch to **Design** view for the DisplayAuthorsTable class.

2. Click the **Author** node in the **Data Sources** window—it should change to a drop-down list. Open the drop-down by clicking the down arrow and ensure that the DataGridView option is selected—this is the GUI control that will be used to display and interact with the data.

3. Drag the **Author** node from the **Data Sources** window onto the Form in **Design** view.

The IDE creates a DataGridView (Fig. 18.17) with the correct column names and a **BindingNavigator** (authorBindingNavigator) that contains Buttons for moving between entries, adding entries, deleting entries and saving changes to the database. The IDE also generates a **BindingSource** (authorBindingSource), which handles the transfer of data between the data source and the data-bound controls on the Form. Nonvisual components such as the BindingSource and the non-visual aspects of the BindingNavigator appear in the component tray—the gray region below the Form in **Design** view. We use the default names for automatically generated components throughout this chapter to show exactly what the IDE creates. To make the **DataGridView** occupy the entire window, select the DataGridView, then use the **Properties** window to set the Dock property to Fill.

Step 3: Connecting the *BooksDataContext* to the *authorBindingSource*

The final step is to connect the BooksDataContext (created with the LINQ to SQL classes in Section 18.5.1) to the authorBindingSource (created earlier in this section), so that the application can interact with the database. Figure 18.18 shows the small amount of code needed to obtain data from the database and to save any changes that the user makes to the data back into the database.

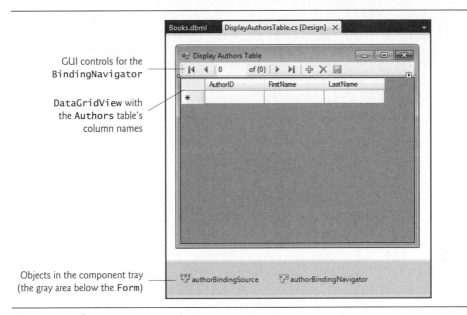

Fig. 18.17 | Component tray holds nonvisual components in **Design** view.

```
1   // Fig. 18.18: DisplayAuthorsTable.cs
2   // Displaying data from a database table in a DataGridView.
3   using System;
4   using System.Linq;
5   using System.Windows.Forms;
6
7   namespace DisplayTable
8   {
9      public partial class DisplayAuthorsTable : Form
10     {
11        // constructor
12        public DisplayAuthorsTable()
13        {
14           InitializeComponent();
15        } // end constructor
16
17        // LINQ to SQL data context
18        private BooksDataContext database = new BooksDataContext();
19
20        // load data from database into DataGridView
21        private void DisplayAuthorsTable_Load( object sender, EventArgs e )
22        {
23           // use LINQ to order the data for display
24           authorBindingSource.DataSource =
25              from author in database.Authors
26              orderby author.AuthorID
27              select author;
28        } // end method DisplayAuthorsTable_Load
```

Fig. 18.18 | Displaying data from a database table in a **DataGridView**. (Part 1 of 2.)

```
29
30          // click event handler for the Save Button in the
31          // BindingNavigator saves the changes made to the data
32          private void authorBindingNavigatorSaveItem_Click(
33             object sender, EventArgs e )
34          {
35             Validate(); // validate input fields
36             authorBindingSource.EndEdit(); // indicate edits are complete
37             database.SubmitChanges(); // write changes to database file
38          } // end method authorBindingNavigatorSaveItem_Click
39       } // end class DisplayAuthorsTable
40    } // end namespace DisplayTable
```

AuthorID	FirstName	LastName
1	Harvey	Deitel
2	Paul	Deitel
3	Greg	Ayer
4	Dan	Quirk

Fig. 18.18 | Displaying data from a database table in a `DataGridView`. (Part 2 of 2.)

As mentioned in Section 18.4, a DataContext object is used to interact with the database. The BooksDataContext class was automatically generated by the IDE when you created the LINQ to SQL classes to allow access to the Books database. Line 18 creates an object of this class named database.

Create the Form's Load handler by double clicking the Form's title bar in **Design** view. We allow data to move between the DataContext and the BindingSource by creating a LINQ query that extracts data from the BooksDataContext's Authors property (lines 25–27), which corresponds to the Authors table in the database. The authorBindingSource's **DataSource property** (line 24) is set to the results of this query. The authorBinding-Source uses the DataSource to extract data from the database and to populate the DataGridView.

Step 4: Saving Modifications Back to the Database
If the user modifies the data in the DataGridView, we'd also like to save the modifications in the database. By default, the BindingNavigator's **Save Data** Button (🖫) is disabled. To enable it, right click this Button's icon and select **Enabled**. Then, double click the icon to create its Click event handler.

Saving the data entered into the DataGridView back to the database is a three-step process (lines 35–37). First, all controls on the form are validated (line 35)—if any of the controls have event handlers for the Validating event, those execute. You typically handle this event to determine whether a control's contents are valid. Second, line 36 calls **EndEdit** on the authorBindingSource, which forces it to save any pending changes in the BooksDataContext. Finally, line 37 calls SubmitChanges on the BooksDataContext to store the changes in the database. For efficiency, LINQ to SQL saves only data that has changed.

Step 5: Configuring the Database File to Persist Changes
When you run the program in debug mode, the database file is overwritten with the original database file each time you execute the program. This allows you to test your program with the original content until it works correctly. When you run the program in release mode (*Ctrl + F5*), changes you make to the database persist automatically; however, if you change the code, the next time you run the program, the database will be restored to its original version. To persist changes for all executions, select the database in the **Solution Explorer** and set the **Copy to Output Directory** property in the **Properties** window to **Copy if newer**.

18.6 Dynamically Binding Query Results

Now that you've seen how to display an entire database table in a DataGridView, we show how to perform several different queries and display the results in a DataGridView. The **Display Query Results** application (Fig. 18.19) allows the user to select a query from the ComboBox at the bottom of the window, then displays the results of the query.

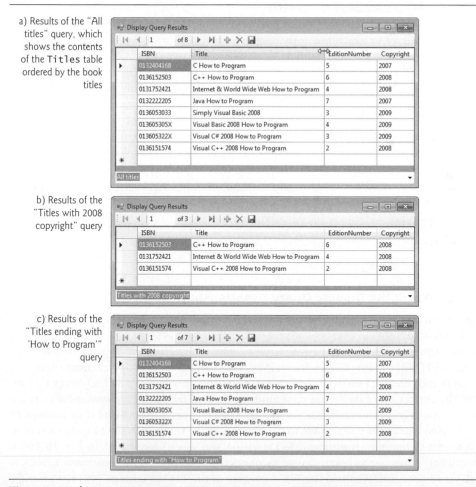

a) Results of the "All titles" query, which shows the contents of the Titles table ordered by the book titles

b) Results of the "Titles with 2008 copyright" query

c) Results of the "Titles ending with 'How to Program'" query

Fig. 18.19 | Sample execution of the Display Query Results application.

18.6.1 Creating the Display Query Results GUI

Perform the following steps to build the **Display Query Results** application's GUI.

Step 1: Creating the Project
First, create a new **Windows Forms Application** named `DisplayQueryResult`. Rename the source file to `TitleQueries.cs`. Set the Form's **Text** property to `Display Query Results`.

Step 2: Creating the LINQ to SQL Classes
Follow the steps in Section 18.5.1 to add the `Books` database to the project and generate the LINQ to SQL classes.

Step 3: Creating a `DataGridView` to Display the `Titles` Table
Follow *Steps 1* and *2* in Section 18.5.2 to create the data source and the `DataGridView`. In this example, select the `Title` class (rather than the `Author` class) as the data source, and drag the **Title** node from the **Data Sources** window onto the form.

Step 4: Adding a `ComboBox` to the Form
In **Design** view, add a `ComboBox` named `queriesComboBox` below the `DataGridView` on the Form. Users will select which query to execute from this control. Set the `ComboBox`'s `Dock` property to `Bottom` and the `DataGridView`'s `Dock` property to `Fill`.

Next, you'll add the names of the queries to the `ComboBox`. Open the `ComboBox`'s **String Collection Editor** by right clicking the `ComboBox` and selecting **Edit Items**. You can also access the **String Collection Editor** from the `ComboBox`'s smart tag menu. A **smart tag menu** provides you with quick access to common properties you might set for a control (such as the `Multiline` property of a `TextBox`), so you can set these properties directly in **Design** view, rather than in the **Properties** window. You can open a control's smart tag menu by clicking the small arrowhead (▶) that appears in the control's upper-right corner in **Design** view when the control is selected. In the **String Collection Editor**, add the following three items to `queriesComboBox`—one for each of the queries we'll create:

1. `All titles`

2. `Titles with 2008 copyright`

3. `Titles ending with "How to Program"`

18.6.2 Coding the Display Query Results Application

Next you must write code that executes the appropriate query each time the user chooses a different item from `queriesComboBox`. Double click `queriesComboBox` in **Design** view to generate a `queriesComboBox_SelectedIndexChanged` event handler (Fig. 18.20, lines 44–78) in the `TitleQueries.cs` file. In the event handler, add a `switch` statement (lines 48–75) to change the `titleBindingSource`'s `DataSource` property to a LINQ query that returns the correct set of data. The data bindings created by the IDE *automatically* update the `titleDataGridView` *each time* we change its `DataSource`. The **MoveFirst method** of the `BindingSource` (line 77) moves to the first row of the result each time a query executes. The results of the queries in lines 53–55, 61–64 and 70–73 are shown in Fig. 18.19(a), (b) and (c), respectively. [*Note:* As we mentioned previously, in the generated LINQ to SQL classes, the IDE renamed the `Title` column of the `Titles` table as `Title1` to avoid a naming conflict with the class `Title`.]

Customizing the Form's Load Event Handler
Create the TitleQueries_Load event handler (lines 20–28) by double clicking the title bar
in **Design** view. Line 23 sets the Log property of the BooksDataContext to Console.Out.
This causes the program to output to the console the SQL query that is sent to the database
for each LINQ query. When the Form loads, it should display the complete list of books from
the Titles table, sorted by title. Rather than defining the same LINQ query as in lines 53–
55, we can programmatically cause the queriesComboBox_SelectedIndexChanged event
handler to execute simply by setting the queriesComboBox's SelectedIndex to 0 (line 27).

```
 1   // Fig. 18.20: TitleQueries.cs
 2   // Displaying the result of a user-selected query in a DataGridView.
 3   using System;
 4   using System.Linq;
 5   using System.Windows.Forms;
 6
 7   namespace DisplayQueryResult
 8   {
 9      public partial class TitleQueries : Form
10      {
11         public TitleQueries()
12         {
13            InitializeComponent();
14         } // end constructor
15
16         // LINQ to SQL data context
17         private BooksDataContext database = new BooksDataContext();
18
19         // load data from database into DataGridView
20         private void TitleQueries_Load( object sender, EventArgs e )
21         {
22            // write SQL to standard output stream
23            database.Log = Console.Out;
24
25            // set the ComboBox to show the default query that
26            // selects all books from the Titles table
27            queriesComboBox.SelectedIndex = 0;
28         } // end method TitleQueries_Load
29
30         // Click event handler for the Save Button in the
31         // BindingNavigator saves the changes made to the data
32         private void titleBindingNavigatorSaveItem_Click(
33            object sender, EventArgs e )
34         {
35            Validate(); // validate input fields
36            titleBindingSource.EndEdit(); // indicate edits are complete
37            database.SubmitChanges(); // write changes to database file
38
39            // when saving, return to "all titles" query
40            queriesComboBox.SelectedIndex = 0;
41         } // end method titleBindingNavigatorSaveItem_Click
42
```

Fig. 18.20 | Displaying the result of a user-selected query in a DataGridView. (Part 1 of 2.)

```
43          // loads data into titleBindingSource based on user-selected query
44          private void queriesComboBox_SelectedIndexChanged(
45              object sender, EventArgs e )
46          {
47              // set the data displayed according to what is selected
48              switch ( queriesComboBox.SelectedIndex )
49              {
50                  case 0: // all titles
51                      // use LINQ to order the books by title
52                      titleBindingSource.DataSource =
53                          from book in database.Titles
54                          orderby book.Title1
55                          select book;
56                      break;
57                  case 1: // titles with 2008 copyright
58                      // use LINQ to get titles with 2008
59                      // copyright and sort them by title
60                      titleBindingSource.DataSource =
61                          from book in database.Titles
62                          where book.Copyright == "2008"
63                          orderby book.Title1
64                          select book;
65                      break;
66                  case 2: // titles ending with "How to Program"
67                      // use LINQ to get titles ending with
68                      // "How to Program" and sort them by title
69                      titleBindingSource.DataSource =
70                          from book in database.Titles
71                          where book.Title1.EndsWith( "How to Program" )
72                          orderby book.Title1
73                          select book;
74                      break;
75              } // end switch
76
77              titleBindingSource.MoveFirst(); // move to first entry
78          } // end method queriesComboBox_SelectedIndexChanged
79      } // end class TitleQueries
80  } // end namespace DisplayQueryResult
```

Fig. 18.20 | Displaying the result of a user-selected query in a `DataGridView`. (Part 2 of 2.)

Saving Changes

Follow the instructions in the previous example to add a handler for the `BindingNavigator`'s **Save Data** Button (lines 32–41). Note that, except for changes to the names, the three lines are identical. The last statement (line 40) displays the results of the `All titles` query in the `DataGridView`.

18.7 Retrieving Data from Multiple Tables with LINQ

In this section, we concentrate on LINQ to SQL features that simplify querying and combining data from multiple tables. The **Joining Tables with LINQ** application (Fig. 18.21) uses LINQ to SQL to combine and organize data from multiple tables, and shows the results of queries that perform the following tasks:

- Get a list of all the authors and the ISBNs of the books they've authored, sorted by last name then first name (Fig. 18.21(a)).

- Get a list of all the authors and the titles of the books they've authored, sorted by last name then first; for each author sort the titles alphabetically (Fig. 18.21(b)).

- Get a list of all the book titles grouped by author, sorted by last name then first; for a given author sort the titles alphabetically (Fig. 18.21(c)).

a) List of authors and the ISBNs of the books they've authored; sort the authors by last name then first name

b) List of authors and the titles of the book's they've authored; sort the authors by last name then first name; for a given author, sort the titles alphabetically

c) List of titles grouped by author; sort the authors by last name then first name; for a given author, sort the titles alphabetically

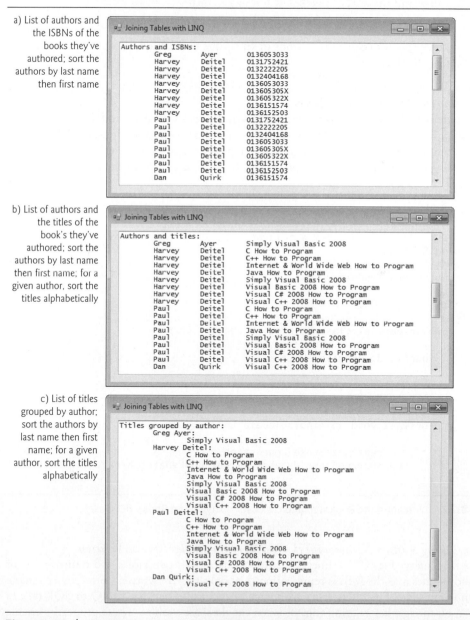

Fig. 18.21 | Outputs from the **Joining Tables with LINQ** application.

GUI for the Joining Tables with LINQ Application
For this example (Fig. 18.22–Fig. 18.25), create a Windows Forms application named
JoinQueries and rename the Form.cs file as JoiningTableData.cs. We set the following
properties for the outputTextBox:

- Font property: Set to Lucida Console to display the output in a fixed-width font.

- Anchor property: Set to Top, Bottom, Left, Right so that you can resize the window and the outputTextBox will resize accordingly.

- Scrollbars property: Set to Vertical, so that you can scroll through the output.

Follow the steps from previous sections to set up the connection to the database and the
LINQ to SQL classes.

*Creating the **BooksDataContext***
The code combines data from the three tables in the Books database and displays the relationships between the book titles and authors in three different ways. It uses LINQ to SQL classes that have been created using the same steps as the first two examples. As in previous examples, the BooksDataContext object (Fig. 18.22, line 19) allows the program to interact with the database.

```
 1    // Fig. 18.22: JoiningTableData.cs
 2    // Using LINQ to perform a join and aggregate data across tables.
 3    using System;
 4    using System.Linq;
 5    using System.Windows.Forms;
 6
 7    namespace JoinQueries
 8    {
 9       public partial class JoiningTableData : Form
10       {
11          public JoiningTableData()
12          {
13             InitializeComponent();
14          } // end constructor
15
16          private void JoiningTableData_Load(object sender, EventArgs e)
17          {
18             // create database connection
19             BooksDataContext database = new BooksDataContext();
20
```

Fig. 18.22 | Creating the BooksDataContext for querying the Books database.

Combining Author Names with the ISBNs of the Books They've Written
The first query (Fig. 18.23, lines 23–26) joins data from two tables and returns a list of
author names and the ISBNs representing the books they've written, sorted by LastName
then FirstName. The query takes advantage of the properties that LINQ to SQL creates
based on foreign-key relationships between the database's tables. These properties enable
you to easily combine data from related rows in multiple tables.

```
21              // get authors and ISBNs of each book they co-authored
22              var authorsAndISBNs =
23                  from author in database.Authors
24                  from book in author.AuthorISBNs
25                  orderby author.LastName, author.FirstName
26                  select new { author.FirstName, author.LastName, book.ISBN };
27
28              outputTextBox.AppendText( "Authors and ISBNs:" );
29
30              // display authors and ISBNs in tabular format
31              foreach ( var element in authorsAndISBNs )
32              {
33                  outputTextBox.AppendText(
34                      String.Format( "\r\n\t{0,-10} {1,-10} {2,-10}",
35                          element.FirstName, element.LastName, element.ISBN ) );
36              } // end foreach
37
```

Fig. 18.23 | Getting a list of authors and the ISBNs of the books they've authored.

The first from clause (line 23) gets one author from the Authors table. The second from clause (line 24) uses the generated AuthorISBNs property of the Author class to get only the rows in the AuthorISBN table that link to the current author—that is, the ones that have the same AuthorID as the current author. The combined result of the two from clauses is a collection of all the authors and the ISBNs of the books they've authored. The two from clauses introduce two range variables into the scope of this query—other clauses can access both range variables to combine data from multiple tables. Line 26 combines the FirstName and LastName of an author from the Authors table with a corresponding ISBN from the AuthorISBNs table. This line creates a new anonymous type that contains these three properties.

Anonymous Types

As you know, anonymous types allow you to create simple classes used to store data without writing a class definition. An anonymous type declaration (line 26)—known formally as an anonymous object-creation expression—is similar to an object initializer (Section 10.16). The anonymous type declaration begins with the keyword new followed by a member-initializer list in braces ({}). No class name is specified after the new keyword. The compiler generates a class definition based on the anonymous object-creation expression. This class contains the properties specified in the member-initializer list—First-Name, LastName and ISBN. All properties of an anonymous type are public. Anonymous type properties are read-only—you cannot modify a property's value once the object is created. Each property's type is inferred from the values assigned to it. The class definition is generated automatically by the compiler, so you don't know the class's type name (hence the term anonymous type). Thus, you must use implicitly typed local variables to store references to objects of anonymous types (e.g., line 31). Though we are not using it here, the compiler defines a ToString method when creating the anonymous type's class definition. The method returns a string in curly braces containing a comma-separated list of *PropertyName* = *value* pairs. The compiler also provides an Equals method, which compares the properties of the anonymous object that calls the method and the anonymous object that it receives as an argument.

Combining Author Names with the Titles of the Books They've Written

The second query (Fig. 18.24, lines 40–45) gives similar output, but uses the foreign-key relationships to go one step further and get the title of each book that an author wrote. The first from clause (line 40) gets one title from the Titles table. The second from clause (line 41) uses the generated AuthorISBNs property of the Title class to get only the rows in the AuthorISBN table that link to the current title—that is, the ones that have the same ISBN as the current title. Each of those book objects contains an Author property that represents the foreign-key relationship between the AuthorISBNs table and the Authors table. This Author property gives us access to the names of the authors for the current book.

```
38            // get authors and titles of each book they co-authored
39            var authorsAndTitles =
40                from title in database.Titles
41                from book in title.AuthorISBNs
42                let author = book.Author
43                orderby author.LastName, author.FirstName, title.Title1
44                select new { author.FirstName, author.LastName,
45                    title.Title1 };
46
47            outputTextBox.AppendText( "\r\n\r\nAuthors and titles:" );
48
49            // display authors and titles in tabular format
50            foreach ( var element in authorsAndTitles )
51            {
52                outputTextBox.AppendText(
53                    String.Format( "\r\n\t{0,-10} {1,-10} {2}",
54                        element.FirstName, element.LastName, element.Title1 ) );
55            } // end foreach
56
```

Fig. 18.24 | Getting a list of authors and the titles of the books they've authored.

Line 42 uses the let query operator, which allows you to declare a new variable in a LINQ query—usually to create a shorter name for an expression. The variable can be accessed in later statements just like a range variable. The author variable created in the let clause refers to book.Author. The select clause (lines 44–45) uses the author and title variables introduced earlier in the query to get the FirstName and LastName of each author from the Authors table and the title of each book from the Titles table.

Organizing Book Titles by Author

Most queries return results with data arranged in a relational-style table of rows and columns. The last query (Fig. 18.25, lines 60–66) returns hierarchical results. Each element in the results contains the name of an Author and a list of Titles that the author wrote. The LINQ query does this by using a nested query in the select clause. The outer query iterates over the authors in the database. The inner query takes a specific author and retrieves all titles that the author worked on. The select clause (lines 62–66) creates an anonymous type with two properties:

- The property `Name` (line 62) combines each author's name, separating the first and last names by a space.

- The property `Titles` (line 63) receives the result of the nested query, which returns the title of each book written by the current author.

In this case, we're providing names for each property in the new anonymous type. When you create an anonymous type, you can specify the name for each property by using the format *name = value*.

```
57              // get authors and titles of each book
58              // they co-authored; group by author
59              var titlesByAuthor =
60                  from author in database.Authors
61                  orderby author.LastName, author.FirstName
62                  select new { Name = author.FirstName + " " + author.LastName,
63                      Titles =
64                          from book in author.AuthorISBNs
65                          orderby book.Title.Title1
66                          select book.Title.Title1 };
67
68              outputTextBox.AppendText( "\r\n\r\nTitles grouped by author:" );
69
70              // display titles written by each author, grouped by author
71              foreach ( var author in titlesByAuthor )
72              {
73                  // display author's name
74                  outputTextBox.AppendText( "\r\n\t" + author.Name + ":" );
75
76                  // display titles written by that author
77                  foreach ( var title in author.Titles )
78                  {
79                      outputTextBox.AppendText( "\r\n\t\t" + title );
80                  } // end inner foreach
81              } // end outer foreach
82          } // end method JoiningTableData_Load
83      } // end class JoiningTableData
84  } // end namespace JoinQueries
```

Fig. 18.25 | Getting a list of titles grouped by authors.

The nested `foreach` statements (lines 71–81) use the properties of the anonymous type created by the query to output the hierarchical results. The outer loop displays the author's name and the inner loop displays the titles of all the books written by that author.

Notice the expression `book.Title.Title1` used in the inner `orderby` and `select` clauses (lines 65–66). This is due to the database having a `Title` column in the `Titles` table, and is another example of following foreign-key relationships. (Recall that the IDE renamed the `Title` column in the LINQ to SQL classes to avoid a naming conflict with the generated `Title` class.) The range variable `book` iterates over the rows of the `Author-ISBN` for the current author's books. Each book's `Title` property contains the corresponding row from the `Titles` table for that book. The `Title1` in the expression returns the `Title` column (the title of the book) from that row of the `Titles` table in the database.

18.8 Creating a Master/Detail View Application

Figure 18.26 demonstrates a so-called **master/detail view**—one part of the GUI (the master) allows you to select an entry, and another part (the details) displays detailed information about that entry. In this example, if you select an author from the **Author:** ComboBox, the application displays the details of the books written by that author (Fig. 18.26(b)). If you select a book title from the **Title:** ComboBox, the application displays the co-authors of that book (Fig. 18.26(c)).

a) **Master/Detail** application when it begins execution before an author or title is selected; no results are displayed in the DataGridView until the user makes a selection from one of the ComboBoxes

b) Select **Harvey Deitel** from the **Author:** drop-down list to view books he's co-authored

c) Select **C++ How to Program** from the **Title:** drop-down to view the authors who wrote that book

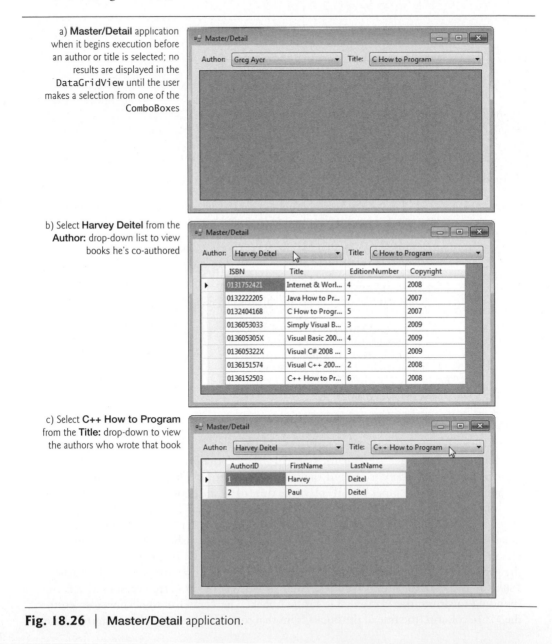

Fig. 18.26 | Master/Detail application.

18.8.1 Creating the Master/Detail GUI

You've seen that the IDE can automatically generate the `BindingSource`, `BindingNavigator` and GUI elements when you drag a data source onto the `Form`. While this works for simple applications, those with more complex operations involve writing more substantial amounts of code. Before explaining the code, we list the steps required to create the GUI.

Step 1: Creating the Project
Create a new **Windows Forms Application** called `MasterDetail`. Name the source file `Details.cs` and set the `Form`'s `Text` property to **Master/Detail**.

Step 2: Creating LINQ to SQL Classes
Follow the instructions in Section 18.5.1 to add the `Books` database and create the LINQ to SQL classes to interact with the database.

Step 3: Creating GUI Elements
Add two `Labels` and two `ComboBoxes` to the top of the `Form`. Position them as shown in Fig. 18.27. The `Label` and `ComboBox` on the left should be named `authorLabel` and `authorComboBox`, respectively. The `Label` and `ComboBox` on the right should be named `titleLabel` and `titleComboBox`. Set the `Text` properties of the `Labels` to `Author:` and `Title:`, respectively. Also change the `DropDownStyle` properties of the `ComboBoxes` from `DropDown` to `DropDownList`—this prevents the user from being able to type in the control.

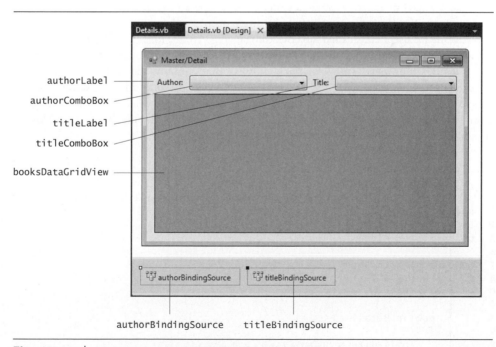

Fig. 18.27 | Finished design of **Master/Detail** application.

Next, create a `DataGridView` called `booksDataGridView` to hold the details that are displayed. Unlike previous examples, do not automatically create it by dragging a data source from the **Data Sources** window—this example sets the data source programmatically. Instead, drag the DataGridView from the **Toolbox**. Resize the DataGridView so that it fills the remainder of the Form. Because this control is only for *viewing* data, set its Read-Only property to True using the **Properties** window.

Finally, we need to add two BindingSources from the **Data** section of the **Toolbox**, one for information from the Titles table and one for information from the Authors table. Name these titleBindingSource and authorBindingSource, respectively. As in the previous examples, these appear in the component tray. These BindingSources are used as data sources for the DataGridView—the data source switches between them, depending on whether we want to view a list of Titles or a list of Authors. With the GUI creation complete, we can now write the code to provide the master/detail functionality.

18.8.2 Coding the Master/Detail Application

Nested Class AuthorBinding

As you saw in Fig. 18.26, the **Author:** ComboBox displays each author's full name. This example uses data binding to display the names in the ComboBox. When you bind a collection of objects to a ComboBox's DataSource property, the ComboBox normally displays the result of calling ToString on each object in the collection. If the String representation is not appropriate, you can specify *one* property of each object in the collection that should be displayed. In this example, we want to display each author's first and last name.

Recall that the author's name is stored as *two* separate fields in the database, so the auto-generated Author class does not have single property that returns the full name. For this reason, we use a class called AuthorBinding (Fig. 18.28, lines 21–25) to help display the author's full name. Class AuthorBinding's Name property stores an author's full name, and the Author property stores the Author object that contains the author's information from the database. Class AuthorBinding is intended for use only in this example, so we defined it inside class Details—it's a so-called **nested class**. Class definitions may be nested inside other classes when they're intended to be used only by their enclosing classes—that is, they're not meant for use by other programs.

```
1   // Fig. 18.28: Details.cs
2   // Using a DataGridView to display details based on a selection.
3   using System;
4   using System.Linq;
5   using System.Windows.Forms;
6
7   namespace MasterDetail
8   {
9      public partial class Details : Form
10     {
11        public Details()
12        {
13           InitializeComponent();
14        } // end constructor
15
```

Fig. 18.28 | Nested class AuthorBinding in class Details. (Part 1 of 2.)

```
16          // connection to database
17          private BooksDataContext database = new BooksDataContext();
18
19          // this class helps us display each author's first
20          // and last name in the authors drop-down list
21          private class AuthorBinding
22          {
23             public Author Author { get; set; } // contained Author object
24             public string Name { get; set; } // author's full name
25          } // end class AuthorBinding
26
```

Fig. 18.28 | Nested class `AuthorBinding` in class `Details`. (Part 2 of 2.)

Configuring the Data Sources
The `ComboBox`'s **`DisplayMember` property** is set to the `String` "Name" (Fig. 18.29, line 31), which tells the `ComboBox` to use the `Name` property of the objects in its `DataSource` to determine what text to display for each item. The `DataSource` in this case is the result of the LINQ query in lines 35–38, which creates an `AuthorBinding` object for each author. The `authorComboBox` will contain the `Name` of each author in the query result. Recall from Section 10.16 that object initializers (like lines 37–38) can initialize an object without explicitly calling a constructor.

```
27          // initialize data sources when the Form is loaded
28          private void Details_Load( object sender, EventArgs e )
29          {
30             // display AuthorBinding.Name
31             authorComboBox.DisplayMember = "Name";
32
33             // set authorComboBox's DataSource to the list of authors
34             authorComboBox.DataSource =
35                from author in database.Authors
36                orderby author.LastName, author.FirstName
37                select new AuthorBinding { Author = author,
38                   Name = author.FirstName + " " + author.LastName };
39
40             // display Title.Title1
41             titleComboBox.DisplayMember = "Title1";
42
43             // set titleComboBox's DataSource to the list of titles
44             titleComboBox.DataSource =
45                from title in database.Titles
46                orderby title.Title1
47                select title;
48
49             // initially, display no "detail" data
50             booksDataGridView.DataSource = null;
51          } // end method Details_Load
52
```

Fig. 18.29 | Configuring the `ComboBox`es' and `DataGridView`'s data sources.

For the titleComboBox, we specify that each book's title should be displayed (line 41). The LINQ query in lines 45–47 returns a sorted list of Title objects and assigns it to the titleComboBox's DataSource.

Initially, we don't want to display any data in the DataGridView. However, when you set a ComboBox's DataSource, the control's SelectedIndexChanged event handler is called. To prevent this data from being displayed when the program first loads, we explicitly set the DataGridView's DataSource property to null (line 50).

The *BindingSource* of a *DataGridView*

Simple GUI elements like ComboBoxes can work directly from a data source, such as the result of a LINQ to SQL query. However, a DataGridView requires a BindingSource as its DataSource. While building the GUI, you created two BindingSource objects—one for displaying a list of Authors and one for displaying a list of Titles. You can change the columns and data displayed in the DataGridView merely by changing its DataSource between the two BindingSource objects. The DataGridView automatically determines the column names it needs to display from its BindingSource and refreshes itself when the BindingSource changes.

Method *authorComboBox_SelectedIndexChanged*

The authorComboBox_SelectedIndexChanged event handler (Fig. 18.30) performs three distinct operations. First, it retrieves the selected Author (lines 58–59) from the authorComboBox. The ComboBox's SelectedItem property returns an object, so we convert the SelectedItem property's value to the type AuthorBinding—recall that the ComboBox's DataSource was set to a collection of AuthorBinding objects. Then, the event handler accesses the AuthorBinding's Author property to retrieve the wrapped Author object.

```
53        // display titles that were co-authored by the selected author
54        private void authorComboBox_SelectedIndexChanged(
55           object sender, EventArgs e )
56        {
57           // get the selected Author object from the ComboBox
58           Author currentAuthor =
59              ( ( AuthorBinding ) authorComboBox.SelectedItem ).Author;
60
61           // set titleBindingSource's DataSource to the
62           // list of titles written by the selected author
63           titleBindingSource.DataSource =
64              from book in currentAuthor.AuthorISBNs
65              select book.Title;
66
67           // display the titles in the DataGridView
68           booksDataGridView.DataSource = titleBindingSource;
69        } // end method authorComboBox_SelectedIndexChanged
70
```

Fig. 18.30 | Displaying the books for the selected author.

Next, the event handler uses LINQ to retrieve the Title objects representing books that the currentAuthor worked on (lines 64–65). The results of the LINQ query are assigned to the DataSource property of titleBindingSource (line 63). The event handler sets the titleBindingSource because we want to display Title objects associated with the currentAuthor. Finally, the DataGridView's DataSource is assigned titleBinding-Source to display the books this author wrote (line 68).

Method titleComboBox_SelectedIndexChanged

The titleComboBox_SelectedIndexChanged event handler (Fig. 18.31) is nearly identical to authorComboBox_SelectedIndexChanged. Line 76 gets the selected Title from the ComboBox. Lines 80–82 set the authorsBindingSource's DataSource to the list of Authors for the current book. Finally, the DataGridView's DataSource is assigned authorBinding-Source to display the authors who wrote this book (line 85).

```
71          // display the authors of the selected title
72          private void titleComboBox_SelectedIndexChanged(
73             object sender, EventArgs e )
74          {
75             // get the selected Title object from the ComboBox
76             Title currentTitle = ( Title ) titleComboBox.SelectedItem;
77
78             // set authorBindingSource's DataSource to the
79             // list of authors for the selected title
80             authorBindingSource.DataSource =
81                from book in currentTitle.AuthorISBNs
82                select book.Author;
83
84             // display the authors in the DataGridView
85             booksDataGridView.DataSource = authorBindingSource;
86          } // end method titleComboBox_SelectedIndexChanged
87       } // end class Details
88    } // end namespace MasterDetail
```

Fig. 18.31 | Displaying the authors of the selected book.

18.9 Address Book Case Study

Our next example (Fig. 18.32) implements a simple AddressBook application that enables users to perform the following tasks on the database AddressBook.mdf (which is included in the directory with this chapter's examples):

- Insert new contacts
- Find contacts whose last names begin with the specified letters
- Update existing contacts
- Delete contacts

We populated the database with six fictional contacts.

Rather than displaying a database table in a DataGridView, this application presents the details of one contact at a time in several TextBoxes. The BindingNavigator at the top of the window allows you to control which *row* of the table is displayed at any given time. The BindingNavigator also allows you to add a contact, delete a contact and save changes to a contact. When you run the application, experiment with the BindingNavigator's controls. The CD- or DVD-like buttons of the BindingNavigator allow you to change the currently displayed row. Adding a row clears the `TextBoxes` and sets the `TextBox` to the right of **Address ID** to zero. When you save a new entry, the **Address ID** field is automatically changed from zero to a unique number by the database.

Recall from Section 18.5 that to allow changes to the database to *persist* between executions of the application, you can run the program in release mode (*Ctrl* + *F5*).

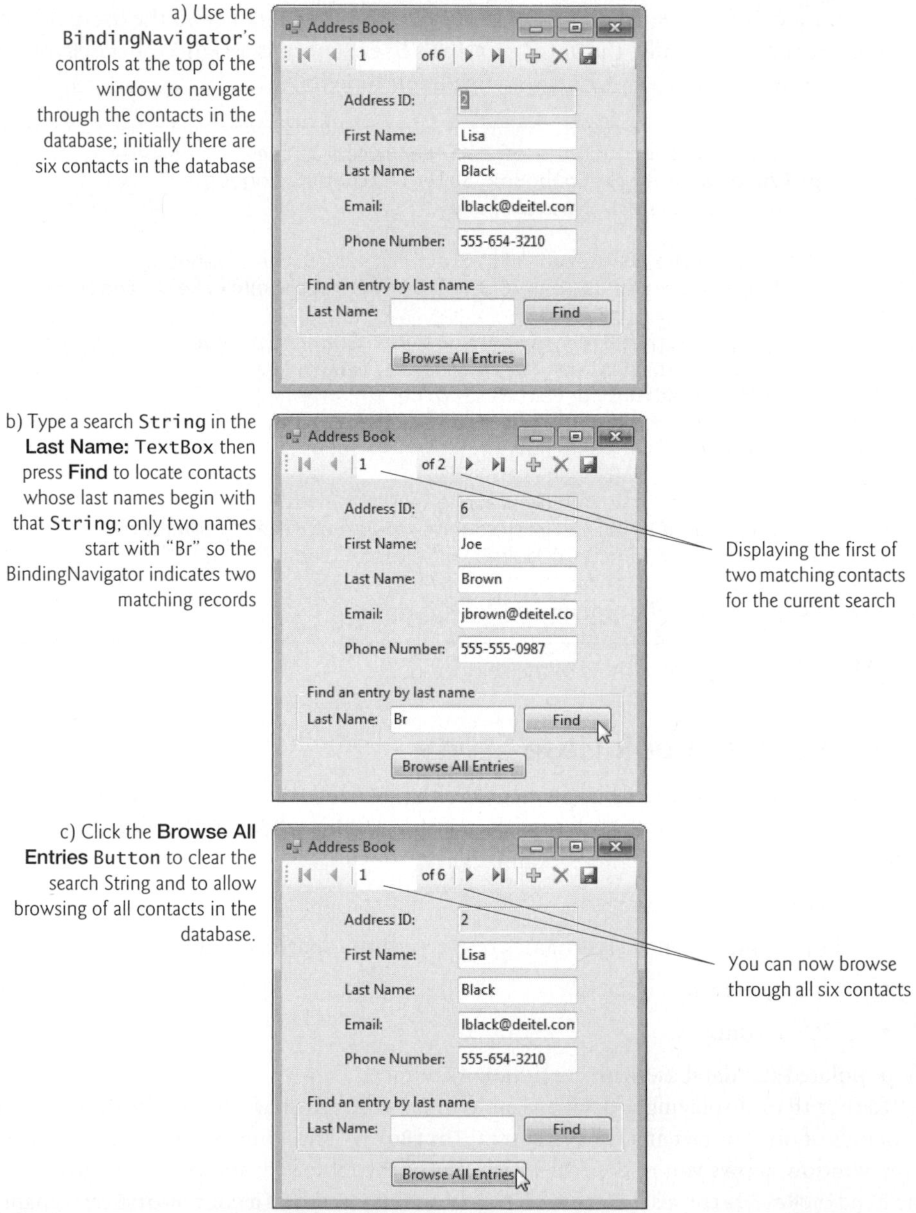
a) Use the BindingNavigator's controls at the top of the window to navigate through the contacts in the database; initially there are six contacts in the database
Address Book
1 of 6
Address ID: 2
First Name: Lisa
Last Name: Black
Email: lblack@deitel.com
Phone Number: 555-654-3210
Find an entry by last name
Last Name:
Find
Browse All Entries
b) Type a search String in the Last Name: TextBox then press Find to locate contacts whose last names begin with that String; only two names start with "Br" so the BindingNavigator indicates two matching records
Address Book
1 of 2
Address ID: 6
First Name: Joe
Last Name: Brown
Email: jbrown@deitel.co
Phone Number: 555-555-0987
Find an entry by last name
Last Name: Br
Find
Browse All Entries
Displaying the first of two matching contacts for the current search
c) Click the Browse All Entries Button to clear the search String and to allow browsing of all contacts in the database.
Address Book
1 of 6
Address ID: 2
First Name: Lisa
Last Name: Black
Email: lblack@deitel.com
Phone Number: 555-654-3210
Find an entry by last name
Last Name:
Find
Browse All Entries
You can now browse through all six contacts

Fig. 18.32 | Manipulating an address book.

18.9.1 Creating the Address Book Application's GUI

We discuss the application's code momentarily. First we show the steps to create this application.

Step 1: Creating the Project
Create a new **Windows Forms Application** named AddressBook, set the Form's filename to Contacts.cs, then set the Form's **Text** property to Address Book.

Step 2: Creating LINQ to SQL Classes and Data Source
Follow the instructions in Section 18.5.1 to add a database to the project and generate the LINQ to SQL classes. For this example, add the AddressBook database and name the file AddressBook.dbml. You must also add the Address table as a data source, as we did with the Authors table in *Step 1* of Section 18.5.2.

Step 3: Displaying the Details of Each Row
In the earlier sections, you dragged an object from the **Data Sources** window to the Form to create a DataGridView that was bound to the data in that object. The IDE allows you to specify the type of control(s) that it will create when you drag and drop an object from the **Data Sources** window onto a Form. In **Design** view, click the Address node in the **Data Sources** window. Note that this becomes a drop-down list when you select it. Click the down arrow to view the items in the list. The item to the left of **DataGridView** is initially highlighted in blue, because the default control that's bound to a table is a DataGridView. Select the **Details** option (Fig. 18.33) in the drop-down list to indicate that the IDE should create a set of Label/TextBox pairs for each column-name/column-value pair when you drag and drop Address onto the Form.

Fig. 18.33 | Specifying that an Address should be displayed as a set of Labels and TextBoxes.

Step 4: Dragging the Address Data-Source Node to the Form
Drag the Address node from the **Data Sources** window to the Form. This automatically creates a BindingNavigator and the Labels and TextBoxes corresponding to the columns of the database table. The fields may be placed out of order, with the Email at the top. Reorder the components, using **Design** view, so they're in the proper order shown in Fig. 18.32.

Step 5: Making the AddressID TextBox ReadOnly
The AddressID column of the Addresses table is an autoincremented identity column, so users should not be allowed to edit the values in this column. Select the TextBox for the AddressID and set its ReadOnly property to True using the **Properties** window.

Step 6: Adding Controls to Allow Users to Specify a Last Name to Locate
While the BindingNavigator allows you to browse the address book, it would be more convenient to be able to find a specific entry by last name. To add this functionality to the application, we must create controls to allow the user to enter a last name and provide event handlers to perform the search.

Add a Label named findLabel, a TextBox named findTextBox, and a Button named findButton. Place these controls in a GroupBox named findGroupBox, then set its Text property to **Find an entry by last name**. Set the Text property of the Label to Last Name: and set the Text property of the Button to Find.

Step 7: Allowing the User to Return to Browsing All Rows of the Database
To allow users to return to browsing all the contacts after searching for contacts with a specific last name, add a Button named browseAllButton below the findGroupBox. Set the Text property of browseAllButton to **Browse All Entries**.

18.9.2 Coding the Address Book Application

Method RefreshContacts
As we showed in previous examples, we must connect the addressBindingSource that controls the GUI with the AddressBookDataContext that interacts with the database. In this example, we do this in the RefreshContacts method (Fig. 18.34, lines 21–31), which is called from several other methods in the application. Method RefreshContacts sets the addressBindingSource's DataSource property to the result of a LINQ query on the Addresses table. We created a private method in this example, because there are three locations in the program where we need to update the addressBindingSource's Data-Source property.

```
 1   // Fig. 18.34: Contact.cs
 2   // Manipulating an address book.
 3   using System;
 4   using System.Linq;
 5   using System.Windows.Forms;
 6
 7   namespace AddressBook
 8   {
 9      public partial class Contacts : Form
10      {
11         public Contacts()
12         {
13            InitializeComponent();
14         } // end constructor
15
16         // LINQ to SQL data context
17         private AddressBookDataContext database =
18            new AddressBookDataContext();
19
```

Fig. 18.34 | Creating the BooksDataContext and defining method RefreshContacts for use in other methods. (Part 1 of 2.)

```
20          // fill our addressBindingSource with all rows, ordered by name
21          private void RefreshContacts()
22          {
23              // use LINQ to create a data source from the database
24              addressBindingSource.DataSource =
25                  from address in database.Addresses
26                  orderby address.LastName, address.FirstName
27                  select address;
28
29              addressBindingSource.MoveFirst(); // go to the first result
30              findTextBox.Clear(); // clear the Find TextBox
31          } // end method RefreshContacts
32
```

Fig. 18.34 | Creating the `BooksDataContext` and defining method `RefreshContacts` for use in other methods. (Part 2 of 2.)

Method Contacts_Load

Method `Contacts_Load` (Fig. 18.35) calls `RefreshContacts` (line 36) so that the first record is displayed when the application starts. As before, you create the `Load` event handler by double clicking the `Form`'s title bar.

```
33          // when the form loads, fill it with data from the database
34          private void Contacts_Load( object sender, EventArgs e )
35          {
36              RefreshContacts(); // fill binding with data from database
37          } // end method Contacts_Load
38
```

Fig. 18.35 | Calling `RefreshContacts` to fill the `TextBox`es when the application loads.

Method addressBindingNavigatorSaveItem_Click

Method `addressBindingNavigatorSaveItem_Click` (Fig. 18.36) saves the changes to the database when the `BindingNavigator`'s save `Button` is clicked. (Remember to enable this button in the `BindingNavigator`.) We call `RefreshContacts` after saving to re-sort the data and move back to the first element.

```
39          // Click event handler for the Save Button in the
40          // BindingNavigator saves the changes made to the data
41          private void addressBindingNavigatorSaveItem_Click(
42              object sender, EventArgs e )
43          {
44              Validate(); // validate input fields
45              addressBindingSource.EndEdit(); // indicate edits are complete
46              database.SubmitChanges(); // write changes to database file
47
48              RefreshContacts(); // change back to initial unfiltered data
49          } // end method addressBindingNavigatorSaveItem_Click
50
```

Fig. 18.36 | Saving changes to the database when the user clicks the **Save Data** Button.

The AddressBook database requires values for the first name, last name, phone number and e-mail. We did not check for errors to simplify the code—if a field is empty when you attempt to save, a SqlException exception (namespace System.Data.SqlClient) occurs.

Method *findButton_Click*

Method findButton_Click (Fig. 18.37) uses LINQ (lines 57–60) to select only people whose last names start with the characters entered in the findTextBox. The query sorts the results by last name then first name. When you enter a last name and click **Find**, the BindingNavigator allows the user to browse only the rows containing the matching last names. This is because the data source bound to the Form's controls (the result of the LINQ query) has changed and now contains only a limited number of rows.

```
51        // use LINQ to create a data source that contains only people
52        // with last names that start with the specified text
53        private void findButton_Click( object sender, EventArgs e )
54        {
55            // use LINQ to create a data source from the database
56            addressBindingSource.DataSource =
57               from address in database.Addresses
58               where address.LastName.StartsWith( findTextBox.Text )
59               orderby address.LastName, address.FirstName
60               select address;
61
62            addressBindingSource.MoveFirst(); // go to first result
63        } // end method findButton_Click
64
```

Fig. 18.37 | Finding the contacts whose last names begin with a specified String.

Method *browseAllButton_Click*

Method browseAllButton_Click (Fig. 18.38) allows users to return to browsing all the rows after searching for specific rows. Double click browseAllButton to create a Click event handler. Have the event handler call RefreshContacts (line 68) to restore the data source to the full list of people and clear the findTextBox.

```
65        // reload addressBindingSource with all rows
66        private void browseButton_Click( object sender, EventArgs e )
67        {
68            RefreshContacts(); // change back to initial unfiltered data
69        } // end method browseButton_Click
70    } // end class Contacts
71 } // end namespace AddressBook
```

Fig. 18.38 | Allowing the user to browse all contacts.

18.10 Tools and Web Resources

Our extensive LINQ Resource Center at www.deitel.com/LINQ contains many links to additional information, including blogs by Microsoft LINQ team members, sample chapters, tutorials, videos, downloads, FAQs, forums, webcasts and other resource sites.

A useful tool for learning LINQ is LINQPad (www.linqpad.net), which allows you to execute and view the results of any C# or Visual Basic expression, including LINQ queries. It also supports connecting to a SQL Server database and querying it using SQL and LINQ to SQL.

18.11 Wrap-Up

This chapter introduced the relational database model, LINQ to SQL and the IDE's visual programming tools for working with databases. You examined the contents of a simple Books database and learned about the relationships among the tables in the database. You used LINQ and the LINQ to SQL classes generated by the IDE to retrieve data from, add new data to, delete data from and update data in a SQL Server Express database.

We discussed the LINQ to SQL classes automatically generated by the IDE, such as the DataContext class that controls interactions with the database. You learned how to use the IDE's tools to connect to databases and to generate LINQ to SQL classes based on a database's schema. You then used the IDE's drag-and-drop capabilities to automatically generate GUIs for displaying and manipulating database data.

In the next chapter, we demonstrate how to build web applications using Microsoft's ASP.NET technology. We introduce the concept of a three-tier application, which is divided into three pieces that can reside on the same computer or be distributed among separate computers across a network such as the Internet. One of these tiers—the information tier—typically stores data in a database.

Web App Development
with ASP.NET

OBJECTIVES

In this chapter you'll learn:

- Web application development using ASP.NET.

- To handle the events from a Web Form's controls.

- To use validation controls to ensure that data is in the correct format before it's sent from a client to the server.

- To maintain user-specific information.

- To create a data-driven web application using ASP.NET and LINQ to SQL.

… the challenges are for the designers of these applications: to forget what we think we know about the limitations of the Web, and begin to imagine a wider, richer range of possibilities. It's going to be fun.
—Jesse James Garrett

If any man will draw up his case, and put his name at the foot of the first page, I will give him an immediate reply. Where he compels me to turn over the sheet, he must wait my leisure.
—Lord Sandwich

19.1 Introduction

In this chapter, we introduce **web-application development** with Microsoft's **ASP.NET** technology. Web-based applications create web content for web-browser clients.

We present several examples that demonstrate web-application development using **Web Forms**, **web controls** (also called **ASP.NET server controls**) and Visual C# programming. Web Form files have the file-name extension **.aspx** and contain the web page's GUI. You customize Web Forms by adding web controls including labels, textboxes, images, buttons and other GUI components. The Web Form file represents the web page that is sent to the client browser. We often refer to Web Form files as **ASPX files**.

An ASPX file created in Visual Studio has a corresponding class written in a .NET language—we use Visual C# in this book. This class contains event handlers, initialization code, utility methods and other supporting code. The file that contains this class is called the **code-behind file** and provides the ASPX file's programmatic implementation.

To develop the code and GUIs in this chapter, we used Microsoft's **Visual Web Developer 2010 Express**—a free IDE designed for developing ASP.NET web applications. The full version of Visual Studio 2010 includes the functionality of Visual Web Developer, so the instructions we present for Visual Web Developer also apply to Visual Studio 2010. The database example (Section 19.8) also requires SQL Server 2008 Express. See the *Before You Begin* section of the book for additional information on this software.

In Chapter 27, we present several additional web-application development topics, including:

- master pages to maintain a uniform look-and-feel across the Web Forms in a web application

- creating password-protected websites with registration and login capabilities

- using the **Web Site Administration Tool** to specify which parts of a website are password protected

- using ASP.NET AJAX to quickly and easily improve the user experience for your web applications, giving them responsiveness comparable to that of desktop applications.

19.2 Web Basics

In this section, we discuss what occurs when a user requests a web page in a browser. In its simplest form, a *web page* is nothing more than an *HTML (HyperText Markup Language) document* (with the extension .html or .htm) that describes to a web browser the document's content and how to format it.

HTML documents normally contain *hyperlinks* that link to different pages or to other parts of the same page. When the user clicks a hyperlink, a **web server** locates the requested web page and sends it to the user's web browser. Similarly, the user can type the *address of a web page* into the browser's *address field* and press *Enter* to view the specified page.

Web development tools like Visual Web Developer typically use a "stricter" version of HTML, called *XHTML (Extensible HyperText Markup Language)*, which is based on XML (Chapter 26). ASP.NET produces web pages as XHTML documents.

URIs and URLs

URIs (Uniform Resource Identifiers) identify resources on the Internet. URIs that start with http:// are called *URLs (Uniform Resource Locators)*. Common URLs refer to files, directories or server-side code that performs tasks such as database lookups, Internet searches and business application processing. If you know the URL of a publicly available resource anywhere on the web, you can enter that URL into a web browser's address field and the browser can access that resource.

Parts of a URL

A URL contains information that directs a browser to the resource that the user wishes to access. Web servers make such resources available to web clients. Popular web servers include Microsoft's Internet Information Services (IIS) and Apache's HTTP Server.

Let's examine the components of the URL

```
http://www.deitel.com/books/downloads.html
```

The http:// indicates that the HyperText Transfer Protocol (HTTP) should be used to obtain the resource. HTTP is the web protocol that enables clients and servers to communicate. Next in the URL is the server's fully qualified **hostname** (www.deitel.com)—the name of the web server computer on which the resource resides. This computer is referred to as the **host**, because it houses and maintains resources. The hostname www.deitel.com is translated into an **IP (Internet Protocol) address**—a numerical value that uniquely identifies the server on the Internet. A **Domain Name System (DNS) server** maintains a database of hostnames and their corresponding IP addresses, and performs the translations automatically.

The remainder of the URL (/books/downloads.html) specifies the resource's location (/books) and name (downloads.html) on the web server. The location could represent an actual directory on the web server's file system. For *security* reasons, however, the location is typically a *virtual directory*. The web server translates the virtual directory into a real location on the server, thus hiding the resource's true location.

Making a Request and Receiving a Response

When given a URL, a web browser uses HTTP to retrieve the web page found at that address. Figure 19.1 shows a web browser sending a request to a web server. Figure 19.2 shows the web server responding to that request.

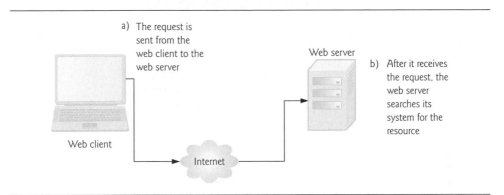

Fig. 19.1 | Client requesting a resource from a web server.

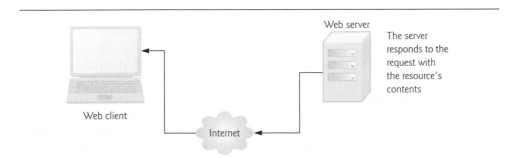

Fig. 19.2 | Client receiving a response from the web server.

19.3 Multitier Application Architecture

Web-based applications are **multitier applications** (sometimes referred to as *n*-tier applications). Multitier applications divide functionality into separate **tiers** (that is, logical groupings of functionality). Although tiers can be located on the *same* computer, the tiers of web-based applications commonly reside on *separate* computers for security and scalability. Figure 19.3 presents the basic architecture of a three-tier web-based application.

Information Tier

The **information tier** (also called the **bottom tier**) maintains the application's data. This tier typically stores data in a relational database management system. For example, a retail store might have a database for storing product information, such as descriptions, prices and quantities in stock. The same database also might contain customer information, such as user names, billing addresses and credit card numbers. This tier can contain multiple databases, which together comprise the data needed for an application.

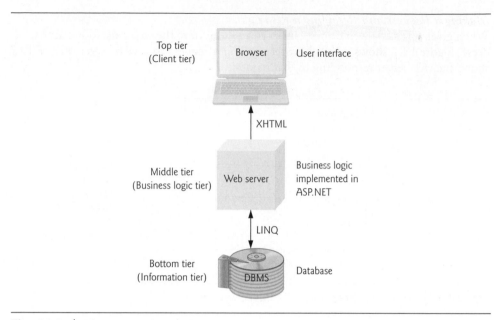

Fig. 19.3 | Three-tier architecture.

Business Logic

The **middle tier** implements **business logic**, **controller logic** and **presentation logic** to control interactions between the application's clients and its data. The middle tier acts as an intermediary between data in the information tier and the application's clients. The middle-tier controller logic processes client requests (such as requests to view a product catalog) and retrieves data from the database. The middle-tier presentation logic then processes data from the information tier and presents the content to the client. Web applications typically present data to clients as web pages.

Business logic in the middle tier enforces *business rules* and ensures that data is reliable before the server application updates the database or presents the data to users. Business rules dictate how clients can and cannot access application data, and how applications process data. For example, a business rule in the middle tier of a retail store's web-based application might ensure that all product quantities remain positive. A client request to set a negative quantity in the bottom tier's product information database would be rejected by the middle tier's business logic.

Client Tier

The **client tier**, or **top tier**, is the application's user interface, which gathers input and displays output. Users interact directly with the application through the user interface (typically viewed in a web browser), keyboard and mouse. In response to user actions (for example, clicking a hyperlink), the client tier interacts with the middle tier to make requests and to retrieve data from the information tier. The client tier then displays to the user the data retrieved from the middle tier. The client tier never directly interacts with the information tier.

19.4 Your First Web Application

Our first example displays the web server's time of day in a browser window (Fig. 19.4). When this application executes—that is, a web browser requests the application's web page—the web server executes the application's code, which gets the current time and displays it in a Label. The web server then returns the result to the web browser that made the request, and the web browser renders the web page containing the time. We executed this application in both the Internet Explorer and Firefox web browsers to show you that the web page renders identically in each.

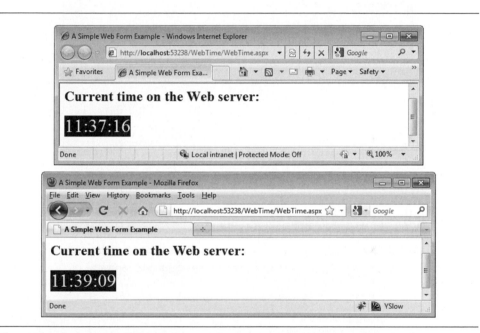

Fig. 19.4 | WebTime web application running in both Internet Explorer and Firefox.

Testing the Application in Your Default Web Browser
To test this application in your default web browser, perform the following steps:

1. Open Visual Web Developer.
2. Select **Open Web Site...** from the **File** menu.
3. In the **Open Web Site** dialog (Fig. 19.5), ensure that **File System** is selected, then navigate to this chapter's examples, select the WebTime folder and click the **Open Button**.
4. Select WebTime.aspx in the **Solution Explorer**, then type *Ctrl* + *F5* to execute the web application.

Testing the Application in a Selected Web Browser
If you wish to execute the application in another web browser, you can copy the web page's address from your default browser's address field and paste it into another browser's address field, or you can perform the following steps:

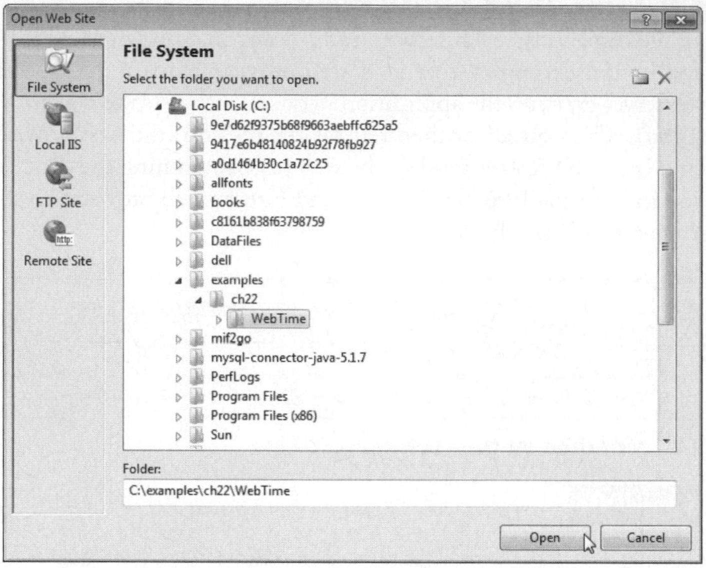

Fig. 19.5 | Open Web Site dialog.

1. In the **Solution Explorer**, right click WebTime.aspx and select **Browse With...** to display the **Browse With** dialog (Fig. 19.6).

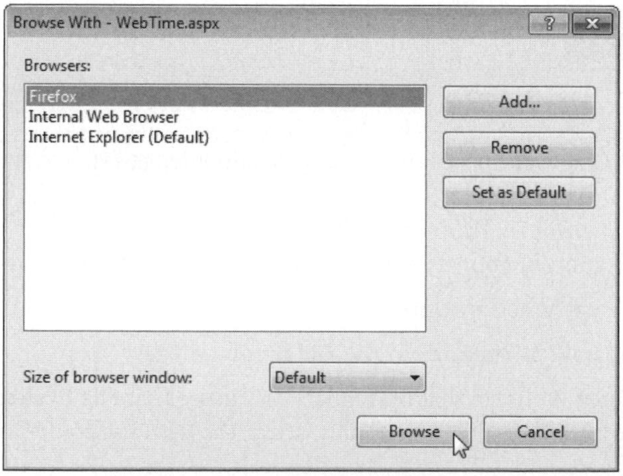

Fig. 19.6 | Selecting another web browser to execute the web application.

2. From the **Browsers** list, select the browser in which you'd like to test the web application and click the **Browse** Button.

If the browser you wish to use is not listed, you can use the **Browse With** dialog to add items to or remove items from the list of web browsers.

19.4.1 Building the WebTime Application

Now that you've tested the application, let's create it in Visual Web Developer.

Step 1: Creating the Web Site Project
Select **File > New Web Site...** to display the **New Web Site** dialog (Fig. 19.7). In the left column of this dialog, ensure that **Visual C#** is selected, then select **ASP.NET** Empty Web Site in the middle column. At the bottom of the dialog you can specify the location and name of the web application.

Fig. 19.7 | Creating an **ASP.NET Web Site** in Visual Web Developer.

The **Web location:** ComboBox provides the following options:

- **File System:** Creates a new website for testing on your local computer. Such websites execute in Visual Web Developer's built-in ASP.NET Development Server and can be accessed only by web browsers running on the same computer. You can later "publish" your website to a production web server for access via a local network or the Internet. Each example in this chapter uses the **File System** option, so select it now.

- **HTTP:** Creates a new website on an IIS web server and uses HTTP to allow you to put your website's files on the server. IIS is Microsoft's software that is used to run production websites. If you own a website and have your own web server, you might use this to build a new website directly on that server computer. You must be an Administrator on the computer running IIS to use this option.

- **FTP:** Uses File Transfer Protocol (FTP) to allow you to put your website's files on the server. The server administrator must first create the website on the server for you. FTP is commonly used by so-called "hosting providers" to allow website owners to share a server computer that runs many websites.

Change the name of the web application from WebSite1 to WebTime, then click **OK** to create the website.

Step 2: Adding a Web Form to the Website and Examining the Solution Explorer
A **Web Form** represents one page in a web application—we'll often use the terms "page" and "Web Form" interchangeably. A Web Form contains a web application's GUI. To create the WebTime.aspx Web Form:

1. Right click the project name in the **Solution Explorer** and select **Add New Item...** to display the **Add New Item** dialog (Fig. 19.8).

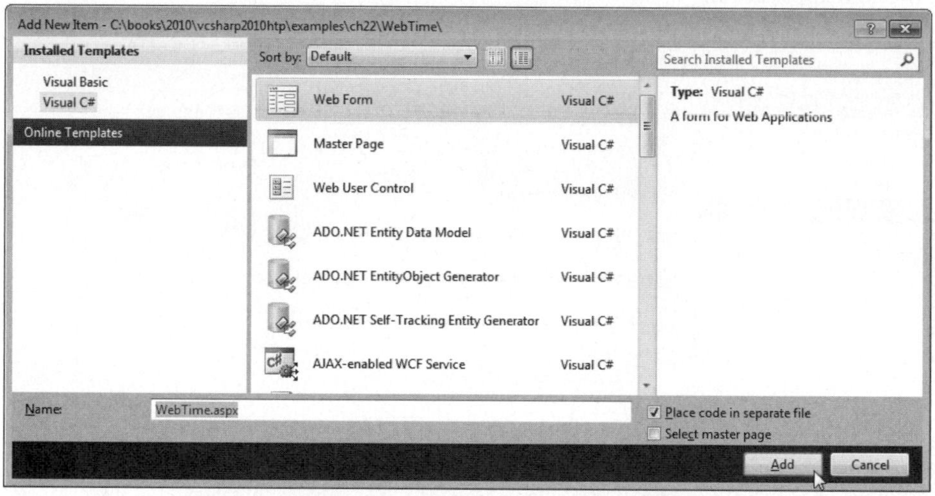

Fig. 19.8 | Adding a new **Web Form** to the website with the **Add New Item** dialog.

2. In the left column, ensure that **Visual C#** is selected, then select **Web Form** in the middle column.

3. In the **Name:** TextBox, change the file name to WebTime.aspx, then click the **Add** Button.

After you add the Web Form, the IDE opens it in **Source** view by default (Fig. 19.9). This view displays the markup for the Web Form. As you become more familiar with ASP.NET and building web sites in general, you might use **Source** view to perform high precision adjustments to your design or to program in the JavaScript language that executes in web browsers. For the purposes of this chapter, we'll keep things simple by working exclusively in **Design** mode. To switch to **Design** mode, you can click the **Design** Button at the bottom of the code editor window.

The Solution Explorer
The **Solution Explorer** (Fig. 19.10) shows the contents of the website. We expanded the node for WebTime.aspx to show you its code-behind file WebTime.aspx.cs. Visual Web Developer's **Solution Explorer** contains several buttons that differ from Visual C# Express. The **Copy Web Site** button opens a dialog that allows you to move the files in this project to another location, such as a remote web server. This is useful if you're developing the application on your local computer but want to make it available to the public from a different location. The **ASP.NET Configuration** button takes you to a web page called the **Web Site Administra-**

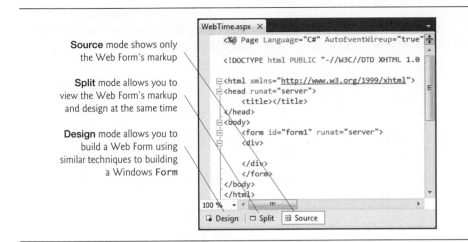

Source mode shows only the Web Form's markup

Split mode allows you to view the Web Form's markup and design at the same time

Design mode allows you to build a Web Form using similar techniques to building a Windows Form

Fig. 19.9 | Web Form in **Source** view.

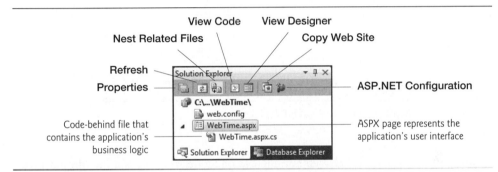

View Code   View Designer

Nest Related Files   Copy Web Site

Refresh

Properties   ASP.NET Configuration

Code-behind file that contains the application's business logic

ASPX page represents the application's user interface

Fig. 19.10 | **Solution Explorer** window for an **Empty Web Site** project after adding the Web Form WebTime.aspx.

tion Tool, where you can manipulate various settings and security options for your application. The **Nest Related Files** button organizes each Web Form and its code-behind file.

If the ASPX file is not open in the IDE, you can open it in **Design** mode three ways:

- double click it in the **Solution Explorer** then select the **Design** tab
- select it in the **Solution Explorer** and click the **View Designer** () Button
- right click it in the **Solution Explorer** and select **View Designer**

To open the code-behind file in the code editor, you can

- double click it in the **Solution Explorer**
- select the ASPX file in the **Solution Explorer**, then click the **View Code** (⊡) Button
- right click the code-behind file in the **Solution Explorer** and select **Open**

The Toolbox
Figure 19.11 shows the **Toolbox** displayed in the IDE when the project loads. Part (a) displays the beginning of the **Standard** list of web controls, and part (b) displays the remain-

ing web controls and the list of other control groups. We discuss specific controls listed in Fig. 19.11 as they're used throughout the chapter. Many of the controls have similar or identical names to Windows Forms controls presented earlier in the book.

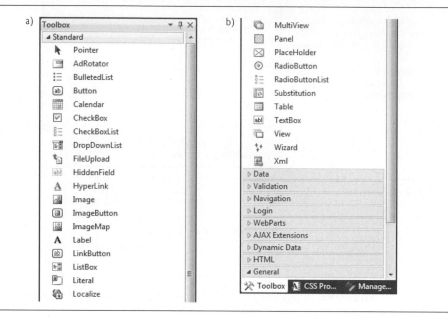

Fig. 19.11 | **Toolbox** in Visual Web Developer.

The Web Forms Designer

Figure 19.12 shows the initial Web Form in **Design** mode. You can drag and drop controls from the **Toolbox** onto the Web Form. You can also type at the current cursor location to add so-called static text to the web page. In response to such actions, the IDE generates the appropriate markup in the ASPX file.

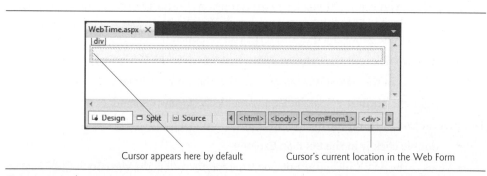

Fig. 19.12 | **Design** mode of the Web Forms Designer.

Step 3: Changing the Title of the Page

Before designing the Web Form's content, you'll change its title to A Simple Web Form Example. This title will be displayed in the web browser's title bar (see Fig. 19.4). It's typically also used by search engines like Google and Bing when they index real websites for searching. Every page should have a title. To change the title:

1. Ensure that the ASPX file is open in **Design** view.

2. View the Web Form's properties by selecting **DOCUMENT**, which represents the Web Form, from the drop-down list in the **Properties** window.

3. Modify the **Title** property in the **Properties** window by setting it to A Simple Web Form Example.

Designing a Page

Designing a Web Form is similar to designing a Windows Form. To add controls to the page, drag-and-drop them from the **Toolbox** onto the Web Form in **Design** view. The Web Form and each control are objects that have properties, methods and events. You can set these properties visually using the **Properties** window or programmatically in the code-behind file. You can also type text directly on a Web Form at the cursor location.

Controls and other elements are placed sequentially on a Web Form one after another in the order in which you drag-and-drop them onto the Web Form. The cursor indicates the insertion point in the page. If you want to position a control between existing text or controls, you can drop the control at a specific position between existing page elements. You can also rearrange controls with drag-and-drop actions in **Design** view. The positions of controls and other elements are relative to the Web Form's upper-left corner. This type of layout is known as relative positioning and it allows the browser to move elements and resize them based on the size of the browser window. Relative positioning is the default, and we'll use it throughout this chapter.

For precise control over the location and size of elements, you can use absolute positioning in which controls are located exactly where you drop them on the Web Form. If you wish to use absolute positioning:

1. Select **Tools > Options....**, to display the **Options** dialog.

2. If it isn't checked already, check the **Show all settings** checkbox.

3. Next, expand the **HTML Designer > CSS Styling** node and ensure that the checkbox labeled **Change positioning to absolute for controls added using Toolbox, paste or drag and drop** is selected.

Step 4: Adding Text and a **Label**

You'll now add some text and a **Label** to the Web Form. Perform the following steps to add the text:

1. Ensure that the Web Form is open in **Design** mode.

2. Type the following text at the current cursor location:

   Current time on the Web server:

3. Select the text you just typed, then select **Heading 2** from the **Block Format** Combo-Box (Fig. 19.13) to format this text as a heading that will appear in a larger bold font. In more complex pages, headings help you specify the relative importance of parts of that content—like sections in a book chapter.

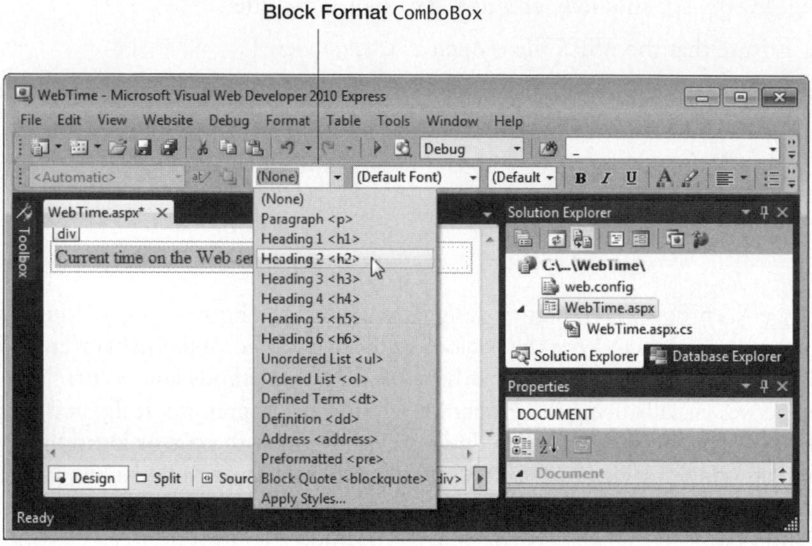

Block Format ComboBox

Fig. 19.13 | Changing the text to **Heading 2** heading.

4. Click to the right of the text you just typed and press the *Enter* key to start a new paragraph in the page. The Web Form should now appear as in Fig. 19.14.

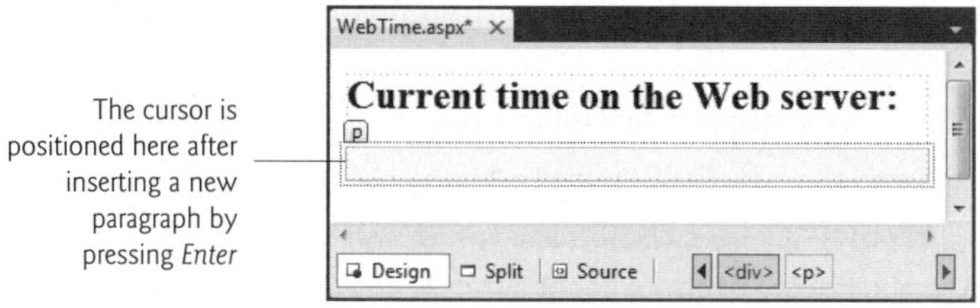

The cursor is positioned here after inserting a new paragraph by pressing *Enter*

Fig. 19.14 | WebTime.aspx after inserting text and a new paragraph.

5. Next, drag a Label control from the **Toolbox** into the new paragraph or double click the Label control in the **Toolbox** to insert the Label at the current cursor position.

6. Using the **Properties** window, set the Label's (ID) property to timeLabel. This specifies the variable name that will be used to programmatically change the Label's Text.

7. Because, the Label's Text will be set programmatically, delete the current value of the Label's Text property. When a Label does not contain text, its name is displayed in square brackets in **Design** view (Fig. 19.15) as a placeholder for design and layout purposes. This text is not displayed at execution time.

Label control ——————

Fig. 19.15 | `WebTime.aspx` after adding a `Label`.

Step 5: Formatting the Label

Formatting in a web page is performed with CSS (Cascading Style Sheets). The details of CSS are beyond the scope of this book. However, it's easy to use CSS to format text and elements in a Web Form via the tools built into Visual Web Developer. In this example, we'd like to change the `Label`'s background color to black, its foreground color yellow and make its text size larger. To format the `Label`, perform the following steps:

1. Click the `Label` in **Design** view to ensure that it's selected.

2. Select **View > Other Windows > CSS Properties** to display the **CSS Properties** window at the left side of the IDE (Fig. 19.16).

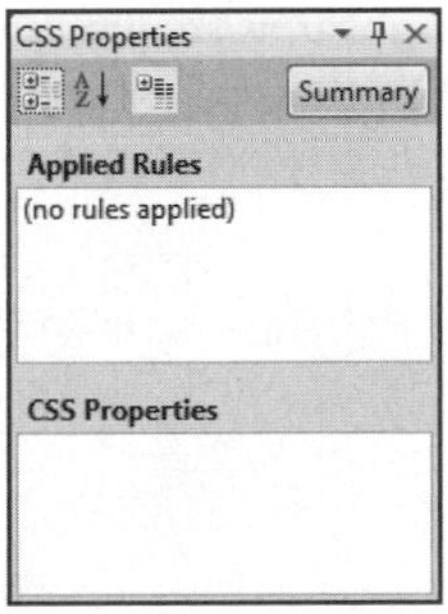

Fig. 19.16 | **CSS Properties** window.

3. Right click in the **Applied Rules** box and select **New Style...** to display the **New Style** dialog (Fig. 19.17).

4. Type the new style's name—`.timeStyle`—in the **Selector:** ComboBox. Styles that apply to specific elements must be named with a dot (.) preceding the name. Such a style is called a CSS class.

5. Each item you can set in the **New Style** dialog is known as a CSS attribute. To change `timeLabel`'s foreground color, select the **Font** category from the **Category** list, then select the yellow color swatch for the **color** attribute.

6. Next, change the **font-size** attribute to `xx-large`.

7. To change `timeLabel`'s background color, select the **Background** category, then select the black color swatch for the **background-color** attribute.

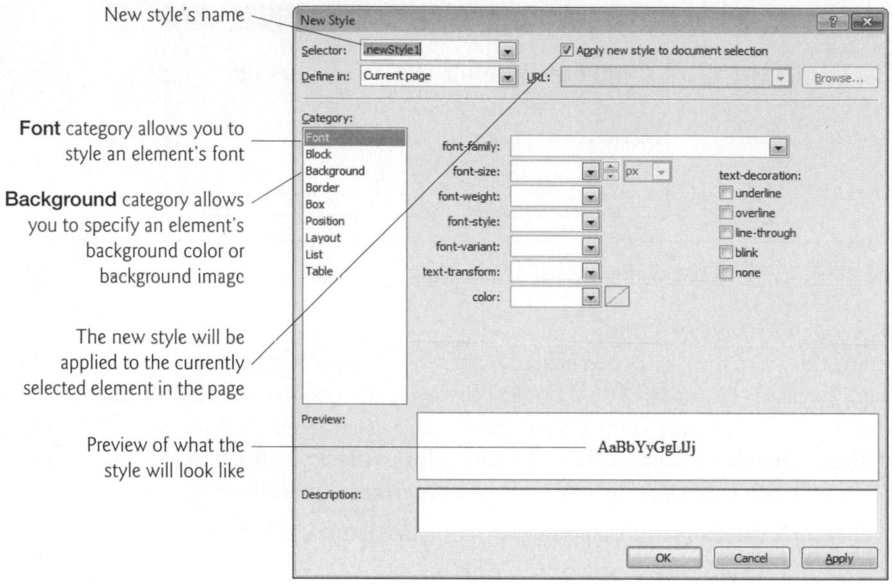
New style's name
Font category allows you to style an element's font
Background category allows you to specify an element's background color or background image
The new style will be applied to the currently selected element in the page
Preview of what the style will look like
New Style
Selector: .newStyle1
Apply new style to document selection
Define in: Current page
URL:
Browse...
Category:
Font
Block
Background
Border
Box
Position
Layout
List
Table
font-family:
font-size:
px
font-weight:
font-style:
font-variant:
text-transform:
color:
text-decoration:
underline
overline
line-through
blink
none
Preview:
AaBbYyGgLlJj
Description:
OK
Cancel
Apply

Fig. 19.17 | **New Style** dialog.

The **New Style** dialog should now appear as shown in (Fig. 19.18). Click the **OK** `Button` to apply the style to the `timeLabel` so that it appears as shown in Fig. 19.19. Also, notice that the `Label`'s `CssClass` property is now set to `timeStyle` in the **Properties** window.

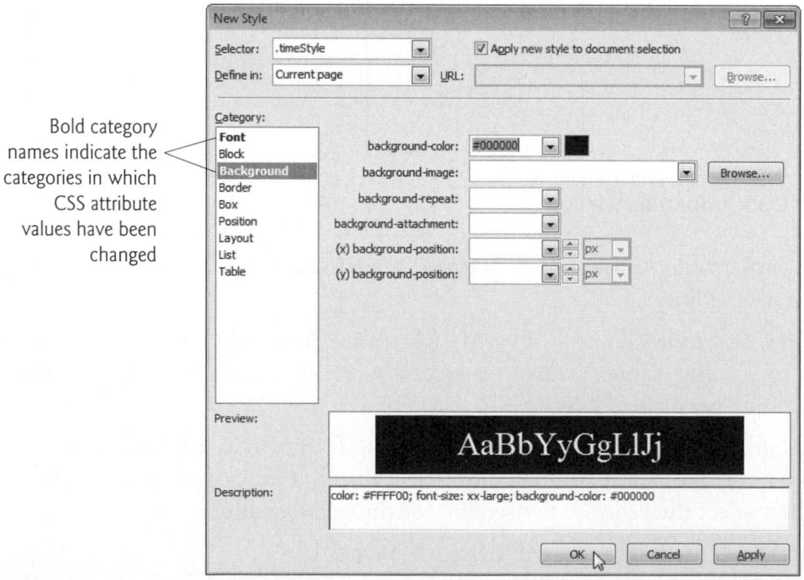
Bold category names indicate the categories in which CSS attribute values have been changed
New Style
Selector: .timeStyle
Apply new style to document selection
Define in: Current page
URL:
Browse...
Category:
Font
Block
Background
Border
Box
Position
Layout
List
Table
background-color: #000000
background-image:
Browse...
background-repeat:
background-attachment:
(x) background-position:
px
(y) background-position:
px
Preview:
AaBbYyGgLlJj
Description:
color: #FFFF00; font-size: xx-large; background-color: #000000
OK
Cancel
Apply

Fig. 19.18 | **New Style** dialog after changing the Label's style.

Fig. 19.19 | **Design** view after changing the Label's style.

Step 6: Adding Page Logic

Now that you've designed the GUI, you'll write code in the code-behind file to obtain the server's time and display it on the Label. Open WebTime.aspx.cs by double clicking it in the **Solution Explorer**. In this example, you'll add an event handler to the code-behind file to handle the Web Form's **Init event**, which occurs when the page is requested by a web browser. The event handler for this event—named **Page_Init**—initialize the page. The only initialization required for this example is to set the timeLabel's Text property to the time on the web server computer. The code-behind file initally contains a Page_Load event handler. To create the Page_Init event handler, simply rename Page_Load as Page_Init. Then complete the event handler by inserting the following code in its body:

```
// display the server's current time in timeLabel
timeLabel.Text = DateTime.Now.ToString("hh:mm:ss");
```

Step 7: Setting the Start Page and Running the Program

To ensure that WebTime.aspx loads when you execute this application, right click it in the **Solution Explorer** and select **Set As Start Page**. You can now run the program in one of several ways. At the beginning of Fig. 19.4, you learned how to view the Web Form by typing *Ctrl + F5*. You can also right click an ASPX file in the **Solution Explorer** and select **View in Browser**. Both of these techniques execute the ASP.NET Development Server, open your default web browser and load the page into the browser, thus running the web application. The development server stops when you exit Visual Web Developer.

    If problems occur when running your application, you can run it in debug mode by selecting **Debug > Start Debugging**, by clicking the **Start Debugging** Button () or by typing *F5* to view the web page in a web browser with debugging enabled. You cannot debug a web application unless debugging is explicitly enabled in the application's **Web.config** file—a file that is generated when you create an ASP.NET web application. This file stores the application's configuration settings. You'll rarely need to manually modify Web.config. The first time you select **Debug > Start Debugging** in a project, a dialog appears and asks whether you want the IDE to modify the Web.config file to enable debugging. After you click **OK**, the IDE executes the application. You can stop debugging by selecting **Debug > Stop Debugging**.

    Regardless of how you execute the web application, the IDE will compile the project before it executes. In fact, ASP.NET compiles your web page whenever it changes between HTTP requests. For example, suppose you browse the page, then modify the ASPX file or add code to the code-behind file. When you reload the page, ASP.NET recompiles the page on the server before returning the response to the browser. This important behavior ensures that clients always see the latest version of the page. You can manually compile an entire website by selecting **Build Web Site** from the **Debug** menu in Visual Web Developer.

19.4.2 Examining WebTime.aspx's Code-Behind File

Figure 19.20 presents the code-behind file WebTime.aspx.cs. Line 5 begins the declaration of class WebTime. In Visual C#, a class declaration can span multiple source-code files—the separate portions of the class declaration in each file are known as **partial classes**. The **partial modifier** indicates that the code-behind file is part of a larger class. Like Windows Forms applications, the rest of the class's code is generated for you based on your visual interactions to create the application's GUI in **Design** mode. That code is stored in other source code files as partial classes with the same name. The compiler assembles all the partial classes that have the same into a single class declaration.

Line 5 indicates that WebTime inherits from class **Page** in namespace **System.Web.UI**. This namespace contains classes and controls for building web-based applications. Class Page represents the default capabilities of each page in a web application—all pages inherit directly or indirectly from this class.

Lines 8–12 define the Page_Init event handler, which initializes the page in response to the page's Init event. The only initialization required for this page is to set the timeLabel's Text property to the time on the web server computer. The statement in line 11 retrieves the current time (DateTime.Now) and formats it as *hh:mm:ss*. For example, 9 AM is formatted as 09:00:00, and 2:30 PM is formatted as 02:30:00. As you'll see, variable timeLabel represents an ASP.NET Label control. The ASP.NET controls are defined in namespace **System.Web.UI.WebControls**.

```
1   // Fig. 19.20: WebTime.aspx.cs
2   // Code-behind file for a page that displays the web server's time.
3   using System;
4
5   public partial class WebTime : System.Web.UI.Page
6   {
7      // initializes the contents of the page
8      protected void Page_Init( object sender, EventArgs e )
9      {
10        // display the server's current time in timeLabel
11        timeLabel.Text = DateTime.Now.ToString( "hh:mm:ss" );
12     } // end method Page_Init
13  } // end class WebTime
```

Fig. 19.20 | Code-behind file for a page that displays the web server's time.

19.5 Standard Web Controls: Designing a Form

This section introduces some of the web controls located in the **Standard** section of the **Toolbox** (Fig. 19.11). Figure 19.21 summarizes the controls used in the next example.

A Form Gathering User Input
Figure 19.22 depicts a form for gathering user input. This example does not perform any tasks—that is, no action occurs when the user clicks **Register**. As an exercise, you could

Web control	Description
TextBox	Gathers user input and displays text.
Button	Triggers an event when clicked.
HyperLink	Displays a hyperlink.
DropDownList	Displays a drop-down list of choices from which a user can select an item.
RadioButtonList	Groups radio buttons.
Image	Displays images (for example, PNG, GIF and JPG).

Fig. 19.21 | Commonly used web controls.

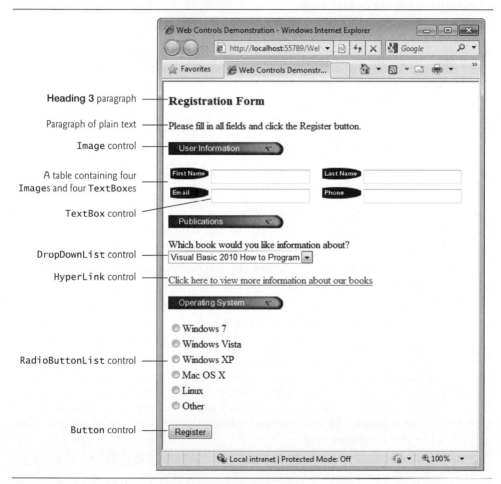

Fig. 19.22 | Web Form that demonstrates web controls.

provide the functionality. Here we focus on the steps for adding these controls to a Web Form and for setting their properties. Subsequent examples demonstrate how to handle the events of many of these controls. To execute this application:

1. Select **Open Web Site...** from the **File** menu.

2. In the **Open Web Site** dialog, ensure that **File System** is selected, then navigate to this chapter's examples, select the `WebControls` folder and click the **Open** Button.

3. Select `WebControls.aspx` in the **Solution Explorer**, then type *Ctrl + F5* to execute the web application in your default web browser.

Creating the Web Site

To begin, follow the steps in Section 19.4.1 to create an **Empty Web Site** named `WebControls`, then add a Web Form named `WebControls.aspx` to the project. Set the document's `Title` property to `"Web Controls Demonstration"`. To ensure that `WebControls.aspx` loads when you execute this application, right click it in the **Solution Explorer** and select **Set As Start Page**.

Adding the Images to the Project

The images used in this example are located in the `images` folder with this chapter's examples. Before you can display images in the Web Form, they must be added to your project. To add the `images` folder to your project:

1. Open Windows Explorer.

2. Locate and open this chapter's examples folder (`ch22`).

3. Drag the `images` folder from Windows Explorer into Visual Web Developer's **Solution Explorer** window and drop the folder on the name of your project.

The IDE will automatically copy the folder and its contents into your project.

Adding Text and an Image to the Form

Next, you'll begin creating the page. Perform the following steps:

1. First create the page's heading. At the current cursor position on the page, type the text `"Registration Form"`, then use the **Block Format** ComboBox in the IDE's toolbar to change the text to **Heading 3** format.

2. Press *Enter* to start a new paragraph, then type the text `"Please fill in all fields and click the Register button"`.

3. Press *Enter* to start a new paragraph, then double click the **Image** control in the **Toolbox**. This control inserts an image into a web page, at the current cursor position. Set the Image's (ID) property to `userInformationImage`. The **ImageUrl** property specifies the location of the image to display. In the **Properties** window, click the ellipsis for the `ImageUrl` property to display the **Select Image** dialog. Select the `images` folder under **Project folders:** to display the list of images. Then select the image `user.png`.

4. Click **OK** to display the image in **Design** view, then click to the right of the Image and press *Enter* to start a new paragraph.

Adding a Table to the Form

Form elements are often placed in tables for layout purposes—like the elements that represent the first name, last name, e-mail and phone information in Fig. 19.22. Next, you'll create a table with two rows and two columns in **Design** mode.

1. Select **Table > Insert Table** to display the **Insert Table** dialog (Fig. 19.23). This dialog allows you to configure the table's options.

2. Under **Size**, ensure that the values of **Rows** and **Columns** are both 2—these are the default values.

3. Click **OK** to close the **Insert Table** dialog and create the table.

By default, the contents of a table cell are aligned vertically in the middle of the cell. We changed the vertical alignment of all cells in the table by setting the `valign` property to `top` in the **Properties** window. This causes the content in each table cell to align with the top of the cell. You can set the `valign` property for each table cell individually or by selecting all the cells in the table at once, then changing the `valign` property's value.

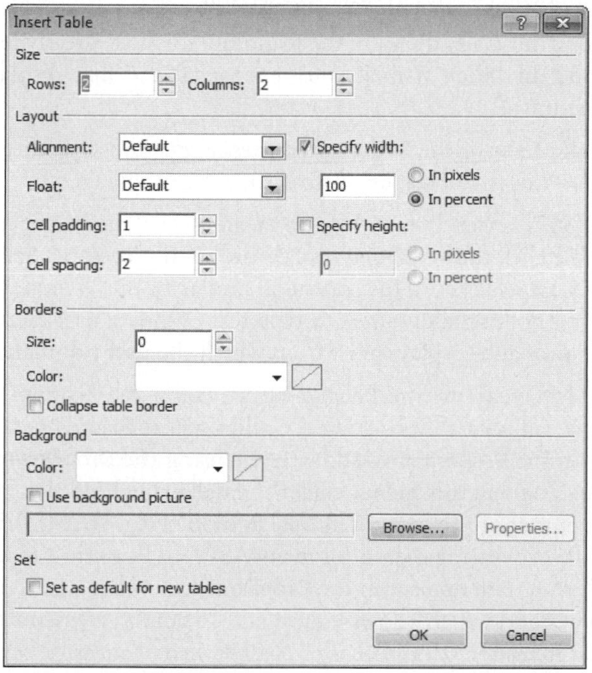

Fig. 19.23 | **Insert Table** dialog.

After creating the table, controls and text can be added to particular cells to create a neatly organized layout. Next, add `Image` and `TextBox` controls to each the four table cells as follows:

1. Click the table cell in the first row and first column of the table, then double click the `Image` control in the **Toolbox**. Set its (ID) property to `firstNameImage` and set its `ImageUrl` property to the image `fname.png`.

2. Next, double click the `TextBox` control in the **Toolbox**. Set its (ID) property to `firstNameTextBox`. As in Windows Forms, a **TextBox** control allows you to obtain text from the user and display text to the user

3. Repeat this process in the first row and second column, but set the Image's (ID) property to lastNameImage and its ImageUrl property to the image lname.png, and set the TextBox's (ID) property to lastNameTextBox.

4. Repeat *Steps 1* and *2* in the second row and first column, but set the Image's (ID) property to emailImage and its ImageUrl property to the image email.png, and set the TextBox's (ID) property to emailTextBox.

5. Repeat *Steps 1* and *2* in the second row and second column, but set the Image's (ID) property to phoneImage and its ImageUrl property to the image phone.png, and set the TextBox's (ID) property to phoneTextBox.

Creating the Publications Section of the Page

This section contains an Image, some text, a DropDownList control and a HyperLink control. Perform the following steps to create this section:

1. Click below the table, then use the techniques you've already learned in this section to add an Image named publicationsImage that displays the publications.png image.

2. Click to the right of the Image, then press *Enter* and type the text "Which book would you like information about?" in the new paragraph.

3. Hold the *Shift* key and press *Enter* to create a new line in the current paragraph, then double click the **DropDownList** control in the **Toolbox**. Set its (ID) property to booksDropDownList. This control is similar to the Windows Forms ComboBox control, but doesn't allow users to type text. When a user clicks the drop-down list, it expands and displays a list from which the user can make a selection.

4. You can add items to the DropDownList using the **ListItem Collection Editor**, which you can access by clicking the ellipsis next to the DropDownList's Items property in the **Properties** window, or by using the **DropDownList Tasks** smart-tag menu. To open this menu, click the small arrowhead that appears in the upper-right corner of the control in **Design** mode (Fig. 19.24). Visual Web Developer displays smart-tag menus for many ASP.NET controls to facilitate common tasks. Clicking **Edit Items...** in the **DropDownList Tasks** menu opens the **ListItem Collection Editor**, which allows you to add ListItem elements to the DropDownList. Add items for "Visual Basic 2010 How to Program", "Visual C# 2010 How to Program", "Java How to Program" and "C++ How to Program" by clicking the **Add** Button four times. For each item, select it, then set its Text property to one of the four book titles.

5. Click to the right of the DropDownList and press *Enter* to start a new paragraph, then double click the **HyperLink** control in the **Toolbox** to add a hyperlink to the

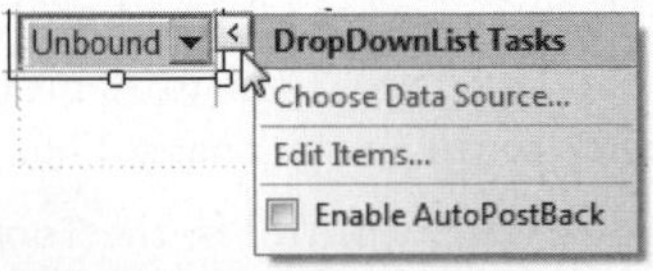

Fig. 19.24 | **DropDownList Tasks** smart-tag menu.

web page. Set its (ID) property to booksHyperLink and its Text property to "Click here to view more information about our books". Set the **NavigateUrl** property to http://www.deitel.com. This specifies the resource or web page that will be requested when the user clicks the HyperLink. Setting the **Target** property to _blank specifies that the requested web page should open in a new browser window. By default, HyperLink controls cause pages to open in the same browser window.

Completing the Page

Next you'll create the **Operating System** section of the page and the **Register** Button. This section contains a **RadioButtonList** control, which provides a series of radio buttons from which the user can select only one. The **RadioButtonList Tasks** smart-tag menu provides an **Edit Items...** link to open the **ListItem Collection Editor** so that you can create the items in the list. Perform the following steps:

1. Click to the right of the HyperLink control and press *Enter* to create a new paragraph, then add an Image named osImage that displays the os.png image.

2. Click to the right of the Image and press *Enter* to create a new paragraph, then add a RadioButtonList. Set its (ID) property to osRadioButtonList. Use the **ListItem Collection Editor** to add the items shown in Fig. 19.22.

3. Finally, click to the right of the RadioButtonList and press *Enter* to create a new paragraph, then add a **Button**. A Button web control represents a button that triggers an action when clicked. Set its (ID) property to registerButton and its Text property to Register. As stated earlier, clicking the **Register** button in this example does not do anything.

You can now execute the application (*Ctrl* + *F5*) to see the Web Form in your browser.

19.6 Validation Controls

This section introduces a different type of web control, called a **validation control** or **validator**, which determines whether the data in another web control is in the proper format. For example, validators can determine whether a user has provided information in a required field or whether a zip-code field contains exactly five digits. Validators provide a mechanism for validating user input on the client. When the page is sent to the client, the validator is converted into JavaScript that performs the validation in the client web browser. JavaScript is a scripting language that enhances the functionality of web pages and is typically executed on the client. Unfortunately, some client browsers might not support scripting or the user might disable it. For this reason, you should always perform validation on the server. ASP.NET validation controls can function on the client, on the server or both.

Validating Input in a Web Form

The Web Form in Fig. 19.25 prompts the user to enter a name, e-mail address and phone number. A website could use a form like this to collect contact information from visitors. After the user enters any data, but before the data is sent to the web server, validators ensure that the user *entered a value in each field* and that the e-mail address and phone-number values are in an acceptable format. In this example, (555) 123-4567, 555-123-4567 and 123-4567 are all considered valid phone numbers. Once the data is submitted, the web server responds by displaying a message that repeats the submitted information. A real business application would typically store the submitted data in a database or in a file on the server. We simply send the data back to the client to demonstrate that the server received the data. To execute this application:

1. Select **Open Web Site…** from the **File** menu.

2. In the **Open Web Site** dialog, ensure that **File System** is selected, then navigate to this chapter's examples, select the `Validation` folder and click the **Open Button**.

3. Select `Validation.aspx` in the **Solution Explorer**, then type *Ctrl + F5* to execute the web application in your default web browser.

a) Initial Web Form

b) Web Form after the user presses the **Submit Button** without having entered any data in the **TextBox**es; each **TextBox** is followed by an error message that was displayed by a validation control

`RequiredFieldValidator` controls

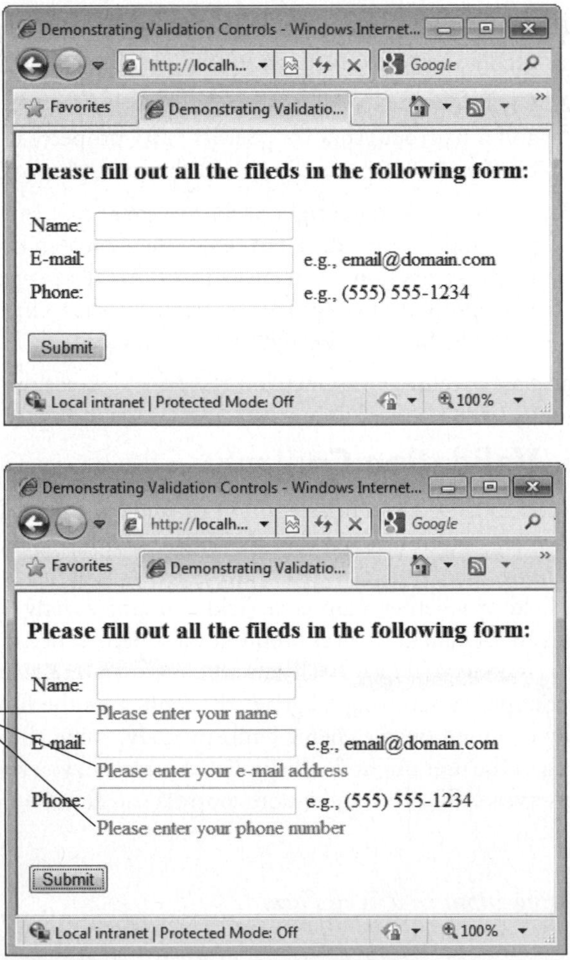

Fig. 19.25 | Validators in a Web Form that retrieves user contact information. (Part 1 of 2.)

c) Web Form after the user enters a name, an invalid e-mail address and an invalid phone number in the TextBoxes, then presses the **Submit** Button; the validation controls display error messages in response to the invalid e-mail and phone number values

RegularExpressionValidator controls

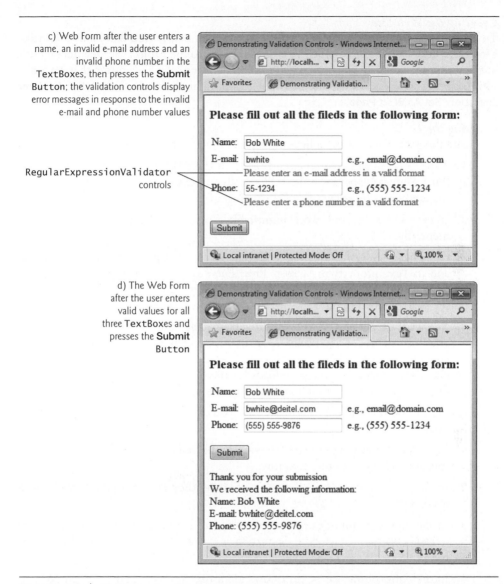

d) The Web Form after the user enters valid values for all three TextBoxes and presses the **Submit** Button

Fig. 19.25 | Validators in a Web Form that retrieves user contact information. (Part 2 of 2.)

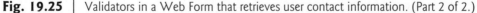

In the sample output:

- Fig. 19.25(a) shows the initial Web Form
- Fig. 19.25(b) shows the result of submitting the form before typing any data in the TextBoxes
- Fig. 19.25(c) shows the results after entering data in each TextBox, but specifying an invalid e-mail address and invalid phone number
- Fig. 19.25(d) shows the results after entering valid values for all three TextBoxes and submitting the form.

Creating the Web Site

To begin, follow the steps in Section 19.4.1 to create an **Empty Web Site** named Valida-tion, then add a Web Form named Validation.aspx to the project. Set the document's Title property to "Demonstrating Validation Controls". To ensure that Valida-tion.aspx loads when you execute this application, right click it in the **Solution Explorer** and select **Set As Start Page**.

Creating the GUI

To create the page, perform the following steps:

1. Type "Please fill out all the fields in the following form:", then use the **Block Format** ComboBox in the IDE's toolbar to change the text to **Heading 3** for-mat and press *Enter* to create a new paragraph.

2. Insert a three row and two column table. You'll add elements to the table mo-mentarily.

3. Click below the table and add a Button. Set its (ID) property to submitButton and its Text property to Submit. Press *Enter* to create a new paragraph. By de-fault, a Button control in a Web Form sends the contents of the form back to the server for processing.

4. Add a Label. Set its (ID) property to outputLabel and clear its Text property—you'll set it programmatically when the user clicks the submitButton. Set the outputLabel's **Visible** property to false, so the Label does not appear in the client's browser when the page loads for the first time. You'll programmatically display this Label after the user submits valid data.

Next you'll add text and controls to the table you created in *Step 2* above. Perform the following steps:

1. In the left column, type the text "Name:" in the first row, "E-mail:" in the second row and "Phone:" in the third row.

2. In the right column of the first row, add a TextBox and set its (ID) property to nameTextBox.

3. In the right column of the second row, add a TextBox and set its (ID) property to emailTextBox. Then type the text "e.g., email@domain.com" to the right of the TextBox.

4. In the right column of the third row, add a TextBox and set its (ID) property to phoneTextBox. Then type the text "e.g., (555) 555-1234" to the right of the TextBox.

Using RequiredFieldValidator Controls

We use three **RequiredFieldValidator** controls (found in the **Validation** section of the **Toolbox**) to ensure that the name, e-mail address and phone number TextBoxes are not empty when the form is submitted. A RequiredFieldValidator makes an input control a required field. If such a field is empty, validation fails. Add a RequiredFieldValidator as follows:

1. Click to the right of the nameTextBox in the table and press *Enter* to move to the next line.

2. Add a `RequiredFieldValidator`, set its `(ID)` to `nameRequiredFieldValidator` and set the `ForeColor` property to Red.

3. Set the validator's **ControlToValidate** property to `nameTextBox` to indicate that this validator verifies the `nameTextBox`'s contents.

4. Set the validator's **ErrorMessage** property to "`Please enter your name`". This is displayed on the Web Form only if the validation fails.

5. Set the validator's **Display** property to `Dynamic`, so the validator occupies space on the Web Form only when validation fails. When this occurs, space is allocated dynamically, causing the controls below the validator to shift downward to accommodate the `ErrorMessage`, as seen in Fig. 19.25(a)–(c).

Repeat these steps to add two more `RequiredFieldValidator`s in the second and third rows of the table. Set their `(ID)` properties to `emailRequiredFieldValidator` and `phoneRequiredFieldValidator`, respectively, and set their `ErrorMessage` properties to "`Please enter your email address`" and "`Please enter your phone number`", respectively.

Using *RegularExpressionValidator Controls*

This example also uses two **RegularExpressionValidator** controls to ensure that the e-mail address and phone number entered by the user are in a valid format. Visual Web Developer provides several *predefined* regular expressions that you can simply select to take advantage of this powerful validation control. Add a `RegularExpressionValidator` as follows:

1. Click to the right of the `emailRequiredFieldValidator` in the second row of the table and add a `RegularExpressionValidator`, then set its `(ID)` to `emailRegularExpressionValidator` and its `ForeColor` property to Red.

2. Set the `ControlToValidate` property to `emailTextBox` to indicate that this validator verifies the `emailTextBox`'s contents.

3. Set the validator's `ErrorMessage` property to "`Please enter an e-mail address in a valid format`".

4. Set the validator's `Display` property to `Dynamic`, so the validator occupies space on the Web Form only when validation fails.

Repeat the preceding steps to add another `RegularExpressionValidator` in the third row of the table. Set its `(ID)` property to `phoneRegularExpressionValidator` and its `ErrorMessage` property to "`Please enter a phone number in a valid format`", respectively.

A `RegularExpressionValidator`'s **ValidationExpression** property specifies the regular expression that validates the `ControlToValidate`'s contents. Clicking the ellipsis next to property `ValidationExpression` in the **Properties** window displays the **Regular Expression Editor** dialog, which contains a list of **Standard expressions** for phone numbers, zip codes and other formatted information. For the `emailRegularExpressionValidator`, we selected the standard expression **Internet e-mail address**. If the user enters text in the `emailTextBox` that does not have the correct format and either clicks in a different text box or attempts to submit the form, the `ErrorMessage` text is displayed in red.

For the `phoneRegularExpressionValidator`, we selected **U.S. phone number** to ensure that a phone number contains an optional three-digit area code either in parentheses and followed by an optional space or without parentheses and followed by a required hyphen. After an optional area code, a phone number must contain three digits, a hyphen and another four digits. For example, (555) 123-4567, 555-123-4567 and 123-4567 are all valid phone numbers.

Submitting the Web Form's Contents to the Server
If all five validators are successful (that is, each TextBox is filled in, and the e-mail address and phone number provided are valid), clicking the **Submit** button sends the form's data to the server. As shown in Fig. 19.25(d), the server then responds by displaying the submitted data in the outputLabel.

Examining the Code-Behind File for a Web Form That Receives User Input
Figure 19.26 shows the code-behind file for this application. Notice that this code-behind file does not contain any implementation related to the validators. We say more about this soon. In this example, we respond to the page's **Load** event to process the data submitted by the user. Like the Init event, the Load event occurs each time the page loads into a web browser—the difference is that on a postback, you cannot access the posted data in the controls. The event handler for this event is **Page_Load** (lines 8–33). The event handler for the Load event is created for you when you add a new Web Form. To complete the event handler, insert the code from Fig. 19.26.

```
1    // Fig. 19.26: Validation.aspx.cs
2    // Code-behind file for the form demonstrating validation controls.
3    using System;
4
5    public partial class Validation : System.Web.UI.Page
6    {
7       // Page_Load event handler executes when the page is loaded
8       protected void Page_Load( object sender, EventArgs e )
9       {
10         // if this is not the first time the page is loading
11         // (i.e., the user has already submitted form data)
12         if ( IsPostBack )
13         {
14            Validate(); // validate the form
15
16            // if the form is valid
17            if ( IsValid )
18            {
19               // retrieve the values submitted by the user
20               string name = nameTextBox.Text;
21               string email = emailTextBox.Text;
22               string phone = phoneTextBox.Text;
23
24               // show the the submitted values
25               outputLabel.Text = "Thank you for your submission<br/>" +
26                  "We received the following information:<br/>";
27               outputLabel.Text +=
28                  String.Format( "Name: {0}{1}E-mail:{2}{1}Phone:{3}",
29                     name, "<br/>", email, phone );
```

Fig. 19.26 | Code-behind file for the form demonstrating validation controls. (Part 1 of 2.)

```
30                      outputLabel.Visible = true; // display the output message
31              } // end if
32          } // end if
33      } // end method Page_Load
34  } // end class Validation
```

Fig. 19.26 | Code-behind file for the form demonstrating validation controls. (Part 2 of 2.)

Differentiating Between the First Request to a Page and a Postback

Web programmers using ASP.NET often design their web pages so that the current page reloads when the user submits the form; this enables the program to receive input, process it as necessary and display the results in the same page when it's loaded the second time. These pages usually contain a form that, when submitted, sends the values of all the controls to the server and causes the current page to be requested again. This event is known as a **postback**. Line 12 uses the **IsPostBack** property of class Page to determine whether the page is being loaded due to a postback. The first time that the web page is requested, IsPostBack is false, and the page displays only the form for user input. When the postback occurs (from the user clicking **Submit**), IsPostBack is true.

Server-Side Web Form Validation

Server-side Web Form validation must be implemented programmatically. Line 14 calls the current Page's **Validate** method to validate the information in the request. This validates the information as specified by the validation controls in the Web Form. Line 17 uses the **IsValid** property of class Page to check whether the validation succeeded. If this property is set to true (that is, validation succeeded and the Web Form is valid), then we display the Web Form's information. Otherwise, the web page loads without any changes, except any validator that failed now displays its ErrorMessage.

Processing the Data Entered by the User

Lines 20–22 retrieve the values of nameTextBox, emailTextBox and phoneTextBox. When data is posted to the web server, the data that the user entered is accessible to the web application through the web controls' properties. Next, lines 25–29 set outputLabel's Text to display a message that includes the name, e-mail and phone information that was submitted to the server. In lines 25, 26 and 29, notice the use of <br/> rather than \n to start new lines in the outputLabel—
 is the markup for a line break in a web page. Line 30 sets the outputLabel's Visible property to true, so the user can see the thank-you message and submitted data when the page reloads in the client web browser.

19.7 Session Tracking

Originally, critics accused the Internet and e-business of failing to provide the customized service typically experienced in "brick-and-mortar" stores. To address this problem, businesses established mechanisms by which they could *personalize* users' browsing experiences, tailoring content to individual users. Businesses achieve this level of service by tracking each customer's movement through the Internet and combining the collected data with information provided by the consumer, including billing information, personal preferences, interests and hobbies.

Personalization

Personalization makes it possible for businesses to communicate effectively with their customers and also improves users' ability to locate desired products and services. Companies that provide content of particular interest to users can establish relationships with customers and build on those relationships over time. Furthermore, by targeting consumers with personal offers, recommendations, advertisements, promotions and services, businesses create customer loyalty. Websites can use sophisticated technology to allow visitors to customize home pages to suit their individual needs and preferences. Similarly, online shopping sites often store personal information for customers, tailoring notifications and special offers to their interests. Such services encourage customers to visit sites more frequently and make purchases more regularly.

Privacy

A trade-off exists between personalized business service and protection of privacy. Some consumers embrace tailored content, but others fear the possible adverse consequences if the info they provide to businesses is released or collected by tracking technologies. Consumers and privacy advocates ask: What if the business to which we give personal data sells or gives that information to another organization without our knowledge? What if we do not want our actions on the Internet—a supposedly anonymous medium—to be tracked and recorded by unknown parties? What if unauthorized parties gain access to sensitive private data, such as credit-card numbers or medical history? These are questions that must be addressed by programmers, consumers, businesses and lawmakers alike.

Recognizing Clients

To provide personalized services to consumers, businesses must be able to recognize clients when they request information from a site. As we have discussed, the request/response system on which the web operates is facilitated by HTTP. Unfortunately, HTTP is a *stateless protocol*—it *does not* provide information that would enable web servers to maintain state information regarding particular clients. This means that web servers cannot determine whether a request comes from a particular client or whether the same or different clients generate a series of requests.

To circumvent this problem, sites can provide mechanisms by which they identify individual clients. A session represents a unique client on a website. If the client leaves a site and then returns later, the client will still be recognized as the same user. When the user closes the browser, the session typically ends. To help the server distinguish among clients, each client must identify itself to the server. Tracking individual clients is known as **session tracking**. One popular session-tracking technique uses cookies (discussed in Section 19.7.1); another uses ASP.NET's HttpSessionState object (used in Section 19.7.2). Additional session-tracking techniques are beyond this book's scope.

19.7.1 Cookies

Cookies provide you with a tool for personalizing web pages. A cookie is a piece of data stored by web browsers in a small text file on the user's computer. A cookie maintains information about the client during and between browser sessions. The first time a user visits the website, the user's computer might receive a cookie from the server; this cookie is then reactivated each time the user revisits that site. The collected information is intended to be an anonymous record containing data that is used to personalize the user's future visits to the site. For example, cookies in a shopping application might store unique identifiers for users. When a user adds items to an online shopping cart or performs another task resulting in a request to the web server, the server receives a cookie containing the user's unique identifier. The server then uses the unique identifier to locate the shopping cart and perform any necessary processing.

In addition to identifying users, cookies also can indicate users' shopping preferences. When a Web Form receives a request from a client, the Web Form can examine the cookie(s) it sent to the client during previous communications, identify the user's preferences and immediately display products of interest to the client.

Every HTTP-based interaction between a client and a server includes a header containing information either about the request (when the communication is from the client to the server) or about the response (when the communication is from the server to the client). When a Web Form receives a request, the header includes information such as the request type and any cookies that have been sent previously from the server to be stored on the client machine. When the server formulates its response, the header information contains any cookies the server wants to store on the client computer and other information, such as the MIME type of the response.

The **expiration date** of a cookie determines how long the cookie remains on the client's computer. If you do not set an expiration date for a cookie, the web browser maintains the cookie for the duration of the browsing session. Otherwise, the web browser maintains the cookie until the expiration date occurs. Cookies are deleted when they **expire**.

Portability Tip 19.1

Users may disable cookies in their web browsers to help ensure their privacy. Such users will experience difficulty using web applications that depend on cookies to maintain state information.

19.7.2 Session Tracking with `HttpSessionState`

The next web application demonstrates session tracking using the .NET class **Http-SessionState**. When you execute this application, the `Options.aspx` page (Fig. 19.27(a)), which is the application's **Start Page**, allows the user to select a programming language from a group of radio buttons. [Note: You might need to right click `Options.aspx` in the **Solution Explorer** and select **Set As Start Page** before running this application.] When the user clicks **Submit**, the selection is sent to the web server for processing. The web server uses an `HttpSessionState` object to store the chosen language and the ISBN number for one of our books on that topic. Each user that visits the site has a unique `HttpSessionState` object, so the selections made by one user are maintained separately from all other users. After storing the selection, the server returns the page to the browser (Fig. 19.27(b)) and displays the user's selection and some information about the user's unique session (which we show just for demonstration purposes). The page also includes links that allow the user to choose between selecting another programming language or viewing the `Recommenda-tions.aspx` page (Fig. 19.27(e)), which lists recommended books pertaining to the programming language(s) that the user selected previously. If the user clicks the link for book recommendations, the information stored in the user's unique `HttpSessionState` object is read and used to form the list of recommendations. To test this application:

1. Select **Open Web Site...** from the **File** menu.

2. In the **Open Web Site** dialog, ensure that **File System** is selected, then navigate to this chapter's examples, select the Sessions folder and click the **Open** Button.

3. Select Options.aspx in the **Solution Explorer**, then type *Ctrl + F5* to execute the web application in your default web browser.

Creating the Web Site

To begin, follow the steps in Section 19.4.1 to create an **Empty Web Site** named Sessions, then add two Web Forms named Options.aspx and Recommendations.aspx to the project. Set the Options.aspx document's Title property to "Sessions" and the Recommendations.aspx document's Title property to "Book Recommendations". To ensure that Options.aspx is the first page to load for this application, right click it in the **Solution Explorer** and select **Set As Start Page**.

a) User selects a language from the Options.aspx page, then presses **Submit** to send the selection to the server

b) Options.aspx page is updated to hide the controls for selecting a language and to display the user's selection; the user clicks the hyperlink to return to the list of languages and make another selection

Fig. 19.27 | ASPX file that presents a list of programming languages. (Part 1 of 2.)

c) User selects another language from the Options.aspx page, then presses **Submit** to send the selection to the server

d) Options.aspx page is updated to hide the controls for selecting a language and to display the user's selection; the user clicks the hyperlink to get a list of book recommendations

e) Recommendations.aspx displays the list of recommended books based on the user's selections

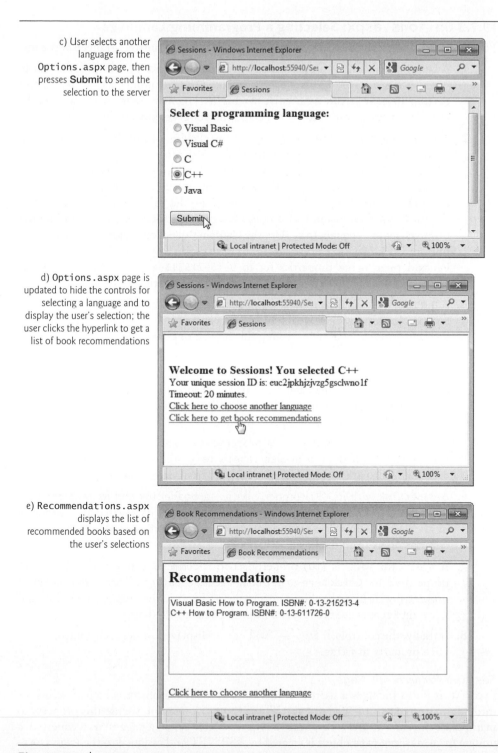

Fig. 19.27 | ASPX file that presents a list of programming languages. (Part 2 of 2.)

19.7.3 `Options.aspx`: Selecting a Programming Language

The `Options.aspx` page Fig. 19.27(a) contains the following controls arranged vertically:

1. A `Label` with its (ID) property set to `promptLabel` and its `Text` property set to `"Select a programming language:"`. We used the techniques shown in *Step 5* of Section 19.4.1 to create a CSS style for this label named `.labelStyle`, and set the style's `font-size` attribute to `large` and the `font-weight` attribute to `bold`.

2. The user selects a programming language by clicking one of the radio buttons in a `RadioButtonList`. Each radio button has a `Text` property and a `Value` property. The `Text` property is displayed next to the radio button and the `Value` property represents a value that is sent to the server when the user selects that radio button and submits the form. In this example, we'll use the `Value` property to represent the ISBN for the recommended book. Create a `RadioButtonList` with its (ID) property set to `languageList`. Use the **ListItem Collection Editor** to add five radio buttons with their `Text` properties set to `Visual Basic`, `Visual C#`, `C`, `C++` and `Java`, and their `Value` properties set to `0-13-215213-4`, `0-13-605322-X`, `0-13-512356-2`, `0-13-611726-0` and `0-13-605306-8`, respectively

3. A `Button` with its (ID) property set to `submitButton` and its `Text` property set to `Submit`. In this example, we'll handle this `Button`'s `Click` event. You can create its event handler by double clicking the `Button` in **Design** view.

4. A `Label` with its (ID) property set to `responseLabel` and its `Text` property set to `"Welcome to Sessions!"`. This `Label` should be placed immediately to the right of the `Button` so that the `Label` appears at the top of the page when we hide the preceding controls on the page. Reuse the CSS style you created in *Step 1* by setting this `Label`'s `CssClass` property to `labelStyle`.

5. Two more `Label`s with their (ID) properties set to `idLabel` and `timeoutLabel`, respectively. Clear the text in each `Label`'s `Text` property—you'll set these programmatically with information about the current user's session.

6. A `HyperLink` with its (ID) property set to `languageLink` and its `Text` property set to `"Click here to choose another language"`. Set its `NavigateUrl` property by clicking the ellipsis next to the property in the **Properties** window and selecting `Options.aspx` from the **Select URL** dialog.

7. A `HyperLink` with its (ID) property set to `recommendationsLink` and its `Text` property set to `"Click here to get book recommendations"`. Set its `NavigateUrl` property by clicking the ellipsis next to the property in the **Properties** window and selecting `Recommendations.aspx` from the **Select URL** dialog.

8. Initially, the controls in *Steps 4–7* will not be displayed, so set each control's `Visible` property to `false`.

Session *Property of a* **Page**

Every Web Form includes a user-specific `HttpSessionState` object, which is accessible through property **Session** of class `Page`. Throughout this section, we use this property to manipulate the current user's `HttpSessionState` object. When a page is first requested, a unique `HttpSessionState` object is created by ASP.NET and assigned to the Page's `Session` property.

Code-Behind File for **Options.aspx**
Fig. 19.28 presents the code-behind file for the Options.aspx page. When this page is requested, the Page_Load event handler (lines 10–40) executes before the response is sent to the client. Since the first request to a page is not a postback, the code in lines 16–39 *does not* execute the first time the page loads.

```
 1    // Fig. 19.28: Options.aspx.cs
 2    // Processes user's selection of a programming language by displaying
 3    // links and writing information in a Session object.
 4    using System;
 5
 6    public partial class Options : System.Web.UI.Page
 7    {
 8       // if postback, hide form and display links to make additional
 9       // selections or view recommendations
10       protected void Page_Load( object sender, EventArgs e )
11       {
12          if ( IsPostBack )
13          {
14             // user has submitted information, so display message
15             // and appropriate hyperlinks
16             responseLabel.Visible = true;
17             idLabel.Visible = true;
18             timeoutLabel.Visible = true;
19             languageLink.Visible = true;
20             recommendationsLink.Visible = true;
21
22             // hide other controls used to make language selection
23             promptLabel.Visible = false;
24             languageList.Visible = false;
25             submitButton.Visible = false;
26
27             // if the user made a selection, display it in responseLabel
28             if ( languageList.SelectedItem != null )
29                responseLabel.Text += " You selected " +
30                   languageList.SelectedItem.Text;
31             else
32                responseLabel.Text += " You did not select a language.";
33
34             // display session ID
35             idLabel.Text = "Your unique session ID is: " + Session.SessionID;
36
37             // display the timeout
38             timeoutLabel.Text = "Timeout: " + Session.Timeout + " minutes.";
39          } // end if
40       } // end method Page_Load
41
42       // record the user's selection in the Session
43       protected void submitButton_Click( object sender, EventArgs e )
44       {
```

Fig. 19.28 | Process user's selection of a programming language by displaying links and writing information in an HttpSessionState object. (Part 1 of 2.)

```
45          // if the user made a selection
46          if ( languageList.SelectedItem != null )
47             // add name/value pair to Session
48             Session.Add( languageList.SelectedItem.Text,
49                languageList.SelectedItem.Value );
50       } // end method submitButton_Click
51   } // end class Options
```

Fig. 19.28 | Process user's selection of a programming language by displaying links and writing information in an HttpSessionState object. (Part 2 of 2.)

Postback Processing

When the user presses **Submit**, a postback occurs. The form is submitted to the server and Page_Load executes. Lines 16–20 display the controls shown in Fig. 19.27(b) and lines 23–25 hide the controls shown in Fig. 19.27(a). Next, lines 28–32 ensure that the user selected a language and, if so, display a message in the responseLabel indicating the selection. Otherwise, the message "You did not select a language" is displayed.

The ASP.NET application contains information about the HttpSessionState object (property Session of the Page object) for the current client. The object's **SessionID** property (displayed in line 35) contains the **unique session ID**—a sequence of random letters and numbers. The first time a client connects to the web server, a unique session ID is created for that client and a temporary cookie is written to the client so the server can identify the client on subsequent requests. When the client makes additional requests, the client's session ID from that temporary cookie is compared with the session IDs stored in the web server's memory to retrieve the client's HttpSessionState object. HttpSessionState property **Timeout** (displayed in line 38) specifies the maximum amount of time that an HttpSessionState object can be inactive before it's discarded. By default, if the user does not interact with this web application for 20 minutes, the HttpSessionState object is discarded by the server and a new one will be created if the user interacts with the application again. Figure 19.29 lists some common HttpSessionState properties.

Properties	Description
Count	Specifies the number of key/value pairs in the Session object.
IsNewSession	Indicates whether this is a new session (that is, whether the session was created during loading of this page).
Keys	Returns a collection containing the Session object's keys.
SessionID	Returns the session's unique ID.
Timeout	Specifies the maximum number of minutes during which a session can be inactive (that is, no requests are made) before the session expires. By default, this property is set to 20 minutes.

Fig. 19.29 | HttpSessionState properties.

Method submitButton_Click

In this example, we wish to store the user's selection in an HttpSessionState object when the user clicks the **Submit** Button. The submitButton_Click event handler (lines 43–50) adds a key/value pair to the HttpSessionState object for the current user, specifying the language chosen and the ISBN number for a book on that language. The HttpSession-State object is a dictionary—a data structure that stores **key/value pairs**. A program uses the key to store and retrieve the associated value in the dictionary. We cover dictionaries in more depth in Chapter 23.

The key/value pairs in an HttpSessionState object are often referred to as **session items**. They're placed in an HttpSessionState object by calling its **Add** method. If the user made a selection (line 46), lines 48–49 get the selection and its corresponding value from the languageList by accessing its SelectedItem's Text and Value properties, respectively, then call HttpSessionState method Add to add this name/value pair as a session item in the HttpSessionState object (Session).

If the application adds a session item that has the same name as an item previously stored in the HttpSessionState object, the session item is replaced—session item names *must* be unique. Another common syntax for placing a session item in the HttpSessionState object is Session[*Name*] = *Value*. For example, we could have replaced lines 48–49 with

```
Session[ languageList.SelectedItem.Text ] =
    languageList.SelectedItem.Value
```

Software Engineering Observation 19.1

A Web Form should not use instance variables to maintain client state information, because each new request or postback is handled by a new instance of the page. Instead, maintain client state information in HttpSessionState objects, because such objects are specific to each client.

Software Engineering Observation 19.2

A benefit of using HttpSessionState objects (rather than cookies) is that they can store any type of object (not just Strings) as attribute values. This provides you with increased flexibility in determining the type of state information to maintain for clients.

19.7.4 Recommendations.aspx: Displaying Recommendations Based on Session Values

After the postback of Options.aspx, the user may request book recommendations. The book-recommendations hyperlink forwards the user to the page Recommendations.aspx (Fig. 19.27(e)) to display the recommendations based on the user's language selections. The page contains the following controls arranged vertically:

1. A Label with its (ID) property set to recommendationsLabel and its Text property set to "Recommendations". We created a CSS style for this label named .label-Style, and set the font-size attribute to x-large and the font-weight attribute to bold. (See *Step 5* in Section 19.4.1 for information on creating a CSS style.)

2. A ListBox with its (ID) property set to booksListBox. We created a CSS style for this label named .listBoxStyle. In the **Position** category, we set the width attribute to 450px and the height attribute to 125px. The px indicates that the measurement is in pixels.

3. A HyperLink with its (ID) property set to languageLink and its Text property set to "Click here to choose another language". Set its NavigateUrl property

by clicking the ellipsis next to the property in the **Properties** window and selecting Options.aspx from the **Select URL** dialog. When the user clicks this link, the Options.aspx page will be reloaded. Requesting the page in this manner *is not* considered a postback, so the original form in Fig. 19.27(a) will be displayed.

Code-Behind File for *Recommendations.aspx*

Figure 19.30 presents the code-behind file for Recommendations.aspx. Event handler Page_Init (lines 8–29) retrieves the session information. If a user has not selected a language in the Options.aspx page, the HttpSessionState object's **Count** property will be 0 (line 11). This property provides the number of session items contained in a HttpSessionState object. If the Count is 0, then we display the text **No Recommendations** (line 22), clear the ListBox and hide it (lines 23–24), and update the Text of the HyperLink back to Options.aspx (line 27).

```
1   // Fig. 19.30: Recommendations.aspx.cs
2   // Creates book recommendations based on a Session object.
3   using System;
4
5   public partial class Recommendations : System.Web.UI.Page
6   {
7      // read Session items and populate ListBox with recommendations
8      protected void Page_Init( object sender, EventArgs e )
9      {
10        // determine whether Session contains any information
11        if ( Session.Count != 0 )
12        {
13           // display Session's name-value pairs
14           foreach ( string keyName in Session.Keys )
15              booksListBox.Items.Add( keyName +
16                 " How to Program. ISBN#: " + Session[ keyName ] );
17        } // end if
18        else
19        {
20           // if there are no session items, no language was chosen, so
21           // display appropriate message and clear and hide booksListBox
22           recommendationsLabel.Text = "No Recommendations";
23           booksListBox.Items.Clear();
24           booksListBox.Visible = false;
25
26           // modify languageLink because no language was selected
27           languageLink.Text = "Click here to choose a language";
28        } // end else
29     } // end method Page_Init
30  } // end class Recommendations
```

Fig. 19.30 | Session data used to provide book recommendations to the user.

If the user chose at least one language, the loop in lines 14–16 iterates through the HttpSessionState object's keys (line 14) by accessing the HttpSessionState's **Keys** property, which returns a collection containing all the keys in the session. Lines 15–16 concatenate the keyName, the String " How to Program. ISBN#: " and the key's corresponding value, which is returned by Session(keyName). This String is the recommendation that is added to the ListBox.

19.8 Case Study: Database-Driven ASP.NET Guestbook

Many websites allow users to provide feedback about the website in a guestbook. Typically, users click a link on the website's home page to request the guestbook page. This page usually consists of a form that contains fields for the user's name, e-mail address, message/feedback and so on. Data submitted on the guestbook form is then stored in a database located on the server.

In this section, we create a guestbook Web Form application. The GUI (Fig. 19.31) contains a **GridView** data control, which displays all the entries in the guestbook in tabular format. This control is located in the **Toolbox**'s **Data** section. We explain how to create and configure this data control shortly. The GridView displays **abc** in **Design** mode to indicate data that will be retrieved from a data source at runtime. You'll learn how to create and configure the GridView shortly.

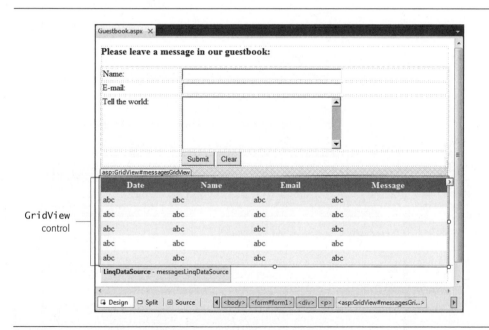

Fig. 19.31 | Guestbook application GUI in **Design** mode.

The Guestbook Database
The application stores the guestbook information in a SQL Server database called Guestbook.mdf located on the web server. (We provide this database in the databases folder with this chapter's examples.) The database contains a single table named Messages.

Testing the Application
To test this application:

    1. Select **Open Web Site...** from the **File** menu.

2. In the **Open Web Site** dialog, ensure that **File System** is selected, then navigate to this chapter's examples, select the Guestbook folder and click the **Open** Button.

3. Select Guestbook.aspx in the **Solution Explorer**, then type *Ctrl* + *F5* to execute the web application in your default web browser.

Figure 19.32(a) shows the user submitting a new entry. Figure 19.32(b) shows the new entry as the last row in the GridView.

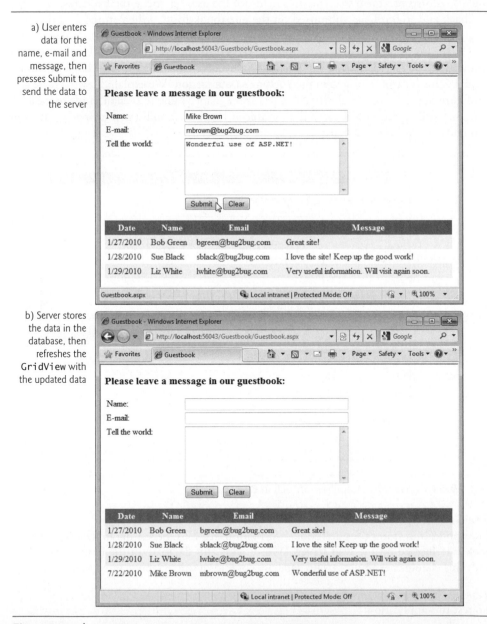

Fig. 19.32 | Sample execution of the **Guestbook** application.

19.8.1 Building a Web Form that Displays Data from a Database

You'll now build this GUI and set up the data binding between the GridView control and the database. Many of these steps are similar to those performed in Chapter 18 to access and interact with a database in a Windows application. We discuss the code-behind file in Section 19.8.2. To build the guestbook application, perform the following steps:

Step 1: Creating the Web Site
To begin, follow the steps in Section 19.4.1 to create an **Empty Web Site** named Guestbook then add a Web Form named Guestbook.aspx to the project. Set the document's Title property to "Guestbook". To ensure that Guestobook.aspx loads when you execute this application, right click it in the **Solution Explorer** and select **Set As Start Page**.

Step 2: Creating the Form for User Input
In **Design** mode, add the text Please leave a message in our guestbook:, then use the **Block Format** ComboBox in the IDE's toolbar to change the text to **Heading 3** format. Insert a table with four rows and two columns, configured so that the text in each cell aligns with the top of the cell. Place the appropriate text (see Fig. 19.31) in the top three cells in the table's left column. Then place TextBoxes named nameTextBox, emailTextBox and messageText-Box in the top three table cells in the right column. Configure the TextBoxes as follows:

- Set the nameTextBox's width to 300px.
- Set the emailTextBox's width to 300px.
- Set the messageTextBox's width to 300px and height to 100px. Also set this control's TextMode property to MultiLine so the user can type a message containing multiple lines of text.

Finally, add Buttons named submitButton and clearButton to the bottom-right table cell. Set the buttons' Text properties to Submit and Clear, respectively. We discuss the buttons' event handlers when we present the code-behind file. You can create these event handlers now by double clicking each Button in **Design** view.

Step 3: Adding a GridView Control to the Web Form
Add a GridView named messagesGridView that will display the guestbook entries. This control appears in the **Data** section of the **Toolbox**. The colors for the GridView are specified through the **Auto Format...** link in the **GridView Tasks** smart-tag menu that opens when you place the GridView on the page. Clicking this link displays an **AutoFormat** dialog with several choices. In this example, we chose **Professional**. We show how to set the GridView's data source (that is, where it gets the data to display in its rows and columns) shortly.

Step 4: Adding a Database to an ASP.NET Web Application
To use a SQL Server Express database file in an ASP.NET web application, you must first add the file to the project's App_Data folder. For security reasons, this folder can be accessed only by the web application on the server—clients cannot access this folder over a network. The web application interacts with the database on behalf of the client.

The **Empty Web Site** template does not create the App_Data folder. To create it, right click the project's name in the **Solution Explorer**, then select **Add ASP.NET Folder > App_Data**. Next, add the Guestbook.mdf file to the App_Data folder. You can do this in one of two ways:

- Drag the file from Windows Explorer and drop it on the App_Data folder.

- Right click the App_Data folder in the **Solution Explorer** and select **Add Existing Item...** to display the **Add Existing Item** dialog, then navigate to the databases folder with this chapter's examples, select the Guestbook.mdf file and click **Add**. [*Note:* Ensure that **Data Files** is selected in the ComboBox above or next to the **Add Button** in the dialog; otherwise, the database file will not be displayed in the list of files.]

Step 5: Creating the LINQ to SQL Classes
As in Chapter 18, you'll use LINQ to interact with the database. To create the LINQ to SQL classes for the Guestbook database:

1. Right click the project in the **Solution Explorer** and select **Add New Item...** to display the **Add New Item** dialog.

2. In the dialog, select **LINQ to SQL Classes**, enter Guestbook.dbml as the **Name**, and click **Add**. A dialog appears asking if you would like to put your new LINQ to SQL classes in the App_Code folder; click **Yes**. The IDE will create an App_Code folder and place the LINQ to SQL classes information in that folder.

3. In the **Database Explorer** window, drag the Guestbook database's Messages table from the **Database Explorer** onto the **Object Relational Designer**. Finally, save your project by selecting **File > Save All**.

Step 6: Binding the GridView to the Messages Table of the Guestbook Database
You can now configure the GridView to display the database's data.

1. In the **GridView Tasks** smart-tag menu, select **<New data source...>** from the **Choose Data Source** ComboBox to display the **Data Source Configuration Wizard** dialog.

2. In this example, we use a **LinqDataSource** control that allows the application to interact with the Guestbook.mdf database through LINQ. Select **LINQ**, then set the ID of the data source to messagesLinqDataSource and click **OK** to begin the **Configure Data Source** wizard.

3. In the **Choose a Context Object** screen, ensure that GuestbookDataContext is selected in the ComboBox, then click **Next >**.

4. The **Configure Data Selection** screen (Fig. 19.33) allows you to specify which data the LinqDataSource should retrieve from the data context. Your choices on this page design a Select LINQ query. The **Table** drop-down list identifies a table in the data context. The Guestbook data context contains one table named Messages, which is selected by default. *If you haven't saved your project* since creating your LINQ to SQL classes (*Step 5*), the list of tables *will not appear*. In the **Select** pane, ensure that the checkbox marked with an asterisk (*) is selected to indicate that you want to retrieve all the columns in the Messages table.

5. Click the **Advanced...** button, then select the **Enable the LinqDataSource to perform automatic inserts** CheckBox and click **OK**. This configures the LinqDataSource control to automatically insert new data into the database when new data is inserted in the data context. We discuss inserting new guestbook entries based on users' form submissions shortly.

6. Click **Finish** to complete the wizard.

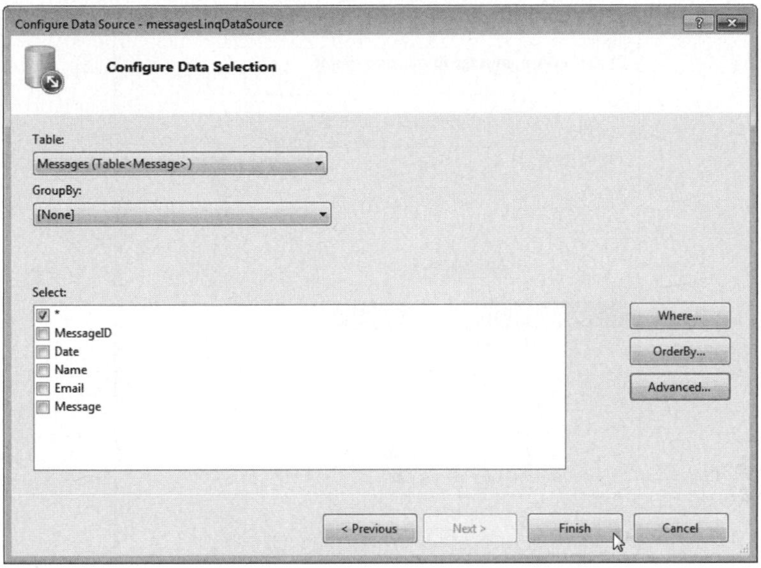

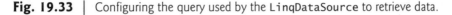

Fig. 19.33 | Configuring the query used by the LinqDataSource to retrieve data.

A control named messagesLinqDataSource now appears on the Web Form directly below the GridView (Fig. 19.34). It's represented in **Design** mode as a gray box containing its type and name. It will *not* appear on the web page—the gray box simply provides a way to manipulate the control visually through **Design** mode—similar to how the objects in the component tray are used in **Design** mode for a Windows Forms application.

The GridView now has column headers that correspond to the columns in the Messages table. The rows each contain either a number (which signifies an autoincremented column) or **abc** (which indicates string data). The actual data from the Guestbook.mdf database file will appear in these rows when you view the ASPX file in a web browser.

Step 7: Modifying the Columns of the Data Source Displayed in the GridView
It's not necessary for site visitors to see the MessageID column when viewing past guestbook entries—this column is merely a unique primary key required by the Messages table within the database. So, let's modify the GridView to prevent this column from displaying on the Web Form. We'll also modify the column **Message1** to read **Message**.

1. In the **GridView Tasks** smart tag menu, click **Edit Columns** to display the **Fields** dialog (Fig. 19.35).

2. Select **MessageID** in the **Selected fields** pane, then click the ☒ Button. This removes the MessageID column from the GridView.

3. Next select **Message1** in the **Selected fields** pane and change its HeaderText property to Message. The IDE renamed this field to prevent a naming conflict in the LINQ to SQL classes.

4. Click **OK** to return to the main IDE window, then set the Width property of the GridView to 650px.

The GridView should now appear as shown in Fig. 19.31.

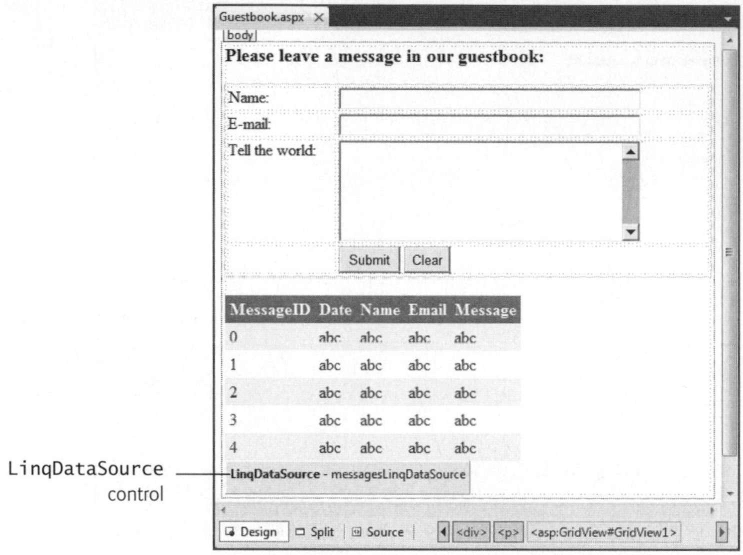

Fig. 19.34 | **Design** mode displaying LinqDataSource control for a GridView.

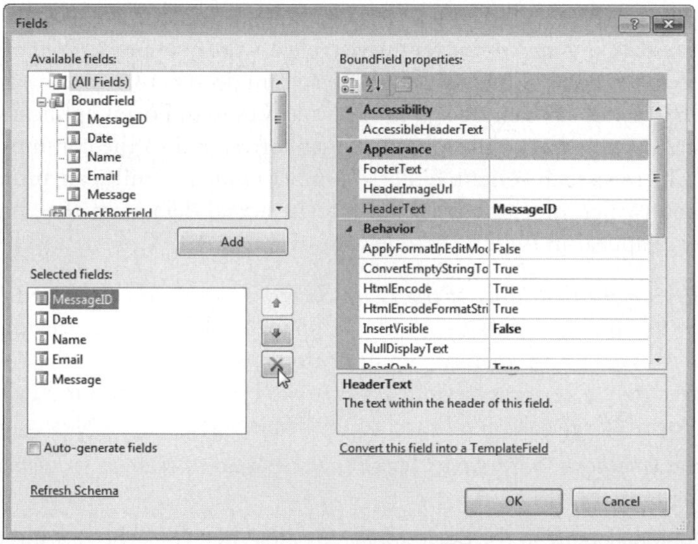

Fig. 19.35 | Removing the MessageID column from the GridView.

19.8.2 Modifying the Code-Behind File for the Guestbook Application

After building the Web Form and configuring the data controls used in this example, double click the **Submit** and **Clear** buttons in **Design** view to create their corresponding Click event handlers in the code-behind file (Fig. 19.36). The IDE generates empty event handlers, so we must add the appropriate code to make these buttons work properly. The event handler for clearButton (lines 37–42) clears each TextBox by setting its Text property to an empty string. This resets the form for a new guestbook submission.

```
 1    // Fig. 19.36: Guestbook.aspx.cs
 2    // Code-behind file that defines event handlers for the guestbook.
 3    using System;
 4    using System.Collections.Specialized; // for class ListDictionary
 5
 6    public partial class Guestbook : System.Web.UI.Page
 7    {
 8       // Submit Button adds a new guestbook entry to the database,
 9       // clears the form and displays the updated list of guestbook entries
10       protected void submitButton_Click( object sender, EventArgs e )
11       {
12          // create dictionary of parameters for inserting
13          ListDictionary insertParameters = new ListDictionary();
14
15          // add current date and the user's name, e-mail address
16          // and message to dictionary of insert parameters
17          insertParameters.Add( "Date", DateTime.Now.ToShortDateString() );
18          insertParameters.Add( "Name", nameTextBox.Text );
19          insertParameters.Add( "Email", emailTextBox.Text );
20          insertParameters.Add( "Message1", messageTextBox.Text );
21
22          // execute an INSERT LINQ statement to add a new entry to the
23          // Messages table in the Guestbook data context that contains the
24          // current date and the user's name, e-mail address and message
25          messagesLinqDataSource.Insert( insertParameters );
26
27          // clear the TextBoxes
28          nameTextBox.Text = String.Empty;
29          emailTextBox.Text = String.Empty;
30          messageTextBox.Text = String.Empty;
31
32          // update the GridView with the new database table contents
33          messagesGridView.DataBind();
34       } // submitButton_Click
35
36       // Clear Button clears the Web Form's TextBoxes
37       protected void clearButton_Click( object sender, EventArgs e )
38       {
39          nameTextBox.Text = String.Empty;
40          emailTextBox.Text = String.Empty;
41          messageTextBox.Text = String.Empty;
42       } // clearButton_Click
43    } // end class Guestbook
```

Fig. 19.36 | Code-behind file for the guestbook application.

Lines 10–34 contain submitButton's event-handling code, which adds the user's information to the Guestbook database's Messages table. To use the values of the TextBoxes on the Web Form as the parameter values inserted into the database, we must create a **ListDictionary** of insert parameters that are key/value pairs.

Line 13 creates a `ListDictionary` object—a set of key/value pairs that is implemented as a linked list and is intended for dictionaries that store 10 or fewer keys. Lines 17–20 use the `ListDictionary`'s `Add` method to store key/value pairs that represent each of the four insert parameters—the current date and the user's name, e-mail address, and message. The keys must match the names of the columns of the `Messages` table in the `.dbml` file. Invoking the `LinqDataSource` method `Insert` (line 25) inserts the data in the data context, adding a row to the `Messages` table and automatically updating the database. We pass the `ListDictionary` object as an argument to the `Insert` method to specify the insert parameters. After the data is inserted into the database, lines 28–30 clear the Text-Boxes, and line 33 invokes `messagesGridView`'s **DataBind method** to refresh the data that the `GridView` displays. This causes `messagesLinqDataSource` (the `GridView`'s source) to execute its `Select` command to obtain the `Messages` table's newly updated data.

19.9 Case Study: ASP.NET AJAX

In Chapter 27, Web App Development with ASP.NET: A Deeper Look, you learn the difference between a traditional web application and an **Ajax (Asynchronous JavaScript and XML) web application**. You also learn how to use **ASP.NET AJAX** to quickly and easily improve the user experience for your web applications, giving them responsiveness comparable to that of desktop applications. To demonstrate ASP.NET AJAX capabilities, you enhance the validation example by displaying the submitted form information without reloading the entire page. The only modifications to this web application appear in `Validation.aspx` file. You use Ajax-enabled controls to add this feature.

19.10 Case Study: Password-Protected Books Database Application

In Chapter 27, we also include a web application case study in which a user logs into a password-protected website to view a list of publications by a selected author. The application consists of several pages and provides website registration and login capabilities. You'll learn about ASP.NET master pages, which allow you to specify a common look-and-feel for all the pages in your app. We also introduce the **Web Site Administration Tool** and use it to configure the portions of the application that can be accessed only by users who are logged into the website.

19.11 Wrap-Up

In this chapter, we introduced web-application development using ASP.NET and Visual Web Developer 2010 Express. We began by discussing the simple HTTP transactions that take place when you request and receive a web page through a web browser. You then learned about the three tiers (that is, the client or top tier, the business logic or middle tier and the information or bottom tier) that comprise most web applications.

Next, we explained the role of ASPX files (that is, Web Form files) and code-behind files, and the relationship between them. We discussed how ASP.NET compiles and executes web applications so that they can be displayed in a web browser. You also learned how to build an ASP.NET web application using Visual Web Developer.

The chapter demonstrated several common ASP.NET web controls used for displaying text and images on a Web Form. We also discussed validation controls, which allow you to ensure that user input on a web page satisfies certain requirements.

We discussed the benefits of maintaining a user's state information across multiple pages of a website. We then demonstrated how you can include such functionality in a web application by using session tracking with `HttpSessionState` objects.

Finally, we built a guestbook application that allows users to submit comments about a website. You learned how to save the user input in a SQL Server database and how to display past submissions on the web page. In Chapter 20, we discuss how to create methods that can order array elements in ascending or descending order, and that can search for values in arrays.

20

Searching and Sorting

OBJECTIVES

In this chapter you'll learn:

- To search for a given value in an array using the linear search and binary search algorithm.

- To sort arrays using the iterative selection and insertion sort algorithms.

- To sort arrays using the recursive merge sort algorithm.

- To determine the efficiency of searching and sorting algorithms.

With sobs and tears
he sorted out
Those of the largest size …
—Lewis Carroll

Attempt the end, and never
stand to doubt;
Nothing's so hard, but
search will find it out.
—Robert Herrick

It is an immutable law in
business that words are
words, explanations are
explanations, promises are
promises — but only
performance is reality.
—Harold S. Green

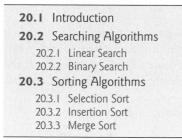

20.1 Introduction

Searching data involves determining whether a value (referred to as the **search key**) is present in the data and, if so, finding the value's location. Two popular search algorithms are the simple linear search and the faster, but more complex, binary search. **Sorting** places data in order, based on one or more **sort keys**. A list of names could be sorted alphabetically, bank accounts could be sorted by account number, employee payroll records could be sorted by social security number and so on. This chapter introduces two simple sorting algorithms, the selection sort and the insertion sort, along with the more efficient, but more complex, merge sort. Figure 20.1 summarizes the searching and sorting algorithms discussed in this book.

Chapter	Algorithm	Location
Searching Algorithms:		
20	Linear Search	Section 20.2.1
	Binary Search	Section 20.2.2
23	BinarySearch method of class Array	Fig. 23.3
	Contains method of classes List<T> and Stack<T>	Fig. 23.4
	ContainsKey method of class Dictionary<K, T>	Fig. 23.7
Sorting Algorithms:		
20	Selection Sort	Section 20.3.1
	Insertion Sort	Section 20.3.2
	Recursive Merge Sort	Section 20.3.3
20, 23	Sort method of classes Array and List<T>	Figs. 20.4, 23.3–23.4

Fig. 20.1 | Searching and sorting capabilities in this text.

20.2 Searching Algorithms

Looking up a phone number, accessing a website and checking the definition of a word in a dictionary all involve searching large amounts of data. The next two sections discuss two common search algorithms—one that is easy to program yet relatively inefficient and one that is relatively efficient but more complex to program.

20.2.1 Linear Search

The **linear search algorithm** searches each element in an array sequentially. If the search key does not match an element in the array, the algorithm tests each element and, when the end of the array is reached, informs the user that the search key is not present. If the search key is in the array, the algorithm tests each element until it finds one that matches the search key and returns the index of that element.

As an example, consider an array containing the following values

34	56	2	10	77	51	93	30	5	52

and a method that is searching for 51. Using the linear search algorithm, the method first checks whether 34 matches the search key. It does not, so the algorithm checks whether 56 matches the search key. The method continues moving through the array sequentially, testing 2, then 10, then 77. When the method tests 51, which matches the search key, the method returns the index 5, which is the location of 51 in the array. If, after checking every array element, the method determines that the search key does not match any element in the array, the method returns a sentinel value (e.g., -1). If there are duplicate values in the array, linear search returns the index of the first element in the array that matches the search key.

Figure 20.2 declares class `LinearArray`. This class has a `private` instance variable `data` (an array of `int`s), and a `static` `Random` object named `generator` to fill the array with randomly generated `int`s. When an object of class `LinearArray` is instantiated, the constructor (lines 12–19) creates and initializes the array `data` with random `int`s in the range 10–99.

```
 1    // Fig. 20.2: LinearArray.cs
 2    // Class that contains an array of random integers and a method
 3    // that searches that array sequentially.
 4    using System;
 5
 6    public class LinearArray
 7    {
 8       private int[] data; // array of values
 9       private static Random generator = new Random();
10
11       // create array of given size and fill with random integers
12       public LinearArray( int size )
13       {
14          data = new int[ size ]; // create space for array
15
16          // fill array with random ints in range 10-99
17          for ( int i = 0; i < size; i++ )
18             data[ i ] = generator.Next( 10, 100 );
19       } // end LinearArray constructor
20
21       // perform a linear search on the data
22       public int LinearSearch( int searchKey )
```

Fig. 20.2 | Class that contains an array of random integers and a method that searches that array sequentially. (Part 1 of 2.)

```
23      {
24          // loop through array sequentially
25          for ( int index = 0; index < data.Length; index++ )
26              if ( data[ index ] == searchKey )
27                  return index; // return index of integer
28
29          return -1; // integer was not found
30      } // end method LinearSearch
31
32      // method to output values in array
33      public override string ToString()
34      {
35          string temporary = string.Empty;
36
37          // iterate through array
38          foreach ( int element in data )
39              temporary += element + " ";
40
41          temporary += "\n"; // add newline character
42          return temporary;
43      } // end method ToString
44  } // end class LinearArray
```

Fig. 20.2 | Class that contains an array of random integers and a method that searches that array sequentially. (Part 2 of 2.)

Lines 22–30 perform the linear search. The search key is passed to parameter searchKey. Lines 25–27 loop through the elements in the array. Line 26 compares each element in the array with searchKey. If the values are equal, line 27 returns the index of the element. If the loop ends without finding the value, line 29 returns -1. Lines 33–43 declare method ToString, which returns a string representation of the array for printing.

Figure 20.3 creates LinearArray object searchArray containing an array of 10 ints (line 13) and allows the user to search the array for specific elements. Lines 17–18 prompt the user for the search key and store it in searchInt. Lines 21–37 loop until the user enters the sentinel value -1. The array holds ints from 10–99 (line 18 of Fig. 20.2). Line 24 calls the LinearSearch method to determine whether searchInt is in the array. If searchInt is found, LinearSearch returns the position of the element, which the method outputs in lines 27–29. If searchInt is not in the array, LinearSearch returns -1, and the method notifies the user (lines 31–32). Lines 35–36 retrieve the next integer from the user.

Efficiency of Linear Search

Searching algorithms all accomplish the same goal—finding an element that matches a given search key, if such an element exists. Many things, however, differentiate search algorithms from one another. The major difference is the amount of effort required to

```
 1   // Fig. 20.3: LinearSearchTest.cs
 2   // Sequentially search an array for an item.
 3   using System;
 4
 5   public class LinearSearchTest
 6   {
 7      public static void Main( string[] args )
 8      {
 9         int searchInt; // search key
10         int position; // location of search key in array
11
12         // create array and output it
13         LinearArray searchArray = new LinearArray( 10 );
14         Console.WriteLine( searchArray ); // print array
15
16         // input first int from user
17         Console.Write( "Please enter an integer value (-1 to quit): " );
18         searchInt = Convert.ToInt32( Console.ReadLine() );
19
20         // repeatedly input an integer; -1 terminates the application
21         while ( searchInt != -1 )
22         {
23            // perform linear search
24            position = searchArray.LinearSearch( searchInt );
25
26            if ( position != -1 ) // integer was not found
27               Console.WriteLine(
28                  "The integer {0} was found in position {1}.\n",
29                  searchInt, position );
30            else // integer was found
31               Console.WriteLine( "The integer {0} was not found.\n",
32                  searchInt );
33
34            // input next int from user
35            Console.Write( "Please enter an integer value (-1 to quit): " );
36            searchInt = Convert.ToInt32( Console.ReadLine() );
37         } // end while
38      } // end Main
39   } // end class LinearSearchTest
```

```
64 90 84 62 28 68 55 27 78 73

Please enter an integer value (-1 to quit): 78
The integer 78 was found in position 8.

Please enter an integer value (-1 to quit): 64
The integer 64 was found in position 0.

Please enter an integer value (-1 to quit): 65
The integer 65 was not found.

Please enter an integer value (-1 to quit): -1
```

Fig. 20.3 | Sequentially search an array for an item.

complete the search. One way to describe this effort is with **Big O notation**, which is a measure of the worst-case runtime for an algorithm—that is, how hard an algorithm may have to work to solve a problem. For searching and sorting algorithms, this is particularly dependent on how many elements there are in the data set and the algorithm used.

Suppose an algorithm is designed to test whether the first element of an array is equal to the second element. If the array has 10 elements, this algorithm requires one comparison. If the array has 1,000 elements, this algorithm still requires one comparison. In fact, this algorithm is completely independent of the number of elements in the array, and is thus said to have a **constant runtime**, which is represented in Big O notation as $O(1)$. An algorithm that is $O(1)$ does not necessarily require only one comparison. $O(1)$ just means that the number of comparisons is *constant*—it does not grow as the size of the array increases. An algorithm that tests whether the first element of an array is equal to any of the next three elements is still $O(1)$, even though it requires three comparisons.

An algorithm that tests whether the first element of an array is equal to *any* of the other elements of the array will require at most $n - 1$ comparisons, where n is the number of elements in the array. If the array has 10 elements, this algorithm requires up to nine comparisons. If the array has 1,000 elements, this algorithm requires up to 999 comparisons. As n grows larger, the n part of the expression "dominates," and subtracting one becomes inconsequential. Big O is designed to highlight these dominant terms and ignore terms that become unimportant as n grows. For this reason, an algorithm that requires a total of $n - 1$ comparisons (such as the one we described earlier) is said to be $O(n)$. An $O(n)$ algorithm is referred to as having a **linear runtime**. $O(n)$ is often pronounced "on the order of n" or more simply "order n."

Now suppose you have an algorithm that tests whether *any* element of an array is duplicated elsewhere in the array. The first element must be compared with every other element in the array. The second element must be compared with every other element except the first (it was already compared to the first). The third element must be compared with every other element except the first two. In the end, this algorithm will end up making $(n - 1) + (n - 2) + \ldots + 2 + 1$ or $n^2/2 - n/2$ comparisons. As n increases, the n^2 term dominates and the n term becomes inconsequential. Again, Big O notation highlights the n^2 term, leaving $n^2/2$. But as we'll soon see, constant factors are omitted in Big O notation.

Big O is concerned with how an algorithm's runtime grows in relation to the number of items processed. Suppose an algorithm requires n^2 comparisons. With four elements, the algorithm will require 16 comparisons; with eight elements, the algorithm will require 64 comparisons. With this algorithm, doubling the number of elements quadruples the number of comparisons. Consider a similar algorithm requiring $n^2/2$ comparisons. With four elements, the algorithm will require eight comparisons; with eight elements, 32 comparisons. Again, doubling the number of elements quadruples the number of comparisons. Both of these algorithms grow as the square of n, so Big O ignores the constant, and both algorithms are considered to be $O(n^2)$, referred to as **quadratic runtime** and pronounced "on the order of n-squared" or more simply "order n-squared."

When n is small, $O(n^2)$ algorithms (running on today's billions-of-operations-per-second personal computers) will not noticeably affect performance. But as n grows, you'll start to notice the performance degradation. An $O(n^2)$ algorithm running on a million-element array would require a trillion "operations" (where each could actually require several machine instructions to execute). This could require many minutes to execute. A billion-element array would require a quintillion operations, a number so large that the algorithm could take decades! $O(n^2)$ algorithms are easy to write, as you'll see shortly. You'll also see algorithms with more favorable Big O measures. These efficient algorithms often take more cleverness and effort to create, but their superior performance can be well worth the extra effort, especially as n gets large and algorithms are compounded into larger applications.

The linear search algorithm runs in $O(n)$ time. The worst case in this algorithm is that every element must be checked to determine whether the search item exists in the array. If the size of the array is doubled, the number of comparisons that the algorithm must perform is also doubled. Linear search can provide outstanding performance if the element matching the search key happens to be at or near the front of the array. But we seek algorithms that perform well, on average, across all searches, including those where the element matching the search key is near the end of the array.

Linear search is the easiest search algorithm to program, but it can be slow compared to other search algorithms. If an application needs to perform many searches on large arrays, it may be better to implement a different, more efficient algorithm, such as the binary search, which we present in the next section.

Performance Tip 20.1

Sometimes the simplest algorithms perform poorly. Their virtue is that they're easy to program, test and debug. Sometimes more complex algorithms are required to realize maximum performance.

20.2.2 Binary Search

The **binary search algorithm** is more efficient than the linear search algorithm, but it requires that the array be sorted. The first iteration of this algorithm tests the middle element in the array. If this matches the search key, the algorithm ends. Assuming the array is sorted in ascending order, if the search key is less than the middle element, the search key cannot match any element in the second half of the array and the algorithm continues with only the first half of the array (i.e., the first element up to, but not including, the middle element). If the search key is greater than the middle element, the search key cannot match any element in the first half of the array, and the algorithm continues with only the second half of the array (i.e., the element after the middle element through the last element). Each iteration tests the middle value of the remaining portion of the array, called a **subarray**. A subarray can have no elements, or it can encompass the entire array. If the search key does not match the element, the algorithm eliminates half of the remaining elements. The algorithm ends by either finding an element that matches the search key or reducing the subarray to zero size.

As an example, consider the sorted 15-element array

| | 2 | 3 | 5 | 10 | 27 | 30 | 34 | 51 | 56 | 65 | 77 | 81 | 82 | 93 | 99 | |

and a search key of 65. An application implementing the binary search algorithm would first check whether 51 is the search key (because 51 is the middle element of the array). The search key (65) is larger than 51, so 51 is "discarded" (i.e., eliminated from consideration) along with the first half of the array (all elements smaller than 51.) Next, the algorithm checks whether 81 (the middle element of the remainder of the array) matches the search key. The search key (65) is smaller than 81, so 81 is discarded along with the elements larger than 81. After just two tests, the algorithm has narrowed the number of values to check to three (56, 65 and 77). The algorithm then checks 65 (which indeed matches the search key) and returns the index of the array element containing 65. This algorithm required just three comparisons to determine whether the search key matched an element of the array. Using a linear search algorithm would have required 10 comparisons. [*Note:* In this example, we have chosen to use an array with 15 elements so that there will always be an obvious middle element in the array. With an even number of elements, the middle of the array lies between two elements. We implement the algorithm to choose the higher of the two elements.]

Figure 20.4 declares class BinaryArray. This class is similar to LinearArray—it has a private instance variable data (an array of ints), a static Random object named generator to fill the array with randomly generated ints, a constructor, a search method (BinarySearch), a RemainingElements method (which creates a string containing the elements not yet searched) and a ToString method. Lines 12–21 declare the constructor. After initializing the array with random ints from 10–99 (lines 17–18), line 20 calls method Array.Sort on the array data. Method **Sort** is a static method of class Array that sorts the elements in an array in ascending order. Recall that the binary search algorithm works only on sorted arrays.

```
1   // Fig. 20.4: BinaryArray.cs
2   // Class that contains an array of random integers and a method
3   // that uses binary search to find an integer.
4   using System;
5
6   public class BinaryArray
7   {
8      private int[] data; // array of values
9      private static Random generator = new Random();
10
11     // create array of given size and fill with random integers
12     public BinaryArray( int size )
13     {
14        data = new int[ size ]; // create space for array
15
16        // fill array with random ints in range 10-99
17        for ( int i = 0; i < size; i++ )
18           data[ i ] = generator.Next( 10, 100 );
19
20        Array.Sort( data );
21     } // end BinaryArray constructor
22
23     // perform a binary search on the data
24     public int BinarySearch( int searchElement )
25     {
26        int low = 0; // low end of the search area
27        int high = data.Length - 1; // high end of the search area
28        int middle = ( low + high + 1 ) / 2; // middle element
29        int location = -1; // return value; -1 if not found
```

Fig. 20.4 | Class that contains an array of random integers and a method that uses binary search to find an integer. (Part 1 of 2.)

```
30
31      do // loop to search for element
32      {
33         // print remaining elements of array
34         Console.Write( RemainingElements( low, high ) );
35
36         // output spaces for alignment
37         for ( int i = 0; i < middle; i++ )
38            Console.Write( "   " );
39
40         Console.WriteLine( " * " ); // indicate current middle
41
42         // if the element is found at the middle
43         if ( searchElement == data[ middle ] )
44            location = middle; // location is the current middle
45
46         // middle element is too high
47         else if ( searchElement < data[ middle ] )
48            high = middle - 1; // eliminate the higher half
49         else // middle element is too low
50            low = middle + 1; // eliminate the lower half
51
52         middle = ( low + high + 1 ) / 2; // recalculate the middle
53      } while ( ( low <= high ) && ( location == -1 ) );
54
55      return location; // return location of search key
56   } // end method BinarySearch
57
58   // method to output certain values in array
59   public string RemainingElements( int low, int high )
60   {
61      string temporary = string.Empty;
62
63      // output spaces for alignment
64      for ( int i = 0; i < low; i++ )
65         temporary += "   ";
66
67      // output elements left in array
68      for ( int i = low; i <= high; i++ )
69         temporary += data[ i ] + " ";
70
71      temporary += "\n";
72      return temporary;
73   } // end method RemainingElements
74
75   // method to output values in array
76   public override string ToString()
77   {
78      return RemainingElements( 0, data.Length - 1 );
79   } // end method ToString
80 } // end class BinaryArray
```

Fig. 20.4 | Class that contains an array of random integers and a method that uses binary search to find an integer. (Part 2 of 2.)

Lines 24–56 declare method BinarySearch. The search key is passed into parameter searchElement (line 24). Lines 26–28 calculate the low end index, high end index and middle index of the portion of the array that the application is currently searching. At the beginning of the method, the low end is 0, the high end is the length of the array minus 1 and the middle is the average of these two values. Line 29 initializes the location of the element to -1—the value that will be returned if the element is not found. Lines 31–53 loop until low is greater than high (this occurs when the element is not found) or location does not equal -1 (indicating that the search key was found). Line 43 tests whether the value in the middle element is equal to searchElement. If this is true, line 44 assigns middle to location. Then the loop terminates, and location is returned to the caller. Each iteration of the loop tests a single value (line 43) and eliminates half of the remaining values in the array (line 48 or 50).

Lines 22–40 of Fig. 20.5 loop until the user enters -1. For each other number the user enters, the application performs a binary search to determine whether the number matches an element in the array. The first line of output from this application is the array of ints, in increasing order. When the user instructs the application to search for 72, the application first tests the middle element (indicated by * in the sample output of Fig. 20.5), which is 52. The search key is greater than 52, so the application eliminates from consideration the first half of the array and tests the middle element from the second half. The search key is smaller than 82, so the application eliminates from consideration the second half of the subarray, leaving only three elements. Finally, the application checks 72 (which matches the search key) and returns the index 9.

```
1   // Fig. 20.5: BinarySearchTest.cs
2   // Using binary search to locate an item in an array.
3   using System;
4
5   public class BinarySearchTest
6   {
7      public static void Main( string[] args )
8      {
9         int searchInt; // search key
10        int position; // location of search key in array
11
12        // create array and output it
13        BinaryArray searchArray = new BinaryArray( 15 );
14        Console.WriteLine( searchArray );
15
16        // prompt and input first int from user
17        Console.Write( "Please enter an integer value (-1 to quit): " );
18        searchInt = Convert.ToInt32( Console.ReadLine() );
19        Console.WriteLine();
20
21        // repeatedly input an integer; -1 terminates the application
22        while ( searchInt != -1 )
23        {
24           // use binary search to try to find integer
25           position = searchArray.BinarySearch( searchInt );
```

Fig. 20.5 | Using binary search to locate an item in an array. (Part 1 of 2.)

```
26
27            // return value of -1 indicates integer was not found
28            if ( position == -1 )
29               Console.WriteLine( "The integer {0} was not found.\n",
30                  searchInt );
31            else
32               Console.WriteLine(
33                  "The integer {0} was found in position {1}.\n",
34                  searchInt, position);
35
36            // prompt and input next int from user
37            Console.Write( "Please enter an integer value (-1 to quit): " );
38            searchInt = Convert.ToInt32( Console.ReadLine() );
39            Console.WriteLine();
40         } // end while
41      } // end Main
42   } // end class BinarySearchTest
```

```
12 17 22 25 30 39 40 52 56 72 76 82 84 91 93

Please enter an integer value (-1 to quit): 72

12 17 22 25 30 39 40 52 56 72 76 82 84 91 93
                        *
                        56 72 76 82 84 91 93
                                    *
                        56 72 76
                            *
The integer 72 was found in position 9.

Please enter an integer value (-1 to quit): 13

12 17 22 25 30 39 40 52 56 72 76 82 84 91 93
                    *
12 17 22 25 30 39 40
            *
12 17 22
    *
12
*
The integer 13 was not found.

Please enter an integer value (-1 to quit): -1
```

Fig. 20.5 | Using binary search to locate an item in an array. (Part 2 of 2.)

Efficiency of Binary Search

In the worst-case scenario, searching a sorted array of 1,023 elements will take only 10 comparisons when using a binary search. Repeatedly dividing 1,023 by 2 (because after each comparison, we are able to eliminate half of the array) and rounding down (because we also remove the middle element) yields the values 511, 255, 127, 63, 31, 15, 7, 3, 1 and 0. The number 1023 ($2^{10} - 1$) is divided by 2 only 10 times to get the value 0, which indicates that there are no more elements to test. Dividing by 2 is equivalent to one comparison in the binary search algorithm. Thus, an array of 1,048,575 ($2^{20} - 1$) elements takes a maximum of 20 comparisons to find the key, and an array of one billion elements (which is less than $2^{30} - 1$) takes a maximum of 30 comparisons to find the key. This is a tremendous improvement in performance over the linear search. For a one-billion-element array, this is a difference between an average of 500 million comparisons for the linear search and a maximum of only 30 comparisons for the binary search! The maximum number of comparisons needed for the binary search of any sorted array is the exponent of the first power of 2 greater than the number of elements in the array, which is represented as $\log_2 n$. All logarithms grow at roughly the same rate, so in Big O notation the base can be omitted. This results in a big O of *O(log n)* for a binary search, which is also known as **logarithmic runtime**.

20.3 Sorting Algorithms

Sorting data (i.e., placing the data in some particular order, such as ascending or descending) is one of the most important computing applications. A bank sorts all checks by account number so that it can prepare individual bank statements at the end of each month. Telephone companies sort their lists of accounts by last name and, further, by first name to make it easy to find phone numbers. Virtually every organization must sort some data—often, massive amounts of it. Sorting data is an intriguing, compute-intensive problem that has attracted substantial research efforts.

It's important to understand about sorting that the end result—the sorted array—will be the same no matter which (correct) algorithm you use to sort the array. The choice of algorithm affects only the runtime and memory use of the application. The rest of the chapter introduces three common sorting algorithms. The first two—selection sort and insertion sort—are simple to program, but inefficient. The last—merge sort—is much faster than selection sort and insertion sort but more difficult to program. We focus on sorting arrays of simple-type data, namely `int`s. It's possible to sort arrays of objects as well—we discuss this in Chapter 23, Collections.

20.3.1 Selection Sort

Selection sort is a simple, but inefficient, sorting algorithm. The first iteration of the algorithm selects the smallest element in the array and swaps it with the first element. The second iteration selects the second-smallest element (which is the smallest of the remaining elements) and swaps it with the second element. The algorithm continues until the last iteration selects the second-largest element and, if necessary, swaps it with the second-to-last element, leaving the largest element in the last position. After the ith iteration, the smallest i elements of the array will be sorted in increasing order in the first i positions of the array.

As an example, consider the array

| 34 | 56 | 4 | 10 | 77 | 51 | 93 | 30 | 5 | 52 |

An application that implements selection sort first determines the smallest element (4) of this array, which is contained in index 2 (i.e., position 3). The application swaps 4 with 34, resulting in

| 4 | 56 | 34 | 10 | 77 | 51 | 93 | 30 | 5 | 52 |

The application then determines the smallest value of the remaining elements (all elements except 4), which is 5, contained in index 8. The application swaps 5 with 56, resulting in

| 4 | 5 | 34 | 10 | 77 | 51 | 93 | 30 | 56 | 52 |

On the third iteration, the application determines the next smallest value (10) and swaps it with 34.

| 4 | 5 | 10 | 34 | 77 | 51 | 93 | 30 | 56 | 52 |

The process continues until the array is fully sorted.

| 4 | 5 | 10 | 30 | 34 | 51 | 52 | 56 | 77 | 93 |

After the first iteration, the smallest element is in the first position. After the second iteration, the two smallest elements are in order in the first two positions. After the third iteration, the three smallest elements are in order in the first three positions.

Figure 20.6 declares class SelectionSort, which has an instance variable data (an array of ints) and a static Random object generator to generate random integers to fill the array. When an object of class SelectionSort is instantiated, the constructor (lines 12–19) creates and initializes array data with random ints in the range 10–99.

```
1   // Fig. 20.6: SelectionSort.cs
2   // Class that creates an array filled with random integers.
3   // Provides a method to sort the array with selection sort.
4   using System;
5
6   public class SelectionSort
7   {
8      private int[] data; // array of values
9      private static Random generator = new Random();
10
11     // create array of given size and fill with random integers
12     public SelectionSort( int size )
13     {
14        data = new int[ size ]; // create space for array
15
16        // fill array with random ints in range 10-99
17        for ( int i = 0; i < size; i++ )
18           data[ i ] = generator.Next( 10, 100 );
19     } // end SelectionSort constructor
20
21     // sort array using selection sort
22     public void Sort()
23     {
24        int smallest; // index of smallest element
25
26        // loop over data.Length - 1 elements
27        for ( int i = 0; i < data.Length - 1; i++ )
28        {
29           smallest = i; // first index of remaining array
30
31           // loop to find index of smallest element
32           for ( int index = i + 1; index < data.Length; index++ )
33              if ( data[ index ] < data[ smallest ] )
34                 smallest = index;
```

Fig. 20.6 | Class that creates an array filled with random integers. Provides a method to sort the array with selection sort. (Part 1 of 2.)

```
35
36            Swap( i, smallest ); // swap smallest element into position
37            PrintPass( i + 1, smallest ); // output pass of algorithm
38         } // end outer for
39      } // end method Sort
40
41      // helper method to swap values in two elements
42      public void Swap( int first, int second )
43      {
44         int temporary = data[ first ]; // store first in temporary
45         data[ first ] = data[ second ]; // replace first with second
46         data[ second ] = temporary; // put temporary in second
47      } // end method Swap
48
49      // print a pass of the algorithm
50      public void PrintPass( int pass, int index )
51      {
52         Console.Write( "after pass {0}: ", pass );
53
54         // output elements through the selected item
55         for ( int i = 0; i < index; i++ )
56            Console.Write( data[ i ] + "  " );
57
58         Console.Write( data[ index ] + "* " ); // indicate swap
59
60         // finish outputting array
61         for ( int i = index + 1; i < data.Length; i++ )
62            Console.Write( data[ i ] + "  " );
63
64         Console.Write( "\n                " ); // for alignment
65
66         // indicate amount of array that is sorted
67         for( int j = 0; j < pass; j++ )
68            Console.Write( "--  " );
69         Console.WriteLine( "\n" ); // skip a line in output
70      } // end method PrintPass
71
72      // method to output values in array
73      public override string ToString()
74      {
75         string temporary = string.Empty;
76
77         // iterate through array
78         foreach ( int element in data )
79            temporary += element + "  ";
80
81         temporary += "\n"; // add newline character
82         return temporary;
83      } // end method ToString
84   } // end class SelectionSort
```

Fig. 20.6 | Class that creates an array filled with random integers. Provides a method to sort the array with selection sort. (Part 2 of 2.)

Lines 22–39 declare the Sort method. Line 24 declares variable smallest, which will store the index of the smallest element in the remaining array. Lines 27–38 loop data.Length - 1 times. Line 29 initializes the index of the smallest element to the current item. Lines 32–34 loop over the remaining elements in the array. For each of these elements, line 33 compares its value to the value of the smallest element. If the current element is smaller than the smallest element, line 34 assigns the current element's index to smallest. When this loop finishes, smallest will contain the index of the smallest element in the remaining array. Line 36 calls method Swap (lines 42–47) to place the smallest remaining element in the next spot in the array.

Line 10 of Fig. 20.7 creates a SelectionSort object with 10 elements. Line 13 implicitly calls method ToString to output the unsorted object. Line 15 calls method Sort (lines 22–39 of Fig. 20.6), which sorts the elements using selection sort. Then lines 17–18 output the sorted object. The output uses dashes to indicate the portion of the array that is sorted after each pass (lines 67–68). An asterisk is placed next to the position of the element that was swapped with the smallest element on that pass. On each pass, the element next to the asterisk and the element above the rightmost set of dashes were the two values that were swapped.

```
 1   // Fig. 20.7: SelectionSortTest.cs
 2   // Testing the selection sort class.
 3   using System;
 4
 5   public class SelectionSortTest
 6   {
 7      public static void Main( string[] args )
 8      {
 9         // create object to perform selection sort
10         SelectionSort sortArray = new SelectionSort( 10 );
11
12         Console.WriteLine( "Unsorted array:" );
13         Console.WriteLine( sortArray ); // print unsorted array
14
15         sortArray.Sort(); // sort array
16
17         Console.WriteLine( "Sorted array:" );
18         Console.WriteLine( sortArray ); // print sorted array
19      } // end Main
20   } // end class SelectionSortTest
```

```
Unsorted array:
86  97  83  45  19  31  86  13  57  61

after pass 1: 13  97  83  45  19  31  86  86* 57  61
              --

after pass 2: 13  19  83  45  97* 31  86  86  57  61
              --  --

after pass 3: 13  19  31  45  97  83* 86  86  57  61
              --  --  --
```

Fig. 20.7 | Testing the selection sort class. (Part 1 of 2.)

```
after pass 4: 13  19  31  45* 97  83  86  86  57  61
              --  --  --  --

after pass 5: 13  19  31  45  57  83  86  86  97* 61
              --  --  --  --  --

after pass 6: 13  19  31  45  57  61  86  86  97  83*
              --  --  --  --  --  --

after pass 7: 13  19  31  45  57  61  83  86  97  86*
              --  --  --  --  --  --  --

after pass 8: 13  19  31  45  57  61  83  86* 97  86
              --  --  --  --  --  --  --  --

after pass 9: 13  19  31  45  57  61  83  86  86  97*
              --  --  --  --  --  --  --  --  --

Sorted array:
13  19  31  45  57  61  83  86  86  97
```

Fig. 20.7 | Testing the selection sort class. (Part 2 of 2.)

Efficiency of Selection Sort

The selection sort algorithm runs in $O(n^2)$ time. Method Sort in lines 22–39 of Fig. 20.6, which implements the selection sort algorithm, contains nested for loops. The outer for loop (lines 27–38) iterates over the first $n - 1$ elements in the array, swapping the smallest remaining element to its sorted position. The inner for loop (lines 32–34) iterates over each element in the remaining array, searching for the smallest. This loop executes $n - 1$ times during the first iteration of the outer loop, $n - 2$ times during the second iteration, then $n - 3, \ldots, 3, 2, 1$. This inner loop will iterate a total of $n(n - 1) / 2$ or $(n^2 - n)/2$. In Big O notation, smaller terms drop out and constants are ignored, leaving a final Big O of $O(n^2)$.

20.3.2 Insertion Sort

Insertion sort is another simple, but inefficient, sorting algorithm. Its first iteration takes the second element in the array and, if it's less than the first, swaps them. The second iteration looks at the third element and inserts it in the correct position with respect to the first two elements, so all three elements are in order. At the ith iteration of this algorithm, the first i elements in the original array will be sorted.

Consider as an example the following array, which is identical to the array used in the discussions of selection sort and merge sort.

| 34 | 56 | 4 | 10 | 77 | 51 | 93 | 30 | 5 | 52 |

An application that implements the insertion sort algorithm first looks at the first two elements of the array, 34 and 56. These are already in order, so the application continues (if they were out of order, it would swap them).

In the next iteration, the application looks at the third value, 4. This value is less than 56, so the application stores 4 in a temporary variable and moves 56 one element to the right. The application then checks and determines that 4 is less than 34, so it moves 34 one element to the right. The application has now reached the beginning of the array, so it places 4 in the zeroth position. The array now is

| 4 | 34 | 56 | 10 | 77 | 51 | 93 | 30 | 5 | 52 |

In the next iteration, the application stores the value 10 in a temporary variable. Then the application compares 10 to 56 and moves 56 one element to the right because it's larger than 10. The application then compares 10 to 34, moving 34 one element to the right. When the application compares 10 to 4, it observes that 10 is larger than 4 and places 10 in element 1. The array now is

| 4 | 10 | 34 | 56 | 77 | 51 | 93 | 30 | 5 | 52 |

Using this algorithm, at the *i*th iteration, the original array's first *i* elements are sorted, but they may not be in their final locations—smaller values may be located later in the array.

Figure 20.8 declares the InsertionSort class. Lines 22–46 declare the Sort method. Line 24 declares variable insert, which holds the element to be inserted while the other elements are moved. Lines 27–45 loop through data.Length - 1 items in the array. In each iteration, line 30 stores in variable insert the value of the element that will be inserted in the sorted portion of the array. Line 33 declares and initializes variable moveItem, which keeps track of where to insert the element. Lines 36–41 loop to locate the correct position to insert the element. The loop will terminate either when the application reaches the front of the array or when it reaches an element that is less than the value to be inserted. Line 39 moves an element to the right, and line 40 decrements the position at which to insert the next element. After the loop ends, line 43 inserts the element in place. Figure 20.9 is the same as Fig. 20.7 except that it creates and uses an InsertionSort object. The output of this application uses dashes to indicate the portion of the array that is sorted after each pass (lines 66–67 of Fig. 20.8). An asterisk is placed next to the element that was inserted in place on that pass.

```
1   // Fig. 20.8: InsertionSort.cs
2   // Class that creates an array filled with random integers.
3   // Provides a method to sort the array with insertion sort.
4   using System;
5
6   public class InsertionSort
7   {
8      private int[] data; // array of values
9      private static Random generator = new Random();
10
11     // create array of given size and fill with random integers
12     public InsertionSort( int size )
13     {
14        data = new int[ size ]; // create space for array
15
16        // fill array with random ints in range 10-99
17        for ( int i = 0; i < size; i++ )
18           data[ i ] = generator.Next( 10, 100 );
19     } // end InsertionSort constructor
20
21     // sort array using insertion sort
22     public void Sort()
23     {
```

Fig. 20.8 | Class that creates an array filled with random integers. Provides a method to sort the array with insertion sort. (Part 1 of 3.)

```
24        int insert; // temporary variable to hold element to insert
25
26        // loop over data.Length - 1 elements
27        for ( int next = 1; next < data.Length; next++ )
28        {
29           // store value in current element
30           insert = data[ next ];
31
32           // initialize location to place element
33           int moveItem = next;
34
35           // search for place to put current element
36           while ( moveItem > 0 && data[ moveItem - 1 ] > insert )
37           {
38              // shift element right one slot
39              data[ moveItem ] = data[ moveItem - 1 ];
40              moveItem--;
41           } // end while
42
43           data[ moveItem ] = insert; // place inserted element
44           PrintPass( next, moveItem ); // output pass of algorithm
45        } // end for
46     } // end method Sort
47
48     // print a pass of the algorithm
49     public void PrintPass( int pass, int index )
50     {
51        Console.Write( "after pass {0}: ", pass );
52
53        // output elements till swapped item
54        for ( int i = 0; i < index; i++ )
55           Console.Write( data[ i ] + "  " );
56
57        Console.Write( data[ index ] + "* " ); // indicate swap
58
59        // finish outputting array
60        for ( int i = index + 1; i < data.Length; i++ )
61           Console.Write( data[ i ] + "  " );
62
63        Console.Write( "\n                 " ); // for alignment
64
65        // indicate amount of array that is sorted
66        for( int i = 0; i <= pass; i++ )
67           Console.Write( "--  " );
68        Console.WriteLine( "\n" ); // skip a line in output
69     } // end method PrintPass
70
71     // method to output values in array
72     public override string ToString()
73     {
74        string temporary = string.Empty;
```

Fig. 20.8 | Class that creates an array filled with random integers. Provides a method to sort the array with insertion sort. (Part 2 of 3.)

```
75
76          // iterate through array
77          foreach ( int element in data )
78              temporary += element + "  ";
79
80          temporary += "\n"; // add newline character
81          return temporary;
82      } // end method ToString
83  } // end class InsertionSort
```

Fig. 20.8 | Class that creates an array filled with random integers. Provides a method to sort the array with insertion sort. (Part 3 of 3.)

```
1   // Fig. 20.9: InsertionSortTest.cs
2   // Testing the insertion sort class.
3   using System;
4
5   public class InsertionSortTest
6   {
7       public static void Main( string[] args )
8       {
9           // create object to perform insertion sort
10          InsertionSort sortArray = new InsertionSort( 10 );
11
12          Console.WriteLine( "Unsorted array:" );
13          Console.WriteLine( sortArray ); // print unsorted array
14
15          sortArray.Sort(); // sort array
16
17          Console.WriteLine( "Sorted array:" );
18          Console.WriteLine( sortArray ); // print sorted array
19      } // end Main
20  } // end class InsertionSortTest
```

```
Unsorted array:
12  27  36  28  33  92  11  93  59  62

after pass 1: 12  27* 36  28  33  92  11  93  59  62
                  --  --

after pass 2: 12  27  36* 28  33  92  11  93  59  62
                  --  --  --

after pass 3: 12  27  28* 36  33  92  11  93  59  62
                  --  --  --  --

after pass 4: 12  27  28  33* 36  92  11  93  59  62
                  --  --  --  --  --

after pass 5: 12  27  28  33  36  92* 11  93  59  62
                  --  --  --  --  --  --
```

Fig. 20.9 | Testing the insertion sort class. (Part 1 of 2.)

```
after pass 6: 11* 12  27  28  33  36  92  93  59  62
              --  --  --  --  --  --  --

after pass 7: 11  12  27  28  33  36  92  93* 59  62
              --  --  --  --  --  --  --  --

after pass 8: 11  12  27  28  33  36  59* 92  93  62
              --  --  --  --  --  --  --  --  --

after pass 9: 11  12  27  28  33  36  59  62* 92  93
              --  --  --  --  --  --  --  --  --  --

Sorted array:
11  12  27  28  33  36  59  62  92  93
```

Fig. 20.9 | Testing the insertion sort class. (Part 2 of 2.)

Efficiency of Insertion Sort

The insertion sort algorithm also runs in $O(n^2)$ time. Like selection sort, the implementation of insertion sort (lines 22–46 of Fig. 20.8) contains nested loops. The `for` loop (lines 27–45) iterates `data.Length - 1` times, inserting an element in the appropriate position in the elements sorted so far. For the purposes of this application, `data.Length - 1` is equivalent to $n - 1$ (as `data.Length` is the size of the array). The `while` loop (lines 36–41) iterates over the preceding elements in the array. In the worst case, this `while` loop will require $n - 1$ comparisons. Each individual loop runs in $O(n)$ time. In Big O notation, nested loops mean that you must multiply the number of iterations of each loop. For each iteration of an outer loop, there will be a certain number of iterations of the inner loop. In this algorithm, for each $O(n)$ iterations of the outer loop, there will be $O(n)$ iterations of the inner loop. Multiplying these values results in a Big O of $O(n^2)$.

20.3.3 Merge Sort

Merge sort is an efficient sorting algorithm but is conceptually more complex than selection sort and insertion sort. The merge sort algorithm sorts an array by splitting it into two equal-sized subarrays, sorting each subarray and merging them in one larger array. With an odd number of elements, the algorithm creates the two subarrays such that one has one more element than the other.

The implementation of merge sort in this example is recursive. The base case is an array with one element. A one-element array is, of course, sorted, so merge sort immediately returns when it's called with a one-element array. The recursion step splits an array in two approximately equal-length pieces, recursively sorts them and merges the two sorted arrays in one larger, sorted array.

Suppose the algorithm has already merged smaller arrays to create sorted arrays A:

4	10	34	56	77

and B:

5	30	51	52	93

Merge sort combines these two arrays in one larger, sorted array. The smallest element in A is 4 (located in the zeroth element of A). The smallest element in B is 5 (located in the zeroth element of B). In order to determine the smallest element in the larger array, the algorithm compares 4 and 5. The value from A is smaller, so 4 becomes the first element in the merged array. The algorithm continues by comparing 10 (the second element in A) to 5 (the first element in B). The value from B is smaller, so 5 becomes the second element in the larger array. The algorithm continues by comparing 10 to 30, with 10 becoming the third element in the array, and so on.

Lines 22–25 of Fig. 20.10 declare the Sort method. Line 24 calls method SortArray with 0 and data.Length - 1 as the arguments—these are the beginning and ending indices of the array to be sorted. These values tell method SortArray to operate on the entire array.

```
1   // Fig. 20.10: MergeSort.cs
2   // Class that creates an array filled with random integers.
3   // Provides a method to sort the array with merge sort.
4   using System;
5
6   public class MergeSort
7   {
8      private int[] data; // array of values
9      private static Random generator = new Random();
10
11     // create array of given size and fill with random integers
12     public MergeSort( int size )
13     {
14        data = new int[ size ]; // create space for array
15
16        // fill array with random ints in range 10-99
17        for ( int i = 0; i < size; i++ )
18           data[ i ] = generator.Next( 10, 100 );
19     } // end MergeSort constructor
20
21     // calls recursive SortArray method to begin merge sorting
22     public void Sort()
23     {
24        SortArray( 0, data.Length - 1 ); // sort entire array
25     } // end method Sort
26
27     // splits array, sorts subarrays and merges subarrays into sorted array
28     private void SortArray( int low, int high )
29     {
30        // test base case; size of array equals 1
31        if ( ( high - low ) >= 1 ) // if not base case
32        {
33           int middle1 = ( low + high ) / 2; // calculate middle of array
34           int middle2 = middle1 + 1; // calculate next element over
35
36           // output split step
37           Console.WriteLine( "split:   " + Subarray( low, high ) );
38           Console.WriteLine( "         " + Subarray( low, middle1 ) );
39           Console.WriteLine( "         " + Subarray( middle2, high ) );
40           Console.WriteLine();
```

Fig. 20.10 | Class that creates an array filled with random integers. Provides a method to sort the array with merge sort. (Part 1 of 3.)

```
41
42            // split array in half; sort each half (recursive calls)
43            SortArray( low, middle1 ); // first half of array
44            SortArray( middle2, high ); // second half of array
45
46            // merge two sorted arrays after split calls return
47            Merge( low, middle1, middle2, high );
48         } // end if
49      } // end method SortArray
50
51      // merge two sorted subarrays into one sorted subarray
52      private void Merge( int left, int middle1, int middle2, int right )
53      {
54         int leftIndex = left; // index into left subarray
55         int rightIndex = middle2; // index into right subarray
56         int combinedIndex = left; // index into temporary working array
57         int[] combined = new int[ data.Length ]; // working array
58
59         // output two subarrays before merging
60         Console.WriteLine( "merge:   " + Subarray( left, middle1 ) );
61         Console.WriteLine( "         " + Subarray( middle2, right ) );
62
63         // merge arrays until reaching end of either
64         while ( leftIndex <= middle1 && rightIndex <= right )
65         {
66            // place smaller of two current elements into result
67            // and move to next space in arrays
68            if ( data[ leftIndex ] <= data[ rightIndex ] )
69               combined[ combinedIndex++ ] = data[ leftIndex++ ];
70            else
71               combined[ combinedIndex++ ] = data[ rightIndex++ ];
72         } // end while
73
74         // if left array is empty
75         if ( leftIndex == middle2 )
76            // copy in rest of right array
77            while ( rightIndex <= right )
78               combined[ combinedIndex++ ] = data[ rightIndex++ ];
79         else // right array is empty
80            // copy in rest of left array
81            while ( leftIndex <= middle1 )
82               combined[ combinedIndex++ ] = data[ leftIndex++ ];
83
84         // copy values back into original array
85         for ( int i = left; i <= right; i++ )
86            data[ i ] = combined[ i ];
87
88         // output merged array
89         Console.WriteLine( "         " + Subarray( left, right ) );
90         Console.WriteLine();
91      } // end method Merge
```

Fig. 20.10 | Class that creates an array filled with random integers. Provides a method to sort the array with merge sort. (Part 2 of 3.)

```
92
93        // method to output certain values in array
94        public string Subarray( int low, int high )
95        {
96            string temporary = string.Empty;
97
98            // output spaces for alignment
99            for ( int i = 0; i < low; i++ )
100               temporary += "   ";
101
102           // output elements left in array
103           for ( int i = low; i <= high; i++ )
104               temporary += " " + data[ i ];
105
106           return temporary;
107       } // end method Subarray
108
109       // method to output values in array
110       public override string ToString()
111       {
112           return Subarray( 0, data.Length - 1 );
113       } // end method ToString
114   } // end class MergeSort
```

Fig. 20.10 | Class that creates an array filled with random integers. Provides a method to sort the array with merge sort. (Part 3 of 3.)

Method SortArray is declared in lines 28–49. Line 31 tests the base case. If the size of the array is 1, the array is already sorted, so the method simply returns immediately. If the size of the array is greater than 1, the method splits the array in two, recursively calls method SortArray to sort the two subarrays and merges them. Line 43 recursively calls method SortArray on the first half of the array, and line 44 recursively calls method Sort-Array on the second half of the array. When these two method calls return, each half of the array has been sorted. Line 47 calls method Merge (lines 52–91) on the two halves of the array to combine the two sorted arrays in one larger sorted array.

Lines 64–72 in method Merge loop until the application reaches the end of either subarray. Line 68 tests which element at the beginning of the arrays is smaller. If the element in the left array is smaller or equal, line 69 places it in position in the combined array. If the element in the right array is smaller, line 71 places it in position in the combined array. When the while loop has completed (line 72), one entire subarray is placed in the combined array, but the other subarray still contains data. Line 75 tests whether the left array has reached the end. If so, lines 77–78 fill the combined array with the remaining elements of the right array. If the left array has not reached the end, then the right array has, and lines 81–82 fill the combined array with the remaining elements of the left array. Finally, lines 85–86 copy the combined array into the original array. Figure 20.11 creates and uses a MergeSort object. The output from this application displays the splits and merges performed by merge sort, showing the progress of the sort at each step of the algorithm.

```
 1   // Fig. 20.11: MergeSortTest.cs
 2   // Testing the merge sort class.
 3   using System;
 4
 5   public class MergeSortTest
 6   {
 7      public static void Main( string[] args )
 8      {
 9         // create object to perform merge sort
10         MergeSort sortArray = new MergeSort( 10 );
11
12         // print unsorted array
13         Console.WriteLine( "Unsorted: {0}\n", sortArray );
14
15         sortArray.Sort(); // sort array
16
17         // print sorted array
18         Console.WriteLine( "Sorted: {0}", sortArray );
19      } // end Main
20   } // end class MergeSortTest
```

```
Unsorted:   36 38 81 93 85 72 31 11 33 74

split:      36 38 81 93 85 72 31 11 33 74
            36 38 81 93 85
                           72 31 11 33 74

split:      36 38 81 93 85
            36 38 81
                    93 85

split:      36 38 81
            36 38
                  81

split:      36 38
            36
               38

merge:      36
               38
            36 38

merge:      36 38
                  81
            36 38 81

split:            93 85
                  93
                     85

merge:            93
                     85
                  85 93

merge:      36 38 81
                     85 93
            36 38 81 85 93
```

Fig. 20.11 | Testing the merge sort class. (Part 1 of 2.)

```
split:                      72 31 11 33 74
                            72 31 11
                                     33 74

split:                      72 31 11
                            72 31
                                  11

split:                      72 31
                            72
                               31

merge:                      72
                               31
                            31 72

merge:                      31 72
                                  11
                            11 31 72

split:                              33 74
                                    33
                                       74

merge:                              33
                                       74
                                    33 74

merge:                      11 31 72
                                       33 74
                            11 31 33 72 74

merge:       36 38 81 85 93
                            11 31 33 72 74
             11 31 33 36 38 72 74 81 85 93

Sorted:      11 31 33 36 38 72 74 81 85 93
```

Fig. 20.11 | Testing the merge sort class. (Part 2 of 2.)

Efficiency of Merge Sort

Merge sort is a far more efficient algorithm than either insertion sort or selection sort when sorting large sets of data. Consider the first (nonrecursive) call to method SortArray. This results in two recursive calls to method SortArray with subarrays each approximately half the size of the original array, and a single call to method Merge. This call to method Merge requires, at worst, $n-1$ comparisons to fill the original array, which is $O(n)$. (Recall that each element in the array can be chosen by comparing one element from each of the subarrays.) The two calls to method SortArray result in four more recursive calls to SortArray, each with a subarray approximately a quarter the size of the original array, along with two calls to method Merge. These two calls to method Merge each require, at worst, $n/2 - 1$ comparisons for a total number of comparisons of $(n/2 - 1) + (n/2 - 1) = n - 2$, which is $O(n)$. This process continues, each call to SortArray generating two additional calls to method SortArray and a call to Merge, until the algorithm has split the array into one-element subarrays. At each level, $O(n)$ comparisons are required to merge the subarrays. Each level splits the size of the arrays in half, so doubling the size of the array requires only one more level. Quadrupling the size of the array requires only two more levels. This pattern is logarithmic and results in $\log_2 n$ levels. This results in a total efficiency of **$O(n \log n)$**.

20.4 Summary of the Efficiency of Searching and Sorting Algorithms

Figure 20.12 summarizes many of the searching and sorting algorithms covered in this book and lists the Big O of each. Figure 20.13 lists the Big O values covered in this chapter, along with a number of values for n to highlight the differences in the growth rates.

Algorithm	Location	Big O
Searching Algorithms:		
Linear Search	Section 20.2.1	$O(n)$
Binary Search	Section 20.2.2	$O(\log n)$
Sorting Algorithms:		
Selection Sort	Section 20.3.1	$O(n^2)$
Insertion Sort	Section 20.3.2	$O(n^2)$
Merge Sort	Section 20.3.3	$O(n \log n)$

Fig. 20.12 | Searching and sorting algorithms with Big O values.

$n =$	$O(\log n)$	$O(n)$	$O(n \log n)$	$O(n^2)$
1	0	1	0	1
2	1	2	2	4
3	1	3	3	9
4	1	4	4	16
5	1	5	5	25
10	1	10	10	100
100	2	100	200	10000
1,000	3	1000	3000	10^6
1,000,000	6	1000000	6000000	10^{12}
1,000,000,000	9	1000000000	9000000000	10^{18}

Fig. 20.13 | Number of comparisons for common Big O notations.

20.5 Wrap-Up

In this chapter, you learned how to search for items in arrays and how to sort arrays so that their elements are arranged in order. We discussed linear search and binary search, and selection sort, insertion sort and merge sort. You learned that linear search can operate on any set of data, but that binary search requires the data to be sorted first. You also learned that the simplest searching and sorting algorithms can exhibit poor performance. We introduced Big O notation—a measure of the efficiency of algorithms—and used it to compare the efficiency of the algorithms we discussed. In the next chapter, you'll learn about dynamic data structures that can grow or shrink at execution time.

21

Data Structures

OBJECTIVES

In this chapter you'll learn:

- To form linked data structures using references, self-referential classes and recursion.

- How boxing and unboxing enable simple-type values to be used where **objects** are expected in a program.

- To create and manipulate dynamic data structures, such as linked lists, queues, stacks and binary trees.

- Various important applications of linked data structures.

- To create reusable data structures with classes, inheritance and composition.

Much that I bound,
I could not free;
Much that I freed
returned to me.
—Lee Wilson Dodd

There is always room at the
top.
—Daniel Webster

I think that I shall never see
A poem lovely as a tree.
—Joyce Kilmer

21.1 Introduction

This chapter continues our four-chapter treatment of data structures. Most of the **data structures** that we have studied thus far have had fixed sizes, such as one- and two-dimensional arrays. Previously, we also introduced the dynamically resizable `List<T>` collection (Chapter 9). This chapter enhances our discussion of **dynamic data structures** that grow and shrink at execution time. Linked lists are collections of data items "lined up in a row" or "chained together"—users can make insertions and deletions anywhere in a linked list. Stacks are important in compilers and operating systems; insertions and deletions are made at only one end—its **top**. Queues represent waiting lines; insertions are made at the back (also referred to as the **tail**) of a queue, and deletions are made from the front (also referred to as the **head**) of a queue. **Binary trees** facilitate high-speed searching and sorting of data, efficient elimination of duplicate data items, representation of file-system directories and compilation of expressions into machine language. These data structures have many other interesting applications as well.

We'll discuss each of these major types of data structures and implement programs that create and manipulate them. We use classes, inheritance and composition to create and package these data structures for reusability and maintainability. In Chapter 22, we introduce generics, which allow you to declare data structures that can be automatically adapted to contain data of any type. In Chapter 23, we discuss C#'s predefined collection classes that implement various data structures.

The chapter examples are practical programs that will be useful in more advanced courses and in industrial applications. The programs focus on reference manipulation.

21.2 Simple-Type `struct`s, Boxing and Unboxing

The data structures we discuss in this chapter store `object` references. However, as you'll soon see, we're able to store both simple- and reference-type values in these data structures. This section discusses the mechanisms that enable simple-type values to be manipulated as objects.

Simple-Type `struct`s

Each simple type (see Appendix B, Simple Types) has a corresponding **struct** in namespace `System` that declares the simple type. These structs are called `Boolean`, `Byte`, `SByte`, `Char`, `Decimal`, `Double`, `Single`, `Int32`, `UInt32`, `Int64`, `UInt64`, `Int16` and `UInt16`. Types declared with keyword `struct` are implicitly value types.

Simple types are actually aliases for their corresponding `structs`, so a variable of a simple type can be declared using either the keyword for that simple type or the `struct` name—e.g., `int` and `Int32` are interchangeable. The methods related to a simple type are located in the corresponding `struct` (e.g., method `Parse`, which converts a `string` to an `int` value, is located in `struct Int32`). Refer to the documentation for the corresponding `struct` type to see the methods available for manipulating values of that type.

Boxing and Unboxing Conversions

Simple types and other `structs` inherit from class **ValueType** in namespace `System`. Class `ValueType` inherits from class `object`. Thus, any simple-type value can be assigned to an object variable; this is referred to as a **boxing conversion** and enables simple types to be used anywhere `objects` are expected. In a boxing conversion, the simple-type value is copied into an object so that the simple-type value can be manipulated as an `object`. Boxing conversions can be performed either *explicitly* or *implicitly* as shown in the following statements:

```
int i = 5; // create an int value
object object1 = ( object ) i; // explicitly box the int value
object object2 = i; // implicitly box the int value
```

After executing the preceding code, both `object1` and `object2` refer to two different objects that contain a copy of the integer value in `int` variable `i`.

An **unboxing conversion** can be used to explicitly convert an `object` reference to a simple value, as shown in the following statement:

```
int int1 = ( int ) object1; // explicitly unbox the int value
```

Explicitly attempting to unbox an `object` reference that does not refer to the correct simple value type causes an **InvalidCastException**.

In Chapters 22 and 23, we discuss C#'s generics and generic collections. As you'll see, generics eliminate the overhead of boxing and unboxing conversions by enabling us to create and use collections of specific value types.

21.3 Self-Referential Classes

A **self-referential class** contains a reference member that refers to an object of the same class type. For example, the class declaration in Fig. 21.1 defines the shell of a self-referential class named `Node`. This type has two properties—integer `Data` and `Node` reference `Next`. `Next` references an object of type `Node`, an object of the same type as the one being declared here—hence, the term "self-referential class." `Next` is referred to as a **link** (i.e., `Next` can be used to "tie" an object of type `Node` to another object of the same type).

```
1   // Fig. 21.1: Fig21_01.cs
2   // Self-referential Node class declaration.
3   class Node
4   {
5      public int Data { get; set; } // store integer data
6      public Node Next { get; set; } // store reference to next Node
7
```

Fig. 21.1 | Self-referential `Node` class declaration. (Part 1 of 2.)

```
 8       public Node( int dataValue )
 9       {
10          Data = dataValue;
11       } // end constructor
12    } // end class node
```

Fig. 21.1 | Self-referential Node class declaration. (Part 2 of 2.)

Self-referential objects can be linked together to form useful data structures, such as lists, queues, stacks and trees. Figure 21.2 illustrates two self-referential objects linked together to form a linked list. A backslash (representing a null reference) is placed in the link member of the second self-referential object to indicate that the link does not refer to another object. The backslash is for illustration purposes; it does *not* correspond to the backslash character in C#. A null link normally indicates the end of a data structure.

Fig. 21.2 | Self-referential class objects linked together.

Common Programming Error 21.1

Not setting the link in the last node of a list to null is a logic error.

Creating and maintaining dynamic data structures requires **dynamic memory allocation**—a program's ability to obtain more memory space at execution time to hold new nodes and to release space no longer needed. As you learned in Section 10.9, C# programs do not explicitly release dynamically allocated memory—rather, the CLR performs automatic garbage collection.

The new operator is essential to dynamic memory allocation. Operator new takes as an operand the type of the object being dynamically allocated and returns a reference to an object of that type. For example, the statement

```
Node nodeToAdd = new Node( 10 );
```

allocates the appropriate amount of memory to store a Node and stores a reference to this object in nodeToAdd. If no memory is available, new throws an OutOfMemoryException. The constructor argument 10 specifies the Node object's data.

The following sections discuss lists, stacks, queues and trees. These data structures are created and maintained with dynamic memory allocation and self-referential classes.

Good Programming Practice 21.1

When creating a large number of objects, test for an OutOfMemoryException. Perform appropriate error processing if the requested memory is not allocated.

21.4 Linked Lists

A **linked list** is a linear collection (i.e., a sequence) of self-referential class objects, called **nodes**, connected by reference links—hence, the term "linked" list. A program accesses a linked list via a reference to the first node of the list. Each subsequent node is accessed via the link-reference member stored in the previous node. By convention, the link reference in the last node of a list is set to null to mark the end of the list. Data is stored in a linked list dynamically—that is, each node is created as necessary. A node can contain data of any type, including references to objects of other classes. Stacks and queues are also linear data structures—in fact, they're constrained versions of linked lists. Trees are nonlinear data structures.

Lists of data can be stored in arrays, but linked lists provide several advantages. A linked list is appropriate when the number of data elements to be represented in the data structure is unpredictable. Unlike a linked list, the size of a conventional C# array cannot be altered, because the array size is fixed at creation time. Conventional arrays can become full, but linked lists become full only when the system has insufficient memory to satisfy dynamic memory allocation requests.

Performance Tip 21.1

An array can be declared to contain more elements than the number of items expected, possibly wasting memory. Linked lists provide better memory utilization in these situations, because they can grow and shrink at execution time.

Programmers can maintain linked lists in sorted order simply by inserting each new element at the proper point in the list (locating the proper insertion point does take time). They do not need to move existing list elements.

Performance Tip 21.2

The elements of an array are stored contiguously in memory to allow immediate access to any array element—the address of any element can be calculated directly from its index. Linked lists do not afford such immediate access to their elements—an element can be accessed only by traversing the list from the front.

Normally linked-list nodes are not stored contiguously in memory. Rather, the nodes are logically contiguous. Figure 21.3 illustrates a linked list with several nodes.

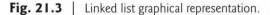

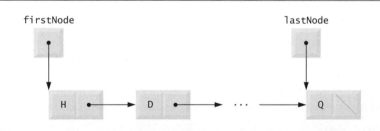

Fig. 21.3 | Linked list graphical representation.

Performance Tip 21.3

Using linked data structures and dynamic memory allocation (instead of arrays) for data structures that grow and shrink at execution time can save memory. Keep in mind, however, that reference links occupy space, and dynamic memory allocation incurs the overhead of method calls.

Linked-List Implementation

Figures 21.4–21.5 use an object of our List class to manipulate a list of miscellaneous object types. Class ListTest's Main method (Fig. 21.5) creates a list of objects, inserts objects at the beginning of the list using List method InsertAtFront, inserts objects at the end of the list using List method InsertAtBack, deletes objects from the front of the list using List method RemoveFromFront and deletes objects from the end of the list using List method Remove-FromBack. After each insert and delete operation, the program invokes List method Display to output the current list contents. If an attempt is made to remove an item from an empty list, an EmptyListException occurs. A detailed discussion of the program follows.

Performance Tip 21.4

Insertion and deletion in a sorted array can be time consuming—all the elements following the inserted or deleted element must be shifted appropriately.

The program consists of four classes—ListNode (Fig. 21.4, lines 8–30), List (lines 33–147), EmptyListException (lines 150–172) and ListTest (Fig. 21.5). The classes in Fig. 21.4 create a linked-list library (defined in namespace LinkedListLibrary) that can be reused throughout this chapter. You should place the code of Fig. 21.4 in its own class library project, as we described in Section 15.13.

```
 1   // Fig. 21.4: LinkedListLibrary.cs
 2   // ListNode, List and EmptyListException class declarations.
 3   using System;
 4
 5   namespace LinkedListLibrary
 6   {
 7      // class to represent one node in a list
 8      class ListNode
 9      {
10         // automatic read-only property Data
11         public object Data { get; private set; }
12
13         // automatic property Next
14         public ListNode Next { get; set; }
15
16         // constructor to create ListNode that refers to dataValue
17         // and is last node in list
18         public ListNode( object dataValue )
19            : this( dataValue, null )
20         {
21         } // end default constructor
22
23         // constructor to create ListNode that refers to dataValue
24         // and refers to next ListNode in List
25         public ListNode( object dataValue, ListNode nextNode )
26         {
27            Data = dataValue;
28            Next = nextNode;
29         } // end constructor
30      } // end class ListNode
```

Fig. 21.4 | ListNode, List and EmptyListException class declarations. (Part 1 of 4.)

```
31
32      // class List declaration
33      public class List
34      {
35          private ListNode firstNode;
36          private ListNode lastNode;
37          private string name; // string like "list" to display
38
39          // construct empty List with specified name
40          public List( string listName )
41          {
42              name = listName;
43              firstNode = lastNode = null;
44          } // end constructor
45
46          // construct empty List with "list" as its name
47          public List()
48              : this( "list" )
49          {
50          } // end default constructor
51
52          // Insert object at front of List. If List is empty,
53          // firstNode and lastNode will refer to same object.
54          // Otherwise, firstNode refers to new node.
55          public void InsertAtFront( object insertItem )
56          {
57              if ( IsEmpty() )
58                  firstNode = lastNode = new ListNode( insertItem );
59              else
60                  firstNode = new ListNode( insertItem, firstNode );
61          } // end method InsertAtFront
62
63          // Insert object at end of List. If List is empty,
64          // firstNode and lastNode will refer to same object.
65          // Otherwise, lastNode's Next property refers to new node.
66          public void InsertAtBack( object insertItem )
67          {
68              if ( IsEmpty() )
69                  firstNode = lastNode = new ListNode( insertItem );
70              else
71                  lastNode = lastNode.Next = new ListNode( insertItem );
72          } // end method InsertAtBack
73
74          // remove first node from List
75          public object RemoveFromFront()
76          {
77              if ( IsEmpty() )
78                  throw new EmptyListException( name );
79
80              object removeItem = firstNode.Data; // retrieve data
81
```

Fig. 21.4 | ListNode, List and EmptyListException class declarations. (Part 2 of 4.)

```
 82            // reset firstNode and lastNode references
 83            if ( firstNode == lastNode )
 84               firstNode = lastNode = null;
 85            else
 86               firstNode = firstNode.Next;
 87
 88            return removeItem; // return removed data
 89         } // end method RemoveFromFront
 90
 91         // remove last node from List
 92         public object RemoveFromBack()
 93         {
 94            if ( IsEmpty() )
 95               throw new EmptyListException( name );
 96
 97            object removeItem = lastNode.Data; // retrieve data
 98
 99            // reset firstNode and lastNode references
100            if ( firstNode == lastNode )
101               firstNode = lastNode = null;
102            else
103            {
104               ListNode current = firstNode;
105
106               // loop while current node is not lastNode
107               while ( current.Next != lastNode )
108                  current = current.Next; // move to next node
109
110               // current is new lastNode
111               lastNode = current;
112               current.Next = null;
113            } // end else
114
115            return removeItem; // return removed data
116         } // end method RemoveFromBack
117
118         // return true if List is empty
119         public bool IsEmpty()
120         {
121            return firstNode == null;
122         } // end method IsEmpty
123
124         // output List contents
125         public void Display()
126         {
127            if ( IsEmpty() )
128            {
129               Console.WriteLine( "Empty " + name );
130            } // end if
131            else
132            {
133               Console.Write( "The " + name + " is: " );
```

Fig. 21.4 | ListNode, List and EmptyListException class declarations. (Part 3 of 4.)

```
134
135                ListNode current = firstNode;
136
137                // output current node data while not at end of list
138                while ( current != null )
139                {
140                    Console.Write( current.Data + " " );
141                    current = current.Next;
142                } // end while
143
144                Console.WriteLine( "\n" );
145            } // end else
146        } // end method Display
147    } // end class List
148
149    // class EmptyListException declaration
150    public class EmptyListException : Exception
151    {
152        // parameterless constructor
153        public EmptyListException()
154            : base( "The list is empty" )
155        {
156            // empty constructor
157        } // end EmptyListException constructor
158
159        // one-parameter constructor
160        public EmptyListException( string name )
161            : base( "The " + name + " is empty" )
162        {
163            // empty constructor
164        } // end EmptyListException constructor
165
166        // two-parameter constructor
167        public EmptyListException( string exception, Exception inner )
168            : base( exception, inner )
169        {
170            // empty constructor
171        } // end EmptyListException constructor
172    } // end class EmptyListException
173 } // end namespace LinkedListLibrary
```

Fig. 21.4 | ListNode, List and EmptyListException class declarations. (Part 4 of 4.)

Class ListNode

Encapsulated in each List object is a linked list of ListNode objects. Class ListNode (Fig. 21.4, lines 8–30) contains two properties—Data and Next. Data can refer to any object. [*Note:* Typically, a data structure will contain data of only one type, or data of any type derived from one base type.] In this example, we use data of various types derived from object to demonstrate that our List class can store data of any type. Next stores a reference to the next ListNode object in the linked list. The ListNode constructors (lines 18–21 and 25–29) enable us to initialize a ListNode that will be placed at the end of a List or before a specific ListNode in a List, respectively.

Class List

Class List (lines 33–147) contains private instance variables firstNode (a reference to the first ListNode in a List) and lastNode (a reference to the last ListNode in a List). The constructors (lines 40–44 and 47–50) initialize both references to null and enable us to specify the List's name for output purposes. InsertAtFront (lines 55–61), InsertAt-Back (lines 66–72), RemoveFromFront (lines 75–89) and RemoveFromBack (lines 92–116) are the primary methods of class List. Method IsEmpty (lines 119–122) is a **predicate method** that determines whether the list is empty (i.e., the reference to the first node of the list is null). Predicate methods typically test a condition and do not modify the object on which they're called. If the list is empty, method IsEmpty returns true; otherwise, it returns false. Method Display (lines 125–146) displays the list's contents. A detailed discussion of class List's methods follows Fig. 21.5.

Class EmptyListException

Class EmptyListException (lines 150–172) defines an exception class that we use to indicate illegal operations on an empty List.

Class ListTest

Class ListTest (Fig. 21.5) uses the linked-list library to create and manipulate a linked list. [*Note:* In the project containing Fig. 21.5, you must add a reference to the class library containing the classes in Fig. 21.4. If you use our existing example, you may need to update this reference.] Line 11 creates a new List object and assigns it to variable list. Lines 14–17 create data to add to the list. Lines 20–27 use List insertion methods to insert these values and use List method Display to output the contents of list after each insertion. The values of the simple-type variables are implicitly boxed in lines 20, 22 and 24 where object references are expected. The code inside the try block (lines 33–50) removes objects via List deletion methods, outputs each removed object and outputs list after every deletion. If there's an attempt to remove an object from an empty list, the catch at lines 51–54 catches the EmptyListException and displays an error message.

```
 1   // Fig. 21.5: ListTest.cs
 2   // Testing class List.
 3   using System;
 4   using LinkedListLibrary;
 5
 6   // class to test List class functionality
 7   class ListTest
 8   {
 9      public static void Main( string[] args )
10      {
11         List list = new List(); // create List container
12
13         // create data to store in List
14         bool aBoolean = true;
15         char aCharacter = '$';
16         int anInteger = 34567;
17         string aString = "hello";
18
```

Fig. 21.5 | Testing class List. (Part 1 of 3.)

```
19        // use List insert methods
20        list.InsertAtFront( aBoolean );
21        list.Display();
22        list.InsertAtFront( aCharacter );
23        list.Display();
24        list.InsertAtBack( anInteger );
25        list.Display();
26        list.InsertAtBack( aString );
27        list.Display();
28
29        // use List remove methods
30        object removedObject;
31
32        // remove data from list and display after each removal
33        try
34        {
35           removedObject = list.RemoveFromFront();
36           Console.WriteLine( removedObject + " removed" );
37           list.Display();
38
39           removedObject = list.RemoveFromFront();
40           Console.WriteLine( removedObject + " removed" );
41           list.Display();
42
43           removedObject = list.RemoveFromBack();
44           Console.WriteLine( removedObject + " removed" );
45           list.Display();
46
47           removedObject = list.RemoveFromBack();
48           Console.WriteLine( removedObject + " removed" );
49           list.Display();
50        } // end try
51        catch ( EmptyListException emptyListException )
52        {
53           Console.Error.WriteLine( "\n" + emptyListException );
54        } // end catch
55     } // end Main
56  } // end class ListTest
```

```
The list is: True

The list is: $ True

The list is: $ True 34567

The list is: $ True 34567 hello

$ removed
The list is: True 34567 hello

True removed
The list is: 34567 hello
```

Fig. 21.5 | Testing class List. (Part 2 of 3.)

```
hello removed
The list is: 34567

34567 removed
Empty list
```

Fig. 21.5 | Testing class `List`. (Part 3 of 3.)

Method *InsertAtFront*

Over the next several pages, we discuss each of the methods of class `List` in detail. Method `InsertAtFront` (Fig. 21.4, lines 55–61) places a new node at the front of the list. The method consists of three steps:

1. Call `IsEmpty` to determine whether the list is empty (line 57).

2. If the list is empty, set both `firstNode` and `lastNode` to refer to a new `ListNode` initialized with `insertItem` (line 58). The `ListNode` constructor at lines 18–21 of Fig. 21.4 calls the `ListNode` constructor at lines 25–29, which sets property `Data` to refer to the `object` passed as the first argument and sets the `Next` property's reference to `null`.

3. If the list is not empty, the new node is "linked" into the list by setting `firstNode` to refer to a new `ListNode` object initialized with `insertItem` and `firstNode` (line 60). When the `ListNode` constructor (lines 25–29) executes, it sets property `Data` to refer to the `object` passed as the first argument and performs the insertion by setting the `Next` reference to the `ListNode` passed as the second argument.

In Fig. 21.6, part (a) shows a list and a new node during the `InsertAtFront` operation before the new node is linked into the list. The dashed lines and arrows in part (b) illustrate *Step 3* of the `InsertAtFront` operation, which enables the node containing 12 to become the new list front.

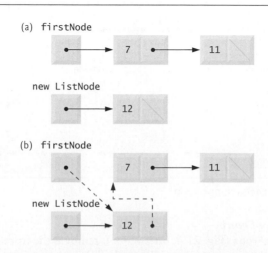

Fig. 21.6 | `InsertAtFront` operation.

Performance Tip 21.5

After locating the insertion point for a new item in a sorted linked list, inserting an element in the list is fast—only two references have to be modified. All existing nodes remain at their current locations in memory.

*Method **InsertAtBack***

Method InsertAtBack (Fig. 21.4, lines 66–72) places a new node at the back of the list. The method consists of three steps:

1. Call IsEmpty to determine whether the list is empty (line 68).

2. If the list is empty, set both firstNode and lastNode to refer to a new ListNode initialized with insertItem (lines 68–69). The ListNode constructor at lines 18–21 calls the ListNode constructor at lines 25–29, which sets property Data to refer to the object passed as the first argument and sets the Next reference to null.

3. If the list is not empty, link the new node into the list by setting lastNode and lastNode.Next to refer to a new ListNode object initialized with insertItem (line 71). When the ListNode constructor (lines 18–21) executes, it calls the constructor at lines 25–29, which sets property Data to refer to the object passed as an argument and sets the Next reference to null.

In Fig. 21.7, part (a) shows a list and a new node during the InsertAtBack operation before the new node has been linked into the list. The dashed lines and arrows in part (b) illustrate *Step 3* of method InsertAtBack, which enables a new node to be added to the end of a list that is not empty.

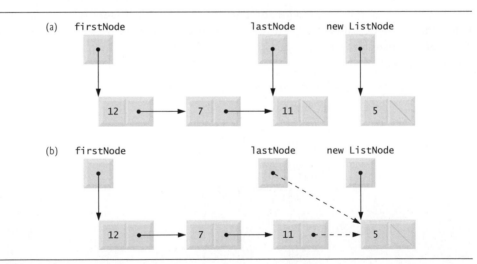

Fig. 21.7 | InsertAtBack operation.

*Method **RemoveFromFront***

Method RemoveFromFront (Fig. 21.4, lines 75–89) removes the front node of the list and returns a reference to the removed data. The method throws an EmptyListException (line 78) if the programmer tries to remove a node from an empty list. Otherwise, the method returns a reference to the removed data. After determining that a List is not empty, the method consists of four steps to remove the first node:

1. Assign firstNode.Data (the data being removed from the list) to variable removeItem (line 80).

2. If the objects to which firstNode and lastNode refer are the same object, the list has only one element, so the method sets firstNode and lastNode to null (line 84) to remove the node from the list (leaving the list empty).

3. If the list has more than one node, the method leaves reference lastNode as is and assigns firstNode.Next to firstNode (line 86). Thus, firstNode references the node that was previously the second node in the List.

4. Return the removeItem reference (line 88).

In Fig. 21.8, part (a) illustrates a list before a removal operation. The dashed lines and arrows in part (b) show the reference manipulations.

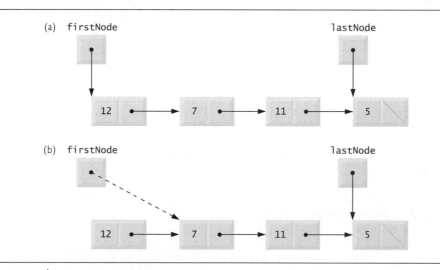

Fig. 21.8 | RemoveFromFront operation.

Method RemoveFromBack

Method RemoveFromBack (Fig. 21.4, lines 92–116) removes the last node of a list and returns a reference to the removed data. The method throws an EmptyListException (line 95) if the program attempts to remove a node from an empty list. The method consists of several steps:

1. Assign lastNode.Data (the data being removed from the list) to variable removeItem (line 97).

2. If firstNode and lastNode refer to the same object (line 100), the list has only one element, so the method sets firstNode and lastNode to null (line 101) to remove that node from the list (leaving the list empty).

3. If the list has more than one node, create ListNode variable current and assign it firstNode (line 104).

4. Now "walk the list" with `current` until it references the node before the last node. The `while` loop (lines 107–108) assigns `current.Next` to `current` as long as `current.Next` is not equal to `lastNode`.

5. After locating the second-to-last node, assign `current` to `lastNode` (line 111) to update which node is last in the list.

6. Set `current.Next` to `null` (line 112) to remove the last node from the list and terminate the list at the current node.

7. Return the `removeItem` reference (line 115).

In Fig. 21.9, part (a) illustrates a list before a removal operation. The dashed lines and arrows in part (b) show the reference manipulations.

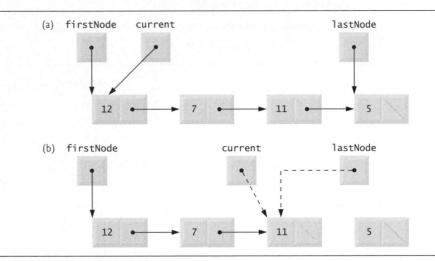

Fig. 21.9 | RemoveFromBack operation.

Method `Display`

Method `Display` (Fig. 21.4, lines 125–146) first determines whether the list is empty (line 127). If so, `Display` displays a `string` consisting of the string `"Empty "` and the list's `name`, then returns control to the calling method. Otherwise, `Display` outputs the data in the list. The method writes a `string` consisting of the string `"The "`, the list's `name` and the string `" is: "`. Then line 135 creates `ListNode` variable `current` and initializes it with `firstNode`. While `current` is not `null`, there are more items in the list. Therefore, the method displays `current.Data` (line 140), then assigns `current.Next` to `current` (line 141) to move to the next node in the list.

Linear and Circular Singly Linked and Doubly Linked Lists

The kind of linked list we have been discussing is a **singly linked list**—it begins with a reference to the first node, and each node contains a reference to the next node "in sequence." This list terminates with a node whose reference member has the value `null`. A singly linked list may be traversed in only one direction.

A **circular, singly linked list** (Fig. 21.10) begins with a reference to the first node, and each node contains a reference to the next node. The "last node" does not contain a `null`

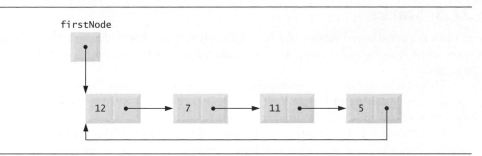

Fig. 21.10 | Circular, singly linked list.

reference; rather, the reference in the last node points back to the first node, thus closing the "circle."

A **doubly linked list** (Fig. 21.11) allows traversals both forward and backward. Such a list is often implemented with two "start references"—one that refers to the first element of the list to allow front-to-back traversal of the list and one that refers to the last element to allow back-to-front traversal. Each node has both a forward reference to the next node in the list and a backward reference to the previous node. If your list contains an alphabetized telephone directory, for example, a search for someone whose name begins with a letter near the front of the alphabet might begin from the front of the list. A search for someone whose name begins with a letter near the end of the alphabet might begin from the back.

In a **circular, doubly linked list** (Fig. 21.12), the forward reference of the last node refers to the first node, and the backward reference of the first node refers to the last node, thus closing the "circle."

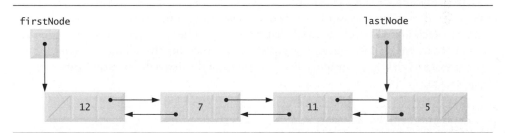

Fig. 21.11 | Doubly linked list.

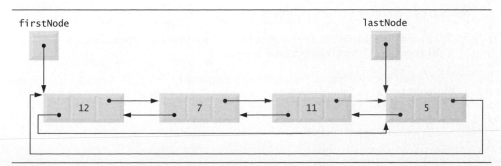

Fig. 21.12 | Circular, doubly linked list.

21.5 Stacks

A **stack** is a constrained version of a linked list—it receives new nodes and releases nodes only at the top. For this reason, a stack is referred to as a **last-in, first-out (LIFO)** data structure.

The primary operations to manipulate a stack are **push** and **pop**. Operation push adds a new node to the top of the stack. Operation pop removes a node from the top of the stack and returns the data item from the popped node.

Stacks have many interesting applications. For example, when a program calls a method, the called method must know how to return to its caller, so the return address is pushed onto the method-call stack. If a series of method calls occurs, the successive return values are pushed onto the stack in last-in, first-out order so that each method can return to its caller. Stacks support recursive method calls in the same manner that they do conventional nonrecursive method calls.

The System.Collections namespace contains class Stack for implementing and manipulating stacks that can grow and shrink during program execution.

In our next example, we take advantage of the close relationship between lists and stacks to implement a stack class by reusing a list class. We demonstrate two different forms of reusability. First, we implement the stack class by inheriting from class List of Fig. 21.4. Then we implement an identically performing stack class through composition by including a List object as a private member of a stack class.

Stack Class That Inherits from *List*

The program of Figs. 21.13 and 21.14 creates a stack class by inheriting from class List of Fig. 21.4 (line 8 of Fig. 21.3). We want the stack to have methods Push, Pop, IsEmpty and Display. Essentially, these are the methods InsertAtFront, RemoveFromFront, IsEmpty and Display of class List. Of course, class List contains other methods (such as InsertAtBack and RemoveFromBack) that we would rather not make accessible through the public interface of the stack. It is important to remember that all methods in the public interface of class List are also public methods of the derived class StackInheritance (Fig. 21.13).

```
1   // Fig. 21.13: StackInheritanceLibrary.cs
2   // Implementing a stack by inheriting from class List.
3   using LinkedListLibrary;
4
5   namespace StackInheritanceLibrary
6   {
7      // class StackInheritance inherits class List's capabilities
8      public class StackInheritance : List
9      {
10         // pass name "stack" to List constructor
11         public StackInheritance()
12            : base( "stack" )
13         {
14         } // end constructor
15
```

Fig. 21.13 | Implementing a stack by inheriting from class List. (Part 1 of 2.)

```
16              // place dataValue at top of stack by inserting
17              // dataValue at front of linked list
18              public void Push( object dataValue )
19              {
20                  InsertAtFront( dataValue );
21              } // end method Push
22
23              // remove item from top of stack by removing
24              // item at front of linked list
25              public object Pop()
26              {
27                  return RemoveFromFront();
28              } // end method Pop
29          } // end class StackInheritance
30      } // end namespace StackInheritanceLibrary
```

Fig. 21.13 | Implementing a stack by inheriting from class List. (Part 2 of 2.)

The implementation of each StackInheritance method calls the appropriate List method—method Push calls InsertAtFront, method Pop calls RemoveFromFront. Class StackInheritance does not define methods IsEmpty and Display, because StackInheritance inherits these methods from class List into StackInheritance's public interface. Class StackInheritance uses namespace LinkedListLibrary (Fig. 21.4); thus, the class library that defines StackInheritance must have a reference to the LinkedListLibrary class library.

StackInheritanceTest's Main method (Fig. 21.14) uses class StackInheritance to create a stack of objects called stack (line 12). Lines 15–18 define four values that will be pushed onto the stack and popped off it. The program pushes onto the stack (lines 21, 23, 25 and 27) a bool containing true, a char containing '$', an int containing 34567 and a string containing "hello". An infinite while loop (lines 33–38) pops the elements from the stack. When the stack is empty, method Pop throws an EmptyListException, and the program displays the exception's stack trace, which shows the program-execution stack at the time the exception occurred. The program uses method Display (inherited by StackInheritance from class List) to output the contents of the stack after each operation. Class StackInheritanceTest uses namespace LinkedListLibrary (Fig. 21.4) and namespace StackInheritanceLibrary (Fig. 21.13); thus, the solution for class StackInheritanceTest must have references to both class libraries.

```
1   // Fig. 21.14: StackInheritanceTest.cs
2   // Testing class StackInheritance.
3   using System;
4   using StackInheritanceLibrary;
5   using LinkedListLibrary;
6
7   // demonstrate functionality of class StackInheritance
8   class StackInheritanceTest
9   {
```

Fig. 21.14 | Testing class StackInheritance. (Part 1 of 3.)

```
10      public static void Main( string[] args )
11      {
12          StackInheritance stack = new StackInheritance();
13
14          // create objects to store in the stack
15          bool aBoolean = true;
16          char aCharacter = '$';
17          int anInteger = 34567;
18          string aString = "hello";
19
20          // use method Push to add items to stack
21          stack.Push( aBoolean );
22          stack.Display();
23          stack.Push( aCharacter );
24          stack.Display();
25          stack.Push( anInteger );
26          stack.Display();
27          stack.Push( aString );
28          stack.Display();
29
30          // remove items from stack
31          try
32          {
33              while ( true )
34              {
35                  object removedObject = stack.Pop();
36                  Console.WriteLine( removedObject + " popped" );
37                  stack.Display();
38              } // end while
39          } // end try
40          catch ( EmptyListException emptyListException )
41          {
42              // if exception occurs, write stack trace
43              Console.Error.WriteLine( emptyListException.StackTrace );
44          } // end catch
45      } // end Main
46  } // end class StackInheritanceTest
```

```
The stack is: True

The stack is: $ True

The stack is: 34567 $ True

The stack is: hello 34567 $ True

hello popped
The stack is: 34567 $ True

34567 popped
The stack is: $ True

$ popped
The stack is: True
```

Fig. 21.14 | Testing class StackInheritance. (Part 2 of 3.)

```
True popped
Empty stack
   at LinkedListLibrary.List.RemoveFromFront()
      in C:\examples\ch21\Fig21_04\LinkedListLibrary\
      LinkedListLibrary\LinkedListLibrary.cs:line 78
   at StackInheritanceLibrary.StackInheritance.Pop()
      in C:\examples\ch21\Fig21_13\StackInheritanceLibrary\
      StackInheritanceLibrary\StackInheritance.cs:line 27
   at StackInheritanceTest.Main(String[] args)
      in C:\examples\ch21\Fig21_14\StackInheritanceTest\
      StackInheritanceTest\StackInheritanceTest.cs:line 35
```

Fig. 21.14 | Testing class StackInheritance. (Part 3 of 3.)

Stack Class That Contains a Reference to a List

Another way to implement a stack class is by reusing a list class through composition. The class in Fig. 21.15 uses a private object of class List (line 10) in the declaration of class StackComposition. Composition enables us to hide the methods of class List that should not be in our stack's public interface by providing public interface methods only to the required List methods. This class implements each stack method by delegating its work to an appropriate List method. StackComposition's methods call List methods Insert-AtFront, RemoveFromFront, IsEmpty and Display. In this example, we do not show class StackCompositionTest, because the only difference in this example is that we change the name of the stack class from StackInheritance to StackComposition.

```
 1   // Fig. 21.15: StackCompositionLibrary.cs
 2   // StackComposition declaration with composed List object.
 3   using LinkedListLibrary;
 4
 5   namespace StackCompositionLibrary
 6   {
 7      // class StackComposition encapsulates List's capabilities
 8      public class StackComposition
 9      {
10         private List stack;
11
12         // construct empty stack
13         public StackComposition()
14         {
15            stack = new List( "stack" );
16         } // end constructor
17
18         // add object to stack
19         public void Push( object dataValue )
20         {
21            stack.InsertAtFront( dataValue );
22         } // end method Push
23
```

Fig. 21.15 | StackComposition class encapsulates functionality of class List. (Part 1 of 2.)

```
24          // remove object from stack
25          public object Pop()
26          {
27             return stack.RemoveFromFront();
28          } // end method Pop
29
30          // determine whether stack is empty
31          public bool IsEmpty()
32          {
33             return stack.IsEmpty();
34          } // end method IsEmpty
35
36          // output stack contents
37          public void Display()
38          {
39             stack.Display();
40          } // end method Display
41       } // end class StackComposition
42    } // end namespace StackCompositionLibrary
```

Fig. 21.15 | StackComposition class encapsulates functionality of class List. (Part 2 of 2.)

21.6 Queues

Another commonly used data structure is the queue. A queue is similar to a checkout line in a supermarket—the cashier services the person at the beginning of the line first. Other customers enter the line only at the end and wait for service. Queue nodes are removed only from the head (or front) of the queue and are inserted only at the tail (or end). For this reason, a queue is a **first-in, first-out** (**FIFO**) data structure. The insert and remove operations are known as **enqueue** and **dequeue**.

Queues have many uses in computer systems. Computers with only a single processor can service only one application at a time. Each application requiring processor time is placed in a queue. The application at the front of the queue is the next to receive service. Each application gradually advances to the front as the applications before it receive service.

Queues are also used to support **print spooling**. For example, a single printer might be shared by all users of a network. Many users can send print jobs to the printer, even when the printer is already busy. These print jobs are placed in a queue until the printer becomes available. A program called a **spooler** manages the queue to ensure that as each print job completes, the next one is sent to the printer.

Information packets also wait in queues in computer networks. Each time a packet arrives at a network node, it must be routed to the next node along the path to the packet's final destination. The routing node routes one packet at a time, so additional packets are enqueued until the router can route them.

A file server in a computer network handles file-access requests from many clients throughout the network. Servers have a limited capacity to service requests from clients. When that capacity is exceeded, client requests wait in queues.

Queue Class That Inherits from List

The program of Figs. 21.16 and 21.17 creates a queue class by inheriting from a list class. We want the QueueInheritance class (Fig. 21.16) to have methods Enqueue, Dequeue,

IsEmpty and Display. Essentially, these are the methods InsertAtBack, RemoveFrom-Front, IsEmpty and Display of class List. Of course, the list class contains other methods (such as InsertAtFront and RemoveFromBack) that we would rather not make accessible through the public interface to the queue class. Remember that all methods in the public interface of the List class are also public methods of the derived class QueueInheritance.

The implementation of each QueueInheritance method calls the appropriate List method—method Enqueue calls InsertAtBack and method Dequeue calls RemoveFrom-Front. Calls to IsEmpty and Display invoke the base-class versions that were inherited from class List into QueueInheritance's public interface. Class QueueInheritance uses namespace LinkedListLibrary (Fig. 21.4); thus, the class library for QueueInheritance must have a reference to the LinkedListLibrary class library.

```
 1   // Fig. 21.16: QueueInheritanceLibrary.cs
 2   // Implementing a queue by inheriting from class List.
 3   using LinkedListLibrary;
 4
 5   namespace QueueInheritanceLibrary
 6   {
 7      // class QueueInheritance inherits List's capabilities
 8      public class QueueInheritance : List
 9      {
10         // pass name "queue" to List constructor
11         public QueueInheritance()
12            : base( "queue" )
13         {
14         } // end constructor
15
16         // place dataValue at end of queue by inserting
17         // dataValue at end of linked list
18         public void Enqueue( object dataValue )
19         {
20            InsertAtBack( dataValue );
21         } // end method Enqueue
22
23         // remove item from front of queue by removing
24         // item at front of linked list
25         public object Dequeue()
26         {
27            return RemoveFromFront();
28         } // end method Dequeue
29      } // end class QueueInheritance
30   } // end namespace QueueInheritanceLibrary
```

Fig. 21.16 | Implementing a queue by inheriting from class List.

Class QueueInheritanceTest's Main method (Fig. 21.17) creates a QueueInheritance object called queue. Lines 15–18 define four values that will be enqueued and dequeued. The program enqueues (lines 21, 23, 25 and 27) a bool containing true, a char containing '$', an int containing 34567 and a string containing "hello". Class QueueInheritanceTest uses namespace LinkedListLibrary and namespace QueueInheritanceLibrary; thus, the solution for class StackInheritanceTest must have references to both class libraries.

```
 1   // Fig. 21.17: QueueTest.cs
 2   // Testing class QueueInheritance.
 3   using System;
 4   using QueueInheritanceLibrary;
 5   using LinkedListLibrary;
 6
 7   // demonstrate functionality of class QueueInheritance
 8   class QueueTest
 9   {
10      public static void Main( string[] args )
11      {
12         QueueInheritance queue = new QueueInheritance();
13
14         // create objects to store in the queue
15         bool aBoolean = true;
16         char aCharacter = '$';
17         int anInteger = 34567;
18         string aString = "hello";
19
20         // use method Enqueue to add items to queue
21         queue.Enqueue( aBoolean );
22         queue.Display();
23         queue.Enqueue( aCharacter );
24         queue.Display();
25         queue.Enqueue( anInteger );
26         queue.Display();
27         queue.Enqueue( aString );
28         queue.Display();
29
30         // use method Dequeue to remove items from queue
31         object removedObject = null;
32
33         // remove items from queue
34         try
35         {
36            while ( true )
37            {
38               removedObject = queue.Dequeue();
39               Console.WriteLine( removedObject + " dequeued" );
40               queue.Display();
41            } // end while
42         } // end try
43         catch ( EmptyListException emptyListException )
44         {
45            // if exception occurs, write stack trace
46            Console.Error.WriteLine( emptyListException.StackTrace );
47         } // end catch
48      } // end Main
49   } // end class QueueTest
```

Fig. 21.17 | Testing class QueueInheritance. (Part 1 of 2.)

```
The queue is: True

The queue is: True $

The queue is: True $ 34567

The queue is: True $ 34567 hello

True dequeued
The queue is: $ 34567 hello

$ dequeued
The queue is: 34567 hello

34567 dequeued
The queue is: hello

hello dequeued
Empty queue
   at LinkedListLibrary.List.RemoveFromFront()
      in C:\examples\ch21\Fig21_04\LinkedListLibrary\
      LinkedListLibrary\LinkedListLibrary.cs:line 78
   at QueueInheritanceLibrary.QueueInheritance.Dequeue()
      in C:\examples\ch21\Fig21_16\QueueInheritanceLibrary\
      QueueInheritanceLibrary\QueueInheritance.cs:line 28
   at QueueTest.Main(String[] args)
      in C:\examples\ch21\Fig21_17\QueueTest\
      QueueTest\QueueTest.cs:line 38
```

Fig. 21.17 | Testing class QueueInheritance. (Part 2 of 2.)

An infinite while loop (lines 36–41) dequeues the elements from the queue in FIFO order. When there are no objects left to dequeue, method Dequeue throws an Empty-ListException, and the program displays the exception's stack trace, which shows the program-execution stack at the time the exception occurred. The program uses method Display (inherited from class List) to output the contents of the queue after each operation. Class QueueInheritanceTest uses namespace LinkedListLibrary (Fig. 21.4) and namespace QueueInheritanceLibrary (Fig. 21.16); thus, the solution for class QueueInheritanceTest must have references to both class libraries.

21.7 Trees

Linked lists, stacks and queues are **linear data structures** (i.e., **sequences**). A **tree** is a non-linear, two-dimensional data structure with special properties. Tree nodes contain two or more links.

Basic Terminology
With binary trees (Fig. 21.18), each tree node contains two links (none, one or both of which may be null). The **root node** is the first node in a tree. Each link in the root node refers to a **child**. The **left child** is the first node in the **left subtree**, and the **right child** is the first node in the **right subtree**. The children of a specific node are called **siblings**. A node with no children is called a **leaf node**. Computer scientists normally draw trees from the root node down—exactly the opposite of the way most trees grow in nature.

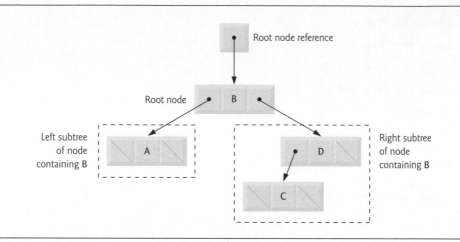

Fig. 21.18 | Binary-tree graphical representation.

 Common Programming Error 21.2

Not setting to null the links in leaf nodes of a tree is a common logic error.

Binary Search Trees

In our binary-tree example, we create a special binary tree called a **binary search tree**. A binary search tree (with no duplicate node values) has the characteristic that the values in any left subtree are less than the value in the subtree's **parent node**, and the values in any right subtree are greater than the value in the subtree's parent node. Figure 21.19 illustrates a binary search tree with 9 integer values. The shape of the binary search tree that corresponds to a set of data can depend on the order in which the values are inserted into the tree.

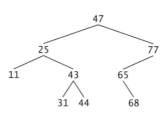

Fig. 21.19 | Binary search tree containing 9 values.

21.7.1 Binary Search Tree of Integer Values

The application of Figs. 21.20 and 21.21 creates a binary search tree of integers and traverses it (i.e., walks through all its nodes) in three ways—using recursive **inorder, preorder** and **postorder** traversals. The program generates 10 random numbers and inserts each into the tree. Figure 21.20 defines class Tree in namespace BinaryTreeLibrary for reuse purposes. Figure 21.21 defines class TreeTest to demonstrate class Tree's functionality. Method Main of class TreeTest instantiates an empty Tree object, then randomly generates 10 integers and inserts each value in the binary tree by calling `Tree` method `Insert-Node`. The program then performs preorder, inorder and postorder traversals of the tree. We'll discuss these traversals shortly.

```cs
 1    // Fig. 21.20: BinaryTreeLibrary.cs
 2    // Declaration of class TreeNode and class Tree.
 3    using System;
 4
 5    namespace BinaryTreeLibrary
 6    {
 7       // class TreeNode declaration
 8       class TreeNode
 9       {
10          // automatic property LeftNode
11          public TreeNode LeftNode { get; set; }
12
13          // automatic property Data
14          public int Data { get; set; }
15
16          // automatic property RightNode
17          public TreeNode RightNode { get; set; }
18
19          // initialize Data and make this a leaf node
20          public TreeNode( int nodeData )
21          {
22             Data = nodeData;
23             LeftNode = RightNode = null; // node has no children
24          } // end constructor
25
26          // insert TreeNode into Tree that contains nodes;
27          // ignore duplicate values
28          public void Insert( int insertValue )
29          {
30             if ( insertValue < Data ) // insert in left subtree
31             {
32                // insert new TreeNode
33                if ( LeftNode == null )
34                   LeftNode = new TreeNode( insertValue );
35                else // continue traversing left subtree
36                   LeftNode.Insert( insertValue );
37             } // end if
38             else if ( insertValue > Data ) // insert in right subtree
39             {
40                // insert new TreeNode
41                if ( RightNode == null )
42                   RightNode = new TreeNode( insertValue );
43                else // continue traversing right subtree
44                   RightNode.Insert( insertValue );
45             } // end else if
46          } // end method Insert
47       } // end class TreeNode
48
```

Fig. 21.20 | Declaration of class `TreeNode` and class `Tree`. (Part 1 of 3.)

```
49    // class Tree declaration
50    public class Tree
51    {
52       private TreeNode root;
53
54       // construct an empty Tree of integers
55       public Tree()
56       {
57          root = null;
58       } // end constructor
59
60       // Insert a new node in the binary search tree.
61       // If the root node is null, create the root node here.
62       // Otherwise, call the insert method of class TreeNode.
63       public void InsertNode( int insertValue )
64       {
65          if ( root == null )
66             root = new TreeNode( insertValue );
67          else
68             root.Insert( insertValue );
69       } // end method InsertNode
70
71       // begin preorder traversal
72       public void PreorderTraversal()
73       {
74          PreorderHelper( root );
75       } // end method PreorderTraversal
76
77       // recursive method to perform preorder traversal
78       private void PreorderHelper( TreeNode node )
79       {
80          if ( node != null )
81          {
82             // output node Data
83             Console.Write( node.Data + " " );
84
85             // traverse left subtree
86             PreorderHelper( node.LeftNode );
87
88             // traverse right subtree
89             PreorderHelper( node.RightNode );
90          } // end if
91       } // end method PreorderHelper
92
93       // begin inorder traversal
94       public void InorderTraversal()
95       {
96          InorderHelper( root );
97       } // end method InorderTraversal
98
99       // recursive method to perform inorder traversal
100      private void InorderHelper( TreeNode node )
101      {
```

Fig. 21.20 | Declaration of class TreeNode and class Tree. (Part 2 of 3.)

```
102            if ( node != null )
103            {
104                // traverse left subtree
105                InorderHelper( node.LeftNode );
106
107                // output node data
108                Console.Write( node.Data + " " );
109
110                // traverse right subtree
111                InorderHelper( node.RightNode );
112            } // end if
113        } // end method InorderHelper
114
115        // begin postorder traversal
116        public void PostorderTraversal()
117        {
118            PostorderHelper( root );
119        } // end method PostorderTraversal
120
121        // recursive method to perform postorder traversal
122        private void PostorderHelper( TreeNode node )
123        {
124            if ( node != null )
125            {
126                // traverse left subtree
127                PostorderHelper( node.LeftNode );
128
129                // traverse right subtree
130                PostorderHelper( node.RightNode );
131
132                // output node Data
133                Console.Write( node.Data + " " );
134            } // end if
135        } // end method PostorderHelper
136    } // end class Tree
137 } // end namespace BinaryTreeLibrary
```

Fig. 21.20 | Declaration of class TreeNode and class Tree. (Part 3 of 3.)

```
1  // Fig. 21.21: TreeTest.cs
2  // Testing class Tree with a binary tree.
3  using System;
4  using BinaryTreeLibrary;
5
6  // class TreeTest declaration
7  public class TreeTest
8  {
9      // test class Tree
10     public static void Main( string[] args )
11     {
12         Tree tree = new Tree();
13         int insertValue;
```

Fig. 21.21 | Testing class Tree with a binary tree. (Part 1 of 2.)

```
14
15          Console.WriteLine( "Inserting values: " );
16          Random random = new Random();
17
18          // insert 10 random integers from 0-99 in tree
19          for ( int i = 1; i <= 10; i++ )
20          {
21              insertValue = random.Next( 100 );
22              Console.Write( insertValue + " " );
23
24              tree.InsertNode( insertValue );
25          } // end for
26
27          // perform preorder traversal of tree
28          Console.WriteLine( "\n\nPreorder traversal" );
29          tree.PreorderTraversal();
30
31          // perform inorder traversal of tree
32          Console.WriteLine( "\n\nInorder traversal" );
33          tree.InorderTraversal();
34
35          // perform postorder traversal of tree
36          Console.WriteLine( "\n\nPostorder traversal" );
37          tree.PostorderTraversal();
38          Console.WriteLine();
39      } // end Main
40  } // end class TreeTest
```

```
Inserting values:
39 69 94 47 50 72 55 41 97 73

Preorder traversal
39 69 47 41 50 55 94 72 73 97

Inorder traversal
39 41 47 50 55 69 72 73 94 97

Postorder traversal
41 55 50 47 73 72 97 94 69 39
```

Fig. 21.21 | Testing class Tree with a binary tree. (Part 2 of 2.)

Class TreeNode (lines 8–47 of Fig. 21.20) is a self-referential class containing three properties—LeftNode and RightNode of type TreeNode and Data of type int. Initially, every TreeNode is a leaf node, so the constructor (lines 20–24) initializes references Left-Node and RightNode to null. We discuss TreeNode method Insert (lines 28–46) shortly.

Class Tree (lines 50–136 of Fig. 21.20) manipulates objects of class TreeNode. Class Tree has as private data root (line 52)—a reference to the root node of the tree. The class contains public method InsertNode (lines 63–69) to insert a new node in the tree and public methods PreorderTraversal (lines 72–75), InorderTraversal (lines 94–97) and PostorderTraversal (lines 116–119) to begin traversals of the tree. Each of these methods calls a separate recursive utility method to perform the traversal operations on the internal representation of the tree. The Tree constructor (lines 55–58) initializes root to null to indicate that the tree initially is empty.

Tree method `InsertNode` (lines 63–69) first determines whether the tree is empty. If so, line 66 allocates a new `TreeNode`, initializes the node with the integer being inserted in the tree and assigns the new node to `root`. If the tree is not empty, `InsertNode` calls `TreeNode` method `Insert` (lines 28–46), which recursively determines the location for the new node in the tree and inserts the node at that location. *A node can be inserted only as a leaf node in a binary search tree.*

The `TreeNode` method `Insert` compares the value to insert with the `data` value in the root node. If the insert value is less than the root-node data, the program determines whether the left subtree is empty (line 33). If so, line 34 allocates a new `TreeNode`, initializes it with the integer being inserted and assigns the new node to reference `LeftNode`. Otherwise, line 36 recursively calls `Insert` for the left subtree to insert the value into the left subtree. If the insert value is greater than the root-node data, the program determines whether the right subtree is empty (line 41). If so, line 42 allocates a new `TreeNode`, initializes it with the integer being inserted and assigns the new node to reference `RightNode`. Otherwise, line 44 recursively calls `Insert` for the right subtree to insert the value in the right subtree.

Methods `InorderTraversal`, `PreorderTraversal` and `PostorderTraversal` call helper methods `InorderHelper` (lines 100–113), `PreorderHelper` (lines 78–91) and `PostorderHelper` (lines 122–135), respectively, to traverse the tree and display the node values. The purpose of the helper methods in class `Tree` is to allow the programmer to start a traversal without needing to obtain a reference to the `root` node first, then call the recursive method with that reference. Methods `InorderTraversal`, `PreorderTraversal` and `PostorderTraversal` simply take `private` variable `root` and pass it to the appropriate helper method to initiate a traversal of the tree. For the following discussion, we use the binary search tree shown in Fig. 21.22.

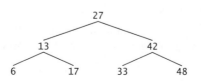

Fig. 21.22 | Binary search tree.

Inorder Traversal Algorithm

Method `InorderHelper` (lines 100–113) defines the steps for an inorder traversal. Those steps are as follows:

1. If the argument is `null`, do not process the tree.

2. Traverse the left subtree with a call to `InorderHelper` (line 105).

3. Process the value in the node (line 108).

4. Traverse the right subtree with a call to `InorderHelper` (line 111).

The inorder traversal does not process the value in a node until the values in that node's left subtree are processed. The inorder traversal of the tree in Fig. 21.22 is

```
6  13  17  27  33  42  48
```

The inorder traversal of a binary search tree displays the node values in ascending order. The process of creating a binary search tree actually sorts the data (when coupled with an inorder traversal)—thus, this process is called the **binary-tree sort**.

Preorder Traversal Algorithm

Method `PreorderHelper` (lines 78–91) defines the steps for a preorder traversal. Those steps are as follows:

1. If the argument is `null`, do not process the tree.
2. Process the value in the node (line 83).
3. Traverse the left subtree with a call to `PreorderHelper` (line 86).
4. Traverse the right subtree with a call to `PreorderHelper` (line 89).

The preorder traversal processes the value in each node as the node is visited. After processing the value in a given node, the preorder traversal processes the values in the left subtree, then the values in the right subtree. The preorder traversal of the tree in Fig. 21.22 is

```
27 13 6 17 42 33 48
```

Postorder Traversal Algorithm

Method `PostorderHelper` (lines 122–135) defines the steps for a postorder traversal. Those steps are as follows:

1. If the argument is `null`, do not process the tree.
2. Traverse the left subtree with a call to `PostorderHelper` (line 127).
3. Traverse the right subtree with a call to `PostorderHelper` (line 130).
4. Process the value in the node (line 133).

The postorder traversal processes the value in each node after the values of all that node's children are processed. The postorder traversal of the tree in Fig. 21.22 is

```
6 17 13 33 48 42 27
```

Duplicate Elimination

A binary search tree facilitates **duplicate elimination.** While building a tree, the insertion operation recognizes attempts to insert a duplicate value, because a duplicate follows the same "go left" or "go right" decisions on each comparison as the original value did. Thus, the insertion operation eventually compares the duplicate with a node containing the same value. At this point, the insertion operation might simply discard the duplicate value.

Searching a binary tree for a value that matches a key value is fast, especially for **tightly packed** binary trees. In a tightly packed binary tree, each level contains about twice as many elements as the previous level. Figure 21.22 is a tightly packed binary tree. A binary search tree with n elements has a minimum of $\log_2 n$ levels. Thus, at most $\log_2 n$ comparisons are required either to find a match or to determine that no match exists. Searching a (tightly packed) 1000-element binary search tree requires at most 10 comparisons, because $2^{10} > 1000$. Searching a (tightly packed) 1,000,000-element binary search tree requires at most 20 comparisons, because $2^{20} > 1,000,000$.

Level-Order Traversal
A **level-order traversal of a binary tree** visits the nodes of the tree row by row, starting at the root-node level. On each level of the tree, a level-order traversal visits the nodes from left to right.

21.7.2 Binary Search Tree of IComparable Objects

The binary-tree example in Section 21.7.1 works nicely when all the data is of type int. Suppose that you want to manipulate a binary tree of doubles. You could rewrite the TreeNode and Tree classes with different names and customize the classes to manipulate doubles. Similarly, for each data type you could create customized versions of classes TreeNode and Tree. This proliferates code, and can become difficult to manage and maintain.

Ideally, we'd like to define the binary tree's functionality once and reuse it for many types. Languages like C# provide polymorphic capabilities that enable all objects to be manipulated in a uniform manner. Using such capabilities enables us to design a more flexible data structure. C# provides these capabilities with generics (Chapter 22).

In our next example, we take advantage of C#'s polymorphic capabilities by implementing TreeNode and Tree classes that manipulate objects of any type that implements interface **IComparable** (namespace System). It is imperative that we be able to compare objects stored in a binary search, so we can determine the path to the insertion point of a new node. Classes that implement IComparable define method **CompareTo**, which compares the object that invokes the method with the object that the method receives as an argument. The method returns an int value less than zero if the calling object is less than the argument object, zero if the objects are equal and a positive value if the calling object is greater than the argument object. Also, both the calling and argument objects must be of the same data type; otherwise, the method throws an ArgumentException.

Figures 21.23–21.24 enhance the program of Section 21.7.1 to manipulate IComparable objects. One restriction on the new versions of classes TreeNode and Tree is that each Tree object can contain objects of only one type (e.g., all strings or all doubles). If a program attempts to insert multiple types in the same Tree object, ArgumentExceptions will occur. We modified only five lines of code in class TreeNode (lines 14, 20, 28, 30 and 38) and one line of code in class Tree (line 63) to enable processing of IComparable objects. Except for lines 30 and 38, all other changes simply replaced int with IComparable. Lines 30 and 38 previously used the < and > operators to compare the value being inserted with the value in a given node. These lines now compare IComparable objects via the interface's CompareTo method, then test the method's return value to determine whether it is less than zero (the calling object is less than the argument object) or greater than zero (the calling object is greater than the argument object), respectively. [*Note:* If this class were written using generics, the type of data, int or IComparable, could be replaced at compile time by any other type that implements the necessary operators and methods.]

```
1    // Fig. 21.23: BinaryTreeLibrary2.cs
2    // Declaration of class TreeNode and class Tree.
3    using System;
```

Fig. 21.23 | Declaration of class TreeNode and class Tree. (Part 1 of 4.)

```
4
5    namespace BinaryTreeLibrary2
6    {
7       // class TreeNode declaration
8       class TreeNode
9       {
10          // automatic property LeftNode
11          public TreeNode LeftNode { get; set; }
12
13          // automatic property Data
14          public IComparable Data { get; set; }
15
16          // automatic property RightNode
17          public TreeNode RightNode { get; set; }
18
19          // initialize Data and make this a leaf node
20          public TreeNode( IComparable nodeData )
21          {
22             Data = nodeData;
23             LeftNode = RightNode = null; // node has no children
24          } // end constructor
25
26          // insert TreeNode into Tree that contains nodes;
27          // ignore duplicate values
28          public void Insert( IComparable insertValue )
29          {
30             if ( insertValue.CompareTo(Data) < 0 ) // insert in left subtree
31             {
32                // insert new TreeNode
33                if ( LeftNode == null )
34                   LeftNode = new TreeNode( insertValue );
35                else // continue traversing left subtree
36                   LeftNode.Insert( insertValue );
37             } // end if
38             else if ( insertValue.CompareTo( Data ) > 0 ) // insert in right
39             {
40                // insert new TreeNode
41                if ( RightNode == null )
42                   RightNode = new TreeNode( insertValue );
43                else // continue traversing right subtree
44                   RightNode.Insert( insertValue );
45             } // end else if
46          } // end method Insert
47       } // end class TreeNode
48
49       // class Tree declaration
50       public class Tree
51       {
52          private TreeNode root;
53
54          // construct an empty Tree of IComparable objects
55          public Tree()
56          {
```

Fig. 21.23 | Declaration of class TreeNode and class Tree. (Part 2 of 4.)

```
57              root = null;
58          } // end constructor
59
60          // Insert a new node in the binary search tree.
61          // If the root node is null, create the root node here.
62          // Otherwise, call the insert method of class TreeNode.
63          public void InsertNode( IComparable insertValue )
64          {
65              if ( root == null )
66                  root = new TreeNode( insertValue );
67              else
68                  root.Insert( insertValue );
69          } // end method InsertNode
70
71          // begin preorder traversal
72          public void PreorderTraversal()
73          {
74              PreorderHelper( root );
75          } // end method PreorderTraversal
76
77          // recursive method to perform preorder traversal
78          private void PreorderHelper( TreeNode node )
79          {
80              if ( node != null )
81              {
82                  // output node Data
83                  Console.Write( node.Data + " " );
84
85                  // traverse left subtree
86                  PreorderHelper( node.LeftNode );
87
88                  // traverse right subtree
89                  PreorderHelper( node.RightNode );
90              } // end if
91          } // end method PreorderHelper
92
93          // begin inorder traversal
94          public void InorderTraversal()
95          {
96              InorderHelper( root );
97          } // end method InorderTraversal
98
99          // recursive method to perform inorder traversal
100         private void InorderHelper( TreeNode node )
101         {
102             if ( node != null )
103             {
104                 // traverse left subtree
105                 InorderHelper( node.LeftNode );
106
107                 // output node data
108                 Console.Write( node.Data + " " );
109
```

Fig. 21.23 | Declaration of class TreeNode and class Tree. (Part 3 of 4.)

```
110              // traverse right subtree
111              InorderHelper( node.RightNode );
112           } // end if
113        } // end method InorderHelper
114
115        // begin postorder traversal
116        public void PostorderTraversal()
117        {
118           PostorderHelper( root );
119        } // end method PostorderTraversal
120
121        // recursive method to perform postorder traversal
122        private void PostorderHelper( TreeNode node )
123        {
124           if ( node != null )
125           {
126              // traverse left subtree
127              PostorderHelper( node.LeftNode );
128
129              // traverse right subtree
130              PostorderHelper( node.RightNode );
131
132              // output node Data
133              Console.Write( node.Data + " " );
134           } // end if
135        } // end method PostorderHelper
136     } // end class Tree
137  } // end namespace BinaryTreeLibrary
```

Fig. 21.23 | Declaration of class `TreeNode` and class `Tree`. (Part 4 of 4.)

Class `TreeTest` (Fig. 21.24) creates three `Tree` objects to store `int`, `double` and `string` values, all of which the .NET Framework defines as `IComparable` types. The program populates the trees with the values in arrays `intArray` (line 12), `doubleArray` (line 13) and `stringArray` (lines 14–15), respectively.

```
1   // Fig. 21.24: TreeTest.cs
2   // Testing class Tree with IComparable objects.
3   using System;
4   using BinaryTreeLibrary2;
5
6   // class TreeTest declaration
7   public class TreeTest
8   {
9      // test class Tree
10     public static void Main( string[] args )
11     {
12        int[] intArray = { 8, 2, 4, 3, 1, 7, 5, 6 };
13        double[] doubleArray = { 8.8, 2.2, 4.4, 3.3, 1.1, 7.7, 5.5, 6.6 };
14        string[] stringArray = { "eight", "two", "four",
15           "three", "one", "seven", "five", "six" };
```

Fig. 21.24 | Testing class `Tree` with `IComparable` objects. (Part 1 of 3.)

```
16
17        // create int Tree
18        Tree intTree = new Tree();
19        PopulateTree( intArray, intTree, "intTree" );
20        TraverseTree( intTree, "intTree" );
21
22        // create double Tree
23        Tree doubleTree = new Tree();
24        PopulateTree( doubleArray, doubleTree, "doubleTree" );
25        TraverseTree( doubleTree, "doubleTree" );
26
27        // create string Tree
28        Tree stringTree = new Tree();
29        PopulateTree( stringArray, stringTree, "stringTree" );
30        TraverseTree( stringTree, "stringTree" );
31     } // end Main
32
33     // populate Tree with array elements
34     private static void PopulateTree( Array array, Tree tree, string name )
35     {
36        Console.WriteLine( "\n\n\nInserting into " + name + ":" );
37
38        foreach ( IComparable data in array )
39        {
40           Console.Write( data + " " );
41           tree.InsertNode( data );
42        } // end foreach
43     } // end method PopulateTree
44
45     // perform traversals
46     private static void TraverseTree( Tree tree, string treeType )
47     {
48        // perform preorder traversal of tree
49        Console.WriteLine( "\n\nPreorder traversal of " + treeType );
50        tree.PreorderTraversal();
51
52        // perform inorder traversal of tree
53        Console.WriteLine( "\n\nInorder traversal of " + treeType );
54        tree.InorderTraversal();
55
56        // perform postorder traversal of tree
57        Console.WriteLine( "\n\nPostorder traversal of " + treeType );
58        tree.PostorderTraversal();
59     } // end method TraverseTree
60  } // end class TreeTest
```

```
Inserting into intTree:
8 2 4 3 1 7 5 6

Preorder traversal of intTree
8 2 1 4 3 7 5 6

Inorder traversal of intTree
1 2 3 4 5 6 7 8
```

Fig. 21.24 | Testing class Tree with IComparable objects. (Part 2 of 3.)

```
Postorder traversal of intTree
1 3 6 5 7 4 2 8

Inserting into doubleTree:
8.8 2.2 4.4 3.3 1.1 7.7 5.5 6.6

Preorder traversal of doubleTree
8.8 2.2 1.1 4.4 3.3 7.7 5.5 6.6

Inorder traversal of doubleTree
1.1 2.2 3.3 4.4 5.5 6.6 7.7 8.8

Postorder traversal of doubleTree
1.1 3.3 6.6 5.5 7.7 4.4 2.2 8.8


Inserting into stringTree:
eight two four three one seven five six

Preorder traversal of stringTree
eight two four five three one seven six

Inorder traversal of stringTree
eight five four one seven six three two

Postorder traversal of stringTree
five six seven one three four two eight
```

Fig. 21.24 | Testing class `Tree` with `IComparable` objects. (Part 3 of 3.)

Method `PopulateTree` (lines 34–43) receives as arguments an `Array` containing the initializer values for the `Tree`, a `Tree` in which the array elements will be placed and a `string` representing the `Tree` name, then inserts each `Array` element into the `Tree`. Method `TraverseTree` (lines 46–59) receives as arguments a `Tree` and a `string` representing the `Tree` name, then outputs the preorder, inorder and postorder traversals of the `Tree`. The inorder traversal of each `Tree` outputs the data in sorted order regardless of the data type stored in the `Tree`. Our polymorphic implementation of class `Tree` invokes the appropriate data type's `CompareTo` method to determine the path to each value's insertion point by using the standard binary-search-tree insertion rules. Also, notice that the `Tree` of `strings` appears in alphabetical order.

21.8 Wrap-Up

In this chapter, you learned that simple types are value-type `structs` but can still be used anywhere `objects` are expected in a program due to boxing and unboxing conversions. You learned that linked lists are collections of data items that are "linked together in a chain." You also learned that a program can perform insertions and deletions anywhere in a linked list (though our implementation performed insertions and deletions only at the ends of the list). We demonstrated that the stack and queue data structures are constrained versions of lists. For stacks, you saw that insertions and deletions are made only at the top—so stacks are known as last-in, first out (LIFO) data structures. For queues, which represent waiting lines, you saw that insertions are made at the tail and deletions are made from the head—so queues are known as first-in, first out (FIFO) data structures. We also presented the binary tree data structure. You saw a binary search tree that facilitated high-speed searching and sorting of data and efficient duplicate elimination. In the next chapter, we introduce generics, which allow you to declare a family of classes and methods that implement the same functionality on *any* type.

22

Generics

...our special individuality, as distinguished from our generic humanity.
—Oliver Wendell Holmes, Sr.

Every man of genius sees the world at a different angle from his fellows.
—Havelock Ellis

Born under one law, to another bound.
—Lord Brooke

OBJECTIVES

In this chapter you'll learn:

- To create generic methods that perform identical tasks on arguments of different types.

- To create a generic Stack class that can be used to store objects of any class or interface type.

- To understand how to overload generic methods with nongeneric methods or with other generic methods.

- To understand the new() constraint of a type parameter.

- To apply multiple constraints to a type parameter.

Outline

22.1 Introduction

In Chapter 21, we presented data structures that stored and manipulated object references. This chapter continues our multi-chapter discussion on data structures. You could store any object in our data structures. One inconvenient aspect of storing object references occurs when retrieving them from a collection. An application normally needs to process specific types of objects. As a result, the object references obtained from a collection typically need to be downcast to an appropriate type to allow the application to process the objects correctly. In addition, data of value types (e.g., int and double) must be boxed to be manipulated with object references, which increases the overhead of processing such data. Most importantly, processing all data as type object limits the C# compiler's ability to perform type checking.

Though we can easily create data structures that manipulate any type of data as objects (as we did in Chapter 21), it would be nice if we could detect type mismatches at compile time—this is known as **compile-time type safety**. For example, if a Stack should store only int values, attempting to push a string onto that Stack should cause a compile-time error. Similarly, a Sort method should be able to compare elements that are all guaranteed to have the same type. If we create type-specific versions of class Stack class and method Sort, the C# compiler would certainly be able to ensure compile-time type safety. However, this would require that we create many copies of the same basic code.

This chapter discusses **generics**, which provide the means to create the general models mentioned above. **Generic methods** enable you to specify, with a single method declaration, a set of related methods. **Generic classes** enable you to specify, with a single class declaration, a set of related classes. Similarly, **generic interfaces** enable you to specify, with a single interface declaration, a set of related interfaces. Generics provide compile-time type safety. [*Note:* You can also implement generic structs and delegates.] So far in this book, we've used the generic types List (Chapter 9) and Dictionary (Chapter 17).

We can write a generic method for sorting an array of objects, then invoke the generic method separately with an int array, a double array, a string array and so on, to sort each different type of array. The compiler performs **type checking** to ensure that the array passed to the sorting method contains only elements of the correct type. We can write a single generic Stack class that manipulates a stack of objects, then instantiate Stack objects for a stack of ints, a stack of doubles, a stack of strings and so on. The compiler performs type checking to ensure that the Stack stores only elements of the correct type.

This chapter presents examples of generic methods and generic classes. It also considers the relationships between generics and other C# features, such as overloading. Chapter 23, Collections, discusses the .NET Framework's generic and nongeneric collections classes. A collection is a data structure that maintains a group of related objects or values. The .NET Framework collection classes use generics to allow you to specify the exact types of object that a particular collection will store.

22.2 Motivation for Generic Methods

Overloaded methods are often used to perform similar operations on different types of data. To understand the motivation for generic methods, let's begin with an example (Fig. 22.1) that contains three overloaded DisplayArray methods (lines 23–29, lines 32–38 and lines 41–47). These methods display the elements of an int array, a double array and a char array, respectively. Soon, we'll reimplement this program more concisely and elegantly using a single generic method.

```csharp
1   // Fig. 22.1: OverloadedMethods.cs
2   // Using overloaded methods to display arrays of different types.
3   using System;
4
5   class OverloadedMethods
6   {
7      static void Main( string[] args )
8      {
9         // create arrays of int, double and char
10        int[] intArray = { 1, 2, 3, 4, 5, 6 };
11        double[] doubleArray = { 1.1, 2.2, 3.3, 4.4, 5.5, 6.6, 7.7 };
12        char[] charArray = { 'H', 'E', 'L', 'L', 'O' };
13
14        Console.WriteLine( "Array intArray contains:" );
15        DisplayArray( intArray ); // pass an int array argument
16        Console.WriteLine( "Array doubleArray contains:" );
17        DisplayArray( doubleArray ); // pass a double array argument
18        Console.WriteLine( "Array charArray contains:" );
19        DisplayArray( charArray ); // pass a char array argument
20     } // end Main
21
22     // output int array
23     private static void DisplayArray( int[] inputArray )
24     {
25        foreach ( int element in inputArray )
26           Console.Write( element + " " );
27
28        Console.WriteLine( "\n" );
29     } // end method DisplayArray
30
31     // output double array
32     private static void DisplayArray( double[] inputArray )
33     {
34        foreach ( double element in inputArray )
35           Console.Write( element + " " );
36
37        Console.WriteLine( "\n" );
38     } // end method DisplayArray
```

Fig. 22.1 | Using overloaded methods to display arrays of different types. (Part 1 of 2.)

```
39
40        // output char array
41        private static void DisplayArray( char[] inputArray )
42        {
43           foreach ( char element in inputArray )
44              Console.Write( element + " " );
45
46           Console.WriteLine( "\n" );
47        } // end method DisplayArray
48     } // end class OverloadedMethods
```

```
Array intArray contains:
1 2 3 4 5 6

Array doubleArray contains:
1.1 2.2 3.3 4.4 5.5 6.6 7.7

Array charArray contains:
H E L L O
```

Fig. 22.1 | Using overloaded methods to display arrays of different types. (Part 2 of 2.)

The program begins by declaring and initializing three arrays—six-element int array intArray (line 10), seven-element double array doubleArray (line 11) and five-element char array charArray (line 12). Then, lines 14–19 output the arrays.

When the compiler encounters a method call, it attempts to locate a method declaration that has the same method name and parameters that match the argument types in the method call. In this example, each DisplayArray call exactly matches one of the DisplayArray method declarations. For example, line 15 calls DisplayArray with intArray as its argument. At compile time, the compiler determines argument intArray's type (i.e., int[]), attempts to locate a method named DisplayArray that specifies a single int[] parameter (which it finds at lines 23–29) and sets up a call to that method. Similarly, when the compiler encounters the DisplayArray call at line 17, it determines argument doubleArray's type (i.e., double[]), then attempts to locate a method named DisplayArray that specifies a single double[] parameter (which it finds at lines 32–38) and sets up a call to that method. Finally, when the compiler encounters the DisplayArray call at line 19, it determines argument charArray's type (i.e., char[]), then attempts to locate a method named DisplayArray that specifies a single char[] parameter (which it finds at lines 41–47) and sets up a call to that method.

Study each DisplayArray method. Note that the array element type (int, double or char) appears in two locations in each method—the method header (lines 23, 32 and 41) and the foreach statement header (lines 25, 34 and 43). If we replace the element types in each method with a generic name (such as T for "type") then all three methods would look like the one in Fig. 22.2. It appears that if we can replace the array element type in each of the three methods with a single "generic type parameter," then we should be able to declare one DisplayArray method that can display the elements of *any* array. The method in Fig. 22.2 will not compile, because its syntax is not correct. We declare a generic DisplayArray method with the proper syntax in Fig. 22.3.

```
 1   private static void DisplayArray( T[] inputArray )
 2   {
 3      foreach ( T element in inputArray )
 4         Console.Write( element + " " );
 5
 6      Console.WriteLine( "\n" );
 7   } // end method DisplayArray
```

Fig. 22.2 | `DisplayArray` method in which actual type names are replaced by convention with the generic name T.

22.3 Generic-Method Implementation

If the operations performed by several overloaded methods are identical for each argument type, the overloaded methods can be more compactly and conveniently coded using a generic method. You can write a single generic-method declaration that can be called at different times with arguments of different types. Based on the types of the arguments passed to the generic method, the compiler handles each method call appropriately.

Figure 22.3 reimplements the application of Fig. 22.1 using a generic `DisplayArray` method (lines 24–30). Note that the `DisplayArray` method calls in lines 16, 18 and 20 are identical to those of Fig. 22.1, the outputs of the two applications are identical and the code in Fig. 22.3 is 17 lines shorter than that in Fig. 22.1. As illustrated in Fig. 22.3, generics enable us to create and test our code once, then reuse it for many different types of data. This demonstrates the expressive power of generics.

```
 1   // Fig. 22.3: GenericMethod.cs
 2   // Using overloaded methods to display arrays of different types.
 3   using System;
 4   using System.Collections.Generic;
 5
 6   class GenericMethod
 7   {
 8      public static void Main( string[] args )
 9      {
10         // create arrays of int, double and char
11         int[] intArray = { 1, 2, 3, 4, 5, 6 };
12         double[] doubleArray = { 1.1, 2.2, 3.3, 4.4, 5.5, 6.6, 7.7 };
13         char[] charArray = { 'H', 'E', 'L', 'L', 'O' };
14
15         Console.WriteLine( "Array intArray contains:" );
16         DisplayArray( intArray ); // pass an int array argument
17         Console.WriteLine( "Array doubleArray contains:" );
18         DisplayArray( doubleArray ); // pass a double array argument
19         Console.WriteLine( "Array charArray contains:" );
20         DisplayArray( charArray ); // pass a char array argument
21      } // end Main
22
```

Fig. 22.3 | Using a generic method to display arrays of different types. (Part 1 of 2.)

```
23        // output array of all types
24        private static void DisplayArray< T >( T[] inputArray )
25        {
26           foreach ( T element in inputArray )
27              Console.Write( element + " " );
28
29           Console.WriteLine( "\n" );
30        } // end method DisplayArray
31     } // end class GenericMethod
```

```
Array intArray contains:
1 2 3 4 5 6

Array doubleArray contains:
1.1 2.2 3.3 4.4 5.5 6.6 7.7

Array charArray contains:
H E L L O
```

Fig. 22.3 | Using a generic method to display arrays of different types. (Part 2 of 2.)

Line 24 begins method DisplayArray's declaration. All generic method declarations have a **type-parameter list** delimited by angle brackets (<T> in this example) that follows the method's name. Each type-parameter list contains one or more **type parameters**, separated by commas. A type parameter is an identifier that's used in place of actual type names. The type parameters can be used to declare the return type, the parameter types and the local variable types in a generic method declaration; the type parameters act as placeholders for **type arguments** that represent the types of data that will be passed to the generic method. A generic method's body is declared like that of any other method. Note that the type-parameter names throughout the method declaration must match those declared in the type-parameter list. For example, line 26 declares element in the foreach statement as type T, which matches the type parameter (T) declared in line 24. Also, a type parameter can be declared only once in the type-parameter list but can appear more than once in the method's parameter list. Type-parameter names need not be unique among different generic methods.

> **Common Programming Error 22.1**
>
> *If you forget to include the type-parameter list when declaring a generic method, the compiler will not recognize the type-parameter names when they're encountered in the method. This results in compilation errors.*

Method DisplayArray's type-parameter list (line 24) declares type parameter T as the placeholder for the array-element type that DisplayArray will output. Note that T appears in the parameter list as the array-element type (line 24). The foreach statement header (line 26) also uses T as the element type. These are the same two locations where the overloaded DisplayArray methods of Fig. 22.1 specified int, double or char as the element type. The remainder of DisplayArray is identical to the version presented in Fig. 22.1.

Good Programming Practice 22.1

It's recommended that type parameters be specified as individual capital letters. Typically, a type parameter that represents the type of an element in an array (or other collection) is named E for "element" or T for "type."

As in Fig. 22.1, the program of Fig. 22.3 begins by declaring and initializing six-element int array intArray (line 11), seven-element double array doubleArray (line 12) and five-element char array charArray (line 13). Then each array is output by calling DisplayArray (lines 16, 18 and 20)—once with argument intArray, once with argument doubleArray and once with argument charArray.

When the compiler encounters a method call such as line 16, it analyzes the set of methods (both nongeneric and generic) that might match the method call, looking for a method that best matches the call. If there are no matching methods, or if there's more than one best match, the compiler generates an error. If you have any uncertainty on which of your methods will be called, the complete details of method-call resolution can be found in Section 14.5.5.1 of the Ecma C# Language Specification

```
www.ecma-international.org/publications/standards/Ecma-334.htm
```

or Section 7.5.3 of the Microsoft C# Language Specification 4

```
bit.ly/CSharp4Spec
```

In the case of line 16, the compiler determines that the best match occurs if the type parameter T in lines 24 and 26 of method DisplayArray's declaration is replaced with the type of the elements in the method call's argument intArray (i.e., int). Then, the compiler sets up a call to DisplayArray with the int as the **type argument** for the type parameter T. This is known as the **type-inferencing** process. The same process is repeated for the calls to method DisplayArray in lines 18 and 20.

Common Programming Error 22.2

If the compiler cannot find a single nongeneric or generic method declaration that's a best match for a method call, or if there are multiple best matches, a compilation error occurs.

You can also use **explicit type arguments** to indicate the exact type that should be used to call a generic function. For example, line 16 could be written as

```
DisplayArray< int >( intArray ); // pass an int array argument
```

The preceding method call explicitly provides the type argument (int) that should be used to replace type parameter T in lines 24 and 26 of the DisplayArray method's declaration.

For each variable declared with a type parameter, the compiler also determines whether the operations performed on such a variable are allowed for all types that the type parameter can assume. The only operation performed on the array elements in this example is to output the string representation of the elements. Line 27 performs an implicit boxing conversion for every value-type array element and an implicit ToString call on every array element. Since all objects have a ToString method, the compiler is satisfied that line 27 performs a valid operation for any array element.

By declaring DisplayArray as a generic method in Fig. 22.3, we eliminated the need for the overloaded methods of Fig. 22.1, saving 17 lines of code and creating a reusable method that can output the string representations of the elements in *any* one-dimensional array, not just arrays of `int`, `double` or `char` elements.

22.4 Type Constraints

In this section, we present a generic `Maximum` method that determines and returns the largest of its three arguments (all of the same type). The generic method in this example uses the type parameter to declare both the method's return type and its parameters. Normally, when comparing values to determine which one is greater, you would use the > operator. However, this operator is not overloaded for use with every type that's built into the Framework Class Library or that might be defined by extending those types. Generic code is restricted to performing operations that are guaranteed to work for every possible type. Thus, an expression like `variable1 < variable2` is not allowed unless the compiler can ensure that the operator < is provided for every type that will ever be used in the generic code. Similarly, you cannot call a method on a generic-type variable unless the compiler can ensure that all types that will ever be used in the generic code support that method.

IComparable<T> Interface

It's possible to compare two objects of the same type if that type implements the generic interface **IComparable<T>** (of namespace `System`). A benefit of implementing interface `IComparable<T>` is that `IComparable<T>` objects can be used with the sorting and searching methods of classes in the `System.Collections.Generic` namespace—we discuss those methods in Chapter 23. The structures in the Framework Class Library that correspond to the simple types all implement this interface. For example, the structure for simple type `double` is `Double` and the structure for simple type `int` is `Int32`—both `Double` and `Int32` implement the `IComparable<T>` interface. Types that implement `IComparable<T>` must declare a `CompareTo` method for comparing objects. For example, if we have two `ints`, `int1` and `int2`, they can be compared with the expression:

```
int1.CompareTo( int2 )
```

Method `CompareTo` must return 0 if the objects are equal, a negative integer if `int1` is less than `int2` or a positive integer if `int1` is greater than `int2`. It's the responsibility of the programmer who declares a type that implements `IComparable<T>` to define method `CompareTo` such that it compares the contents of two objects of that type and returns the appropriate result.

Specifying Type Constraints

Even though `IComparable` objects can be compared, they cannot be used with generic code by default, because not all types implement interface `IComparable<T>`. However, we can restrict the types that can be used with a generic method or class to ensure that they meet certain requirements. This feature—known as a **type constraint**—restricts the type of the argument supplied to a particular type parameter. Figure 22.4 declares method `Maximum` (lines 20–34) with a type constraint that requires each of the method's arguments to be of type `IComparable<T>`. This restriction is important, because not all objects can be compared. However, all `IComparable<T>` objects are guaranteed to have a `CompareTo` method that can be used in method `Maximum` to determine the largest of its three arguments.

```
 1   // Fig. 22.4: MaximumTest.cs
 2   // Generic method Maximum returns the largest of three objects.
 3   using System;
 4
 5   class MaximumTest
 6   {
 7      public static void Main( string[] args )
 8      {
 9         Console.WriteLine( "Maximum of {0}, {1} and {2} is {3}\n",
10            3, 4, 5, Maximum( 3, 4, 5 ) );
11         Console.WriteLine( "Maximum of {0}, {1} and {2} is {3}\n",
12            6.6, 8.8, 7.7, Maximum( 6.6, 8.8, 7.7 ) );
13         Console.WriteLine( "Maximum of {0}, {1} and {2} is {3}\n",
14            "pear", "apple", "orange",
15            Maximum( "pear", "apple", "orange" ) );
16      } // end Main
17
18      // generic function determines the
19      // largest of the IComparable objects
20      private static T Maximum< T >( T x, T y, T z )
21         where T : IComparable< T >
22      {
23         T max = x; // assume x is initially the largest
24
25         // compare y with max
26         if ( y.CompareTo( max ) > 0 )
27            max = y; // y is the largest so far
28
29         // compare z with max
30         if ( z.CompareTo( max ) > 0 )
31            max = z; // z is the largest
32
33         return max; // return largest object
34      } // end method Maximum
35   } // end class MaximumTest
```

```
Maximum of 3, 4 and 5 is 5

Maximum of 6.6, 8.8 and 7.7 is 8.8

Maximum of pear, apple and orange is pear
```

Fig. 22.4 | Generic method Maximum returns the largest of three objects.

Generic method Maximum uses type parameter T as the return type of the method (line 20), as the type of method parameters x, y and z (line 20), and as the type of local variable max (line 23). Generic method Maximum's **where** clause (after the parameter list in line 21) specifies the type constraint for type parameter T. In this case, the clause where T : IComparable<T> indicates that this method requires the type argument to implement interface IComparable<T>. If no type constraint is specified, the default type constraint is object.

C# provides several kinds of type constraints. A **class constraint** indicates that the type argument must be an object of a specific base class or one of its subclasses. An **interface**

constraint indicates that the type argument's class must implement a specific interface. The type constraint in line 20 is an interface constraint, because IComparable<T> is an interface. You can specify that the type argument must be a reference type or a value type by using the **reference-type constraint (class)** or the **value-type constraint (struct)**, respectively. Finally, you can specify a **constructor constraint—new()**—to indicate that the generic code can use operator new to create new objects of the type represented by the type parameter. If a type parameter is specified with a constructor constraint, the type argument's class must provide a public parameterless or default constructor to ensure that objects of the class can be created without passing constructor arguments; otherwise, a compilation error occurs.

It's possible to apply **multiple constraints** to a type parameter. To do so, simply provide a comma-separated list of constraints in the where clause. If you have a class constraint, reference-type constraint or value-type constraint, it must be listed first—only one of these types of constraints can be used for each type parameter. Interface constraints (if any) are listed next. The constructor constraint is listed last (if there is one).

Analyzing the Code

Method Maximum assumes that its first argument (x) is the largest and assigns it to local variable max (line 23). Next, the if statement at lines 26–27 determines whether y is greater than max. The condition invokes y's CompareTo method with the expression y.CompareTo(max). If y is greater than max, then y is assigned to variable max (line 27). Similarly, the statement at lines 30–31 determines whether z is greater than max. If so, line 31 assigns z to max. Then, line 33 returns max to the caller.

In Main (lines 7–16), line 10 calls Maximum with the integers 3, 4 and 5. Generic method Maximum is a match for this call, but its arguments must implement interface IComparable<T> to ensure that they can be compared. Type int is a synonym for struct Int32, which implements interface IComparable<int>. Thus, ints (and other simple types) are valid arguments to method Maximum.

Line 12 passes three double arguments to Maximum. Again, this is allowed because double is a synonym for the Double struct, which implements IComparable<double>. Line 15 passes Maximum three strings, which are also IComparable<string> objects. Note that we intentionally placed the largest value in a different position in each method call (lines 10, 12 and 15) to show that the generic method always finds the maximum value, regardless of its position in the argument list and regardless of the inferred type argument.

22.5 Overloading Generic Methods

A generic method may be **overloaded**. Each overloaded method must have a unique signature (as discussed in Chapter 7). A class can provide two or more generic methods with the same name but different method parameters. For example, we could provide a second version of generic method DisplayArray (Fig. 22.3) with the additional parameters lowIndex and highIndex that specify the portion of the array to output.

A generic method can be overloaded by nongeneric methods with the same method name. When the compiler encounters a method call, it searches for the method declaration that best matches the method name and the argument types specified in the call. For example, generic method DisplayArray of Fig. 22.3 could be overloaded with a version specific to strings that outputs the strings in neat, tabular format. If the compiler cannot match a method call to either a nongeneric method or a generic method, or if there's ambiguity due to multiple possible matches, the compiler generates an error.

22.6 Generic Classes

The concept of a data structure (e.g., a stack) that contains data elements can be understood independently of the element type it manipulates. A generic class provides a means for describing a class in a type-independent manner. We can then instantiate type-specific versions of the generic class. This capability is an opportunity for software reusability.

With a generic class, you can use a simple, concise notation to indicate the actual type(s) that should be used in place of the class's type parameter(s). At compilation time, the compiler ensures your code's type safety, and the runtime system replaces type parameters with type arguments to enable your client code to interact with the generic class.

One generic Stack class, for example, could be the basis for creating many Stack classes (e.g., "Stack of double," "Stack of int," "Stack of char," "Stack of Employee"). Figure 22.5 presents a generic Stack class declaration. This class should not be confused with the class Stack from namespace System.Collections.Generics. A generic class declaration is similar to a nongeneric class declaration, except that the class name is followed by a type-parameter list (line 5) and, optionally, one or more constraints on its type parameter. Type parameter T represents the element type the Stack will manipulate. As with generic methods, the type-parameter list of a generic class can have one or more type parameters separated by commas. Type parameter T is used throughout the Stack class declaration (Fig. 22.5) to represent the element type. Class Stack declares variable elements as an array of type T (line 8). This array (created at line 21) will store the Stack's elements. [*Note:* This example implements a Stack as an array. As you've seen in Chapter 21, Stacks also are commonly implemented as linked lists.]

```
1   // Fig. 22.5: Stack.cs
2   // Generic class Stack.
3   using System;
4
5   class Stack< T >
6   {
7      private int top; // location of the top element
8      private T[] elements; // array that stores stack elements
9
10     // parameterless constructor creates a stack of the default size
11     public Stack()
12        : this( 10 ) // default stack size
13     {
14        // empty constructor; calls constructor at line 18 to perform init
15     } // end stack constructor
16
17     // constructor creates a stack of the specified number of elements
18     public Stack( int stackSize )
19     {
```

Fig. 22.5 | Generic class Stack. (Part I of 2.)

```
20          if ( stackSize > 0 ) // validate stackSize
21             elements = new T[ stackSize ]; // create stackSize elements
22          else
23             throw new ArgumentException( "Stack size must be positive." );
24
25          top = -1; // stack initially empty
26       } // end stack constructor
27
28       // push element onto the stack; if unsuccessful,
29       // throw FullStackException
30       public void Push( T pushValue )
31       {
32          if ( top == elements.Length - 1 ) // stack is full
33             throw new FullStackException( string.Format(
34                "Stack is full, cannot push {0}", pushValue ) );
35
36          ++top; // increment top
37          elements[ top ] = pushValue; // place pushValue on stack
38       } // end method Push
39
40       // return the top element if not empty,
41       // else throw EmptyStackException
42       public T Pop()
43       {
44          if ( top == -1 ) // stack is empty
45             throw new EmptyStackException( "Stack is empty, cannot pop" );
46
47          --top; // decrement top
48          return elements[ top + 1 ]; // return top value
49       } // end method Pop
50    } // end class Stack
```

Fig. 22.5 | Generic class Stack. (Part 2 of 2.)

Class Stack has two constructors. The parameterless constructor (lines 11–15) passes the default stack size (10) to the one-argument constructor, using the syntax this (line 12) to invoke another constructor in the same class. The one-argument constructor (lines 18–26) validates the stackSize argument and creates an array of the specified stackSize (if it's greater than 0) or throws an exception, otherwise.

Method Push (lines 30–38) first determines whether an attempt is being made to push an element onto a full Stack. If so, lines 33–34 throw a FullStackException (declared in Fig. 22.6). If the Stack is not full, line 36 increments the top counter to indicate the new top position, and line 37 places the argument in that location of array elements.

Method Pop (lines 42–49) first determines whether an attempt is being made to pop an element from an empty Stack. If so, line 45 throws an EmptyStackException (declared in Fig. 22.7). Otherwise, line 47 decrements the top counter to indicate the new top position, and line 48 returns the original top element of the Stack.

Classes FullStackException (Fig. 22.6) and EmptyStackException (Fig. 22.7) each provide a parameterless constructor, a one-argument constructor of exception classes (as discussed in Section 13.8) and a two-argument constructor for creating a new exception using an existing one. The parameterless constructor sets the default error message while the other two constructors set custom error messages.

```
1   // Fig. 22.6: FullStackException.cs
2   // FullStackException indicates a stack is full.
3   using System;
4
5   class FullStackException : Exception
6   {
7      // parameterless constructor
8      public FullStackException() : base( "Stack is full" )
9      {
10        // empty constructor
11     } // end FullStackException constructor
12
13     // one-parameter constructor
14     public FullStackException( string exception ) : base( exception )
15     {
16        // empty constructor
17     } // end FullStackException constructor
18
19     // two-parameter constructor
20     public FullStackException( string exception, Exception inner )
21        : base( exception, inner )
22     {
23        // empty constructor
24     } // end FullStackException constructor
25  } // end class FullStackException
```

Fig. 22.6 | FullStackException indicates a stack is full.

```
1   // Fig. 22.7: EmptyStackException.cs
2   // EmptyStackException indicates a stack is empty.
3   using System;
4
5   class EmptyStackException : Exception
6   {
7      // parameterless constructor
8      public EmptyStackException() : base( "Stack is empty" )
9      {
10        // empty constructor
11     } // end EmptyStackException constructor
12
13     // one-parameter constructor
14     public EmptyStackException( string exception ) : base( exception )
15     {
16        // empty constructor
17     } // end EmptyStackException constructor
18
```

Fig. 22.7 | EmptyStackException indicates a stack is empty. (Part 1 of 2.)

```
19       // two-parameter constructor
20       public EmptyStackException( string exception, Exception inner )
21          : base( exception, inner )
22       {
23          // empty constructor
24       } // end EmptyStackException constructor
25    } // end class EmptyStackException
```

Fig. 22.7 | EmptyStackException indicates a stack is empty. (Part 2 of 2.)

As with generic methods, when a generic class is compiled, the compiler performs type checking on the class's type parameters to ensure that they can be used with the code in the generic class. The constraints determine the operations that can be performed on the type parameters. The runtime system replaces the type parameters with the actual types at runtime. For class Stack (Fig. 22.5), no type constraint is specified, so the default type constraint, object, is used. The scope of a generic class's type parameter is the entire class.

Now, let's consider an application (Fig. 22.8) that uses the Stack generic class. Lines 13–14 declare variables of type Stack<double> (pronounced "Stack of double") and Stack<int> (pronounced "Stack of int"). The types double and int are the Stack's type arguments. The compiler replaces the type parameters in the generic class so that the compiler can perform type checking. Method Main instantiates objects doubleStack of size 5 (line 18) and intStack of size 10 (line 19), then calls methods TestPushDouble (lines 28–48), TestPopDouble (lines 51–73), TestPushInt (lines 76–96) and TestPopInt (lines 99–121) to manipulate the two Stacks in this example.

```
1     // Fig. 22.8: StackTest.cs
2     // Testing generic class Stack.
3     using System;
4
5     class StackTest
6     {
7        // create arrays of doubles and ints
8        private static double[] doubleElements =
9           new double[]{ 1.1, 2.2, 3.3, 4.4, 5.5, 6.6 };
10       private static int[] intElements =
11          new int[]{ 1, 2, 3, 4, 5, 6, 7, 8, 9, 10, 11 };
12
13       private static Stack< double > doubleStack; // stack stores doubles
14       private static Stack< int > intStack; // stack stores int objects
15
16       public static void Main( string[] args )
17       {
18          doubleStack = new Stack< double >( 5 ); // stack of doubles
19          intStack = new Stack< int >( 10 ); // stack of ints
20
21          TestPushDouble(); // push doubles onto doubleStack
22          TestPopDouble(); // pop doubles from doubleStack
23          TestPushInt(); // push ints onto intStack
24          TestPopInt(); // pop ints from intStack
25       } // end Main
```

Fig. 22.8 | Testing generic class Stack. (Part 1 of 4.)

```
26
27      // test Push method with doubleStack
28      private static void TestPushDouble()
29      {
30         // push elements onto stack
31         try
32         {
33            Console.WriteLine( "\nPushing elements onto doubleStack" );
34
35            // push elements onto stack
36            foreach ( var element in doubleElements )
37            {
38               Console.Write( "{0:F1} ", element );
39               doubleStack.Push( element ); // push onto doubleStack
40            } // end foreach
41         } // end try
42         catch ( FullStackException exception )
43         {
44            Console.Error.WriteLine();
45            Console.Error.WriteLine( "Message: " + exception.Message );
46            Console.Error.WriteLine( exception.StackTrace );
47         } // end catch
48      } // end method TestPushDouble
49
50      // test Pop method with doubleStack
51      private static void TestPopDouble()
52      {
53         // pop elements from stack
54         try
55         {
56            Console.WriteLine( "\nPopping elements from doubleStack" );
57
58            double popValue; // store element removed from stack
59
60            // remove all elements from stack
61            while ( true )
62            {
63               popValue = doubleStack.Pop(); // pop from doubleStack
64               Console.Write( "{0:F1} ", popValue );
65            } // end while
66         } // end try
67         catch ( EmptyStackException exception )
68         {
69            Console.Error.WriteLine();
70            Console.Error.WriteLine( "Message: " + exception.Message );
71            Console.Error.WriteLine( exception.StackTrace );
72         } // end catch
73      } // end method TestPopDouble
74
75      // test Push method with intStack
76      private static void TestPushInt()
77      {
```

Fig. 22.8 | Testing generic class `Stack`. (Part 2 of 4.)

```
78          // push elements onto stack
79          try
80          {
81              Console.WriteLine( "\nPushing elements onto intStack" );
82
83              // push elements onto stack
84              foreach ( var element in intElements )
85              {
86                  Console.Write( "{0} ", element );
87                  intStack.Push( element ); // push onto intStack
88              } // end foreach
89          } // end try
90          catch ( FullStackException exception )
91          {
92              Console.Error.WriteLine();
93              Console.Error.WriteLine( "Message: " + exception.Message );
94              Console.Error.WriteLine( exception.StackTrace );
95          } // end catch
96      } // end method TestPushInt
97
98      // test Pop method with intStack
99      private static void TestPopInt()
100     {
101         // pop elements from stack
102         try
103         {
104             Console.WriteLine( "\nPopping elements from intStack" );
105
106             int popValue; // store element removed from stack
107
108             // remove all elements from stack
109             while ( true )
110             {
111                 popValue = intStack.Pop(); // pop from intStack
112                 Console.Write( "{0} ", popValue );
113             } // end while
114         } // end try
115         catch ( EmptyStackException exception )
116         {
117             Console.Error.WriteLine();
118             Console.Error.WriteLine( "Message: " + exception.Message );
119             Console.Error.WriteLine( exception.StackTrace );
120         } // end catch
121     } // end method TestPopInt
122 } // end class StackTest
```

```
Pushing elements onto doubleStack
1.1 2.2 3.3 4.4 5.5 6.6
Message: Stack is full, cannot push 6.6
   at Stack`1.Push(T pushValue) in
      C:\Examples\ch22\Fig22_05_08\Stack\Stack\Stack.cs:line 36
   at StackTest.TestPushDouble() in
      C:\Examples\ch22\Fig22_05_08\Stack\Stack\StackTest.cs:line 39
```

Fig. 22.8 | Testing generic class Stack. (Part 3 of 4.)

```
Popping elements from doubleStack
5.5 4.4 3.3 2.2 1.1

Message: Stack is empty, cannot pop
   at Stack`1.Pop() in
      C:\Examples\ch22\Fig22_05_08\Stack\Stack\Stack.cs:line 47
   at StackTest.TestPopDouble() in
      C:\Examples\ch22\Fig22_05_08\Stack\Stack\StackTest.cs:line 63

Pushing elements onto intStack
1 2 3 4 5 6 7 8 9 10 11
Message: Stack is full, cannot push 11
   at Stack`1.Push(T pushValue) in
      C:\Examples\ch22\Fig22_05_08\Stack\Stack\Stack.cs:line 36
   at StackTest.TestPushInt() in
      C:\Examples\ch22\Fig22_05_08\Stack\Stack\StackTest.cs:line 87

Popping elements from intStack
10 9 8 7 6 5 4 3 2 1
Message: Stack is empty, cannot pop
   at Stack`1.Pop() in
      C:\Examples\ch22\Fig22_05_08\Stack\Stack\Stack.cs:line 47
   at StackTest.TestPopInt() in
      C:\Examples\ch22\Fig22_05_08\Stack\Stack\StackTest.cs:line 111
```

Fig. 22.8 | Testing generic class `Stack`. (Part 4 of 4.)

Method `TestPushDouble` (lines 28–48) invokes method `Push` to place the `double` values 1.1, 2.2, 3.3, 4.4 and 5.5 stored in array `doubleElements` onto `doubleStack`. The `foreach` statement terminates when the test program attempts to `Push` a sixth value onto `doubleStack` (which is full, because `doubleStack` can store only five elements). In this case, the method throws a `FullStackException` (Fig. 22.6) to indicate that the `Stack` is full. Lines 42–47 catch this exception and display the message and stack-trace information. The stack trace indicates the exception that occurred and shows that `Stack` method `Push` generated the exception at line 36 of the file `Stack.cs` (Fig. 22.5). The trace also shows that method `Push` was called by `StackTest` method `TestPushDouble` at line 39 of `StackTest.cs`. This information enables you to determine the methods that were on the method-call stack at the time that the exception occurred. Because the program catches the exception, the C# runtime environment considers the exception to have been handled, and the program can continue executing.

Method `TestPopDouble` (lines 51–73) invokes `Stack` method `Pop` in an infinite `while` loop to remove all the values from the stack. Note in the output that the values are popped off in last-in, first-out order—this, of course, is the defining characteristic of stacks. The `while` loop (lines 61–65) continues until the stack is empty. An `EmptyStackException` occurs when an attempt is made to pop from the empty stack. This causes the program to proceed to the `catch` block (lines 67–72) and handle the exception, so the program can continue executing. When the test program attempts to `Pop` a sixth value, the `doubleStack` is empty, so method `Pop` throws an `EmptyStackException`.

Method `TestPushInt` (lines 76–96) invokes `Stack` method `Push` to place values onto `intStack` until it's full. Method `TestPopInt` (lines 99–121) invokes `Stack` method `Pop` to remove values from intStack until it's empty. Once again, note that the values pop off in last-in, first-out order.

Creating Generic Methods to Test Class Stack< T >

Note that the code in methods TestPushDouble and TestPushInt is almost identical for pushing values onto a Stack<double> or a Stack<int>, respectively. Similarly the code in methods TestPopDouble and TestPopInt is almost identical for popping values from a Stack<double> or a Stack<int>, respectively. This presents another opportunity to use generic methods. Figure 22.9 declares generic method TestPush (lines 33–54) to perform the same tasks as TestPushDouble and TestPushInt in Fig. 22.8—that is, Push values onto a Stack<T>. Similarly, generic method TestPop (lines 57–79) performs the same tasks as TestPopDouble and TestPopInt in Fig. 22.8—that is, Pop values off a Stack<T>. Note that the output of Fig. 22.9 precisely matches the output of Fig. 22.8.

```
1   // Fig. 22.9: StackTest.cs
2   // Testing generic class Stack.
3   using System;
4   using System.Collections.Generic;
5
6   class StackTest
7   {
8       // create arrays of doubles and ints
9       private static double[] doubleElements =
10          new double[] { 1.1, 2.2, 3.3, 4.4, 5.5, 6.6 };
11      private static int[] intElements =
12          new int[] { 1, 2, 3, 4, 5, 6, 7, 8, 9, 10, 11 };
13
14      private static Stack< double > doubleStack; // stack stores doubles
15      private static Stack< int > intStack; // stack stores int objects
16
17      public static void Main( string[] args )
18      {
19          doubleStack = new Stack< double >( 5 ); // stack of doubles
20          intStack = new Stack< int >( 10 ); // stack of ints
21
22          // push doubles onto doubleStack
23          TestPush( "doubleStack", doubleStack, doubleElements );
24          // pop doubles from doubleStack
25          TestPop( "doubleStack", doubleStack );
26          // push ints onto intStack
27          TestPush( "intStack", intStack, intElements );
28          // pop ints from intStack
29          TestPop( "intStack", intStack );
30      } // end Main
31
32      // test Push method
33      private static void TestPush< T >( string name, Stack< T > stack,
34          IEnumerable< T > elements )
35      {
```

Fig. 22.9 | Testing generic class Stack. (Part 1 of 3.)

```
36          // push elements onto stack
37          try
38          {
39              Console.WriteLine( "\nPushing elements onto " + name );
40
41              // push elements onto stack
42              foreach ( var element in elements )
43              {
44                  Console.Write( "{0} ", element );
45                  stack.Push( element ); // push onto stack
46              } // end foreach
47          } // end try
48          catch ( FullStackException exception )
49          {
50              Console.Error.WriteLine();
51              Console.Error.WriteLine( "Message: " + exception.Message );
52              Console.Error.WriteLine( exception.StackTrace );
53          } // end catch
54      } // end method TestPush
55
56      // test Pop method
57      private static void TestPop< T >( string name, Stack< T > stack )
58      {
59          // push elements onto stack
60          try
61          {
62              Console.WriteLine( "\nPopping elements from " + name );
63
64              T popValue; // store element removed from stack
65
66              // remove all elements from stack
67              while ( true )
68              {
69                  popValue = stack.Pop(); // pop from stack
70                  Console.Write( "{0} ", popValue );
71              } // end while
72          } // end try
73          catch ( EmptyStackException exception )
74          {
75              Console.Error.WriteLine();
76              Console.Error.WriteLine( "Message: " + exception.Message );
77              Console.Error.WriteLine( exception.StackTrace );
78          } // end catch
79      } // end TestPop
80  } // end class StackTest
```

```
Pushing elements onto doubleStack
1.1 2.2 3.3 4.4 5.5 6.6
Message: Stack is full, cannot push 6.6
   at Stack`1.Push(T pushValue) in
      C:\Examples\ch22\Fig22_09\Stack\Stack\Stack.cs:line 36
   at StackTest.TestPush[T](String name, Stack`1 stack, IEnumerable`1
      elements) in C:\Examples\ch22\Fig22_09\Stack\Stack\StackTest.cs:line 45
```

Fig. 22.9 | Testing generic class Stack. (Part 2 of 3.)

```
Popping elements from doubleStack
5.5 4.4 3.3 2.2 1.1

Message: Stack is empty, cannot pop
   at Stack`1.Pop() in
      C:\Examples\ch22\Fig22_09\Stack\Stack\Stack.cs:line 47
   at StackTest.TestPop[T](String name, Stack`1 stack) in
      C:\Examples\ch22\Fig22_09\Stack\Stack\StackTest.cs:line 69

Pushing elements onto intStack
1 2 3 4 5 6 7 8 9 10 11
Message: Stack is full, cannot push 11
   at Stack`1.Push(T pushValue) in
      C:\Examples\ch22\Fig22_09\Stack\Stack\Stack.cs:line 36
   at StackTest.TestPush[T](String name, Stack`1 stack, IEnumerable`1
      elements) in C:\Examples\ch22\Fig22_09\Stack\Stack\StackTest.cs:line 45

Popping elements from intStack
10 9 8 7 6 5 4 3 2 1
Message: Stack is empty, cannot pop
   at Stack`1.Pop() in
      C:\Examples\ch22\Fig22_09\Stack\Stack\Stack.cs:line 47
   at StackTest.TestPop[T](String name, Stack`1 stack) in
      C:\Examples\ch22\Fig22_09\Stack\Stack\StackTest.cs:line 69
```

Fig. 22.9 | Testing generic class Stack. (Part 3 of 3.)

Method Main (lines 17–30) creates the Stack<double> (line 19) and Stack<int> (line 20) objects. Lines 23–29 invoke generic methods TestPush and TestPop to test the Stack objects.

Generic method TestPush (lines 33–54) uses type parameter T (specified at line 33) to represent the data type stored in the Stack. The generic method takes three arguments—a string that represents the name of the Stack object for output purposes, an object of type Stack<T> and an IEnumerable<T> that contains the elements that will be Pushed onto Stack<T>. Note that the compiler enforces consistency between the type of the Stack and the elements that will be pushed onto the Stack when Push is invoked, which is the type argument of the generic method call. Generic method TestPop (lines 57–79) takes two arguments—a string that represents the name of the Stack object for output purposes and an object of type Stack<T>.

22.7 Wrap-Up

This chapter introduced generics. We discussed how generics ensure compile-time type safety by checking for type mismatches at compile time. You learned that the compiler will allow generic code to compile only if all operations performed on the type parameters in the generic code are supported for all types that could be used with the generic code. You also learned how to declare generic methods and classes using type parameters. We demonstrated how to use a type constraint to specify the requirements for a type parameter—a key component of compile-time type safety. We discussed several kinds of type constraints, including reference-type constraints, value-type constraints, class constraints, interface constraints and constructor constraints. We also discussed how to implement multiple type constraints for a type parameter. Finally, we showed how generics improve code reuse. In the next chapter, we demonstrate the .NET Framework Class Library's collection classes, interfaces and algorithms. Collection classes are pre-built data structures that you can reuse in your applications, saving you time.

23

Collections

The shapes a bright
container can contain!
—Theodore Roethke

*The shapes a bright
container can contain!*
—Theodore Roethke

*I think this is the most
extraordinary collection of
talent, of human
knowledge, that has ever
been gathered together at
the White House—with the
possible exception of when
Thomas Jefferson dined
alone.*
—John F. Kennedy

OBJECTIVES

In this chapter you'll learn:

- The nongeneric and generic collections that are provided by the .NET Framework.

- To use class **Array**'s **static** methods to manipulate arrays.

- To use enumerators to "walk through" a collection.

- To use the **foreach** statement with the .NET collections.

- To use nongeneric collection classes **ArrayList**, **Stack**, and **Hashtable**.

- To use generic collection classes **SortedDictionary** and **LinkedList**.

23.1 Introduction

Chapter 21 discussed how to create and manipulate data structures. The discussion was "low level," in the sense that we painstakingly created each element of each data structure dynamically with new and modified the data structures by directly manipulating their elements and references to their elements. For the vast majority of applications, there's no need to build custom data structures. Instead, you can use the prepackaged data-structure classes provided by the .NET Framework. These classes are known as **collection classes**—they store collections of data. Each instance of one of these classes is a **collection** of items. Some examples of collections are the cards you hold in a card game, the songs stored in your computer, the real-estate records in your local registry of deeds (which map book numbers and page numbers to property owners), and the players on your favorite sports team.

Collection classes enable programmers to store sets of items by using existing data structures, without concern for how they're implemented. This is a nice example of code reuse. Programmers can code faster and expect excellent performance, maximizing execution speed and minimizing memory consumption. In this chapter, we discuss the collection interfaces that list the capabilities of each collection type, the implementation classes and the **enumerators** that "walk through" collections.

The .NET Framework provides three namespaces dedicated to collections. Namespace **System.Collections** contains collections that store references to objects. We included these because there's a large amount of legacy code in industry that uses these collections. Most new applications should use the collections in the **System.Collections.Generic** namespace, which contains generic classes—such as the List<T> and Dictionary<K, V> classes you learned previously—to store collections of specific types. The **System.Collections.Specialized** namespace contains several collections that support specific types, such as strings and bits. You can learn more about this namespace at msdn.microsoft.com/en-us/library/system.collections.specialized.aspx. The collections in these namespaces provide standardized, reusable components; you do not need to write your own collection classes. These collections are written for broad reuse. They're tuned for rapid execution and for efficient use of memory. As new data structures and algorithms are developed that fit this framework, a large base of programmers already will be familiar with the interfaces and algorithms implemented by those data structures.

23.2 Collections Overview

All collection classes in the .NET Framework implement some combination of the collection interfaces. These interfaces declare the operations to be performed generically on various types of collections. Figure 23.1 lists some of the interfaces of the .NET Framework collections. All the interfaces in Fig. 23.1 are declared in namespace `System.Collections` and have generic analogs in namespace `System.Collections.Generic`. Implementations of these interfaces are provided within the framework. Programmers may also provide implementations specific to their own requirements.

Interface	Description
ICollection	The interface from which interfaces IList and IDictionary inherit. Contains a Count property to determine the size of a collection and a CopyTo method for copying a collection's contents into a traditional array.
IList	An ordered collection that can be manipulated like an array. Provides an indexer for accessing elements with an int index. Also has methods for searching and modifying a collection, including Add, Remove, Contains and IndexOf.
IDictionary	A collection of values, indexed by an arbitrary "key" object. Provides an indexer for accessing elements with an object index and methods for modifying the collection (e.g., Add, Remove). IDictionary property Keys contains the objects used as indices, and property Values contains all the stored objects.
IEnumerable	An object that can be enumerated. This interface contains exactly one method, GetEnumerator, which returns an IEnumerator object (discussed in Section 23.3). ICollection extends IEnumerable, so all collection classes implement IEnumerable directly or indirectly.

Fig. 23.1 | Some common collection interfaces.

In earlier versions of C#, the .NET Framework primarily provided the collection classes in the `System.Collections` and `System.Collections.Specialized` namespaces. These classes stored and manipulated `object` references. You could store any `object` in a collection. One inconvenient aspect of storing `object` references occurs when retrieving them from a collection. An application normally needs to process specific types of objects. As a result, the `object` references obtained from a collection typically need to be downcast to an appropriate type to allow the application to process the objects correctly.

The .NET Framework also includes the `System.Collections.Generic` namespace, which uses the generics capabilities we introduced in Chapter 22. Many of these classes are simply generic counterparts of the classes in namespace `System.Collections`. This means that you can specify the exact type that will be stored in a collection. You also receive the benefits of compile-time type checking—the compiler ensures that you're using appropriate types with your collection and, if not, issues compile-time error messages. Also, once you specify the type stored in a collection, any item you retrieve from the collection will have the correct type. This eliminates the need for explicit type casts that can throw `InvalidCastExceptions` at execution time if the referenced object is not of the appropriate type. This also eliminates the overhead of explicit casting, improving efficiency and type safety. Generic collections are especially useful for storing `struct`s, since they eliminate the overhead of boxing and unboxing.

This chapter demonstrates collection classes **Array**, **ArrayList**, **Stack**, **Hashtable**, generic **SortedDictionary**, and generic **LinkedList**—plus built-in array capabilities. Namespace `System.Collections` provides several other data structures, including **BitArray** (a collection of true/false values), **Queue** and **SortedList** (a collection of key/value pairs that are sorted by key and can be accessed either by key or by index). Figure 23.2 summarizes many of the collection classes. We also discuss the IEnumerator interface. Collection classes can create enumerators that allow programmers to walk through the collections. Although these enumerators have different implementations, they all implement the IEnumerator interface so that they can be processed polymorphically. As we'll soon see, the foreach statement is simply a convenient notation for using an enumerator. In the next section, we begin our discussion by examining enumerators and the capabilities for array manipulation. [*Note:* Collection classes directly or indirectly implement ICollection and IEnumerable (or their generic equivalents ICollection<T> and IEnumerable<T> for generic collections).]

Class	Implements	Description
System namespace:		
Array	IList	The base class of all conventional arrays. See Section 23.3.
System.Collections namespace:		
ArrayList	IList	Mimics conventional arrays, but will grow or shrink as needed to accommodate the number of elements. See Section 23.4.1.
BitArray	ICollection	A memory-efficient array of bools.
Hashtable	IDictionary	An unordered collection of key/value pairs that can be accessed by key. See Section 23.4.3.
Queue	ICollection	A first-in, first-out collection. See Section 21.6.
SortedList	IDictionary	A collection of key/value pairs that are sorted by key and can be accessed either by key or by index.
Stack	ICollection	A last-in, first-out collection. See Section 23.4.2.
System.Collections.Generic namespace:		
Dictionary< K, V >	IDictionary< K, V >	A generic, unordered collection of key/value pairs that can be accessed by key. See Section 17.4.
LinkedList< T >	ICollection< T >	A doubly linked list. See Section 23.5.2.
List< T >	IList< T >	A generic ArrayList. Section 9.4.
Queue< T >	ICollection< T >	A generic Queue.
SortedDictionary< K, V >	IDictionary< K, V >	A Dictionary that sorts the data by the keys in a binary tree. See Section 23.5.1.
SortedList< K, V >	IDictionary< K, V >	A generic SortedList.
Stack< T >	ICollection< T >	A generic Stack. See .

Fig. 23.2 | Some collection classes of the .NET Framework.

23.3 Class Array and Enumerators

Chapter 8 presented basic array-processing capabilities. All arrays implicitly inherit from abstract base class Array (namespace System); this class defines property Length, which specifies the number of elements in the array. In addition, class Array provides static methods that provide algorithms for processing arrays. Typically, class Array overloads these methods—for example, Array method Reverse can reverse the order of the elements in an entire array or can reverse the elements in a specified range of elements in an array. For a complete list of class Array's static methods visit:

> msdn.microsoft.com/en-us/library/system.array.aspx

Figure 23.3 demonstrates several static methods of class Array.

```csharp
 1   // Fig. 23.3: UsingArray.cs
 2   // Array class static methods for common array manipulations.
 3   using System;
 4   using System.Collections;
 5
 6   // demonstrate algorithms of class Array
 7   public class UsingArray
 8   {
 9      private static int[] intValues = { 1, 2, 3, 4, 5, 6 };
10      private static double[] doubleValues = { 8.4, 9.3, 0.2, 7.9, 3.4 };
11      private static int[] intValuesCopy;
12
13      // method Main demonstrates class Array's methods
14      public static void Main( string[] args )
15      {
16         intValuesCopy = new int[ intValues.Length ]; // defaults to zeroes
17
18         Console.WriteLine( "Initial array values:\n" );
19         PrintArrays(); // output initial array contents
20
21         // sort doubleValues
22         Array.Sort( doubleValues );
23
24         // copy intValues into intValuesCopy
25         Array.Copy( intValues, intValuesCopy, intValues.Length );
26
27         Console.WriteLine( "\nArray values after Sort and Copy:\n" );
28         PrintArrays(); // output array contents
29         Console.WriteLine();
30
31         // search for 5 in intValues
32         int result = Array.BinarySearch( intValues, 5 );
33         if ( result >= 0 )
34            Console.WriteLine( "5 found at element {0} in intValues",
35               result );
36         else
37            Console.WriteLine( "5 not found in intValues" );
38
```

Fig. 23.3 | Array class used to perform common array manipulations. (Part 1 of 2.)

```
39        // search for 8763 in intValues
40        result = Array.BinarySearch( intValues, 8763 );
41        if ( result >= 0 )
42           Console.WriteLine( "8763 found at element {0} in intValues",
43              result );
44        else
45           Console.WriteLine( "8763 not found in intValues" );
46     } // end Main
47
48     // output array content with enumerators
49     private static void PrintArrays()
50     {
51        Console.Write( "doubleValues: " );
52
53        // iterate through the double array with an enumerator
54        IEnumerator enumerator = doubleValues.GetEnumerator();
55
56        while ( enumerator.MoveNext() )
57           Console.Write( enumerator.Current + " " );
58
59        Console.Write( "\nintValues: " );
60
61        // iterate through the int array with an enumerator
62        enumerator = intValues.GetEnumerator();
63
64        while ( enumerator.MoveNext() )
65           Console.Write( enumerator.Current + " " );
66
67        Console.Write( "\nintValuesCopy: " );
68
69        // iterate through the second int array with a foreach statement
70        foreach ( var element in intValuesCopy )
71           Console.Write( element + " " );
72
73        Console.WriteLine();
74     } // end method PrintArrays
75  } // end class UsingArray
```

```
Initial array values:

doubleValues: 8.4 9.3 0.2 7.9 3.4
intValues: 1 2 3 4 5 6
intValuesCopy: 0 0 0 0 0 0

Array values after Sort and Copy:

doubleValues: 0.2 3.4 7.9 8.4 9.3
intValues: 1 2 3 4 5 6
intValuesCopy: 1 2 3 4 5 6

5 found at element 4 in intValues
8763 not found in intValues
```

Fig. 23.3 | Array class used to perform common array manipulations. (Part 2 of 2.)

The using directives in lines 3–4 include the namespaces System (for classes Array and Console) and System.Collections (for interface IEnumerator, which we discuss shortly). References to the assemblies for these namespaces are implicitly included in every application, so we do not need to add any new references to the project file.

Our test class declares three static array variables (lines 9–11). The first two lines initialize intValues and doubleValues to an int and double array, respectively. Static variable intValuesCopy is intended to demonstrate the Array's Copy method, so it's left with the default value null—it does not yet refer to an array.

Line 16 initializes intValuesCopy to an int array with the same length as array int-Values. Line 19 calls the PrintArrays method (lines 49–74) to output the initial contents of all three arrays. We discuss the PrintArrays method shortly. We can see from the output of Fig. 23.3 that each element of array intValuesCopy is initialized to the default value 0.

Line 22 uses static Array method **Sort** to sort array doubleValues. When this method returns, the array contains its original elements sorted in ascending order. The elements in the array must implement the IComparable interface.

Line 25 uses static Array method **Copy** to copy elements from array intValues to array intValuesCopy. The first argument is the array to copy (intValues), the second argument is the destination array (intValuesCopy) and the third argument is an int representing the number of elements to copy (in this case, intValues.Length specifies all elements).

Lines 32 and 40 invoke static Array method **BinarySearch** to perform binary searches on array intValues. Method BinarySearch receives the *sorted* array in which to search and the key for which to search. The method returns the index in the array at which it finds the key (or a negative number if the key was not found). BinarySearch assumes that it receives a sorted array. Its behavior on an unsorted array is unpredictable. Chapter 20 discussed binary searching in detail.

Method PrintArrays (lines 49–74) uses class Array's methods to loop though each array. The GetEnumerator method (line 54) obtains an enumerator for array doubleValues. Recall that Array implements the **IEnumerable** interface. All arrays inherit implicitly from Array, so both the int[] and double[] array types implement IEnumerable interface method **GetEnumerator**, which returns an enumerator that can iterate over the collection. Interface **IEnumerator** (which all enumerators implement) defines methods **MoveNext** and **Reset** and property **Current**. MoveNext moves the enumerator to the next element in the collection. The first call to MoveNext positions the enumerator at the first element of the collection. MoveNext returns true if there's at least one more element in the collection; otherwise, the method returns false. Method Reset positions the enumerator before the first element of the collection. Methods MoveNext and Reset throw an **InvalidOperationException** if the contents of the collection are modified in any way after the enumerator is created. Property Current returns the object at the current location in the collection.

> ### Common Programming Error 23.1
> *If a collection is modified after an enumerator is created for that collection, the enumerator immediately becomes invalid—any methods called on the enumerator after this point throw InvalidOperationExceptions. For this reason, enumerators are said to be "fail fast."*

When an enumerator is returned by the GetEnumerator method in line 54, it's initially positioned *before* the first element in Array doubleValues. Then when line 56 calls MoveNext in the first iteration of the while loop, the enumerator advances to the first element in `doubleValues`. The `while` statement in lines 56–57 loops over each element until the enumerator passes the end of `doubleValues` and `MoveNext` returns `false`. In each iteration, we use the enumerator's `Current` property to obtain and output the current array element. Lines 62–65 iterate over array `intValues`.

Notice that `PrintArrays` is called twice (lines 19 and 28), so `GetEnumerator` is called twice on `doubleValues`. The `GetEnumerator` method (lines 54 and 62) always returns an enumerator positioned before the first element. Also notice that the `IEnumerator` property `Current` is read-only. Enumerators cannot be used to modify the contents of collections, only to obtain the contents.

Lines 70–71 use a `foreach` statement to iterate over the collection elements like an enumerator. In fact, the `foreach` statement behaves exactly like an enumerator. Both loop over the elements of an array one by one in consecutive order. Neither allows you to modify the elements during the iteration. This is not a coincidence. The `foreach` statement implicitly obtains an enumerator via the `GetEnumerator` method and uses the enumerator's `MoveNext` method and `Current` property to traverse the collection, just as we did explicitly in lines 54–57. For this reason, we can use the `foreach` statement to iterate over *any* collection that implements the `IEnumerable` interface—not just arrays. We demonstrate this functionality in the next section when we discuss class `ArrayList`.

Other `static Array` methods include **Clear** (to set a range of elements to 0, `false` or `null`, as appropriate), **CreateInstance** (to create a new array of a specified type), **IndexOf** (to locate the first occurrence of an object in an array or portion of an array), **LastIndexOf** (to locate the last occurrence of an object in an array or portion of an array) and **Reverse** (to reverse the contents of an array or portion of an array).

23.4 Nongeneric Collections

The `System.Collections` namespace in the .NET Framework Class Library is the primary source for nongeneric collections. These classes provide standard implementations of many of the data structures discussed in Chapter 21 with collections that store references of type `object`. In this section, we demonstrate classes `ArrayList`, `Stack` and `Hashtable`.

23.4.1 Class ArrayList

In most programming languages, conventional arrays have a fixed size—they cannot be changed dynamically to conform to an application's execution-time memory requirements. In some applications, this fixed-size limitation presents a problem for programmers. They must choose between using fixed-size arrays that are large enough to store the maximum number of elements the application may require and using dynamic data structures that can grow and shrink the amount of memory required to store data in response to the changing requirements of an application at execution time.

The .NET Framework's **ArrayList** collection class mimics the functionality of conventional arrays and provides dynamic resizing of the collection through the class's methods. At any time, an `ArrayList` contains a certain number of elements less than or equal to its **capacity**—the number of elements currently reserved for the `ArrayList`. An application can manipulate the capacity with `ArrayList` property `Capacity`. [*Note:* New applications should use the generic `List<T>` class introduced in Chapter 9.]

Performance Tip 23.1

As with linked lists, inserting additional elements into an ArrayList *whose current size is less than its capacity is a fast operation.*

Performance Tip 23.2

It's a slow operation to insert an element into an ArrayList *that needs to grow larger to accommodate a new element. An* ArrayList *that's at its capacity must have its memory reallocated and the existing values copied into it.*

Performance Tip 23.3

If storage is at a premium, use method **TrimToSize** *of class* ArrayList *to trim an Array-List to its exact size. This will optimize an* ArrayList's *memory use. Be careful—if the application needs to insert additional elements, the process will be slower, because the Ar-rayList must grow dynamically (trimming leaves no room for growth).*

ArrayLists store references to objects. All classes derive from class object, so an ArrayList can contain objects of any type. Figure 23.4 lists some useful methods and properties of class ArrayList.

Method or property	Description
Add	Adds an object to the ArrayList and returns an int specifying the index at which the object was added.
Capacity	Property that gets and sets the number of elements for which space is currently reserved in the ArrayList.
Clear	Removes all the elements from the ArrayList.
Contains	Returns true if the specified object is in the ArrayList; otherwise, returns false.
Count	Read-only property that gets the number of elements stored in the ArrayList.
IndexOf	Returns the index of the first occurrence of the specified object in the ArrayList.
Insert	Inserts an object at the specified index.
Remove	Removes the first occurrence of the specified object.
RemoveAt	Removes an object at the specified index.
RemoveRange	Removes a specified number of elements starting at a specified index in the ArrayList.
Sort	Sorts the ArrayList.
TrimToSize	Sets the Capacity of the ArrayList to the number of elements the ArrayList currently contains (Count).

Fig. 23.4 | Some methods and properties of class ArrayList.

Figure 23.5 demonstrates class ArrayList and several of its methods. Class ArrayList belongs to the System.Collections namespace (line 4). Lines 8–11 declare two arrays of strings (colors and removeColors) that we'll use to fill two ArrayList objects. Recall from Section 10.11 that constants must be initialized at compile time, but readonly variables can be initialized at execution time. Arrays are objects created at execution time, so we declare colors and removeColors with readonly—not const—to make them unmodifiable. When the application begins execution, we create an ArrayList with an initial capacity of one element and store it in variable list (line 16). The foreach statement in lines 19–20 adds the five elements of array colors to list via ArrayList's **Add** method, so list grows to accommodate these new elements. Line 24 uses ArrayList's overloaded constructor to create a new ArrayList initialized with the contents of array removeColors, then assigns it to variable removeList. This constructor can initialize the contents of an ArrayList with the elements of any ICollection passed to it. Many of the collection classes have such a constructor. Notice that the constructor call in line 24 performs the task of lines 19–20.

```
1   // Fig. 23.5: ArrayListTest.cs
2   // Using class ArrayList.
3   using System;
4   using System.Collections;
5
6   public class ArrayListTest
7   {
8      private static readonly string[] colors =
9         { "MAGENTA", "RED", "WHITE", "BLUE", "CYAN" };
10     private static readonly string[] removeColors =
11        { "RED", "WHITE", "BLUE" };
12
13     // create ArrayList, add colors to it and manipulate it
14     public static void Main( string[] args )
15     {
16        ArrayList list = new ArrayList( 1 ); // initial capacity of 1
17
18        // add the elements of the colors array to the ArrayList list
19        foreach ( var color in colors )
20           list.Add( color ); // add color to the ArrayList list
21
22        // add elements in the removeColors array to
23        // the ArrayList removeList with the ArrayList constructor
24        ArrayList removeList = new ArrayList( removeColors );
25
26        Console.WriteLine( "ArrayList: " );
27        DisplayInformation( list ); // output the list
28
29        // remove from ArrayList list the colors in removeList
30        RemoveColors( list, removeList );
31
32        Console.WriteLine( "\nArrayList after calling RemoveColors: " );
33        DisplayInformation( list ); // output list contents
34     } // end Main
35
```

Fig. 23.5 | Using class ArrayList. (Part I of 2.)

```
36        // displays information on the contents of an array list
37        private static void DisplayInformation( ArrayList arrayList )
38        {
39           // iterate through array list with a foreach statement
40           foreach ( var element in arrayList )
41              Console.Write( "{0} ", element ); // invokes ToString
42
43           // display the size and capacity
44           Console.WriteLine( "\nSize = {0}; Capacity = {1}",
45              arrayList.Count, arrayList.Capacity );
46
47           int index = arrayList.IndexOf( "BLUE" );
48
49           if ( index != -1 )
50              Console.WriteLine( "The array list contains BLUE at index {0}.",
51                 index );
52           else
53              Console.WriteLine( "The array list does not contain BLUE." );
54        } // end method DisplayInformation
55
56        // remove colors specified in secondList from firstList
57        private static void RemoveColors( ArrayList firstList,
58           ArrayList secondList )
59        {
60           // iterate through second ArrayList like an array
61           for ( int count = 0; count < secondList.Count; count++ )
62              firstList.Remove( secondList[ count ] );
63        } // end method RemoveColors
64     } // end class ArrayListTest
```

```
ArrayList:
MAGENTA RED WHITE BLUE CYAN
Size = 5; Capacity = 8
The array list contains BLUE at index 3.

ArrayList after calling RemoveColors:
MAGENTA CYAN
Size = 2; Capacity = 8
The array list does not contain BLUE.
```

Fig. 23.5 | Using class ArrayList. (Part 2 of 2.)

Line 27 calls method DisplayInformation (lines 37–54) to output the contents of the list. This method uses a foreach statement to traverse the elements of an ArrayList. As we discussed in Section 23.3, the foreach statement is a convenient shorthand for calling ArrayList's GetEnumerator method and using an enumerator to traverse the elements of the collection. Also, line 40 infers that the iteration variable's type is object because class ArrayList is nongeneric and stores references to objects.

We use properties **Count** and **Capacity** (line 45) to display the current number and the maximum number of elements that can be stored without allocating more memory to the ArrayList. The output of Fig. 23.5 indicates that the ArrayList has capacity 8.

In line 47, we invoke method **IndexOf** to determine the position of the string "BLUE" in arrayList and store the result in local variable index. IndexOf returns -1 if the element is not found. The if statement in lines 49–53 checks if index is -1 to determine whether arrayList contains "BLUE". If it does, we output its index. ArrayList also provides method **Contains**, which simply returns true if an object is in the ArrayList, and false otherwise. Method Contains is preferred if we do not need the index of the element.

> **Performance Tip 23.4**
>
> *ArrayList methods IndexOf and Contains each perform a linear search, which is a costly operation for large ArrayLists. If the ArrayList is sorted, use ArrayList method BinarySearch to perform a more efficient search. Method BinarySearch returns the index of the element, or a negative number if the element is not found.*

After method DisplayInformation returns, we call method RemoveColors (lines 57–63) with the two ArrayLists. The for statement in lines 61–62 iterates over ArrayList secondList. Line 62 uses an indexer to access an ArrayList element—by following the ArrayList reference name with square brackets ([]) containing the desired index of the element. An ArgumentOutOfRangeException occurs if the specified index is not both greater than 0 and less than the number of elements currently stored in the ArrayList (specified by the ArrayList's Count property).

We use the indexer to obtain each of secondList's elements, then remove each one from firstList with the **Remove** method. This method deletes a specified item from an ArrayList by performing a linear search and removing (only) the first occurrence of the specified object. All subsequent elements shift toward the beginning of the ArrayList to fill the emptied position.

After the call to RemoveColors, line 33 again outputs the contents of list, confirming that the elements of removeList were, indeed, removed.

23.4.2 Class Stack

The Stack class implements a stack data structure and provides much of the functionality that we defined in our own implementation in Section 21.5. Refer to that section for a discussion of stack data-structure concepts. We created a test application in Fig. 21.14 to demonstrate the StackInheritance data structure that we developed. We adapt Fig. 21.14 in Fig. 23.6 to demonstrate the .NET Framework collection class Stack. [*Note:* New applications requiring a stack class should use the generic Stack<T> class.]

```
1   // Fig. 23.6: StackTest.cs
2   // Demonstrating class Stack.
3   using System;
4   using System.Collections;
5
6   public class StackTest
7   {
8      public static void Main( string[] args )
9      {
10        Stack stack = new Stack(); // create an empty Stack
11
12        // create objects to store in the stack
13        bool aBoolean = true;
```

Fig. 23.6 | Demonstrating class Stack. (Part I of 3.)

```
14            char aCharacter = '$';
15            int anInteger = 34567;
16            string aString = "hello";
17
18            // use method Push to add items to (the top of) the stack
19            stack.Push( aBoolean );
20            PrintStack( stack );
21            stack.Push( aCharacter );
22            PrintStack( stack );
23            stack.Push( anInteger );
24            PrintStack( stack );
25            stack.Push( aString );
26            PrintStack( stack );
27
28            // check the top element of the stack
29            Console.WriteLine( "The top element of the stack is {0}\n",
30               stack.Peek() );
31
32            // remove items from stack
33            try
34            {
35               while ( true )
36               {
37                  object removedObject = stack.Pop();
38                  Console.WriteLine( removedObject + " popped" );
39                  PrintStack( stack );
40               } // end while
41            } // end try
42            catch ( InvalidOperationException exception )
43            {
44               // if exception occurs, output stack trace
45               Console.Error.WriteLine( exception );
46            } // end catch
47         } // end Main
48
49         // display the contents of a stack
50         private static void PrintStack( Stack stack )
51         {
52            if ( stack.Count == 0 )
53               Console.WriteLine( "stack is empty\n" ); // the stack is empty
54            else
55            {
56               Console.Write( "The stack is: " );
57
58               // iterate through the stack with a foreach statement
59               foreach ( var element in stack )
60                  Console.Write( "{0} ", element ); // invokes ToString
61
62               Console.WriteLine( "\n" );
63            } // end else
64         } // end method PrintStack
65      } // end class StackTest
```

Fig. 23.6 | Demonstrating class Stack. (Part 2 of 3.)

```
The stack is: True

The stack is: $ True

The stack is: 34567 $ True

The stack is: hello 34567 $ True

The top element of the stack is hello

hello popped
The stack is: 34567 $ True

34567 popped
The stack is: $ True

$ popped
The stack is: True

True popped
stack is empty

System.InvalidOperationException: Stack empty.
   at System.Collections.Stack.Pop()
   at StackTest.Main(String[] args) in C:\examples\ch23\
      fig23_06\StackTest\StackTest.cs:line 37
```

Fig. 23.6 | Demonstrating class Stack. (Part 3 of 3.)

The using directive in line 4 allows us to use the Stack class with its unqualified name from the System.Collections namespace. Line 10 creates a Stack. As one might expect, class Stack has methods **Push** and **Pop** to perform the basic stack operations.

Method Push takes an object as an argument and inserts it at the top of the Stack. If the number of items on the Stack (the Count property) is equal to the capacity at the time of the Push operation, the Stack grows to accommodate more objects. Lines 19–26 use method Push to add four elements (a bool, a char, an int and a string) to the stack and invoke method PrintStack (lines 50–64) after each Push to output the contents of the stack. Notice that this nongeneric Stack class can store only references to objects, so each of the value-type items—the bool, the char and the int—is implicitly boxed before it's added to the Stack. (Namespace System.Collections.Generic provides a generic Stack class that has many of the same methods and properties used in Fig. 23.6. This version eliminates the overhead of boxing and unboxing simple types.)

Method PrintStack (lines 50–64) uses Stack property Count (implemented to fulfill the contract of interface ICollection) to obtain the number of elements in stack. If the stack is not empty (i.e., Count is not equal to 0), we use a foreach statement to iterate over the stack and output its contents by implicitly invoking the ToString method of each element. The foreach statement implicitly invokes Stack's GetEnumerator method, which we could have called explicitly to traverse the stack via an enumerator.

Method **Peek** returns the value of the top stack element but does not remove the element from the Stack. We use Peek at line 30 to obtain the top object of the Stack, then output that object, implicitly invoking the object's ToString method. An InvalidOperationException occurs if the Stack is empty when the application calls Peek. (We do not need an exception-handling block because we know the stack is not empty here.)

Method Pop takes no arguments—it removes and returns the object currently on top of the Stack. An infinite loop (lines 35–40) pops objects off the stack and outputs them until the stack is empty. When the application calls Pop on the empty stack, an Invalid-OperationException is thrown. The catch block (lines 42–46) outputs the exception, implicitly invoking the InvalidOperationException's ToString method to obtain its error message and stack trace.

Common Programming Error 23.2

Attempting to Peek or Pop an empty Stack (a Stack whose Count property is 0) causes an InvalidOperationException.

Although Fig. 23.6 does not demonstrate it, class Stack also has method **Contains**, which returns true if the Stack contains the specified object, and returns false otherwise.

23.4.3 Class Hashtable

When an application creates objects of new or existing types, it needs to manage those objects efficiently. This includes sorting and retrieving objects. Sorting and retrieving information with arrays is efficient if some aspect of your data directly matches the key value and if those keys are unique and tightly packed. If you have 100 employees with nine-digit social security numbers and you want to store and retrieve employee data by using the social security number as a key, it would nominally require an array with 1,000,000,000 elements, because there are 1,000,000,000 unique nine-digit numbers. If you have an array that large, you could get high performance storing and retrieving employee records by simply using the social security number as the array index, but it would be a large waste of memory.

Many applications have this problem—either the keys are of the wrong type (i.e., not nonnegative integers), or they're of the right type but are sparsely spread over a large range.

What is needed is a high-speed scheme for converting keys such as social security numbers and inventory part numbers to unique array indices. Then, when an application needs to store something, the scheme could convert the application key rapidly to an index and the record of information could be stored at that location in the array. Retrieval occurs the same way—once the application has a key for which it wants to retrieve the data record, the application simply applies the conversion to the key, which produces the array index where the data resides in the array and retrieves the data.

The scheme we describe here is the basis of a technique called **hashing**, in which we store data in a data structure called a **hash table**. Why the name? Because, when we convert a key into an array index, we literally scramble the bits, making a "hash" of the number. The number actually has no real significance beyond its usefulness in storing and retrieving this particular data record.

A glitch in the scheme occurs when there are **collisions** (i.e., two different keys "hash into" the same cell, or element, in the array). Since we cannot sort two different data records to the same space, we need to find an alternative home for all records beyond the first that hash to a particular array index. One scheme for doing this is to "hash again" (i.e., to reapply the hashing transformation to the key to provide a next candidate cell in the array). The hashing process is designed so that with just a few hashes, an available cell will be found.

Another scheme uses one hash to locate the first candidate cell. If the cell is occupied, successive cells are searched linearly until an available cell is found. Retrieval works the same way—the key is hashed once, the resulting cell is checked to determine whether it contains the desired data. If it does, the search is complete. If it does not, successive cells are searched linearly until the desired data is found.

The most popular solution to hash-table collisions is to have each cell of the table be a hash "bucket"—typically, a linked list of all the key/value pairs that hash to that cell. This is the solution that the .NET Framework's **Hashtable** class implements.

The **load factor** affects the performance of hashing schemes. The load factor is the ratio of the number of objects stored in the hash table to the total number of cells of the hash table. As this ratio gets higher, the chance of collisions tends to increase.

> **Performance Tip 23.5**
>
> *The load factor in a hash table is a classic example of a **space/time trade-off**: By increasing the load factor, we get better memory utilization, but the application runs slower due to increased hashing collisions. By decreasing the load factor, we get better application speed because of reduced hashing collisions, but we get poorer memory utilization because a larger portion of the hash table remains empty.*

Computer-science students study hashing schemes in courses called "Data Structures" and "Algorithms." Recognizing the value of hashing, the .NET Framework provides class Hashtable to enable programmers to easily employ hashing in applications.

This concept is profoundly important in our study of object-oriented programming. Classes encapsulate and hide complexity (i.e., implementation details) and offer user-friendly interfaces. Crafting classes to do this properly is one of the most valued skills in the field of object-oriented programming.

A **hash function** performs a calculation that determines where to place data in the hash table. The hash function is applied to the key in a key/value pair of objects. Class Hashtable can accept any object as a key. For this reason, class object defines method **GetHashCode**, which all objects inherit. Most classes that are candidates to be used as keys in a hash table override this method to provide one that performs efficient hash-code calculations for a specific type. For example, a string has a hash-code calculation that's based on the contents of the string. Figure 23.7 uses a Hashtable to count the number of occurrences of each word in a string. [*Note:* New applications should use generic class Dictionary<K, V> (introduced in Section 17.4) rather than Hashtable.]

```
1   // Fig. 23.7: HashtableTest.cs
2   // Application counts the number of occurrences of each word in a string
3   // and stores them in a hash table.
4   using System;
5   using System.Text.RegularExpressions;
6   using System.Collections;
7
8   public class HashtableTest
9   {
```

Fig. 23.7 | Application counts the number of occurrences of each word in a string and stores them in a hash table. (Part 1 of 3.)

```
10          public static void Main( string[] args )
11          {
12             // create hash table based on user input
13             Hashtable table = CollectWords();
14
15             // display hash-table content
16             DisplayHashtable( table );
17          } // end Main
18
19          // create hash table from user input
20          private static Hashtable CollectWords()
21          {
22             Hashtable table = new Hashtable(); // create a new hash table
23
24             Console.WriteLine( "Enter a string: " ); // prompt for user input
25             string input = Console.ReadLine(); // get input
26
27             // split input text into tokens
28             string[] words = Regex.Split( input, @"\s+" );
29
30             // processing input words
31             foreach ( var word in words )
32             {
33                string wordKey = word.ToLower(); // get word in lowercase
34
35                // if the hash table contains the word
36                if ( table.ContainsKey( wordKey ) )
37                {
38                   table[ wordKey ] = ( ( int ) table[ wordKey ] ) + 1;
39                } // end if
40                else
41                   // add new word with a count of 1 to hash table
42                   table.Add( wordKey, 1 );
43             } // end foreach
44
45             return table;
46          } // end method CollectWords
47
48          // display hash-table content
49          private static void DisplayHashtable( Hashtable table )
50          {
51             Console.WriteLine( "\nHashtable contains:\n{0,-12}{1,-12}",
52                "Key:", "Value:" );
53
54             // generate output for each key in hash table
55             // by iterating through the Keys property with a foreach statement
56             foreach ( var key in table.Keys )
57                Console.WriteLine( "{0,-12}{1,-12}", key, table[ key ] );
58
59             Console.WriteLine( "\nsize: {0}", table.Count );
60          } // end method DisplayHashtable
61       } // end class HashtableTest
```

Fig. 23.7 | Application counts the number of occurrences of each word in a `string` and stores them in a hash table. (Part 2 of 3.)

```
Enter a string:
As idle as a painted ship upon a painted ocean

Hashtable contains:
Key:          Value:
ocean         1
a             2
as            2
ship          1
upon          1
painted       2
idle          1

size: 7
```

Fig. 23.7 | Application counts the number of occurrences of each word in a string and stores them in a hash table. (Part 3 of 3.)

Lines 4–6 contain using directives for namespaces System (for class Console), System.Text.RegularExpressions (for class Regex) and System.Collections (for class Hashtable). Class HashtableTest declares three static methods. Method CollectWords (lines 20–46) inputs a string and returns a Hashtable in which each value stores the number of times that word appears in the string and the word is used for the key. Method DisplayHashtable (lines 49–60) displays the Hashtable passed to it in column format. The Main method (lines 10–17) simply invokes CollectWords (line 13), then passes the Hashtable returned by CollectWords to DisplayHashtable in line 16.

Method CollectWords (lines 20–46) begins by initializing local variable table with a new Hashtable (line 22) that has a default maximum load factor of 1.0. When the Hashtable reaches the specified load factor, the capacity is increased automatically. (This implementation detail is invisible to clients of the class.) Lines 24–25 prompt the user and input a string. We use static method Split of class Regex in line 28 to divide the string by its whitespace characters. This creates an array of "words," which we then store in local variable words.

Lines 31–43 loop over every element of array words. Each word is converted to lowercase with string method **ToLower**, then stored in variable wordKey (line 33). Then line 36 calls Hashtable method **ContainsKey** to determine whether the word is in the hash table (and thus has occurred previously in the string). If the Hashtable does not contain an entry for the word, line 42 uses Hashtable method **Add** to create a new entry in the hash table, with the lowercase word as the key and an object containing 1 as the value. Autoboxing occurs when the application passes integer 1 to method Add, because the hash table stores both the key and value in references of type object.

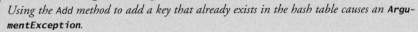

> **Common Programming Error 23.3**
> *Using the Add method to add a key that already exists in the hash table causes an **Argu-mentException**.*

If the word is already a key in the hash table, line 38 uses the Hashtable's indexer to obtain and set the key's associated value (the word count) in the hash table. We first downcast the value obtained by the get accessor from an object to an int. This unboxes the value so that we can increment it by 1. Then, when we use the indexer's set accessor to assign the key's associated value, the incremented value is implicitly reboxed so that it can be stored in the hash table.

Notice that invoking the get accessor of a Hashtable indexer with a key that does not exist in the hash table obtains a null reference. Using the set accessor with a key that does not exist in the hash table creates a new entry, as if you had used the Add method.

Line 45 returns the hash table to the Main method, which then passes it to method DisplayHashtable (lines 49–60), which displays all the entries. This method uses read-only property **Keys** (line 56) to get an ICollection that contains all the keys. Because ICollection extends IEnumerable, we can use this collection in the foreach statement in lines 56–57 to iterate over the keys of the hash table. This loop accesses and outputs each key and its value in the hash table using the iteration variable and table's get accessor. Each key and its value is displayed in a field width of -12. The negative field width indicates that the output is left justified. A hash table is not sorted, so the key/value pairs are not displayed in any particular order. Line 59 uses Hashtable property **Count** to get the number of key/value pairs in the Hashtable.

Lines 56–57 could have also used the foreach statement with the Hashtable object itself, instead of using the Keys property. If you use a foreach statement with a Hashtable object, the iteration variable will be of type **DictionaryEntry**. The enumerator of a Hashtable (or any other class that implements **IDictionary**) uses the DictionaryEntry structure to store key/value pairs. This structure provides properties Key and Value for retrieving the key and value of the current element. If you do not need the key, class Hashtable also provides a read-only **Values** property that gets an ICollection of all the values stored in the Hashtable. We can use this property to iterate through the values stored in the Hashtable without regard for where they're stored.

Problems with Nongeneric Collections

In the word-counting application of Fig. 23.7, our Hashtable stores its keys and data as object references, even though we store only string keys and int values by convention. This results in some awkward code. For example, line 38 was forced to unbox and box the int data stored in the Hashtable every time it incremented the count for a particular key. This is inefficient. A similar problem occurs in line 56—the iteration variable of the foreach statement is an object reference. If we need to use any of its string-specific methods, we need an explicit downcast.

This can cause subtle bugs. Suppose we decide to improve the readability of Fig. 23.7 by using the indexer's set accessor instead of the Add method to add a key/value pair in line 42, but accidentally type:

```
table[ wordKey ] = wordKey; // initialize to 1
```

This statement will create a new entry with a string key and string value instead of an int value of 1. Although the application will compile correctly, this is clearly incorrect. If a word appears twice, line 38 will try to downcast this string to an int, causing an InvalidCastException at execution time. The error that appears at execution time will indicate that the problem is at line 38, where the exception occurred, *not* at line 42. This makes the error more difficult to find and debug, especially in large software applications where the exception may occur in a different file—and even in a different assembly.

23.5 Generic Collections

The System.Collections.Generic namespace contains generic classes that allow us to create collections of specific types. As you saw in Fig. 23.2, many of the classes are simply generic versions of nongeneric collections. A couple of classes implement new data structures. Here, we demonstrate generic collections SortedDictionary and LinkedList.

23.5.1 Generic Class SortedDictionary

A **dictionary** is the general term for a collection of key/value pairs. A hash table is one way to implement a dictionary. The .NET Framework provides several implementations of dictionaries, both generic and nongeneric, all of which implement the IDictionary interface (described in Fig. 23.1). The application in Fig. 23.8 is a modification of Fig. 23.7 that uses the generic class **SortedDictionary**. Generic class SortedDictionary does not use a hash table, but instead stores its key/value pairs in a binary search tree. (We discuss binary trees in depth in Section 21.7.) As the class name suggests, the entries in Sorted-Dictionary are sorted in the tree by key. When the key implements generic interface IComparable<T>, the SortedDictionary uses the results of IComparable<T> method CompareTo to sort the keys. Notice that despite these implementation details, we use the same public methods, properties and indexers with classes Hashtable and SortedDictionary in the same ways. In fact, except for the generic-specific syntax, Fig. 23.8 looks remarkably similar to Fig. 23.7. This is the beauty of object-oriented programming.

```
1   // Fig. 23.12: SortedDictionaryTest.cs
2   // Application counts the number of occurrences of each word in a string
3   // and stores them in a generic sorted dictionary.
4   using System;
5   using System.Text.RegularExpressions;
6   using System.Collections.Generic;
7
8   public class SortedDictionaryTest
9   {
10     public static void Main( string[] args )
11     {
12        // create sorted dictionary based on user input
13        SortedDictionary< string, int > dictionary = CollectWords();
14
15        // display sorted dictionary content
16        DisplayDictionary( dictionary );
17     } // end Main
18
19     // create sorted dictionary from user input
20     private static SortedDictionary< string, int > CollectWords()
21     {
22        // create a new sorted dictionary
23        SortedDictionary< string, int > dictionary =
24           new SortedDictionary< string, int >();
25
```

Fig. 23.8 | Application counts the number of occurrences of each word in a string and stores them in a generic sorted dictionary. (Part I of 2.)

```
26              Console.WriteLine( "Enter a string: " ); // prompt for user input
27              string input = Console.ReadLine(); // get input
28
29              // split input text into tokens
30              string[] words = Regex.Split( input, @"\s+" );
31
32              // processing input words
33              foreach ( var word in words )
34              {
35                  string wordKey = word.ToLower(); // get word in lowercase
36
37                  // if the dictionary contains the word
38                  if ( dictionary.ContainsKey( wordKey ) )
39                  {
40                      ++dictionary[ wordKey ];
41                  } // end if
42                  else
43                      // add new word with a count of 1 to the dictionary
44                      dictionary.Add( wordKey, 1 );
45              } // end foreach
46
47              return dictionary;
48          } // end method CollectWords
49
50          // display dictionary content
51          private static void DisplayDictionary< K, V >(
52              SortedDictionary< K, V > dictionary )
53          {
54              Console.WriteLine( "\nSorted dictionary contains:\n{0,-12}{1,-12}",
55                  "Key:", "Value:" );
56
57              // generate output for each key in the sorted dictionary
58              // by iterating through the Keys property with a foreach statement
59              foreach ( K key in dictionary.Keys )
60                  Console.WriteLine( "{0,-12}{1,-12}", key, dictionary[ key ] );
61
62              Console.WriteLine( "\nsize: {0}", dictionary.Count );
63          } // end method DisplayDictionary
64      } // end class SortedDictionaryTest
```

```
Enter a string:
We few, we happy few, we band of brothers

Sorted dictionary contains:
Key:        Value:
band        1
brothers    1
few,        2
happy       1
of          1
we          3

size: 6
```

Fig. 23.8 | Application counts the number of occurrences of each word in a `string` and stores them in a generic sorted dictionary. (Part 2 of 2.)

Line 6 contains a using directive for the System.Collections.Generic namespace, which contains class SortedDictionary. The generic class SortedDictionary takes two type arguments—the first specifies the type of key (i.e., string) and the second the type of value (i.e., int). We have simply replaced the word Hashtable in line 13 and lines 23–24 with SortedDictionary<string, int> to create a dictionary of int values keyed with strings. Now, the compiler can check and notify us if we attempt to store an object of the wrong type in the dictionary. Also, because the compiler now knows that the data structure contains int values, there's no longer any need for the downcast in line 40. This allows line 40 to use the much more concise prefix increment (++) notation. These changes result in code that can be checked for type safety at compile time.

Static method DisplayDictionary (lines 51–63) has been modified to be completely generic. It takes type parameters K and V. These parameters are used in line 52 to indicate that DisplayDictionary takes a SortedDictionary with keys of type K and values of type V. We use type parameter K again in line 59 as the type of the iteration key. This use of generics is a marvelous example of code reuse. If we decide to change the application to count the number of times each character appears in a string, method DisplayDictionary could receive an argument of type SortedDictionary<char, int> without modification. The key-value pairs displayed are now ordered by key, as shown in Fig. 23.8.

Performance Tip 23.6

Because class SortedDictionary keeps its elements sorted in a binary tree, obtaining or inserting a key/value pair takes O(log n) *time, which is fast compared to linear searching, then inserting.*

Common Programming Error 23.4

Invoking the get accessor of a SortedDictionary indexer with a key that does not exist in the collection causes a **KeyNotFoundException**. *This behavior is different from that of the Hashtable indexer's get accessor, which would return* null.

23.5.2 Generic Class LinkedList

The generic **LinkedList** class is a doubly linked list—we can navigate the list both backward and forward with nodes of generic class **LinkedListNode**. Each node contains property **Value** and read-only properties **Previous** and **Next**. The Value property's type matches LinkedList's single type parameter because it contains the data stored in the node. The Previous property gets a reference to the preceding node in the linked list (or null if the node is the first of the list). Similarly, the Next property gets a reference to the subsequent reference in the linked list (or null if the node is the last of the list). We demonstrate a few linked-list manipulations in Fig. 23.9.

```
1   // Fig. 23.9: LinkedListTest.cs
2   // Using LinkedLists.
3   using System;
4   using System.Collections.Generic;
5
```

Fig. 23.9 | Using LinkedLists. (Part 1 of 4.)

```
 6   public class LinkedListTest
 7   {
 8      private static readonly string[] colors = { "black", "yellow",
 9         "green", "blue", "violet", "silver" };
10      private static readonly string[] colors2 = { "gold", "white",
11         "brown", "blue", "gray" };
12
13      // set up and manipulate LinkedList objects
14      public static void Main( string[] args )
15      {
16         LinkedList< string > list1 = new LinkedList< string >();
17
18         // add elements to first linked list
19         foreach ( var color in colors )
20            list1.AddLast( color );
21
22         // add elements to second linked list via constructor
23         LinkedList< string > list2 = new LinkedList< string >( colors2 );
24
25         Concatenate( list1, list2 ); // concatenate list2 onto list1
26         PrintList( list1 ); // display list1 elements
27
28         Console.WriteLine( "\nConverting strings in list1 to uppercase\n" );
29         ToUppercaseStrings( list1 ); // convert to uppercase string
30         PrintList( list1 ); // display list1 elements
31
32         Console.WriteLine( "\nDeleting strings between BLACK and BROWN\n" );
33         RemoveItemsBetween( list1, "BLACK", "BROWN" );
34
35         PrintList( list1 ); // display list1 elements
36         PrintReversedList( list1 ); // display list in reverse order
37      } // end Main
38
39      // display list contents
40      private static void PrintList< T >( LinkedList< T > list )
41      {
42         Console.WriteLine( "Linked list: " );
43
44         foreach ( T value in list )
45            Console.Write( "{0} ", value );
46
47         Console.WriteLine();
48      } // end method PrintList
49
50      // concatenate the second list on the end of the first list
51      private static void Concatenate< T >( LinkedList< T > list1,
52         LinkedList< T > list2 )
53      {
54         // concatenate lists by copying element values
55         // in order from the second list to the first list
56         foreach ( T value in list2 )
57            list1.AddLast( value ); // add new node
58      } // end method Concatenate
```

Fig. 23.9 | Using LinkedLists. (Part 2 of 4.)

```
59
60     // locate string objects and convert to uppercase
61     private static void ToUppercaseStrings( LinkedList< string > list )
62     {
63        // iterate over the list by using the nodes
64        LinkedListNode< string > currentNode = list.First;
65
66        while ( currentNode != null )
67        {
68           string color = currentNode.Value; // get value in node
69           currentNode.Value = color.ToUpper(); // convert to uppercase
70
71           currentNode = currentNode.Next; // get next node
72        } // end while
73     } // end method ToUppercaseStrings
74
75     // delete list items between two given items
76     private static void RemoveItemsBetween< T >( LinkedList< T > list,
77        T startItem, T endItem )
78     {
79        // get the nodes corresponding to the start and end item
80        LinkedListNode< T > currentNode = list.Find( startItem );
81        LinkedListNode< T > endNode = list.Find( endItem );
82
83        // remove items after the start item
84        // until we find the last item or the end of the linked list
85        while ( ( currentNode.Next != null ) &&
86           ( currentNode.Next != endNode ) )
87        {
88           list.Remove( currentNode.Next ); // remove next node
89        } // end while
90     } // end method RemoveItemsBetween
91
92     // display reversed list
93     private static void PrintReversedList< T >( LinkedList< T > list )
94     {
95        Console.WriteLine( "Reversed List:" );
96
97        // iterate over the list by using the nodes
98        LinkedListNode< T > currentNode = list.Last;
99
100       while ( currentNode != null )
101       {
102          Console.Write( "{0} ", currentNode.Value );
103          currentNode = currentNode.Previous; // get previous node
104       } // end while
105
106       Console.WriteLine();
107    } // end method PrintReversedList
108 } // end class LinkedListTest
```

Fig. 23.9 | Using LinkedLists. (Part 3 of 4.)

```
Linked list:
black yellow green blue violet silver gold white brown blue gray

Converting strings in list1 to uppercase

Linked list:
BLACK YELLOW GREEN BLUE VIOLET SILVER GOLD WHITE BROWN BLUE GRAY

Deleting strings between BLACK and BROWN

Linked list:
BLACK BROWN BLUE GRAY
Reversed List:
GRAY BLUE BROWN BLACK
```

Fig. 23.9 | Using LinkedLists. (Part 4 of 4.)

The using directive in line 4 allows us to use the LinkedList class by its unqualified name. Lines 16–23 create LinkedLists list1 and list2 of strings and fill them with the contents of arrays colors and colors2, respectively. LinkedList is a generic class that has one type parameter for which we specify the type argument string in this example (lines 16 and 23). We demonstrate two ways to fill the lists. In lines 19–20, we use the foreach statement and method **AddLast** to fill list1. The AddLast method creates a new LinkedListNode (with the given value available via the Value property) and appends this node to the end of the list. There's also an **AddFirst** method that inserts a node at the beginning of the list. Line 23 invokes the constructor that takes an IEnumerable<string> parameter. All arrays implicitly inherit from the generic interfaces IList and IEnumerable with the type of the array as the type argument, so the string array colors2 implements IEnumerable<string>. The type parameter of this generic IEnumerable matches the type parameter of the generic LinkedList object. This constructor call copies the contents of the array colors2 to list2.

Line 25 calls generic method Concatenate (lines 51–58) to append all elements of list2 to the end of list1. Line 26 calls method PrintList (lines 40–48) to output list1's contents. Line 29 calls method ToUppercaseStrings (lines 61–73) to convert each string element to uppercase, then line 30 calls PrintList again to display the modified strings. Line 33 calls method RemoveItemsBetween (lines 76–90) to remove the elements between "BLACK" and "BROWN"—not including either. Line 35 outputs the list again, then line 36 invokes method PrintReversedList (lines 93–107) to display the list in reverse order.

Generic method Concatenate (lines 51–58) iterates over list2 with a foreach statement and calls method AddLast to append each value to the end of list1. The LinkedList class's enumerator loops over the values of the nodes, not the nodes themselves, so the iteration variable has type T. Notice that this creates a new node in list1 for each node in list2. One LinkedListNode cannot be a member of more than one LinkedList. If you want the same data to belong to more than one LinkedList, you must make a copy of the node for each list to avoid InvalidOperationExceptions.

Generic method PrintList (lines 40–48) similarly uses a foreach statement to iterate over the values in a LinkedList, and outputs them. Method ToUppercaseStrings (lines 61–73) takes a linked list of strings and converts each string value to uppercase. This method replaces the strings stored in the list, so we cannot use an enumerator (via a foreach statement) as in the previous two methods. Instead, we obtain the first LinkedListNode via the First property (line 64), and use a while statement to loop through the list (lines 66–72). Each iteration of the while statement obtains and updates the contents of currentNode via property Value, using string method **ToUpper** to create an uppercase version of string color. At the end of each iteration, we move the current node to the next node in the list by assigning currentNode to the node obtained by its own Next property (line 71). The Next property of the last node of the list gets null, so when the while statement iterates past the end of the list, the loop exits.

Notice that it does not make sense to declare ToUppercaseStrings as a generic method, because it uses the string-specific methods of the values in the nodes. Methods PrintList (lines 40–48) and Concatenate (lines 51–58) do not need to use any string-specific methods, so they can be declared with generic type parameters to promote maximal code reuse.

Generic method RemoveItemsBetween (lines 76–90) removes a range of items between two nodes. Lines 80–81 obtain the two "boundary" nodes of the range by using method **Find**. This method performs a linear search on the list and returns the first node that contains a value equal to the passed argument. Method Find returns null if the value is not found. We store the node preceding the range in local variable currentNode and the node following the range in endNode.

The while statement in lines 85–89 removes all the elements between currentNode and endNode. On each iteration of the loop, we remove the node following currentNode by invoking method **Remove** (line 88). Method Remove takes a LinkedListNode, splices that node out of the LinkedList, and fixes the references of the surrounding nodes. After the Remove call, currentNode's Next property now gets the node *following* the node just removed, and that node's Previous property now gets currentNode. The while statement continues to loop until there are no nodes left between currentNode and endNode, or until currentNode is the last node in the list. (There's also an overloaded version of method Remove that performs a linear search for the specified value and removes the first node in the list that contains it.)

Method PrintReversedList (lines 93–107) displays the list backward by navigating the nodes manually. Line 98 obtains the last element of the list via the **Last** property and stores it in currentNode. The while statement in lines 100–104 iterates through the list backward by moving the currentNode reference to the previous node at the end of each iteration, then exiting when we move past the beginning of the list. Note how similar this code is to lines 64–72, which iterated through the list from the beginning to the end.

23.6 Covariance and Contravariance for Generic Types

A new feature in Visual C# 2010 is *covariance* and *contravariance* of generic interface and delegate types. To understand these concepts, we'll consider them in the context of arrays, which have always been covariant and contravariant in C#.

Covariance in Arrays
Recall our Employee class hierarchy from Section 12.5, which consisted of the base class Employee and the derived classes SalariedEmployee, CommissionEmployee and Base-PlusCommissionEmployee. Assuming the declarations

```
SalariedEmployee[] salariedEmployees = {
   new SalariedEmployee( "Bob", "Blue", "111-11-1111", 800M ),
   new SalariedEmployee( "Rachel", "Red", "222-22-2222", 1234M ) };
Employee[] employees;
```

we can write the following statement:

```
employees = salariedEmployees;
```

Even though the array type `SalariedEmployee[]` does *not* derive from the array type `Employee[]`, the preceding assignment *is* allowed because class `SalariedEmployee` is a derived class of `Employee`.

Similarly, suppose we have the following method, which displays the `string` representation of each `Employee` in its `employees` array parameter:

```
void PrintEmployees( Employee[] employees )
```

We can call this method with the array of `SalariedEmployees`, as in:

```
PrintEmployees( salariedEmployees );
```

and the method will correctly display the `string` representation of each `SalariedEmployee` object in the argument array. Assigning an array of a derived-class type to an array variable of a base-class type is an example of **covariance**.

Covariance in Generic Types

Covariance now also works with several *generic interface and delegate types*, including `IEnumerable<T>`. Arrays and generic collections implement the `IEnumerable<T>` interface. Using the `salariedEmployees` array declared previously, consider the following statement:

```
IEnumerable< Employee > employees = salariedEmployees;
```

Prior to Visual C# 2010, this generated a compilation error. Interface `IEnumerable<T>` is now covariant, so the preceding statement *is* allowed. If we modify method `PrintEmployees` as in:

```
void PrintEmployees( IEnumerable< Employee > employees )
```

we can call `PrintEmployees` with the array of `SalariedEmployee` objects, because that array implements the interface `IEnumerable<SalariedEmployee>` and because a `SalariedEmployee` *is an* `Employee` and because `IEnumerable<T>` is covariant. Covariance like this works *only* with *reference* types that are related by a class hierarchy.

Contravariance in Arrays

Previously, we showed that an array of a derived-class type (`salariedEmployees`) can be assigned to an array variable of a base-class type (`employees`). Now, consider the following statement, which has *always* worked in C#:

```
SalariedEmployee[] salariedEmployees2 =
   ( SalariedEmployee[] ) employees;
```

Based on the previous statements, we know that the `Employee` array variable `employees` currently refers to an array of `SalariedEmployees`. Using a cast operator to assign `employees`—an array of base-class-type elements—to `salariedEmployees2`—an array of derived-class-type elements—is an example of contravariance. The preceding cast will fail at runtime if `employees` is *not* an array of `SalariedEmployees`.

Contravariance in Generic Types

To understand **contravariance** in generic types, consider a SortedSet of SalariedEmployees. Class **SortedSet<T>** maintains a set of objects in sorted order—no duplicates are allowed. The objects placed in a SortedSet *must* implement the **IComparable<T> interface**. For classes that *do not* implement this interface, you can still compare their objects using an object that implements the **IComparer<T> interface**. This interface's *Compare* method compares its two arguments and returns 0 if they're equal, a negative integer if the first object is less than the second, or a positive integer if the first object is greater than the second.

Our Employee hierarchy classes do not implement IComparable<T>. Let's assume we wish to sort Employees by social security number. We can implement the following class to compare any two Employees:

```
class EmployeeComparer : IComparer< Employee >
{
   int IComparer< Employee >.Compare( Employee a, Employee b)
   {
      return a.SocialSecurityNumber.CompareTo(
         b.SocialSecurityNumber );
   } // end method Compare
} // end class EmployeeComparer
```

Method Compare returns the result of comparing the two Employees social security numbers using string method CompareTo.

Now consider the following statement, which creates a SortedSet:

```
SortedSet< SalariedEmployee > set =
   new SortedSet< SalariedEmployee >( new EmployeeComparer() );
```

When the type argument does not implement IComparable<T>, you must supply an appropriate IComparer<T> object to compare the objects that will be placed in the SortedSet. Since, we're creating a SortedSet of SalariedEmployees, the compiler expects the IComparer<T> object to implement the IComparer<SalariedEmployee>. Instead, we provided an object that implements IComparer<Employee>. The compiler allows us to provide an IComparer for a base-class type where an IComparer for a derived-class type is expected because interface IComparer<T> supports contravariance.

Web Resources

For a list of covariant and contravariant interface types in .NET 4, visit

```
msdn.microsoft.com/en-us/library/dd799517.aspx#VariantList
```

It's also possible to create your own variant types. For information on this, visit

```
msdn.microsoft.com/en-us/library/dd997386.aspx
```

23.7 Wrap-Up

This chapter introduced the .NET Framework collection classes. You learned about the hierarchy of interfaces that many of the collection classes implement. You saw how to use class Array to perform array manipulations. You learned that the System.Collections and System.Collections.Generic namespaces contain many nongeneric and generic collection classes, respectively. We presented the nongeneric classes ArrayList, Stack and

Hashtable as well as generic classes SortedDictionary and LinkedList. In doing so, we discussed data structures in greater depth. We discussed dynamically expanding collections, hashing schemes, and two implementations of a dictionary. You saw the advantages of generic collections over their nongeneric counterparts.

You also learned how to use enumerators to traverse these data structures and obtain their contents. We demonstrated the foreach statement with many of the classes of the Framework Class Library, and explained that this works by using enumerators "behind-the-scenes" to traverse the collections.

24

GUI with Windows Presentation Foundation

OBJECTIVES

In this chapter you'll learn:

- To mark up data using XML.

- To define a WPF GUI with Extensible Application Markup Language (XAML).

- To handle WPF user-interface events.

- To use WPF's commands feature to handle common application tasks such as cut, copy and paste.

- To customize the look-and-feel of WPF GUIs using styles and control templates.

- To use data binding to display data in WPF controls.

My function is to present old masterpieces in modern frames.
—Rudolf Bing

Instead of being a static one-time event, bonding is a process, a dynamic and continuous one.
—Julius Segal

...they do not declare but only hint.
—Friedrich Nietzsche

Science is the knowledge of consequences, and dependence of one fact upon another.
—Thomas Hobbes

Here form is content, content is form.
—Samuel Beckett

24.1 Introduction

In Chapters 14–15, you built GUIs using Windows Forms. In this chapter, you'll build GUIs using **Windows Presentation Foundation (WPF)**—Microsoft's newer framework for GUI, graphics, animation and multimedia. In Chapter 25, WPF Graphics and Multimedia, you'll learn how to incorporate 2D graphics, 3D graphics, animation, audio and video in WPF applications. In Chapter 29, Silverlight and Rich Internet Applications, we'll demonstrate how to use Silverlight (a subset of WPF for web applications) to create Internet applications.

We begin with an introduction to WPF. Next, we discuss an important tool for creating WPF applications called **XAML** (pronounced "zammel")—**Extensible Application Markup Language**. XAML is a descriptive markup language that can be used to define and arrange GUI controls without any C# code. Its syntax is **XML** (**Extensible Markup Language**), a widely supported standard for describing data that is commonly used to exchange that data between applications over the Internet. We present an introduction to XML in Sections 24.3–24.5. Section 24.6 demonstrates how to define a WPF GUI with XAML. Sections 24.7–24.10 demonstrate the basics of creating a WPF GUI—layout, controls and events. You'll also learn new capabilities that are available in WPF controls and event handling.

WPF allows you to easily customize the look-and-feel of a GUI beyond what is possible in Windows Forms. Sections 24.11–24.14 demonstrate several techniques for manipulating the appearance of your GUIs. WPF also allows you to create data-driven GUIs that interact with many types of data. We demonstrate how to do this in Section 24.15.

24.2 Windows Presentation Foundation (WPF)

Previously, you often had to use multiple technologies to build client applications. If a Windows Forms application required video and audio capabilities, you needed to incorporate an additional technology such as Windows Media Player. Likewise, if your application required 3D graphics capabilities, you had to incorporate a separate technology such as Direct3D. WPF provides a single platform capable of handling both of these requirements, and more. It enables you to use one technology to build applications containing GUI, images, animation, 2D or 3D graphics, audio and video capabilities. In this chapter and Chapters 25 and 29, we demonstrate each of these capabilities.

WPF can interoperate with existing technologies. For example, you can include WPF controls in Windows Forms applications to incorporate multimedia content (such as audio or video) without converting the entire application to WPF, which could be a costly and time-consuming process. You can also use Windows Forms controls in WPF applications.

WPF's ability to use the acceleration capabilities of your computer's graphics hardware increases your applications' performance. In addition, WPF generates **vector-based graphics** and is **resolution independent**. Vector-based graphics are defined, not by a grid of pixels as **raster-based graphics** are, but rather by mathematical models. An advantage of vector-based graphics is that when you change the resolution, there is no loss of quality. Hence, the graphics become portable to a great variety of devices. Moreover, your applications won't appear smaller on higher-resolution screens. Instead, they'll remain the same size and display sharper. Chapter 25 presents more information about vector-based graphics and resolution independence.

Building a GUI with WPF is similar to building a GUI with Windows Forms—you drag-and-drop predefined controls from the **Toolbox** onto the design area. Many WPF controls correspond directly to those in Windows Forms. Just as in a Windows Forms application, the functionality is event driven. Many of the Windows Forms events you're familiar with are also in WPF. A WPF Button, for example, is similar to a Windows Forms Button, and both raise Click events.

There are several important differences between the two technologies, though. The WPF layout scheme is different. WPF properties and events have more capabilities. Most notably, WPF allows designers to define the appearance and content of a GUI without any C# code by defining it in XAML, a descriptive **markup** language (that is, a text-based notation for describing something).

Introduction to XAML

In Windows Forms, when you use the designer to create a GUI, the IDE generates code statements that create and configure the controls. In WPF, it generates XAML markup (that is, a text-based notation for describing data). Because markup is designed to be readable by both humans and computers, you can also manually write XAML markup to define GUI controls. When you compile your WPF application, a XAML compiler generates code to create and configure controls based on your XAML markup. This technique of defining *what* the GUI should contain without specifying *how* to generate it is an example of **declarative programming**.

XAML allows designers and programmers to work together more efficiently. Without writing any code, a graphic designer can edit the look-and-feel of an application using a design tool, such as Microsoft's **Expression Blend**—a XAML graphic design program. A programmer can import the XAML markup into Visual Studio and focus on coding the logic that gives an application its functionality. Even if you're working alone, however, this separation of front-end appearance from back-end logic improves your program's organization and makes it easier to maintain. XAML is an essential component of WPF programming.

Because XAML is implemented with XML, it's important that you understand the basics of XML before we continue our discussion of XAML and WPF GUIs.

24.3 XML Basics

The Extensible Markup Language was developed in 1996 by the **World Wide Web Consortium's (W3C's)** XML Working Group. XML is a widely supported standard for describing data that is commonly used to exchange that data between applications over the Internet. It permits document authors to create markup for virtually any type of information. This enables them to create entirely new markup languages for describing any type of data, such as mathematical formulas, software-configuration instructions, chemical molecular structures, music, news, recipes and financial reports. XML describes data in a way that both human beings and computers can understand.

Figure 24.1 is a simple XML document that describes information for a baseball player. We focus on lines 5–11 to introduce basic XML syntax. You'll learn about the other elements of this document in Section 24.4.

```
 I    <?xml version = "1.0"?>
 2    <!-- Fig. 24.1: player.xml -->
 3    <!-- Baseball player structured with XML -->
 4
 5    <player>
 6       <firstName>John</firstName>
 7
 8       <lastName>Doe</lastName>
 9
10       <battingAverage>0.375</battingAverage>
 II   </player>
```

Fig. 24.1 | XML that describes a baseball player's information.

XML documents contain text that represents content (that is, data), such as John (line 6), and **elements** that specify the document's structure, such as firstName (line 6). XML documents delimit elements with **start tags** and **end tags**. A start tag consists of the element name in **angle brackets** (for example, <player> and <firstName> in lines 5 and 6, respectively). An end tag consists of the element name preceded by a **forward slash** (/) in angle brackets (for example, </firstName> and </player> in lines 6 and 11, respectively). An element's start and end tags enclose text that represents a piece of data (for example, the firstName of the player—John—in line 6, which is enclosed by the <firstName> start tag and and </firstName> end tag) or other elements (for example, the firstName, lastName, and battingAverage elements in the player element). Every XML document must have exactly one **root element** that contains all the other elements. In Fig. 24.1, player (lines 5–11) is the root element.

Some XML-based markup languages include XHTML (Extensible HyperText Markup Language—HTML's replacement for marking up web content), MathML (for mathematics), VoiceXML™ (for speech), CML (Chemical Markup Language—for chemistry) and XBRL (Extensible Business Reporting Language—for financial data exchange). ODF (Open Document Format—developed by Sun Microsystems) and OOXML (Office Open XML—developed by Microsoft as a replacement for the old proprietary Microsoft Office formats) are two competing standards for electronic office documents such as spreadsheets, presentations, and word processing documents. These markup languages are called XML **vocabularies** and provide a means for describing particular types of data in standardized, structured ways.

Massive amounts of data are currently stored on the Internet in a variety of formats (for example, databases, web pages, text files). Based on current trends, it's likely that much of this data, especially that which is passed between systems, will soon take the form of XML. Organizations see XML as the future of data encoding. Information-technology groups are planning ways to integrate XML into their systems. Industry groups are developing custom XML vocabularies for most major industries that will allow computer-based business applications to communicate in common languages. For example, web services, which we discuss in Chapter 28, allow web-based applications to exchange data seamlessly through standard protocols based on XML. Also, web services are described by an XML vocabulary called WSDL (Web Services Description Language).

The next generation of the Internet and World Wide Web is being built on a foundation of XML, which enables the development of more sophisticated web-based applications. XML allows you to assign meaning to what would otherwise be random pieces of data. As a result, programs can "understand" the data they manipulate. For example, a web browser might view a street address listed on a simple HTML web page as a string of characters without any real meaning. In an XML document, however, this data can be clearly identified (that is, marked up) as an address. A program that uses the document can recognize this data as an address and provide links to a map of that location, driving directions from that location or other location-specific information. Likewise, an application can recognize names of people, dates, ISBN numbers and any other type of XML-encoded data. Based on this data, the application can present users with other related information, providing a richer, more meaningful user experience.

Viewing and Modifying XML Documents

XML documents are portable. Viewing or modifying an XML document—a text file, usually with the `.xml` file-name extension—does not require special software, although many software tools exist, and new ones are frequently released that make it more convenient to develop XML-based applications. Most text editors can open XML documents for viewing and editing. Visual C# Express includes an XML editor that provides *IntelliSense*. The editor also checks that the document is well formed and is valid if a schema (discussed shortly) is present. Also, most web browsers can display an XML document in a formatted manner that shows its structure. We demonstrate this using Internet Explorer in Section 24.4. One important characteristic of XML is that it's both human readable and machine readable.

Processing XML Documents

Processing an XML document requires software called an **XML parser** (or **XML processor**). A parser makes the document's data available to applications. While reading the contents of an XML document, a parser checks that the document follows the syntax rules specified by the W3C's XML Recommendation (`www.w3.org/XML`). XML syntax requires a single root element, a start tag and end tag for each element and properly nested tags (that is, the end tag for a nested element must appear before the end tag of the enclosing element). Furthermore, XML is case sensitive, so the proper capitalization must be used in elements. A document that conforms to this syntax is a **well-formed XML document**, and is syntactically correct. We present fundamental XML syntax in Section 24.4. If an XML parser can process an XML document successfully, that XML document is well formed. Parsers can provide access to XML-encoded data in well-formed documents only—if a document is not well-formed, the parser will report an error to the user or calling application.

Often, XML parsers are built into software such as Visual Studio or available for download over the Internet. Popular parsers include **Microsoft XML Core Services (MSXML)**, the .NET Framework's `XmlReader` **class**, the Apache Software Foundation's **Xerces** (available from `xerces.apache.org`) and the open-source **Expat XML Parser** (available from `expat.sourceforge.net`).

Validating XML Documents

An XML document can optionally reference a **Document Type Definition (DTD)** or a **W3C XML Schema** (referred to simply as a "schema" for the rest of this book) that defines the XML document's proper structure. When an XML document references a DTD or a schema, some parsers (called **validating parsers**) can use the DTD/schema to check that it has the appropriate structure. If the XML document conforms to the DTD/schema (that is, the document has the appropriate structure), the XML document is **valid**. For example, if in Fig. 24.1 we were referencing a DTD that specifies that a `player` element must have `firstName`, `lastName` and `battingAverage` elements, then omitting the `lastName` element (line 8) would cause the XML document `player.xml` to be invalid. The XML document would still be well formed, however, because it follows proper XML syntax (that is, it has one root element, and each element has a start and an end tag). By definition, a valid XML document is well formed. Parsers that cannot check for document conformity against DTDs/schemas are **nonvalidating parsers**—they determine only whether an XML document is well formed.

For more information about validation, DTDs and schemas, as well as the key differences between these two types of structural specifications, see Chapter 26. For now, schemas are XML documents themselves, whereas DTDs are not. As you'll learn in Chapter 26, this difference presents several advantages in using schemas over DTDs.

Software Engineering Observation 24.1

DTDs and schemas are essential for business-to-business (B2B) transactions and mission-critical systems. Validating XML documents ensures that disparate systems can manipulate data structured in standardized ways and prevents errors caused by missing or malformed data.

Formatting and Manipulating XML Documents

XML documents contain only data, not formatting instructions, so applications that process XML documents must decide how to manipulate or display each document's data. For example, a PDA (personal digital assistant) may render an XML document differently than a wireless phone or a desktop computer. You can use **Extensible Stylesheet Language (XSL)** to specify rendering instructions for different platforms. We discuss XSL in Chapter 26.

XML-processing programs can also search, sort and manipulate XML data using technologies such as XSL. Some other XML-related technologies are XPath (XML Path Language—a language for accessing parts of an XML document), XSL-FO (XSL Formatting Objects—an XML vocabulary used to describe document formatting) and XSLT (XSL Transformations—a language for transforming XML documents into other documents). We present XSLT and XPath in Chapter 26. We'll also present new C# features that greatly simplify working with XML in your code. With these features, XSLT and similar technologies are not needed while coding in C#, but they remain relevant on platforms where C# and .NET are not available.

24.4 Structuring Data

In Fig. 24.2, we present an XML document that marks up a simple article using XML. The line numbers shown are for reference only and are not part of the XML document.

```
 I   <?xml version = "1.0"?>
 2   <!-- Fig. 24.2: article.xml -->
 3   <!-- Article structured with XML -->
 4
 5   <article>
 6      <title>Simple XML</title>
 7
 8      <date>July 24, 2008</date>
 9
10      <author>
11         <firstName>John</firstName>
12         <lastName>Doe</lastName>
13      </author>
14
15      <summary>XML is pretty easy.</summary>
16
17      <content>
18         In this chapter, we present a wide variety of examples that use XML.
19      </content>
20   </article>
```

Fig. 24.2 | XML used to mark up an article.

This document begins with an **XML declaration** (line 1), which identifies the document as an XML document. The **version attribute** specifies the XML version to which the document conforms. The current XML standard is version 1.0. Though the W3C released a version 1.1 specification in February 2004, this newer version is not yet widely supported. The W3C may continue to release new versions as XML evolves to meet the requirements of different fields.

Some XML documents also specify an **encoding attribute** in the XML declaration. An encoding specifies how characters are stored in memory and on disk—historically, the way an uppercase "A" was stored on one computer architecture was different than the way it was stored on a different computer architecture. Appendix F discusses Unicode, which specifies encodings that can describe characters in any written language. An introduction to different encodings in XML can be found at the website bit.ly/EncodeXMLData.

Portability Tip 24.1
Documents should include the XML declaration to identify the version of XML used. A document that lacks an XML declaration might be assumed erroneously to conform to the latest version of XML—in which case, errors could result.

Common Programming Error 24.1

Placing whitespace characters before the XML declaration is an error.

XML comments (lines 2–3), which begin with <!-- and end with -->, can be placed almost anywhere in an XML document. XML comments can span to multiple lines—an end marker on each line is not needed; the end marker can appear on a subsequent line, as long as there is exactly one end marker (-->) for each begin marker (<!--). Comments are used in XML for documentation purposes. Line 4 is a blank line. As in a C# program, blank lines, whitespaces and indentation are used in XML to improve readability. Later you'll see that the blank lines are normally ignored by XML parsers.

Common Programming Error 24.2

In an XML document, each start tag must have a matching end tag; omitting either tag is an error. Soon, you'll learn how such errors are detected.

Common Programming Error 24.3

XML is case sensitive. Using different cases for the start-tag and end-tag names for the same element is a syntax error.

In Fig. 24.2, article (lines 5–20) is the root element. The lines that precede the root element (lines 1–4) are the XML **prolog**. In an XML prolog, the XML declaration must appear before the comments and any other markup.

The elements we used in the example do not come from any specific markup language. Instead, we chose the element names and markup structure that best describe our particular data. You can invent whatever elements make sense for the particular data you're dealing with. For example, element title (line 6) contains text that describes the article's title (for example, Simple XML). Similarly, date (line 8), author (lines 10–13), firstName (line 11), lastName (line 12), summary (line 15) and content (lincs 17–19) contain text that describes the date, author, the author's first name, the author's last name, a summary and the content of the document, respectively. XML element and attribute names can be of any length and may contain letters, digits, underscores, hyphens and periods. However, they must begin with either a letter or an underscore, and they should not begin with "xml" in any combination of uppercase and lowercase letters (for example, XML, Xml, xMl), as this is reserved for use in the XML standards.

Common Programming Error 24.4

Using a whitespace character in an XML element name is an error.

Good Programming Practice 24.1

XML element names should be meaningful to humans and should not use abbreviations.

XML elements are **nested** to form hierarchies—with the root element at the top of the hierarchy. This allows document authors to create parent/child relationships between data. For example, elements title, date, author, summary and content are nested within article. Elements firstName and lastName are nested within author.

> **Common Programming Error 24.5**
> *Nesting XML tags improperly is a syntax error—it causes an XML document to not be well-formed. For example, <x><y>hello</x></y> is an error, because the </y> tag must precede the </x> tag.*

Any element that contains other elements (for example, article or author) is a **container element**. Container elements also are called **parent elements**. Elements nested inside a container element are **child elements** (or children) of that container element.

Viewing an XML Document in Internet Explorer

The XML document in Fig. 24.2 is simply a text file named article.xml. This document does not contain formatting information for the article. The reason is that XML is a technology for describing the structure of data. Formatting and displaying data from an XML document are application-specific issues. For example, when the user loads article.xml in Internet Explorer (IE), MSXML (Microsoft XML Core Services) parses and displays the document's data. Internet Explorer uses a built-in **style sheet** to format the data. The resulting format of the data (Fig. 24.3) is similar to the format of the listing in Fig. 24.2. In Chapter 26, we show how to create style sheets to transform your XML data into various formats suitable for display.

Note the minus sign (–) and plus sign (+) in the screenshots of Fig. 24.3. Although these symbols are not part of the XML document, Internet Explorer places them next to every container element. A minus sign indicates that Internet Explorer is displaying the container element's child elements. Clicking the minus sign next to an element collapses that element (that is, causes Internet Explorer to hide the container element's children and replace the minus sign with a plus sign). Conversely, clicking the plus sign next to an element expands that element (that is, causes Internet Explorer to display the container element's children and replace the plus sign with a minus sign). This behavior is similar to viewing the directory structure using Windows Explorer. In fact, a directory structure

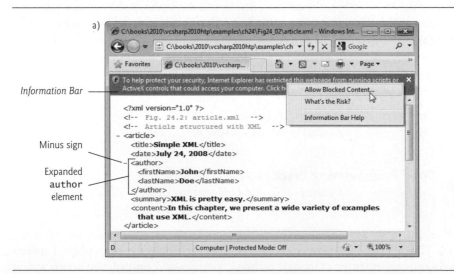

Fig. 24.3 | article.xml displayed by Internet Explorer. (Part 1 of 2.)

b)

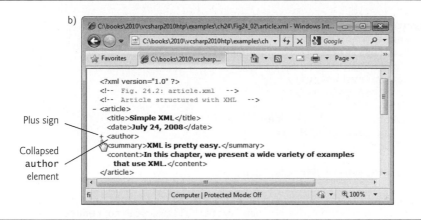

Plus sign

Collapsed author element

Fig. 24.3 | `article.xml` displayed by Internet Explorer. (Part 2 of 2.)

often is modeled as a series of tree structures, in which the **root** of a tree represents a drive letter (for example, C:), and **nodes** in the tree represent directories. Parsers often store XML data as tree structures to facilitate efficient manipulation.

[*Note:* By default Internet Explorer displays all the XML elements in expanded view, and clicking the minus sign (Fig. 24.3(a)) does not do anything. So, by default, you won't be able to collapse the element. To enable this functionality, right click the *Information Bar* just below the **Address** field and select **Allow Blocked Content....** Then click **Yes** in the popup window that appears.]

XML Markup for a Business Letter

Now that we have seen a simple XML document, let's examine a more complex one that marks up a business letter (Fig. 24.4). Again, we begin the document with the XML declaration (line 1) that states the XML version to which the document conforms.

```
 1   <?xml version = "1.0"?>
 2   <!-- Fig. 24.4: letter.xml -->
 3   <!-- Business letter marked up as XML -->
 4
 5   <!DOCTYPE letter SYSTEM "letter.dtd">
 6
 7   <letter>
 8      <contact type = "sender">
 9         <name>Jane Doe</name>
10         <address1>Box 12345</address1>
11         <address2>15 Any Ave.</address2>
12         <city>Othertown</city>
13         <state>Otherstate</state>
14         <zip>67890</zip>
15         <phone>555-4321</phone>
16         <flag gender = "F" />
17      </contact>
```

Fig. 24.4 | Business letter marked up as XML. (Part 1 of 2.)

```
18
19      <contact type = "receiver">
20          <name>John Doe</name>
21          <address1>123 Main St.</address1>
22          <address2></address2>
23          <city>Anytown</city>
24          <state>Anystate</state>
25          <zip>12345</zip>
26          <phone>555-1234</phone>
27          <flag gender = "M" />
28      </contact>
29
30      <salutation>Dear Sir:</salutation>
31
32      <paragraph>It is our privilege to inform you about our new database
33          managed with XML. This new system allows you to reduce the
34          load on your inventory list server by having the client machine
35          perform the work of sorting and filtering the data.
36      </paragraph>
37
38      <paragraph>Please visit our website for availability
39          and pricing.
40      </paragraph>
41
42      <closing>Sincerely,</closing>
43      <signature>Ms. Jane Doe</signature>
44  </letter>
```

Fig. 24.4 | Business letter marked up as XML. (Part 2 of 2.)

Line 5 specifies that this XML document references a DTD. Recall from Section 24.3 that DTDs define the structure of the data for an XML document. For example, a DTD specifies the elements and parent/child relationships between elements permitted in an XML document.

Error-Prevention Tip 24.1

An XML document is not required to reference a DTD, but validating XML parsers can use a DTD to ensure that the document has the proper structure.

Portability Tip 24.2

Validating an XML document helps guarantee that independent developers will exchange data in a standardized form that conforms to the DTD.

The DTD reference (line 5) contains three items: the name of the root element that the DTD specifies (letter); the keyword **SYSTEM** (which denotes an **external DTD**—a DTD declared in a separate file, as opposed to a DTD declared locally in the same file); and the DTD's name and location (that is, letter.dtd in the same directory as the XML document). DTD document file names typically end with the **.dtd** extension. We discuss DTDs and letter.dtd in detail in Chapter 26.

Root element letter (lines 7–44 of Fig. 24.4) contains the child elements contact, contact, salutation, paragraph, paragraph, closing and signature. Besides being placed between tags, data also can be placed in **attributes**—name/value pairs that appear within the angle brackets of start tags. Elements can have any number of attributes (separated by spaces) in their start tags, provided all the attribute names are unique. The first contact element (lines 8–17) has an attribute named type with **attribute value** "sender", which indicates that this contact element identifies the letter's sender. The second contact element (lines 19–28) has attribute type with value "receiver", which indicates that this contact element identifies the letter's recipient. Like element names, attribute names are case sensitive, can be of any length, may contain letters, digits, underscores, hyphens and periods, and must begin with either a letter or an underscore character. A contact element stores various items of information about a contact, such as the contact's name (represented by element name), address (represented by elements address1, address2, city, state and zip), phone number (represented by element phone) and gender (represented by attribute gender of element flag). Element salutation (line 30) marks up the letter's salutation. Lines 32–40 mark up the letter's body using two paragraph elements. Elements closing (line 42) and signature (line 43) mark up the closing sentence and the author's "signature," respectively.

Common Programming Error 24.6

Failure to enclose attribute values in double ("") or single (' ') quotes is a syntax error.

Line 16 introduces the **empty element** flag. An empty element contains no content. However, it may sometimes contain data in the form of attributes. Empty element flag contains an attribute that indicates the gender of the contact (represented by the parent contact element). Document authors can close an empty element either by placing a slash immediately preceding the right angle bracket, as shown in line 16, or by explicitly writing an end tag, as in line 22:

```
<address2></address2>
```

Line 22 can also be written as:

```
<address2/>
```

The address2 element in line 22 is empty, because there is no second part to this contact's address. However, we must include this element to conform to the structural rules specified in the XML document's DTD—letter.dtd (which we present in Chapter 26). This DTD specifies that each contact element must have an address2 child element (even if it's empty). In Chapter 26, you'll learn how DTDs indicate that certain elements are required while others are optional.

24.5 XML Namespaces

XML allows document authors to create custom elements. This extensibility can result in **naming collisions**—elements with identical names that represent different things—when combining content from multiple sources. For example, we may use the element book to mark up data about a Deitel publication. A stamp collector may use the element book to mark up data about a book of stamps. Using both of these elements in the same document could create a naming collision, making it difficult to determine which kind of data each element contains.

An XML **namespace** is a collection of element and attribute names. Like C# namespaces, XML namespaces provide a means for document authors to unambiguously refer to elements that have the same name (that is, prevent collisions). For example,

```
<subject>Math</subject>
```

and

```
<subject>Cardiology</subject>
```

use element subject to mark up data. In the first case, the subject is something one studies in school, whereas in the second case, the subject is a field of medicine. Namespaces can differentiate these two subject elements. For example,

```
<school:subject>Math</school:subject>
```

and

```
<medical:subject>Cardiology</medical:subject>
```

Both school and medical are **namespace prefixes**. A document author places a namespace prefix and colon (:) before an element name to specify the namespace to which that element belongs. Document authors can create their own namespace prefixes using virtually any name except the reserved namespace prefixes xml and xmlns. In the subsections that follow, we demonstrate how document authors ensure that namespaces are unique.

Common Programming Error 24.7

Attempting to create a namespace prefix named xml in any mixture of uppercase and lowercase letters is a syntax error—the xml namespace prefix is reserved for internal use by XML itself.

Differentiating Elements with Namespaces

Figure 24.5 uses namespaces to differentiate two distinct elements—the file element related to a text file and the file document related to an image file.

```
1   <?xml version = "1.0"?>
2   <!-- Fig. 24.5: namespace.xml -->
3   <!-- Demonstrating namespaces -->
4
5   <text:directory
6      xmlns:text = "urn:deitel:textInfo"
7      xmlns:image = "urn:deitel:imageInfo">
8
9      <text:file filename = "book.xml">
10        <text:description>A book list</text:description>
11     </text:file>
12
13     <image:file filename = "funny.jpg">
14        <image:description>A funny picture</image:description>
15        <image:size width = "200" height = "100" />
16     </image:file>
17  </text:directory>
```

Fig. 24.5 | XML namespaces demonstration. (Part 1 of 2.)

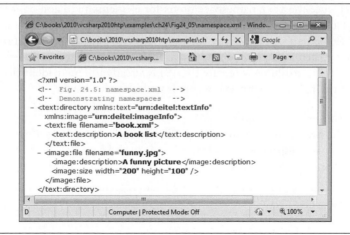

Fig. 24.5 | XML namespaces demonstration. (Part 2 of 2.)

Lines 6–7 use the XML-namespace reserved attribute `xmlns` to create two namespace prefixes—`text` and `image`. Creating a namespace prefix is similar to using a `using` statement in C#—it allows you to access XML elements from a given namespace. Each namespace prefix is bound to a series of characters called a **Uniform Resource Identifier** (**URI**) that uniquely identifies the namespace. Document authors create their own namespace prefixes and URIs. A URI is a way to identify a resource, typically on the Internet. Two popular types of URI are **Uniform Resource Name** (**URN**) and **Uniform Resource Locator** (**URL**).

To ensure that namespaces are unique, document authors must provide unique URIs. In this example, we use the text `urn:deitel:textInfo` and `urn:deitel:imageInfo` as URIs. These URIs employ the URN scheme frequently used to identify namespaces. Under this naming scheme, a URI begins with `"urn:"`, followed by a unique series of additional names separated by colons. These URIs are not guaranteed to be unique—the idea is simply that creating a long URI in this way makes it unlikely that two authors will use the same namespace.

Another common practice is to use URLs, which specify the location of a file or a resource on the Internet. For example, `http://www.deitel.com` is the URL that identifies the home page of the Deitel & Associates website. Using URLs for domains that you own guarantees that the namespaces are unique, because the domain names (for example, `www.deitel.com`) are guaranteed to be unique. For example, lines 5–7 could be rewritten as

```
<text:directory
    xmlns:text = "http://www.deitel.com/xmlns-text"
    xmlns:image = "http://www.deitel.com/xmlns-image">
```

where URLs related to the Deitel & Associates, Inc. domain name serve as URIs to identify the `text` and `image` namespaces. The parser does not visit these URLs, nor do these URLs need to refer to actual web pages. Each simply represents a unique series of characters used to differentiate URI names. In fact, any string can represent a namespace. For example, our `image` namespace URI could be `hgjfkdlsa4556`, in which case our prefix assignment would be

```
xmlns:image = "hgjfkdlsa4556"
```

Lines 9–11 use the `text` namespace prefix for elements `file` and `description`. The end tags must also specify the namespace prefix `text`. Lines 13–16 apply namespace prefix `image` to the elements `file`, `description` and `size`. Attributes do not require namespace prefixes, because each attribute is already part of an element that specifies the namespace prefix. For example, attribute `filename` (line 9) is already uniquely identified by being in the context of the `filename` start tag, which is prefixed with `text`.

Specifying a Default Namespace
To eliminate the need to place namespace prefixes in each element, document authors may specify a **default namespace** for an element and its children. Figure 24.6 demonstrates using a default namespace (`urn:deitel:textInfo`) for element `directory`.

```
1   <?xml version = "1.0"?>
2   <!-- Fig. 24.6: defaultnamespace.xml -->
3   <!-- Using default namespaces -->
4
5   <directory xmlns = "urn:deitel:textInfo"
6      xmlns:image = "urn:deitel:imageInfo">
7
8      <file filename = "book.xml">
9         <description>A book list</description>
10     </file>
11
12     <image:file filename = "funny.jpg">
13        <image:description>A funny picture</image:description>
14        <image:size width = "200" height = "100" />
15     </image:file>
16  </directory>
```

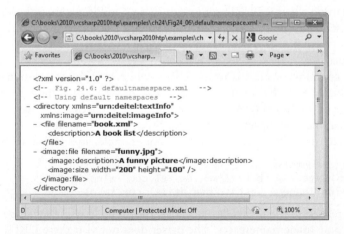

Fig. 24.6 | Default namespace demonstration.

Line 5 defines a default namespace using attribute `xmlns` with a URI as its value. Once we define this default namespace, child elements which do not specify a prefix belong to the default namespace. Thus, element `file` (lines 8–10) is in the default namespace urn:deitel:textInfo. Compare this to lines 9–11 of Fig. 24.5, where we had to prefix the file and description element names with the namespace prefix text.

> **Common Programming Error 24.8**
> *The default namespace can be overridden at any point in the document with another xmlns attribute. All direct and indirect children of the element with the xmlns attribute use the new default namespace.*

The default namespace applies to the directory element and all elements that are not qualified with a namespace prefix. However, we can use a namespace prefix to specify a different namespace for particular elements. For example, the file element in lines 12–15 includes the image namespace prefix, indicating that this element is in the urn:deitel:imageInfo namespace, not the default namespace.

Namespaces in XML Vocabularies
XML-based languages, such as XML Schema, Extensible Stylesheet Language (XSL) and BizTalk (www.microsoft.com/biztalk), often use namespaces to identify their elements. Each vocabulary defines special-purpose elements that are grouped in namespaces. These namespaces help prevent naming collisions between predefined and user-defined elements.

24.6 Declarative GUI Programming Using XAML

A XAML document defines the appearance of a WPF application. Figure 24.7 is a simple XAML document that defines a window that displays Welcome to WPF!

```
1   <!-- Fig. 24.7: XAMLIntroduction.xaml -->
2   <!-- A simple XAML document. -->
3
4   <!-- the Window control is the root element of the GUI -->
5   <Window x:Class="XAMLIntroduction.MainWindow"
6       xmlns="http://schemas.microsoft.com/winfx/2006/xaml/presentation"
7       xmlns:x="http://schemas.microsoft.com/winfx/2006/xaml"
8       Title="A Simple Window" Height="150" Width="250">
9
10      <!-- a layout container -->
11      <Grid Background="Gold">
12
13          <!-- a Label control -->
14          <Label HorizontalAlignment="Center" VerticalAlignment="Center">
15              Welcome to WPF!
16          </Label>
17      </Grid>
18  </Window>
```

Fig. 24.7 | A simple XAML document.

Since XAML documents are XML documents, a XAML document consists of many nested elements, delimited by start tags and end tags. As with any other XML document, each XAML document must contain a single root element. Just as in XML, data is placed as nested content or in attributes.

Two standard namespaces must be defined in every XAML document so that the XAML compiler can interpret your markup—the **presentation XAML namespace**, which defines WPF-specific elements and attributes, and the **standard XAML namespace**, which defines elements and attributes that are standard to all types of XAML documents. Usually, the presentation XAML namespace (`http://schemas.microsoft.com/winfx/2006/xaml/presentation`) is defined as the default namespace (line 6), and the standard XAML namespace (`http://schemas.microsoft.com/winfx/2006/xaml`) is mapped to the namespace prefix x (line 7). These are both automatically included in the Window element's start tag when you create a WPF application.

WPF **controls** are represented by elements in XAML markup. The root element of the XAML document in Fig. 24.7 is a `Window` control (lines 5–18), which defines the application's window—this corresponds to the Form control in Windows Forms.

The `Window` start tag (line 5) also defines another important attribute, **x:Class**, which specifies the class name of the associated code-behind class that provides the GUI's functionality (line 5). The x: signifies that the Class attribute is located in the standard XAML namespace. A XAML document must have an associated code-behind file to handle events.

Using attributes, you can define a control's properties in XAML. For example, the Window's Title, Width and Height properties are set in line 8. A Window's Title specifies the text that is displayed in the Window's title bar. The Width and Height properties apply to a control of any type and specify the control's width and height, respectively, using machine-independent pixels.

Window is a **content control** (a control derived from class **ContentControl**), meaning it can have exactly one child element or text content. You'll almost always set a **layout container** (a control derived from the **Panel** class) as the child element so that you can host multiple controls in a Window. A layout container such as a Grid (lines 11–17) can have many child elements, allowing it to contain many controls. In Section 24.8, you'll use content controls and layout containers to arrange a GUI.

Like Window, a **Label**—corresponding to the Label control in Windows Forms—is also a ContentControl. It's generally used to display text.

24.7 Creating a WPF Application in Visual C# Express

To create a new WPF application, open the **New Project** dialog (Fig. 24.8) and select **WPF Application** from the list of template types. The IDE for a WPF application looks nearly identical to that of a Windows Forms application. You'll recognize the familiar **Toolbox**, **Design** view, **Solution Explorer** and **Properties** window.

XAML View
There are differences, however. One is the new **XAML view** (Fig. 24.9) that appears when you open a XAML document. This view is linked to the **Design** view and the **Properties** window. When you edit content in the **Design** view, the **XAML** view automatically updates, and vice versa. Likewise, when you edit properties in the **Properties** window, the **XAML** view automatically updates, and vice versa.

Fig. 24.8 | **New Project** dialog.

Fig. 24.9 | **XAML** view.

Generated Files
When you create a WPF application, four files are generated and can be viewed in the **Solution Explorer**. **App.xaml** defines the Application object and its settings. The most noteworthy setting is the **StartupUri** attribute, which defines the XAML document that executes first when the Application loads (MainWindow.xaml by default). **App.xaml.cs** is its code-behind class and handles application-level events. MainWindow.xaml defines the application window, and MainWindow.xaml.cs is its code-behind class, which handles the window's events. The file name of the code-behind class is always the file name of the associated XAML document followed by the .cs file-name extension.

Setting XAML Indent Size and Displaying Line Numbers
We use three-space indents in our code. To ensure that your code appears the same as the book's examples, change the tab spacing for XAML documents to three spaces (the default is four). Select **Tools > Options** and ensure that the **Show all settings** checkbox is checked. In **Text Editor > XAML > Tabs** change the **Tab and indent size** to 3. You should also configure the **XAML** editor to display line numbers by checking the **Line numbers** checkbox in **Text Editor > XAML > General**. You're now ready to create your first WPF application.

GUI Design

Creating a WPF application in Visual C# Express is similar to creating a Windows Forms application. You can drag-and-drop controls onto the **Design** view of your WPF GUI. A control's properties can be edited in the **Properties** window.

Because XAML is easy to understand and edit, it's often less difficult to manually edit your GUI's XAML markup than to do everything through the IDE. In some cases, you must manually write XAML markup in order to take full advantage of the features that are offered in WPF. Nevertheless, the visual programming tools in Visual Studio are often handy, and we'll point out the situations in which they might be useful as they occur.

24.8 Laying Out Controls

In Windows Forms, a control's size and location are specified explicitly. In WPF, a control's size should be specified as a range of possible values rather than fixed values, and its location specified relative to those of other controls. This scheme, in which you specify how controls share the available space, is called **flow-based layout**. Its advantage is that it enables your GUIs, if designed properly, to be aesthetically pleasing, no matter how a user might resize the application. Likewise, it enables your GUIs to be resolution independent.

24.8.1 General Layout Principles

Layout refers to the size and positioning of controls. The WPF layout scheme addresses both of these in a flow-based fashion and can be summarized by two fundamental principles with regard to a control's size and position.

Size of a Control

Unless necessary, a control's size should not be defined explicitly. Doing so often creates a design that looks pleasing when it first loads, but deteriorates when the application is resized or the content updates. Thus, in addition to the Width and Height properties associated with every control, all WPF controls have the **MinWidth**, **MinHeight**, **MaxHeight** and **MaxWidth** properties. If the Width and Height properties are both Auto (which is the default when they are not specified in the XAML code), you can use these minimum and maximum properties to specify a range of acceptable sizes for a control. Its size will automatically adjust as the size of its container changes.

Position of a Control

A control's position should not be defined in absolute terms. Instead, it should be specified based on its position relative to the layout container in which it's included and the other controls in the same container. All controls have three properties for doing this—**Margin**, **HorizontalAlignment** and **VerticalAlignment**. Margin specifies how much space to put around a control's edges. The value of Margin is a comma-separated list of four integers, representing the left, top, right and bottom margins. Additionally, you can specify two integers, which it interprets as the left–right and top–bottom margins. If you specify just one integer, it uses the same margin on all four sides.

HorizontalAlignment and VerticalAlignment specify how to align a control within its layout container. Valid options of HorizontalAlignment are Left, Center, Right and Stretch. Valid options of VerticalAlignment are Top, Center, Bottom and Stretch. Stretch means that the object will occupy as much space as possible.

Other Layout Properties

A control can have other layout properties specific to the layout container in which it's contained. We'll discuss these as we examine the specific layout containers. WPF provides many controls for laying out a GUI. Figure 24.10 lists several of them.

Control	Description
Layout containers (derived from Panel)	
Grid	Layout is defined by a grid of rows and columns, depending on the Row-Definitions and ColumnDefinitions properties. Elements are placed into cells.
Canvas	Layout is coordinate based. Element positions are defined explicitly by their distance from the top and left edges of the Canvas.
StackPanel	Elements are arranged in a single row or column, depending on the Orientation property.
DockPanel	Elements are positioned based on which edge they're docked to. If the LastChildFill property is True, the last element gets the remaining space in the middle.
WrapPanel	A wrapping StackPanel. Elements are arranged sequentially in rows or columns (depending on the Orientation), each row or column wrapping to start a new one when it reaches the WrapPanel's right or bottom edge, respectively.
Content controls (derived from ContentControl)	
Border	Adds a background or a border to the child element.
GroupBox	Surrounds the child element with a titled box.
Window	The application window. Also the root element.
Expander	Puts the child element in a titled area that collapses to display just the header and expands to display the header and the content.

Fig. 24.10 | Common controls used for layout.

24.8.2 Layout in Action

Figure 24.11 shows the XAML document and the GUI display of a painter application. Note the use of Margin, HorizontalAlignment and VerticalAlignment throughout the markup. This example introduces several WPF controls that are commonly used for layout, as well as a few other basic ones.

The controls in this application look similar to Windows Forms controls. WPF **RadioButton**s function as mutually exclusive options, just like their Windows Forms counterparts. However, a WPF RadioButton does not have a Text property. Instead, it's a ContentControl, meaning it can have exactly one child or text content. This makes the control more versatile, enabling it to be labeled by an image or other item. In this example, each RadioButton is labeled by plain text (for example, lines 33–34). A WPF **Button** behaves like a Windows Forms Button but is a ContentControl. As such, a WPF Button can display any single element as its content, not just text. Lines 59–63 define the two buttons seen in the Painter application. You can drag and drop controls onto the WPF designer and create their event handlers, just as you do in the Windows Forms designer.

```xml
 1   <!-- Fig. 24.11: MainWindow.xaml -->
 2   <!-- XAML of a painter application. -->
 3   <Window x:Class="Painter.MainWindow"
 4      xmlns="http://schemas.microsoft.com/winfx/2006/xaml/presentation"
 5      xmlns:x="http://schemas.microsoft.com/winfx/2006/xaml"
 6      Title="Painter" Height="340" Width="350" Background="Beige">
 7
 8      <!-- creates a Grid -->
 9      <Grid>
10         <!-- defines columns -->
11         <Grid.ColumnDefinitions>
12            <ColumnDefinition Width="Auto" /> <!-- defines a column -->
13            <ColumnDefinition Width="*" /> <!-- defines a column -->
14         </Grid.ColumnDefinitions>
15
16         <!-- creates a Canvas -->
17         <Canvas Grid.Column="1" Margin="0" Name="paintCanvas"
18            Background="White" MouseMove="paintCanvas_MouseMove"
19            MouseLeftButtonDown="paintCanvas_MouseLeftButtonDown"
20            MouseLeftButtonUp="paintCanvas_MouseLeftButtonUp"
21            MouseRightButtonDown="paintCanvas_MouseRightButtonDown"
22            MouseRightButtonUp="paintCanvas_MouseRightButtonUp"/>
23
24         <!-- creates a StackPanel-->
25         <StackPanel Margin="3">
26            <!-- creates a GroupBox for color options -->
27            <GroupBox Grid.ColumnSpan="1" Header="Color" Margin="3"
28               HorizontalAlignment="Stretch" VerticalAlignment="Top">
29               <StackPanel Margin="3" HorizontalAlignment="Left"
30                  VerticalAlignment="Top">
31
32                  <!-- creates RadioButtons for selecting color -->
33                  <RadioButton Name="redRadioButton" Margin="3"
34                     Checked="redRadioButton_Checked">Red</RadioButton>
35                  <RadioButton Name="blueRadioButton" Margin="3"
36                     Checked="blueRadioButton_Checked">Blue</RadioButton>
37                  <RadioButton Name="greenRadioButton" Margin="3"
38                     Checked="greenRadioButton_Checked">Green</RadioButton>
39                  <RadioButton Name="blackRadioButton" IsChecked="True"
40                     Checked="blackRadioButton_Checked" Margin="3">Black
41                  </RadioButton>
42               </StackPanel>
43            </GroupBox>
44
45            <!-- creates GroupBox for size options -->
46            <GroupBox Header="Size" Margin="3">
47               <StackPanel Margin="3">
```

Fig. 24.11 | XAML of a painter application. (Part 1 of 2.)

```
48                    <RadioButton Name="smallRadioButton" Margin="3"
49                       Checked="smallRadioButton_Checked">Small</RadioButton>
50                    <RadioButton Name="mediumRadioButton" IsChecked="True"
51                       Checked="mediumRadioButton_Checked" Margin="3">Medium
52                    </RadioButton>
53                    <RadioButton Name="largeRadioButton" Margin="3"
54                       Checked="largeRadioButton_Checked">Large</RadioButton>
55                 </StackPanel>
56              </GroupBox>
57
58              <!-- creates a Button-->
59              <Button Height="23" Name="undoButton" Width="75"
60                 Margin="3,10,3,3" Click="undoButton_Click">Undo</Button>
61
62              <Button Height="23" Name="clearButton" Width="75"
63                 Margin="3" Click="clearButton_Click">Clear</Button>
64           </StackPanel>
65        </Grid>
66     </Window>
```

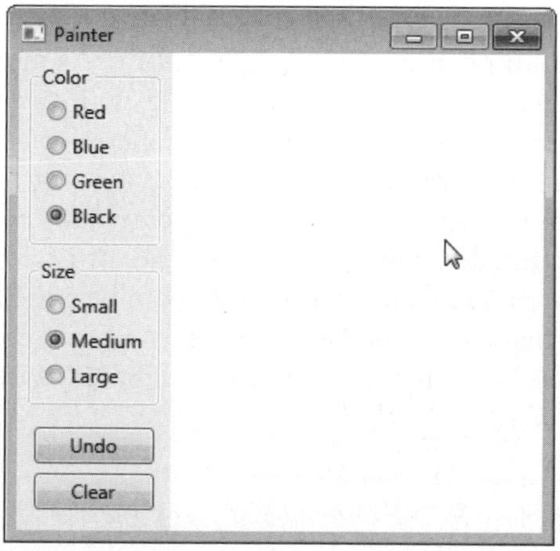

Fig. 24.11 | XAML of a painter application. (Part 2 of 2.)

GroupBox *Control*

A WPF **GroupBox** arranges controls and displays just as a Windows Forms GroupBox would, but using one is slightly different. The **Header** property replaces the Windows Forms version's Text property. In addition, a GroupBox is a ContentControl, so to place multiple controls in it, you must place them in a layout container (for example, lines 27–43).

StackPanel *Control*

In the Painter application, we organized each GroupBox's RadioButtons by placing them in **StackPanel**s (for example, lines 29–42). A StackPanel is the simplest of layout containers. It arranges its content either vertically or horizontally, depending on its **Orientation** property's setting. The default Orientation is Vertical, which is used by every StackPanel in the Painter example.

Grid Control

The Painter Window's contents are contained within a **Grid**—a flexible, all-purpose layout container. A Grid organizes controls into a user-defined number of rows and columns (one row and one column by default). You can define a Grid's rows and columns by setting its **RowDefinitions** and **ColumnDefinitions** properties, whose values are a collection of **RowDefinition** and **ColumnDefinition** objects, respectively. Because these properties do not take string values, they cannot be specified as attributes in the Grid tag. Another syntax is used instead. A class's property can be defined in XAML as a nested element with the name *ClassName.PropertyName*. For example, the Grid.ColumnDefinitions element in lines 11–14 sets the Grid's ColumnDefinitions property and defines two columns, which separate the options from the painting area, as shown in Fig. 24.11.

You can specify the Width of a ColumnDefinition and the Height of a RowDefinition with an explicit size, a relative size (using *) or Auto. Auto makes the row or column only as big as it needs to be to fit its contents. The setting * specifies the size of a row or column with respect to the Grid's other rows and columns. For example, a column with a Height of 2* would be twice the size of a column that is 1* (or just *). A Grid first allocates its space to the rows and columns whose sizes are defined explicitly or determined automatically. The remaining space is divided among the other rows and columns. By default, all Widths and Heights are set to *, so every cell in the grid is of equal size. In the Painter application, the first column is just wide enough to fit the controls, and the rest of the space is allotted to the painting area (lines 12–13). If you resize the Painter window, you'll notice that only the width of the paintable area increases or decreases.

If you click the ellipsis button next to the RowDefinitions or ColumnDefinitions property in the **Properties** window, the **Collection Editor** window will appear. This tool can be used to add, remove, reorder, and edit the properties of rows and columns in a Grid. In fact, any property that takes a collection as a value can be edited in a version of the **Collection Editor** specific to that collection. For example, you could edit the Items property of a ComboBox (that is, drop-down list) in such a way. The ColumnDefinitions **Collection Editor** is shown in Fig. 24.12.

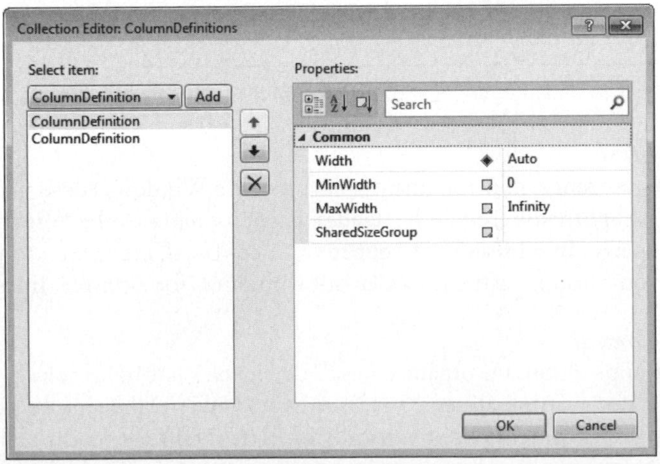

Fig. 24.12 | Using the **Collection Editor**.

The control properties we've introduced so far look and function just like their Windows Forms counterparts. To indicate which cell of a Grid a control belongs in, however, you use the **Grid.Row** and **Grid.Column** properties. These are known as **attached properties**—they're defined by a different control than that to which they're applied. In this case, Row and Column are defined by the Grid itself but applied to the controls contained in the Grid (for example, line 17). To specify the number of rows or columns that a control spans, you can use the **Grid.RowSpan** or **Grid.ColumnSpan** attached properties, respectively (for example, line 27). By default, a control spans the entire Grid, unless the Grid.Row or Grid.Column property is set, in which case the control spans only the specified row or column by default.

Canvas Control

The painting area of the Painter application is a **Canvas** (lines 17–22), another layout container. A Canvas allows users to position controls by defining explicit coordinates. Controls in a Canvas have the attached properties, **Canvas.Left** and **Canvas.Top**, which specify the control's coordinate position based on its distance from the Canvas's left and top borders, respectively. If two controls overlap, the one with the greater **Canvas.ZIndex** displays in the foreground. If this property is not defined for the controls, then the last control added to the canvas displays in the foreground.

Layout in Design Mode

As you're creating your GUI in **Design** mode, you'll notice many helpful layout features. For example, as you resize a control, its width and height are displayed. In addition, snaplines appear as necessary to help you align the edges of elements. These lines will also appear when you move controls around the design area.

When you select a control, margin lines that extend from the control to the edges of its container appear, as shown in Fig. 24.13. If a line extends to the edge of the container, then the distance between the control and that edge is fixed. If it displays as a small hollow circle, then the distance between the control and that edge is dynamic and changes as its surroundings change. You can toggle between the two by clicking on the circle.

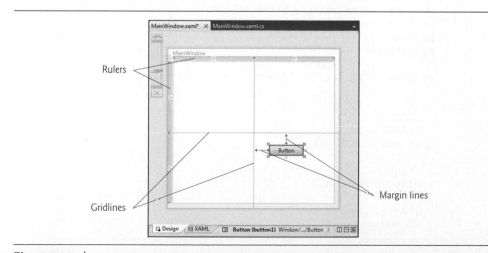

Fig. 24.13 | Margin lines and gridlines in **Design** view.

Furthermore, the **Design** view also helps you use a Grid. As shown in Fig. 24.13, when you select a control in a Grid, the Grid's rulers appear to the left and on top of it. The widths and heights of each column and row, respectively, appear on the rulers. Gridlines that outline the Grid's rows and columns also appear, helping you align and position the Grid's elements. You can also create more rows and columns by clicking where you want to separate them on the ruler.

24.9 Event Handling

Basic event handling in WPF is almost identical to Windows Forms event handling, but there is a fundamental difference, which we'll explain later in this section. We'll use the Painter example to introduce WPF event handling. Figure 24.14 provides the code-behind class for the Painter Window. As in Windows Forms GUIs, when you double click a control, the IDE automatically generates an event handler for that control's primary event. The IDE also adds an attribute to the control's XAML element specifying the event name and the name of the event handler that responds to the event. For example, in line 34, the attribute

```
Checked="redRadioButton_Checked"
```

specifies that the redRadioButton's Checked event handler is redRadioButton_Checked.

```
1   // Fig. 24.14: MainWindow.xaml.cs
2   // Code-behind for MainWindow.xaml.
3   using System.Windows;
4   using System.Windows.Controls;
5   using System.Windows.Input;
6   using System.Windows.Media;
7   using System.Windows.Shapes;
8
9   namespace Painter
10  {
11     public partial class MainWindow : Window
12     {
13        private int diameter = Sizes.MEDIUM; // set diameter of circle
14        private Brush brushColor = Brushes.Black; // set the drawing color
15        private bool shouldErase = false; // specify whether to erase
16        private bool shouldPaint = false; // specify whether to paint
17
18        private enum Sizes // size constants for diameter of the circle
19        {
20           SMALL = 4,
21           MEDIUM = 8,
22           LARGE = 10
23        } // end enum Sizes
24
25        // constructor
26        public MainWindow()
27        {
28           InitializeComponent();
29        } // end constructor
```

Fig. 24.14 | Code-behind class for Painter. (Part 1 of 4.)

```
30
31      // paints a circle on the Canvas
32      private void PaintCircle( Brush circleColor, Point position )
33      {
34         Ellipse newEllipse = new Ellipse(); // create an Ellipse
35
36         newEllipse.Fill = circleColor; // set Ellipse's color
37         newEllipse.Width = diameter; // set its horizontal diameter
38         newEllipse.Height = diameter; // set its vertical diameter
39
40         // set the Ellipse's position
41         Canvas.SetTop( newEllipse, position.Y );
42         Canvas.SetLeft( newEllipse, position.X );
43
44         paintCanvas.Children.Add( newEllipse );
45      } // end method PaintCircle
46
47      // handles paintCanvas's MouseLeftButtonDown event
48      private void paintCanvas_MouseLeftButtonDown( object sender,
49         MouseButtonEventArgs e )
50      {
51         shouldPaint = true; // OK to draw on the Canvas
52      } // end method paintCanvas_MouseLeftButtonDown
53
54      // handles paintCanvas's MouseLeftButtonUp event
55      private void paintCanvas_MouseLeftButtonUp( object sender,
56         MouseButtonEventArgs e )
57      {
58         shouldPaint = false; // do not draw on the Canvas
59      } // end method paintCanvas_MouseLeftButtonUp
60
61      // handles paintCanvas's MouseRightButtonDown event
62      private void paintCanvas_MouseRightButtonDown( object sender,
63         MouseButtonEventArgs e )
64      {
65         shouldErase = true; // OK to erase the Canvas
66      } // end method paintCanvas_MouseRightButtonDown
67
68      // handles paintCanvas's MouseRightButtonUp event
69      private void paintCanvas_MouseRightButtonUp( object sender,
70         MouseButtonEventArgs e )
71      {
72         shouldErase = false; // do not erase the Canvas
73      } // end method paintCanvas_MouseRightButtonUp
74
75      // handles paintCanvas's MouseMove event
76      private void paintCanvas_MouseMove( object sender,
77         MouseEventArgs e )
78      {
79         if ( shouldPaint )
80         {
81            // draw a circle of selected color at current mouse position
82            Point mousePosition = e.GetPosition( paintCanvas );
```

Fig. 24.14 | Code-behind class for Painter. (Part 2 of 4.)

```
83                   PaintCircle( brushColor, mousePosition );
84              } // end if
85              else if ( shouldErase )
86              {
87                  // erase by drawing circles of the Canvas's background color
88                  Point mousePosition = e.GetPosition( paintCanvas );
89                  PaintCircle( paintCanvas.Background, mousePosition );
90              } // end else if
91          } // end method paintCanvas_MouseMove
92
93          // handles Red RadioButton's Checked event
94          private void redRadioButton_Checked( object sender,
95              RoutedEventArgs e )
96          {
97              brushColor = Brushes.Red;
98          } // end method redRadioButton_Checked
99
100         // handles Blue RadioButton's Checked event
101         private void blueRadioButton_Checked( object sender,
102             RoutedEventArgs e )
103         {
104             brushColor = Brushes.Blue;
105         } // end method blueRadioButton_Checked
106
107         // handles Green RadioButton's Checked event
108         private void greenRadioButton_Checked( object sender,
109             RoutedEventArgs e )
110         {
111             brushColor = Brushes.Green;
112         } // end method greenRadioButton_Checked
113
114         // handles Black RadioButton's Checked event
115         private void blackRadioButton_Checked( object sender,
116             RoutedEventArgs e )
117         {
118             brushColor = Brushes.Black;
119         } // end method blackRadioButton_Checked
120
121         // handles Small RadioButton's Checked event
122         private void smallRadioButton_Checked( object sender,
123             RoutedEventArgs e )
124         {
125             diameter = ( int ) Sizes.SMALL;
126         } // end method smallRadioButton_Checked
127
128         // handles Medium RadioButton's Checked event
129         private void mediumRadioButton_Checked( object sender,
130             RoutedEventArgs e )
131         {
132             diameter = ( int ) Sizes.MEDIUM;
133         } // end method mediumRadioButton_Checked
134
```

Fig. 24.14 | Code-behind class for Painter. (Part 3 of 4.)

```
135          // handles Large RadioButton's Checked event
136          private void largeRadioButton_Checked( object sender,
137             RoutedEventArgs e )
138          {
139             diameter = ( int ) Sizes.LARGE;
140          } // end method largeRadioButton_Checked
141
142          // handles Undo Button's Click event
143          private void undoButton_Click( object sender, RoutedEventArgs e )
144          {
145             int count = paintCanvas.Children.Count;
146
147             // if there are any shapes on Canvas remove the last one added
148             if ( count > 0 )
149                paintCanvas.Children.RemoveAt( count - 1 );
150          } // end method undoButton_Click
151
152          // handles Clear Button's Click event
153          private void clearButton_Click( object sender, RoutedEventArgs e )
154          {
155             paintCanvas.Children.Clear(); // clear the canvas
156          } // end method clearButton_Click
157       } // end class MainWindow
158    } // end namespace Painter
```

Fig. 24.14 | Code-behind class for `Painter`. (Part 4 of 4.)

The `Painter` application "draws" by placing colored circles on the `Canvas` at the mouse pointer's position as you drag the mouse. The `PaintCircle` method (lines 32–45 in Fig. 24.14) creates the circle by defining an `Ellipse` object (lines 34–38), and positions it using the **`Canvas.SetTop`** and **`Canvas.SetLeft`** methods (lines 41–42), which change the circle's `Canvas.Left` and `Canvas.Top` attached properties, respectively.

The **`Children`** property stores a list (of type **`UIElementCollection`**) of a layout container's child elements. This allows you to edit the layout container's child elements with C# code as you would any other implementation of the `IEnumerable` interface. You can add an element to the container by calling the **`Add`** method of the `Children` list (for example, line 44). The **Undo** and **Clear** buttons work by invoking the **RemoveAt** and **Clear** methods of the Children list (lines 149 and 155), respectively.

Just as with a Windows Forms RadioButton, a WPF RadioButton has a Checked event. Lines 94–140 handle the **Checked** event for each of the RadioButtons in this example, which change the color and the size of the circles painted on the Canvas. The Button control's **Click** event also functions the same in WPF as it did in Windows Forms. Lines 143–156 handle the **Undo** and **Clear** Buttons. The event-handler declarations look almost identical to how they would look in a Windows Forms application, except that the event-arguments object (e) is a RoutedEventArgs object instead of an EventArgs object. We'll explain why later in this section.

Mouse and Keyboard Events

WPF has built-in support for keyboard and mouse events that is nearly identical to the support in Windows Forms. Painter uses the **MouseMove** event of the paintable Canvas to paint and erase (lines 76–91). A control's MouseMove event is triggered whenever the mouse moves while within the boundaries of the control. Information for the event is passed to the event handler using a **MouseEventArgs** object, which contains mouse-specific information. The **GetPosition** method of MouseEventArgs, for example, returns the current position of the mouse relative to the control that triggered the event (for example, lines 82 and 88). Mouse-Move works exactly the same as it does in Windows Forms. [*Note:* Much of the functionality in our sample Painter application is already provided by the WPF InkCanvas control. We chose not to use this control so we could demonstrate various other WPF features.]

WPF has additional mouse events. Painter also uses the **MouseLeftButtonDown** and **MouseLeftButtonUp** events to toggle painting on and off (lines 48–59), and the **Mouse-RightButtonDown** and **MouseRightButtonUp** events to toggle erasing on and off (lines 62–73). All of these events pass information to the event handler using the **MouseButtonEvent-Args** object, which has properties specific to a mouse button (for example, ButtonState or ClickCount) in addition to mouse-specific ones. These events are new to WPF and are more specific versions of MouseUp and MouseDown (which are still available in WPF). A summary of commonly used mouse and keyboard events is provided in Fig. 24.15.

Common mouse and keyboard events

Mouse Events with an Event Argument of Type MouseEventArgs	
MouseMove	Raised when you move the mouse within a control's boundaries.

Mouse Events with an Event Argument of Type MouseButtonEventArgs	
MouseLeftButtonDown	Raised when the left mouse button is pressed.
MouseLeftButtonUp	Raised when the left mouse button is released.
MouseRightButtonDown	Raised when the right mouse button is pressed.
MouseRightButtonUp	Raised when the right mouse button is released.

Mouse Events with an Event Argument of Type MouseWheelEventArgs	
MouseWheel	Raised when the mouse wheel is rotated.

Fig. 24.15 | Common mouse and keyboard events. (Part 1 of 2.)

Common mouse and keyboard events
Keyboard Events with an Event Argument of Type KeyEventArgs
KeyDown   Raised when a key is pressed.
KeyUp   Raised when a key is released.

Fig. 24.15 | Common mouse and keyboard events. (Part 2 of 2.)

Routed Events

WPF events have a significant distinction from their Windows Forms counterparts—they can travel either up (from child to parent) or down (from parent to child) the containment hierarchy—the hierarchy of nested elements defined within a control. This is called **event routing**, and all WPF events are **routed events**.

The event-arguments object that is passed to the event handler of a WPF Button's Click event or a RadioButton's Check event is of the type **RoutedEventArgs**. All event-argument objects in WPF are of type RoutedEventArgs or one of its subclasses. As an event travels up or down the hierarchy, it may be useful to stop it before it reaches the end. When the **Handled** property of the RoutedEventArgs parameter is set to true, event handlers ignore the event. It may also be useful to know the source where the event was first triggered. The **Source** property stores this information. You can learn more about the benefits of routed events at bit.ly/RoutedEvents.

Figures 24.16 and 24.17 show the XAML and code-behind for a program that demonstrates event routing. The program contains two GroupBoxes, each with a Label inside (lines 15–28 in Fig. 24.16). One group handles a left-mouse-button press with Mouse-LeftButtonUp, and the other with PreviewMouseLeftButtonUp. As the event travels up or down the containment hierarchy, a log of where the event has traveled is displayed in a **TextBox** (line 30). The WPF TextBox functions just like its Windows Forms counterpart.

```
1    <!-- Fig. 24.16: MainWindow.xaml -->
2    <!-- Routed-events example (XAML). -->
3    <Window x:Class="RoutedEvents.MainWindow"
4       xmlns="http://schemas.microsoft.com/winfx/2006/xaml/presentation"
5       xmlns:x="http://schemas.microsoft.com/winfx/2006/xaml"
6       Title="Routed Events" Height="300" Width="300"
7       Name="routedEventsWindow">
8       <Grid>
9          <Grid.RowDefinitions>
10            <RowDefinition Height="Auto" />
11            <RowDefinition Height="Auto" />
12            <RowDefinition Height="*" />
13         </Grid.RowDefinitions>
14
15         <GroupBox Name="tunnelingGroupBox" Grid.Row="0" Header="Tunneling"
16            Margin="5" PreviewMouseLeftButtonUp="Tunneling">
17            <Label Margin="5" HorizontalAlignment="Center"
18               Name="tunnelingLabel" PreviewMouseLeftButtonUp="Tunneling">
```

Fig. 24.16 | Routed-events example (XAML). (Part 1 of 2.)

```
19                    Click Here
20               </Label>
21          </GroupBox>
22
23          <GroupBox Name="bubblingGroupBox" Grid.Row="1" Header="Bubbling"
24             Margin="5" MouseLeftButtonUp="Bubbling">
25             <Label Margin="5" MouseLeftButtonUp="Bubbling"
26                Name="bubblingLabel" HorizontalAlignment="Center">Click Here
27             </Label>
28          </GroupBox>
29
30          <TextBox Name="logTextBox" Grid.Row="2" Margin="5" />
31       </Grid>
32    </Window>
```

Fig. 24.16 | Routed-events example (XAML). (Part 2 of 2.)

```
1    // Fig. 24.17: MainWindow.xaml.cs
2    // Routed-events example (code-behind).
3    using System.Windows;
4    using System.Windows.Controls;
5    using System.Windows.Input;
6
7    namespace RoutedEvents
8    {
9       public partial class MainWindow : Window
10      {
11         int bubblingEventStep = 1; // step counter for Bubbling
12         int tunnelingEventStep = 1; // step counter for Tunneling
13         string tunnelingLogText = string.Empty; // temporary Tunneling log
14
15         public RoutedEventsWindow()
16         {
17            InitializeComponent();
18         } // end constructor
19
20         // PreviewMouseUp is a tunneling event
21         private void Tunneling( object sender, MouseButtonEventArgs e )
22         {
23            // append step number and sender
24            tunnelingLogText = string.Format( "{0}({1}): {2}\n",
25               tunnelingLogText, tunnelingEventStep,
26               ( ( Control ) sender ).Name );
27            ++tunnelingEventStep; // increment counter
28
29            // execution goes from parent to child, ending with the source
30            if ( e.Source.Equals( sender ) )
31            {
32               tunnelingLogText = string.Format(
33                  "This is a tunneling event:\n{0}", tunnelingLogText );
34               logTextBox.Text = tunnelingLogText; // set logTextBox text
```

Fig. 24.17 | Routed-events example (code-behind). (Part 1 of 2.)

```
35                tunnelingLogText = string.Empty; // clear temporary log
36                tunnelingEventStep = 1; // reset counter
37             } // end if
38          } // end method Tunneling
39
40          // MouseUp is a bubbling event
41          private void Bubbling( object sender, MouseButtonEventArgs e )
42          {
43             // execution goes from child to parent, starting at the source
44             if ( e.Source.Equals( sender ) )
45             {
46                logTextBox.Clear(); // clear the logTextBox
47                bubblingEventStep = 1; // reset counter
48                logTextBox.Text = "This is a bubbling event:\n";
49             } // end if
50
51             // append step number and sender
52             logTextBox.Text = string.Format( "{0}({1}): {2}\n",
53                logTextBox.Text, bubblingEventStep,
54                ( ( Control ) sender ).Name );
55             ++bubblingEventStep;
56          } // end method Bubbling
57       } // end class RoutedEventsWindow
58    } // end namespace RoutedEvents
```

Fig. 24.17 | Routed-events example (code-behind). (Part 2 of 2.)

There are three types of routed events—**direct events**, **bubbling events** and **tunneling events**. Direct events are like ordinary Windows Forms events—they do not travel up or down the containment hierarchy. Bubbling events start at the Source and travel up the hierarchy ending at the root (Window) or until you set Handled to true. Tunneling events start at the top and travel down the hierarchy until they reach the Source or Handled is true. To help you distinguish tunneling events from bubbling events, WPF prefixes the names of tunneling events with Preview. For example, **PreviewMouseLeftButtonDown** is the tunneling version of MouseLeftButtonDown, which is a bubbling event.

If you click the **Click Here** Label in the **Tunneling** GroupBox, the click is handled first by the GroupBox, then by the contained Label. The event handler that responds to the click handles the **PreviewMouseLeftButtonUp** event—a tunneling event. The Tunneling method (lines 21–38 in Fig. 24.17) handles the events of both the GroupBox and the Label. An event handler can handle events for many controls. Simply select each control then use the events tab in the **Properties** window to select the appropriate event handler for the corresponding event of each control. If you click the other Label, the click is handled first by the Label, then by the containing GroupBox. The Bubbling method (lines 41–56) handles the MouseLeftButtonUp events of both controls.

24.10 Commands and Common Application Tasks

In Windows Forms, event handling is the only way to respond to user actions. WPF provides an alternate technique called a **command**—an action or a task that may be triggered by many different user interactions. In Visual Studio, for example, you can cut, copy and paste code. You can execute these tasks through the **Edit** menu, a toolbar or keyboard shortcuts. To program this functionality in WPF, you can define a single command for each task, thus centralizing the handling of common tasks—this is not easily done in Windows Forms.

Commands also enable you to synchronize a task's availability to the state of its corresponding controls. For example, users should be able to copy something only if they have content selected. When you define the copy command, you can specify this as a requirement. As a result, if the user has no content selected, then the menu item, toolbar item and keyboard shortcut for copying are all automatically disabled.

Commands are implementations of the **ICommand** interface. When a command is executed, the **Execute** method is called. However, the command's execution logic (that is, how it should execute) is not defined in its Execute method. You must specify this logic when implementing the command. An ICommand's **CanExecute** method works in the same way. The logic that specifies when a command is enabled and disabled is not determined by the CanExecute method and must instead be specified by responding to an appropriate event. Class RoutedCommand is the standard implementation of ICommand. Every Routed-Command has a Name and a collection of **InputGestures** (that is, keyboard shortcuts) associated with it. RoutedUICommand is an extension of RoutedCommand with a Text property, which specifies the default text to display on a GUI element that triggers the command.

WPF provides a command library of built-in commands. These commands have their standard keyboard shortcuts already associated with them. For example, Copy is a built-in command and has *Ctrl-C* associated with it. Figure 24.18 provides a list of some common built-in commands, separated by the classes in which they're defined.

Common built-in commands from the WPF command library			
ApplicationCommands properties			
New	Open	Save	Close
Cut	Copy	Paste	
EditingCommands properties			
ToggleBold	ToggleItalic	ToggleUnderline	
MediaCommands properties			
Play	Stop	Rewind	FastForward
IncreaseVolume	DecreaseVolume	NextTrack	PreviousTrack

Fig. 24.18 | Common built-in commands from the WPF command library.

Figures 24.19 and 24.20 are the XAML markup and C# code for a simple text-editor application that allows users to format text into bold and italics, and also to cut, copy and paste text. The example uses the **RichTextBox** control (line 49), which allows users to enter, edit and format text. We use this application to demonstrate several built-in commands from the command library.

```
 1    <!-- Fig. 24.19: MainWindow.xaml -->
 2    <!-- Creating menus and toolbars, and using commands (XAML). -->
 3    <Window x:Class="TextEditor.MainWindow"
 4       xmlns="http://schemas.microsoft.com/winfx/2006/xaml/presentation"
 5       xmlns:x="http://schemas.microsoft.com/winfx/2006/xaml"
 6       Title="Text Editor" Height="300" Width="300">
 7
 8       <Window.CommandBindings> <!-- define command bindings -->
 9          <!-- bind the Close command to handler -->
10          <CommandBinding Command="Close" Executed="closeCommand_Executed" />
11       </Window.CommandBindings>
12
13       <Grid> <!-- define the GUI -->
14          <Grid.RowDefinitions>
15             <RowDefinition Height="Auto" />
16             <RowDefinition Height="Auto" />
17             <RowDefinition Height="*" />
18          </Grid.RowDefinitions>
19
20          <Menu Grid.Row="0"> <!-- create the menu -->
21             <!-- map each menu item to corresponding command -->
22             <MenuItem Header="File">
23                <MenuItem Header="Exit" Command="Close" />
24             </MenuItem>
25             <MenuItem Header="Edit">
26                <MenuItem Header="Cut" Command="Cut" />
27                <MenuItem Header="Copy" Command="Copy" />
28                <MenuItem Header="Paste" Command="Paste" />
29                <Separator /> <!-- separates groups of menu items -->
30                <MenuItem Header="Bold" Command="ToggleBold"
31                   FontWeight="Bold" />
32                <MenuItem Header="Italic" Command="ToggleItalic"
33                   FontStyle="Italic" />
34             </MenuItem>
35          </Menu>
36
37          <ToolBar Grid.Row="1"> <!-- create the toolbar -->
38             <!-- map each toolbar item to corresponding command -->
39             <Button Command="Cut">Cut</Button>
40             <Button Command="Copy">Copy</Button>
41             <Button Command="Paste">Paste</Button>
42             <Separator /> <!-- separates groups of toolbar items -->
43             <Button FontWeight="Bold" Command="ToggleBold">Bold</Button>
44             <Button FontStyle="Italic" Command="ToggleItalic">
45                Italic</Button>
46          </ToolBar>
```

Fig. 24.19 | Creating menus and toolbars, and using commands (XAML). (Part 1 of 2.)

```
47
48          <!-- display editable, formattable text -->
49          <RichTextBox Grid.Row="2" Margin="5" />
50      </Grid>
51  </Window>
```

Fig. 24.19 | Creating menus and toolbars, and using commands (XAML). (Part 2 of 2.)

```
 1  // Fig. 24.20: MainWindow.xaml.cs
 2  // Code-behind class for a simple text editor.
 3  using System.Windows;
 4  using System.Windows.Input;
 5
 6  namespace TextEditor
 7  {
 8      public partial class MainWindow : Window
 9      {
10          public MainWindow()
11          {
12              InitializeComponent();
13          } // end constructor
14
15          // exit the application
16          private void closeCommand_Executed( object sender,
17              ExecutedRoutedEventArgs e )
18          {
19              Application.Current.Shutdown();
20          } // end method closeCommand_Executed
21      } // end class MainWindow
22  } // end namespace TextEditor
```

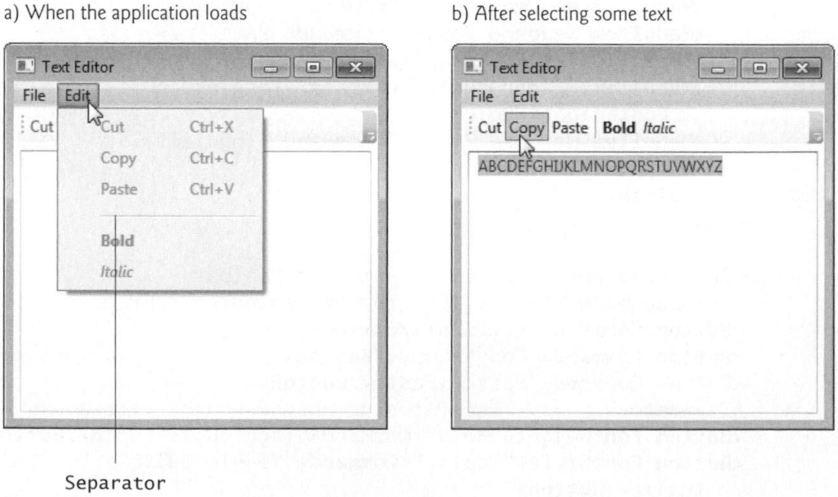

a) When the application loads

b) After selecting some text

Separator

Fig. 24.20 | Code-behind class for a simple text editor. (Part 1 of 2.)

c) After copying some text

Fig. 24.20 | Code-behind class for a simple text editor. (Part 2 of 2.)

A command is executed when it's triggered by a command source. For example, the Close command is triggered by a MenuItem (line 23 in Fig. 24.19). The Cut command has two sources, a MenuItem and a ToolBar Button (lines 26 and 39, respectively). A command can have many sources.

To make use of a command, you must create a **command binding**—a link between a command and the methods containing its application logic. You can declare a command binding by creating a **CommandBinding** object in XAML and setting its Command property to the name of the associated command (line 10). A command binding raises the **Executed** and **PreviewExecuted** events (bubbling and tunneling versions of the same event) when its associated command is executed. You program the command's functionality into an event handler for one of these events. In line 10, we set the Executed attribute to a method name, telling the program that the specified method (closeCommand_Executed) handles the command binding's Executed event.

In this example, we demonstrate the use of a command binding by implementing the Close command. When it executes, it shuts down the application. The method that executes this task is **Application.Current.Shutdown**, as shown in line 19 of Fig. 24.20.

You can also use a command binding to specify the application logic for determining when a command should be enabled or disabled. You can do so by handling either the **CanExecute** or **PreviewCanExecute** (bubbling and tunneling versions of the same events) events in the same way that you handle the Executed or PreviewExecuted events. Because we do not define such a handler for the Close command in its command binding, it's always enabled. Command bindings should be defined within the **Window.Command-Bindings** element (for example, lines 8–11).

The only time a command binding is not necessary is when a control has built-in functionality for dealing with a command. A Button or MenuItem linked to the Cut, Copy, or Paste commands is an example (for example, lines 26–28 and lines 39–41). As Fig. 24.20(a) shows, all three commands are disabled when the application loads. If you select some text, the Cut and Copy commands are enabled, as shown in Fig. 24.20(b).

Once you have copied some text, the Paste command is enabled, as evidenced by Fig. 24.20(c). We did not have to define any associated command bindings or event handlers to implement these commands. The ToggleBold and ToggleItalic commands are also implemented without any command bindings.

Menus and Toolbars

The text editor uses menus and toolbars. The **Menu** control creates a menu containing **MenuItem**s. MenuItems can be top-level menus such as **File** or **Edit** (lines 22 and 25 in Fig. 24.19), submenus, or items in a menu, which function like Buttons (for example, lines 26–28). If a MenuItem has nested MenuItems, then it's a top-level menu or a submenu. Otherwise, it's an item that executes an action via either an event or a command. MenuItems are content controls and thus can display any single GUI element as content.

A **ToolBar** is a single row or column (depending on the Orientation property) of options. A ToolBar's Orientation is a read-only property that gets its value from the parent **ToolBarTray**, which can host multiple ToolBars. If a ToolBar has no parent ToolBarTray, as is the case in this example, its Orientation is Horizontal by default. Unlike elements in a Menu, a ToolBar's child elements are not of a specific type. A ToolBar usually contains Buttons, CheckBoxes, ComboBoxes, RadioButtons and Separators, but any WPF control can be used. ToolBars overwrite the look-and-feel of their child elements with their own specifications, so that the controls look seamless together. You can override the default specifications to create your own look-and-feel. Lines 37–46 define the text editor's ToolBar.

Menus and ToolBars can incorporate **Separators** (for example, lines 29 and 42) that differentiate groups of MenuItems or controls. In a Menu, a Separator displays as a horizontal bar—as shown between the **Paste** and **Bold** menu options in Fig. 24.20(a). In a horizontal ToolBar, it displays as a short vertical bar—as shown in Fig. 24.20(b). You can use Separators in any type of control that can contain multiple child elements, such as a StackPanel.

24.11 WPF GUI Customization

One advantage of WPF over Windows Forms is the ability to customize controls. WPF provides several techniques to customize the look and behavior of controls. The simplest takes full advantage of a control's properties. The value of a control's **Background** property, for example, is a brush (i.e, Brush object). This allows you to create a gradient or an image and use it as the background rather than a solid color. For more information about brushes, see Section 25.5. In addition, many controls that allowed only text content in Windows Forms are ContentControls in WPF, which can host any type of content—including other controls. The caption of a WPF Button, for example, could be an image or even a video.

In Section 24.12, we demonstrate how to use styles in WPF to achieve a uniform look-and-feel. In Windows Forms, if you want to make all your Buttons look the same, you have to manually set properties for every Button, or copy and paste. To achieve the same result in WPF, you can define the properties once as a style and apply the style to each Button. This is similar to the CSS/XHTML implementation of styles. XHTML specifies the content and structure of a website, and CSS defines styles that specify the presentation of elements in a website. For more information on CSS and XHTML, see Chapters 19 and 27, and visit our XHTML and CSS Resource Centers at www.deitel.com/xhtml/ and www.deitel.com/css21/, respectively.

Styles are limited to modifying a control's look-and-feel through its properties. In Section 24.14, we introduce control templates, which offer you the freedom to define a control's appearance by modifying its visual structure. With a custom control template, you can completely strip a control of all its visual settings and rebuild it to look exactly the way you like, while maintaining its existing functionality. A Button with a custom control template might look structurally different from a default Button, but it still functions the same as any other Button.

If you want to change only the appearance of an element, a style or control template should suffice. However, you can also create entirely new custom controls that have their own functionality, properties, methods and events. We demonstrate how to create a custom control in Section 29.4.3.

24.12 Using Styles to Change the Appearance of Controls

Once defined, a **WPF style** is a collection of property-value and event-handler definitions that can be reused. Styles enable you to eliminate repetitive code or markup. For example, if you want to change the look-and-feel of the standard Button throughout a section of your application, you can define a style and apply it to all the Buttons in that section. Without styles, you have to set the properties for each individual Button. Furthermore, if you later decided that you wanted to tweak the appearance of these Buttons, you would have to modify your markup or code several times. By using a style, you can make the change only once in the style and it's automatically be applied to any control which uses that style.

Styles are **WPF resources**. A resource is an object that is defined for an entire section of your application and can be reused multiple times. A resource can be as simple as a property or as complex as a control template. Every WPF control can hold a collection of resources that can be accessed by any element down the containment hierarchy. In a way, this is similar in approach to the concept of variable scope that you learned about in Chapter 7. For example, if you define a style as a resource of a Window, then any element in the Window can use that style. If you define a style as a resource of a layout container, then only the elements of the layout container can use that style. You can also define application-level resources for an Application object in the App.xaml file. These resources can be accessed in any file in the application.

Figure 24.21 provides the XAML markup and Fig. 24.22 provides the C# code for a color-chooser application. This example demonstrates styles and introduces the Slider user input control.

```
1   <!-- Fig. 24.21: MainWindow.xaml -->
2   <!-- Color chooser application showing the use of styles (XAML). -->
3   <Window x:Class="ColorChooser.MainWindow"
4       xmlns="http://schemas.microsoft.com/winfx/2006/xaml/presentation"
5       xmlns:x="http://schemas.microsoft.com/winfx/2006/xaml"
6       Title="Color Chooser" Height="150" Width="500">
7
```

Fig. 24.21 | Color-chooser application showing the use of styles (XAML). (Part 1 of 3.)

```
8    <Window.Resources> <!-- define Window's resources -->
9       <Style x:Key="SliderStyle"> <!-- define style for Sliders -->
10
11          <!-- set properties for Sliders -->
12          <Setter Property="Slider.Width" Value="256" />
13          <Setter Property="Slider.Minimum" Value="0" />
14          <Setter Property="Slider.Maximum" Value="255" />
15          <Setter Property="Slider.IsSnapToTickEnabled" Value="True" />
16          <Setter Property="Slider.VerticalAlignment" Value="Center" />
17          <Setter Property="Slider.HorizontalAlignment" Value="Center" />
18          <Setter Property="Slider.Value" Value="0" />
19          <Setter Property="Slider.AutoToolTipPlacement"
20             Value="TopLeft" />
21
22          <!-- set event handler for ValueChanged event -->
23          <EventSetter Event="Slider.ValueChanged"
24             Handler="slider_ValueChanged" />
25       </Style>
26    </Window.Resources>
27
28    <Grid Margin="5"> <!-- define GUI -->
29       <Grid.RowDefinitions>
30          <RowDefinition />
31          <RowDefinition />
32          <RowDefinition />
33          <RowDefinition />
34       </Grid.RowDefinitions>
35       <Grid.ColumnDefinitions>
36          <ColumnDefinition Width="Auto" />
37          <ColumnDefinition Width="Auto" />
38          <ColumnDefinition Width="50" />
39          <ColumnDefinition />
40       </Grid.ColumnDefinitions>
41
42       <!-- define Labels for Sliders -->
43       <Label Grid.Row="0" Grid.Column="0" HorizontalAlignment="Right"
44          VerticalAlignment="Center">Red:</Label>
45       <Label Grid.Row="1" Grid.Column="0" HorizontalAlignment="Right"
46          VerticalAlignment="Center">Green:</Label>
47       <Label Grid.Row="2" Grid.Column="0" HorizontalAlignment="Right"
48          VerticalAlignment="Center">Blue:</Label>
49       <Label Grid.Row="3" Grid.Column="0" HorizontalAlignment="Right"
50          VerticalAlignment="Center">Alpha:</Label>
51
52       <!-- define Label that displays the color -->
53       <Label Name="colorLabel" Grid.RowSpan="4" Grid.Column="3"
54          Margin="10" />
55
56       <!-- define Sliders and apply style to them -->
57       <Slider Name="redSlider" Grid.Row="0" Grid.Column="1"
58          Style="{StaticResource SliderStyle}"
59          Value="{Binding Text, ElementName=redBox}" />`
60       <Slider Name="greenSlider" Grid.Row="1" Grid.Column="1"
```

Fig. 24.21 | Color-chooser application showing the use of styles (XAML). (Part 2 of 3.)

```
61                Style="{StaticResource SliderStyle}"
62                Value="{Binding Text, ElementName=greenBox}"/>
63          <Slider Name="blueSlider" Grid.Row="2" Grid.Column="1"
64                Style="{StaticResource SliderStyle}"
65                Value="{Binding Text, ElementName=blueBox}"/>
66          <Slider Name="alphaSlider" Grid.Row="3" Grid.Column="1"
67                Style="{StaticResource SliderStyle}"
68                Value="{Binding Text, ElementName=alphaBox}" />
69
70          <TextBox Name="redBox" Grid.Row="0" Grid.Column="2"
71                Text="{Binding Value, ElementName=redSlider}"/>
72          <TextBox Name="greenBox" Grid.Row="1" Grid.Column="2"
73                Text="{Binding Value, ElementName=greenSlider}"/>
74          <TextBox Name="blueBox" Grid.Row="2" Grid.Column="2"
75                Text="{Binding Value, ElementName=blueSlider}"/>
76          <TextBox Name="alphaBox" Grid.Row="3" Grid.Column="2"
77                Text="{Binding Value, ElementName=alphaSlider}"/>
78       </Grid>
79    </Window>
```

Fig. 24.21 | Color-chooser application showing the use of styles (XAML). (Part 3 of 3.)

```
1   // Fig. 24.22: MainWindow.xaml.cs
2   // Color chooser application showing the use of styles (code-behind).
3   using System.Windows;
4   using System.Windows.Media;
5
6   namespace ColorChooser
7   {
8      public partial class MainWindow : Window
9      {
10         public MainWindow()
11         {
12            InitializeComponent();
13            alphaSlider.Value = 255; // override Value from style
14         } // constructor
15
16         // handles the ValueChanged event for the Sliders
17         private void slider_ValueChanged( object sender,
18            RoutedPropertyChangedEventArgs< double > e )
19         {
20            // generates new color
21            SolidColorBrush backgroundColor = new SolidColorBrush();
22            backgroundColor.Color = Color.FromArgb(
23               ( byte ) alphaSlider.Value, ( byte ) redSlider.Value,
24               ( byte ) greenSlider.Value, ( byte ) blueSlider.Value );
25
26            // set colorLabel's background to new color
27            colorLabel.Background = backgroundColor;
28         } // end method slider_ValueChanged
29      } // end class MainWindow
30   } // end namespace ColorChooser
```

Fig. 24.22 | Color-chooser application showing the use of styles (code-behind). (Part 1 of 2.)

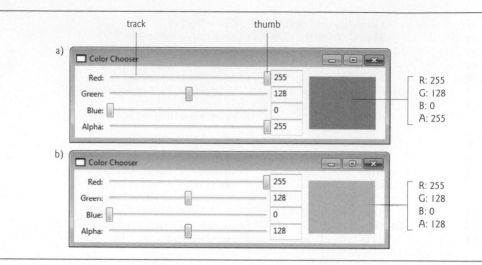

Fig. 24.22 | Color-chooser application showing the use of styles (code-behind). (Part 2 of 2.)

RGBA Colors

The color-chooser application uses the RGBA color system. Every color is represented by its red, green and blue color values, each ranging from 0 to 255, where 0 denotes no color and 255 full color. For example, a color with a red value of 0 would contain no red component. The alpha value (A)—which also ranges from 0 to 255—represents a color's opacity, with 0 being completely transparent and 255 completely opaque. The two colors in Fig. 24.22's sample outputs have the same RGB values, but the color displayed in Fig. 24.22(b) is semitransparent.

Slider Controls

The color-chooser GUI uses four **Slider** controls that change the RGBA values of a color displayed by a Label. Next to each Slider is a TextBox that displays the Slider's current value. You can also type a number in a TextBox to update the value of the corresponding Slider. A Slider is a numeric user input control that allows users to drag a "thumb" along a track to select the value. Whenever the user moves a Slider, the application generates a new color, the corresponding TextBox is updated and the Label displays the new color as its background. The new color is generated by using class Color's FromArgb method, which returns a color based on the four RGBA byte values you pass it (Fig. 24.22, lines 22–24). The color is then applied as the Background of the Label. Similarly, changing the value of a Text-Box updates the thumb of the corresponding Slider to reflect the change, which then updates the Label with the new color. We discuss the updates of the TextBoxes shortly.

Style for the Sliders

Styles can be defined as a resource of any control. In the color-chooser application, we defined the style as a resource of the entire Window. We also could have defined it as a resource of the Grid. To define resources for a control, you set a control's **Resources** property. Thus, to define a resource for a Window, as we did in this example, you would use Window.Resources (lines 8–26 in Fig. 24.21). To define a resource for a Grid, you would use Grid.Resources.

Style objects can be defined in XAML using the **Style** element. The x:Key attribute (i.e., attribute Key from the standard XAML namespace) must be set in every style (or other resource) so that it can be referenced later by other controls (line 9). The children of a Style element set properties and define event handlers. A **Setter** sets a property to a specific value (e.g., line 12, which sets the styled Slider's Width property to 256). An **EventSetter** specifies the method that responds to an event (e.g., lines 23–24, which specifies that method slider_ValueChanged handles the Slider's ValueChanged event).

The Style in the color-chooser example (SliderStyle) primarily uses Setters. It lays out the color Sliders by specifying the Width, HorizontalAlignment and VerticalAlignment properties (lines 12, 16 and 17). It also sets the Minimum and Maximum properties, which determine a Slider's range of values (lines 13–14). In line 18, the default Value is set to 0. IsSnapToTickEnabled is set to True, meaning that only values that fall on a "tick" are allowed (line 15). By default, each tick is separated by a value of 1, so this setting makes the styled Slider accept only integer values. Lastly, the style also sets the AutoToolTipPlacement property, which specifies where a Slider's tooltip should appear, if at all.

Although the Style defined in the color-chooser example is clearly meant for Sliders, it can be applied to any control. Styles are not control specific. You can make all controls of one type use the same default style by setting the style's **TargetType** attribute to the control type. For example, if we wanted all of the Window's Sliders to use a Style, we would add TargetType="Slider" to the Style's start tag.

Using a Style
To apply a style to a control, you create a **resource binding** between a control's Style property and the Style resource. You can create a resource binding in XAML by specifying the resource in a **markup extension**—an expression enclosed in curly braces ({}). The form of a markup extension calling a resource is {*ResourceType ResourceKey*} (for example, {StaticResource SliderStyle} in Fig. 24.21, line 58).

Static and Dynamic Resources
There are two types of resources. **Static resources** are applied at initialization time only. **Dynamic resources** are applied every time the resource is modified by the application. To use a style as a static resource, use StaticResource as the type in the markup extension. To use a style as a dynamic resource, use DynamicResource as the type. Because styles don't normally change during runtime, they are usually used as static resources. However, using one as a dynamic resource is sometimes necessary, such as when you wish to enable users to customize a style at runtime.

In this application, we apply SliderStyle as a static resource to each Slider (lines 58, 61, 64 and 67). Once you apply a style to a control, the **Design** view and **Properties** window update to display the control's new appearance settings. If you then modify the control through the **Properties** window, the control itself is updated, not the style.

Element-to-Element Bindings
In this application, we use a new feature of WPF called **element-to-element binding** in which a property of one element is always equal to a property of another element. This enables us to declare in XAML that each TextBox's Text property should always have the value of the corresponding Slider's Value property, and that each Slider's Value property should always have the value of the corresponding TextBox's Text property. Once

these bindings are defined, changing a Slider updates the corresponding TextBox and vice versa. In Fig. 24.21, lines 59, 62, 65 and 68 each use a Binding markup extension to bind a Slider's Value property to the Text property of the appropriate TextBox. Similary, lines 71, 73, 75 and 77 each use a Binding markup extension to bind a TextBox's Text property to the Value property of the appropriate Slider.

Programmatically Changing the Alpha Slider's *Value*
As shown in Fig. 24.23, the Slider that adjusts the alpha value in the color-chooser example starts with a value of 255, whereas the R, G and B Sliders' values start at 0. The Value property is defined by a Setter in the style to be 0 (line 18 in Fig. 24.21). This is why the R, G and B values are 0. The Value property of the alpha Slider is programmatically defined to be 255 (line 13 in Fig. 24.22), but it could also be set locally in the XAML. Because a local declaration takes precedence over a style setter, the alpha Slider's value would start at 255 when the application loads.

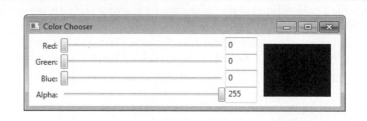

Fig. 24.23 | GUI of the color-chooser application at initialization.

Dependency Properties
Most WPF properties, though they might look and behave exactly like ordinary ones, are in fact **dependency properties**. Such properties have built-in support for change notification—that is, an application knows and can respond to changes in property values. In addition, they support inheritance down the control-containment hierarchy. For example, when you specify FontSize in a Window, every control in the Window inherits it as the default FontSize. You can also specify a control's property in one of its child elements. This is how attached properties work.

A control's properties may be set at many different levels in WPF, so instead of holding a fixed value, a dependency property's value is determined during execution by a value-determination system. If a property is defined at several levels at once, then the current value is the one defined at the level with the highest precedence. A style, for example, overwrites the default appearance of a control, because it takes higher precedence. A summary of the levels, in order from highest to lowest precedence, is shown in Fig. 24.24.

Levels of value determination system	
Animation	The value is defined by an active animation. For more information about animation, see Chapter 25.

Fig. 24.24 | Levels of value determination from highest to lowest precedence. (Part 1 of 2.)

Levels of value determination system	
Local declaration	The value is defined as an attribute in XAML or set in code. This is how ordinary properties are set.
Trigger	The value is defined by an active trigger. For more information about triggers, see Section 24.14.
Style	The value is defined by a setter in a style.
Inherited value	The value is inherited from a definition in a containing element.
Default value	The value is not explicitly defined.

Fig. 24.24 | Levels of value determination from highest to lowest precedence. (Part 2 of 2.)

24.13 Customizing Windows

For over a decade, the standard design of an application window has remained practically the same—a framed rectangular box with a header in the top left and a set of buttons in the top right for minimizing, maximizing and closing the window. Cutting-edge applications, however, have begun to use custom windows that diverge from this standard to create a more interesting look.

WPF lets you do this more easily. To create a custom window, set the **WindowStyle** property to None. This removes the standard frame around your Window. To make your Window irregularly shaped, you set the **AllowsTransparency** property to True and the Background property to Transparent. If you then add controls, only the space within the boundaries of those controls behaves as part of the window. This works because a user cannot interact with any part of a Window that is transparent. You still define your Window as a rectangle with a width and a height, but when a user clicks in a transparent part of the Window, it behaves as if the user clicked outside the Window's boundaries—that is, the window does not respond to the click.

Figure 24.25 is the XAML markup that defines a GUI for a circular digital clock. The Window's WindowStyle is set to None and AllowsTransparency is set to True (line 7). In this example, we set the background to be an image using an ImageBrush (lines 10–12). The background image is a circle with a drop shadow surrounded by transparency. Thus, the Window appears circular.

```
1   <!-- Fig. 24.25: MainWindow.xaml -->
2   <!-- Creating custom windows and using timers (XAML). -->
3   <Window x:Class="Clock.MainWindow"
4       xmlns="http://schemas.microsoft.com/winfx/2006/xaml/presentation"
5       xmlns:x="http://schemas.microsoft.com/winfx/2006/xaml"
6       Title="Clock" Name="clockWindow" Height="118" Width="118"
7       WindowStyle="None" AllowsTransparency="True"
8       MouseLeftButtonDown="clockWindow_MouseLeftButtonDown">
9
10      <Window.Background> <!-- Set background image -->
11          <ImageBrush ImageSource="images/circle.png" />
12      </Window.Background>
```

Fig. 24.25 | Creating custom windows and using timers (XAML). (Part 1 of 2.)

```
13
14      <Grid>
15          <TextBox Name="timeTextBox" Margin="0,42,0,0"
16              Background="Transparent" TextAlignment="Center"
17              FontWeight="Bold" Foreground="White" FontSize="16"
18              BorderThickness="0" Cursor="Arrow" Focusable="False" />
19      </Grid>
20   </Window>
```

Fig. 24.25 | Creating custom windows and using timers (XAML). (Part 2 of 2.)

The time is displayed in the center of the window in a TextBox (lines 15–18). Its Background is set to Transparent so that the text displays directly on the circular background (line 16). We configured the text to be size 16, bold, and white by setting the FontSize, FontWeight, and Foreground properties. The Cursor property is set to Arrow, so that the mouse cursor doesn't change when it moves over the time (line 18). Setting Focusable to False disables the user's ability to select the text (line 18).

When you create a custom window, there's no built-in functionality for doing the simple tasks that normal windows do. For example, there is no way for the user to move, resize, minimize, maximize, or close a window unless you write the code to enable these features. You can move the clock around, because we implemented this functionality in the Window's code-behind class (Fig. 24.26). Whenever the left mouse button is held down on the clock (handled by the MouseLeftButtonDown event), the Window is dragged around using the **DragMove** method (lines 27–31). Because we did not define how to close or minimize the Window, the only way to shut down the clock is to press *Alt-F4*—this is a feature built into Windows.

```
 1   // Fig. 24.26: MainWindow.xaml.cs
 2   // Creating custom windows and using timers (code-behind).
 3   using System;
 4   using System.Windows;
 5   using System.Windows.Input;
 6
 7   namespace Clock
 8   {
 9      public partial class MainWindow : Window
10      {
11         // create a timer to control clock
12         private System.Windows.Threading.DispatcherTimer timer =
13            new System.Windows.Threading.DispatcherTimer();
```

Fig. 24.26 | Creating custom windows and using timers (code-behind). (Part 1 of 2.)

```
14
15          // constructor
16          public MainWindow()
17          {
18              InitializeComponent();
19
20              timer.Interval = TimeSpan.FromSeconds( 1 ); // tick every second
21              timer.IsEnabled = true; // enable timer
22
23              timer.Tick += timer_Tick;
24          } // end constructor
25
26          // drag Window when the left mouse button is held down
27          private void clockWindow_MouseLeftButtonDown( object sender,
28              MouseButtonEventArgs e )
29          {
30              this.DragMove(); // moves the window
31          } // end method clockWindow_MouseLeftButtonDown
32
33          // update the time when the timer ticks
34          private void timer_Tick( object sender, EventArgs e )
35          {
36              DateTime currentTime = DateTime.Now; // get the current time
37
38              // display the time as hh:mm:ss
39              timeTextBox.Text = currentTime.ToLongTimeString();
40          } // end method timer_Tick
41      } // end class MainWindow
42  } // end namespace Clock
```

Fig. 24.26 | Creating custom windows and using timers (code-behind). (Part 2 of 2.)

The clock works by getting the current time every second and displaying it in the TextBox. To do this, the clock uses a **DispatcherTimer** object (of the Windows.Threading namespace), which raises the **Tick** event repeatedly at a prespecified time interval. Since the DispatcherTimer is defined in the C# code rather than the XAML, we need to specify the method to handle the Tick event in the C# code. Line 23 assigns method timer_Tick to the Tick event's delegate. This adds a new EventHandler—which takes a method name as an argument—to the specified event. After it is declared, you must specify the interval between Ticks by setting the **Interval** property, which takes a TimeSpan as its value. **TimeSpan** has several class methods for instantiating a TimeSpan object, including From-Seconds, which defines a TimeSpan lasting the number of seconds you pass to the method. Line 20 creates a one-second TimeSpan and sets it as the DispatcherTimer's Interval. A DispatcherTimer is disabled by default. Until you enable it by setting the **IsEnabled** property to true (line 21), it will not Tick. In this example, the Tick event handler gets the current time and displays it in the TextBox.

You may recall that the Timer component provided the same capabilities in Windows Forms. A similar object that you can drag-and-drop onto your GUI doesn't exist in WPF. Instead, you must create a DispatcherTimer object, as illustrated in this example.

24.14 Defining a Control's Appearance with Control Templates

We now update the clock example to include buttons for minimizing and closing the application. We also introduce **control templates**—a powerful tool for customizing the look-and-feel of your GUIs. As previously mentioned, a custom control template can redefine the appearance of any control without changing its functionality. In Windows Forms, if you want to create a round button, you have to create a new control and simulate the functionality of a Button. With control templates, you can simply redefine the visual elements that compose the Button control and still use the preexisting functionality.

All WPF controls are **lookless**—that is, a control's properties, methods and events are coded into the control's class, but its appearance is not. Instead, the appearance of a control is determined by a control template, which is a hierarchy of visual elements. Every control has a built-in default control template. All of the GUIs discussed so far have used these default templates.

The hierarchy of visual elements defined by a control template can be represented as a tree, called a control's **visual tree**. Figure 24.27(b) shows the visual tree of a default Button (Fig. 24.28). This is a more detailed version of the same Button's **logical tree**, which is shown in Fig. 24.27(a). A logical tree depicts how a control is a defined, whereas a visual tree depicts how a control is graphically rendered.

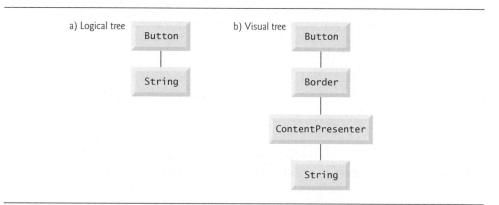

Fig. 24.27 | The logical and visual trees for a default Button.

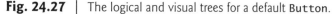

Fig. 24.28 | The default Button.

A control's logical tree always mirrors its definition in XAML. For example, you'll notice that the Button's logical tree, which comprises only the Button and its string caption, exactly represents the hierarchy outlined by its XAML definition, which is

```
<Button>
   Click Me
</Button>
```

To actually render the Button, WPF displays a ContentPresenter with a Border around it. These elements are included in the Button's visual tree. A **ContentPresenter** is an object used to display a single element of content on the screen. It's often used in a template to specify where to display content.

In the updated clock example, we create a custom control template (named Button-Template) for rendering Buttons and apply it to the two Buttons in the application. The XAML markup is shown in Fig. 24.29. Like a style, a control template is usually defined as a resource, and applied by binding a control's **Template** property to the control template using a resource binding (for example, lines 47 and 52). After you apply a control template to a control, the Design view will update to display the new appearance of the control. The Properties window remains unchanged, since a control template does not modify a control's properties.

```
1   <!-- Fig. 24.29: MainWindow.xaml -->
2   <!-- Using control templates (XAML). -->
3   <Window x:Class="Clock.MainWindow"
4      xmlns="http://schemas.microsoft.com/winfx/2006/xaml/presentation"
5      xmlns:x="http://schemas.microsoft.com/winfx/2006/xaml"
6      Title="Clock" Name="clockWindow" Height="118" Width="118"
7      WindowStyle="None" AllowsTransparency="True"
8      MouseLeftButtonDown="clockWindow_MouseLeftButtonDown">
9
10     <Window.Resources>
11        <!-- control template for Buttons -->
12        <ControlTemplate x:Key="ButtonTemplate" TargetType="Button">
13           <Border Name="Border" BorderThickness="2" CornerRadius="2"
14              BorderBrush="RoyalBlue">
15
16              <!-- Template binding to Button.Content -->
17              <ContentPresenter Margin="0" Width="8"
18                 Content="{TemplateBinding Content}" />
19           </Border>
20
21           <ControlTemplate.Triggers>
22              <!-- if mouse is over the button -->
23              <Trigger Property="IsMouseOver" Value="True">
24                 <!-- make the background blue -->
25                 <Setter TargetName="Border" Property="Background"
26                    Value="LightBlue" />
27              </Trigger>
28           </ControlTemplate.Triggers>
29        </ControlTemplate>
30     </Window.Resources>
31
32     <Window.Background> <!-- Set background image -->
33        <ImageBrush ImageSource="images/circle.png" />
34     </Window.Background>
35
36     <Grid>
37        <Grid.RowDefinitions>
```

Fig. 24.29 | Using control templates (XAML). (Part 1 of 2.)

```
38              <RowDefinition Height="Auto" />
39              <RowDefinition />
40          </Grid.RowDefinitions>
41
42          <StackPanel Grid.Row="0" Orientation="Horizontal"
43              HorizontalAlignment="Right">
44
45              <!-- these buttons use the control template -->
46              <Button Name="minimizeButton" Margin="0" Focusable="False"
47                  IsTabStop="False" Template="{StaticResource ButtonTemplate}"
48                  Click="minimizeButton_Click">
49                  <Image Source="images/minimize.png" Margin="0" />
50              </Button>
51              <Button Name="closeButton" Margin="1,0,0,0" Focusable="False"
52                  IsTabStop="False" Template="{StaticResource ButtonTemplate}"
53                  Click="closeButton_Click">
54                  <Image Source="images/close.png" Margin="0"/>
55              </Button>
56          </StackPanel>
57
58          <TextBox Name="timeTextBox" Grid.Row="1" Margin="0,30,0,0"
59              Background="Transparent" TextAlignment="Center"
60              FontWeight="Bold" Foreground="White" FontSize="16"
61              BorderThickness="0" Cursor="Arrow" Focusable="False" />
62      </Grid>
63  </Window>
```

Fig. 24.29 | Using control templates (XAML). (Part 2 of 2.)

To define a control template in XAML, you create a **ControlTemplate** element. Just as with a style, you must specify the control template's x:Key attribute so you can reference it later (line 12). You must also set the **TargetType** attribute to the type of control for which the template is designed (line 12). Inside the ControlTemplate element, you can build the control using any WPF visual element (lines 13–19). In this example, we replace the default Border and ContentPresenter with our own custom ones.

Sometimes, when defining a control template, it may be beneficial to use the value of one of the templated control's properties. For example, if you want several controls of different sizes to use the same control template, you may need to use the values of their Width and Height properties in the template. WPF allows you to do this with a **template binding**, which can be created in XAML with the markup extension, {TemplateBinding *PropertyName*}. To bind a property of an element in a control template to one of the properties of the templated control (that is, the control that the template is applied to), you need to set the appropriate markup extension as the value of that property. In ButtonTemplate, we bind the **Content** property of a ContentPresenter to the Content property of the templated Button (line 18). The nested element of a ContentControl is the value of its Content property. Thus, the images defined in lines 49 and 54 are the Content of the Buttons and are displayed by the ContentPresenters in their respective control templates. You can also create template bindings to a control's events.

Often you'll use a combination of control templates, styles and local declarations to define the appearance of your application. Recall that a control template defines the default appearance of a control and thus has a lower precedence than a style in dependency property-value determination.

Triggers

The control template for Buttons used in the updated clock example defines a **trigger**, which changes a control's appearance when that control enters a certain state. For example, when your mouse is over the clock's minimize or close Buttons, the Button is highlighted with a light blue background, as shown in Fig. 24.29(b). This simple change in appearance is caused by a trigger that fires whenever the IsMouseOver property becomes True.

A trigger must be defined in the **Style.Triggers** or **ControlTemplate.Triggers** element of a style or a control template, respectively (for example, lines 21–28). You can create a trigger by defining a **Trigger** object. The **Property** and **Value** attributes define the state when a trigger is active. Setters nested in the Trigger element are carried out when the trigger is fired. When the trigger no longer applies, the changes are removed. A Setter's **TargetName** property specifies the name of the element that the Setter applies to (for example, line 25).

Lines 23–27 define the IsMouseOver trigger for the minimize and close Buttons. When the mouse is over the Button, **IsMouseOver** becomes True, and the trigger becomes active. The trigger's Setter makes the background of the Border in the control template temporarily light blue. When the mouse exits the boundaries of the Button, IsMouseOver becomes False. Thus, the Border's background returns to its default setting, which in this case is transparent.

Functionality

Figure 24.30 shows the code-behind class for the clock application. Although the custom control template makes the Buttons in this application look different, it doesn't change how they behave. Lines 3–40 remain unchanged from the code in the first clock example (Fig. 24.26). The functionality for the minimize and close Buttons is implemented in the same way as any other button—by handling the Click event (lines 43–47 and 50–53 of Fig. 24.30, respectively). To minimize the window, we set the **WindowState** of the Window to **WindowState.Minimized** (line 46).

```
1   // Fig. 24.30: MainWindow.xaml.cs
2   // Using control templates (code-behind).
3   using System;
4   using System.Windows;
5   using System.Windows.Input;
```

Fig. 24.30 | Using control templates (code-behind). (Part 1 of 2.)

```
 6
 7   namespace Clock
 8   {
 9      public partial class MainWindow : Window
10      {
11         // creates a timer to control clock
12         private System.Windows.Threading.DispatcherTimer timer =
13            new System.Windows.Threading.DispatcherTimer();
14
15         // constructor
16         public MainWindow()
17         {
18            InitializeComponent();
19
20            timer.Interval = TimeSpan.FromSeconds( 1 ); // tick every second
21            timer.IsEnabled = true; // enable timer
22
23            timer.Tick += timer_Tick;
24         } // end constructor
25
26         // drag Window when the left mouse button is held down
27         private void clockWindow_MouseLeftButtonDown( object sender,
28            MouseButtonEventArgs e )
29         {
30            this.DragMove();
31         } // end method clockWindow_MouseLeftButtonDown
32
33         // update the time when the timer ticks
34         private void timer_Tick( object sender, EventArgs e )
35         {
36            DateTime currentTime = DateTime.Now; // get the current time
37
38            // display the time as hh:mm:ss
39            timeTextBox.Text = currentTime.ToLongTimeString();
40         } // end method timer_Tick
41
42         // minimize the application
43         private void minimizeButton_Click( object sender,
44            RoutedEventArgs e )
45         {
46            this.WindowState = WindowState.Minimized; // minimize window
47         } // end method minimizeButton_Click
48
49         // close the application
50         private void closeButton_Click( object sender, RoutedEventArgs e )
51         {
52            Application.Current.Shutdown(); // shut down application
53         } // end method closeButton_Click
54      } // end class MainWindow
55   } // end namespace Clock
```

Fig. 24.30 | Using control templates (code-behind). (Part 2 of 2.)

24.15 Data-Driven GUIs with Data Binding

Often, an application needs to edit and display data. WPF provides a comprehensive model for allowing GUIs to interact with data.

Bindings

A **data binding** is a pointer to data, represented by a **Binding** object. WPF allows you to create a binding to a broad range of data types. At the simplest level, you could create a binding to a single property. Often, however, it's useful to create a binding to a data object—an object of a class with properties that describe the data. You can also create a binding to objects like arrays, collections and data in an XML document. The versatility of the WPF data model even allows you to bind to data represented by LINQ statements.

Like other binding types, a data binding can be created declaratively in XAML markup with a markup extension. To declare a data binding, you must specify the data's source. If it's another element in the XAML markup, use property **ElementName**. Otherwise, use **Source**. Then, if you're binding to a specific data point of the source, such as a property of a control, you must specify the **Path** to that piece of information. Use a comma to separate the binding's property declarations. For example, to create a binding to a control's property, you would use {Binding ElementName=*ControlName*, Path=*PropertyName*}.

Figure 24.31 presents the XAML markup of a book-cover viewer that lets the user select from a list of books, and displays the cover of the currently selected book. The list of books is presented in a **ListView** control (lines 15–24), which displays a set of data as items in a selectable list. Its current selection can be retrieved from the **SelectedItem** property. A large image of the currently selected book's cover is displayed in an Image control (lines 27–28), which automatically updates when the user makes a new selection. Each book is represented by a Book object, which has four string properties:

1. ThumbImage—the full path to the small cover image of the book.

2. LargeImage—the full path to the large cover image of the book.

3. Title—the title of the book.

4. ISBN—the 10-digit ISBN of the book.

```
1   <!-- Fig. 24.31: MainWindow.xaml -->
2   <!-- Using data binding (XAML). -->
3   <Window x:Class="BookViewer.MainWindow"
4       xmlns="http://schemas.microsoft.com/winfx/2006/xaml/presentation"
5       xmlns:x="http://schemas.microsoft.com/winfx/2006/xaml"
6       Title="Book Viewer" Height="400" Width="600">
7
8       <Grid> <!-- define GUI -->
9           <Grid.ColumnDefinitions>
10              <ColumnDefinition Width="Auto" />
11              <ColumnDefinition />
12          </Grid.ColumnDefinitions>
13
14          <!-- use ListView and GridView to display data -->
15          <ListView Grid.Column="0" Name="booksListView" MaxWidth="250">
```

Fig. 24.31 | Using data binding (XAML). (Part 1 of 2.)

```
16          <ListView.View>
17            <GridView>
18              <GridViewColumn Header="Title" Width="100"
19                  DisplayMemberBinding="{Binding Path=Title}" />
20              <GridViewColumn Header="ISBN" Width="80"
21                  DisplayMemberBinding="{Binding Path=ISBN}" />
22            </GridView>
23          </ListView.View>
24        </ListView>
25
26        <!-- bind to selected item's full-size image -->
27        <Image Grid.Column="1" Source="{Binding ElementName=booksListView,
28            Path=SelectedItem.LargeImage}" Margin="5" />
29      </Grid>
30    </Window>
```

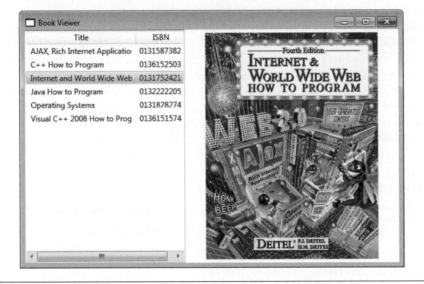

Fig. 24.31 | Using data binding (XAML). (Part 2 of 2.)

Class Book also contains a constructor that initializes a Book and sets each of its properties. The full source code of the Book class is not presented here but you can view it in the IDE by opening this example's project.

To synchronize the book cover that's being displayed with the currently selected book, we bind the Image's Source property to the file location of the currently selected book's large cover image (lines 27–28). The Binding's ElementName property is the name of the selector control, booksListView. The Path property is SelectedItem.LargeImage. This indicates that the binding should be linked to the LargeImage property of the Book object that is currently booksListView's SelectedItem.

Some controls have built-in support for data binding, and a separate Binding object doesn't need to be created. A ListView, for example, has a built-in **ItemsSource** property that specifies the data source from which the items of the list are determined. There is no need to create a binding—instead, you can just set the ItemsSource property as you would any other property. When you set ItemsSource to a collection of data, the objects in the collection automatically become the items in the list. Figure 24.32 presents the code-behind class for the book-cover viewer. When the Window is created, a collection of six Book objects is initialized (lines 17–31) and set as the ItemsSource of the booksListView, meaning that each item displayed in the selector is one of the Books.

```
1   // Fig. 24.32: MainWindow.xaml.cs
2   // Using data binding (code-behind).
3   using System.Collections.Generic;
4   using System.Windows;
5
6   namespace BookViewer
7   {
8      public partial class MainWindow : Window
9      {
10         private List< Book > books = new List< Book >();
11
12         public MainWindow()
13         {
14            InitializeComponent();
15
16            // add Book objects to the List
17            books.Add( new Book( "AJAX, Rich Internet Applications, " +
18               "and Web Development for Programmers", "0131587382",
19               "images/small/ajax.jpg", "images/large/ajax.jpg" ) );
20            books.Add( new Book( "C++ How to Program", "0136152503",
21               "images/small/cppHTP6e.jpg", "images/large/cppHTP6e.jpg" ) );
22            books.Add( new Book(
23               "Internet and World Wide Web How to Program", "0131752421",
24               "images/small/iw3htp4.jpg", "images/large/iw3htp4.jpg" ) );
25            books.Add( new Book( "Java How to Program", "0132222205",
26               "images/small/jhtp7.jpg", "images/large/jhtp7.jpg" ) );
27            books.Add( new Book( "Operating Systems", "0131828274",
28               "images/small/os3e.jpg", "images/large/os3e.jpg" ) );
29            books.Add( new Book( "Visual C++ 2008 How to Program",
30               "0136151574", "images/small/vcpp2008htp2e.jpg",
31               "images/large/vcpp2008htp2e.jpg" ) );
32
33            booksListView.ItemsSource = books; // bind data to the list
34         } // end constructor
35      } // end class MainWindow
36   } // end namespace BookViewer
```

Fig. 24.32 | Using data binding (code-behind).

Displaying Data in the ListView
For a ListView to display objects in a useful manner, you must specify how. For example, if you don't specify how to display each Book, the ListView simply displays the result of the item's ToString method, as shown in Fig. 24.33.

There are many ways to format the display of a ListView. One such method is to display each item as a row in a tabular grid, as shown in Fig. 24.31. This can be achieved by setting a **GridView** as the View property of a ListView (lines 16–23). A GridView consists

Fig. 24.33 | `ListView` display with no data template.

of many **GridViewColumns**, each representing a property. In this example, we define two columns, one for **Title** and one for **ISBN** (lines 18–19 and 20–21, respectively). A `Grid-ViewColumn`'s `Header` property specifies what to display as its header. The values displayed in each column are determined by its **DisplayMemberBinding** property. We set the **Title** column's `DisplayMemberBinding` to a `Binding` object that points to the `Title` property (line 19), and the **ISBN** column's to one that points to the `ISBN` property (line 21). Neither of the `Binding`s has a specified `ElementName` or `Source`. Because the `ListView` has already specified the data source (line 33 of Fig. 24.32), the two data bindings inherit this source, and we do not need specify it again.

Data Templates
A much more powerful technique for formatting a `ListView` is to specify a template for displaying each item in the list. This template defines how to display bound data and is called a **data template**. Figure 24.34 is the XAML markup that describes a modified version of the book-cover viewer GUI. Each book, instead of being displayed as a row in a table, is represented by a small thumbnail of its cover image with its title and ISBN. Lines 11–32 define the data template (that is, a **DataTemplate** object) that specifies how to display a `Book` object. Note the similarity between the structure of a data template and that of a control template. If you define a data template as a resource, you apply it by using a resource binding, just as you would a style or control template. To apply a data template to items in a `ListView`, use the **ItemTemplate** property (for example, line 43).

```
1   <!-- Fig. 24.34: MainWindow.xaml -->
2   <!-- Using data templates (XAML). -->
3   <Window x:Class="BookViewer.MainWindow"
4      xmlns="http://schemas.microsoft.com/winfx/2006/xaml/presentation"
5      xmlns:x="http://schemas.microsoft.com/winfx/2006/xaml"
6      Title="Book Viewer" Height="400" Width="600" Name="bookViewerWindow">
7
8      <Window.Resources> <!-- Define Window's resources -->
9
10        <!-- define data template -->
11        <DataTemplate x:Key="BookTemplate">
12           <Grid MaxWidth="250" Margin="3">
13              <Grid.ColumnDefinitions>
14                 <ColumnDefinition Width="Auto" />
15                 <ColumnDefinition />
16              </Grid.ColumnDefinitions>
17
```

Fig. 24.34 | Using data templates (XAML). (Part 1 of 3.)

```
18              <!-- bind image source -->
19              <Image Grid.Column="0" Source="{Binding Path=ThumbImage}"
20                 Width="50" />
21
22              <StackPanel Grid.Column="1">
23                 <!-- bind Title and ISBN -->
24                 <TextBlock Margin="3,0" Text="{Binding Path=Title}"
25                    FontWeight="Bold" TextWrapping="Wrap" />
26                 <StackPanel Margin="3,0" Orientation="Horizontal">
27                    <TextBlock Text="ISBN: " />
28                    <TextBlock Text="{Binding Path=ISBN}" />
29                 </StackPanel>
30              </StackPanel>
31           </Grid>
32        </DataTemplate>
33     </Window.Resources>
34
35     <Grid> <!-- define GUI -->
36        <Grid.ColumnDefinitions>
37           <ColumnDefinition Width="Auto" />
38           <ColumnDefinition />
39        </Grid.ColumnDefinitions>
40
41        <!-- use ListView and template to display data -->
42        <ListView Grid.Column="0" Name="booksListView"
43           ItemTemplate="{StaticResource BookTemplate}" />
44
45        <!-- bind to selected item's full-size image -->
46        <Image Grid.Column="1" Source="{Binding ElementName=booksListView,
47           Path=SelectedItem.LargeImage}" Margin="5" />
48     </Grid>
49  </Window>
```

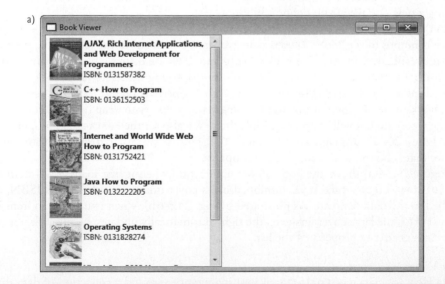

Fig. 24.34 | Using data templates (XAML). (Part 2 of 3.)

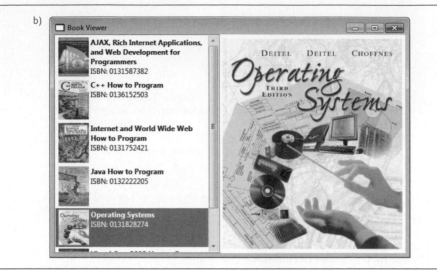

Fig. 24.34 | Using data templates (XAML). (Part 3 of 3.)

A data template uses data bindings to specify how to display data. Once again, we can omit the data binding's ElementName and Source properties, because its source has already been specified by the ListView (line 33 of Fig. 24.32). The same principle can be applied in other scenarios as well. If you bind an element's **DataContext** property to a data source, then its child elements can access data within that source without your having to specify it again. In other words, if a binding already has a context (i.e, a DataContext has already been defined by a parent), it automatically inherits the data source. For example, if you bind a data source to the DataContext property of a Grid, then any data binding created in the Grid uses that source by default. You can, however, override this source by explicitly defining a new one when you define a binding.

In the BookTemplate data template, lines 19–20 of Fig. 24.34 define an Image whose Source is bound to the Book's ThumbImage property, which stores the relative file path to the thumbnail cover image. The Book's Title and ISBN are displayed to the right of the book using **TextBlocks**—lightweight controls for displaying text. The TextBlock in lines 24–25 displays the Book's Title because the Text property is bound to it. Because some of the books' titles are long, we set the TextWrapping property to Wrap (line 25) so that, if the title is too long, it will wrap to multiple lines. We also set the FontWeight property to Bold. Lines 26–29 display two additional TextBlocks, one that displays ISBN:, and another that is bound to the Book's ISBN property.

Figure 24.34(a) shows the book-viewer application when it first loads. Each item in the ListView is represented by a thumbnail of its cover image, its title and its ISBN, as specified in the data template. As illustrated by Fig. 24.34(b), when you select an item in the ListView, the large cover image on the right automatically updates, because it's bound to the SelectedItem property of the list.

Data Views
A **data view** (of class type **CollectionView**) is a wrapper around a collection of data that can provide us with multiple "views" of the same data based on how we filter, sort and

group the data. A default view is automatically created in the background every time a data binding is created. To retrieve the data view, use the **CollectionViewSource.GetDefaultView** method and pass it the source of your data binding. For example, to retrieve the default view of bookListView in the book-viewer application, you would use CollectionViewSource.GetDefaultView(bookListView.ItemsSource).

You can then modify the view to create the exact view of the data that you want to display. The methods of filtering, sorting and grouping data are beyond the scope of this book. For more information, see msdn.microsoft.com/en-us/library/ms752347.aspx#what_are_collection_views.

Asynchronous Data Binding

Sometimes you may wish to create asynchronous data bindings that don't hold up your application while data is being transmitted. To do this, you set the **IsAsync** property of a data binding to True (it's False by default). Often, however, it's not the transmission but the instantiation of data that is the most expensive operation. An asynchronous data binding does not provide a solution for instantiating data asynchronously. To do so, you must use a **data provider**, a class that can create or retrieve data. There are two types of data providers, **XmlDataProvider** (for XML) and **ObjectDataProvider** (for data objects). Both can be declared as resources in XAML markup. If you set a data provider's **IsAsynchronous** property to True, the provider will run in the background. Creating and using data providers is beyond the scope of this book. See msdn.microsoft.com/en-us/library/aa480224.aspx for more information.

24.16 Wrap-Up

In this chapter, we discussed some basic XML terminology and introduced the concepts of markup, XML vocabularies and XML parsers (validating and nonvalidating). We then demonstrated how to describe and structure data in XML, illustrating these points with examples marking up an article and a business letter. Next, we discussed XML namespaces and namespace prefixes. You learned that each namespace has a unique name that provides a means for document authors to refer unambiguously to elements with the same name (that is, prevent naming collisions) from different namespaces. We presented examples of defining two namespaces in the same document, as well as setting the default namespace for a document.

Many of today's commercial applications provide GUIs that are easy to use and manipulate. The demand for sophisticated and user-friendly GUIs makes GUI design an essential programming skill. In Chapters 14–15, we showed you how to create GUIs with Windows Forms. In this chapter, we demonstrated how to create GUIs with WPF. You learned how to design a WPF GUI with XAML markup and how to give it functionality in a C# code-behind class. We presented WPF's new flow-based layout scheme, in which a control's size and position are both defined relatively. You learned not only to handle events just as you did in a Windows Forms application, but also to implement WPF commands when you want multiple user interactions to execute the same task. We demonstrated the flexibility WPF offers for customizing the look-and-feel of your GUIs. You learned how to use styles, control templates and triggers to define a control's appearance. The chapter concluded with a demonstration of how to create data-driven GUIs with data bindings and data templates.

But WPF is not merely a GUI-building platform. Chapter 25 explores some of the many other capabilities of WPF, showing you how to incorporate 2D and 3D graphics, animation and multimedia into your WPF applications. Chapter 29 demonstrates how to create Internet applications using a subset of WPF's features that are available in the Silverlight runtime, which executes as a plug-in for several popular browsers and platforms.

24.17 Web Resources

There is a tremendous amount of material on the web to help you learn more about WPF. Check out our Windows Presentation Foundation Resource Center

```
www.deitel.com/wpf/
```

for the latest WPF articles, books, sample chapters, tutorials, webcasts, blogs and more.

25

WPF Graphics and Multimedia

Nowadays people's visual imagination is so much more sophisticated, so much more developed, particularly in young people, that now you can make an image which just slightly suggests something, they can make of it what they will.
—Robert Doisneau

In shape, it is perfectly elliptical. In texture, it is smooth and lustrous. In color, it ranges from pale alabaster to warm terra cotta.
—Sydney J Harris, "Tribute to an Egg"

OBJECTIVES

In this chapter you'll learn:

- To manipulate fonts.

- To draw basic WPF shapes.

- To use WPF brushes to customize the `Fill` or `Background` of an object.

- To use WPF transforms to reposition or reorient GUI elements.

- To completely customize the look of a control while maintaining its functionality.

- To animate the properties of a GUI element.

- To transform and animate 3-D objects.

- To use speech synthesis and recognition.

25.1 Introduction

This chapter overviews WPF's graphics and multimedia capabilities, including two-dimensional and three-dimensional shapes, fonts, transformations, animations, audio and video. WPF integrates drawing and animation features that were previously available only in special libraries (such as DirectX). The graphics system in WPF is designed to use your computer's graphics hardware to reduce the load on the CPU.

WPF graphics use resolution-independent units of measurement, making applications more uniform and portable across devices. The size properties of graphic elements in WPF are measured in **machine-independent pixels**, where one pixel typically represents 1/96 of an inch—however, this depends on the computer's DPI (dots per inch) setting. The graphics engine determines the correct pixel count so that all users see elements of the same size on all devices.

Graphic elements are rendered on screen using a **vector-based** system in which calculations determine how to size and scale each element, allowing graphic elements to be preserved across any rendering size. This produces smoother graphics than the so-called **raster-based** systems, in which the precise pixels are specified for each graphical element. Raster-based graphics tend to degrade in appearance as they're scaled larger. Vector-based graphics appear smooth at any scale. Graphic elements other than images and video are drawn using WPF's vector-based system, so they look good at any screen resolution.

The basic 2-D shapes are `Lines`, `Rectangles` and `Ellipses`. WPF also has controls that can be used to create custom shapes or curves. `Brushes` can be used to fill an element with solid colors, complex patterns, gradients, images or videos, allowing for unique and interesting visual experiences. WPF's robust animation and transform capabilities allow you to further customize GUIs. Transforms reposition and reorient graphic elements.

WPF also includes 3-D modeling and rendering capabilities. In addition, 2-D manipulations can be applied to 3-D objects as well. You can find more information on WPF in our WPF Resource Center at `www.deitel.com/wpf/`. The chapter ends with an introduction to speech synthesis and recognition.

25.2 Controlling Fonts

This section introduces how to control fonts by modifying the font properties of a **Text-Block** control in the XAML code. Figure 25.1 shows how to use `TextBlocks` and how to change the properties to control the appearance of the displayed text.

```
1   <!-- Fig. 25.1: MainWindow.xaml -->
2   <!-- Formatting fonts in XAML code. -->
3   <Window x:Class="UsingFonts.MainWindow"
4      xmlns="http://schemas.microsoft.com/winfx/2006/xaml/presentation"
5      xmlns:x="http://schemas.microsoft.com/winfx/2006/xaml"
6      Title="UsingFonts" Height="120" Width="400">
7
8      <StackPanel>
9         <!-- make a font bold using the FontWeight property -->
10        <TextBlock FontFamily="Arial" FontSize="12" FontWeight="Bold">
11           Arial 12 point bold.</TextBlock>
12
13        <!-- if no font size is specified, default is 12 -->
14        <TextBlock FontFamily="Times New Roman">
15           Times New Roman 12 point plain.</TextBlock>
16
17        <!-- specifying a different font size and using FontStyle -->
18        <TextBlock FontFamily="Courier New" FontSize="16"
19           FontStyle="Italic" FontWeight="Bold">
20           Courier New 16 point bold and italic.
21        </TextBlock>
22
23        <!-- using Overline and Baseline TextDecorations -->
24        <TextBlock>
25           <TextBlock.TextDecorations>
26              <TextDecoration Location="OverLine" />
27              <TextDecoration Location="Baseline" />
28           </TextBlock.TextDecorations>
29           Default font with overline and baseline.
30        </TextBlock>
31
32        <!-- using Strikethrough and Underline TextDecorations -->
33        <TextBlock>
34           <TextBlock.TextDecorations>
35              <TextDecoration Location="Strikethrough" />
36              <TextDecoration Location="Underline" />
37           </TextBlock.TextDecorations>
38           Default font with strikethrough and underline.
39        </TextBlock>
40     </StackPanel>
41  </Window>
```

Fig. 25.1 | Formatting fonts in XAML code.

The text that you want to display in the TextBlock is placed between the TextBlock tags. The **FontFamily** property defines the font of the displayed text. This property can be set to any font. Lines 10, 14 and 18 define the separate TextBlock fonts to be Arial, Times

New Roman and Courier New, respectively. If the font is not specified or is not available, the default font, Segoe UI for Windows Vista/Windows 7, is used (lines 24 and 33).

The **FontSize** property defines the text size measured in points. When no FontSize is specified, the property is set to the default value of 12 (this is actually determined by System.MessageFontSize). The font sizes are defined in lines 10 and 18. In lines 14, 24 and 33, the FontSize is not defined so the default is used.

TextBlocks have various properties that can further modify the font. Lines 10 and 19 set the **FontWeight** property to Bold to make the font thicker. This property can be set either to a numeric value (1–999) or to a predefined descriptive value—such as Light or UltraBold—to define the thickness of the text. You can use the **FontStyle** property to make the text either Italic or Oblique—which is simply a more emphasized italic. Line 19 sets the FontStyle property to Italic.

You can also define **TextDecorations** for a TextBlock to draw a horizontal line through the text. **Overline** and **Baseline**—shown in the fourth TextBlock of Fig. 25.1—create lines above the text and at the base of the text, respectively (lines 26–27). **Strikethrough** and **Underline**—shown in the fifth TextBlock—create lines through the middle of the text and under the text, respectively (lines 35–36). The Underline option leaves a small amount of space between the text and the line, unlike the Baseline. The **Location** property of the **TextDecoration** class defines which decoration you want to apply.

25.3 Basic Shapes

WPF has several built-in shapes. The BasicShapes example (Fig. 25.2) shows you how to display Lines, Rectangles and Ellipses.

```
1   <!-- Fig. 25.2: MainWindow.xaml -->
2   <!-- Drawing basic shapes in XAML. -->
3   <Window x:Class="BasicShapes.MainWindow"
4       xmlns="http://schemas.microsoft.com/winfx/2006/xaml/presentation"
5       xmlns:x="http://schemas.microsoft.com/winfx/2006/xaml"
6       Title="BasicShapes" Height="200" Width="500">
7       <Canvas>
8          <!-- Rectangle with fill but no stroke -->
9          <Rectangle Canvas.Left="90" Canvas.Top="30" Width="150" Height="90"
10            Fill="Blue" />
11
12         <!-- Lines defined by starting points and ending points-->
13         <Line X1="90" Y1="30" X2="110" Y2="40" Stroke="Black" />
14         <Line X1="90" Y1="120" X2="110" Y2="130" Stroke="Black" />
15         <Line X1="240" Y1="30" X2="260" Y2="40" Stroke="Black" />
16         <Line X1="240" Y1="120" X2="260" Y2="130" Stroke="Black" />
17
18         <!-- Rectangle with stroke but no fill -->
19         <Rectangle Canvas.Left="110" Canvas.Top="40" Width="150"
20            Height="90" Stroke="Black" />
21
22         <!-- Ellipse with fill and no stroke -->
23         <Ellipse Canvas.Left="280" Canvas.Top="75" Width="100" Height="50"
24            Fill="Red" />
```

Fig. 25.2 | Drawing basic shapes in XAML. (Part 1 of 2.)

```
25          <Line X1="380" Y1="55" X2="380" Y2="100" Stroke="Black" />
26          <Line X1="280" Y1="55" X2="280" Y2="100" Stroke="Black" />
27
28          <!-- Ellipse with stroke and no fill -->
29          <Ellipse Canvas.Left="280" Canvas.Top="30" Width="100" Height="50"
30             Stroke="Black" />
31      </Canvas>
32  </Window>
```

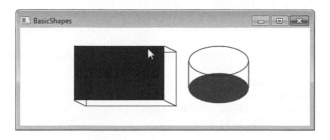

Fig. 25.2 | Drawing basic shapes in XAML. (Part 2 of 2.)

The first shape drawn uses the **Rectangle** object to create a filled rectangle in the window. Notice that the layout control is a Canvas allowing us to use coordinates to position the shapes. To specify the upper-left corner of the Rectangle at lines 9–10, we set the Canvas.Left and Canvas.Top properties to 90 and 30, respectively. We then set the Width and Height properties to 150 and 90, respectively, to specify the size. To define the Rectangle's color, we use the **Fill** property (line 10). You can assign any Color or Brush to this property. Rectangles also have a **Stroke** property, which defines the color of the outline of the shape (line 20). If either the Fill or the Stroke is not specified, that property will be rendered transparently. For this reason, the blue Rectangle in the window has no outline, while the second Rectangle drawn has only an outline (with a transparent center). Shape objects have a **StrokeThickness** property which defines the thickness of the outline. The default value for StrokeThickness is 1 pixel.

A **Line** is defined by its two endpoints—X1, Y1 and X2, Y2. Lines have a Stroke property that defines the color of the line. In this example, the lines are all set to have black Strokes (lines 13–16 and 25–26).

To draw a circle or ellipse, you can use the **Ellipse** control. The placement and size of an Ellipse is defined like a Rectangle—with the Canvas.Left and Canvas.Top properties for the upper-left corner, and the Width and Height properties for the size (line 23). Together, the Canvas.Left, Canvas.Top, Width and Height of an Ellipse define a "bounding rectangle" in which the Ellipse touches the center of each side of the rectangle. To draw a circle, provide the same value for the Width and Height properties. As with Rectangles, having an unspecified Fill property for an Ellipse makes the shape's fill transparent (lines 29–30).

25.4 Polygons and Polylines

There are two shape controls for drawing multisided shapes—**Polyline** and **Polygon**. Polyline draws a series of connected lines defined by a set of points, while Polygon does the same but connects the start and end points to make a closed figure. The application DrawPolygons (Fig. 25.3) allows you to click anywhere on the Canvas to define points for one of three shapes. You select which shape you want to display by selecting one of the RadioButtons in the second column. The difference between the **Filled Polygon** and the **Polygon** options is that the former has a Fill property specified while the latter does not.

```
1   <!-- Fig. 25.3: MainWindow.xaml -->
2   <!-- Defining Polylines and Polygons in XAML. -->
3   <Window x:Class="DrawPolygons.MainWindow"
4      xmlns="http://schemas.microsoft.com/winfx/2006/xaml/presentation"
5      xmlns:x="http://schemas.microsoft.com/winfx/2006/xaml"
6      Title="DrawPolygons" Height="400" Width="450" Name="mainWindow">
7      <Grid>
8         <Grid.ColumnDefinitions>
9            <ColumnDefinition />
10           <ColumnDefinition Width="Auto" />
11        </Grid.ColumnDefinitions>
12
13        <!-- Canvas contains two polygons and a polyline -->
14        <!-- only the shape selected by the radio button is visible -->
15        <Canvas Name="drawCanvas" Grid.Column="0" Background="White"
16           MouseDown="drawCanvas_MouseDown">
17           <Polyline Name="polyLine" Stroke="Black"
18              Visibility="Collapsed" />
19           <Polygon Name="polygon" Stroke="Black" Visibility="Collapsed" />
20           <Polygon Name="filledPolygon" Fill="DarkBlue"
21              Visibility="Collapsed" />
22        </Canvas>
23
24        <!-- StackPanel containing the RadioButton options -->
25        <StackPanel Grid.Column="1" Orientation="Vertical"
26           Background="WhiteSmoke">
27           <GroupBox Header="Select Type" Margin="10">
28              <StackPanel>
29                 <!-- Polyline option -->
30                 <RadioButton Name="lineRadio" Margin="5"
31                    Checked="lineRadio_Checked">Polyline</RadioButton>
32
33                 <!-- unfilled Polygon option -->
34                 <RadioButton Name="polygonRadio" Margin="5"
35                    Checked="polygonRadio_Checked">Polygon</RadioButton>
36
37                 <!-- filled Polygon option -->
38                 <RadioButton Name="filledPolygonRadio" Margin="5"
39                    Checked="filledPolygonRadio_Checked">
40                    Filled Polygon</RadioButton>
41              </StackPanel>
42           </GroupBox>
43
44           <!-- Button clears the shape from the canvas -->
45           <Button Name="clearButton" Click="clearButton_Click"
46              Margin="5">Clear</Button>
```

Fig. 25.3 | Defining Polylines and Polygons in XAML. (Part 1 of 2.)

```
47              </StackPanel>
48          </Grid>
49      </Window>
```

a) Application with the Polyline option selected   b) Application with the Filled Polygon option selected

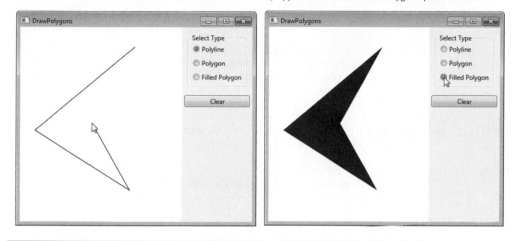

Fig. 25.3 | Defining Polylines and Polygons in XAML. (Part 2 of 2.)

The code defines a two-column GUI (lines 9–10). The first column contains a Canvas (lines 15–22) that the user interacts with to create the points of the selected shape. Embedded in the Canvas are a Polyline (lines 17–18) and two Polygons—one with a Fill (lines 20–21) and one without (line 19). The **Visibility** of a control can be set to **Visible**, **Collapsed** or **Hidden**. This property is initially set to Collapsed for all three shapes (lines 18, 19 and 21), because we'll display only the shape that corresponds to the selected RadioButton. The difference between Hidden and Collapsed is that a Hidden object occupies space in the GUI but is not visible, while a Collapsed object has a Width and Height of 0. As you can see, Polyline and Polygon objects have Fill and Stroke properties like the simple shapes we discussed earlier.

The RadioButtons (lines 30–40) allow you to select which shape appears in the Canvas. There is also a Button (lines 45–46) that clears the shape's points to allow you to start over. The code-behind file for this application is shown in Fig. 25.4.

```
 1      // Fig. 25.4: MainWindow.xaml.cs
 2      // Drawing Polylines and Polygons.
 3      using System.Windows;
 4      using System.Windows.Input;
 5      using System.Windows.Media;
 6
 7      namespace DrawPolygons
 8      {
 9          public partial class MainWindow : Window
10          {
```

Fig. 25.4 | Drawing Polylines and Polygons. (Part 1 of 3.)

```
11      // stores the collection of points for the multisided shapes
12      private PointCollection points = new PointCollection();
13
14      // initialize the points of the shapes
15      public MainWindow()
16      {
17         InitializeComponent();
18
19         polyLine.Points = points; // assign Polyline points
20         polygon.Points = points; // assign Polygon points
21         filledPolygon.Points = points; // assign filled Polygon points
22      } // end constructor
23
24      // adds a new point when the user clicks on the canvas
25      private void drawCanvas_MouseDown( object sender,
26         MouseButtonEventArgs e )
27      {
28         // add point to collection
29         points.Add( e.GetPosition( drawCanvas ) );
30      } // end method drawCanvas_MouseDown
31
32      // when the clear Button is clicked
33      private void clearButton_Click( object sender, RoutedEventArgs e )
34      {
35         points.Clear(); // clear the points from the collection
36      } // end method clearButton_Click
37
38      // when the user selects the Polyline
39      private void lineRadio_Checked( object sender, RoutedEventArgs e )
40      {
41         // Polyline is visible, the other two are not
42         polyLine.Visibility = Visibility.Visible;
43         polygon.Visibility = Visibility.Collapsed;
44         filledPolygon.Visibility = Visibility.Collapsed;
45      } // end method lineRadio_Checked
46
47      //  when the user selects the Polygon
48      private void polygonRadio_Checked( object sender,
49         RoutedEventArgs e )
50      {
51         // Polygon is visible, the other two are not
52         polyLine.Visibility = Visibility.Collapsed;
53         polygon.Visibility = Visibility.Visible;
54         filledPolygon.Visibility = Visibility.Collapsed;
55      } // end method polygonRadio_Checked
56
57      // when the user selects the filled Polygon
58      private void filledPolygonRadio_Checked( object sender,
59         RoutedEventArgs e )
60      {
61         // filled Polygon is visible, the other two are not
62         polyLine.Visibility = Visibility.Collapsed;
63         polygon.Visibility = Visibility.Collapsed;
```

Fig. 25.4 | Drawing Polylines and Polygons. (Part 2 of 3.)

```
64              filledPolygon.Visibility = Visibility.Visible;
65          } // end method filledPolygonRadio_Checked
66      } // end class MainWindow
67  } // end namespace DrawPolygons
```

Fig. 25.4 | Drawing Polylines and Polygons. (Part 3 of 3.)

To allow the user to specify a variable number of points, line 12 declares a **Point-Collection**, which is a collection that stores Point objects. This keeps track of each mouse-click location. The collection's **Add** method adds new points to the end of the collection. When the application executes, we set the **Points** property (lines 19–21) of each shape to reference the PointCollection instance variable created in line 12.

We created a MouseDown event handler to capture mouse clicks on the Canvas (lines 25–30). When the user clicks the mouse on the Canvas, the mouse coordinates are recorded (line 29) and the points collection is updated. Since the Points property of each of the three shapes has a reference to our PointCollection object, the shapes are automatically updated with the new Point. The Polyline and Polygon shapes connect the Points based on the ordering in the collection.

Each RadioButton's Checked event handler sets the corresponding shape's Visibility property to Visible and sets the other two to Collapsed to display the correct shape in the Canvas. For example, the lineRadio_Checked event handler (lines 39–45) makes polyLine Visible (line 42) and makes polygon and filledPolygon Collapsed (lines 43–44). The other two RadioButton event handlers are defined similarly in lines 48–55 and lines 58–65.

The clearButton_Click event handler erases the stored collection of Points (line 35). The **Clear** method of the PointCollection points erases its elements.

25.5 Brushes

Brushes change an element's graphic properties, such as the Fill, Stroke or Background. A SolidColorBrush fills the element with the specified color. To customize elements further, you can use ImageBrushes, VisualBrushes and gradient brushes. Run the Using-Brushes application (Fig. 25.5) to see Brushes applied to TextBlocks and Ellipses.

```
 1  <!-- Fig. 25.5: MainWindow.xaml -->
 2  <!-- Applying brushes to various XAML elements. -->
 3  <Window x:Class="UsingBrushes.MainWindow"
 4      xmlns="http://schemas.microsoft.com/winfx/2006/xaml/presentation"
 5      xmlns:x="http://schemas.microsoft.com/winfx/2006/xaml"
 6      Title="UsingBrushes" Height="450" Width="700">
 7      <Grid>
 8          <Grid.RowDefinitions>
 9              <RowDefinition />
10              <RowDefinition />
11              <RowDefinition />
12          </Grid.RowDefinitions>
13
```

Fig. 25.5 | Applying brushes to various XAML elements. (Part 1 of 3.)

```
14         <Grid.ColumnDefinitions>
15            <ColumnDefinition />
16            <ColumnDefinition />
17         </Grid.ColumnDefinitions>
18
19         <!-- TextBlock with a SolidColorBrush -->
20         <TextBlock FontSize="100" FontWeight="999">
21            <TextBlock.Foreground>
22               <SolidColorBrush Color="#5F2CAE" />
23            </TextBlock.Foreground>
24            Color
25         </TextBlock>
26
27         <!-- Ellipse with a SolidColorBrush (just a Fill) -->
28         <Ellipse Grid.Column="1" Height="100" Width="300" Fill="#5F2CAE" />
29
30         <!-- TextBlock with an ImageBrush -->
31         <TextBlock Grid.Row="1" FontSize="100" FontWeight="999">
32            <TextBlock.Foreground>
33               <!-- Flower image as an ImageBrush -->
34               <ImageBrush ImageSource="flowers.jpg" />
35            </TextBlock.Foreground>
36            Image
37         </TextBlock>
38
39         <!-- Ellipse with an ImageBrush -->
40         <Ellipse Grid.Row="1" Grid.Column="1" Height="100" Width="300">
41            <Ellipse.Fill>
42               <ImageBrush ImageSource="flowers.jpg" />
43            </Ellipse.Fill>
44         </Ellipse>
45
46         <!-- TextBlock with a MediaElement as a VisualBrush -->
47         <TextBlock Grid.Row="2" FontSize="100" FontWeight="999">
48            <TextBlock.Foreground>
49               <!-- VisualBrush with an embedded MediaElement-->
50               <VisualBrush>
51                  <VisualBrush.Visual>
52                     <MediaElement Source="nasa.wmv" />
53                  </VisualBrush.Visual>
54               </VisualBrush>
55            </TextBlock.Foreground>
56            Video
57         </TextBlock>
58
59         <!-- Ellipse with a MediaElement as a VisualBrush -->
60         <Ellipse Grid.Row="2" Grid.Column="1" Height="100" Width="300">
61            <Ellipse.Fill>
62               <VisualBrush>
63                  <VisualBrush.Visual>
64                     <MediaElement Source="nasa.wmv" IsMuted="True"/>
65                  </VisualBrush.Visual>
66               </VisualBrush>
```

Fig. 25.5 | Applying brushes to various XAML elements. (Part 2 of 3.)

```
67            </Ellipse.Fill>
68         </Ellipse>
69      </Grid>
70   </Window>
```

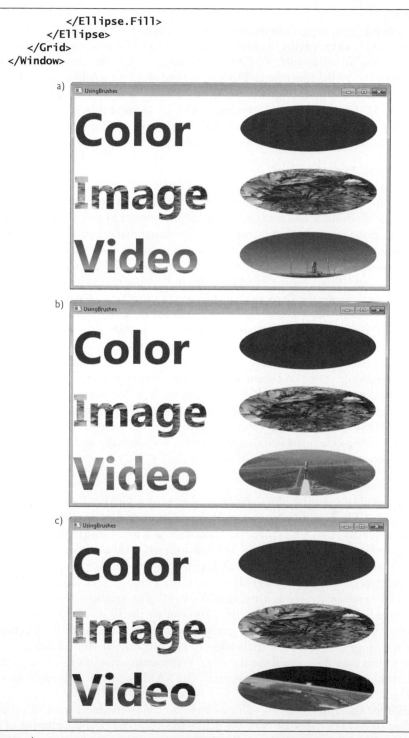

Fig. 25.5 | Applying brushes to various XAML elements. (Part 3 of 3.)

ImageBrush

An **ImageBrush** paints an image into the property it is assigned to (such as a Background). For instance, the TextBlock with the text "Image" and the Ellipse next to it are both filled with the same flower picture. To fill the text, we can assign the ImageBrush to the Foreground property of the TextBlock. The **Foreground** property specifies the fill for the text itself while the **Background** property specifies the fill for the area surrounding the text. Notice in lines 32–35 we apply the ImageBrush with its **ImageSource** set to the file we want to display (the image file must be included in the project). We can also assign the brush to the Fill of the Ellipse (lines 41–43) to display the image inside the shape.

VisualBrush and MediaElement

This example displays a video in a TextBlock's Foreground and an Ellipse's Fill. To use audio or video in a WPF application, you use the **MediaElement** control. Before using a video file in your application, add it to your Visual Studio project by first selecting the **Add Existing Item...** option in the **Project** menu. In the file dialog that appears, find and select the video you want to use. In the drop-down menu next to the **File Name** TextBox, you must change the selection to **All Files (*.*)** to be able to find your file. Once you have selected your file, click **Add**. Select the newly added video in the **Solution Explorer**. Then, in the **Properties** window, change the **Copy to Output Directory** property to **Copy if newer**. This tells the project to copy your video to the project's output directory where it can directly reference the file. You can now set the **Source** property of your MediaElement to the video. In the UsingBrushes application, we use nasa.wmv (line 52 and 64).

We use the **VisualBrush** element to display a video in the desired controls. Lines 50–54 define the Brush with a MediaElement assigned to its **Visual** property. In this property you can completely customize the look of the brush. By assigning the video to this property, we can apply the brush to the Foreground of the TextBlock (lines 48–55) and the Fill of the Ellipse (lines 61–67) to play the video inside the controls. Notice that the Fill of the third Row's elements is different in each screen capture in Fig. 25.5. This is because the video is playing inside the two elements.

Gradients

A **gradient** is a gradual transition through two or more colors. Gradients can be applied as the background or fill for various elements. There are two types of gradients in WPF—LinearGradientBrush and RadialGradientBrush. The **LinearGradientBrush** transitions through colors along a straight path. The **RadialGradientBrush** transitions through colors radially outward from a specified point. Linear gradients are discussed in the UsingGradients example, which displays a gradient across the window. This was created by applying a LinearGradientBrush to a Rectangle's Fill. The gradient starts white and transitions linearly to black from left to right. You can set the RGBA values of the start and end colors to change the look of the gradient. The values entered in the TextBoxes must be in the range 0–255 for the application to run properly. If you set either color's alpha value to less than 255, you'll see the text "Transparency test" in the background, showing that the Rectangle is semitransparent. The XAML code for this application is shown in Fig. 25.6.

The GUI for this application contains a single Rectangle with a LinearGradient-Brush applied to its Fill (lines 20–30). We define the **StartPoint** and **EndPoint** of the gradient in line 22. You must assign **logical points** to these properties, meaning the *x-* and

```
 1    <!-- Fig. 25.6: MainWindow.xaml -->
 2    <!-- Defining gradients in XAML. -->
 3    <Window x:Class="UsingGradients.MainWindow"
 4       xmlns="http://schemas.microsoft.com/winfx/2006/xaml/presentation"
 5       xmlns:x="http://schemas.microsoft.com/winfx/2006/xaml"
 6       Title="UsingGradients" Height="200" Width="450">
 7       <Grid>
 8          <Grid.RowDefinitions>
 9             <RowDefinition />
10             <RowDefinition Height="Auto" />
11             <RowDefinition Height="Auto" />
12             <RowDefinition Height="Auto" />
13          </Grid.RowDefinitions>
14
15          <!-- TextBlock in the background to show transparency -->
16          <TextBlock FontSize="30" HorizontalAlignment="Center"
17             VerticalAlignment="Center">Transparency test</TextBlock>
18
19          <!-- sample rectangle with linear gradient fill -->
20          <Rectangle>
21             <Rectangle.Fill>
22                <LinearGradientBrush StartPoint="0,0" EndPoint="1,0">
23                   <!-- gradient stop can define a color at any offset -->
24                   <GradientStop x:Name="startGradient" Offset="0.0"
25                      Color="White" />
26                   <GradientStop x:Name="stopGradient" Offset="1.0"
27                      Color="Black" />
28                </LinearGradientBrush>
29             </Rectangle.Fill>
30          </Rectangle>
31
32          <!-- shows which TextBox corresponds with which ARGB value-->
33          <StackPanel Grid.Row="1" Orientation="Horizontal">
34             <TextBlock Width="75" Margin="5">Alpha:</TextBlock>
35             <TextBlock Width="75" Margin="5">Red:</TextBlock>
36             <TextBlock Width="75" Margin="5">Green:</TextBlock>
37             <TextBlock Width="75" Margin="5">Blue:</TextBlock>
38          </StackPanel>
39
40          <!-- GUI to select the color of the first GradientStop -->
41          <StackPanel Grid.Row="2" Orientation="Horizontal">
42             <TextBox Name="fromAlpha" Width="75" Margin="5">255</TextBox>
43             <TextBox Name="fromRed" Width="75" Margin="5">255</TextBox>
44             <TextBox Name="fromGreen" Width="75" Margin="5">255</TextBox>
45             <TextBox Name="fromBlue" Width="75" Margin="5">255</TextBox>
46             <Button Name="fromButton" Width="75" Margin="5"
47                Click="fromButton_Click">Start Color</Button>
48          </StackPanel>
49
50          <!-- GUI to select the color of second GradientStop -->
51          <StackPanel Grid.Row="3" Orientation="Horizontal">
52             <TextBox Name="toAlpha" Width="75" Margin="5">255</TextBox>
53             <TextBox Name="toRed" Width="75" Margin="5">0</TextBox>
```

Fig. 25.6 | Defining gradients in XAML. (Part 1 of 2.)

```
54              <TextBox Name="toGreen" Width="75" Margin="5">0</TextBox>
55              <TextBox Name="toBlue" Width="75" Margin="5">0</TextBox>
56              <Button Name="toButton" Width="75" Margin="5"
57                 Click="toButton_Click">End Color</Button>
58          </StackPanel>
59       </Grid>
60    </Window>
```

a) The application immediately after it is loaded   b) The application after changing the start and end colors

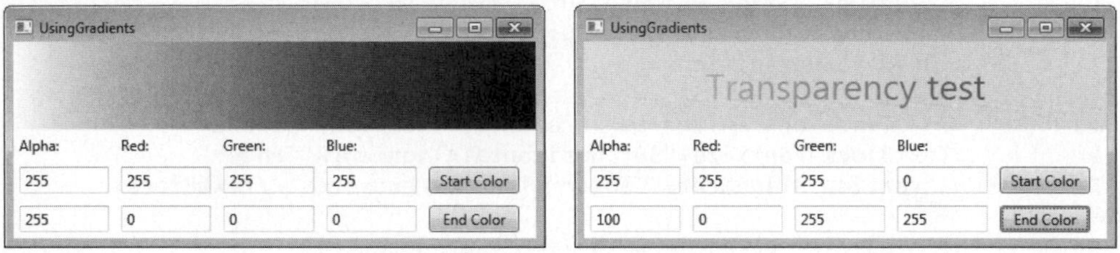

Fig. 25.6 | Defining gradients in XAML. (Part 2 of 2.)

y-coordinates take values between 0 and 1, inclusive. Logical points are used to reference locations in the control independent of the actual size. The point (0,0) represents the top-left corner while the point (1,1) represents the bottom-right corner. The gradient will transition linearly from the start to the end—for RadialGradientBrush, the StartPoint represents the center of the gradient.

A gradient is defined using GradientStop controls. A **GradientStop** defines a single color along the gradient. You can define as many stops as you want by embedding them in the brush element. A GradientStop is defined by its Offset and Color properties. The **Color** property defines the color you want the gradient to transition to—lines 25 and 27 indicate that the gradient transitions through white and black. The **Offset** property defines where along the linear transition you want the color to appear. You can assign any double value between 0 and 1, inclusive, which represent the start and end of the gradient. In the example we use 0.0 and 1.0 offsets (lines 24 and 26), indicating that these colors appear at the start and end of the gradient (which were defined in line 22), respectively. The code in Fig. 25.7 allows the user to set the Colors of the two stops.

When fromButton is clicked, we use the Text properties of the corresponding Text-Boxes to obtain the RGBA values and create a new color. We then assign it to the Color property of startGradient (lines 21–25). When the toButton is clicked, we do the same for stopGradient's Color (lines 32–36).

```
1    // Fig. 25.7: MainWindow.xaml.cs
2    // Customizing gradients.
3    using System;
4    using System.Windows;
5    using System.Windows.Media;
6
```

Fig. 25.7 | Customizing gradients. (Part 1 of 2.)

```
 7    namespace UsingGradients
 8    {
 9       public partial class MainWindow : Window
10       {
11          // constructor
12          public MainWindow()
13          {
14             InitializeComponent();
15          } // end constructor
16
17          // change the starting color of the gradient when the user clicks
18          private void fromButton_Click( object sender, RoutedEventArgs e )
19          {
20             // change the color to use the ARGB values specified by user
21             startGradient.Color = Color.FromArgb(
22                Convert.ToByte( fromAlpha.Text ),
23                Convert.ToByte( fromRed.Text ),
24                Convert.ToByte( fromGreen.Text ),
25                Convert.ToByte( fromBlue.Text ) );
26          } // end method fromButton_Click
27
28          // change the ending color of the gradient when the user clicks
29          private void toButton_Click( object sender, RoutedEventArgs e )
30          {
31             // change the color to use the ARGB values specified by user
32             stopGradient.Color = Color.FromArgb(
33                Convert.ToByte( toAlpha.Text ),
34                Convert.ToByte( toRed.Text ),
35                Convert.ToByte( toGreen.Text ),
36                Convert.ToByte( toBlue.Text ) );
37          } // end method toButton_Click
38       } // end class MainWindow
39    } // end namespace UsingGradients
```

Fig. 25.7 | Customizing gradients. (Part 2 of 2.)

25.6 Transforms

A **transform** can be applied to any UI element to reposition or reorient the graphic. There are several types of transforms. Here we discuss **TranslateTransform**, **RotateTransform**, **SkewTransform** and **ScaleTransform**. A TranslateTransform moves an object to a new location. A RotateTransform rotates the object around a point and by a specified RotationAngle. A SkewTransform skews (or shears) the object. A ScaleTransform scales the object's *x*- and *y*-coordinate points by different specified amounts. See Section 25.7 for an example using a SkewTransform and a ScaleTransform.

The next example draws a star using the Polygon control and uses RotateTransforms to create a circle of randomly colored stars. Figure 25.8 shows the XAML code and a sample output. Lines 10–11 define a Polygon in the shape of a star. The Polygon's Points property is defined here in a new syntax. Each Point in the collection is defined with a comma separating the *x*- and *y*- coordinates. A single space separates each Point. We defined ten Points in the collection. The code-behind file is shown in Fig. 25.9.

```
1   <!-- Fig. 25.8: MainWindow.xaml -->
2   <!-- Defining a Polygon representing a star in XAML. -->
3   <Window x:Class="DrawStars.MainWindow"
4      xmlns="http://schemas.microsoft.com/winfx/2006/xaml/presentation"
5      xmlns:x="http://schemas.microsoft.com/winfx/2006/xaml"
6      Title="DrawStars" Height="330" Width="330" Name="DrawStars">
7      <Canvas Name="mainCanvas"> <!-- Main canvas of the application -->
8
9         <!-- Polygon with points that make up a star -->
10        <Polygon Name="star" Fill="Green" Points="205,150 217,186 259,186
11           223,204 233,246 205,222 177,246 187,204 151,186 193,186" />
12     </Canvas>
13  </Window>
```

Fig. 25.8 | Defining a `Polygon` representing a star in XAML.

```
1   // Fig. 25.9: MainWindow.xaml.cs
2   // Applying transforms to a Polygon.
3   using System;
4   using System.Windows;
5   using System.Windows.Media;
6   using System.Windows.Shapes;
7
8   namespace DrawStars
9   {
10     public partial class MainWindow : Window
11     {
12        // constructor
13        public MainWindow()
14        {
15           InitializeComponent();
16
17           Random random = new Random(); // get random values for colors
18
19           // create 18 more stars
20           for ( int count = 0; count < 18; count++ )
21           {
```

Fig. 25.9 | Applying transforms to a `Polygon`. (Part 1 of 2.)

```
22              Polygon newStar = new Polygon(); // create a polygon object
23              newStar.Points = star.Points; // copy the points collection
24
25              byte[] colorValues = new byte[ 4 ]; // create a Byte array
26              random.NextBytes( colorValues ); // create four random values
27              newStar.Fill = new SolidColorBrush( Color.FromArgb(
28                 colorValues[ 0 ], colorValues[ 1 ], colorValues[ 2 ],
29                 colorValues[ 3 ] ) ); // creates a random color brush
30
31              // apply a rotation to the shape
32              RotateTransform rotate =
33                 new RotateTransform( count * 20, 150, 150 );
34              newStar.RenderTransform = rotate;
35              mainCanvas.Children.Add( newStar );
36          } // end for
37       } // end constructor
38    } // end class MainWindow
39 } // end namespace DrawStars
```

Fig. 25.9 | Applying transforms to a `Polygon`. (Part 2 of 2.)

In the code-behind, we replicate star 18 times and apply a different RotateTransform to each to get the circle of Polygons shown in the screen capture of Fig. 25.8. Each iteration of the loop duplicates star by creating a new Polygon with the same set of points (lines 22–23). To generate the random colors for each star, we use the Random class's **NextBytes** method, which assigns a random value in the range 0–255 to each element in its Byte array argument. Lines 25–26 define a four-element Byte array and supply the array to the NextBytes method. We then create a new Brush with a color that uses the four randomly generated values as its RGBA values (lines 27–29).

To apply a rotation to the new Polygon, we set the **RenderTransform** property to a new RotateTransform object (lines 32–34). Each iteration of the loop assigns a new rotation-angle value by using the control variable multiplied by 20 as the RotationAngle argument. The first argument in the RotateTransform's constructor is the angle by which to rotate the object. The next two arguments are the x- and y-coordinates of the point of rotation. The center of the circle of stars is the point (150,150) because all 18 stars were rotated about that point. Each new shape is added as a new Child element to mainCanvas (line 35) so it can be rendered on screen.

25.7 WPF Customization: A Television GUI

In Chapter 24, we introduced several techniques for customizing the appearance of WPF controls. We revisit them in this section, now that we have a basic understanding of how to create and manipulate 2-D graphics in WPF. You'll learn to apply combinations of shapes, brushes and transforms to define every aspect of a control's appearance and to create graphically sophisticated GUIs.

This case study models a television. The GUI depicts a 3-D-looking environment featuring a TV that can be turned on and off. When it is on, the user can play, pause and stop the TV's video. When the video plays, a semitransparent reflection plays simultaneously on what appears to be a flat surface in front of the screen (Fig. 25.10).

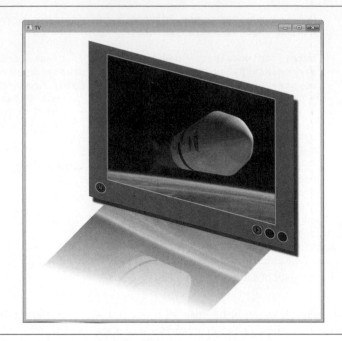

Fig. 25.10 | GUI representing a television.

The TV GUI may appear overwhelmingly complex, but it's actually just a basic WPF GUI built using controls with modified appearances. This example demonstrates the use of **WPF bitmap effects** to apply simple visual effects to some of the GUI elements. In addition, it introduces **opacity masks**, which can be used to hide parts of an element. Other than these two new concepts, the TV application is created using only the WPF elements and concepts that you've already learned. Figure 25.11 presents the XAML markup and a screen capture of the application when it first loads. The video used in this case study is a public-domain NASA video entitled *Animation: To the Moon* and can be downloaded from the NASA website (www.nasa.gov/multimedia/hd/index.html).

```
1   <!-- Fig. 25.11: MainWindow.xaml -->
2   <!-- TV GUI showing the versatility of WPF customization. -->
3   <Window x:Class="TV.MainWindow"
4      xmlns="http://schemas.microsoft.com/winfx/2006/xaml/presentation"
5      xmlns:x="http://schemas.microsoft.com/winfx/2006/xaml"
6      Title="TV" Height="720" Width="720">
7      <Window.Resources>
8         <!-- define template for play, pause and stop buttons -->
9         <ControlTemplate x:Key="RadioButtonTemplate"
10           TargetType="RadioButton">
11           <Grid>
12              <!-- create a circular border -->
13              <Ellipse Width="25" Height="25" Fill="Silver" />
```

Fig. 25.11 | TV GUI showing the versatility of WPF customization (XAML). (Part 1 of 5.)

```
14
15          <!-- create an "illuminated" background -->
16          <Ellipse Name="backgroundEllipse" Width="22" Height="22">
17              <Ellipse.Fill> <!-- enabled and unchecked state -->
18                  <RadialGradientBrush> <!-- red "light" -->
19                      <GradientStop Offset="0" Color="Red" />
20                      <GradientStop Offset="1.25" Color="Black" />
21                  </RadialGradientBrush>
22              </Ellipse.Fill>
23          </Ellipse>
24
25          <!-- display button image -->
26          <ContentPresenter Content="{TemplateBinding Content}" />
27      </Grid>
28
29      <!-- change appearance when state changes -->
30      <ControlTemplate.Triggers>
31          <!-- disabled state -->
32          <Trigger Property="RadioButton.IsEnabled" Value="False">
33              <Setter TargetName="backgroundEllipse" Property="Fill">
34                  <Setter.Value>
35                      <RadialGradientBrush> <!-- dim "light" -->
36                          <GradientStop Offset="0" Color="LightGray" />
37                          <GradientStop Offset="1.25" Color="Black" />
38                      </RadialGradientBrush>
39                  </Setter.Value>
40              </Setter>
41          </Trigger>
42
43          <!-- checked state -->
44          <Trigger Property="RadioButton.IsChecked" Value="True">
45              <Setter TargetName="backgroundEllipse" Property="Fill">
46                  <Setter.Value>
47                      <RadialGradientBrush> <!-- green "light" -->
48                          <GradientStop Offset="0" Color="LimeGreen" />
49                          <GradientStop Offset="1.25" Color="Black" />
50                      </RadialGradientBrush>
51                  </Setter.Value>
52              </Setter>
53          </Trigger>
54      </ControlTemplate.Triggers>
55  </ControlTemplate>
56  </Window.Resources>
57
58  <!-- define the GUI -->
59  <Canvas>
60      <!-- define the "TV" -->
61      <Border Canvas.Left="150" Height="370" Width="490"
62          Canvas.Top="20" Background="DimGray">
63          <Grid>
64              <Grid.RowDefinitions>
65                  <RowDefinition />
```

Fig. 25.11 | TV GUI showing the versatility of WPF customization (XAML). (Part 2 of 5.)

```
66                       <RowDefinition Height="Auto" />
67                   </Grid.RowDefinitions>
68
69                   <!-- define the screen -->
70                   <Border Margin="0,20,0,10" Background="Black"
71                      HorizontalAlignment="Center" VerticalAlignment="Center"
72                      BorderThickness="2" BorderBrush="Silver" CornerRadius="2">
73                      <MediaElement Height="300" Width="400"
74                         Name="videoMediaElement" Source="Video/future_nasa.wmv"
75                         LoadedBehavior="Manual" Stretch="Fill" />
76                   </Border>
77
78                   <!-- define the play, pause, and stop buttons -->
79                   <StackPanel Grid.Row="1" HorizontalAlignment="Right"
80                      Orientation="Horizontal">
81                      <RadioButton Name="playRadioButton" IsEnabled="False"
82                         Margin="0,0,5,15"
83                         Template="{StaticResource RadioButtonTemplate}"
84                         Checked="playRadioButton_Checked">
85                         <Image Height="20" Width="20"
86                            Source="Images/play.png" Stretch="Uniform" />
87                      </RadioButton>
88                      <RadioButton Name="pauseRadioButton" IsEnabled="False"
89                         Margin="0,0,5,15"
90                         Template="{StaticResource RadioButtonTemplate}"
91                         Checked="pauseRadioButton_Checked">
92                         <Image Height="20" Width="20"
93                            Source="Images/pause.png" Stretch="Uniform" />
94                      </RadioButton>
95                      <RadioButton Name="stopRadioButton" IsEnabled="False"
96                         Margin="0,0,15,15"
97                         Template="{StaticResource RadioButtonTemplate}"
98                         Checked="stopRadioButton_Checked">
99                         <Image Height="20" Width="20"
100                           Source="Images/stop.png" Stretch="Uniform" />
101                     </RadioButton>
102                  </StackPanel>
103
104                  <!-- define the power button -->
105                  <CheckBox Name="powerCheckBox" Grid.Row="1" Width="25"
106                     Height="25" HorizontalAlignment="Left"
107                     Margin="15,0,0,15" Checked="powerCheckBox_Checked"
108                     Unchecked="powerCheckBox_Unchecked">
109                     <CheckBox.Template> <!-- set the template -->
110                        <ControlTemplate TargetType="CheckBox">
111                           <Grid>
112                              <!-- create a circular border -->
113                              <Ellipse Width="25" Height="25"
114                                 Fill="Silver" />
115
116                              <!-- create an "illuminated" background -->
117                              <Ellipse Name="backgroundEllipse" Width="22"
118                                 Height="22">
```

Fig. 25.11 | TV GUI showing the versatility of WPF customization (XAML). (Part 3 of 5.)

```
119                          <Ellipse.Fill> <!-- unchecked state -->
120                              <RadialGradientBrush> <!-- dim "light" -->
121                                  <GradientStop Offset="0"
122                                      Color="LightGray" />
123                                  <GradientStop Offset="1.25"
124                                      Color="Black" />
125                              </RadialGradientBrush>
126                          </Ellipse.Fill>
127                      </Ellipse>
128
129                      <!-- display power-button image-->
130                      <Image Source="Images/power.png" Width="20"
131                          Height="20" />
132                  </Grid>
133
134                  <!-- change appearance when state changes -->
135                  <ControlTemplate.Triggers>
136                      <!-- checked state -->
137                      <Trigger Property="CheckBox.IsChecked"
138                          Value="True">
139                          <Setter TargetName="backgroundEllipse"
140                              Property="Fill">
141                              <Setter.Value> <!-- green "light" -->
142                                  <RadialGradientBrush>
143                                      <GradientStop Offset="0"
144                                          Color="LimeGreen" />
145                                      <GradientStop Offset="1.25"
146                                          Color="Black" />
147                                  </RadialGradientBrush>
148                              </Setter.Value>
149                          </Setter>
150                      </Trigger>
151                  </ControlTemplate.Triggers>
152              </ControlTemplate>
153          </CheckBox.Template>
154      </CheckBox>
155  </Grid>
156
157  <!-- skew "TV" to give a 3-D appearance -->
158  <Border.RenderTransform>
159      <SkewTransform AngleY="15" />
160  </Border.RenderTransform>
161
162  <!-- apply shadow effect to "TV" -->
163  <Border.Effect>
164      <DropShadowEffect Color="Gray" ShadowDepth="15" />
165  </Border.Effect>
166  </Border>
167
168  <!-- define reflection -->
169  <Border Canvas.Left="185" Canvas.Top="410" Height="300"
170      Width="400">
171      <Rectangle Name="reflectionRectangle">
```

Fig. 25.11 | TV GUI showing the versatility of WPF customization (XAML). (Part 4 of 5.)

```
172            <Rectangle.Fill>
173               <!-- create a reflection of the video -->
174               <VisualBrush
175                  Visual="{Binding ElementName=videoMediaElement}">
176                  <VisualBrush.RelativeTransform>
177                     <ScaleTransform ScaleY="-1" CenterY="0.5" />
178                  </VisualBrush.RelativeTransform>
179               </VisualBrush>
180            </Rectangle.Fill>
181
182            <!-- make reflection more transparent the further it gets
183               from the screen -->
184            <Rectangle.OpacityMask>
185               <LinearGradientBrush StartPoint="0,0" EndPoint="0,1">
186                  <GradientStop Color="Black" Offset="-0.25" />
187                  <GradientStop Color="Transparent" Offset="0.5" />
188               </LinearGradientBrush>
189            </Rectangle.OpacityMask>
190         </Rectangle>
191
192         <!-- skew reflection to look 3-D -->
193         <Border.RenderTransform>
194            <SkewTransform AngleY="15" AngleX="-45" />
195         </Border.RenderTransform>
196      </Border>
197   </Canvas>
198 </Window>
```

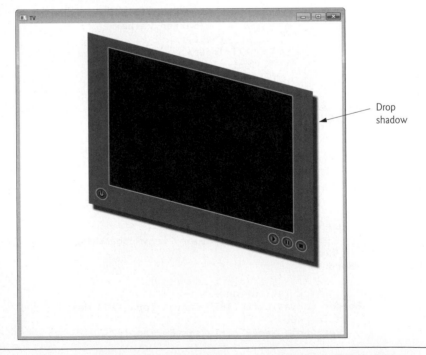

Drop shadow

Fig. 25.11 | TV GUI showing the versatility of WPF customization (XAML). (Part 5 of 5.)

WPF Effects

WPF allows you to apply graphical effects to any GUI element. There are two predefined effects—the **DropShadowEffect**, which gives an element a shadow as if a light were shining at it (Fig. 25.11, lines 163–165), and the **BlurEffect**, which makes an element's appearance blurry. The System.Windows.Media.Effects namespace also contains the more generalized ShaderEffect class, which allows you to build and use your own custom shader effects. For more information on the ShaderEffect class, visit Microsoft's developer center.

> bit.ly/ShaderEffect

You can apply an effect to any element by setting its Effect property. Each Effect has its own unique properties. For example, DropShadowEffect's ShadowDepth property specifies the distance from the element to the shadow (line 164), while a BlurEffect's KernelType property specifies the type of blur filter it uses and its Radius property specifies the filter's size.

Creating Buttons on the TV

The representations of TV buttons in this example are not Button controls. The play, pause, and stop buttons are RadioButtons, and the power button is a CheckBox. Lines 9–55 and 110–152 define the ControlTemplates used to render the RadioButtons and CheckBox, respectively. The two templates are defined similarly, so we discuss only the RadioButton template in detail.

In the background of each button are two circles, defined by Ellipse objects. The larger Ellipse acts as a border (line 13). The smaller Ellipse is colored by a RadialGradientBrush. The gradient is a light color in the center and becomes black as it extends farther out. This makes it appear to be a source of light (lines 16–23). The content of the RadioButton is then applied on top of the two Ellipses (line 26).

The images used in this example are transparent outlines of the play, pause, and stop symbols on a black background. When the button is applied over the RadialGradientBrush, it appears to be illuminated. In its default state (enabled and unchecked), each playback button glows red. This represents the TV being on, with the playback option not active. When the application first loads, the TV is off, so the playback buttons are disabled. In this state, the background gradient is gray. When a playback option is active (i.e., RadioButton is checked), it glows green. The latter two deviations in appearance when the control changes states are defined by triggers (lines 30–54).

The power button, represented by a CheckBox, behaves similarly. When the TV is off (i.e., CheckBox is unchecked), the control is gray. When the user presses the power button and turns the TV on (i.e., CheckBox becomes checked), the control turns green. The power button is never disabled.

Creating the TV Interface

The TV panel is represented by a beveled Border with a gray background (lines 61–166). Recall that a Border is a ContentControl and can host only one direct child element. Thus, all of the Border's elements are contained in a Grid layout container. Nested within the TV panel is another Border with a black background containing a MediaElement control (lines 70–76). This portrays the TV's screen. The power button is placed in the bottom-left corner, and the playback buttons are bound in a StackPanel in the bottom-right corner (lines 79–154).

Creating the Reflection of the TV Screen

Lines 169–196 define the GUI's video reflection using a Rectangle element nested in a Border. The Rectangle's Fill is a VisualBrush that is bound to the MediaElement (lines 172–180). To invert the video, we define a ScaleTransform and specify it as the RelativeTransform property, which is common to all brushes (lines 176–178). You can invert an element by setting the **ScaleX** or **ScaleY**—the amounts by which to scale the respective coordinates—property of a ScaleTransform to a negative number. In this example, we set ScaleY to -1 and CenterY to 0.5, inverting the VisualBrush vertically centered around the midpoint. The **CenterX** and **CenterY** properties specify the point from which the image expands or contracts. When you scale an image, most of the points move as a result of the altered size. The center point is the only point that stays at its original location when ScaleX and ScaleY are set to values other than 1.

To achieve the semitransparent look, we applied an opacity mask to the Rectangle by setting the **OpacityMask** property (lines 184–189). The mask uses a LinearGradientBrush that changes from black near the top to transparent near the bottom. When the gradient is applied as an opacity mask, the gradient translates to a range from completely opaque, where it is black, to completely transparent. In this example, we set the Offset of the black GradientStop to -0.25, so that even the opaque edge of the mask is slightly transparent. We also set the Offset of the transparent GradientStop to 0.5, indicating that only the top half of the Rectangle (or bottom half of the movie) should display.

Skewing the GUI Components to Create a 3-D Look

When you draw a three-dimensional object on a two-dimensional plane, you are creating a 2-D projection of that 3-D environment. For example, to represent a simple box, you draw three adjoining parallelograms. Each face of the box is actually a flat, skewed rectangle rather than a 2-D view of a 3-D object. You can apply the same concept to create simple 3-D-looking GUIs without using a 3-D engine.

In this case study, we applied a SkewTransform to the TV representation, skewing it vertically by 15 degrees clockwise from the *x*-axis (lines 158–160). The reflection is then skewed vertically by 15 degrees clockwise from the *x*-axis and horizontally by 45 degrees clockwise from the *y*-axis (lines 193–195). Thus the GUI becomes a 2-D **orthographic projection** of a 3-D space with the axes 105, 120, and 135 degrees from each other, as shown in Fig. 25.12. Unlike a **perspective projection**, an orthographic projection does not show depth. Thus, the TV GUI does not present a realistic 3-D view, but rather a graphical representation. In Section 25.9, we present a 3-D object in perspective.

Examining the Code-Behind Class

Figure 25.13 presents the code-behind class that provides the functionality for the TV application. When the user turns on the TV (i.e., checks the powerCheckBox), the reflection is made visible and the playback options are enabled (lines 16–26). When the user turns off the TV, the MediaElement's Close method is called to close the media. In addition, the reflection is made invisible and the playback options are disabled (lines 29–45).

Whenever one of the RadioButtons that represent each playback option is checked, the MediaElement executes the corresponding task (lines 48–66). The methods that execute these tasks are built into the MediaElement control. Playback can be modified programmatically only if the LoadedBehavior is Manual (line 75 in Fig. 25.11).

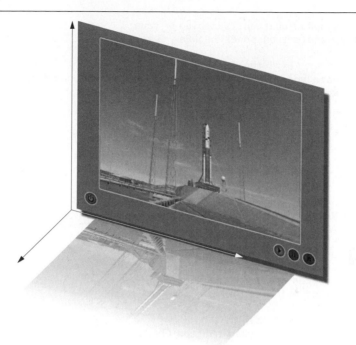

Fig. 25.12 | The effect of skewing the TV application's GUI components.

```
1   // Fig. 25.13: MainWindow.xaml.cs
2   // TV GUI showing the versatility of WPF customization (code-behind).
3   using System.Windows;
4
5   namespace TV
6   {
7      public partial class MainWindow : Window
8      {
9         // constructor
10        public MainWindow()
11        {
12           InitializeComponent();
13        } // end constructor
14
15        // turns "on" the TV
16        private void powerCheckBox_Checked( object sender,
17           RoutedEventArgs e )
18        {
19           // render the reflection visible
20           reflectionRectangle.Visibility = Visibility.Visible;
21
22           // enable play, pause, and stop buttons
23           playRadioButton.IsEnabled = true;
24           pauseRadioButton.IsEnabled = true;
```

Fig. 25.13 | TV GUI showing the versatility of WPF customization (code-behind). (Part 1 of 2.)

```
25        stopRadioButton.IsEnabled = true;
26     } // end method powerCheckBox_Checked
27
28     // turns "off" the TV
29     private void powerCheckBox_Unchecked( object sender,
30        RoutedEventArgs e )
31     {
32        // shut down the screen
33        videoMediaElement.Close();
34
35        // hide the reflection
36        reflectionRectangle.Visibility = Visibility.Hidden;
37
38        // disable the play, pause, and stop buttons
39        playRadioButton.IsChecked = false;
40        pauseRadioButton.IsChecked = false;
41        stopRadioButton.IsChecked = false;
42        playRadioButton.IsEnabled = false;
43        pauseRadioButton.IsEnabled = false;
44        stopRadioButton.IsEnabled = false;
45     } // end method powerCheckBox_Unchecked
46
47     // plays the video
48     private void playRadioButton_Checked( object sender,
49        RoutedEventArgs e )
50     {
51        videoMediaElement.Play();
52     } // end method playRadioButton_Checked
53
54     // pauses the video
55     private void pauseRadioButton_Checked( object sender,
56        RoutedEventArgs e )
57     {
58        videoMediaElement.Pause();
59     } // end method pauseRadioButton_Checked
60
61     // stops the video
62     private void stopRadioButton_Checked( object sender,
63        RoutedEventArgs e )
64     {
65        videoMediaElement.Stop();
66     } // end method stopRadioButton_Checked
67     } // end class MainWindow
68  } // end namespace TV
```

Fig. 25.13 | TV GUI showing the versatility of WPF customization (code-behind). (Part 2 of 2.)

25.8 Animations

An animation in WPF applications simply means a transition of a property from one value to another in a specified amount of time. Most graphic properties of a control can be animated. The UsingAnimations example (Fig. 25.14) shows a video's size being animated. A MediaElement along with two input TextBoxes—one for Width and one for Height—and an animate Button are created in the GUI. When you click the animate Button, the video's Width and Height properties animate to the values typed in the corresponding TextBoxes by the user.

As you can see, the animations create a smooth transition from the original Height and Width to the new values. Lines 31–43 define a **Storyboard** element embedded in the Button's click event Trigger. A Storyboard contains embedded animation elements. When the Storyboard begins executing (line 30), all embedded animations execute. A Storyboard has two important properties—**TargetName** and **TargetProperty**. The TargetName (line 31) specifies which control to animate. The TargetProperty specifies which property of the animated control to change. In this case, the Width (line 34) and Height (line 40) are the TargetProperties, because we're changing the size of the video. Both the TargetName and TargetProperty can be defined in the Storyboard or in the animation element itself.

```
1   <!-- Fig. 25.14: MainWindow.xaml -->
2   <!-- Animating graphic elements with Storyboards. -->
3   <Window x:Class="UsingAnimations.MainWindow"
4      xmlns="http://schemas.microsoft.com/winfx/2006/xaml/presentation"
5      xmlns:x="http://schemas.microsoft.com/winfx/2006/xaml"
6      Title="UsingAnimations" Height="400" Width="500">
7      <Grid>
8         <Grid.ColumnDefinitions>
9            <ColumnDefinition />
10           <ColumnDefinition Width="Auto" />
11        </Grid.ColumnDefinitions>
12
13        <MediaElement Name="video" Height="100" Width="100" Stretch="Fill"
14           Source="newfractal.wmv" /> <!-- Animated video -->
15
16        <StackPanel Grid.Column="1">
17           <!-- TextBox will contain the new Width for the video -->
18           <TextBlock Margin="5,0,0,0">Width:</TextBlock>
19           <TextBox Name="widthValue" Width="75" Margin="5">100</TextBox>
20
21           <!-- TextBox will contain the new Height for the video -->
22           <TextBlock Margin="5,0,0,0">Height:</TextBlock>
23           <TextBox Name="heightValue" Width="75" Margin="5">100</TextBox>
24
25           <!-- When clicked, rectangle animates to the input values -->
26           <Button Width="75" Margin="5">Animate
27              <Button.Triggers> <!-- Use trigger to call animation -->
28                 <!-- When button is clicked -->
29                 <EventTrigger RoutedEvent="Button.Click">
30                    <BeginStoryboard> <!-- Begin animation -->
31                       <Storyboard Storyboard.TargetName="video">
32                          <!-- Animates the Width -->
33                          <DoubleAnimation Duration="0:0:2"
34                             Storyboard.TargetProperty="Width"
35                             To="{Binding ElementName=widthValue,
36                             Path=Text}" />
37
```

Fig. 25.14 | Animating the width and height of a video. (Part 1 of 2.)

```
38                         <!-- Animates the Height -->
39                         <DoubleAnimation Duration="0:0:2"
40                             Storyboard.TargetProperty="Height"
41                             To="{Binding ElementName=heightValue,
42                             Path=Text}" />
43                     </Storyboard>
44                 </BeginStoryboard>
45             </EventTrigger>
46         </Button.Triggers>
47     </Button>
48   </StackPanel>
49   </Grid>
50 </Window>
```

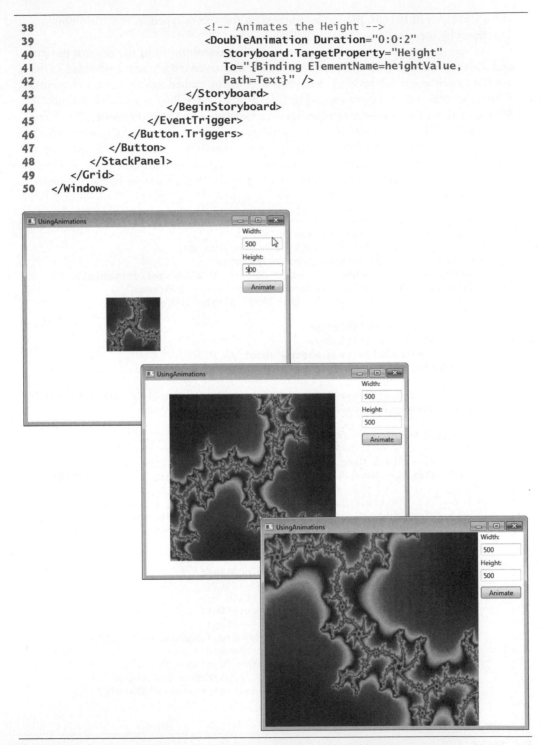

Fig. 25.14 | Animating the width and height of a video. (Part 2 of 2.)

To animate a property, you can use one of several animation classes available in WPF. We use the `DoubleAnimation` for the size properties—PointAnimations and Color-Animations are two other commonly used animation classes. A **DoubleAnimation** animates properties of type `Double`. The `Width` and `Height` animations are defined in lines 33–36 and 39–42, respectively. Lines 35–36 define the **To** property of the `Width` animation, which specifies the value of the `Width` at the end of the animation. We use data binding to set this to the value in the `widthValue` TextBox. The animation also has a **Duration** property that specifies how long the animation takes. Notice in line 33 that we set the `Duration` of the `Width` animation to 0:0:2, meaning the animation takes 0 hours, 0 minutes and 2 seconds. You can specify fractions of a second by using a decimal point. Hour and minute values must be integers. Animations also have a **From** property which defines a constant starting value of the animated property.

Since we're animating the video's `Width` and `Height` properties separately, it is not always displayed at its original width and height. In line 13, we define the `MediaElement`'s **Stretch** property. This is a property for graphic elements and determines how the media stretches to fit the size of its enclosure. This property can be set to **None**, **Uniform**, **UniformToFill** or **Fill**. None allows the media to stay at its native size regardless of the container's size. `Uniform` resizes the media to its largest possible size while maintaining its native **aspect ratio**. A video's aspect ratio is the proportion between its width and height. Keeping this ratio at its original value ensures that the video does not look "stretched." `UniformToFill` resizes the media to completely fill the container while still keeping its aspect ratio—as a result, it could be **cropped**. When an image or video is cropped, the pieces of the edges are cut off from the media in order to fit the shape of the container. `Fill` forces the media to be resized to the size of the container (aspect ratio is not preserved). In the example, we use `Fill` to show the changing size of the container.

25.9 (Optional) 3-D Objects and Transforms

WPF has substantial three-dimensional graphics capabilities. Once a 3-D shape is created, it can be manipulated using 3-D transforms and animations. This section requires an understanding of 3-D analytical geometry. Readers without a strong background in these geometric concepts can still enjoy this section. We overview several advanced WPF 3-D capabilities.

The next example creates a rotating pyramid. The user can change the axis of rotation to see all sides of the object. The XAML code for this application is shown in Fig. 25.15.

The first step in creating a 3-D object is to create a **Viewport3D** control (lines 29–76). The viewport represents the 2-D view the user sees when the application executes. This control defines a rendering surface for the content and contains content that represents the 3-D objects to render.

```
1    <!-- Fig. 25.15: MainWindow.xaml -->
2    <!-- Animating a 3-D object. -->
3    <Window x:Class="Application3D.MainWindow"
4        xmlns="http://schemas.microsoft.com/winfx/2006/xaml/presentation"
5        xmlns:x="http://schemas.microsoft.com/winfx/2006/xaml"
6        Title="Application3D" Height="300" Width="300">
7        <Grid>
```

Fig. 25.15 | Animating a 3-D object. (Part 1 of 3.)

```
 8          <Grid.RowDefinitions>
 9             <RowDefinition />
10             <RowDefinition Height="Auto" />
11          </Grid.RowDefinitions>
12
13          <Grid.Triggers>
14             <!-- when the window has loaded, begin the animation -->
15             <EventTrigger RoutedEvent="Grid.Loaded">
16                <BeginStoryboard>
17                   <Storyboard Storyboard.TargetName="rotation"
18                      RepeatBehavior="Forever">
19
20                      <!-- rotate the object 360 degrees -->
21                      <DoubleAnimation Storyboard.TargetProperty="Angle"
22                         To="360" Duration="0:0:3" />
23                   </Storyboard>
24                </BeginStoryboard>
25             </EventTrigger>
26          </Grid.Triggers>
27
28          <!-- viewport window for viewing the 3D object -->
29          <Viewport3D>
30             <Viewport3D.Camera>
31                <!-- camera represents what user sees -->
32                <PerspectiveCamera x:Name="camera" Position="6,0,1"
33                   LookDirection="-1,0,0" UpDirection="0,0,1" />
34             </Viewport3D.Camera>
35
36             <!-- defines the 3-D content in the viewport -->
37             <ModelVisual3D>
38                <ModelVisual3D.Content>
39                   <Model3DGroup>
40
41                      <!-- two light sources to illuminate the objects-->
42                      <DirectionalLight Color="White" Direction="-1,0,0" />
43                      <DirectionalLight Color="White" Direction="0,0,-1" />
44
45                      <GeometryModel3D>
46                         <!-- rotate the geometry about the z-axis -->
47                         <GeometryModel3D.Transform>
48                            <RotateTransform3D>
49                               <RotateTransform3D.Rotation>
50                                  <AxisAngleRotation3D x:Name="rotation"
51                                     Angle="0" Axis="0,0,1" />
52                               </RotateTransform3D.Rotation>
53                            </RotateTransform3D>
54                         </GeometryModel3D.Transform>
55
56                         <!-- defines the pyramid -->
57                         <GeometryModel3D.Geometry>
58                            <MeshGeometry3D Positions="1,1,0 1,-1,0 -1,1,0
59                               -1,-1,0 0,0,2" TriangleIndices="0,4,1 2,4,0
```

Fig. 25.15 | Animating a 3-D object. (Part 2 of 3.)

```
60                              3,4,2 3,1,4 2,0,1 3,2,1"
61                              TextureCoordinates="0,0 1,0 0,1 1,1 0,0" />
62                      </GeometryModel3D.Geometry>
63
64                      <!-- defines the surface of the object -->
65                      <GeometryModel3D.Material>
66                          <DiffuseMaterial>
67                              <DiffuseMaterial.Brush>
68                                  <ImageBrush ImageSource="cover.png" />
69                              </DiffuseMaterial.Brush>
70                          </DiffuseMaterial>
71                      </GeometryModel3D.Material>
72                  </GeometryModel3D>
73              </Model3DGroup>
74          </ModelVisual3D.Content>
75      </ModelVisual3D>
76      </Viewport3D>
77
78      <!-- RadioButtons to change the axis of rotation -->
79      <GroupBox Grid.Row="1" Header="Axis of rotation">
80          <StackPanel Orientation="Horizontal"
81              HorizontalAlignment="Center">
82              <RadioButton Name="xRadio" Margin="5"
83                  Checked="xRadio_Checked">x-axis</RadioButton>
84              <RadioButton Name="yRadio" Margin="5"
85                  Checked="yRadio_Checked">y-axis</RadioButton>
86              <RadioButton Name="zRadio" Margin="5"
87                  Checked="zRadio_Checked">z-axis</RadioButton>
88          </StackPanel>
89      </GroupBox>
90      </Grid>
91  </Window>
```

Fig. 25.15 | Animating a 3-D object. (Part 3 of 3.)

Create a **ModelVisual3D** object (lines 37–75) to define a 3-D object in a Viewport3D control. ModelVisual3D's **Content** property contains the shapes you wish to define in your space. To add multiple objects to the Content, embed them in a **Model3DGroup** element.

Creating the 3-D Object

3-D objects in WPF are modeled as sets of triangles, because you need a minimum of three points to make a flat surface. Every surface must be created or approximated as a collection of triangles. For this reason, shapes with flat surfaces (like cubes) are relatively simple to create, while curved surfaces (like spheres) are extremely complex. To make more complicated 3-D elements, you can use 3-D application development tools such as Electric Rain's ZAM 3D (erain.com/products/zam3d/DefaultPDC.asp), which generates the XAML markup.

Use the **GeometryModel3D** element to define a shape (lines 45–72). This control creates and textures your 3-D model. First we discuss this control's **Geometry** property (lines 57–62). Use the **MeshGeometry3D** control (lines 58–61) to specify the exact shape of the object you want to create in the Geometry property. To create the object, you need two collections—one is a set of points to represent the vertices, and the other uses those vertices to specify the triangles that define the shape. These collections are assigned to the **Positions** and **TriangleIndices** properties of MeshGeometry3D, respectively. The points that we assigned to the Positions attribute (lines 58–59) are shown in a 3-D space in Fig. 25.16. The view in the figure does not directly correspond to the view of the pyramid shown in the application. In the application, if you change the camera's Position (as you'll soon learn) to "5,5,5", LookDirection to "-1,-1,-1" and UpDirection to "0,1,0", you'll see the pyramid in the same orientation as in Fig. 25.16.

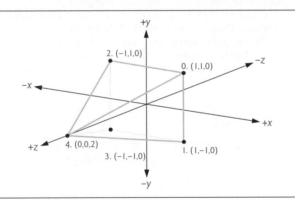

Fig. 25.16 | 3-D points making up a pyramid with a square base.

The points are labeled in the order they're defined in the Positions collection. For instance, the text 0. (1,1,0) in the diagram refers to the first defined point, which has an index of 0 in the collection. Points in 3-D are defined with the notation "(*x*-coordinate, *y*-coordinate, *z*-coordinate)." With these points, we can define the triangles that we use to model the 3-D shape. The TriangleIndices property specifies the three corners of each individual triangle in the collection. The first element in the collection defined in line 59 is (0,4,1). This indicates that we want to create a triangle with corners at points 0, 4 and 1 defined in the Positions collection. You can see this triangle in Fig. 25.16 (the frontmost triangle in the picture). We can define all the sides of the pyramid by defining the rest of the triangles. Note also that while the pyramid has five flat surfaces, there are six triangles defined, because we need two triangles to create the pyramid's square base.

The order in which you define the triangle's corners dictates which side is considered the "front" versus the "back." Suppose you want to create a flat square in your viewport.

This can be done using two triangles, as shown in Fig. 25.17. If you want the surface facing toward you to be the "front," you must define the corners in counterclockwise order. So, to define the lower-left triangle, you need to define the triangle as "0,1,3". The upper-right triangle needs to be "1,2,3". By default, the "front" of the triangle is drawn with your defined `Material` (described in the next section) while the "back" is made transparent. Therefore, the order in which you define the triangle's vertices is significant.

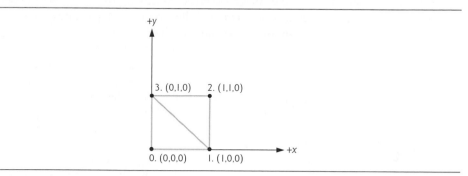

Fig. 25.17 | Defining two triangles to create a square in 3-D space.

Using a Brush on the Surface of a 3-D Object
By defining the **Material** property of the GeometryModel3D, we can specify what type of brush to use when painting each surface of the 3-D object. There are several different controls you can use to set the `Material` property. Each control gives a different "look" to the surface. Figure 25.18 describes the available controls.

3-D material controls	
DiffuseMaterial	Creates a "flat" surface that reflects light evenly in all directions.
SpecularMaterial	Creates a glossy-looking material. It creates a surface similar to that of metal or glass.
EmissiveMaterial	Creates a glowing surface that generates its own light (this light does not act as a light source for other objects).
MaterialGroup	Allows you to combine multiple materials, which are layered in the order they're added to the group.

Fig. 25.18 | 3-D material controls.

In the example, we use the **DiffuseMaterial** control. We can assign the brushes described in Section 25.5 to the material's **Brush** property to define how to paint the 3-D object's surface. We use an ImageBrush with cover.png as its source (line 68) to draw an image on the pyramid.

Notice in line 61 of Fig. 25.15 that we define the **TextureCoordinates** of the 3-D object. This property takes a PointCollection and determines how the Material is mapped onto the object's surfaces. If this property is not defined, the brush may not render correctly on the surface. The TextureCoordinates property defines which point on the image is mapped onto which vertex—an intersection of two or more edges—of the object.

Notice we assigned the String "0,0 1,0 0,1 1,1 0,0" to the TextureCoordinates property. This String is translated into a PointCollection containing Points (0,0), (1,0), (0,1), (1,1) and (0,0). These points are logical points—as described in Section 25.5—on the image. The five points defined here correspond directly to the five points defined in the Positions collection. The image's top-left corner (0,0)—defined first in Texture-Coordinates—is mapped onto the first point in the Positions collection (1,1,0). The bottom-right corner (1,1) of the image—defined fourth in TextureCoordinates—is mapped onto the fourth point in the Positions collection (-1,-1,0). The other two corners are also mapped accordingly to the second and third points. This makes the image fully appear on the bottom surface of the pyramid, since that face is rectangular.

If a point is shared by two adjacent sides, you may not want to map the same point of the image to that particular vertex for the two different sides. To have complete control over how the brush is mapped onto the surfaces of the object, you may need to define a vertex more than once in the Positions collection.

Defining a Camera and a Light Source

The **Camera** property of Viewport3D (lines 30–34) defines a virtual camera for viewing the defined 3-D space. In this example, we use a **PerspectiveCamera** to define what the user sees. We must set the camera's **Position**, **LookDirection** and **UpDirection** (lines 32–33). The Position property requires a **Point3D** object which defines a 3-D point, while the LookDirection and UpDirection require **Vector3D** objects which define vectors in 3-D space. 3-D vectors are defined by an x-, a y- and a z-component (defined in that order in the XAML markup). For instance, the vector applied to the UpDirection is written as "0,0,1" (line 33) and represents a vector with an x- and y-component of 0, and a z-component of 1. This vector points in the positive direction of the z-axis.

The Position defines the location of the camera in the 3-D space. The LookDirection defines the direction in which the camera is pointed. The UpDirection defines the orientation of the camera by specifying the upward direction in the viewport. If the UpDirection in this example were set to "0,0,-1" then the pyramid would appear "upside-down" in the viewport.

Unlike 2-D objects, a 3-D object needs a virtual light source so the camera can actually "see" the 3-D scene. In the Model3DGroup, which groups all of the ModelVisual3D's objects, we define two **DirectionalLight** objects (lines 42–43) to illuminate the pyramid. This control creates uniform rays of light pointing in the direction specified by the **Direction** property. This property receives a vector that points in the direction of the light. You can also define the **Color** property to change the light's color.

Animating the 3-D Object

As with 2-D animations, there is a set of 3-D animations that can be applied to 3-D objects. Lines 47–54 define the **Transform** property of the GeometryModel3D element that models a pyramid. We use the **RotateTransform3D** control to implement a rotation of the pyramid. We then use the **AxisAngleRotation3D** to strictly define the transform's rotation (lines 50–51). The **Angle** and **Axis** properties can be modified to customize the transform. The Angle is initially set to 0 (that is, not rotated) and the Axis of rotation to the z-axis, represented by the vector defined as "0,0,1" (line 51).

To animate the rotation, we created a Storyboard that modifies the Angle property of the AxisAngleRotation3D (lines 17–23). Notice we set the **RepeatBehavior** of the Storyboard to **Forever** (line 18), indicating that the animation repeats continuously while the window is open. This Storyboard is set to begin when the page loads (line 15).

The application contains RadioButtons at the bottom of the window that change the axis of rotation. The code-behind for this functionality appears in Fig. 25.19.

With each RadioButton's Checked event, we change the Axis of rotation to the appropriate Vector3D. We also change the Position of the PerspectiveCamera to give a better view of the rotating object. For instance, when xButton is clicked, we change the axis of rotation to the *x*-axis (line 19) and the camera's position to give a better view (line 20).

```
1   // Fig. 25.19: MainWindow.xaml.cs
2   // Changing the axis of rotation for a 3-D animation.
3   using System.Windows;
4   using System.Windows.Media.Media3D;
5
6   namespace Application3D
7   {
8      public partial class MainWindow : Window
9      {
10        // constructor
11        public MainWindow()
12        {
13           InitializeComponent();
14        } // end constructor
15
16        // when user selects xRadio, set axis of rotation
17        private void xRadio_Checked( object sender, RoutedEventArgs e )
18        {
19           rotation.Axis = new Vector3D( 1, 0, 0 ); // set rotation axis
20           camera.Position = new Point3D( 6, 0, 0 ); // set camera position
21        } // end method xRadio_Checked
22
23        // when user selects yRadio, set axis of rotation
24        private void yRadio_Checked( object sender, RoutedEventArgs e )
25        {
26           rotation.Axis = new Vector3D( 0, 1, 0 ); // set rotation axis
27           camera.Position = new Point3D( 6, 0, 0 ); // set camera position
28        } // end method yRadio_Checked
29
30        // when user selects zRadio, set axis of rotation
31        private void zRadio_Checked( object sender, RoutedEventArgs e )
32        {
33           rotation.Axis = new Vector3D( 0, 0, 1 ); // set rotation axis
34           camera.Position = new Point3D( 6, 0, 1 ); // set camera position
35        } // end method zRadio_Checked
36     } // end class MainWindow
37  } // end namespace Application3D
```

Fig. 25.19 | Changing the axis of rotation for a 3-D animation.

25.10 Speech Synthesis and Speech Recognition

Speech-based interfaces make computers easier to use for people with disabilities (and others). **Speech synthesizers**, or **text-to-speech** (TTS) **systems**, read text out loud and are an ideal method for communicating information to sight-impaired individuals. **Speech recognizers**, or **speech-to-text (STT) systems**, transform human speech (input through a microphone) into text and are a good way to gather input or commands from users who have difficulty with keyboards and mice. .NET 4.0 provides powerful tools for working with speech synthesis and recognition. The program shown in Figs. 25.20–25.21 provides explanations of the various kinds of programming tips found in this book using an STT system (and the mouse) as input and a TTS system (and text) as output.

Our speech application's GUI (Fig. 25.20) consists of a vertical StackPanel containing a TextBox, a Button and a series of horizontal StackPanels containing Images and TextBlocks that label those Images.

```
1   <!-- Fig. 25.20: MainWindow.xaml -->
2   <!-- Text-To-Speech and Speech-To-Text -->
3   <Window x:Class="SpeechApp.MainWindow"
4      xmlns="http://schemas.microsoft.com/winfx/2006/xaml/presentation"
5      xmlns:x="http://schemas.microsoft.com/winfx/2006/xaml"
6      Title="Speech App" Height="580" Width="350">
7      <Grid>
8         <StackPanel Orientation="Vertical">
9            <TextBox x:Name="SpeechBox" Text="Enter text to speak here"/>
10           <Button x:Name="SpeechButton"
11              Content="Click to hear the text above."
12              Click="SpeechButton_Click" />
13           <StackPanel Orientation="Horizontal"
14              HorizontalAlignment="center">
15              <Image Source="images/CPE_100h.gif" Name="ErrorImage"
16                 MouseDown="Image_MouseDown" />
17              <Image Source="images/EPT_100h.gif" Name="PreventionImage"
18                 MouseDown="Image_MouseDown" />
19              <Image Source="images/GPP_100h.gif"
20                 Name="GoodPracticesImage" MouseDown="Image_MouseDown" />
21           </StackPanel>
22           <StackPanel Orientation="Horizontal"
23              HorizontalAlignment="Center">
24              <TextBlock Width="110" Text="Common Programming Errors"
25                 TextWrapping="wrap" TextAlignment="Center"/>
26              <TextBlock Width="110" Text="Error-Prevention Tips"
27                 TextWrapping="wrap" TextAlignment="Center" />
28              <TextBlock Width="110" Text="Good Programming Practices"
29                 TextWrapping="wrap" TextAlignment="Center"/>
30           </StackPanel>
31           <StackPanel Orientation="Horizontal"
32              HorizontalAlignment="center">
33              <Image Source="images/GUI_100h.gif"
34                 Name="LookAndFeelImage" MouseDown="Image_MouseDown" />
35              <Image Source="images/PERF_100h.gif"
36                 Name="PerformanceImage" MouseDown="Image_MouseDown" />
37              <Image Source="images/PORT_100h.gif"
38                 Name="PortabilityImage" MouseDown="Image_MouseDown" />
39           </StackPanel>
```

Fig. 25.20 | Text-To-Speech and Speech-To-Text (XAML). (Part 1 of 2.)

```
40                  <StackPanel Orientation="Horizontal"
41                     HorizontalAlignment="Center">
42                     <TextBlock Width="110" Text="Look-and-Feel Observations"
43                        TextWrapping="wrap" TextAlignment="Center"/>
44                     <TextBlock Width="110" Text="Performance Tips"
45                        TextWrapping="wrap" TextAlignment="Center" />
46                     <TextBlock Width="110" Text="Portability Tips"
47                        TextWrapping="wrap" TextAlignment="Center"/>
48                  </StackPanel>
49                  <Image Source="images/SEO_100h.gif" Height="100" Width="110"
50                     Name="ObservationsImage" MouseDown="Image_MouseDown" />
51                  <TextBlock Width="110" Text="Software Engineering
52                     Observations" TextWrapping="wrap" TextAlignment="Center" />
53                  <TextBlock x:Name="InfoBlock" Margin="5"
54                     Text="Click an icon or say its name to view details."
55                     TextWrapping="Wrap"/>
56               </StackPanel>
57            </Grid>
58         </Window>
```

Fig. 25.20 | Text-To-Speech and Speech-To-Text (XAML). (Part 2 of 2.)

Figure 25.21 provides the speech application's functionality. The user either clicks an Image or speaks its name into a microphone, then the GUI displays a text description of the concept which that image or phrase represents, and a speech synthesizer speaks this description. To use .NET's speech synthesis and recognition classes, you must add a reference to System.Speech to the project as follows:

1. Right click the project name in the **Solution Explorer** then select **Add Reference....**

2. On the .NET tab of the **Add Reference** dialog, locate and select System.Speech and click **OK**.

You must also import the **System.Speech.Synthesis** and **System.Speech.Recognition** namespaces (lines 5–6).

```
 1  // Fig. 25.21: MainWindow.xaml.cs
 2  // Text-To-Speech and Speech-To-Text
 3  using System;
 4  using System.Collections.Generic;
 5  using System.Speech.Synthesis;
 6  using System.Speech.Recognition;
 7  using System.Windows;
 8  using System.Windows.Controls;
 9
10  namespace SpeechApp
11  {
12     public partial class MainWindow : Window
13     {
14        // listens for speech input
15        private SpeechRecognizer listener = new SpeechRecognizer();
16
17        // gives the listener choices of possible input
18        private Grammar myGrammar;
19
20        // sends speech output to the speakers
21        private SpeechSynthesizer talker = new SpeechSynthesizer();
22
23        // keeps track of which description is to be printed and spoken
24        private string displayString;
25
26        // maps images to their descriptions
27        private Dictionary< Image, string > imageDescriptions =
28           new Dictionary< Image, string >();
29
30        // maps input phrases to their descriptions
31        private Dictionary< string, string > phraseDescriptions =
32           new Dictionary< string, string >();
33
34        public MainWindow()
35        {
36           InitializeComponent();
37
38           // define the input phrases
39           string[] phrases = { "Good Programming Practices",
40              "Software Engineering Observations", "Performance Tips",
41              "Portability Tips", "Look-And-Feel Observations",
42              "Error-Prevention Tips", "Common Programming Errors" };
43
44           // add the phrases to a Choices collection
45           Choices theChoices = new Choices( phrases );
46
```

Fig. 25.21 | Text-To-Speech and Speech-To-Text code-behind. (Part 1 of 3.)

```
47              // build a Grammar around the Choices and set up the
48              // listener to use this grammar
49              myGrammar = new Grammar( new GrammarBuilder( theChoices ) );
50              listener.Enabled = true;
51              listener.LoadGrammar( myGrammar );
52              myGrammar.SpeechRecognized += myGrammar_SpeechRecognized;
53
54              // define the descriptions for each icon/phrase
55              string[] descriptions = {
56                 "Good Programming Practices highlight " +
57                    "techniques for writing programs that are clearer, more " +
58                    "understandable, more debuggable, and more maintainable.",
59                 "Software Engineering Observations highlight " +
60                    "architectural and design issues that affect the " +
61                    "construction of complex software systems.",
62                 "Performance Tips highlight opportunities " +
63                    "for improving program performance.",
64                 "Portability Tips help students write " +
65                    "portable code that can execute on different platforms.",
66                 "Look-and-Feel Observations highlight " +
67                    "graphical user interface conventions. These " +
68                    "observations help students design their own graphical " +
69                    "user interfaces in conformance with industry standards.",
70                 "Error-Prevention Tips tell people how to " +
71                    "test and debug their programs. Many of the tips also " +
72                    "describe aspects of creating programs that " +
73                    "reduce the likelihood of 'bugs' and thus simplify the " +
74                    "testing and debugging process.",
75                 "Common Programming Errors focus the " +
76                    "students' attention on errors commonly made by " +
77                    "beginning programmers. This helps students avoid " +
78                    "making the same errors. It also helps reduce the long " +
79                    "lines outside instructors' offices during " +
80                    "office hours!" };
81
82           // map each image to its corresponding description
83           imageDescriptions.Add( GoodPracticesImage, descriptions[ 0 ] );
84           imageDescriptions.Add( ObservationsImage, descriptions[ 1 ] );
85           imageDescriptions.Add( PerformanceImage, descriptions[ 2 ] );
86           imageDescriptions.Add( PortabilityImage, descriptions[ 3 ] );
87           imageDescriptions.Add( LookAndFeelImage, descriptions[ 4 ] );
88           imageDescriptions.Add( PreventionImage, descriptions[ 5 ] );
89           imageDescriptions.Add( ErrorImage, descriptions[ 6 ] );
90
91           // loop through the phrases and descriptions and map accordingly
92           for ( int index = 0; index <= 6; ++index )
93              phraseDescriptions.Add( phrases[ index ],
94                 descriptions[ index ] );
95
96           talker.Rate = -4; // slows down the speaking rate
97        } // end constructor
98
```

Fig. 25.21 | Text-To-Speech and Speech-To-Text code-behind. (Part 2 of 3.)

```
 99          // when the user clicks on the speech-synthesis button, speak the
100          // contents of the related text box
101          private void SpeechButton_Click( object sender, RoutedEventArgs e )
102          {
103             talker.SpeakAsync( SpeechBox.Text );
104          } // end method SpeechButton_Click
105
106          private void Image_MouseDown( object sender,
107             System.Windows.Input.MouseButtonEventArgs e )
108          {
109             // use the image-to-description dictionary to get the
110             // appropriate description for the clicked image
111             displayString = imageDescriptions[ (Image) sender ];
112             DisplaySpeak();
113          } // end method Image_MouseDown
114
115          // when the listener recognizes a phrase from the grammar, set the
116          // display string and call DisplaySpeak
117          void myGrammar_SpeechRecognized(
118             object sender, RecognitionEventArgs e )
119          {
120             // Use the phrase-to-description dictionary to get the
121             // appropriate description for the spoken phrase
122             displayString = phraseDescriptions[ e.Result.Text ];
123
124             // Use the dispatcher to call DisplaySpeak
125             this.Dispatcher.BeginInvoke(
126                new Action( DisplaySpeak ) );
127          } // end method myGrammar_SpeechRecognized
128
129          // Set the appropriate text block to the display string
130          // and order the synthesizer to speak it
131          void DisplaySpeak()
132          {
133             InfoBlock.Text = displayString;
134             talker.SpeakAsync( displayString );
135          } // end method DisplaySpeak
136       } // end class MainWindow
137    } // end namespace SpeechApp
```

Fig. 25.21 | Text-To-Speech and Speech-To-Text code-behind. (Part 3 of 3.)

Instance Variables

You can now add instance variables of types **SpeechRecognizer**, **Grammar** and **Speech-Synthesizer** (lines 15, 18 and 21). The SpeechRecognizer class has several ways to recognize input phrases. The most reliable involves building a Grammar containing the exact phrases that the SpeechRecognizer can receive as spoken input. The SpeechSynthesizer object speaks text, using one of several voices. Variable displayString (line 24) keeps track of the description that will be displayed and spoken. Lines 27–28 and 31–32 declare two objects of type **Dictionary** (namespace System.Collections.Generic). A Dictionary is a collection of key/value pairs, in which each key has a corresponding value. The Dictionary imageDescriptions contains pairs of Images and strings, and the Dictionary phraseDescriptions contains pairs of strings and strings. These Dictionary objects associate each input phrase and each clickable Image with the corresponding description phrase to be displayed and spoken.

Constructor

In the constructor (lines 34–97), the application initializes the input phrases and places them in a **Choices** collection (lines 39–45). A Choices collection is used to build a Grammar (lines 49–51). Line 52 registers the listener for the Grammar's SpeechRecognized event. Lines 55–80 create an array of the programming-tip descriptions. Lines 83–89 add each image and its corresponding description to the imageDescriptions Dictionary. Lines 92–94 add each programming-tip name and corresponding description to the phraseDescriptions Dictionary. Finally, line 96 sets the SpeechSynthesizer object's Rate property to -4 to slow down the default rate of speech.

Method SpeechButton_Click

Method SpeechButton_Click (lines 101–104) calls the SpeechSynthesizer's Speak-Async method to speak the contents of SpeechBox. SpeechSynthesizers also have a Speak method, which is not asynchronous, and SpeakSsml and SpeakSsmlAsynch, methods specifically for use with Speech Synthesis Markup Language (SSML)—an XML vocabulary created particularly for TTS systems. For more information on SSML, visit www.xml.com/pub/a/2004/10/20/ssml.html.

Method Image_MouseDown

Method Image_MouseDown (lines 106–113) handles the MouseDown events for all the Image objects. When the user clicks an Image, the program casts sender to type Image, then passes the results as input into the imageDescriptions Dictionary to retrieve the corresponding description string. This string is assigned to displayString (line 111). We then call DisplaySpeak to display displayString at the bottom of the window and cause the SpeechSynthesizer to speak it.

Method myGrammar_SpeechRecognized

Method myGrammar_SpeechRecognized (lines 117–127) is called whenever the Speech-Recognizer detects that one of the input phrases defined in myGrammar was spoken. The Result property of the RecognitionEventArgs parameter contains the recognized text. We use the phraseDescriptions Dictionary object to determine which description to display (line 122). We cannot call DisplaySpeak directly here, because GUI events and the SpeechRecognizer events operate on different **threads**—they are processes being executed in parallel, independently from one another and without access to each other's methods. Every method that modifies the GUI must be called via the GUI thread of execution. To do this, we use a **Dispatcher** object (lines 125–126) to invoke the method. The method to call must be wrapped in a so-called delegate object. An Action delegate object represents a method with no parameters.

Method DisplaySpeak

Method DisplaySpeak (lines 131–135) outputs displayString to the screen by updating InfoBlock's Text property and to the speakers by calling the SpeechSynthesizer's SpeakAsync method.

25.11 Wrap-Up

In this chapter you learned how to manipulate graphic elements in your WPF application. We introduced how to control fonts using the properties of TextBlocks. You learned to change the TextBlock's FontFamily, FontSize, FontWeight and FontStyle in XAML. We also demonstrated the TextDecorations Underline, Overline, Baseline and Strikethrough. Next, you learned how to create basic shapes such as Lines, Rectangles and Ellipses. You set the Fill and Stroke of these shapes. We then discussed an application that created a Polyline and two Polygons. These controls allow you to create multisided objects using a set of Points in a PointCollection.

You learned that there are several types of brushes for customizing an object's Fill. We demonstrated the SolidColorBrush, the ImageBrush, the VisualBrush and the LinearGradientBrush. Though the VisualBrush was used only with a MediaElement, this brush has a wide range of capabilities.

We explained how to apply transforms to an object to reposition or reorient any graphic element. You used transforms such as the TranslateTransform, the RotateTransform, the SkewTransform and the ScaleTransform to manipulate various controls.

The television GUI application used ControlTemplates and BitmapEffects to create a completely customized 3-D-looking television set. You saw how to use ControlTemplates to customize the look of RadioButtons and CheckBoxes. The application also included an opacity mask, which can be used on any shape to define the opaque or transparent regions of the control. Opacity masks are particularly useful with images and video where you cannot change the Fill to directly control transparency.

We showed how animations can be applied to transition properties from one value to another. Common 2-D animation types include DoubleAnimations, PointAnimations and ColorAnimations.

You learned how to create a 3-D space using a Viewport3D control. You saw how to model 3-D objects as sets of triangles using the MeshGeometry3D control. The ImageBrush, which was previously applied to a 2-D object, was used to display a book-cover image on the surface of the 3-D pyramid using GeometryModel3D's mapping techniques. We discussed how to include lighting and camera objects in your Viewport3D to modify the view shown in the application. We showed how similar transforms and animations are in 2-D and 3-D.

Finally, we introduced the speech synthesis and speech recognition APIs. You learned how to make the computer speak text and how to receive voice input. You also learned how to create a Grammar of phrases that the user can speak to control the program. In Chapter 26, we discuss XML and LINQ to XML.

26

XML and LINQ to XML

Like everything metaphysical, the harmony between thought and reality is to be found in the grammar of the language.
—Ludwig Wittgenstein

I played with an idea, and grew willful; tossed it into the air; transformed it; let it escape and recaptured it; made it iridescent with fancy, and winged it with paradox.
—Oscar Wilde

OBJECTIVES

In this chapter you'll learn:

- To specify and validate an XML document's structure.

- To create and use simple XSL style sheets to render XML document data.

- To use the Document Object Model (DOM) to manipulate XML in C# programs.

- To use LINQ to XML to extract and manipulate data from XML documents.

- To create new XML documents using the classes provided by the .NET Framework.

- To work with XML namespaces in your C# code.

- To transform XML documents into XHTML using class `XslCompiledTransform`.

26.1 Introduction

In Chapter 24, we began our introduction to XML to help explain the syntax of XAML (eXtensible Application Markup Language). You learned the syntax of XML, how to use XML namespaces and were introduced to the concept of DTDs and schemas. In this chapter, you learn how to create your own DTDs (Section 26.2) and schemas (Section 26.3) to validate your XML documents.

The .NET Framework uses XML extensively. Many of the configuration files that Visual Studio creates—such as those that represent project settings—use XML format. XML is also used heavily in serialization, as you'll see in Chapter 28, Web Services. You've already used XAML—an XML vocabulary used for creating user interfaces—in Chapters 24–25. XAML is also used in Chapter 29, Silverlight and Rich Internet Applications.

Sections 26.4–26.8 demonstrate techniques for working with XML documents in C# applications. Visual C# provides language features and .NET Framework classes for working with XML. **LINQ to XML** provides a convenient way to manipulate data in XML documents using the same LINQ syntax you used on arrays and collections in Chapter 9. LINQ to XML also provides a set of classes for easily navigating and creating XML documents in your code.

26.2 Document Type Definitions (DTDs)

Document Type Definitions (DTDs) are one of two techniques you can use to specify XML document structure. Section 26.3 presents W3C XML Schema documents, which provide an improved method of specifying XML document structure.

Software Engineering Observation 26.1

XML documents can have many different structures, and for this reason an application cannot be certain whether a particular document it receives is complete, ordered properly, and not missing data. DTDs and schemas (Section 26.3) solve this problem by providing an extensible way to describe XML document structure. Applications should use DTDs or schemas to confirm whether XML documents are valid.

Software Engineering Observation 26.2

*Many organizations and individuals are creating DTDs and schemas for a broad range of applications. These collections—called **repositories**—are available free for download from the web (e.g., www.xml.org, www.oasis-open.org).*

Creating a Document Type Definition
Figure 24.4 presented a simple business letter marked up with XML. Recall that line 5 of
`letter.xml` references a DTD—`letter.dtd` (Fig. 26.1). This DTD specifies the business
letter's element types and attributes and their relationships to one another.

```
 1   <!-- Fig. 26.1: letter.dtd        -->
 2   <!-- DTD document for letter.xml -->
 3
 4   <!ELEMENT letter ( contact+, salutation, paragraph+,
 5      closing, signature )>
 6
 7   <!ELEMENT contact ( name, address1, address2, city, state,
 8      zip, phone, flag )>
 9   <!ATTLIST contact type CDATA #IMPLIED>
10
11   <!ELEMENT name ( #PCDATA )>
12   <!ELEMENT address1 ( #PCDATA )>
13   <!ELEMENT address2 ( #PCDATA )>
14   <!ELEMENT city ( #PCDATA )>
15   <!ELEMENT state ( #PCDATA )>
16   <!ELEMENT zip ( #PCDATA )>
17   <!ELEMENT phone ( #PCDATA )>
18   <!ELEMENT flag EMPTY>
19   <!ATTLIST flag gender (M | F) "M">
20
21   <!ELEMENT salutation ( #PCDATA )>
22   <!ELEMENT closing ( #PCDATA )>
23   <!ELEMENT paragraph ( #PCDATA )>
24   <!ELEMENT signature ( #PCDATA )>
```

Fig. 26.1 | Document Type Definition (DTD) for a business letter.

A DTD describes the structure of an XML document and enables an XML parser to
verify whether an XML document is valid (i.e., whether its elements contain the proper
attributes and appear in the proper sequence). DTDs allow users to check document structure and to exchange data in a standardized format. A DTD expresses the set of rules for
document structure by specifying what attributes and other elements may appear inside a
given element.

Common Programming Error 26.1
*For documents validated with DTDs, any document that uses elements, attributes or re-
lationships not explicitly defined by a DTD is an invalid document.*

Defining Elements in a DTD
The **ELEMENT element type declaration** in lines 4–5 defines the rules for element `letter`.
In this case, `letter` contains one or more `contact` elements, one `salutation` element, one
or more paragraph elements, one `closing` element and one `signature` element, in that
sequence. The **plus sign (+) occurrence indicator** specifies that the DTD allows one or
more occurrences of an element. Other occurrence indicators include the **asterisk** (*),
which indicates an optional element that can occur zero or more times, and the **question**

mark (?), which indicates an optional element that can occur at most once (i.e., zero or one occurrence). If an element does not have an occurrence indicator, the DTD allows exactly one occurrence.

The contact element type declaration (lines 7–8) specifies that a contact element contains child elements name, address1, address2, city, state, zip, phone and flag—in that order. The DTD requires exactly one occurrence of each of these elements.

Defining Attributes in a DTD

Line 9 uses the **ATTLIST attribute-list declaration** to define an attribute named type for the contact element. Keyword **#IMPLIED** specifies that the type attribute of the contact element is optional—a missing type attribute will not invalidate the document. Other keywords that can be used in place of #IMPLIED in an ATTLIST declaration include #RE-QUIRED and #FIXED. Keyword **#REQUIRED** specifies that the attribute must be present in the element, and keyword **#FIXED** specifies that the attribute (if present) must have the given fixed value. For example,

```
<!ATTLIST address zip CDATA #FIXED "01757">
```

indicates that attribute zip (if present in element address) must have the value 01757 for the document to be valid. If the attribute is not present, then the parser, by default, uses the fixed value that the ATTLIST declaration specifies. You can supply a default value instead of one of these keywords. Doing so makes the attribute optional, but the default value will be used if the attribute's value is not specified.

Character Data vs. Parsed Character Data

Keyword **CDATA** (line 9) specifies that attribute type contains **character data** (i.e., a string). A parser will pass such data to an application without modification.

Software Engineering Observation 26.3

DTD syntax cannot describe an element's (or attribute's) type. For example, a DTD cannot specify that a particular element or attribute can contain only integer data.

Keyword **#PCDATA** (line 11) specifies that an element (e.g., name) may contain **parsed character data** (i.e., data that is processed by an XML parser). Elements with parsed character data cannot contain markup characters, such as less than (<), greater than (>) or ampersand (&). The document author should replace any markup character in a #PCDATA element with the character's corresponding **character entity reference**. For example, the character entity reference < should be used in place of the less-than symbol (<), and the character entity reference > should be used in place of the greater-than symbol (>). A document author who wishes to use a literal ampersand should use the entity reference & instead—parsed character data can contain ampersands (&) only for inserting entities. The final two entities defined by XML are ' and ", representing the single (') and double (") quote characters, respectively.

Common Programming Error 26.2

Using markup characters (e.g., <, > and &) in parsed character data is an error. Use character entity references (e.g., <, > and & instead).

Defining Empty Elements in a DTD

Line 18 defines an empty element named flag. Keyword **EMPTY** specifies that the element does not contain any data between its start and end tags. Empty elements commonly describe data via attributes. For example, flag's data appears in its gender attribute (line 19). Line 19 specifies that the gender attribute's value must be one of the enumerated values (M or F) enclosed in parentheses and delimited by a vertical bar (|) meaning "or." Line 19 also indicates that gender has a default value of M.

Well-Formed Documents vs. Valid Documents

Recall that a well-formed document is syntactically correct (i.e., each start tag has a corresponding end tag, the document contains only one root element, and so on), and a valid document contains the proper elements with the proper attributes in the proper sequence. An XML document cannot be valid unless it is well formed.

Visual Studio can validate XML documents against both DTDs and schemas. You do not have to create a project to use this facility—simply open the XML file in Visual Studio as in Fig. 26.2. If the DTD or schema referenced in the XML document can be retrieved, Visual Studio will automatically validate the XML. If the XML file does not validate, Visual Studio will display a warning just as it does with errors in your C# code. Visit www.w3.org/XML/Schema for a list of additional validation tools.

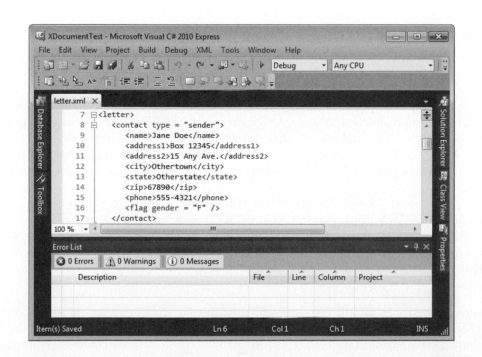

Fig. 26.2 | An XML file open in the Visual C# IDE. (Part 1 of 2.)

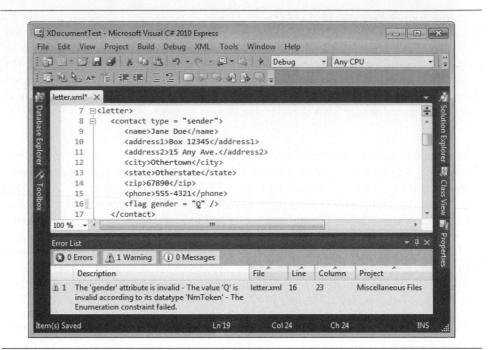

Fig. 26.2 | An XML file open in the Visual C# IDE. (Part 2 of 2.)

26.3 W3C XML Schema Documents

In this section, we introduce schemas for specifying XML document structure and validating XML documents. Many developers in the XML community believe that DTDs are not flexible enough to meet today's programming needs. For example, DTDs lack a way of indicating what specific type of data (e.g., numeric, text) an element can contain, and DTDs are not themselves XML documents, making it difficult to manipulate them programmatically. These and other limitations have led to the development of schemas.

Unlike DTDs, schemas use XML syntax and are actually XML documents that programs can manipulate. Like DTDs, schemas are used by validating parsers to validate documents.

In this section, we focus on the W3C's **XML Schema** vocabulary. For the latest information on XML Schema, visit www.w3.org/XML/Schema. For tutorials on XML Schema concepts beyond what we present here, visit www.w3schools.com/schema/default.asp.

A DTD describes an XML document's structure, not the content of its elements. For example,

> `<quantity>`5`</quantity>`

contains character data. If the document that contains element `quantity` references a DTD, an XML parser can validate the document to confirm that this element indeed does contain PCDATA content. However, the parser cannot validate that the content is numeric; DTDs do not provide this capability. So, unfortunately, the parser also considers

> `<quantity>`hello`</quantity>`

to be valid. An application that uses the XML document containing this markup should test that the data in element `quantity` is numeric and take appropriate action if it is not.

XML Schema enables schema authors to specify that element `quantity`'s data must be numeric or, even more specifically, an integer. A parser validating the XML document against this schema can determine that 5 conforms and `hello` does not. An XML document that conforms to a schema document is **schema valid**, and one that does not conform is **schema invalid**. Schemas are XML documents and therefore must themselves be valid.

Validating Against an XML Schema Document

Figure 26.3 shows a schema-valid XML document named `book.xml`, and Fig. 26.4 shows the pertinent XML Schema document (`book.xsd`) that defines the structure for `book.xml`. By convention, schemas use the **.xsd** extension. Recall that Visual Studio can perform schema validation if it can locate the schema document. Visual Studio can locate a schema if it is specified in the XML document, is in the same solution or is simply open in Visual Studio at the same time as the XML document. To validate the schema document itself (i.e., `book.xsd`) and produce the output shown in Fig. 26.4, we used an online XSV (XML Schema Validator) provided by the W3C at

    `www.w3.org/2001/03/webdata/xsv`

These tools enforce the W3C's specifications regarding XML Schemas and schema validation. Figure 26.3 contains markup describing several books. The `books` element (line 5) has the namespace prefix `deitel` (declared in line 5), indicating that the `books` element is a part of the namespace `http://www.deitel.com/booklist`.

```
 1   <?xml version = "1.0"?>
 2   <!-- Fig. 26.3: book.xml -->
 3   <!-- Book list marked up as XML -->
 4
 5   <deitel:books xmlns:deitel = "http://www.deitel.com/booklist">
 6      <book>
 7         <title>Visual Basic 2008 How to Program</title>
 8      </book>
 9
10      <book>
11         <title>Visual C# 2008 How to Program, 3/e</title>
12      </book>
13
14      <book>
15         <title>Java How to Program, 7/e</title>
16      </book>
17
18      <book>
19         <title>C++ How to Program, 6/e</title>
20      </book>
21
22      <book>
23         <title>Internet and World Wide Web How to Program, 4/e</title>
24      </book>
25   </deitel:books>
```

Fig. 26.3 | Schema-valid XML document describing a list of books.

Creating an XML Schema Document

Figure 26.4 presents the XML Schema document that specifies the structure of book.xml (Fig. 26.3). This document defines an XML-based language (i.e., a vocabulary) for writing XML documents about collections of books. The schema defines the elements, attributes and parent-child relationships that such a document can (or must) include. The schema also specifies the type of data that these elements and attributes may contain.

```
 1   <?xml version = "1.0"?>
 2   <!-- Fig. 26.4: book.xsd          -->
 3   <!-- Simple W3C XML Schema document -->
 4
 5   <schema xmlns = "http://www.w3.org/2001/XMLSchema"
 6      xmlns:deitel = "http://www.deitel.com/booklist"
 7      targetNamespace = "http://www.deitel.com/booklist">
 8
 9      <element name = "books" type = "deitel:BooksType"/>
10
11      <complexType name = "BooksType">
12         <sequence>
13            <element name = "book" type = "deitel:SingleBookType"
14               minOccurs = "1" maxOccurs = "unbounded"/>
15         </sequence>
16      </complexType>
17
18      <complexType name = "SingleBookType">
19         <sequence>
20            <element name = "title" type = "string"/>
21         </sequence>
22      </complexType>
23   </schema>
```

Fig. 26.4 | XML Schema document for book.xml.

Root element **schema** (Fig. 26.4, lines 5–23) contains elements that define the structure of an XML document such as book.xml. Line 5 specifies as the default namespace the standard W3C XML Schema namespace URI—**http://www.w3.org/2001/XMLSchema**. This namespace contains predefined elements (e.g., root element schema) that comprise the XML Schema vocabulary—the language used to write an XML Schema document.

Portability Tip 26.1
W3C XML Schema authors specify URI http://www.w3.org/2001/XMLSchema *when referring to the XML Schema namespace. This namespace contains predefined elements that comprise the XML Schema vocabulary. Specifying this URI ensures that validation tools correctly identify XML Schema elements and do not confuse them with those defined by document authors.*

Line 6 binds the URI http://www.deitel.com/booklist to namespace prefix deitel. As we discuss momentarily, the schema uses this namespace to differentiate names created by us from names that are part of the XML Schema namespace. Line 7 also specifies http://www.deitel.com/booklist as the **targetNamespace** of the schema. This attribute identifies the namespace of the XML vocabulary that this schema defines. The targetNamespace of book.xsd is the same as the namespace referenced in line 5 of book.xml (Fig. 26.3). This is what "connects" the XML document with the schema that defines its structure. When an XML schema validator examines book.xml and book.xsd, it will recognize that book.xml uses elements and attributes from the http://www.deitel.com/booklist namespace. The validator also will recognize that this namespace is the one defined in book.xsd (i.e., the schema's targetNamespace). Thus the validator knows where to look for the structural rules for the elements and attributes used in book.xml.

Defining an Element in XML Schema
In XML Schema, the **element** tag (line 9) defines an element to be included in an XML document that conforms to the schema. In other words, element specifies the actual *elements* that can be used to mark up data. Line 9 defines the books element, which we use as the root element in book.xml (Fig. 26.3). Attributes **name** and **type** specify the element's name and type, respectively. An element's type attribute indicates the data type that the element may contain. Possible types include XML Schema–defined types (e.g., string, double) and user-defined types (e.g., BooksType, which is defined in lines 11–16). Figure 26.5 lists several of XML Schema's many built-in types. For a complete list of built-in types, see Section 3 of the specification found at www.w3.org/TR/xmlschema-2.

In this example, books is defined as an element of type deitel:BooksType (line 9). BooksType is a user-defined type (lines 11–16) in the http://www.deitel.com/booklist namespace and therefore must have the namespace prefix deitel. It is not an existing XML Schema type.

Two categories of types exist in XML Schema—**simple types** and **complex types**. They differ only in that simple types cannot contain attributes or child elements and complex types can.

A user-defined type that contains attributes or child elements must be defined as a complex type. Lines 11–16 use element **complexType** to define BooksType as a complex type that has a child element named book. The sequence element (lines 12–15) allows you to specify the sequential order in which child elements must appear. The element (lines 13–14) nested within the complexType element indicates that a BooksType element (e.g., books) can contain child elements named book of type deitel:SingleBookType (defined in lines 18–22). Attribute **minOccurs** (line 14), with value 1, specifies that elements of type BooksType must contain a minimum of one book element. Attribute **maxOccurs** (line 14), with value **unbounded**, specifies that elements of type BooksType may have any number of book child elements. Both of these attributes have default values of 1.

Lines 18–22 define the complex type `SingleBookType`. An element of this type contains a child element named `title`. Line 20 defines element `title` to be of simple type `string`. Recall that elements of a simple type cannot contain attributes or child elements. The `schema` end tag (`</schema>`, line 23) declares the end of the XML Schema document.

A Closer Look at Types in XML Schema

Every element in XML Schema has a type. Types include the built-in types provided by XML Schema (Fig. 26.5) or user-defined types (e.g., `SingleBookType` in Fig. 26.4).

Type	Description	Ranges or structures	Examples
string	A character string.		`hello`
boolean	True or false.	`true`, `false`	`true`
decimal	A decimal numeral.	$i * (10^n)$, where i is an integer and n is an integer that is less than or equal to zero.	`5, -12, -45.78`
float	A floating-point number.	$m * (2^e)$, where m is an integer whose absolute value is less than 2^{24} and e is an integer in the range -149 to 104. Plus three additional numbers: positive infinity (`INF`), negative infinity (`-INF`) and not-a-number (`NaN`).	`0, 12, -109.375, NaN`
double	A floating-point number.	$m * (2^e)$, where m is an integer whose absolute value is less than 2^{53} and e is an integer in the range -1075 to 970. Plus three additional numbers: positive infinity, negative infinity and not-a-number.	`0, 12, -109.375, NaN`
long	A whole number.	-9223372036854775808 to 9223372036854775807, inclusive.	`1234567890, -1234567890`
int	A whole number.	-2147483648 to 2147483647, inclusive.	`1234567890, -1234567890`
short	A whole number.	-32768 to 32767, inclusive.	`12, -345`
date	A date consisting of a year, month and day.	yyyy-mm with an optional dd and an optional time zone, where yyyy is four digits long and mm and dd are two digits long. The time zone is specified as +hh:mm or -hh:mm, giving an offset in hours and minutes.	`2008-07-25+01:00`
time	A time consisting of hours, minutes and seconds.	hh:mm:ss with an optional time zone, where hh, mm and ss are two digits long.	`16:30:25-05:00`

Fig. 26.5 | Some XML Schema types.

Every simple type defines a **restriction** on an XML Schema-defined type or a restriction on a user-defined type. Restrictions limit the possible values that an element can hold.

Complex types are divided into two groups—those with **simple content** and those with **complex content**. Both can contain attributes, but only complex content can contain child elements. Complex types with simple content must extend or restrict some other existing type. Complex types with complex content do not have this limitation. We demonstrate complex types with each kind of content in the next example.

The schema in Fig. 26.6 creates simple types and complex types. The XML document in Fig. 26.7 (`laptop.xml`) follows the structure defined in Fig. 26.6 to describe parts of a laptop computer. A document such as `laptop.xml` that conforms to a schema is known as an **XML instance document**—the document is an instance (i.e., example) of the schema.

```
 1   <?xml version = "1.0"?>
 2   <!-- Fig. 26.6: computer.xsd -->
 3   <!-- W3C XML Schema document -->
 4
 5   <schema xmlns = "http://www.w3.org/2001/XMLSchema"
 6      xmlns:computer = "http://www.deitel.com/computer"
 7      targetNamespace = "http://www.deitel.com/computer">
 8
 9      <simpleType name = "gigahertz">
10         <restriction base = "decimal">
11            <minInclusive value = "2.1"/>
12         </restriction>
13      </simpleType>
14
15      <complexType name = "CPU">
16         <simpleContent>
17            <extension base = "string">
18               <attribute name = "model" type = "string"/>
19            </extension>
20         </simpleContent>
21      </complexType>
22
23      <complexType name = "portable">
24         <all>
25            <element name = "processor" type = "computer:CPU"/>
26            <element name = "monitor" type = "int"/>
27            <element name = "CPUSpeed" type = "computer:gigahertz"/>
28            <element name = "RAM" type = "int"/>
29         </all>
30         <attribute name = "manufacturer" type = "string"/>
31      </complexType>
32
33      <element name = "laptop" type = "computer:portable"/>
34   </schema>
```

Fig. 26.6 | XML Schema document defining simple and complex types.

Line 5 (Fig. 26.6) declares the default namespace as the standard XML Schema namespace—any elements without a prefix are assumed to be in the XML Schema namespace. Line 6 binds the namespace prefix `computer` to the namespace `http://www.deitel.com/computer`. Line 7 identifies this namespace as the `targetNamespace`—the namespace being defined by the current XML Schema document.

To design the XML elements for describing laptop computers, we first create a simple type in lines 9–13 using the **simpleType** element. We name this simpleType gigahertz because it will be used to describe the clock speed of the processor in gigahertz. Simple types are restrictions of a type typically called a **base type**. For this simpleType, line 10 declares the base type as decimal, and we restrict the value to be at least 2.1 by using the **minInclusive** element in line 11.

Next, we declare a complexType named CPU that has **simpleContent** (lines 16–20). Remember that a complex type with simple content can have attributes but not child elements. Also recall that complex types with simple content must extend or restrict some XML Schema type or user-defined type. The **extension** element with attribute **base** (line 17) sets the base type to string. In this complexType, we extend the base type string with an attribute. The **attribute** element (line 18) gives the complexType an attribute of type string named model. Thus an element of type CPU must contain string text (because the base type is string) and may contain a model attribute that is also of type string.

Last, we define type portable, which is a complexType with complex content (lines 23–31). Such types are allowed to have child elements and attributes. The element **all** (lines 24–29) encloses elements that must each be included once in the corresponding XML instance document. These elements can be included in any order. This complex type holds four elements—processor, monitor, CPUSpeed and RAM. They're given types CPU, int, gigahertz and int, respectively. When using types CPU and gigahertz, we must include the namespace prefix computer, because these user-defined types are part of the computer namespace (http://www.deitel.com/computer)—the namespace defined in the current document (line 7). Also, portable contains an attribute defined in line 30. The **attribute** element indicates that elements of type portable contain an attribute of type string named manufacturer.

Line 33 declares the actual element that uses the three types defined in the schema. The element is called laptop and is of type portable. We must use the namespace prefix computer in front of portable.

We have now created an element named laptop that contains child elements processor, monitor, CPUSpeed and RAM, and an attribute manufacturer. Figure 26.7 uses the laptop element defined in the computer.xsd schema. We used Visual Studio's built-in schema validation to ensure that this XML instance document adheres to the schema's structural rules.

```xml
1   <?xml version = "1.0"?>
2   <!-- Fig. 26.7: laptop.xml                      -->
3   <!-- Laptop components marked up as XML -->
4
5   <computer:laptop xmlns:computer = "http://www.deitel.com/computer"
6       manufacturer = "IBM">
7
8       <processor model = "Centrino">Intel</processor>
9       <monitor>17</monitor>
10      <CPUSpeed>2.4</CPUSpeed>
11      <RAM>256</RAM>
12  </computer:laptop>
```

Fig. 26.7 | XML document using the laptop element defined in computer.xsd.

Line 5 declares namespace prefix `computer`. The `laptop` element requires this prefix because it is part of the `http://www.deitel.com/computer` namespace. Line 6 sets the laptop's `manufacturer` attribute, and lines 8–11 use the elements defined in the schema to describe the laptop's characteristics.

Automatically Creating Schemas using Visual Studio

Visual Studio includes a tool that allows you to create a schema from an existing XML document, using the document as a template. With an XML document open, select **XML > Create Schema** to use this feature. A new schema file opens that conforms to the standards of the XML document. You can now save it and add it to the project.

> **Good Programming Practice 26.1**
> *The schema generated by Visual Studio is a good starting point, but you should refine the restrictions and types it specifies so they're appropriate for your XML documents.*

26.4 Extensible Stylesheet Language and XSL Transformations

Extensible Stylesheet Language (XSL) documents specify how programs are to render XML document data. XSL is a group of three technologies—**XSL-FO** (**XSL Formatting Objects**), **XPath** (**XML Path Language**) and **XSLT** (**XSL Transformations**). XSL-FO is a vocabulary for specifying formatting, and XPath is a string-based language of expressions used by XML and many of its related technologies for effectively and efficiently locating structures and data (such as specific elements and attributes) in XML documents.

The third portion of XSL—XSL Transformations (XSLT)—is a technology for transforming XML documents into other documents—i.e., transforming the structure of the XML document data to another structure. XSLT provides elements that define rules for transforming one XML document to produce a different XML document. This is useful when you want to use data in multiple applications or on multiple platforms, each of which may be designed to work with documents written in a particular vocabulary. For example, XSLT allows you to convert a simple XML document to an **XHTML** (**Extensible HyperText Markup Language**) document that presents the XML document's data (or a subset of the data) formatted for display in a web browser. (See Fig. 26.8 for a sample "before" and "after" view of such a transformation.) XHTML is the W3C technical recommendation that replaces HTML for marking up web content. For more information on XHTML, visit `www.deitel.com/xhtml/`.

Transforming an XML document using XSLT involves two tree structures—the **source tree** (i.e., the XML document to be transformed) and the **result tree** (i.e., the XML document to be created). XPath is used to locate parts of the source-tree document that match **templates** defined in an **XSL style sheet**. When a match occurs (i.e., a node matches a template), the matching template executes and adds its result to the result tree. When there are no more matches, XSLT has transformed the source tree into the result tree. The XSLT does not analyze every node of the source tree; it selectively navigates the source tree using XSLT's `select` and `match` attributes. For XSLT to function, the source tree must be properly structured. Schemas, DTDs and validating parsers can validate document structure before using XPath and XSLTs.

A Simple XSL Example

Figure 26.8 lists an XML document that describes various sports. The output shows the result of the transformation (specified in the XSLT template of Fig. 26.9) rendered by Internet Explorer 7. Right click with the page open in Internet Explorer and select **View Source** to view the generated XHTML.

```
1   <?xml version = "1.0"?>
2   <?xml-stylesheet type = "text/xsl" href = "sports.xsl"?>
3
4   <!-- Fig. 26.8: sports.xml -->
5   <!-- Sports Database -->
6
7   <sports>
8      <game id = "783">
9         <name>Cricket</name>
10
11         <paragraph>
12            More popular among Commonwealth nations.
13         </paragraph>
14      </game>
15
16      <game id = "239">
17         <name>Baseball</name>
18
19         <paragraph>
20            More popular in America.
21         </paragraph>
22      </game>
23
24      <game id = "418">
25         <name>Soccer (Futbol)</name>
26
27         <paragraph>
28            Most popular sport in the world.
29         </paragraph>
30      </game>
31   </sports>
```

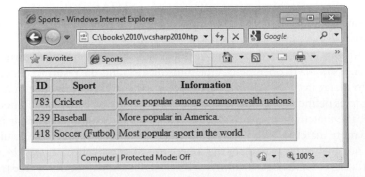

Fig. 26.8 | XML document that describes various sports.

To perform transformations, an XSLT processor is required. Popular XSLT processors include Microsoft's MSXML, the Apache Software Foundation's **Xalan** (xalan.apache.org) and the XslCompiledTransform class from the .NET Framework that we use in Section 26.8. The XML document shown in Fig. 26.8 is transformed into an XHTML document by MSXML when the document is loaded in Internet Explorer. MSXML is both an XML parser and an XSLT processor.

Line 2 (Fig. 26.8) is a **processing instruction** (**PI**) that references the XSL style sheet sports.xsl (Fig. 26.9). A processing instruction is embedded in an XML document and provides application-specific information to whichever XML processor the application uses. In this particular case, the processing instruction specifies the location of an XSLT document with which to transform the XML document. The characters **<?** and **?>** (line 2, Fig. 26.8) delimit a processing instruction, which consists of a **PI target** (e.g., xml-stylesheet) and a **PI value** (e.g., type = "text/xsl" href = "sports.xsl"). The PI value's type attribute specifies that sports.xsl is a text/xsl file (i.e., a text file containing XSL content). The href attribute specifies the name and location of the style sheet to apply—in this case, sports.xsl in the current directory.

Software Engineering Observation 26.4

XSL enables document authors to separate data presentation (specified in XSL documents) from data description (specified in XML documents).

Figure 26.9 shows the XSL document for transforming the structured data of the XML document of Fig. 26.8 into an XHTML document for presentation. By convention, XSL documents have the file-name extension **.xsl**.

```
 1   <?xml version = "1.0"?>
 2   <!-- Fig. 26.9: sports.xsl -->
 3   <!-- A simple XSLT transformation -->
 4
 5   <!-- reference XSL style sheet URI -->
 6   <xsl:stylesheet version = "1.0"
 7      xmlns:xsl = "http://www.w3.org/1999/XSL/Transform">
 8
 9      <xsl:output method = "xml" omit-xml-declaration = "no"
10         doctype-system =
11            "http://www.w3c.org/TR/xhtml11/DTD/xhtml11-strict.dtd"
12         doctype-public = "-//W3C//DTD XHTML 1.0 Strict//EN"/>
13
14      <xsl:template match = "/"> <!-- match root element -->
15
16      <html xmlns = "http://www.w3.org/1999/xhtml">
17         <head>
18            <title>Sports</title>
19         </head>
20
21         <body>
22            <table border = "1" style = "background-color: wheat">
23               <thead>
```

Fig. 26.9 | XSLT that creates elements and attributes in an XHTML document. (Part 1 of 2.)

```
24                   <tr>
25                      <th>ID</th>
26                      <th>Sport</th>
27                      <th>Information</th>
28                   </tr>
29                </thead>
30
31                <!-- insert each name and paragraph element value -->
32                <!-- into a table row. -->
33                <xsl:for-each select = "/sports/game">
34                   <tr>
35                      <td><xsl:value-of select = "@id"/></td>
36                      <td><xsl:value-of select = "name"/></td>
37                      <td><xsl:value-of select = "paragraph"/></td>
38                   </tr>
39                </xsl:for-each>
40             </table>
41          </body>
42       </html>
43
44    </xsl:template>
45 </xsl:stylesheet>
```

Fig. 26.9 | XSLT that creates elements and attributes in an XHTML document. (Part 2 of 2.)

Lines 6–7 begin the XSL style sheet with the **stylesheet** start tag. Attribute **version** specifies the XSLT version to which this document conforms. Line 7 binds namespace prefix **xsl** to the W3C's XSLT URI (i.e., http://www.w3.org/1999/XSL/Transform).

Lines 9–12 use element **xsl:output** to write an XHTML document type declaration (DOCTYPE) to the result tree (i.e., the XML document to be created). The DOCTYPE identifies XHTML as the type of the resulting document. Attribute method is assigned "xml", which indicates that XML is being output to the result tree. (Recall that XHTML is a type of XML.) Attribute **omit-xml-declaration** specifies whether the transformation should write the XML declaration to the result tree. In this case, we do not want to omit the XML declaration, so we assign to this attribute the value "no". Attributes doctype-system and doctype-public write the DOCTYPE DTD information to the result tree.

XSLT uses **templates** (i.e., **xsl:template** elements) to describe how to transform particular nodes from the source tree to the result tree. A template is applied to nodes that are specified in the match attribute. Line 14 uses the **match** attribute to select the **document root** (i.e., the conceptual part of the document that contains the root element and everything below it) of the XML source document (i.e., sports.xml). The **XPath character /** (a forward slash) is used as a separator between element names. Recall that XPath is a string-based language used to locate parts of an XML document easily. In XPath, a leading forward slash specifies that we are using **absolute addressing** (i.e., we are starting from the root and defining paths down the source tree). In the XML document of Fig. 26.8, the child nodes of the document root are the two processing-instruction nodes (lines 1–2), the two comment nodes (lines 4–5) and the sports element node (lines 7–31). The template in Fig. 26.9, line 14, matches a node (i.e., the document root), so the contents of the template are now added to the result tree.

The XSLT processor writes the XHTML in lines 16–29 (Fig. 26.9) to the result tree exactly as it appears in the XSL document. Now the result tree consists of the DOCTYPE definition and the XHTML code from lines 16–29. Lines 33–39 use element **xsl:for-each** to iterate through the source XML document, searching for game elements. The xsl:for-each element is similar to C#'s foreach statement. Attribute **select** is an XPath expression that specifies the nodes (called the **node set**) on which the xsl:for-each operates. Again, the first forward slash means that we are using absolute addressing. The forward slash between sports and game indicates that game is a child node of sports. Thus, the xsl:for-each finds game nodes that are children of the sports node. The XML document sports.xml contains only one sports node, which is also the document root element. After finding the elements that match the selection criteria, the xsl:for-each processes each element with the code in lines 34–38 (these lines produce one row in an XHTML table each time they execute) and places the result of lines 34–38 in the result tree.

Line 35 uses element **value-of** to retrieve attribute id's value and place it in a td element in the result tree. The XPath symbol @ specifies that id is an attribute node of the game **context node** (i.e., the current node being processed). Lines 36–37 place the name and paragraph element values in td elements and insert them in the result tree. When an XPath expression has no beginning forward slash, the expression uses **relative addressing**. Omitting the beginning forward slash tells the **xsl:value-of select** statements to search for name and paragraph elements that are children of the context node, not the root node. Owing to the last XPath expression selection, the current context node is game, which indeed has an id attribute, a name child element and a paragraph child element.

Using XSLT to Sort and Format Data

Figure 26.10 presents an XML document (sorting.xml) that marks up information about a book. Several elements of the markup describing the book appear out of order (e.g., the element describing Chapter 3 appears before the element describing Chapter 2). We arranged them this way purposely to demonstrate that the XSL style sheet referenced in line 5 (sorting.xsl) can sort the XML file's data for presentation purposes.

```
 1   <?xml version = "1.0"?>
 2   <!-- Fig. 26.10: sorting.xml -->
 3   <!-- XML document containing book information -->
 4
 5   <?xml-stylesheet type = "text/xsl" href = "sorting.xsl"?>
 6
 7   <book isbn = "999-99999-9-X">
 8      <title>Deitel&apos;s XML Primer</title>
 9
10      <author>
11         <firstName>Jane</firstName>
12         <lastName>Blue</lastName>
13      </author>
14
15      <chapters>
16         <frontMatter>
17            <preface pages = "2" />
```

Fig. 26.10 | XML document containing book information. (Part 1 of 2.)

```
18              <contents pages = "5" />
19              <illustrations pages = "4" />
20          </frontMatter>
21
22          <chapter number = "3" pages = "44">Advanced XML</chapter>
23          <chapter number = "2" pages = "35">Intermediate XML</chapter>
24          <appendix number = "B" pages = "26">Parsers and Tools</appendix>
25          <appendix number = "A" pages = "7">Entities</appendix>
26          <chapter number = "1" pages = "28">XML Fundamentals</chapter>
27      </chapters>
28
29      <media type = "CD" />
30  </book>
```

Fig. 26.10 | XML document containing book information. (Part 2 of 2.)

Figure 26.11 presents an XSL document (sorting.xsl) for transforming sorting.xml (Fig. 26.10) to XHTML. Recall that an XSL document navigates a source tree and builds a result tree. In this example, the source tree is XML, and the output tree is XHTML. Line 14 of Fig. 26.11 matches the root element of the document in Fig. 26.10. Line 15 outputs an html start tag to the result tree. The <xsl:apply-templates/> element (line 16) specifies that the XSLT processor is to apply the xsl:templates defined in this XSL document to the current node's (i.e., the document root's) children. The content from the applied templates is output in the html element that ends at line 17. Lines 21–86 specify a template that matches element book. The template indicates how to format the information contained in book elements of sorting.xml (Fig. 26.10) as XHTML.

```
 1  <?xml version = "1.0"?>
 2  <!-- Fig. 26.11: sorting.xsl -->
 3  <!-- Transformation of book information into XHTML -->
 4
 5  <xsl:stylesheet version = "1.0" xmlns = "http://www.w3.org/1999/xhtml"
 6      xmlns:xsl = "http://www.w3.org/1999/XSL/Transform">
 7
 8      <!-- write XML declaration and DOCTYPE DTD information -->
 9      <xsl:output method = "xml" omit-xml-declaration = "no"
10          doctype-system = "http://www.w3.org/TR/xhtml11/DTD/xhtml11.dtd"
11          doctype-public = "-//W3C//DTD XHTML 1.1//EN"/>
12
13      <!-- match document root -->
14      <xsl:template match = "/">
15          <html>
16              <xsl:apply-templates/>
17          </html>
18      </xsl:template>
19
20      <!-- match book -->
21      <xsl:template match = "book">
```

Fig. 26.11 | XSL document that transforms sorting.xml into XHTML. (Part 1 of 3.)

```
22        <head>
23           <title>ISBN <xsl:value-of select = "@isbn"/> -
24              <xsl:value-of select = "title"/></title>
25        </head>
26
27        <body>
28           <h1 style = "color: blue"><xsl:value-of select = "title"/></h1>
29           <h2 style = "color: blue">by
30              <xsl:value-of select = "author/firstName"/>
31              <xsl:text> </xsl:text>
32              <xsl:value-of select = "author/lastName"/>
33           </h2>
34
35           <table style = "border-style: groove; background-color: wheat">
36
37              <xsl:for-each select = "chapters/frontMatter/*">
38                 <tr>
39                    <td style = "text-align: right">
40                       <xsl:value-of select = "name()"/>
41                    </td>
42
43                    <td>
44                       ( <xsl:value-of select = "@pages"/> pages )
45                    </td>
46                 </tr>
47              </xsl:for-each>
48
49              <xsl:for-each select = "chapters/chapter">
50                 <xsl:sort select = "@number" data-type = "number"
51                    order = "ascending"/>
52                 <tr>
53                    <td style = "text-align: right">
54                       Chapter <xsl:value-of select = "@number"/>
55                    </td>
56
57                    <td>
58                       <xsl:value-of select = "text()"/>
59                       ( <xsl:value-of select = "@pages"/> pages )
60                    </td>
61                 </tr>
62              </xsl:for-each>
63
64              <xsl:for-each select = "chapters/appendix">
65                 <xsl:sort select = "@number" data-type = "text"
66                    order = "ascending"/>
67                 <tr>
68                    <td style = "text-align: right">
69                       Appendix <xsl:value-of select = "@number"/>
70                    </td>
71
72                    <td>
73                       <xsl:value-of select = "text()"/>
```

Fig. 26.11 | XSL document that transforms sorting.xml into XHTML. (Part 2 of 3.)

```
74                          ( <xsl:value-of select = "@pages"/> pages )
75                       </td>
76                    </tr>
77                 </xsl:for-each>
78              </table>
79
80              <p style = "color: blue">Pages:
81                 <xsl:variable name = "pagecount"
82                    select = "sum(chapters//*/@pages)"/>
83                 <xsl:value-of select = "$pagecount"/>
84              <br />Media Type: <xsl:value-of select = "media/@type"/></p>
85           </body>
86        </xsl:template>
87     </xsl:stylesheet>
```

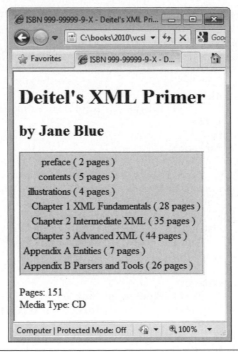

Fig. 26.11 | XSL document that transforms `sorting.xml` into XHTML. (Part 3 of 3.)

Lines 23–24 create the title for the XHTML document. We use the book's ISBN (from attribute `isbn`) and the contents of element `title` to create the string that appears in the browser window's title bar (**ISBN 999-99999-9-X - Deitel's XML Primer**).

Line 28 creates a header element that contains the book's title. Lines 29–33 create a header element that contains the book's author. Because the context node (i.e., the current node being processed) is book, the XPath expression `author/lastName` selects the author's last name, and the expression `author/firstName` selects the author's first name. The `xsl:text` element (line 31) is used to insert literal text. Because XML (and therefore XSLT) ignores whitespace, the author's name would appear as **JaneBlue** without inserting the explicit space.

Line 37 selects each element (indicated by an asterisk) that is a child of element `frontMatter`. Line 40 calls **node-set function name** to retrieve the current node's element name (e.g., `preface`). The current node is the context node specified in the `xsl:for-each` (line 37). Line 44 retrieves the value of the pages attribute of the current node.

Line 49 selects each `chapter` element. Lines 50–51 use element **`xsl:sort`** to sort chapters by number in ascending order. Attribute **`select`** selects the value of attribute `number` in context node `chapter`. Attribute **`data-type`**, with value `"number"`, specifies a numeric sort, and attribute **`order`**, with value `"ascending"`, specifies ascending order. Attribute `data-type` also accepts the value `"text"` (line 65), and attribute `order` also accepts the value `"descending"`. Line 58 uses **node-set function text** to obtain the text between the `chapter` start and end tags (i.e., the name of the chapter). Line 59 retrieves the value of the `pages` attribute of the current node. Lines 64–77 perform similar tasks for each appendix.

Lines 81–82 use an **XSL variable** to store the value of the book's total page count and output the page count to the result tree. Such variables cannot be modified after they're initialized. Attribute **`name`** specifies the variable's name (i.e., `pagecount`), and attribute `select` assigns a value to the variable. Function **`sum`** (line 82) totals the values for all `page` attribute values. The two slashes between `chapters` and `*` indicate a **recursive descent**—the XSLT processor will search for elements that contain an attribute named `pages` in all descendant nodes of `chapters`. The XPath expression

```
//*
```

selects all the nodes in an XML document. Line 83 retrieves the value of the newly created XSL variable `pagecount` by placing a dollar sign in front of its name.

Performance Tip 26.1
Selecting all nodes in a document when it is not necessary slows XSLT processing.

Summary of XSL Style-Sheet Elements

This section's examples used several predefined XSL elements to perform various operations. Figure 26.12 lists commonly used XSL elements. For more information on these elements and XSL in general, see www.w3.org/Style/XSL.

Element	Description
`<xsl:apply-templates>`	Applies the templates of the XSL document to the children of the current node.
`<xsl:apply-templates match = "`*expression*`">`	Applies the templates of the XSL document to the children of the nodes matching *expression*. The value of the attribute match (i.e., *expression*) must be an XPath expression that specifies elements.
`<xsl:template>`	Contains rules to apply when a specified node is matched.

Fig. 26.12 | XSL style-sheet elements. (Part 1 of 2.)

Element	Description
`<xsl:value-of select = "expression">`	Selects the value of an XML element or attribute and adds it to the output tree of the transformation. The required `select` attribute contains an XPath expression.
`<xsl:for-each select = "expression">`	Applies a template to every node selected by the XPath specified by the `select` attribute.
`<xsl:sort select = "expression">`	Used as a child element of an `<xsl:apply-templates>` or `<xsl:for-each>` element. Sorts the nodes selected by the `<xsl:apply-template>` or `<xsl:for-each>` element so that the nodes are processed in sorted order.
`<xsl:output>`	Has various attributes to define the format (e.g., XML, XHTML), version (e.g., 1.0, 2.0), document type and MIME type of the output document. This tag is a top-level element—it can be used only as a child element of an `xsl:stylesheet`.
`<xsl:copy>`	Adds the current node to the output tree.

Fig. 26.12 | XSL style-sheet elements. (Part 2 of 2.)

This section introduced Extensible Stylesheet Language (XSL) and showed how to create XSL transformations to convert XML documents from one format to another. We showed how to transform XML documents to XHTML documents for display in a web browser. In most business applications, XML documents are transferred between business partners and are transformed to other XML vocabularies programmatically. In Section 26.8, we demonstrate how to perform XSL transformations using the `XslCompiledTransform` class provided by the .NET Framework.

26.5 LINQ to XML: Document Object Model (DOM)

Although an XML document is a text file, retrieving data from the document using traditional sequential file-processing techniques is not practical, especially for adding and removing elements dynamically.

On successfully parsing a document, some XML parsers store document data as trees in memory. Figure 26.13 illustrates the tree structure for the document `article.xml` discussed in Fig. 24.2. This hierarchical tree structure is called a **Document Object Model (DOM) tree**, and an XML parser that creates such a tree is known as a **DOM parser**. DOM gets its name from the conversion of an XML document's tree structure into a tree of objects that are then manipulated using an object-oriented programming language such as C#. Each element name (e.g., `article`, `date`, `firstName`) is represented by a node. A node that contains other nodes (called **child nodes** or children) is called a **parent node** (e.g., `author`). A parent node can have many children, but a child node can have only one parent node. Nodes that are peers (e.g., `firstName` and `lastName`) are called **sibling nodes**. A node's **descendant nodes** include its children, its children's children and so on. A node's **ancestor nodes** include its parent, its parent's parent and so on.

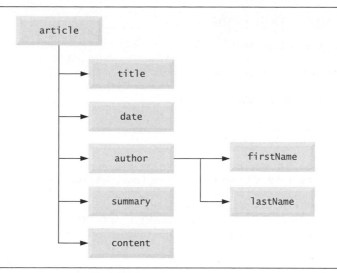

Fig. 26.13 | Tree structure for the document `article.xml`.

The DOM tree has a single **root node**, which contains all the other nodes in the document. For example, the root node of the DOM tree that represents `article.xml` (Fig. 24.2) contains a node for the XML declaration (line 1), two nodes for the comments (lines 2–3) and a node for the XML document's root element `article` (line 5).

Classes for creating, reading and manipulating XML documents are located in the `System.Xml` namespace, which also contains additional namespaces that provide other XML-related operations.

Reading an XML Document with an *XDocument*

Namespace **`System.Xml.Linq`** contains the classes used to manipulate a DOM in .NET. Though LINQ query expressions are not required to use them, the technologies used are collectively referred to as LINQ to XML. Previous versions of the .NET Framework used a different DOM implementation in the `System.Xml` namespace. These classes (such as `XmlDocument`) should generally be avoided in favor of LINQ to XML. In LINQ to XML, the **`XElement`** class represents a DOM element node—an XML document is represented by a tree of `XElement` objects. The **`XDocument`** class represents an entire XML document. Unlike `XElement`s, `XDocument`s cannot be nested. Figure 26.14 uses these classes to load the `article.xml` document (Fig. 24.2) and display its data in a `TextBox`. The program displays a formatted version of its input XML file. If `article.xml` were poorly formatted, such as being all on one line, this application would allow you to convert it into a form that is much easier to understand.

```
1   // Fig. 26.14: XDocumentTestForm.cs
2   // Reading an XML document and displaying it in a TextBox.
3   using System;
4   using System.Xml.Linq;
```

Fig. 26.14 | Reading an XML document and displaying it in a `TextBox`. (Part 1 of 3.)

```csharp
 5   using System.Windows.Forms;
 6
 7   namespace XDocumentTest
 8   {
 9      public partial class XDocumentTestForm : Form
10      {
11         public XDocumentTestForm()
12         {
13            InitializeComponent();
14         } // end constructor
15
16         // read XML document and display its content
17         private void XDocumentTestForm_Load( object sender, EventArgs e )
18         {
19            // load the XML file into an XDocument
20            XDocument xmlFile = XDocument.Load( "article.xml" );
21            int indentLevel = 0; // no indentation for root element
22
23            // print elements recursively
24            PrintElement( xmlFile.Root, indentLevel );
25         } // end method XDocumentTestForm_Load
26
27         // display an element (and its children, if any) in the TextBox
28         private void PrintElement( XElement element, int indentLevel )
29         {
30            // get element name without namespace
31            string name = element.Name.LocalName;
32
33            // display the element's name within its tag
34            IndentOutput( indentLevel ); // indent correct amount
35            outputTextBox.AppendText( '<' + name + ">\n" );
36
37            // check for child elements and print value if none contained
38            if ( element.HasElements )
39            {
40               // print all child elements at the next indentation level
41               foreach ( var child in element.Elements() )
42                  PrintElement( child, indentLevel + 1 );
43            } // end if
44            else
45            {
46               // increase the indentation amount for text elements
47               IndentOutput( indentLevel + 1 );
48
49               // display the text inside this element
50               outputTextBox.AppendText( element.Value.Trim() + '\n' );
51            } // end else
52
53            // display end tag
54            IndentOutput( indentLevel );
55            outputTextBox.AppendText( "</" + name + ">\n" );
56         } // end method PrintElement
```

Fig. 26.14 | Reading an XML document and displaying it in a TextBox. (Part 2 of 3.)

```
57
58          // add the specified amount of indentation to the current line
59          private void IndentOutput( int number )
60          {
61             for ( int i = 0; i < number; i++ )
62                outputTextBox.AppendText( "    " );
63          } // end method IndentOutput
64       } // end class XDocumentTestForm
65    } // end namespace XDocumentTest
```

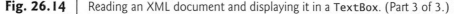

Fig. 26.14 | Reading an XML document and displaying it in a TextBox. (Part 3 of 3.)

To create an XDocument from an existing XML document, we use XDocument's static
Load method, giving the location of the document as an argument (line 20). The returned
XDocument contains a tree representation of the loaded XML file, which is used to navigate
the file's contents. The XDocument's **Root property** (line 24) returns an XElement representing the root element of the XML file.

Method PrintElement (lines 28–56) displays an XElement in outputTextBox.
Because nested elements should be at different indentation levels, PrintElement takes an
int specifying the amount of indentation to use in addition to the XElement it is displaying. Variable indentLevel is passed as an argument to the IndentOutput method
(lines 59–63) to add the correct amount of spacing before the begin (line 35) and end (line
55) tags are displayed.

As you've seen in previous sections, tag and attribute names often have a namespace
prefix. Because the full names consist of two parts (the prefix and name), tag and attribute
names are stored not simply as strings, but as objects of class **XName**. The **Name property**
of an XElement (line 31) returns an XName object containing the tag name and
namespace—we are not interested in the namespace for this example, so we retrieve the
unqualified name using the XName's **LocalName property**.

XElements with and without children are treated differently in the program—this test is performed using the **HasElements property** (line 38). For XElements with children, we use the **Elements method** (line 41) to obtain the children, then iterate through them and recursively print their children by calling PrintElement (line 42). For XElements that do not have children, the text they contain is displayed using the **Value property** (line 50). If used on an element with children, the Value property returns all of the text contained within its descendants, with the tags removed. For simplicity, elements with attributes and those with both elements and text as children are not handled. The indentation is increased by one in both cases to allow for proper formatting.

26.6 LINQ to XML Class Hierarchy

As you saw in the previous section, XElement objects provide several methods for quickly traversing the DOM tree they represent. LINQ to XML provides many other classes for representing different parts of the tree. Figure 26.15 demonstrates the use of these additional classes to navigate the structure of an XML document and display it in a TreeView control. It also shows how to use these classes to get functionality equivalent to the XPath strings introduced in Section 26.4. The file used as a data source (sports.xml) is shown in Fig. 26.8.

```
1   // Fig. 26.15: PathNavigatorForm.cs
2   // Document navigation using XNode.
3   using System;
4   using System.Collections.Generic;
5   using System.Linq;
6   using System.Xml; // for XmlNodeType enumeration
7   using System.Xml.Linq; // for XNode and others
8   using System.Xml.XPath; // for XPathSelectElements
9   using System.Windows.Forms;
10
11  namespace PathNavigator
12  {
13     public partial class PathNavigatorForm : Form
14     {
15        private XNode current; // currently selected node
16        private XDocument document; // the document to navigate
17        private TreeNode tree; // TreeNode used by TreeView control
18
19        public PathNavigatorForm()
20        {
21           InitializeComponent();
22        } // end PathNavigatorForm
23
24        // initialize variables and TreeView control
25        private void PathNavigatorForm_Load( object sender, EventArgs e )
26        {
27           document = XDocument.Load( "sports.xml" ); // load sports.xml
28
```

Fig. 26.15 | Document navigation using XNode. (Part 1 of 6.)

```
29              // current node is the entire document
30              current = document;
31
32              // create root TreeNode and add to TreeView
33              tree = new TreeNode( NodeText( current ) );
34              pathTreeView.Nodes.Add( tree ); // add TreeNode to TreeView
35              TreeRefresh(); // reset the tree display
36          } // end method PathNavigatorForm_Load
37
38          // print the elements of the selected path
39          private void locateComboBox_SelectedIndexChanged(
40              object sender, EventArgs e )
41          {
42              // retrieve the set of elements to output
43              switch ( locateComboBox.SelectedIndex )
44              {
45                  case 0: // print all sports elements
46                      PrintElements( document.Elements( "sports" ) );
47                      break;
48                  case 1: // print all game elements
49                      PrintElements( document.Descendants( "game" ) );
50                      break;
51                  case 2: // print all name elements
52                      PrintElements( document.XPathSelectElements( "//name" ) );
53                      break;
54                  case 3: // print all paragraph elements
55                      PrintElements( document.Descendants( "game" )
56                          .Elements( "paragraph" ) );
57                      break;
58                  case 4: // print game elements with name element of "Cricket"
59                      // use LINQ to XML to retrieve the correct node
60                      var cricket =
61                          from game in document.Descendants( "game" )
62                          where game.Element( "name" ).Value == "Cricket"
63                          select game;
64                      PrintElements( cricket );
65                      break;
66                  case 5: // print all id attributes of game
67                      PrintIDs( document.Descendants( "game" ) );
68                      break;
69              } // end switch
70          } // end method locateComboBox_SelectedIndexChanged
71
72          // traverse to first child
73          private void firstChildButton_Click( object sender, EventArgs e )
74          {
75              // try to convert to an XContainer
76              var container = current as XContainer;
77
78              // if container has children, move to first child
79              if ( container != null && container.Nodes().Any() )
80              {
81                  current = container.Nodes().First(); // first child
```

Fig. 26.15 | Document navigation using XNode. (Part 2 of 6.)

```
82
83              // create new TreeNode for this node with correct label
84              var newNode = new TreeNode( NodeText( current ) );
85              tree.Nodes.Add( newNode ); // add node to TreeNode Nodes list
86              tree = newNode; // move current selection to newNode
87              TreeRefresh(); // reset the tree display
88           } // end if
89           else
90           {
91              // current node is not a container or has no children
92              MessageBox.Show( "Current node has no children.", "Warning",
93                 MessageBoxButtons.OK, MessageBoxIcon.Information );
94           } // end else
95        } // end method firstChildButton_Click
96
97        // traverse to node's parent
98        private void parentButton_Click( object sender, EventArgs e )
99        {
100          // if current node is not the root, move to parent
101          if ( current.Parent != null )
102             current = current.Parent; // get parent node
103          else // node is at top level: move to document itself
104             current = current.Document;
105
106          // move TreeView if it is not already at the root
107          if ( tree.Parent != null )
108          {
109             tree = tree.Parent; // get parent in tree structure
110             tree.Nodes.Clear(); // remove all children
111             TreeRefresh(); // reset the tree display
112          } // end if
113       } // end method parentButton_Click
114
115       // traverse to previous node
116       private void previousButton_Click( object sender, EventArgs e )
117       {
118          // if current node is not first, move to previous node
119          if ( current.PreviousNode != null )
120          {
121             current = current.PreviousNode; // move to previous node
122             var treeParent = tree.Parent; // get parent node
123             treeParent.Nodes.Remove( tree ); // delete current node
124             tree = treeParent.LastNode; // set current display position
125             TreeRefresh(); // reset the tree display
126          } // end if
127          else // current element is first among its siblings
128          {
129             MessageBox.Show( "Current node is first sibling.", "Warning",
130                MessageBoxButtons.OK, MessageBoxIcon.Information );
131          } // end else
132       } // end method previousButton_Click
133
```

Fig. 26.15 | Document navigation using XNode. (Part 3 of 6.)

```csharp
134         // traverse to next node
135         private void nextButton_Click( object sender, EventArgs e )
136         {
137            // if current node is not last, move to next node
138            if ( current.NextNode != null )
139            {
140               current = current.NextNode; // move to next node
141
142               // create new TreeNode to display next node
143               var newNode = new TreeNode( NodeText( current ) );
144               var treeParent = tree.Parent; // get parent TreeNode
145               treeParent.Nodes.Add( newNode ); // add to parent node
146               tree = newNode; // set current position for display
147               TreeRefresh(); // reset the tree display
148            } // end if
149            else // current node is last among its siblings
150            {
151               MessageBox.Show( "Current node is last sibling.", "Warning",
152                  MessageBoxButtons.OK, MessageBoxIcon.Information );
153            } // end else
154         } // end method nextButton_Click
155
156         // update TreeView control
157         private void TreeRefresh()
158         {
159            pathTreeView.ExpandAll(); // expand tree node in TreeView
160            pathTreeView.Refresh(); // force TreeView update
161            pathTreeView.SelectedNode = tree; // highlight current node
162         } // end method TreeRefresh
163
164         // print values in the given collection
165         private void PrintElements( IEnumerable< XElement > elements )
166         {
167            locateTextBox.Clear(); // clear the text area
168
169            // display text inside all elements
170            foreach ( var element in elements )
171               locateTextBox.AppendText( element.Value.Trim() + '\n' );
172         } // end method PrintElements
173
174         // print the ID numbers of all games in elements
175         private void PrintIDs( IEnumerable< XElement > elements )
176         {
177            locateTextBox.Clear(); // clear the text area
178
179            // display "id" attribute of all elements
180            foreach ( var element in elements )
181               locateTextBox.AppendText(
182                  element.Attribute( "id" ).Value.Trim() + '\n' );
183         } // end method PrintIDs
184
```

Fig. 26.15 | Document navigation using XNode. (Part 4 of 6.)

```
185        // returns text used to represent an element in the tree
186        private string NodeText( XNode node )
187        {
188           // different node types are displayed in different ways
189           switch ( node.NodeType )
190           {
191              case XmlNodeType.Document:
192                 // display the document root
193                 return "Document root";
194              case XmlNodeType.Element:
195                 // represent node by tag name
196                 return '<' + ( node as XElement ).Name.LocalName + '>';
197              case XmlNodeType.Text:
198                 // represent node by text stored in Value property
199                 return ( node as XText ).Value;
200              case XmlNodeType.Comment:
201                 // represent node by comment text
202                 return ( node as XComment ).ToString();
203              case XmlNodeType.ProcessingInstruction:
204                 // represent node by processing-instruction text
205                 return ( node as XProcessingInstruction ).ToString();
206              default:
207                 // all nodes in this example are already covered;
208                 // return a reasonable default value for other nodes
209                 return node.NodeType.ToString();
210           } // end switch
211        } // end method NodeText
212     } // end class PathNavigatorForm
213 } // end namespace PathNavigator
```

a) **Path Navigator** form upon loading

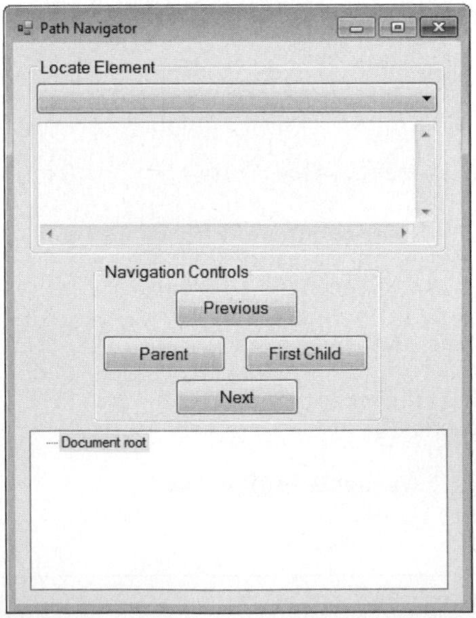

b) The **//name** path is selected

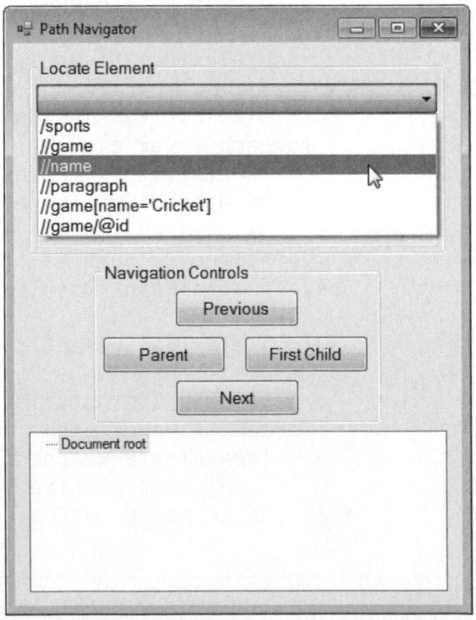

Fig. 26.15 | Document navigation using XNode. (Part 5 of 6.)

c) The **//name** path displays all **name** elements in the document

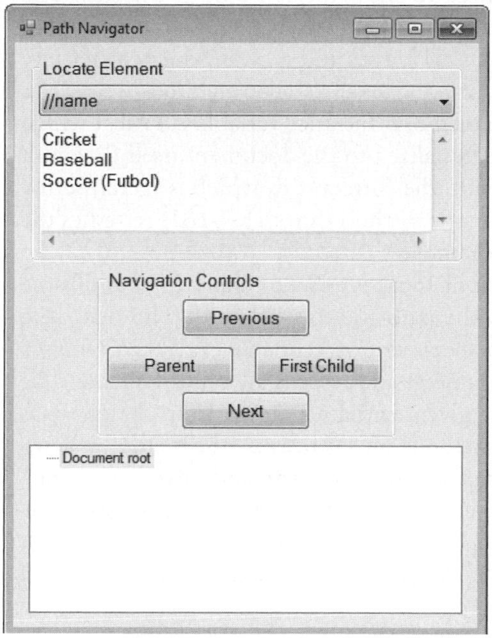

d) The **//game[name='Cricket']** path displays **game** elements with a **name** element containing "Cricket"

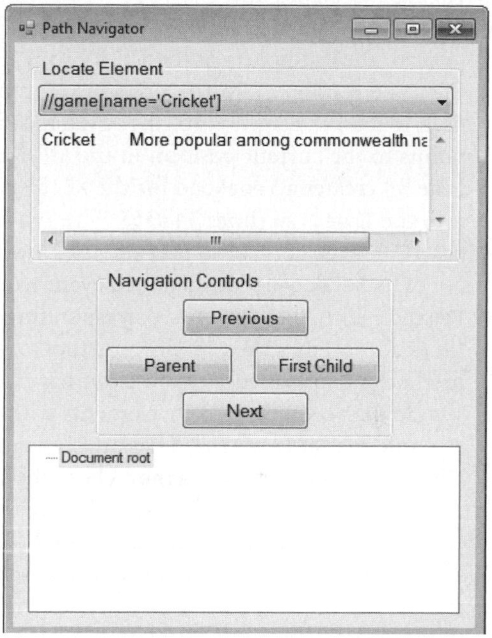

e) The **First Child** button expands the tree to show the first element in that group

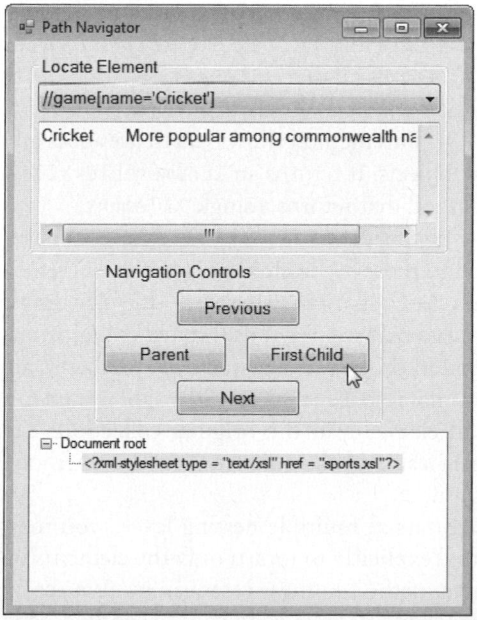

f) The **Next** button lets you view siblings of the current element

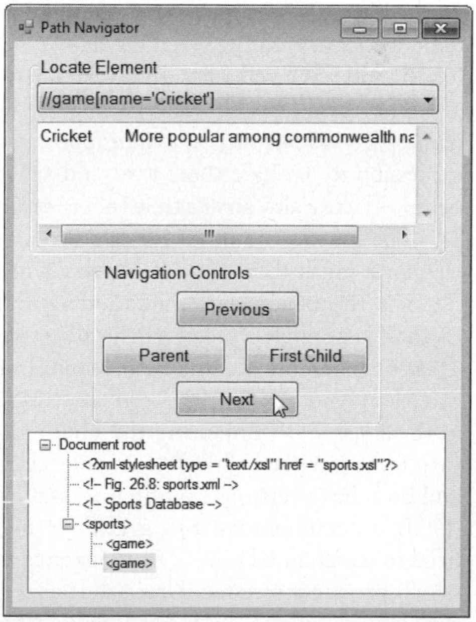

Fig. 26.15 | Document navigation using XNode. (Part 6 of 6.)

The interface for this example allows the user to display selected elements in the TextBox, or to navigate through the DOM tree in the lower TreeView. Initially, the TextBox is blank, and the TreeView is initialized to show the the root of the tree. The ComboBox at the top of the Form contains XPath expressions. These are not used directly—instead, the example uses the LINQ to XML DOM classes and a LINQ query to retrieve the same results. As in the previous example, the XDocument's Load method (line 27) is used to load the contents of the XML file into memory. Instance variable current, which points to the current position in the DOM, is initialized to the document itself (line 30). Line 33 creates a TreeNode for the XElement with the correct text, which is then inserted into the TreeView (lines 34–35). The TreeRefresh method (lines 157–162) refreshes the pathTreeView control so that the user interface updates correctly.

The SelectedIndexChanged event handler of locateComboBox (lines 39–70) fills the TextBox with the elements corresponding to the path the user selected. The first case (lines 45–47) uses the Elements method of the XDocument object document. The Elements method is overloaded—one version has no parameter and returns all child elements. The second version returns only elements with the given tag name. Recall from the previous example that XElement also has an Elements method. This is because the method is actually defined in the **XContainer class**, the base class of XDocument and XElement. XContainer represents nodes in the DOM tree that can contain other nodes. The results of the call to the method Elements are passed to the PrintElements method (lines 165–172). The PrintElements method uses the XElement's Value property (line 171) introduced in the previous example. The Value property returns all text in the current node and its descendants. The text is displayed in locateTextBox.

The second case (lines 48–50) uses the **Descendants method**—another XContainer method common to XElement and XDocument—to get the same results as the XPath double slash (//) operator. In other words, the Descendants method returns all descendant elements with the given tag name, not just direct children. Like Elements, it is overloaded and has a version with no parameter that returns all descendants.

The third case (lines 51–53) uses extension method **XPathSelectElements** from namespace **System.Xml.XPath** (imported at line 8). This method allows you to use an XPath expression to navigate XDocument and XElement objects. It returns an IEnumerable<XElement>. There's also an XPathSelectElement method that returns a single XElement.

The fourth case (lines 54–57) also uses the Descendants method to retrieve all game elements, but it then calls the Elements method to retrieve the child paragraph elements. Because the Descendants method returns an IEnumerable<XElement>, the Elements method is not being called on the XContainer class that we previously stated contains the Elements method. Calling the Elements method in this way is allowed because there's an extension method in the System.Xml.Linq namespace that returns an IEnumerable<XElement> containing the children of all elements in the original collection. To match the interface of the XContainer class, there's also a Descendants extension method, and both have versions that do not take an argument.

In a document where a specific element appears at multiple nesting levels, you may need to use chained calls of the Elements method explicitly to return only the elements in which you are interested. Using the Descendants method in these cases can be a source of subtle bugs—if the XML document's structure changes, your code could silently accept input that the program should not treat as valid. The Descendants method is best used for tags that can appear at any nesting level within the document, such as formatting tags in XHTML, which can occur in many distinct parts of the text.

The fifth case (lines 58–65) retrieves only the game elements with a name element containing "Cricket". To do this, we use a LINQ query (lines 61–63). The Descendants and Elements methods return an IEnumerable<XElement>, so they can be used as the subject of a LINQ query. The where clause (line 62) uses the Element method to retrieve all name elements that are children of the game element the range variable represents. The **Element method**, a member of the XContainer class, returns the first child element with the given tag name or null if no such element exists. The where clause uses the Value property to retrieve the text contained in the element. We do not check for Element returning null because we know that all game elements in sports.xml contain name elements.

The PrintIDs method (lines 175–183) displays the id attributes of the XElement objects passed to it—specifically, the game elements in the document (line 67). To do this, it uses the **Attribute method** of the XElement class (line 182). The Attribute method returns an XAttribute object matching the given attribute name or null if no such object exists. The **XAttribute class** represents an XML attribute—it holds the attribute's name and value. Here, we access its Value property to get a string that contains the attribute's value—it can also be used as an *lvalue* to modify the value.

The Click event handlers for the Buttons in the example are used to update the data displayed in the TreeView. These methods introduce many other classes from the namespace System.Xml.Linq. The entire LINQ to XML class hierarchy is shown in the UML class diagram of Fig. 26.16. XNamespace will be covered in the next section, and **XDocumentType** holds a DTD, which may be defined directly in an XML file rather than externally referenced (as we did in Fig. 24.4, letter.xml).

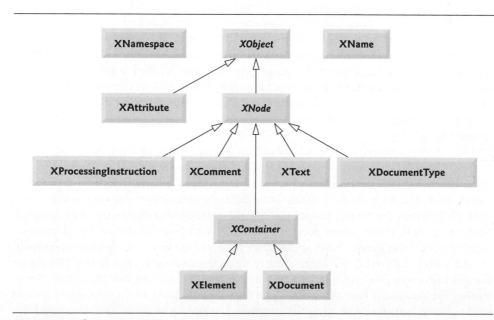

Fig. 26.16 | LINQ to XML class hierarchy diagram.

As you can see from the diagram, the **XNode class** is a common abstract base class of all the node types in an XML document—including elements, text and processing instructions. Because all DOM node classes inherit from XNode, an XNode object can be used to keep track of our current location as we navigate the DOM tree.

The firstChildButton_Click event handler (lines 73–95) uses the as operator to determine whether the current node is an XContainer (line 76). Recall that the as operator attempts to cast the reference to another type, and returns null if it cannot. If current is an XContainer and has children (line 79), we move current to its first child (line 81). These operations use the **Nodes method** of class XContainer, which returns a reference to an object of type IEnumerable<XNode> containing all children of the given XContainer. Line 79 uses the Any extension method introduced in Chapter 9—all of the standard LINQ to Objects methods may be used with the LINQ to XML classes. The event handler then inserts a TreeNode into the TreeView to display the child element that current now references (lines 84–87).

Line 84 uses the NodeText method (lines 186–211) to determine what text to display in the TreeNode. It uses the **NodeType property**, which returns a value of the **XmlNodeType enumeration** from the System.Xml namespace (imported at line 6) indicating the object's node type. Although we call it on an XNode, the NodeType property is actually defined in the **XObject class**. XObject is an abstract base class for all nodes and attributes. The Node-Type property is overridden in the concrete subclasses to return the correct value.

After the node's type has been determined, it is converted to the appropriate type using the as operator, then the correct text is retrieved. For the entire document, it returns the text **Document root** (line 193). For elements, NodeText returns the tag name enclosed in angle brackets (line 196). For text nodes, it uses the contained text. It retrieves this by converting the XNode to an XText object—the **XText class** holds the contents of a text node. XText's **Value property** returns the contained text (line 199)—we could also have used its ToString method. Comments, represented by the **XComment class**, are displayed just as they're written in the XML file using the ToString method of XComment (line 202). The ToString methods of all subclasses of XNode return the XML they and their children (if any) represent with proper indentation. The last type handled is processing instructions, stored in the **XProcessingInstruction class** (line 205)—in this example, the only processing instruction is the XML declaration at the beginning of the file. A default case returning the name of the node type is included for other node types that do not appear in sports.xml (line 209).

The event handlers for the other Buttons are structured similarly to firstChild-Button_Click—each moves current and updates the TreeView accordingly. The parentButton_Click method (lines 98–113) ensures that the current node has a parent—that is, it is not at the root of the XDocument—before it tries to move current to the parent (line 102). It uses the **Parent property** of XObject, which returns the parent of the given XObject or null if the parent does not exist. For nodes at the root of the document, including the root element, XML declaration, header comments and the document itself, Parent with return null. We want to move up to the document root in this case, so we use the **Document property** (also defined in XObject) to retrieve the XDocument representing the document root (line 104). The Document property of an XDocument returns itself. This is consistent with most file systems—attempting to move up a directory from the root will succeed, but not move.

The event handlers for the **Previous** (lines 116–132) and **Next** (lines 135–154) Buttons use the **PreviousNode** (lines 119 and 121) and **NextNode** (lines 138 and 140) properties of XNode, respectively. As their names imply, they return the previous or next sibling node in the tree. If there's no previous or next node, the properties return null.

26.7 LINQ to XML: Namespaces and Creating Documents

As you learned in Chapter 24, XML namespaces provide a technique for preventing collisions between tag names used for different purposes. LINQ to XML provides the **XNamespace class** to enable creation and manipulation of XML namespaces.

Using LINQ to XML to navigate data already stored in an XML document is a common operation, but sometimes it is necessary to create an XML document from scratch. Figure 26.17 uses these features to update an XML document to a new format and combine the data in it with data from a document already in the new format. Figures 26.18 and 26.19 contain the XML files in the old and new formats, respectively. Figure 26.20 displays the file output by the program.

```
1    // Fig. 26.17: XMLCombine.cs
2    // Transforming an XML document and splicing its contents with another.
3    using System;
4    using System.Linq;
5    using System.Xml.Linq;
6
7    class XMLCombine
8    {
9       // namespaces used in XML files
10      private static readonly XNamespace employeesOld =
11         "http://www.deitel.com/employeesold";
12      private static readonly XNamespace employeesNew =
13         "http://www.deitel.com/employeesnew";
14
15      static void Main( string[] args )
16      {
17         // load files from disk
18         XDocument newDocument = XDocument.Load( "employeesNew.xml" );
19         XDocument oldDocument = XDocument.Load( "employeesOld.xml" );
20
21         // convert from old to new format
22         oldDocument = TransformDocument( oldDocument );
23
24         // combine documents and write to output file
25         SaveFinalDocument( newDocument, oldDocument );
26
27         // tell user we have finished
28         Console.WriteLine( "Documents successfully combined." );
29      } // end Main
30
```

Fig. 26.17 | Transforming an XML document and splicing its contents with another. (Part 1 of 2.)

```
31        // convert the given XDocument in the old format to the new format
32        private static XDocument TransformDocument( XDocument document )
33        {
34           // use a LINQ query to fill the new XML root with the correct data
35           var newDocumentRoot = new XElement( employeesNew + "employeelist",
36              from employee in document.Root.Elements()
37              select TransformEmployee( employee ) );
38
39           return new XDocument( newDocumentRoot ); // return new document
40        } // end method TransformDocument
41
42        // transform a single employee's data from old to new format
43        private static XElement TransformEmployee( XElement employee )
44        {
45           // retrieve values from old-format XML document
46           XNamespace old = employeesOld; // shorter name
47           string firstName = employee.Element( old + "firstname" ).Value;
48           string lastName = employee.Element( old + "lastname" ).Value;
49           string salary = employee.Element( old + "salary" ).Value;
50
51           // return new-format element with the correct data
52           return new XElement( employeesNew + "employee",
53              new XAttribute( "name", firstName + " " + lastName ),
54              new XAttribute( "salary", salary ) );
55        } // end method TransformEmployee
56
57        // take two new-format XDocuments and combine
58        // them into one, then save to output.xml
59        private static void SaveFinalDocument( XDocument document1,
60           XDocument document2 )
61        {
62           // create new root element
63           var root = new XElement( employeesNew + "employeelist" );
64
65           // fill with the elements contained in the roots of both documents
66           root.Add( document1.Root.Elements() );
67           root.Add( document2.Root.Elements() );
68
69           root.Save( "output.xml" ); // save document to file
70        } // end method SaveFinalDocument
71     } // end class XMLCombine
```

Fig. 26.17 | Transforming an XML document and splicing its contents with another. (Part 2 of 2.)

```
1     <?xml version="1.0"?>
2     <!-- Fig. 26.18: employeesOld.xml -->
3     <!-- Sample old-format input for the XMLCombine application. -->
4     <employees xmlns="http://www.deitel.com/employeesold">
5        <employeelisting>
6           <firstname>Christopher</firstname>
```

Fig. 26.18 | Sample old-format input for the XMLCombine application. (Part 1 of 2.)

```
 7          <lastname>Green</lastname>
 8          <salary>1460</salary>
 9       </employeelisting>
10       <employeelisting>
11          <firstname>Michael</firstname>
12          <lastname>Red</lastname>
13          <salary>1420</salary>
14       </employeelisting>
15    </employees>
```

Fig. 26.18 | Sample old-format input for the XMLCombine application. (Part 2 of 2.)

```
1    <?xml version="1.0"?>
2    <!-- Fig. 26.19: employeesNew.xml -->
3    <!-- Sample new-format input for the XMLCombine application. -->
4    <employeelist xmlns="http://www.deitel.com/employeesnew">
5       <employee name="Jenn Brown" salary="2300"/>
6       <employee name="Percy Indigo" salary="1415"/>
7    </employeelist>
```

Fig. 26.19 | Sample new-format input for the XMLCombine application.

```
1    <?xml version="1.0" encoding="utf-8"?>
2    <employeelist xmlns="http://www.deitel.com/employeesnew">
3      <employee name="Jenn Brown" salary="2300" />
4      <employee name="Percy Indigo" salary="1415" />
5      <employee name="Christopher Green" salary="1460" />
6      <employee name="Michael Red" salary="1420" />
7    </employeelist>
```

Fig. 26.20 | XML file generated by XMLCombine (Fig. 26.17).

Lines 10–13 of Fig. 26.17 define XNamespace objects for the two namespaces used in the input XML documents. There's an implicit conversion from string to XNamespace.

The TransformDocument method (lines 32–40) converts an XML document from the old format to the new format. It creates a new XElement newDocumentRoot, passing the desired name and child elements as arguments. It then creates and returns a new XDocument, with newDocumentRoot as its root element.

The first argument (line 35) creates an XName object for the tag name using the XNamespace's overloaded + operator—the XName contains the XNamespace from the left operand and the local name given by the string in the right operand. Recall that you can use XName's LocalName property to access the element's unqualified name. The **Namespace property** gives you access to the contained XNamespace object. The second argument is the result of a LINQ query (lines 36–37), which uses the TransformEmployee method to transform each employeelisting entry in the old format (returned by calling the Elements method on the root of the old document) into an employee entry in the new format. When passed a collection of XElements, the XElement constructor adds all members of the collection as children.

The `TransformEmployee` method (lines 43–55) reformats the data for one employee. It does this by retrieving the text contained in the child elements of each of the `employeelisting` entries, then creating a new `employee` element and returning it. The expressions passed to the `Element` method use `XNamespaces`—this is necessary because the elements they're retrieving are in the old namespace. Passing just the tag's local name would cause the `Element` method to return `null`, creating a `NullReferenceException` when the `Value` property was accessed.

Once we've retrieved the values from the original XML document, we add them as attributes to an `employee` element. This is done by creating new `XAttribute` objects with the attribute's name and value, and passing these to the `XElement` constructor (lines 52–54).

The `SaveFinalDocument` method (lines 59–70) merges the two documents and saves them to disk. It first creates a new root element in the correct namespace (line 63). Then it adds the `employee` elements from both documents as children using the **Add method** defined in the `XContainer` class (lines 66–67). The `Add` method, like `XElement`'s constructor, will add all elements if passed a collection. After creating and filling the new root, we save it to disk (line 69).

26.8 XSLT with Class `XslCompiledTransform`

Recall from Section 26.4 that XSL elements define rules for transforming one type of XML document to another type of XML document. We showed how to transform XML documents into XHTML documents and displayed the results in Internet Explorer. MSXML, the XSLT processor used by Internet Explorer, performed the transformations. We now perform a similar task in a C# program.

Performing an XSL Transformation in C# Using the .NET Framework
Figure 26.21 applies the style sheet `sports.xsl` (Fig. 26.9) to the XML document `sports.xml` (Fig. 26.8) programmatically. The result of the transformation is written to an XHTML file on disk and displayed in a text box. Figure 26.21(c) shows the resulting XHTML document (`sports.html`) when you view it in Internet Explorer.

```
1   // Fig. 26.21: TransformTestForm.cs
2   // Applying an XSLT style sheet to an XML Document.
3   using System;
4   using System.IO;
5   using System.Windows.Forms;
6   using System.Xml.Xsl; // contains class XslCompiledTransform
7
8   namespace TransformTest
9   {
10     public partial class TransformTestForm : Form
11     {
12        public TransformTestForm()
13        {
14           InitializeComponent();
15        } // end constructor
16
```

Fig. 26.21 | Applying an XSLT style sheet to an XML document. (Part 1 of 2.)

```
17          // applies the transformation
18          private XslCompiledTransform transformer;
19
20          // initialize variables
21          private void TransformTestForm_Load( object sender, EventArgs e )
22          {
23              transformer = new XslCompiledTransform(); // create transformer
24
25              // load and compile the style sheet
26              transformer.Load( "sports.xsl" );
27          } // end TransformTestForm_Load
28
29          // transform data on transformButton_Click event
30          private void transformButton_Click( object sender, EventArgs e )
31          {
32              // perform the transformation and store the result in new file
33              transformer.Transform( "sports.xml", "sports.html" );
34
35              // read and display the XHTML document's text in a TextBox
36              consoleTextBox.Text = File.ReadAllText( "sports.html" );
37          } // end method transformButton_Click
38      } // end class TransformTestForm
39  } // end namespace TransformTest
```

a) Initial GUI   b) GUI showing transformed raw XHTML

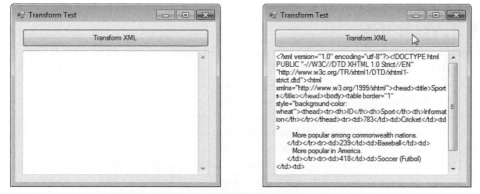

c) Transformed XHTML rendered in Internet Explorer

Fig. 26.21 | Applying an XSLT style sheet to an XML document. (Part 2 of 2.)

Line 6 imports the **System.Xml.Xsl** namespace, which contains class **XslCompiledTransform** for applying XSL style sheets to XML documents. Line 18 declares XslCompiledTransform object transformer, which serves as an XSLT processor to transform XML data from one format to another.

In event handler TransformTestForm_Load (lines 21–27), line 23 creates and initializes transformer. Line 26 calls the XslCompiledTransform object's **Load** method, which loads and parses the style sheet that this application uses. This method takes an argument specifying the name and location of the style sheet—sports.xsl (Fig. 26.9) located in the current directory.

The event handler transformButton_Click (lines 30–37) calls the **Transform** method of class XslCompiledTransform to apply the style sheet (sports.xsl) to sports.xml (line 33). This method takes two string arguments—the first specifies the XML file to which the style sheet should be applied, and the second specifies the file in which the result of the transformation should be stored on disk. Thus the Transform method call in line 33 transforms sports.xml to XHTML and writes the result to disk as the file sports.html. Figure 26.21(c) shows the new XHTML document rendered in Internet Explorer. The output is identical to that of Fig. 26.8—in the current example, though, the XHTML is stored on disk rather than generated dynamically by MSXML.

After applying the transformation, the program displays the content of the new file sports.html in consoleTextBox, as shown in Fig. 26.21(b). Line 36 obtains the text of the file by passing its name to method ReadAllText of the System.IO.File class, which simplifies file-processing tasks on the local system.

26.9 Wrap-Up

In this chapter, we continued our XML introduction from Chapter 24 by demonstrating several technologies related to XML. We discussed how to create DTDs and schemas for specifying and validating the structure of an XML document. We showed how to use various tools to confirm whether XML documents are valid (i.e., conform to a DTD or schema).

You learned how to create and use XSL documents to specify rules for converting XML documents between formats. Specifically, you learned how to format and sort XML data and output it as XHTML for display in a web browser.

The final sections of the chapter presented more advanced uses of XML in C# applications. We demonstrated how to retrieve and display data from an XML document using various .NET classes. We illustrated how a DOM tree represents each element of an XML document as a node in the tree. The chapter also demonstrated loading data from an XML document using the Load method of the XDocument class. We demonstrated the tools LINQ to XML provides for working with namespaces. Finally, we showed how to use the XslCompiledTransform class to perform XSL transformations.

26.10 Web Resources

www.deitel.com/XML/

The Deitel XML Resource Center focuses on the vast amount of free XML content available online, plus some for-sale items. Start your search here for tools, downloads, tutorials, podcasts, wikis, documentation, conferences, FAQs, books, e-books, sample chapters, articles, newsgroups, forums, downloads from CNET's download.com, jobs and contract opportunities, and more that will help you develop XML applications.

27

Web App Development with ASP.NET: A Deeper Look

… the challenges are for the designers of these applications: to forget what we think we know about the limitations of the Web, and begin to imagine a wider, richer range of possibilities. It's going to be fun.
—Jesse James Garrett

If any man will draw up his case, and put his name at the foot of the first page, I will give him an immediate reply. Where he compels me to turn over the sheet, he must wait my leisure.
—Lord Sandwich

OBJECTIVES

In this chapter you'll learn:

- To use the **Web Site Administration Tool** to modify web application configuration settings.

- To restrict access to pages to authenticated users.

- To create a uniform look-and-feel for a website using master pages.

- To use ASP.NET Ajax to improve the user interactivity of your web applications.

27.1 Introduction

In Chapter 19, we introduced ASP.NET and web application development. In this chapter, we introduce several additional ASP.NET web-application development topics, including:

- master pages to maintain a uniform look-and-feel across the Web Forms in a web application

- creating a password-protected website with registration and login capabilities

- using the **Web Site Administration Tool** to specify which parts of a website are password protected

- using ASP.NET Ajax to quickly and easily improve the user experience for your web applications, giving them responsiveness comparable to that of desktop applications.

27.2 Case Study: Password-Protected Books Database Application

This case study presents a web application in which a user logs into a password-protected website to view a list of publications by a selected author. The application consists of several ASPX files. For this application, we'll use the **ASP.NET Web Site** template, which is a starter kit for a small multi-page website. The template uses Microsoft's recommended practices for organizing a website and separating the website's style (look-and-feel) from its content. The default site has two primary pages (**Home** and **About**) and is pre-configured with login and registration capabilities. The template also specifies a common look-and-feel for all the pages in the website—a concept known as a master page.

We begin by examining the features of the default website that is created with the **ASP.NET Web Site** template. Next, we test drive the completed application to demonstrate the changes we made to the default website. Then, we provide step-by-step instructions to guide you through building the application.

27.2.1 Examining the ASP.NET Web Site Template

To test the default website, begin by creating the website that you'll customize in this case study. Perform the following steps:

1. Select **File > New Web Site...** to display the **New Web Site** dialog.

2. In the left column of the **New Web Site** dialog, ensure that **Visual C#** is selected, then select **ASP.NET Web Site** in the middle column.

3. Choose a location for your website, name it Bug2Bug and click **OK** to create it.

Fig. 27.1 shows the website's contents in the **Solution Explorer**.

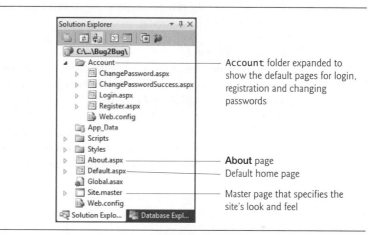

Account folder expanded to show the default pages for login, registration and changing passwords

About page

Default home page

Master page that specifies the site's look and feel

Fig. 27.1 | The default **ASP.NET Web Site** in the **Solution Explorer**.

Executing the Website
You can now execute the website. Select the Default.aspx page in the **Solution Explorer**, then type *Ctrl + F5* to display the default page shown in Fig. 27.2.

Navigation bar contains links to the **Home** and **About** pages

You can customize the content of each page and the look-and-feel of the website

Click this link to log into the website

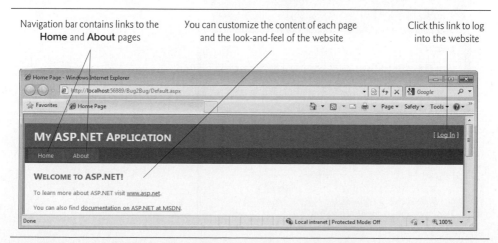

Fig. 27.2 | Default **Home** page of a website created with the **ASP.NET Web Site** template.

Navigation and Pages

The default **ASP.NET Web Site** contains a home page and an about page—so-called **content pages**—that you'll customize in subsequent sections. The navigation bar near the top of the page allows you to switch between these pages by clicking the link for the appropriate page. In Section 27.2.7, you'll add another link to the navigation bar to allow users to browse book information.

As you navigate between the pages, notice that each page has the same look-and-feel. This is typical of professional websites. The site uses a **master page** and cascading style sheets (CSS) to achieve this. A master page defines common GUI elements that are displayed by each page in a set of content pages. Just as C# classes can inherit instance variables and methods from existing classes, content pages can inherit elements from master pages—this is a form of visual inheritance.

Login and Registration Support

Websites commonly provide "membership capabilities" that allow users to register at a website and log in. Often this gives users access to website customization capabilities or premium content. The default **ASP.NET Web Site** is pre-configured to support registration and login capabilities.

In the upper-right corner of each page is a **Log In** link. Click that link to display the **Login** page (Fig. 27.3). If you are already registered with the site, you can log in with your username and password. Otherwise, you can click the **Register** link to display the **Register** page (Fig. 27.4). For the purpose of this case study, we created an account with the username `testuser1` and the password `testuser1`. You do not need to be registered or logged into the default website to view the home and about pages.

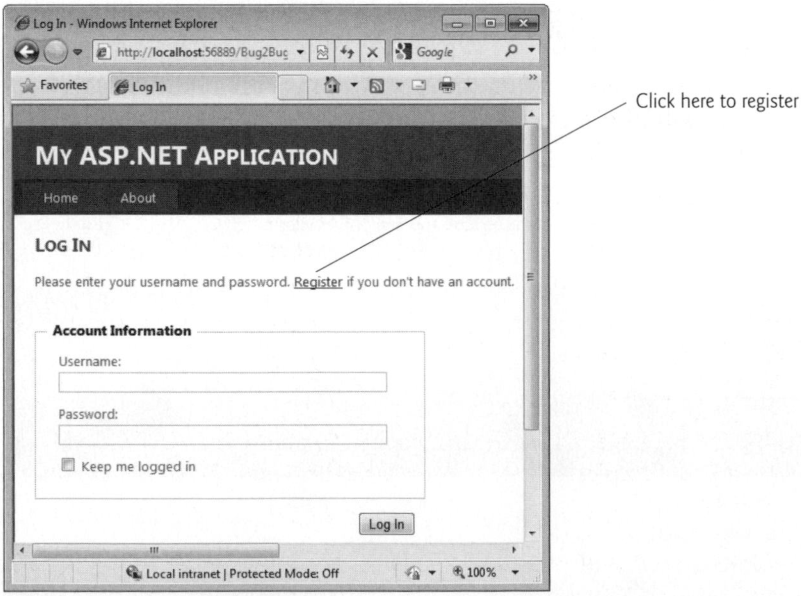

Fig. 27.3 | Login page.

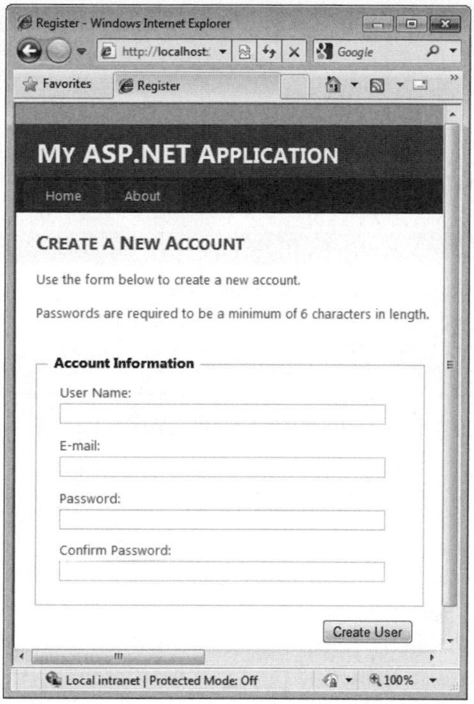

Fig. 27.4 | Register page.

27.2.2 Test-Driving the Completed Application

This example uses a technique known as **forms authentication** to protect a page so that only registered users who are logged into the website can access the page. Such users are known as the site's members. Authentication is a crucial tool for sites that allow only members to enter the site or a portion of the site. In this application, website visitors must log in before they're allowed to view the publications in the Books database.

Let's open the completed Bug2Bug website and execute it so that you can see the authentication functionality in action. Perform the following steps:

1. Close the application you created in Section 27.2.1—you'll reopen this website so that you can customize it in Section 27.2.3.

2. Select **Open Web Site...** from the **File** menu.

3. In the **Open Web Site** dialog, ensure that **File System** is selected, then navigate to this chapter's examples, select the Bug2Bug folder and click the **Open** Button.

4. Select the Default.aspx page then type *Ctrl + F5* to execute the website.

The website appears as shown in Fig. 27.5. Notice that we modified the site's master page so that the top of the page displays an image, the background color of the top of the page is white and the **Log In** link is black. Also, the navigation bar contains a link for the **Books** page that you'll create later in this case study.

Fig. 27.5 | **Home** page for the completed `Bug2Bug` website.

Try to visit the **Books** page by clicking the **Books** link in the navigation bar. Because this page is password protected in the `Bug2Bug` website, the website automatically redirects you to the **Login** page instead—you cannot view the **Books** page without logging in first. If you've not yet registered at the completed `Bug2Bug` website, click the **Register** link to create a new account. If you have registered, log in now.

If you are logging in, when you click the **Log In** Button on the **Log In** page, the website attempts to validate your username and password by comparing them with the usernames and passwords that are stored in a database on the server—this database is created for you with the **ASP.NET Web Site** template. If there is a match, you are **authenticated** (that is, your identity is confirmed) and you're redirected to the **Books** page (Fig. 27.6). If you're registering for the first time, the server ensures that you've filled out the registration form properly and that your password is valid (at least 6 characters), then logs you in and redirects you to the **Books** page.

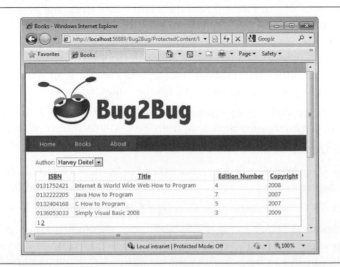

Fig. 27.6 | `Books.aspx` displaying books by Harvey Deitel (by default).

The **Books** page provides a drop-down list of authors and a table containing the ISBNs, titles, edition numbers and copyright years of books in the database. By default, the page displays all the books by Harvey Deitel. Links appear at the bottom of the table that allow you to access additional pages of data—we configured the table to display only four rows of data at a time. When the user chooses an author, a postback occurs, and the page is updated to display information about books written by the selected author (Fig. 27.7).

Fig. 27.7 | `Books.aspx` displaying books by Greg Ayer.

Logging Out of the Website
When you're logged in, the **Log In** link is replaced in the upper-right corner of each page (not shown in Figs. 27.6–27.7) with the message "Welcome *username*" where *username* is replaced with your log in name, and a **Log Out** link. When you click **Log Out**, the website redirects you to the home page (Fig. 27.5).

27.2.3 Configuring the Website

Now that you're familiar with how this application behaves, you'll modify the default website you created in Section 27.2.1. Thanks to the rich functionality of the default website, you'll have to write almost no Visual C# code to create this application. The **ASP.NET Web Site** template hides the details of authenticating users against a database of user names and passwords, displaying appropriate success or error messages and redirecting the user to the correct page based on the authentication results. We now discuss the steps you must perform to create the password-protected books database application.

Step 1: Opening the Website
Open the default website that you created in Section 27.2.1.

1. Select **Open Web Site...** from the **File** menu.

2. In the **Open Web Site** dialog, ensure that **File System** is selected, then navigate to the location where you created your version of the Bug2Bug website and click the **Open** Button.

Step 2: Setting Up Website Folders

For this website, you'll create two new folders—one that will contain the image that is used on all the pages and one that will contain the password-protected page. Password-protected parts of your website are typically placed in a separate folder. As you'll see shortly, you can control access to specific folders in a website.

You can choose any name you like for these folders—we chose Images for the folder that will contain the image and ProtectedContent for the folder that will contain the password-protected **Books** page. To create the folders, perform the following steps:

1. Create an Images folder by right clicking the location of the website in the **Solution Explorer**, selecting **New Folder** and typing the name Images.

2. Create a ProtectedContent folder by right clicking the location of the website in the **Solution Explorer**, selecting **New Folder** and typing the name ProtectedContent.

Step 3: Importing the Website Header Image and the Database File

Next, you'll add an image to the Images folder and the database file to the App_Data folder.

1. In Windows Explorer, locate the folder containing this chapter's examples.

2. Drag the image bug2bug.png from the images folder in Windows Explorer into the Images folder in the **Solution Explorer** to copy the image into the website.

3. Drag the Books.mdf database file from the databases folder in Windows Explorer to the project's App_Data folder. We show how to retrieve data from this database later in the section.

Step 4: Opening the Web Site Administration Tool

In this application, we want to ensure that only authenticated users are allowed to access Books.aspx (created in Section 27.2.5) to view the information in the database. Previously, we created all of our ASPX pages in the web application's root directory. By default, any website visitor (regardless of whether the visitor is authenticated) can view pages in the root directory. ASP.NET allows you to restrict access to particular folders of a website. We do not want to restrict access to the root of the website, however, because users won't be able to view any pages of the website except the login and registration pages. To restrict access to the **Books** page, it must reside in a directory other than the root directory.

You'll now configure the website to allow only authenticated users (that is, users who have logged in) to view the pages in the ProtectedContent folder. Perform the following steps:

1. Select **Website > ASP.NET Configuration** to open the **Web Site Administration Tool** in a web browser (Fig. 27.8). This tool allows you to configure various options that determine how your application behaves.

2. Click either the **Security** link or the **Security** tab to open a web page in which you can set security options (Fig. 27.9), such as the type of authentication the application should use. By default, website users are authenticated by entering username and password information in a web form.

Fig. 27.8 | Web Site Administration Tool for configuring a web application.

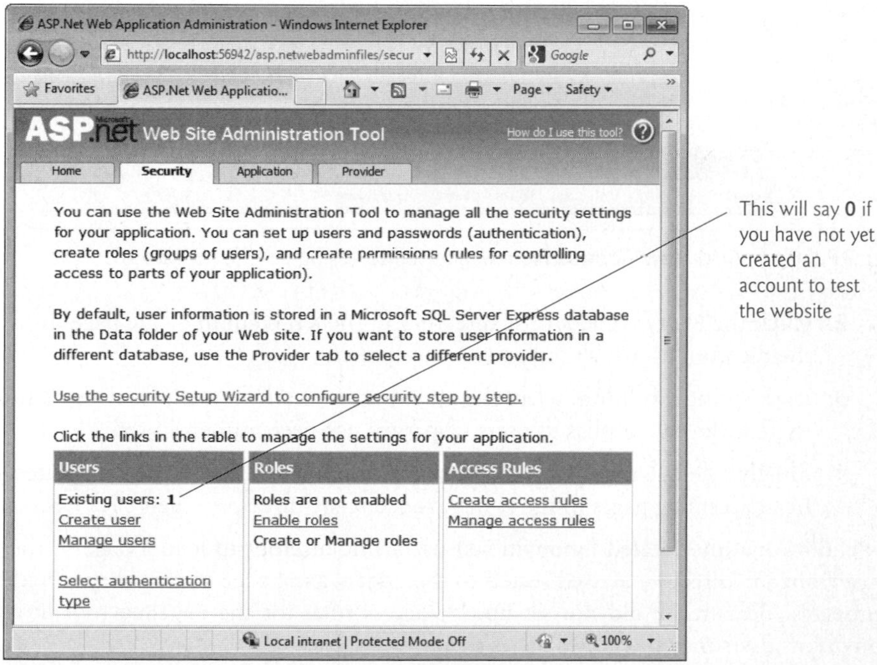

This will say **0** if you have not yet created an account to test the website

ASP.Net Web Application Administration - Windows Internet Explorer

This will say **0** if you have not yet created an account to test the website

Fig. 27.9 | Security page of the Web Site Administration Tool.

Step 5: Configuring the Website's Security Settings

Next, you'll configure the ProtectedContent folder to grant access only to authenticated users—anyone who attempts to access pages in this folder without first logging in will be redirected to the **Login** page. Perform the following steps:

1. Click the **Create access rules** link in the **Access Rules** column of the **Web Site Administration Tool** (Fig. 27.9) to view the **Add New Access Rule** page (Fig. 27.10). This page is used to create an **access rule**—a rule that grants or denies access to a particular directory for a specific user or group of users.

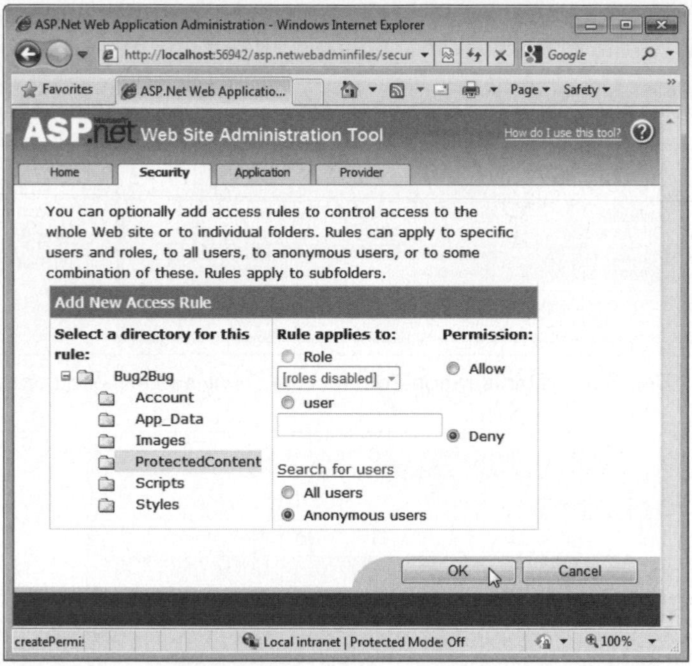

Fig. 27.10 | **Add New Access Rule** page used to configure directory access.

2. Click the `ProtectedContent` directory in the left column of the page to identify the directory to which our access rule applies.

3. In the middle column, select the radio button marked **Anonymous users** to specify that the rule applies to users who have not been authenticated.

4. Finally, select **Deny** in the **Permission** column to prevent unauthenticated users from accessing pages in the `ProtectedContent` directory, then click **OK**.

By default, unauthenticated (anonymous) users who attempt to load a page in the `ProtectedContent` directory are redirected to the `Login.aspx` page so that they can identify themselves. Because we did not set up any access rules for the `Bug2Bug` root directory, anonymous users may still access pages there.

27.2.4 Modifying the Default.aspx and About.aspx Pages

We modified the content of the home (`Default.aspx`) and about (`About.aspx`) pages to replace the default content. To do so, perform the following steps:

1. Double click `Default.aspx` in the **Solution Explorer** to open it, then switch to **Design** view (Fig. 27.11). As you move the cursor over the page, you'll notice that

sometimes the cursor displays as ⊘ to indicate that you cannot edit the part of the page behind the cursor. Any part of a content page that is defined in a master page can be edited only in the master page.

This cursor indicates a part of a content page that cannot be edited because it's inherited from a master page

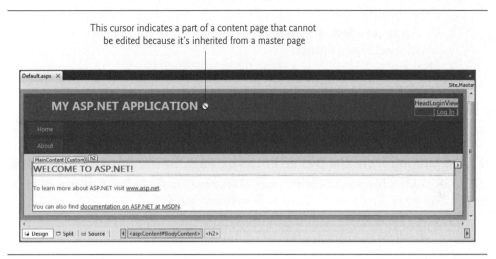

Fig. 27.11 | Default.aspx page in **Design** view.

2. Change the text "Welcome to ASP.NET!" to "Welcome to Our Password-Protected Book Information Site". Note that the text in this heading is actually formatted as small caps text when the page is displayed in a web browser—all of the letters are displayed in uppercase, but the letters that would normally be lowercase are smaller than the first letter in each word.

3. Select the text of the two paragraphs that remain in the page and replace them with "To learn more about our books, click here or click the Books tab in the navigation bar above. You must be logged in to view the Books page." In a later step, you'll link the words "click here" to the **Books** page.

4. Save and close the Default.aspx page.

5. Next, open About.aspx and switch to **Design** view.

6. Change the text "Put content here." to "This is the Bug2Bug password-protected book information database example."

7. Save and close the About.aspx page.

27.2.5 Creating a Content Page That Only Authenticated Users Can Access

We now create the Books.aspx file in the ProtectedContent folder—the folder for which we set an access rule denying access to anonymous users. If an unauthenticated user requests this file, the user will be redirected to Login.aspx. From there, the user can either log in or create a new account, both of which will authenticate the user, then redirect back to Books.aspx. To create the page, perform the following steps:

1. Right click the `ProtectedContent` folder in the **Solution Explorer** and select **Add New Item....** In the resulting dialog, select **Web Form** and specify the file name `Books.aspx`. Ensure that the CheckBox **Select master page** is checked to indicate that this Web Form should be created as a content page that references a master page, then click **Add**.

2. In the **Select a Master Page** dialog, select `Site.master` and click **OK**. The IDE creates the file and opens it.

3. Switch to **Design** view, click in the page to select it, then select **DOCUMENT** from the ComboBox in the **Properties** window.

4. Change the `Title` property of the page to `Books`, then save and close the page

You'll customize this page and create its functionality shortly.

27.2.6 Linking from the `Default.aspx` Page to the `Books.aspx` Page

Next, you'll add a hyperlink from the text "`click here`" in the `Default.aspx` page to the `Books.aspx` page. To do so, perform the following steps:

1. Open the `Default.aspx` page and switch to **Design** view.

2. Select the text "`click here`".

3. Click the **Convert to Hyperlink** (🖳) Button on the toolbar at the top of Visual Web Developer to display the **Hyperlink** dialog. You can enter a URL here, or you can link to another page within the website.

4. Click the **Browse...** Button to display the **Select Project Item** dialog, which allows you to select another page in the website.

5. In the left column, select the `ProtectedContent` directory.

6. In the right column, select `Books.aspx`, then click **OK** to dismiss the **Select Project Item** dialog and click **OK** again to dismiss the **Hyperlink** dialog.

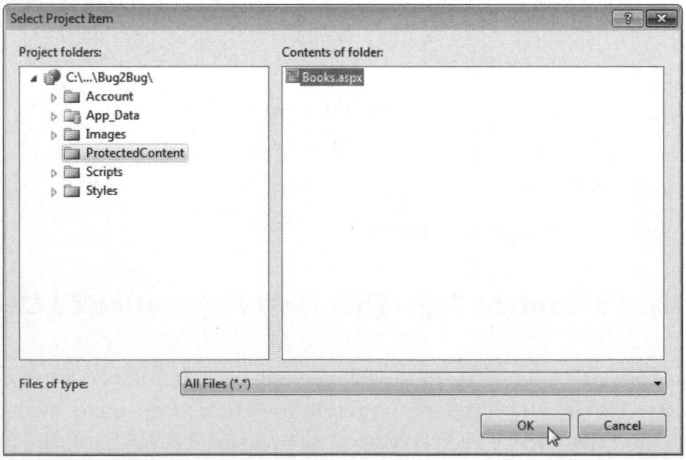

Fig. 27.12 | Selecting the Books.aspx page from the Select Project Item dialog.

Users can now click the **click here** link in the `Default.aspx` page to browse to the `Books.aspx` page. If a user is not logged in, clicking this link will redirect the user to the **Login** page.

27.2.7 Modifying the Master Page (`Site.master`)

Next, you'll modify the website's master page, which defines the common elements we want to appear on each page. A master page is like a base class in a visual inheritance hierarchy, and content pages are like derived classes. The master page contains placeholders for custom content created in each content page. The content pages visually inherit the master page's content, then add content in the areas designated by the master page's placeholders.

For example, it's common to include a **navigation bar** (that is, a series of buttons or menus for navigating a website) on every page of a site. If a site encompasses a large number of pages, adding markup to create the navigation bar for each page can be time consuming. Moreover, if you subsequently modify the navigation bar, every page on the site that uses it must be updated. By creating a master page, you can specify the navigation-bar in one file and have it appear on all the content pages. If the navigation bar changes, only the master page changes—any content pages that use it are updated the next time the page is requested.

In the final version of this website, we modified the master page to include the `Bug2Bug` logo in the header at the top of every page. We also changed the colors of some elements in the header to make them work better with the logo. In particular, we changed the background color from a dark blue to white, and we changed the color of the text for the **Log In** and **Log Out** links to black. The color changes require you to modify the CSS styles for some of the master page's elements. These styles are defined in the file `Site.css`, which is located in the website's `Styles` folder. You will not modify the CSS file directly. Instead, you'll use the tools built into Visual Web Developer to perform these modifications.

Inserting an *Image* in the Header

To display the logo, we'll place an `Image` control in the header of the master page. Each content page based on this master page will include the logo. Perform the following steps to add the `Image`:

1. Open `Site.master` and switch to **Design** view.
2. Delete the text `MY ASP.NET APPLICATION` at the top of the page.
3. In the **Toolbox**, double click **Image** to add an `Image` control where the text used to be.
4. Edit the `Image` control's `ImageUrl` property to point to the `bug2bug.png` image in the `Images` folder.

Customizing the CSS Styles for the Master Page

Our logo image was designed to be displayed against a white background. To change the background color in the header at the top of the page, perform the following steps:

1. Just below the **Design** view is a list of `Buttons` that show you where the cursor is currently located in the master page (Fig. 27.13). These `Buttons` also allow you to select specific elements in the page. Click the **<div.header>** `Button` to select the header portion of the page.

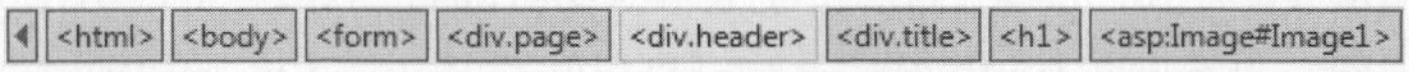

| ◀ | \<html\> | \<body\> | \<form\> | \<div.page\> | \<div.header\> | \<div.title\> | \<h1\> | \<asp:Image#Image1\> |

Fig. 27.13 | Buttons for selecting parts of a page in **Design** view.

2. Select **View > Other Windows > CSS Properties** to display the CSS properties (at the left of the IDE) for the currently selected element (the header of the page).

3. At the top of the **CSS Properties** window, click the **Summary** Button to show only the CSS properties that are currently set for the selected element.

4. Change the background property from #4b6c9e (the hexadecimal value for the current dark blue background) to white and press *Enter*.

5. The **Log In** and **Log Out** links use white text in the default website. Now that the background of the header is white, we need to change the color of these links so they'll be visible. In the upper-right corner of the master page click the **HeadLoginView** control, which is where the **Log In** and **Log Out** links get displayed.

6. Below the **Design** view, click the \<div.loginDisplay\> Button to display the styles for the **HeadLoginView** in the **CSS Properties** window.

7. Change the color property from white to black and press *Enter*.

8. Click inside the box below **HeadLoginView**. Then, below the **Design** view, click the \<a#HeadingLoginStatus\> Button to display the styles for the **Log In/Log Out** link in the **CSS Properties** window

9. Change the color property from white to black and press *Enter*.

10. We chose to make some style changes directly in the Site.css file. On many websites, when you move the mouse over a hyperlink, the color of the link changes. Similarly, once you click a hyperlink, the hyperlink is often displayed in a different color the next time you visit the page to indicate that you've already clicked that link during a previous visit. The predefined styles in this website set the color of the **Log In** link to white for both of these cases. To change these to black, open the Site.css file from the Styles folder in the **Solution Explorer**, then search for the following two styles:

```
.loginDisplay a:visited
.loginDisplay a:hover
```

Change each style's color property from white to black.

11. Save the Site.master and Site.css files.

Adding a Books Link to the Navigation Bar

Currently the navigation bar has only **Home** and **About** links. Next, you'll add a link to the **Books** page. Perform the following steps:

1. In the master page, position the mouse over the navigation bar links, then open the smart-tag menu and click **Edit Menu Items**.

2. In the **Menu Item Editor** dialog, click the **Add a root item** (🔳) Button.

3. Set the new item's Text property to Books and use the up arrow Button to move the new item up so the order of the navigation bar items is Home, Books and About.

4. Set the new item's `NavigateUrl` property to the `Books.aspx` page in the `ProtectedContent` folder.

5. Click **OK**, then save `Site.master` to complete the changes to the master page.

27.2.8 Customizing the Password-Protected `Books.aspx` Page

You are now ready to customize the `Books.aspx` page to display the book information for a particular author.

Generating LINQ to SQL Classes Based on the `Books.mdf` Database

The `Books.aspx` page will provide a `DropDownList` containing authors' names and a `GridView` displaying information about books written by the author selected in the `DropDownList`. A user will select an author from the `DropDownList` to cause the `GridView` to display information about only the books written by the selected author.

To work with the `Books` database through LINQ, we use the same approach as in the **Guestbook** case study (Section 19.8). First you need to generate the LINQ to SQL classes based on the `Books` database, which is provided in the `databases` directory of this chapter's examples folder. Name the file `Books.dbml`. When you drag the tables of the `Books` database from the **Database Explorer** onto the **Object Relational Designer** of `Books.dbml`, you'll find that associations (represented by arrows) between the two tables are automatically generated (Fig. 27.14).

Fig. 27.14 | **Object Relational Designer** for the `Books` database.

To obtain data from this data context, you'll use two `LinqDataSource` controls. In both cases, the `LinqDataSource` control's built-in data selection functionality won't be versatile enough, so the implementation will be slightly different than in Section 19.8. So, we'll use a custom `Select` LINQ statement as the query of a `LinqDataSource`.

Adding a `DropDownList` to Display the Authors' First and Last Names

Now that we have created a `BooksDataContext` class (one of the generated LINQ to SQL classes), we add controls to `Books.aspx` that will display the data on the web page. We first add the `DropDownList` from which users can select an author.

1. Open `Books.aspx` in **Design** mode, then add the text `Author:` and a `DropDownList` control named `authorsDropDownList` in the page's editable content area (which has a white background). The `DropDownList` initially displays the text `Unbound`.

2. Next, we'll bind the list to a data source, so the list displays the author information in the `Authors` table of the `Books` database. Because the **Configure Data**

Source wizard allows us to create LinqDataSources with only simple Select LINQ statements, we cannot use the wizard here. Instead, add a LinqDataSource object below the DropDownList named authorsLinqDataSource.

3. Open the smart-tag menu for the DropDownList and click **Choose Data Source...** to start the **Data Source Configuration Wizard** (Fig. 27.15). Select authorsLinq-DataSource from the **Select a data source** drop-down list in the first screen of the wizard. Then, type Name as the data field to display in the DropDownList and AuthorID as the data field that will be submitted to the server when the user makes a selection. [*Note:* You must manually type these values in because authorsLinqDataSource does not yet have a defined Select query.] When authorsDropDownList is rendered in a web browser, the list items will display the names of the authors, but the underlying values associated with each item will be the AuthorIDs of the authors. Click **OK** to bind the DropDownList to the specified data.

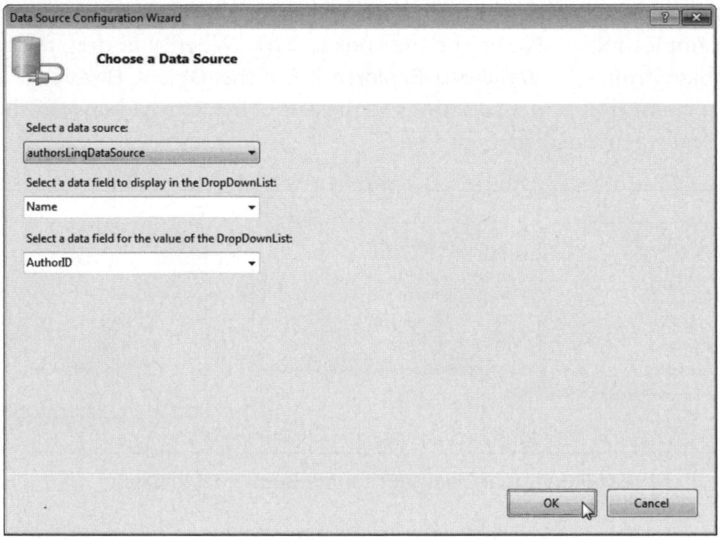

Fig. 27.15 | Choosing a data source for a DropDownList.

4. In the C# code-behind file (Books.aspx.cs), create an instance of BooksData-Context named database as an instance variable.

5. In the **Design** view of Books.aspx, double click authorsLinqDataSource to create an event handler for its **Selecting** event. This event occurs every time the LinqDataSource selects data from its data context, and can be used to implement custom Select queries against the data context. To do so, assign the custom LINQ query to the **Result** property of the event handler's LinqDataSourceSe-lectEventArgs argument. The query results become the data source's data. In this case, we must create a custom anonymous type in the Select clause with properties Name and AuthorID that contain the author's full name and ID. The LINQ query is

```
from author in database.Authors
select new { Name = author.FirstName + " " + author.LastName,
    author.AuthorID };
```

The limitations of the **Configure Data Source** wizard prevent us from using a custom field such as Name (a combination of first name and last name, separated by a space) that isn't one of the database table's existing columns.

6. The last step in configuring the DropDownList on Books.aspx is to set the control's **AutoPostBack** property to True. This property indicates that a postback occurs each time the user selects an item in the DropDownList. As you'll see shortly, this causes the page's GridView (created in the next step) to display new data.

Creating a *GridView to Display the Selected Author's Books*

We now add a GridView to Books.aspx for displaying the book information by the author selected in the authorsDropDownList.

1. Add a GridView named titlesGridView below the other controls in the page's content area.

2. To bind the GridView to data from the Books database, create a LinqDataSource named titlesLinqDataSource beneath the GridView.

3. Select titlesLinqDataSource from the **Choose Data Source** drop-down list in the **GridView Tasks** smart-tag menu. Because titlesLinqDataSource has no defined Select query, the GridView will not automatically be configured.

4. To configure the columns of the GridView to display the appropriate data, select **Edit Columns...** from the **GridView Tasks** smart-tag menu to display the **Fields** dialog (Fig. 27.16).

5. Uncheck the **Auto-generate fields** box to indicate that you'll manually define the fields to display.

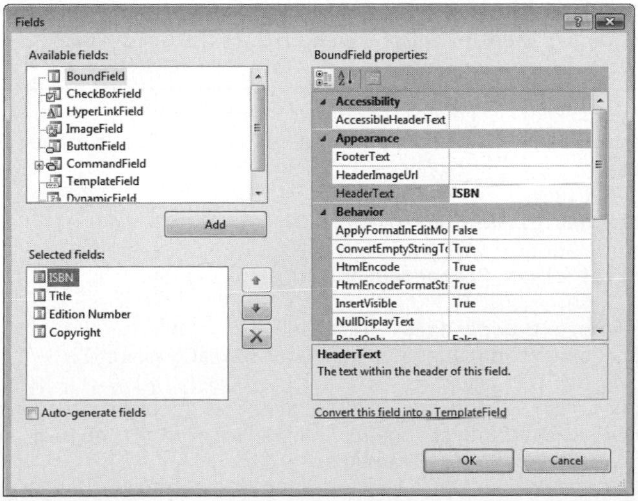

Fig. 27.16 | Creating GridView fields in the **Fields** dialog.

6. Create four BoundFields with the HeaderText ISBN, Title, Edition Number and Copyright, respectively.

7. For the ISBN and Copyright BoundFields, set the SortExpression and Data-Field properties to match the HeaderText. For the Title BoundField, set the SortExpression and DataField properties to Title1 (the IDE renamed the Title column to Title1 to avoid a naming conflict with the table's class—Title). For Edition Number, set the SortExpression and DataField to EditionNumber—the name of the field in the database. The SortExpression specifies to sort by the associated data field when the user chooses to sort by the column. Shortly, we'll enable sorting to allow users to sort this GridView. Click **OK** to close the **Fields** dialog.

8. To specify the Select LINQ query for obtaining the data, double click titles-LinqDataSource to create its Selecting event handler. Assign the custom LINQ query to the LinqDataSourceSelectEventArgs argument's Result property. Use the following LINQ query:

```
from book in database.AuthorISBNs
where book.AuthorID ==
    Convert.ToInt32( authorsDropDownList.SelectedValue )
select book.Title
```

9. The GridView needs to update every time the user makes a new author selection. To implement this, double click the DropDownList to create an event handler for its SelectedIndexChanged event. You can make the GridView update by invoking its DataBind method.

Code-Behind File for the Books Page

Figure 27.17 shows the code for the completed code-behind file. Line 10 defines the data context object that is used in the LINQ queries. Lines 13–20 and 23–31 define the two LinqDataSource's Selecting events. Lines 34–38 define the authorsDropDownList's SelectedIndexChanged event handler, which updates the GridView.

```
1   // Fig. 27.17: ProtectedContent_Books.aspx.cs
2   // Code-behind file for the password-protected Books page.
3   using System;
4   using System.Linq;
5   using System.Web.UI.WebControls;
6
7   public partial class ProtectedContent_Books : System.Web.UI.Page
8   {
9      // data context queried by data sources
10     BooksDataContext database = new BooksDataContext();
11
12     // specify the Select query that creates a combined first and last name
13     protected void authorsLinqDataSource_Selecting( object sender,
14        LinqDataSourceSelectEventArgs e )
15     {
```

Fig. 27.17 | Code-behind file for the password-protected **Books** page. (Part 1 of 2.)

```
16          e.Result =
17             from author in database.Authors
18             select new { Name = author.FirstName + " " + author.LastName,
19                author.AuthorID };
20       } // end method authorsLinqDataSource_Selecting
21
22       // specify the Select query that gets the specified author's books
23       protected void titlesLinqDataSource_Selecting( object sender,
24          LinqDataSourceSelectEventArgs e )
25       {
26          e.Result =
27             from book in database.AuthorISBNs
28             where book.AuthorID ==
29                Convert.ToInt32( authorsDropDownList.SelectedValue )
30             select book.Title;
31       } // end method titlesLinqDataSource_Selecting
32
33       // refresh the GridView when a different author is selected
34       protected void authorsDropDownList_SelectedIndexChanged(
35          object sender, EventArgs e )
36       {
37          titlesGridView.DataBind(); // update the GridView
38       } // end method authorsDropDownList_SelectedIndexChanged
39    } // end class ProtectedContent_Books
```

Fig. 27.17 | Code-behind file for the password-protected **Books** page. (Part 2 of 2.)

Configuring the GridView to Enable Sorting and Paging

Now that the GridView is tied to a data source, we modify several of the control's properties to adjust its appearance and behavior.

1. In **Design** view, use the GridView's sizing handles to set the width to 580px.

2. Next, in the **GridView Tasks** smart-tag menu, check **Enable Sorting** so that the column headings in the GridView become hyperlinks that allow users to sort the data in the GridView using the sort expressions specified by each column. For example, clicking the Titles heading in the web browser will cause the displayed data to appear sorted in alphabetical order. Clicking this heading a second time will cause the data to be sorted in reverse alphabetical order. ASP.NET hides the details required to achieve this functionality.

3. Finally, in the **GridView Tasks** smart-tag menu, check **Enable Paging**. This causes the GridView to split across multiple pages. The user can click the numbered links at the bottom of the GridView control to display a different page of data. GridView's **PageSize** property determines the number of entries per page. Set the **PageSize** property to 4 using the **Properties** window so that the GridView displays only four books per page. This technique for displaying data makes the site more readable and enables pages to load more quickly (because less data is displayed at one time). As with sorting data in a GridView, you do not need to add any code to achieve paging functionality. Figure 27.18 displays the completed Books.aspx file in **Design** mode.

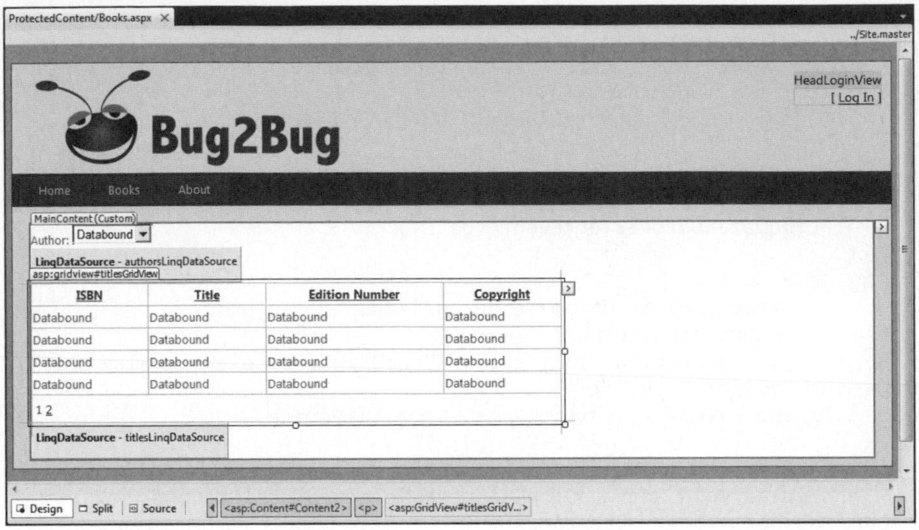

Fig. 27.18 | Completed `Books.aspx` page in **Design** mode.

27.3 ASP.NET Ajax

In this section, you learn the difference between a traditional web application and an **Ajax (Asynchronous JavaScript and XML) web application**. You also learn how to use **ASP.NET Ajax** to quickly and easily improve the user experience for your web applications. To demonstrate ASP.NET Ajax capabilities, you enhance the validation example of Section 19.6 by displaying the submitted form information without reloading the entire page. The only modifications to this web application appear in the `Validation.aspx` file. You use Ajax-enabled controls to add this feature.

27.3.1 Traditional Web Applications

Figure 27.19 presents the typical interactions between the client and the server in a traditional web application, such as one that uses a user registration form. The user first fills in the form's fields, then submits the form (Fig. 27.19, *Step 1*). The browser generates a request to the server, which receives the request and processes it (*Step 2*). The server generates and sends a response containing the exact page that the browser renders (*Step 3*), which causes the browser to load the new page (*Step 4*) and temporarily makes the browser window blank. The client *waits* for the server to respond and *reloads the entire page* with the data from the response (*Step 4*). While such a **synchronous request** is being processed on the server, the user cannot interact with the web page. Frequent long periods of waiting, due perhaps to Internet congestion, have led some users to refer to the World Wide Web as the "World Wide Wait." If the user interacts with and submits another form, the process begins again (*Steps 5–8*).

This model was designed for a web of hypertext documents—what some people call the "brochure web." As the web evolved into a full-scale applications platform, the model shown in Fig. 27.19 yielded "choppy" user experiences. Every full-page refresh required users to reload the full page. Users began to demand a more responsive model.

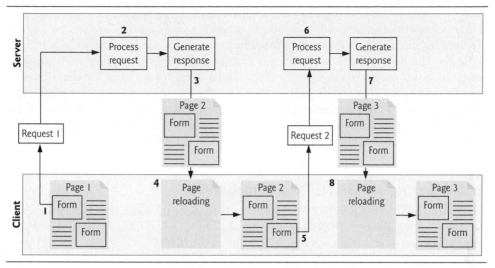

Fig. 27.19 | Traditional web application reloading the page for every user interaction.

27.3.2 Ajax Web Applications

Ajax web applications add a layer between the client and the server to manage communication between the two (Fig. 27.20). When the user interacts with the page, the client requests information from the server (*Step 1*). The request is intercepted by the ASP.NET Ajax controls and sent to the server as an **asynchronous request** (*Step 2*)—the user can continue interacting with the application in the client browser while the server processes the request. Other user interactions could result in additional requests to the server (*Steps 3*

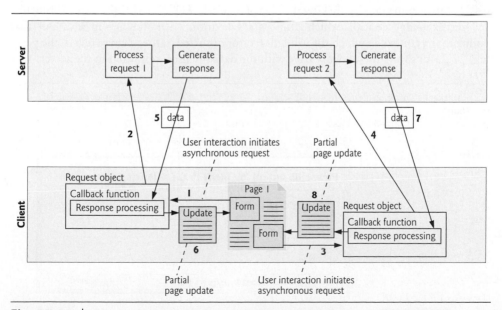

Fig. 27.20 | Ajax-enabled web application interacting with the server asynchronously.

and *4*). Once the server responds to the original request (*Step 5*), the ASP.NET Ajax control that issued the request calls a client-side function to process the data returned by the server. This function—known as a **callback function**—uses **partial-page updates** (*Step 6*) to display the data in the existing web page *without reloading the entire page*. At the same time, the server may be responding to the second request (*Step 7*) and the client browser may be starting another partial-page update (*Step 8*). The callback function updates only a designated part of the page. Such partial-page updates help make web applications more responsive, making them feel more like desktop applications. The web application does not load a new page while the user interacts with it. In the following section, you use ASP.NET Ajax controls to enhance the `Validation.aspx` page.

27.3.3 Testing an ASP.NET Ajax Application

To demonstrate ASP.NET Ajax capabilities we'll enhance the **Validation** application from Section 19.6 by adding ASP.NET Ajax controls. There are no C# code modifications to this application—all of the changes occur in the `.aspx` file.

Testing the Application in Your Default Web Browser

To test this application in your default web browser, perform the following steps:

1. Select **Open Web Site...** from the Visual Web Developer **File** menu.
2. In the **Open Web Site** dialog, select **File System**, then navigate to this chapter's examples, select the `ValidationAjax` folder and click the **Open** `Button`.
3. Select `Validation.aspx` in the **Solution Explorer**, then type *Ctrl + F5* to execute the web application in your default web browser.

Figure 27.21 shows a sample execution of the enhanced application. In Fig. 27.21(a), we show the contact form split into two tabs via the `TabContainer` Ajax control. You can switch between the tabs by clicking the title of each tab. Fig. 27.21(b) shows a `ValidatorCalloutExtender` control, which displays a validation error message in a callout that points to the control in which the validation error occurred, rather than as text in the page. Fig. 27.21(c) shows the updated page with the data the user submitted to the server.

a) Entering a name on the **Name** tab then clicking the **Contact** tab

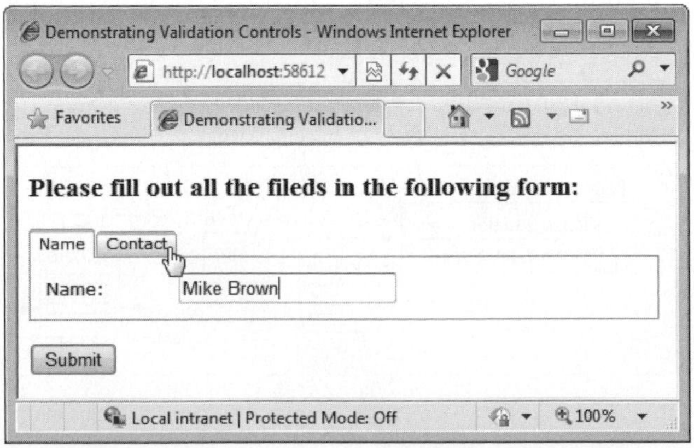

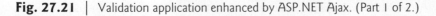

Fig. 27.21 | Validation application enhanced by ASP.NET Ajax. (Part 1 of 2.)

b) Entering an e-mail address in an incorrect format and pressing the *Tab* key to move to the next input field causes a callout to appear informing the user to enter an e-mail address in a valid format

Please fill out all the fileds in the following form:

Name | Contact

E-mail: mbrown

Phone: (555) 555-1234

Please enter an e-mail address in a valid format

Submit

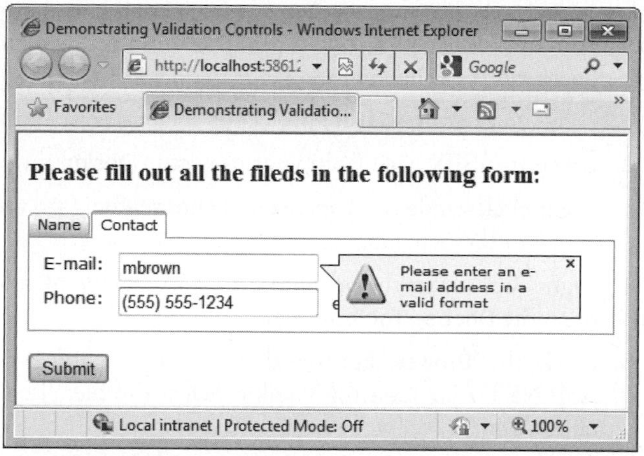

c) After filling out the form properly and clicking the **Submit** button, the submitted data is displayed at the bottom of the page with a partial page update

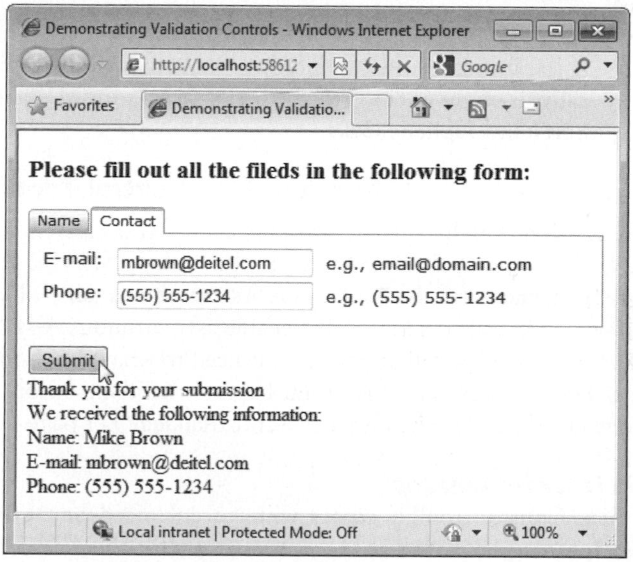

Please fill out all the fileds in the following form:

Name | Contact

E-mail: mbrown@deitel.com   e.g., email@domain.com

Phone: (555) 555-1234   e.g., (555) 555-1234

Submit
Thank you for your submission
We received the following information:
Name: Mike Brown
E-mail: mbrown@deitel.com
Phone: (555) 555-1234

Fig. 27.21 | Validation application enhanced by ASP.NET Ajax. (Part 2 of 2.)

27.3.4 The ASP.NET Ajax Control Toolkit

You'll notice that there is a tab of basic **AJAX Extensions** controls in the **Toolbox**. Microsoft also provides the **ASP.NET Ajax Control Toolkit** as part of the ASP.NET Ajax Library

```
ajax.codeplex.com
```

The toolkit contains many more Ajax-enabled, rich GUI controls. Click the **Download** Button to begin the download. The toolkit does not come with an installer, so you must extract the contents of the toolkit's ZIP file to your hard drive. Note the location where you extracted the files as you'll need this information to add the ASP.NET Ajax Controls to your **Toolbox.**

Adding the ASP.NET Ajax Controls to the Toolbox
You should add controls from the Ajax Control Toolkit to the **Toolbox** in Visual Web Developer (or in Visual Studio), so you can drag and drop controls onto your Web Forms. To do so, perform the following steps:

1. Open an existing website project or create a new website project.

2. Open an ASPX page from your project in **Design** mode.

3. Right click inside the **Toolbox** and choose **Add Tab**, then type ASP.NET Ajax Library in the new tab.

4. Right click under the new **ASP.NET Ajax Library** tab and select **Choose Items...** to open the **Choose Toolbox Items** dialog.

5. Click the **Browse** Button then locate the folder where you extracted the ASP.NET Ajax Control Toolkit. Select the file AjaxControlToolkit.dll then click **Open**.

6. Click **OK** to close dialog. The controls from the Ajax Control Toolkit now appear in the **Toolbox**'s **ASP.NET Ajax Library** tab.

7. If the control names are not in alphabetical order, you can sort them alphabetically, by right clicking in the list of Ajax Control Toolkit controls and selecting **Sort Items Alphabetically**.

27.3.5 Using Controls from the Ajax Control Toolkit

In this section, you'll enhance the application you created in Section 19.6 by adding ASP.NET Ajax controls. The key control in every ASP.NET Ajax-enabled application is the **ScriptManager** (in the **Toolbox**'s **AJAX Extensions** tab), which manages the JavaScript client-side code (called scripts) that enable asynchronous Ajax functionality. A benefit of using ASP.NET Ajax is that you do not need to know JavaScript to be able to use these scripts. The ScriptManager is meant for use with the controls in the **Toolbox**'s **AJAX Extensions** tab. There can be only one ScriptManager per page.

ToolkitScriptManager
The Ajax Control Toolkit comes with an enhanced ScriptManager called the **ToolkitScriptManager**, which manages the scripts for the ASP. NET Ajax Toolkit controls. This one should be used in any page with controls from the ASP. NET Ajax Toolkit.

> **Common Programming Error 27.1**
> *Putting more than one ScriptManager and/or ToolkitScriptManager control on a Web Form causes the application to throw an InvalidOperationException when the page is initialized.*

Open the Validation website you created in Section 19.6. Then drag a ToolkitScriptManager from the **ASP.NET Ajax Library** tab in the **Toolbox** to the top of the page— a script manager must appear before any controls that use the scripts it manages.

Grouping Information in Tabs Using the TabContainer Control
The **TabContainer control** enables you to group information into tabs that are displayed only if they're selected. The information in an unselected tab won't be displayed until the

user selects that tab. To demonstrate a `TabContainer` control, let's split the form into two tabs—one in which the user can enter the name and one in which the user can enter the e-mail address and phone number. Perform the following steps:

1. Click to the right of the text **Please fill out all the fields in the following form:** and press *Enter* to create a new paragraph.

2. Drag a `TabContainer` control from the **ASP.NET Ajax Library** tab in the **Toolbox** into the new paragraph. This creates a container for hosting tabs. Set the TabContainer's `Width` property to 450px.

3. To add a tab, open the **TabContainer Tasks** smart-tag menu and select **Add Tab Panel**. This adds a **TabPanel** object—representing a tab—to the `TabContainer`. Do this again to add a second tab.

4. You must change each TabPanel's `HeaderText` property by editing the ASPX page's markup. To do so, click the `TabContainer` to ensure that it's selected, then switch to **Split** view in the design window. In the highlighted markup that corresponds to the `TabContainer`, locate `HeaderText="TabPanel1"` and change `"TabPanel1"` to `"Name"`, then locate `HeaderText="TabPanel2"` and change `"TabPanel2"` to `"Contact"`. Switch back to **Design** view. In **Design** view, you can navigate between tabs by clicking the tab headers. You can drag-and-drop elements into the tab as you would anywhere else.

5. Click in the **Name** tab's body, then insert a one row and two column table. Take the text and controls that are currently in the **Name:** row of the original table and move them to the table in the **Name** tab.

6. Switch to the **Contact** tab, click in its body, then insert a two-row-by-two-column table. Take the text and controls that are currently in the **E-mail:** and **Phone:** rows of the original table and move them to the table in the **Contact** tab.

7. Delete the original table that is currently below the `TabContainer`.

Partial-Page Updates Using the `UpdatePanel` *Control*

The **UpdatePanel control** eliminates full-page refreshes by isolating a section of a page for a partial-page update. In this example, we'll use a partial-page update to display the user's information that is submitted to the server.

To implement a partial-page update, perform the following steps:

1. Click to the left of the **Submit** Button and press *Enter* to create a new paragraph above it. Then click in the new paragraph and drag an UpdatePanel control from the **AJAX Extensions** tab in the **Toolbox** to your form.

2. Then, drag into the UpdatePanel the control(s) to update and the control that triggers the update. For this example, drag the outputLabel and the submitButton into the UpdatePanel.

3. To specify when an UpdatePanel should update, you need to define an **UpdatePanel trigger**. Select the UpdatePanel, then click the ellipsis button next to the control's `Triggers` property in the **Properties** window. In the **UpdatePanel-Trigger Collection** dialog that appears (Fig. 27.22), click **Add** to add an **Async-PostBackTrigger**. Set the `ControlID` property to submitButton and the

EventName property to Click. Now, when the user clicks the **Submit** button, the UpdatePanel intercepts the request and makes an asynchronous request to the server instead. Then the response is inserted in the outputLabel element, and the UpdatePanel reloads the label to display the new text without refreshing the entire page. Click **OK** to close the dialog.

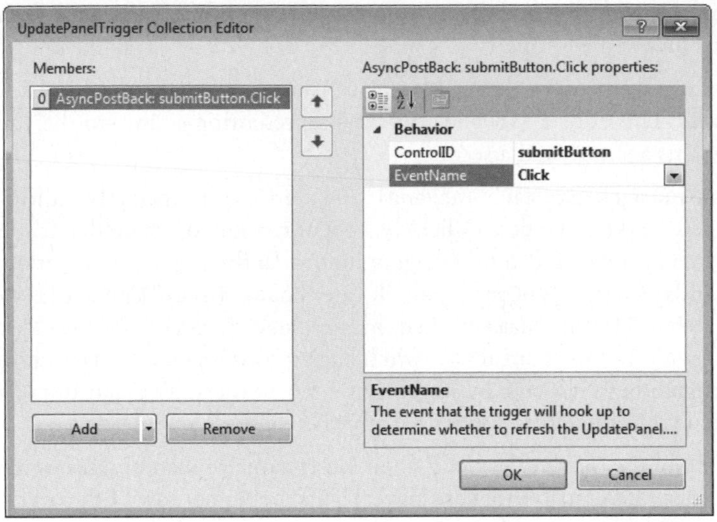

Fig. 27.22 | Creating a trigger for an UpdatePanel.

Adding Ajax Functionality to ASP.NET Validation Controls Using Ajax Extenders
Several controls in the Ajax Control Toolkit are **extenders**—components that enhance the functionality of regular ASP.NET controls. In this example, we use **ValidatorCallout-Extender controls** that enhance the ASP.NET validation controls by displaying error messages in small yellow callouts next to the input fields, rather than as text in the page.

You can create a ValidatorCalloutExtender by opening any validator control's smart-tag menu and clicking **Add Extender...** to display the **Extender Wizard** dialog (Fig. 27.23). Next, choose ValidatorCalloutExtender from the list of available extenders. The extender's ID is chosen based on the ID of the validation control you're extending, but you can rename it if you like. Click **OK** to create the extender. Do this for each of the validation controls in this example.

Changing the Display Property of the Validation Controls
The ValidatorCalloutExtenders display error messages with a nicer look-and-feel, so we no longer need the validator controls to display these messages on their own. For this reason, set each validation control's Display property to None.

Running the Application
When you run this application, the TabContainer will display whichever tab was last displayed in the ASPX page's **Design** view. Ensure that the **Name** tab is displayed, then select Validation.aspx in the **Solution Explorer** and type *Ctrl* + *F5* to execute the application.

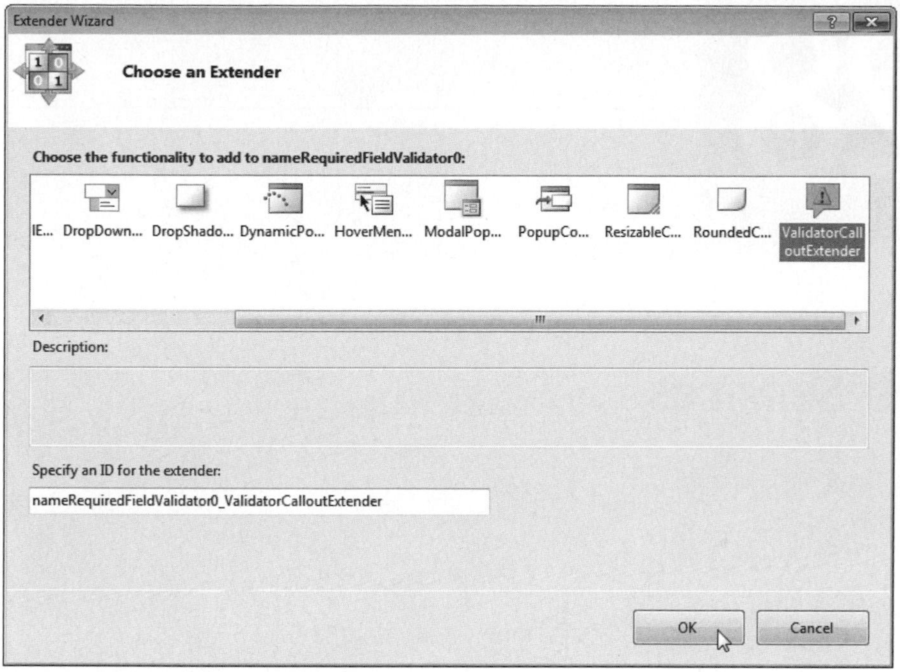

Fig. 27.23 | Creating a control extender using the **Extender Wizard**.

Additional ASP.NET Information

The Ajax Control Toolkit contains many other extenders and independent controls. You can check them out at www.asp.net/ajax/ajaxcontroltoolkit/samples/. For more information on ASP.NET Ajax, check out our ASP.NET Ajax Resource Center at

> www.deitel.com/aspdotnetajax

27.4 Wrap-Up

In this chapter, we presented a case study in which we built a password-protected web application that requires users to log in before accessing information from the Books database. You used the **Web Site Administration Tool** to configure the application to prevent anonymous users from accessing the book information. We used the **ASP.NET Web Site** template, which provides login and registration capabilities for a website. You also learned to create a uniform look-and-feel for a website with a master page.

Finally, you learned the difference between a traditional web application and an Ajax web application. We introduced ASP.NET AJAX and Microsoft's Ajax Control Toolkit. You learned how to build an Ajax-enabled web application by using a ScriptManager and the Ajax-enabled controls of the Ajax Extensions package and the Ajax Control Toolkit.

In the next chapter, we introduce web services, which allow methods on one machine to call methods on other machines via common data formats and protocols, such as XML and HTTP. You will learn how web services promote software reusability and interoperability across multiple computers on a network such as the Internet.

28

Web Services

OBJECTIVES

In this chapter you'll learn:

- How to create WCF web services.

- How XML, JSON, XML-Based Simple Object Access Protocol (SOAP) and Representational State Transfer Architecture (REST) enable WCF web services.

- The elements that comprise WCF web services, such as service references, service endpoints, service contracts and service bindings.

- How to create a client that consumes a WCF web service.

- How to use WCF web services with Windows and web applications.

- How to use session tracking in WCF web services to maintain state information for the client.

- How to pass user-defined types to a WCF web service.

28.1 Introduction

This chapter introduces **Windows Communication Foundation (WCF)** services. WCF is a set of technologies for building distributed systems in which system components communicate with one another over networks. In earlier versions of .NET, the various types of communication used different technologies and programming models. WCF uses a common framework for all communication between systems, so you need to learn only one programming model to use WCF.

This chapter focuses on WCF web services, which promote software reusability in distributed systems that typically execute across the Internet. A **web service** is a class that allows its methods to be called by methods on other machines via common data formats and protocols, such as XML (see Chapter 26), JSON (Section 28.5) and HTTP. In .NET, the over-the-network method calls are commonly implemented through **Simple Object Access Protocol (SOAP)** or the **Representational State Transfer (REST)** architecture. SOAP is an XML-based protocol describing how to mark up requests and responses so that they can be sent via protocols such as HTTP. SOAP uses a standardized XML-based format to enclose data in a message that can be sent between a client and a server. REST is a network architecture that uses the web's traditional request/response mechanisms such as GET and POST requests. REST-based systems do not require data to be wrapped in a special message format.

We build the WCF web services presented in this chapter in Visual Web Developer 2010 Express, and we create client applications that invoke these services using both Visual C# 2010 Express and Visual Web Developer 2010 Express. Full versions of Visual Studio 2010 include the functionality of both Express editions.

Requests to and responses from web services created with Visual Web Developer are typically transmitted via SOAP or REST, so any client capable of generating and processing SOAP or REST messages can interact with a web service, regardless of the language in which the web service is written. We say more about SOAP and REST in Section 28.3 and Section 28.4, respectively.

28.2 WCF Services Basics

Microsoft's Windows Communication Foundation (WCF) was created as a single platform to encompass many existing communication technologies. WCF increases productivity, because you learn only one straightforward programming model. Each WCF service has three key components—addresses, bindings and contracts (usually called the ABCs of a WCF service):

- An **address** represents the service's location (also known as its **endpoint**), which includes the protocol (for example, HTTP) and network address (for example, www.deitel.com) used to access the service.

- A **binding** specifies how a client communicates with the service (for example, SOAP, REST, and so on). Bindings can also specify other options, such as security constraints.

- A **contract** is an interface representing the service's methods and their return types. The service's contract allows clients to interact with the service.

The machine on which the web service resides is referred to as a **web service host**. The client application that accesses the web service sends a method call over a network to the web service host, which processes the call and returns a response over the network to the application. This kind of distributed computing benefits systems in various ways. For example, an application without direct access to data on another system might be able to retrieve this data via a web service. Similarly, an application lacking the processing power necessary to perform specific computations could use a web service to take advantage of another system's superior resources.

28.3 Simple Object Access Protocol (SOAP)

The Simple Object Access Protocol (SOAP) is a platform-independent protocol that uses XML to make remote procedure calls, typically over HTTP. Each request and response is packaged in a **SOAP message**—an XML message containing the information that a web service requires to process the message. SOAP messages are written in XML so that they're computer readable, human readable and platform independent. Most **firewalls**—security barriers that restrict communication among networks—allow HTTP traffic to pass through, so that clients can browse the Internet by sending requests to and receiving responses from web servers. Thus, SOAP-based services can send and receive SOAP messages over HTTP connections with few limitations.

SOAP supports an extensive set of types. The **wire format** used to transmit requests and responses must support all types passed between the applications. SOAP types include the primitive types (for example, `int`), as well as `DateTime`, `XmlNode` and others. SOAP can also transmit arrays of these types. In Section 28.11, you'll see that you can also transmit user-defined types in SOAP messages.

When a program invokes a method of a SOAP web service, the request and all relevant information are packaged in a SOAP message enclosed in a **SOAP envelope** and sent to the server on which the web service resides. When the web service receives this SOAP message, it parses the XML representing the message, then processes the message's contents. The message specifies the method that the client wishes to execute and the arguments the client passed to that method. Next, the web service calls the method with the specified arguments (if any) and sends the response back to the client in another SOAP message. The client parses the response to retrieve the method's result. In Section 28.6, you'll build and consume a basic SOAP web service.

28.4 Representational State Transfer (REST)

Representational State Transfer (REST) refers to an architectural style for implementing web services. Such web services are often called **RESTful web services**. Though REST itself is not a standard, RESTful web services are implemented using web standards. Each operation in a RESTful web service is identified by a unique URL. Thus, when the server receives a request, it immediately knows what operation to perform. Such web services can be used in a program or directly from a web browser. The results of a particular operation may be cached locally by the browser when the service is invoked with a `GET` request. This can make subsequent requests for the same operation faster by loading the result directly from the browser's cache. Amazon's web services (`aws.amazon.com`) are RESTful, as are many others.

RESTful web services are alternatives to those implemented with SOAP. Unlike SOAP-based web services, the request and response of REST services are not wrapped in envelopes. REST is also not limited to returning data in XML format. It can use a variety of formats, such as XML, JSON, HTML, plain text and media files. In Sections 28.7–28.8, you'll build and consume basic RESTful web services.

28.5 JavaScript Object Notation (JSON)

JavaScript Object Notation (JSON) is an alternative to XML for representing data. JSON is a text-based data-interchange format used to represent objects in JavaScript as collections of name/value pairs represented as `Strings`. It is commonly used in Ajax applications. JSON is a simple format that makes objects easy to read, create and parse, and allows programs to transmit data efficiently across the Internet because it is much less verbose than XML. Each JSON object is represented as a list of property names and values contained in curly braces, in the following format:

```
{ propertyName1 : value1, propertyName2 : value2 }
```

Arrays are represented in JSON with square brackets in the following format:

```
[ value1, value2, value3 ]
```

Each value in an array can be a string, a number, a JSON object, `true`, `false` or `null`. To appreciate the simplicity of JSON data, examine this representation of an array of address-book entries

```
[ { first: 'Cheryl', last: 'Black' },
  { first: 'James', last: 'Blue' },
  { first: 'Mike', last: 'Brown' },
  { first: 'Meg', last: 'Gold' } ]
```

Many programming languages now support the JSON data format.

28.6 Publishing and Consuming SOAP-Based WCF Web Services

This section presents our first example of **publishing** (enabling for client access) and **consuming** (using) a web service. We begin with a SOAP-based web service.

28.6.1 Creating a WCF Web Service

To build a SOAP-based WCF web service in Visual Web Developer, you first create a project of type **WCF Service**. SOAP is the default protocol for WCF web services, so no special configuration is required to create them. Visual Web Developer then generates files for the WCF service code, an **SVC file** (`Service.svc`, which provides access to the service), and a **Web.config** file (which specifies the service's binding and behavior).

Visual Web Developer also generates code files for the **WCF service class** and any other code that is part of the WCF service implementation. In the service class, you define the methods that your WCF web service makes available to client applications.

28.6.2 Code for the `WelcomeSOAPXMLService`

Figures 28.1 and 28.2 present the code-behind files for the `WelcomeSOAPXMLService` WCF web service that you'll build in Section 28.6.3. When creating services in Visual Web Developer, you work almost exclusively in the code-behind files. The service provides a method that takes a name (represented as a `string`) as an argument and appends it to the welcome message that is returned to the client. We use a parameter in the method definition to demonstrate that a client can send data to a web service.

Figure 28.1 is the service's interface, which describes the service's contract—the set of methods and properties the client uses to access the service. The **ServiceContract** attribute (line 6) exposes a class that implements this interface as a WCF web service. The **OperationContract** attribute (line 10) exposes the `Welcome` method to clients for remote calls. Optional parameters can be assigned to these contracts to change the data format and method behavior, as we'll show in later examples.

Figure 28.2 defines the class that implements the interface declared as the `Service-Contract`. Lines 7–12 define the method `Welcome`, which returns a `string` welcoming you to WCF web services. Next, we build the web service from scratch.

```
 1   // Fig. 28.1: IWelcomeSOAPXMLService.cs
 2   // WCF web service interface that returns a welcome message through SOAP
 3   // protocol and XML data format.
 4   using System.ServiceModel;
 5
 6   [ServiceContract]
 7   public interface IWelcomeSOAPXMLService
 8   {
 9      // returns a welcome message
10      [OperationContract]
11      string Welcome( string yourName );
12   } // end interface IWelcomeSOAPXMLService
```

Fig. 28.1 | WCF web-service interface that returns a welcome message through SOAP protocol and XML format.

```
 1   // Fig. 28.2: WelcomeSOAPXMLService.cs
 2   // WCF web service that returns a welcome message using SOAP protocol and
 3   // XML data format.
 4   public class WelcomeSOAPXMLService : IWelcomeSOAPXMLService
 5   {
 6      // returns a welcome message
 7      public string Welcome( string yourName )
 8      {
 9         return string.Format(
10            "Welcome to WCF Web Services with SOAP and XML, {0}!",
11            yourName );
12      } // end method Welcome
13   } // end class WelcomeSOAPXMLService
```

Fig. 28.2 | WCF web service that returns a welcome message through the SOAP protocol and XML format.

28.6.3 Building a SOAP WCF Web Service

In the following steps, you create a **WCF Service** project for the WelcomeSOAPXMLService and test it using the built-in ASP.NET Development Server that comes with Visual Web Developer Express and Visual Studio.

Step 1: Creating the Project
To create a project of type **WCF Service**, select **File > New Web Site...** to display the **New Web Site** dialog (Fig. 28.3). Select the **WCF Service** template. Select **File System** from the **Location** drop-down list to indicate that the files should be placed on your local hard disk. By default, Visual Web Developer places files on the local machine in a directory named WCFService1. Rename this folder to WelcomeSOAPXMLService. We modified the default path as well. Click **OK** to create the project.

Step 2: Examining the Newly Created Project
After you create the project, the code-behind file Service.cs, which contains code for a simple web service, is displayed by default. If the code-behind file is not open, open it by double clicking the file in the **App_Code** directory listed in the **Solution Explorer**. By

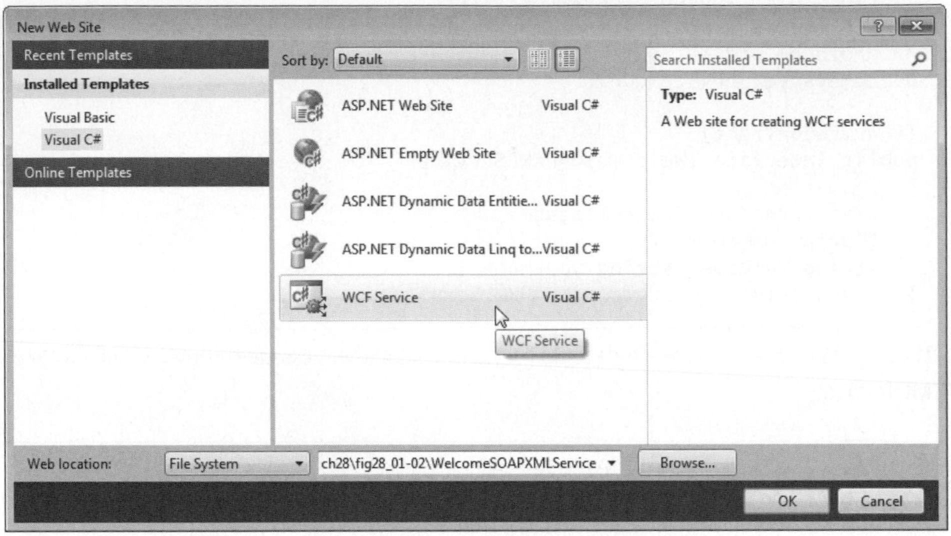

Fig. 28.3 | Creating a **WCF Service** in Visual Web Developer.

default, a new code-behind file implements an interface named IService. This interface (in the file IService.cs) is marked with the ServiceContract and OperationContract attributes. In addition, the IService.cs file defines a class named CompositeType with a DataContract attribute (discussed in Section 28.8). The interface contains two sample service methods named GetData and GetDataUsingContract. The Service.cs contains the code that defines these methods.

Step 3: Modifying and Renaming the Code-Behind File
To create the WelcomeSOAPXMLService service developed in this section, modify IService.cs and Service.cs by replacing the sample code provided by Visual Web Developer with the code from the IWelcomeSOAPXMLService and WelcomeSOAPXMLService files (Figs. 28.1 and 28.2, respectively). Then rename the files to IWelcomeSOAPXMLService.cs and WelcomeSOAPXMLService.cs by right clicking each file in the Solution Explorer and choosing **Rename**.

Step 4: Examining the SVC File
The Service.svc file, when accessed through a web browser, provides information about the web service. However, if you open the SVC file on disk, it contains only

```
<%@ ServiceHost Language="C#" Debug="true" Service="Service"
    CodeBehind="~/App_Code/Service.cs" %>
```

to indicate the programming language in which the web service's code-behind file is written, the Debug attribute (enables a page to be compiled for debugging), the name of the service and the code-behind file's location. When you request the SVC page in a web browser, WCF uses this information to dynamically generate the WSDL document.

Step 5: Modifying the SVC File

If you change the code-behind file name or the class name that defines the web service, you must modify the SVC file accordingly. Thus, after defining class `WelcomeSOAPXMLService` in the code-behind file `WelcomeSOAPXMLService.cs`, modify the SVC file as follows:

```
<%@ ServiceHost Language="C#" Debug="true"
    Service="WelcomeSOAPXMLService"
    CodeBehind="~/App_Code/WelcomeSOAPXMLService.cs" %>
```

28.6.4 Deploying the `WelcomeSOAPXMLService`

You can choose **Build Web Site** from the **Build** menu to ensure that the web service compiles without errors. You can also test the web service directly from Visual Web Developer by selecting **Start Debugging** from the **Debug** menu. The first time you do this, the **Debugging Not Enabled** dialog appears. Click **OK** if you want to enable debugging. Next, a browser window opens and displays information about the service. This information is generated dynamically when the SVC file is requested. Figure 28.4 shows a web browser displaying the `Service.svc` file for the `WelcomeSOAPXMLService` WCF web service.

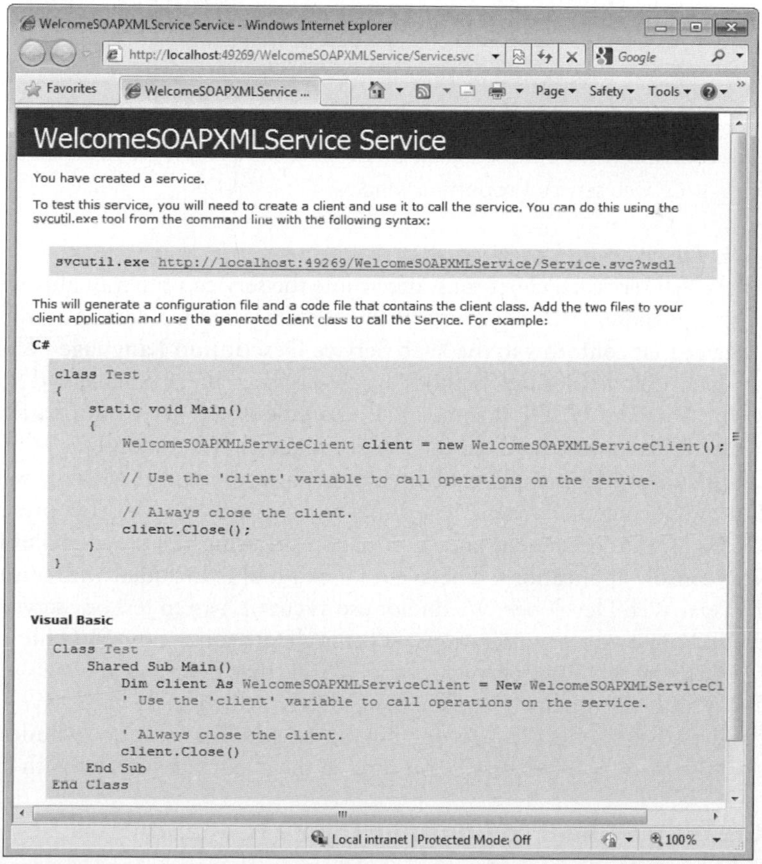

Fig. 28.4 | SVC file rendered in a web browser.

Once the service is running, you can also access the SVC page from your browser by typing a URL of the following form in a web browser:

> `http://localhost:`*portNumber*`/`*virtualPath*`/Service.svc`

(See the actual URL in Fig. 28.4.) By default, the ASP.NET Development Server assigns a random port number to each website it hosts. You can change this behavior by going to the **Solution Explorer** and clicking on the project name to view the **Properties** window (Fig. 28.5). Set the **Use dynamic ports** property to **False** and set the **Port number** property to the port number that you want to use, which can be any unused TCP port. Generally, you don't do this for web services that will be deployed to a real web server. You can also change the service's virtual path, perhaps to make the path shorter or more readable.

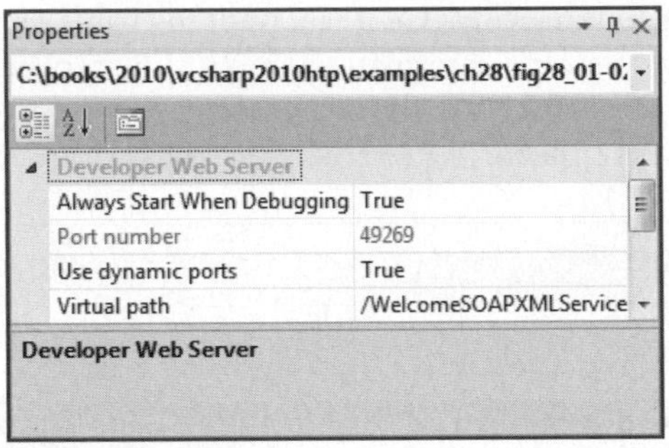

Fig. 28.5 | WCF web service **Properties** window.

Web Services Description Language

To consume a web service, a client must determine the service's functionality and how to use it. For this purpose, web services normally contain a **service description**. This is an XML document that conforms to the **Web Service Description Language** (WSDL)—an XML vocabulary that defines the methods a web service makes available and how clients interact with them. The WSDL document also specifies lower-level information that clients might need, such as the required formats for requests and responses.

WSDL documents help applications determine how to interact with the web services described in the documents. When viewed in a web browser, an SVC file presents a link to the service's WSDL document and information on using the utility **svcutil.exe** to generate test console applications. The svcutil.exe tool is included with Visual Studio 2010 and Visual Web Developer. We do not use svcutil.exe to test our services, opting instead to build our own test applications. When a client requests the SVC file's URL followed by ?wsdl, the server autogenerates the WSDL that describes the web service and returns the WSDL document. Copy the SVC URL (which ends with .svc) from the browser's address field in Fig. 28.4, as you'll need it in the next section to build the client application. Also, leave the web service running so the client can interact with it.

28.6.5 Creating a Client to Consume the `WelcomeSOAPXMLService`

Now that you've defined and deployed the web service, let's consume it from a client application. A .NET web-service client can be any type of .NET application, such as a Windows application, a console application or a web application. You can enable a client application to consume a web service by **adding a service reference** to the client. Figure 28.6 diagrams the parts of a client for a SOAP-based web service after a service reference has been added. [*Note*: This section discusses building a client application in Visual C# 2010 Express, but the discussion also applies to Visual Web Developer 2010 Express.]

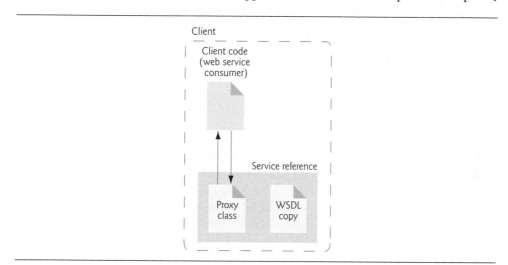

Fig. 28.6 | .NET WCF web-service client after a web-service reference has been added.

An application that consumes a SOAP-based web service actually consists of two parts—a proxy class representing the web service and a client application that accesses the web service via a proxy object (that is, an instance of the proxy class). A **proxy class** handles all the "plumbing" required for service method calls (that is, the networking details and the formation of SOAP messages). Whenever the client application calls a web service's method, the application actually calls a corresponding method in the proxy class. This method has the same name and parameters as the web service's method that is being called, but formats the call to be sent as a request in a SOAP message. The web service receives this request as a SOAP message, executes the method call and sends back the result as another SOAP message. When the client application receives the SOAP message containing the response, the proxy class deserializes it and returns the results as the return value of the web-service method that was called. Figure 28.7 depicts the interactions among the client code, proxy class and web service. The proxy class is not shown in the project unless you click the **Show All Files** button in the **Solution Explorer**.

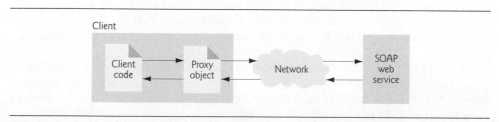

Fig. 28.7 | Interaction between a web-service client and a SOAP web service.

Many aspects of web-service creation and consumption—such as generating WSDL files and proxy classes—are handled by Visual Web Developer, Visual C# 2010 and WCF. Although developers are relieved of the tedious process of creating these files, they can still modify the files if necessary. This is required only when developing advanced web services—none of our examples require modifications to these files.

We now create a client and generate a proxy class that allows the client to access the WelcomeSOAPXMLService web service. First create a Windows application named WelcomeSOAPXMLClient in Visual C# 2010, then perform the following steps.

Step 1: Opening the Add Service Reference Dialog
Right click the project name in the **Solution Explorer** and select **Add Service Reference...** to display the **Add Service Reference** dialog.

Step 2: Specifying the Web Service's Location
In the dialog, enter the URL of WelcomeSOAPXMLService's .svc file (that is, the URL you copied from Fig. 28.4) in the **Address** field and click **Go**. When you specify the service you want to consume, the IDE accesses the web service's WSDL information and copies it into a WSDL file that is stored in the client project's Service References folder. This file is visible when you view all of your project's files in the **Solution Explorer**. [*Note:* A copy of the WSDL file provides the client application with local access to the web service's description. To ensure that the WSDL file is up to date, Visual C# 2010 provides an **Update Service Reference** option (available by right clicking the service reference in the **Solution Explorer**), which updates the files in the Service References folder.]

Many companies that provide web services simply distribute the exact URLs at which their web services can be accessed. The **Add Service Reference** dialog also allows you to search for services on your local machine or on the Internet.

Step 3: Renaming the Service Reference's Namespace
In the **Add Service Reference** dialog, rename the service reference's namespace by changing the **Namespace** field to ServiceReference.

Step 4: Adding the Service Reference
Click the **Ok** button to add the service reference.

Step 5: Viewing the Service Reference in the Solution Explorer
The **Solution Explorer** should now contain a **Service References** folder with a node showing the namespace you specified in *Step 3*.

28.6.6 Consuming the WelcomeSOAPXMLService

The application in Fig. 28.8 uses the WelcomeSOAPXMLService service to send a welcome message. You are already familiar with Visual C# applications that use Labels, TextBoxes and Buttons, so we focus our discussions on the web-services concepts in this chapter's applications.

Line 11 defines a new ServiceReference.WelcomeSOAPXMLServiceClient proxy object named client. The event handler uses this object to call methods of the WelcomeSOAPXMLService web service. Line 22 invokes the WelcomeSOAPXMLService web service's Welcome method. The call is made via the local proxy object client, which then communicates with the web service on the client's behalf. If you're using the downloaded exam-

```
1   // Fig. 28.8: WelcomeSOAPXML.cs
2   // Client that consumes the WelcomeSOAPXMLService.
3   using System;
4   using System.Windows.Forms;
5
6   namespace WelcomeSOAPXMLClient
7   {
8      public partial class WelcomeSOAPXML : Form
9      {
10        // declare a reference to web service
11        private ServiceReference.WelcomeSOAPXMLServiceClient client;
12
13        public WelcomeSOAPXML()
14        {
15           InitializeComponent();
16           client = new ServiceReference.WelcomeSOAPXMLServiceClient();
17        } // end constructor
18
19        // creates welcome message from text input and web service
20        private void submitButton_Click( object sender, EventArgs e )
21        {
22           MessageBox.Show( client.Welcome( textBox.Text ), "Welcome" );
23        } // end method submitButton_Click
24     } // end class WelcomeSOAPXML
25   } // end namespace WelcomeSOAPXMLClient
```

a) User inputs name and clicks **Submit** to send it to the web service

b) Message returned by the web service

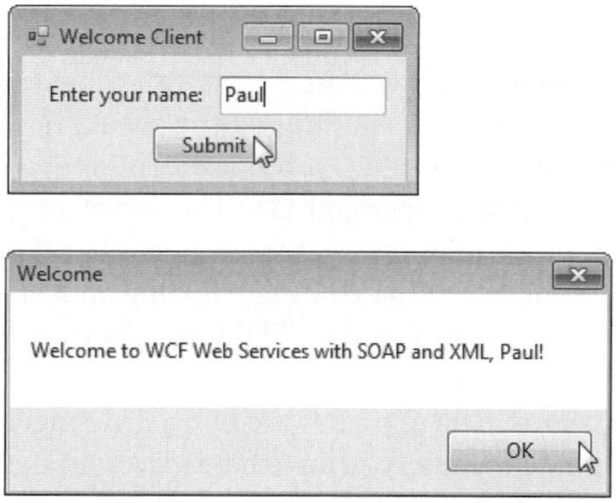

Fig. 28.8 | Client that consumes the `WelcomeSOAPXMLService`.

ples from this chapter, you may need to regenerate the proxy by removing the service reference, then adding it again, because ASP.NET Development Server may use a different port number on your computer. To do so, right click ServiceReference in the **Service References** folder in the **Solution Explorer** and select option **Delete**. Then follow the instructions in Section 28.6.5 to add the service reference to the project.

When the application runs, enter your name and click the **Submit** button. The application invokes the Welcome service method to perform the appropriate task and return the result, then displays the result in a MessageBox.

28.7 Publishing and Consuming REST-Based XML Web Services

In the previous section, we used a proxy object to pass data to and from a WCF web service using the SOAP protocol. In this section, we access a WCF web service using the REST architecture. We modify the IWelcomeSOAPXMLService example to return data in plain XML format. You can create a **WCF Service** project as you did in Section 28.6 to begin.

28.7.1 HTTP get and post Requests

The two most common **HTTP request types** (also known as **request methods**) are get and post. A **get request** typically gets (or retrieves) information from a server. Common uses of get requests are to retrieve a document or an image, or to fetch search results based on a user-submitted search term. A **post request** typically posts (or sends) data to a server. Common uses of post requests are to send form data or documents to a server.

An HTTP request often posts data to a **server-side form handler** that processes the data. For example, when a user performs a search or participates in a web-based survey, the web server receives the information specified in the XHTML form as part of the request. *Both* types of requests can be used to send form data to a web server, yet each request type sends the information differently.

A get request sends information to the server in the URL. For example, in the following URL

```
www.google.com/search?q=deitel
```

search is the name of Google's server-side form handler, q is the name of a *variable* in Google's search form and deitel is the search term. A ? separates the **query string** from the rest of the URL in a request. A *name/value* pair is passed to the server with the *name* and the *value* separated by an equals sign (=). If more than one *name/value* pair is submitted, each pair is separated by an ampersand (&). The server uses data passed in a query string to retrieve an appropriate resource from the server. The server then sends a **response** to the client. A get request may be initiated by submitting an XHTML form whose method attribute is set to "get", or by typing the URL (possibly containing a query string) directly into the browser's address bar.

A post request sends form data as part of the HTTP message, not as part of the URL. A get request typically limits the query string (that is, everything to the right of the ?) to a specific number of characters. For example, Internet Explorer restricts the entire URL to no more than 2083 characters. Typically, large amounts of information should be sent using the post method. The post method is also sometimes preferred because it *hides* the submitted data from the user by embedding it in an HTTP message. If a form submits hidden input values along with user-submitted data, the post method might generate a URL like www.searchengine.com/search. The form data still reaches the server for processing, but the user does not see the exact information sent.

28.7.2 Creating a REST-Based XML WCF Web Service

Step 1: Adding the WebGet Attribute

IWelcomeRESTXMLService interface (Fig. 28.9) is a modified version of the IWelcome-SOAPXMLService interface. The Welcome method's **WebGet** attribute (line 12) maps a method to a unique URL that can be accessed via an HTTP get operation programmatically or in a web browser. To use the WebGet attribute, we import the System.ServiceModel.Web namespace (line 5). WebGet's **UriTemplate** property (line 12) specifies the URI format that is used to invoke the method. You can access the Welcome method in a web browser by appending text that matches the UriTemplate definition to the end of the service's location, as in http://localhost:*portNumber*/WelcomeRESTXMLService/Service.svc/welcome/ Paul. WelcomeRESTXMLService (Fig. 28.10) is the class that implements the IWelcomeRESTXMLService interface; it is similar to the WelcomeSOAPXMLService class (Fig. 28.2).

```
 1   // Fig. 28.9: IWelcomeRESTXMLService.cs
 2   // WCF web service interface. A class that implements this interface
 3   // returns a welcome message through REST architecture and XML data format
 4   using System.ServiceModel;
 5   using System.ServiceModel.Web;
 6
 7   [ServiceContract]
 8   public interface IWelcomeRESTXMLService
 9   {
10      // returns a welcome message
11      [OperationContract]
12      [WebGet( UriTemplate = "/welcome/{yourName}" )]
13      string Welcome( string yourName );
14   } // end interface IWelcomeRESTXMLService
```

Fig. 28.9 | WCF web-service interface. A class that implements this interface returns a welcome message through REST architecture and XML data format.

```
 1   // Fig. 28.10: WelcomeRESTXMLService.cs
 2   // WCF web service that returns a welcome message using REST architecture
 3   // and XML data format.
 4   public class WelcomeRESTXMLService : IWelcomeRESTXMLService
 5   {
 6      // returns a welcome message
 7      public string Welcome( string yourName )
 8      {
 9         return string.Format( "Welcome to WCF Web Services"
10            + " with REST and XML, {0}!", yourName );
11      } // end method Welcome
12   } // end class WelcomeRESTXMLService
```

Fig. 28.10 | WCF web service that returns a welcome message using REST architecture and XML data format.

Step 2: Modifying the **Web.config** File
Figure 28.11 shows part of the default Web.config file modified to use REST architecture. The **endpointBehaviors** element (lines 16–20) in the behaviors element indicates that this web service endpoint will be accessed using the web programming model (REST).

The nested **webHttp** element specifies that clients communicate with this service using the standard HTTP request/response mechanism. The **protocolMapping** element (lines 22–24) in the system.serviceModel element, changes the default protocol for communicating with this web service (normally SOAP) to **webHttpBinding**, which is used for REST-based HTTP requests.

```
 1   <system.serviceModel>
 2      <behaviors>
 3         <serviceBehaviors>
 4            <behavior>
 5               <!-- To avoid disclosing metadata information, set the
 6                    value below to false and remove the metadata
 7                    endpoint above before deployment -->
 8               <serviceMetadata httpGetEnabled="true"/>
 9               <!-- To receive exception details in faults for debugging
10                    purposes, set the value below to true.  Set to false
11                    before deployment to avoid disclosing exception
12                    information -->
13               <serviceDebug includeExceptionDetailInFaults="false"/>
14            </behavior>
15         </serviceBehaviors>
16         <endpointBehaviors>
17            <behavior>
18               <webHttp/>
19            </behavior>
20         </endpointBehaviors>
21      </behaviors>
22      <protocolMapping>
23         <add scheme="http" binding="webHttpBinding"/>
24      </protocolMapping>
25      <serviceHostingEnvironment multipleSiteBindingsEnabled="true"/>
26   </system.serviceModel>
```

Fig. 28.11 | WelcomeRESTXMLService Web.config file.

Figure 28.12 tests the WelcomeRESTXMLService's Welcome method in a web browser. The URL specifies the location of the Service.svc file and uses the URI template to invoke method Welcome with the argument Bruce. The browser displays the XML data response from WelcomeRESTXMLService. Next, you'll learn how to consume this service.

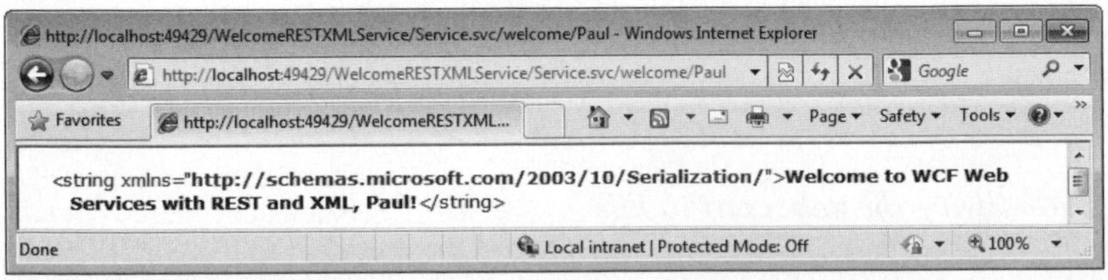

Fig. 28.12 | Response from WelcomeRESTXMLService in XML data format.

28.7.3 Consuming a REST-Based XML WCF Web Service

WelcomeRESTXMLFo(Fig. 28.13) uses the System.Net namespace's **WebClient** class (line 13) to invoke the web service and receive its response. In lines 23–25, we register a handler for the WebClient's DownloadStringCompleted event.

```csharp
 1   // Fig. 28.13: WelcomeRESTXML.cs
 2   // Client that consumes the WelcomeRESTXMLService.
 3   using System;
 4   using System.Net;
 5   using System.Windows.Forms;
 6   using System.Xml.Linq;
 7
 8   namespace WelcomeRESTXMLClient
 9   {
10      public partial class WelcomeRESTXML : Form
11      {
12         // object to invoke the WelcomeRESTXMLService
13         private WebClient client = new WebClient();
14
15         private XNamespace xmlNamespace = XNamespace.Get(
16            "http://schemas.microsoft.com/2003/10/Serialization/" );
17
18         public WelcomeRESTXML()
19         {
20            InitializeComponent();
21
22            // add DownloadStringCompleted event handler to WebClient
23            client.DownloadStringCompleted +=
24               new DownloadStringCompletedEventHandler(
25               client_DownloadStringCompleted );
26         } // end constructor
27
28         // get user input and pass it to the web service
29         private void submitButton_Click( object sender, EventArgs e )
30         {
31            // send request to WelcomeRESTXMLService
32            client.DownloadStringAsync( new Uri(
33               "http://localhost:49429/WelcomeRESTXMLService/Service.svc/" +
34               "welcome/" + textBox.Text ) );
35         } // end method submitButton_Click
36
37         // process web service response
38         private void client_DownloadStringCompleted(
39            object sender, DownloadStringCompletedEventArgs e )
40         {
41            // check if any error occurred in retrieving service data
42            if ( e.Error == null )
43            {
44               // parse the returned XML string (e.Result)
45               XDocument xmlResponse = XDocument.Parse( e.Result );
46
```

Fig. 28.13 | Client that consumes the WelcomeRESTXMLService. (Part 1 of 2.)

```
47                    // get the <string> element's value
48                    MessageBox.Show( xmlResponse.Element(
49                       xmlNamespace + "string" ).Value, "Welcome" );
50               } // end if
51           } // end method client_DownloadStringCompleted
52       } // end class WelcomeRESTXML
53   } // end namespace WelcomeRESTXMLClient
```

a) User inputs name

b) Message sent from **WelcomeRESTXMLService**

Fig. 28.13 | Client that consumes the `WelcomeRESTXMLService`. (Part 2 of 2.)

In this example, we process the WebClient's **DownloadStringCompleted** event, which occurs when the client receives the completed response from the web service. Lines 32–34 call the client object's **DownloadStringAsync** method to invoke the web service asynchronously. (There's also a synchronous DownloadString method that does not return until it receives the response.) The method's argument (i.e., the URL to invoke the web service) must be specified as an object of class **Uri**. Class Uri's constructor receives a string representing a uniform resource identifier. [*Note:* The URL's port number must match the one issued to the web service by the ASP.NET Development Server.] When the call to the web service completes, the WebClient object raises the DownloadStringCompleted event. Its event handler has a parameter e of type **DownloadStringCompletedEventArgs** which contains the information returned by the web service. We can use this variable's properties to get the returned XML document (**e.Result**) and any errors that may have occurred during the process (**e.Error**). We then parse the XML response using XDocument method Parse (line 45). In lines 15–16, we specify the XML message's namespace (seen in Fig. 28.12), and use it to parse the service's XML response to display our welcome string in a MessageBox (lines 48–49).

28.8 Publishing and Consuming REST-Based JSON Web Services

We now build a RESTful web service that returns data in JSON format.

28.8.1 Creating a REST-Based JSON WCF Web Service

By default, a web-service method with the WebGet attribute returns data in XML format. In Fig. 28.14, we modify the WelcomeRESTXMLService to return data in JSON format by setting WebGet's **ResponseFormat** property to WebMessageFormat.Json (line 13). (WebMessageFormat.XML is the default value.) For JSON serialization to work properly, the objects being converted to JSON must have Public properties. This enables the JSON serialization to create name/value pairs representing each Public property and its corresponding value. The previous examples return `String` objects containing the responses. Even though `Strings` are objects, `Strings` do not have any `Public` properties that represent their contents. So, lines 19–25 define a `TextMessage` class that encapsulates a `String` value and defines a `Public` property `Message` to access that value. The **DataContract** attribute (line 19) exposes the `TextMessage` class to the client access. Similarly, the **DataMember** attribute (line 23) exposes a property of this class to the client. This property will appear in the JSON object as a name/value pair. Only `DataMembers` of a `DataContract` are serialized.

```
 1    // Fig. 28.14: IWelcomeRESTJSONService.cs
 2    // WCF web service interface that returns a welcome message through REST
 3    // architecture and JSON format.
 4    using System.Runtime.Serialization;
 5    using System.ServiceModel;
 6    using System.ServiceModel.Web;
 7
 8    [ServiceContract]
 9    public interface IWelcomeRESTJSONService
10    {
11       // returns a welcome message
12       [OperationContract]
13       [WebGet( ResponseFormat = WebMessageFormat.Json,
14          UriTemplate = "/welcome/{yourName}" )]
15       TextMessage Welcome( string yourName );
16    } // end interface IWelcomeRESTJSONService
17
18    // class to encapsulate a string to send in JSON format
19    [DataContract]
20    public class TextMessage
21    {
22       // automatic property message
23       [DataMember]
24       public string Message {get; set; }
25    } // end class TextMessage
```

Fig. 28.14 | WCF web-service interface that returns a welcome message through REST architecture and JSON format.

Figure 28.15 shows the implementation of the interface of Fig. 28.14. The `Welcome` method (lines 7–15) returns a `TextMessage` object, reflecting the changes we made to the interface class. This object is automatically serialized in JSON format (as a result of line 13 in Fig. 28.14) and sent to the client.

```
 1    // Fig. 28.15: WelcomeRESTJSONService.cs
 2    // WCF web service that returns a welcome message through REST
 3    // architecture and JSON format.
 4    public class WelcomeRESTJSONService : IWelcomeRESTJSONService
 5    {
```

Fig. 28.15 | WCF web service that returns a welcome message through REST architecture and JSON format. (Part 1 of 2.)

```
 6        // returns a welcome message
 7        public TextMessage Welcome( string yourName )
 8        {
 9            // add welcome message to field of TextMessage object
10            TextMessage message = new TextMessage();
11            message.Message = string.Format(
12                "Welcome to WCF Web Services with REST and JSON, {0}!",
13                yourName );
14            return message;
15        } // end method Welcome
16    } // end class WelcomeRESTJSONService
```

Fig. 28.15 | WCF web service that returns a welcome message through REST architecture and JSON format. (Part 2 of 2.)

We can once again test the web service using a web browser, by accessing the Service.svc file (http://localhost:49745/WelcomeRESTJSONService/Service.svc) and appending the URI template (welcome/*yourName*) to the address. The response prompts you to download a file called *yourName*, which is a text file. If you save it to disk, the file will have the .json extension. This contains the JSON formatted data. By opening the file in a text editor such as Notepad (Fig. 28.16), you can see the service response as a JSON object. Notice that the property named Message has the welcome message as its value.

Fig. 28.16 | Response from WelcomeRESTJSONService in JSON data format.

28.8.2 Consuming a REST-Based JSON WCF Web Service

We mentioned earlier that all types passed to and from web services can be supported by REST. Custom types that are sent to or from a REST web service are converted to XML or JSON data format. This process is referred to as **XML serialization** or **JSON serialization**, respectively. In Fig. 28.17, we consume the WelcomeRESTJSONService service using an object of the System.Runtime.Serialization.Json library's **DataContractJsonSerializer** class (lines 44–45). The TextMessage class (lines 57–61) maps the JSON response's fields for the DataContractJsonSerializer to deserialize. We add the **Serializable** attribute (line 57) to the TextMessage class to recognize it as a valid serializable object we can convert to and from JSON format. Also, this class on the client must have public data or properties that match the public data or properties in the corresponding class from the web service. Since we want to convert the JSON response into a Text-Message object, we set the DataContractJsonSerializer's type parameter to TextMessage (line 45). In line 48, we use the System.Text namespace's Encoding.Unicode.GetBytes method to convert the JSON response to a Unicode encoded byte array, and encapsulate the byte array in a MemoryStream object so we can read data from the array using stream semantics. The bytes in the MemoryStream object are read by the DataContractJsonSerializer and deserialized into a TextMessage object (lines 47–48).

```
1    // Fig. 28.17: WelcomeRESTJSONForm.cs
2    // Client that consumes the WelcomeRESTJSONService.
3    using System;
4    using System.IO;
5    using System.Net;
6    using System.Runtime.Serialization.Json;
7    using System.Text;
8    using System.Windows.Forms;
9
10   namespace WelcomeRESTJSONClient
11   {
12      public partial class WelcomeRESTJSONForm : Form
13      {
14         // object to invoke the WelcomeRESTJSONService
15         private WebClient client = new WebClient();
16
17         public WelcomeRESTJSONForm()
18         {
19            InitializeComponent();
20
21            // add DownloadStringCompleted event handler to WebClient
22            client.DownloadStringCompleted+=
23               new DownloadStringCompletedEventHandler(
24                  client_DownloadStringCompleted );
25         } // end constructor
26
27         // get user input and pass it to the web service
28         private void submitButton_Click( object sender, EventArgs e )
29         {
30            // send request to WelcomeRESTJSONService
31            client.DownloadStringAsync( new Uri(
32               "http://localhost:49579/WelcomeRESTJSONService/Service.svc/"
33               + "welcome/" + textBox.Text ) );
34         } // end method submitButton_Click
35
36         // process web service response
37         private void client_DownloadStringCompleted(
38            object sender, DownloadStringCompletedEventArgs e )
39         {
40            // check if any error occurred in retrieving service data
41            if ( e.Error == null )
42            {
43               // deserialize response into a TextMessage object
44               DataContractJsonSerializer JSONSerializer =
45                  new DataContractJsonSerializer( typeof( TextMessage ) );
46               TextMessage message =
47                  ( TextMessage ) JSONSerializer.ReadObject( new
48                  MemoryStream( Encoding.Unicode.GetBytes( e.Result ) ) );
49
```

Fig. 28.17 | Client that consumes the WelcomeRESTJSONService. (Part 1 of 2.)

```
50              // display Message text
51              MessageBox.Show( message.Message, "Welcome" );
52           } // end if
53        } // end method client_DownloadStringCompleted
54     } // end class WelcomeRESTJSONForm
55
56     // TextMessage class representing a JSON object
57     [Serializable]
58     public class TextMessage
59     {
60        public string Message;
61     } // end class TextMessage
62  } // end namespace WelcomeRESTJSONClient
```

a) User inputs name.   b) Message sent from WelcomeRESTJSONService.

Fig. 28.17 | Client that consumes the WelcomeRESTJSONService. (Part 2 of 2.)

28.9 Blackjack Web Service: Using Session Tracking in a SOAP-Based WCF Web Service

In Chapter 19, we described the advantages of maintaining information about users to personalize their experiences. In particular, we discussed session tracking using HttpSessionState objects. Next, we incorporate session tracking into a SOAP-based WCF web service.

Suppose a client application needs to call several methods from the same web service, possibly several times each. In such a case, it can be beneficial for the web service to maintain state information for the client. Session tracking eliminates the need for information about the client to be passed between the client and the web service multiple times. For example, a web service providing access to local restaurant reviews would benefit from storing the client user's street address. Once the user's address is stored in a session variable, web service methods can return personalized, localized results without requiring that the address be passed in each method call. This not only improves performance but also requires less effort on your part—less information is passed in each method call.

28.9.1 Creating a Blackjack Web Service

Web services store session information to provide more intuitive functionality. Our next example is a SOAP-based web service that assists programmers in developing a blackjack card game. The web service provides methods to deal a card and to evaluate a hand of cards. After presenting the web service, we use it to serve as the dealer for a game of blackjack. The blackjack web service creates a session variable to maintain a unique deck of cards for each client application. Several clients can use the service at the same time, but method calls made by a specific client use only the deck stored in that client's session. Our example uses a simple subset of casino blackjack rules:

> *Two cards each are dealt to the dealer and the player. The player's cards are dealt face up. Only the dealer's first card is dealt face up. Each card has a value. A card numbered 2 through 10 is worth its face value. Jacks, queens and kings each count as 10. Aces can count as 1 or 11—whichever value is more beneficial to the player (as we'll soon see). If the sum of the player's two initial cards is 21 (that is, the player was dealt a card valued at 10 and an ace, which counts as 11 in this situation), the player has "blackjack" and immediately wins the game. Otherwise, the player can begin taking additional cards one at a time. These cards are dealt face up, and the player decides when to stop taking cards. If the player "busts" (that is, the sum of the player's cards exceeds 21), the game is over, and the player loses. When the player is satisfied with the current set of cards, the player "stays" (that is, stops taking cards), and the dealer's hidden card is revealed. If the dealer's total is 16 or less, the dealer must take another card; otherwise, the dealer must stay. The dealer must continue to take cards until the sum of the dealer's cards is greater than or equal to 17. If the dealer exceeds 21, the player wins. Otherwise, the hand with the higher point total wins. If the dealer and the player have the same point total, the game is a "push" (that is, a tie), and no one wins.*

The Blackjack WCF web service's interface (Fig. 28.18) uses a ServiceContract with the **SessionMode** property set to Required (line 5). This means the service requires sessions to execute correctly. By default, the SessionMode property is set to Allowed. It can also be set to NotAllowed to disable sessions.

```
 1   // Fig. 28.18: IBlackjackService.cs
 2   // Blackjack game WCF web service interface.
 3   using System.ServiceModel;
 4
 5   [ServiceContract( SessionMode = SessionMode.Required )]
 6   public interface IBlackjackService
 7   {
 8      // deals a card that has not been dealt
 9      [OperationContract]
10      string DealCard();
11
12      // creates and shuffle the deck
13      [OperationContract]
14      void Shuffle();
15
16      // calculates value of a hand
17      [OperationContract]
18      int GetHandValue( string dealt );
19   } // end interface IBlackjackService
```

Fig. 28.18 | Blackjack game WCF web-service interface.

The web-service class (Fig. 28.19) provides methods to deal a card, shuffle the deck and determine the point value of a hand. For this example, we want a separate object of the BlackjackService class to handle each client session, so we can maintain a unique deck for each client. To do this, we must specify this behavior in the **ServiceBehavior** attribute (line 7). Setting the ServiceBehavior's **InstanceContextMode** property to

PerSession creates a new instance of the class for each session. The InstanceContextMode property can also be set to PerCall or Single. PerCall uses a new object of the web-service class to handle every method call to the service. Single uses the same object of the web-service class to handle all calls to the service.

```
1    // Fig. 28.19: BlackjackService.cs
2    // Blackjack game WCF web service.
3    using System;
4    using System.Collections.Generic;
5    using System.ServiceModel;
6
7    [ServiceBehavior( InstanceContextMode = InstanceContextMode.PerSession )]
8    public class BlackjackService : IBlackjackService
9    {
10       // create persistent session deck of cards object
11       List< string > deck = new List< string >();
12
13       // deals card that has not yet been dealt
14       public string DealCard()
15       {
16          string card = deck[ 0 ]; // get first card
17          deck.RemoveAt( 0 ); // remove card from deck
18          return card;
19       } // end method DealCard
20
21       // creates and shuffles a deck of cards
22       public void Shuffle()
23       {
24          Random randomObject = new Random(); // generates random numbers
25
26          deck.Clear(); // clears deck for new game
27
28          // generate all possible cards
29          for ( int face = 1; face <= 13; face++ ) // loop through faces
30             for ( int suit = 0; suit <= 3; suit++ ) // loop through suits
31                deck.Add( face + " " + suit ); // add card (string) to deck
32
33          // shuffles deck by swapping each card with another card randomly
34          for ( int i = 0; i < deck.Count; i++ )
35          {
36             // get random index
37             int newIndex = randomObject.Next( deck.Count - 1 );
38
39             // save current card in temporary variable
40             string temporary = deck[ i ];
41             deck[ i ] = deck[ newIndex ]; // copy randomly selected card
42
43             // copy current card back into deck
44             deck[ newIndex ] = temporary;
45          } // end for
46       } // end method Shuffle
47
```

Fig. 28.19 | Blackjack game WCF web service. (Part 1 of 2.)

```
48        // computes value of hand
49        public int GetHandValue( string dealt )
50        {
51           // split string containing all cards
52           string[] cards = dealt.Split( '\t' ); // get array of cards
53           int total = 0; // total value of cards in hand
54           int face; // face of the current card
55           int aceCount = 0; // number of aces in hand
56
57           // loop through the cards in the hand
58           foreach ( var card in cards )
59           {
60              // get face of card
61              face = Convert.ToInt32(
62                 card.Substring( 0, card.IndexOf( ' ' ) ) );
63
64              switch ( face )
65              {
66                 case 1: // if ace, increment aceCount
67                    ++aceCount;
68                    break;
69                 case 11: // if jack add 10
70                 case 12: // if queen add 10
71                 case 13: // if king add 10
72                    total += 10;
73                    break;
74                 default: // otherwise, add value of face
75                    total += face;
76                    break;
77              } // end switch
78           } // end foreach
79
80           // if there are any aces, calculate optimum total
81           if ( aceCount > 0 )
82           {
83              // if it is possible to count one ace as 11, and the rest
84              // as 1 each, do so; otherwise, count all aces as 1 each
85              if ( total + 11 + aceCount - 1 <= 21 )
86                 total += 11 + aceCount - 1;
87              else
88                 total += aceCount;
89           } // end if
90
91           return total;
92        } // end method GetHandValue
93     } // end class BlackjackService
```

Fig. 28.19 | Blackjack game WCF web service. (Part 2 of 2.)

We represent each card as a string consisting of a digit (that is, 1–13) representing the card's face (for example, ace through king), followed by a space and a digit (that is, 0–3) representing the card's suit (for example, clubs, diamonds, hearts or spades). For example, the jack of hearts is represented as "11 2", and the two of clubs as "2 0". After deploying the web service, we create a Windows Forms application that uses the Black-jackService's methods to implement a blackjack game.

Method DealCard

Method DealCard (lines 14–19) removes a card from the deck and sends it to the client. Without using session tracking, the deck of cards would need to be passed back and forth with each method call. Using session state makes the method easy to call (it requires no arguments) and avoids the overhead of sending the deck over the network multiple times.

This method manipulates the current user's deck (the List of strings defined at line 11). From the user's deck, DealCard obtains the current top card (line 16), removes the top card from the deck (line 17) and returns the card's value as a string (line 18).

Method Shuffle

Method Shuffle (lines 22–46) fills and shuffles the List representing a deck of cards. Lines 29–31 generate strings in the form "*face suit*" to represent each card in a deck. Lines 34–45 shuffle the deck by swapping each card with a randomly selected other card.

Method GetHandValue

Method GetHandValue (lines 49–92) determines the total value of cards in a hand by trying to attain the highest score possible without going over 21. Recall that an ace can be counted as either 1 or 11, and all face cards count as 10.

As you'll see in Fig. 28.20, the client application maintains a hand of cards as a string in which each card is separated by a tab character. Line 52 of Fig. 28.19 tokenizes the hand of cards (represented by dealt) into individual cards by calling string method Split and passing to it the tab character. Split uses the delimiter characters to separate tokens in the string. Lines 58–78 count the value of each card. Lines 61–62 retrieve the first integer—the face—and use that value in the switch statement (lines 64–77). If the card is an ace, the method increments variable aceCount (line 67). We discuss how this variable is used shortly. If the card is an 11, 12 or 13 (jack, queen or king), the method adds 10 to the total value of the hand (line 72). If the card is anything else, the method increases the total by that value (line 75).

Because an ace can represent 1 or 11, additional logic is required to process aces. Lines 81–89 process the aces after all the other cards. If a hand contains several aces, only one ace can be counted as 11 (if two aces each are counted as 11, the hand would have a losing value of at least 22). The condition in line 85 determines whether counting one ace as 11 and the rest as 1 results in a total that does not exceed 21. If this is possible, line 86 adjusts the total accordingly. Otherwise, line 88 adjusts the total, counting each ace as 1.

Method GetHandValue maximizes the value of the current cards without exceeding 21. Imagine, for example, that the dealer has a 7 and receives an ace. The new total could be either 8 or 18. However, GetHandValue always maximizes the value of the cards without going over 21, so the new total is 18.

Modifying the web.config File

To allow this web service to perform session tracking, you must modify the web.config file to include the following element in the system.serviceModel element:s

```
<protocolMapping>
   <add scheme="http" binding="wsHttpBinding"/>
</protocolMapping>
```

28.9.2 Consuming the Blackjack Web Service

We use our blackjack web service in a Windows application (Fig. 28.20). This application uses an instance of BlackjackServiceClient (declared in line 14 and created in line 48) to represent the dealer. The web service keeps track of the cards dealt to the player and the dealer. As in Section 28.6.5, you must add a service reference to your project so it can access the service. The images for this example are provided with the chapter's examples.

Each player has 11 PictureBoxes—the maximum number of cards that can be dealt without exceeding 21 (that is, four aces, four twos and three threes). These PictureBoxes are placed in a List (lines 51–73), so we can index the List during the game to determine which PictureBox should display a particular card image. The images are located in the blackjack_images directory with this chapter's examples. Drag this directory from Windows Explorer into your project. In the **Solution Explorer**, select all the files in that folder and set their **Copy to Output Directory** property to **Copy if newer**.

GameOver Method

Method GameOver (lines 169–202) shows an appropriate message in the status PictureBox and displays the final point totals of both the dealer and the player. These values are obtained by calling the web service's GetHandValue method in lines 194 and 196. Method GameOver receives as an argument a member of the GameStatus enumeration (defined in lines 31–37). The enumeration represents whether the player tied, lost or won the game; its four members are PUSH, LOSE, WIN and BLACKJACK.

```
 I   // Fig. 28.20: Blackjack.cs
 2   // Blackjack game that uses the BlackjackService web service.
 3   using System;
 4   using System.Drawing;
 5   using System.Windows.Forms;
 6   using System.Collections.Generic;
 7   using System.Resources;
 8
 9   namespace BlackjackClient
10   {
11      public partial class Blackjack : Form
12      {
13         // reference to web service
14         private ServiceReference.BlackjackServiceClient dealer;
15
16         // string representing the dealer's cards
17         private string dealersCards;
18
19         // string representing the player's cards
20         private string playersCards;
21
22         // list of PictureBoxes for card images
23         private List< PictureBox > cardBoxes;
24         private int currentPlayerCard; // player's current card number
25         private int currentDealerCard; // dealer's current card number
26
```

Fig. 28.20 | Blackjack game that uses the BlackjackService web service. (Part I of 9.)

```
27          private ResourceManager pictureLibrary =
28              BlackjackClient.Properties.Resources.ResourceManager;
29
30          // enum representing the possible game outcomes
31          public enum GameStatus
32          {
33              PUSH, // game ends in a tie
34              LOSE, // player loses
35              WIN, // player wins
36              BLACKJACK // player has blackjack
37          } // end enum GameStatus
38
39          public Blackjack()
40          {
41              InitializeComponent();
42          } // end constructor
43
44          // sets up the game
45          private void Blackjack_Load( object sender, EventArgs e )
46          {
47              // instantiate object allowing communication with web service
48              dealer = new ServiceReference.BlackjackServiceClient();
49
50              // put PictureBoxes into cardBoxes List
51              cardBoxes = new List<PictureBox>(); // create list
52              cardBoxes.Add( pictureBox1 );
53              cardBoxes.Add( pictureBox2 );
54              cardBoxes.Add( pictureBox3 );
55              cardBoxes.Add( pictureBox4 );
56              cardBoxes.Add( pictureBox5 );
57              cardBoxes.Add( pictureBox6 );
58              cardBoxes.Add( pictureBox7 );
59              cardBoxes.Add( pictureBox8 );
60              cardBoxes.Add( pictureBox9 );
61              cardBoxes.Add( pictureBox10 );
62              cardBoxes.Add( pictureBox11 );
63              cardBoxes.Add( pictureBox12 );
64              cardBoxes.Add( pictureBox13 );
65              cardBoxes.Add( pictureBox14 );
66              cardBoxes.Add( pictureBox15 );
67              cardBoxes.Add( pictureBox16 );
68              cardBoxes.Add( pictureBox17 );
69              cardBoxes.Add( pictureBox18 );
70              cardBoxes.Add( pictureBox19 );
71              cardBoxes.Add( pictureBox20 );
72              cardBoxes.Add( pictureBox21 );
73              cardBoxes.Add( pictureBox22 );
74          } // end method Blackjack_Load
75
76          // deals cards to dealer while dealer's total is less than 17,
77          // then computes value of each hand and determines winner
78          private void DealerPlay()
79          {
```

Fig. 28.20 | Blackjack game that uses the BlackjackService web service. (Part 2 of 9.)

```
 80              // reveal dealer's second card
 81              string[] cards = dealersCards.Split( '\t' );
 82              DisplayCard( 1, cards[1] );
 83
 84              string nextCard;
 85
 86              // while value of dealer's hand is below 17,
 87              // dealer must take cards
 88              while ( dealer.GetHandValue( dealersCards ) < 17 )
 89              {
 90                 nextCard = dealer.DealCard(); // deal new card
 91                 dealersCards += '\t' + nextCard; // add new card to hand
 92
 93                 // update GUI to show new card
 94                 MessageBox.Show( "Dealer takes a card" );
 95                 DisplayCard( currentDealerCard, nextCard );
 96                 ++currentDealerCard;
 97              } // end while
 98
 99              int dealersTotal = dealer.GetHandValue( dealersCards );
100              int playersTotal = dealer.GetHandValue( playersCards );
101
102              // if dealer busted, player wins
103              if ( dealersTotal > 21 )
104              {
105                 GameOver( GameStatus.WIN );
106              } // end if
107              else
108              {
109                 // if dealer and player have not exceeded 21,
110                 // higher score wins; equal scores is a push.
111                 if ( dealersTotal > playersTotal ) // player loses game
112                    GameOver( GameStatus.LOSE );
113                 else if ( playersTotal > dealersTotal ) // player wins game
114                    GameOver( GameStatus.WIN );
115                 else // player and dealer tie
116                    GameOver( GameStatus.PUSH );
117              } // end else
118        } // end method DealerPlay
119
120        // displays card represented by cardValue in specified PictureBox
121        public void DisplayCard( int card, string cardValue )
122        {
123           // retrieve appropriate PictureBox
124           PictureBox displayBox = cardBoxes[ card ];
125
126           // if string representing card is empty,
127           // set displayBox to display back of card
128           if ( string.IsNullOrEmpty( cardValue ) )
129           {
130              displayBox.Image =
131                 ( Image ) pictureLibrary.GetObject( "cardback" );
```

Fig. 28.20 | Blackjack game that uses the BlackjackService web service. (Part 3 of 9.)

```
132                return;
133            } // end if
134
135            // retrieve face value of card from cardValue
136            string face =
137                cardValue.Substring( 0, cardValue.IndexOf( ' ' ) );
138
139            // retrieve the suit of the card from cardValue
140            string suit =
141                cardValue.Substring( cardValue.IndexOf( ' ' ) + 1 );
142
143            char suitLetter; // suit letter used to form image file name
144
145            // determine the suit letter of the card
146            switch ( Convert.ToInt32( suit ) )
147            {
148                case 0: // clubs
149                    suitLetter = 'c';
150                    break;
151                case 1: // diamonds
152                    suitLetter = 'd';
153                    break;
154                case 2: // hearts
155                    suitLetter = 'h';
156                    break;
157                default: // spades
158                    suitLetter = 's';
159                    break;
160            } // end switch
161
162            // set displayBox to display appropriate image
163            displayBox.Image = ( Image ) pictureLibrary.GetObject(
164                "_" + face + suitLetter );
165        } // end method DisplayCard
166
167        // displays all player cards and shows
168        // appropriate game status message
169        public void GameOver( GameStatus winner )
170        {
171            string[] cards = dealersCards.Split( '\t' );
172
173            // display all the dealer's cards
174            for ( int i = 0; i < cards.Length; i++ )
175                DisplayCard( i, cards[ i ] );
176
177            // display appropriate status image
178            if ( winner == GameStatus.PUSH ) // push
179                statusPictureBox.Image =
180                    ( Image ) pictureLibrary.GetObject( "tie" );
181            else if ( winner == GameStatus.LOSE ) // player loses
182                statusPictureBox.Image =
183                    ( Image ) pictureLibrary.GetObject( "lose" );
```

Fig. 28.20 | Blackjack game that uses the BlackjackService web service. (Part 4 of 9.)

```
184              else if ( winner == GameStatus.BLACKJACK )
185                  // player has blackjack
186                  statusPictureBox.Image =
187                     ( Image ) pictureLibrary.GetObject( "blackjack" );
188              else // player wins
189                  statusPictureBox.Image =
190                     ( Image ) pictureLibrary.GetObject( "win" );
191
192              // display final totals for dealer and player
193              dealerTotalLabel.Text =
194                 "Dealer: " + dealer.GetHandValue( dealersCards );
195              playerTotalLabel.Text =
196                 "Player: " + dealer.GetHandValue( playersCards );
197
198              // reset controls for new game
199              stayButton.Enabled = false;
200              hitButton.Enabled = false;
201              dealButton.Enabled = true;
202           } // end method GameOver
203
204           // deal two cards each to dealer and player
205           private void dealButton_Click( object sender, EventArgs e )
206           {
207              string card; // stores a card temporarily until added to a hand
208
209              // clear card images
210              foreach ( PictureBox cardImage in cardBoxes )
211                 cardImage.Image = null;
212
213              statusPictureBox.Image = null; // clear status image
214              dealerTotalLabel.Text = string.Empty; // clear dealer total
215              playerTotalLabel.Text = string.Empty; // clear player total
216
217              // create a new, shuffled deck on the web service host
218              dealer.Shuffle();
219
220              // deal two cards to player
221              playersCards = dealer.DealCard(); // deal first card to player
222              DisplayCard( 11, playersCards ); // display card
223              card = dealer.DealCard(); // deal second card to player
224              DisplayCard( 12, card ); // update GUI to display new card
225              playersCards += '\t' + card; // add second card to player's hand
226
227              // deal two cards to dealer, only display face of first card
228              dealersCards = dealer.DealCard(); // deal first card to dealer
229              DisplayCard( 0, dealersCards ); // display card
230              card = dealer.DealCard(); // deal second card to dealer
231              DisplayCard( 1, string.Empty ); // display card face down
232              dealersCards += '\t' + card; // add second card to dealer's hand
233
234              stayButton.Enabled = true; // allow player to stay
235              hitButton.Enabled = true; // allow player to hit
236              dealButton.Enabled = false; // disable Deal Button
```

Fig. 28.20 | Blackjack game that uses the BlackjackService web service. (Part 5 of 9.)

```
237
238            // determine the value of the two hands
239            int dealersTotal = dealer.GetHandValue( dealersCards );
240            int playersTotal = dealer.GetHandValue( playersCards );
241
242            // if hands equal 21, it is a push
243            if ( dealersTotal == playersTotal && dealersTotal == 21 )
244               GameOver( GameStatus.PUSH );
245            else if ( dealersTotal == 21 ) // if dealer has 21, dealer wins
246               GameOver( GameStatus.LOSE );
247            else if ( playersTotal == 21 ) // player has blackjack
248               GameOver( GameStatus.BLACKJACK );
249
250            // next dealer card has index 2 in cardBoxes
251            currentDealerCard = 2;
252
253            // next player card has index 13 in cardBoxes
254            currentPlayerCard = 13;
255         } // end method dealButton
256
257         // deal another card to player
258         private void hitButton_Click( object sender, EventArgs e )
259         {
260            string card = dealer.DealCard(); // deal new card
261            playersCards += '\t' + card; // add new card to player's hand
262
263            DisplayCard( currentPlayerCard, card ); // display card
264            ++currentPlayerCard;
265
266            // determine the value of the player's hand
267            int total = dealer.GetHandValue( playersCards );
268
269            // if player exceeds 21, house wins
270            if ( total > 21 )
271               GameOver( GameStatus.LOSE );
272            else if ( total == 21 ) // if player has 21, dealer's turn
273            {
274               hitButton.Enabled = false;
275               DealerPlay();
276            } // end if
277         } // end method hitButton_Click
278
279         // play the dealer's hand after the player chooses to stay
280         private void stayButton_Click( object sender, EventArgs e )
281         {
282            stayButton.Enabled = false; // disable Stay Button
283            hitButton.Enabled = false; // disable Hit Button
284            dealButton.Enabled = true; // enable Deal Button
285            DealerPlay(); // player chose to stay, so play the dealer's hand
286         } // end method stayButton_Click
287      } // end class Blackjack
288 } // end namespace BlackjackClient
```

Fig. 28.20 | Blackjack game that uses the BlackjackService web service. (Part 6 of 9.)

a) Initial cards dealt to the player and the dealer when the user presses the **Deal** button.

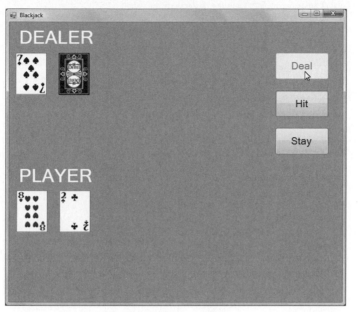

b) Cards after the player presses the **Hit** button once, then the **Stay** button. In this case, the player wins the game with a higher total than the dealer.

Fig. 28.20 | Blackjack game that uses the BlackjackService web service. (Part 7 of 9.)

c) Cards after the player presses the **Hit** button once, then the **Stay** button. In this case, the player busts (exceeds 21) and the dealer wins the game.

d) Cards after the player presses the **Deal** button. In this case, the player wins with Blackjack because the first two cards are an ace and a card with a value of 10 (a jack in this case).

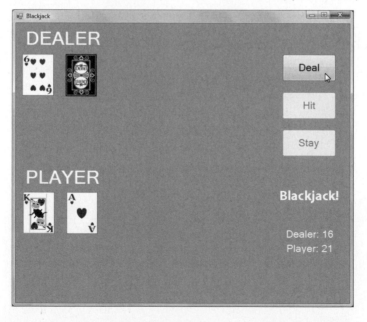

Fig. 28.20 | Blackjack game that uses the BlackjackService web service. (Part 8 of 9.)

e) Cards after the player presses the **Stay** button. In this case, the player and dealer push—
they have the same card total.

Fig. 28.20 | Blackjack game that uses the `BlackjackService` web service. (Part 9 of 9.)

dealButton_Click *Method*

When the player clicks the **Deal** button, the event handler (lines 205–255) clears the
`PictureBox`es and the `Label`s displaying the final point totals. Line 218 shuffles the deck
by calling the web service's `Shuffle` method, then the player and dealer receive two cards
each (returned by calls to the web service's `DealCard` method in lines 221, 223, 228 and
230). Lines 239–240 evaluate both the dealer's and player's hands by calling the web service's `GetHandValue` method. If the player and the dealer both obtain scores of 21, the program calls method `GameOver`, passing `GameStatus.PUSH`. If only the player has 21 after the
first two cards are dealt, the program passes `GameStatus.BLACKJACK` to method `GameOver`.
If only the dealer has 21, the program passes `GameStatus.LOSE` to method `GameOver`.

hitButton_Click *Method*

If `dealButton_Click` does not call `GameOver`, the player can take more cards by clicking
the **Hit** button. The event handler for this button is in lines 258–277. Each time a player
clicks **Hit**, the program deals the player one more card (line 260), displaying it in the GUI.
Line 267 evaluates the player's hand. If the player exceeds 21, the game is over, and the
player loses. If the player has exactly 21, the player cannot take any more cards, and method `DealerPlay` (lines 78–118) is called, causing the dealer to keep taking cards until the
dealer's hand has a value of 17 or more (lines 88–97). If the dealer exceeds 21, the player
wins (line 105); otherwise, the values of the hands are compared, and `GameOver` is called
with the appropriate argument (lines 111–116).

hitButton_Click Method

Clicking the **Stay** button indicates that a player does not want to be dealt another card. The event handler for this button (lines 280–286) disables the **Hit** and **Stay** buttons, then calls method `DealerPlay`.

DisplayCard Method

Method `DisplayCard` (lines 121–165) updates the GUI to display a newly dealt card. The method takes as arguments an integer representing the index of the `PictureBox` in the `List` that must have its image set, and a `string` representing the card. An empty `string` indicates that we wish to display the card face down. If method `DisplayCard` receives a `string` that's not empty, the program extracts the face and suit from the `string` and uses this information to find the correct image. The `switch` statement (lines 146–160) converts the number representing the suit to an `int` and assigns the appropriate character literal to `suitLetter` (c for clubs, d for diamonds, h for hearts and s for spades). The character in `suitLetter` is used to complete the image's file name (lines 163–164).

28.10 Airline Reservation Web Service: Database Access and Invoking a Service from ASP.NET

Our prior examples accessed web services from Windows Forms applications. You can just as easily use web services in ASP.NET web applications. In fact, because web-based businesses are becoming increasingly prevalent, it is common for web applications to consume web services. Figures 28.21 and 28.22 present the interface and class, respectively, for an airline reservation service that receives information regarding the type of seat a customer wishes to reserve, checks a database to see if such a seat is available and, if so, makes a reservation. Later in this section, we present an ASP.NET web application that allows a customer to specify a reservation request, then uses the airline reservation web service to attempt to execute the request. The code and database used in this example are provided with the chapter's examples.

```
 1   // Fig. 28.21: IReservationService.cs
 2   // Airline reservation WCF web service interface.
 3   using System.ServiceModel;
 4
 5   [ServiceContract]
 6   public interface IReservationService
 7   {
 8      // reserves a seat
 9      [OperationContract]
10      bool Reserve( string seatType, string classType );
11   } // end interface IReservationService
```

Fig. 28.21 | Airline reservation WCF web-service interface.

```
 1   // Fig. 28.22: ReservationService.cs
 2   // Airline reservation WCF web service.
 3   using System.Linq;
```

Fig. 28.22 | Airline reservation WCF web service. (Part 1 of 2.)

```
4
5   public class ReservationService : IReservationService
6   {
7      // create ticketsDB object to access Tickets database
8      private TicketsDataContext ticketsDB = new TicketsDataContext();
9
10     // checks database to determine whether matching seat is available
11     public bool Reserve( string seatType, string classType )
12     {
13        //  LINQ query to find seats matching the parameters
14        var result =
15           from seat in ticketsDB.Seats
16           where ( seat.Taken == false ) && ( seat.Type == seatType ) &&
17              ( seat.Class == classType )
18           select seat;
19
20        // get first available seat
21        Seat firstAvailableSeat = result.FirstOrDefault();
22
23        // if seat is available seats, mark it as taken
24        if ( firstAvailableSeat != null )
25        {
26           firstAvailableSeat.Taken = true; // mark the seat as taken
27           ticketsDB.SubmitChanges(); // update
28           return true; // seat was reserved
29        } // end if
30
31        return false; // no seat was reserved
32     } // end method Reserve
33  } // end class ReservationService
```

Fig. 28.22 | Airline reservation WCF web service. (Part 2 of 2.)

In Chapter 18, you learned how to use LINQ to SQL to extract data from a database. We added the Tickets.mdf database and corresponding LINQ to SQL classes to create a DataContext object (line 8) for our ticket reservation system. Tickets.mdf database contains the Seats table with four columns—the seat number (1–10), the seat type (Window, Middle or Aisle), the class (Economy or First) and a column containing either 1 (true) or 0 (false) to indicate whether the seat is taken.

This web service has a single method—Reserve (Fig. 28.22, lines 11–32)—which searches a seat database (Tickets.mdf) to locate a seat matching a user's request. If it finds an appropriate seat, Reserve updates the database, makes the reservation and returns true; otherwise, no reservation is made, and the method returns false. The statements in lines 14–18 and lines 24–29, which query and update the database, use LINQ to SQL.

Reserve receives two parameters—a string representing the seat type (that is, Window, Middle or Aisle) and a string representing the class type (that is, Economy or First). Lines 15–18 retrieve the seat numbers of any available seats matching the requested seat and class type with the results of a query. Line 21 gets the first matching seat (or null if there is not one). If there is a matching seat (line 24), the web service reserves the that seat. Line 26 marks the seat as taken and line 27 submits the changes to the database. Method Reserve returns true (line 28) to indicate that the reservation was successful. If there are no matching seats, `Reserve` returns `false` (line 31) to indicate that no seats matched the user's request.

Creating a Web Form to Interact with the Airline Reservation Web Service
Figure 28.23 shows an ASP.NET page through which users can select seat types. This page allows users to reserve a seat on the basis of its class (`Economy` or `First`) and location (`Aisle`, `Middle` or `Window`) in a row of seats. The page then uses the airline reservation web service to carry out user requests. If the database request is not successful, the user is instructed to modify the request and try again. When you create this ASP.NET application, remember to add a service reference to the `ReservationService`.

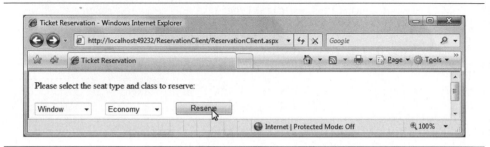

Fig. 28.23 | ASPX file that takes reservation information.

This page defines two `DropDownList` objects and a `Button`. One `DropDownList` displays all the seat types from which users can select (`Aisle`, `Middle`, `Window`). The second provides choices for the class type. Users click the `Button` named `reserveButton` to submit requests after making selections from the `DropDownLists`. The page also defines an initially blank `Label` named `errorLabel`, which displays an appropriate message if no seat matching the user's selection is available. The code-behind file is shown in Fig. 28.24.

```
 1   // Fig. 28.24: ReservationClient.aspx.cs
 2   // ReservationClient code behind file.
 3   using System;
 4
 5   public partial class ReservationClient : System.Web.UI.Page
 6   {
 7      // object of proxy type used to connect to ReservationService
 8      private ServiceReference.ReservationServiceClient ticketAgent =
 9         new ServiceReference.ReservationServiceClient();
10
11      // attempt to reserve the selected type of seat
12      protected void reserveButton_Click( object sender, EventArgs e )
13      {
14         // if the ticket is reserved
15         if ( ticketAgent.Reserve( seatList.SelectedItem.Text,
16            classList.SelectedItem.Text ) )
17         {
```

Fig. 28.24 | `ReservationClient` code-behind file. (Part 1 of 2.)

```
18              // hide other controls
19              instructionsLabel.Visible = false;
20              seatList.Visible = false;
21              classList.Visible = false;
22              reserveButton.Visible = false;
23              errorLabel.Visible = false;
24
25              // display message indicating success
26              Response.Write( "Your reservation has been made. Thank you." );
27          } // end if
28          else // service method returned false, so signal failure
29          {
30              // display message in the initially blank errorLabel
31              errorLabel.Text = "This type of seat is not available. " +
32                  "Please modify your request and try again.";
33          } // end else
34      } // end method reserveButton_Click
35  } // end class ReservationClient
```

Fig. 28.24 | ReservationClient code-behind file. (Part 2 of 2.)

Lines 8–9 of Fig. 28.24 creates a ReservationServiceClient proxy object. When the user clicks **Reserve** (Fig. 28.25(a)), the reserveButton_Click event handler (lines 12–34 of Fig. 28.24) executes, and the page reloads. The event handler calls the web service's Reserve method and passes to it the selected seat and class type as arguments (lines 15–16). If Reserve returns true, the application hides the GUI controls and displays a message thanking the user for making a reservation (line 26); otherwise, the application notifies the user that the type of seat requested is not available and instructs the user to try again (lines

a) Selecting a seat

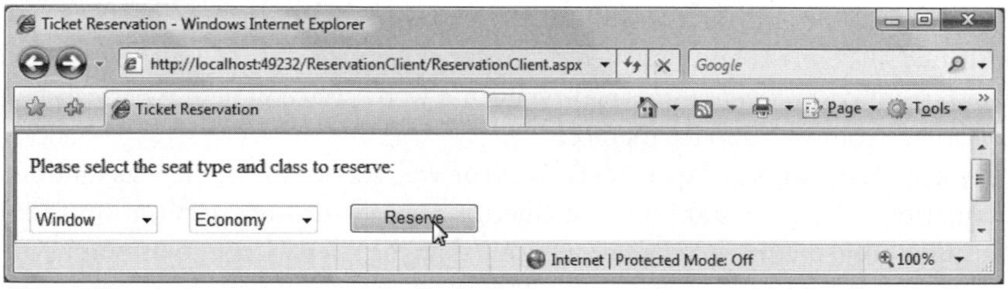

b) Seat is reserved successfully

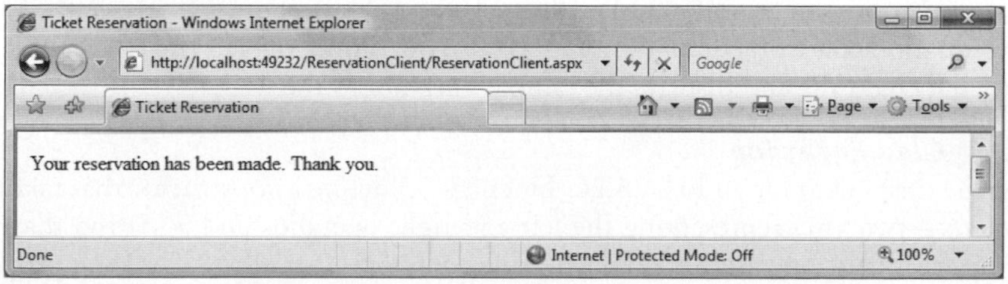

Fig. 28.25 | Ticket reservation web-application sample execution. (Part 1 of 2.)

c) Attempting to reserve another seat

d) No seats match the requested type and class

Fig. 28.25 | Ticket reservation web-application sample execution. (Part 2 of 2.)

31–32). You can use the techniques presented in Chapter 19 to build this ASP.NET Web Form. Figure 28.25 shows several user interactions with this web application.

28.11 Equation Generator: Returning User-Defined Types

With the exception of the `WelcomeRESTJSONService` (Fig. 28.15), the web services we've demonstrated all received and returned primitive-type instances. It is also possible to process instances of complete user-defined types in a web service. These types can be passed to or returned from web-service methods.

This section presents an `EquationGenerator` web service that generates random arithmetic equations of type `Equation`. The client is a math-tutoring application that inputs information about the mathematical question that the user wishes to attempt (addition, subtraction or multiplication) and the skill level of the user (1 specifies equations using numbers from 1 to 10, 2 specifies equations involving numbers from 10 to 100, and 3 specifies equations containing numbers from 100 to 1000). The web service then generates an equation consisting of random numbers in the proper range. The client application receives the `Equation` and displays the sample question to the user.

Defining Class `Equation`
We define class `Equation` in Fig. 28.26. Lines 33–53 define a constructor that takes three arguments—two `int`s representing the left and right operands and a `string` that represents the arithmetic operation to perform. The constructor sets the `Equation`'s properties, then calculates the appropriate result. The parameterless constructor (lines 26–30) calls the three-argument constructor (lines 33–53) and passes default values.

```csharp
1   // Fig. 28.26: Equation.cs
2   // Class Equation that contains information about an equation.
3   using System.Runtime.Serialization;
4
5   [DataContract]
6   public class Equation
7   {
8      // automatic property to access the left operand
9      [DataMember]
10     private int Left { get; set; }
11
12     // automatic property to access the right operand
13     [DataMember]
14     private int Right { get; set; }
15
16     // automatic property to access the result of applying
17     // an operation to the left and right operands
18     [DataMember]
19     private int Result { get; set; }
20
21     // automatic property to access the operation
22     [DataMember]
23     private string Operation { get; set; }
24
25     // required default constructor
26     public Equation()
27        : this( 0, 0, "add" )
28     {
29        // empty body
30     } // end default constructor
31
32     // three-argument constructor for class Equation
33     public Equation( int leftValue, int rightValue, string type )
34     {
35        Left = leftValue;
36        Right = rightValue;
37
38        switch ( type ) // perform appropriate operation
39        {
40           case "add": // addition
41              Result = Left + Right;
42              Operation = "+";
43              break;
44           case "subtract": // subtraction
45              Result = Left - Right;
46              Operation = "-";
47              break;
48           case "multiply": // multiplication
49              Result = Left * Right;
50              Operation = "*";
51              break;
52        } // end switch
53     } // end three-argument constructor
```

Fig. 28.26 | Class Equation that contains information about an equation. (Part 1 of 2.)

```
54
55      // return string representation of the Equation object
56      public override string ToString()
57      {
58         return string.Format( "{0} {1} {2} = {4}", Left, Operation,
59            Right, Result );
60      } // end method ToString
61
62      // property that returns a string representing left-hand side
63      [DataMember]
64      private string LeftHandSide
65      {
66         get
67         {
68            return string.Format( "{0} {1} {2}", Left, Operation, Right );
69         } // end get
70         set
71         {
72            // empty body
73         } // end set
74      } // end property LeftHandSide
75
76      // property that returns a string representing right-hand side
77      [DataMember]
78      private string RightHandSide
79      {
80         get
81         {
82            return Result.ToString();
83         } // end get
84         set
85         {
86            // empty body
87         } // end set
88      } // end property RightHandSide
89   } // end class Equation
```

Fig. 28.26 | Class Equation that contains information about an equation. (Part 2 of 2.)

Class Equation defines properties LeftHandSide (lines 64–74), RightHandSide (lines 78–88), Left (line 10), Right (line 14), Result (line 19) and Operation (line 23). The web service client does not need to modify the values of properties LeftHandSide and RightHandSide. However, a property can be serialized only if it has both a get and a set accessor—even if the set accessor has an empty body. Each property is preceded by the DataMember attribute to indicate that it should be serialized. LeftHandSide (lines 64–74) returns a string representing everything to the left of the equals (=) sign in the equation, and RightHandSide (lines 78–88) returns a string representing everything to the right of the equals (=) sign. Left (line 10) returns the int to the left of the operator (known as the left operand), and Right (lines 14) returns the int to the right of the operator (known as the right operand). Result (line 19) returns the solution to the equation, and Operation (line 23) returns the operator in the equation. The client in this case study does not use the RightHandSide property, but we included it in case future clients choose to use it. Method ToString (lines 56–60) returns a string representation of the equation.

28.11.1 Creating the REST-Based XML EquationGenerator Web Service

Figures 28.27 and 28.28 present the interface and class for the EquationGeneratorService web service, which creates random, customized Equations. This web service contains only method GenerateEquation (lines 9–26 of Fig. 28.28), which takes two parameters—a string representing the mathematical operation ("add", "subtract" or "multiply") and a string representing the difficulty level. When line 25 of Fig. 28.28 returns the Equation, it is serialized as XML by default and sent to the client. We'll do this with JSON as well in Section 28.11.3. Recall from Section 28.7.2 that you must modify the Web.config file to enable REST support as well.

```
 1   // Fig. 28.27: IEquationGeneratorService.cs
 2   // WCF REST service interface to create random equations based on a
 3   // specified operation and difficulty level.
 4   using System.ServiceModel;
 5   using System.ServiceModel.Web;
 6
 7   [ServiceContract]
 8   public interface IEquationGeneratorService
 9   {
10      // method to generate a math equation
11      [OperationContract]
12      [WebGet( UriTemplate = "equation/{operation}/{level}" )]
13      Equation GenerateEquation( string operation, string level );
14   } // end interface IEquationGeneratorService
```

Fig. 28.27 | WCF REST service interface to create random equations based on a specified operation and difficulty level.

```
 1   // Fig. 28.28: EquationGeneratorService.cs
 2   // WCF REST service to create random equations based on a
 3   // specified operation and difficulty level.
 4   using System;
 5
 6   public class EquationGeneratorService : IEquationGeneratorService
 7   {
 8      // method to generate a math equation
 9      public Equation GenerateEquation( string operation, string level )
10      {
11         // calculate maximum and minimum number to be used
12         int maximum =
13            Convert.ToInt32( Math.Pow( 10, Convert.ToInt32( level ) ) );
14         int minimum =
15            Convert.ToInt32( Math.Pow( 10, Convert.ToInt32( level ) - 1 ) );
16
```

Fig. 28.28 | WCF REST service to create random equations based on a specified operation and difficulty level. (Part 1 of 2.)

```
17          Random randomObject = new Random(); // generate random numbers
18
19          // create Equation consisting of two random
20          // numbers in the range minimum to maximum
21          Equation newEquation = new Equation(
22             randomObject.Next( minimum, maximum ),
23             randomObject.Next( minimum, maximum ), operation );
24
25          return newEquation;
26       } // end method GenerateEquation
27    } // end class EquationGeneratorService
```

Fig. 28.28 | WCF REST service to create random equations based on a specified operation and difficulty level. (Part 2 of 2.)

28.11.2 Consuming the REST-Based XML EquationGenerator Web Service

The MathTutor application (Fig. 28.29) calls the EquationGenerator web service's GenerateEquation method to create an Equation object. The tutor then displays the left-hand side of the Equation and waits for user input.

The default setting for the difficulty level is 1, but the user can change this by choosing a level from the RadioButtons in the GroupBox labeled **Difficulty**. Clicking any of the levels invokes the corresponding RadioButton's CheckedChanged event handler (lines 112–133), which sets integer level to the level selected by the user. Although the default setting for the question type is **Addition**, the user also can change this by selecting one of the RadioButtons in the GroupBox labeled **Operation**. Doing so invokes the corresponding operation's event handlers in lines 88–109, which assigns to string operation the string corresponding to the user's selection.

```
1    // Fig. 28.29: MathTutor.cs
2    // Math tutor using EquationGeneratorServiceXML to create equations.
3    using System;
4    using System.Net;
5    using System.Windows.Forms;
6    using System.Xml.Linq;
7
8    namespace MathTutorXML
9    {
10      public partial class MathTutor : Form
11      {
12         private string operation = "add"; // the default operation
13         private int level = 1; // the default difficulty level
14         private string leftHandSide; // the left side of the equation
15         private int result; // the answer
16         private XNamespace xmlNamespace =
17            XNamespace.Get( "http://schemas.datacontract.org/2004/07/" );
18
```

Fig. 28.29 | Math tutor using EquationGeneratorServiceXML to create equations. (Part 1 of 4.)

```
19          // object used to invoke service
20          private WebClient service = new WebClient();
21
22          public MathTutor()
23          {
24             InitializeComponent();
25
26             // add DownloadStringCompleted event handler to WebClient
27             service.DownloadStringCompleted +=
28                new DownloadStringCompletedEventHandler(
29                service_DownloadStringCompleted );
30          } // end constructor
31
32          // generates new equation when user clicks button
33          private void generateButton_Click( object sender, EventArgs e )
34          {
35             // send request to EquationGeneratorServiceXML
36             service.DownloadStringAsync( new Uri(
37                "http://localhost:49732/EquationGeneratorServiceXML" +
38                "/Service.svc/equation/" + operation + "/" + level ) );
39          } // end method generateButton_Click
40
41          // process web service response
42          private void service_DownloadStringCompleted(
43             object sender, DownloadStringCompletedEventArgs e )
44          {
45             // check if any errors occurred in retrieving service data
46             if ( e.Error == null )
47             {
48                // parse response and get LeftHandSide and Result values
49                XDocument xmlResponse = XDocument.Parse( e.Result );
50                leftHandSide = xmlResponse.Element(
51                   xmlNamespace + "Equation" ).Element(
52                   xmlNamespace + "LeftHandSide" ).Value;
53                result = Convert.ToInt32( xmlResponse.Element(
54                   xmlNamespace + "Equation" ).Element(
55                   xmlNamespace + "Result" ).Value );
56
57                // display left side of equation
58                questionLabel.Text = leftHandSide;
59                okButton.Enabled = true; // enable okButton
60                answerTextBox.Enabled = true; // enable answerTextBox
61             } // end if
62          } // end method client_DownloadStringCompleted
63
64          // check user's answer
65          private void okButton_Click( object sender, EventArgs e )
66          {
67             if ( !string.IsNullOrEmpty( answerTextBox.Text ) )
68             {
```

Fig. 28.29 | Math tutor using EquationGeneratorServiceXML to create equations. (Part 2 of 4.)

```
69              // get user's answer
70              int userAnswer = Convert.ToInt32( answerTextBox.Text );
71
72              // determine whether user's answer is correct
73              if ( result == userAnswer )
74              {
75                 questionLabel.Text = string.Empty; // clear question
76                 answerTextBox.Clear(); // clear answer
77                 okButton.Enabled = false; // disable OK button
78                 MessageBox.Show( "Correct! Good job!", "Result" );
79              } // end if
80              else
81              {
82                 MessageBox.Show( "Incorrect. Try again.", "Result" );
83              } // end else
84           } // end if
85        } // end method okButton_Click
86
87        // set the operation to addition
88        private void additionRadioButton_CheckedChanged( object sender,
89           EventArgs e )
90        {
91           if ( additionRadioButton.Checked )
92              operation = "add";
93        } // end method additionRadioButton_CheckedChanged
94
95        // set the operation to subtraction
96        private void subtractionRadioButton_CheckedChanged( object sender,
97           EventArgs e )
98        {
99           if ( subtractionRadioButton.Checked )
100             operation = "subtract";
101       } // end method subtractionRadioButton_CheckedChanged
102
103       // set the operation to multiplication
104       private void multiplicationRadioButton_CheckedChanged(
105          object sender, EventArgs e )
106       {
107          if ( multiplicationRadioButton.Checked )
108             operation = "multiply";
109       } // end method multiplicationRadioButton_CheckedChanged
110
111       // set difficulty level to 1
112       private void levelOneRadioButton_CheckedChanged( object sender,
113          EventArgs e )
114       {
115          if ( levelOneRadioButton.Checked )
116             level = 1;
117       } // end method levelOneRadioButton_CheckedChanged
118
```

Fig. 28.29 | Math tutor using EquationGeneratorServiceXML to create equations. (Part 3 of 4.)

```
119            // set difficulty level to 2
120            private void levelTwoRadioButton_CheckedChanged( object sender,
121               EventArgs e )
122            {
123               if ( levelTwoRadioButton.Checked )
124                  level = 2;
125            } // end method levelTwoRadioButton_CheckedChanged
126
127            // set difficulty level to 3
128            private void levelThreeRadioButton_CheckedChanged( object sender,
129               EventArgs e )
130            {
131               if ( levelThreeRadioButton.Checked )
132                  level = 3;
133            } // end method levelThreeRadioButton_CheckedChanged
134         } // end class MathTutor
135      } // end namespace MathTutorXML
```

a) Generating a level 1 addition equation

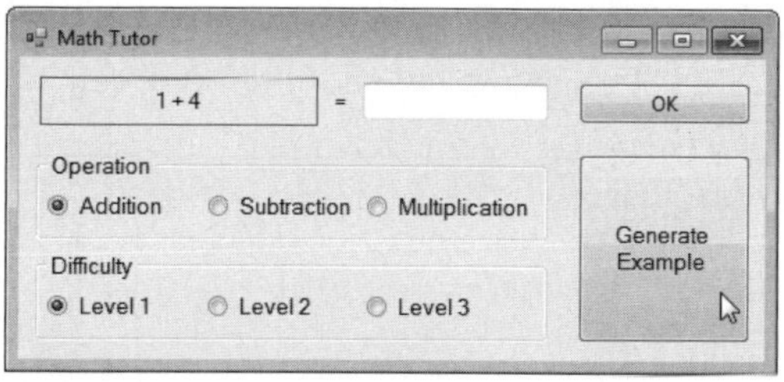

b) Answering the question incorrectly

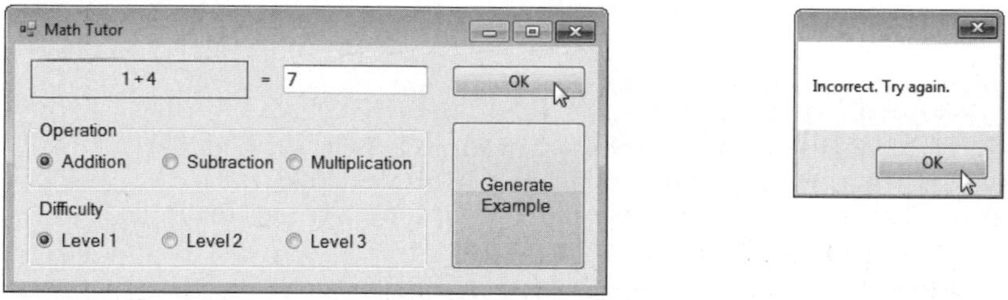

c) Answering the question correctly

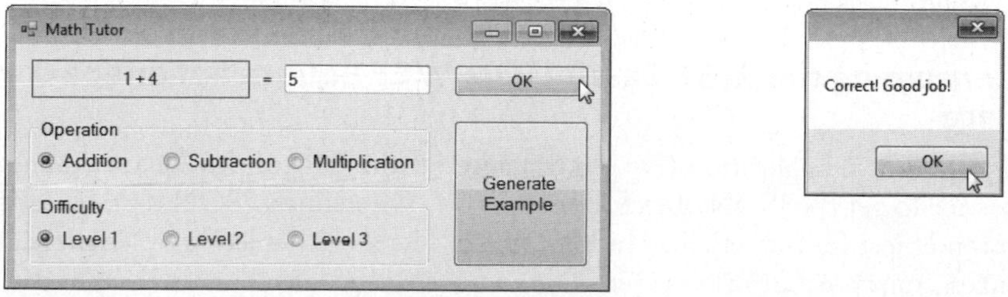

Fig. 28.29 | Math tutor using EquationGeneratorServiceXML to create equations. (Part 4 of 4.)

Line 20 defines the WebClient that is used to invoke the web service. Event handler generateButton_Click (lines 33–39) invokes EquationGeneratorService method GenerateEquation (line 36–38) asynchronously using the web service's UriTemplate specified at line 12 in Fig. 28.27. When the response arrives, the DownloadStringCompleted event handler (lines 42–62) parses the XML response (line 49), uses XDocument's Element method to obtain the left side of the equation (lines 50–52) and stores the result (lines 53–55). We define the XML response's namespace in lines 16–17 as an XNamespace to parse the XML response. Then, the handler displays the left-hand side of the equation in questionLabel (line 58) and enables okButton so that the user can enter an answer. When the user clicks **OK**, okButton_Click (lines 65–85) checks whether the user provided the correct answer.

28.11.3 Creating the REST-Based JSON WCF EquationGenerator Web Service

You can set the web service to return JSON data instead of XML. Figure 28.30 is a modified IEquationGeneratorService interface for a service that returns an Equation in JSON format. The ResponseFormat property (line 12) is added to the WebGet attribute and set to WebMessageFormat.Json. We don't show the implementation of this interface here, because it is identical to that of Fig. 28.28. This shows how flexible WCF can be.

```
1   // Fig. 28.30: IEquationGeneratorService.cs
2   // WCF REST service interface to create random equations based on a
3   // specified operation and difficulty level.
4   using System.ServiceModel;
5   using System.ServiceModel.Web;
6
7   [ServiceContract]
8   public interface IEquationGeneratorService
9   {
10     // method to generate a math equation
11     [OperationContract]
12     [WebGet( ResponseFormat = WebMessageFormat.Json,
13        UriTemplate = "equation/{operation}/{level}" )]
14     Equation GenerateEquation( string operation, string level );
15   } // end interface IEquationGeneratorService
```

Fig. 28.30 | WCF REST service interface to create random equations based on a specified operation and difficulty level.

28.11.4 Consuming the REST-Based JSON WCF EquationGenerator Web Service

A modified MathTutor application (Fig. 28.31) accesses the URI of the EquationGenerator web service to get the JSON object (lines 35–37). We define a JSON representation of an Equation object for the serializer in Fig. 28.32. The JSON object is deserialized using the System.Runtime.Serialization.Json namespace's DataContractJsonSerializer (lines 48–49) and converted into an Equation object. We use the LeftHandSide field of the deserialized object (line 55) to display the left side of the equation and the Result field (line 67) to obtain the answer.

```
 1   // Fig. 28.31: MathTutorForm.cs
 2   // Math tutor using EquationGeneratorServiceJSON to create equations.
 3   using System;
 4   using System.IO;
 5   using System.Net;
 6   using System.Runtime.Serialization.Json;
 7   using System.Text;
 8   using System.Windows.Forms;
 9
10   namespace MathTutorJSON
11   {
12      public partial class MathTutorForm : Form
13      {
14         private string operation = "add"; // the default operation
15         private int level = 1; // the default difficulty level
16         private Equation currentEquation;  // represents the Equation
17
18         // object used to invoke service
19         private WebClient service = new WebClient();
20
21         public MathTutorForm()
22         {
23            InitializeComponent();
24
25            // add DownloadStringCompleted event handler to WebClient
26            service.DownloadStringCompleted +=
27               new DownloadStringCompletedEventHandler(
28                  service_DownloadStringCompleted );
29         } // end constructor
30
31         // generates new equation when user clicks button
32         private void generateButton_Click( object sender, EventArgs e )
33         {
34            // send request to EquationGeneratorServiceJSON
35            service.DownloadStringAsync( new Uri(
36               "http://localhost:50238/EquationGeneratorServiceJSON" +
37               "/Service.svc/equation/" + operation + "/" + level ) );
38         } // end method generateButton_Click
39
40         // process web service response
41         private void service_DownloadStringCompleted(
42            object sender, DownloadStringCompletedEventArgs e )
43         {
44            // check if any errors occurred in retrieving service data
45            if ( e.Error == null )
46            {
47               // deserialize response into an Equation object
48               DataContractJsonSerializer JSONSerializer =
49                  new DataContractJsonSerializer( typeof( Equation ) );
50               currentEquation =
51                  ( Equation ) JSONSerializer.ReadObject( new
52                  MemoryStream( Encoding.Unicode.GetBytes( e.Result ) ) );
```

Fig. 28.31 | Math tutor using EquationGeneratorServiceJSON. (Part 1 of 4.)

```
53
54              // display left side of equation
55              questionLabel.Text = currentEquation.LeftHandSide;
56              okButton.Enabled = true; // enable okButton
57              answerTextBox.Enabled = true; // enable answerTextBox
58           } // end if
59        } // end method client_DownloadStringCompleted
60
61        // check user's answer
62        private void okButton_Click( object sender, EventArgs e )
63        {
64           if ( !string.IsNullOrEmpty( answerTextBox.Text ) )
65           {
66              // determine whether user's answer is correct
67              if ( currentEquation.Result ==
68                 Convert.ToInt32( answerTextBox.Text ) )
69              {
70                 questionLabel.Text = string.Empty; // clear question
71                 answerTextBox.Clear(); // clear answer
72                 okButton.Enabled = false; // disable OK button
73                 MessageBox.Show( "Correct! Good job!", "Result" );
74              } // end if
75              else
76              {
77                 MessageBox.Show( "Incorrect. Try again.", "Result" );
78              } // end else
79           } // end if
80        } // end method okButton_Click
81
82        // set the operation to addition
83        private void additionRadioButton_CheckedChanged( object sender,
84           EventArgs e )
85        {
86           if ( additionRadioButton.Checked )
87              operation = "add";
88        } // end method additionRadioButton_CheckedChanged
89
90        // set the operation to subtraction
91        private void subtractionRadioButton_CheckedChanged( object sender,
92           EventArgs e )
93        {
94           if ( subtractionRadioButton.Checked )
95              operation = "subtract";
96        } // end method subtractionRadioButton_CheckedChanged
97
98        // set the operation to multiplication
99        private void multiplicationRadioButton_CheckedChanged(
100          object sender, EventArgs e )
101       {
102          if ( multiplicationRadioButton.Checked )
103             operation = "multiply";
104       } // end method multiplicationRadioButton_CheckedChanged
```

Fig. 28.31 | Math tutor using EquationGeneratorServiceJSON. (Part 2 of 4.)

```
105
106          // set difficulty level to 1
107          private void levelOneRadioButton_CheckedChanged( object sender,
108             EventArgs e )
109          {
110             if ( levelOneRadioButton.Checked )
111                level = 1;
112          } // end method levelOneRadioButton_CheckedChanged
113
114          // set difficulty level to 2
115          private void levelTwoRadioButton_CheckedChanged( object sender,
116             EventArgs e )
117          {
118             if ( levelTwoRadioButton.Checked )
119                level = 2;
120          } // end method levelTwoRadioButton_CheckedChanged
121
122          // set difficulty level to 3
123          private void levelThreeRadioButton_CheckedChanged( object sender,
124             EventArgs e )
125          {
126             if ( levelThreeRadioButton.Checked )
127                level = 3;
128          } // end method levelThreeRadioButton_CheckedChanged
129       } // end class MathTutorForm
130    } // end namespace MathTutorJSON
```

a) Generating a level 2 multiplication equation

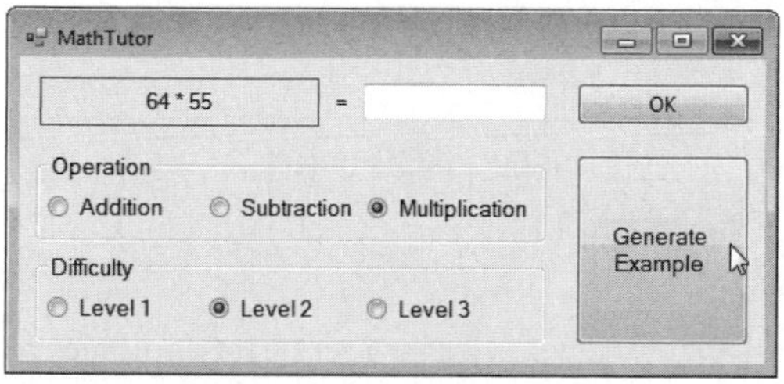

b) Answering the question incorrectly

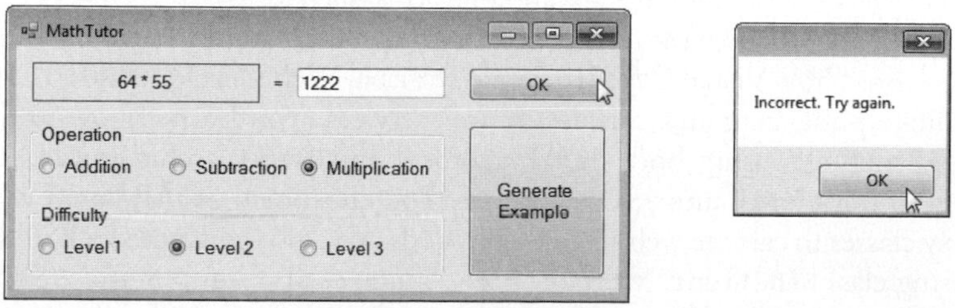

Fig. 28.31 | Math tutor using EquationGeneratorServiceJSON. (Part 3 of 4.)

c) Answering the question correctly

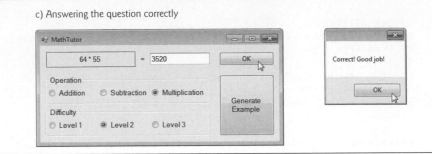

Fig. 28.31 | Math tutor using `EquationGeneratorServiceJSON`. (Part 4 of 4.)

```
 1   // Fig. 28.32: Equation.cs
 2   // Equation class representing a JSON object.
 3   using System;
 4
 5   namespace MathTutorJSON
 6   {
 7      [Serializable]
 8      class Equation
 9      {
10         public int Left = 0;
11         public string LeftHandSide = null;
12         public string Operation = null;
13         public int Result = 0;
14         public int Right = 0;
15         public string RightHandSide = null;
16      } // end class Equation
17   } // end namespace MathTutorJSON
```

Fig. 28.32 | `Equation` class representing a JSON object.

28.12 Wrap-Up

This chapter introduced WCF web services—a set of technologies for building distributed systems in which system components communicate with one another over networks. You learned that a web service is a class that allows client software to call the web service's methods remotely via common data formats and protocols, such as XML, JSON, HTTP, SOAP and REST. We also discussed several benefits of distributed computing with web services.

We discussed how Visual C# 2010 Express, Visual Web Developer 2010 Express, and WCF facilitate publishing and consuming web services. You learned how to define web services and methods using both SOAP protocol and REST architecture, and how to return data in both XML and JSON formats. You consumed SOAP-based web services using proxy classes to call the web service's methods. You also consumed REST-based web services using class `WebClient`. We built both Windows applications and ASP.NET web applications as web-service clients. After explaining the mechanics of web services through our `Welcome` examples, we demonstrated more sophisticated web services that use session tracking, database access and user-defined types.

28.13 Deitel Web Services Resource Centers

To learn more about web services, check out our web services Resource Centers at:

```
www.deitel.com/WebServices/
www.deitel.com/RESTWebServices/
```

You'll find articles, samples chapters and tutorials that discuss XML, web-services specifications, SOAP, WSDL, UDDI, .NET web services, consuming XML web services and web-services architecture. You'll learn how to build your own Yahoo! maps mashups and applications that work with the Yahoo! Music Engine. You'll find information about Amazon's web services including the Amazon E-Commerce Service (ECS), Amazon historical pricing, Amazon Mechanical Turk, Amazon S3 (Simple Storage Service) and the Scalable Simple Queue Service (SQS). You'll learn how to use web services from several other companies including eBay, Google and Microsoft. You'll find REST web services best practices and guidelines. You'll also learn how to use REST web services with other technologies including SOAP, Rails, Windows Communication Foundation (WCF) and more. You can view the complete list of Deitel Resource Centers at www.deitel.com/ResourceCenters.html.

Silverlight and Rich Internet Applications

OBJECTIVES

In this chapter you'll learn:

- How Silverlight relates to WPF.

- To use Silverlight controls to create Rich Internet Applications.

- To create custom Silverlight controls.

- To use animation for enhanced GUIs.

- To display and manipulate images.

- To use Silverlight with Flickr's web services to build an online photo-searching application.

- To create Silverlight deep zoom applications.

- To include audio and video in Silverlight applications.

*Had I the heavens'
embroidered cloths,
Enwrought with gold and
silver light.*
—William Butler Yeats

*This world is but a canvas
to our imaginations.*
—Henry David Thoreau

*Something deeply hidden
had to be behind things.*
—Albert Einstein

*Individuality of expression
is the beginning and end of
all art.*
—Johann Wolfgang von Goethe

29.1 Introduction

Silverlight™ is Microsoft's platform for building **Rich Internet Applications (RIAs)**—web applications comparable in responsiveness and rich user interactivity to desktop applications. Silverlight is a robust, cross-platform, cross-browser implementation of the .NET platform that competes with RIA technologies such as Adobe Flash and Flex and Sun's JavaFX, and complements Microsoft's ASP.NET and ASP.NET AJAX (which we discussed in Chapter 27). Developers familiar with programming WPF applications are able to adapt quickly to creating Silverlight applications.

The "sizzle" of Silverlight is **multimedia**—the use of images, graphics, animation, sound and video to make applications "come alive." Silverlight includes strong multimedia support, including state-of-the-art high-definition video streaming. WPF and Silverlight, through the .NET class libraries, provide extensive multimedia facilities that enable you to start developing powerful multimedia applications immediately. Among these facilities is **deep zoom**, which allows the user to view high-resolution images over the web as if the images were stored on the local computer. Users can interactively "explore" a high-resolution image by zooming in and out and panning—while maintaining the original image's quality. Silverlight supports deep zoom images up to one billion by one billion pixels in size!

[*Note:* The **WeatherViewer** and **FlickrViewer** examples require web service API keys from WeatherBug and Flickr, respectively, before you can execute them. See Sections 29.4–29.5 for details.]

29.2 Platform Overview

Silverlight runs as a browser plug-in for Internet Explorer, Firefox and Safari on recent versions of Microsoft Windows and Mac OS X. The system requirements for the runtime can be found at `www.microsoft.com/silverlight/faq/#sys-req`. Silverlight is also available on Linux systems via the Mono Project's Moonlight (`mono-project.com/Moonlight`).

Like WPF applications, Silverlight applications consist of user interfaces described in XAML and code-behind files containing application logic. The XAML used in Silverlight is a subset of that used in WPF.

The subset of the .NET Framework available in Silverlight includes APIs for collections, input/output, generics, multithreading, globalization, XML, LINQ and more. It also includes APIs for interacting with JavaScript and the elements in a web page, and APIs for local storage data to help you create more robust web-based applications.

Silverlight is an implementation of the .NET Platform, so you can create Silverlight applications in .NET languages such as Visual C#, Visual Basic, IronRuby and Iron-Python. This makes it easy for .NET programmers to create applications that run in a web browser.

Silverlight's graphics and GUI capabilities are a subset of the Windows Presentation Foundation (WPF) framework. Some capabilities supported in Silverlight include GUI controls, layout management, graphics, animation and multimedia. There are also styles and template-based "skinning" capabilities to manage the look-and-feel of a Silverlight user interface. Like WPF, Silverlight provides a powerful data-binding model that makes it easy to display data from objects, collections, databases, XML and even other GUI controls. Silverlight also provides rich networking support, enabling you to write browser-based applications that invoke web services and use other networking technologies.

29.3 Silverlight Runtime and Tools Installation

Silverlight runs in web browsers as a plug-in. To view websites programmed in Silverlight, you need the **Silverlight Runtime** plug-in from `www.silverlight.net/getstarted/`. After installing the plug-in, go to Microsoft's Silverlight Showcase (`www.silverlight.net/showcase/`) to try some sample applications.

The examples in this chapter were built using the Silverlight 4 SDK, which is available from

```
bit.ly/SilverlightDownload
```

and Visual Web Developer 2010 Express, which is available from:

```
www.microsoft.com/express/web/
```

Additional information about Silverlight is available at:

```
www.silverlight.net
```

29.4 Building a Silverlight WeatherViewer Application

Silverlight is a subset of WPF, so the two share many capabilities. Since Silverlight produces Internet applications instead of desktop applications, the setup of a Silverlight project is different from that of WPF.

A Silverlight application created with the **Silverlight Application** project template has two XAML files—`MainPage.xaml` and `App.xaml`. `MainPage.xaml` defines the application's GUI, and its code-behind file `MainPage.xaml.cs` declares the GUI event handlers and other methods required by the application. `App.xaml` declares your application's shared resources that can be applied to various GUI elements. The code-behind file `App.xaml.cs` defines application-level event handlers, such as an event handler for unhandled exceptions. Content in the `App.xaml` and `App.xaml.cs` files can be used by all the application's pages. We do not use `App.xaml` and `App.xaml` in this chapter. In Visual Web Developer 2010 and Visual Studio 2010 there is also a **Silverlight Navigation Application** project template for creating multipage Silverlight applications. We do not cover this template.

Differences Between WPF and Silverlight
To create a new Silverlight project in Visual Web Developer Express, select **File > New Project...**. In the **Installed Templates** pane under **Visual C#**, select the **Silverlight** option. Then in the **Templates** window, select **Silverlight Application**. After entering your project's name (WeatherViewer) and selecting its location, click **OK**. A **New Silverlight Application** dialog appears, asking how you would like to host your application. Ensure that the **Host the Silverlight application in a new Web site** option is selected. In the **New Web project type** drop-down menu, select **ASP.NET Web Application Project**. Keep the default project name and click **OK**.

MainPage.xaml
The MainPage.xaml file displayed in the XAML tab of Visual Studio (Fig. 29.1) is similar to the default XAML file for a WPF application. In a WPF application, the root XAML element is a Window. In Silverlight, the root element is a **UserControl**. The default User-Control has a class name specified with the **x:Class** attribute (line 1), specifies the namespaces (lines 2–5) to provide access to the Silverlight controls throughout the XAML, and has a width and height of 400 and 300 pixels, respectively. These numbers are system-independent pixel measurements, where each pixel represents 1/96th of an inch. Lines 9–11 are the default Grid layout container. Unlike a WPF application, the default Grid's **x:Name** (the name used in code that manipulates the control) and Background attributes are set by default in a Silverlight application.

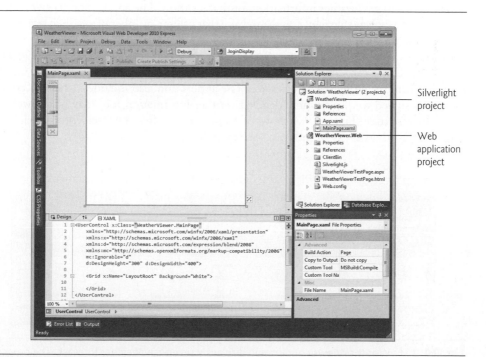

Fig. 29.1 | New Silverlight application in Visual Studio.

.xap File

A compiled Silverlight application is packaged by the IDE as a `.xap` file containing the application and its supporting resources (such as images or other files used by the application). The web page that hosts the Silverlight application references the Silverlight plug-in and the application's `.xap` file. The Silverlight plug-in then executes the application. The test web application that was created for you contains the file `WeatherViewerTest-Page.aspx`, which loads and executes the Silverlight application.

A Silverlight application must be hosted in a web page. The **Web Application Project** is used to test the Silverlight application in a web browser. Building the solution automatically copies the compiled application into the **Web Application Project**. You can then test it using the built-in web server in Visual Studio. After the application is built in the IDE, this part of the application contains the `.xap` file that was described in the preceding paragraph.

Desiging Silverlight User Interfaces

As in WPF, you can use the **Design** view and the **Properties** window to design your user Silverlight interfaces, but the Visual Studio designer for WPF and Silverlight is not as robust as that provided by Microsoft Expression Blend. Expression Blend is beyond the scope of this chapter. Trial versions are available from `www.microsoft.com/expression/`.

Introduction to the WeatherViewer Application

Our **WeatherViewer** application (Fig. 29.2) allows the user to input a zip code and invokes a web service to get weather information for that location. The application receives weather data from `www.weatherbug.com`—a website that offers a number of weather-related web services, including some that return XML data. To run this example on your computer, you need to register for your own WeatherBug API key at `weather.weatherbug.com/desktop-weather/api.html`. This application uses LINQ to XML to process the weather data that is returned by the web service. The application also includes a custom control that we designed to display more detailed weather information for a day of the week selected by the user. Figure 29.2 shows the application after the user enters a zip code (Fig. 29.2(a)) then clicks Monday to see its weather details (Fig. 29.2(b)).

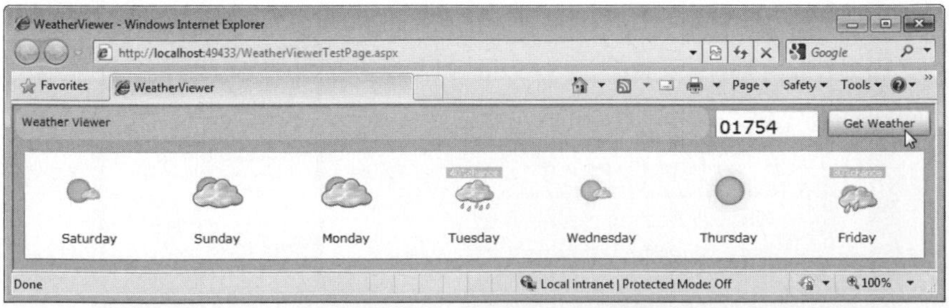

Fig. 29.2 | **WeatherViewer** application displays a seven-day weather forecast. The program can also display detailed information for a selected day. (Part 1 of 2.)

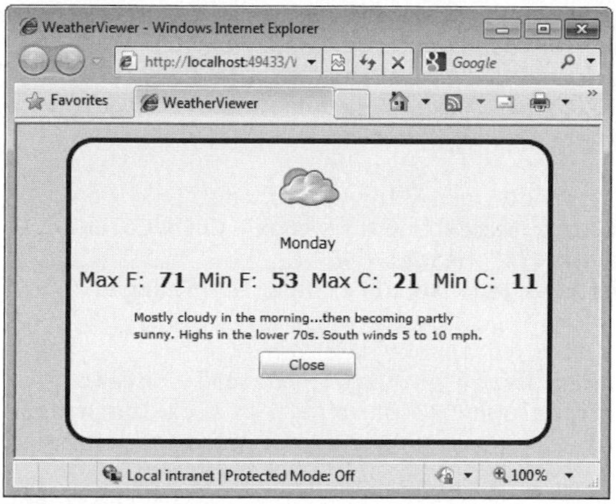

Fig. 29.2 | **WeatherViewer** application displays a seven-day weather forecast. The program can also display detailed information for a selected day. (Part 2 of 2.)

29.4.1 GUI Layout

The layout controls of WPF described in Chapter 24—Grid, StackPanel and Canvas— are also available in Silverlight. The XAML for the layout of the **WeatherViewer** application is shown in Fig. 29.3. This application uses nested Grid controls to lay out its elements.

```
1   <!-- Fig. 29.3: MainPage.xaml -->
2   <!-- WeatherViewer displays day-by-day weather data (XAML). -->
3   <UserControl xmlns:Weather="clr-namespace:WeatherViewer"
4      x:Class="WeatherViewer.MainPage"
5      xmlns="http://schemas.microsoft.com/winfx/2006/xaml/presentation"
6      xmlns:x="http://schemas.microsoft.com/winfx/2006/xaml"
7      xmlns:d="http://schemas.microsoft.com/expression/blend/2008"
8      xmlns:mc="http://schemas.openxmlformats.org/markup-compatibility/2006"
9      mc:Ignorable="d">
10
11   <Grid x:Name="LayoutRoot" Background="LightSkyBlue">
12      <Grid.RowDefinitions>
13         <RowDefinition Height="35" />
14         <RowDefinition x:Name="messageRow" Height="0" />
15         <RowDefinition />
16      </Grid.RowDefinitions>
17
18      <!-- Grid contains border, textbox and search button -->
19      <Grid>
20         <Grid.ColumnDefinitions>
21            <ColumnDefinition />
22            <ColumnDefinition Width="110" />
23            <ColumnDefinition Width="110" />
24         </Grid.ColumnDefinitions>
25
```

Fig. 29.3 | **WeatherViewer** displays day-by-day weather data (XAML). (Part 1 of 3.)

```
26            <!-- Border containing the title "Weather Viewer" -->
27            <Border Grid.Column="0" CornerRadius="10"
28               Background="LightGray" Margin="2">
29               <TextBlock Text="Weather Viewer" Padding="6" />
30            </Border>
31
32            <!-- zip code goes into this text box -->
33            <TextBox x:Name="inputTextBox" Grid.Column="1" FontSize="18"
34               Margin="4" Height="40"
35               TextChanged="inputTextBox_TextChanged" />
36
37            <!-- Click to invoke web service -->
38            <Button x:Name="getWeatherButton" Content="Get Weather"
39               Grid.Column="2" Margin="4" Click="getWeatherButton_Click" />
40         </Grid>
41
42         <!-- Border to contain text block which shows error messages -->
43         <Border x:Name="messageBorder" Background="White"
44            Grid.Row="1" Padding="8">
45            <TextBlock x:Name="messageBlock" FontSize="14"
46               HorizontalAlignment="Left" Foreground="Red"/>
47         </Border>
48
49         <!-- Contains weather images for several upcoming days -->
50         <ListBox x:Name="forecastList" Grid.Row="2" Margin="10"
51            SelectionChanged="forecastList_SelectionChanged">
52            <ListBox.ItemsPanel>
53               <ItemsPanelTemplate>
54                  <!-- Arrange items horizontally -->
55                  <StackPanel Orientation="Horizontal" />
56               </ItemsPanelTemplate>
57            </ListBox.ItemsPanel>
58
59            <ListBox.ItemTemplate>
60               <DataTemplate>
61                  <!-- Represents item for a single day -->
62                  <StackPanel Width="120" Orientation="Vertical"
63                     HorizontalAlignment="Center">
64                     <!-- Displays image for a single day -->
65                     <Image Source="{Binding WeatherImage}"
66                        Margin="5" Width="55" Height="58" />
67
68                     <!-- Displays the day of the week -->
69                     <TextBlock Text="{Binding DayOfWeek}"
70                        TextAlignment="Center" FontSize="12"
71                        Margin="5" TextWrapping="Wrap" />
72                  </StackPanel>
73               </DataTemplate>
74            </ListBox.ItemTemplate>
75         </ListBox>
76
```

Fig. 29.3 | WeatherViewer displays day-by-day weather data (XAML). (Part 2 of 3.)

```
77          <!-- Custom control for displaying detailed information -->
78          <Weather:WeatherDetailsView x:Name="completeDetails"
79             Visibility="Collapsed" Grid.RowSpan="3" />
80       </Grid>
81    </UserControl>
```

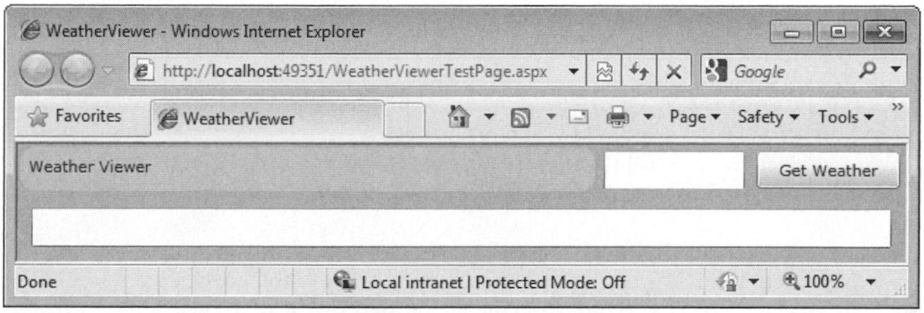

Fig. 29.3 | **WeatherViewer** displays day-by-day weather data (XAML). (Part 3 of 3.)

Lines 12–16 contain the RowDefinitions of the main Grid. Lines 20–24 contain the ColumnDefinitions of a nested Grid which displays the top row of the page containing the light gray title Border, the search TextBox and the search Button, as shown in Fig. 29.3.

Line 28 defines the Border's **Margin** property, which specifies the amount of space between the Border and any adjacent elements. Lines 43–47 define a Border that contains a TextBlock in which we display an error message if the user enters an invalid zip code. Lines 49–75 define the ListBox used on the main page to display each day's weather image. Line 55 defines the StackPanel that is used as a template by the ListBox's Items-Panel, allowing the ListBox's items to display horizontally. Lines 62–72 define a Stack-Panel for each individual item, displaying the weather Image and the TextBlock containing the day of the week in a vertical orientation. Lines 65 and 69 bind data from the web service's XML response to the two elements that display weather information.

Lines 78–79 create a WeatherDetailsView custom control element. The code for the custom control is shown in Section 29.4.3. This control's Visibility property is initially set to Collapsed, so it is not visible when the page loads. The Visibility of a control defines whether it is rendered on the screen. We also set the Grid.RowSpan property to 3. By taking up two rows, the GUI is blocked when the custom control is displayed, so the user can no longer interact with the main page until the control is closed. Notice that WeatherDetailsView is in the namespace Weather. This namespace (defined in line 3 of the XAML file) allows you to use the custom control in the application. The custom control must be referenced through the namespace since it is not a pre-defined control. If we did not define the namespace, there would be no way to reference WeatherDetailsView.

29.4.2 Obtaining and Displaying Weather Forecast Data

The **WeatherViewer** example uses Silverlight's web services, LINQ to XML and data-binding capabilities. The application's code-behind file appears in Fig. 29.4. You must insert your WeatherBug API key in line 18 in place of "YOUR API KEY HERE".

```
 1    // Fig. 29.4: MainPage.xaml.cs
 2    // WeatherViewer displays day-by-day weather data (code-behind).
 3    using System;
 4    using System.Linq;
 5    using System.Net;
 6    using System.Text.RegularExpressions;
 7    using System.Windows;
 8    using System.Windows.Controls;
 9    using System.Windows.Input;
10    using System.Xml.Linq;
11
12    namespace WeatherViewer
13    {
14       public partial class MainPage : UserControl
15       {
16          // object to invoke weather forecast web service
17          private WebClient weatherService = new WebClient();
18          private const string APIKey = "YOUR API KEY HERE";
19          private const int messageRowHeight = 35;
20
21          // constructor
22          public MainPage()
23          {
24             InitializeComponent();
25
26             weatherService.DownloadStringCompleted +=
27                new DownloadStringCompletedEventHandler(
28                   weatherService_DownloadStringCompleted );
29          } // end constructor
30
31          // process getWeatherButton's Click event
32          private void getWeatherButton_Click(
33             object sender, RoutedEventArgs e )
34          {
35             // make sure the input string contains a five-digit number
36             if ( Regex.IsMatch( inputTextBox.Text, @"\d{5}" ) )
37             {
38                string zipcode =
39                   Regex.Match( inputTextBox.Text, @"\d{5}" ).ToString();
40
41                // URL to pass to the WebClient to get our weather, complete
42                // with API key. OutputType=1 specifies XML data is needed.
43                string forecastURL =
44                   "http://" + APIKey + ".api.wxbug.net/" +
45                   "getForecastRSS.aspx?ACode=" + APIKey +
46                   "&ZipCode=" + zipcode + "&OutputType=1";
47
48                // asynchronously invoke the web service
49                weatherService.DownloadStringAsync( new Uri( forecastURL ) );
50
51                // set the cursor to the wait symbol
52                this.Cursor = Cursors.Wait;
53             } // end if
```

Fig. 29.4 | **WeatherViewer** displays day-by-day weather data (code-behind). (Part 1 of 4.)

```
54          else // if input string does not contain a five-digit number,
55          {    // output an error message and do nothing else
56             messageBlock.Text = "Please enter a valid zipcode.";
57             messageRow.Height = new GridLength( messageRowHeight );
58             messageBorder.Width = forecastList.ActualWidth;
59          } // end else
60       } // end method getWeatherButton_Click
61
62       // when download is complete for web service result
63       private void weatherService_DownloadStringCompleted( object sender,
64          DownloadStringCompletedEventArgs e )
65       {
66          if ( e.Error == null )
67             DisplayWeatherForecast( e.Result );
68
69          this.Cursor = Cursors.Arrow; // arrow cursor
70       } // end method weatherService_DownloadStringCompleted
71
72       // display the received weather data
73       private void DisplayWeatherForecast( string xmlData )
74       {
75          // parse the XML data for use with LINQ
76          XDocument weatherXML = XDocument.Parse( xmlData );
77
78          XNamespace weatherNamespace =
79             XNamespace.Get( "http://www.aws.com/aws" );
80
81          // find out if the data describes the same zipcode the user
82          // entered and get the location information via LINQ to XML
83          var locationInformation =
84             from item in weatherXML.Descendants(
85                weatherNamespace + "location" )
86             select item;
87
88          string xmlZip = string.Empty;
89          string xmlCity = string.Empty;
90          string xmlState = string.Empty;
91
92          foreach ( var item in locationInformation )
93          {
94             xmlZip = item.Element( weatherNamespace + "zip" ).Value;
95             xmlCity = item.Element( weatherNamespace + "city" ).Value;
96             xmlState = item.Element( weatherNamespace + "state" ).Value;
97          } // end for
98
99          // if the zipcodes don't match, display the data anyway,
100         // but display a message informing them of it
101         if ( !xmlZip.Equals( inputTextBox.Text ) )
102         {
103            messageBlock.Text = "Zipcode not valid; " +
104               "displaying data for closest valid match: " +
105               xmlCity + ", " + xmlState + ", " + xmlZip;
106            messageRow.Height = new GridLength( messageRowHeight );
```

Fig. 29.4 | **WeatherViewer** displays day-by-day weather data (code-behind). (Part 2 of 4.)

```
107            messageBorder.Width = forecastList.ActualWidth;
108         } // end if
109
110      // store all the data into WeatherData objects
111      var weatherInformation =
112         from item in weatherXML.Descendants(
113            weatherNamespace + "forecast" )
114         select new WeatherData
115         {
116            DayOfWeek =
117               item.Element( weatherNamespace + "title" ).Value,
118            WeatherImage = "http://img.weather.weatherbug.com/" +
119               "forecast/icons/localized/65x55/en/trans/" +
120               ( ( item.Element( weatherNamespace + "image" ).Value).
121                  Substring( 51 ).Replace( ".gif", ".png" ) ),
122            MaxTemperatureF =
123               item.Element( weatherNamespace + "high" ).Value,
124            MaxTemperatureC = convertToCelsius(
125               item.Element( weatherNamespace + "high" ).Value),
126            MinTemperatureF =
127               item.Element( weatherNamespace + "low" ).Value,
128            MinTemperatureC = convertToCelsius(
129               item.Element( weatherNamespace + "low" ).Value),
130            Description =
131               item.Element( weatherNamespace + "prediction" ).Value
132         }; // end LINQ to XML that creates WeatherData objects
133
134      // bind forecastList.ItemSource to the weatherInformation
135      forecastList.ItemsSource = weatherInformation;
136   } // end method DisplayWeatherForecast
137
138   // convert the temperature into Celsius if it's a number;
139   // cast as Integer to avoid long decimal values
140   string convertToCelsius( string fahrenheit )
141   {
142      if ( fahrenheit != "--" )
143         return ( ( Int32.Parse( fahrenheit ) - 32) *
144            5 / 9 ).ToString();
145
146      return fahrenheit;
147   } // end methodconvertToCelsius
148
149   // show details of the selected day
150   private void forecastList_SelectionChanged(
151      object sender, SelectionChangedEventArgs e )
152   {
153      // specify the WeatherData object containing the details
154      if ( forecastList.SelectedItem != null )
155         completeDetails.DataContext = forecastList.SelectedItem;
156
157      // show the complete weather details
158      completeDetails.Visibility = Visibility.Visible;
159   } // end method forecastList_SelectionChanged
```

Fig. 29.4 | **WeatherViewer** displays day-by-day weather data (code-behind). (Part 3 of 4.)

```
160
161        // remove displayed weather information when input zip code changes
162        private void inputTextBox_TextChanged( object sender,
163           TextChangedEventArgs e )
164        {
165           forecastList.ItemsSource = null;
166
167           // also clear the message by getting rid of its row
168           messageRow.Height = new System.Windows.GridLength( 0 );
169        } // end method inputTextBox_TextChanged
170     } // end class MainPage
171  } // end namespace WeatherViewer
```

Fig. 29.4 | **WeatherViewer** displays day-by-day weather data (code-behind). (Part 4 of 4.)

The code for the main page of the **WeatherViewer** invokes the WeatherBug web service and binds all the necessary data to the proper elements of the page. Notice that we imported the System.Xml.Linq namespace (line 10), which enables the LINQ to XML that is used in the example. You must also add a reference to the System.Xml.Linq assembly to the WeatherViewer Silverlight project. To do so, right click the **WeatherViewer** project in the **Solution Explorer** and select **Add Reference...**. In the dialog that appears, locate the assembly System.Xml.Linq in the **.NET** tab and click **OK**.

This application also uses the class WeatherData (line 114) that includes all the necessary weather information for a single day of the week. We created this class for you. It contains six weather information properties—DayOfWeek, WeatherImage, MaxTemperatureF, MinTemperatureF, MaxTemperatureC, MinTemperatureC and Description. To add the code for this class to the project, right click the **WeatherViewer** project in the **Solution Explorer** and select **Add > Existing Item...**. Find the file WeatherData.cs in this chapter's examples folder and click **OK**. We use this class to bind the necessary information to the ListBox and the custom control in our application.

Using the **WebClient** Class to Invoke a Web Service

The application's method for handling the getWeatherButton click grabs the zip code entered by the user in the TextBox and checks it against a regular-expression pattern to make sure it contains a five-digit number (line 36). If so, we store the five-digit number (lines 38–39). Next, we format the web service URL with the zip code (lines 43–46) and asynchronously invoke the web service (line 49). We use the WebClient class to use the web service and retrieve the desired information. We registered the event handler that handles the response in 26–28.

Line 49 calls the weatherService object's DownloadStringAsync method to invoke the web service. The web service's location must be specified as an object of class Uri. Class Uri's constructor receives a String representing a uniform resource identifier, such as "http://www.deitel.com". In this example, the web service is invoked asynchronously. When the web service returns its result, the WebClient object raises the DownloadString-Completed event. Its event handler (lines 63–70) has a parameter e of type Download-StringCompletedEventArgs which contains information returned by the web service. We can use this variable's properties to get the returned XML (e.Result) and any errors that may have occurred during the process (e.Error).

Using LINQ to XML to Process the Weather Data

Once the WebClient has received the response, the application checks for an error (line 66). If there is no error, the application calls the DisplayWeatherForecast method (defined in lines 73–136).The XML that the service returns contains information about the location the user specified, which can be used for error-checking. If the user enters an incorrect zip code, the service will simply provide data for the correct zip code which is the closest match to the one the user entered. A sample of the web service's XML response appears in Fig. 29.5. The web service returns XML data that describes the high and low temperatures for the corresponding city over a period of several days. The data for each day also contains a link to an image that represents the weather for that day and a brief text description of the weather.

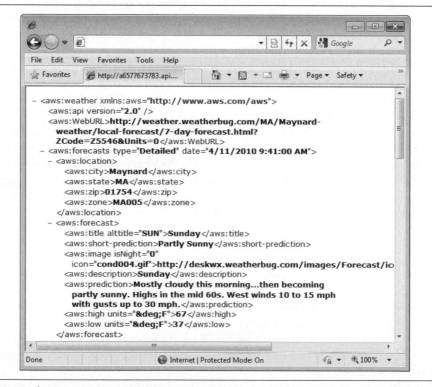

Fig. 29.5 | Sample web service XML response.

We use class XDocument's **Parse** method (line 76) to convert a string—containing the contents of the XML response—to an XDocument to use in the LINQ to XML queries (lines 83–86 and 111–132). Lines 78–79 get the namespace for the XML returned by the web service. Each XML element in the response must be qualified with that name.

Error-Prevention Tip 29.1

When invoking a web service that returns XML, ensure that the namespace you specify in your code precisely matches the namespace specified in the returned XML. Otherwise, the elements in the returned XML will not be recognized in your code.

The first query pulls information from the document about the location the XML describes, which can be compared against the input string (line 101) to determine whether they denote the same location; if not, the input string is not a valid zip code, so we display an error message. We still display the data that is returned. The second query gathers the weather information and sets the corresponding values for a WeatherData object. The query gathers more information from the XML than is initially displayed on the main page of the application. This is because the selected object is also passed to the custom control where more detailed information about the weather is displayed. Also, the returned XML data only provides temperatures in Fahrenheit—getting them in Celsius would require a second invocation of the service with different parameters. As such, the program has a convertToCelsius method (lines 140–147) which converts a Fahrenheit temperature to Celsius as long as the temperature is numerical rather than two dashes "--" (the default when a temperature is not returned). If this is the case, convertToCelsius does nothing. The returned XML does not always provide both a maximum and minimum temperature for one day.

Using Data Binding to Display the Weather Data

We bind the results of the weatherInformation LINQ query (an IEnumerable<T> containing WeatherData objects) to the ListBox (line 135). This displays the summary of the weather forecast. When the user selects a particular day, we bind the WeatherData object for the selected day to the custom control, which displays the details for that day. The ListBox's SelectionChanged event handler (lines 150–159) sets the DataContext of our custom control (line 155) to the WeatherData object for the selected day. The method also changes the custom control's Visibility to Visible, so the user can see the weather details.

29.4.3 Custom Controls

There are many ways to customize controls in Silverlight, including WPF's Styles and ControlTemplates. As with WPF, if deeper customization is desired, you can create **custom controls** by using the UserControl element as a template. The **WeatherViewer** example creates a custom control that displays detailed weather information for a particular day of the week. The control has a simple GUI and is displayed when you change your selection in the ListBox on the main page.

To add a new UserControl to the project, right click the project in the **Solution Explorer** and select **Add > New Item...**. Select the **Silverlight User Control** template and name the file WeatherDetailsView (Fig. 29.6).

Once added to the project, the UserControl can be coded similar to any other Silverlight application. The XAML code for the custom control's GUI appears in Fig. 29.7. This control contains two StackPanels embedded in a Grid. Since the aquamarine Rectangle (lines 12–13) in the background has an Opacity of 0.8, you can see that the control is treated as another element "on top of" the main page. Figure 29.8 shows the code-behind file for this control. The Button's Click event handler collapses the control, so the user can continue interacting with the main page of the application.

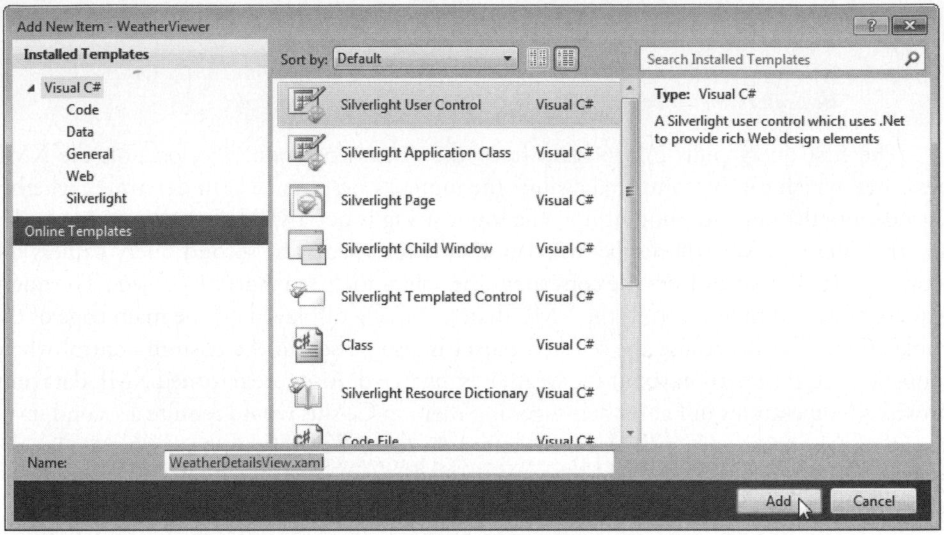

Fig. 29.6 | Adding a new `UserControl` to a Silverlight application.

```
 1   <!-- Fig. 29.7: WeatherDetailsView.xaml -->
 2   <!-- WeatherViewer's WeatherDetailsView custom control (XAML). -->
 3   <UserControl x:Class="WeatherViewer.WeatherDetailsView"
 4      xmlns="http://schemas.microsoft.com/winfx/2006/xaml/presentation"
 5      xmlns:x="http://schemas.microsoft.com/winfx/2006/xaml"
 6      xmlns:d="http://schemas.microsoft.com/expression/blend/2008"
 7      xmlns:mc="http://schemas.openxmlformats.org/markup-compatibility/2006"
 8      mc:Ignorable="d">
 9
10      <Grid x:Name="LayoutRoot" Background="White">
11         <!-- Background semitransparent rectangle -->
12         <Rectangle HorizontalAlignment="Stretch" Fill="Aquamarine"
13            VerticalAlignment="Stretch" Opacity="0.8" />
14
15         <!-- Border containing all the elements of the control -->
16         <Border CornerRadius="20" Background="AliceBlue"
17            BorderBrush="Blue" BorderThickness="4"
18            Width="400" MinHeight="175" MaxHeight="250">
19
20            <!-- StackPanel contains all the displayed weather info -->
21            <StackPanel>
22               <!-- The day's weather image -->
23               <Image Source="{Binding WeatherImage}" Margin="5" Width="55"
24                  Height="58" />
25               <!-- Day of the week -->
26               <TextBlock Text="{Binding DayOfWeek}" Margin="5"
27                  TextAlignment="Center" FontSize="12"
28                  TextWrapping="Wrap" />
29               <!-- Displays the temperature info in C and F -->
```

Fig. 29.7 | `WeatherViewer`'s `WeatherDetailsView` custom control (XAML). (Part 1 of 2.)

```
30                  <StackPanel HorizontalAlignment="Center"
31                     Orientation="Horizontal">
32                     <TextBlock Text="Max F:" Margin="5" FontSize="16" />
33                     <TextBlock Text="{Binding MaxTemperatureF}"
34                        Margin="5" FontSize="16" FontWeight="Bold" />
35                     <TextBlock Text="Min F:" Margin="5" FontSize="16" />
36                     <TextBlock Text="{Binding MinTemperatureF}"
37                        Margin="5" FontSize="16" FontWeight="Bold" />
38                     <TextBlock Text="Max C:" Margin="5" FontSize="16" />
39                     <TextBlock Text="{Binding MaxTemperatureC}"
40                        Margin="5" FontSize="16" FontWeight="Bold" />
41                     <TextBlock Text="Min C:" Margin="5" FontSize="16" />
42                     <TextBlock Text="{Binding MinTemperatureC}"
43                        Margin="5" FontSize="16" FontWeight="Bold" />
44                  </StackPanel>
45                  <!-- A description of the day's predicted weather -->
46                  <TextBlock Text="{Binding Description}" FontSize="10"
47                     HorizontalAlignment="Center" MaxWidth="300"
48                     TextWrapping="Wrap" Margin="5"/>
49
50                  <!-- Closes the control to go back to the main page -->
51                  <Button x:Name="closeButton" Content="Close" Width="80"
52                     Click="closeButton_Click" />
53               </StackPanel>
54            </Border>
55         </Grid>
56   </UserControl>
```

Fig. 29.7 | WeatherViewer's `WeatherDetailsView` custom control (XAML). (Part 2 of 2.)

```
1    // Fig. 29.8: WeatherDetailsView.xaml.cs
2    // WeatherViewer's WeatherDetailsView custom control (code-behind).
3    using System.Windows;
4    using System.Windows.Controls;
5
```

Fig. 29.8 | WeatherViewer's `WeatherDetailsView` custom control (code-behind). (Part 1 of 2.)

```
 6    namespace WeatherViewer
 7    {
 8       public partial class WeatherDetailsView : UserControl
 9       {
10          // constructor
11          public WeatherDetailsView()
12          {
13             InitializeComponent();
14          } // end constructor
15
16          // close the details view
17          private void closeButton_Click( object sender, RoutedEventArgs e )
18          {
19             this.Visibility = Visibility.Collapsed;
20          } // end method closeButton_Click
21       } // end class WeatherDetailsView
22    } // end namespace WeatherViewer
```

Fig. 29.8 | **WeatherViewer**'s `WeatherDetailsView` custom control (code-behind). (Part 2 of 2.)

29.5 Animations and the FlickrViewer

Animations in Silverlight are defined in `Storyboards`, which are created as `Resources` of a layout control and contain one or more animation elements. When a `Storyboard`'s `Begin` method is called, its animations are applied. Silverlight has several animation types, including `DoubleAnimations`, `PointAnimations`, and `ColorAnimations`.

FlickrViewer Example

Our **FlickrViewer** example (a sample screen capture is shown in Fig. 29.9) uses a web service provided by the public photo-sharing site Flickr. The application allows you to search by tag for photos that users worldwide have uploaded to Flickr. **Tagging**—or labeling content—is part of the collaborative nature of social networking. A **tag** is any user-generated word or phrase that helps organize web content. Tagging items with self-chosen words or phrases creates a strong identification of the content. Flickr uses tags on uploaded files to improve its photo-search service, giving the user better results. To run this example on your computer, *you need to obtain your own Flickr API key at* `www.flickr.com/services/api/keys/` *and add it to the* `MainPage.xaml.cs` *file* (which we discuss shortly). This key is a unique string of characters and numbers that enables Flickr to track usage of their APIs.

The application shows you thumbnails of the first 20 (or fewer if there are not 20) public results (as specified in the URL that invokes the web service) and allows you to click a thumbnail to view its full-sized image. As you change your selection, the application animates out the previously selected image and animates in the new selection. The `Border` shrinks until the current `Image` is no longer visible, then expands to display the new selected `Image`.

As shown in Fig. 29.9, you can type one or more tags (e.g., "`deitel flowers`") into the application's `TextBox`. When you click the **Search** `Button`, the application invokes the Flickr web service, which responds with an XML document containing links to the photos that match the tags. The application parses the XML and displays thumbnails of these photos. The application's XAML is shown in Fig. 29.10.

Fig. 29.9 | FlickrViewer allows users to search photos by tag.

```
 1   <!-- Fig. 29.10: MainPage.xaml -->
 2   <!-- FlickrViewer allows users to search for tagged photos (XAML). -->
 3   <UserControl x:Class="FlickrViewer.MainPage"
 4      xmlns="http://schemas.microsoft.com/winfx/2006/xaml/presentation"
 5      xmlns:x="http://schemas.microsoft.com/winfx/2006/xaml"
 6      xmlns:d="http://schemas.microsoft.com/expression/blend/2008"
 7      xmlns:mc="http://schemas.openxmlformats.org/markup-compatibility/2006"
 8      mc:Ignorable="d">
 9
10      <Grid x:Name="LayoutRoot" Background="White">
11         <Grid.RowDefinitions>
12            <!-- Defines the rows of the main grid -->
13            <RowDefinition Height="Auto" />
14            <RowDefinition x:Name="imageRow" />
15            <RowDefinition Height="Auto" />
16         </Grid.RowDefinitions>
17
18         <Grid.Resources> <!-- Contains the page's animations -->
19
20            <!-- Enlarges the Border to display a new image -->
21            <Storyboard x:Name="animateIn"
22               Storyboard.TargetName="largeCoverImage"
23               Completed="animateIn_Completed">
24               <DoubleAnimation x:Name="animate"
25                  Storyboard.TargetProperty="Height" Duration="0:0:0.75" >
```

Fig. 29.10 | FlickrViewer allows users to search for tagged photos (XAML). (Part 1 of 3.)

```
26              <DoubleAnimation.EasingFunction>
27                 <ElasticEase Springiness="10"/>
28              </DoubleAnimation.EasingFunction>
29           </DoubleAnimation>
30        </Storyboard>
31
32        <!-- Collapses the Border in preparation for a new image -->
33        <Storyboard x:Name="animateOut"
34           Storyboard.TargetName="largeCoverImage"
35           Completed="animateOut_Completed">
36           <DoubleAnimation Storyboard.TargetProperty="Height" To="60"
37              Duration="0:0:0.25" />
38        </Storyboard>
39
40        <!-- Rotates the Search button in three dimensions -->
41        <Storyboard x:Name="buttonRotate"
42           Storyboard.TargetName="buttonProjection">
43           <DoubleAnimation x:Name="rotX"
44              Storyboard.TargetProperty="RotationX" Duration="0:0:0.5" />
45           <DoubleAnimation x:Name="rotY"
46              Storyboard.TargetProperty="RotationY" Duration="0:0:0.5" />
47           <DoubleAnimation x:Name="rotZ"
48              Storyboard.TargetProperty="RotationZ" Duration="0:0:0.5" />
49        </Storyboard>
50     </Grid.Resources>
51
52     <!-- Contains the search box and button for user interaction -->
53     <StackPanel Grid.Row="0" Orientation="Horizontal">
54        <TextBox x:Name="searchBox" Width="150" />
55        <Button x:Name="searchButton" Content="Search" Width="75"
56           Click="searchButton_Click">
57           <!-- We must declare and name the button's projection in
58              order to rotate it -->
59           <Button.Projection>
60              <PlaneProjection x:Name="buttonProjection" />
61           </Button.Projection>
62        </Button>
63     </StackPanel>
64
65     <!-- Border that contains the large main image -->
66     <Border Grid.Row="1" x:Name="largeCoverImage" Height="60"
67        BorderBrush="Black" BorderThickness="10" CornerRadius="10"
68        Padding="20" Margin="10" HorizontalAlignment="Center">
69        <Border.Background>
70           <LinearGradientBrush StartPoint="0,0" EndPoint="0,1">
71              <GradientStop Offset="0" Color="Black" />
72              <GradientStop Offset="1" Color="LightGray" />
73           </LinearGradientBrush>
74        </Border.Background>
75
76        <!-- Displays the image that the user selected -->
77        <Image Source="{Binding}" Stretch="Uniform" />
78     </Border>
```

Fig. 29.10 | FlickrViewer allows users to search for tagged photos (XAML). (Part 2 of 3.)

```
79
80            <!-- Listbox displays thumbnails of the search results -->
81            <ListBox x:Name="thumbsListBox" Grid.Row="2"
82               HorizontalAlignment="Center"
83               SelectionChanged="thumbsListBox_SelectionChanged">
84               <ListBox.ItemsPanel>
85                  <ItemsPanelTemplate>
86                     <StackPanel Orientation="Horizontal"/>
87                  </ItemsPanelTemplate>
88               </ListBox.ItemsPanel>
89
90               <ListBox.ItemTemplate>
91                  <DataTemplate>
92                     <Image Source="{Binding}" Margin="10" />
93                  </DataTemplate>
94               </ListBox.ItemTemplate>
95            </ListBox>
96         </Grid>
97      </UserControl>
```

Fig. 29.10 | **FlickrViewer** allows users to search for tagged photos (XAML). (Part 3 of 3.)

Lines 18–50 define the Grid's Resources, which contain three Storyboard elements to facilitate various animations. The animateIn Storyboard (lines 21–30) contains a DoubleAnimation that animates the Height property of the largeCoverImage's Border. Though this animation is a From/To/By animation, the To property is not set. We set this value in the C# code to allow the border to fill the available space in the window regardless of the browser window size. Lines 26–28 contain an **EasingFunction**. Silverlight animations provide smooth, linear change of an item's attribute over a set period of time, but an EasingFunction allows animations to follow other patterns. This particular EasingFunction, ElasticEase, will cause animateIn to oscillate like it is attached to a spring. The animateOut Storyboard (lines 33–38) shrinks the Border until the image inside is no longer visible. Storyboards can also contain multiple animations; the buttonRotate Storyboard (lines 41–49) will rotate the button in all three dimensions when it's clicked, but a separate DoubleAnimation must be declared for each dimension. Like animateIn, buttonRotate's To property is set programmatically.

The rest of the layout is similar to that of the **WeatherViewer**. Lines 11–16 define the main Grid's three rows. The first row contains a StackPanel with an embedded search TextBox and a Button (lines 53–63). To give the three-dimensional buttonRotate animation a target, the Button's Projection must be declared and named; an item's Projection lets you control its rotation in three dimensions. The second row contains the Border with an embedded Image (lines 66–78) to display the large version of the selected thumbnail. The third row contains the ListBox (lines 81–95), which displays the thumbnails of the photos returned from Flickr. This ListBox is organized and coded in the same way as in the **WeatherViewer**, except that the DataTemplate contains only one Image—one of the photos returned by the web service. The screen capture in Fig. 29.10 shows the empty layout of the **FlickrViewer** before the user enters a search query.

The C# code for the application can be seen in Fig. 29.11. This example uses web services and LINQ to XML.

```csharp
1   // Fig. 29.11: MainPage.xaml.cs
2   // FlickrViewer allows users to search for photos (code-behind).
3   using System;
4   using System.Linq;
5   using System.Net;
6   using System.Net.NetworkInformation;
7   using System.Windows;
8   using System.Windows.Controls;
9   using System.Xml.Linq;
10
11  namespace FlickrViewer
12  {
13     public partial class MainPage : UserControl
14     {
15        // Flickr API key
16        private const string KEY = "YOUR API KEY HERE";
17
18        // object used to invoke Flickr web service
19        private WebClient flickr = new WebClient();
20
21        // constructor
22        public MainPage()
23        {
24           InitializeComponent();
25           flickr.DownloadStringCompleted +=
26              new DownloadStringCompletedEventHandler(
27                 flickr_DownloadStringCompleted );
28        } // end constructor
29
30        // when the photo selection has changed
31        private void thumbsListBox_SelectionChanged( object sender,
32           SelectionChangedEventArgs e )
33        {
34           // set the height back to a value so that it can be animated
35           largeCoverImage.Height = largeCoverImage.ActualHeight;
36
37           animateOut.Begin(); // begin shrinking animation
38        } // end method thumbsListBox_SelectionChanged
39
```

Fig. 29.11 | FlickrViewer allows users to search for tagged photos (code-behind). (Part 1 of 3.)

```
40        // this makes sure that the border will resize with the window
41        private void animateIn_Completed( object sender, EventArgs e )
42        {
43            largeCoverImage.Height = double.NaN; // image height = *
44        } // end method animateIn_Completed
45
46        // once the nested image is no longer visible
47        private void animateOut_Completed( object sender, EventArgs e )
48        {
49            if ( thumbsListBox.SelectedItem != null )
50            {
51                // grab the URL of the selected item's full image
52                string photoURL =
53                    thumbsListBox.SelectedItem.ToString().Replace(
54                    "_t.jpg", ".jpg" );
55
56                largeCoverImage.DataContext = photoURL;
57
58                animate.To = imageRow.ActualHeight - 20;
59                animateIn.Begin();
60            } // end if
61        } // end method animateOut_Completed
62
63        // begin the search when the user clicks the search button
64        private void searchButton_Click( object sender, RoutedEventArgs e )
65        {
66            // if network is available, get images
67            if ( NetworkInterface.GetIsNetworkAvailable() )
68            {
69                // Flickr's web service URL for searches
70                var flickrURL = string.Format(
71                    "http://api.flickr.com/services/rest/?" +
72                    "method=flickr.photos.search&api_key={0}&tags={1}" +
73                    "&tag_mode=all&per_page=20&privacy_filter=1", KEY,
74                    searchBox.Text.Replace( " ", "," ) );
75
76                // invoke the web service
77                flickr.DownloadStringAsync( new Uri( flickrURL ) );
78
79                // disable the search button
80                searchButton.Content = "Loading...";
81                searchButton.IsEnabled = false;
82
83                flipButton(); // start 3D Button rotation animation
84            } // end if
85            else
86                MessageBox.Show( "ERROR: Network not available!" );
87        } // end method searchButton_Click
88
89        // once we have received the XML file from Flickr
90        private void flickr_DownloadStringCompleted( object sender,
91            DownloadStringCompletedEventArgs e )
92        {
```

Fig. 29.11 | FlickrViewer allows users to search for tagged photos (code-behind). (Part 2 of 3.)

```
93          searchButton.Content = "Search";
94          searchButton.IsEnabled = true;
95
96          if ( e.Error == null )
97          {
98             // parse the data with LINQ
99             XDocument flickrXML = XDocument.Parse( e.Result );
100
101            // gather information on all photos
102            var flickrPhotos =
103               from photo in flickrXML.Descendants( "photo" )
104               let id = photo.Attribute( "id" ).Value
105               let secret = photo.Attribute( "secret" ).Value
106               let server = photo.Attribute( "server" ).Value
107               let farm = photo.Attribute( "farm" ).Value
108               select string.Format(
109                  "http://farm{0}.static.flickr.com/{1}/{2}_{3}_t.jpg",
110                  farm, server, id, secret);
111
112            // set thumbsListBox's item source to the URLs we received
113            thumbsListBox.ItemsSource = flickrPhotos;
114         } // end if
115      } // end method flickr_DownloadStringCompleted
116
117      // perform 3D Button rotation animation
118      void flipButton()
119      {
120         // give all the animations a new goal
121         rotX.To = buttonProjection.RotationX + 360;
122         rotY.To = buttonProjection.RotationY + 360;
123         rotZ.To = buttonProjection.RotationZ + 360;
124
125         buttonRotate.Begin(); // start the animation
126      } // end method flipButton
127   } // end class MainPage
128 } // end namespace FlickrViewer
```

Fig. 29.11 | **FlickrViewer** allows users to search for tagged photos (code-behind). (Part 3 of 3.)

The library `System.Net.NetworkInformation` contains tools to check the status of the network. Using the `NetworkInterface.GetIsNetworkAvailable` function (line 67), the program attempts to connect to Flickr only if connected to a network (lines 67–84) and simply displays an error message otherwise (lines 85–86).

Line 16 defines a constant `String` for the API key that is required to use the Flickr API. To run this application insert your Flickr API key here.

Recall that the `To` property of the `DoubleAnimation` in the `animateIn` Storyboard is set programatically. Line 58 sets the `To` property to the `Height` of the page's second row (minus 20 to account for the `Border`'s `Margin`), animating the `Height` to the largest possible value while keeping the `Border` completely visible on the page.

For animations to function properly, the properties being animated must contain numeric values—relative values "*" and "Auto" do not work. So before `animateOut` begins, we assign the value `largeImageCover.ActualHeight` to the `Border`'s `Height` (line

35). When the Border is not being animated, we want it to take up as much space as possible on screen while still being resizable based on the changing size of the browser window. Line 43 resets the Border's Height back to Double.NaN, which allows the border to be resized with the window.

Notice that when you click a new picture that you have not previously viewed, the Border's Height increases without displaying a new picture inside. This is because the animation begins before the application can download the entire image. The picture is not displayed until its download is complete. If you click the thumbnail of an image you've viewed previously, it displays properly, because the image has already been downloaded to your system and cached by the browser. Viewing the image again causes it to be loaded from the browser's cache rather than over the web.

Lines 102–110 of Fig. 29.11 use a LINQ query to gather the necessary information from the attributes of the photo elements in the XML returned by the web service. A sample of the XML response is shown in Fig. 29.12. The four values collected are required to form the URL to the online photos. The thumbnail URLs are created in lines 108–110 in the LINQ query's select clause. The "_t" before the ".jpg" in each URL indicates that we want the thumbnail of the photo rather than the full-sized file. These URLs are passed to the ItemsSource property of thumbsListBox, which displays all the thumbnails at the bottom of the page. To load the large Image, use the URL of the thumbnail and remove the "_t" from the link (lines 52–54), then change the source of the Image element in the Border (line 56). Notice that the data binding in lines 77 and 92 of Fig. 29.10 use the simple "{Binding}" syntax. This works because we're binding a single String to the object rather than an object with several properties.

```xml
1   <?xml version="1.0" encoding="utf-8" ?>
2   <rsp stat="ok">
3      <photos page="1" pages="1" perpage="20" total="5">
4         <photo id="2608518732" owner="8832668@N04" secret="76dab8eb42"
5            server="3185" farm="4" title="Red Flowers 1" ispublic="1"
6            isfriend="0" isfamily="0" />
7         <photo id="2608518654" owner="8832668@N04" secret="57d35c8f64"
8            server="3293" farm="4" title="Lavender Flowers" ispublic="1"
9            isfriend="0" isfamily="0" />
10        <photo id="2608518890" owner="8832668@N04" secret="98fcb5fb42"
11           server="3121" farm="4" title="Yellow Flowers" ispublic="1"
12           isfriend="0" isfamily="0" />
13        <photo id="2608518370" owner="8832668@N04" secret="0099e12778"
14           server="3076" farm="4" title="Fuscia Flowers" ispublic="1"
15           isfriend="0" isfamily="0" />
16        <photo id="2607687273" owner="8832668@N04" secret="4b630e31ba"
17           server="3283" farm="4" title="Red Flowers 2" ispublic="1"
18           isfriend="0" isfamily="0" />
19     </photos>
20  </rsp>
```

Fig. 29.12 | Sample XML response from the Flickr APIs.

Method flipButton (lines 118–126) activates the buttonRotate Storyboard. The method sets the To property in all three dimensions to 360 degrees greater than its current value. When we call the Storyboard's Begin method, the button rotates 360 degrees in each dimension.

Out-of-Browser Experience

Silverlight's **out-of-browser experiences** enable you to configure a Silverlight application so that any user can download a local copy of it and place a shortcut to it on their desktop and in their **Start** menu. To configure the FlickerViewer application for an out-of-browser experience, perform the following steps:

1. Right click the **FlickerViewer** project in the **Solution Explorer** and select **Properties**.

2. Ensure that **Enable running application out of the browser** is checked.

3. Click the **Out-of-Browser Settings...** button.

4. In the **Out-of-Browser Settings** dialog (Fig. 29.13), you can configure the application's settings, including the window's title, width and height. You can also specify the shortcut name, the application's description and icons to represent your application. In this case, we kept the default settings, but set the width and height of the window.

5. Click **OK** to save your settings.

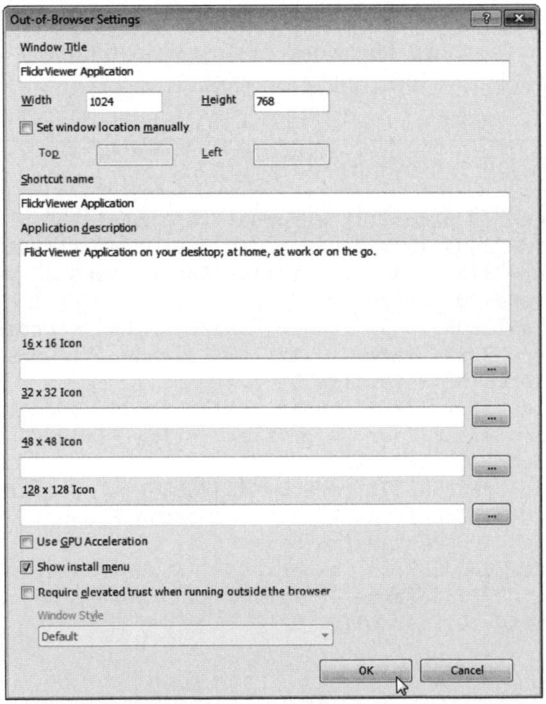

Fig. 29.13 | **Out-of-Browser Settings** dialog.

Once you've configured the application for an out-of-browser experience, the user can right click the application in the browser to see the menu in Fig. 29.14. Selecting **Install**

FlickrViewer onto this computer... presents you with a dialog that allows you to choose where you want the shortcut for the application to be installed. After clicking **OK**, the application will execute in its own window. In the future, you can run the Silverlight application from its shortcut.

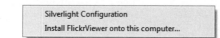

Fig. 29.14 | Right-click menu for a Silverlight application that supports an out-of-browser experience.

29.6 Images and Deep Zoom

One feature in Silverlight that is not in WPF is the `MultiScaleImage`. In most desktop applications, you'll have no trouble viewing and zooming in on a high-resolution image. Doing this over the Internet is problematic, however, because transferring large images usually takes significant time, which prevents web-based applications from having the feel of desktop applications.

This problem is addressed by Silverlight's **deep zoom** capabilities, which use `MultiScaleImages` to allow you to zoom far into an image in a web browser while maintaining quality. One of the best demonstrations of this technology is the Hard Rock Cafe's memorabilia page (`memo.hardrock.com`), which uses Silverlight's deep zoom capabilities to display a large collage of rock and roll memorabilia. You can zoom in on any individual item to see its high-resolution image. The photographs were taken at such high resolution that you can actually see fingerprints on the surfaces of some of the guitars!

Deep zoom works by sending only the necessary image data for the part of the image you are viewing to your machine. To split an image or collage of images into the Silverlight-ready format used by `MultiScaleImages`, you use the **Deep Zoom Composer** (available from `www.microsoft.com/uk/wave/software-deepzoom.aspx`). The original images are split into smaller pieces to support various zoom levels. This enables the server to send smaller chunks of the picture rather than the entire file. If you zoom in close to an image, the server sends only the small section that you are viewing at its highest available resolution (which depends on the resolution of the original image). If you zoom out, the server sends only a lower-resolution version of the image. In either case, the server sends just enough data to give the user a rich image-viewing experience.

A `MultiScaleImage`'s `Source` is an XML document—created by Deep Zoom Composer. The `MultiScaleImage` uses the data in the XML to display an image or collage of images. A **`MultiScaleSubImage`** of a `MultiScaleImage` contains information on a single image in a collage.

The DeepZoomCoverCollage Example
Our **DeepZoomCoverCollage** application contains a high-resolution collage of 12 of our book covers. You can zoom in and out and pan the image with simple keystroke and mouse-click combinations. Figure 29.15 shows screen captures of the application.

Figure 29.15(a) shows the application when it's first loaded with all 12 cover images displayed. Eight large images and three tiny images are clearly visible. One cover is hidden within one of these eleven covers. Test-run the program to see if you can find it. Figure 29.15(b) shows the application after we've zoomed in closely on the leftmost small

a)

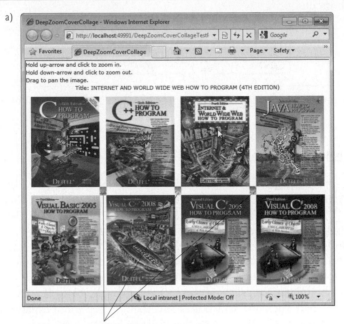

Small images nested among larger images in the collage

b)

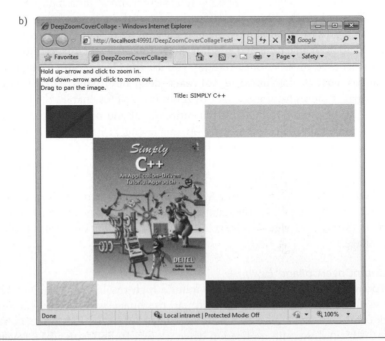

Fig. 29.15 | Main page of the **DeepZoomCoverCollage**. (Part 1 of 2.)

c)

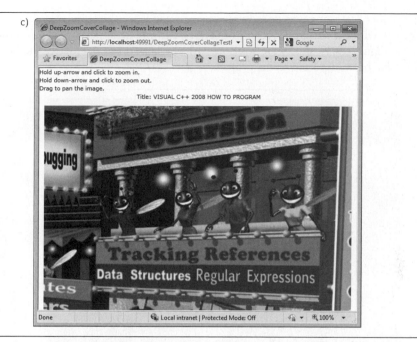

Fig. 29.15 | Main page of the **DeepZoomCoverCollage**. (Part 2 of 2.)

cover image. As you can see in the second screen capture, the small cover image still comes up clearly, because it was originally created in the Deep Zoom Composer with a high-resolution image. Figure 29.15(c) shows the application with an even deeper zoom on a different cover. Rather than being pixelated, the image displays the details of the original picture.

29.6.1 Getting Started With Deep Zoom Composer

To create the collection of files that is used by `MultiScaleImage`, you need to import the image or set of images into Deep Zoom Composer. When you first open the program, create a new project through the **File** menu, and specify the project's **Name** and **Location**. We named the project **CoverCollage**. Figure 29.16 shows the **New Project** dialog.

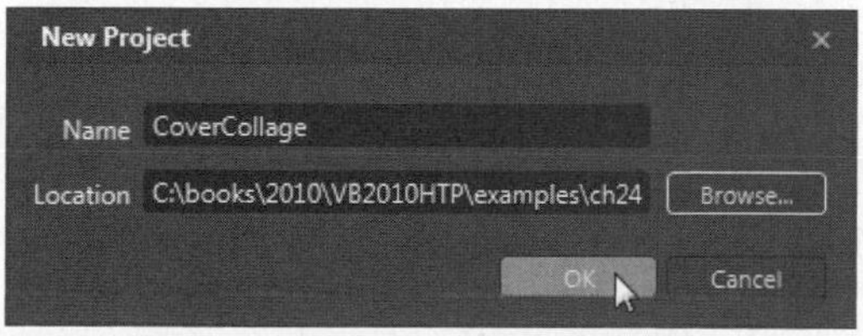

Fig. 29.16 | Deep Zoom Composer's **New Project** dialog.

The **Import** tab in Deep Zoom Composer is displayed by default. It enables you to add the image(s) that you want in the collage. Click the **Add Image...** button to add your images. (We provided our book-cover images with this chapter's examples in the **Cover**

Images folder.) Once you've added your images, you'll see their thumbnails on the right side of the window. A larger version of the selected image appears in the middle of the window. Figure 29.17 shows the window with the **Import** tab open after the book-cover images have been imported to the project.

Fig. 29.17 | Deep Zoom Composer showing the imported image files.

For our **CoverCollage** example, we use high-resolution `.jpg` images. Deep Zoom Composer also supports `.tif`, `.bmp` and `.png` formats. After importing the images, you can go to the **Compose** tab to organize them on your collage.

Drag the thumbnail of each desired image onto the main canvas of the window. When you drag a file into the collage, its thumbnail is grayed out in the side bar and you cannot add it to the collage again. Figure 29.18 shows what the composer looks like, once you bring files into the project.

When images are in the composition, you can move the images to the canvas and resize them to be as large or small as you want. Deep Zoom Composer has features such as snapping and alignment tools that help you lay out the images. Yellow pins throughout the collage in Fig. 29.18(a) indicate that there are small images at those locations. You can zoom in on the composition by scrolling the mouse wheel to see the smaller image. Figure 29.18(b) shows the smaller cover marked by one of the pins. A small screen in the bottom-left corner shows the entire collage and a white rectangle indicating the view displayed in the window.

The panel on the right showing all the images also has a **Layer View** option, which indicates the layer ordering of all the composition's images. This view is used to control the order of overlapping images. The layers can be rearranged to allow you to place certain images on top of others.

Fig. 29.18 | Deep Zoom Composer showing the editable composition.

Once you have a completed collage, go to the **Export** tab to export the files to be used by a `MultiScaleImage` in your application. Figure 29.19 shows the contents of the window when the **Export** tab is open.

You'll need to name the project. For this example, select the **Custom** tab, then name the project `CoverCollageCollection` and keep the default **Export Location**. The files are

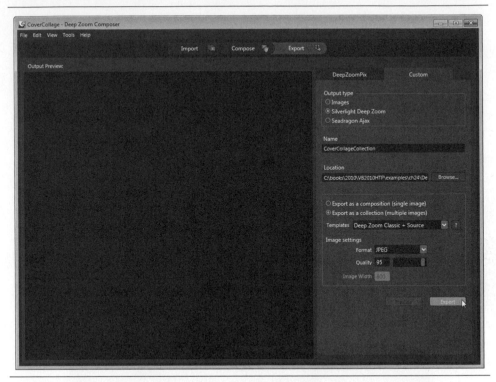

Fig. 29.19 | Deep Zoom Composer's exporting capabilities.

exported to a new folder inside the directory that you created earlier for the Deep Zoom Composer project. By default, Deep Zoom Composer selects the **Export as Collection** option using a JPEG file format. By exporting as a collection instead of a composition, subimage information is included in the output XML files. Keep the JPEG **Quality** at 95— lower values result in smaller file sizes and lower-quality images. From **Templates**, select the **Deep Zoom Classic + Source** option, then click **Export**. Once the project is done exporting, you'll be ready to import these files into a Silverlight project and use them to create a deep zoom application.

29.6.2 Creating a Silverlight Deep Zoom Application

Deep zoom images are created in Silverlight Projects by using the `MultiScaleImage` element, which takes an XML file as its source. A `MultiScaleImage` can be treated in the XAML code similar to a simple `Image` element. Previously, we showed you screen captures of the `DeepZoomCoverCollage` example. Figure 29.20 is the XAML code that produces the layout of this application.

```
1   <!-- Fig. 29.20: MainPage.xaml -->
2   <!-- DeepZoomCoverCollage employs Silverlight's deep zoom (XAML). -->
3   <UserControl x:Class="DeepZoomCoverCollage.MainPage"
```

Fig. 29.20 | **DeepZoomCoverCollage** employs Silverlight's deep zoom (XAML). (Part 1 of 2.)

```
4         xmlns="http://schemas.microsoft.com/winfx/2006/xaml/presentation"
5         xmlns:x="http://schemas.microsoft.com/winfx/2006/xaml"
6         xmlns:d="http://schemas.microsoft.com/expression/blend/2008"
7         xmlns:mc="http://schemas.openxmlformats.org/markup-compatibility/2006"
8         mc:Ignorable="d" KeyDown="mainPage_KeyDown" KeyUp="mainPage_KeyUp">
9
10        <Grid x:Name="LayoutRoot" Background="White">
11
12           <!-- instructions on how to interact with the page -->
13           <StackPanel Orientation="Vertical">
14              <TextBlock Text="Hold up-arrow and click to zoom in." />
15              <TextBlock Text="Hold down-arrow and click to zoom out." />
16              <TextBlock Text="Drag to pan the image."  />
17
18              <!-- book title -->
19              <TextBlock x:Name="titleTextBlock" Text="Title:"
20                 HorizontalAlignment="Center" />
21
22              <!-- deep zoom collage that was created in composer -->
23              <MultiScaleImage x:Name="Image" Margin="10"
24                 Source="/GeneratedImages/dzc_output.xml"
25                 MouseLeave="Image_MouseLeave" MouseMove="Image_MouseMove" />
26                 MouseLeftButtonDown="Image_MouseLeftButtonDown"
27                 MouseLeftButtonUp="Image_MouseLeftButtonUp" />
28           </StackPanel>
29        </Grid>
30     </UserControl>
```

Fig. 29.20 | DeepZoomCoverCollage employs Silverlight's deep zoom (XAML). (Part 2 of 2.)

The main page contains only a StackPanel with TextBlocks that display instructions, a TextBlock to display the selected book's title and the MultiScaleImage to display the collage we created in the previous section. To use the collage, you must add the entire GeneratedImages folder to your Silverlight project. If you kept the default Deep Zoom Composer export location, this folder can be found in the CoverCollage project's folder under the subfolder \Exported Data\covercollagecollection\DeepZoomProject-Site\ClientBin\. Copy the GeneratedImages folder into the ClientBin folder of the web application project by dragging it from Windows Explorer onto that folder in the **Solution Explorer**. If the CoverCollageCollection folder was copied correctly, you should see a GeneratedImages folder (Fig. 29.21). You can now refer to this collection in your application.

Once the necessary files are in the project, they can be used by the MultiScaleImage element that displays the deep zoom image. Line 24 of Fig. 29.20 defines the source of the MultiScaleImage to "/GeneratedImages/dzc_output.xml". The source address in this case is relative to the **ClientBin**, meaning that the application searches for the given path in the **ClientBin** folder of the project. Now that the MultiScaleImage is ready, we can program the application's event handlers for zooming and panning the image, and for displaying a book's title when its cover is clicked (Fig. 29.22). We use a LINQ query to find the title of the cover image the user selects. We have several instance variables that help us determine which operation is to occur when you click the mouse.

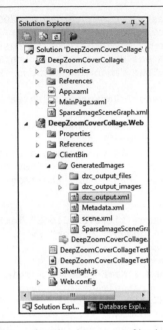

Fig. 29.21 | **Solution Explorer** after the deep zoom files have been added to the project.

```
1   // Fig. 29.22: MainPage.xaml.cs
2   // DeepZoomCoverCollage employs Silverlight's deep zoom (code-behind).
3   using System;
4   using System.IO;
5   using System.Linq;
6   using System.Windows;
7   using System.Windows.Controls;
8   using System.Windows.Input;
9   using System.Xml.Linq;
10
11  namespace DeepZoomCoverCollage
12  {
13     public partial class MainPage : UserControl
14     {
15        private const double ZOOMFACTOR = 2.0;
16
17        private bool zoomIn = false; // true if Up button is pressed
18        private bool zoomOut = false; // true if Down button is pressed
19        private bool mouseDown = false; // true if mouse button is down
20        private Point currentPosition; // position of viewport when clicked
21        private Point dragOffset; // mouse offset used for panning
22
23        // constructor
24        public DeepZoomCoverCollagePage()
25        {
```

Fig. 29.22 | **DeepZoomCoverCollage** employs Silverlight's deep zoom (code-behind). (Part 1 of 4.)

```
26                InitializeComponent();
27          } // end constructor
28
29          //  when a key is pressed, set the correct variables to true
30          private void mainPage_KeyDown( object sender, KeyEventArgs e )
31          {
32             if ( e.Key == Key.Up ) // button pressed is Up
33             {
34                zoomIn = true; // prepare to zoom in
35             } // end if
36             else if ( e.Key == Key.Down ) // button pressed is Down
37             {
38                zoomOut = true; // prepare to zoom out
39             } // end else if
40          } // end method mainPage_KeyDown
41
42          // when a key is released, set the correct variables to false
43          private void mainPage_KeyUp( object sender, KeyEventArgs e )
44          {
45             if ( e.Key == Key.Up ) // button released is Up
46             {
47                zoomIn = false; // don't zoom in
48             } // end if
49             else if ( e.Key == Key.Down ) // button released is Down
50             {
51                zoomOut = false; // don't zoom out
52             } // end else if
53          } // end method mainPage_KeyUp
54
55          // when the mouse leaves the area of the image we don't want to pan
56          private void Image_MouseLeave( object sender, MouseEventArgs e )
57          {
58             mouseDown = false; // if mouse leaves area, no more panning
59          } // end method Image_MouseLeave
60
61          // handle events when user clicks the mouse
62          private void Image_MouseLeftButtonDown( object sender,
63             MouseButtonEventArgs e )
64          {
65             mouseDown = true; // mouse button is down
66             currentPosition = Image.ViewportOrigin; // viewport position
67             dragOffset = e.GetPosition( Image ); // mouse position
68
69             // logical position (between 0 and 1) of mouse
70             Point click = Image.ElementToLogicalPoint( dragOffset );
71
72             if ( zoomIn ) // zoom in when Up key is pressed
73             {
74                Image.ZoomAboutLogicalPoint( ZOOMFACTOR, click.X, click.Y );
75             } // end if
```

Fig. 29.22 | **DeepZoomCoverCollage** employs Silverlight's deep zoom (code-behind). (Part 2 of 4.)

```
76          else if ( zoomOut ) // zoom out when Down key is pressed
77          {
78              Image.ZoomAboutLogicalPoint( 1 / ZOOMFACTOR,
79                  click.X, click.Y );
80          } // end else if
81
82          // determine which book cover was pressed to display the title
83          int index = SubImageIndex( click );
84
85          if ( index > -1 )
86          {
87              titleTextBlock.Text = string.Format(
88                  "Title: {0}", GetTitle( index ) );
89          }
90          else // user clicked a blank space
91          {
92              titleTextBlock.Text = "Title:";
93          } // end else
94      } // end method Image_MouseLeftButtonDown
95
96      // if the mouse button is released, we don't want to pan anymore
97      private void Image_MouseLeftButtonUp( object sender,
98          MouseButtonEventArgs e )
99      {
100         mouseDown = false; // no more panning
101     } // end method Image_MouseLeftButtonUp
102
103     // handle when the mouse moves: panning
104     private void Image_MouseMove( object sender, MouseEventArgs e )
105     {
106         // if no zoom occurs, we want to pan
107         if ( mouseDown && !zoomIn && !zoomOut )
108         {
109             Point click = new Point(); // records point to move to
110             click.X = currentPosition.X - Image.ViewportWidth * (
111                 e.GetPosition( Image ).X - dragOffset.X ) /
112                 Image.ActualWidth;
113             click.Y = currentPosition.Y - Image.ViewportWidth * (
114                 e.GetPosition( Image ).Y - dragOffset.Y ) /
115                 Image.ActualWidth;
116             Image.ViewportOrigin = click; // pans the image
117         } // end if
118     } // end method Image_MouseMove
119
120     // returns the index of the clicked subimage
121     private int SubImageIndex( Point click )
122     {
123         // go through images such that images on top are processed first
124         for ( int i = Image.SubImages.Count - 1; i >= 0; i-- )
125         {
```

Fig. 29.22 | DeepZoomCoverCollage employs Silverlight's deep zoom (code-behind). (Part 3 of 4.)

```
126              // select a single subimage
127              MultiScaleSubImage subImage = Image.SubImages[ i ];
128
129              // create a rect around the area of the cover
130              double scale = 1 / subImage.ViewportWidth;
131              Rect area = new Rect( -subImage.ViewportOrigin.X * scale,
132                 -subImage.ViewportOrigin.Y * scale, scale, scale /
133                 subImage.AspectRatio );
134
135              if ( area.Contains( click ) )
136              {
137                 return i; // return the index of the clicked cover
138              } // end if
139           } // end for
140           return -1; // if no cover was clicked, return -1
141        } // end method SubImageIndex
142
143        // returns the title of the subimage with the given index
144        private string GetTitle( int index )
145        {
146           // XDocument that contains info on all subimages in the collage
147           XDocument xmlDocument =
148              XDocument.Load( "SparseImageSceneGraph.xml" );
149
150           // LINQ to XML to find the title based on index of clicked image
151           var bookTitle =
152              from info in xmlDocument.Descendants( "SceneNode" )
153              let order = Convert.ToInt32( info.Element( "ZOrder" ).Value )
154              where order == index + 1
155              select info.Element( "FileName" ).Value;
156
157           string title = bookTitle.Single(); // gets book title
158
159           // only want title of book, not the rest of the file name
160           title = Path.GetFileName( title );
161
162           // make slight changes to the file name
163           title = title.Replace( ".jpg", string.Empty );
164           title = title.Replace( "pp", "++" );
165           title = title.Replace( "sharp", "#" );
166
167           // display the title on the page
168           return title.ToUpper();
169        } // end method GetTitle
170     } // end class MainPage
171  } // end namespace DeepZoomCoverCollage
```

Fig. 29.22 | DeepZoomCoverCollage employs Silverlight's deep zoom (code-behind). (Part 4 of 4.)

Zooming a MultiScaleImage

To zoom in or out with a MultiScaleImage, we call its **ZoomAboutLogicalPoint** method (lines 74 and 78–79), which takes a zoom factor, an *x*-coordinate and a *y*-coordinate as parameters. A zoom factor of 1 keeps the image at its current size. Values less than 1 zoom out and values greater than 1 zoom in. The method zooms toward or away from the coordinates passed to the method. The coordinates need to be absolute points divided by the entire collage's `Width`. To convert the absolute coordinates raised by a mouse event to these coordinates, we use `MultiScaleImage`'s **`ElementToLogicalPoint`** method (line 70), which takes the `Point`'s absolute coordinates as parameters.

Panning a *MultiScaleImage*

The viewport of a `MultiScaleImage` represents the portion of the image that is rendered on screen. To pan, change the **`ViewportOrigin`** property of the `MultiScaleImage` (line 116). By keeping track of the offset between where the user initially clicked (line 67) and where the user has dragged the mouse, we can calculate where we need to move the origin (lines 110–115) to shift the image. Figures 29.23–29.24 demonstrate what values are returned by various `MultiScaleImage` properties. Assume the "container" of Fig. 29.23 is the viewport while the "image" is the entire collage.

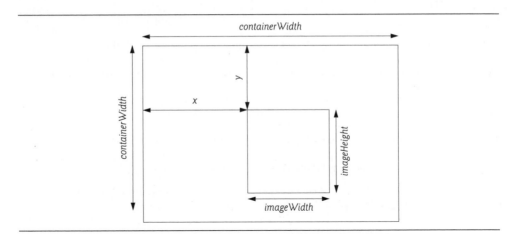

Fig. 29.23 | Various values used to by `MultiScaleImage`'s properties.

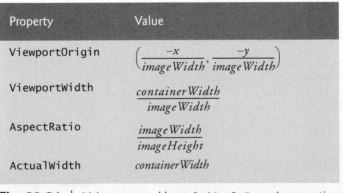

Property	Value
ViewportOrigin	$\left(\dfrac{-x}{imageWidth}, \dfrac{-y}{imageWidth} \right)$
ViewportWidth	$\dfrac{containerWidth}{imageWidth}$
AspectRatio	$\dfrac{imageWidth}{imageHeight}$
ActualWidth	$containerWidth$

Fig. 29.24 | Values returned by `MultiScaleImage`'s properties.

To determine the new *x*-coordinate of the ViewportOrigin, we first find the difference between the *x*-coordinates of the current mouse position (e.GetPosition(Image).X) and the mouse position where the user initially clicked (dragOffset.X), which we'll refer to as the mouse offset. To convert this value to one we can use for the ViewportOrigin, we need to divide it by the width of the collage. The MultiScaleImage's **ViewportWidth** returns the ratio of the viewport's width and the collage's width. A MultiScaleImage's **ActualWidth** property returns the width of the piece of the collage rendered on-screen (viewport's width). Multiplying the mouse offset by the ViewportWidth and dividing by the ActualWidth returns the ratio of the mouse offset and the collage's width. We then subtract this value from the ViewportOrigin's original *x*-coordinate to obtain the new value. A similar calculation is performed for the *y*-coordinate (keep in mind we still use ActualWidth in this calculation since ViewportOrigin's coordinates are given in terms of the width).

Determining the Title of the Clicked Cover

To determine a clicked image's book title requires the SparseImageSceneGraph.xml file created by Deep Zoom Composer. In the **Solution Explorer**, find this XML file in the collection folder we imported and drag the file to your Silverlight deep zoom project so that you can use it in a LINQ query later in the application. The file contains information on where each subimage is located in the collage.

To determine which cover the user clicked, we create a **Rect** object (lines 131–133) for each subimage that represents the on-screen area that the image occupies. A Rect defines a rectangular area on the page. If the Point returned by the mouse-click event is inside the Rect, the user clicked the cover in that Rect. We can use Rect method **Contains** to determine whether the click was inside the rectangle. If a cover was clicked, method SubImageIndex returns the index of the subimage. Otherwise the method returns -1.

A MultiScaleSubImage's properties return the same ratios as a MultiScaleImage's properties (Figs. 29.23–29.24), except that the "container" represents the entire collage while the "image" represents the subimage. Since the ElementToLogicalPoint method of a MultiScaleImage control returns points based on a scaled coordinate system with the origin at the top-left corner of the collage, we want to create Rect objects using the same coordinate system. By dividing the subimage's ViewportOrigin by the subimage's ViewportWidth, we obtain coordinates for the top-left corner of the Rect. To find the Rect's Width, we take the inverse of the subimage's ViewportWidth. We can then use the subimage's AspectRatio to obtain the Height from the Width.

Next, we use the subimage's index in a LINQ to XML query (in method GetTitle) to locate the subimage's information in the SparseImageSceneGraph.xml document (lines 151–155). Each subimage in the collage has a unique numeric ZOrder property, which corresponds to the order in which the images are rendered on screen—the cover with a ZOrder of 1 is drawn first (behind the rest of the covers), while the cover with a ZOrder of 12 is drawn last (on top of all other covers). This ordering also corresponds to the order of the subimages in the collection Image.SubImages and therefore corresponds with the index that we found in the SubImageIndex method. To determine which cover was clicked, we can compare the returned index with the ZOrder of each subimage in the collection using our LINQ to XML query. We add 1 to the returned index (line 154), because the indices in a collection start at 0 while the ZOrder properties of the subimages start at 1. We then obtain and return the title from the subimage's original file name (lines 157–

168) and display the title above the deep zoom image (lines 87–88). If none of the covers were clicked, then no title is displayed (line 92).

29.7 Audio and Video

Silverlight uses the MediaElement control to embed audio or video files into your application. A MediaElement's source can be a file stored with the Silverlight application or a source on the Internet. MediaElement supports playback in many formats. For a list, see:

> msdn.microsoft.com/en-us/library/cc189080(VS.95).aspx

Silverlight supports high-definition video. Microsoft's Expression Encoder can be used to convert files into a supported format. Other encoders that can convert to Windows media format will work as well, including the free online media encoder at

> media-convert.com/

MediaElements can be in one of the following states—Buffering, Closed, Paused, Opening, Playing or Stopped. A MediaElement's state is determined by its **CurrentState** property. When in the Buffering state, the MediaElement is loading the media in preparation for playback. When in the Closed state, the MediaElement contains no media and displays a transparent frame.

Our **VideoSelector** application (Fig. 29.25) shows some of Silverlight's media-playing capabilities. This application obtains its video sources from a user-created XML file and displays small previews of those videos on the left side of the screen. When you click a preview, the application loads that video in the application's main area. The application plays the audio only for the video in the main area.

```
 1   <!-- Fig. 29.25: MainPage.xaml -->
 2   <!-- VideoSelector lets users watch several videos at once (XAML). -->
 3   <UserControl x:Class="VideoSelector.MainPage"
 4      xmlns="http://schemas.microsoft.com/winfx/2006/xaml/presentation"
 5      xmlns:x="http://schemas.microsoft.com/winfx/2006/xaml"
 6      xmlns:d="http://schemas.microsoft.com/expression/blend/2008"
 7      xmlns:mc="http://schemas.openxmlformats.org/markup-compatibility/2006"
 8      mc:Ignorable="d">
 9
10      <Grid x:Name="LayoutRoot" Background="White">
11         <Grid.ColumnDefinitions> <!-- Defines the page's two columns -->
12            <ColumnDefinition Width="Auto" />
13            <ColumnDefinition />
14         </Grid.ColumnDefinitions>
15
16         <Grid.Resources> <!-- Contains the page's animations -->
17
18            <!-- Fades the main screen in, displaying the new video -->
19            <Storyboard x:Name="fadeIn" Storyboard.TargetName="screen">
20               <DoubleAnimation Storyboard.TargetProperty="Opacity"
21                  From="0" To="1" Duration="0:0:0.5" />
22            </Storyboard>
```

Fig. 29.25 | VideoSelector lets users watch several videos at once (XAML). (Part 1 of 2.)

```
23
24          <!-- Fades the main screen out when a new video is selected -->
25          <Storyboard x:Name="fadeOut" Storyboard.TargetName="screen"
26             Completed="fadeOut_Completed">
27             <DoubleAnimation Storyboard.TargetProperty="Opacity"
28                From="1" To="0" Duration="0:0:0.5" />
29          </Storyboard>
30       </Grid.Resources>
31
32       <!-- ListBox containing all available videos -->
33       <ListBox x:Name="previewListBox"
34          SelectionChanged="previewListBox_SelectionChanged">
35          <ListBox.ItemsPanel>
36             <ItemsPanelTemplate>
37                <StackPanel Orientation="Vertical" />
38             </ItemsPanelTemplate>
39          </ListBox.ItemsPanel>
40       </ListBox>
41
42       <!-- Rectangle object with a video brush showing the main video -->
43       <Rectangle x:Name="screen" Grid.Column="1">
44          <Rectangle.Fill>
45             <VideoBrush x:Name="brush" Stretch="Uniform" />
46          </Rectangle.Fill>
47       </Rectangle>
48    </Grid>
49 </UserControl>
```

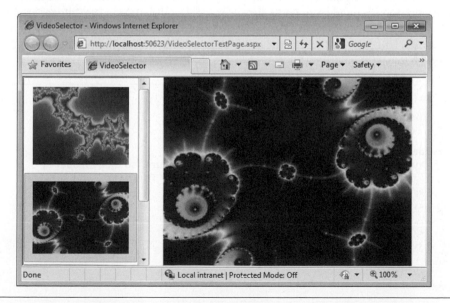

Fig. 29.25 | **VideoSelector** lets users watch several videos at once (*XAML*). (Part 2 of 2.)

The videos for this example were downloaded from the Wikimedia Commons website (commons.wikimedia.org) and are in the public domain. This site contains many images and sound and video files that you can use in your programs—not all items are in the public domain. The videos in the screen capture in Fig. 29.25 were obtained under the science videos section at

`commons.wikimedia.org/wiki/Category:Science_videos`

The files were `.ogg` files that we converted to `.wmv` files using the online video converter at `media-convert.com/`.

The application displays one preview video on the side of the page for each source defined in a user-created XML file (discussed shortly). The GUI contains a `Grid` with two `Columns`. The first `Column` contains a `ListBox` that allows you to scroll through previews of the videos (lines 33–40). The second `Column` contains a `Rectangle` element with a `VideoBrush` for its `Fill` (lines 43–47). A **VideoBrush** displays a video as a graphics object's `Fill`—similar to an `ImageBrush`. The `SetSource` method of `VideoBrush` takes a `Media-Element` as a parameter and sets the video to be played in the brush.

The `Grid` element contains two `Storyboard Resources`, which contain the main video's fade-in and fade-out animations (lines 19–29). These animations are `DoubleAni-mations` that target the `Opacity` property of the `Rectangle` that displays the video. To make the `Rectangle` display the selected video, we'll change the `VideoBrush`'s source to the video the user clicks.

When the page loads, the application performs several initialization tasks. It first loads a new `MediaElement` for each source that is included in the `sources.xml` file (Fig. 29.26). We query this XML file using LINQ to XML. To specify your own list of videos, you must edit our `sources.xml` file, or create a new one and add it to the project. To do this, open a new XML file by right clicking the application project—in this case **VideoSelector**—in the **Solution Explorer** and go to **Add > New Item...**. Select **Visual C#** in the **Categories** section of the window, then select **XML File** in the **Templates** section. Change the file's **Name** to **sources.xml** and click **Add**. Open the file to begin editing it. The sample file in Fig. 29.26 shows the format required to list the sources of the desired videos.

```
 1   <?xml version="1.0" encoding="utf-8" ?>
 2
 3   <!-- Fig. 29.26: sources.xml -->
 4   <!-- VideoSelector's list of video sources. -->
 5   <videos>
 6     <video> <!-- each video child contains a uri source property -->
 7        <uri>/newfractal.wmv</uri> <!-- source for first video -->
 8     </video>
 9     <video>
10        <uri>/fractal.wmv</uri> <!-- source for second video -->
11     </video>
12     <video>
13        <uri>/bailey.wmv</uri> <!-- source for third video -->
14     </video>
15   </videos>
```

Fig. 29.26 | VideoSelector's list of video sources.

The XML document defines a `videos` element that may contain any number of `video` elements. Each `video` element contains a `url` element whose value is the source URL for the corresponding MediaElement. Simply replace the value in the url tag(s) with the path to your video(s). These videos also need to be included in your **Web Project**'s **ClientBin** if you want to play them from the same location as the Silverlight application. If your source URLs link to online videos, then you'll need to change the UrlKind in line 31 (Fig. 29.27). To add the local files, right click the **ClientBin** folder in the **Web Project** associated with your Silverlight application (**VideoSelector.Web**) in the **Solution Explorer** and select **Add > Existing Item....** Locate the videos you want to add and click **Add**. Now that we've added the necessary files to the project, we can continue with the code-behind file shown in Fig. 29.27.

The **VideoSelector** uses LINQ to XML to determine which videos to display in the side bar. Line 22 defines the XDocument that loads sources.xml. Lines 25–35 contain a LINQ query that gets each video element from the XML file. For each video element that has a non-empty url element, the query creates a new MediaElement with that url as its relative Source. If your video is in the same location as the application or any subdirectory of that location, you may use a relative Source value. Otherwise, you need to use an absolute Source, which specifies the full path of the video. We set each element's Width, Margin and **IsMuted** properties to specify how the videos appear and perform when the application loads. Setting a MediaElement's IsMuted property to true (line 34) mutes its audio—the default value is False—so that we do not hear the audio from all videos at once. We then assign the videos to the ItemsSource (line 38) of the ListBox to display the preview videos.

```
1   // Fig. 29.27: VideoSelector.xaml.cs
2   // VideoSelector lets users watch several videos (code-behind).
3   using System;
4   using System.Linq;
5   using System.Windows;
6   using System.Windows.Controls;
7   using System.Windows.Media;
8   using System.Xml.Linq;
9
10  namespace VideoSelector
11  {
12     public partial class VideoSelectorPage : UserControl
13     {
14        private MediaElement currentVideo = new MediaElement();
15
16        // constructor
17        public VideoSelectorPage()
18        {
19           InitializeComponent();
20
21           // sources.xml contains the sources for all the videos
22           XDocument sources = XDocument.Load( "sources.xml" );
23
24           // LINQ to XML to create new MediaElements
25           var videos =
26              from video in sources.Descendants( "video" )
27              where video.Element( "uri" ).Value != string.Empty
```

Fig. 29.27 | **VideoSelector** lets users watch several videos at once. (Part 1 of 2.)

```
28              select new MediaElement()
29              {
30                  Source = new Uri( video.Element( "uri" ).Value,
31                      UriKind.Relative ),
32                  Width = 150,
33                  Margin = new Thickness( 10 ),
34                  IsMuted = true
35              };
36
37          // send all videos to the ListBox
38          previewListBox.ItemsSource = videos;
39      } // end constructor
40
41      // when the user makes a new selection
42      private void previewListBox_SelectionChanged( object sender,
43          SelectionChangedEventArgs e )
44      {
45          fadeOut.Begin(); // begin fade out animation
46      } // end method previewListBox_SelectionChanged
47
48      // change the video if there is a new selection
49      private void fadeOut_Completed( object sender, EventArgs e )
50      {
51          // if there is a selection
52          if ( previewListBox.SelectedItem != null )
53          {
54              // grab the new video to be played
55              MediaElement newVideo =
56                  ( MediaElement ) previewListBox.SelectedItem;
57
58              // if new video has finished playing, restart it
59              if ( newVideo.CurrentState == MediaElementState.Paused )
60              {
61                  newVideo.Stop();
62                  newVideo.Play();
63              } // end if
64
65              currentVideo.IsMuted = true; // mute the old video
66              newVideo.IsMuted = false; // play audio for main video
67
68              currentVideo = newVideo; // set the currently playing video
69              brush.SetSource( newVideo ); // set source of video brush
70          } // end if
71
72          fadeIn.Begin(); // begin fade in animation
73      } // end method fadeOut_Completed
74  } // end class VideoSelectorPage
75 } // end namespace VideoSelector
```

Fig. 29.27 | **VideoSelector** lets users watch several videos at once. (Part 2 of 2.)

The application uses previewListBox's SelectionChanged event handler to determine which video the user wants to view in the main area. When this event occurs, we begin the fade-out animation (line 45). After the fade-out animation completes, the application determines which video was clicked by grabbing previewListBox's SelectedItem object and stores it in a MediaElement variable (lines 55–56).

When a video has finished playing, it is placed in the Paused state. Lines 59–63 ensure that the selected video is restarted if it is in this state. We then mute the audio of the old video and enable the audio of the selected video (lines 65 and 66 respectively). Next, we set the source for the VideoBrush of the Rectangle's Fill to the selected video (line 69). Finally, we begin the fade-in animation to show the new video in the main area (line 72).

29.8 Wrap-Up

In this chapter, you learned how to use Silverlight (a cross-platform, cross-browser subset of .NET) to build Rich Internet Applications (RIAs) in Visual Web Developer 2010 Express. We began by introducing the **WeatherViewer** application to portray some of the key features of a new Silverlight application. Silverlight and WPF have similar programming environments with slight minor variations. The GUI of any Silverlight page is created by a XAML file in the project. All event handlers and other methods are created in the code-behind files.

With the **WeatherViewer** example, we showed that you can use web services, LINQ to XML and data binding to create a web application with desktoplike capabilities. We also showed you how to create a custom control by using a UserControl as a template. Unlike Styles and ControlTemplates, custom controls allow you to manipulate the control's functionality rather than just the visual aspects. The GUI and code-behind of a custom control are created in their own .xaml and .xaml.cs files.

We showed you our **FlickrViewer** example, which, similar to the **WeatherViewer**, shows how to use web services to enhance the capabilities of your application—specifically in this example with the Image control. This application combines a web service—provided by Flickr—and animations to create a photo-searching website. We also introduced Silverlight's out-of-browser experience capabilities.

You learned about Silverlight's deep zoom capabilities. You saw how to use Deep Zoom Composer and Silverlight to create your own deep zoom application. We showed how to implement zooming, panning, and subimage recognition in the code-behind file of your application using MultiScaleImage and MultiScaleSubImage.

Silverlight supports audio and video playback using the MediaElement control. This control supports embedding Windows media format files into the application. We introduced our **VideoSelector** application to show how to program MediaElements in your application. The example also showed the VideoBrush control being applied to the Fill of a Rectangle (applicable to any graphics object) to display the video within the graphic. In the next chapter, we begin presenting our object-oriented design case study.

30

ATM Case Study, Part 1: Object-Oriented Design with the UML

OBJECTIVES

In this chapter you'll learn:

- A simple object-oriented design methodology.
- What a requirements document is.
- To identify classes and class attributes from a requirements document.
- To identify objects' states, activities and operations from a requirements document.
- To determine the collaborations among objects in a system.
- To work with various UML diagrams to graphically model an object-oriented system.

Action speaks louder than words but not nearly as often.
—Mark Twain

Always design a thing by considering it in its next larger context.
—Eliel Saarinen

Oh, life is a glorious cycle of song.
—Dorothy Parker

The Wright brothers' design ... allowed them to survive long enough to learn how to fly.
—Michael Potts

30.1 Introduction

Now we begin the optional portion of our object-oriented design and implementation case study. In this chapter and Chapter 31, you'll design and implement an object-oriented automated teller machine (ATM) software system. The case study provides you with a concise, carefully paced, complete design and implementation experience. In Sections 30.2–30.7 and 31.2–31.3, you'll perform the steps of an object-oriented design (OOD) process using the UML while relating these steps to the concepts discussed in Chapters 3–12. In this chapter, you'll work with six popular types of UML diagrams to graphically represent the design. In Chapter 31, you'll tune the design with inheritance, then fully implement the ATM in a C# console application (Section 31.4).

This is not an exercise; rather, it's an end-to-end learning experience that concludes with a detailed walkthrough of the complete C# code that implements our design. It will acquaint you with the kinds of substantial problems encountered in industry. These chapters can be studied as a continuous unit after you've completed the introduction to object-oriented programming in Chapters 3 and 10–12.

30.2 Examining the ATM Requirements Document

We begin our design process by presenting a **requirements document** that specifies the overall purpose of the ATM system and *what* it must do. Throughout the case study, we refer to the requirements document to determine precisely what functionality the system must include.

Requirements Document

A small local bank intends to install a new automated teller machine (ATM) to allow users (i.e., bank customers) to perform basic financial transactions (Fig. 30.1). For simplicity, each user can have only one account at the bank. ATM users should be able to view their account balance, withdraw cash (i.e., take money out of an account) and deposit funds (i.e., place money into an account).

The user interface of the automated teller machine contains the following hardware components:

- a screen that displays messages to the user
- a keypad that receives numeric input from the user
- a cash dispenser that dispenses cash to the user
- a deposit slot that receives deposit envelopes from the user

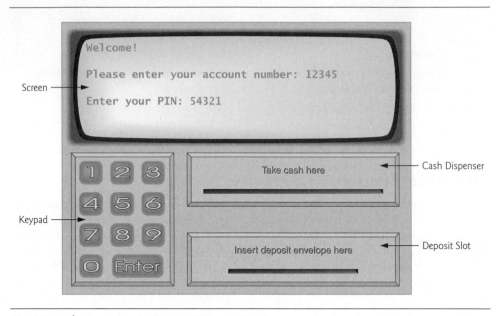

Fig. 30.1 | Automated teller machine user interface.

The cash dispenser begins each day loaded with 500 $20 bills. [*Note:* Owing to the limited scope of this case study, certain elements of the ATM described here simplify various aspects of a real ATM. For example, a real ATM typically contains a device that reads a user's account number from an ATM card, whereas this ATM asks the user to type an account number on the keypad (which you'll simulate with your personal computer's keypad). Also, a real ATM usually prints a paper receipt at the end of a session, but all output from this ATM appears on the screen.]

The bank wants you to develop software to perform the financial transactions initiated by bank customers through the ATM. The bank will integrate the software with the ATM's hardware at a later time. The software should simulate the functionality of the hardware devices (e.g., cash dispenser, deposit slot) in software components, but it need not concern itself with how these devices perform their duties. The ATM hardware has not been developed yet, so instead of writing your software to run on the ATM, you should develop a first version of the software to run on a personal computer. This version should use the computer's monitor to simulate the ATM's screen and the computer's keyboard to simulate the ATM's keypad.

An ATM session consists of authenticating a user (i.e., proving the user's identity) based on an account number and personal identification number (PIN), followed by creating and executing financial transactions. To authenticate a user and perform transactions, the ATM must interact with the bank's account information database. [*Note:* A database is an organized collection of data stored on a computer.] For each bank account, the database stores an account number, a PIN and a balance indicating the amount of money in the account. [*Note:* The bank plans to build only one ATM, so we do not need to worry about multiple ATMs accessing the database at the same time. Furthermore, we assume that the bank does not make any changes to the information in the database while a user is accessing the ATM. Also, any business system like an ATM faces reasonably complicated security issues that go well beyond the scope of a first- or second-semester programming course. We make the simplifying assumption, however, that the bank trusts the ATM to access and manipulate the information in the database without significant security measures.]

Upon approaching the ATM, the user should experience the following sequence of events (see Fig. 30.1):

1. The screen displays a welcome message and prompts the user to enter an account number.

2. The user enters a five-digit account number, using the keypad.

3. For authentication purposes, the screen prompts the user to enter the PIN (personal identification number) associated with the specified account number.

4. The user enters a five-digit PIN, using the keypad.

5. If the user enters a valid account number and the correct PIN for that account, the screen displays the main menu (Fig. 30.2). If the user enters an invalid account number or an incorrect PIN, the screen displays an appropriate message, then the ATM returns to *Step 1* to restart the authentication process.

After the ATM authenticates the user, the main menu (Fig. 30.2) displays a numbered option for each of the three types of transactions: balance inquiry (option 1), withdrawal (option 2) and deposit (option 3). The main menu also displays an option that allows the user to exit the system (option 4). The user then chooses either to perform a transaction (by entering 1, 2 or 3) or to exit the system (by entering 4). If the user enters an invalid option, the screen displays an error message, then redisplays the main menu.

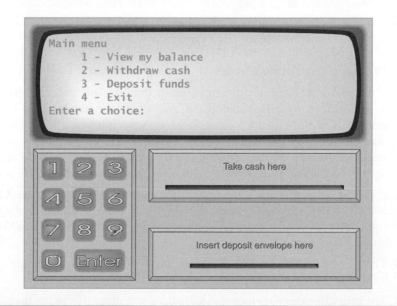

Fig. 30.2 | ATM main menu.

If the user enters 1 to make a balance inquiry, the screen displays the user's account balance. To do so, the ATM must retrieve the balance from the bank's database.

The following actions occur when the user enters 2 to make a withdrawal:

1. The screen displays a menu (shown in Fig. 30.3) containing standard withdrawal amounts: $20 (option 1), $40 (option 2), $60 (option 3), $100 (option 4) and $200 (option 5). The menu also contains option 6, which allows the user to cancel the transaction.

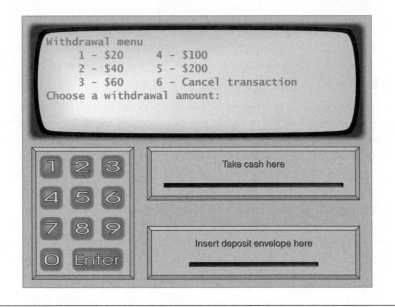

Fig. 30.3 | ATM withdrawal menu.

2. The user enters a menu selection (1–6) using the keypad.

3. If the withdrawal amount chosen is greater than the user's account balance, the screen displays a message stating this and telling the user to choose a smaller amount. The ATM then returns to *Step 1*. If the withdrawal amount chosen is less than or equal to the user's account balance (i.e., an acceptable withdrawal amount), the ATM proceeds to *Step 4*. If the user chooses to cancel the transaction (option 6), the ATM displays the main menu (Fig. 30.2) and waits for user input.

4. If the cash dispenser contains enough cash to satisfy the request, the ATM proceeds to *Step 5*. Otherwise, the screen displays a message indicating the problem and telling the user to choose a smaller withdrawal amount. The ATM then returns to *Step 1*.

5. The ATM debits (i.e., subtracts) the withdrawal amount from the user's account balance in the bank's database.

6. The cash dispenser dispenses the desired amount of money to the user.

7. The screen displays a message reminding the user to take the money.

The following actions occur when the user enters 3 (from the main menu) to make a deposit:

1. The screen prompts the user to enter a deposit amount or to type 0 (zero) to cancel the transaction.

2. The user enters a deposit amount or 0, using the keypad. [*Note:* The keypad does not contain a decimal point or a dollar sign, so the user cannot type a real dollar amount (e.g., $147.25). Instead, the user must enter a deposit amount as a number of cents (e.g., 14725). The ATM then divides this number by 100 to obtain a number representing a dollar amount (e.g., 14725 ÷ 100 = 147.25).]

3. If the user specifies a deposit amount, the ATM proceeds to *Step 4*. If the user chooses to cancel the transaction (by entering 0), the ATM displays the main menu (Fig. 30.2) and waits for user input.

4. The screen displays a message telling the user to insert a deposit envelope into the deposit slot.

5. If the deposit slot receives a deposit envelope within two minutes, the ATM credits (i.e., adds) the deposit amount to the user's account balance in the bank's database. [*Note:* This money is not immediately available for withdrawal. The bank first must verify the amount of cash in the deposit envelope, and any checks in the envelope must clear (i.e., money must be transferred from the check writer's account to the check recipient's account). When either of these events occurs, the bank appropriately updates the user's balance stored in its database. This occurs independently of the ATM system.] If the deposit slot does not receive a deposit envelope within two minutes, the screen displays a message that the system has canceled the transaction due to inactivity. The ATM then displays the main menu and waits for user input.

After the system successfully executes a transaction, the system should redisplay the main menu (Fig. 30.2) so that the user can perform additional transactions. If the user chooses to exit the system (by entering option 4), the screen should display a thank-you message, then display the welcome message for the next user.

Analyzing the ATM System

The preceding statement presented a simplified requirements document. Typically, such a document is the result of a detailed process of **requirements gathering** that might include interviews with potential users of the system and specialists in fields related to the system. For example, a systems analyst who is hired to prepare a requirements document for banking software (e.g., the ATM system described here) might interview financial experts and people who have used ATMs to gain a better understanding of *what* the software must do. The analyst would use the information gained to compile a list of **system requirements** to guide systems designers.

The process of requirements gathering is a key task of the first stage of the software life cycle. The **software life cycle** specifies the stages through which software evolves from the time it's conceived to the time it's retired from use. These stages typically include analysis, design, implementation, testing and debugging, deployment, maintenance and retirement. Several software life-cycle models exist, each with its own preferences and specifications for when and how often software engineers should perform the various stages. **Waterfall models** perform each stage once in succession, whereas **iterative models** may repeat one or more stages several times throughout a product's life cycle.

The analysis stage of the software life cycle focuses on precisely defining the problem to be solved. When designing any system, one must certainly *solve the problem right*, but of equal importance, one must *solve the right problem*. Systems analysts collect the requirements that indicate the specific problem to solve. Our requirements document describes our simple ATM system in sufficient detail that you do not need to go through an extensive analysis stage—it has been done for you.

To capture what a proposed system should do, developers often employ a technique known as **use case modeling**. This process identifies the **use cases** of the system, each of which represents a different capability that the system provides to its clients. For example, ATMs typically have several use cases, such as "View Account Balance," "Withdraw Cash," "Deposit Funds," "Transfer Funds Between Accounts" and "Buy Postage Stamps." The simplified ATM system we build in this case study requires only the first three use cases (Fig. 30.4).

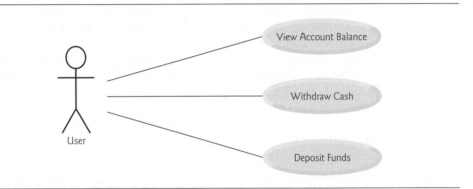

Fig. 30.4 | Use case diagram for the ATM system from the user's perspective.

Each use case describes a typical scenario in which the user uses the system. You have already read descriptions of the ATM system's use cases in the requirements document; the lists of steps required to perform each type of transaction (i.e., balance inquiry, withdrawal and deposit) actually described the three use cases of our ATM—"View Account Balance," "Withdraw Cash" and "Deposit Funds."

Use Case Diagrams
We now introduce the first of several UML diagrams in our ATM case study. We create a **use case diagram** to model the interactions between a system's clients (in this case study, bank customers) and the system. The goal is to show the kinds of interactions users have with a system without providing the details—these are shown in other UML diagrams (which we present throughout the case study). Use case diagrams are often accompanied by informal text that describes the use cases in more detail—like the text that appears in the requirements document. Use case diagrams are produced during the analysis stage of the software life cycle. In larger systems, use case diagrams are simple but indispensable tools that help system designers focus on satisfying the users' needs.

Figure 30.4 shows the use case diagram for our ATM system. The stick figure represents an **actor**, which defines the roles that an external entity—such as a person or another system—plays when interacting with the system. For our automated teller machine, the actor is a User who can view an account balance, withdraw cash and deposit funds using the ATM. The User is not an actual person, but instead comprises the roles that a real person—when playing the part of a User—can play while interacting with the ATM. A use case diagram can include multiple actors. For example, the use case diagram for a real bank's ATM system might also include an actor named Administrator who refills the cash dispenser each day.

We identify the actor in our system by examining the requirements document, which states, "ATM users should be able to view their account balance, withdraw cash and deposit funds." The actor in each of the three use cases is simply the User who interacts with the ATM. An external entity—a real person—plays the part of the User to perform financial transactions. Figure 30.4 shows one actor, whose name, User, appears below the actor in the diagram. The UML models each use case as an oval connected to an actor with a solid line.

Software engineers (more precisely, systems designers) must analyze the requirements document, or a set of use cases, and design the system before programmers implement it in a particular programming language. During the analysis stage, systems designers focus on understanding the requirements document to produce a high-level specification that describes *what* the system is supposed to do. The output of the design stage—a **design specification**—should specify *how* the system should be constructed to satisfy these requirements. In the next several Software Engineering Case Study sections, we perform the steps of a simple OOD process on the ATM system to produce a design specification containing a collection of UML diagrams and supporting text. Recall that the UML is designed for use with any OOD process. Many such processes exist, the best known being the Rational Unified Process™ (RUP) developed by Rational Software Corporation (now a division of IBM). RUP is a rich process for designing "industrial-strength" applications. For this case study, we present a simplified design process.

Designing the ATM System

We now begin the design stage of our ATM system. A **system** is a set of components that interact to solve a problem. For example, to perform the ATM system's designated tasks, our ATM system has a user interface (Fig. 30.1), contains software that executes financial transactions and interacts with a database of bank-account information. **System structure** describes the system's objects and their interrelationships. **System behavior** describes how the system changes as its objects interact with one another. Every system has both structure and behavior—designers must specify both. There are several distinct types of system structures and behaviors. For example, the interactions among objects in the system differ from those between the user and the system, yet both constitute a portion of the system behavior.

The UML 2 specifies 13 diagram types for documenting system models. Each diagram type models a distinct characteristic of a system's structure or behavior—six relate to system structure and seven to system behavior. We list here only the six types of diagrams used in our case study—of which one (the class diagram) models system structure and five model system behavior. We overview the remaining seven UML diagram types in Appendix E, UML 2: Additional Diagram Types.

1. **Use case diagrams**, such as the one in Fig. 30.4, model the interactions between a system and its external entities (actors) in terms of use cases (system capabilities, such as "View Account Balance," "Withdraw Cash" and "Deposit Funds").

2. **Class diagrams**, which you'll study in Section 30.3, model the classes, or "building blocks," used in a system. Each noun, or "thing," described in the requirements document is a candidate to be a class in the system (e.g., "account," "keypad"). Class diagrams help us specify the structural relationships between parts of the system. For example, the ATM system class diagram will, among other things, specify that the ATM is physically composed of a screen, a keypad, a cash dispenser and a deposit slot.

3. **State machine diagrams**, which you'll study in Section 30.5, model the ways in which an object changes state. An object's **state** is indicated by the values of all its attributes at a given time. When an object changes state, it may subsequently behave differently in the system. For example, after validating a user's PIN, the ATM transitions from the "user not authenticated" state to the "user authenticated" state, at which point the ATM allows the user to perform financial transactions (e.g., view account balance, withdraw cash, deposit funds).

4. **Activity diagrams**, which you'll also study in Section 30.5, model an object's **activity**—the object's workflow (sequence of events) during program execution. An activity diagram models the actions the object performs and specifies the order in which it performs them. For example, an activity diagram shows that the ATM must obtain the balance of the user's account (from the bank's account-information database) before the screen can display the balance to the user.

5. **Communication diagrams** (called collaboration diagrams in earlier versions of the UML) model the interactions among objects in a system, with an emphasis on *what* interactions occur. You'll learn in Section 30.7 that these diagrams show which objects must interact to perform an ATM transaction. For example, the ATM must communicate with the bank's account-information database to retrieve an account balance.

6. **Sequence diagrams** also model the interactions among the objects in a system, but unlike communication diagrams, they emphasize *when* interactions occur. You'll learn in Section 30.7 that these diagrams help show the order in which interactions occur in executing a financial transaction. For example, the screen prompts the user to enter a withdrawal amount before cash is dispensed.

In Section 30.3, we continue designing our ATM system by identifying the classes from the requirements document. We accomplish this by extracting key nouns and noun phrases from the requirements document. Using these classes, we develop our first draft of the class diagram that models the structure of our ATM system.

Web Resources

We've created an extensive UML Resource Center that contains many links to additional information, including introductions, tutorials, blogs, books, certification, conferences, developer tools, documentation, e-books, FAQs, forums, groups, UML in Java, podcasts, security, tools, downloads, training courses, videos and more. We encourage you to browse our UML Resource Center at www.deitel.com/UML/ to learn more.

Self-Review Exercises

30.1 Suppose we enabled a user of our ATM system to transfer money between two bank accounts. Modify the use case diagram of Fig. 30.4 to reflect this change.

30.2 _____ model the interactions among objects in a system with an emphasis on *when* these interactions occur.
  a) Class diagrams
  b) Sequence diagrams
  c) Communication diagrams
  d) Activity diagrams

30.3 Which of the following choices lists stages of a typical software life cycle in sequential order?
  a) design, analysis, implementation, testing
  b) design, analysis, testing, implementation
  c) analysis, design, testing, implementation
  d) analysis, design, implementation, testing

30.3 Identifying the Classes in the ATM Requirements Document

Now we begin designing the ATM system. In this section, we identify the classes that are needed to build the ATM system by analyzing the nouns and noun phrases that appear in the requirements document. We introduce UML class diagrams to model the relationships between these classes. This is an important first step in defining the structure of our system.

Identifying the Classes in a System

We begin our object-oriented design (OOD) process by identifying the classes required to build the ATM system. We'll eventually describe these classes using UML class diagrams and implement these classes in C#. First, we review the requirements document of Section 30.2 and find key nouns and noun phrases to help us identify classes that comprise the ATM system. We may decide that some of these nouns and noun phrases are attributes of other classes in the system. We may also conclude that some of the nouns and noun phrases do not correspond to parts of the system and thus should not be modeled at all. Additional classes may become apparent to us as we proceed through the design process. Figure 30.5 lists the nouns and noun phrases in the requirements document.

Nouns and noun phrases in the requirements document		
bank	money / funds	account number
ATM	screen	PIN
user	keypad	bank database
customer	cash dispenser	balance inquiry

Fig. 30.5 | Nouns and noun phrases in the requirements document.

Nouns and noun phrases in the requirements document		
transaction	$20 bill / cash	withdrawal
account	deposit slot	deposit
balance	deposit envelope	

Fig. 30.5 | Nouns and noun phrases in the requirements document.

We create classes only for the nouns and noun phrases that have significance in the ATM system. We do not need to model "bank" as a class, because the bank is not a part of the ATM system—the bank simply wants us to build the ATM. "User" and "customer" also represent entities outside of the system—they're important because they interact with our ATM system, but we do not need to model them as classes in the ATM system. Recall that we modeled an ATM user (i.e., a bank customer) as the actor in the use case diagram of Fig. 30.4.

We do not model "$20 bill" or "deposit envelope" as classes. These are physical objects in the real world, but they're not part of what is being automated. We can adequately represent the presence of bills in the system using an attribute of the class that models the cash dispenser. (We assign attributes to classes in Section 30.4.) For example, the cash dispenser maintains a count of the number of bills it contains. The requirements document does not say anything about what the system should do with deposit envelopes after it receives them. We can assume that simply acknowledging the receipt of an envelope—an **operation** performed by the class that models the deposit slot—is sufficient to represent the presence of an envelope in the system. (We assign operations to classes in Section 30.6.)

In our simplified ATM system, representing various amounts of "money," including the "balance" of an account, as attributes of other classes seems most appropriate. Likewise, the nouns "account number" and "PIN" represent significant pieces of information in the ATM system. They're important attributes of a bank account. They do not, however, exhibit behaviors. Thus, we can most appropriately model them as attributes of an account class.

Though the requirements document frequently describes a "transaction" in a general sense, we do not model the broad notion of a financial transaction at this time. Instead, we model the three types of transactions (i.e., "balance inquiry," "withdrawal" and "deposit") as individual classes. These classes possess specific attributes needed to execute the transactions they represent. For example, a withdrawal needs to know the amount of money the user wants to withdraw. A balance inquiry, however, does not require any additional data if the user is authenticated. Furthermore, the three transaction classes exhibit unique behaviors. A withdrawal involves dispensing cash to the user, whereas a deposit involves receiving a deposit envelope from the user. [*Note:* In Section 31.3, we "factor out" common features of all transactions into a general "transaction" class using the object-oriented concepts of abstract classes and inheritance.]

We determine the classes for our system based on the remaining nouns and noun phrases from Fig. 30.5. Each of these refers to one or more of the following:

- ATM

- screen

- keypad

- cash dispenser

- deposit slot

- account

- bank database

- balance inquiry

- withdrawal

- deposit

The elements of this list are likely to be classes we'll need to implement our system, although it's too early in our design process to claim that this list is complete.

We can now model our system's classes based on the list we've created. We capitalize class names in the design process—a UML convention—as we'll do when we write the C# code that implements our design. If the name of a class contains more than one word, we run the words together and capitalize each word (e.g., `MultipleWordName`). Using these conventions, we create classes `ATM`, `Screen`, `Keypad`, `CashDispenser`, `DepositSlot`, `Account`, `BankDatabase`, `BalanceInquiry`, `Withdrawal` and `Deposit`. We construct our system using all of these classes as building blocks. Before we begin building the system, however, we must gain a better understanding of how the classes relate to one another.

Modeling Classes

The UML enables us to model, via **class diagrams**, the classes in the ATM system and their interrelationships. Figure 30.6 represents class `ATM`. In the UML, each class is modeled as a rectangle with three compartments. The top compartment contains the name of the class, centered horizontally and appearing in boldface. The middle compartment contains the class's attributes. (We discuss attributes in Sections 30.4–30.5.) The bottom compartment contains the class's operations (discussed in Section 30.6). In Fig. 30.6, the middle and bottom compartments are empty, because we've not yet determined this class's attributes and operations.

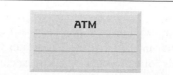

Fig. 30.6 | Representing a class in the UML using a class diagram.

Class diagrams also show the relationships between the classes of the system. Figure 30.7 shows how our classes `ATM` and `Withdrawal` relate to one another. For the moment, we choose to model only this subset of the ATM classes for simplicity. We present a more complete class diagram later in this section. Notice that the rectangles representing classes in this diagram are not subdivided into compartments. The UML allows the suppression of class attributes and operations in this manner, when appropriate, to create more readable diagrams. Such a diagram is said to be an **elided diagram**—one in which some information, such as the contents of the second and third compartments, is not modeled. We'll place information in these compartments in Sections 30.4–30.6.

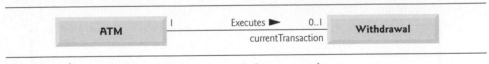

Fig. 30.7 | Class diagram showing an association among classes.

In Fig. 30.7, the solid line that connects the two classes represents an **association**—a relationship between classes. The numbers near each end of the line are **multiplicity** values, which indicate how many objects of each class participate in the association. In this case, following the line from one end to the other reveals that, at any given moment, one ATM object participates in an association with either zero or one Withdrawal objects—zero if the current user is not performing a transaction or has requested a different type of transaction, and one if the user has requested a withdrawal. The UML can model many types of multiplicity. Figure 30.8 explains the multiplicity types.

Symbol	Meaning
0	None
1	One
m	An integer value
0..1	Zero or one
m, n	m or n
$m..n$	At least m, but not more than n
*	Any nonnegative integer (zero or more)
0..*	Zero or more (identical to *)
1..*	One or more

Fig. 30.8 | Multiplicity types.

An association can be named. For example, the word Executes above the line connecting classes ATM and Withdrawal in Fig. 30.7 indicates the name of that association. This part of the diagram reads "one object of class ATM executes zero or one objects of class Withdrawal." association names are directional, as indicated by the filled arrowhead—so it would be improper, for example, to read the preceding association from right to left as "zero or one objects of class Withdrawal execute one object of class ATM."

The word currentTransaction at the Withdrawal end of the association line in Fig. 30.7 is a **role name**, which identifies the role the Withdrawal object plays in its relationship with the ATM. A role name adds meaning to an association between classes by identifying the role a class plays in the context of an association. A class can play several roles in the same system. For example, in a college personnel system, a person may play the role of "professor" when relating to students. The same person may take on the role of "colleague" when participating in a relationship with another professor, and "coach" when coaching student athletes. In Fig. 30.7, the role name currentTransaction indicates that the Withdrawal object participating in the Executes association with an object of class ATM represents the transaction currently being processed by the ATM. In other contexts, a Withdrawal object may take on other roles (e.g., the previous transaction). Notice that we do not specify a role name for the ATM end of the Executes association. Role names are often omitted in class diagrams when the meaning of an association is clear without them.

In addition to indicating simple relationships, associations can specify more complex relationships, such as objects of one class being composed of objects of other classes. Consider a real-world automated teller machine. What "pieces" does a manufacturer put together to build a working ATM? Our requirements document tells us that the ATM is composed of a screen, a keypad, a cash dispenser and a deposit slot.

In Fig. 30.9, the **solid diamonds** attached to the association lines of class ATM indicate that class ATM has a **composition** relationship with classes Screen, Keypad, CashDispenser and DepositSlot. Composition implies a whole/part relationship. The class that has the composition symbol (the solid diamond) on its end of the association line is the whole (in this case, ATM), and the classes on the other end of the association lines are the parts—in this case, classes Screen, Keypad, CashDispenser and DepositSlot. The compositions in Fig. 30.9 indicate that an object of class ATM is formed from one object of class Screen, one object of class CashDispenser, one object of class Keypad and one object of class DepositSlot—the ATM "has a" screen, a keypad, a cash dispenser and a deposit slot. The **has-a relationship** defines composition. (We'll see in the Software Engineering Case Study section in Section 31.3 that the *is-a* relationship defines inheritance.)

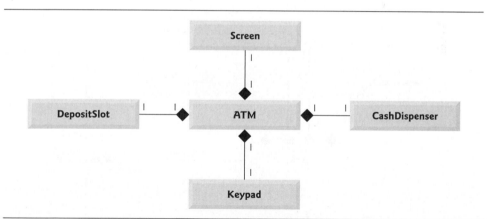

Fig. 30.9 | Class diagram showing composition relationships.

According to the UML specification, composition relationships have the following properties:

1. Only one class in the relationship can represent the whole (i.e., the diamond can be placed on only one end of the association line). For example, either the screen is part of the ATM or the ATM is part of the screen, but the screen and the ATM cannot both represent the whole in the relationship.

2. The parts in the composition relationship exist only as long as the whole, and the whole is responsible for creating and destroying its parts. For example, the act of constructing an ATM includes manufacturing its parts. Furthermore, if the ATM is destroyed, its screen, keypad, cash dispenser and deposit slot are also destroyed.

3. A part may belong to only one whole at a time, although the part may be removed and attached to another whole, which then assumes responsibility for the part.

The solid diamonds in our class diagrams indicate composition relationships that fulfill these three properties. If a *has-a* relationship does not satisfy one or more of these criteria, the UML specifies that hollow diamonds be attached to the ends of association lines to indicate **aggregation**—a weaker form of composition. For example, a personal computer and a computer monitor participate in an aggregation relationship—the computer "has a" monitor, but the two parts can exist independently, and the same monitor can be attached to multiple computers at once, thus violating the second and third properties of composition.

Figure 30.10 shows a class diagram for the ATM system. This diagram models most of the classes that we identified earlier in this section, as well as the associations between them that we can infer from the requirements document. [*Note:* Classes `BalanceInquiry` and `Deposit` participate in associations similar to those of class `Withdrawal`, so we've chosen to omit them from this diagram for simplicity. In Section 31.3, we expand our class diagram to include all the classes in the ATM system.]

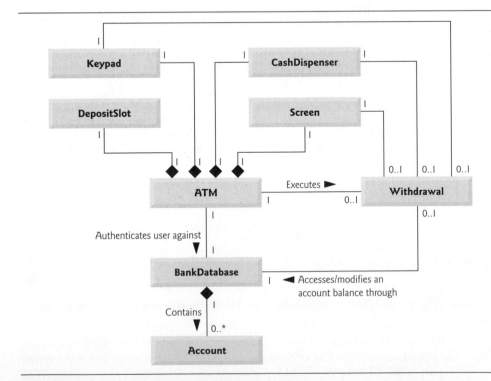

Fig. 30.10 | Class diagram for the ATM system model.

Figure 30.10 presents a graphical model of the structure of the ATM system. This class diagram includes classes `BankDatabase` and `Account` and several associations that were not present in either Fig. 30.7 or Fig. 30.9. The class diagram shows that class `ATM` has a **one-to-one relationship** with class `BankDatabase`—one `ATM` object authenticates users against one `BankDatabase` object. In Fig. 30.10, we also model the fact that the bank's database contains information about many accounts—one object of class `BankDatabase` participates in a composition relationship with zero or more objects of class `Account`. Recall from Fig. 30.8 that the multiplicity value 0..* at the `Account` end of the association between class `BankDatabase` and class `Account` indicates that zero or more objects of class `Account` take part in the association. Class `BankDatabase` has a **one-to-many relationship** with class `Account`—the `BankDatabase` can contain many `Accounts`. Similarly, class `Account` has a **many-to-one relationship** with class `BankDatabase`—there can be many `Accounts` in the `BankDatabase`. Recall from Fig. 30.8 that the multiplicity value * is identical to 0..]

Figure 30.10 also indicates that if the user is performing a withdrawal, "one object of class `Withdrawal` accesses/modifies an account balance through one object of class `BankDatabase`." We could have created an association directly between class `Withdrawal` and class `Account`. The requirements document, however, states that the "ATM must interact with the bank's account-information database" to perform transactions. A bank account contains sensitive information, and systems engineers must always consider the security of personal data when designing a system. Thus, only the `BankDatabase` can access and manipulate an account directly. All other parts of the system must interact with the database to retrieve or update account information (e.g., an account balance).

The class diagram in Fig. 30.10 also models associations between class `Withdrawal` and classes `Screen`, `CashDispenser` and `Keypad`. A withdrawal transaction includes prompting the user to choose a withdrawal amount and receiving numeric input. These actions require the use of the screen and the keypad, respectively. Dispensing cash to the user requires access to the cash dispenser.

Classes `BalanceInquiry` and `Deposit`, though not shown in Fig. 30.10, take part in several associations with the other classes of the ATM system. Like class `Withdrawal`, each of these classes associates with classes `ATM` and `BankDatabase`. An object of class `BalanceInquiry` also associates with an object of class `Screen` to display the balance of an account to the user. Class `Deposit` associates with classes `Screen`, `Keypad` and `DepositSlot`. Like withdrawals, deposit transactions require use of the screen and the keypad to display prompts and receive inputs, respectively. To receive a deposit envelope, an object of class `Deposit` associates with an object of class `DepositSlot`.

We've identified our ATM system's classes, although we may discover others as we proceed with the design and implementation. In Section 30.4, we determine each class's attributes, and in Section 30.5, we use these attributes to examine how the system changes over time.

Self-Review Exercises

30.4   Suppose we have a class `Car` that represents a car. Think of some of the different pieces that a manufacturer would put together to produce a whole car. Create a class diagram (similar to Fig. 30.9) that models some of the composition relationships of class `Car`.

30.5 Suppose we have a class `File` that represents an electronic document in a stand-alone, non-networked computer represented by class `Computer`. What sort of association exists between class `Computer` and class `File`?

    a) Class `Computer` has a one-to-one relationship with class `File`.

    b) Class `Computer` has a many-to-one relationship with class `File`.

    c) Class `Computer` has a one-to-many relationship with class `File`.

    d) Class `Computer` has a many-to-many relationship with class `File`.

30.6 State whether the following statement is *true* or *false*. If *false*, explain why: A UML class diagram in which a class's second and third compartments are not modeled is said to be an elided diagram.

30.7 Modify the class diagram of Fig. 30.10 to include class `Deposit` instead of class `Withdrawal`.

30.4 Identifying Class Attributes

In the previous section, we began the first stage of an object-oriented design (OOD) for our ATM system—analyzing the requirements document and identifying the classes needed to implement the system. We listed the nouns and noun phrases in the requirements document and identified a separate class for each one that plays a significant role in the ATM system. We then modeled the classes and their relationships in a UML class diagram (Fig. 30.10). Classes have attributes (data) and operations (behaviors). Class attributes are implemented in C# programs as instance variables and properties, and class operations are implemented as methods and properties. In this section, we determine many of the attributes needed in the ATM system. In Section 30.5, we examine how these attributes represent an object's state. In Section 30.6, we determine the operations for our classes.

Identifying Attributes

Consider the attributes of some real-world objects: A person's attributes include height, weight and whether the person is left-handed, right-handed or ambidextrous. A radio's attributes include its station setting, its volume setting and its AM or FM setting. A car's attributes include its speedometer and odometer readings, the amount of gas in its tank and what gear it is in. A personal computer's attributes include its manufacturer (e.g., Dell, Gateway, Sun, Apple or IBM), type of screen (e.g., LCD or CRT), main memory size and hard-disk size.

We can identify many attributes of the classes in our system by looking for descriptive words and phrases in the requirements document. For each one we find that plays a significant role in the ATM system, we create an attribute and assign it to one or more of the classes identified in Section 30.3. We also create attributes to represent any additional data that a class may need, as such needs become clear throughout the design process.

Figure 30.11 lists the words or phrases from the requirements document that describe each class. For example, the requirements document describes the steps taken to obtain a "withdrawal amount," so we list "amount" next to class `Withdrawal`.

Figure 30.11 leads us to create one attribute of class `ATM`. Class `ATM` maintains information about the state of the ATM. The phrase "user is authenticated" describes a state of the ATM (we discuss states in detail in Section 30.5), so we include `userAuthenticated` as a `bool` **attribute** (i.e., an attribute that has a value of either `true` or `false`). This attribute indicates whether the ATM has successfully authenticated the current user—`user-Authenticated` must be `true` for the system to allow the user to perform transactions and

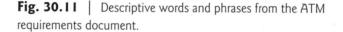

Class	Descriptive words and phrases
ATM	user is authenticated
BalanceInquiry	account number
Withdrawal	account number
	amount
Deposit	account number
	amount
BankDatabase	[no descriptive words or phrases]
Account	account number
	PIN
	balance
Screen	[no descriptive words or phrases]
Keypad	[no descriptive words or phrases]
CashDispenser	begins each day loaded with 500 $20 bills
DepositSlot	[no descriptive words or phrases]

Fig. 30.11 | Descriptive words and phrases from the ATM requirements document.

access account information. This attribute helps ensure the security of the data in the system.

Classes `BalanceInquiry`, `Withdrawal` and `Deposit` share one attribute. Each transaction involves an "account number" that corresponds to the account of the user making the transaction. We assign integer attribute `accountNumber` to each transaction class to identify the account to which an object of the class applies.

Descriptive words and phrases in the requirements document also suggest some differences in the attributes required by each transaction class. The requirements document indicates that to withdraw cash or deposit funds, users must enter a specific "amount" of money to be withdrawn or deposited, respectively. Thus, we assign to classes `Withdrawal` and `Deposit` an attribute `amount` to store the value supplied by the user. The amounts of money related to a withdrawal and a deposit are defining characteristics of these transactions that the system requires for them to take place. Recall that C# represents monetary amounts with type `decimal`. Class `BalanceInquiry` does not need additional data to perform its task—it requires only an account number to indicate the account whose balance should be retrieved.

Class `Account` has several attributes. The requirements document states that each bank account has an "account number" and a "PIN," which the system uses for identifying accounts and authenticating users. We assign to class `Account` two integer attributes: `accountNumber` and `pin`. The requirements document also specifies that an account maintains a "balance" of the amount of money in the account, and that the money the user deposits does not become available for a withdrawal until the bank verifies the amount of cash in the deposit envelope and any checks in the envelope clear. An account must still record the amount of money that a user deposits, however. Therefore, we decide that an account should represent a balance using two `decimal` attributes—`availableBalance` and totalBalance. Attribute availableBalance tracks the amount of money that a user can withdraw from the account. Attribute totalBalance refers to the total amount of money that the user has "on deposit" (i.e., the amount of money available, plus the amount of cash deposits waiting to be verified or the amount of checks waiting to be cleared). For example, suppose an ATM user deposits $50.00 in cash into an empty account. The totalBalance attribute would increase to $50.00 to record the deposit, but the availableBalance would remain at $0 until a bank employee counts the amount of cash in the envelope and confirms the total. [*Note:* We assume that the bank updates the availableBalance attribute of an Account soon after the ATM transaction occurs, in response to confirming that $50 worth of cash was found in the deposit envelope. We assume that this update occurs through a transaction that a bank employee performs using a bank system other than the ATM. Thus, we do not discuss this transaction in our case study.]

Class CashDispenser has one attribute. The requirements document states that the cash dispenser "begins each day loaded with 500 $20 bills." The cash dispenser must keep track of the number of bills it contains to determine whether enough cash is on hand to satisfy withdrawal requests. We assign to class CashDispenser integer attribute count, which is initially set to 500.

For real problems in industry, there is no guarantee that requirements documents will be rich enough and precise enough for the object-oriented systems designer to determine all the attributes, or even all the classes. The need for additional classes, attributes and behaviors may become clear as the design process proceeds. As we progress through this case study, we too will continue to add, modify and delete information about the classes in our system.

Modeling Attributes

The class diagram in Fig. 30.12 lists some of the attributes for the classes in our system—the descriptive words and phrases in Fig. 30.11 helped us identify these attributes. For simplicity, Fig. 30.12 does not show the associations among classes—we showed these in Fig. 30.10. Systems designers commonly do this. Recall that in the UML, a class's attributes are placed in the middle compartment of the class's rectangle. We list each attribute's name and type separated by a colon (:), followed in some cases by an equal sign (=) and an initial value.

Consider the userAuthenticated attribute of class ATM:

```
userAuthenticated : bool = false
```

This attribute declaration contains three pieces of information about the attribute. The **attribute name** is userAuthenticated. The **attribute type** is bool. In C#, an attribute can be represented by a simple type, such as bool, int, double or decimal, or a class type. We have chosen to model only simple-type attributes in Fig. 30.12—we discuss the reasoning behind this decision shortly.

We can also indicate an initial value for an attribute. Attribute userAuthenticated in class ATM has an initial value of false. This indicates that the system initially does not consider the user to be authenticated. If an attribute has no initial value specified, only its name and type (separated by a colon) are shown. For example, the accountNumber attribute of class BalanceInquiry is an int. Here we show no initial value, because the value of this attribute is a number that we do not yet know. This number will be determined at execution time based on the account number entered by the current ATM user.

Fig. 30.12 | Classes with attributes.

Figure 30.12 does not contain attributes for classes Screen, Keypad and DepositSlot. These are important components of our system for which our design process simply has not yet revealed any attributes. We may discover some, however, in the remaining phases of design or when we implement these classes in C#. This is perfectly normal.

> ### Software Engineering Observation 30.1
> *Early in the design process, classes often lack attributes (and operations). Such classes should not be eliminated, however, because attributes (and operations) may become evident in the later phases of design and implementation.*

Fig. 30.12 also does not include attributes for class BankDatabase. We have chosen to include only simple-type attributes in Fig. 30.12 (and in similar class diagrams throughout the case study). A class-type attribute is modeled more clearly as an association (in particular, a composition) between the class with the attribute and the attribute's own class. For example, the class diagram in Fig. 30.10 indicates that class BankDatabase participates in a composition relationship with zero or more Account objects. From this composition, we can determine that when we implement the ATM system in C#, we'll be required to create an attribute of class BankDatabase to hold zero or more Account objects. Similarly, we'll assign attributes to class ATM that correspond to its composition relationships with classes Screen, Keypad, CashDispenser and DepositSlot. These composition-based attributes would be redundant if modeled in Fig. 30.12, because the compositions modeled in Fig. 30.10 already convey the fact that the database contains information about zero or more accounts and that an ATM is composed of a screen, keypad, cash dispenser and deposit slot. Software developers typically model these whole/part relationships as composition associations rather than as attributes required to implement the relationships.

The class diagram in Fig. 30.12 provides a solid basis for the structure of our model, but the diagram is not complete. In Section 30.5 we identify the states and activities of the objects in the model, and in Section 30.6 we identify the operations that the objects perform. As we present more of the UML and object-oriented design, we'll continue to strengthen the structure of our model.

Self-Review Exercises

30.8 We typically identify the attributes of the classes in our system by analyzing the _____ in the requirements document.
   a) nouns and noun phrases
   b) descriptive words and phrases
   c) verbs and verb phrases
   d) All of the above

30.9 Which of the following is not an attribute of an airplane?
   a) length
   b) wingspan
   c) fly
   d) number of seats

30.10 Describe the meaning of the following attribute declaration of class CashDispenser in the class diagram in Fig. 30.12:

```
count : int = 500
```

30.5 Identifying Objects' States and Activities

In the previous section, we identified many of the class attributes needed to implement the ATM system and added them to the class diagram in Fig. 30.12. In this section, we show how these attributes represent an object's state. We identify some key states that our objects may occupy and discuss how objects change state in response to various events occurring in the system. We also discuss the workflow, or **activities**, that various objects perform in the ATM system. We present the activities of BalanceInquiry and Withdrawal transaction objects in this section.

State Machine Diagrams
Each object in a system goes through a series of discrete states. An object's state at a given point in time is indicated by the values of its attributes at that time. **State machine diagrams** model key states of an object and show under what circumstances the object changes state. Unlike the class diagrams presented in earlier case study sections, which focused primarily on the *structure* of the system, state machine diagrams model some of the *behavior* of the system.

Figure 30.13 is a simple state machine diagram that models two of the states of an object of class ATM. The UML represents each state in a state machine diagram as a **rounded rectangle** with the name of the state placed inside it. A **solid circle** with an attached stick arrowhead designates the **initial state**. Recall that we modeled this state information as the `bool` attribute `userAuthenticated` in the class diagram of Fig. 30.12. This attribute is initialized to `false`, or the "User not authenticated" state, according to the state machine diagram.

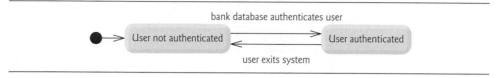

Fig. 30.13 | State machine diagram for some of the states of the ATM object.

The arrows with stick arrowheads indicate **transitions** between states. An object can transition from one state to another in response to various events that occur in the system. The name or description of the event that causes a transition is written near the line that corresponds to the transition. For example, the ATM object changes from the "User not authenticated" state to the "User authenticated" state after the bank database authenticates the user. Recall from the requirements document that the database authenticates a user by comparing the account number and PIN entered by the user with those of the corresponding account in the database. If the database indicates that the user has entered a valid account number and the correct PIN, the ATM object transitions to the "User authenticated" state and changes its `userAuthenticated` attribute to the value `true`. When the user exits the system by choosing the "exit" option from the main menu, the ATM object returns to the "User not authenticated" state in preparation for the next ATM user.

Software Engineering Observation 30.2

Software designers do not generally create state machine diagrams showing every possible state and state transition for all attributes—there are simply too many of them. State machine diagrams typically show only the most important or complex states and state transitions.

Activity Diagrams

Like a state machine diagram, an activity diagram models aspects of system behavior. Unlike a state machine diagram, an activity diagram models an object's workflow (sequence of tasks) during application execution. An activity diagram models the actions to perform and in what order the object will perform them. The activity diagram in Fig. 30.14 models the actions involved in executing a `BalanceInquiry` transaction. We assume that a `BalanceInquiry` object has already been initialized and assigned a valid account number (that of the current user), so the object knows which balance to retrieve. The diagram includes the actions that occur after the user selects a balance inquiry from the main menu and before the ATM returns the user to the main menu—a `BalanceInquiry` object does not perform or initiate these actions, so we do not model them here. The diagram begins with the retrieval of the available balance of the user's account from the database. Next, the `BalanceInquiry` retrieves the total balance of the account. Finally, the transaction displays the balances on the screen.

The UML represents an action in an activity diagram as an action state, which is modeled by a rectangle with its left and right sides replaced by arcs curving outward. Each

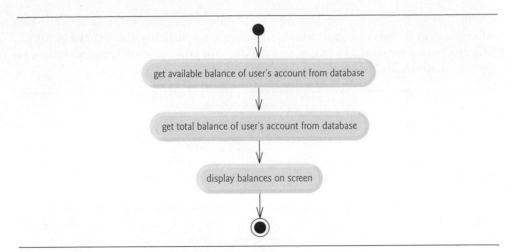

Fig. 30.14 | Activity diagram for a `BalanceInquiry` transaction.

action state contains an action expression—for example, "get available balance of user's account from database"—that specifies an action to perform. An arrow with a stick arrowhead connects two action states, indicating the order in which the actions represented by the action states occur. The solid circle (at the top of Fig. 30.14) represents the activity's initial state—the beginning of the workflow before the object performs the modeled actions. In this case, the transaction first executes the "get available balance of user's account from database" action expression. Second, the transaction retrieves the total balance. Finally, the transaction displays both balances on the screen. The solid circle enclosed in an open circle (at the bottom of Fig. 30.14) represents the final state—the end of the workflow after the object performs the modeled actions.

Figure 30.15 shows an activity diagram for a `Withdrawal` transaction. We assume that a `Withdrawal` object has been assigned a valid account number. We do not model the user selecting a withdrawal from the main menu or the ATM returning the user to the main menu, because these are not actions performed by a `Withdrawal` object. The transaction first displays a menu of standard withdrawal amounts (Fig. 30.3) and an option to cancel the transaction. The transaction then inputs a menu selection from the user. The activity flow now arrives at a decision symbol. This point determines the next action based on the associated guard conditions. If the user cancels the transaction, the system displays an appropriate message. Next, the cancellation flow reaches a merge symbol, where this activity flow joins the transaction's other possible activity flows (which we discuss shortly). A merge can have any number of incoming transition arrows, but only one outgoing transition arrow. The decision at the bottom of the diagram determines whether the transaction should repeat from the beginning. When the user has canceled the transaction, the guard condition "cash dispensed or user canceled transaction" is true, so control transitions to the activity's final state.

If the user selects a withdrawal amount from the menu, `amount` (an attribute of class `Withdrawal` originally modeled in Fig. 30.12) is set to the value chosen by the user. The transaction next gets the available balance of the user's account (i.e., the `availableBalance` attribute of the user's `Account` object) from the database. The activity flow then arrives at another decision. If the requested withdrawal amount exceeds the user's available balance, the system displays an appropriate error message informing the user of the

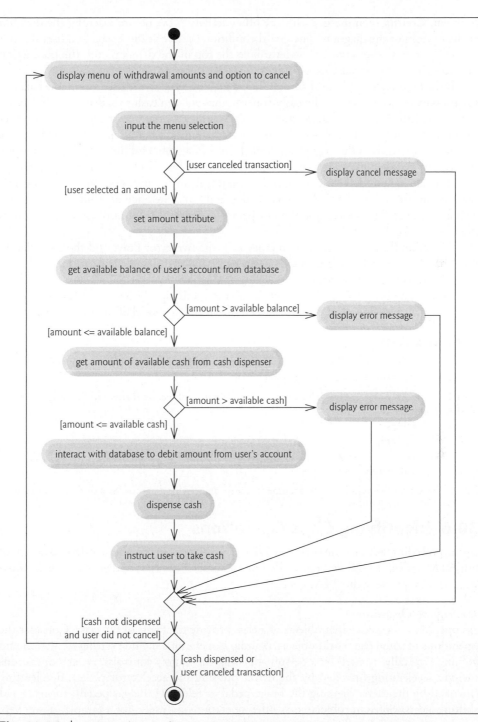

Fig. 30.15 | Activity diagram for a `Withdrawal` transaction.

problem. Control then merges with the other activity flows before reaching the decision at the bottom of the diagram. The guard condition "cash not dispensed and user did not cancel" is true, so the activity flow returns to the top of the diagram, and the transaction prompts the user to input a new amount.

If the requested withdrawal amount is less than or equal to the user's available balance, the transaction tests whether the cash dispenser has enough cash to satisfy the withdrawal request. If it does not, the transaction displays an appropriate error message and passes through the merge before reaching the final decision. Cash was not dispensed, so the activity flow returns to the beginning of the activity diagram, and the transaction prompts the user to choose a new amount. If sufficient cash is available, the transaction interacts with the database to debit the withdrawal amount from the user's account (i.e., subtract the amount from *both* the `availableBalance` and `totalBalance` attributes of the user's `Account` object). The transaction then dispenses the desired amount of cash and instructs the user to take the cash.

The main flow of activity next merges with the two error flows and the cancellation flow. In this case, cash was dispensed, so the activity flow reaches the final state.

We've taken the first steps in modeling the behavior of the ATM system and have shown how an object's attributes affect the object's activities. In Section 30.6, we investigate the operations of our classes to create a more complete model of the system's behavior.

Self-Review Exercises

30.11 State whether the following statement is *true* or *false*, and if *false*, explain why: State machine diagrams model structural aspects of a system.

30.12 An activity diagram models the _____ that an object performs and the order in which it performs them.
  a) actions
  b) attributes
  c) states
  d) state transitions

30.13 Based on the requirements document, create an activity diagram for a deposit transaction.

30.6 Identifying Class Operations

In the preceding sections, we performed the first few steps in the object-oriented design of our ATM system. In this section, we determine some of the class operations (or behaviors) needed to implement the ATM system.

Identifying Operations

An operation is a service that objects of a class provide to clients of the class. Consider the operations of some real-world objects. A radio's operations include setting its station and volume (typically invoked by a person adjusting the radio's controls). A car's operations include accelerating (invoked by the driver pressing the accelerator pedal), decelerating (invoked by the driver pressing the brake pedal or releasing the gas pedal), turning, and shifting gears. Software objects can offer operations as well—for example, a software graphics object might offer operations for drawing a circle, drawing a line and drawing a square. A spreadsheet software object might offer operations like printing the spreadsheet, totaling the elements in a row or column and graphing information in the spreadsheet as a bar chart or pie chart.

We can derive many of the operations of the classes in our ATM system by examining the verbs and verb phrases in the requirements document. We then relate each of these to particular classes in our system. The verbs and verb phrases in Fig. 30.16 help us determine the operations of our classes.

Class	Verbs and verb phrases
ATM	executes financial transactions
BalanceInquiry	[none in the requirements document]
Withdrawal	[none in the requirements document]
Deposit	[none in the requirements document]
BankDatabase	authenticates a user, retrieves an account balance, credits an account, debits an account
Account	retrieves an account balance, credits a deposit amount to an account, debits a withdrawal amount to an account
Screen	displays a message to the user
Keypad	receives numeric input from the user
CashDispenser	dispenses cash, indicates whether it contains enough cash to satisfy a withdrawal request
DepositSlot	receives a deposit envelope

Fig. 30.16 | Verbs and verb phrases for each class in the ATM system.

Modeling Operations

To identify operations, we examine the verb phrases listed for each class in Fig. 30.16. The "executes financial transactions" phrase associated with class ATM implies that class ATM instructs transactions to execute. Therefore, classes BalanceInquiry, Withdrawal and Deposit each need an operation to provide this service to the ATM. We place this operation (which we have named Execute) in the third compartment of the three transaction classes in the updated class diagram of Fig. 30.17. During an ATM session, the ATM object will invoke the Execute operation of each transaction object to tell it to execute.

The UML represents operations (which are implemented as methods in C#) by listing the operation name, followed by a comma-separated list of parameters in parentheses, a colon and the return type:

operationName(*parameter1*, *parameter2*, ..., *parameterN*) : *returnType*

Each parameter in the comma-separated parameter list consists of a parameter name, followed by a colon and the parameter type:

parameterName : *parameterType*

For the moment, we do not list the parameters of our operations—we'll identify and model the parameters of some of the operations shortly. For some of the operations, we do not yet know the return types, so we also omit them from the diagram. These omissions are perfectly normal at this point. As our design and implementation proceed, we'll add the remaining return types.

ATM
userAuthenticated : bool = false

BalanceInquiry
accountNumber : int
Execute()

Withdrawal
accountNumber : int amount : decimal
Execute()

Deposit
accountNumber : int amount : decimal
Execute()

BankDatabase
AuthenticateUser() : bool GetAvailableBalance() : decimal GetTotalBalance() : decimal Credit() Debit()

Account

accountNumber : int
pin : int
«property» AvailableBalance :
    decimal {readOnly}
«property» TotalBalance :
    decimal {readOnly}

ValidatePIN() : bool Credit() Debit()

Screen
DisplayMessage()

Keypad
GetInput() : int

CashDispenser
billCount : int = 500
DispenseCash() IsSufficientCashAvailable() : bool

DepositSlot
IsDepositEnvelopeReceived() : bool

Fig. 30.17 | Classes in the ATM system with attributes and operations.

Operations of Class BankDatabase and Class Account

Figure 30.16 lists the phrase "authenticates a user" next to class BankDatabase—the database is the object that contains the account information necessary to determine whether the account number and PIN entered by a user match those of an account at the bank. Therefore, class BankDatabase needs an operation that provides an authentication service to the ATM. We place the operation AuthenticateUser in the third compartment of class BankDatabase (Fig. 30.17). However, an object of class Account, not class BankDatabase, stores the account number and PIN that must be accessed to authenticate a user, so class Account must provide a service to validate a PIN obtained through user input against a PIN stored in an Account object. Therefore, we add a ValidatePIN operation to class Account. We specify a return type of bool for the AuthenticateUser and ValidatePIN operations. Each operation returns a value indicating either that the operation was successful in performing its task (i.e., a return value of `true`) or that it was not successful (i.e., a return value of `false`).

Figure 30.16 lists several additional verb phrases for class `BankDatabase`: "retrieves an account balance," "credits an account" and "debits an account." Like "authenticates a user," these remaining phrases refer to services that the database must provide to the ATM, because the database holds all the account data used to authenticate a user and perform ATM transactions. However, objects of class `Account` actually perform the operations to which these phrases refer. Thus, class `BankDatabase` and class `Account` both need operations that correspond to each of these phrases. Recall from Section 30.3 that, because a bank account contains sensitive information, we do not allow the ATM to access accounts directly. The database acts as an intermediary between the ATM and the account data, preventing unauthorized access. As we'll see in Section 30.7, class `ATM` invokes the operations of class `BankDatabase`, each of which in turn invokes corresponding operations (which are `get` accessors of read-only properties) in class `Account`.

The phrase "retrieves an account balance" suggests that classes `BankDatabase` and `Account` each need an operation that gets the balance. However, recall that we created two attributes in class `Account` to represent a balance—`availableBalance` and `totalBalance`. A balance inquiry requires access to both balance attributes so that it can display them to the user, but a withdrawal needs to check only the value of `availableBalance`. To allow objects in the system to obtain these balance attributes individually from a specific `Account` object in the `BankDatabase`, we add operations `GetAvailableBalance` and `GetTotalBalance` to the third compartment of class `BankDatabase` (Fig. 30.17). We specify a return type of `decimal` for each of these operations, because the balances that they retrieve are of type `decimal`.

Once the `BankDatabase` knows which `Account` to access, it must be able to obtain each balance attribute individually from that `Account`. For this purpose, we could add operations `GetAvailableBalance` and `GetTotalBalance` to the third compartment of class `Account` (Fig. 30.17). However, in C#, simple operations such as getting the value of an attribute are typically performed by a property's `get` accessor (at least when that particular class "owns" the underlying attribute). This design is for a C# application, so, rather than modeling operations `GetAvailableBalance` and `GetTotalBalance`, we model decimal properties `AvailableBalance` and `TotalBalance` in class `Account`. Properties are placed in the second compartment of a class diagram. These properties replace the `availableBalance` and `totalBalance` attributes that we modeled for class `Account` previously. Recall that a property's accessors are implied—thus, they're not modeled in a class diagram. Figure 30.16 does not mention the need to set the balances, so Fig. 30.17 shows properties `AvailableBalance` and `TotalBalance` as read-only properties (i.e., they have only `get` accessors). To indicate a read-only property in the UML, we follow the property's type with "`{readOnly}`."

You may be wondering why we modeled `AvailableBalance` and `TotalBalance` *properties* in class `Account`, but modeled `GetAvailableBalance` and `GetTotalBalance` *operations* in class `BankDatabase`. Since there can be many `Account` objects in the `BankDatabase`, the ATM must specify which `Account` to access when invoking `BankDatabase` operations `GetAvailableBalance` and `GetTotalBalance`. The ATM does this by passing an account-number argument to each `BankDatabase` operation. The `get` accessors of the properties you've seen in C# code cannot receive arguments. Thus, we modeled

GetAvailableBalance and GetTotalBalance as operations in class BankDatabase so that we could specify parameters to which the ATM can pass arguments. Also, the underlying balance attributes are not owned by the BankDatabase, so get accessors are not appropriate here. We discuss the parameters for the BankDatabase operations shortly.

The phrases "credits an account" and "debits from an account" indicate that classes BankDatabase and Account must perform operations to update an account during deposits and withdrawals, respectively. We therefore assign Credit and Debit operations to classes BankDatabase and Account. You may recall that crediting an account (as in a deposit) adds an amount only to the Account's total balance. Debiting an account (as in a withdrawal), on the other hand, subtracts the amount from both the total and available balances. We hide these implementation details inside class Account. This is a good example of encapsulation and information hiding.

If this were a real ATM system, classes BankDatabase and Account would also provide a set of operations to allow another banking system to update a user's account balance after either confirming or rejecting all or part of a deposit. Operation ConfirmDepositAmount, for example, would add an amount to the Account's available balance, thus making deposited funds available for withdrawal. Operation RejectDepositAmount would subtract an amount from the Account's total balance to indicate that a specified amount, which had recently been deposited through the ATM and added to the Account's total balance, was invalidated (or checks may have "bounced"). The bank would invoke operation Reject-DepositAmount after determining either that the user failed to include the correct amount of cash or that any checks did not clear (i.e., they "bounced"). While adding these operations would make our system more complete, we do not include them in our class diagrams or implementation because they're beyond the scope of the case study.

Operations of Class *Screen*

Class Screen "displays a message to the user" at various times in an ATM session. All visual output occurs through the screen of the ATM. The requirements document describes many types of messages (e.g., a welcome message, an error message, a thank-you message) that the screen displays to the user. The requirements document also indicates that the screen displays prompts and menus to the user. However, a prompt is really just a message describing what the user should input next, and a menu is essentially a type of prompt consisting of a series of messages (i.e., menu options) displayed consecutively. Therefore, rather than provide class Screen with an individual operation to display each type of message, prompt and menu, we simply create one operation that can display any message specified by a parameter. We place this operation (DisplayMessage) in the third compartment of class Screen in our class diagram (Fig. 30.17). We do not worry about the parameter of this operation at this time—we model the parameter momentarily.

Operations of Class *Keypad*

From the phrase "receives numeric input from the user" listed by class Keypad in Fig. 30.16, we conclude that class Keypad should perform a GetInput operation. Because the ATM's keypad, unlike a computer keyboard, contains only the numbers 0–9, we specify that this operation returns an integer value. Recall from the requirements document that in different situations, the user may be required to enter a different type of number (e.g., an account number, a PIN, the number of a menu option, a deposit amount as a number of cents). Class Keypad simply obtains a numeric value for a client of the class—

it does not determine whether the value meets any specific criteria. Any class that uses this operation must verify that the user entered appropriate numbers and, if not, display error messages via class Screen. [*Note:* When we implement the system, we simulate the ATM's keypad with a computer keyboard, and for simplicity, we assume that the user does not enter nonnumeric input using keys on the computer keyboard that do not appear on the ATM's keypad.]

Operations of Class CashDispenser and Class DepositSlot

Figure 30.16 lists "dispenses cash" for class CashDispenser. Therefore, we create operation DispenseCash and list it under class CashDispenser in Fig. 30.17. Class CashDispenser also "indicates whether it contains enough cash to satisfy a withdrawal request." Thus, we include IsSufficientCashAvailable, an operation that returns a value of type bool, in class CashDispenser. Figure 30.16 also lists "receives a deposit envelope" for class DepositSlot. The deposit slot must indicate whether it received an envelope, so we place the operation IsDepositEnvelopeReceived, which returns a bool value, in the third compartment of class DepositSlot. [*Note:* A real hardware deposit slot would most likely send the ATM a signal to indicate that an envelope was received. We simulate this behavior, however, with an operation in class DepositSlot that class ATM can invoke to find out whether the deposit slot received an envelope.]

Operations of Class ATM

We do not list any operations for class ATM at this time. We're not yet aware of any services that class ATM provides to other classes in the system. When we implement the system in C#, however, operations of this class, and additional operations of the other classes in the system, may become apparent.

Identifying and Modeling Operation Parameters

So far, we have not been concerned with the parameters of our operations—we have attempted to gain only a basic understanding of the operations of each class. Let's now take a closer look at some operation parameters. We identify an operation's parameters by examining what data the operation requires to perform its assigned task.

Consider the AuthenticateUser operation of class BankDatabase. To authenticate a user, this operation must know the account number and PIN supplied by the user. Thus we specify that operation AuthenticateUser takes int parameters userAccountNumber and userPIN, which the operation must compare to the account number and PIN of an Account object in the database. We prefix these parameter names with user to avoid confusion between the operation's parameter names and the attribute names that belong to class Account. We list these parameters in the class diagram in Fig. 30.18, which models only class BankDatabase. [*Note:* It is perfectly normal to model only one class in a class diagram. In this case, we're most concerned with examining the parameters of this particular class, so we omit the other classes. In class diagrams later in the case study, parameters are no longer the focus of our attention, so we omit the parameters to save space. Remember, however, that the operations listed in these diagrams still have parameters.]

Recall that the UML models each parameter in an operation's comma-separated parameter list by listing the parameter name, followed by a colon and the parameter type. Figure 30.18 thus specifies, for example, that operation AuthenticateUser takes two parameters—userAccountNumber and userPIN, both of type int.

BankDatabase
AuthenticateUser(userAccountNumber : int, userPIN : int) : bool GetAvailableBalance(userAccountNumber : int) : decimal GetTotalBalance(userAccountNumber : int) : decimal Credit(userAccountNumber : int, amount : decimal) Debit(userAccountNumber : int, amount : decimal)

Fig. 30.18 | Class BankDatabase with operation parameters.

Class BankDatabase operations GetAvailableBalance, GetTotalBalance, Credit and Debit also each require a userAccountNumber parameter to identify the account to which the database must apply the operations, so we include these parameters in the class diagram. In addition, operations Credit and Debit each require a decimal parameter amount to specify the amount of money to be credited or debited, respectively.

The class diagram in Fig. 30.19 models the parameters of class Account's operations. Operation ValidatePIN requires only a userPIN parameter, which contains the user-specified PIN to be compared with the PIN associated with the account. Like their counterparts in class BankDatabase, operations Credit and Debit in class Account each require a decimal parameter amount that indicates the amount of money involved in the operation. Class Account's operations do not require an account-number parameter—each can be invoked only on the Account object in which they're executing, so including a parameter to specify an Account is unnecessary.

Account
accountNumber : int pin : int «property» AvailableBalance : decimal {readOnly} «property» TotalBalance : decimal {readOnly}
ValidatePIN(userPIN: int) : bool Credit(amount : decimal) Debit(amount : decimal)

Fig. 30.19 | Class Account with operation parameters.

Figure 30.20 models class Screen with a parameter for operation DisplayMessage. This operation requires only string parameter message, which is the text to be displayed.

Screen
DisplayMessage(message : string)

Fig. 30.20 | Class Screen with an operation parameter.

The class diagram in Fig. 30.21 specifies that operation `DispenseCash` of class `CashDispenser` takes `decimal` parameter `amount` to indicate the amount of cash (in dollars) to be dispensed. Operation `IsSufficientCashAvailable` also takes `decimal` parameter `amount` to indicate the amount of cash in question.

CashDispenser
billCount : int = 500
DispenseCash(amount : decimal) IsSufficientCashAvailable(amount : decimal) : bool

Fig. 30.21 | Class `CashDispenser` with operation parameters.

We don't discuss parameters for operation `Execute` of classes `BalanceInquiry`, `Withdrawal` and `Deposit`, operation `GetInput` of class `Keypad` and operation `IsDepositEnvelopeReceived` of class `DepositSlot`. At this point in our design process, we cannot determine whether these operations require additional data to perform their tasks, so we leave their parameter lists empty. As we progress through the case study, we may decide to add parameters to these operations.

In this section, we have determined many of the operations performed by the classes in the ATM system. We have identified the parameters and return types of some of the operations. As we continue our design process, the number of operations belonging to each class may vary—we might find that new operations are needed or that some current operations are unnecessary—and we might determine that some of our class operations need additional parameters and different return types. Again, all of this is perfectly normal.

Self-Review Exercises

30.14 Which of the following is not a behavior?
   a) reading data from a file
   b) displaying output
   c) text output
   d) obtaining input from the user

30.15 If you were to add to the ATM system an operation that returns the `amount` attribute of class `Withdrawal`, how and where would you specify this operation in the class diagram of Fig. 30.17?

30.16 Describe the meaning of the following operation listing that might appear in a class diagram for an object-oriented design of a calculator:

```
Add( x : int, y : int ) : int
```

30.7 Identifying Collaboration Among Objects

When two objects communicate with each other to accomplish a task, they're said to **collaborate**. A **collaboration** consists of an object of one class sending a **message** to an object of another class. Messages are sent in C# via method calls. In this section, we concentrate on the collaborations (interactions) among the objects in our ATM system.

In the previous section, we determined many of the operations of the classes in our system. In this section, we concentrate on the messages that invoke these operations. To identify the collaborations in the system, we return to the requirements document of Section 30.2. Recall that this document specifies the activities that occur during an ATM session (e.g., authenticating a user, performing transactions). The steps used to describe how the system must perform each of these tasks are our first indication of the collaborations in our system. As we proceed through this and the remaining Software Engineering Case Study sections, we may discover additional collaborations.

Identifying the Collaborations in a System

We begin to identify the collaborations in the system by carefully reading the sections of the requirements document that specify what the ATM should do to authenticate a user and to perform each transaction type. For each action or step described in the requirements document, we decide which objects in our system must interact to achieve the desired result. We identify one object as the sending object (i.e., the object that sends the message) and another as the receiving object (i.e., the object that offers that operation to clients of the class). We then select one of the receiving object's operations (identified in Section 30.6) that must be invoked by the sending object to produce the proper behavior. For example, the ATM displays a welcome message when idle. We know that an object of class Screen displays a message to the user via its DisplayMessage operation. Thus, we decide that the system can display a welcome message by employing a collaboration between the ATM and the Screen in which the ATM sends a DisplayMessage message to the Screen by invoking the DisplayMessage operation of class Screen. [*Note:* To avoid repeating the phrase "an object of class...," we refer to each object simply by using its class name preceded by an article (e.g., "a," "an" or "the")—for example, "the ATM" refers to an object of class ATM.]

Figure 30.22 lists the collaborations that can be derived from the requirements document. For each sending object, we list the collaborations in the order in which they're discussed in the requirements document. We list each collaboration involving a unique sender, message and recipient only once, even though the collaboration may occur several times during an ATM session. For example, the first row in Fig. 30.22 indicates that the ATM collaborates with the Screen whenever the ATM needs to display a message to the user.

An object of class...	sends the message...	to an object of class...
ATM	DisplayMessage	Screen
	GetInput	Keypad
	AuthenticateUser	BankDatabase
	Execute	BalanceInquiry
	Execute	Withdrawal
	Execute	Deposit
BalanceInquiry	GetAvailableBalance	BankDatabase
	GetTotalBalance	BankDatabase
	DisplayMessage	Screen

Fig. 30.22 | Collaborations in the ATM system. (Part 1 of 2.)

An object of class...	sends the message...	to an object of class...
Withdrawal	DisplayMessage	Screen
	GetInput	Keypad
	GetAvailableBalance	BankDatabase
	IsSufficientCashAvailable	CashDispenser
	Debit	BankDatabase
	DispenseCash	CashDispenser
Deposit	DisplayMessage	Screen
	GetInput	Keypad
	IsDepositEnvelopeReceived	DepositSlot
	Credit	BankDatabase
BankDatabase	ValidatePIN	Account
	AvailableBalance (get)	Account
	TotalBalance (get)	Account
	Debit	Account
	Credit	Account

Fig. 30.22 | Collaborations in the ATM system. (Part 2 of 2.)

Let's consider the collaborations in Fig. 30.22. Before allowing a user to perform any transactions, the ATM must prompt the user to enter an account number, then a PIN. It accomplishes each of these tasks by sending a DisplayMessage message to the Screen. Both of these actions refer to the same collaboration between the ATM and the Screen, which is already listed in Fig. 30.22. The ATM obtains input in response to a prompt by sending a GetInput message to the Keypad. Next the ATM must determine whether the user-specified account number and PIN match those of an account in the database. It does so by sending an AuthenticateUser message to the BankDatabase. Recall that the Bank-Database cannot authenticate a user directly—only the user's Account (i.e., the Account that contains the account number specified by the user) can access the user's PIN to authenticate the user. Figure 30.22 therefore lists a collaboration in which the Bank-Database sends a ValidatePIN message to an Account.

After the user is authenticated, the ATM displays the main menu by sending a series of DisplayMessage messages to the Screen and obtains input containing a menu selection by sending a GetInput message to the Keypad. We have already accounted for these collaborations. After the user chooses a type of transaction to perform, the ATM executes the transaction by sending an Execute message to an object of the appropriate transaction class (i.e., a BalanceInquiry, a Withdrawal or a Deposit). For example, if the user chooses to perform a balance inquiry, the ATM sends an Execute message to a BalanceInquiry.

Further examination of the requirements document reveals the collaborations involved in executing each transaction type. A BalanceInquiry retrieves the amount of money available in the user's account by sending a GetAvailableBalance message to the BankDatabase, which sends a get message to an Account's AvailableBalance property to access the available balance. Similarly, the BalanceInquiry retrieves the amount of money on deposit by sending a GetTotalBalance message to the BankDatabase, which sends a get message to an Account's TotalBalance property to access the total balance on deposit.

To display both measures of the user's balance at the same time, the `BalanceInquiry` sends `DisplayMessage` messages to the `Screen`.

A `Withdrawal` sends `DisplayMessage` messages to the `Screen` to display a menu of standard withdrawal amounts (i.e., $20, $40, $60, $100, $200). The `Withdrawal` sends a `GetInput` message to the `Keypad` to obtain the user's menu selection. Next, the `Withdrawal` determines whether the requested withdrawal amount is less than or equal to the user's account balance. The `Withdrawal` obtains the amount of money available in the user's account by sending a `GetAvailableBalance` message to the `BankDatabase`. The `Withdrawal` then tests whether the cash dispenser contains enough cash by sending an `IsSufficientCashAvailable` message to the `CashDispenser`. A `Withdrawal` sends a `Debit` message to the `BankDatabase` to decrease the user's account balance. The `BankDatabase` in turn sends the same message to the appropriate `Account`. Recall that debiting an `Account` decreases both the total balance and the available balance. To dispense the requested amount of cash, the `Withdrawal` sends a `DispenseCash` message to the `CashDispenser`. Finally, the `Withdrawal` sends a `DisplayMessage` message to the `Screen`, instructing the user to take the cash.

A `Deposit` responds to an `Execute` message first by sending a `DisplayMessage` message to the `Screen` to prompt the user for a deposit amount. The `Deposit` sends a `GetInput` message to the `Keypad` to obtain the user's input. The `Deposit` then sends a `DisplayMessage` message to the `Screen` to tell the user to insert a deposit envelope. To determine whether the deposit slot received an incoming deposit envelope, the `Deposit` sends an `IsDepositEnvelopeReceived` message to the `DepositSlot`. The `Deposit` updates the user's account by sending a `Credit` message to the `BankDatabase`, which subsequently sends a `Credit` message to the user's `Account`. Recall that crediting an `Account` increases the total balance but not the available balance.

Interaction Diagrams

Now that we have identified a set of possible collaborations between the objects in our ATM system, let us graphically model these interactions. The UML provides several types of **interaction diagrams** that model the behavior of a system by modeling how objects interact with one another. The **communication diagram** emphasizes *which objects* participate in collaborations. [*Note:* Communication diagrams were called **collaboration diagrams** in earlier versions of the UML.] Like the communication diagram, the **sequence diagram** shows collaborations among objects, but it emphasizes *when* messages are sent between objects.

Communication Diagrams

Figure 30.23 shows a communication diagram that models the ATM executing a `BalanceInquiry`. Objects are modeled in the UML as rectangles containing names in the form `objectName : ClassName`. In this example, which involves only one object of each type, we disregard the object name and list only a colon followed by the class name. Specifying the name of each object in a communication diagram is recommended when modeling multiple objects of the same type. Communicating objects are connected with solid lines, and messages are passed between objects along these lines in the direction shown by arrows with filled arrowheads. The name of the message, which appears next to the arrow, is the name of an operation (i.e., a method) belonging to the receiving object—think of the name as a service that the receiving object provides to sending objects (its "clients").

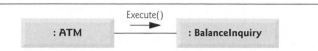

Fig. 30.23 | Communication diagram of the ATM executing a balance inquiry.

The filled arrow in Fig. 30.23 represents a message—or **synchronous call**—in the UML and a method call in C#. This arrow indicates that the flow of control is from the sending object (the ATM) to the receiving object (a BalanceInquiry). Since this is a synchronous call, the sending object cannot send another message, or do anything at all, until the receiving object processes the message and returns control (and possibly a return value) to the sending object. The sender just waits. For example, in Fig. 30.23, the ATM calls method Execute of a BalanceInquiry and cannot send another message until Execute finishes and returns control to the ATM. [*Note:* If this were an **asynchronous call**, represented by a stick arrowhead, the sending object would not have to wait for the receiving object to return control—it would continue sending additional messages immediately following the asynchronous call. Such calls are beyond the scope of this book.]

Sequence of Messages in a Communication Diagram

Figure 30.24 shows a communication diagram that models the interactions among objects in the system when an object of class BalanceInquiry executes. We assume that the object's accountNumber attribute contains the account number of the current user. The collaborations in Fig. 30.24 begin after the ATM sends an Execute message to a BalanceInquiry (i.e., the interaction modeled in Fig. 30.23). The number to the left of a message name indicates the order in which the message is passed. The **sequence of messages** in a communication diagram progresses in numerical order from least to greatest. In this diagram, the numbering starts with message 1 and ends with message 3. The Balance-Inquiry first sends a GetAvailableBalance message to the BankDatabase (message 1), then sends a GetTotalBalance message to the BankDatabase (message 2). Within the parentheses following a message name, we can specify a comma-separated list of the names of the arguments sent with the message (i.e., arguments in a C# method call)—the BalanceInquiry passes attribute accountNumber with its messages to the BankDatabase to indicate which Account's balance information to retrieve. Recall from Fig. 30.18 that operations GetAvailableBalance and GetTotalBalance of class BankDatabase each require a parameter to identify an account. The BalanceInquiry next displays the available balance and the total balance to the user by passing a DisplayMessage message to the Screen (message 3) that includes a parameter indicating the message to be displayed.

Figure 30.24 models two additional messages passing from the BankDatabase to an Account (message 1.1 and message 2.1). To provide the ATM with the two balances of the user's Account (as requested by messages 1 and 2), the BankDatabase must send get messages to the Account's AvailableBalance and TotalBalance properties. A message passed within the handling of another message is called a **nested message**. The UML recommends using a decimal numbering scheme to indicate nested messages. For example, message 1.1 is the first message nested in message 1—the BankDatabase sends the get message to the Account's AvailableBalance property during BankDatabase's processing of a GetAvailableBalance message. [*Note:* If the BankDatabase needed to pass a second nested message while processing message 1, it would be numbered 1.2.] A message may

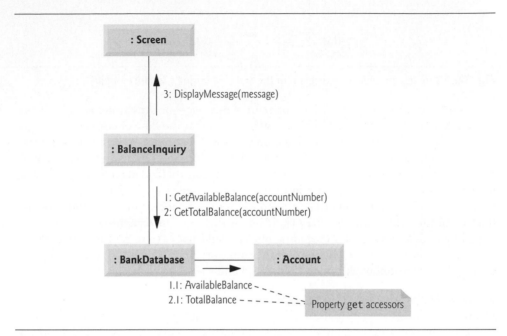

Fig. 30.24 | Communication diagram for executing a `BalanceInquiry`.

be passed only when all the nested messages from the previous message have been passed. For example, the `BalanceInquiry` passes message 3 to the `Screen` only after messages 2 and 2.1 have been passed, in that order.

The nested numbering scheme used in communication diagrams helps clarify precisely when and in what context each message is passed. For example, if we numbered the five messages in Fig. 30.24 using a flat numbering scheme (i.e., 1, 2, 3, 4, 5), someone looking at the diagram might not be able to determine that `BankDatabase` passes the `get` message to an `Account`'s `AvailableBalance` property (message 1.1) *during* the `BankDatabase`'s processing of message 1, as opposed to *after* completing the processing of message 1. The nested decimal numbers make it clear that the `get` message (message 1.1) is passed to an `Account`'s `AvailableBalance` property within the handling of the `GetAvailableBalance` message (message 1) by the `BankDatabase`.

Sequence Diagrams
Communication diagrams emphasize the participants in collaborations but model their timing a bit awkwardly. A sequence diagram helps model the timing of collaborations more clearly. Figure 30.25 shows a sequence diagram modeling the sequence of interactions that occur when a `Withdrawal` executes. The dotted line extending down from an object's rectangle is that object's **lifeline**, which represents the progression of time. Actions typically occur along an object's lifeline in chronological order from top to bottom—an action near the top happens before one near the bottom.

Message passing in sequence diagrams is similar to message passing in communication diagrams. An arrow with a filled arrowhead extending from the sending object to the receiving object represents a message between two objects. The arrowhead points to an activation on the receiving object's lifeline. An **activation**, shown as a thin vertical rect-

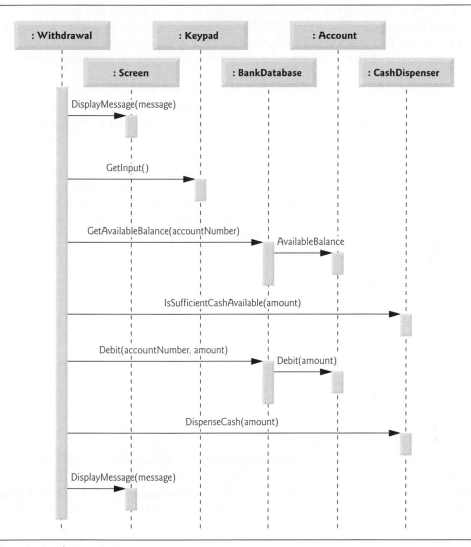

Fig. 30.25 | Sequence diagram that models a `Withdrawal` executing.

angle, indicates that an object is executing. When an object returns control, a return message, represented as a dashed line with a stick arrowhead, extends from the activation of the object returning control to the activation of the object that initially sent the message. To eliminate clutter, we omit the return-message arrows—the UML allows this practice to make diagrams more readable. Like communication diagrams, sequence diagrams can indicate message parameters between the parentheses following a message name.

The sequence of messages in Fig. 30.25 begins when a `Withdrawal` prompts the user to choose a withdrawal amount by sending a `DisplayMessage` message to the `Screen`. The `Withdrawal` then sends a `GetInput` message to the `Keypad`, which obtains input from the user. We have already modeled the control logic involved in a `Withdrawal` in the activity diagram of Fig. 30.15, so we do not show this logic in the sequence diagram of Fig. 30.25.

Instead, we model the best-case scenario, in which the balance of the user's account is greater than or equal to the chosen withdrawal amount, and the cash dispenser contains a sufficient amount of cash to satisfy the request. You can model control logic in a sequence diagram with UML frames (which are not covered in this case study). For a quick overview of UML frames, visit www.agilemodeling.com/style/frame.htm.

After obtaining a withdrawal amount, the Withdrawal sends a GetAvailableBalance message to the BankDatabase, which in turn sends a get message to the Account's AvailableBalance property. Assuming that the user's account has enough money available to permit the transaction, the Withdrawal next sends an IsSufficientCashAvailable message to the CashDispenser. Assuming that there is enough cash available, the Withdrawal decreases the balance of the user's account (both the total balance and the available balance) by sending a Debit message to the BankDatabase. The BankDatabase responds by sending a Debit message to the user's Account. Finally, the Withdrawal sends a DispenseCash message to the CashDispenser and a DisplayMessage message to the Screen, telling the user to remove the cash from the machine.

We have identified collaborations among objects in the ATM system and modeled some of these collaborations using UML interaction diagrams—communication diagrams and sequence diagrams. In the next section, we enhance the structure of our model to complete a preliminary object-oriented design; then we begin implementing the ATM system in C#.

Self-Review Exercises

30.1   A(n) _____ consists of an object of one class sending a message to an object of another class.

    a) association
    b) aggregation
    c) collaboration
    d) composition

30.2   Which form of interaction diagram emphasizes *what* collaborations occur? Which form emphasizes *when* collaborations occur?

30.3   Create a sequence diagram that models the interactions among objects in the ATM system that occur when a Deposit executes successfully. Explain the sequence of messages modeled by the diagram.

30.8 Wrap-Up

In this chapter, you learned how to work from a detailed requirements document to develop an object-oriented design. You worked with six popular types of UML diagrams to graphically model an object-oriented automated teller machine software system. In Chapter 31, we tune the design using inheritance, then completely implement the design in a C# console application.

Answers to Self-Review Exercises

30.1   Figure 30.26 contains a use case diagram for a modified version of our ATM system that also allows users to transfer money between accounts.

30.2   b.

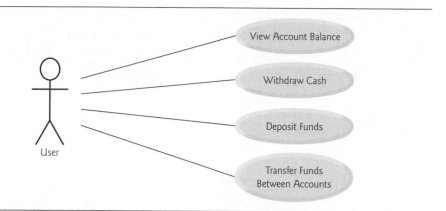

Fig. 30.26 | Use case diagram for a modified version of our ATM system that also allows users to transfer money between accounts.

30.3 d.

30.4 Figure 30.27 presents a class diagram that shows some of the composition relationships of a class Car.

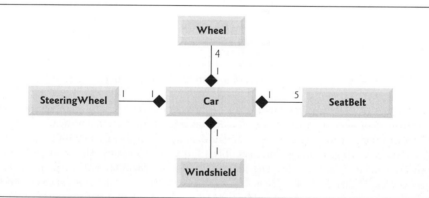

Fig. 30.27 | Class diagram showing some composition relationships of a class Car.

30.5 c. In a computer network, this relationship could be many-to-many.

30.6 True.

30.7 Figure 30.28 presents a class diagram for the ATM including class Deposit instead of class Withdrawal (as in Fig. 30.10). Class Deposit does not associate with class CashDispenser but does associate with class DepositSlot.

30.8 b.

30.9 c. Fly is an operation or behavior of an airplane, not an attribute.

30.10 This declaration indicates that attribute count is an int with an initial value of 500; count keeps track of the number of bills available in the CashDispenser at any given time.

30.11 False. State machine diagrams model some of the behaviors of a system.

30.12 a.

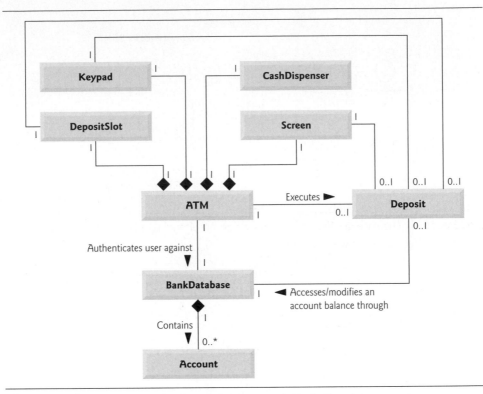

Fig. 30.28 | Class diagram for the ATM system model including class Deposit.

30.13 Figure 30.29 presents an activity diagram for a deposit transaction. The diagram models the actions that occur after the user chooses the deposit option from the main menu and before the ATM returns the user to the main menu. Recall that part of receiving a deposit amount from the user involves converting an integer number of cents to a dollar amount. Also recall that crediting a deposit amount to an account involves increasing only the totalBalance attribute of the user's Account object. The bank updates the availableBalance attribute of the user's Account object only after confirming the amount of cash in the deposit envelope and after the enclosed checks clear— this occurs independently of the ATM system.

30.14 c.

30.15 An operation that retrieves the amount attribute of class Withdrawal would typically be implemented as a get accessor of a property of class Withdrawal. The following would replace attribute amount in the attribute (i.e., second) compartment of class Withdrawal:

«property» Amount : decimal {readOnly}

30.16 This is an operation named Add that takes int parameters x and y and returns an int value. This operation would most likely sum its parameters x and y and return the result.

30.17 c.

30.18 Communication diagrams emphasize *what* collaborations occur. Sequence diagrams emphasize *when* collaborations occur.

30.19 Figure 30.30 presents a sequence diagram that models the interactions between objects in the ATM system that occur when a Deposit executes successfully. It indicates that a Deposit first

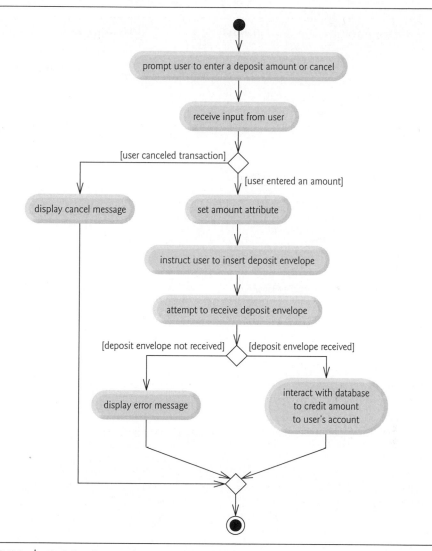

Fig. 30.29 | Activity diagram for a Deposit transaction.

sends a DisplayMessage message to the Screen (to ask the user to enter a deposit amount). Next, the Deposit sends a GetInput message to the Keypad to receive the amount the user will be depositing. The Deposit then prompts the user (to insert a deposit envelope) by sending a DisplayMessage message to the Screen. The Deposit next sends an IsDepositEnvelopeReceived message to the DepositSlot to confirm that the deposit envelope has been received by the ATM. Finally, the Deposit increases the total balance (but not the available balance) of the user's Account by sending a Credit message to the BankDatabase. The BankDatabase responds by sending the same message to the user's Account.

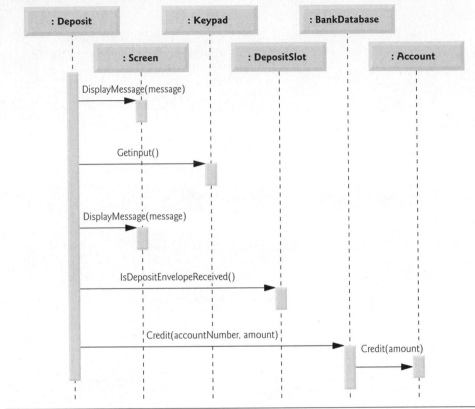

Fig. 30.30 | Sequence diagram that models a Deposit executing.

31

ATM Case Study, Part 2: Implementing an Object-Oriented Design

You can't work in the abstract.
—I. M. Pei

To generalize means to think.
—Georg Wilhelm Friedrich Hegel

We are all gifted. That is our inheritance.
—Ethel Waters

Let me walk through the fields of paper touching with my wand dry stems and stunted butterflies…
—Denise Levertov

OBJECTIVES

In this chapter you'll learn:

- Incorporate inheritance into the design of the ATM.

- Incorporate polymorphism into the design of the ATM.

- Fully implement in C# the UML-based object-oriented design of the ATM software.

- Study a detailed code walkthrough of the ATM software system that explains the implementation issues.

31.1 Introduction

In Chapter 30, we developed an object-oriented design for our ATM system. In this chapter, we took a deeper look at the details of programming with classes. We now begin implementing our object-oriented design by converting class diagrams to C# code. In the final case study section (Section 31.3), we modify the code to incorporate the object-oriented concepts of inheritance and polymorphism. We present the full C# code implementation in Section 31.4.

31.2 Starting to Program the Classes of the ATM System

Visibility
We now apply access modifiers to the members of our classes. In Chapter 4, we introduced access modifiers `public` and `private`. Access modifiers determine the **visibility**, or accessibility, of an object's attributes and operations to other objects. Before we can begin implementing our design, we must consider which attributes and methods of our classes should be `public` and which should be `private`.

In Chapter 4, we observed that attributes normally should be `private` and that methods invoked by clients of a class should be `public`. Methods that are called only by other methods of the class as "utility functions," however, should be `private`. The UML employs **visibility markers** for modeling the visibility of attributes and operations. Public visibility is indicated by placing a plus sign (+) before an operation or an attribute; a minus sign (–) indicates private visibility. Figure 31.1 shows our updated class diagram with visibility markers included. [*Note:* We do not include any operation parameters in Fig. 31.1. This is perfectly normal. Adding visibility markers does not affect the parameters already modeled in the class diagrams of Figs. 30.18–30.21.]

Navigability
Before we begin implementing our design in C#, we introduce an additional UML notation. The class diagram in Fig. 31.2 further refines the relationships among classes in the ATM system by adding navigability arrows to the association lines. **Navigability arrows** (represented as arrows with stick arrowheads in the class diagram) indicate in which direction an association can be traversed and are based on the collaborations modeled in communication and sequence diagrams (see Section 30.7). When implementing a system designed using the

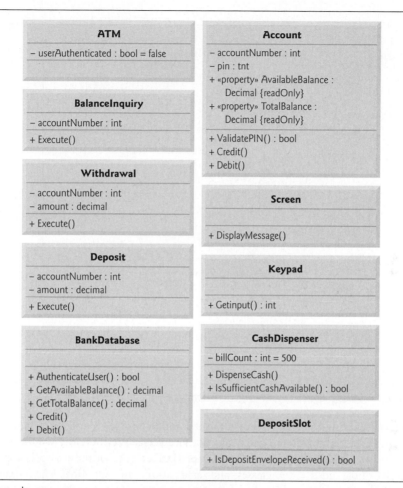

Fig. 31.1 | Class diagram with visibility markers.

UML, programmers use navigability arrows to help determine which objects need references to other objects. For example, the navigability arrow pointing from class ATM to class Bank-Database indicates that we can navigate from the former to the latter, thereby enabling the ATM to invoke the BankDatabase's operations. However, since Fig. 31.2 does not contain a navigability arrow pointing from class BankDatabase to class ATM, the BankDatabase cannot access the ATM's operations. Associations in a class diagram that have navigability arrows at both ends or do not have navigability arrows at all indicate **bidirectional navigability**—navigation can proceed in either direction across the association.

The class diagram of Fig. 31.2 omits classes BalanceInquiry and Deposit to keep the diagram simple. The navigability of the associations in which these classes participate closely parallels the navigability of class Withdrawal's associations. Recall that Balance-Inquiry has an association with class Screen. We can navigate from class BalanceInquiry to class Screen along this association, but we cannot navigate from class Screen to class BalanceInquiry. Thus, if we were to model class BalanceInquiry in Fig. 31.2, we would place a navigability arrow at class Screen's end of this association. Also recall that class

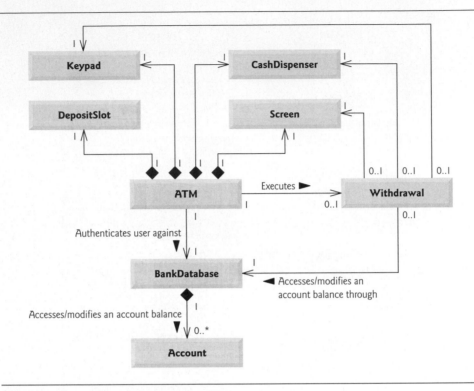

Fig. 31.2 | Class diagram with navigability arrows.

`Deposit` associates with classes `Screen`, `Keypad` and `DepositSlot`. We can navigate from class `Deposit` to each of these classes, but not vice versa. We therefore would place navigability arrows at the `Screen`, `Keypad` and `DepositSlot` ends of these associations. [*Note:* We model these additional classes and associations in our final class diagram in Section 31.3, after we have simplified the structure of our system by incorporating the object-oriented concept of inheritance.]

Implementing the ATM System from Its UML Design

We're now ready to begin implementing the ATM system. We first convert the classes in the diagrams of Fig. 31.1 and 31.2 into C# code. This code will represent the "skeleton" of the system. In Section 31.3, we modify the code to incorporate the object-oriented concept of inheritance. In Section 31.4, we present the complete working C# code that implements our object-oriented design.

As an example, we begin to develop the code for class `Withdrawal` from our design of class `Withdrawal` in Fig. 31.1. We use this figure to determine the attributes and operations of the class. We use the UML model in Fig. 31.2 to determine the associations among classes. We follow these four guidelines for each class:

1. Use the name located in the first compartment of a class in a class diagram to declare the class as a `public` class with an empty parameterless constructor—we include this constructor simply as a placeholder to remind us that most classes will need one or more constructors. In Section 31.4.10, when we complete a working

version of this class, we add any necessary arguments and code to the body of the constructor. Class `Withdrawal` initially yields the code in Fig. 31.3.

```
1   // Fig. 31.3: Withdrawal.cs
2   // Class Withdrawal represents an ATM withdrawal transaction
3   public class Withdrawal
4   {
5      // parameterless constructor
6      public Withdrawal()
7      {
8         // constructor body code
9      } // end constructor
10  } // end class Withdrawal
```

Fig. 31.3 | Initial C# code for class `Withdrawal` based on Figs. 31.1 and 31.2.

2. Use the attributes located in the class's second compartment to declare the instance variables. The `private` attributes `accountNumber` and `amount` of class `Withdrawal` yield the code in Fig. 31.4.

```
1   // Fig. 31.4: Withdrawal.cs
2   // Class Withdrawal represents an ATM withdrawal transaction
3   public class Withdrawal
4   {
5      // attributes
6      private int accountNumber; // account to withdraw funds from
7      private decimal amount; // amount to withdraw from account
8
9      // parameterless constructor
10     public Withdrawal()
11     {
12        // constructor body code
13     } // end constructor
14  } // end class Withdrawal
```

Fig. 31.4 | Incorporating `private` variables for class `Withdrawal` based on Figs. 31.1–31.2.

3. Use the associations described in the class diagram to declare references to other objects. According to Fig. 31.2, `Withdrawal` can access one object of class `Screen`, one object of class `Keypad`, one object of class `CashDispenser` and one object of class `BankDatabase`. Class `Withdrawal` must maintain references to these objects to send messages to them, so lines 10–13 of Fig. 31.5 declare the appropriate references as `private` instance variables. In the implementation of class `Withdrawal` in Section 31.4.10, a constructor initializes these instance variables with references to the actual objects.

4. Use the operations located in the third compartment of Fig. 31.1 to declare the shells of the methods. If we have not yet specified a return type for an operation, we declare the method with return type `void`. Refer to the class diagrams of Figs. 30.18–30.21 to declare any necessary parameters. Adding the `public` operation `Execute` (which has an empty parameter list) in class `Withdrawal` yields the code in lines 23–26 of Fig. 31.6. [*Note:* We code the bodies of the methods when we implement the complete ATM system.]

Software Engineering Observation 31.1

Many UML modeling tools can convert UML-based designs into C# code, considerably speeding up the implementation process.

```
1   // Fig. 31.5: Withdrawal.cs
2   // Class Withdrawal represents an ATM withdrawal transaction
3   public class Withdrawal
4   {
5      // attributes
6      private int accountNumber; // account to withdraw funds from
7      private decimal amount; // amount to withdraw
8
9      // references to associated objects
10     private Screen screen; // ATM's screen
11     private Keypad keypad; // ATM's keypad
12     private CashDispenser cashDispenser; // ATM's cash dispenser
13     private BankDatabase bankDatabase; // account-information database
14
15     // parameterless constructor
16     public Withdrawal()
17     {
18        // constructor body code
19     } // end constructor
20  } // end class Withdrawal
```

Fig. 31.5 | Incorporating `private` reference handles for the associations of class `Withdrawal` based on Figs. 31.1 and 31.2.

```
1   // Fig. 31.6: Withdrawal.cs
2   // Class Withdrawal represents an ATM withdrawal transaction
3   public class Withdrawal
4   {
5      // attributes
6      private int accountNumber; // account to withdraw funds from
7      private decimal amount; // amount to withdraw
8
9      // references to associated objects
10     private Screen screen; // ATM's screen
11     private Keypad keypad; // ATM's keypad
12     private CashDispenser cashDispenser; // ATM's cash dispenser
13     private BankDatabase bankDatabase; // account-information database
14
15     // parameterless constructor
16     public Withdrawal()
17     {
```

Fig. 31.6 | C# code incorporating method `Execute` in class `Withdrawal` based on Figs. 31.1 and 31.2. (Part 1 of 2.)

```
18          // constructor body code
19      } // end constructor
20
21      // operations
22      // perform transaction
23      public void Execute()
24      {
25          // Execute method body code
26      } // end method Execute
27  } // end class Withdrawal
```

Fig. 31.6 | C# code incorporating method `Execute` in class `Withdrawal` based on Figs. 31.1 and 31.2. (Part 2 of 2.)

This concludes our discussion of the basics of generating class files from UML diagrams. In the next section, we demonstrate how to modify the code in Fig. 31.6 to incorporate the object-oriented concepts of inheritance and polymorphism, which we presented in Chapters 11 and 12, respectively.

Self-Review Exercises

31.1 State whether the following statement is *true* or *false*, and if *false*, explain why: If an attribute of a class is marked with a minus sign (-) in a class diagram, the attribute is not directly accessible outside of the class.

31.2 In Fig. 31.2, the association between the ATM and the Screen indicates:
   a) that we can navigate from the Screen to the ATM.
   b) that we can navigate from the ATM to the Screen.
   c) Both a and b; the association is bidirectional.
   d) None of the above.

31.3 Write C# code to begin implementing the design for class Account.

31.3 Incorporating Inheritance and Polymorphism into the ATM System

We now revisit our ATM system design to see how it might benefit from inheritance and polymorphism. To apply inheritance, we first look for commonality among classes in the system. We create an inheritance hierarchy to model similar classes in an elegant and efficient manner that enables us to process objects of these classes polymorphically. We then modify our class diagram to incorporate the new inheritance relationships. Finally, we demonstrate how the inheritance aspects of our updated design are translated into C# code.

In Section 30.3, we encountered the problem of representing a financial transaction in the system. Rather than create one class to represent all transaction types, we created three distinct transaction classes—BalanceInquiry, Withdrawal and Deposit—to represent the transactions that the ATM system can perform. The class diagram of Fig. 31.7 shows the attributes and operations of these classes. They have one private attribute (accountNumber) and one public operation (Execute) in common. Each class requires attribute accountNumber to specify the account to which the transaction applies. Each class contains operation Execute, which the ATM invokes to perform the transaction. Clearly, BalanceInquiry, Withdrawal and Deposit represent *types of* transactions.

Figure 31.7 reveals commonality among the transaction classes, so using inheritance to factor out the common features seems appropriate for designing these classes. We place the common functionality in base class `Transaction` and derive classes `BalanceInquiry`, `Withdrawal` and `Deposit` from `Transaction` (Fig. 31.8).

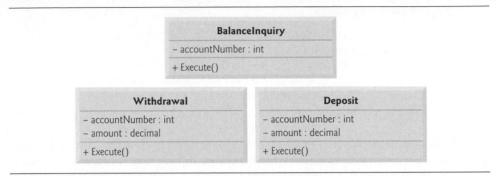

Fig. 31.7 | Attributes and operations of classes `BalanceInquiry`, `Withdrawal` and `Deposit`.

The UML specifies a relationship called a **generalization** to model inheritance. Figure 31.8 is the class diagram that models the inheritance relationship between base class `Transaction` and its three derived classes. The arrows with triangular hollow arrowheads indicate that classes `BalanceInquiry`, `Withdrawal` and `Deposit` are derived from class `Transaction` by inheritance. Class `Transaction` is said to be a generalization of its derived classes. The derived classes are said to be **specializations** of class `Transaction`.

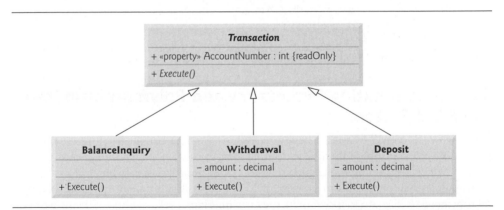

Fig. 31.8 | Class diagram modeling the generalization (i.e., inheritance) relationship between the base class `Transaction` and its derived classes `BalanceInquiry`, `Withdrawal` and `Deposit`.

As Fig. 31.7 shows, classes `BalanceInquiry`, `Withdrawal` and `Deposit` share private `int` attribute `accountNumber`. We'd like to factor out this common attribute and place it in the base class `Transaction`. However, recall that a base class's private attributes are not accessible in derived classes. The derived classes of `Transaction` require access to attribute `accountNumber` so that they can specify which `Account` to process in the `BankDatabase`. A derived class can access the `public` and `protected` members of its base class. However, the derived classes in this case do not need to modify attribute accountNumber—they need only to access its value. For this reason, we have chosen to replace private attribute accountNumber in our model with the public read-only property AccountNumber. Since this is a read-only property, it provides only a get accessor to access the account number. Each derived class inherits this property, enabling the derived class to access its account number as needed to execute a transaction. We no longer list accountNumber in the second compartment of each derived class, because the three derived classes inherit property AccountNumber from Transaction.

According to Fig. 31.7, classes BalanceInquiry, Withdrawal and Deposit also share operation Execute, so base class Transaction should contain public operation Execute. However, it does not make sense to implement Execute in class Transaction, because the functionality that this operation provides depends on the specific type of the actual transaction. We therefore declare Execute as an **abstract operation** in base class Transaction—it will become an abstract method in the C# implementation. This makes Transaction an abstract class and forces any class derived from Transaction that must be a concrete class (i.e., BalanceInquiry, Withdrawal and Deposit) to implement the operation Execute to make the derived class concrete. The UML requires that we place abstract class names and abstract operations in italics. Thus, in Fig. 31.8, Transaction and Execute appear in italics for the Transaction class; Execute is not italicized in derived classes BalanceInquiry, Withdrawal and Deposit. Each derived class overrides base class Transaction's Execute operation with an appropriate concrete implementation. Fig. 31.8 includes operation Execute in the third compartment of classes BalanceInquiry, Withdrawal and Deposit, because each class has a different concrete implementation of the overridden operation.

A derived class can inherit interface and implementation from a base class. Compared to a hierarchy designed for implementation inheritance, one designed for interface inheritance tends to have its functionality lower in the hierarchy—a base class signifies one or more operations that should be defined by each class in the hierarchy, but the individual derived classes provide their own implementations of the operation(s). The inheritance hierarchy designed for the ATM system takes advantage of this type of inheritance, which provides the ATM with an elegant way to execute all transactions "in the general" (i.e., polymorphically). Each class derived from Transaction inherits some implementation details (e.g., property AccountNumber), but the primary benefit of incorporating inheritance into our system is that the derived classes share a common interface (e.g., abstract operation Execute). The ATM can aim a Transaction reference at any transaction, and when the ATM invokes the operation Execute through this reference, the version of Execute specific to that transaction runs (polymorphically) automatically (due to polymorphism). For example, suppose a user chooses to perform a balance inquiry. The ATM aims a Transaction reference at a new object of class BalanceInquiry, which the C# compiler allows because a BalanceInquiry *is a* Transaction. When the ATM uses this reference to invoke Execute, BalanceInquiry's version of Execute is called (polymorphically).

This polymorphic approach also makes the system easily extensible. Should we wish to create a new transaction type (e.g., funds transfer or bill payment), we would simply create an additional Transaction derived class that overrides the Execute operation with a version appropriate for the new transaction type. We would need to make only minimal changes to the system code to allow users to choose the new transaction type from the main menu and for the ATM to instantiate and execute objects of the new derived class. The ATM could execute transactions of the new type using the current code, because it executes all transactions identically (through polymorphism).

An abstract class like Transaction is one for which the programmer never intends to (and, in fact, cannot) instantiate objects. An abstract class simply declares common attributes and behaviors for its derived classes in an inheritance hierarchy. Class Transaction defines the concept of what it means to be a transaction that has an account number and can be executed. You may wonder why we bother to include abstract operation Execute in class Transaction if Execute lacks a concrete implementation. Conceptually, we include this operation because it is the defining behavior of all transactions—executing. Technically, we must include operation Execute in base class Transaction so that the ATM (or any other class) can invoke each derived class's overridden version of this operation polymorphically via a Transaction reference.

Derived classes BalanceInquiry, Withdrawal and Deposit inherit property Account-Number from base class Transaction, but classes Withdrawal and Deposit contain the additional attribute amount that distinguishes them from class BalanceInquiry. Classes Withdrawal and Deposit require this additional attribute to store the amount of money that the user wishes to withdraw or deposit. Class BalanceInquiry has no need for such an attribute and requires only an account number to execute. Even though two of the three Transaction derived classes share the attribute amount, we do not place it in base class Transaction—we place only features common to *all* the derived classes in the base class, so derived classes do not inherit unnecessary attributes (and operations).

Figure 31.9 presents an updated class diagram of our model that incorporates inheritance and introduces abstract base class Transaction. We model an association between class ATM and class Transaction to show that the ATM, at any given moment, either is executing a transaction or is not (i.e., zero or one objects of type Transaction exist in the system at a time). Because a Withdrawal is a type of Transaction, we no longer draw an association line directly between class ATM and class Withdrawal—derived class Withdrawal inherits base class Transaction's association with class ATM. Derived classes BalanceInquiry and Deposit also inherit this association, which replaces the previously omitted associations between classes BalanceInquiry and Deposit, and class ATM. Note again the use of triangular hollow arrowheads to indicate the specializations (i.e., derived classes) of class Transaction, as indicated in Fig. 31.8.

We also add an association between Transaction and BankDatabase (Fig. 31.9). All Transactions require a reference to the BankDatabase so that they can access and modify account information. Each Transaction derived class inherits this reference, so we no longer model the association between Withdrawal and BankDatabase. The association between class Transaction and the BankDatabase replaces the previously omitted associations between classes BalanceInquiry and Deposit, and the BankDatabase.

We include an association between class Transaction and the Screen because all Transactions display output to the user via the Screen. Each derived class inherits this association. Therefore, we no longer include the association previously modeled between Withdrawal and the Screen. Class Withdrawal still participates in associations with the CashDispenser and the Keypad, however—these associations apply to derived class Withdrawal but not to derived classes BalanceInquiry and Deposit, so we do not move these associations to base class Transaction.

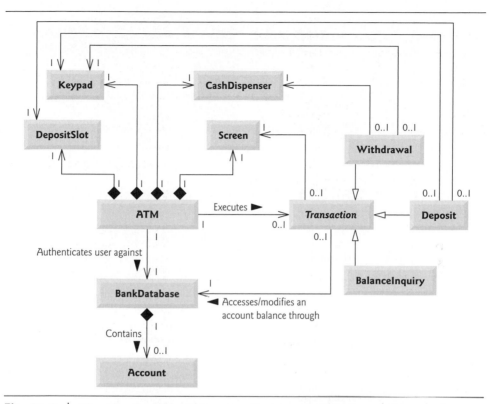

Fig. 31.9 | Class diagram of the ATM system (incorporating inheritance). Abstract class name `Transaction` appears in italics.

Our class diagram incorporating inheritance (Fig. 31.9) also models classes `Deposit` and `BalanceInquiry`. We show associations between `Deposit` and both the `DepositSlot` and the `Keypad`. Class `BalanceInquiry` takes part in only those associations inherited from class `Transaction`—a `BalanceInquiry` interacts only with the `BankDatabase` and the `Screen`.

The modified class diagram in Fig. 31.10 includes abstract base class `Transaction`. This abbreviated diagram does not show inheritance relationships (these appear in Fig. 31.9), but instead shows the attributes and operations after we have employed inheritance in our system. Abstract class name `Transaction` and abstract operation name `Execute` in class `Transaction` appear in italics. To save space, we do not include those attributes shown by associations in Fig. 31.9—we do, however, include them in the C# implementation. We also omit all operation parameters—incorporating inheritance does not affect the parameters already modeled in Figs. 30.18–30.21.

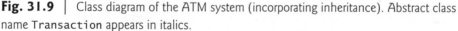

Software Engineering Observation 31.2

A complete class diagram shows all the associations among classes, and all the attributes and operations for each class. When the number of class attributes, operations and associations is substantial (as in Figs. 31.9 and 31.10), a good practice that promotes readability is to divide this information between two class diagrams—one focusing on associations and the other on attributes and operations.

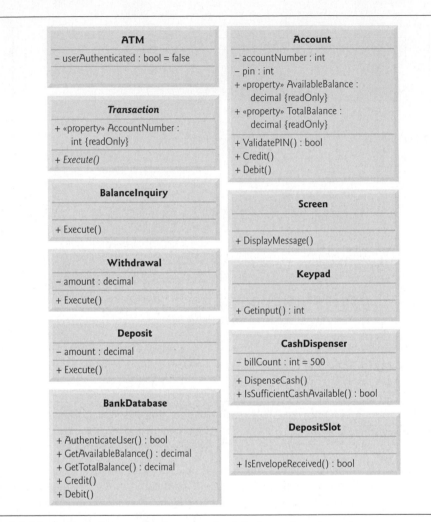

Fig. 31.10 | Class diagram after incorporating inheritance into the system.

Implementing the ATM System Design Incorporating Inheritance

In the previous section, we began implementing the ATM system design in C#. We now incorporate inheritance, using class Withdrawal as an example.

1. If a class A is a generalization of class B, then class B is derived from (and is a specialization of) class A. For example, abstract base class Transaction is a generalization of class Withdrawal. Thus, class Withdrawal is derived from (and is a specialization of) class Transaction. Figure 31.11 contains the shell of class Withdrawal, in which the class definition indicates the inheritance relationship between Withdrawal and Transaction (line 3).

2. If class A is an abstract class and class B is derived from class A, then class B must implement the abstract operations of class A if class B is to be a concrete class. For example, class Transaction contains abstract operation Execute, so class Withdrawal

```
 1   // Fig. 31.11: Withdrawal.cs
 2   // Class Withdrawal represents an ATM withdrawal transaction.
 3   public class Withdrawal : Transaction
 4   {
 5      // code for members of class Withdrawal
 6   } // end class Withdrawal
```

Fig. 31.11 | C# code for shell of class `Withdrawal`.

must implement this operation if we want to instantiate `Withdrawal` objects. Figure 31.12 contains the portions of the C# code for class `Withdrawal` that can be inferred from Fig. 31.9 and Fig. 31.10. Class `Withdrawal` inherits property `AccountNumber` from base class `Transaction`, so `Withdrawal` does not declare this property. Class `Withdrawal` also inherits references to the `Screen` and the `BankDatabase` from class `Transaction`, so we do not include these references in our code. Figure 31.10 specifies attribute `amount` and operation `Execute` for class `Withdrawal`. Line 6 of Fig. 31.12 declares an instance variable for attribute `amount`. Lines 17–20 declare the shell of a method for operation `Execute`. Recall that derived class `Withdrawal` must provide a concrete implementation of the abstract method `Execute` from base class `Transaction`. The keypad and cash-`Dispenser` references (lines 7–8) are instance variables whose need is apparent from class `Withdrawal`'s associations in Fig. 31.9—in the C# implementation of this class in Section 31.4.10, a constructor initializes these references to actual objects.

We discuss the polymorphic processing of `Transactions` in Section 31.4.1 of the ATM implementation. Class `ATM` performs the actual polymorphic call to method `Execute` at line 99 of Fig. 31.26.

```
 1   // Fig. 31.12: Withdrawal.cs
 2   // Class Withdrawal represents an ATM withdrawal transaction.
 3   public class Withdrawal : Transaction
 4   {
 5      // attributes
 6      private decimal amount; // amount to withdraw
 7      private Keypad keypad; // reference to keypad
 8      private CashDispenser cashDispenser; // reference to cash dispenser
 9
10      // parameterless constructor
11      public Withdrawal()
12      {
13         // constructor body code
14      } // end constructor
15
16      // method that overrides Execute
17      public override void Execute()
18      {
19         // Execute method body code
20      } // end method Execute
21   } // end class Withdrawal
```

Fig. 31.12 | C# code for class `Withdrawal` based on Figs. 31.9 and 31.10.

Self-Review Exercises

31.4 The UML uses an arrow with a _____ to indicate a generalization relationship.
a) solid filled arrowhead
b) triangular hollow arrowhead
c) diamond-shaped hollow arrowhead
d) stick arrowhead

31.5 State whether the following statement is *true* or *false*, and if *false*, explain why: The UML requires that we underline abstract class names and abstract operation names.

31.6 Write C# code to begin implementing the design for class Transaction specified in Figures 31.9 and 12.22. Be sure to include private references based on class Transaction's associations. Also, be sure to include properties with public get accessors for any of the private instance variables that the derived classes must access to perform their tasks.

31.4 ATM Case Study Implementation

This section contains the complete working implementation of the ATM system. The implementation comprises 655 lines of C# code. We consider the 11 classes in the order in which we identified them in Section 30.3 (with the exception of Transaction, which was introduced in Section 31.3 as the base class of classes BalanceInquiry, Withdrawal and Deposit):

- ATM

- Screen

- Keypad

- CashDispenser

- DepositSlot

- Account

- BankDatabase

- Transaction

- BalanceInquiry

- Withdrawal

- Deposit

We apply the guidelines discussed in Sections 31.2–31.3 to code these classes based on how we modeled them in the UML class diagrams of Figs. 31.9–31.10. To develop the bodies of class methods, we refer to the activity diagrams presented in Section 30.5 and the communication and sequence diagrams presented in Section 30.6. Our ATM design does not specify all the program logic and may not specify all the attributes and operations required to complete the ATM implementation. This is a normal part of the object-oriented design process. As we implement the system, we complete the program logic and add attributes and behaviors as necessary to construct the ATM system specified by the requirements document in Section 30.2.

We conclude the discussion by presenting a test harness (ATMCaseStudy in Section 31.4.12) that creates an object of class ATM and starts it by calling its Run method. Recall that we are developing a first version of the ATM system that runs on a personal computer and uses the keyboard and monitor to approximate the ATM's keypad and screen. Also, we simulate the actions of the ATM's cash dispenser and deposit slot. We attempt to implement the system so that real hardware versions of these devices could be integrated without significant code changes. [*Note:* For the purpose of this simulation, we have provided two predefined accounts in class BankDatabase. The first account has the account number 12345 and the PIN 54321. The second account has the account number 98765 and the PIN 56789. You should use these accounts when testing the ATM.]

31.4.1 Class ATM

Class ATM (Fig. 31.13) represents the ATM as a whole. Lines 5–11 implement the class's attributes. We determine all but one of these attributes from the UML class diagrams of Figs. 31.9–31.10. Line 5 declares the bool attribute userAuthenticated from Fig. 31.10. Line 6 declares an attribute not found in our UML design—int attribute currentAccountNumber, which keeps track of the account number of the current authenticated user. Lines 7–11 declare reference-type instance variables corresponding to the ATM class's associations modeled in the class diagram of Fig. 31.9. These attributes allow the ATM to access its parts (i.e., its Screen, Keypad, CashDispenser and DepositSlot) and interact with the bank's account information database (i.e., a BankDatabase object).

Lines 14–20 declare an enumeration that corresponds to the four options in the ATM's main menu (i.e., balance inquiry, withdrawal, deposit and exit). Lines 23–32 declare class ATM's constructor, which initializes the class's attributes. When an ATM object is first created, no user is authenticated, so line 25 initializes userAuthenticated to false. Line 26 initializes currentAccountNumber to 0 because there is no current user yet. Lines 27–30 instantiate new objects to represent the parts of the ATM. Recall that class ATM has composition relationships with classes Screen, Keypad, CashDispenser and DepositSlot, so class ATM is responsible for their creation. Line 31 creates a new BankDatabase. As you'll soon see, the BankDatabase creates two Account objects that can be used to test the ATM. [*Note:* If this were a real ATM system, the ATM class would receive a reference to an existing database object created by the bank. However, in this implementation, we are only simulating the bank's database, so class ATM creates the BankDatabase object with which it interacts.]

```
 1   // ATM.cs
 2   // Represents an automated teller machine.
 3   public class ATM
 4   {
 5      private bool userAuthenticated; // true if user is authenticated
 6      private int currentAccountNumber; // user's account number
 7      private Screen screen; // reference to ATM's screen
 8      private Keypad keypad; // reference to ATM's keypad
 9      private CashDispenser cashDispenser; // ref to ATM's cash dispenser
10      private DepositSlot depositSlot; // reference to ATM's deposit slot
11      private BankDatabase bankDatabase; // ref to account info database
12
13      // enumeration that represents main menu options
14      private enum MenuOption
15      {
```

Fig. 31.13 | Class ATM represents the ATM. (Part 1 of 4.)

```
16          BALANCE_INQUIRY = 1,
17          WITHDRAWAL = 2,
18          DEPOSIT = 3,
19          EXIT_ATM = 4
20      } // end enum MenuOption
21
22      // parameterless constructor initializes instance variables
23      public ATM()
24      {
25          userAuthenticated = false; // user is not authenticated to start
26          currentAccountNumber = 0; // no current account number to start
27          screen = new Screen(); // create screen
28          keypad = new Keypad(); // create keypad
29          cashDispenser = new CashDispenser(); // create cash dispenser
30          depositSlot = new DepositSlot(); // create deposit slot
31          bankDatabase = new BankDatabase(); // create account info database
32      } // end constructor
33
34      // start ATM
35      public void Run()
36      {
37          // welcome and authenticate users; perform transactions
38          while ( true ) // infinite loop
39          {
40              // loop while user is not yet authenticated
41              while ( !userAuthenticated )
42              {
43                  screen.DisplayMessageLine( "\nWelcome!" );
44                  AuthenticateUser(); // authenticate user
45              } // end while
46
47              PerformTransactions(); // for authenticated user
48              userAuthenticated = false; // reset before next ATM session
49              currentAccountNumber = 0; // reset before next ATM session
50              screen.DisplayMessageLine( "\nThank you! Goodbye!" );
51          } // end while
52      } // end method Run
53
54      // attempt to authenticate user against database
55      private void AuthenticateUser()
56      {
57          // prompt for account number and input it from user
58          screen.DisplayMessage( "\nPlease enter your account number: " );
59          int accountNumber = keypad.GetInput();
60
61          // prompt for PIN and input it from user
62          screen.DisplayMessage( "\nEnter your PIN: " );
63          int pin = keypad.GetInput();
64
65          // set userAuthenticated to boolean value returned by database
66          userAuthenticated =
67              bankDatabase.AuthenticateUser( accountNumber, pin );
68
```

Fig. 31.13 | Class ATM represents the ATM. (Part 2 of 4.)

```
69          // check whether authentication succeeded
70          if ( userAuthenticated )
71             currentAccountNumber = accountNumber; // save user's account #
72          else
73             screen.DisplayMessageLine(
74                "Invalid account number or PIN. Please try again." );
75       } // end method AuthenticateUser
76
77       // display the main menu and perform transactions
78       private void PerformTransactions()
79       {
80          Transaction currentTransaction; // transaction being processed
81          bool userExited = false; // user has not chosen to exit
82
83          // loop while user has not chosen exit option
84          while ( !userExited )
85          {
86             // show main menu and get user selection
87             int mainMenuSelection = DisplayMainMenu();
88
89             // decide how to proceed based on user's menu selection
90             switch ( ( MenuOption ) mainMenuSelection )
91             {
92                // user chooses to perform one of three transaction types
93                case MenuOption.BALANCE_INQUIRY:
94                case MenuOption.WITHDRAWAL:
95                case MenuOption.DEPOSIT:
96                   // initialize as new object of chosen type
97                   currentTransaction =
98                      CreateTransaction( mainMenuSelection );
99                   currentTransaction.Execute(); // execute transaction
100                  break;
101               case MenuOption.EXIT_ATM: // user chose to terminate session
102                  screen.DisplayMessageLine( "\nExiting the system..." );
103                  userExited = true; // this ATM session should end
104                  break;
105               default: // user did not enter an integer from 1-4
106                  screen.DisplayMessageLine(
107                     "\nYou did not enter a valid selection. Try again." );
108                  break;
109            } // end switch
110         } // end while
111      } // end method PerformTransactions
112
113      // display the main menu and return an input selection
114      private int DisplayMainMenu()
115      {
116         screen.DisplayMessageLine( "\nMain menu:" );
117         screen.DisplayMessageLine( "1 - View my balance" );
118         screen.DisplayMessageLine( "2 - Withdraw cash" );
119         screen.DisplayMessageLine( "3 - Deposit funds" );
120         screen.DisplayMessageLine( "4 - Exit\n" );
121         screen.DisplayMessage( "Enter a choice: " );
```

Fig. 31.13 | Class ATM represents the ATM. (Part 3 of 4.)

```
122          return keypad.GetInput(); // return user's selection
123       } // end method DisplayMainMenu
124
125       // return object of specified Transaction derived class
126       private Transaction CreateTransaction( int type )
127       {
128          Transaction temp = null; // null Transaction reference
129
130          // determine which type of Transaction to create
131          switch ( ( MenuOption ) type )
132          {
133             // create new BalanceInquiry transaction
134             case MenuOption.BALANCE_INQUIRY:
135                temp = new BalanceInquiry( currentAccountNumber,
136                   screen, bankDatabase);
137                break;
138             case MenuOption.WITHDRAWAL: // create new Withdrawal transaction
139                temp = new Withdrawal( currentAccountNumber, screen,
140                   bankDatabase, keypad, cashDispenser);
141                break;
142             case MenuOption.DEPOSIT: // create new Deposit transaction
143                temp = new Deposit( currentAccountNumber, screen,
144                   bankDatabase, keypad, depositSlot);
145                break;
146          } // end switch
147
148          return temp;
149       } // end method CreateTransaction
150    } // end class ATM
```

Fig. 31.13 | Class ATM represents the ATM. (Part 4 of 4.)

Implementing the Operation

The class diagram of Fig. 31.10 does not list any operations for class ATM. We now implement one operation (i.e., public method) in class ATM that allows an external client of the class (i.e., class ATMCaseStudy; Section 31.4.12) to tell the ATM to run. ATM method Run (lines 35–52) uses an infinite loop (lines 38–51) to repeatedly welcome a user, attempt to authenticate the user and, if authentication succeeds, allow the user to perform transactions. After an authenticated user performs the desired transactions and exits, the ATM resets itself, displays a goodbye message and restarts the process for the next user. We use an infinite loop here to simulate the fact that an ATM appears to run continuously until the bank turns it off (an action beyond the user's control). An ATM user can exit the system, but cannot turn off the ATM completely.

Inside method Run's infinite loop, lines 41–45 cause the ATM to repeatedly welcome and attempt to authenticate the user as long as the user has not been authenticated (i.e., the condition !userAuthenticated is true). Line 43 invokes method DisplayMessageLine of the ATM's screen to display a welcome message. Like Screen method DisplayMessage designed in the case study, method DisplayMessageLine (declared in lines 14–17 of Fig. 31.14) displays a message to the user, but this method also outputs a newline after displaying the message. We add this method during implementation to give class Screen's clients more control over the placement of displayed messages. Line 44 invokes class ATM's private utility method AuthenticateUser (declared in lines 55–75) to attempt to authenticate the user.

Authenticating the User
We refer to the requirements document to determine the steps necessary to authenticate the user before allowing transactions to occur. Line 58 of method AuthenticateUser invokes method DisplayMessage of the ATM's screen to prompt the user to enter an account number. Line 59 invokes method GetInput of the ATM's keypad to obtain the user's input, then stores this integer in local variable accountNumber. Method AuthenticateUser next prompts the user to enter a PIN (line 62), and stores the PIN in local variable pin (line 63). Next, lines 66–67 attempt to authenticate the user by passing the accountNumber and pin entered by the user to the bankDatabase's AuthenticateUser method. Class ATM sets its userAuthenticated attribute to the bool value returned by this method—userAuthenticated becomes true if authentication succeeds (i.e., the accountNumber and pin match those of an existing Account in bankDatabase) and remains false otherwise. If userAuthenticated is true, line 71 saves the account number entered by the user (i.e., accountNumber) in the ATM attribute currentAccountNumber. The other methods of class ATM use this variable whenever an ATM session requires access to the user's account number. If userAuthenticated is false, lines 73–74 call the screen's DisplayMessageLine method to indicate that an invalid account number and/or PIN was entered, so the user must try again. We set currentAccountNumber only after authenticating the user's account number and the associated PIN—if the database cannot authenticate the user, currentAccountNumber remains 0.

After method Run attempts to authenticate the user (line 44), if userAuthenticated is still false (line 41), the while loop body (lines 41–45) executes again. If userAuthenticated is now true, the loop terminates, and control continues with line 47, which calls class ATM's private utility method PerformTransactions.

Performing Transactions
Method PerformTransactions (lines 78–111) carries out an ATM session for an authenticated user. Line 80 declares local variable Transaction, to which we assign a BalanceInquiry, Withdrawal or Deposit object representing the ATM transaction currently being processed. We use a Transaction variable here to allow us to take advantage of polymorphism. Also, we name this variable after the role name included in the class diagram of Fig. 30.7—currentTransaction. Line 81 declares another local variable—a bool called userExited that keeps track of whether the user has chosen to exit. This variable controls a while loop (lines 84–110) that allows the user to execute an unlimited number of transactions before choosing to exit. Within this loop, line 87 displays the main menu and obtains the user's menu selection by calling ATM utility method DisplayMainMenu (declared in lines 114–123). This method displays the main menu by invoking methods of the ATM's screen and returns a menu selection obtained from the user through the ATM's keypad. Line 87 stores the user's selection, returned by DisplayMainMenu, in local variable mainMenuSelection.

After obtaining a main menu selection, method PerformTransactions uses a switch statement (lines 90–109) to respond to the selection appropriately. If mainMenuSelection is equal to the underlying value of any of the three enum members representing transaction types (i.e., if the user chose to perform a transaction), lines 97–98 call utility method

CreateTransaction (declared in lines 126–149) to return a newly instantiated object of the type that corresponds to the selected transaction. Variable currentTransaction is assigned the reference returned by method CreateTransaction, then line 99 invokes method Execute of this transaction to execute it. We discuss Transaction method Execute and the three Transaction derived classes shortly. We assign to the Transaction variable currentTransaction an object of one of the three Transaction derived classes so that we can execute transactions. For example, if the user chooses to perform a balance inquiry, (MenuOption) mainMenuSelection (line 90) matches the case label MenuOption.BALANCE_INQUIRY, and CreateTransaction returns a BalanceInquiry object (lines 97–98). Thus, currentTransaction refers to a BalanceInquiry and invoking currentTransaction.Execute() (line 99) results in BalanceInquiry's version of Execute being called polymorphically.

Creating Transactions

Method CreateTransaction (lines 126–149) uses a switch statement (lines 131–146) to instantiate a new Transaction derived class object of the type indicated by the parameter type. Recall that method PerformTransactions passes mainMenuSelection to method CreateTransaction only when mainMenuSelection contains a value corresponding to one of the three transaction types. So parameter type (line 126) receives one of the values MenuOption.BALANCE_INQUIRY, MenuOption.WITHDRAWAL or MenuOption.DEPOSIT. Each case in the switch statement instantiates a new object by calling the appropriate Transaction derived class constructor. Each constructor has a unique parameter list, based on the specific data required to initialize the derived class object. A BalanceInquiry (lines 135–136) requires only the account number of the current user and references to the ATM's screen and the bankDatabase. In addition to these parameters, a Withdrawal (lines 139–140) requires references to the ATM's keypad and cashDispenser, and a Deposit (lines 143–144) requires references to the ATM's keypad and depositSlot. We discuss the transaction classes in detail in Sections 31.4.8–31.4.11.

After executing a transaction (line 99 in method PerformTransactions), userExited remains false, and the while loop in lines 84–110 repeats, returning the user to the main menu. However, if a user does not perform a transaction and instead selects the main menu option to exit, line 103 sets userExited to true, causing the condition in line 84 of the while loop (!userExited) to become false. This while is the final statement of method PerformTransactions, so control returns to line 47 of the calling method Run. If the user enters an invalid main menu selection (i.e., not an integer in the range 1–4), lines 106–107 display an appropriate error message, userExited remains false (as set in line 81) and the user returns to the main menu to try again.

When method PerformTransactions returns control to method Run, the user has chosen to exit the system, so lines 48–49 reset the ATM's attributes userAuthenticated and currentAccountNumber to false and 0, respectively, to prepare for the next ATM user. Line 50 displays a goodbye message to the current user before the ATM welcomes the next user.

31.4.2 Class Screen

Class Screen (Fig. 31.14) represents the screen of the ATM and encapsulates all aspects of displaying output to the user. Class Screen simulates a real ATM's screen with the computer monitor and outputs text messages using standard console output methods

Console.Write and Console.WriteLine. In the design portion of this case study, we endowed class Screen with one operation—DisplayMessage. For greater flexibility in displaying messages to the Screen, we now declare three Screen methods—DisplayMessage, DisplayMessageLine and DisplayDollarAmount.

```csharp
 1   // Screen.cs
 2   // Represents the screen of the ATM
 3   using System;
 4
 5   public class Screen
 6   {
 7      // displays a message without a terminating carriage return
 8      public void DisplayMessage( string message )
 9      {
10         Console.Write( message );
11      } // end method DisplayMessage
12
13      // display a message with a terminating carriage return
14      public void DisplayMessageLine( string message )
15      {
16         Console.WriteLine( message );
17      } // end method DisplayMessageLine
18
19      // display a dollar amount
20      public void DisplayDollarAmount( decimal amount )
21      {
22         Console.Write( "{0:C}", amount );
23      } // end method DisplayDollarAmount
24   } // end class Screen
```

Fig. 31.14 | Class Screen represents the screen of the ATM.

Method DisplayMessage (lines 8–11) takes a string as an argument and prints it to the screen using Console.Write. The cursor stays on the same line, making this method appropriate for displaying prompts to the user. Method DisplayMessageLine (lines 14–17) does the same using Console.WriteLine, which outputs a newline to move the cursor to the next line. Finally, method DisplayDollarAmount (lines 20–23) outputs a properly formatted dollar amount (e.g., $1,234.56). Line 22 uses method Console.Write to output a decimal value formatted as currency with a dollar sign, two decimal places and commas to increase the readability of large dollar amounts.

31.4.3 Class Keypad

Class Keypad (Fig. 31.15) represents the keypad of the ATM and is responsible for receiving all user input. Recall that we are simulating this hardware, so we use the computer's keyboard to approximate the keypad. We use method Console.ReadLine to obtain keyboard input from the user. A computer keyboard contains many keys not found on the ATM's keypad. We assume that the user presses only the keys on the computer keyboard that also appear on the keypad—the keys numbered 0–9 and the *Enter* key.

```
1   // Keypad.cs
2   // Represents the keypad of the ATM.
3   using System;
4
5   public class Keypad
6   {
7      // return an integer value entered by user
8      public int GetInput()
9      {
10         return Convert.ToInt32( Console.ReadLine() );
11     } // end method GetInput
12  } // end class Keypad
```

Fig. 31.15 | Class Keypad represents the ATM's keypad.

Method GetInput (lines 8–11) invokes Convert method ToInt32 to convert the input returned by Console.ReadLine (line 10) to an int value. [*Note:* Method ToInt32 can throw a FormatException if the user enters non-integer input. Because the real ATM's keypad permits only integer input, we simply assume that no exceptions will occur. See Chapter 13 for information on catching and processing exceptions.] Recall that ReadLine obtains all the input used by the ATM. Class Keypad's GetInput method simply returns the integer input by the user. If a client of class Keypad requires input that satisfies some particular criteria (i.e., a number corresponding to a valid menu option), the client must perform the appropriate error checking.

31.4.4 Class CashDispenser

Class CashDispenser (Fig. 31.16) represents the cash dispenser of the ATM. Line 6 declares constant INITIAL_COUNT, which indicates the number of $20 bills in the cash dispenser when the ATM starts (i.e., 500). Line 7 implements attribute billCount (modeled in Fig. 31.10), which keeps track of the number of bills remaining in the CashDispenser at any time. The constructor (lines 10–13) sets billCount to the initial count. [*Note:* We assume that the process of adding more bills to the CashDispenser and updating the bill-Count occur outside the ATM system.] Class CashDispenser has two public methods—DispenseCash (lines 16–21) and IsSufficientCashAvailable (lines 24–31). The class trusts that a client (i.e., Withdrawal) calls method DispenseCash only after establishing that sufficient cash is available by calling method IsSufficientCashAvailable. Thus, DispenseCash simulates dispensing the requested amount of cash without checking whether sufficient cash is available.

```
1   // CashDispenser.cs
2   // Represents the cash dispenser of the ATM
3   public class CashDispenser
4   {
5      // the default initial number of bills in the cash dispenser
6      private const int INITIAL_COUNT = 500;
7      private int billCount; // number of $20 bills remaining
```

Fig. 31.16 | Class CashDispenser represents the ATM's cash dispenser. (Part 1 of 2.)

```
 8
 9       // parameterless constructor initializes billCount to INITIAL_COUNT
10       public CashDispenser()
11       {
12          billCount = INITIAL_COUNT; // set billCount to INITIAL_COUNT
13       } // end constructor
14
15       // simulates dispensing the specified amount of cash
16       public void DispenseCash( decimal amount )
17       {
18          // number of $20 bills required
19          int billsRequired = ( ( int ) amount ) / 20;
20          billCount -= billsRequired;
21       } // end method DispenseCash
22
23       // indicates whether cash dispenser can dispense desired amount
24       public bool IsSufficientCashAvailable( decimal amount )
25       {
26          // number of $20 bills required
27          int billsRequired = ( ( int ) amount ) / 20;
28
29          // return whether there are enough bills available
30          return ( billCount >= billsRequired );
31       } // end method IsSufficientCashAvailable
32    } // end class CashDispenser
```

Fig. 31.16 | Class `CashDispenser` represents the ATM's cash dispenser. (Part 2 of 2.)

Method `IsSufficientCashAvailable` (lines 24–31) has a parameter amount that specifies the amount of cash in question. Line 27 calculates the number of $20 bills required to dispense the specified amount. The ATM allows the user to choose only withdrawal amounts that are multiples of $20, so we convert amount to an integer value and divide it by 20 to obtain the number of `billsRequired`. Line 30 returns true if the Cash-Dispenser's `billCount` is greater than or equal to `billsRequired` (i.e., enough bills are available) and `false` otherwise (i.e., not enough bills). For example, if a user wishes to withdraw $80 (i.e., `billsRequired` is 4), but only three bills remain (i.e., `billCount` is 3), the method returns `false`.

Method `DispenseCash` (lines 16–21) simulates cash dispensing. If our system were hooked up to a real hardware cash dispenser, this method would interact with the hardware device to physically dispense the cash. Our simulated version of the method simply decreases the `billCount` of bills remaining by the number required to dispense the specified amount (line 20). It is the responsibility of the client of the class (i.e., `Withdrawal`) to inform the user that cash has been dispensed—`CashDispenser` does not interact directly with `Screen`.

31.4.5 Class `DepositSlot`

Class `DepositSlot` (Fig. 31.17) represents the deposit slot of the ATM. This class simulates the functionality of a real hardware deposit slot. `DepositSlot` has no attributes and only one method—`IsDepositEnvelopeReceived` (lines 7–10)—which indicates whether a deposit envelope was received.

```
 1   // DepositSlot.cs
 2   // Represents the deposit slot of the ATM
 3   public class DepositSlot
 4   {
 5      // indicates whether envelope was received (always returns true,
 6      // because this is only a software simulation of a real deposit slot)
 7      public bool IsDepositEnvelopeReceived()
 8      {
 9         return true; // deposit envelope was received
10      } // end method IsDepositEnvelopeReceived
11   } // end class DepositSlot
```

Fig. 31.17 | Class DepositSlot represents the ATM's deposit slot.

Recall from the requirements document that the ATM allows the user up to two minutes to insert an envelope. The current version of method IsDepositEnvelopeReceived simply returns true immediately (line 9), because this is only a software simulation, so we assume that the user inserts an envelope within the required time frame. If an actual hardware deposit slot were connected to our system, method IsDepositEnvelopeReceived would be implemented to wait for a maximum of two minutes to receive a signal from the hardware deposit slot indicating that the user has indeed inserted a deposit envelope. If IsDepositEnvelopeReceived were to receive such a signal within two minutes, the method would return true. If two minutes were to elapse and the method still had not received a signal, then the method would return false.

31.4.6 Class Account

Class Account (Fig. 31.25) represents a bank account. Each Account has four attributes (modeled in Fig. 31.10)—accountNumber, pin, availableBalance and totalBalance. Lines 5–8 implement these attributes as private instance variables. For each of the instance variables accountNumber, availableBalance and totalBalance, we provide a property with the same name as the attribute, but starting with a capital letter. For example, property AccountNumber corresponds to the accountNumber attribute modeled in Fig. 31.10. Clients of this class do not need to modify the accountNumber instance variable, so AccountNumber is declared as a read-only property (i.e., it provides only a get accessor).

```
 1   // Account.cs
 2   // Class Account represents a bank account.
 3   public class Account
 4   {
 5      private int accountNumber; // account number
 6      private int pin; // PIN for authentication
 7      private decimal availableBalance; // available withdrawal amount
 8      private decimal totalBalance; // funds available + pending deposit
 9
10      // four-parameter constructor initializes attributes
11      public Account( int theAccountNumber, int thePIN,
12         decimal theAvailableBalance, decimal theTotalBalance )
13      {
```

Fig. 31.18 | Class Account represents a bank account. (Part 1 of 2.)

```
14              accountNumber = theAccountNumber;
15              pin = thePIN;
16              availableBalance = theAvailableBalance;
17              totalBalance = theTotalBalance;
18          } // end constructor
19
20          // read-only property that gets the account number
21          public int AccountNumber
22          {
23              get
24              {
25                  return accountNumber;
26              } // end get
27          } // end property AccountNumber
28
29          // read-only property that gets the available balance
30          public decimal AvailableBalance
31          {
32              get
33              {
34                  return availableBalance;
35              } // end get
36          } // end property AvailableBalance
37
38          // read-only property that gets the total balance
39          public decimal TotalBalance
40          {
41              get
42              {
43                  return totalBalance;
44              } // end get
45          } // end property TotalBalance
46
47          // determines whether a user-specified PIN matches PIN in Account
48          public bool ValidatePIN( int userPIN )
49          {
50              return ( userPIN == pin );
51          } // end method ValidatePIN
52
53          // credits the account (funds have not yet cleared)
54          public void Credit( decimal amount )
55          {
56              totalBalance += amount; // add to total balance
57          } // end method Credit
58
59          // debits the account
60          public void Debit( decimal amount )
61          {
62              availableBalance -= amount; // subtract from available balance
63              totalBalance -= amount; // subtract from total balance
64          } // end method Debit
65      } // end class Account
```

Fig. 31.18 | Class Account represents a bank account. (Part 2 of 2.)

Class `Account` has a constructor (lines 11–18) that takes an account number, the PIN established for the account, the initial available balance and the initial total balance as arguments. Lines 14–17 assign these values to the class's attributes (i.e., instance variables). `Account` objects would normally be created externally to the ATM system. However, in this simulation, the `Account` objects are created in the `BankDatabase` class (Fig. 31.19).

public *Read-Only Properties of Class* Account

Read-only property `AccountNumber` (lines 21–27) provides access to an `Account`'s `accountNumber` instance variable. We include this property in our implementation so that a client of the class (e.g., `BankDatabase`) can identify a particular `Account`. For example, `BankDatabase` contains many `Account` objects, and it can access this property on each of its `Account` objects to locate the one with a specific account number.

Read-only properties `AvailableBalance` (lines 30–36) and `TotalBalance` (lines 39–45) allow clients to retrieve the values of `private decimal` instance variables `availableBalance` and `totalBalance`, respectively. Property `AvailableBalance` represents the amount of funds available for withdrawal. Property `TotalBalance` represents the amount of funds available, plus the amount of deposited funds pending confirmation of cash in deposit envelopes or clearance of checks in deposit envelopes.

public *Methods of Class* Account

Method `ValidatePIN` (lines 48–51) determines whether a user-specified PIN (i.e., parameter `userPIN`) matches the PIN associated with the account (i.e., attribute `pin`). Recall that we modeled this method's parameter `userPIN` in the UML class diagram of Fig. 31.9. If the two PINs match, the method returns `true`; otherwise, it returns `false`.

Method `Credit` (lines 54–57) adds an amount of money (i.e., parameter `amount`) to an `Account` as part of a deposit transaction. This method adds the `amount` only to instance variable `totalBalance` (line 56). The money credited to an account during a deposit does not become available immediately, so we modify only the total balance. We assume that the bank updates the available balance appropriately at a later time, when the amount of cash in the deposit envelope has be verified and the checks in the deposit envelope have cleared. Our implementation of class `Account` includes only methods required for carrying out ATM transactions. Therefore, we omit the methods that some other bank system would invoke to add to instance variable `availableBalance` to confirm a deposit or to subtract from attribute `totalBalance` to reject a deposit.

Method `Debit` (lines 60–64) subtracts an amount of money (i.e., parameter `amount`) from an `Account` as part of a withdrawal transaction. This method subtracts the `amount` from both instance variable `availableBalance` (line 62) and instance variable `totalBalance` (line 63), because a withdrawal affects both balances.

31.4.7 Class BankDatabase

Class `BankDatabase` (Fig. 31.19) models the bank database with which the ATM interacts to access and modify a user's account information. We determine one reference-type attribute for class `BankDatabase` based on its composition relationship with class `Account`. Recall from Fig. 31.9 that a `BankDatabase` is composed of zero or more objects of class `Account`. Line 5 declares attribute `accounts`—an array that will store `Account` objects—to implement this composition relationship. Class `BankDatabase` has a parameterless constructor (lines 8–

15) that initializes accounts with new Account objects (lines 13–14). The Account constructor (Fig. 31.25, lines 11–18) has four parameters—the account number, the PIN assigned to the account, the initial available balance and the initial total balance.

```csharp
1   // BankDatabase.cs
2   // Represents the bank account information database
3   public class BankDatabase
4   {
5      private Account[] accounts; // array of the bank's Accounts
6
7      // parameterless constructor initializes accounts
8      public BankDatabase()
9      {
10        // create two Account objects for testing and
11        // place them in the accounts array
12        accounts = new Account[ 2 ]; // create accounts array
13        accounts[ 0 ] = new Account( 12345, 54321, 1000.00M, 1200.00M );
14        accounts[ 1 ] = new Account( 98765, 56789, 200.00M, 200.00M );
15     } // end constructor
16
17     // retrieve Account object containing specified account number
18     private Account GetAccount( int accountNumber )
19     {
20        // loop through accounts searching for matching account number
21        foreach ( Account currentAccount in accounts )
22        {
23           if ( currentAccount.AccountNumber == accountNumber )
24              return currentAccount;
25        } // end foreach
26
27        // account not found
28        return null;
29     } // end method GetAccount
30
31     // determine whether user-specified account number and PIN match
32     // those of an account in the database
33     public bool AuthenticateUser( int userAccountNumber, int userPIN)
34     {
35        // attempt to retrieve the account with the account number
36        Account userAccount = GetAccount( userAccountNumber );
37
38        // if account exists, return result of Account function ValidatePIN
39        if ( userAccount != null )
40           return userAccount.ValidatePIN( userPIN ); // true if match
41        else
42           return false; // account number not found, so return false
43     } // end method AuthenticateUser
44
45     // return available balance of Account with specified account number
46     public decimal GetAvailableBalance( int userAccountNumber )
47     {
```

Fig. 31.19 | Class BankDatabase represents the bank's account information database. (Part 1 of 2.)

```
48          Account userAccount = GetAccount( userAccountNumber );
49          return userAccount.AvailableBalance;
50       } // end method GetAvailableBalance
51
52       // return total balance of Account with specified account number
53       public decimal GetTotalBalance( int userAccountNumber )
54       {
55          Account userAccount = GetAccount(userAccountNumber);
56          return userAccount.TotalBalance;
57       } // end method GetTotalBalance
58
59       // credit the Account with specified account number
60       public void Credit( int userAccountNumber, decimal amount )
61       {
62          Account userAccount = GetAccount( userAccountNumber );
63          userAccount.Credit( amount );
64       } // end method Credit
65
66       // debit the Account with specified account number
67       public void Debit( int userAccountNumber, decimal amount )
68       {
69          Account userAccount = GetAccount( userAccountNumber );
70          userAccount.Debit( amount );
71       } // end method Debit
72    } // end class BankDatabase
```

Fig. 31.19 | Class BankDatabase represents the bank's account information database. (Part 2 of 2.)

Recall that class BankDatabase serves as an intermediary between class ATM and the actual Account objects that contain users' account information. Thus, methods of class BankDatabase invoke the corresponding methods and properties of the Account object belonging to the current ATM user.

private *Utility Method* GetAccount
We include private utility method GetAccount (lines 18–29) to allow the BankDatabase to obtain a reference to a particular Account within the accounts array. To locate the user's Account, the BankDatabase compares the value returned by property AccountNumber for each element of accounts to a specified account number until it finds a match. Lines 21–25 traverse the accounts array. If currentAccount's account number equals the value of parameter accountNumber, the method returns currentAccount. If no account has the given account number, then line 28 returns null.

public *Methods*
Method AuthenticateUser (lines 33–43) proves or disproves the identity of an ATM user. This method takes a user-specified account number and a user-specified PIN as arguments and indicates whether they match the account number and PIN of an Account in the database. Line 36 calls method GetAccount, which returns either an Account with userAccount-Number as its account number or null to indicate that userAccountNumber is invalid. If GetAccount returns an Account object, line 40 returns the bool value returned by that ob-

ject's ValidatePIN method. BankDatabase's AuthenticateUser method does not perform the PIN comparison itself—rather, it forwards userPIN to the Account object's ValidatePIN method to do so. The value returned by Account method ValidatePIN (line 40) indicates whether the user-specified PIN matches the PIN of the user's Account, so method AuthenticateUser simply returns this value (line 40) to the client of the class (i.e., ATM).

The BankDatabase trusts the ATM to invoke method AuthenticateUser and receive a return value of true before allowing the user to perform transactions. BankDatabase also trusts that each Transaction object created by the ATM contains the valid account number of the current authenticated user and that this account number is passed to the remaining BankDatabase methods as argument userAccountNumber. Methods GetAvailableBalance (lines 46–50), GetTotalBalance (lines 53–57), Credit (lines 60–64) and Debit (lines 67–71) therefore simply retrieve the user's Account object with utility method GetAccount, then invoke the appropriate Account method on that object. We know that the calls to GetAccount within these methods will never return null, because userAccountNumber must refer to an existing Account. GetAvailableBalance and GetTotalBalance return the values returned by the corresponding Account properties. Also, methods Credit and Debit simply redirect parameter amount to the Account methods they invoke.

31.4.8 Class Transaction

Class Transaction (Fig. 31.20) is an abstract base class that represents the notion of an ATM transaction. It contains the common features of derived classes BalanceInquiry, Withdrawal and Deposit. This class expands on the "skeleton" code first developed in Section 31.2. Line 3 declares this class to be abstract. Lines 5–7 declare the class's private instance variables. Recall from the class diagram of Fig. 31.10 that class Transaction contains the property AccountNumber that indicates the account involved in the Transaction. Line 5 implements the instance variable accountNumber to maintain the AccountNumber property's data. We derive attributes screen (implemented as instance variable userScreen in line 6) and bankDatabase (implemented as instance variable database in line 7) from class Transaction's associations, modeled in Fig. 31.9. All transactions require access to the ATM's screen and the bank's database.

Class Transaction has a constructor (lines 10–16) that takes the current user's account number and references to the ATM's screen and the bank's database as arguments. Because Transaction is an abstract class (line 3), this constructor is never called directly to instantiate Transaction objects. Instead, this constructor is invoked by the constructors of the Transaction derived classes via constructor initializers.

Class Transaction has three public read-only properties—AccountNumber (lines 19–25), UserScreen (lines 28–34) and Database (lines 37–43). Derived classes of Transaction inherit these properties and use them to gain access to class Transaction's private instance variables. We chose the names of the UserScreen and Database properties for clarity—we wanted to avoid property names that are the same as the class names Screen and BankDatabase, which can be confusing.

Class Transaction also declares abstract method Execute (line 46). It does not make sense to provide an implementation for this method in class Transaction, because a generic transaction cannot be executed. Thus, we declare this method to be abstract, forcing each Transaction concrete derived class to provide its own implementation that executes the particular type of transaction.

```
1   // Transaction.cs
2   // Abstract base class Transaction represents an ATM transaction.
3   public abstract class Transaction
4   {
5      private int accountNumber; // account involved in the transaction
6      private Screen userScreen; // reference to ATM's screen
7      private BankDatabase database; // reference to account info database
8
9      // three-parameter constructor invoked by derived classes
10     public Transaction( int userAccount, Screen theScreen,
11        BankDatabase theDatabase )
12     {
13        accountNumber = userAccount;
14        userScreen = theScreen;
15        database = theDatabase;
16     } // end constructor
17
18     // read-only property that gets the account number
19     public int AccountNumber
20     {
21        get
22        {
23           return accountNumber;
24        } // end get
25     } // end property AccountNumber
26
27     // read-only property that gets the screen reference
28     public Screen UserScreen
29     {
30        get
31        {
32           return userScreen;
33        } // end get
34     } // end property UserScreen
35
36     // read-only property that gets the bank database reference
37     public BankDatabase Database
38     {
39        get
40        {
41           return database;
42        } // end get
43     } // end property Database
44
45     // perform the transaction (overridden by each derived class)
46     public abstract void Execute(); // no implementation here
47  } // end class Transaction
```

Fig. 31.20 | abstract base class Transaction represents an ATM transaction.

31.4.9 Class BalanceInquiry

Class BalanceInquiry (Fig. 31.21) inherits from Transaction and represents an ATM balance inquiry transaction (line 3). BalanceInquiry does not have any attributes of its own, but it inherits Transaction attributes accountNumber, screen and bankDatabase, which are accessible through Transaction's public read-only properties. The BalanceInquiry constructor (lines 6–8) takes arguments corresponding to these attributes and forwards them to Transaction's constructor by invoking the constructor initializer with keyword base (line 8). The body of the constructor is empty.

Class BalanceInquiry overrides Transaction's abstract method Execute to provide a concrete implementation (lines 11–27) that performs the steps involved in a balance inquiry. Lines 14–15 obtain the specified Account's available balance by invoking the GetAvailableBalance method of the inherited property Database. Line 15 uses the inherited property AccountNumber to get the account number of the current user. Line 18 retrieves the specified Account's total balance. Lines 21–26 display the balance information on the ATM's screen using the inherited property UserScreen. Recall that DisplayDollarAmount takes a decimal argument and outputs it to the screen formatted as a dollar amount with a dollar sign. For example, if a user's available balance is 1000.50M, line 23 outputs $1,000.50. Line 26 inserts a blank line of output to separate the balance information from subsequent output (i.e., the main menu repeated by class ATM after executing the BalanceInquiry).

```
1   // BalanceInquiry.cs
2   // Represents a balance inquiry ATM transaction
3   public class BalanceInquiry : Transaction
4   {
5       // five-parameter constructor initializes base class variables
6       public BalanceInquiry( int userAccountNumber,
7           Screen atmScreen, BankDatabase atmBankDatabase )
8           : base( userAccountNumber, atmScreen, atmBankDatabase ) {}
9
10      // performs transaction; overrides Transaction's abstract method
11      public override void Execute()
12      {
13          // get the available balance for the current user's Account
14          decimal availableBalance =
15              Database.GetAvailableBalance( AccountNumber );
16
17          // get the total balance for the current user's Account
18          decimal totalBalance = Database.GetTotalBalance( AccountNumber );
19
20          // display the balance information on the screen
21          UserScreen.DisplayMessageLine( "\nBalance Information:" );
22          UserScreen.DisplayMessage( " - Available balance: " );
23          UserScreen.DisplayDollarAmount( availableBalance );
24          UserScreen.DisplayMessage( "\n - Total balance: " );
25          UserScreen.DisplayDollarAmount( totalBalance );
26          UserScreen.DisplayMessageLine( "" );
27      } // end method Execute
28  } // end class BalanceInquiry
```

Fig. 31.21 | Class BalanceInquiry represents a balance inquiry ATM transaction.

31.4.10 Class Withdrawal

Class Withdrawal (Fig. 31.22) extends Transaction and represents an ATM withdrawal transaction. This class expands on the "skeleton" code for this class developed in

Fig. 31.11. Recall from the class diagram of Fig. 31.9 that class Withdrawal has one attribute, amount, which line 5 declares as a decimal instance variable. Figure 31.9 models associations between class Withdrawal and classes Keypad and CashDispenser, for which lines 6–7 implement reference attributes keypad and cashDispenser, respectively. Line 10 declares a constant corresponding to the cancel menu option.

```
1   // Withdrawal.cs
2   // Class Withdrawal represents an ATM withdrawal transaction.
3   public class Withdrawal : Transaction
4   {
5      private decimal amount; // amount to withdraw
6      private Keypad keypad; // reference to Keypad
7      private CashDispenser cashDispenser; // reference to cash dispenser
8
9      // constant that corresponds to menu option to cancel
10     private const int CANCELED = 6;
11
12     // five-parameter constructor
13     public Withdrawal( int userAccountNumber, Screen atmScreen,
14        BankDatabase atmBankDatabase, Keypad atmKeypad,
15        CashDispenser atmCashDispenser )
16        : base( userAccountNumber, atmScreen, atmBankDatabase )
17     {
18        // initialize references to keypad and cash dispenser
19        keypad = atmKeypad;
20        cashDispenser = atmCashDispenser;
21     } // end constructor
22
23     // perform transaction, overrides Transaction's abstract method
24     public override void Execute()
25     {
26        bool cashDispensed = false; // cash was not dispensed yet
27
28        // transaction was not canceled yet
29        bool transactionCanceled = false;
30
31        // loop until cash is dispensed or the user cancels
32        do
33        {
34           // obtain the chosen withdrawal amount from the user
35           int selection = DisplayMenuOfAmounts();
36
37           // check whether user chose a withdrawal amount or canceled
38           if ( selection != CANCELED )
39           {
40              // set amount to the selected dollar amount
41              amount = selection;
42
43              // get available balance of account involved
44              decimal availableBalance =
45                 Database.GetAvailableBalance( AccountNumber );
46
```

Fig. 31.22 | Class Withdrawal represents an ATM withdrawal transaction. (Part 1 of 3.)

```
47              // check whether the user has enough money in the account
48              if ( amount <= availableBalance )
49              {
50                  // check whether the cash dispenser has enough money
51                  if ( cashDispenser.IsSufficientCashAvailable( amount ) )
52                  {
53                      // debit the account to reflect the withdrawal
54                      Database.Debit( AccountNumber, amount );
55
56                      cashDispenser.DispenseCash( amount ); // dispense cash
57                      cashDispensed = true; // cash was dispensed
58
59                      // instruct user to take cash
60                      UserScreen.DisplayMessageLine(
61                          "\nPlease take your cash from the cash dispenser." );
62                  } // end innermost if
63                  else // cash dispenser does not have enough cash
64                      UserScreen.DisplayMessageLine(
65                          "\nInsufficient cash available in the ATM." +
66                          "\n\nPlease choose a smaller amount." );
67              } // end middle if
68              else // not enough money available in user's account
69                  UserScreen.DisplayMessageLine(
70                      "\nInsufficient cash available in your account." +
71                      "\n\nPlease choose a smaller amount." );
72          } // end outermost if
73          else
74          {
75              UserScreen.DisplayMessageLine( "\nCanceling transaction..." );
76              transactionCanceled = true; // user canceled the transaction
77          } // end else
78      } while ( ( !cashDispensed ) && ( !transactionCanceled ) );
79   } // end method Execute
80
81   // display a menu of withdrawal amounts and the option to cancel;
82   // return the chosen amount or 6 if the user chooses to cancel
83   private int DisplayMenuOfAmounts()
84   {
85      int userChoice = 0; // variable to store return value
86
87      // array of amounts to correspond to menu numbers
88      int[] amounts = { 0, 20, 40, 60, 100, 200 };
89
90      // loop while no valid choice has been made
91      while ( userChoice == 0 )
92      {
93          // display the menu
94          UserScreen.DisplayMessageLine( "\nWithdrawal options:" );
95          UserScreen.DisplayMessageLine( "1 - $20" );
96          UserScreen.DisplayMessageLine( "2 - $40" );
97          UserScreen.DisplayMessageLine( "3 - $60" );
98          UserScreen.DisplayMessageLine( "4 - $100" );
99          UserScreen.DisplayMessageLine( "5 - $200" );
```

Fig. 31.22 | Class Withdrawal represents an ATM withdrawal transaction. (Part 2 of 3.)

```
100              UserScreen.DisplayMessageLine( "6 - Cancel transaction" );
101              UserScreen.DisplayMessage(
102                 "\nChoose a withdrawal option (1-6): " );
103
104              // get user input through keypad
105              int input = keypad.GetInput();
106
107              // determine how to proceed based on the input value
108              switch ( input )
109              {
110                 // if the user chose a withdrawal amount (i.e., option
111                 // 1, 2, 3, 4, or 5), return the corresponding amount
112                 // from the amounts array
113                 case 1: case 2: case 3: case 4: case 5:
114                    userChoice = amounts[ input ]; // save user's choice
115                    break;
116                 case CANCELED: // the user chose to cancel
117                    userChoice = CANCELED; // save user's choice
118                    break;
119                 default:
120                    UserScreen.DisplayMessageLine(
121                       "\nInvalid selection. Try again." );
122                    break;
123              } // end switch
124          } // end while
125
126          return userChoice;
127      } // end method DisplayMenuOfAmounts
128 } // end class Withdrawal
```

Fig. 31.22 | Class `Withdrawal` represents an ATM withdrawal transaction. (Part 3 of 3.)

Class `Withdrawal`'s constructor (lines 13–21) has five parameters. It uses the constructor initializer to pass parameters `userAccountNumber`, `atmScreen` and `atmBankDatabase` to base class `Transaction`'s constructor to set the attributes that `Withdrawal` inherits from `Transaction`. The constructor also takes references `atmKeypad` and `atmCashDispenser` as parameters and assigns them to reference-type attributes `keypad` and `cashDispenser`, respectively.

Overriding abstract Method Execute

Class `Withdrawal` overrides `Transaction`'s abstract method `Execute` with a concrete implementation (lines 24–79) that performs the steps involved in a withdrawal. Line 26 declares and initializes a local bool variable `cashDispensed`. This variable indicates whether cash has been dispensed (i.e., whether the transaction has completed successfully) and is initially false. Line 29 declares and initializes to false a bool variable `transactionCanceled` to indicate that the transaction has not yet been canceled by the user.

Lines 32–78 contain a do...while statement that executes its body until cash is dispensed (i.e., until `cashDispensed` becomes true) or until the user chooses to cancel (i.e., until `transactionCanceled` becomes true). We use this loop to continuously return the user to the start of the transaction if an error occurs (i.e., the requested withdrawal amount is greater than the user's available balance or greater than the amount of cash in the cash dispenser). Line 35 displays a menu of withdrawal amounts and obtains a user selection by calling private utility method DisplayMenuOfAmounts (declared in lines 83–127). This method displays the menu of amounts and returns either an int withdrawal amount or an int constant CANCELED to indicate that the user has chosen to cancel the transaction.

Displaying Options With private Utility Method DisplayMenuOfAmounts

Method DisplayMenuOfAmounts (lines 83–127) first declares local variable userChoice (initially 0) to store the value that the method will return (line 85). Line 88 declares an integer array of withdrawal amounts that correspond to the amounts displayed in the withdrawal menu. We ignore the first element in the array (index 0), because the menu has no option 0. The while statement at lines 91–124 repeats until userChoice takes on a value other than 0. We will see shortly that this occurs when the user makes a valid selection from the menu. Lines 94–102 display the withdrawal menu on the screen and prompt the user to enter a choice. Line 105 obtains integer input through the keypad. The switch statement at lines 108–123 determines how to proceed based on the user's input. If the user selects 1, 2, 3, 4 or 5, line 114 sets userChoice to the value of the element in the amounts array at index input. For example, if the user enters 3 to withdraw $60, line 114 sets userChoice to the value of amounts[3]—i.e., 60. Variable userChoice no longer equals 0, so the while at lines 91–124 terminates, and line 126 returns userChoice. If the user selects the cancel menu option, line 117 executes, setting userChoice to CANCELED and causing the method to return this value. If the user does not enter a valid menu selection, lines 120–121 display an error message, and the user is returned to the withdrawal menu.

The if statement at line 38 in method Execute determines whether the user has selected a withdrawal amount or chosen to cancel. If the user cancels, line 75 displays an appropriate message to the user before control is returned to the calling method—ATM method PerformTransactions. If the user has chosen a withdrawal amount, line 41 assigns local variable selection to instance variable amount. Lines 44–45 retrieve the available balance of the current user's Account and store it in a local decimal variable availableBalance. Next, the if statement at line 48 determines whether the selected amount is less than or equal to the user's available balance. If it is not, lines 69–71 display an error message. Control then continues to the end of the do…while statement, and the loop repeats because both cashDispensed and transactionCanceled are still false. If the user's balance is high enough, the if statement at line 51 determines whether the cash dispenser has enough money to satisfy the withdrawal request by invoking the cashDispenser's IsSufficientCashAvailable method. If this method returns false, lines 64–66 display an error message, and the do…while statement repeats. If sufficient cash is available, the requirements for the withdrawal are satisfied, and line 54 debits the user's account in the database by amount. Lines 56–57 then instruct the cash dispenser to dispense the cash to the user and set cashDispensed to true. Finally, lines 60–61 display a message to the user to take the dispensed cash. Because cashDispensed is now true, control continues after the do…while statement. No additional statements appear below the loop, so the method returns control to class ATM.

31.4.11 Class Deposit

Class Deposit (Fig. 31.23) inherits from Transaction and represents an ATM deposit transaction. Recall from the class diagram of Fig. 31.10 that class Deposit has one attribute, amount, which line 5 declares as a decimal instance variable. Lines 6–7 create reference attributes keypad and depositSlot that implement the associations between class Deposit and classes Keypad and DepositSlot, modeled in Fig. 31.9. Line 10 declares a constant CANCELED that corresponds to the value a user enters to cancel a deposit transaction.

```
1    // Deposit.cs
2    // Represents a deposit ATM transaction.
3    public class Deposit : Transaction
4    {
5       private decimal amount; // amount to deposit
6       private Keypad keypad; // reference to the Keypad
7       private DepositSlot depositSlot; // reference to the deposit slot
8
9       // constant representing cancel option
10      private const int CANCELED = 0;
11
12      // five-parameter constructor initializes class's instance variables
13      public Deposit( int userAccountNumber, Screen atmScreen,
14         BankDatabase atmBankDatabase, Keypad atmKeypad,
15         DepositSlot atmDepositSlot )
16         : base( userAccountNumber, atmScreen, atmBankDatabase )
17      {
18         // initialize references to keypad and deposit slot
19         keypad = atmKeypad;
20         depositSlot = atmDepositSlot;
21      } // end five-parameter constructor
22
23      // perform transaction; overrides Transaction's abstract method
24      public override void Execute()
25      {
26         amount = PromptForDepositAmount(); // get deposit amount from user
27
28         // check whether user entered a deposit amount or canceled
29         if ( amount != CANCELED )
30         {
31            // request deposit envelope containing specified amount
32            UserScreen.DisplayMessage(
33               "\nPlease insert a deposit envelope containing " );
34            UserScreen.DisplayDollarAmount( amount );
35            UserScreen.DisplayMessageLine( " in the deposit slot." );
36
37            // retrieve deposit envelope
38            bool envelopeReceived = depositSlot.IsDepositEnvelopeReceived();
39
40            // check whether deposit envelope was received
41            if ( envelopeReceived )
42            {
43               UserScreen.DisplayMessageLine(
44                  "\nYour envelope has been received.\n" +
45                  "The money just deposited will not be available " +
46                  "until we \nverify the amount of any " +
47                  "enclosed cash, and any enclosed checks clear." );
```

Fig. 31.23 | Class Deposit represents an ATM deposit transaction. (Part 1 of 2.)

```
48
49                    // credit account to reflect the deposit
50                    Database.Credit( AccountNumber, amount );
51                } // end inner if
52                else
53                    UserScreen.DisplayMessageLine(
54                        "\nYou did not insert an envelope, so the ATM has " +
55                        "canceled your transaction." );
56            } // end outer if
57            else
58                UserScreen.DisplayMessageLine( "\nCanceling transaction..." );
59        } // end method Execute
60
61        // prompt user to enter a deposit amount to credit
62        private decimal PromptForDepositAmount()
63        {
64            // display the prompt and receive input
65            UserScreen.DisplayMessage(
66                "\nPlease input a deposit amount in CENTS (or 0 to cancel): " );
67            int input = keypad.GetInput();
68
69            // check whether the user canceled or entered a valid amount
70            if ( input == CANCELED )
71                return CANCELED;
72            else
73                return input / 100.00M;
74        } // end method PromptForDepositAmount
75    } // end class Deposit
```

Fig. 31.23 | Class Deposit represents an ATM deposit transaction. (Part 2 of 2.)

Class Deposit contains a constructor (lines 13–21) that passes three parameters to base class Transaction's constructor using a constructor initializer. The constructor also has parameters atmKeypad and atmDepositSlot, which it assigns to the corresponding reference instance variables (lines 19–20).

Overriding abstract Method Execute
Method Execute (lines 24–59) overrides abstract method Execute in base class Transaction with a concrete implementation that performs the steps required in a deposit transaction. Line 26 prompts the user to enter a deposit amount by invoking private utility method PromptForDepositAmount (declared in lines 62–74) and sets attribute amount to the value returned. Method PromptForDepositAmount asks the user to enter a deposit amount as an integer number of cents (because the ATM's keypad does not contain a decimal point; this is consistent with many real ATMs) and returns the decimal value representing the dollar amount to be deposited.

Getting Deposit Amount with private Utility Method PromptForDepositAmount
Lines 65–66 in method PromptForDepositAmount display a message asking the user to input a deposit amount as a number of cents or "0" to cancel the transaction. Line 67 receives the user's input from the keypad. The if statement at lines 70–73 determines whether the user has entered a deposit amount or chosen to cancel. If the user chooses to cancel, line 71 returns constant CANCELED. Otherwise, line 73 returns the deposit amount

after converting the int number of cents to a dollar-and-cents amount by dividing by the decimal literal 100.00M. For example, if the user enters 125 as the number of cents, line 73 returns 125 divided by 100.00M, or 1.25—125 cents is $1.25.

The if statement at lines 29–58 in method Execute determines whether the user has chosen to cancel the transaction instead of entering a deposit amount. If the user cancels, line 58 displays an appropriate message, and the method returns. If the user enters a deposit amount, lines 32–35 instruct the user to insert a deposit envelope with the correct amount. Recall that Screen method DisplayDollarAmount outputs a decimal value formatted as a dollar amount (including the dollar sign).

Line 38 sets a local bool variable to the value returned by depositSlot's IsDepositEnvelopeReceived method, indicating whether a deposit envelope has been received. Recall that we coded method IsDepositEnvelopeReceived (lines 7–10 of Fig. 31.17) to always return true, because we are simulating the functionality of the deposit slot and assume that the user always inserts an envelope in a timely fashion (i.e., within the two-minute time limit). However, we code method Execute of class Deposit to test for the possibility that the user does not insert an envelope—good software engineering demands that programs account for all possible return values. Thus, class Deposit is prepared for future versions of IsDepositEnvelopeReceived that could return false. Lines 43–50 execute if the deposit slot receives an envelope. Lines 43–47 display an appropriate message to the user. Line 50 credits the user's account in the database with the deposit amount. Lines 53–55 execute if the deposit slot does not receive a deposit envelope. In this case, we display a message stating that the ATM has canceled the transaction. The method then returns without crediting the user's account.

31.4.12 Class ATMCaseStudy

Class ATMCaseStudy (Fig. 31.24) simply allows us to start, or "turn on," the ATM and test the implementation of our ATM system model. Class ATMCaseStudy's Main method (lines 6–10) simply instantiates a new ATM object named theATM (line 8) and invokes its Run method (line 9) to start the ATM.

```
1    // ATMCaseStudy.cs
2    // Application for testing the ATM case study.
3    public class ATMCaseStudy
4    {
5       // Main method is the application's entry point
6       public static void Main( string[] args )
7       {
8          ATM theATM = new ATM();
9          theATM.Run();
10      } // end method Main
11   } // end class ATMCaseStudy
```

Fig. 31.24 | Class ATMCaseStudy starts the ATM.

31.5 Wrap-Up

In this chapter, you used inheritance to tune the design of the ATM software system, and you fully implemented the ATM in C#. Congratulations on completing the entire ATM case study! We hope you found this experience to be valuable and that it reinforced many of the object-oriented programming concepts that you've learned.

Answers to Self-Review Exercises

31.1 True. The minus sign (–) indicates private visibility.

31.2 b.

31.3 The design for class Account yields the code in Fig. 31.25. We public auto-implemented properties AvailableBalance and TotalBalance to store the data that methods Credit and Debit, will manipulate.

```csharp
1   // Fig. 31.25: Account.cs
2   // Class Account represents a bank account.
3   public class Account
4   {
5      private int accountNumber; // account number
6      private int pin; // PIN for authentication
7
8      // automatic read-only property AvailableBalance
9      public decimal AvailableBalance { get; private set; }
10
11     // automatic read-only property TotalBalance
12     public decimal TotalBalance { get; private set; }
13
14     // parameterless constructor
15     public Account()
16     {
17        // constructor body code
18     } // end constructor
19
20     // validates user PIN
21     public bool ValidatePIN()
22     {
23        // ValidatePIN method body code
24     } // end method ValidatePIN
25
26     // credits the account
27     public void Credit()
28     {
29        // Credit method body code
30     } // end method Credit
31
32     // debits the account
33     public void Debit()
34     {
35        // Debit method body code
36     } // end method Debit
37   } // end class Account
```

Fig. 31.25 | C# code for class Account based on Figs. 31.1 and 31.2.

31.4 b.

31.5 False. The UML requires that we italicize abstract class names and operation names.

31.6 The design for class Transaction yields the code in Fig. 31.26. In the implementation, a constructor initializes private instance variables userScreen and database to actual objects, and read-only properties UserScreen and Database access these instance variables. These properties allow classes derived from Transaction to access the ATM's screen and interact with the bank's database. We chose the names of the UserScreen and Database properties for clarity—we wanted to avoid property names that are the same as the class names Screen and BankDatabase, which can be confusing.

```csharp
1   // Fig. 31.26: Transaction.cs
2   // Abstract base class Transaction represents an ATM transaction.
3   public abstract class Transaction
4   {
5      private int accountNumber; // indicates account involved
6      private Screen userScreen; // ATM's screen
7      private BankDatabase database; // account info database
8
9      // parameterless constructor
10     public Transaction()
11     {
12        // constructor body code
13     } // end constructor
14
15     // read-only property that gets the account number
16     public int AccountNumber
17     {
18        get
19        {
20           return accountNumber;
21        } // end get
22     } // end property AccountNumber
23
24     // read-only property that gets the screen reference
25     public Screen UserScreen
26     {
27        get
28        {
29           return userScreen;
30        } // end get
31     } // end property UserScreen
32
33     // read-only property that gets the bank database reference
34     public BankDatabase Database
35     {
36        get
37        {
38           return database;
39        } // end get
40     } // end property Database
41
42     // perform the transaction (overridden by each derived class)
43     public abstract void Execute();
44  } // end class Transaction
```

Fig. 31.26 | C# code for class Transaction based on Figures 31.9 and 31.10.

Operator Precedence Chart

Operators are shown in decreasing order of precedence from top to bottom with each level of precedence separated by a horizontal line. The associativity of the operators is shown in the right column.

Operator	Type	Associativity
.	member access	left-to-right
()	method call	
[]	element access	
++	postfix increment	
--	postfix decrement	
new	object creation	
typeof	get System.Type object for a type	
sizeof	get size in bytes of a type	
checked	checked evaluation	
unchecked	unchecked evaluation	
+	unary plus	right-to-left
-	unary minus	
!	logical negation	
~	bitwise complement	
++	prefix increment	
--	prefix decrement	
(*type*)	cast	

Fig. A.1 | Operator precedence chart (Part 1 of 2.).

Operator	Type	Associativity
*	multiplication	left-to-right
/	division	
%	remainder	
+	addition	left-to-right
-	subtraction	
>>	right shift	left-to-right
<<	left shift	
<	less than	left-to-right
>	greater than	
<=	less than or equal to	
>=	greater than or equal to	
is	type comparison	
as	type conversion	
!=	is not equal to	left-to-right
==	is equal to	
&	logical AND	left-to-right
^	logical XOR	left-to-right
|	logical OR	left-to-right
&&	conditional AND	left-to-right
||	conditional OR	left-to-right
??	null coalescing	right-to-left
?:	conditional	right-to-left
=	assignment	right-to-left
*=	multiplication assignment	
/=	division assignment	
%=	remainder assignment	
+=	addition assignment	
-=	subtraction assignment	
<<=	left shift assignment	
>>=	right shift assignment	
&=	logical AND assignment	
^=	logical XOR assignment	
|=	logical OR assignment	

Fig. A.1 | Operator precedence chart (Part 2 of 2.).

Simple Types

Type	Size in bits	Value range	Standard
bool	8	true or false	
byte	8	0 to 255, inclusive	
sbyte	8	−128 to 127, inclusive	
char	16	'\u0000' to '\uFFFF' (0 to 65535), inclusive	Unicode
short	16	−32768 to 32767, inclusive	
ushort	16	0 to 65535, inclusive	
int	32	−2,147,483,648 to 2,147,483,647, inclusive	
uint	32	0 to 4,294,967,295, inclusive	
float	32	*Approximate negative range:* −3.4028234663852886E+38 to −1.40129846432481707E−45 *Approximate positive range:* 1.40129846432481707E−45 to 3.4028234663852886E+38 *Other supported values:* positive and negative zero positive and negative infinity not-a-number (NaN)	IEEE 754 IEC 60559
long	64	−9,223,372,036,854,775,808 to 9,223,372,036,854,775,807, inclusive	
ulong	64	0 to 18,446,744,073,709,551,615, inclusive	

Fig. B.1 | Simple types. (Part 1 of 2.)

Type	Size in bits	Value range	Standard
double	64	*Approximate negative range:* −1.7976931348623157E+308 to −4.94065645841246544E−324 *Approximate positive range:* 4.94065645841246544E−324 to 1.7976931348623157E+308 *Other supported values:* positive and negative zero positive and negative infinity not-a-number (NaN)	IEEE 754 IEC 60559
decimal	128	*Negative range:* −79,228,162,514,264,337,593,543,950,335 (−7.9E+28) to −1.0E−28 *Positive range:* 1.0E−28 to 79,228,162,514,264,337,593,543,950,335 (7.9E+28)	

Fig. B.1 | Simple types. (Part 2 of 2.)

Additional Simple Type Information

- This appendix is based on information from Sections 4.1.4–4.1.8 of Microsoft's version of the *C# Language Specification* and Sections 11.1.4–11.1.8 of the ECMA-334 (the ECMA version of the *C# Language Specification*). These documents are available from the following websites:

  ```
  msdn.microsoft.com/en-us/vcsharp/aa336809.aspx
  www.ecma-international.org/publications/standards/Ecma-334.htm
  ```

- Values of type float have seven digits of precision.

- Values of type double have 15–16 digits of precision.

- Values of type decimal are represented as integer values that are scaled by a power of 10. Values between −1.0 and 1.0 are represented exactly to 28 digits.

- For more information on IEEE 754 visit grouper.ieee.org/groups/754/. For more information on Unicode, see Appendix F.

ASCII Character Set

	0	1	2	3	4	5	6	7	8	9
0	nul	soh	stx	etx	eot	enq	ack	bel	bs	ht
1	nl	vt	ff	cr	so	si	dle	dc1	dc2	dc3
2	dc4	nak	syn	etb	can	em	sub	esc	fs	gs
3	rs	us	sp	!	"	#	$	%	&	'
4	(	)	*	+	,	-	.	/	0	1
5	2	3	4	5	6	7	8	9	:	;
6	<	=	>	?	@	A	B	C	D	E
7	F	G	H	I	J	K	L	M	N	O
8	P	Q	R	S	T	U	V	W	X	Y
9	Z	[	\	]	^	_	'	a	b	c
10	d	e	f	g	h	i	j	k	l	m
11	n	o	p	q	r	s	t	u	v	w
12	x	y	z	{	|	}	~	del		

Fig. C.1 | ASCII Character Set.

The digits at the left of the table are the left digits of the decimal equivalent (0–127) of the character code, and the digits at the top of the table are the right digits of the character code. For example, the character code for "F" is 70, and the character code for "&" is 38.

Most users of this book are interested in the ASCII character set used to represent English characters on many computers. The ASCII character set is a subset of the Unicode character set used by C# to represent characters from most of the world's languages. For more information on the Unicode character set, see Appendix F.

D

Number Systems

Objectives

In this appendix you'll learn:

- To understand basic number systems concepts, such as base, positional value and symbol value.

- To understand how to work with numbers represented in the binary, octal and hexadecimal number systems.

- To abbreviate binary numbers as octal numbers or hexadecimal numbers.

- To convert octal numbers and hexadecimal numbers to binary numbers.

- To convert back and forth between decimal numbers and their binary, octal and hexadecimal equivalents.

- To understand binary arithmetic and how negative binary numbers are represented using two's complement notation.

Here are only numbers ratified.
—William Shakespeare

Nature has some sort of arithmetic-geometrical coordinate system, because nature has all kinds of models. What we experience of nature is in models, and all of nature's models are so beautiful. It struck me that nature's system must be a real beauty, because in chemistry we find that the associations are always in beautiful whole numbers— there are no fractions.
—Richard Buckminster Fuller

D.1 Introduction

In this appendix, we introduce the key number systems that programmers use, especially when they're working on software projects that require close interaction with machine-level hardware. Projects like this include operating systems, computer networking software, compilers, database systems and applications requiring high performance.

When we write an integer such as 227 or –63 in a program, the number is assumed to be in the decimal (base 10) number system. The digits in the decimal number system are 0, 1, 2, 3, 4, 5, 6, 7, 8 and 9. The lowest digit is 0 and the highest digit is 9—one less than the base of 10. Internally, computers use the binary (base 2) number system. The binary number system has only two digits, namely 0 and 1. Its lowest digit is 0 and its highest digit is 1—one less than the base of 2.

As we'll see, binary numbers tend to be much longer than their decimal equivalents. Programmers who work in assembly languages and in high-level languages like C# that enable programmers to reach down to the machine level, find it cumbersome to work with binary numbers. So two other number systems—the octal number system (base 8) and the hexadecimal number system (base 16)—are popular primarily because they make it convenient to abbreviate binary numbers.

In the octal number system, the digits range from 0 to 7. Because both the binary number system and the octal number system have fewer digits than the decimal number system, their digits are the same as the corresponding digits in decimal.

The hexadecimal number system poses a problem because it requires 16 digits—a lowest digit of 0 and a highest digit with a value equivalent to decimal 15 (one less than the base of 16). By convention, we use the letters A through F to represent the hexadecimal digits corresponding to decimal values 10 through 15. Thus in hexadecimal we can have numbers like 876 consisting solely of decimal-like digits, numbers like 8A55F consisting of digits and letters and numbers like FFE consisting solely of letters. Occasionally, a hexadecimal number spells a common word such as FACE or FEED—this can appear strange to programmers accustomed to working with numbers. The digits of the binary, octal, decimal and hexadecimal number systems are summarized in Fig. D.1–Fig. D.2.

Each of these number systems uses positional notation—each position in which a digit is written has a different positional value. For example, in the decimal number 937 (the 9, the 3 and the 7 are referred to as symbol values), we say that the 7 is written in the ones position, the 3 is written in the tens position and the 9 is written in the hundreds position. Each of these positions is a power of the base (base 10) and that these powers begin at 0 and increase by 1 as we move left in the number (Fig. D.3).

Binary digit	Octal digit	Decimal digit	Hexadecimal digit
0	0	0	0
1	1	1	1
	2	2	2
	3	3	3
	4	4	4
	5	5	5
	6	6	6
	7	7	7
		8	8
		9	9
			A (decimal value of 10)
			B (decimal value of 11)
			C (decimal value of 12)
			D (decimal value of 13)
			E (decimal value of 14)
			F (decimal value of 15)

Fig. D.1 | Digits of the binary, octal, decimal and hexadecimal number systems.

Attribute	Binary	Octal	Decimal	Hexadecimal
Base	2	8	10	16
Lowest digit	0	0	0	0
Highest digit	1	7	9	F

Fig. D.2 | Comparing the binary, octal, decimal and hexadecimal number systems.

Positional values in the decimal number system			
Decimal digit	9	3	7
Position name	Hundreds	Tens	Ones
Positional value	100	10	1
Positional value as a power of the base (10)	10^2	10^1	10^0

Fig. D.3 | Positional values in the decimal number system.

For longer decimal numbers, the next positions to the left would be the thousands position (10 to the 3rd power), the ten-thousands position (10 to the 4th power), the hundred-thousands position (10 to the 5th power), the millions position (10 to the 6th power), the ten-millions position (10 to the 7th power) and so on.

In the binary number 101, the rightmost 1 is written in the ones position, the 0 is written in the twos position and the leftmost 1 is written in the fours position. Each position is a power of the base (base 2) and that these powers begin at 0 and increase by 1 as we move left in the number (Fig. D.4). So, $101 = 1 * 2^2 + 0 * 2^1 + 1 * 2^0 = 4 + 0 + 1 = 5$.

Positional values in the binary number system			
Binary digit	1	0	1
Position name	Fours	Twos	Ones
Positional value	4	2	1
Positional value as a power of the base (2)	2^2	2^1	2^0

Fig. D.4 | Positional values in the binary number system.

For longer binary numbers, the next positions to the left would be the eights position (2 to the 3rd power), the sixteens position (2 to the 4th power), the thirty-twos position (2 to the 5th power), the sixty-fours position (2 to the 6th power) and so on.

In the octal number 425, we say that the 5 is written in the ones position, the 2 is written in the eights position and the 4 is written in the sixty-fours position. Each of these positions is a power of the base (base 8) and that these powers begin at 0 and increase by 1 as we move left in the number (Fig. D.5).

Positional values in the octal number system			
Decimal digit	4	2	5
Position name	Sixty-fours	Eights	Ones
Positional value	64	8	1
Positional value as a power of the base (8)	8^2	8^1	8^0

Fig. D.5 | Positional values in the octal number system.

For longer octal numbers, the next positions to the left would be the five-hundred-and-twelves position (8 to the 3rd power), the four-thousand-and-ninety-sixes position (8 to the 4th power), the thirty-two-thousand-seven-hundred-and-sixty-eights position (8 to the 5th power) and so on.

In the hexadecimal number 3DA, we say that the A is written in the ones position, the D is written in the sixteens position and the 3 is written in the two-hundred-and-fifty-sixes position. Each of these positions is a power of the base (base 16) and that these powers begin at 0 and increase by 1 as we move left in the number (Fig. D.6).

For longer hexadecimal numbers, the next positions to the left would be the four-thousand-and-ninety-sixes position (16 to the 3rd power), the sixty-five-thousand-five-hundred-and-thirty-sixes position (16 to the 4th power) and so on.

Positional values in the hexadecimal number system			
Decimal digit	3	D	A
Position name	Two-hundred-and-fifty-sixes	Sixteens	Ones
Positional value	256	16	1
Positional value as a power of the base (16)	16^2	16^1	16^0

Fig. D.6 | Positional values in the hexadecimal number system.

D.2 Abbreviating Binary Numbers as Octal and Hexadecimal Numbers

The main use for octal and hexadecimal numbers in computing is for abbreviating lengthy binary representations. Figure D.7 highlights the fact that lengthy binary numbers can be expressed concisely in number systems with higher bases than the binary number system.

Decimal number	Binary representation	Octal representation	Hexadecimal representation
0	0	0	0
1	1	1	1
2	10	2	2
3	11	3	3
4	100	4	4
5	101	5	5
6	110	6	6
7	111	7	7
8	1000	10	8
9	1001	11	9
10	1010	12	A
11	1011	13	B
12	1100	14	C
13	1101	15	D
14	1110	16	E
15	1111	17	F
16	10000	20	10

Fig. D.7 | Decimal, binary, octal and hexadecimal equivalents.

A particularly important relationship that both the octal number system and the hexadecimal number system have to the binary system is that the bases of octal and hexadecimal (8 and 16 respectively) are powers of the base of the binary number system (base 2). Consider the following 12-digit binary number and its octal and hexadecimal equivalents. See if you can determine how this relationship makes it convenient to abbreviate binary numbers in octal or hexadecimal. The answer follows the numbers.

Binary number	Octal equivalent	Hexadecimal equivalent
100011010001	4321	8D1

To see how the binary number converts easily to octal, simply break the 12-digit binary number into groups of three consecutive bits each and write those groups over the corresponding digits of the octal number as follows:

100	011	010	001
4	3	2	1

The octal digit you have written under each group of three bits corresponds precisely to the octal equivalent of that 3-digit binary number, as shown in Fig. D.7.

The same kind of relationship can be observed in converting from binary to hexadecimal. Break the 12-digit binary number into groups of four consecutive bits each and write those groups over the corresponding digits of the hexadecimal number as follows:

1000	1101	0001
8	D	1

Notice that the hexadecimal digit you wrote under each group of four bits corresponds precisely to the hexadecimal equivalent of that 4-digit binary number as shown in Fig. D.7.

D.3 Converting Octal and Hexadecimal Numbers to Binary Numbers

In the previous section, we saw how to convert binary numbers to their octal and hexadecimal equivalents by forming groups of binary digits and simply rewriting them as their equivalent octal digit values or hexadecimal digit values. This process may be used in reverse to produce the binary equivalent of a given octal or hexadecimal number.

For example, the octal number 653 is converted to binary simply by writing the 6 as its 3-digit binary equivalent 110, the 5 as its 3-digit binary equivalent 101 and the 3 as its 3-digit binary equivalent 011 to form the 9-digit binary number 110101011.

The hexadecimal number FAD5 is converted to binary simply by writing the F as its 4-digit binary equivalent 1111, the A as its 4-digit binary equivalent 1010, the D as its 4-digit binary equivalent 1101 and the 5 as its 4-digit binary equivalent 0101 to form the 16-digit 1111101011010101.

D.4 Converting from Binary, Octal or Hexadecimal to Decimal

We are accustomed to working in decimal, and therefore it is often convenient to convert a binary, octal, or hexadecimal number to decimal to get a sense of what the number is "really" worth. Our diagrams in Section D.1 express the positional values in decimal. To convert a number to decimal from another base, multiply the decimal equivalent of each digit by its positional value and sum these products. For example, the binary number 110101 is converted to decimal 53, as shown in Fig. D.8.

Converting a binary number to decimal					
Postional values:	32	16	8	4	2	1
Symbol values:	1	1	0	1	0	1
Products:	1*32=32	1*16=16	0*8=0	1*4=4	0*2=0	1*1=1
Sum:	= 32 + 16 + 0 + 4 + 0s + 1 = 53					

Fig. D.8 | Converting a binary number to decimal.

To convert octal 7614 to decimal 3980, we use the same technique, this time using appropriate octal positional values, as shown in Fig. D.9.

Converting an octal number to decimal			
Positional values:	512	64	8	1
Symbol values:	7	6	1	4
Products	7*512=3584	6*64=384	1*8=8	4*1=4
Sum:	= 3584 + 384 + 8 + 4 = 3980			

Fig. D.9 | Converting an octal number to decimal.

To convert hexadecimal AD3B to decimal 44347, we use the same technique, this time using appropriate hexadecimal positional values, as shown in Fig. D.10.

Converting a hexadecimal number to decimal			
Postional values:	4096	256	16	1
Symbol values:	A	D	3	B
Products	A*4096=40960	D*256=3328	3*16=48	B*1=11
Sum:	= 40960 + 3328 + 48 + 11 = 44347			

Fig. D.10 | Converting a hexadecimal number to decimal.

D.5 Converting from Decimal to Binary, Octal or Hexadecimal

The conversions in Section D.4 follow naturally from the positional notation conventions. Converting from decimal to binary, octal, or hexadecimal also follows these conventions.

Suppose we wish to convert decimal 57 to binary. We begin by writing the positional values of the columns right to left until we reach a column whose positional value is greater than the decimal number. We do not need that column, so we discard it. Thus, we first write:

Positional values:	64	32	16	8	4	2	1

Then we discard the column with positional value 64, leaving:

Positional values:		32	16	8	4	2	1

Next we work from the leftmost column to the right. We divide 32 into 57 and observe that there is one 32 in 57 with a remainder of 25, so we write 1 in the 32 column. We divide 16 into 25 and observe that there is one 16 in 25 with a remainder of 9 and write 1 in the 16 column. We divide 8 into 9 and observe that there is one 8 in 9 with a remainder of 1. The next two columns each produce quotients of 0 when their positional values are divided into 1, so we write 0s in the 4 and 2 columns. Finally, 1 into 1 is 1, so we write 1 in the 1 column. This yields:

Positional values:	32	16	8	4	2	1
Symbol values:	1	1	1	0	0	1

and thus decimal 57 is equivalent to binary 111001.

To convert decimal 103 to octal, we begin by writing the positional values of the columns until we reach a column whose positional value is greater than the decimal number. We do not need that column, so we discard it. Thus, we first write:

Positional values:	512	64	8	1

Then we discard the column with positional value 512, yielding:

Positional values:		64	8	1

Next we work from the leftmost column to the right. We divide 64 into 103 and observe that there is one 64 in 103 with a remainder of 39, so we write 1 in the 64 column. We divide 8 into 39 and observe that there are four 8s in 39 with a remainder of 7 and write 4 in the 8 column. Finally, we divide 1 into 7 and observe that there are seven 1s in 7 with no remainder, so we write 7 in the 1 column. This yields:

Positional values:	64	8	1
Symbol values:	1	4	7

and thus decimal 103 is equivalent to octal 147.

To convert decimal 375 to hexadecimal, we begin by writing the positional values of the columns until we reach a column whose positional value is greater than the decimal number. We do not need that column, so we discard it. Thus, we first write:

Positional values:	4096	256	16	1

Then we discard the column with positional value 4096, yielding:

Positional values:		256	16	1

Next we work from the leftmost column to the right. We divide 256 into 375 and observe that there is one 256 in 375 with a remainder of 119, so we write 1 in the 256 column. We divide 16 into 119 and observe that there are seven 16s in 119 with a remainder of 7 and write 7 in the 16 column. Finally, we divide 1 into 7 and observe that there are seven 1s in 7 with no remainder, so we write 7 in the 1 column. This yields:

```
Positional values:   256      16       1
Symbol values:        1        7       7
```

and thus decimal 375 is equivalent to hexadecimal 177.

D.6 Negative Binary Numbers: Two's Complement Notation

The discussion so far in this appendix has focused on positive numbers. In this section, we explain how computers represent negative numbers using *two's complement notation*. First we explain how the two's complement of a binary number is formed, then we show why it represents the negative value of the given binary number.

Consider a machine with 32-bit integers. Suppose

```
int value = 13;
```

The 32-bit representation of value is

```
00000000 00000000 00000000 00001101
```

To form the negative of value we first form its *one's complement* by applying C#'s bitwise complement operator (~):

```
onesComplementOfValue = ~value;
```

Internally, ~value is now value with each of its bits reversed—ones become zeros and zeros become ones, as follows:

```
value:
00000000 00000000 00000000 00001101

~value  (i.e., value's ones complement):
11111111 11111111 11111111 11110010
```

To form the two's complement of value, simply add 1 to value's one's complement. Thus

```
Two's complement of value:
11111111 11111111 11111111 11110011
```

Now if this is in fact equal to −13, we should be able to add it to binary 13 and obtain a result of 0. Let us try this:

```
 00000000 00000000 00000000 00001101
+11111111 11111111 11111111 11110011
------------------------------------
 00000000 00000000 00000000 00000000
```

The carry bit coming out of the leftmost column is discarded and we indeed get 0 as a result. If we add the one's complement of a number to the number, the result would be all 1s. The key to getting a result of all zeros is that the twos complement is one more than the one's complement. The addition of 1 causes each column to add to 0 with a carry of 1. The carry keeps moving leftward until it is discarded from the leftmost bit, and thus the resulting number is all zeros.

Computers actually perform a subtraction, such as

```
x = a - value;
```

by adding the two's complement of value to a, as follows:

```
x = a + (~value + 1);
```

Suppose a is 27 and value is 13 as before. If the two's complement of value is actually the negative of value, then adding the two's complement of value to a should produce the result 14. Let us try this:

```
a (i.e., 27)          00000000 00000000 00000000 00011011
+(~value + 1)        +11111111 11111111 11111111 11110011
                     -------------------------------------
                      00000000 00000000 00000000 00001110
```

which is indeed equal to 14.

E
UML 2: Additional Diagram Types

E.1 Introduction

If you read the Software Engineering Case Study in Chapters 30–31, you should now have a comfortable grasp of the UML diagram types that we use to model our ATM system. The case study is intended for use in first- or second-semester courses, so we limit our discussion to a concise subset of the UML. The UML 2 provides a total of 13 diagram types. The end of Section 30.2 summarizes the six diagram types that we use in the case study. This appendix lists and briefly defines the seven remaining diagram types.

E.2 Additional Diagram Types

The following are the seven diagram types that we have chosen not to use in our Software Engineering Case Study.

- **Object diagrams** model a "snapshot" of the system by modeling a system's objects and their relationships at a specific point in time. Each object represents an instance of a class from a class diagram, and several objects may be created from one class. For our ATM system, an object diagram could show several distinct Account objects side by side, illustrating that they're all part of the bank's account database.

- **Component diagrams** model the **artifacts** and **components**—resources (which include source files)—that make up the system.

- **Deployment diagrams** model the rsystem's runtime requirements (such as the computer or computers on which the system will reside), memory requirements, or other devices the system requires during execution.

- **Package diagrams** model the hierarchical structure of **packages** (which are groups of classes) in the system at compile time and the relationships that exist between the packages.

- **Composite structure diagrams** model the internal structure of a complex object at runtime. New in UML 2, they allow system designers to hierarchically decompose a complex object into smaller parts. Composite structure diagrams are beyond the scope of our case study. They're more appropriate for larger industrial applications, which exhibit complex groupings of objects at execution time.

- **Interaction overview diagrams**, new in UML 2, provide a summary of control flow in the system by combining elements of several types of behavioral diagrams (e.g., activity diagrams, sequence diagrams).

- **Timing diagrams**, also new in UML 2, model the timing constraints imposed on stage changes and interactions between objects in a system.

To learn more about these diagrams and advanced UML topics, please visit www.uml.org and our UML Resource Center at www.deitel.com/UML.

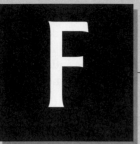

Unicode®

Objectives

In this appendix you'll learn:

- The mission of the Unicode Consortium.
- The design basis of Unicode.
- The three Unicode encoding forms: UTF-8, UTF-16 and UTF-32.
- Characters and glyphs.
- The advantages and disadvantages of using Unicode.

F.1 Introduction

The use of inconsistent character **encodings** (i.e., numeric values associated with characters) in the developing of global software products causes serious problems, because computers process information as numbers. For instance, the character "a" is converted to a numeric value so that a computer can manipulate that piece of data. Many countries and corporations have developed their own encoding systems that are incompatible with the encoding systems of other countries and corporations. For example, the Microsoft Windows operating system assigns the value 0xC0 to the character "A with a grave accent"; the Apple Macintosh operating system assigns that same value to an upside-down question mark. This results in the misrepresentation and possible corruption of data when it is not processed as intended.

In the absence of a widely implemented universal character-encoding standard, global software developers had to **localize** their products extensively before distribution. Localization includes the language translation and cultural adaptation of content. The process of localization usually includes significant modifications to the source code (such as the conversion of numeric values and the underlying assumptions made by programmers), which results in increased costs and delays releasing the software. For example, some English-speaking programmers might design global software products assuming that a single character can be represented by one byte. However, when those products are localized for Asian markets, the programmer's assumptions are no longer valid; thus, the majority, if not the entirety, of the code needs to be rewritten. Localization is necessary with each release of a version. By the time a software product is localized for a particular market, a newer version, which needs to be localized as well, may be ready for distribution. As a result, it is cumbersome and costly to produce and distribute global software products in a market where there is no universal character-encoding standard.

In response to this situation, the **Unicode Standard**, an encoding standard that facilitates the production and distribution of software, was created. The Unicode Standard outlines a specification to produce consistent encoding of the world's characters and symbols. Software products that handle text encoded in the Unicode Standard need to be localized, but the localization process is simpler and more efficient, because the numeric values need not be converted and the assumptions made by programmers about the character encoding are universal. The Unicode Standard is maintained by a nonprofit organization called the **Unicode Consortium**, whose members include Apple, IBM, Microsoft, Oracle, Sun Microsystems, Sybase and many others.

When the Consortium envisioned and developed the Unicode Standard, they wanted an encoding system that was **universal**, **efficient**, **uniform** and **unambiguous**. A universal encoding system encompasses all commonly used characters. An efficient encoding system allows text files to be parsed easily. A uniform encoding system assigns fixed values to all characters. An unambiguous encoding system represents a given character in a consistent manner. These four terms are referred to as the Unicode Standard **design basis**.

F.2 Unicode Transformation Formats

Although Unicode incorporates the limited ASCII character set (i.e., a collection of characters), it encompasses a more comprehensive character set. In ASCII each character is represented by a byte containing 0s and 1s. One byte is capable of storing the binary numbers from 0 to 255. Each character is assigned a number between 0 and 255; thus, ASCII-based systems can support only 256 characters, a tiny fraction of world's characters. Unicode extends the ASCII character set by encoding the vast majority of the world's characters. The Unicode Standard encodes all of those characters in a uniform numerical space from 0 to 10FFFF hexadecimal. An implementation will express these numbers in one of several transformation formats, choosing the one that best fits the particular application at hand.

Three such formats are in use, called **UTF-8**, **UTF-16** and **UTF-32**, depending on the size of the units—in bits—being used. UTF-8, a variable-width encoding form, requires one to four bytes to express each Unicode character. UTF-8 data consists of 8-bit bytes (sequences of one, two, three or four bytes depending on the character being encoded) and is well suited for ASCII-based systems, where there is a predominance of one-byte characters (ASCII represents characters as one byte). Currently, UTF-8 is widely implemented in UNIX systems and in databases.

The variable-width UTF-16 encoding form expresses Unicode characters in units of 16 bits (i.e., as two adjacent bytes, or a short integer in many machines). Most characters of Unicode are expressed in a single 16-bit unit. However, characters with values above FFFF hexadecimal are expressed with an ordered pair of 16-bit units called **surrogates**. Surrogates are 16-bit integers in the range D800 through DFFF, which are used solely for the purpose of "escaping" into higher-numbered characters. Approximately one million characters can be expressed in this manner. Although a surrogate pair requires 32 bits to represent characters, it is space efficient to use these 16-bit units. Surrogates are rare characters in current implementations. Many string-handling implementations are written in terms of UTF-16. [*Note:* Details and sample code for UTF-16 handling are available on the Unicode Consortium website at www.unicode.org.]

Implementations that require significant use of rare characters or entire scripts encoded above FFFF hexadecimal should use UTF-32, a 32-bit, fixed-width encoding form that usually requires twice as much memory as UTF-16 encoded characters. The major advantage of the fixed-width UTF-32 encoding form is that it expresses all characters uniformly, so it is easy to handle in arrays.

There are few guidelines that state when to use a particular encoding form. The best encoding form to use depends on computer systems and business protocols, not on the data itself. Typically, the UTF-8 encoding form should be used where computer systems and business protocols require data to be handled in 8-bit units, particularly in legacy systems being upgraded, because it often simplifies changes to existing programs. For this reason, UTF-8 has become the encoding form of choice on the Internet. Likewise, UTF-16 is the encoding form of choice on Microsoft Windows applications. UTF-32 is likely to become more widely used in the future, as more characters are encoded with values above FFFF hexadecimal. Also, UTF-32 requires less sophisticated handling than UTF-16 in the presence of surrogate pairs. Figure F.1 shows the different ways in which the three encoding forms handle character encoding.

Character	UTF-8	UTF-16	UTF-32
Latin Capital Letter A	0x41	0x0041	0x00000041
Greek Capital Letter Alpha	0xCD 0x91	0x0391	0x00000391
CJK Unified Ideograph-4e95	0xE4 0xBA 0x95	0x4E95	0x00004E95
Old Italic Letter A	0xF0 0x80 0x83 0x80	0xDC00 0xDF00	0x00010300

Fig. F.1 | Correlation between the three encoding forms.

F.3 Characters and Glyphs

The Unicode Standard consists of characters, written components (i.e., alphabetic letters, numerals, punctuation marks, accent marks, and so on) that can be represented by numeric values. Examples of characters include: U+0041 Latin capital letter A. In the first character representation, U+*yyyy* is a **code value**, in which U+ refers to Unicode code values, as opposed to other hexadecimal values. The *yyyy* represents a four-digit hexadecimal number of an encoded character. Code values are bit combinations that represent encoded characters. Characters are represented with **glyphs**, various shapes, fonts and sizes for displaying characters. There are no code values for glyphs in the Unicode Standard. Examples of glyphs are shown in Fig. F.2.

The Unicode Standard encompasses the alphabets, ideographs, syllabaries, punctuation marks, **diacritics**, mathematical operators and so on that comprise the written languages and scripts of the world. A diacritic is a special mark added to a character to distinguish it from another letter or to indicate an accent (e.g., in Spanish, the tilde "~" above the character "n"). Currently, Unicode provides code values for 94,140 character representations, with more than 880,000 code values reserved for future expansion.

Fig. F.2 | Various glyphs of the character A.

F.4 Advantages/Disadvantages of Unicode

The Unicode Standard has several significant advantages that promote its use. One is its impact on the performance of the international economy. Unicode standardizes the characters for the world's writing systems to a uniform model that promotes transferring and sharing data. Programs developed using such a schema maintain their accuracy, because each character has a single definition (i.e., *a* is always U+0061, % is always U+0025). This enables corporations to manage the high demands of international markets by processing different writing systems at the same time. Also, all characters can be managed in an identical manner, thus avoiding any confusion caused by different character-code architectures. Moreover, managing data in a consistent manner eliminates data corruption, because data can be sorted, searched and manipulated via a consistent process.

Another advantage of the Unicode Standard is portability (i.e., the ability to execute software on disparate computers or with disparate operating systems). Most operating systems, databases, programming languages and web browsers currently support, or are planning to support, Unicode. Additionally, Unicode includes more characters than any other character set in common use (although it does not yet include all of the world's characters).

A disadvantage of the Unicode Standard is the amount of memory required by UTF-16 and UTF-32. ASCII character sets are 8 bits in length, so they require less storage than the default 16-bit Unicode character set. However, the **double-byte character set (DBCS)** and the **multibyte character set (MBCS)** that encode Asian characters (ideographs) require two to four bytes, respectively. In such instances, the UTF-16 or the UTF-32 encoding forms may be used with little hindrance to memory and performance.

F.5 Using Unicode

Visual Studio uses Unicode UTF-16 encoding to represent all characters. Figure F.3 uses C# to display the text "Welcome to Unicode!" in eight different languages: English, French, German, Japanese, Portuguese, Russian, Spanish and Traditional Chinese.

The first welcome message (lines 19–23) contains the hexadecimal codes for the English text. The **Code Charts** page on the Unicode Consortium website contains a document that lists the code values for the **Basic Latin** block (or category), which includes the English alphabet. The hexadecimal codes in lines 19–21 equate to "Welcome." When using Unicode characters in C#, the format \u*yyyy* is used, where *yyyy* represents the hexadecimal Unicode encoding. For example, the letter "W" (in "Welcome") is denoted by \u0057.

```
1   // Fig. G.3: UnicodeForm.cs
2   // Unicode enconding demonstration.
3   using System;
4   using System.Windows.Forms;
5
6   namespace UnicodeDemo
7   {
8      public partial class UnicodeForm : Form
9      {
10         public UnicodeForm()
11         {
12            InitializeComponent();
13         }
14
15         // assign Unicode strings to each Label
16         private void UnicodeForm_Load( object sender, EventArgs e )
17         {
18            // English
19            char[] english = { '\u0057', '\u0065', '\u006C',
20               '\u0063', '\u006F', '\u006D', '\u0065', '\u0020',
21               '\u0074', '\u006F', '\u0020' };
22            englishLabel.Text = new string( english ) +
23               "Unicode" + '\u0021';
24
```

Fig. F.3 | Windows application demonstrating Unicode encoding. (Part 1 of 3.)

```
25              // French
26              char[] french = { '\u0042', '\u0069', '\u0065',
27                  '\u006E', '\u0076', '\u0065', '\u006E', '\u0075',
28                  '\u0065', '\u0020', '\u0061', '\u0075', '\u0020' };
29              frenchLabel.Text = new string( french ) +
30                  "Unicode" + '\u0021';
31
32              // German
33              char[] german = { '\u0057', '\u0069', '\u006C',
34                  '\u006B', '\u006F', '\u006D', '\u006D', '\u0065',
35                  '\u006E', '\u0020', '\u007A', '\u0075', '\u0020' };
36              germanLabel.Text = new string( german ) +
37                  "Unicode" + '\u0021';
38
39              // Japanese
40              char[] japanese = { '\u3078',  '\u3087', '\u3045',
41                  '\u3053', '\u305D', '\u0021' };
42              japaneseLabel.Text = "Unicode" + new string( japanese );
43
44              // Portuguese
45              char[] portuguese = { '\u0053', '\u0065', '\u006A',
46                  '\u0061', '\u0020', '\u0062', '\u0065', '\u006D',
47                  '\u0020', '\u0076', '\u0069', '\u006E', '\u0064',
48                  '\u006F', '\u0020', '\u0061', '\u0020' };
49              portugueseLabel.Text = new string( portuguese ) +
50                  "Unicode" + '\u0021';
51
52              // Russian
53              char[] russian = { '\u0414', '\u043E', '\u0431',
54                  '\u0440', '\u043E', '\u0020', '\u043F', '\u043E',
55                  '\u0436', '\u0430', '\u043B', '\u043E', '\u0432',
56                  '\u0430', '\u0442', '\u044A', '\u0020', '\u0432', '\u0020' };
57              russianLabel.Text = new string( russian ) +
58                  "Unicode" + '\u0021';
59
60              // Spanish
61              char[] spanish = { '\u0042', '\u0069', '\u0065',
62                  '\u006E', '\u0076', '\u0065', '\u006E', '\u0069',
63                  '\u0064', '\u006F', '\u0020', '\u0061', '\u0020' };
64              spanishLabel.Text = new string( spanish ) +
65                  "Unicode" + '\u0021';
66
67              // Simplified Chinese
68              char[] chinese = { '\u6B22', '\u8FCE', '\u4F7F',
69                  '\u7528', '\u0020' };
70              chineseLabel.Text = new string( chinese ) +
71                  "Unicode" + '\u0021';
72          } // end method UnicodeForm_Load
73      } // end class UnicodeForm
74  } // end namespace UnicodeDemo
```

Fig. F.3 | Windows application demonstrating Unicode encoding. (Part 2 of 3.)

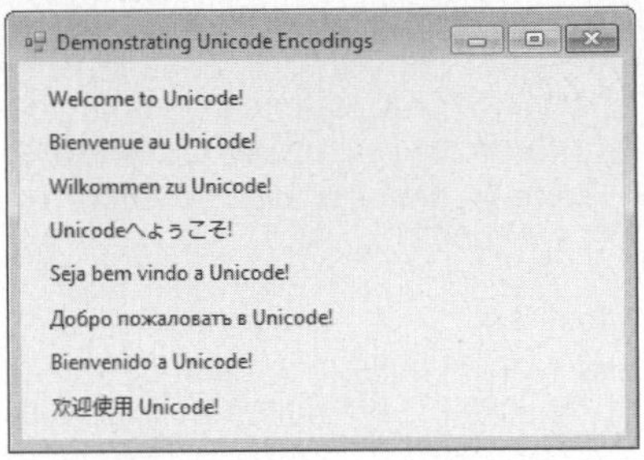

Welcome to Unicode!

Bienvenue au Unicode!

Wilkommen zu Unicode!

Unicodeへようこそ!

Seja bem vindo a Unicode!

Добро пожаловать в Unicode!

Bienvenido a Unicode!

欢迎使用 Unicode!

Fig. F.3 | Windows application demonstrating Unicode encoding. (Part 3 of 3.)

Line 9 contains the hexadecimal for the *space* character (\u0020). The hexadecimal value for the word "to" is on line 21, and the word "Unicode" is on line 23. "Unicode" is not encoded because it is a registered trademark and has no equivalent translation in most languages. Line 23 also contains the \u0021 notation for the exclamation mark (!).

The remaining welcome messages (lines 26–71) contain the hexadecimal codes for the other seven languages. The code values used for the French, German, Portuguese and Spanish text are located in the **Basic Latin** block, the code values used for the Traditional Chinese text are located in the **CJK Unified Ideographs** block, the code values used for the Russian text are located in the **Cyrillic** block and the code values used for the Japanese text are located in the **Hiragana** block.

[*Note:* To render the Asian characters in an application under Windows XP, you need to install the proper language files on your computer. To do this, open the **Regional Options** dialog from the **Control Panel** (**Start > Settings > Control Panel**). At the bottom of the **General** tab is a list of languages. Check the **Japanese** and the **Traditional Chinese** checkboxes and press **Apply**. Follow the directions of the install wizard to install the languages. For more information, visit www.unicode.org/help/display_problems.html.]

F.6 Character Ranges

The Unicode Standard assigns code values, which range from 0000 (**Basic Latin**) to E007F (**Tags**), to the written characters of the world. Currently, there are code values for 94,140 characters. To simplify the search for a character and its associated code value, the Unicode Standard generally groups code values by **script** and function (i.e., Latin characters are grouped in a block, mathematical operators are grouped in another block, and so on). As a rule, a script is a single writing system that is used for multiple languages (e.g., the Latin script is used for English, French, Spanish, and so on). The **Code Charts** page on the Unicode Consortium website lists all the defined blocks and their respective code values. Figure F.4 lists some blocks (scripts) from the website and their range of code values.

Script	Range of code values
Arabic	U+0600–U+06FF
Basic Latin	U+0000–U+007F

Fig. F.4 | Some character ranges. (Part 1 of 2.)

Script	Range of code values
Bengali (India)	U+0980–U+09FF
Cherokee (Native America)	U+13A0–U+13FF
CJK Unified Ideographs (East Asia)	U+4E00–U+9FAF
Cyrillic (Russia and Eastern Europe)	U+0400–U+04FF
Ethiopic	U+1200–U+137F
Greek	U+0370–U+03FF
Hangul Jamo (Korea)	U+1100–U+11FF
Hebrew	U+0590–U+05FF
Hiragana (Japan)	U+3040–U+309F
Khmer (Cambodia)	U+1780–U+17FF
Lao (Laos)	U+0E80–U+0EFF
Mongolian	U+1800–U+18AF
Myanmar	U+1000–U+109F
Ogham (Ireland)	U+1680–U+169F
Runic (Germany and Scandinavia)	U+16A0–U+16FF
Sinhala (Sri Lanka)	U+0D80–U+0DFF
Telugu (India)	U+0C00–U+0C7F
Thai	U+0E00–U+0E7F

Fig. F.4 | Some character ranges. (Part 2 of 2.)

Using the Visual C# 2010 Debugger

Objectives

In this chapter you'll learn:

- To use breakpoints to pause program execution and allow you to examine the values of variables.

- To set, disable and remove breakpoints.

- To use the **Continue** command to continue execution from a breakpoint.

- To use the **Locals** window to view and modify variable values.

- To use the **Watch** window to evaluate expressions.

- To use the **Step Into**, **Step Out** and **Step Over** commands to execute a program line by line.

- To use **Just My Code**™ debugging.

We are built to make mistakes, coded for error.
—Lewis Thomas

What we anticipate seldom occurs; what we least expect generally happens.
—Benjamin Disraeli

It is one thing to show a man that he is in error, and another to put him in possession of truth.
—John Locke

He can run but he can't hide.
—Joe Louis

And so shall I catch the fly.
—William Shakespeare

G.1 Introduction

In this appendix, you'll learn about tools and techniques that can be used to address compilation errors and logic errors. Syntax errors are a type of **compilation error**—an error that prevents code from compiling. Logic errors, also called **bugs**, do not prevent a program from compiling successfully, but can cause a running program to produce erroneous results or terminate prematurely. Most compiler vendors, like Microsoft, package their IDEs with a tool called a **debugger**. Debuggers allow you to monitor the execution of your programs to locate and remove logic errors. A program must successfully compile before it can be used in the debugger. The debugger allows you to suspend program execution, examine and set variable values and much more. In this appendix, we introduce the Visual C# 2010 IDE and debugger features for fixing errors in your programs.

G.2 Breakpoints and the Continue Command

While compilation errors can be found automatically by the compiler, it can be much more difficult to determine the cause of logic errors. To help with this, we investigate the concept of **breakpoints**. Breakpoints are special markers that can be set at any executable line of code. They cannot be placed on comments or whitespace. When a running program reaches a breakpoint, execution pauses, allowing you to examine the values of variables to help determine whether logic errors exist. For example, you can examine the value of a variable that stores a calculation's result to determine whether the calculation was performed correctly. You can also examine the value of an expression.

To illustrate the debugger features, we use the program in Figs. G.1–G.2 that creates and manipulates an Account (Fig. G.1) object. This example is based on concepts from Chapter 4, so it does not use features that are presented after Chapter 4. Execution begins in Main (lines 8–41 of Fig. G.2). Line 10 creates an Account object with an initial balance of $50.00. Account's constructor (lines 10–13 of Fig. G.1) accepts one argument, which specifies the Account's initial balance. Lines 13–14 of Fig. G.2 output the initial account balance using Account property Balance. Lines 18–20 prompt the user for and input the withdrawalAmount. Lines 22–24 subtract the withdrawal amount from the Account's balance using its Debit method. Line 27 displays the new balance. Next, lines 30–40 perform similar steps to credit the account.

```
1   // Fig. G.1: Account.cs
2   // Account class with a Debit method that withdraws money from account.
3   using System;
4
5   public class Account
6   {
7      private decimal balance; // instance variable that stores the balance
8
9      // constructor
10     public Account( decimal initialBalance )
11     {
12        Balance = initialBalance; // set balance using property
13     } // end Account constructor
14
15     // credits (adds) an amount to the account
16     public void Credit( decimal amount )
17     {
18        Balance = Balance + amount; // add amount to balance
19     } // end method Credit
20
21     // debit (subtracts) an amount from the account
22     public void Debit( decimal amount )
23     {
24        if ( amount > Balance )
25           Console.WriteLine( "Debit amount exceeded account balance." );
26
27        if ( amount <= Balance )
28           Balance = Balance - amount; // subtract amount from balance
29     } // end method Debit
30
31     // property to get the balance
32     public decimal Balance
33     {
34        get
35        {
36           return balance;
37        } // end get
38        set
39        {
40           // validate that value is greater than or equal to 0;
41           // if it is not, balance is left unchanged
42           if ( value >= 0 )
43              balance = value;
44        } // end set
45     } // end property Balance
46  } // end class Account
```

Fig. G.1 | Account class with a Debit method that withdraws money from account.

```
1   // Fig. G.2: AccountTest.cs
2   // Creating and manipulating an Account object.
3   using System;
```

Fig. G.2 | Creating and manipulating an Account object. (Part 1 of 2.)

```
4
5    public class AccountTest
6    {
7        // Main method begins execution of C# application
8        public static void Main( string[] args )
9        {
10           Account account1 = new Account( 50.00M ); // create Account object
11
12           // display initial balance of account object
13           Console.WriteLine( "account1 balance: {0:C}",
14               account1.Balance );
15
16           decimal withdrawalAmount; // withdrawal amount entered by user
17
18           Console.Write( "Enter withdrawal amount for account1: " );
19           // obtain user input
20           withdrawalAmount = Convert.ToDecimal( Console.ReadLine() );
21
22           Console.WriteLine( "\nsubtracting {0:C} from account1 balance",
23               withdrawalAmount );
24           account1.Debit( withdrawalAmount ); // subtract amount from account1
25
26           // display balance
27           Console.WriteLine( "account1 balance: {0:C}", account1.Balance );
28           Console.WriteLine();
29
30           Console.Write( "Enter credit amount for account1: " );
31           // obtain user input
32           decimal creditAmount = Convert.ToDecimal( Console.ReadLine() );
33
34           Console.WriteLine( "\nadding {0:C} to account1 balance",
35               creditAmount );
36           account1.Credit( creditAmount );
37
38           // display balance
39           Console.WriteLine( "account1 balance: {0:C}", account1.Balance );
40           Console.WriteLine();
41       } // end Main
42   } // end AccountTest
```

```
account1 balance: $50.00
Enter withdrawal amount for account1: 25

subtracting $25.00 from account1 balance
account1 balance: $25.00

Enter credit amount for account1: 33

adding $33.00 to account1 balance
account1 balance: $58.00
```

Fig. G.2 | Creating and manipulating an Account object. (Part 2 of 2.)

In the following steps, you'll use breakpoints and debugger commands to examine variable withdrawalAmount's value (declared in Fig. G.2) while the program executes.

1. *Inserting breakpoints in Visual C#.* First, ensure that AccountTest.cs is open in the IDE's code editor. To insert a breakpoint, left click inside the **margin indicator bar** (the gray margin at the left of the code window in Fig. G.3) next to the line of code at which you wish to break, or right click that line of code and select **Breakpoint > Insert Breakpoint**. Additionally, you can also press *F9* when your cursor is on the line to toggle the breakpoint. You may set as many breakpoints as you like. Set breakpoints at lines 18, 24 and 41 of your code. [*Note:* If you have not already done so, have the code editor display line numbers by opening **Tools > Options...**, navigating to **Text Editor > C#** and selecting the **Line numbers** checkbox.] A solid circle appears in the margin indicator bar where you clicked, and the entire code statement is highlighted, indicating that breakpoints have been set (Fig. G.3). When the program runs, the debugger suspends execution at any line that contains a breakpoint. The program then enters **break mode**. Breakpoints can be set before running a program, both in break mode and during execution. To show a list of all breakpoints in a project, select **Debug > Windows > Breakpoints**. This feature is available only in the full version of Visual Studio 2010.

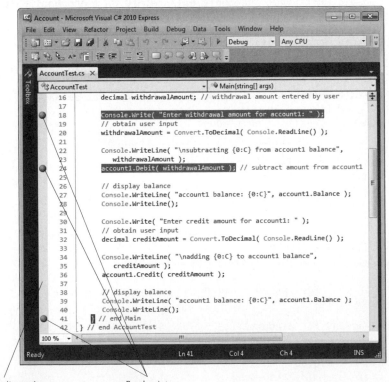

Margin indicator bar   Breakpoints

Fig. G.3 | Setting breakpoints.

2. *Beginning the debugging process.* After setting breakpoints in the code editor, select **Build > Build Solution** to compile the program, then select **Debug > Start Debugging** (or press the *F5* key) to begin the debugging process. While debugging a console application, the **Command Prompt** window appears (Fig. G.4), allowing program interaction (input and output).

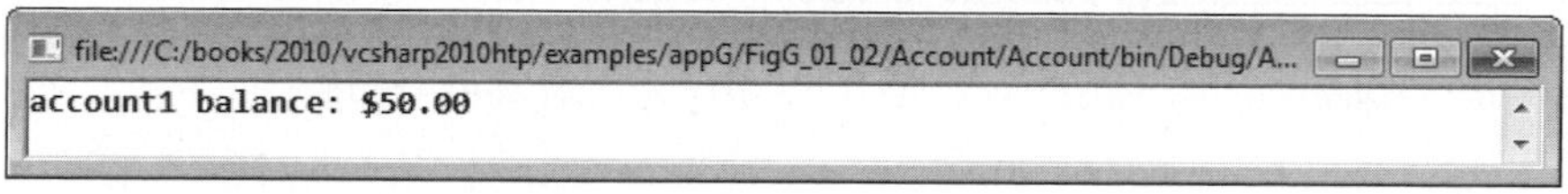

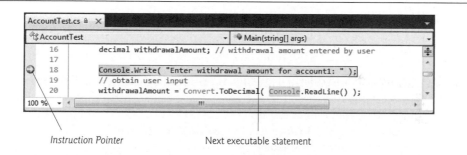

Fig. G.4 | Account program running.

3. *Examining program execution.* Program execution pauses at the first breakpoint (line 18), and the IDE becomes the active window (Fig. G.5). The yellow arrow to the left of line 18, also called the *Instruction Pointer*, indicates that this line contains the next statement to execute. The IDE also highlights the line as well.

Fig. G.5 | Program execution suspended at the first breakpoint.

4. *Using the Continue command to resume execution.* To resume execution, select **Debug > Continue** (or press the *F5* key). The **Continue command** executes the statements from the current point in the program to the next breakpoint or the end of Main, whichever comes first. It is also possible to drag the *Instruction Pointer* to another line in the same method to resume execution starting at that position. Here, we use the **Continue** command, and the program continues executing and pauses for input at line 20. Enter 25 in the **Command Prompt** window as the withdrawal amount. When you press *Enter*, the program executes until it stops at the next breakpoint (line 24). Notice that when you place the mouse pointer over the variable name withdrawalAmount, its value is displayed in a *Quick Info* box (Fig. G.6). As you'll see, this can help you spot logic errors in your programs.

5. *Continuing program execution.* Use the **Debug > Continue** command to execute line 24. The program then asks you to input a credit (deposit) amount. Enter 33, then press *Enter*. The program displays the result of its calculation (Fig. G.7).

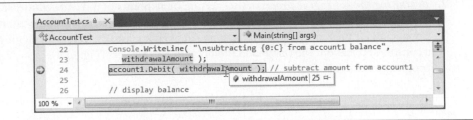

Fig. G.6 | *Quick Info* box displays value of variable `withdrawalAmount`.

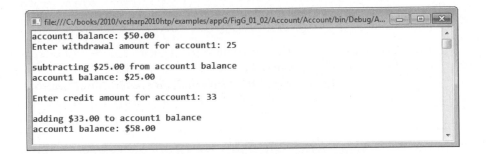

Fig. G.7 | Sample execution of `Account.exe` in debug mode.

6. *Disabling a breakpoint.* To **disable a breakpoint**, right click a line of code in which the breakpoint has been set and select **Breakpoint > Disable Breakpoint**. The disabled breakpoint is indicated by a hollow circle (Fig. G.8)—the breakpoint can be reenabled by right clicking the line marked by the hollow circle and selecting **Breakpoint > Enable Breakpoint**.

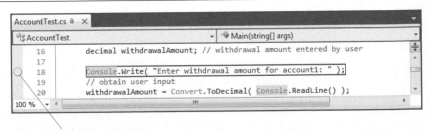

Disabled breakpoint

Fig. G.8 | Disabled breakpoint.

7. *Removing a breakpoint.* To remove a breakpoint that you no longer need, right click the line of code on which the breakpoint has been set and select **Breakpoint > Delete Breakpoint**. You also can remove a breakpoint by clicking the circle in the margin indicator bar or pressing *F9* when the cursor is on the line.

8. *Finishing program execution.* Select **Debug > Continue** to execute the program to completion. Then delete all the breakpoints.

G.3 *DataTips* and Visualizers

You already know how to use the *Quick Info* window to view a variable's value. However, often you may want to check the status of an object. For example, you may want to check the Text value of a TextBox control. When you hover the mouse over a reference-type variable while debugging, the **DataTip** window appears (Fig. G.9). When you hover over the + sign in the *DataTip*, the *DataTip* window gives information about the object's data. There are some limitations—references must be instance variables or local variables, and expressions involving method calls cannot be evaluated.

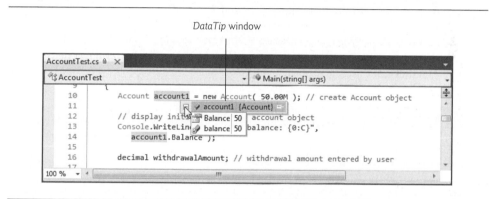

Fig. G.9 | A *DataTip* displayed for the account1 variable.

For the Account object, this means that you can see the balance inside it (as well as the Balance property used to access it). Just like the *Quick Info* window, you can also change the value of a property or variable inside it by clicking on one of the values listed, then typing the new value.

DataTips do not intuitively display information for all variables. For example, a variable representing an XML document cannot be viewed in its natural form using most debugging tools. For such types, **visualizers** can be useful. Visualizers are specialized windows to view certain types of data. They are shown through *DataTip* windows by clicking the small magnifying glass next to a variable name. There are three predefined visualizers—advanced programmers may create additional ones. The **Text Visualizer** lets you see string values with all their formatting included. The **XML Visualizer** formats XML objects into a color-coded format. Finally, the **HTML Visualizer** parses HTML code (in string or XML form) into a web page, which is displayed in the small window.

G.4 The Locals and Watch Windows

In the preceding section, you learned how to use the *Quick Info* and *DataTip* features to examine the variable's value. In this section, you'll learn how to use the **Locals window** to view all variables that are in use while your program is running. You'll also use the **Watch window** to examine the values of expressions.

1. *Inserting breakpoints.* Set a breakpoint at line 24 (Fig. G.10) in the source code by left clicking in the margin indicator bar to the left of line 24. Use the same technique to set breakpoints at lines 27 and 28 as well.

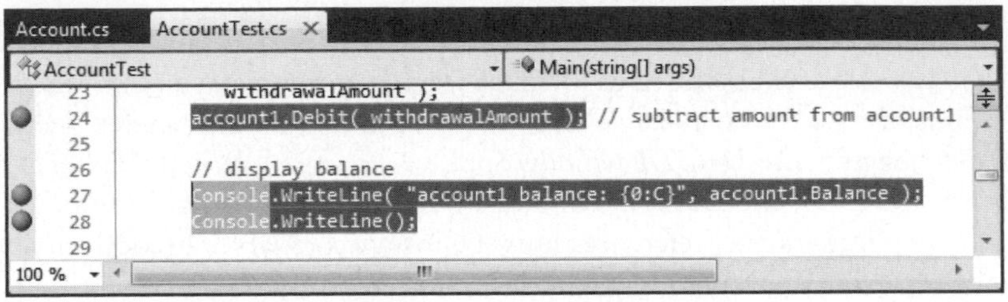

Fig. G.10 | Setting breakpoints at lines 24, 27 and 28.

2. *Starting debugging.* Select **Debug > Start Debugging**. Type 25 at the **Enter withdrawal amount for account1:** prompt (Fig. G.11) and press *Enter*. The program executes until the breakpoint at line 24.

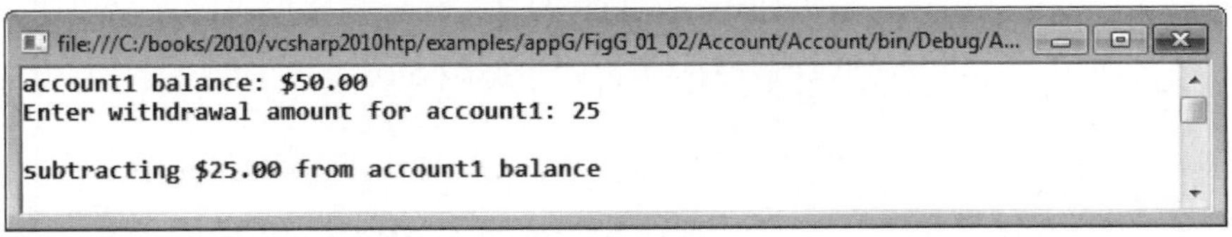

Fig. G.11 | Entering the withdrawal amount before the breakpoint is reached.

3. *Suspending program execution.* When the program reaches line 24, the IDE suspends program execution and switches the program into break mode (Fig. G.12). At this point, the statement in line 20 (Fig. G.2) has input the `withdrawalAmount` that you entered (25), the statement in lines 22–23 has output that the program is subtracting that amount from the `account1` balance and the statement in line 24 is the next statement that executes.

4. *Examining data.* Once the program enters break mode, you can explore the local variable values using the **Locals** window. If this window is not displayed, select **Debug > Windows > Locals**. Click the plus to the left of `account1` in the **Locals** window's **Name** column (Fig. G.13). This allows you to view each of `account1`'s instance variable values individually, including the value for `balance` (50). The **Locals** window displays a class' properties as data, which is why you see both the `Balance` property and the `balance` instance variable in the window. In addition, the current value of local variable `withdrawalAmount` (25) is displayed.

5. *Evaluating arithmetic and boolean expressions.* You can evaluate arithmetic and `bool` expressions using the **Watch** window. Select **Debug > Windows > Watch** to display the window (Fig. G.14). In the **Name** column's first row (which should be blank initially), type `(withdrawalAmount + 10) * 5`, then press *Enter*. The value 175 is displayed (Fig. G.14). In the **Name** column's next row in the **Watch**

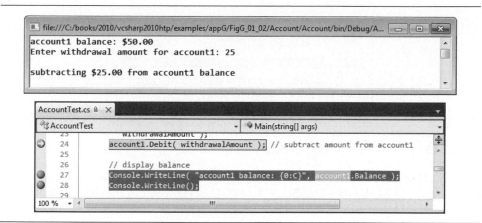

Fig. G.12 | Program execution pauses when debugger reaches the breakpoint at line 24.

Fig. G.13 | Examining local variables.

window, type withdrawalAmount == 200, then press *Enter*. This expression determines whether the value contained in withdrawalAmount is 200. Expressions containing the == symbol are boolean expressions. The value returned is false (Fig. G.14), because withdrawalAmount does not currently contain the value 200.

6. *Resuming execution.* Select **Debug > Continue** to resume execution. Line 24 executes, subtracting the account with the withdrawal amount, and the program enters break mode again at line 27. Select **Debug > Windows > Locals**. The updated balance instance variable and Balance property value are now displayed (Fig. G.15). The values in red in the window are those that have just been modified.

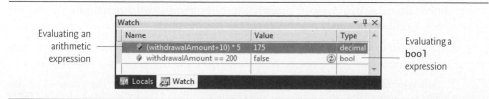

Fig. G.14 | Examining the values of expressions.

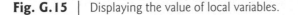

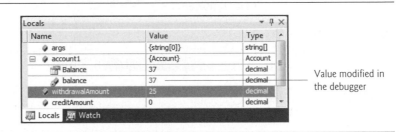

Updated value of the `balance` variable appears in red on the screen

Fig. G.15 | Displaying the value of local variables.

7. *Modifying values.* Based on the value input by the user (25), the account balance output by the program should be 25. However, you can use the **Locals** window to change variable values during program execution. This can be valuable for experimenting with different values and for locating logic errors in programs. In the **Locals** window, click the **Value** field in the `balance` row to select the value 25. Type 37, then press *Enter*. The debugger changes the value of `balance` (and the `Balance` property as well), then displays its new value in red (Fig. G.16). Now select **Debug > Continue** to execute lines 27–28. Notice that the new value of `balance` is displayed in the **Command Prompt** window.

Value modified in the debugger

Fig. G.16 | Modifying the value of a variable.

8. *Stopping the debugging session.* Select **Debug > Stop Debugging**. Delete all breakpoints, which can be done by pressing *Shift + F5*.

G.5 Controlling Execution Using the Step Into, Step Over, Step Out and Continue Commands

Sometimes you need to execute a program line by line to find and fix logic errors. Stepping through a portion of your program this way can help you verify that a method's code executes correctly. The commands you learn in this section allow you to execute a method line by line, execute all of a method's statements or execute only its remaining statements (if you have already executed some statements in the method).

1. *Setting a breakpoint.* Set a breakpoint at line 24 by left clicking in the margin indicator bar.

2. *Starting the debugger.* Select **Debug > Start Debugging**. Enter the value 25 at the **Enter withdrawal amount for account1:** prompt. Program execution halts when the program reaches the breakpoint at line 24.

3. *Using the Step Into command.* The **Step Into** command executes the next statement in the program and immediately halts. If the statement to execute is a method call, control transfers to the called method. The **Step Into** command allows you to follow execution into a method and confirm its execution by individually executing each statement inside the method. Select **Debug > Step Into** (or press *F11*) to enter class Account's Debit method (Fig. G.17).

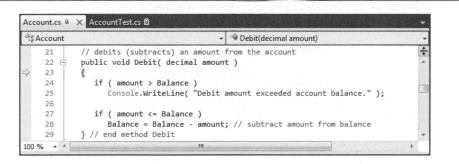

Fig. G.17 | Stepping into the Debit method.

4. *Using the Step Over command.* Select **Debug > Step Over** (or press *F10*) to enter the Debit method's body and transfer control to line 25. The **Step Over** command behaves like the **Step Into** command when the next statement to execute does not contain a method call or access a property. You'll see how the **Step Over** command differs from the **Step Into** command in *Step 10*.

5. *Using the Step Out command.* Select **Debug > Step Out** or press *Shift-F11* to execute the remaining statements in the method and return control to the calling method. Often, in lengthy methods, you may want to look at a few key lines of code, then continue debugging the caller's code. The **Step Out** command executes the remainder of a method and returns to the caller.

6. *Setting a breakpoint.* Set a breakpoint at line 28 of Fig. G.2. This breakpoint is used in the next step.

7. *Using the Continue command.* Select **Debug > Continue** to execute until the next breakpoint is reached at line 20. This feature saves time when you do not want to step line by line through many lines of code to reach the next breakpoint.

8. *Stopping the debugger.* Select **Debug > Stop Debugging** to stop debugging.

9. *Starting the debugger.* Before we can demonstrate the next debugger feature, you must restart the debugger. Start it, as you did in *Step 2*, and enter the same value (25). The debugger pauses execution at line 24.

10. *Using the Step Over command.* Select **Debug > Step Over** (Fig. G.18). Recall that this command behaves like the **Step Into** command when the next statement to execute does not contain a method call. If the next statement to execute contains a method call, the called method executes in its entirety (without pausing execution at any statement inside the method—unless there is a breakpoint in the

method), and the arrow advances to the next executable line (after the method call) in the current method. In this case, the debugger executes line 24 in Main (Fig. G.2), which calls the Debit method. Then the debugger pauses execution at line 27, the next executable statement.

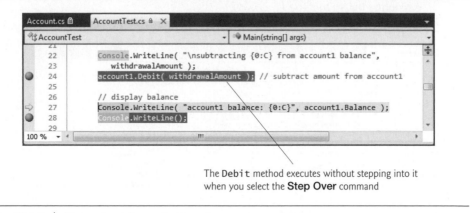

The Debit method executes without stepping into it when you select the **Step Over** command

Fig. G.18 │ Using the debugger's **Step Over** command.

> **11.** *Stopping the debugger.* Select **Debug > Stop Debugging**. Remove all remaining breakpoints.

G.6 Other Debugging Features

Visual C# 2010 provides many other debugging features that simplify the testing and debugging process. We discuss some of these features in this section.

G.6.1 Exception Assistant

You can run a program by selecting either **Debug > Start Debugging** or **Debug > Start Without Debugging**. If you select the option **Debug > Start Debugging** and the runtime environment detects uncaught exceptions, the application pauses, and a window called the **Exception Assistant** appears, indicating where the exception occurred, the exception type and links to helpful information on handling the exception. We discuss the **Exception Assistant** in detail in Section 13.3.3.

G.6.2 Just My Code™ Debugging

Throughout this book, we produce increasingly substantial programs that often include a combination of code written by the programmer and code generated by Visual Studio. The IDE-generated code can be difficult to understand—fortunately, you rarely need to look at this code. Visual Studio 2010 provides a debugging feature called **Just My Code**™ that allows programmers to test and debug only the portion of the code they have written. When this option is enabled, the debugger always steps over method calls to methods of classes that you did not write.

To enable this option, in the **Options** dialog, select the **Debugging** category to view the available debugging tools and options. Then click the checkbox that appears next to the **Enable Just My Code (Managed only)** option (Fig. G.19) to enable or disable this feature.

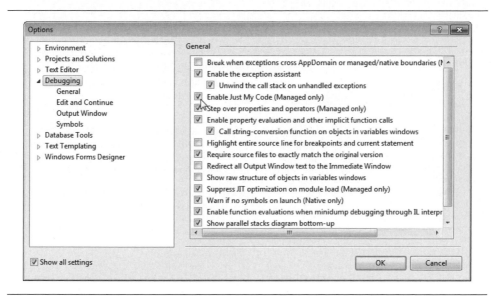

Fig. G.19 | Enabling the **Just My Code** debugging feature in Visual C#.

G.6.3 Other Debugger Features

You can learn more about the Visual Studio 2010 debugger at

```
msdn.microsoft.com/en-us/library/sc65sadd.aspx
```

Index